Handbook of Psychiatric Measures

HANDBOOK OF PSYCHIATRIC MEASURES

TASK FORCE FOR THE HANDBOOK
OF PSYCHIATRIC MEASURES

A. John Rush Jr., M.D.
Harold Alan Pincus, M.D.
Michael B. First, M.D.
Deborah Blacker, M.D., Sc.D.
Jean Endicott, Ph.D.
Samuel J. Keith, M.D.
Katharine A. Phillips, M.D.
Neal D. Ryan, M.D.
G. Richard Smith Jr., M.D.
Ming T. Tsuang, M.D., Ph.D., D.Sc.
Thomas A. Widiger, Ph.D.
Deborah A. Zarin, M.D.

Published by the American Psychiatric Association ■ Washington, DC

Copyright © 2000 American Psychiatric Association
ALL RIGHTS RESERVED
Manufactured in the United States of America on acid-free paper

First Edition   03   02   4   3

American Psychiatric Association
1400 K Street, N.W.
Washington, DC   20005
www.psych.org

Library of Congress Cataloging-in-Publication Data
American Psychiatric Association. Task Force for the Handbook of Psychiatric Measures.
    Handbook of psychiatric measures / Task Force for the Handbook of Psychiatric
Measures ; A. John Rush, Jr. . . . [et al.].-- 1st ed.
        p. ; cm.
Includes bibliographical references and indexes.
ISBN 0-89042-415-2 (casebound : alk. paper)
    1. Psychiatric rating scales--Handbooks, manuals, etc. 2. Mental
illness--Diagnosis--Handbooks, manuals, etc. I. Rush, A. John. II. Title.
    [DNLM: 1. Psychiatric Status Rating Scales--Handbooks. 2. Mental
Disorders--diagnosis--Handbooks. WM 34 A512 2000]
RC473.P78 A46 2000
616.89'075--dc21   00-024851

British Library Cataloguing in Publication Data
A CIP record is available from the British Library.

Contents

Task Force for the Handbook of Psychiatric Measures

A. John Rush Jr., M.D.
Chairperson

Harold Alan Pincus, M.D.
Director, Diagnosis and Assessment Projects

Michael B. First, M.D.
Editor

Deborah A. Zarin, M.D.
Director of Methodology

Deborah Blacker, M.D., Sc.D., *Special Adviser*

Jean Endicott, Ph.D.

Samuel J. Keith, M.D.

Katharine A. Phillips, M.D.

Neal D. Ryan, M.D.

G. Richard Smith Jr., M.D., *Vice-Chairperson*

Ming T. Tsuang, M.D., Ph.D., D.Sc.

Thomas A. Widiger, Ph.D.

Laurie E. McQueen, M.S.S.W.
Project Manager, Diagnosis and Assessment Projects

Ruth Ross, M.A.
Science Editor

Yoshie Satake, B.A.
Program Coordinator, Diagnosis and Assessment Projects

Jennifer F. Powell, B.A.
Program Coordinator, Diagnosis and Assessment Projects

PRINCIPAL CONTRIBUTORS

Diagnostic Interviews for Adults

Andrew E. Skodol, M.D.
Columbia University College of Physicians and Surgeons
New York State Psychiatric Institute

Donna S. Bender, Ph.D.
New York State Psychiatric Institute

General Psychiatric Symptoms Measures

Robert S. Goldman, Ph.D.
Hillside Hospital

Delbert Robinson, M.D.
Hillside Hospital

Brett S. Grube, Ph.D.
Queen Hospital Center

Robin A. Hanks, Ph.D.
Wayne State University—Detroit, Michigan

David S. Nichols, Ph.D.
Oregon State Hospital—Portland

Katherine Putnam, Ph.D.
University of Wisconsin–Madison

Deborah J. Walder, B.A.
Emory University

John M. Kane, M.D.
Hillside Hospital

Mental Health Status, Functioning, and Disabilities Measures

Janet B. W. Williams, D.S.W.
Columbia University College of Physicians and Surgeons
New York State Psychiatric Institute

General Health Status, Functional, and Disabilities Measures

Anthony F. Lehman, M.D., M.S.P.H.
University of Maryland–Baltimore

Susan T. Azrin, M.A.
University of Maryland–College Park

Richard W. Goldberg, Ph.D.
University of Maryland–Baltimore

Quality of Life Measures

Judith Rabkin, Ph.D.
Columbia University
New York State Psychiatric Institute

Glenn Wagner, Ph.D.
New York State Psychiatric Institute

Kenneth W. Griffin, Ph.D.
Weill Medical College of Cornell University

Adverse Effects Measures

Nina R. Schooler, Ph.D.
Hillside Hospital
North Shore–Long Island Jewish Health System

K. N. R. Chengappa, M.D.
University of Pittsburgh
Western Psychiatric Institute and Clinic

Patient Perceptions of Care Measures

Gregory B. Teague, Ph.D.
University of South Florida

Practitioner and System Evaluation

Richard R. Owen, M.D.
University of Arkansas for Medical Sciences
VA HSR&D Center for Mental Healthcare and
  Outcomes Research
Central Arkansas Veterans Healthcare Systems

Carol R. N. Thrush, M.A.
University of Arkansas for Medical Sciences

Stress and Life Events Measures

William S. Shaw, Ph.D.
University of California–San Diego

Joel E. Dimsdale, M.D.
University of California–San Diego

Thomas L. Patterson, Ph.D.
University of California–San Diego

Family and Relational Issues Measures

Stephen C. Messer, Ph.D.
George Washington University
Children's National Medical Center

David Reiss, M.D.
George Washington University Medical Center

Suicide Risk Measures

Kenneth J. Tardiff, M.D., M.P.H.
Cornell Medical College–New York Hospital

Andrew C. Leon, Ph.D.
Cornell Medical College–New York Hospital

Peter Marzuk, M.D.
Cornell Medical College–New York Hospital

Child and Adolescent Measures for Diagnosis and Screening

Laurence L. Greenhill, M.D.
New York State Psychiatric Institute

Joan Malcolm, Ph.D.
New York State Psychiatric Institute

Symptom-Specific Measures for Disorders Usually First Diagnosed in Infancy, Childhood, or Adolescence

Laurie S. Miller, Ph.D.
New York University Child Study Center

Dimitra Kamboukos, M.A.
University of Southern Florida

Child and Adolescent Measures of Functional Status

Barbara J. Burns, Ph.D.
Duke University Medical Center

Krista Kutash, Ph.D.
University of South Florida

Behavioral Measures for Cognitive Disorders

Constantine G. Lyketsos, M.D., M.H.S.
Johns Hopkins University

Martin Steinberg, M.D.
Johns Hopkins University

Neuropsychiatric Measures for Cognitive Disorders

David P. Salmon, Ph.D.
University of California–San Diego

Substance Use Disorders Measures

Bruce J. Rounsaville, M.D.
Yale University School of Medicine

James Poling, Ph.D.
Yale University School of Medicine

Psychotic Disorders Measures

Diana O. Perkins, M.D., M.P.H.
University of North Carolina–Chapel Hill

T. Scott Stroup, M.D., M.P.H.
University of North Carolina–Chapel Hill

Jeffrey A. Lieberman, M.D.
University of North Carolina–Chapel Hill

Mood Disorders Measures

Kimberly A. Yonkers, M.D.
Yale University School of Medicine

Jacqueline Samson, Ph.D.
Harvard Medical School
McLean Hospital

Anxiety Disorders Measures

M. Katherine Shear, M.D.
University of Pittsburgh
Western Psychiatric Institute and Clinic

Ulrike Feske, Ph.D.
University of Pittsburgh
Western Psychiatric Institute and Clinic

Charlotte Brown, Ph.D.
University of Pittsburgh
Western Psychiatric Institute and Clinic

Duncan B. Clark, M.D., Ph.D.
University of Pittsburgh
Western Psychiatric Institute and Clinic

Oommen Mammen, M.D.
University of Pittsburgh
Western Psychiatric Institute and Clinic

Joseph Scotti, Ph.D.
West Virginia University

Somatoform and Factitious Disorders and Malingering Measures

Katharine A. Phillips, M.D.
Butler Hospital

Brian Fallon, M.D.
Columbia Hospital

Dissociative Disorders Measures

Frank W. Putnam, M.D.
University of Cincinnati
Children's Hospital Medical Center

Jennie Noll, Ph.D.
University of Southern California

Marlene Steinberg, M.D.
University of Massachusetts Medical Center

Sexual Disorders Measures

Leonard R. Derogatis, Ph.D.
Clinical Psychometric Research

Peter J. Fagan, Ph.D.
Johns Hopkins University

Julia G. Strand, Ph.D.
Johns Hopkins University

Eating Disorders Measures

Kathleen M. Pike, Ph.D.
Columbia University

Sara L. Wolk, M.A., Ed.M.
New York State Psychiatric Institute

Marci Gluck, Ph.D.
Yeshiva University

B. Timothy Walsh, M.D.
Columbia University

Sleep Disorders Measures

Ruth Benca, M.D., Ph.D.
University of Wisconsin–Madison

Thomas Kwapil, Ph.D.
University of North Carolina–Greensboro

Impulse-Control Disorders Measures

Eric Hollander, M.D.
Mt. Sinai School of Medicine

Lisa Cohen, Ph.D.
Beth Israel Medical Center

Lorraine Simon, M.A.
Mt. Sinai School of Medicine

Personality Disorders, Personality Traits, and Defense Mechanisms Measures

Arthur L. Kaye, Ph.D.
Westwood Group—Richmond, Virginia

M. Tracie Shea, Ph.D.
Brown University School of Medicine

COMMITTEE ON PSYCHIATRIC DIAGNOSIS AND ASSESSMENT

David J. Kupfer, M.D., Chairperson (1998–2000)

A. John Rush Jr., M.D., Chairperson (1994–1998)

Lori L. Altshuler, M.D., Member (1995–1998)

Frederick G. Guggenheim, M.D., Member (1993–1999)

Katharine A. Phillips, M.D., Member (1994–2000)

David Shaffer, M.D., Member (1994–1999)

Hagop S. Akiskal, M.D., Consultant (1998–1999)

Joseph Biederman, M.D., Consultant (1996–1999)

Jack D. Barchas, M.D., Corresponding Member (1996–1999)

Jorge A. Costa e Silva, M.D., Corresponding Member (1996–1999)

Charles T. Kaelber, M.D., Corresponding Member (1996–1999)

T. Bedirhan Ustun, M.D., Corresponding Member (1996–1999)

Janet B. W. Williams, D.S.W., Corresponding Member (1996–1999)

Louis A. Moench, M.D., Assembly Liaison (1995–1999)

Acknowledgments

From the beginning, the development of the *Handbook of Psychiatric Measures* has relied on the collaborative efforts of many individuals. Their commitment to this project and tremendous efforts have made publication of this volume possible. Members of the Task Force for the Handbook of Psychiatric Measures, administrative staff, and principal contributors are listed on pp. xv–xviii, and advisers are listed on pp. 751–756.

The process and structure of the project were developed by the Task Force for the *Handbook of Psychiatric Measures*. We would like to thank the members of the task force for their contributions and the direction they provided in the development of the handbook. Deborah Blacker played a special role in ensuring that the process applied the highest level of methodologic and quality standards. We appreciate the many months of hard work by the principal contributors and cocontributors. Their careful research and thoughtful evaluation of the measures made the handbook a reality. The development of the handbook would not have been possible without the dedicated, persistent, and superb efforts of Laurie McQueen, who kept all of us informed, connected, and on track. Ruth Ross deserves our special thanks for editing and ensuring a consistent format throughout the handbook.

We would also like to acknowledge the Hogg Foundation, Austin, Texas, which provided financial support for the development of the handbook.

Many individuals within the American Psychiatric Association merit our appreciation. We would like to thank Melvin Sabshin, former medical director of the American Psychiatric Association, who provided much support and advice when this project was in its infancy, and the presidents and assembly speakers of the association for their enthusiasm for this project. Steven Mirin, medical director, has provided valuable assistance in the final stages of the project. The efforts of Kathleen Dempsey, chief financial officer, Jack White, and the staff in the business administration office are appreciated. We would also like to thank Ron McMillen, Claire Reinberg, Pam Harley, Bob Pursell, Pam Anderson, and Jane Hoover Davenport of the publishing group for their assistance and expertise in the production of the *Handbook of Psychiatric Measures*. We are appreciative of Sam Guze and the Council on Research and the members of the Committee on Psychiatric Diagnosis and Assessment for their ongoing support of this endeavor.

The entire staff of the office of research, and especially Jennifer Powell and Yoshie Satake, deserve our special thanks for all of their work throughout this project.

A. John Rush Jr., M.D., *Chairperson, Task Force for the Handbook of Psychiatric Measures*

Harold Alan Pincus, M.D., *Director, Diagnosis and Assessment Projects*

Michael B. First, M.D., *Editor*

Cautionary Statement

The evaluations of psychiatric measures included in this volume are offered to assist clinicians in selecting such measures for use in their practice or in understanding the results of research studies. These measures cannot serve as the only method to assess or determine a diagnosis for an individual nor should they be used as the sole basis for clinical decision making. Rather, in selected situations, they have the potential to provide additional information that may inform the clinical judgment of the practitioner. The proper interpretation of the results of these measures requires both clinical training and consideration of a variety of other factors. A particular result, in and of itself, is never sufficient to determine clinical judgments such as the diagnosis of a specific mental disorder, propensity to violence or self-injury, or legal or other nonmedical standards of disability or competence.

Measures were included or not included in this volume for various reasons, such as potential clinical utility, common usage in research and/or clinical settings, and space considerations. The inclusion of a measure within this volume does not represent the American Psychiatric Association's endorsement or promotion of that measure. Likewise, the exclusion of a measure from this volume does not imply that the measure is not suitable for use in clinical practice or research. This manual is not intended to be a comprehensive and exhaustive encyclopedia of all available measures for psychiatric–mental health practice or research.

The reader should also be aware that many of the measures herein have specific training requirements to which users must adhere to achieve the stated results.

Introduction

Harold Alan Pincus, M.D.
A. John Rush Jr., M.D.
Michael B. First, M.D.
Laurie E. McQueen, M.S.S.W.

PURPOSES

This handbook was compiled and designed primarily for clinicians who work in mental health or primary care settings. Its purpose is to inform clinicians about the selection, use, and interpretation of formal assessments (whether structured interviews, self-report questionnaires, or ratings by clinicians or significant others) and to assist them in evaluating the potential utility of such measurement tools in clinical practice. Because of its clinical focus, this manual is not designed to be an encyclopedia of all available measures in all relevant domains. Rather, the focus is on providing clinicians with a basic introduction to the potential roles, opportunities, and risks and benefits in the use of assessment, evaluation, and outcome measures in the routine clinical care of patients with mental disorders.

Clinical decision making should be informed by a wide range of data beyond that included in a multiaxial DSM-IV diagnosis. Although a comprehensive clinical assessment (as described in the American Psychiatric Association's *Practice Guideline for Psychiatric Evaluation of Adults* [1995]) is essential, there are important reasons why clinicians may find the systematic use of structured measures beneficial to their practices. As described in Chapter 3 and discussed in the "Clinical Utility" section of the text describing each instrument in this manual, measures can be useful

- To screen for, and thus identify, individuals who need treatment, monitoring, or other intervention (e.g., use in an unselected general medical setting)
- To assist in diagnosis according to DSM-IV or a similar system
- To assess clinical features beyond diagnosis to inform the initial selection of treatments and/or level of care (e.g., severity and social supports)
- To monitor beneficial and/or adverse effects of treatment
- For other purposes that may not directly influence treatment decisions (e.g., to determine prognosis)
- For administrative purposes (e.g., to inform disability and/or other benefit determinations, for forensic evaluation and/or documentation, to assess the performance of health care delivery systems, and for other administrative uses)

In selecting, applying, and interpreting a measure, however, clinicians must be knowledgeable about the nuances of measurement, including not only the psychometric properties of an instrument (e.g., its reliability or validity) but, even more importantly, the factors that affect the clinical utility of the measure. For example, as discussed in Chapter 3, the use of an instrument to screen for a particular condition in a population with a low incidence of that condition, especially when the instrument has a high false-positive rate, can lead to increased risks and costs (e.g., pursuing unneeded further testing or interventions) without corresponding benefits. Similarly, when making a psychiatric diagnosis, the clinical utility of a lengthy structured diagnostic interview is considerably reduced if the presentation is so straightforward that the diagnosis is obvious. On the other hand, for patients with complex clinical presentations, structured interviewing or the use of specific symptom assessment tools may provide additional data on which to base a diagnosis or may provide critical information for treatment planning.

This handbook is also written for policy makers and planners (e.g., medical directors and administrators in managed-care or public health systems) to help them better understand and properly use clinical measures to assess an individual provider's performance as well as the performance of groups of providers in health care delivery systems. Recently, a plethora of "homegrown" measures that have not been formally evaluated for either reliability or validity have nevertheless been implemented in various care systems and used to guide policy. However, without proper testing, evaluation, and an understanding of the context in which these measures are being used, the results may be inappropriately applied and the conclusions drawn may be invalid. It is also important for clinicians to be aware of the suitability of the measures that are now being used in systems of care to evaluate practitioners' performance and how norms are established by system administrators.

Another purpose for this volume is to assist both clinicians and policy makers in understanding the available literature with regard to the evaluation of treatment efficacy and service system delivery interventions. Scaled assessments, structured interviewing, and other methods are invariably used to gauge the effectiveness of treatments or to measure the effectiveness of programmatic revisions (e.g., health systems research). Familiarity with the instruments used and awareness of their strengths and limitations are crucial to allow both clinicians and policy makers to interpret the validity of such literature.

Finally, in this volume we attempt to identify research areas in which knowledge is lacking. Identification of research needs has the potential to focus instrument developers' efforts on the questions of highest significance to practitioners and/or policy makers. A variety of works that attempt to synthesize the ever-growing array of symptom, disability, functioning, and system performance measurements are available to researchers. Some of these sources (e.g., *The Thirteenth Mental Measurements Yearbook* [Impara and Plake 1998]) are published yearly. This handbook is not intended to be as comprehensive as these sources, but the evidence-based process used in its development has revealed important gaps in the field; these gaps are noted in the "Current Status and Future Research Needs for Assessment" sections that conclude the introductions of the various chapters. Therefore, we hope that this volume will be a stimulus to research.

Caveats in the Use of the Manual

This handbook is not meant to be comprehensive. Literally thousands of measures appear in the literature. Given the limited size of this volume and our hope that it will be both informative and user-friendly, it was not possible to include any more than a cursory description of a selection of measures to illustrate principles and approaches in the use of measures. Neither is the handbook intended as an endorsement of any particular measure. The appropriateness of a given measure depends on its specific use and context. Several widely used measures were included to advise readers on their limitations and inappropriate applications. The decision to include a measure in this volume was based almost exclusively on the likelihood that the measure may be useful or is likely to be encountered in the literature or used in clinical practice. Furthermore, inclusion or exclusion of a type of measure in this handbook does not imply that any individual or group of health professionals does or does not possess the training or experience to administer or interpret a particular measure. Again, individual clinicians vary in their degree of expertise and training in the use of measures.

Because the area of psychiatric measurement is an ever-evolving body of knowledge, up-and-coming measures that have yet to be fully evaluated in a wide range of populations could not always be included given both space limitations and the limited availability of published data. Thus, in this volume we do not attempt to define the field of measurement. Instead, we hope that this work will serve as a stimulus for clinicians to learn more about this area. In future revisions of this handbook, we anticipate that some measures included in this volume will be dropped and some measures that were left out will be added.

It is important to note that we do not recommend the use of formal measures in all clinical circumstances. Rather, clinicians who are informed about the properties of measures and the clinical contexts in which measures may be useful need to make informed decisions as to when, whether, and how to employ such measures in their clinical practices. Of particular importance is a careful consideration of the relevance of specific cultural, ethnic, gender, social, and age factors to the selection of standardized interviews and rating scales and the interpretation of their results (see Chapter 5). Formal measurements should always be used within the context of the clinical situation and with an eye toward the degree to which the measurement is either informative or uninformative in regard to specific clinical problems or situations. Even if formal measures are used, they cannot in any way replace clinical judgment. On the other hand, formal measurement may provide an additional perspective and further information that, in certain circumstances, will improve the knowledge base on which clinicians must exercise clinical judgment and therapeutic decision making.

It is not possible to measure all elements or components that enter into clinical decision making. The hopes, pains, suffering, and disabilities of patients with mental illnesses cannot be entirely translated into any scaled number. Individuals also differ substantially in the degree of importance they attach to certain elements of their treatment (e.g., dry mouth represents a much greater cost of treatment to a professional singer than to someone whose livelihood is less dependent on clear and articulate vocalization). As always, clinicians are confronted with the issue of taking group-based data and individually tailoring and managing it to optimally diagnose and treat individuals' illnesses. This translation requires not only scientific knowledge and, where indicated, appropriate measurement but also a solid therapeutic alliance and constant consideration of the entire biopsychosocial context of an individual patient. Thus, the information supplied in this volume is not intended to imply that the personal and emotionally relevant aspects of the management of individuals with mental illness can or should be reduced to scaled ratings.

However, as will be apparent after even a cursory glance through this volume, the state of the art of measurement has advanced remarkably over the past 30 years. We believe, therefore, that this body of information should be provided to practitioners and should be updated, in a timely fashion, so that the best of the currently available scientific evidence can be properly used by practitioners to produce optimal outcomes for patients and their families and for those responsible for paying for services.

Finally, some may view the expanding role of measures in clinical practice as controversial. On the one hand, the increased use of measures may represent a positive change in improving patient care. On the other hand, there is the potential risk of setting standards and expectations for the use of measures that may not be fully justified. Assessment tools are misused, for example, when their results become the sole basis for determining whether a practitioner properly managed a patient's care. The American Psychiatric Association is clearly not recommending that measurements be used uniformly in all clinical situations. In fact, such a recommendation would be contrary to the scientific knowledge base presented in this handbook. There is reason to believe that the indiscriminate use of measures across all clinical circumstances will increase costs without improving the efficient use of resources and without substantially benefiting the population. Furthermore, the collection of these measures in this handbook should under no circumstances be viewed as defining a standard of care. Readers are advised to refer to the cautionary statement on p. xxi.

The following final caveat is offered to those wishing to codify and simplify the complex intellectual activities required to deliver optimal medical and psychiatric services. An overall judgment as to the appropriateness, quality, and relevance of the procedure selected cannot be gleaned from any single measurement, whether of blood loss, level of disability resulting or reduced, or symptomatic status after the intervention. This judgment is complex in all situations. For example, a measure of the amount of blood lost during a surgical procedure does not inform us whether the procedure was well or poorly performed or indicated or not indicated. Furthermore, even a poor outcome in the course of surgery may well have been the best possible outcome given the circumstances under which the procedure was performed and the baseline health of the patient.

However, measurements can be used to clarify or evaluate some particular aspect of the total situation. Thus, the decision to allow or disallow continued services for an individual who has substantially benefited from prior services is a judgment call based not on the measurements to date but on the probability that the individual will continue to benefit from additional services to be rendered or that the previous advances will be maintained only by continued treatment. This decision requires some judgment on the likelihood of further benefits with further services—a judgment that cannot be made by computers or determined entirely on the basis of group data. Rather, it must be made on an individual patient-by-patient basis. Although this judgment may be informed by prior measurement and further informed by additional evaluation and measurement, the decision itself cannot be rendered by a computer algorithm that is inherently designed to establish the likelihood of further group benefit for the group as a whole. An individual- rather than a group-based judgment is required.

The true art of medical and psychiatric practice involves the blending of group-based information, tailored to and interpreted for individuals, with patient-specific data. We hope that this volume provides information, elements, tools, and a conceptual basis to guide and help clinicians who are confronted on a daily basis with this dilemma between individual- and group-based decision making.

Preparation of the Handbook

The process of developing this handbook was modeled from the outset on the DSM-IV revision process. All decisions involved in the preparation of the handbook, from the selection of measures to be included in the handbook to the discussion of the advantages and disadvantages of each of the selected measures, were to be primarily informed by a comprehensive review of the available literature. Work on developing the principles of the handbook was begun in the fall of 1995. The American Psychiatric Association appointed a task force to develop the overall structure of the handbook, to establish criteria for inclusion of measures and the process for literature review and data collection, and to oversee the preparation of the chapters of the handbook. The task force identified 59 principal and co-principal contributors (henceforth referred to as contributors), who were given the task of conducting the literature reviews. In most cases, contributors, who were not themselves measure developers, were invited to participate. In a few domains, it was not possible to find someone with enough expertise to be a contributor who was not also a test developer. In such cases, oversight from the task force served to minimize any potential bias that might influence the choice of measures or the content of the reviews.

A methods conference was held in March 1996 to present the overall structure of the handbook to the contributors. Specific task force members served as consultants to the contributors for each domain to provide guidance on methodology and to facilitate discussions of boundary issues and cross-cutting issues between chapters and groups of disorders.

The first task undertaken by the contributors was determining which measures would be included in the handbook. They compiled lists of candidate measures for each of their domains. The initial list was drawn from the following sources: 1) the contributors', consultants', and task force members' knowledge of and experience with available measures, 2) the results of a Medline/PsychLit literature search of measures in that domain, and 3) perusal of existing review books of measures. Questions occasionally arose concerning to which domain a particular measure best belonged (e.g., does the Minnesota Multiphasic Personality Inventory belong in the chapter on measures of general symptoms or the chapter on personality disorders?). In such cases, task force members made decisions on boundary issues after consultation with the relevant contributors.

Candidate measures were considered for inclusion on this initial list only if they met the following basic criteria:

- The measure is available in English.
- The information being measured is restricted to either verbal, written, or cognitive performance data obtained directly from the patient (or an informant). Examples of measures include questionnaires; interviews; and verbal, paper and pencil, and performance tests. Measures that rely on the assessment of body fluids, imaging techniques, and other measures of physiological functioning are not included in the handbook.
- The measure can be administered, by and large, by a psychiatrist in an office setting. Tests that require special equipment (other than computers), highly spe-

cialized training, or an extraordinary amount of time (e.g., several hours) to administer are generally excluded.

- At a minimum, there is sufficient peer-reviewed material available regarding psychometric properties to allow for a fair evaluation of the measure. In most cases, at least two articles reporting psychometric data were required, although, in some cases, a single article sufficed if it was sufficiently comprehensive (e.g., if it included extensive reliability and validity data on a large number of clinically relevant subjects).

The initial lists of measures were reviewed by advisers from the field who provided their opinions about whether to include or exclude the measures on the basis of the scope of the project and the criteria provided. The advisers also suggested relevant measures that may have been omitted. Advisers for each domain were identified by the task force and the contributors for their expertise in the domains addressed in the handbook. This group was composed of clinicians, researchers, health systems administrators, and policy makers and included measure developers.

After developing this initial list, the next (and perhaps most difficult) step was to winnow the options down to a final list of measures to be included for each domain. Several considerations went into this determination. First and foremost was the practical consideration of page limitations. One of the primary goals of the handbook project was to produce a clinician-friendly guide that would be useful for everyday practice. We understood from the outset that this requirement meant that the handbook could not provide a comprehensive review of every available measure. The handbook's target size of approximately 700 total pages restricted the total number of measures to be included to no more than approximately 240 and precluded an in-depth appraisal of each measure. Given these tight constraints, contributors were provided with suggested targets for the number of measures that could be included in their domains; the number could be increased or decreased on the basis of the actual number of clinically relevant measures in the domain.

The final selection of measures also took into consideration the availability of adequate empirical evidence and the importance of the measure for psychiatric clinical practice, interpreting clinical trials, quality assurance, utilization review, or reimbursement decision making. Evidence included use in the literature (citations in studies and references in textbooks) and the judgment of the contributors, advisers, and the task force that the measure is either widely used by clinicians or third-party payers or that the measure is up-and-coming (i.e., even though it is currently not in wide use, it is likely to be a highly important scale in the future).

Contributors conducted a comprehensive literature review for each measure on the final list. Data were eligible for consideration only if they were published or had been accepted for publication in a peer-reviewed journal. Unpublished data sets, pharmaceutical company data, and other such material were excluded. In addition, copies of the measures, any user's guides, and important articles were requested from the measures' authors. Relevant articles included those presenting psychometric data (e.g., reliability and internal consistency), those comparing measures with each other and with external validators, and those presenting data regarding the clinical utility of a measure. The output of the literature review process was standardized by having the contributors prepare an extraction sheet for each relevant article according to a specified format. Data from these extraction sheets were then collected and summarized in an evidence table that provided the basis for the handbook text describing the measure.

Input from the field was requested and provided at many different phases of the project. As noted previously, advisers for each domain received the initial list of measures drawn up by the contributors and were asked to comment on the proposed measures and suggest any relevant measures that might have been left out. Advisers were then asked to review drafts of both the introductory text for each domain and the text sections on the specific measures. Their comments and suggestions were used as the basis for the revision of each chapter.

To increase the utility of the handbook, after final decisions were made about which measures would be included, an effort was made to obtain permission from copyright holders to reprint as many measures as possible on an accompanying CD-ROM. In all, permission was granted by copyright holders for inclusion of 108 measures on the CD-ROM—over 900 pages. To increase its usefulness, the CD-ROM also contains the complete text of the handbook, with links to the measures included.

The final product, the *Handbook of Psychiatric Measures*, is the work of many individuals who have given of their time and their expertise to see this project to fruition. It is our hope and expectation that this manual will be an invaluable resource and tool for clinicians and other mental health professionals in the care of their patients.

REFERENCES

American Psychiatric Association: Practice Guideline for the Psychiatric Evaluation of Adults. Washington, DC, American Psychiatric Association, 1995

Impara JC, Plake BS (eds): The Thirteenth Mental Measurements Yearbook, 13th Edition. Buros Institute of Mental Measurements, 1998

Introduction to the Handbook

CHAPTER 1

Organization and Use of the Handbook

Michael B. First, M.D.

The handbook begins with several introductory chapters that present the rationale for the handbook and provide background on the use of measures in specific contexts. These chapters address the nature of measures and limitations in their use; psychometric properties of measures (specifically concepts of reliability and validity); ethnic, cultural, and socioeconomic factors that influence the use and interpretation of measures; and considerations in choosing a measure for a particular clinical or health care systems context.

The remainder of the handbook covers particular measures, organized by domain. General measures that cut across disorders are presented first. They include diagnostic interviews, measures of severity and psychiatric and general medical functioning, measures of quality of life, and other measures, such as those used to rate adverse effects, patient satisfaction, and stress or life events and measures for practitioner and system evaluation. The subsequent disorder-specific sections are organized according to their order in DSM-IV: childhood disorders (with sections on child diagnostic and specific symptom measures as well as child functional measures), cognitive disorders, substance use disorders, psychotic disorders, mood disorders, anxiety disorders, somatoform and factitious disorders (including pain), dissociative disorders, sexual disorders, eating disorders, sleep disorders, impulse-control disorders, and personality disorders and traits (including coping styles and defenses).

Accompanying the handbook is a CD-ROM that includes complete copies of many of the measures discussed in the handbook. A list of measures included on the CD-ROM is provided in Appendix C. See the "About the CD-ROM" section at the end of this chapter for more information about the contents of the CD-ROM.

The handbook includes five appendixes: a list of advisers and consultants to the handbook, the DSM-IV-TR Classification, a list of measures available on the CD-ROM, an index of measures, and an index of abbreviations for measures.

OVERVIEW TEXT FOR EACH CHAPTER

Each chapter of the handbook begins with a brief introductory overview of the organization of the chapter and relevant assessment issues that apply to all of the measures presented in that chapter. The overview is divided into four main sections: Introduction, Using Measures in This Domain, Guide to the Selection of Measures, and Current Status and Future Research Needs for Assessment.

The introduction is generally divided into three subsections: Major Domains, Organization, and Relevant Measures Included Elsewhere in the Handbook. The major construct to be assessed in the chapter is first described, and, depending on the domain, important subdomains are also described (e.g., Chapter 24, "Mood Disorders Measures," is divided into measures for depression and measures for mania). The Organization section includes a table that lists the measures included in the chapter, provides a brief descriptive summary of each measure, and indicates on which pages the description of the measure can be found. This table also indicates which measures are included on the CD-ROM that accompanies the handbook. The third subsection references measures relevant to the construct that are included in other chapters of the handbook (e.g., the introduction to Chapter 14, "Stress and Life Events Measures," refers the reader to the measures included in Chapter 27, "Dissociative Disorders Measures," and to the section on posttraumatic stress disorder in Chapter 25, "Anxiety Disorders Measures").

The section Using Measures in This Domain is divided into three subsections: Goals of Assessment, Implementation Issues, and Issues in Interpreting Psychometric Data. The subsection Goals of Assessment presents the common assessment goals specific to the domain covered in the chapter. For example, in Chapter 20, "Behavioral Measures for Cognitive Disorders," the Goals of Assessment section describes how general behavioral measures are used to screen for behavioral symptoms during an evaluation or routine follow-up, to monitor response to treatment, or to guide decisions regarding the need for services. It also discusses the use of burden measures with dementia caregivers to assess the need for respite care or other services, to assess the need for direct services to the caregiver, and to monitor the patient's response to treatment. The next subsection describes implementation issues relevant to measures in the domain (e.g., the need to employ parent *and* child measures in the assessment of childhood disorders in young children). The subsection Issues in Interpreting Psychometric Data addresses domain-specific issues that are important in understanding and evaluating the data contained in the Psychometric Properties section for each measure (e.g., evaluating the significance of correlations between instruments that contain different definitions of the underlying construct). Specific cultural, ethnic, and gender considerations relevant to assessment issues and interpretation of data are included in both the Implementation Issues and Issues in Interpreting Psychometric Data subsections.

The next section, Guide to the Selection of Measures, briefly summarizes which measures may be appropriate for each of the stated assessment needs and indicates their overall strengths and weaknesses. Other measures that serve the same purpose or that explore the same domain in more detail but that could not be included in the handbook may be mentioned here (e.g., in Chapter 6, "Diagnostic Interviews for Adults," instruments that were developed for specialized patient populations or for specific purposes, such as the Diagnostic Interview for Genetic Studies, are mentioned and referenced). Similarly, newly developed measures that look promising but whose psychometric properties have not yet been fully evaluated are mentioned in this section.

The final section of the overview text, Current Status and Future Research Needs for Assessment, summarizes the overall strengths and weaknesses of existing measures and describes areas of needed focus for the future (e.g., the need for instruments to be developed for a particular population or setting).

The introductory text concludes with a list of references and suggested readings that apply across the domain.

TEXT SECTIONS FOR EACH MEASURE

The discussion of each individual measure is divided into six sections: Goals, Description, Practical Issues, Psychometric Properties, Clinical Utility, and References and Suggested Readings. In general, if a particular type of information is omitted, it should be assumed that supporting data are not available. For example, if translations are not mentioned in the Practical Issues section, it implies that no non-English versions are known to exist. Similarly, the omission of psychometric data regarding test-retest reliability indicates that such information is unknown.

Goals

The Goals section discusses the construct being assessed by the measure, including how the construct is defined or operationalized by the authors of the measure. In most cases, the construct is defined using readily understandable terms and concepts (e.g., a measure of whether the clinical presentation meets the diagnostic criteria for major depressive disorder as defined by DSM-IV or a measure of the severity of anxiety as evidenced by the number and intensity of characteristic cognitive and somatic symptoms). When the construct is defined in terms of a particular theoretical orientation or perspective, that information is presented in this section (e.g., the five-factor model of personality is discussed in the Goals section of the NEO Personality Inventory—Revised [NEO-PI-R] in Chapter 32, "Personality Disorders, Personality Traits, and Defense Mechanisms Measures"). In some cases, the developmental history of the measure is relevant to understanding the construct, particularly in situations in which the authors' main goal in developing a particular measure was to correct one or more deficiencies in existing measures.

The authors' intended uses of the measure, in both clinical and nonclinical settings, are also presented in this section. Goals that are directly related to the clinical management of individual patients are noted first (e.g., diagnosis, identifying those who need treatment, assessing current clinical status, assessing functional state, and monitoring beneficial or adverse effects of treatment), followed by other potential nonclinical uses (e.g., assessing status or outcome in psychiatric research, determining resource allocation, evaluating treatment efficacy systemwide, and measuring patient satisfaction with care).

Description

The Description section describes various aspects of the measure, including its format (e.g., fully structured vs. semistructured and all items administered vs. skip-out formats), method of administration (e.g., self-report vs. clinician or layperson administered and patient vs. informant as source of information), and organization (e.g., total number of items and anchor points or range of answers per item). Sample items that illustrate wording and format are provided for most measures. The range of possible overall scores and subscale scores is presented, and some guidance regarding interpretation of scores is provided. In some cases, recommendations (from either the measure's authors or the chapter authors) are made regarding the significance of a particular cutoff score (e.g., a score above 10 indicates clinically significant depression). In other cases, mean scores for clinically meaningful groups of test subjects (e.g., for a depression severity measure, mean scores for patients with diagnoses of major depressive disorder vs. psychiatrically healthy subjects) may be presented to provide a rough guideline. Sources of normative data (as well as the demographic characteristics of the normative sample) are also referenced in this section.

One complication in describing certain instruments is that multiple versions of the measure may exist. In some cases, the versions represent successive improvements by the same authors in which additional items are added (or dropped). In other cases, much briefer versions of the same measure, which purportedly measure the identical construct, have been developed. Finally, for some measures, different authors have developed different versions, usually customized for a particular application (e.g., at least four DSM-IV versions of the Schedule for Affective Disorders and Schizophrenia for School-Age Children [K-SADS], a diagnostic interview for childhood disorders, are available). In most such situations, after a brief presentation of the various versions, psychometric and other data are presented on the single most widely used (or most studied) version.

Practical Issues

The Practical Issues section lists administration time and training requirements. Also included are how and where to obtain the test and the cost (including copyright issues), available translations, available computer-administered versions, and whether telephone administration has been reported. This information was verified as this book was being written, but is of course subject to change. Please contact test owners for updated information. Unless otherwise indicated, the author of the test should be contacted regarding how to obtain available foreign language translations.

All measures included in this handbook, except those in the public domain, are protected by copyright. Unless otherwise mentioned in this section (e.g., "the test may be freely copied without contacting the author" or "the test is in the public domain"), measures can be reprinted, photocopied, or printed from the CD-ROM that accompanies this handbook only after obtaining written permission from the copyright holder. Users should always contact the copyright holder to inquire about copyright restrictions and to obtain permission for reuse of the material. Many of the measures reviewed in this handbook are included on the accompanying CD-ROM, and some are available for use without any additional permission. However, inclusion of a measure on the CD-ROM does not indicate that readers can use it without permission from the copyright holder.

Psychometric Properties

The Psychometric Properties section provides statistics on the reliability and validity of the measure on the basis of available literature (see Chapter 2, "Psychometric Properties: Concepts of Reliability and Validity," for a detailed discussion of these concepts and for definitions of the terms mentioned in the following). For measures for which a large body of psychometric data is available, space considerations necessitated that the data be presented in aggregated form, giving the range of statistics across studies. The section on reliability typically begins with data on internal consistency, usually reported as Cronbach's alpha. In some cases, other forms of internal consistency (e.g., split-half reliability) are reported. Diagnostic agreement among different raters is then reported as joint reliability (multiple raters using the same source of information) and/or test-retest reliability (different raters making independent ratings at different times) over a particular time interval. For self-report measures, the same measure is administered to the same subject at different times.

The discussion of psychometric data on the measure's validity typically begins with comparisons with other measures that are purported to measure the same construct (concurrent or procedural validity). The ability of the measure to discriminate between individuals with and without the construct (discriminant validity) is usually presented next, often as significant differences in means between an affected and a control group (either nonpatients or those with a different disorder). Studies demonstrating other types of validity (e.g., construct validity, predictive validity, or sensitivity to change) are presented next. Studies that focus on factor analytic techniques are included only if their results are clinically relevant (e.g., a factor analytic study supporting the validity of a measure's subscales). P values and other indicators of statistical significance are not reported; in general, unless otherwise stated, correlations, differences in means, and other statistics are reported only if they are statistically significant.

Clinical Utility

The Clinical Utility section describes the potential clinical utility and limitations of the measure in particular settings and populations. For each type of potential clinical application, the extent and quality of the psychometric data, as well as practical issues such as the impact of the measure's length and complexity or training requirements for use of the instrument, are considered.

References and Suggested Readings

The most important references concerning the measure are included in the References and Suggested Readings section. Most measures have a key reference, usually by the measure's authors, that describes the measure and provides some of the basic psychometric data. Important studies referred to in the Psychometric Properties section may also be included here.

ABOUT THE CD-ROM

Accompanying the handbook is a CD-ROM that includes complete copies of measures that are either in the public domain or for which permission to reprint in this handbook was granted from the copyright holders. In all, 108 measures are included on the CD-ROM—over 900 pages. A list of the measures included on the CD-ROM is provided in Appendix C. The tables of measures that introduce each chapter also indicate which measures are included on the CD-ROM. The measures on the CD-ROM can be viewed on the computer screen or printed out. (Please note that some measures have copyright restrictions on further use; see the "Practical Issues" section for each measure in the handbook for more information about copyright restrictions.)

The CD-ROM also includes the complete, unabridged text of the *Handbook of Psychiatric Measures*, in fully searchable form. The electronic version is replete with links and cross-references, including links from the text of the handbook to the actual measures being discussed.

CHAPTER 2

Psychometric Properties: Concepts of Reliability and Validity

Deborah Blacker, M.D., Sc.D.
Jean Endicott, Ph.D.

INTRODUCTION

The term *psychometric,* which originally meant "mind measuring," is now used more generally to describe the performance characteristics of many types of measures. The two principal psychometric properties of a measure are reliability and validity. Although these words have overlapping meanings in common usage, in the context of evaluating measures they are distinct. To be useful, methods of classification should be reliable (i.e., consistent and repeatable even if performed by different raters at different times or under different conditions) and they should be valid (i.e., accurate in representing the true state of nature).

Most of the measures in this book are designed in part to improve the reliability and validity of patient assessment over what might be accomplished in a standard clinical interview. Thus, an evaluation of their reliability and validity is key to judging the potential value of each measure for a particular purpose. The purpose of this introductory chapter is to help the reader derive maximum benefit from the descriptive material provided on each measure by fostering an understanding of reliability and validity, their various forms, and the statistics that are used to assess them. The focus is conceptual rather than technical. Readers who wish to conduct a reliability or validity study or to understand how the statistics are used and calculated should consult a textbook of statistics, psy-

chometrics, or research methodology (e.g., Fava and Rosenbaum 1992; Hulley and Cummings 1988; Lord and Novick 1968; Nunnally 1978; Tsuang et al. 1995).

Background: Constructs and Their Assessment

The measures described in this book are aimed at assessing one or more constructs, each of which may have a single domain or multiple domains and subdomains. These domains may be conceptualized as substantially related or as independent, in which case they are often referred to as dimensions or axes. Many measures yield separate scores for multiple domains or dimensions, and the reliability and validity of each subscore can be assessed in addition to the reliability and validity of the total score.

In psychiatric practice and research, a broad range of constructs is assessed, including diagnoses, signs and symptoms, severity, impairment, family functioning, quality of life, and many others. Two broad approaches may be used to measure these constructs. *Categorical classification* is a qualitative assessment of the presence or absence of a given attribute (e.g., whether an individual should be committed on the basis of dangerousness to self or others) or the selection of the category best suited to a given individual among a finite number of options (e.g., assigning a diagnosis). The most frequent categorical classification used in psychiatry is diagnosis. Others include appropriateness for medication treatment, need for hospitalization, and eligibility for disability payments.

Continuous measures provide a quantitative assessment (e.g., along a continuum of intensity, frequency, or severity) of a specific attribute in a given individual. The most frequently used continuous measures in psychiatry assess symptom severity and functional status. A broad range of other attributes, including quality of life, patient satisfaction, and personality traits, are also generally measured continuously.

Categorical and continuous measurement, although conceptually distinct, are not entirely separable. First, ordinal classification, which uses a finite, ordered set of categories (e.g., unaffected, mild, moderate, and severe), stands between the two. The line between ordinal and continuous measures is ill-defined, although a putatively ordinal scale with 10 or more points is effectively continuous. Second, a cut point can be used with any continuous (or ordinal) scale to indicate a threshold for membership in a corresponding category. For instance, individuals with Mini-Mental State Exam (MMSE) (p. 422) scores below 24 may be considered to have dementia and those with Global Assessment Scale (GAS) (p. 96) ratings below 60 may be considered psychiatrically impaired. Quantitative thresholds are also embedded in most categorical diagnoses (e.g., five symptoms of depression are required to be present over a period of at least 2 weeks to make a DSM-IV diagnosis of major depressive episode).

Reliability and Validity and Their Relationship

Reliability refers to the consistency or repeatability with which subjects are discriminated from one another and is largely empirical. In the categorical context, it refers to whether we can agree on the classification of each individual. In the continuous context, it refers to whether we can agree on the assignment of a given score. It can also be seen as precision (i.e., whether a measure yields a ballpark estimate or a very finely graded score). Validity refers to conformity with truth or a gold standard that can stand for truth. In the categorical context, it refers to whether an instrument can make correct classifications. In the continuous context, it refers to accuracy, or whether the score we assign can be said to represent the true state of nature.

Reliability is sometimes said to put an upper limit on validity because the "noise" of poor reliability makes it hard to detect a valid "signal." However, reliability problems can be overcome to an extent by using repeated measures, canceling out some of the random error by av-

eraging or combining data from several assessments with the same unreliable measure (e.g., multiple diagnosticians). Unfortunately, improved reliability in no way guarantees improved validity. In fact, it is possible to improve reliability at the expense of validity. For example, an instrument for diagnosing personality disorders might focus on overt behaviors rather than inner thoughts and feelings to achieve higher reliability; however, in the process, it may lose some of the most valid information about personality. Even with clinically trained raters, it is particularly difficult to achieve reliability on items that require subjective clinical judgment (e.g., feelings evoked in the examiner); nonetheless, when used by experienced diagnosticians, such items may contribute substantially to valid diagnoses. With lay raters, reliability may be improved by using a highly structured diagnostic instrument that does not allow follow-up questions to clarify discrepancies or observations about patient responses; however, this approach may be less valid than an expert clinical interview. Because raters may differ in their ability to recognize that a patient's answer to a particular question is inaccurate due to a misunderstanding, restricted probing increases the likelihood that different raters will reach similar conclusions. However, a more open approach will allow the subset of raters with greater sensitivity to reach more accurate conclusions.

RELIABILITY

The reliability of a measure is the consistency or precision with which it can discriminate one subject from another. Although consistency and repeatability are the core of reliability, the focus is consistent discrimination, not merely agreement. Thus, the percentage of agreement between raters or occasions is not an index of reliability because it ignores variability among the subjects and fails to take into account chance agreement. For instance, imagine an effort to identify cases of schizophrenia in a primary care sample, in which the prevalence of schizophrenia would be expected to be extremely low. If two raters each assess 100 patients, and each identifies 2 entirely different cases of schizophrenia, they will agree on the diagnosis (nonschizophrenia) 98% of the time, even though they have no agreement whatsoever on which individuals have schizophrenia.

In the following sections the three standard forms of reliability—internal consistency, interrater reliability, and test-retest reliability—are described. When available, each of these forms of reliability is reported for each measure in this book, both for the measure as a whole and for any important subscales.

Internal Consistency

Internal consistency is a measure of agreement among the individual components of a measure. It is a measure of reliability because each item is viewed as a single measurement of the underlying construct; thus, the coherence of the items suggests that each of them is measuring the same thing (and hence that all of them are). Internal consistency is higher to the extent that the items are measuring a single dimension. The most frequently reported statistic is Cronbach's alpha (Cronbach 1951), which measures the degree to which the items covary with one another. Kuder-Richardson split-half reliability (Kuder and Richardson 1937), which measures the agreement between two halves of the scale, may also be reported, especially in older studies. Item-total correlation (i.e., the correlation of each item with the total score) is also sometimes used as an indicator of reliability. However, some modestly correlated items may be included in a scale because they are integral to the construct. For instance, in a measure of the positive symptoms of schizophrenia, extremely bizarre symptoms such as voices carrying on a running commentary may show only modest correlations with the total score but may be retained because they are very strongly associated with the disease when they occur.

One limitation of internal consistency as a way of judging a measure is that it depends on the internal consistency of the construct that the measure purports to assess. For instance, to the extent that neurovegetative and psychotic symptoms of mania are not perfectly correlated, the internal consistency of an overall mania measure may be decreased. When a measure assesses a multidimensional construct, the internal consistency of each relevant subscale may provide more useful information than the overall internal consistency. Partly for this reason, internal consistency provides a limited measure of reliability. However, because it can be easily estimated from a single administration of the measure, it is particularly suitable as a quick initial assessment of performance or as a periodic reassessment during ongoing use.

Joint and Test-Retest Reliability

Joint (also called interrater or interjudge) reliability is a measure of agreement between two or more observers evaluating the same series of subjects and using the same information. Estimates may vary with assessment conditions. In particular, a paradigm in which both raters watch the same high-quality videotaped interview is likely to achieve higher reliability than one in which an interview is conducted by one novice rater, with the other observing.

Test-retest reliability is a measure of agreement between evaluations at two points in time. Unlike joint reliability, it is suitable for self-report measures. For interviews or other rater assessments, two different raters are employed. In either case, test-retest evaluations measure reliability only to the extent that the subject's true condition remains stable in the time interval. It is critical to select a time interval short enough that little or no change occurs during the interval but also long enough that respondents are unlikely to recall their answers to the original interview. In practice, no interval satisfies these conditions for attributes that fluctuate over brief time periods (e.g., state anxiety), and compromises are inevitable. Moreover, even if patients' conditions remain the same, their answers to a given question may vary on the basis of their understanding of the question, how comfortable they feel giving a certain answer, how the interviewer phrased—or read—the question and follow-up, and so on.

Joint reliability tends to be higher than test-retest reliability because all information is shared; it is likely to overestimate the true reliability of the measure. Because the test-retest situation more closely reflects the clinical problems associated with serial evaluations by multiple clinicians, to the extent that concerns about change during the interval can be eliminated, it is generally a more useful indicator of reliability in practice.

Joint and test-retest reliability are both assessed by using the same statistics. For categorical measures, the statistic of choice is the kappa coefficient, which is a measure of agreement corrected for chance agreement (Fleiss 1981). A kappa of 1 would indicate perfect reliability, and a kappa of 0 only chance agreement. It is sometimes said that a kappa above 0.8 can be considered excellent, 0.7–0.8 good, 0.5–0.7 fair, and less than 0.5 poor. However, the need for reliability varies with the clinical context: settings in which small differences are clinically important may require very high reliability, whereas for other purposes fair to good reliability may be adequate.

For ordinal measures, weighted kappa (Cohen 1968) adjusts the level of disagreement on the basis of the distance between the two ratings. For example, a disagreement between mild and moderate is given less weight than one between mild and severe. For continuous measures, intraclass correlation coefficients (ICCs) are the statistic of choice (Shrout and Fleiss 1979). Of note, weighted kappa (given the proper weights) has been shown to be equivalent to the ICC (Fleiss and Cohen 1973). Like kappa, ICCs range from 0 to 1 and can be interpreted similarly.

Especially in older studies, other types of reliability statistics may be reported. Common ones include Yule's Y and Scott's pi, both of which, like kappa, are measures of agreement corrected for chance; they can be interpreted much as kappa would be. Less appropriately, percentage of agreement itself may be reported; as noted earlier, this statistic may overestimate reliability because it fails to correct for chance agreement. For continuous measures, a simple correlation coefficient rather than an ICC may be reported. This statistic too may overestimate reliability because it fails to take into account systematic biases (e.g., two raters can be perfectly correlated even if one consistently gives a score that is 5 points higher).

When interpreting reliability data, it is important to bear in mind that the reported reliability of a measure depends on several factors extrinsic to the measure itself. First, as with any statistic, reliability estimates on the basis of a small study may be inaccurate. Second, observed reliability depends not only on the subjects but also on testing conditions (e.g., a dark, noisy, or uncomfortable room may decrease reliability) and the rater's current status (e.g., an emotionally distracted or poorly trained rater will decrease reliability). On the whole, because of extensive rater training and optimal testing conditions, published reliability data tend to overestimate the reliability that can be obtained in ordinary clinical practice.

In addition, observed reliability depends on the nature of the sample on which the measure was tested. In particular, a large fraction of difficult cases (e.g., individuals near a diagnostic threshold or resistant to being interviewed) will diminish observed reliability. Furthermore, because greater effort is required to make relatively fine distinctions, reliability tends to be higher in samples with high variability. It is therefore particularly risky to generalize a reliability estimate from a heterogeneous population (e.g., a mixed group of psychiatric patients and healthy individuals) to a homogeneous population (e.g., a community survey, in which severe mental illness is rare). Thus, when selecting an instrument to be used in a certain population, reliability data from a similar population should be obtained whenever possible.

VALIDITY

The validity of a measure is the degree to which the diagnosis, category, rating, or score it yields is a reflection of the true state of nature. Although reliability is an empirical question, validity is partly theoretical; for many constructs measured in psychiatry, there is no absolute truth. Even so, some measures yield more useful and meaningful data than others, so that assessment of validity is of great value. Quantitative assessments of validity are possible to the extent that there is agreement on an appropriate gold standard or other criterion of accuracy against which the measure can be tested. Another indication of the validity of a measure is the degree to which it conveys information "beyond the score" (i.e., the expected correlates of the construct under study, often referred to as external validators).

A variety of terms are used to describe different aspects of validity. Because these aspects of validity have indistinct boundaries, and the terms describing them are not always used consistently by different authors, they are not generally used in this volume; however, validity data covering all of these areas are included. Basically, validity includes whether the items appear to assess the construct in question (sometimes called face validity) and provide good coverage of the relevant domain(s) (sometimes called content validity), whether the measure agrees with a gold standard or criterion of accuracy (sometimes called criterion, predictive, or concurrent validity), and whether the measure correlates as expected with external validators (sometimes called construct validity, which may include convergent, divergent, and discriminant validity, along with sensitivity to change).

Assessing the Items and Their Coverage of the Domain

A critical first step in deciding whether a measure is valid is deciding whether it appears to do what it claims to do, sometimes referred to as face validity (i.e., do the items, on their face, appear to be valid assessments of the construct in question?). In a related vein, it is critical to determine whether the items provide good coverage of the domain and subdomains of the construct, sometimes referred to as content validity. For instance, a measure of the symptoms of schizophrenia needs to include items that assess both positive and negative symptoms. The assessment of content validity is fundamentally qualitative and depends on a careful inspection of each item by someone who thoroughly understands the intent of the measure. In addition, quantitative techniques such as factor analysis (Kim and Mueller 1978) are sometimes used to assess which items pertain to each relevant subdomain. However, factor analysis provides no information about what critical items may be missing, and the results may vary substantially depending on the sample used.

A careful review of the items is essential for individuals considering use of a measure. The user must feel comfortable with the specific questions and their wording. In addition, it is critical to see precisely what is being measured; although a test may purport to measure a construct of interest, the developers may have conceptualized that construct very differently. For instance, a measure of insight may define insight in either psychoanalytic or neurological terms.

Assessing Validity With a Gold Standard

When a gold standard or other criterion of accuracy is available, a comparison with this standard is critical to assessing the measure's validity. This type of validity is sometimes referred to as criterion, predictive, or concurrent validity. For example, does a lay-administered diagnostic instrument make diagnoses consistent with those made by experienced clinicians? Does a school entrance exam predict good performance in school? Does a new brief mental status test score correlate with an established neuropsychological test?

When comparing continuous measures with a gold standard, a correlation coefficient is the statistic most often reported. For categorical variables such as diagnoses (or continuous measures with a cut point), sensitivity and specificity (Hulley and Cummings 1988; Zarin and Earls 1993) are the statistics of choice. Sensitivity refers to the test's ability to identify true cases, or its true positive rate. For instance, primary care physicians may have poor sensitivity in diagnosing major depressive disorder because they focus on mood symptoms rather than neurovegeta-

tive signs and thus miss many cases of depression. Specificity is the test's accuracy in identifying noncases, or one minus the false-positive rate. For example, lay interviewers may have poor specificity in diagnosing schizophrenia because they fail to discriminate between unusual experiences and abnormal ones and thus tend to overdiagnose psychosis.

The other key terms to understand concerning validity against a gold standard are positive predictive value and negative predictive value. Positive predictive value is the probability (in a given population) that a positive test result corresponds to a true case, and negative predictive value is the probability (in a given population) that a negative test result corresponds to a noncase. Positive and negative predictive value are characteristics of the test in a given population and are highly dependent on base rates; when the base rate of the disorder is low, a high false-positive rate will be observed even when using a test with very high specificity. For instance, the positive predictive value of virtually any test of psychosis in a community mental health center, where psychosis is common, would be very high, but it would be quite low in a community survey, where psychosis is rare.

Sensitivity and specificity are said to be properties of the measure itself, but they may also vary in different populations, especially if there are differing numbers of cases near a diagnostic or other threshold. For example, a measure that appears very sensitive in detecting depression in a setting in which all cases are severe may miss cases in a population that has a mixture of severe and mild cases.

Trade-offs between sensitivity and specificity are inevitable. In general, the more sensitive a test, the less specific it is. This trade-off is easiest to see when a threshold or cutoff score is used to define a true case: as the cutoff is lowered, sensitivity rises but specificity falls. For example, if we were trying to detect cases of severe depression by using a simple checklist and we set the threshold for a positive diagnosis very low, we would capture most of the cases—high sensitivity—but only at the expense of many false cases—low specificity. On the other hand, if we increased our threshold to decrease the number of false-positive results, we would inevitably miss true cases that deserved attention. This reasoning applies equally to an explicit cutoff score (e.g., 15 on the Hamilton Rating Scale for Depression [Ham-D] [p. 526]) or an implicit threshold (e.g., presence of five depressive symptoms almost every day for 2 weeks). Receiver operating characteristic (ROC) analysis, which plots the sensitivity and specificity of a scale as a function of the cutoff value, can help determine the optimal cutoff for a given purpose (Kraemer 1992; Murphy et al. 1987; Zarin and Earls 1993). This optimum depends on the base rate of the disorder and the impact of false-positive and false-negative results, as described in Chapter 3, "Considerations in Choosing, Using, and Interpreting a Measure for a Particular Clinical Context."

Although measuring validity against a gold standard provides a concrete and readily interpretable assessment of validity, the method is limited by the appropriateness of the gold standard as a stand-in for "truth." Before reported sensitivity, specificity, and the like are accepted as true indicators of the validity of a measure, it is critical to evaluate the adequacy of the gold standard. It is sometimes said that there are no gold standards in psychiatry. Few instruments can be validated on the basis of a definitive biological test, and many instruments designed in part to compensate for clinician fallibility must nonetheless be validated by a clinician interview. In some domains, there is a kind of circularity in which a handful of instruments, which often have many items in common, are validated against one another. However, when a reasonable gold standard is available, it can be quite helpful in establishing the validity of a measure. For example, the long form of an established instrument may properly be used to validate a shorter and thus more efficient form. For many constructs, a well-established instrument or procedure may be accepted as a standard validator; for example, the Structured Clinical Interview for DSM-IV (SCID) (p. 49) and the Schedule for Affective Disorders and Schizophrenia (SADS) (p. 58) serve as benchmarks for new diagnostic instruments. Overall, the optimal gold standard is generally whatever provides the most accurate and complete information. For instance, a proposed gold standard for diagnostic instruments is the LEAD standard—Longitudinal observation by Experts using All available Data as sources of information (Spitzer 1983)—which incorporates expert clinical evaluation, longitudinal data, medical records, family history, and any other sources of information. Analogous maximally complete data may be used to validate measures of other constructs (e.g., a compliance measure would be validated against a complete assessment on the basis of a clinician interview, pill counts, and urine or blood tests).

Assessing Validity Without a Gold Standard

When an adequate gold standard is not available, or whenever additional validity data are desired, one can compare the measure with external validators, which is sometimes referred to as construct validity (Cronbach and Meehl 1955). External validators are attributes that bear a well-characterized relationship to the construct under study but are "beyond the score" (i.e., are not measured directly by the instrument). Instruments that purport to measure a given construct are validated on the basis of their ability to identify individuals with the expected attributes. The line between a gold standard and an external validator is ill-defined, but on the whole gold standards represent fairly clear alternative ways to measure a construct (e.g., an established instrument measuring the same thing or a clinical exam for a self-report), whereas external validators are less directly related.

External validators used to validate psychiatric diagnostic criteria and the diagnostic instruments that aim to operationalize them include course of illness, family history, and treatment response (Robins and Guze 1970). Thus, for example, depression measures, when compared with schizophrenia measures, are expected to identify more individuals with a remitting course, a family history of major mood disorders, and a good response to antidepressant therapy. A broad range of external validators have been used to validate measures of different constructs. For instance, sociopathy would be expected to be associated with a significant criminal record, so that the construct validity of a sociopathy scale might be addressed by looking at whether the number of arrests and convictions for crime rises with an increased score on the scale.

Two special cases of assessing validity by using external validators are worth noting because of their clinical relevance. One is discriminant validity, which examines a measure's ability to discriminate between populations that are expected to differ on the construct of interest. For example, does a disability measure correctly separate individuals living in the community from those in a halfway house? Although such discriminations are important in clinical practice, the true test of a measure is its ability to discriminate at the margins. A study of discriminant validity is more clearly relevant if it includes the types of cases encountered in clinical practice (e.g., psychotic depression vs. schizoaffective disorder) rather than more easily discriminated populations (e.g., psychotic depression vs. psychiatric health). Another special case is sensitivity to change; the fact that a measure shows expected changes (e.g., an improvement with an efficacious treatment or a decrement with a progressive disease) can be a strong validator. However, before assuming that such a measure will serve to follow patients over time, sensitivity to change data must be reviewed carefully. First, the amount of change observed must be clinically relevant. Some instruments are able to detect large changes but may not demonstrate utility in measuring the smaller changes expected in routine practice. Second, the range of scores in which change can be observed must be relevant in a given setting. For instance, some mental status measures readily show decline in the early stages of dementia but not once the illness has become more severe; such measures are said to demonstrate a floor effect (i.e., progressive severity below a minimum score on the scale ["the floor"] cannot be detected by the scale). On the other hand, other mental status measures may perform well in the middle or late stages but cannot detect early decline, especially in highly educated individuals, because of a ceiling effect (i.e., the "true" initial score was above the ceiling, so that, even though decline has occurred, no change is detected).

Another technique sometimes used to assess validity without a gold standard is factor analysis (Kim and Mueller 1978). First, it is used to examine whether the intercorrelations among items demonstrate the expected structure for the construct (e.g., do the items from a schizophrenia measure "load on" [tend to be statistically associated with] factors related to both positive and negative symptoms?). Second, one can include not only items from the measure but also items from other instruments that measure similar and dissimilar constructs. The items from the construct under study are expected to load on the same factors as items from measures of similar constructs (sometimes called convergent validity) and on different factors from measures of different constructs (sometimes called divergent validity). For example, one would expect items from a schizophrenia measure to load with items from positive and negative symptom scales and not with items from a depression scale. However, the results of a factor analysis should be interpreted with caution, because they depend on the specific sample studied, the specific items included, and the details of the analysis itself.

Assessing validity in areas in which there are few established measures and for which a gold standard or criterion of accuracy cannot be established is difficult. The assessment of the validity of the measure is essentially a joint measure of the validity of the measure and the validity of the construct itself. For this reason, it is most problematic when it is most needed—for measures of newer, less validated constructs. Moreover, the various external validators may not all yield the same answer about the optimal measure or optimal definition of a construct (Kendler 1990). Nonetheless, by triangulating between a better definition of the construct, better ways to measure it, and better exploration of how it operates in clinical practice and research, the field moves to greater validity over time.

REFERENCES AND SUGGESTED READINGS

Cohen J: Weighted kappa: nominal scale agreement with provision for scaled disagreement or partial credit. Psychol Bull 70:213–220, 1968

Cronbach LJ: Coefficient alpha and the internal structure of tests. Psychometrika 16:297–334, 1951

Cronbach L, Meehl P: Construct validity in psychological tests. Psychol Bull 42:281–301, 1955

Fava M, Rosenbaum JF (eds): Research Designs and Methods in Psychiatry. Amsterdam, Elsevier, 1992

Fleiss JL: Statistical Methods for Rates and Proportions, 2nd Edition. New York, Wiley, 1981

Fleiss JL, Cohen J: The equivalence of weighted kappa and the intraclass correlation coefficient as measures of reliability. Educ Psychol Measmt 33:613–619, 1973

Hulley SB, Cummings SR: Designing Clinical Research: An Epidemiologic Approach. Baltimore, MD, Williams & Wilkins, 1988

Kendler KS: Toward a scientific nosology: strengths and limitations. Arch Gen Psychiatry 47:969–973, 1990

Kim JO, Mueller CW: Introduction to Factor Analysis: What It Is and How to Do It. Newbury Park, CA, Sage, 1978

Kraemer HC: Evaluating Medical Tests: Objective and Quantitative Guidelines. Newbury Park, CA, Sage, 1992

Kuder GF, Richardson MW: The theory of the estimation of test reliability. Psychometrika 2:151–160, 1937

Lord FM, Novick MR: Statistical Theories of Mental Test Scores. Reading, MA, Addison-Wesley, 1968

Murphy JM, Berwick DM, Weinstein MC, et al: Performance of screening and diagnostic tests: application of receiver operating characteristic analysis. Arch Gen Psychiatry 44:550–555, 1987

Nunnally JC: Psychometric Theory, 2nd Edition. New York, McGraw-Hill, 1978

Robins E, Guze SB: Establishment of diagnostic validity in psychiatric illness: its application to schizophrenia. Am J Psychiatry 126:983–987, 1970

Shrout PE, Fleiss JL: Intraclass correlations: uses in assessing rater reliability. Psychol Bull 86:420–428, 1979

Spitzer RL: Psychiatric diagnosis: are clinicians still necessary? Compr Psychiatry 24:399–411, 1983

Tsuang MT, Tohen M, Zahner GEP: Textbook in Psychiatric Epidemiology. New York, Wiley, 1995

Zarin DA, Earls F: Diagnostic decision making in psychiatry. Am J Psychiatry 150:197–206, 1993

Considerations in Choosing, Using, and Interpreting a Measure for a Particular Clinical Context

Deborah A. Zarin, M.D.

The use of measures in clinical practice can yield many benefits. However, the decision to use a particular measure in a specific clinical context can be complicated. The clinical utility of the measures discussed in this book is governed by the same principles that guide the use of diagnostic tests in all areas of medicine. The utility of any measure depends on the likely benefits (e.g., obtaining critical information), the likely adverse effects or costs (e.g., dollar costs and the negative consequences of false results), and the benefits and costs of alternative clinical strategies (e.g., using a different measure or not using a formal measure) (Eddy 1996; Weinstein et al. 1980; Zarin and Earl 1993). This chapter reviews general principles of testing as they relate to the decision to use a particular measure and summarize a logical process for making decisions about the clinical use of measures.

GENERAL COMMENTS ON USES OF MEASURES

Benefits to Individual Patients

The use of formal measures in clinical practice can improve the collection, synthesis, and reporting of information as compared with the use of unstructured clinical examinations. Specifically, formal measures can

- Ensure that relevant topics are covered in appropriate depth and decrease the likelihood of omitting impor-

tant domains of information. Some broad measures provide a mechanism for covering domains that are not under active consideration by the clinician (e.g., a broad diagnostic interview). These measures have advantages and disadvantages that are similar to those of other screening tests used in general medicine (e.g., a Chem 20).

- Categorize and/or quantify symptoms according to an agreed-upon system (e.g., a DSM-IV diagnosis or a symptom rating scale score).
- Provide consistency of assessment across time and across examiners and provide a standardized "language" for communication among professionals and with patients. For example, a DSM-IV diagnosis made on the basis of a structured interview or a score on a symptom rating scale has a consistent meaning.

Potential Costs for Individual Patients

The use of measures also entails costs. Direct costs include clinician and patient time (which might have been spent more beneficially in other ways) and any other costs associated with the measure (e.g., for materials or scoring). Indirect costs are more difficult to itemize but reflect a variety of potential negative consequences of using formal measures. For example, the use of measures may lead to suboptimal clinical decisions if the results are false (e.g., as in the case of a false-positive diagnosis). Even if the results are accurate, the quality of clinical care delivered based on the use of a formal measure may be diminished. For example, if clinicians begin to overvalue constructs or items that are easy to measure and are included in formal measures (e.g., suicidal behavior), they may consequently undervalue constructs that are difficult to measure but nonetheless clinically important (e.g., demoralization). Alternatively, data from formal measures (especially if they are quantified) may convey a greater degree of precision or certainty than is appropriate. For example, a quantifiable change in a rating scale score may convey more certainty about meaningful clinical change than is the case.

Potential Benefits for the Field

Clinical decision making may be improved by the availability and use of measures if the measures lead to the collection of more accurate information and if they improve the ability to communicate "clinical rules." For example, the widespread use in research studies and clinical practice of DSM diagnoses that are based on standardized assessments improves the ability of clinicians to determine which patients are likely to benefit from tested treatment strategies. The routine use of measures may also lead to advances in the field in less direct ways. For example, the routine use of structured (and perhaps quantified) measures in clinical practice may increase the likelihood that certain potentially important patterns will be detected, leading to the development of testable research hypotheses.

Potential Effects on the Doctor-Patient Relationship

The potential impact of a formal measure on the doctor-patient relationship should be considered before its use. Formal measures may be helpful or harmful to this relationship, depending on the clinical context and the specific attributes of the measure. In some situations, measures with broad coverage of symptoms may increase the patient's sense of having been carefully and thoroughly evaluated. Furthermore, measures (especially self-report questionnaires) may help both clinicians and patients address sensitive or embarrassing topics (e.g., drug use, binge eating, and sexual side effects). However, in other contexts, some patients may experience measures as a barrier to or an intrusion on the relationship with the clinician.

POTENTIAL USES OF MEASURES

When deciding whether to use a particular measure, it is important to consider its potential uses. The discussion of each measure in this handbook includes a description of the potential uses of the measure. The psychometric properties and other features of the measure are considered in the context of these potential uses. There are many ways to categorize the potential uses of measures or other tests. The categories listed in the following section are those used throughout this book.

Clinical Uses

Clinical uses are those designed to improve the care of individual patients and include the following categories:

- *Screening* is done to identify individuals in a target population who may need treatment, monitoring, or other intervention. Examples of target populations are an unselected community sample, a general medical population, or patients in a general psychiatric clinic. A variety of conditions (e.g., any psychiatric diagnosis, a particular diagnosis or symptom, or an adverse drug effect such as tardive dyskinesia) may be the focus of screening.
- *Diagnosis* according to DSM-IV or a similar system results in the categorization of a patient's condition according to an agreed-upon classification system.
- *Clinical features* beyond those needed to determine a diagnosis may be assessed to inform clinical decisions such as the selection of treatment and the level of care needed. Examples of clinical features include severity and characteristics of specific symptoms and aspects of functional capacity.
- *Beneficial and adverse effects* of treatments are monitored in order to make ongoing decisions about the need to continue or change the patient's treatment. One can assess for the presence and severity of symptoms, behaviors, or functional capacities that are the target of treatment interventions or other features of the patient's status that may change over time or be affected by treatment (e.g., monitoring the course of tardive dyskinesia).
- *Other uses* of measures may not directly affect treatment decisions but may be considered clinically important. For example, a measure could be used to assess prognosis.

Administrative Uses

Administrative uses are those designed to provide information that can be used to make administrative decisions, to improve the functioning of health care systems, or to aid in system planning and resource allocation. Examples include disability and forensic evaluations, health system quality assurance activities, and cost-effectiveness studies. Although the focus of this chapter is the clinical use of measures, many of the same principles apply to the use of measures for administrative purposes.

Use in Interpreting Research Studies

Clinicians rely on research studies to guide the selection of treatments and other interventions for their patients. The ability to properly interpret research reports is critical to this process. This handbook contains some measures that are primarily used in research settings to determine eligibility for studies, characterize subjects, and track changes in clinical status over the course of the study. Information is provided about each measure to enable clinicians to determine 1) whether the study is generalizable to their patients (i.e., was the study population similar enough to their clinical population?) and 2) the nature of the changes observed.

PRACTICAL ISSUES TO CONSIDER IN CHOOSING A MEASURE

Many features of a measure may affect its use. These features need to be considered in light of the intended use of the measure, the population in which it would be used, and other features of the setting. The practical issues discussed in the following should be considered.

Clinician Time

The clinician time needed to administer, score, and interpret a measure is highly variable. The availability of time and the alternative ways in which that time could have been used (i.e., the opportunity cost) need to be considered.

Patient Time

The patient time needed is also highly variable and is also associated with an opportunity cost.

Training Requirements

Training requirements for interviewers or evaluators vary across measures. Some require little training, whereas others require intensive training (e.g., a training course may be required or recommended).

Assessment of Psychometric Properties in Light of Potential Uses

The psychometric properties of measures were discussed in Chapter 2. This chapter focuses on ways in which a measure's psychometric properties may affect its functioning in a specific clinical context.

What Is the Purpose of the Measure in This Context?

Measures in this book are organized according to the construct(s) that they assess (e.g., diagnosis, severity of mood disorder, and functional status). The clinical utility of a measure, however, is generally determined by the degree to which it may inform a specific clinical decision (Weinstein et al. 1980). Clinical decisions are frequently made on the basis of a categorization of a patient into one of two or more groups (for continuous measures, this classification may mean determining whether the patient falls above or below an established cutoff point). Patients are categorized implicitly, rather than explicitly, in many cases. Examples include categorizing depressed patients into those who are likely or not likely to respond to an antidepressant medication and categorizing patients in crisis into those who require hospitalization and those who do not.* In this sense, measures can be thought of as discriminating one group of patients from another. In the previous examples, the "groups" are antidepressant responders versus nonresponders and patients who need hospitalization versus those who do not. In many clinical situations, a third "uncertain" group is also identified (e.g., patients for whom more information would be needed to determine whether they should receive an antidepressant). Many such decisions actually involve determining whether a patient falls above or below a cut-

---

*Although clinical decisions are generally made for individual patients, it is helpful to think about a group (or population) of similar patients. For example, when making decisions about one depressed patient, it may be helpful to think of 100 depressed patients with the same characteristics; some of these would be best treated with an antidepressant medication and some would be best treated without an antidepressant. The proportions of these two subgroups can be thought of as the probability that the one patient would benefit from an antidepressant.

off point on a continuous scale. For example, the hospitalization decision may be made on the basis of a scale of acute suicidal risk that specifies what risk warrants hospitalization.

The first step in considering the psychometric properties of a measure is to determine whether the groups that the measure is designed to discriminate between are relevant to the current clinical context. For example, if the clinical context entails determining whether the patient requires hospitalization, a measure that determines diagnosis or overall symptom severity (even with a high degree of accuracy) may not be helpful.

What Is the Expected Consequence, in Terms of True and False Results, of Using the Measure in This Context?

Figure 3–1 illustrates the results when a typical diagnostic test is used in two populations, one with a 50% prevalence of the target disorder and one with a 20% prevalence (Zarin and Earl 1993). Each curve represents the typical distribution of test scores in a population: the curve above the horizontal line is what might be expected in a population of those with the disorder and the curve below the horizontal line is typical for a population without the disorder. Thus, the vertical axis indicates the number of individuals with a particular test result; the region above the horizontal axis indicates the number of individuals with the target disorder who have the test result, and the region below the horizontal line indicates the number of individuals without the target disorder. For any diagnostic test, it is important to establish a cut point, above which individuals are considered to have a positive test result (i.e., to the right of the line) and below which individuals are considered to have a negative test result (i.e., to the left of the line). Four areas are therefore identified by the horizontal axis, the cutoff line, and the curves; these areas are labeled as true- and false-positive results and true- and false-negative results. Because the curves for those with and without the disorder overlap, there is no perfect cutoff score. Any placement of the cutoff line will result in some false results, although the relative sizes of the areas will vary.

What Groups Does the Measure Tend to Classify Correctly?

The *sensitivity* of a measure indicates the percentage of those with the disorder who are correctly classified. The *specificity* indicates the percentage without the disorder

who are correctly classified. The errors may be random or systematic. For example, a measure may correctly categorize individuals with severe disorders and do less well in categorizing individuals with less severe disorders. The nondisordered group may include individuals without any disorder and those with closely related disorders. Measures may be better at classifying some of these individuals and worse at classifying others. For example, measures may be particularly good at classifying those with a certain pattern of symptoms or those with particular sociodemographic characteristics (e.g., age, gender, and education). In other words, the specific features of the curves in Figure 3–1 depend on the characteristics of the group with disorders (above the horizontal axis) and the group without disorders (below the axis).

When considering the use of a measure for a particular context, it is thus important to determine the characteristics of the patient and the nature of the discrimination being sought. A diagnostic measure of depression could be used in a variety of age, gender, and socioeconomic groups, all of which may affect the accuracy of the measure. For example, it could be used to screen for depression among seemingly psychiatrically healthy individuals (i.e., discriminating between depression and no diagnosis), to identify depressed individuals who meet criteria for major depressive disorder (i.e., distinguishing between major depressive disorder and other mood disorders such as dysthymic disorder), or to distinguish between depression and dementia in an elderly group. In each example, knowledge of the types of patients who are likely to be falsely categorized would be helpful, in addition to summary knowledge of the sensitivity and specificity of the measure, including the characteristics of the population in which the sensitivity and specificity were derived.

What Are the Likely Rates of False-Positive and False-Negative Results in the Intended Clinical Context?

The sensitivity and specificity are reported, when available and applicable, for each measure in the handbook. (Refer to the section in Chapter 2 titled "Assessing Validity With a Gold Standard" [p. 11] for more information about these psychometric properties.) However, knowing the sensitivity and specificity of a measure is not enough to evaluate whether a measure will be useful in a clinical situation. Clinical decisions typically require knowledge of the positive predictive value and negative predictive value of a measure. In clinical situations, one knows the test result and needs to know the likelihood that, given a positive test, the patient has the disorder (or, given a negative test, the likelihood that the patient does not have the disorder). Table 3–1 shows the relationships among these statistics.

The sensitivity can be determined by examining the operation of the test entirely within the group with the disorder (i.e., looking only at the left column). The specificity can be determined by examining the operation of the test entirely within the group without the disorder (i.e., looking only at the right column). In general, sensitivity and specificity do not vary with the prevalence of the condition (or the relative mix between the two columns); this feature makes them relatively stable, which is why they tend to be reported. As noted previously, however, the nature of the groups with and without disorders (sometimes referred to as features of the case mix) can affect the sensitivity and specificity. The *predictive values* require an examination of both groups with and without disorders and thus depend, in part, on the relative sizes of the two groups; in other words, the prevalence of the condition affects the predictive values. Therefore, the clinician must consider the prevalence of the condition in the specific clinical context to determine the likely predictive values (and the likely false-positive and false-negative rates). When the prevalence in the intended setting is very different from the prevalence in the setting in which the psychometric properties were determined, the false-positive and false-negative rates could be very different. Figure 3–1 demonstrates the effect of prevalence. Note that as the prevalence decreases, the size of the false-positive area increases (and the relative size of the false-negative area decreases).

TABLE 3–1 ■ Relationships among test characteristics

	DISORDER PRESENT	DISORDER NOT PRESENT
Test +	A	B
Test −	C	D

Note. 1 minus the positive predictive value is the false-positive rate, and 1 minus the negative predictive value is the false-negative rate.

Sensitivity: A/(A + C)

Specificity: B/(B + D)

Positive predictive value: A/(A + B)

Negative predictive value: D/(C + D)

FIGURE 3–1 ■ Results of a typical diagnostic test when applied to populations with different prevalences of disorder

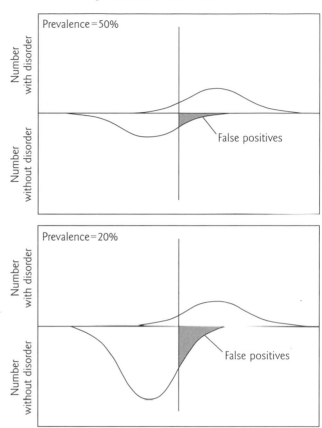

Source. Reprinted from Zarin DA, Earls F: "Diagnostic Decision Making in Psychiatry." *Am J Psychiatry* 150:197–206, 1993. Used with permission.

What Are the Likely Consequences of True and False Results?

The ultimate decision about a measure's utility depends on how the information will affect clinical decisions and outcome for the patient. Are patients with true-positive results better off than they would have been without the information? What about those with true-negative results? Conversely, are those with false-positive and false-negative results likely to experience adverse consequences? Specific features of the clinical situation determine the answers. For example, if one were screening for a condition with moderate morbidity and an excellent, low-risk treatment, the consequences of true-positive results would be good (i.e., receiving a highly effective treatment) and the consequences of false-positive results would be minimal (i.e., receiving an unnecessary but low-risk treatment). Those with false-negative results would not receive treatment, but the condition has only moderate morbidity. On the other hand, if one were screening for a condition with high morbidity and no available treatment (e.g., Huntington's disease), the value of a limited or true-positive result may be questionable, and the adverse consequences of a false-positive result may be high. Because most measures can be used in many different contexts, it is not possible to determine, in general, whether their use would be beneficial for an individual patient. When using continuous measures with cutoff points, it is possible to change the cutoff to optimize the operation of the measure in a specific clinical context.

ALTERATIONS IN THE CONTEXT IN WHICH THE MEASURE IS USED

Many features of the clinical context affect the utility of the measure. To the extent that these features differ between the test populations and the intended clinical situation, the clinician will need to assess the likely effect on the rates and consequences of true and false results.

Prevalence is one such feature. Effective prevalence may vary because of the setting (e.g., a psychiatric clinic vs. a general medical clinic vs. the community) or because of the clinical stage at which the measure is used. For example, a diagnostic measure for substance use could be used at intake in a psychiatric setting or only after the clinician has examined the patient and suspects a substance use disorder; the prevalence in the latter group would likely be much higher than that in the former.

The *cutoff* used also affects the rates of true and false results. If the cutoff line in Figure 3–1 is moved to the left or right, the relative sizes of the areas change, reflecting a trade-off between sensitivity and specificity. Therefore, it is important to know what cutoff was used when the psychometric properties were determined; if a different cutoff is to be used clinically, then the new psychometric properties should be considered. The optimal cutoff varies with the specific factors of the clinical situation because it depends on the consequences of true- and false-positive and true- and false-negative results. It may sometimes make sense to change the cutoff to account for changes in prevalence or in the specific use of the test.

In addition to prevalence, populations may vary with regard to sociodemographic features (e.g., age, gender, and educational status), specific characteristics of the group with disorders (e.g., severity and pattern of co-morbidities), and specific characteristics of the group without disorders (e.g., prevalence and pattern of other disorders). All of these characteristics may affect the expected rates of true and false results. It is thus important to consider how similar the target patient (or target group) is to the population that was studied because important differences will affect the accuracy of the test results for the target population.

Alternative Means of Obtaining the Clinical Information

Alternatives to the use of a particular formal measure include a clinical evaluation without the use of any formal measure, the use of a different measure, or the use of the same measure with a different informant (e.g., self-report, clinician, or family member). The benefits and costs associated with use of the best alternative should be compared with the benefits and costs associated with use of the measure under consideration. Simply knowing that a measure has excellent psychometric properties is not sufficient to determine its utility because it may or may not be better than available alternative clinical strategies.

Checklist for Use in Assessing Clinical Utility

The clinical utility of a measure is defined as the degree to which a strategy that involves use of the measure leads to better decisions (or outcomes) than a strategy that does not involve use of the measure. Sometimes a measure may also have utility for other clinical reasons (e.g., a measure of prognosis may be helpful to the patient and clinician without altering any treatment decisions).

The following checklist can be used in considering the use of a measure:

- Likely use(s) of the measure
- Practicality for that use
- Likely proportions of true and false results for the intended use
- Clinical consequences of true and false results
- Alternative means of obtaining the clinical information
- Comparison of "balance sheet" with available alternatives

REFERENCES AND SUGGESTED READINGS

Eddy D: Clinical Decision Making. London, Jones & Bartlett, 1996

Sackett D, Haynes R, Guyatt G, et al: Clinical Epidemiology: A Basic Science for Clinical Medicine. Boston, MA, Little, Brown, 1991

Weinstein MC, Fineberg HV, Elstein AS, et al: Clinical Decision Analysis. Philadelphia, PA, WB Saunders, 1980

Zarin D, Earl F: Diagnostic decision making in psychiatry. Am J Psychiatry 50:197–206, 1993

Considerations in Choosing, Using, and Interpreting Measures for Health Care Systems

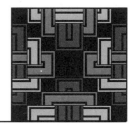

G. Richard Smith Jr., M.D.

INTRODUCTION

This chapter describes a new arena for mental health measurement, namely the assessment of systems of care and of patients within systems of care. As health care systems become more highly organized, this type of assessment is becoming increasingly routine as systems attempt to maintain or improve the quality of the care they provide. The goal of this chapter is to acquaint readers with the terms and concepts used in this area and to promote a common understanding of potentially confusing terms. The chapter serves as an introduction for several of the later chapters in this book, including Chapter 12, "Patient Perceptions of Care Measures," and Chapter 13, "Practitioner and System Evaluation." The chapter begins with an organizing framework and then moves to a discussion of the domains and levels of measurement. Next, the types of assessments and the potential uses of these assessments are described. Finally, important design issues, properties of measurement tools, and practical issues are presented.

ORGANIZING FRAMEWORK

Table 4–1 and Table 4–2 present a general organizing framework for measurement of systems of care and of patients within systems of care. Specific to this type of mea-

TABLE 4–1 ■ General organizing framework for measures

SOURCE OF INFORMATION	USE OF INFORMATION	
	PATIENT LEVEL	SYSTEM LEVEL
Patient level	Type A	Type B
System level	Type C	Type D

surement is the notion of needing to specify the level of measurement. Table 4–1 seeks to distinguish between the source of the information (from patients or from the system of care) and the use of the information (to inform about a specific patient or about a system of care). Type A measures use information from the individual patient as the source of data and provide data about that particular patient. Most of the measures described in this book are Type A measures. Type B measures use information from specific patients as the source of data but provide information about the system of care. Type B measures are usually Type A measures that collect data in a manner that is representative of a particular system of care.

Type C measures are typically derived from information management systems (e.g., computerized pharmacy records) that are maintained to assist in the operation of health care systems. This information originates at the system of care level but can be attributed to a specific patient. Finally, Type D measures neither use in-

TABLE 4–2 ■ Types of assessments covered in this handbook

	DOMAINS OF MEASUREMENT							
	SYSTEM LEVEL				PATIENT LEVEL			
TYPES OF ASSESSMENT	ACCESS TO CARE	PATIENT CHARACTERISTICS	PROCESS OF CARE	OUTCOMES OF CARE	PATIENT CHARACTERISTICS	PROCESS OF CARE	OUTCOMES OF CARE	SATISFACTION WITH CARE
General health	Not covered in handbook	Not covered in handbook	Not covered in handbook	Usually aggregates of patient-level assessment (Chapter 9)	Not covered in handbook	Not covered in handbook	Chapter 9	Chapter 12
General mental health	Not covered in handbook	Usually diagnostic frequencies from administrative databases or aggregates of patient-level data (Chapters 6, 7, and 17)	Not covered in handbook	Usually aggregates of patient-level assessment (Chapter 8)	Broadly covered throughout handbook	Not covered in handbook	Covered throughout handbook	Chapter 12
Disease specific	Not covered in handbook	Aggregate of patient-level assessment (Chapter 13)	Aggregate of patient-level assessment (Chapter 13)	Usually aggregates of patient-level assessment (many measures in Section III and some in Chapter 13)	Broadly covered throughout handbook	Chapter 13	Some measures in Chapter 13 and some in Section III	Not covered in handbook

formation on specific patients as the source of the information nor provide information about specific patients. An example of this type of measure is hospital readmission rates.

Generally, data specific to a particular patient are referred to as patient-level data, whereas system-level data are often reflective of the entire system but not of any individual patient. Patient-level data can be and often are aggregated to reflect the system of care. To be representative of the system of care, the patient-level data must be obtained in a systematic manner that allows use of statistical approaches to reflect the entire system of care. The most straightforward approach is to obtain data on every patient in the system and then use a summary statistic to describe the population under care. However, it is often impractical to obtain or even try to obtain data on every patient. In most cases, statistical sampling approaches are used to assess a group of patients who are considered to be representative of the population.

DOMAINS AND LEVELS OF MEASUREMENT

As shown in Table 4–2, there are four categories of measurement under the system level of organization: access to care, patient characteristics, process of care, and patient outcomes of care. These four aspects are described in the following discussion. Two additional aspects of systems are often included in assessments of how well a system functions: the structure of care and the cost of care. The structure of care refers to the structural aspects of care such as whether the health care organization has a charter and bylaws or whether nonflammable anesthetics are used in the operating rooms. The costs of care often refer to the direct costs of care, or the amount of money required to operate the system of care. Neither the structure nor the costs of care have direct patient components and are therefore beyond the scope of this handbook.

Access to care refers to whether a person in need of care enters care. Access to care does not measure the need for care, only whether a person enters care. Multiple patient factors, such as motivation for treatment, and multiple system factors, such as the availability of appointment times or the convenience of clinical locations, affect the accessibility of a system. Access to care is mea-

sured on a system-level basis, not a patient-level basis (i.e., a given patient either enters or does not enter care). Usually, access is reported as treated prevalence rates such as 6 people receiving care per year of the 100 in the covered population (sometimes called penetration rates in the managed-care industry). Although access to care is not usually broken into subcategories, it could be subdivided as access to care for general health treatment (e.g., the ability to obtain primary care), access to care for general mental health treatment (e.g., programs in which diagnoses are often not important), and access to disease-specific care for a certain diagnosis. Data concerning access to care are often obtained from administrative data sets such as billing records. At other times, surveys are fielded to determine the percentage of eligible people who receive care in a given year.

Patient characteristics refer to the aspects of the person receiving care or, on a system level, to the collective aspects of the people receiving care. Information about patient characteristics is often used to determine the relative difficulty of treating the population of people under care. Patient characteristics may be assessed via survey research approaches to understand the characteristics of the entire group of people receiving care in a system or assessed as an aggregate of individual patient-level data. Patient characteristics include standard sociodemographic information such as age, race, gender, education, and income. The clinical status of the person or persons is also considered a patient characteristic. Relevant information concerning clinical status often depends on the disorder or disorders under consideration. Factors that make up the case mix characteristics for the population are also included. These case mix characteristics are usually disease specific and include factors that predict response to treatment. For example, in major depressive disorder, case mix factors might include previous response to treatment, comorbid substance dependence or abuse, and the presence of a personality disorder. Data concerning patient characteristics are most often collected directly from the patient via patient self-report. For some patients, such as those with psychotic disorders or children, these characteristics are often obtained via an interview. Some system evaluations allow the clinician and others to report patient characteristics. For conditions such as schizophrenia, family members or others who know the patient well report patient characteristics.

Processes of care, or patient treatment approaches in clinical settings, include data such as what type and what dose of medication the patient received, whether the patient received psychotherapy and at what frequency during a specific period, and whether the patient was admitted to the hospital and for how many days. Therefore, these types of data include health care utilization information (e.g., hospital days and outpatient visits) and clinical processes (e.g., medication dosage). In highly automated health care systems, the health care utilization information is often obtained from automated management information systems such as billing systems or accounting systems. Increasingly, pharmacy management systems are also able to provide process of care information about medication type and dosages. However, most of the time, utilization information and clinical information are obtained via a chart abstraction system or from patient self-report. Process of care information may thus be assessed at the system level or at the patient level and then aggregated from the patient level to the system level. The clinician is asked to provide this information relatively rarely.

Data about *patient outcomes of care* refer to how well or poorly the patient is doing relative to the primary disorder for which the patient is receiving care. The outcomes may be general health outcomes such as general physical health, social health, or disability. Patient outcomes may also be assessed in terms of generic mental health such as global levels of anxiety or dysphoria or a total count of symptoms of mental illness. However, increasingly patient outcomes are being assessed relative to a specific disease or disorder for which the patient is receiving care. Disease-specific assessment allows for in-depth data acquisition about multiple aspects of the disorder of interest while avoiding irrelevant questions about symptoms unrelated to that condition. For example, although it is important to assess anticipatory anxiety in patients with panic disorder, that symptom has little relevance for patients with major depressive disorder. For the vast majority of disorders, the patient outcomes of care are assessed from the patient's perspective by asking the patient direct questions through either interviews or self-report questionnaires. Occasionally, someone who knows the patient well, such as a family member for a patient who has, or has had, psychotic disorders or a parent for a young child, is asked about the patient's status. Patient outcomes may be assessed via survey research approaches such as trained interviewers who visit the patient in his or her home or telephone interviewers who use computer-assisted interviews to reflect the outcomes

of a system of care. Alternatively, individual patient-level outcomes obtained in the clinical setting may be aggregated to reflect the system of care. Clinicians are rarely asked about patient outcomes because high-quality data may be obtained directly from patients, and data derived from patients are assumed to have higher validity than data derived from clinicians.

The same variables used to assess patient characteristics at the system level (described earlier) are used to assess patient characteristics at the patient level; however, each patient is assessed, and the data can be attributed to the particular patient. Similarly, process of care data and patient outcomes data are often the same variables as used in system-level assessment; however, the data are collected in a manner reflective of a given patient as well as of the population of patients under care.

Data on *patient satisfaction* are often collected in health care settings and are most frequently patient-level data. These data are usually then aggregated to reflect the population under care. Patient satisfaction may be assessed through a variety of instruments and from at least three perspectives, as described in the following section.

TYPES OF ASSESSMENTS

Health system outcomes assessments can be subdivided into three categories: general health, general mental health, and disease- or disorder-specific assessment. General health assessment, often called health status assessment, is concerned with the patient's overall health. Traditionally, this category has included physical health, mental health, social health, health perceptions, and disability as defined by the World Health Organization in 1948 (World Health Organization 1948). Chapter 9, "General Health Status, Functioning, and Disabilities Measures," describes these assessments.

General mental health assessment can be a subset of general health status assessment or a separate construct. Mental health research has a long history of using general mental health assessments; in other settings these assessments are often referred to as general symptom inventories, such as the Symptom Checklist–90—Revised (SCL-90-R) (p. 81). The concept refers to assessing the general symptoms of people with mental disorders. Usually, one inventory covers all symptoms; therefore, the instrument must be broadly based and typically collects only modestly detailed information. Although mental health clinicians have long relied on this type of measurement, the field is increasingly moving away from using only general mental health status assessment to a strategy that combines a general approach with a disease-specific approach.

Disease- or disorder-specific health status assessment is an innovation modeled on other areas of medicine in which health status assessment across diseases is not helpful (e.g., using a common assessment approach for both hip fracture and asthma). Similarly, when detailed patient characteristics, process of care information, and/or patient outcomes data are needed, the disease-specific characteristics of two different disorders, such as panic disorder and schizophrenia, far outweigh their similarities and therefore require different measurement tools. Disease-specific assessment allows for in-depth data collection of variables unique to the disorder and to the person without burdening the patient with irrelevant questions. Disease-specific assessment is thus usually much more thorough for a given disorder yet less broadly applicable. For instance, the assessment for a substance use disorder includes substantial detail about substance dependence and abuse but has very little if any applicability to patients with major depressive disorder without comorbid substance use disorder. Examples of disease-specific assessments for major depressive disorder include the Inventory of Depressive Symptomatology (IDS) (p. 529) and the Depression Outcomes Module (DOM) (p. 213).

The following sections provide examples of the types of measurement instruments that fit into cells in Table 4–2 and indicate where they are described in this handbook. The types of measurement instruments not covered in this handbook are also described.

System-Level Access to Care

All approaches to assessing system-level access to care require survey research techniques; such instruments are not covered in this manual.

System-Level Patient Characteristics

General Health Patient Characteristics　　Data about generic factors that affect the outcomes of all health care (e.g., income, education, and social support) may be reflective of the population as a whole but not of a given patient. They are often obtained from administrative databases. Instruments that assess general health patient characteristics are not covered in this handbook.

General Mental Health Patient Characteristics　　System-level data for general mental health patient characteristics are usually diagnostic frequencies from administrative data sets. Alternatively, these data are obtained by aggregating patient-level data from measures covered in Chapter 6, "Diagnostic Interviews for Adults," Chapter 7, "General Psychiatric Symptoms Measures," and Chapter 17, "Child and Adolescent Measures for Diagnosis and Screening."

Disease-Specific Patient Characteristics

Factors that affect the outcomes of a particular disorder and are unique to the patient (e.g., previous response to pharmacotherapy or the presence of a comorbid personality disorder in a patient with major depressive disorder) are patient specific; therefore, when used at the system level, they are an aggregate of patient-level data. These measures are covered in Chapter 13 and throughout Section III.

System-Level Process of Care Variables

General Health Process of Care　　Examples include process of care factors that affect general health (e.g., immunization rates and fecal occult blood screening). Such measures are not covered in this handbook.

General Mental Health Process of Care　　Factors relevant to the process of care for all mental disorders (e.g., screening for substance abuse and the use of a diagnostic system) are included in this category. Examples include counts of mental health services provided without regard to diagnosis (e.g., number of patients receiving any form of psychotherapy). Such measures are not covered in this handbook.

Disease-Specific Process of Care　　Disease-specific process of care factors are elements of care that should be addressed in the treatment of a particular disorder (e.g., whether a patient with depression is suicidal or whether a patient with panic disorder is given medication to block panic attacks). Usually, system-level, disease-specific process of care data are aggregate patient-level data. Examples include the Depression Outcomes Module (DOM) (p. 213) and the Schizophrenia Outcomes Module (SCHIZOM) (p. 218).

System-Level Outcomes of Care

General Health Outcomes of Care   Examples include efforts to assess how well the system is performing in enhancing the health or maintaining the health of the people it covers through survey research techniques or the aggregation of individual reports of general health. General health status assessment is covered in Chapter 9, "General Health Status, Functioning, and Disabilities Measures."

General Mental Health Outcomes of Care   General mental health outcomes of care can be assessed via survey research approaches (e.g., to determine whether a Medicaid population is being well served by a managed-care contract) or through the aggregation of general mental health status assessment of people receiving care in the system. Although survey research approaches are not included in this volume, general mental health status assessment is covered in Chapter 8, "Mental Health Status, Functioning, and Disabilities Measures."

Disease-Specific Outcomes of Care   Information regarding disease-specific outcomes of care may be obtained through survey research approaches or an aggregation of outcome data from patients receiving care for a particular condition (e.g., major depressive disorder or schizophrenia). Many of the measures included in Section III can be administered using a survey research methodology, and the four outcomes modules from Chapter 13 can also be used for this purpose.

Patient-Level Patient Characteristics

General Health Patient Characteristics   Examples include demographic characteristics. Such measures are not covered in this handbook.

General Mental Health Patient Characteristics   Examples include global measures of dysphoria or anxiety for a specific patient. Often a global measure of dysphoria is also an outcomes measure. Demographic characteristics are more general and therefore are usually covered in general health instruments, but they obviously affect mental health as well. Many of the categories are not mutually exclusive. These measures are covered throughout this handbook.

Disease-Specific Patient Characteristics   Examples relate to a specific patient with a specific disorder (e.g., prognostic factors for recovery in a patient with major depressive disorder or cocaine dependence). These measures are covered in Chapter 13 and broadly in Section III.

Patient-Level Process of Care

General Health Process of Care   Examples are whether a specific patient was immunized for influenza or had a Papanicolaou test. Such measures are not covered in this handbook.

General Mental Health Process of Care   Examples are whether a psychiatric outpatient receives a comprehensive diagnostic evaluation on the initial visit or whether a patient with major depressive disorder is receiving adequate doses of an antidepressant. Such measures are not covered in this handbook.

Disease-Specific Process of Care   Examples are whether a patient with schizophrenia receives assertive community treatment or whether a patient with substance abuse participates in intensive outpatient treatment. Some measures in Chapter 13 collect these data.

Patient-Level Outcomes of Care

General Health Outcomes of Care   Examples are whether a patient with hypertension has a diastolic blood pressure below 90 mm Hg or whether a patient with congestive heart failure is able to walk up a flight of stairs. General health status and functional scales are covered in Chapter 9.

General Mental Health Outcomes of Care   Examples are whether a patient with breast carcinoma has symptoms of anxiety 6 months after a mastectomy or whether a patient in psychotherapy has depressive symptoms. These measures are covered throughout this handbook.

Disease-Specific Outcomes of Care   Examples are whether a patient with panic disorder develops anticipatory anxiety or whether a patient with substance abuse develops legal problems. Some of the measures are covered in Chapter 13, and others are covered throughout Section III.

Patient-Level Satisfaction With Care

Patient-level satisfaction with care refers to how satisfied a particular patient or group of patients is with the care received. Although satisfaction measures generally relate to overall judgments about health care, some instruments are more applicable to specific health care settings (e.g., mental health settings and dialysis units). These measures are covered in Chapter 12.

POTENTIAL USES OF MEASUREMENTS

There are numerous potential uses for measures that assess systems of care and patients within systems of care in health care settings today. Potential uses include efforts to enhance quality, to increase efficiency or to control costs, to introduce innovation, and to demonstrate accountability.

There are two types of quality enhancement efforts: quality assurance and quality improvement. Quality assurance usually involves a retrospective analysis of some aspect of care. These studies often focus mainly on the processes of care, usually at the patient level. For instance, a quality assurance study could be done to determine the percentage of patients with suicidal ideation who were evaluated for major depressive disorder and substance use disorders. Measurement tools from both the system-level and patient-level categories are appropriate for quality assurance efforts.

Quality improvement is a prospective effort that may involve elements of patient characteristics, process of care, and/or outcomes of care. These efforts may occur at the system or the patient level. For example, a clinic may seek to improve the outcomes of patients with major depressive disorder by increasing the number of patients who are receiving guideline-concordant pharmacotherapy for their depression. Such an approach would require the use of assessment tools, sometimes called outcomes modules, that measure patient characteristics (e.g., diagnostic assessment of depression), process of care (e.g., medication type, dosage, and frequency), and patient outcomes (e.g., depression diagnosis, depression severity, and disease-specific disability). Measurement tools of this type are described in Chapter 13.

There is a great demand in today's health care system to improve efficiency and control costs. Studies to understand how to control costs often need to relate diagnosis to health care utilization; they therefore involve assessments of patient characteristics and of the process of care. For example, assessments of both are necessary to understand how hospital days of care used by patients with schizophrenia relate to whether they are also re-ceiving assertive case management. Efficiency studies frequently focus on hospital-based treatment pathways for a particular disorder (e.g., how the length of stay for patients receiving electroconvulsive therapy for major depressive disorder can be reduced). These types of studies require some assessment of patient characteristics (diagnosis) (Chapter 7 and Section III) and process of care (utilization) (Chapter 13).

Innovation efforts are frequently efforts to improve outcomes and typically require the implementation of outcomes management systems. These systems seek to provide clinical information, usually for patients with a given disorder, in a manner analogous to that used in financial information systems. In other words, just as one would maintain financial accountability with an accounting system, one would maintain clinical accountability with a clinical information system. Clinical accountability requires the assessment of patient characteristics, processes of care, and outcomes of care, which are the components of outcomes modules. For example, a community mental health center might operate an outcomes management system for patients with major depressive disorder to learn about the care it provides and the outcomes it produces. Tools for this type of system are found in Chapter 13.

Four types of accountability demonstrations are increasingly being required in today's health care environment: population monitoring, accreditation, outcomes monitoring, and provider profiling. Population monitoring is often instituted at the behest of some health or health care authority (e.g., a state Medicaid director). This effort seeks to determine whether the mental health status of a population is enhanced or maintained by a contract with a managed-care company. Population surveys of this type are done most efficiently at the system of care level by monitoring the general mental health status of the population. Tools for this type of assessment are covered in Chapter 7 and Chapter 8.

Several accrediting organizations have recently begun to require health care systems to provide the results of systematic assessment of performance measures (often patient outcomes measures) to receive accreditation. An example of this type of assessment is the number of patients with major depressive disorder who are discharged from a hospital on a guideline-concordant dose of medication. Patient outcomes modules are found in Chapter 13. Health care providers are increasingly seeking to monitor their own practices, most often through an outcomes management system, as described previously. Tools for this type of assessment are found in Chapter 13.

Finally, many managed-care organizations and other provider groups, such as large hospital systems, undertake provider profiling in an effort to decrease costs or improve care within their systems. Although this approach often involves only an assessment of utilization, more sophisticated systems also assess the degree of severity of the patients' symptoms (patient characteristics) and the outcomes of care to better differentiate among providers. These measures are found in Chapter 13.

MEASUREMENT DESIGN ISSUES

Several measurement design issues are important in assessment of systems of care and of patients within systems of care, including whether the measurement is appropriate to the purpose, the perspective of the person providing the assessment (i.e., the source of the information), and the assessment strategy. Whether the measurement is appropriate to the purpose is critical to obtaining value from the study being conducted. For example, if the intent of the study is to assess patient outcomes for a certain disorder, then a disease-specific assessment for that disorder must be used; a general mental health assessment alone would therefore not meet the needs of the study.

The source of the assessment is an important consideration and includes the patient, family members, and providers. The patient is the strongly preferred source of information, especially concerning outcomes, functioning, and quality of life. In fact, in most outcomes evaluations, it is presumed that the patient is the source of the information and that other sources are used only if there is substantial justification for doing so. The next most desirable source of information concerning patient health status and functioning, if the patient is unavailable or unable to provide the information, is a family member or another person with close personal knowledge of the patient's day-to-day functioning. At times, for patients with psychotic disorders, such as schizophrenia, and cognitive impairment disorders, such as dementia, family members are the only source available to provide health status information. Although providers of care, such as physicians, have long been the source of most information about a patient's health

status, the current work in fields such as accountability and quality of care rely on patient self-report over clinician report, which may be misinformed at best and biased at worst.

Assessment strategies are essential for successful evaluations of health systems. Two issues are key to this area: the external validity of the data and clinically meaningful follow-up time points. External validity refers to what degree the data obtained are generalizable to the population of interest. The goal is to have data that are reflective of the group or population of patients who are receiving care in the system. Therefore, the data reported must be from the entire population or from a representative sample of the population. Because it is rarely feasible to report on an entire population, a sample of the population is usually the solution. One type of sample is the convenience sample, which usually is used in an attempt to measure an entire population when only a percentage of the population is assessed. Because this type of sample is extremely prone to bias, the standard for a convenience sample to be representative of the population is often 70%–80% of the population. Operationally, this level of participation is very difficult to achieve. The second type of sample is a representative sample, in which patients are scientifically sampled to be a part of the study. Much lower percentages of the population can have scientific validity if patients are properly chosen. The key point of this latter type of sample is that it must be representative of the population of interest.

Meaningful follow-up at clinically relevant time points is important in seeking to understand the relationship of patient characteristics, processes of care, and outcomes of care within a system. For example, substantial clinical improvement in a patient with major depressive disorder would not be expected to occur by the end of the first week of treatment but would be expected to occur after 3 months of treatment. Programs often seek to collect outcomes data at points when patients are changing from one part of a system of care to another (e.g., hospital discharge); if this change occurs after the first week of treatment for major depressive disorder, little is gained from the assessment. Clinically meaningful assessment time points vary by condition. Patients with major depressive and panic disorders are often assessed at 3-month intervals, those with substance abuse are often assessed at 6-month intervals, and those with more chronic conditions in which change is very slow, such as schizophrenia, may require intervals of 9–18 months.

ASSESSMENT OF MEASUREMENT PROPERTIES IN LIGHT OF POTENTIAL USES

There are several key issues concerning measures chosen for the assessment of systems of care and of patients within systems of care, including the psychometric properties of the measurement tools, the comprehensiveness of the assessment tools, the costs of the assessment, and the feasibility of the assessment strategy. Necessary psychometric properties are demonstrated validity and reliability, as discussed in Chapter 2, "Psychometric Properties: Concepts of Reliability and Validity." Measures in this arena must also be sensitive to clinically important change. For example, an assessment tool for depression should be able to detect when a patient goes into remission from the disorder, not simply whether his or her symptoms have improved. The comprehensiveness of the assessment is also important; the broadness or narrowness of the assessment should be determined on the basis of what questions are being asked by the evaluation system. In assessing patients with major depressive disorder, it is much simpler to measure a reduction in depressive symptoms than it is to assess the effectiveness of treatment, given the many effects expected from successful treatment.

Cost of measurement is also an important consideration. Costs include the burden to the patient in terms of time, effort, discomfort, and perhaps travel. Costs to the provider should also be considered and include the operational burden of measurement within the system of care relative to the benefit of the assessment. Finally, the direct costs of measurement are important and include the costs of using the tests themselves, personnel time, and any necessary equipment.

The feasibility of the measurement system should also be considered. For example, can the system actually capture the data needed to be representative of the population of interest? How easy or difficult is it to acquire the data? Can this measurement approach actually be done within the system or will the system of care need to be changed to accommodate the measurement process?

CONCLUSION

In this chapter the assessment of systems of care and of patients within those systems of care has been described. These approaches are multilevel in nature and are focused on whether the system of care had a positive impact on the patients' views of the care received. The approaches differ from the more familiar clinical assessments of patients; however, in the current health care environment, the clinician is well advised to be knowledgeable of these approaches.

REFERENCES

World Health Organization: Constitution of the World Health Organization, in Basic Documents. Geneva, World Health Organization, 1948

Cultural Factors Influencing the Selection, Use, and Interpretation of Psychiatric Measures

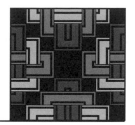

Maritza Rubio-Stipec, M.A.
Madelyn Hsiao-Rei Hicks, M.D.
Ming T. Tsuang, M.D., Ph.D., D.Sc.

INTRODUCTION

As communications improve and populations become more mobile, it is increasingly likely that clinicians trained in one culture will be faced with the challenge of treating persons from other cultural backgrounds. Cross-cultural studies provide important information for clinicians trying to understand how patients from different cultures can vary in the clinical features and communication of their illness and in the factors that affect their risk and outcome. Cross-cultural studies also provide a useful means of comparing the relative effects of biological and environmental factors on the development, course, and outcome of psychiatric disorders. For such studies to be valid, assessment of illness and outcome must take place within the cultural context in which the illness is manifested.

Social, economic, educational, and cultural factors all affect the measurement of psychiatric illness. This chapter focuses specifically on the influence of culture on the assessment of psychiatric illness and outcomes. Various approaches that are used to take culture into account in research and clinical assessment are surveyed, and suggestions for clinicians on how to address the impact of cultural differences on clinical assessment are provided.

ETHNIC AND CULTURAL ISSUES IN PSYCHIATRIC ASSESSMENT

An awareness of the cultural frame of reference is essential in correctly differentiating between pathological and nonpathological variants of behavior, belief, or experience particular to the individual's culture. Appendix I of DSM-IV recommends that clinicians assess cultural factors in four specific areas to formulate an appropriate diagnosis and intervention for the patient:

1. Cultural identity of the individual
2. Cultural explanations of the individual's illness
3. Cultural factors regarding the social environment and level of functioning
4. Cultural factors in the relationship between the individual and the clinician

It is important to consider these four areas when selecting assessment instruments or interpreting published research involving different ethnic groups. Such attention to the sociocultural framework of the study population and the researcher is necessary because consonance between the instruments used for case identification or outcome measurement and the cultural framework of the study population lends validity to the findings. Key ways in which cultural and socioeconomic factors are relevant to psychiatric measurement are described in the following sections.

Cultural Identity, Acculturation, and Classification

Cultural identity is generally a powerful indicator of commonly recognized values, themes, and social histories, all of which contribute to an individual's social context and experience of illness. One way to approach the issue of measuring cultural identity, particularly among immigrant populations, is by assessing acculturation. Some measurements of acculturation use a linear scale on which the immigrant is rated as more acculturated or less acculturated to the host culture, whereas others measure acculturation on a multidimensional scale, on the basis of positive and negative ways of relating to both the original and the host cultures (e.g., Berry et al. 1986).

Cultural identity can vary significantly among the cultural subgroups within a country (McKenney et al. 1993). Clinicians must be aware that even within a given population of immigrants the manner and degree of acculturation can vary considerably, in part because of the variation between subgroups or cohorts of a population that are based on differences in education, gender, age, class, and social history. Intergenerational cultural differences and conflicts can be important sources of stress in the patient's family life.

To the extent that such acculturation factors influence the experience and manifestation of mental illness, they are potentially important for research and clinical psychiatry. For example, family and genetic studies typically use the same diagnostic criteria for all members of a pedigree, regardless of generation. Hence, people from different generations in the same family could be classified differently not because they have different underlying diagnoses but because the manifestation of an illness varies from generation to generation. The result could be the impaired identification of phenotypes and increased phenotypic heterogeneity in psychiatric genetic research on immigrant populations. For example, phenotypic heterogeneity has been associated with age in different studies dealing with immigrant populations, and it is unclear to what extent assessment instruments tap the manifestation of an illness with the same level of accuracy in all generations (Tsuang 1993; Tsuang and Faraone 1995).

Cultural Factors in the Experience and Manifestation of Illness

The experience and manifestation of psychiatric illness can vary in different cultures and social contexts. This variation is often of major concern for clinicians with patients from other cultures. Cross-cultural variation in symptoms and illness categories is expressed in three basic ways. First, the appropriate categorization of phenomena as pathological or nonpathological can differ. Second, the content or clustering of pathological symptoms may vary. Third, there may be different idioms of distress (Nichter 1981) that are culturally valid ways to label, experience, and express the distress associated with normal experiences and illness.

Awareness of these three potential sources of cross-cultural variation is important to avoid misclassification when assessing and measuring illness in a patient. For example, when scales are used to measure symptoms, it is important to adjust for potential differences in the pathological thresholds among populations. Otherwise, results may be misinterpreted, leading to under- or over-labeling of pathology. An example is provided by the Minnesota Multiphasic Personality Inventory (MMPI) (p. 89), a psychological test widely used to clarify diagnosis. Although average black Americans have been found to have higher baseline scores than whites on a variety of scales, including the schizophrenia scale, the pathological threshold is usually not adjusted (Gynther 1972), which could contribute to an overdiagnosis of disorders such as schizophrenia in black patients. In the clinical setting, psychological tests provide information to supplement the clinical assessment. When psychological testing is used for other purposes, such as the primary method for determining access to jobs, its application can be inappropriate and its impact is often undiluted by other assessment methods. Gottfredson (1994) and Sackett and Wilk (1994) present excellent reviews of the debate among psychologists over the scientific, philosophical, and moral issues of using race-adjusted thresholds to determine normal and pathological scores in psychological test scores used in employee selection.

In addition to possible cross-cultural or cross-ethnic differences in test score thresholds, whether a phenomenon itself is pathological or nonpathological may differ. Beliefs or experiences that could be considered abnormal or even psychotic in someone from mainstream Western culture may be nonpathological representations of reality within other cultural frameworks. For example, nonpathological hallucinations concerning premonitions, voices, or visions can occur within the usual range of experience in many cultures.

An example of the variance of cultural idioms of distress is provided by the cross-cultural variation in social phobia. As defined by DSM-IV, and typical for Western cultures, social phobia involves fear of personal humiliation. In Japan, in contrast, social phobia is manifested as *taijin kyofusho*, in which the phobia is intense fear of humiliating or offending others through one's behavior or appearance, which reflects cultural differences in the orientation of the self to others (Russell 1989). Other examples of culture-specific idioms of distress particular to certain cultures include *nervios* (nerves) in Hispanic populations, *shenjing shuairuo* (neurasthenia) among Chinese, and anorexia nervosa in some Western populations.

Symptom content and themes vary widely from one culture to another. For example, delusions and hallucinations may emphasize the cultural themes of witches in parts of Africa, soul loss in Southeast Asia, or the Central Intelligence Agency in the United States. In cross-cultural studies of depression, feelings of self-blame and guilt have not been found to be universal (Marsella 1978). The somatic experience of depression has also been found to vary; depressed South Indians emphasize symptoms of pain (Raguram et al. 1996), and depressed Hong Kong Chinese express primarily weakness and fatigue, reflecting the culturally acceptable idiom of distress of neurasthenia (Cheung et al. 1981).

The clustering of symptoms has also been found to vary in cultures, raising questions about the criteria used for identifying a diagnostic "case" (Chung and Kagawa-Singer 1995; Guarnaccia et al. 1989b). Lack of attention to any of these cultural factors can result in the over- or underdiagnosis of cases in epidemiological studies and in the misdiagnosis of patients in clinical settings. Moreover, given the lack of a gold standard for psychiatric diagnosis in epidemiology, awareness of cultural variation in psychiatric illness is crucial to avoid misclassification. The presence of under- or overdiagnosis can go undetected unless exploratory investigation is done to determine how psychiatric illness is expressed within the populations of interest.

Culture, Social Context, and Psychiatric Outcomes

Psychiatric outcomes such as dysfunctional behavior, chronic symptoms, impaired role functioning, and in-

creased health service utilization also need to be examined within their social context. Measurements of psychiatric disability, for example, need to be made relevant to the social setting of the patient or the population of interest to reflect differences in gender roles, rural versus urban environments, and developed versus developing countries. Some behaviors that are impairing in one setting may not be impairing in another, resulting in differential case identification.

As another example, social consequences of drinking are important in the diagnosis of alcoholism and also constitute a major focus of treatment outcome research. However, criteria regarding social consequences need to include scenarios that are pertinent to different cultural settings. For example, in countries where few people drive, being arrested for drunk driving is an unlikely social consequence; a question about losing a job because of drinking behavior is less relevant in a setting in which many people are unemployed. Underdiagnosing alcoholism in women and a false finding of lower female–male ratios of alcoholism in areas where fewer women work outside the home are also potential consequences of not ensuring that diagnostic criteria are culturally appropriate and reflect local gender roles. Modifying the criteria so that problems caring for children or doing chores count as social consequences ensures that gender-specific manifestations of alcoholism are recognized.

Help seeking is often measured as an illness-invoked response and has been examined in various cultural groups (Cheung et al. 1984; Freidenberg et al. 1993; Lin et al. 1978; Sue et al. 1991; Van Der Stuyft et al. 1989). The tendency of some groups to underutilize mainstream mental health services can be due to factors such as service inaccessibility, lack of familiarity with the native language, the stigma of mental illness, and cultural beliefs about illness (Chung and Lin 1994; Ying 1990). These factors can lead to delays in treatment and decreased cooperation with treatment recommendations, both of which can contribute to a worsened course of illness. The clinician should therefore be aware of these differences when determining the form of treatment.

Social factors other than culture should also be considered when analyzing illness prevalence and outcome. Socioeconomic level is one such factor. When reading reports of cross-ethnic or cross-cultural comparisons of illness, clinicians should check whether the researchers carefully accounted for the possible impact of socioeconomic level or class. This practice was largely neglected in many public health comparisons of black and white morbidity and mortality in the United States (Navarro 1990), which may thus have biased findings of interracial differences. As discussed by Davis and Proctor (1989), the assessment of patient functioning can be subject to class bias on the part of those interpreting the test results (e.g., lower patient socioeconomic status being interpreted as an indication of higher dysfunction). Furthermore, if ethnicity is associated with lower socioeconomic status, reported ethnic differences might largely reflect differences in socioeconomic status.

Major disruptions in the social history of a population also need to be considered. Psychiatric symptoms in many populations can be specifically related to historical social stressors, while simultaneously being influenced by culture. Therefore, these social factors, language, and idioms of distress have been integrated into instruments developed to investigate posttraumatic stress disorder in such populations. A good example is an instrument developed to evaluate the psychiatric status of Cambodians in the United States, a population profoundly influenced by torture and family separation under the Khmer Rouge regime and the later stresses of escape and migration (Mollica et al. 1987, 1992).

In general, lack of recognition of the effects of class and other social factors can make higher levels of pathology or service underutilization appear natural to certain ethnic or cultural groups, thereby creating an invalid framework for analyzing the effects of culture or social factors in psychiatric illness and outcomes.

Cultural Factors in Communication and Symptom Reporting

Not only the manifestation of symptoms but also the accuracy of reporting can vary from one culture to another. The sanctions each culture gives to specific behaviors are socially defined. Hence, a behavior that is easily endorsed in one setting might never be acknowledged in another. For example, Cheung et al. (1981) found that depressed Chinese patients frequently reported feelings of sadness but only when specifically asked about this symptom, probably due to the severe stigma associated with mental illness in that culture. In South India, greater stigma is associated with psychological symptoms than with somatic symptoms (Raguram et al. 1996). Some groups may find direct questions about experiences that they perceive to be shameful or difficult to be particularly inappropriate. For example, Native Americans who belong to the

Flathead tribe might not answer questions about such subjects when asked in a direct fashion (Good 1993). To minimize the underreporting of symptoms because of stigma, questions about potentially stigmatizing symptoms or situations should be asked in a sensitive way, at an appropriate time, and in an appropriate setting. Assessment instruments can address this potential difficulty by placing such questions in the middle or end of the questionnaire and by including a preface to the query. When interpreting research reports, clinicians should keep in mind that the appropriateness of the research methodology for the community under study may significantly affect the results. Several authors have discussed how to carry out valid and appropriate research in specific ethnic and cultural communities (e.g., Liu 1982; Shore 1977).

CULTURAL FACTORS IN THE DEVELOPMENT AND SELECTION OF ASSESSMENT INSTRUMENTS

Most clinicians do not develop their own assessment instruments or use such instruments in research studies. Nevertheless, having a working understanding of how culture can play a part in the development and selection of instruments will help the clinician to choose appropriate instruments, to recognize their possible limitations, and to interpret the relevance of cross-cultural studies for his or her patient population.

Accurate cross-cultural psychiatric assessment requires a valid and complete description of the symptomatology and its associated impairments. The usual approach is to rely on instruments that have been developed and validated cross-culturally, with proper attention to the coverage of manifestations of illness in that culture, the feasibility and acceptability of the format, the training and ability of interviewers, and psychometric properties such as reliability and validity.

Cultural Validity in the Coverage of Symptoms and Instrument Design

Documentation of local forms of illness can help improve the validity of psychiatric epidemiological surveys to avoid misclassification and inaccurate prevalence rates in those cultures. Such research often combines the use of psychiatric symptom scales and structured diagnostic instruments with qualitative data-gathering methods such as ethnography, interviews about "explanatory models of illness" (Kleinman et al. 1978; Weiss et al. 1995), and interviews with "key informants" in the community (e.g., Ensink and Robertson 1996). Guarnaccia et al. (1989a, 1990) used such methods to elucidate the impact of the Puerto Rican idiom of distress, *nervios* (nerves), on somatization scale results and the impact of *ataques de nervios* (nervous attacks) on the rates of diagnosed panic disorder. Manson et al. (1985) combined qualitative, clinical, and epidemiological methods to clarify the interaction of Hopi illness categories and major depressive disorder.

Instruments designed specifically for cross-cultural use can improve symptom coverage and hence validity. Ideally, researchers from different cultures and settings are involved in the joint development of the instrument so that cultural manifestations of illness are addressed and misclassification avoided. The researchers thereby function as key informants, with expertise in both cultural idioms of distress and psychiatric diagnosis. The instrument next undergoes field trials in different countries to test its adequacy for tapping different manifestations of the illness. The instrument is then modified and improved. An example of multicultural instrument design is the development and widespread implementation of the Composite International Diagnostic Interview (CIDI) by the World Health Organization (p. 61) (Robins et al. 1989).

Because of limited resources and communication difficulties, a more common but also more limited approach is to take an instrument designed in one country and then translate and modify it for use in another country or culture. The coverage of items included in any such instrument may be specific to the setting in which the instrument was developed, reflecting the theoretical orientation of the developers and the patient composition of the original sample. Therefore, particularly for cross-cultural comparisons, replicability of these assessment instruments in different settings is pivotal in lending validity to the findings. Clinicians who read assorted findings on the basis of the same instrument used in different populations should be aware of the limits of their generalizability.

Instrument Administration and Feasibility

Education, language comprehension, social preferences, and the intragroup diversity of the specific group being investigated are important considerations when selecting an assessment instrument for a specific ethnic group. Instruments can either be self-administered or require the use of an interviewer. Self-administered instruments allow the respondent to endorse symptoms privately and are also less costly than other instruments, but they require fluency in the written language in addition to comprehension of the meaning intended by each question. Not everyone who can read can understand the inquiry posed by a question. Migration into the United States is highly correlated with low socioeconomic status, which can be associated with limited literacy. As a result, some immigrant groups may answer a self-administered questionnaire with decreased accuracy. In contrast, for groups such as immigrant students, self-reporting is often more accurate.

Instruments designed for administration by an interviewer require that either a clinician or a nonclinician conduct the interview. Those that require administration by clinicians involve higher personnel costs than those administered by nonclinicians and may not be feasible to use in testing sites that have few clinicians. In addition, instruments that require a judgment on the part of the clinician rely on the interviewer's awareness of different cultural manifestations of the criteria being measured and may thus be subject to interviewer bias.

Interviews designed for administration by nonclinicians usually rely on the respondent's endorsement of instrument items, with minimal judgment by the interviewer. In this case, interviewers read items as written from a structured interview, so the validity and comprehensibility of the items are important. Interviewers should be thoroughly trained in the proper administration of the instrument to increase reliability and, in turn, cross-cultural comparability.

Developing an awareness of their own cultural and class background and biases should be an important part of the training of both clinical and nonclinical interviewers. Interviewers should be sensitive to cultural issues and have the ability to behave with and relate to interviewees appropriately.

Translation and Adaptation of Diagnostic Instruments

The methods used for translating and adapting an instrument can enhance or impair understanding and therefore the reliability and validity of responses. The translation process usually involves translation of the instrument into the target language, reverse translation by a different person into the original language, and then comparison of the two versions for discrepancies. This process is usually followed by a series of modifications and reviews by a bilingual committee. The bilingual committee and pilot test subjects should represent the variety of regions, subcultures, and educational backgrounds present in the target population because of intracultural and class diversity. The instrument should also reflect intergenerational differences in culture and language use.

Translated assessment instruments should maintain cultural equivalency of the construct being measured. A useful model to attain this goal focuses on five dimensions of the translation and adaptation process: semantic equivalence, content equivalence, technical equivalence, criterion equivalence, and conceptual equivalence (Bravo et al. 1991, 1993; Flaherty et al. 1988). The clinician should look for these features when reviewing different assessment instruments.

The meaning of each item should be the same in the language of each culture (a condition known as *semantic equivalence*). The literal translation of seemingly simple, straightforward questions can result in very different meanings to a respondent who operates in a different cultural frame of reference (Kortmann 1990). The content of each item should be relevant to the population under study—that is, it should tap a phenomenon that occurs in and is noted as real by members of that culture (*content equivalence*). For example, a mental state item that inquires "What season is it?" does not tap the same construct in Puerto Rico, a tropical island with no change of seasons, as it does in North America (Bravo et al. 1993). In Puerto Rico, this item would test abstraction on the part of the respondent rather than the intended construct of orientation.

The method of assessment should achieve comparable effects in gathering data in different cultures (*technical equivalence*). For example, lack of reading skills might make a self-administered instrument inappropriate in a specific setting and require an interviewer to read items aloud. Methods should also be equivalent in the degree of self-revelation they elicit in the subject's sociocultural context. The results of a measure should be interpretable according to the norms of each culture (*criterion equivalence*). Testing the validity of an assessment instrument in the relevant setting can be considered an indicator of criterion equivalency. Finally, *conceptual equivalence* is achieved when the same theoretical con-

struct can be evaluated in different cultures. It is the result of meta-analyses of individual, culture-specific findings.

CULTURAL DIFFERENCES IN CLINICAL SETTINGS: SUGGESTIONS FOR CLINICIANS

The increasing ethnic and cultural diversity of the population requires that clinicians be alert and adaptable to the sociocultural issues of their patients to optimize engagement, communication, diagnosis, and treatment. Unaddressed cultural differences between the clinician and patient can lead to difficulties with over- or underdiagnosis, noncompliance with treatment, and mutual frustration when the patient or the clinician does not meet implicit, culturally determined expectations of proper clinical or social behavior. On the other hand, cultural differences can sometimes be advantageous in assessment and treatment. Patients may report symptoms and accept treatment more readily from a sympathetic clinician who is not a member of their community, because they may believe that confidentiality is increased and stigma lessened. How, then, can the clinician address cultural factors relevant to assessment in the clinical setting? The following suggestions summarize the role of cultural factors in assessment discussed previously:

1. Be aware that no one is culture free in the assessment of illness—not patients, clinicians, or researchers. An awareness of one's own professional, cultural, and class background and biases is essential to the correct assessment of mental illness across cultures and classes.

2. As part of a detailed history of the present illness, ask about the patient's "explanatory model"—what he or she believes caused the illness, its nature, and its expected course and treatment (Kleinman 1988). Have factors particular to the patient's social history contributed to the illness (e.g., recent immigration, a history of persecution, war exposure, torture, family stressors, or poverty)? Ask for permission to talk to family or close friends for a more thorough assessment of the social context.

3. Clarify whether the patient's explanation of the illness is a common, culturally accepted explanation or if it indicates a manifestation of psychiatric illness. Expla-

nations can be clarified by asking patients, their families, and their acquaintances about these explanations. Whenever possible, consult with the patient's family and friends and with culturally knowledgeable colleagues regarding their interpretations and the appropriateness of the patient's explanation. Check the psychiatric literature on illness beliefs in the specific culture. Keep in mind that a cultural explanation of illness may be known by many but believed by only some subgroups within a culture because of generational, educational, and intracultural diversity. Although family members and professionals may not ascribe to a culture-specific belief, they may understand it.

4. Do not overattribute symptoms to culture and assume that they do not warrant treatment. Culture can be a red herring in diagnosis (Stein 1985) if its presence is recognized but then misunderstood as the sole cause of the symptoms. For example, acknowledging the cultural context of a psychotic episode does not preclude treating the psychotic symptoms and determining whether depression or a medical illness is a contributing factor. Awareness of the possible roles of culture can be used as the basis for a deeper investigation of the illness and its appropriate treatment. More difficult cross-cultural cases usually involve a complicated knot of social factors in which culture is just one thread that needs to be disentangled for accurate assessment.

5. When using an instrument to assess a patient from another culture, check whether it has been translated, adapted, and validated in that specific culture. If not, use the information it provides judiciously. An instrument developed in a Western culture, or in a different culture that shares the same language as the patient, may use language or concepts that will seem nonsensical to your patient. The instrument might also miss symptoms common to the patient's culture, misclassify cultural idioms of distress, or mislabel a common cultural phenomenon as pathological.

Additional guides for the clinician in formulating cultural issues in psychiatric assessment are included in the "Outline for Cultural Formulation" in Appendix I of DSM-IV (pp. 843–844) and a useful series of case studies of culture-specific illnesses examined within a sociobiopsychological context (Fleming 1996; Lewis-Fernandez 1996a, 1996b).

REFERENCES AND SUGGESTED READINGS

Berry JW, Trimble J, Olmedo E: Assessment of acculturation, in Field Methods in Cross-cultural Research. Edited by Lonner W, Berry J. Beverly Hills, CA, Sage, 1986, pp 291–324

Bravo M, Rubio-Stipec M, Woodbury-Farina MA: Cross-cultural adaptation of a diagnostic instrument: the DIS adaptation in Puerto Rico. Cult Med Psychiatry 15:1–18, 1991

Bravo M, Woodbury-Farina M, Canino G, et al: The translation and cultural adaptation of the Diagnostic Interview Schedule for Children (DISC) in Puerto Rico. Cult Med Psychiatry 17:329–344, 1993

Cheung F, Lau BW, Waldmann E: Somatization among Chinese depressives in general practice. Int J Psychiatry Med 10:361–374, 1981

Cheung F, Lau BWK, Wong S-W: Paths to psychiatric care in Hong Kong. Cult Med Psychiatry 8:207–228, 1984

Chung RC-Y, Kagawa-Singer M: Interpretation of symptom presentation and distress. J Nerv Ment Dis 183:639–648, 1995

Chung R, Lin K-M: Helpseeking behavior among Southeast Asian refugees. Journal of Community Psychology 22:109–120, 1994

Davis LE, Proctor EK: Race, Gender, and Class: Guidelines for Practice with Individuals, Families, and Groups. Englewood Cliffs, NJ, Prentice-Hall, 1989

Ensink K, Robertson B: Indigenous categories of distress and dysfunction in South African Xhosa children and adolescents as described by indigenous healers. Transcultural Psychiatric Research Review 33:137–172, 1996

Flaherty FA, Gaviria FM, Pathak D, et al: Developing instruments for cross-cultural psychiatric research. Journal of Nervous and Psychiatric Disease 176:257–263, 1988

Fleming CM: Cultural formulation of psychiatric diagnosis: case no. 01. An American Indian woman suffering from depression, alcoholism, and childhood trauma. Cult Med Psychiatry 20:145–154, 1996

Freidenberg J, Mulvihill M, Caraballo L: From ethnography to survey: some methodological issues in research on health seeking in East Harlem. Human Organization 52:151–161, 1993

Good BJ: Culture, diagnosis, and comorbidity. Cult Med Psychiatry 16:427–446, 1993

Gottfredson LS: The science and politics of race-norming. Am Psychol 49:955–963, 1994

Guarnaccia PJ, Rubio-Stipec M, Canino G: Ataques de nervios in the Puerto Rican Diagnostic Interview Schedule: the impact of cultural categories on psychiatric epidemiology. Cult Med Psychiatry 13:275–295, 1989a

Guarnaccia PJ, Angel R, Worobey JL: The factor structure of the CES-D in the Hispanic Health and Nutrition Examination Survey: the influences of ethnicity, gender, and language. Soc Sci Med 29:85–94, 1989b

Guarnaccia PJ, Good BJ, Kleinman A: A critical review of epidemiological studies of Puerto Rican mental health. Am J Psychiatry 147:1449–1456, 1990

Gynther MD: White norms and black MMPIs: a prescription for discrimination? Psychol Bull 78:386–402, 1972

Kleinman A: Rethinking Psychiatry: From Cultural Category to Personal Experience. New York, Free Press, 1988

Kleinman A, Eisenberg L, Good B: Culture, illness, and care: clinical lessons from anthropologic and cross-cultural research. Ann Intern Med 88:251–258, 1978

Kortmann F: Psychiatric case finding in Ethiopia: shortcomings of the Self Reporting Questionnaire. Cult Med Psychiatry 14: 381–391, 1990

Lewis-Fernandez R: Cultural formulation of psychiatric diagnosis. Cult Med Psychiatry 20:133–144, 1996a

Lewis-Fernandez R: Cultural formulation of psychiatric diagnosis: case no. 02. Diagnosis and treatment of nervios and ataques in a female Puerto Rican migrant. Cult Med Psychiatry 20:155–163, 1996b

Lin T-Y, Tardiff K, Donetz G, et al: Ethnicity and patterns of help-seeking. Cult Med Psychiatry 2:3–13, 1978

Liu WT (ed): Methodological problems in minority research (Occasional Paper Series, No 7). Pacific/Asian American Mental Health Research Center, 1982

Manson SM, Shore JH, Bloom JD: The depressive experience in American Indian communities: a challenge for psychiatric theory and diagnosis, in Culture and Depression: Studies in the Anthropology and Cross-Cultural Psychiatry of Affect and Disorder. Edited by Kleinman A, Good BJ. Berkeley, CA, University of California Press, 1985, pp 331–368

Marsella AJ: Thoughts on cross-cultural studies on the epidemiology of depression. Cult Med Psychiatry 2:343–357, 1978

McKenney N, Bennett C, Harrison R, et al: Evaluating Racial and Ethnic Reporting in the 1990 Census. Washington, DC, U.S. Bureau of the Census, 1993

Mollica RF, Wyshak G, de Marneffe D, et al: Indochinese version of the Hopkins Symptom Checklist-25: a screening instrument for the psychiatric care of refugees. Am J Psychiatry 144:497–500, 1987

Mollica RF, Caspi-Yavin Y, Bollini P, et al: The Harvard Trauma Questionnaire: validating a cross-cultural instrument for measuring torture, trauma, and posttraumatic stress disorder in Indochinese refugees. J Nerv Ment Dis 180:111–116, 1992

Navarro V: Race or class versus race and class: mortality differentials in the United States. Lancet 336:1238–1240, 1990

Nichter M: Idioms of distress. Alternatives in the expression of psychosocial distress: a case study from South India. Cult Med Psychiatry 5:379–408, 1981

Raguram R, Weiss MG, Channabasavanna SM, et al: Stigma, depression, and somatization in South India. Am J Psychiatry 153:1043–1049, 1996

Robins LN, Helzer J, Croughan J, et al: The NIMH Diagnostic Interview Schedule: its history, characteristics, and validity. Arch Gen Psychiatry 38:381–389, 1981

Robins LN, Wing JK, Wittchen HU, et al: The Composite International Diagnostic Instrument: an epidemiologic instrument suitable for use in conjunction with different diagnostic systems and in different cultures. Arch Gen Psychiatry 45:1069–1077, 1989

Russell JG: Anxiety disorders in Japan: a review of the Japanese literature on shinkeishitsu and taijinkyofusho. Cult Med Psychiatry 13:391–403, 1989

Sackett PR, Wilk SL: Within-group norming and other forms of score adjustment in preemployment testing. Am Psychol 49:929–954, 1994

Shore JH: Psychiatric research issues with American Indians, in Current Perspectives in Cultural Psychiatry. Edited by Foulks EF, Wintrob RM, Westermeyer J, et al. New York, Spectrum, 1977, pp 73–80

Stein HF: The culture of the patient as a red herring in clinical decision making: a case study. Med Anthropol Q 17:2–5, 1985

Sue S, Fujino DC, Hu L, et al: Community mental health services for ethnic minority groups: a test of the cultural responsiveness hypothesis. J Consult Clin Psychol 59:533–540, 1991

Tsuang MT: Genotypes, phenotypes, and the brain: search for connections in schizophrenia. 67th Annual Maudsley Lecture. Br J Psychiatry 163:299–307, 1993

Tsuang MT, Faraone SV: The case for heterogeneity in the etiology of schizophrenia. Schizophr Res 17:161–175, 1995

Van Der Stuyft P, De Muynck A, Schillemans L, et al: Migration, acculturation, and utilization of primary health care. Soc Sci Med 29:53–60, 1989

Weiss MG, Raguram R, Channabasavanna SM: Cultural dimensions of psychiatric diagnosis: a comparison of DSM-III-R and illness explanatory models in South India. Br J Psychiatry 166:353–359, 1995

Ying Y-W: Explanatory models of major depression and implications for help-seeking among immigrant Chinese-American women. Cult Med Psychiatry 14:393–408, 1990

General Measures (Non–Disorder Specific)

CHAPTER 6

Diagnostic Interviews for Adults

Andrew E. Skodol, M.D.
Donna S. Bender, Ph.D.

INTRODUCTION

Major Domains

This chapter includes instruments that are intended to provide some level of structure to the diagnostic assessment process. The primary output of each instrument is a determination of whether the patient's clinical picture meets diagnostic criteria for one of the psychiatric disorders covered by the instrument.

Organization

The interviews included in this chapter are listed in Table 6–1. Interviews that were designed to be used primarily in psychiatric populations (the Structured Clinical Interview for DSM-IV Axis I Disorders [SCID-I], the Schedules for Clinical Assessment in Neuropsychiatry [SCAN], and the Schedule for Affective Disorders and Schizophrenia [SADS]) are listed first, followed by interviews designed for epidemiological studies (the Diagnostic Interview Schedule [DIS] and the Composite International Diagnostic Interview [CIDI]) and then interviews designed for use in primary care settings (the Primary Care Evaluation of Mental Disorders [PRIME-MD] and the Symptom-Driven Diagnostic System for Primary Care [SDDS-PC]).

Diagnostic interviews were first developed to provide reliable diagnoses for clinical research on patients with particular mental disorders. Later, to address the need for reliable data on the prevalence of mental disorders in the general population, interviews were developed for use in epidemiological community studies. Interviews for use in clinical research have generally been intended to be administered by experienced mental health professionals, and those primarily for use in epidemiological research have been designed to be administered by specially trained lay interviewers. The interviews for use in psychiatric populations included here are the SCID-I, the SCAN, and the SADS. Although the DIS and CIDI were specifically designed for epidemiological purposes, both have been used in clinical populations as well.

Mental disorders are present in at least 20% of medical outpatients and are a major source of disability and health care costs. Today, more patients with mental disorders receive care in the primary care sector than in the mental health sector, yet, historically, primary care physicians have failed to diagnose and treat up to 50% of their patients who have mental disorders. Two interviews included here—the PRIME-MD and the SDDS-PC— were developed to address the need for better recognition of mental disorders associated with shifting the delivery of routine mental health care from the psychiatric specialist to the primary care physician.

Relevant Measures Included Elsewhere in the Handbook

Interviews designed exclusively for use in diagnosing personality disorders are covered in Chapter 32. Diagnostic

TABLE 6–1 ■ Diagnostic interviews

Name of Measure	Disorder or Construct Assessed	Format	Pages
Structured Clinical Interview for DSM-IV Axis I Disorders (SCID-I); Patient edition (SCID-I/P); Nonpatient edition (SCID-I/NP); Clinician version (SCID-CV)	Broad coverage of psychiatric diagnoses according to DSM-IV	Clinician-administered, semistructured interview; seven diagnostic modules	49–53
Schedules for Clinical Assessment in Neuropsychiatry (SCAN)	Psychopathology and behavior associated with a broad range of major psychiatric disorders of adult life in dimensional ratings not tied to any single classification system; includes ICD-10 and DSM-IV, among others	SCAN interview text (Present State Examination [PSE10], Item Group Checklist [IGC], and Clinical History Schedule [CHS]), glossary of differential definitions, and CATEGO-5 computer program	53–58
Schedule for Affective Disorders and Schizophrenia (SADS)	Mental disorders as defined by Research Diagnostic Criteria (RDC)	Clinician-administered interview; first section on symptoms and second section on history of mental disorders	58–61
Diagnostic Interview Schedule (DIS) Composite International Diagnostic Interview (CIDI)	Current and lifetime psychiatric disorders according to DSM-IV criteria Expanded DIS for use across cultures; it provides diagnoses according to both ICD-10 and DSM-IV criteria	Highly structured interviews with demographic section and diagnostic modules for administration by laypersons	61–65
Primary Care Evaluation of Mental Disorders (PRIME-MD)*	For use by primary care physicians in diagnosing the mental disorders most commonly seen in adults in primary care settings	1-page Patient Questionnaire (PQ) and 9-page Clinician Evaluation Guide (CEG)	65–68
Symptom-Driven Diagnostic System for Primary Care (SDDS-PC)	Computerized instrument for the detection, diagnosis, and management of mental disorders in primary care practice	29-item patient self-report screening questionnaire, a diagnostic interview guide with an extra module for suicide risk, and a longitudinal tracking form	68–70

*Measure is included on the CD-ROM that accompanies this handbook.

interviews for childhood disorders are covered in Chapter 17.

USING MEASURES IN THIS DOMAIN

Goals of Assessment

The goal of the interviews reviewed in this chapter is to provide reliable methods for making a range of psychiatric diagnoses for research or clinical purposes. They would ordinarily be used as part of an initial comprehensive assessment, although they might be repeated at a later date to determine a change in psychiatric status.

Implementation Issues

Most of the instruments reviewed here are clinician-administered interviews that require experienced clinicians with a knowledge of psychopathology and special training in the use of the interview. However, two of the interviews (DIS and CIDI) are designed to be administered by trained nonclinical or lay interviewers. These interviews have been used in large-scale community surveys of the prevalence of mental disorders, because the number of subjects interviewed is so large that the cost of clinician-administered interviews is prohibitive. The two primary care interviews are hybrid instruments that combine both self-report and follow-up clinician examination designed for use by nonpsychiatric physicians.

Issues in Interpreting Psychometric Data

The instruments included in this chapter differ in the extent of available data on their reliability and validity. Before the advent of diagnostic criteria and the development of structured and semistructured diagnostic interviews, psychiatric diagnosis was notoriously unreliable. Three sources of unreliability (or error variance) have been identified, corresponding to different reasons why clinicians may disagree on a particular patient's diagnosis: 1) they were basing the diagnosis on different types and amounts of information about the patient (*information variance*), 2) they interpreted the information they had differently in terms of its psychopathological significance (*interpretation variance*), or 3) they put the information together differently in arriving at a diagnosis because they used different definitions of disorders (*criterion variance*).

Structured and semistructured diagnostic interviews were designed to reduce information variance (and thus increase reliability) by ensuring that clinicians asked the same or similar questions in the same or similar order in conducting their evaluations. Diagnostic criteria provide standardized definitions of disorders to reduce criterion variance. Interviews vary in the extent to which they focus on rating signs and symptoms of psychopathology versus rating diagnostic criteria. Interviews that focus on rating criteria or use computer programs to generate diagnoses may reduce criterion variance. Reducing interpretation variance is thought to be a function of training in the elements of psychopathology. Interviews that provide detailed glossaries of psychopathology or illustrative user's guides and extensive training programs in their use help to reduce interpretation variance.

Diagnostic reliability is tested in one of two ways: Either two evaluators rate identical interview material (joint reliability) or they each conduct an independent assessment of the patient on two occasions separated by a few days to 1–2 weeks (test-retest reliability). Test-retest reliability is a more stringent test, because even with a structured or semistructured guide to assessment, the patient may give somewhat different answers to the same questions on the two occasions. Different follow-up questions may be asked to probe the significance of a symptom, thus introducing information variance. When there is only one interview (observed, audiotaped, or videotaped), there is only one set of questions and only one answer to each question to be interpreted and rated.

The standard psychometric measure of reliability for categorical diagnoses is Cohen's kappa. Kappa is preferred over a measure such as percentage of agreement because it measures agreement over and above agreement to be expected by chance alone. There are kappa statistics for use when several diagnostic categories are possible, when several clinicians' assessments are being compared, and when disagreements vary in diagnostic importance. Kappa values range from –1.0, which indicates complete disagreement, to 1.0, which indicates perfect agreement. A kappa of 0 indicates agreement no better than chance. As a rule of thumb, kappa values greater than 0.75 indicate excellent agreement beyond chance, values less than 0.40 represent poor agreement, and values in between represent fair to good agreement.

The reliability of a diagnostic interview is influenced by many factors: the questions included and how well they are understood by the patient, the conditions under which the interview is administered, the training of the interviewers and their familiarity with each other, the types of disorders covered and their complexity, and the frequency (base rate) of the diagnoses in the population undergoing evaluation. In general, mental disorders are more reliably assessed when they are severe, as opposed to mild, and when they are currently present, as opposed to present only at some time in the past.

The validity of a diagnostic interview depends on the existence of a gold standard diagnosis with which it can be compared. Unfortunately, no gold standard for psychiatric diagnosis exists. Diagnoses on the basis of unstructured clinical interviews cannot serve as gold standards because their unreliability limits their validity. The validity of a diagnostic interview has typically been tested by comparing one interview with another more established or more face-valid interview or by comparing an interview with a diagnostic assessment that incorporates data from interviews, chart review, other informants, and longitudinal observation. Such an amalgamated diagnosis has been referred to as a "best estimate" diagnosis or the "LEAD standard" (Longitudinal observation by Experts using All available Data as sources of information) when it includes follow-up information. Lay-administered interviews have been compared with clinician-administered interviews on the basis of the premise that the layperson's interview is meant to approximate a clinician's interview and that the latter is the standard against which the former should be compared. The statistics employed for this type of validity determination (called procedural validity) are usually sensitivity, specificity, and positive and negative predictive values, which are discussed in detail in Chapter 2.

A reliable diagnostic interview is not necessarily valid, in the sense that it identifies clinically significant psychopathology useful in treatment planning and prognosis. The validity of any interview is attenuated by unreliability. A fully structured interview that allows no flexibility in the interviewer's questions and elicits yes or no answers may be associated with high reliability, but the diagnoses generated may lack clinical salience. On the other hand, clinicians may believe that their clinical hunches or intuitions about patients are of great value in guiding treatment, but if these judgments are not reproducible (i.e., reliable), they may be idiosyncratic to a particular clinician and thus lack general utility. An ideal diagnostic interview is one developed to strike a balance between reliability and validity.

GUIDE TO THE SELECTION OF MEASURES

The interviews presented here differ in the extent of their coverage of Axis I disorders (i.e., the range of different disorders assessed), the degree of structure imposed (i.e., fully structured interviews that allow virtually no clinical leeway on the part of the interviewer vs. semistructured interviews that require extensive follow-up questioning and application of clinical judgment), and the diagnostic output. Some are wedded to one set of diagnostic criteria, whereas others can generate diagnoses according to multiple types of criteria (e.g., DSM-IV, ICD-10, and Research Diagnostic Criteria). The major limitations of diagnostic interviews are that they are time-consuming and, consequently, expensive to use, especially in the case of clinician-administered interviews. Interviews with a modular structure that permit the interviewer to select only segments that are of particular interest might be more cost-effective. However, versions that are focused on only a subset of diagnoses may miss psychiatric co-

morbidity that might be both clinically and etiologically significant.

Several diagnostic instruments not covered in this chapter have been designed specifically for use in special patient populations. The Diagnostic Interview for Genetic Studies (DIGS) (Nurnberger et al. 1994) and the Semi-Structured Assessment for the Genetics of Alcoholism (SSAGA) (Bucholz et al. 1994) are comprehensive and lengthy instruments designed as diagnostic assessments in genetics studies. For patients with anxiety disorders, the Anxiety Disorders Interview Schedule (ADIS) (DiNardo et al. 1993) provides DSM diagnoses of anxiety disorders by DSM criteria, with additional coverage of mood, somatoform, and substance use disorders. For patients with psychotic and affective symptoms, the Comprehensive Assessment of Symptoms and History (CASH) (Andreasen et al. 1992) provides comprehensive diagnostic information on the basis of current and past psychotic and affective signs and symptoms, premorbid functioning, cognitive functioning, sociodemographic status, treatment history, and course of illness. The Psychiatric Research Interview for Substance and Mental Disorders (PRISM) (Hasin et al. 1996) provides detailed diagnostic information on substance use disorders and also includes sections for major mood, anxiety, and eating disorders; antisocial and borderline personality disorders; and psychotic symptoms.

CURRENT STATUS AND FUTURE RESEARCH NEEDS FOR ASSESSMENT

The reliability of diagnostic interviews has proven somewhat disappointing, at least for certain disorders. Improvements need to be made to reduce interpretation variance, perhaps by developing and disseminating standardized, illustrated definitions of the elements of psychopathology for training purposes.

Most importantly, studies need to be done to investigate whether diagnostic interviews increase the validity of clinical diagnostic evaluation. In other words, do they improve the accurate detection of clinically significant disorders or of comorbid disorders, and does improved diagnostic accuracy result in better outcomes of patient care? Until the benefits of using interview schedules in clinical practice are apparent, the clinician is unlikely to judge them worth the time and effort involved in learning to use them and in administering them.

Two instruments under development are the Mini-International Neuropsychiatric Interview (MINI) (Sheehan and Lecrubier 1994) and the Psychiatric Diagnostic Screening Questionnaire (PDSR) (Zimmerman and Mattia, in press). The MINI is designed to be a brief, structured diagnostic interview for use by health information technicians in clinical and research settings. It has both clinician-rated and patient-rated versions; a total of 120 questions cover 17 current DSM-III-R Axis I disorders. The PDSR is a 90-item self-report questionnaire designed to efficiently screen psychiatric patients for a range of DSM-IV Axis I disorders.

REFERENCES AND SUGGESTED READINGS

Andreasen NC, Flaum M, Arndt S: The Comprehensive Assessment of Symptoms and History (CASH): an instrument for assessing diagnosis and psychopathology. Arch Gen Psychiatry 49:615–623, 1992

Baldessarini RJ, Finkelstein S, Arana GW: The predictive power of diagnostic tests and the effect of prevalence of illness. Arch Gen Psychiatry 40:569–573, 1983

Bucholz KK, Cadoret R, Cloninger CR, et al: A new, semi-structured interview for use in genetic linkage studies: a report of the reliability of the SSAGA. J Stud Alcohol 55:149–158, 1994

DiNardo PA, Moras K, Barlow DH, et al: Reliability of DSM-III-R anxiety disorder categories using the Anxiety Disorders Interview Schedule—Revised (ADIS-R). Arch Gen Psychiatry 50:251–256, 1993

Hasin DS, Skodol AE: Standardized diagnostic interviews for psychiatric research, in The Instruments of Psychiatric Research. Edited by Thompson C. Chichester, England, Wiley, 1989, pp 19–57

Hasin DS, Trautman KD, Miele GM, et al: Psychiatric Research Interview for Substance and Mental Disorders (PRISM): reliability for substance abusers. Am J Psychiatry 153:1195–1201, 1996

Helzer JE: Standardized interviews in psychiatry. Psychiatric Developments 2:161–178, 1983

Nurnberger JI, Blehar MC, Kaufman CA, et al: Diagnostic Interview for Genetic Studies: rationale, unique features, and training. Arch Gen Psychiatry 51:849–859, 1994

Regier DA, Kaelber CT, Rae DS, et al: Limitations of diagnostic criteria and assessment instruments for mental disorders. Arch Gen Psychiatry 55:109–115, 1998

Sheehan DV, Lecrubier Y: Mini-International Neuropsychiatric Interview (MINI). Tampa, FL, University of South Florida, Institute for Research in Psychiatry; Paris, INSERM-Hopital de la Salpetriere, 1994

Shrout PE, Spitzer RL, Fleiss JL: Quantification of agreement in psychiatric diagnosis revisited. Arch Gen Psychiatry 44:172–177, 1987

Williams JBW: Psychiatric classification, in American Psychiatric Press Synopsis of Psychiatry. Edited by Hales RE, Yudofsky SC. Washington, DC, American Psychiatric Press, 1996, pp 211–236

Zimmerman M, Mattia JI: The reliability and validity of a screening questionnaire for 13 DSM-IV disorders (PDSR) in psychiatric outpatients. J Clin Psychiatry, in press

Structured Clinical Interview for DSM-IV Axis I Disorders (SCID-I)

M. B. First, R. L. Spitzer, J. B. W. Williams, and M. Gibbon

GOALS

The Structured Clinical Interview for DSM-IV Axis I Disorders (SCID-I) is a clinician-administered, semi-structured interview for use with psychiatric patients or with nonpatient community subjects who are undergoing evaluation for psychopathology. The SCID-I was developed to provide broad coverage of psychiatric diagnoses according to DSM-IV. It was designed to be more efficient and simpler to use than other existing instruments and, consequently, to require less time for training and administration.

DESCRIPTION

The SCID-I interview begins with an overview section that obtains demographic information, work history, chief complaint, history of present and past periods of psychiatric illness, treatment history, and assessment of current functioning with open-ended questions to elicit responses in the subject's own words. The main body of the SCID-I consists of nine diagnostic modules: Mood Episodes, Psychotic Symptoms, Psychotic Disorders Differential, Mood Disorders Differential, Substance Use, Anxiety, Somatoform Disorders, Eating Disorders, and Adjustment Disorders. Investigators may choose to eliminate one or more modules to focus only on areas of the greatest diagnostic interest. In all, 51 specific DSM-IV Axis I diagnoses are covered by the patient edition (SCID-I/P, version 2.0). An optional module for research disorders (e.g., mixed anxiety depressive disorder and minor depressive disorder) is also included. The interview provides required probe questions and suggested follow-up questions. Liberal use of "skip-out" directions (which enable the interviewer to skip subsequent questions in a section) are employed when a subject fails to meet a critical criterion required for a particular disorder.

Two versions of the measure are available: the SCID-I (research version) (First et al. 1995) and the SCID-CV (clinician version) (First et al. 1997). The SCID-I is intended for use in research settings and includes a wide variety of subtypes and specifiers that may be of use only to researchers with a specialized interest. The SCID-CV covers only the diagnoses most commonly seen in clinical practice, excludes most of the disorder subtypes and specifiers in the research version, and provides simplified Mood and Substance Use Disorders modules. The research version comes in three editions that differ on the basis of the type of subjects being interviewed. The SCID-I/P is the standard SCID-I designed for research subjects identified as psychiatric patients; the SCID-I/NP (nonpatient edition) is for subjects who are not self-identified as psychiatric patients, such as those in community surveys, in family studies, or in primary care or general medical settings, and the SCID-I/P with Psychotic Screen is for psychiatric patients who are unlikely to need a full psychotic disorder assessment (e.g., subjects in a psychotherapy trial). The SCID-I/NP differs from the SCID-I/P in its overview, which does not assume a chief complaint, and in using a screen for psychotic disorders instead of the lengthy and complex Psychotic Disorders Differential module. A separate interview for Axis II Personality Disorders (SCID-II), discussed in Chapter 32, is also available.

Next to each probe question the SCID-I presents the individual diagnostic criteria for each disorder. The interviewer rates each criterion independently on the basis of the probe question and any follow-up questions deemed necessary. In the research version of the SCID-I, each criterion is rated in the right-hand column of the interview booklet as follows: 1 = absent or false, 2 = subthreshold (i.e., present but of subthreshold duration or severity and therefore not counted toward the diagnosis), or 3 = threshold or true (i.e., present and of clinically significant duration or severity).

In the SCID-CV, the required questions, suggested follow-up questions, and diagnostic criteria are supplied in a reusable administration booklet. The ratings of the criteria (in the SCID-CV, they are present [+], absent or subthreshold [–], and inadequate information [?]) and clinical notes are made in a separate one-time-use booklet, the SCID-CV score sheet. Example 6–1 shows item A4 for evaluating insomnia from the SCID-CV. This item appears in the first diagnostic module after the overview, Mood Episodes. At this point, the clinician has already determined that the patient has experienced depressed mood or markedly diminished interest or pleasure most of the day, nearly every day, for at least 2 weeks, either in the past month (a current episode) or at some other time in the past (a lifetime episode), suggesting the possibility of a major depressive episode.

Interviewers are encouraged to use all available sources of information about a subject in making ratings, including chart and informant (e.g., family member) data. The interviewer makes the final decision about whether all the available information, not only the subject's self-report, indicates that a criterion item has been met.

Most diagnoses are made on a lifetime (ever present) and current (meets diagnostic criteria in the past month) basis and are recorded on the summary score sheet at the beginning of the SCID-I. Subthreshold diagnoses can also be noted. Diagnoses are made by the interviewer during the course of the interview; no separate scoring algorithm or program is required. SCID-I scoring takes only a few minutes if all items in the body of the interview have been explored and marked. Evaluation on DSM-IV Axis IV, Psychosocial and Environmental Problems, and a rating on DSM-IV Axis V, Global Assessment of Functioning Scale, complete the diagnostic assessment.

EXAMPLE 6–1 ■ Insomnia item from the Clinician Version of the Structured Clinical Interview for DSM-IV Axis I Disorders. The questions and the criterion item are presented in a reusable administration booklet (top). The ratings are made on a separate score sheet (bottom).

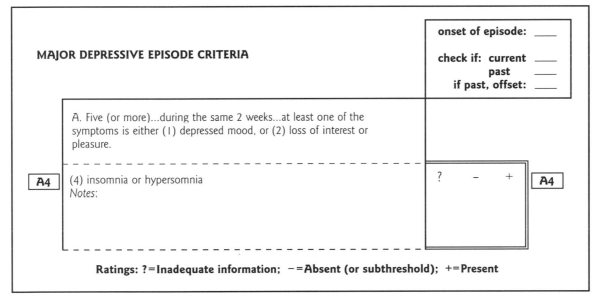

Reprinted with permission from American Psychiatric Press, Inc.

PRACTICAL ISSUES

The ideal SCID-I interviewer is someone with enough clinical experience and knowledge of psychopathology and psychiatric diagnosis to conduct a diagnostic interview without an interview guide. Less experience, knowledge, or skill may necessitate study of general DSM-IV training books or videos before specific SCID-I training.

In addition, training of all SCID-I interviewers must include review of the SCID user's guide, which contains case examples and corresponding samples of scored SCID-I modules. An 11-hour training video that contains both didactic instruction and sample interviews can be ordered by contacting Biometrics Research. Before use in actual clinical or research settings, SCID-I interviews should be practiced, observed by an experienced interviewer, and thoroughly discussed to reduce misunderstandings or errors.

It may take 1 hour or less to administer the SCID in subjects with little or no psychopathology but up to 2–3 hours in those with a complicated history and several comorbid mental disorders. Researchers may obtain the SCID-I research version (all editions), including the user's guide, from

SCID Central—Biometrics Research
New York State Psychiatric Institute, Unit 60
1051 Riverside Drive
New York, NY 10032
Phone: 212-543-5524

Ordering and other information regarding the SCID-I (including information about updates, other studies using the SCID-I, and so forth) is available on the Internet (www.scid8.org). The SCID-CV is published by the American Psychiatric Press and can be ordered by phone (800-368-5777) or over the Internet (www.appi.org). The cost is $65.00 for a set of the user's guide, reusable administration booklet, and package of five score sheets.

A computer-administered version of the SCID-CV (CAS-CV) and SCID-I research version (CAS-RV) are available from Multi-Health Systems of Toronto, Canada (800-456-3003, www.mhs.com). Telephone administration of the SCID-I has been reported. The SCID-I has been translated in its entirety into Danish, Dutch, French, German, Greek, Hebrew, Italian, Portuguese, Russian, Spanish, Swedish, and Turkish. Most of the SCID-I/NP has been translated into Spanish. (Information about availability of these translations is listed on the SCID Web page.)

PSYCHOMETRIC PROPERTIES

Reliability

The joint reliability and test-retest reliability of the SCID-I for DSM-III-R Axis I diagnoses were determined in a variety of populations and nations. In the major multisite test-retest reliability study conducted by the instrument's developers (Williams et al. 1992), the overall reliability was fair to good in patient samples (overall weighted kappa = 0.61) but poor in nonpatients (overall weighted kappa = 0.37). Good to excellent reliability was obtained for diagnoses of bipolar disorder (kappa = 0.84), alcohol abuse or dependence (0.75), other drug abuse or dependence (0.84), anorexia nervosa (0.72), and bulimia nervosa (0.86). Reliability was poor for dysthymia (0.40), agoraphobia without panic disorder (0.43), and social phobia (0.47). Test-retest reliability for specific substance dependence diagnoses was also high. Other studies found fair to good test-retest reliability for panic disorder and its subtypes in an international sample; good joint reliability (kappa > 0.70) for major depressive disorder, generalized anxiety disorder, anxiety disorders, and somatoform disorders in patients over age 55 years; and good reliability for most DSM-III-R disorders except agoraphobia without panic

disorder, obsessive-compulsive disorder, and somatoform disorders in Norwegians. Reliability of the SCID-I for DSM-IV diagnoses has not been determined.

Validity

Few validity studies are relevant to the SCID-I. SCID-I diagnoses of substance abuse in psychiatric inpatients were more sensitive than urine toxicology analyses or admission or discharge diagnoses of substance abuse in identifying those known to have abused substances. More than 85% of patients with known psychotic symptoms revealed all or some of their symptoms during a SCID-I interview. The positive predictive value of a SCID-I–generated diagnosis was high in a sample of homeless mentally ill subjects, but the negative predictive value was low. One study (Steiner et al. 1995) showed generally poor agreement between SCID-I and standard clinical diagnoses, although it was not determined which assessment was more correct.

CLINICAL UTILITY

The SCID-I is the most user-friendly of the clinician-administered interviews and makes diagnoses according to the current DSM nomenclature. It is still a time-consuming procedure, however, and might be most suited for difficult differential diagnoses or in special circumstances such as a forensic evaluation, in which documentation of a thorough assessment of psychopathology and detailed data on the diagnostic criteria met might be desirable. Alternatively, the modular nature of the SCID-I allows a clinician to use it selectively, possibly to confirm a diagnosis suspected after a standard clinical psychiatric diagnostic evaluation. A limitation at the moment is that no data have been published on the SCID-I for DSM-IV disorders.

REFERENCES AND SUGGESTED READINGS

Albanese MJ, Bartel RL, Bruno RF, et al: Comparison of measures used to determine substance abuse in an inpatient psychiatric population. Am J Psychiatry 151:1077–1078, 1994

First MB, Spitzer RL, Williams JBW, et al: Structured Clinical Interview for DSM-IV (SCID-I) (User's Guide and Interview) Research Version. New York, Biometrics Research Department, New York Psychiatric Institute, 1995

First MB, Spitzer RL, Williams JBW, et al: Structured Clinical Interview for DSM-IV—Clinician Version (SCID-CV) (User's Guide and Interview). Washington, DC, American Psychiatric Press, 1997

Segal DL, Hersen M, Van Hasselt VB, et al: Reliability of diagnosis in older psychiatric patients using the Structured Clinical Interview for DSM-III-R. Journal of Psychopathology and Behavioral Assessment 15:347–356, 1993

Segal DL, Hersen M, Van Hasselt VB: Reliability of the Structured Clinical Interview for DSM-III-R: an evaluative review. Compr Psychiatry 35:316–327, 1994

Spitzer RL, Williams JBW, Gibbon M, et al: The Structured Clinical Interview for DSM-III-R (SCID), I: history, rationale, and description. Arch Gen Psychiatry 49:624–629, 1992

Steiner JL, Tebes JK, Sledge W, et al: A comparison of the structured clinical interview for DSM-III-R and clinical diagnoses. J Nerv Ment Dis 183(6):365–369, 1995

Williams JBW, Gibbon M, First MB, et al: The Structured Clinical Interview for DSM-III-R (SCID), II: multisite test-retest reliability. Arch Gen Psychiatry 49:630–636, 1992

Schedules for Clinical Assessment in Neuropsychiatry (SCAN)

World Health Organization

GOALS

The Schedules for Clinical Assessment in Neuropsychiatry (SCAN) (World Health Organization 1994) are a set of instruments and manuals that were developed internationally for the study of psychopathology. The SCAN forms the basis for collaborative studies of the causes, risk factors, outcomes, and consequences of mental disorders. The purpose of the SCAN is to assess, measure, and classify the psychopathology and behavior associated with a broad range of major psychiatric disorders of adult life. The SCAN was designed to provide dimensional ratings of symptoms and syndromes that are not wedded to any single classification or diagnostic system. It can be used to make psychiatric diagnoses according to ICD-10—Diagnostic Criteria for Research (ICD-10-DCR), DSM-IV, and other systems. The SCAN was developed to be a diagnostic "toolbox" from which the user would choose appropriate symptom modules and diagnostic time frames (e.g., current or lifetime). The SCAN is an outgrowth of the Present State Examination (PSE) (Wing et al. 1974), which was first developed in the early 1960s and has undergone nine revisions.

DESCRIPTION

The essential elements of the SCAN system are the SCAN interview text, the glossary of differential definitions, and CATEGO-5, a set of computer programs that process SCAN data and provide output.

The SCAN text contains three components: the 10th edition of the Present State Examination (PSE10), the Item Group Checklist (IGC), and the Clinical History Schedule (CHS). The PSE10 is divided into two parts. Part I consists of 14 sections that cover sociodemographic information; clinical history; physical health; signs and symptoms of somatoform, dissociative, anxiety, mood, eating, alcohol, and other substance use disorders; and a screen for Part II symptoms. Part II consists of 11 sections that cover signs and symptoms of psychotic and cognitive disorders, insight, and manifestations of functional impairment. The aim of the PSE is to discover which of a comprehensive list of signs and symptoms of psychopathology have been present over a designated period and to what degree of severity, by means of a structured, rigorous, clinical cross-examination of the patient. The IGC is a list of 59 signs and symptoms that are rated on the basis of information derived from case records, other clinicians, and informants other than the patient. The CHS is a list of items that describe childhood education, intellectual level, personality disorder, social impairment, and aspects of the clinical course, information that is necessary to assign specific diagnoses according to different diagnostic systems.

The function of the glossary is to support the process of clinical cross-examination. The glossary provides detailed definitions—grounded in the tradition of European phenomenology—of the clinical concepts embodied by each item rated in the interview to allow comparison of subject responses. Clinicians use the glossary to guide their judgments on each item to be rated in the SCAN.

Each individual item in the SCAN interview is accompanied by a main probe question or questions and several optional probe questions. After asking a sufficient number of probe questions, the interviewer rates most items for up to two separate episodes of illness (primary and secondary) on one of four rating scales in the interview. Scale I, the main scale used to rate items, is a 4-point scale: 0 = absent, 1 = present in a minor degree, 2 = present and clinically significant, and 3 = present in severe form. Scale II, also a 4-point scale, is used to rate psychotic symptoms. Scale III (3 points) is used for motor, behavior, affect, and speech items, and Scale IV (3 points) is used to rate the IGC. Other items include their own individual rating scales. An optional attribution scale enables the interviewer to make judgments about the presumed etiology of symptoms if they are believed to be caused by alcohol or other psychoactive substances, somatic treatments, nonpsychiatric medications, intracranial diseases, or other medical conditions. General medical and substance-induced symptoms are exclusions in rule-based diagnostic systems, such as ICD-10 and DSM-IV, but are not specified by the SCAN interview itself.

Example 6–2 displays the questions and items pertaining to sleep problems in the SCAN, which would be asked of every patient. Sleep problems are part of Section 8, Bodily Functions, in Part I of the SCAN. The Bodily Functions section follows Section 6, Depressed Mood and Ideation, and Section 7, Thinking, Concentration, Energy, Interests. The questions are included in a manual, and the ratings are made in a separate code book. Ratings are made using Rating Scale I in the two open boxes (one for each of two possible episodes) to the right of each item. The two dashed-line boxes below the standard boxes are for the optional ratings of attribution.

Three kinds of primary periods of illness (the patient's current condition, viewed from one of three perspectives depending on the clinician's needs or interests) may be rated from the PSE interview: present state (month before examination), present (up to a year before the examination), or lifetime (from onset to examina-

tion). A secondary period may be rated from the PSE, IGC, or both. The secondary period, which occurs earlier than the primary period (the most recent period rated), may be a representative episode more characteristic than the primary period or a lifetime episode, before the onset of the primary period. The dates of periods of symptoms are also indicated for the various items.

In general, SCAN rating rules are conservative (i.e., interviewers are instructed to always rate down to the lesser level of significance or severity, because false-negative results are considered preferable to false-positive results).

CATEGO programs process data entered from the SCAN interviews and produce various outputs: profiles of individual symptoms or IGC items in the Index of Definition (eight levels of confidence in clinically significant symptoms) for ICD-10 and DSM-IV categories, a prediagnostic profile of categories (ignoring exclusion rules of hierarchical classification systems), or a list of items rated as present.

PRACTICAL ISSUES

SCAN interviewers are meant to be well trained in eliciting and evaluating the signs and symptoms of psychopathology, to have thoroughly studied the glossary of differential definitions, and to have undergone SCAN-specific training. However, lay interviewers without previous clinical experience have been trained to administer a brief form of the PSE9 (the predecessor of the PSE10) reliably, and theoretically could be trained to administer the SCAN.

A SCAN training pack contains the glossary itself; other written materials that provide a comprehensive introduction to the SCAN text, the glossary, and the computer programs; and materials for SCAN training courses.

It is estimated that it takes 1.5–2 hours to administer the SCAN; however, it could take considerably longer in an individual with much psychopathology. Part II of the PSE10, which focuses on psychotic symptoms and symptoms of cognitive impairment, can be omitted with patients who are unlikely to have such symptoms or who are negative on the Part II screen at the end of Part I. Skipping Part II shortens the interview.

The SCAN can be administered directly by computer; glossary definitions and ICD-10 and DSM-IV al-

EXAMPLE 6–2 ■ Sleep problem items from the Schedules for Clinical Assessment in Neuropsychiatry. The questions are provided in a manual, and the ratings are made in a separate code book for two possible episodes.

SLEEP PROBLEMS

Have you had any difficulty or disturbance in sleeping during [PERIOD] or have you been sleeping too much?

- *Has the quality of your sleep been as good as usual?*

Use judgement if night or shift work.

- *Do you take sleeping tablets?*

If yes:

Why? What are they? How much do you take? For how long? Who prescribes them? Do you sleep well while taking them?

CUT OFF=> to 8.024   **if no sleep problems, not taking tablets, and not depressed during period.**

If depressed mood:

8.009   *Sleep problem with depressed mood*   □ □

Have the sleep problems been associated mainly with the time you have been depressed?

0   Not specifically associated.
I   Definite association with depressed mood.

If > 2 years consider dysthymia.

8.011   *Delayed sleep*   □ □

What is your usual pattern of sleeping? [When to bed, when wake?]

- *How long ago was it normal for you?*
- *What is/was the problem now/during PERIOD?*

Allow R to answer fully then choose the appropriate items. Do not ask questions R has already answered spontaneously.

- *Is the problem one of falling asleep or of quality?*
- *How long do you lie awake? As much as an hour?*
- *How often does that happen? As much as 3 times a week?*
- *Is the sleep problem distressing?*
- *Has it been going on for as long as a month?*
- *Does it reduce efficiency during the day?*

0   No problem.
I   R complains of delay (at least an hour), not 2.
2   Delay of I hour+, 3+ times a week, at least I month.

If sleep problem judged to be due to physical condition, e.g., pain, psychoactive substance use disorder, medication, neurological disorder, etc., rate attribution of cause using etiology options.

If there is poor quality sleep ask **8.012.**

EXAMPLE 6–2 ■ **Sleep problem items from the Schedules for Clinical Assessment in**
(continued)   **Neuropsychiatry. The questions are provided in a manual, and the**
                  ratings are made in a separate code book for two possible episodes.

8.012   *Poor quality sleep*   ☐ ☐
                                                                       ☐ ☐
        In what way is your sleep unsatisfactory?

        -   *Do you wake feeling sleepy even when you have not lain awake or woken*
            frequently?

        Do not include reasons for disturbed sleep such as nightmares, etc., rated
        elsewhere.

        0   No problem. Good quality sleep.
        I   Sleep is not refreshing (specify in what way).
        2   3+ times a week, for at least a month.

8.013   *Middle insomnia*   ☐ ☐
                                                                       ☐ ☐
        Do you wake during the night?

        -   *For how many hours? How often? For what period of time?*

        0   No problem.
        I   R complains of waking (at least an hour) but not to criterion (2).
        2   Waking for I hour+, 3+ times a week, for I+ month at a time.

8.014   *Early waking*   ☐ ☐
                                                                       ☐ ☐
        What time do you usually wake in the morning when you are sleeping normally?

        -   *Have you been waking much earlier than this?*

        Use frequency and time probes, making due allowance for unusual working
        hours.

        If R has been depressed during period:

        Does/did it happen only when you are depressed?

        0   No problem.
        I   R complains of early waking (at least an hour) but not to criterion (2).
        2   Wakes at least 2 hours early, 3+ times a week, for at least a month.
        3   As (2), but only in association with episode of depression.

8   **Bodily functions**

        8.009   *Sleep problem with depressed mood*   ☐ ☐
                                                                       ☐ ☐

        8.012   *Poor quality sleep*   ☐ ☐
                                                                       ☐ ☐

        8.013   *Middle insomnia*   ☐ ☐
                                                                       ☐ ☐

        8.014   *Early waking*   ☐ ☐
                                                                       ☐ ☐

        8.011   *Delayed sleep*   ☐ ☐
                                                                       ☐ ☐

---

gorithms are easily accessible. In the absence of automated data entry by computer administration, entry of scores of items recorded in the written SCAN code book into the CATEGO system could be extremely time-consuming, because the code book contains more than 1,700 separate ratings for each episode of disorder.

The SCAN has been translated into 13 languages, including Chinese, Danish, Dutch, English, French, German, Greek, Italian, Kannada, Portuguese, Spanish, Turkish, and Yoruba. The most recent English language version (2.0), published by the World Health Organization (WHO), is distributed in the United States by

> American Psychiatric Press
> 1400 K Street, NW
> Washington, DC 20005
> Phone: 800-368-5777
> Internet: www.appi.org

The manual, glossary, and 10 recording booklets are available for $120.00 from the American Psychiatric Press. Additional information and references about the instrument are available from the WHO Web site (www.who.org/msa/mnh/ems/informat/scan/scandes.htm).

It is recommended that SCAN users complete a training course at one of the WHO's Training Centers located throughout the world. More detailed information about training may be found at the Web site.

PSYCHOMETRIC PROPERTIES

Reliability

Early studies of PSE reliability in the 1960s and 1970s demonstrated good to excellent joint reliability (mean kappa values for items and sections between 0.71 and 0.84) but only fair test-retest reliability (mean kappa = 0.41–0.64) for both inpatients and outpatients. In general, ratings of behavior, affect, and speech observed during the interviews were less reliable than ratings of subjective symptoms reported to the interviewer.

Joint reliabilities (intraclass form of kappa) for current SCAN-generated diagnoses of DSM-III-R anxiety and depressive disorders were found to range from 0.30 (obsessive-compulsive disorder) to 0.76 (agoraphobia or panic disorder). The overall intraclass correlation coef-

ficient was 0.67, and the overall reliability of lifetime diagnoses was 0.60.

Validity

The PSE has been used to describe patients and measure change in a wide range of research studies on the epidemiology, causes, and treatment of mental disorders. The PSE was used as the standard in a study that attempted to validate the Composite International Diagnostic Interview (CIDI) (p. 61). Agreement between the SCAN and the SADS (p. 58), another widely used diagnostic interview on individual items, was disappointingly low, but on syndrome classification, diagnostic class, and severity, agreement was statistically significant.

The SCAN has been shown to yield DSM-III-R diagnoses in agreement with those obtained by a modified SADS interview (p. 58) in a sample of 60 inpatients and outpatients and a sample of 62 psychotic patients and their first-degree relatives from five European sites.

CLINICAL UTILITY

The SCAN interview provides a broad information base for the evaluation of psychopathology and could thus be considered potentially valuable to clinicians. Because it is not tied to a single diagnostic system or criteria set, it has the added advantage of flexibility in the diagnostic process.

However, the SCAN is also cumbersome. Adept administration of the interview requires careful study and considerable practice. It is also quite long. Although the glossary is a rich resource for definitions of basic elements of psychopathology, users must study it intensively to become familiar enough with the concepts to eliminate the need to consult it frequently during the interview, which would slow the procedure even more. Some glossary terms and definitions are unfamiliar to clinicians trained in the United States. A diagnosis is not easily obtained from the SCAN. The clinician would either have to review the extensive information gathered and make a clinical diagnosis or have the data entered into the computer program to generate a diagnosis. The version of the SCAN for computer administration may hold the most promise. To date, there is no psychometric information on DSM-IV diagnoses generated by the SCAN.

REFERENCES AND SUGGESTED READINGS

Cooper JE, Copeland JRM, Brown GW, et al: Further studies on interview training and interrater reliability of the Present State Examination (PSE). Psychol Med 7:517–523, 1977

Farmer A, Cosyns P, Leboyer M, et al: A SCAN-SADS comparison study of psychotic subjects and their first-degree relatives. Eur Arch Psychiatry Clin Neurosci 242:352–356, 1993

Luria RE, Berry R: Reliability and descriptive validity of PSE syndromes. Arch Gen Psychiatry 36:1187–1195, 1979

Silverstone PH: SCAN accurately gives diagnoses according to DSM-III-R criteria: validation in psychiatric patients using SADS. International Journal of Methods in Psychiatric Research 3:209–213, 1993

Wing JK, Cooper JE, Sartorius N: The Measurement and Classification of Psychiatric Symptoms. London, Cambridge University Press, 1974

Wing JK, Babor T, Brugha T, et al: SCAN: Schedules for Clinical Assessment in Neuropsychiatry. Arch Gen Psychiatry 47:589–593, 1990

World Health Organization: Schedules for Clinical Assessment in Neuropsychiatry, Version 2.0 Manual. Geneva, World Health Organization, 1994

Schedule for Affective Disorders and Schizophrenia (SADS)

J. Endicott and R. L. Spitzer

GOALS

The Schedule for Affective Disorders and Schizophrenia (SADS) (Endicott and Spitzer 1978) is a semistructured interview for the assessment of mental disorders as defined by the Research Diagnostic Criteria (RDC) (Spitzer et al. 1978), a precursor of DSM-III. RDC cover 23 major diagnostic categories, including schizophrenia, major depressive disorder, manic-depressive disorder, minor depressive disorder, panic disorder, Briquet's disorder, and antisocial personality disorder. Some categories, such as schizophrenia, major depressive disorder, and drug use disorder, also have multiple subtypes.

The SADS was initially developed "in an effort to reduce information variance in both the descriptive and diagnostic evaluation of a subject" for the National Institute of Mental Health (NIMH) Clinical Research Branch Collaborative Program on the Psychobiology of Depression (Endicott and Spitzer 1978, p. 837).

DESCRIPTION

The SADS is a clinician-administered interview for use with psychiatric patients or other subjects who are manifesting psychopathology. It consists of two sections: the first covers the symptoms of current mental disorders, and the second covers the lifetime history of mental disorders before the year preceding the interview. Individual symptoms and other aspects of current affective (mood) disorders (e.g., level of associated impairment), psychotic disorders, and anxiety disorders are rated in detail on scales of severity. Alcohol use, drug use, antisocial personality, and psychosocial functioning are also assessed. Symptoms are rated according to their most severe level during the current episode and at the level they were experienced in the week before the interview. Clinically significant symptoms of lifetime disorders are rated as present or absent.

Individual symptoms are rated on multipoint (usually 6-point) scales, with severity level anchors defined. Clinically significant symptoms are identified with cut points on the scales. After rating symptoms, the interviewer consults the RDC to arrive at appropriate diagnoses by applying the criteria to the clinically significant symptom ratings. (See Example 6–3 for anchor point ranges.)

Example 6–3 depicts the insomnia item from Part I of the SADS, which is asked of all patients, regardless of whether they have acknowledged other symptoms of depression. At this point in the interview, the rater will have explored an overview of the subject's present illness; reviewed recent problems or difficulties; classified the

EXAMPLE 6–3 ■ **Insomnia item from the Schedule for Affective Disorders and Schizophrenia. The vertical ratings are for recording the worst period during the current episode or the past year. The horizontal ratings are for recording the symptom at its worst during the week before the interview.**

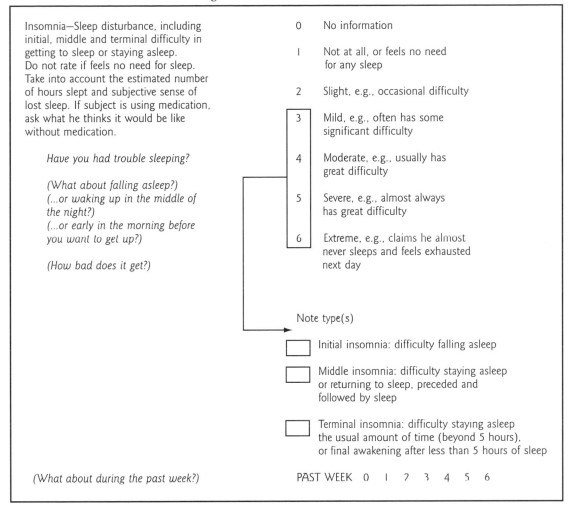

present illness in terms of its mode of onset, duration, and relationship to stressors or to physical illness, drugs, or medications; reviewed the recent treatment history; and inquired about other symptoms of depression and anxiety. Insomnia is rated for the worst period in the current episode and for the week before the interview. A rating of 3 or greater is considered clinically significant. The type of insomnia is also noted.

At the conclusion of the SADS, the interviewer reviews the RDC and determines which criteria have been met by using the information collected during the administration of the SADS. SADS symptom scores can also be combined to yield summary scale scores on symptom dimensions, such as manic syndrome and formal thought disorder.

PRACTICAL ISSUES

SADS interviewers must have clinical experience, particularly in judging psychopathology, and must receive special training in SADS interviewing. Training consists of reading case vignettes for practice in making RDC diagnoses, watching videotapes and making SADS ratings, and administering SADS interviews while being observed by experienced SADS interviewers. A SADS training package is available.

Although it takes only 1 hour or less to administer the SADS to healthy subjects, the interview usually requires 2–3 hours for psychiatric patients. Administration may take place over more than one session. Interviewers also consult available medical records and speak with third-party informants, such as treatment personnel or family members, to make their ratings. SADS scoring is usually done by hand; however, computer scoring programs can be used to derive the summary scale scores for both Parts I and II.

Several specialized versions of the SADS have been developed for various applications:

- SADS-L: a lifetime version that includes only questions pertaining to the lifetime occurrence of symptoms
- SADS-LB: a version with increased coverage for bipolar disorders
- SADS-LA: a version with increased coverage for anxiety disorders
- SADS-LI: a version for assessing interim functioning and diagnoses since prior administration of the SADS
- SADS-C: a change version that includes symptom severity ratings for the week before the interview

The SADS has been translated into 10 languages, and information about the translations may be obtained from Dr. Endicott. Other diagnostic procedures related to the SADS–RDC system include the Family History–RDC (to obtain information on lifetime psychiatric histories of the relatives of subjects) and the Longitudinal Interval Follow-up Evaluation (LIFE) (to document the course of disorders and functioning over time). Copies of the SADS, administration instructions, and training materials are available from

> Jean Endicott, Ph.D.
> Department of Research Assessment and Training
> New York State Psychiatric Institute, Unit 123
> 1051 Riverside Drive
> New York, NY 10032
> Phone: 212-543-5536

PSYCHOMETRIC PROPERTIES

Reliability

Studies using a variety of designs consistently demonstrated good to excellent agreement, except in relation to bipolar II disorder. Test-retest reliability of summary scale scores from Part I of the SADS was excellent. Intraclass correlation coefficients (ICCs) were >0.78, with the exception of anxiety (0.67) and formal thought disorder (0.49). (Test-retest intervals ranged from 48 to 72 hours.) Test-retest reliability of disorders showed good to excellent agreement (kappa > 0.65) for most disorders and subtypes of affective disorders, with the exception of hypomania (kappa = 0.57). Long-interval reliability studies and studies of community subjects yielded lower levels of reliability. Agreement on a diagnosis of major depressive disorder (lifetime) after 18 months was only 0.41 (kappa). Reinterviews with relatives of psychiatric patients after 6 years ($N = 2,155$) found the following kappa values for disorders occurring with a lifetime frequency of at least 5%: 0.57 for major depressive disorder ($n = 519$), 0.33 for hypomania ($n = 100$), 0.69 for alcoholism ($n = 196$), and 0.29 for generalized anxiety disorder ($n = 112$). More severe cases or subjects who had been treated had better reliability of diagnosis over long intervals.

Validity

Disorders diagnosed by SADS and SADS-L were shown to cluster generally within families, and many subtypes of affective disorders were shown to be differentially familial. Differences in the clinical course of bipolar and unipolar depression diagnosed using the SADS as well as prognostic differences between schizoaffective disorder and psychotic depression were demonstrated. SADS item and scale scores were shown to be sensitive to change in placebo-controlled medication studies.

CLINICAL UTILITY

The major limitation of the SADS for clinical purposes is that it is labor intensive in its training requirements and in its administration. Clinicians also sometimes have difficulty adhering to the relatively tight structure of the interview, which is necessary for the valid use of the SADS. Finally, the diagnostic output is in terms of the RDC, which had been used primarily by researchers before the widespread adoption of DSM-III in the early 1980s and which are not equivalent to DSM-IV. On the other hand, many important principles that guide current clinical practice, such as estimating the prognosis (i.e., the course of recovery and relapse) of major depressive disorder and deciding how long patients should continue with maintenance treatment for depression have come from studies that have used the RDC, not DSM-IV.

REFERENCES AND SUGGESTED READINGS

Andreasen NC, Grove WM, Shapiro RW, et al: Reliability of lifetime diagnoses. Arch Gen Psychiatry 38:400–405, 1981

Andreasen NC, McDonald-Scott P, Grove WM, et al: Assessment of reliability in multicenter collaborative research with a videotape approach. Am J Psychiatry 139:876–882, 1982

Bromet EJ, Dunn LO, Connell MM, et al: Long-term reliability of diagnosing lifetime major depression in a community sample. Arch Gen Psychiatry 43:435–440, 1986

Endicott J, Spitzer RL: A diagnostic interview: the Schedule for Affective Disorders and Schizophrenia. Arch Gen Psychiatry 35:837–844, 1978

Spitzer RL, Endicott J, Robins E: Research Diagnostic Criteria: rationale and reliability. Arch Gen Psychiatry 35:773–782, 1978

Diagnostic Interview Schedule (DIS); Diagnostic Interview Schedule—IV (DIS-IV); Composite International Diagnostic Interview (CIDI)

L. N. Robins, J. E. Helzer, J. Croughan, K. S. Ratcliff, L. Marcus, W. Reich, R. Cunningham, T. Gallagher, and World Health Organization

GOALS

The Diagnostic Interview Schedule (DIS) (Robins et al. 1981) was developed for lay interviewers to assess current and lifetime psychiatric disorders according to DSM-III criteria in the large-scale NIMH Epidemiologic Catchment Area Study. It has been revised several times, and the latest version, DIS-IV (Robins et al. 1996), yields diagnoses on the basis of DSM-IV diagnostic criteria. DIS-IV also provides information about symptom duration, remission, and recency and about associated impairment and treatment received.

The DIS is the forerunner of the Composite International Diagnostic Interview (CIDI) (Robins et al. 1988), which was designed to address the need for a psychiatric epidemiologic interview that is applicable across cultures and to provide diagnoses according to both the ICD and DSM criteria. The CIDI enables simultaneous comparisons of diagnostic systems in epidemiological studies. Like the DIS, the CIDI was designed primarily for administration by laypersons.

DESCRIPTION

Both the DIS and the CIDI are highly structured interviews. They are administered by the verbatim reading of questions with a set of predetermined response choices concerning a series of psychopathological symptoms that are arranged in diagnostic sections. Interviewers are discouraged from rephrasing misunderstood questions until they have tried repeating with emphasis the phrase that is apparently being ignored or misunderstood. Clinical exploration of responses is limited to provided probe questions, which typically include requests for specific examples. If a particular symptom is present, the interviewer proceeds through a probe flowchart to determine the severity and the presumed etiology of the symptom. If the symptom is clinically significant (see the later discussion of scoring) and is not attributable to either physical illness or injury (on the basis of a previous medical consultation or subject attribution) or to the use of medicines, drugs, or alcohol, it is then counted toward the determination of a psychiatric diagnosis.

The DIS begins with a demographic section, followed by 19 diagnostic modules, and concludes with an open-ended question about problems the interviewer may not have covered and a section for rating observations of the subject's speech, affect, and behavior. Major DSM-IV Axis I diagnostic groups, such as schizophrenia, schizophreniform, or schizoaffective disorders, depression or dysthymia, alcohol dependence or abuse, and anorexia nervosa or bulimia, are addressed, along with selected childhood disturbances, such as attention-deficit disorder, separation anxiety, and conduct disorder. The DIS also examines one Axis II personality disorder: antisocial personality.

Like the DIS, the CIDI consists of a series of modules beginning with a demographic section. However, the CIDI was designed to accommodate both the ICD-10 and DSM-IV systems, and most of the major ICD and DSM Axis I diagnostic classes are addressed by the most recent CIDI (version 2.1). The 11 diagnostic modules (core module) included in the CIDI roughly correspond to the modules that cover adult Axis I disorders in the DIS, with some modest differences in terminology and content. Thus, the CIDI module that corresponds to the DIS-IV module Somatization/Pain is called Somatoform and Dissociative (Conversion) Disorders, and the CIDI module that corresponds to the DIS-IV module Specific Phobia/Social Phobia/Agoraphobia/Panic is called Phobic and Other Anxiety Disorders. The CIDI does not include modules for disorders of children or antisocial personality. An expanded version of Section L, Substance-Related Disorders, known as the CIDI-Substance Abuse Module (CIDI-SAM), is available.

An alternative version of the CIDI was developed for use in the National Comorbidity Survey (NCS) in the United States in the early 1990s. Commonly known as the UM-CIDI (for the University of Michigan, where the principal investigator of the NCS was located at the time of the survey) (Kessler et al. 1994), this version includes several modifications of the original CIDI that are of special significance for the study of comorbid mental disorders. Importantly, screening or stem questions for all disorders are asked early in the interview, so that respondents will not learn that positive responses lead to substantially more extensive questioning and thus underreport symptoms as the interview progresses. Other changes include the removal of certain skip rules in the CIDI that interfered with the ability to study comorbidity between mental disorders and substance use disorders, improvements in the detail with which age at onset of disorders is evaluated, and the addition of explicit questions about episode comorbidity and timing to establish both temporal and causal priorities between syndromes.

For both the DIS and the CIDI, interviewers proceed through a series of questions formatted according to a flowchart. When the subject answers in the affirmative a question about whether a symptom has ever been experienced, the interviewer asks whether the subject has 1) told a doctor or other professional about the symptom, 2) taken medication for it, or 3) experienced significant interference with life or activities as a result of it. If none of these is true, the symptom is scored 2 and considered not clinically significant. If any of these indicators of clinical significance is positive, the interviewer pursues questions regarding physical illness or injury (coded 4) and medication, drugs, or alcohol (coded 3) as sole causes for the problem. If physical causes do not fully explain every occurrence, the symptom is coded as positive. If a threshold number of symptoms is endorsed positively for a particular disorder, the interviewer then returns to determine prevalence and age at the first and last occurrence of any of these symptoms or episodes. Item scores are entered into a computer program that generates both diagnostic and symptom profiles. The DIS program is written in SAS and the CIDI program in SPSS.

Example 6–4 shows questions that pertain to sleep from the CIDI 2.1. These questions are contained in Section E, Depressive Disorders and Dysthymic Disorder. The questions about sleep problems follow questions about depressed mood and appetite disturbance. Any of the three different types of sleep disturbance lasting at least 2 weeks is sufficient to qualify on a lifetime (column I) and worst period (column II) basis. There is no exclusion for lack of clinical significance or physical causes; these issues are addressed for the depressive episode as a whole rather than for its individual symptoms. The notations to the left of the questions in both the DIS and the CIDI refer to the diagnosis, the diagnostic system, and the specific criterion to which the item applies. They allow the user to compare questions with the specific diagnostic criterion to which they relate and to learn how responses are combined in the scoring programs.

PRACTICAL ISSUES

Both the DIS and the CIDI can be completed in one session and do not require the interviewer to consult additional sources of information such as medical charts or outside informants.

Additions made to version IV of the DIS have increased administration time to approximately 90–120 minutes. However, the modular structure of the instrument allows the interviewer to skip diagnoses that are not of interest for a particular study. The DIS manual also provides instructions for several strategies that can be used to shorten the interview. On average, it takes 75 minutes to administer the CIDI core module. Although some diagnoses can be dropped, the manual cautions

EXAMPLE 6–4 ■ Sleep disturbance items from the Composite International Diagnostic Interview 2.1. The item is first rated on a lifetime basis (I) by using the probe flowchart. All psychiatrically significant (rated 5) symptoms are checked for presence during the episode with the most symptoms (II).

SLEEP PROBLEMS				I EVER IN LIFETIME		II WHEN MOST SX	
				NO	YES	NO	YES
DEP10C6 DP4A4	E8		When you (were feeling depressed/had lost interest/lacked energy), [did you have <u>trouble sleeping</u> almost every night for two weeks or more—either trouble falling asleep, waking in the middle of the night, or waking up too early?]	I	5	I	5
			IF NOT CODED 5, SKIP TO E9				
DEP10S3		A.	[Did you <u>wake up at least two hours before you wanted to</u> every day for at least 2 weeks?]	I	5	I	5
DEP10C6 DP4A4	E9		During a period when you (felt depressed/had lost interest/lacked energy), [were you <u>sleeping too much</u> almost every day?	I	5	I	5

Reprinted with permission from the World Health Organization.

users against doing so, because there is some overlap across modules. For both instruments, the interview can take much longer if a subject is talkative and has extensive psychiatric symptoms.

A computerized version of the CIDI, CIDI-Auto, can be either interviewer or self-administered. There is also a computerized 12-month version that evaluates the presence of disorders only in the past year. A computer-administered version of the DIS is currently being developed.

The CIDI 2.1 has been translated into Arabic, Cantonese, Czech, Dutch, French, German, Greek, Hebrew, Hindi, Italian, Japanese, Kannada, Korean, Lithuanian, Luxembourgish, Mandarin, Nepali, Norwegian, Persian, Polish, Portuguese, Russian, Spanish, and Turkish.

It is recommended that training be conducted by centers or individuals authorized by WHO. Training takes approximately 5 days. Washington University in St. Louis offers weeklong courses for the DIS and for the English version of the CIDI. Several other CIDI training centers have been established throughout the world to accommodate those using versions in other languages. Associated training materials include a manual with mock interview scripts and homework assignments.

After purchasing the DIS-IV or the CIDI 2.1 package, which includes the interview, data entry, and cleaning and scoring programs, the buyer is permitted to reproduce as many copies of the interview as necessary. The DIS-IV is available from

Dr. Lee N. Robins
Washington University School of Medicine
Department of Psychiatry
4940 Children's Place
St. Louis, MO 63110-1093
Phone: 314-362-2469

The DIS-IV costs $50.00 for the interview; $25.00 for the mock interviews and homework; $75.00 for the computer scoring program; and $200.00 for the software for data entry, cleaning, and scoring. CIDI materials are available from

American Psychiatric Press
1400 K Street, NW
Washington, DC 20005
Phone: 800-368-5777
Internet: www.appi.org

The CIDI 2.1 can be downloaded from the WHO Web site (www.who.int/dsa/cat98/men8.htm).

PSYCHOMETRIC PROPERTIES

Reliability

No reliability studies conducted with English-speaking interviewers using the DIS have been published. A test-retest reliability study of an early Spanish DIS yielded kappa values ranging from 0.16 for dysthymia to 0.92 for antisocial personality disorder (test-retest interval was 7 days). A study using the German language DIS version 2 demonstrated test-retest kappa values ranging from 0.52 for phobias to 0.90 for major depressive disorder (test-retest interval was 3 days). In this study, the reliability for individual items was generally high; rates of agreement were less than 75% for only 16 of the items.

WHO field trials found good test-retest reliability for the CIDI (test-retest intervals were 1–6 days). Most diagnoses had agreement rates that exceeded 85%; many were over 90%. Corresponding kappa statistics were somewhat lower, ranging from 0.52 for dysthymia to 0.84 for panic disorder. In terms of joint reliability, the agreement for all diagnoses was over 97%, with kappa coefficients for joint reliability larger than 0.90 in the majority of cases. Only somatization disorder (kappa = 0.67) was found to have less than excellent joint reliability.

Validity

Several validity studies were conducted to test the agreement between DSM diagnoses determined by clinical evaluations and those obtained using the DIS. The patient and community samples varied considerably, as did the types of clinical procedures used. Overall, a wide range of concordance results were found; the strongest agreement occurred for diagnoses of substance use disorders. Examples of the range of agreement (kappa coefficient) for other major disorders were –0.06 to 0.60 for schizophrenia, 0.13 to 0.84 for major depressive disorder, and 0.05 to 0.90 for obsessive-compulsive disorder.

The validity of early versions of the CIDI apparently exceeded that of early versions of the DIS. Validity studies using the CIDI core version 1.0 to determine the instrument's overall diagnostic concordance with both DSM-III-R and ICD-10 yielded good results. Clinicians used DSM and ICD checklists to assess diagnoses in subjects who had been administered the CIDI. Kappa statistics were calculated for overall diagnostic concordance between the DSM-III-R checklist and the CIDI (0.78) and for three diagnostic groups: anxiety or phobic dis-

orders (0.76), depressive disorders (0.84), and substance use disorders (0.83). Similar levels of concordance between ICD-10 diagnostic groups and the CIDI were reported: overall (kappa = 0.77), anxiety or phobic disorders (kappa = 0.73), depressive disorders (kappa = 0.78), and substance use disorders (kappa = 0.83). No reliability or validity studies have yet been published for the latest versions of the DIS or the CIDI.

CLINICAL UTILITY

Although the design of the DIS and the CIDI serves to enhance diagnostic reliability, mental health clinicians may find it difficult to adhere to the rigidly structured nature of these instruments. Also troublesome is a wide range of concordance figures for comparisons between clinicians' diagnoses and laypersons' diagnoses, at least in the case of the DIS. Concordance for the CIDI is better, but the diagnostic groups examined are broader than in the earlier DIS studies and thus would be expected to demonstrate higher agreement on this basis alone. However, the symptom profiles generated may be useful for some purposes. In addition to identifying significant diagnoses, it is possible to determine the historical progression and duration patterns of clinically significant symptoms and disorders.

REFERENCES AND SUGGESTED READINGS

Janca A, Robins LN, Cottler LB, et al: Clinical observation of assessment using the Composite International Diagnostic Interview (CIDI): an analysis of the CIDI field trials—wave II at the St. Louis site. Br J Psychiatry 160:815–818, 1992

Kessler RC, McGonagle KA, Zhao S, et al: Lifetime and 12-month prevalence of DSM-III-R psychiatric disorders in the United States: results from the National Comorbidity Survey. Arch Gen Psychiatry 51:8–19, 1994

Robins LN, Helzer JE, Croughan J, et al: National Institute of Mental Health Diagnostic Interview Schedule. Arch Gen Psychiatry 38:381–389, 1981

Robins LN, Wing J, Wittchen H-U, et al: The Composite International Diagnostic Interview: an epidemiologic instrument suitable for use in conjunction with different diagnostic systems and in different cultures. Arch Gen Psychiatry 45:1069–1077, 1988

Robins LN, Marcus L, Reich W, et al: Diagnostic Interview Schedule, Version IV. St. Louis, MO, Department of Psychiatry, Washington School of Medicine, 1996

Wittchen H-U: Reliability and validity studies of the WHO–Composite International Diagnostic Interview (CIDI): a critical review. J Psychiatr Res 28:57–84, 1994

Wittchen H-U, Robins LN, Cottler LB, et al: Cross-cultural feasibility, reliability, and sources of variance of the Composite International Diagnostic Interview (CIDI). Br J Psychiatry 159:645–653, 1991

World Health Organization: Composite International Diagnostic Interview, Version 2.1. Geneva, World Health Organization, 1993

Primary Care Evaluation of Mental Disorders (PRIME-MD)

R. L. Spitzer, J. B. W. Williams, K. Kroenke, M. Linzer, F. V. deGruy, S. Hahn, and D. Brody

GOALS

The Primary Care Evaluation of Mental Disorders (PRIME-MD) (Spitzer et al. 1994) is an instrument designed to assist the primary care physician in efficiently and accurately diagnosing the mental disorders that are most commonly seen in adults in primary care settings.

DESCRIPTION

PRIME-MD has two components: the one-page Patient Questionnaire (PQ), which is completed by the patient before he or she sees the physician, and the nine-page Clinician Evaluation Guide (CEG), which is a structured interview that the physician uses to follow up on items checked positive on the PQ. The PQ is an initial symptom screen for the mental disorders covered by the CEG. It consists of 25 yes-no questions about signs and symp-

toms experienced by the patient in the past month, plus an item referring to the patient's overall health. Fifteen items cover the majority of somatic complaints seen in primary care, one item refers to abnormal eating behavior, two to symptoms of depression, three to anxiety symptoms, and four to problems with alcohol use. The CEG consists of five diagnostic modules that cover disorders in the DSM-IV (i.e., mood, anxiety, alcohol use, eating, and somatoform disorders) and a diagnostic summary sheet. One or more modules may be administered depending on the patient's responses to the PQ and any other indications the physician may have from the history, the informant report, or the patient's behavior that the patient might have a mental disorder.

Any one item answered affirmatively from the non-somatic symptoms of the PQ would trigger the physician to use the corresponding module of the CEG for diagnostic evaluation. At least three of the somatic symptoms trigger the Somatoform module. Each question in a diagnostic module covers a simplified version of a DSM-IV criterion for a possible current mental disorder. Questions are answered yes or no, after which the physician can determine whether sufficient criteria have been met to warrant a diagnosis.

Example 6–5 provides the screening item for trouble sleeping from the PRIME-MD PQ and the follow-up question from the Mood module of the CEG. The screening item is in the list of somatic symptoms of the PQ and would not necessarily lead the physician to follow up with the questions concerning major depressive disorder. However, the physician may enter the Mood module if he or she suspects depression is the cause of the insomnia. The Somatoform module cautions that physical symptoms that are part of a major depressive disorder (such as insomnia) are not to be considered somatoform.

Of the 16 diagnostic categories covered by the PRIME-MD system, 8 correspond to specific DSM-IV diagnoses: major depressive disorder, partial remission of major depressive disorder, dysthymic disorder, panic disorder, generalized anxiety disorder, bulimia nervosa (purging type), bulimia nervosa (nonpurging type), and multisomatoform disorder (a severe form of undifferentiated somatoform disorder). Five PRIME-MD diagnoses are subthreshold because they are characterized by fewer symptoms than are required for specific diagnoses. The subthreshold diagnoses are minor depressive disorder, anxiety disorder not otherwise specified, probable alcohol abuse or dependence, binge eating disorder, and soma-

EXAMPLE 6–5 ■ Items from the Primary Care Evaluation of Mental Disorders that relate to trouble sleeping. Item 15 (top) is from the self-report Patient Questionnaire. Item 1 (bottom) is from the Mood module of the physician-administered Clinician Evaluation Guide.

INSTRUCTIONS: This questionnaire will help in understanding problems that you may have. It may be necessary to ask you more questions about some of these items. Please make sure to check a box for every item.

During the **PAST MONTH**, have you been bothered **A LOT** by...

	Yes	No
15. trouble sleeping	—	—

MAJOR DEPRESSION

For the last 2 weeks, have you had any of the following problems nearly every day?

1. Trouble falling or staying asleep, or sleeping too much?	Yes	No

Reprinted with permission from Robert L. Spitzer, M.D.

toform disorder not otherwise specified. Finally, three rule-out (R/O) diagnoses are included: R/O bipolar disorder; R/O depressive disorder due to general medical condition, medication, or other drug; and R/O anxiety disorder due to general medical condition, medication, or other drug. The final diagnoses are checked off on a diagnostic summary sheet.

PRACTICAL ISSUES

The PRIME-MD is intended for use by primary care physicians working with the time constraints inherent in a busy office setting. Typically, physicians should have 1–3 hours of specific training in the use of the PRIME-MD system. The PRIME-MD PQ and CEG come with a 13-page instruction manual, which explains how to use the PRIME-MD, discusses reimbursement for the evaluation, and provides definitions of the disorders covered by the system and corresponding treatment options.

In a study of 1,000 primary care patients, the average amount of time spent by the physician administering the CEG to patients who scored positively on the PQ was 8.4 minutes. For patients without a PRIME-MD diagnosis, the average time was 5.6 minutes; for patients who were given a PRIME-MD diagnosis, the average time required was 11.4 minutes. Overall, 95% of the cases required less than 20 minutes.

The PRIME-MD can be administered by desktop computer and by computer over the telephone through use of interactive voice response technology. The PRIME-MD has been translated into a number of languages, including Afrikaner, Chinese, French, German, Philippino, and Spanish. A self-report version of the CEG, the Patient Problem Questionnaire (PPQ), has recently been developed; initial results suggest that its validity is comparable with that of the clinician-administered procedure.

PRIME-MD was developed with the support of, and is under copyright to, Pfizer, Inc. Complimentary copies of PRIME-MD materials can be obtained from

Robert L. Spitzer, M.D.
Biometrics Research Department, Unit 60
New York State Psychiatric Institute
1051 Riverside Drive
New York, NY 10032

A computer-generated telephone version of the PRIME-MD is also available from

John Greist, M.D.
Dean Foundation
2711 Allen Boulevard
Middleton, WI 53562
Phone: 608-827-2300

The PRIME-MD is included on the CD-ROM that accompanies this handbook.

PSYCHOMETRIC PROPERTIES

Reliability

In the PRIME-MD 1000 Study, 431 patients were reinterviewed by mental health professionals to assess the validity of the primary care physicians' PRIME-MD evaluations (Spitzer et al. 1994). Although the instrument itself was not repeated, because of the similarity of the questions asked and the criteria rated in the two assessments, agreement can be viewed as a demonstration of joint reliability. The kappa value for agreement on any psychiatric diagnosis (versus none) was 0.71. The kappa values on individual disorders ranged from a good 0.73 for any eating disorder to a poor 0.15 for minor depressive disorder. Kappa values for major depressive disorder (0.61) and panic disorder (0.60) were satisfactory.

Validity

If the evaluation by the mental health professionals in the PRIME-MD 1000 Study is regarded as a diagnostic criterion standard, then the validity of the PRIME-MD evaluations can be assessed. The sensitivity of the PRIME-MD was very good for detecting any psychiatric diagnosis (0.83) and at least satisfactory for detecting any diagnosis within a particular diagnostic module. For specific diagnoses, the sensitivity ranged from very good (0.81 for probable alcohol abuse or dependence) to poor (0.22 for minor depressive disorder). Specificity was excellent across diagnostic modules (range of 0.92–0.99) and specific diagnoses (range of 0.91–0.96). Overall diagnostic accuracy was generally very good to excellent (range of 0.84–0.96). The PQ itself functioned well as a screen for mental disorders in primary care settings (i.e., had high sensitivity) but did not perform diagnostically as well as the complete PRIME-MD system, primarily because of a higher rate of false-positive diagnosis.

The overall prevalence of mental disorders and specifically of major depressive disorder diagnosed by the PRIME-MD was comparable with that found in previous research studies using more lengthy interview schedules administered by mental health professionals. The construct validity of PRIME-MD diagnoses was supported by the significantly more impaired functioning and greater health care utilization of patients with these diagnoses as compared to patients without them. Impairment was also found in patients who had subthreshold diagnoses, such as minor depressive disorder and anxiety disorder not otherwise specified. Mental disorders were found to be associated with more impairment in health-related quality of life than were common general medical conditions.

CLINICAL UTILITY

The PRIME-MD was specifically designed for use by nonpsychiatric primary care physicians. Because of its simplicity and efficiency in time of administration, it may also be useful as a quick assessment tool for psychiatrists evaluating patients with anxiety, depressive, or somatic symptoms. Its limitations are that it covers only a few of the psychiatric diagnoses encountered in psychiatric settings and it ignores certain aspects of the criteria for the disorders that it does cover, such as the impairment and differential diagnosis criteria. There have been no formal reliability studies of the PRIME-MD. Existing validity data are based on DSM-III-R (not DSM-IV) diagnoses, although there is little reason to expect significant differences for the diagnoses covered.

REFERENCES AND SUGGESTED READINGS

Johnson JG, Spitzer RL, Williams JBW, et al: Psychiatric co-morbidity, health status, and functional impairment associated with alcohol abuse and dependence in primary care patients: findings of the PRIME MD-1000 Study. J Consult Clin Psychol 63:133–140, 1995

Kroenke K, Spitzer RL, Williams JBW, et al: Physical symptoms in primary care: predictors of psychiatric disorders and functional impairment. Arch Fam Med 3:774–779, 1994

Spitzer RL, Williams JBW, Kroenke K, et al: Utility of a new procedure for diagnosing mental disorders in primary care: the PRIME-MD 1000 Study. JAMA 272:1749–1756, 1994

Spitzer RL, Kroenke K, Linzer M, et al: Health-related quality of life in primary care patients with mental disorders: results from the PRIME-MD Study. JAMA 274:1511–1517, 1995

Williams JBW, Spitzer RL, Linzer M, et al: Gender differences in depression in primary care. Am J Obstet Gynecol 173:654–659, 1995

Symptom-Driven Diagnostic System for Primary Care (SDDS-PC)

W. E. Broadhead, M. M. Weissman, C. W. Hoven, J. E. Barrett, R. S. Blacklow, D. V. Sheehan, and M. Olfson

GOALS

The Symptom-Driven Diagnostic System for Primary Care (SDDS-PC) (Olfson et al. 1995; Weissman et al. 1995) was developed as a computerized instrument to improve the detection, diagnosis, and ongoing management of mental disorders in primary care practice.

DESCRIPTION

The SDDS-PC consists of three components: 1) a 29-item patient self-report screening questionnaire, 2) a di-agnostic interview guide consisting of six diagnosis-specific modules and a module for evaluating suicide risk, and 3) a longitudinal tracking form.

The patient screening form contains 26 dichotomously scored (yes or no) symptoms from the DSM-IV categories of major depressive disorder, alcohol dependence, drug dependence, generalized anxiety disorder, obsessive-compulsive disorder, and panic disorder. Three multiple-choice questions assess the degree of occupational and social impairment and the level of overall emotional health. The patient is instructed to report only symptoms experienced in the past month.

The structured diagnostic modules of the SDDS-PC provide interview questions to clarify the implications of symptoms reported on the screening questionnaire and to arrive at a corresponding DSM-IV diagnosis, if warranted. There is a diagnostic module for each of the six symptom areas screened and a Suicide Risk module. The questions clarify the presence and duration of reported symptoms and of other symptoms of the mental disorders in question and assess their impact on functioning. The Suicide Risk module provides questions to elicit information concerning suicidal thoughts, wishes, plans, and previous attempts. Clinical judgment and knowledge of the individual patient, in addition to the patient's responses to the questions, should guide the diagnostic process.

The longitudinal tracking form is a one-page symptom and impairment summary that charts the symptoms of patients who meet diagnostic criteria for a particular disorder or disorders or who have subsyndromal conditions that warrant clinical monitoring. Symptoms can be tracked over the course of 100 patient visits.

The SDDS-PC screen is self-administered in the waiting room. The scoring algorithm is based on a linear modeling approach that precludes manual scoring. Therefore, the answers to the screening questionnaire must be entered into a computer to generate the modular interview questions.

Judgments on the criterion-based questions of the diagnostic modules are also rated dichotomously (yes or no). The scoring algorithms here follow DSM-IV criteria. If patients fail to meet certain required criteria, instructions are given to skip the remaining questions in the module. The computer output is in the form of a DSM-IV diagnosis or a statement of the presence of subsyndromal symptoms.

PRACTICAL ISSUES

The SDDS-PC is intended for use by primary care physicians and nurse practitioners with little or no specific training in its use. No training materials are available.

It takes approximately 5 minutes for patients to complete the screening form. Each diagnostic module can take between 5 and 10 minutes to administer. Direct data entry on an office-based computer is available and saves the time of entering data for scoring from the paper and pencil format. The screening questions can also be administered to patients via a computer-assisted telephone interviewing system.

SDDS-PC materials are protected by copyright and can only be used with permission from Pharmacia & Upjohn Company. Materials, permission, and cost and ordering information may be obtained from

> Charles Barr, M.D., Ph.D.
> Greenstone Healthcare Solutions
> 7000 Portage Road, #9682-203-40
> Kalamazoo, MI 49001-0199
> Phone: 616-833-5357

PSYCHOMETRIC PROPERTIES

Reliability

The reliability of the SDDS-PC has not been tested.

Validity

An initial 62-item version of the patient screening questionnaire was tested in a sample of 937 primary care patients, of whom 388 were reinterviewed face-to-face by trained clinical interviewers using the Structured Clinical Interview for DSM-IV Axis I Disorders (SCID-I) (p. 49). As a result of this study, 16 items that optimized sensitivity, specificity, and positive predictive value for SCID-I diagnoses, while minimizing the number of items used, were selected. These items had sensitivities for specific diagnoses ranging from 0.62 (alcohol abuse or dependence) to 0.90 (major depressive disorder) and specificities ranging from 0.54 (generalized anxiety disorder) to 0.98 (alcohol abuse or dependence). Overall sensitivity for any disorder was 0.92, and overall

specificity was 0.49. Positive predictive values were between 0.21 and 0.54 for all disorders except generalized anxiety disorder (0.05) and obsessive-compulsive disorder (0.05). Four diagnoses that were tested could not be easily identified by using the original pool of screening items: agoraphobia without panic disorder, drug abuse, social phobia, and somatoform disorder. These diagnoses had poor sensitivities or positive predictive values and therefore were eliminated from further consideration. Patients who screened positive on the SDDS-PC had elevated scores on independent depression and drinking scales, had lower Global Assessment Scale (GAS) scores (p. 96), and were more likely to exhibit functional impairments than patients who screened negative on the SDDS-PC.

A cross-validation study was carried out on 775 patients. The operating characteristics of the screening items were attenuated as compared with the results of the initial study; sensitivities were lower for all disorders except suicidal ideation (range of 0.24–0.85). The overall sensitivity for any disorder was 0.88. Positive predictive values were in the same range as in the original study.

In this second sample, a test of agreement between SDDS-PC diagnoses made by primary care physicians and SCID diagnoses made by trained mental health interviewers revealed kappa values ranging from 0.11 (generalized anxiety disorder) to 0.48 (suicidal ideation); the overall kappa for any diagnosis was 0.50. Of the specific disorder diagnoses, only major depressive disorder showed even fair concordance (kappa = 0.47).

In a third validation study, a computerized SDDS-PC had a sensitivity for any DSM-IV disorder diagnosed by a clinical interview of 0.89 and a specificity of 0.70.

CLINICAL UTILITY

The operating characteristics of the SDDS-PC are only fair in primary care settings and have not been tested in mental health settings. It cannot be used without computer scoring. It has limited diagnostic coverage for general use in psychiatric practice. Thus, the SDDS-PC may have limited appeal to psychiatrists as a screening tool in their practices or to primary care physicians in the clinic.

REFERENCES AND SUGGESTED READINGS

Broadhead WE, Leon AC, Weissman MM: Development and validation of the SDDS-PC screen for multiple mental disorders in primary care. Arch Fam Med 4:211–219, 1995

Leon AC, Olfson M, Weissman MM, et al: Brief screens for mental disorders in primary care. J Gen Intern Med 11:426–430, 1996

Olfson M, Weissman M, Broadhead WE: The SDDS-PC: a novel diagnostic procedure for mental disorders in primary care. Primary Psychiatry 2:16–18, 1995

Weissman MM, Olfson M, Leon AC, et al: Brief diagnostic interviews (SDDS-PC) for multiple mental disorders in primary care. Arch Fam Med 4:220–227, 1995

CHAPTER 7

General Psychiatric Symptoms Measures

Robert S. Goldman, Ph.D., Delbert Robinson, M.D., Brett S. Grube, Ph.D., Robin A. Hanks, Ph.D., Katherine Putnam, Ph.D., Deborah J. Walder, B.A., John M. Kane, M.D., and David S. Nichols, Ph.D.

INTRODUCTION

This chapter examines the most commonly used measures of general psychiatric symptoms. Scales that provide relatively brief but comprehensive assessment of psychopathology are emphasized, although the lengthy Minnesota Multiphasic Personality Inventory (MMPI) has been included because of its widespread use. The scales reviewed are intended as screening instruments to identify individuals likely to have psychopathology, not as specific diagnostic measures to identify particular Axis I or Axis II disorders.

Organization

The measures included in this chapter are listed in Table 7–1. The Mental Health Inventory (MHI), the General Health Questionnaire (GHQ), the Crown-Crisp Experiential Index (CCEI), the Symptom Checklist–90—Revised (SCL-90-R), the Brief Symptom Inventory (BSI), and the Behavior and Symptom Identification Scale (BASIS-32) are all relatively brief self-report questionnaires for assessing general psychiatric symptoms. Although its length precludes its use as a quick screening device to detect psychopathology, the MMPI is reviewed because of its role as perhaps the most extensively validated and normed instrument for the general assessment of psychopathology and because more than 100 scales have been derived from it.

Relevant Measures Included Elsewhere in the Handbook

The scales in Chapter 8, "Mental Health Status, Functioning, and Disabilities Measures," are also considered general measures of psychopathology but generally focus on the impact of the psychopathology on the individual's ability to function. Furthermore, unlike the scales included in this chapter, they are primarily intended to be used in psychiatric settings. Scales included in Chapter 9, "General Health Status, Functioning, and Disabilities Measures," assess general psychopathology as a component of overall general health status. Chapter 6, "Diagnostic Interviews for Adults," includes measures that cover a broad range of psychopathology; unlike the scales included in this chapter, however, the instruments in Chapter 6 have been designed to provide specific psychiatric diagnoses. Chapter 17, "Child and Adolescent Measures for Diagnosis and Screening," includes general measures of psychopathology that were specifically designed to be used in child and adolescent populations.

USING MEASURES IN THIS DOMAIN

Each of the self-report measures in this chapter was designed to provide relatively brief (administration time of 5–20 minutes) assessment of several dimensions of be-

TABLE 7–1 ■ General symptom measures

NAME OF MEASURE	DISORDER OR CONSTRUCT ASSESSED	FORMAT	PAGES
Mental Health Inventory (MHI), Alternate form (MHI-5AF)	Level of mental health among psychiatrically healthy samples and screening in general clinical practice for symptoms of psychopathology; MHI-5AF developed for group-level studies	Self-report inventory; 38-, 18-, and 5-item versions.	73–75
General Health Questionnaire (GHQ)	Presence of psychiatric distress as related to general medical illness	Self-administered questionnaire; 60-, 30-, 28-, and 12-item versions	75–79
Crown-Crisp Experiential Index (CCEI)* [often referred to as the Middlesex Hospital Questionnaire (MHQ)]	Rapid quantification of symptoms and traits of psychoneurotic illness and personality disorder	Self-report questionnaire; 48 items	79–81
Symptom Checklist–90—Revised (SCL-90-R)	Measure of outcome or status of psychopathology and quantification of current psychopathology along nine symptom constructs	Self-report inventory; 90 items	81–84
Brief Symptom Inventory (BSI)	Psychological symptom patterns of respondents in community, medical, and psychiatric settings; derived from the SCL-90	Self-report questionnaire; 53 items	84–86
Behavior and Symptom Identification Scale (BASIS-32)*	General mental health functioning and evaluation of change	Structured interview or self-administration; 32 items	86–89
Minnesota Multiphasic Personality Inventory (MMPI, MMPI-2, and MMPI-A)	Clinical diagnosis and assessment of general psychopathology in adults (MMPI and MMPI-2) and adolescents (MMPI-A)	Self-report inventories; 567 items (MMPI-2); 478 items (MMPI-A)	89–92

*Measure is included on the CD-ROM that accompanies this handbook.

havior. In most cases, these measures were intended to provide a baseline assessment of emotional distress for rapid screening before intervention and also to measure the outcome of a particular pharmacological or non-pharmacological therapeutic intervention.

The measures of general psychiatric symptoms were designed as self-report measures to be used as screening instruments. As self-report measures, all the instruments described are susceptible to the questions of validity inherent in self-rating instruments (i.e., because all questions are face valid and inquire about emotional or behavioral difficulties, individuals may exaggerate or minimize their degree of distress). With the exception of the MMPI, none of the scales contain subscales to assess the presence of sophisticated response sets such as social desirability or symptom exaggeration. As such, external validation through informant material or more extensive clinical interviewing may be necessary in selected cases. Furthermore, these scales cannot be used for patients with acute psychosis, intoxication, or dementia.

Because these scales measure general distress, they are typically designed to be factorally complex, measuring several dimensions of psychopathology and functional behavior. These dimensions assess symptoms from broad diagnostic groups such as affective disorder and mood disorder; the results can then be used to determine whether more specific diagnostic instruments are necessary.

GUIDE TO THE SELECTION OF MEASURES

The measures in this chapter provide the clinician and researcher with many brief self-report measures of psychiatric symptomatology to be used before intervention or as an outcome-based assessment after medical or psychiatric interventions. Each measure is psychometrically reliable and has proven validity with respect to detecting general psychiatric distress. The major practical strength of these measures is their brevity, which allows for rapid screening in a wide variety of medical and psychiatric settings. Because these measures were designed to detect general psychiatric distress and therefore have less precision with respect to diagnostic specificity, appropriate supplementary diagnostic instruments may be needed. As with all self-report measures, response bias may affect the veracity of results for particular patients, and clinical correlation may be necessary in many cases.

All of the measures in this chapter function as general screening devices for psychopathology. Both the MHI and the GHQ assess levels of mental health in general clinical practice. The MHI detects symptoms of mental distress among psychiatrically healthy samples as well as in patients with more pronounced psychopathology, whereas the GHQ screens for psychiatric distress that is specifically related to general medical illness. In addition to general screening, the CCEI (often referred to as the Middlesex Hospital Questionnaire) also generates personality profiles, screens for particular psychoneurotic symptoms, and measures change in response to intervention. The SCL-90-R goes further in assessing specific symptoms with nine symptom constructs. The SCL-90-R also provides three global measures. The BSI is a multidimensional symptom inventory derived for brevity from the SCL-90-R. The BASIS-32 allows for the evaluation of change and functioning as a general screening device. The MMPI provides the most comprehensive evaluation among all of the instruments covered in this chapter. It has the advantage of an enormous amount of supporting material to assist in its interpretation, and it is the only measure that attempts to measure test-taking biases such as faking and underreporting.

Mental Health Inventory (MHI)

C. T. Veit and J. E. Ware Jr.

GOALS

The Mental Health Inventory (MHI) (Veit and Ware 1983) is a self-report inventory designed to assess the level of mental health among psychiatrically healthy samples, to provide screening for use in general clinical practice to detect symptoms of psychopathology, and to measure the affective components of psychological distress and well-being. This measure was developed to meet the growing demand for mental health status measures that not only meet minimum psychometric standards but also are brief, inexpensive to administer and score, and easily interpreted.

DESCRIPTION

The MHI has its basis in the General Well-Being (GWB) Schedule developed by Dupuy (1973). The MHI focuses on depression, anxiety, and other affective states such as loss of emotional control; however, it does not include physiological symptoms related to depression and anxiety, such as sleep disturbances, changes in appetite, changes in energy, motor tension, and autonomic hyperactivity.

The self-administered MHI is available in several different versions: a 38-item version fielded in the Health Insurance Experiment; an 18-item version with five subscales of anxiety, depression, loss of behavioral or emotional control, positive affect, and interpersonal ties; and a 5-item version. The 5-item version includes items that best reproduce the total score from the longer version: anxiety, calmness, depression, happiness, and behavioral or emotional control. Regression methods and factor analytic techniques were used to select the 5 items that best reproduced the MHI. An alternate form, the MHI-5AF, was developed to assess general mental health repeatedly in group-level studies.

All versions of the instrument are self-administered and ask how much of the time during the past month the individual has been experiencing various symptoms. A sample item from the MHI-38 (also included in the MHI-5) is provided in Example 7–1. The six possible responses range from "all the time" to "none of the time." The items are bidirectional; some inquire about positive feelings and some about negative feelings. The scoring of items is adjusted so that the highest achievable MHI score shows the least favorable health, and the lowest possible score shows the most favorable health.

PRACTICAL ISSUES

It takes only a few minutes to complete the 5-item version; the 18-item version takes less than 10 minutes, and the longer 38-item version takes between 10 and 20 minutes to complete. All versions of the MHI are available from

>   Rand Corporation
>   1700 Main Street
>   Santa Monica, CA 90407-2138
>   Phone: 310-393-0411, ext. 7002
>   Request publication #N-2190-HHS

Rand Corporation usually grants permission to reproduce and use the MHI-5 and the MHI-5AF with proper attribution.

PSYCHOMETRIC PROPERTIES

Reliability

Internal consistency estimates for the MHI-38 range from 0.83 to 0.91 for scales (Cronbach's alpha) on the basis of the five lower-order factors and from 0.92 to 0.96 for scales on the basis of the two higher-order factors of the MHI. The test-retest reliability coefficients for the MHI-38 are in the range of 0.56–0.64, indicating that a substantial proportion of the reliable variance in these

EXAMPLE 7–1 ■ Sample item from the Mental
                          Health Inventory

| How much time during the past month have you been a very nervous person? |

Reprinted with permission from Rand Corporation.

scales is stable over a 1-year interval. Correlations among the five MHI subscales range from 0.34 for Emotional Ties and Anxiety to 0.75 for Anxiety and Depression.

Item-scale correlations for the MHI-5 range from 0.65 to 0.80; for the MHI-5AF, they range from 0.66 to 0.81. Cronbach's alpha is 0.89 for the MHI-5 and the MHI-5AF.

Validity

To examine the psychometric properties of the instrument, the performance of the MHI-18 was compared in a medical population with two other screening tests, the General Health Questionnaire (GHQ) (p. 75) and the Somatic Symptom Inventory (SSI), using the Diagnostic Interview Schedule (DIS) (p. 61) as the gold standard. These scales were compared by using the entire DIS (i.e., the presence of any current DIS disorder, other than tobacco dependence or psychosexual dysfunction) as well as three different clusters of DIS diagnoses as the diagnostic standard (Weinstein et al. 1989). The three clusters were as follows:

1. *GHQ-related cluster:* the presence of DIS diagnoses specifically related to the face content of the GHQ (major depressive disorder, single episode or recurrent, dysthymic disorder, panic disorder, generalized anxiety disorder, and grief reaction)
2. *Affective disorders:* the presence of any DIS affective disorder (major depressive disorder, single episode or recurrent, dysthymic disorder, mania or bipolar disorder, grief reaction, and atypical bipolar disorder)
3. *Anxiety disorders:* the presence of any anxiety disorder (panic disorder, generalized anxiety disorder, obsessive-compulsive disorder, agoraphobia, social phobia, simple phobia, and agoraphobia with panic attacks)

Using receiver operating characteristic (ROC) curves, analyses revealed statistically significant advantages of the MHI over the GHQ in detecting any DIS disorder, of the MHI over the SSI in detecting the GHQ cluster, of both the GHQ and the MHI over the SSI in detecting an affective disorder, and of the SSI and the MHI over the GHQ in detecting an anxiety disorder.

A similar study examined the specificity and sensitivity of the MHI-5 version (Berwick et al. 1991). ROC curves were calculated for each of four screening scores: the GHQ, the SSI, the MHI-18, and the MHI-5. The criterion diagnoses were four diagnostic clusters derived from the list of all DIS disorders, as described earlier, as well as the diagnosis of major depressive disorder. Examination of the area under the curve and standard errors for each of the four screening scores and for each of the diagnostic clusters indicated that the MHI-5 is equal to the MHI-18 and to the GHQ-30 in detecting any DIS disorder, the GHQ cluster disorders, anxiety disorders, and major depressive disorder. The MHI-5 is inferior to the MHI-18 only for the detection of the full range of affective disorders; it is inferior to the GHQ for no cluster of diagnoses.

The correlation between the MHI-5 and the MHI-5AF is 0.93; the correlation between the MHI-5 and the MHI-32 and between the MHI-5AF and the MHI-32 is 0.96. Correlations between the MHI-5 and the SF-36 Health Survey (p. 128) are Physical Functioning, 0.18; Physical Role Functioning, 0.33; Bodily Pain, 0.35; General Health, 0.40; Vitality, 0.56; Social Functioning, 0.64; and Emotional Role Functioning, 0.61. The correlations between the MHI-5AF and the SF-36 are very similar to those between the MHI-5 and the SF-36.

The scale has been found useful in assessing both older and younger individuals (Zautra et al. 1988). The factor structure of the MHI with older individuals (ages 60–80 years) yields a set of scales similar to those reported for younger populations. However, one factor found in the younger sample, loss of behavioral or emotional control, was replaced with a subset of items denoting suicidal ideation in the older sample.

CLINICAL UTILITY

The MHI is a useful tool for detecting undiagnosed depression and anxiety disorders in primary care patients. It is a brief instrument that is easy to administer and interpret. The MHI-18 has also been shown to be valid with both older and younger patients.

Because of its brevity, the MHI lacks sufficient power to detect a range of psychiatric disorders. It is not appropriate for use with children or psychiatric populations.

REFERENCES AND SUGGESTED READINGS

Berwick DM, Murphy JM, Goldman PA, et al: Performance of a five-item mental health screening test. Med Care 29:169–176, 1991

Dupuy HJ: Developmental Rationale, Substantive Derivative, and Conceptual Relevance of the General Well-Being Schedule. Fairfax, VA, National Center for Health Statistics, 1973

McHorney CA, Ware JE: Construction and validation of an alternate form General Mental Health Scale for the Medical Outcomes Study Short-Form 36-Item Health Survey. Med Care 33:15–28, 1995

Veit CT, Ware JE Jr: The structure of psychological distress and well-being in general populations. J Consult Clin Psychol 51:703–742, 1983

Weinstein MC, Berwick DM, Goldman PA, et al: A comparison of three psychiatric screening tests using receiver operating characteristics (ROC) analysis. Med Care 27:593–607, 1989

Zautra AJ, Guarnaccia CA, Reich JW: Factor structure of mental health measures for older adults. J Consult Clin Psychol 56:514–519, 1988

General Health Questionnaire (GHQ)

D. P. Goldberg

GOALS

The General Health Questionnaire (GHQ) (Goldberg 1972; Goldberg and Williams 1991) was designed to assess for the presence of psychiatric distress related to general medical illness. This measure is not designed for psychiatric diagnosis but rather as a screening device that produces results that could lead to a formal psychiatric interview to determine a diagnosis. The GHQ may be seen as a complement to the formal psychiatric interview typically conducted by a clinician; it is possible to state the number of symptoms at which there is a 95% probability that an individual will meet the criteria for a psychiatric case (threshold score). The authors therefore use a one-dimensional model of psychiatric "caseness" rather than an official diagnosis to explain scores on the GHQ.

The GHQ was developed to evaluate the psychological components of ill health. Specifically, it assesses changes in an individual's ability to carry out functions and the emergence of a new psychological disorder rather than lifelong personality characteristics. Therefore, transitory symptoms that last less than 2 weeks are viewed as psychologically significant on the GHQ.

DESCRIPTION

The GHQ is a paper and pencil, self-administered questionnaire; no formal reading level is specified. A sample item is provided in Example 7–2.

There are four versions of the GHQ: a 60-item, a 30-item, a 28-item, and a 12-item version. The GHQ-30 has been conceptualized as a purer measure of psychological distress than the GHQ-60, because the items from the GHQ-60 that were commonly present in subjects with entirely physical illness were excluded.

The GHQ-28 is a scaled version of the GHQ designed on the basis of results from principal components analysis, indicating a total score with four subscales: Somatic Symptoms (Scale A), Anxiety/Insomnia (Scale B), Social Dysfunction (Scale C), and Severe Depression (D). These subscales represent dimensions of symptomatology rather than distinct diagnoses and are not independent of each other. A brief, 5-item GHQ and a 20-item GHQ have been developed by other investigators, but there is only nominal literature on these versions.

A variety of scoring methods are possible for all versions of the GHQ. The traditional GHQ score is derived by scoring a Likert scale with weights assigned to each position. The same response can also be scored by using a bimodal response scale, so that only pathological deviations from psychiatric health indicate a significant response. The advantage of this scoring model is that a response style of "yea or no saying" (using only either the end answers [1 and 4] or the middle answers [2 and 3] of the scale) is corrected by incorporating the answers into an either-or system. Thus, individuals who prefer to answer only positions 1 and 4 will receive the same score as individuals who choose only positions 2 and 3.

Although the manual presents threshold scores of 11 and 12 for the GHQ-60, 4 and 5 for the GHQ-30, 4 and 5 for the GHQ-28, and 1 or 2 and 3 for the GHQ-12, the clinician should review the extensive body of literature for the appropriate study representing the corresponding patient population.

Most GHQ scores are highly skewed, and there is a significant floor effect. In an attempt to correct for these issues, the CGHQ method of scoring was developed. The CGHQ scoring method looks at the chronicity of symptoms and identifies different individuals than those identified with the GHQ score, which is a general measure of psychiatric distress. The CGHQ scores are typically much less skewed and reduce the floor effect noted with standard GHQ scoring. Some evidence suggests that the CGHQ is more sensitive to psychiatric distress than the GHQ. Validity coefficients from various studies also suggest that these scores correlate better with other measures of psychiatric disorder and there is less of a tendency for decreased scores on retesting. Goldberg and Williams (1991) also suggest that the GHQ can be used to provide an estimate of the prevalence of a certain psychiatric disorder. This use is appropriate if the psychological disorder is regarded as a dimension rather than as a distinct case versus noncase category. A formula to compute this prevalence estimate is given in the manual. This type of analysis may be helpful in avoiding misclassifications in settings with a low prevalence of psychiatric disorders.

PRACTICAL ISSUES

It takes approximately 3–15 minutes to complete the GHQ, depending on the version used. The most recent manual for the GHQ (Goldberg and Williams 1991) is published by

> Nfer-Nelson
> Darville House
> 2 Oxford Road East
> Windsor SL4 1DF United Kingdom

EXAMPLE 7–2 ■ Sample item from the General Health Questionnaire

Have you recently been feeling perfectly well and in good health?

1 = better than usual
2 = same as usual
3 = worse than usual
4 = much worse than usual

Reprinted with permission from Nfer-Nelson.

Phone: 01-753-858-961
Fax: 01-753-856-830

The manual indicates that almost any individual can administer the GHQ with minimal training in scoring. However, the organization of the manual is not user-friendly. Information on administration and scoring is scattered throughout the manual rather than being clearly explained in the chapter devoted to administration and scoring. The manual also sometimes presents voluminous psychometric data without clearly indicating the appropriate demographic information. The administration section of the manual is highly focused on use of the GHQ for research rather than clinical purposes, which may somewhat limit clinical utility. Finally, the manual states that the scale has been translated into 36 different European, Asian, and other languages but does not indicate the specific translations available. On the basis of a review of the literature, there appear to be translations in Chinese, Dutch, French, Italian, Japanese, Norwegian, Spanish, and Yoruba.

PSYCHOMETRIC PROPERTIES

Reliability

A significant number of reliability studies have attempted to assess the internal consistency of various versions of the GHQ. Good internal consistency was demonstrated; Cronbach's alpha coefficients for the GHQ-60, GHQ-30, and GHQ-12 typically ranged from approximately 0.82 to 0.93, and split-half coefficients ranged from 0.78 to 0.95 for all versions. Test-retest reliability appears to be best for the GHQ-28, which was demonstrated to have a coefficient (r) of 0.90, and the other versions typically have coefficients in the range of 0.50–0.90. Test-retest reliability may be variable given that GHQ scores are measuring transient psychiatric distress rather than long-standing psychotic disorders or personality disturbance.

Validity

The manual notes that the GHQ possesses adequate content validity; each test item has been shown to discriminate between respondents who are psychologically distressed and those who are not distressed. Generally, good validity was consistently demonstrated in more than 60 empirical studies. The manual reports the sensitivity and specificity data for all versions of the GHQ up to 1987. Some validity studies have been published since then, the majority of which have results consistent with data noted before 1988.

GHQ and CGHQ scores were shown to correlate with psychiatric diagnoses on the basis of structured interviews, usually from the Present State Examination (PSE) (p. 53) or the Clinical Interview Schedule (CIS) (Goldberg et al. 1970). Total GHQ scores typically correlated with outcome scores from psychiatric structured interviews in the range of $r = 0.65–0.70$. On the basis of more than 60 studies, all versions of the GHQ have sensitivity estimates for psychiatric distress of 80%–84%; estimates for specificity are generally commensurate with these figures for sensitivity if not slightly higher. All versions demonstrated acceptable sensitivity and specificity; the GHQ-60 demonstrated the best specificity (89%). However, the length of the GHQ-60 should be considered when selecting a version for certain clinical populations, because this version may be too long for use as a screening measure for seriously ill or low-functioning patient groups. Sensitivity and specificity figures are generally consistent between the English and non-English versions of the GHQ. In general, sensitivity and specificity figures are best for detecting psychiatric distress in general medical or community samples rather than specific clinical groups.

Construct validity is supported by factor analytic studies and by correlations with predictors regarding external validators. Although the GHQ was not designed to predict subsequent psychopathology (because it is a measure of psychological state rather than trait), some studies have provided evidence for minimal predictive validity. The manual presents studies that found significant correlations between GHQ scores and future medical problems and associated distress.

Factor analytic studies report a wide range of factors depending on the version of the GHQ used in the analysis. For the 60-item version, the number of significant factors ranges from 7 to 19. For the 30-item version, 4–6 factors were typically found, accounting for 48%–50% of the variance. For the GHQ-12, only 2 or 3 factors were generally indicated; 48%–50% of the variance was accounted for by these factors.

On the basis of these studies and other item analyses, the authors report that one main factor and five specific factors are evident in the GHQ. The first and general factor is thought to account for one-third to two-thirds of the variance in the GHQ and is interpreted as indicating the severity of psychological distress. The five subfactors include 1) depression factor (GHQ-30 and GHQ-60); 2) anxiety factor (GHQ-30 and GHQ-60); 3) sleep factor (GHQ-12, GHQ-30, and GHQ-60), which is sometimes subsumed under the two factors mentioned earlier; 4) somatic factor (GHQ-60), which is sometimes subsumed under the depression or anxiety factor; and 5) social functioning factor (GHQ-12, GHQ-30, and GHQ-60).

In general, the GHQ appears to be appropriate for all ages. On the basis of evidence from the manual, age does not appear to have a strong effect on GHQ scores, although some evidence indicates that there is a tendency for women's scores to decline with age, at least until age 65. Men's scores either show no age effect or increase until middle age and then drop until age 65. For both genders, there appears to be an increase in scores after age 75.

The psychometric properties of the GHQ are not unduly affected by social class and gender. Misclassification rates related to sociodemographic factors suggest that the GHQ classified men more accurately than women and white individuals more accurately than black individuals, although these differences were so small that they were not statistically significant. However, other studies have found that classification was actually more accurate for women than for men. Receiver operating characteristic curve analysis found a greater rate of false-negative results in men and more false-positive errors in less educated individuals. Some evidence suggests that lower socioeconomic status is related to higher scores, but this finding is most likely related to general health factors in this group.

The GHQ appears to be sensitive to affective disorders, although the manual notes that it may not be as sensitive to some aspects of anxiety disorders such as phobic symptoms. As noted previously, this measure was designed to detect transient symptoms and therefore should not be used to screen for enduring pathology such as personality traits. Some evidence in the literature suggests that a defensive response bias may result in overestimated psychiatric distress of approximately 6%, but this response style does not appear to affect specificity. False-positive results have also been noted in seriously medically ill individuals.

CLINICAL UTILITY

The GHQ was originally developed in England in 1972 for use in an outpatient psychiatric clinic and validated against individual psychiatric evaluations. However, this measure has now been used in a variety of clinical settings across a variety of cultures. Its strength lies in its brevity and its acceptability to a wide range of clinical groups. The manual states that this measure has been used in approximately 36 languages, with little change in validity coefficients. The authors argue that although labels or categories of psychological disorders may vary among cultures, a universal underlying dimension of psychological distress is common across cultural groups. This measure is helpful in screening for general emotional distress but should not be used as the sole criterion for diagnosis.

Despite the apparent clinical utility of the GHQ, the manual mentions some reports that patient care was not significantly affected by use of this measure in a medical setting. The manual recommends that reporting of results to physicians include actual responses, because a general score from the GHQ may not be as useful to the referring physician as actual responses. The GHQ may also be helpful in teaching medical students how to identify potential psychological distress, because many of the items are very brief, possess good face validity, and are common symptoms in general medical settings. The variety of versions available makes it easy to find an appropriate version for a specific population.

REFERENCES AND SUGGESTED READINGS

Goldberg DP: The Detection of Psychiatric Illness by Questionnaire. Oxford, England, Oxford University Press, 1972

Goldberg D, Williams P: A User's Guide to the General Health Questionnaire. Berkshire, England, Nfer-Nelson, 1991

Goldberg D, Cooper B, Eastwood MR, et al: A standardised psychiatric interview for use in community surveys. British Journal of Preventive and Social Medicine 24:18–23, 1970

Huppert FA, Walters DE, Day NE, et al: The factor structure of the General Health Questionnaire (GHQ-30): a reliability study on 6317 community residents. Br J Psychiatry 155:178–185, 1989

Naughton MJ, Wiklund I: A critical review of dimension-specific measures of health-related quality of life in cross-cultural research. Qual Life Res 2:397–432, 1993

Van Hemert AM, Den Heijer MD, Vorstenbosch M, et al: Detecting psychiatric disorders in medical practice using the General Health Questionnaire: why do cut-off scores vary? Psychol Med 25:165–170, 1995

Crown-Crisp Experiential Index (CCEI) or Middlesex Hospital Questionnaire (MHQ)

S. Crown and A. H. Crisp

GOALS

The Crown-Crisp Experiential Index (CCEI), originally published as the Middlesex Hospital Questionnaire (MHQ) (Crown and Crisp 1966), was designed for the rapid quantification of symptoms and traits of psychoneurotic illness and personality disorder. The CCEI assesses six constructs that correspond to its six subscales: Free-Floating Anxiety (FFA), Phobic Anxiety (PHO), Obsessionality (OBS), Somatic Concomitants of Anxiety (SOM), Depression (DEP), and Hysterical Traits (HYS). The CCEI was designed to generate personality profiles, to screen for psychoneurotic symptoms, and to measure change in response to intervention. The questionnaire was meant for use in clinical research and practice in psychiatry, general medicine, education, industry, and related fields.

DESCRIPTION

The CCEI is a 48-item self-report questionnaire. Questions are numbered, easy-to-read, short sentences that require the subject to check off the response that best applies. Responses are either yes-no or never-often-sometimes choices, and the order of choices varies across questions. A sample question is provided in Example 7–3.

There are eight items for each of the six subscales, and the CCEI is ordered so that one item from each subscale appears in questions 1–8, one from each subscale in questions 9–16, and so forth through questions 41–48.

The CCEI can be scored by summing the scores (0 or 2 for two-choice answers and 0, 1, or 2 for three-choice answers) for each item to provide an overall measure of neuroticism and as a profile by summing the scores separately for each of the six subscales. Thus, total scores can vary from 0 to 96, and subscale scores from 0 to 16; higher scores indicate greater levels of distress. A graph for plotting subscale scores is printed on the back of the questionnaire. This graph includes standardization data for subscales for psychiatrically healthy and clinical samples, which are stratified by gender and geographical origin (i.e., rural vs. suburban). Several validation studies with relatively large sample sizes and a diversity of psychiatrically healthy and clinical populations have been done and are described in the CCEI manual (Crown and Crisp 1979) and later in this section. Means and standard deviations for subscale scores from these studies are provided in the manual and are stratified by age, sex, and psychiatric diagnosis. Although cutoff scores for the CCEI have not been adequately established, in at least one study (Hurwitz et al. 1987), a score of 36 was reported as a cutoff point for the presence of psychological symptoms severe enough to warrant psychiatric treatment.

PRACTICAL ISSUES

The CCEI was designed for brevity and simplicity. It takes 5–10 minutes to complete. It is copyrighted by Crown and Crisp (1979), with all rights reserved. Complete materials include the questionnaire, a manual, and a scoring stencil, which can be obtained from

Hodder Headline (formerly Hodder & Stoughton)
338 Euston Road

EXAMPLE 7–3 ■ **Sample item from the Crown-Crisp Experiential Index**

> 19. Do you sometimes feel really panicky?
>
> No _____ Yes _____

Reprinted with permission from Hodder Headline.

London, NW1 3BH United Kingdom
Phone: 44-171-873-6000
Fax: 44-171-873-6024

The CCEI has been translated into several languages, including Hindi. The CCEI is included on the CD-ROM that accompanies this handbook.

PSYCHOMETRIC PROPERTIES

Reliability

Cronbach's alpha for the total CCEI score in one study ranged from 0.84 (for a combined group of 39 students self-referred for psychiatric care and 385 interns and residents used for comparison) to 0.74 (for the students only). Test-retest reliability coefficients over 4-week and 1-year intervals have ranged from 0.50 for the FFA subscale to 0.84 for the HYS subscale. Split-half reliability coefficients have ranged from 0.35 for the DEP subscale to 0.82 for the FFA subscale. One study compared the means on split halves of subscales and found that only the FFA and HYS subscales were not significantly different. In another study, item-to-subscale correlations were reported; although high coefficients were obtained for items with their own subscales, they were also obtained for items with other subscales, suggesting that items tap dimensions that are not uniquely associated with their own subscales.

Validity

Validity studies of the CCEI have yielded mixed support for its subscale content, and the inclusion of the HYS subscale has been especially criticized. Some investigators have argued that on the basis of its content, this scale is more a measure of interpersonal adjustment or extraversion than of hysteria. In one study, a subgroup analysis revealed a significant correlation of 0.31 between the HYS subscale and Eysenck's measure of extraversion (Eysenck and Eysenck 1994), and the other five CCEI subscales were significantly correlated ($r = 0.73$) with Eysenck's measure of neuroticism.

The discriminative ability of the CCEI has been only partially validated. In general, studies have supported the use of the total scale score to differentiate psychiatrically healthy populations from patient populations and more from less severely ill patient populations (e.g., pa-

tients with schizophrenia from those with anxiety disorders). Investigators in large part have been unable to establish an adequate cutoff score, with some exceptions (e.g., Hurwitz et al. 1979).

Studies of the ability of the CCEI subscales to differentiate between the diagnostic groups to which they correspond have yielded mixed results. In the original validation study by Crown and Crisp (1966), clinicians independently rated patients along symptoms that corresponded to the subscale headings, and all subscales except OBS were found to significantly differentiate patients on the basis of the clinicians' ratings (using Mann-Whitney U tests). In another study (Crisp et al. 1978), the FFA, PHO, OBS, and DEP subscales were found to differentiate anxious and depressed patients from the general population, from those who were designated as not ill by clinical diagnosis, and from patients with anorexia nervosa or schizophrenia. Despite this sensitivity, these subscales usually lacked the specificity or discriminatory capacity to differentiate patients at a more refined level, such as patients with personality disorders from those with affective disorders or anxious patients from depressed patients. Other investigators found that the PHO subscale differentiated patients with anxiety and phobic neuroses from patients with obsessive-compulsive and depressive neuroses, although they also found that no other subscales differentiated patients as intended. Williamson et al. (1976) found that the subscale scores did not differentiate patients rated by psychiatrists as either psychiatrically healthy or unhealthy on corresponding symptom domains, and the investigators concluded that the CCEI lacked both sensitivity and specificity to be used for either screening or profile analysis.

The high intercorrelations among CCEI subscale scores found in some studies have led investigators to conclude that the subscale scores do not measure unique domains of psychoneurotic illness as intended. In addition, factor analyses of the CCEI have typically yielded a large general factor with high loadings of all scale items. Some investigators have proposed that the scale is best used to provide a general measure of psychological distress or demoralization rather than a profile of the subscale domains.

As reported in the CCEI manual, several studies have provided normative data from control groups in England that can be used as a baseline against which to compare data derived from various patient groups. Normative data have been provided from a rural population ranging in age from 17 to 70+ (n = 316 men and 339 women) and from a suburban population ranging in age from 35 to 70 (n = 343 men and 412 women). Mean subscale scores from these groups are provided on the back of the CCEI questionnaire along with scores from a smaller group of inpatients (collapsed across sex) with psychoneurotic illness and from specific clinical groups (stratified by sex) corresponding to the CCEI subscales FFA, PHO, OBS, and DEP, with subsample totals ranging from n = 14 to 144. On examination of the plot of these means, the inpatient and specific clinical groups scored higher than the rural and suburban control groups on all subscales. Although the profile of scores from the rural and suburban groups was remarkably similar, which the authors of the CCEI consider to be relevant to its use as a screening survey, the similarity of men and women across these groups was even more striking. Other normative data have been reported from 1,208 male industrial employees of the UK Atomic Energy Authority ages 42–56 and from undergraduates ages 18–22 (n = 118 men and 189 women). The scores from the industrial and student groups were similar to other control groups, with the exception of the mean HYS subscale score, which was substantially higher in the student group.

CLINICAL UTILITY

Although Crown and Crisp (1979) report in the CCEI manual that one use of this scale is to screen for psychoneurotic traits in various settings, including general medical practice, studies to date have yielded mixed results in this regard. The inability of researchers to establish an adequate cutoff score without substantial error suggests that further examination of the CCEI is needed, although most researchers agree that the scale has strength as a screening instrument for clinically significant psychological distress. The greatest strength of the CCEI lies in its ability to generate a general measure of subjective psychological distress across a wide range of demographic variables and diagnostic groups quickly and easily. Well-established norms for various populations are available, and clinicians should be aware of effects for age and sex. The use of the CCEI as a personality profile has not received adequate support in research studies, because its subscales have not been shown to discrimi-

nate between corresponding diagnoses or clinicians' ratings. Evidence from research studies, including evidence of adequate test-retest stability, has suggested that the CCEI can be used as a measure of change that is sensitive to treatment effects. The CCEI has been widely used in research and epidemiological studies, for which it is well suited.

REFERENCES AND SUGGESTED READINGS

Crisp AH, Gaynor Jones M, Slater P: The Middlesex Hospital Questionnaire: a validity study. Br J Med Psychol 51:269–280, 1978

Crown S, Crisp AH: A short clinical diagnostic self-rating scale for psychoneurotic patients: the Middlesex Hospital Questionnaire (M.H.Q.). Br J Psychiatry 112:917–923, 1966

Crown S, Crisp AH: Manual of the Crown-Crisp Experiential Index. London, Hodder & Stoughton, 1979

Eysenck HJ, Eysenck SBG: Manual for the Eysenck Personality Questionnaire—Revised. London, Hodder & Stoughton, 1994

Hurwitz TA, Nichol H, Beiser M, et al: Validation of the Middlesex Hospital Questionnaire as a self-rating screening instrument for clinically significant psychological stress. Psychiatr J Univ Ott 12:239–241, 1979

Williamson JD, Robinson D, Rowson S: Psychiatric screening and the Middlesex Hospital Questionnaire (MHQ). Int J Soc Psychiatry 22:167–188, 1976

Symptom Checklist–90— Revised (SCL-90-R)

L. R. Derogatis

GOALS

The Symptom Checklist–90—Revised (SCL-90-R) (Derogatis 1994) is intended for use as a quick screening instrument, as a measure of the outcome or status of psychopathology, and as a quantification of current psychopathology along nine symptom constructs: somatization, obsessive-compulsive symptoms, interpersonal sensitivity, depression, anxiety, hostility, phobic-anxiety, paranoid ideation, and psychoticism. The precursor to the SCL-90-R and the Brief Symptom Inventory (BSI) (p. 84), was the Hopkins Symptom Checklist (HSCL), a measure of psychopathology and psychological distress. The comprehensive coverage of symptoms found in the SCL-90-R resulted from the refinement, through psychometric analysis, of the five basic dimensions of the HSCL and through the addition of four new dimensions. The SCL-90-R, the BSI, and their matching clinician rating scales (the Derogatis Psychiatric Rating Scale [Derogatis 1993] and the SCL-90 Analogue Scale) were developed to address the shortcomings of the HSCL. These shortcomings included that the HSCL was a research instrument and norms were never formally derived, its five dimensions were not sufficiently comprehensive in their coverage of the range of contemporary psychopathology, and several of the items were not factorially "pure" measures of the five primary symptom constructs. Finally, an analogous clinical observer's scale was never developed for the HSCL.

The SCL-90-R contains only minor revisions from the SCL-90 (replacement of two items and minor changes to seven other items). It can be difficult to determine which scale is being used in a given published study, because investigators sometimes fail to identify the revised version even when it is clear that they are using it.

DESCRIPTION

The SCL-90-R is a 90-item, single-page (double-sided), self-administered questionnaire. Instructions direct respondents to report how much discomfort each item caused them during the past week, including during the current day. Items are numbered rejoinders to the opening stem "How much were you distressed by . . . ?" Respondents mark one numbered circle for each item on a Likert-type scale of 0 = not at all, 1 = a little bit, 2 = moderately, 3 = quite a bit, and 4 = extremely. A sample SCL-90-R item is provided in Example 7–4. The number of items varies across subscales, and items appear to be sequenced randomly throughout the scale.

EXAMPLE 7–4 ■ Sample item from the Symptom Checklist–90—Revised

> How much were you distressed by hearing voices that other people do not hear?

Reprinted with permission from National Computer Systems (NCS), Minneapolis, MN.

The SCL-90-R yields raw scores and T-values for each of the nine dimensions (i.e., Somatization [SOM], Obsessive-Compulsive [O-C], Interpersonal Sensitivity [INT], Depression [DEP], Anxiety [ANX], Hostility [HOS], Phobic-Anxiety [PHOB], Paranoid Ideation [PAR], and Psychoticism [PSY]). In addition, three global indexes are also easily calculated. The Global Severity Index (GSI) is essentially a mean of all items, and the Positive Symptom Total (PST) and Positive Symptom Distress Index (PSDI) are indices created on the basis of all items endorsed as not at all (0) responses. Hand scoring is relatively simple, and computerized scoring is also available (see next section).

PRACTICAL ISSUES

The SCL-90-R requires a brief introduction and a minimal amount of instruction to ensure validity. It takes about 12–20 minutes to complete. It is copyrighted by Leonard R. Derogatis, with all rights reserved. The measure, manual (Derogatis 1994), and computer versions are available for purchase from

> National Computer Systems (NCS)
> P.O. Box 1416
> Minneapolis, MN 55440
> Phone: 800-431-1421
> Internet: www.ncs.com

A hand scoring starter kit is available for the SCL-90-R from NCS for $104.00; it includes the administration manual, 50 test sheets, 50 gender-keyed normative profile forms, and a plastic overlay answer key. The gender-keyed norms were developed on the basis of nonpatient adults (over age 17), nonpatient adolescents (ages 13–17), psychiatric outpatients, and psychiatric inpatients. A specialized degree in health care with an appropriate license or certificate is considered a minimum requirement for obtaining materials.

A computerized scoring system is also available as part of the Microtest Q software package for an $89.00 annual licensing fee (with no additional charges for discs and so forth). Another option is scoring by NCS, which includes a user-determined style of report. The SCL-90-R is available in Arabic, Chinese, Danish, Dutch, French, German, Hebrew, Italian, Japanese, Korean, Norwegian, Portuguese, Spanish, Swedish, and Vietnamese.

PSYCHOMETRIC PROPERTIES

Reliability

Coefficients of internal consistency (i.e., Cronbach's alpha) have been reported for the SCL-90-R subscales and global indexes across several different patient populations (e.g., control groups, cancer patients, and psychiatric or substance abuse inpatients). For example, alpha coefficients in two studies (one with 209 symptomatic volunteers and another with 103 psychiatric outpatients) ranged from 0.79 to 0.90. Stability coefficients for the SCL-90-R have generally been adequate across a range of patient groups and test-retest intervals. One study with a test-retest interval of 1 week had a range of $r = 0.78$–0.90; a second study with a 10-week interval between tests had correlation coefficients ranging from 0.68 to 0.80.

Validity

Studies have generally supported better convergent than divergent validity for the SCL-90-R. Derogatis et al. (1976) reported correlations between the primary dimensions of the SCL-90-R and three sets of scores from the Minnesota Multiphasic Personality Inventory (MMPI) (p. 89) (i.e., standard clinical scales, Wiggins content scales, and Tryon's cluster analytic scales). The results demonstrated that the nine primary symptom dimensions of the SCL-90-R correlated significantly in a convergent fashion with like score constructs on the MMPI from all three scoring systems.

In a study of 79 inpatient adolescents, the SCL-90-R DEP subscale had a significantly higher correlation ($r = 0.79$) with the Children's Depression Inventory (CDI) (p. 344) than with the Social Maladjustment (SM) scale of the Jessness Inventory ($r = 0.58$). Conversely, the PAR subscale had a significantly higher correlation ($r = 0.65$) with the SM scale than with the CDI ($r = 0.46$).

In a study of 900 psychiatric outpatients, a depression dimension of the SCL-90-R was correlated with the Beck Depression Inventory (BDI) (p. 519) total score ($r = 0.22$) but not with the Beck Anxiety Inventory (BAI) (p. 557) total score ($r = -0.02$). At the same time, a somatic anxiety dimension of the SCL-90-R was correlated with the BAI total score ($r = 0.37$) but not with the BDI total score ($r = -0.03$). In other studies of varied patient groups, correlations between the DEP subscale of the SCL-90-R and the BDI ranged from 0.73 to 0.80, and the correlation between the DEP subscale and the Montgomery-Asberg Depression Scale (MADRS) (p. 531) was 0.81. In at least one study, however, good correlations were obtained between other SCL-90-R subscales and the BDI or MADRS (most ranged from $r = 0.5$ to 0.6).

In a study of 54 outpatients with obsessive-compulsive disorder, the SCL-90-R O-C subscale correlated significantly with other scales that measure obsessive-compulsive disorder, such as the Maudsley Obsessive Compulsive Scale (MOCI) (Hodgson and Rachman 1977) and the Yale-Brown Obsessive Compulsive Scale (Y-BOCS) (p. 572), with correlations (r) ranging from 0.41 to 0.76 for pre- and posttreatment comparisons. However, correlations between the O-C subscale and pre- and posttreatment scores on a behavioral measure and on ratings of target symptoms were nonsignificant in 9 out of 10 instances. It should be noted that the O-C subscale was generally more strongly related to the SCL-90-R DEP and ANX subscales than to other measures of OCD symptoms, indicating questionable divergent validity. In addition, the O-C subscale was highly sensitive to changes after behavioral treatment, although this sensitivity was evident for rituals and not for obsessions.

Several studies have evaluated the diagnostic utility of the SCL-90-R across diverse patient samples by using a variety of gold standards (e.g., DSM-IV diagnosis and the Present State Examination [PSE]). Using the PSE (p. 53) as the diagnostic standard in both psychiatric and medical populations, Peveler and Fairburn (1990) demonstrated a sensitivity of 0.88 and a specificity of 0.80 in the psychiatric sample; for the medical sample the sensitivity was 0.76 and the specificity 0.92. A logistic regression analysis that related GSI scales from the SCL-90-R to the probability of diagnosis by the PSE showed sensitivity and specificity scores of 0.77 and 0.91, respectively, for the psychiatric cohort and 0.72 and 0.87, respectively, for the medical cohort.

Studies by Derogatis et al. have generally found support for nine dimensions corresponding closely to the subscales of the SCL-90-R. Others (e.g., Cyr et al. 1985) have concluded that the SCL-90-R is best considered a unidimensional measure of overall psychological distress. Other factor analytic studies of the SCL-90-R have yielded from six dimensions (depression, somatization, anger or hostility, paranoia-psychoticism, phobic anxiety, and obsessive-compulsive) to two highly correlated dimensions (anxious-depression and paranoid thinking).

CLINICAL UTILITY

The SCL-90-R has received the most support for wide-ranging use as a screening instrument of global psychological distress and, to some extent, as a multidimensional measure of symptom profiles. This scale is economical and easy to administer (Peveler and Fairburn 1990; Wetzler and Marlowe 1993). The SCL-90-R has received much research attention, and norms are available across a wide range of psychiatric and medical patient and nonpatient groups. With discretion on the part of the user, the applications of the SCL-90-R can be diverse. Although the SCL-90-R may be somewhat limited in terms of dimensional and diagnostic precision, it has shown the potential to differentiate broad categories of patients (e.g., affective vs. psychotic) as well as patients from nonpatients. Some evidence has emerged for the sensitivity of the SCL-90-R to changes due to treatment.

REFERENCES AND SUGGESTED READINGS

Cyr JJ, McKenna-Foley JM, Peacock E: Factor structure of the SCL-90-R: is there one? J Pers Assess 49:571–578, 1985

Derogatis LR: Brief Symptom Inventory (BSI): Administration, Scoring, and Procedures Manual, Third Edition. Minneapolis, MN, National Computer Systems, 1993

Derogatis LR: SCL-90-R, Brief Symptom Inventory, and matching clinical rating scales, in Psychological Testing, Treatment Planning, and Outcome Assessment. Edited by Maruish M. New York, Erlbaum, 1994

Derogatis LR, Melisaratos N: The Brief Symptom Inventory: an introductory report. Psychol Med 13:595–605, 1983

Derogatis LR, Lipman RS, Covi L: The SCL-90: an outpatient psychiatric rating scale. Psychopharmacol Bull 9:13–28, 1973

Derogatis LR, Lipman RS, Rickels K, et al: The Hopkins Symptom Checklist (HSCL): a self-report symptom inventory. Behav Sci 19:1–15, 1974

Derogatis LR, Rickels K, Rock AF: The SCL-90 and the MMPI: a step in the validation of a new self-report scale. Br J Psychiatry 128:280–289, 1976

Hodgson RJ, Rachman S: Obsessional-compulsive complaints. Behav Res Ther 15:389–395, 1977

Peveler RC, Fairburn CG: Measurement of neurotic symptoms by self-report questionnaire: validity of the SCL-90-R. Psychol Med 20:873–879, 1990

Wetzler S, Marlowe DB: The diagnosis and assessment of depression, mania, and psychosis by self-report. J Pers Assess 60:1–31, 1993

Brief Symptom Inventory (BSI)

L. R. Derogatis

GOALS

The Brief Symptom Inventory (BSI) (Derogatis 1993), which was derived from the Symptom Checklist–90—Revised (SCL-90-R) (p. 81), is a multidimensional symptom inventory designed to reflect the psychological symptom patterns of respondents in community, medical, and psychiatric settings. An item selection algorithm was used to select items from the SCL-90-R that had the heaviest loadings on the nine primary symptom dimensions to achieve reliable and valid measurement of the same symptom constructs as the SCL-90-R. The test may also be used with adolescents as young as 13 because separate norms for this age group have been developed.

DESCRIPTION

The BSI is a 53-item brief self-report form of the SCL-90-R; it reflects psychopathology and psychological distress in terms of the same nine symptom dimensions and three global indices as the SCL-90-R. Instructions direct respondents to report how much discomfort each item caused them during the past week, including during the current day. Items are numbered rejoinders to the opening stem "How much were you distressed by . . . ?" Each item of the BSI is rated on a 5-point scale of distress (0–4), ranging from 0 = not at all at one pole to 4 = extremely at the other.

After raw scores for the nine symptom dimensions and three global indexes are calculated, they are then converted to standardized T-scores and plotted on the appropriate profile (according to norm group). Like the SCL-90-R, the BSI is scored and profiled in terms of its nine primary symptom dimensions and three global indices of distress. The 3 global indices, 9 dimensions, and 53 items reflect the three principal levels of interpretation of the BSI, descending from general superordinate measures of psychological status, through syndromal representations, to individual symptoms. Four major gender-keyed norms have been developed for the BSI: a community sample of nonpatient psychiatrically healthy subjects, a sample of heterogeneous psychiatric outpatients, a sample of psychiatric inpatients, and a sample of adolescent nonpatient psychiatrically healthy subjects.

PRACTICAL ISSUES

The BSI requires only a brief introduction and a minimal amount of instruction to ensure validity. It usually takes 2–5 minutes for instruction and 8–10 minutes to complete the BSI.

The scale is available for purchase from National Computer Systems, under license from Leonard R. Derogatis, Ph.D.:

> National Computer Systems (NCS)
> P.O. Box 1416
> Minneapolis, MN 55440
> Phone: 800-431-1421
> Internet: www.ncs.com

The BSI can be scored using either SCL-90-R/BSI scoring templates and worksheets or a computerized scoring service available from NCS. Hand scoring materials can be obtained from NCS at a minimal cost. NCS can also provide a profile report (i.e., a graphical presentation of a respondent's scores) and a narrative report (i.e., a text report describing the nature, clinical significance, and meaning of the individual's test performance) for an additional $2.00 for the profile and $7.00–$9.00 for the narrative. The manual (Derogatis 1993) is also available from NCS.

The BSI is available in Arabic, Chinese, Danish, Dutch, French, German, Hebrew, Italian, Japanese, Korean, Norwegian, Portuguese, Spanish, Swedish, and Vietnamese.

PSYCHOMETRIC PROPERTIES

Reliability

On the basis of a sample of 718 psychiatric outpatients, Cronbach's alpha coefficients ranged from 0.71 on the Psychoticism dimension to 0.85 on the Depression dimension. A sample of 60 nonpatient individuals was tested twice across a 2-week interval, and coefficients ranged from 0.68 for Somatization to 0.91 for Phobic Anxiety. The Global Severity Index (GSI) has a stability coefficient of 0.90. Very high correlations between the BSI and the SCL-90-R were found on all nine symptom dimensions for a population of 565 psychiatric outpatients.

Validity

Collectively, the sum of studies using the BSI demonstrates the instrument to be broadly sensitive to the manifestations of psychological distress and interventions across a wide range of contexts. The BSI was used to identify newly diagnosed cancer patients who were likely to manifest clinical levels of psychological distress, both at the time of diagnosis and in the future. The BSI correctly identified 84% of the patients who were actually judged to be clinically distressed 1 year later as potentially problematic. The BSI was also shown to identify approximately 80% of the orthopedic patients referred for consultation to a psychiatrist as positive for psychiatric distress; an 87% confirmation rate (of the 80% identified with psychiatric distress) came from formal psychiatric diagnosis. The BSI has also been used to identify clients at an outpatient drug treatment agency with differential levels of drug abuse. Very strong associations between distress levels on the BSI and levels of drug use, as well as between BSI scores and ultimate case disposition (Royse and Drude 1984), were found. The BSI was used to measure levels of psychological distress in a group of 800 members of a state bar association (Chiles et al. 1990). Smoking, alcohol consumption, and medical status were also evaluated. Among male lawyers, scores on the Somatization, Anxiety, and Depression dimensions discriminated markedly between smokers and nonsmokers. Discriminant function analysis demonstrated that smoking was disproportionately associated with psychological distress and greater alcohol use.

The relationship between the GSI of the BSI and the Global Assessment of Functioning (GAF) Scale (p. 96) was assessed in a sample of 217 psychiatric inpatients. No discernible relationship was found between symptom distress reported by patients (GSI) and global functioning rated by clinicians (GAF).

CLINICAL UTILITY

The BSI may be used as a single, one-time assessment of the patient's clinical status. It may also be used repeatedly to document formal outcomes or quantify pre- and post-treatment responses. This instrument is therefore useful both in screening primary care patients and in planning treatment and evaluating outcome.

The BSI is appropriate for a broad range of individuals, except those with delirium, mental retardation, or florid psychosis. Currently, there are four gender-keyed formal norm groups for the BSI: adult psychiatric outpatients, adult community nonpatients, adult psychiatric inpatients, and adolescent community nonpatients. Two matching rating scales for clinical observers that measure the same psychopathologic constructs are available to quantify clinical judgment concerning patient psychological distress levels: the Derogatis Psychiatric Rating Scale (DPRS) (Derogatis 1993) and the SCL-90 Analogue Scale (Derogatis 1993).

The use of standardized scores enables the clinician to compare an individual's scores with those of a relevant reference group of interest, as well as to make meaningful comparisons of an individual's performance in one domain with that in another. Because of its brevity, the BSI is an effective screening tool to enhance the identification of psychiatric disorders in primary care.

This scale is not appropriate for individuals who are motivated to disguise their answers by either minimizing or exaggerating distress.

REFERENCES AND SUGGESTED READINGS

Chiles JA, Benjamin AH, Cahn TS: Who smokes? why? psychiatric aspects of continued cigarette usage among lawyers in Washington state. Compr Psychiatry 31:176–184, 1990

Derogatis LR: Brief Symptom Inventory (BSI): Administration, Scoring, and Procedures Manual, Third Edition. Minneapolis, MN, National Computer Systems, 1993

Derogatis LR: SCL-90-R, Brief Symptom Inventory, and matching clinical rating scales, in Psychological Testing, Treatment Planning, and Outcome Assessment. Edited by Maruish M. New York, Erlbaum, 1994

Derogatis LR, Derogatis MF: SCL-90-R and the BSI, in Quality of Life and Pharmacoeconomics in Clinical Trials, 2nd Edition. Edited by Spilker B. Philadelphia, PA, Lippincott-Raven, 1996

Piersma HL, Boes JL: Agreement between patient self-report and clinician rating: concurrence between the BSI and the GAF among psychiatric inpatients. J Clin Psychol 51:153–157, 1995

Royse D, Drude K: Screening drug abuse clients with the Brief Symptom Inventory. International Journal of the Addictions 19:849–857, 1984

Behavior and Symptom Identification Scale (BASIS-32)

S. V. *Eisen* and M. C. *Grob*

GOALS

The Behavior and Symptom Identification Scale (BASIS-32) (Eisen et al. 1986) was designed to be a brief but comprehensive outcome measure of mental health treatment from the patient's perspective. It is a broad-based measure of general functioning that allows for the evaluation of change over the course of treatment. It assesses the major symptom and functioning domains that lead to the need for inpatient psychiatric treatment, including mood disturbances, anxiety, suicidality, psychotic symptoms, self-understanding, interpersonal relations, role functioning, daily living skills, impulsivity, and substance abuse. The BASIS-32 was designed to cover behavioral and functioning areas in addition to psychiatric symptoms.

DESCRIPTION

The BASIS-32 was empirically derived from psychiatric inpatients' reports of symptoms and problems that were cluster analyzed to arrive at the 32 items. Respondents are asked to indicate the degree of difficulty they have been experiencing on each item during the past week. The degree of difficulty is rated on a 5-point scale, with 0 = no difficulty, 1 = a little difficulty, 2 = moderate difficulty, 3 = quite a bit of difficulty, and 4 = extreme difficulty. A sample item is provided in Example 7–5.

Subscale and overall mean scores can range from 0 to 4. Scores on the 32 items can be broken down into five subscales: Relation to Self and Others, Daily Living and Role Functioning, Depression and Anxiety, Impulsive and Addictive Behavior, and Psychosis. In addition, an overall average score is computed.

Populations measured include adolescents through adults (ages 14 and up) receiving mental health treatment, excluding geriatric patients with severe dementia.

PRACTICAL ISSUES

Four different data collection procedures have been successfully used to obtain BASIS-32 assessments: structured interviews in which a staff member or volunteer reads the items to patients and elicits their ratings for each

EXAMPLE 7–5 ■ Sample item from the Behavior and Symptom Identification Scale

IN THE PAST WEEK, how much difficulty have you been having in the area of:

2. Household Responsibilities. (For example, shopping, cooking, laundry, cleaning, other chores).

Reprinted with permission from Susan V. Eisen, Ph.D.

item, patient self-administration, telephone interviews, and mailed self-report questionnaires. It takes 5–20 minutes to complete the self-report version. Administration as a structured interview generally takes 15–20 minutes. A BASIS-32 packet is available from

Susan V. Eisen, Ph.D.
Department of Mental Health Services Research
McLean Hospital
115 Mill Street
Belmont, MA 02178
Fax: 617-855-2948

The packet includes sample copies of the measure, an instruction and scoring booklet, and a reference list. The BASIS-32 is also part of a performance measurement system approved by the Joint Commission on Accreditation of Healthcare Organizations. Contact Leslie Cahill, M.A., M.P.H., at 617-855-2190 for more information.

The BASIS-32 is copyrighted by the McLean Hospital Corporation, which has given mental health providers permission to reproduce and use the manual versions of the BASIS-32 to assess outcomes in their own clients or patients. There is no charge for this use. Permission has not been granted for any facility to sell the BASIS-32 to others. However, nonexclusive licensing arrangements for the commercial use of the BASIS-32 by providers and insurance, managed-care, pharmaceutical, software development, and consulting organizations can be made directly with McLean Hospital. Proposals should be submitted in writing to Leslie Cahill, M.A., M.P.H., at the address given earlier.

Currently, a manual version of the BASIS-32 that can be used at intake, during treatment, and/or at follow-up after termination of treatment is available. In addition to the 32 items, it includes demographic and employment information. The manual version of the BASIS-32 can be scored by hand or by computer using the scoring algorithms provided in the instruction booklet. Several automated versions of the BASIS-32 are available from commercial vendors.

The technical report "Use of BASIS-32 for Outcome Assessment of Recipients of Outpatient Mental Health Services," by Eisen, Wilcox, Schaefer, Culhane, and Leif, is available from the Evaluation Center at Human Services Research Institute (HSRI) in Cambridge, Massachusetts (617-876-0426 or www.hsri.org).

The BASIS-32 is included on the CD-ROM that accompanies this handbook.

PSYCHOMETRIC PROPERTIES

Reliability

In a sample of 387 newly admitted psychiatric inpatients, internal consistency (Cronbach's alpha) of the subscales ranged from 0.65 to 0.81, with a full-scale internal consistency of 0.89 (Eisen et al. 1994). In a sample of 407 psychiatric outpatients, Cronbach's alpha coefficients for the subscales ranged from 0.65 to 0.89, with a full-scale internal consistency of 0.95 (Eisen et al. 1999). In an inpatient sample, test-retest reliability coefficients (with a 2- to 3-day interval) ranged from 0.65 to 0.81 for the five subscales. Admission scores were significantly different from those obtained at 6-month follow-up for both the inpatient and outpatient samples, as were scores during the course of hospitalization from admission to discharge.

Validity

Scores on the BASIS-32 items in the inpatient sample were correlated with comparable scales on the Symptom Checklist–90—Revised (SCL-90-R) (p. 81): Depression, 0.63; Impulsivity, 0.53; and Psychoticism, 0.48 (Eisen et al. 1986). For the outpatient sample, scores from the SF-36 Health Survey (p. 128), a 36-item self-report survey designed to measure functional health status, were correlated with BASIS-32 subscale scores. The first three BASIS-32 subscales are all highly correlated with the SF-36 Social Functioning and Mental Health subscales.

Two objective indicators—continued hospitalization or rehospitalization during the 6 months after admission and employment status at follow-up—were compared with patients' subjective reports at a follow-up point 6 months after hospital admission (Eisen et al. 1994). Consistent with their hospital status, patients who were discharged to the community and remained so during the 6 months reported the least difficulty, whereas patients who were hospitalized at the 6-month follow-up point reported the greatest difficulty. Patients who were working reported significantly less difficulty with respect to daily living and role functioning than those who were not working. Correlations were computed between patient self-ratings and ratings by family members at admission on the basis of an earlier version of the scale with 17 areas of symptomatology (Eisen et al. 1986). These correlations ranged from 0.07 to 0.52, with most between 0.20 and 0.40. Correlations were statistically significant in 16 of 17 areas. The correlations between patient and family ratings were higher at follow-up than at admission, with most over 0.30. Three of the five subscales are relatively highly correlated with each other (0.58–0.66).

Relevant BASIS-32 subscale scores for psychiatric inpatients successfully discriminated three diagnostic groups: those with depressive or anxiety disorders, those with substance use disorders, and those with psychotic disorders. The subscores for the outpatient sample were able to discriminate only the depressive or anxiety disorders group.

Comparable participation rates are obtained for self-administered versus interviewer-administered methods. There were differences in reported symptoms between the following groups: adult psychiatric inpatients assigned to be interviewed with the measure (n = 47), those assigned a self-report version of the measure (n = 52), and those allowed to choose between being interviewed with the measure (n = 33) and completing a self-report (n = 18). On two of the five subscales, Relation to Self and Others and Daily Living and Role Functioning, the assigned self-report group reported significantly more difficulty than the group of individuals who chose to be interviewed (Eisen 1995).

CLINICAL UTILITY

The BASIS-32 has been used most extensively with psychiatric hospital inpatients. It has been used to assess the patient's progress during the course of treatment and maintenance over a follow-up period, to assess symptom patterns in different populations (e.g., adolescent and adult substance abuse populations), and to assess the impact of particular treatment cost reimbursement methods on patient outcome (Sederer et al. 1992). However, because of the lack of published studies from other settings, it is not known whether the psychometric properties of the measure are applicable to more diverse populations (Eisen 1996). The BASIS-32 has been shown to be sensitive to changes in symptom distress after treatment. The authors of the scale envision three distinct uses of the BASIS: 1) as an outcome measure for specific populations under study (e.g., alcoholic patients and adolescents), with the potential for identifying good versus poor outcome within specific time frames; 2) as another source of information for the clinician to use in diagnosis and treatment planning; and 3) as a clinical tool for use by the patient and clinician together to help identify, assess, and compare aspects of problem behavior at specified intervals during treatment.

A major strength of this measure is its applicability to a wide range of people receiving mental health treatment. In addition, unlike the SCL-90-R, which includes only symptoms and not difficulties in functioning, the BASIS-32 includes the major symptoms and problems that bring people to inpatient treatment. The measure is simple and brief, so it can be administered by nonprofessional personnel. Another strength of the BASIS-32 is that it allows for group comparisons because assessments are made on the basis of the same problems.

REFERENCES AND SUGGESTED READINGS

Eisen SV: Assessment of subjective distress by patients' self-report versus structured interview. Psychol Rep 76:35–39, 1995

Eisen SV: Behavior and Symptom Identification Scale (BASIS-32), in Outcome Assessment in Clinical Practice. Edited by Sederer LI, Dickey B. Baltimore, MD, Williams & Wilkins, 1996

Eisen SV, Grob MC, Klein AA: BASIS: the development of a self-report measure for psychiatric inpatient evaluation. Psychiatric Hospital 17:165–171, 1986

Eisen SV, Dill DL, Grob MC: Reliability and validity of a brief patient-report instrument for psychiatric outcome evaluation. Hospital and Community Psychiatry 45:242–247, 1994

Eisen SV, Wilcox M, Leff HS, et al: Assessing behavioral health outcomes in outpatient programs: reliability and validity of the BASIS-32. J Behav Health Serv Res 26:5–17, 1999

Sederer LI, Eisen SV, Dill DL, et al: Case-based reimbursement for psychiatric hospital care. Hospital and Community Psychiatry 42:1120–1126, 1992

Minnesota Multiphasic Personality Inventory (MMPI, MMPI-2, and MMPI-A)

S. R. Hathaway and J. C. McKinley

GOALS

The Minnesota Multiphasic Personality Inventories (MMPI, MMPI-2, and MMPI-A) are omnibus self-report inventories primarily designed to aid in clinical diagnosis and in the assessment of general psychopathology in adults (MMPI and MMPI-2) and adolescents (MMPI-A). The original version of the MMPI was developed in the 1940s. The current edition is the MMPI-2 (Butcher et al. 1989), which has been partially revised and restandardized on a contemporary normative sample. The 13 standard clinical and validity scales of the original MMPI (described later) are largely unchanged in the MMPI-2 and MMPI-A.

DESCRIPTION

The MMPI-2 and MMPI-A consist, respectively, of 567 and 478 self-report, true-false items, presented in either a test booklet or on an audiotape. The items are presented in a largely random order, but the first few items are intended to be relatively nonthreatening; in addition, the items keyed for the basic clinical and validity scales are among the first 370 items of the MMPI-2 (and the first 350 of the MMPI-A). A sample question is provided in Example 7–6.

The eight basic syndrome scales are Hypochondriasis (Hs), Depression (D), Hysteria (Hy), Psychopathic Deviate (Pd), Paranoia (Pa), Psychasthenia (Pt), Schizo-

EXAMPLE 7–6 ■ Sample item from the Minnesota Multiphasic Personality Inventory

> I find it hard to keep my mind on a task or job.

Reprinted with permission from National Computer Systems (NCS), Minneapolis, MN.

phrenia (Sc), and Mania (Ma); two additional basic clinical scales are Masculinity-Femininity (Mf) and Social Introversion-Extroversion (Si). There are also three basic validity scales to assess test-taking attitudes: Lie (L), Infrequency (F), and Correction/Defensiveness (K). In keeping with their syndromal character, the eight basic scales are multidimensional, and subscales have been developed to discern characteristic symptomatic trends contributing to the full scale scores. To supplement the interpretation of the basic clinical scales, many additional scales are also routinely scored. Examples include scales developed on the basis of clusters of item content (e.g., Bizarre Mentation, Type A Behavior, and Family Problems); new and experimental scales to address areas such as substance abuse, gender role, and marital disharmony (e.g., Ego Strength, MacAndrew Alcoholism Scale—Revised, Dominance, Overcontrolled Hostility, and Post-Traumatic Stress Disorder); and additional scales to assess response consistency and various test-taking attitudes (e.g., Back-Page Infrequency and Variable Response Inconsistency). An eighth-grade reading level is recommended for the MMPI-2 (seventh grade for the MMPI-A); if the reading requirements pose a problem, clinicians can use the audiotape version.

The MMPI-2 and MMPI-A provide raw and T-scores for each of the basic clinical and validity scales (the T-score is a transformation of the raw scale scores into scales that have the same mean of 50 and standard deviation of 10); fractions of the Correction/Defensiveness (K) scale are added to five of the eight syndrome scales to address over- or underreporting of symptoms. Normative data derived from representative samples of the community of 1,138 men and 1,462 women of diverse ethnic origins gathered from seven states are used to derive the T-scores. The scores for each scale are recorded on forms that display them in a graphic profile (automatically converting the raw scores to T-scores). Hand scoring templates are available; however, there are currently more than 100 scales supported by the test publisher for routine scoring.

PRACTICAL ISSUES

It typically takes 1–1.5 hours to complete the MMPI-2 and MMPI-A. Both versions are copyrighted by the University of Minnesota Press. The MMPI-2 manual (Butcher et al. 1989) provides normative data, supportive

research, and interpretive guidelines. Test materials and computerized scoring and interpretive services for both the MMPI-2 and the MMPI-A are available from

National Computer Systems (NCS)
P.O. Box 1416
Minneapolis, MN 55440
Phone: 800-431-1421
Internet: www.ncs.com

Alternative computer scoring and interpretation are available from

Caldwell Report
1545 Sawtelle Boulevard
Los Angeles, CA 90025
Phone: 310-478-3133

Hand scoring starter kits are available from NCS for $350.00. Each kit includes the manual (Butcher et al. 1989), 10 test item booklets, 50 answer sheets and profile forms, and various scoring templates. Item booklets are available in both English and Spanish from the test publisher. The MMPI and MMPI-2 have also been translated into dozens of other languages. (Contact NCS and the Caldwell Report at the addresses listed for more information.) Purchase of MMPI materials requires evidence of relevant graduate-level education and state licensure.

PSYCHOMETRIC PROPERTIES

Reliability

Internal consistency estimates (Cronbach's alpha) range from 0.34 (Paranoia) to 0.88 (Schizophrenia) for the basic scales, from 0.68 (Type A Behavior) to 0.86 (Cynicism) for the content scales, and from 0.24 (Overcontrolled Hostility) to 0.91 (Post-Traumatic Stress Disorder) for the supplementary scales. Temporal stability coefficients over a median 1-week interval for the MMPI-2 range from 0.58 (Paranoia) to 0.92 (Social Introversion) for the basic scales, from 0.78 (Bizarre Mentation) to 0.91 (Anxiety) for the content scales, and from 0.62 (MacAndrew Alcoholism Scale) to 0.91 (Post-Traumatic Stress Disorder) for the supplementary scales; comparable results are obtained for the MMPI-A.

Validity

A research base accumulated over a period of 60 years and numbering more than 10,000 references supports the validity of the standard MMPI and MMPI-2 scales across a wide range of applications, including psychiatric, general medical, forensic, and vocational assessments (Dahlstrom et al. 1975; Greene 1991). Approaches to the validation of the MMPI and MMPI-2 have been so diverse with respect to the designs and samples employed as to defy concise summarization but have included multivariate analyses, various classification paradigms, and the identification of empirical correlates of items, scales, and profiles of scales. Findings from studies of the MMPI-2 and MMPI-A have mostly been consistent with those from studies of the original MMPI. Investigations have indicated an incremental, albeit modest, contribution to the accuracy of clinical prediction when the MMPI is compared or combined with other sources of clinical information (Butcher et al. 1989; Greene 1991).

Evidence for the convergent validity of the MMPI, MMPI-2, and MMPI-A is generally recognized to be better than that for its discriminant validity. The method of contrasted groups, in which the item responses of a pathological criterion group (e.g., patients with schizophrenia) are contrasted with those of a diverse group of psychiatrically healthy individuals, used for the development of the basic clinical scales has been the subject of criticism on both theoretical and psychometric grounds (Helmes and Reddon 1993). This method of scale construction increased sensitivity but allowed considerable item overlap, giving rise to enhanced correlations among the clinical scales and reduction of specificity and compromising discriminant validity. As a consequence, the test tends to perform better in discriminating between major psychiatric conditions (e.g., across somatoform, anxiety, mood, psychotic, and personality disorder categories) than it does within them. For example, the success of the MMPI in discriminating among patients with somatization disorder and neurological conditions such as multiple sclerosis and closed-head injuries has been less satisfactory than in the discrimination of psychotic and nonpsychotic states (although the availability of empirical documentation of its performance within a wide range of specific clinical populations and settings is itself a positive feature of the test). In addition, the scales vary in their range of sensitivity and specificity; some scales fail to perform as desired. For example, the basic Paranoia scale is generally considered to lack sensitivity for patients manifesting overt paranoid symptomatology, although its specificity is relatively high.

The provision of additional content and supplementary scales has extended the performance of the test in the context of differential diagnosis. The original (basic) clinical scales were derived from clinical constructs recognized in the 1930s, whereas the content and supplementary scales are more closely coordinated with current diagnostic concepts. Not all of these newer scales have been satisfactorily validated at this point, however. In addition, although many of the content scales, such as those for symptomatic anxiety, fears and phobias, obsessiveness, and depression, can augment diagnostic discrimination among these groups, these scales still contain some item overlap and moderately high statistical redundancy.

One feature of the MMPI-2 and MMPI-A that has influenced their adoption for use within both clinical and nonclinical populations is the availability of scales and indexes to evaluate the test-taking attitudes of the persons being assessed. The basic and supplemental validity scales available within the MMPI-2 and MMPI-A have been empirically shown to be relatively successful in identifying a variety of willful or self-deceptive distortions and manipulations (Nichols and Greene 1997).

CLINICAL UTILITY

Like the MMPI, the MMPI-2 and MMPI-A have been used most extensively among psychiatric inpatients and outpatients as screening instruments for a wide variety of mental disorder symptomatology, as measures of clinical prediction and prognosis, and as guidelines for treatment planning. Medical or neurological, forensic, and vocational (rehabilitation and employment screening) applications are also well established for the MMPI and the MMPI-2. For example, scores greater than 70T (i.e., scores transformed onto the T-distribution) on the Hypomania scale are often interpreted as indicating unstable mood, expedient if not impulsive judgment, a tendency to react irritably or oppositionally to the demands of others, an overly energized but poorly focused and nonpersistent approach to tasks, and a heightened activity level that may be associated with clinical symptoms such as hyperactivity, pressured speech, flight of ideas, and grandiosity. However, the interpretation would vary with both the clinical setting and other features of the test profile. In a correctional setting, such a score might place the individual at increased risk of conflict with peers because of his or her intrusiveness and conflict with correctional officers for rule violations, acts of disrespect, or challenges to authority. In a psychiatric setting, such a score might suggest the presence of a mood disorder and the potential benefit of treatment with a mood stabilizer. Although the MMPI-2 and MMPI-A are commonly used to assess global and symptomatic outcomes of treatment, the amount of time required for their administration is considered to be a disadvantage. In addition, these tests are perhaps not well suited for the purpose of closely tracking the response to specific treatments and interventions.

However, considering the range and validity of the information available from the more than 100 available scales, especially when computer scoring is used, the MMPI-2 and MMPI-A are an economic and efficient way to augment a clinical assessment. The MMPI and MMPI-2 have a substantial research base to support the validity of a wide variety of clinical applications. This research encompasses a broad range of psychiatric, medical, disability, and psychiatrically healthy (nonclinical) groups, addresses an equally diverse range of clinical issues, and provides normative data for a considerable number of particular populations (Butcher et al. 1989; Greene 1991), thereby providing clinicians and research investigators with information that may have relevance to their specific needs. The MMPI, MMPI-2, and MMPI-A are especially suitable for use when an assessment of the accuracy (e.g., honesty) of the person's self-report is questionable and/or considered to be an important component of the evaluation. For example, scores greater than 65T on the L scale are often interpreted as indicating a conscious reluctance to admit to even minor faults and shortcomings and a desire to present oneself as unusually virtuous, responsible, and controlled. (However, immigrants, clergy, persons of low intelligence, and groups isolated from the dominant culture may produce elevated scores for other reasons.) The many available language translations of the MMPI-2 and MMPI-A are helpful in obtaining scores for refugees and immigrants from many parts of the world.

Interpretation of the MMPI-2 and MMPI-A findings, however, is more complex than the appearance of the score profiles might suggest (Greene 1991). One should not interpret the scale titles literally. For example, elevations on the Schizophrenia scale are commonly found in a variety of disorders, including borderline personality disorder, schizotypal personality disorder, and even major depressive disorder and some anxiety disorders. Thus, elevations should not be interpreted as indicating clinical diagnoses in the absence of supportive information concerning setting, demographics, and other scale scores. The research literature available for these tests is perhaps most useful in decreasing an overly optimistic, naive test interpretation that can occur with instruments that have experienced less empirical scrutiny. The prediction of low-frequency events, such as suicide, are especially problematic, and these tests should not be used in isolation for this purpose.

REFERENCES AND SUGGESTED READINGS

Butcher JN, Dahlstrom WG, Graham JR, et al: Minnesota Multiphasic Personality-2 (MMPI-2): Manual for Administration and Scoring. Minneapolis, MN, University of Minnesota Press, 1989

Dahlstrom WG, Welsh GS, Dahlstrom LE: MMPI Handbook, Vol II: Research Applications. Minneapolis, MN, University of Minnesota Press, 1975

Greene RL: MMPI/MMPI-2: An Interpretive Manual. Boston, MA, Allyn & Bacon, 1991

Helmes E, Reddon JR: A perspective on developments in assessing psychopathology: a critical review of the MMPI and MMPI-2. Psychol Bull 113:453–471, 1993

Nichols DS, Greene RL: Dimensions of deception in personality assessment: the example of the MMPI-2. J Pers Assess 68:251–266, 1997

CHAPTER 8

Mental Health Status, Functioning, and Disabilities Measures

Janet B. W. Williams, D.S.W.

INTRODUCTION

Major Domains

In this chapter, instruments for measuring global mental health status, functioning, and disabilities are reviewed. Although the instruments described cover different aspects of these domains, they are all designed to be used with clinical populations, and they all assess global aspects of functioning. With the exception of the Life Skills Profile (LSP), the Multnomah Community Ability Scale (MCAS), and the Sheehan Disability Scale, these instruments were all designed for specific populations, although the latter two may be useful for patients with other diagnoses as well. The Global Assessment Scale (GAS) and the Clinical Global Impressions (CGI) Scale require a rater to summarize overall symptoms and functioning into a single score. The other scales require ratings of several specific behaviors, and the final score then reflects a summary judgment.

Organization

The instruments can be divided into two groups: those useful for general purposes and those developed for specific diagnoses. Within these two groups, some scales are designed to be administered by a clinician or trained other, some may be self-administered, and some may be either clinician or self-administered.

The scales (Table 8–1) designed for general use include the GAS, the CGI, the Health of the Nation Out-come Scales (HoNOS), and the Social Adjustment Scale (SAS). The GAS, the Global Assessment of Functioning (GAF) Scale, and the similar Social and Occupational Functioning Assessment Scale (SOFAS) all reflect summary judgments of functioning in two or three areas combined (psychological, social, and occupational). The widely used CGI measures the severity of an illness and improvement (or deterioration) over time. The newly published HoNOS, available in both clinician-rated and patient-completion forms, measures aspects of both mental health and social functioning. The SAS measures role performance in six major areas of social functioning and also comes in interview and self-report forms.

The MCAS, which assesses psychiatric disability in four major areas of functioning, is designed to be used in chronically mentally ill adults who are living in the community. The LSP, designed for use with adults with schizophrenia, rates five areas of disability that affect survival and adaptation in the community, assessed independently of psychiatric "symptoms." Finally, the Shee-han Disability Scale, clinician or self-rated, is designed to assess disability in work, social, and home life due to psychiatric symptoms, especially manic, anxiety, phobic, and depressive symptoms.

Relevant Measures Included Elsewhere in the Handbook

This chapter includes scales that were designed to measure health status, functioning, and disability in indi-

TABLE 8–1 ■ Mental health status measures

Name of measure	Disorder or construct assessed	Format	Pages
Global Assessment Scale (GAS)* Global Assessment of Functioning (GAF) Scale Social and Occupational Functioning Assessment Scale (SOFAS)	GAS: Overall psychosocial functioning (psychological symptoms and social and occupational functioning) during a specified period GAF: Similar to GAS but includes rating point of 0 to be used when there are insufficient data to make a rating; comprises Axis V of the DSM-IV multiaxial system SOFAS: Social and occupational functioning; includes impairments due to both physical and mental disorders; can be used to track progress in rehabilitation independent of the severity of psychological symptoms	Clinician-rated, 100-point, single-item scale	96–100
Clinical Global Impressions (CGI) Scale*	Severity of illness, change over time, and efficacy of medication	Clinician rated; three global scales: Severity of Illness, Global Improvement (may also be rated by patient), and Efficacy Index	100–102
Multnomah Community Ability Scale (MCAS)*	Level of functioning of chronically mentally ill patients in community mental health programs	Completed by case manager; 17 items	102–104
Health of the Nation Outcome Scales (HoNOS)*	Problems in personal mental health and social functioning	Clinician rated (also available in version for completion by patients); 12 severity rating scales of 5 points each	104–107
Life Skills Profile (LSP)*	Functioning and disability in adults with schizophrenia	Rater administered; 39 items	107–109
Social Adjustment Scale (SAS) Self-report version (SAS-SR)	Social functioning	Semistructured or self-report; 48 items	109–113
Sheehan Disability Scale*	Effect of panic, anxiety, phobic, or depressive symptoms on work, social, and home life	Self-rated or clinician rated; 3 items	113–115

*Measure is included on the CD-ROM that accompanies this handbook.

viduals who have symptoms of psychological dysfunction. Scales designed to measure health status, functioning, and disability primarily in general medical settings (e.g., Sickness Impact Profile [p. 126], SF-36 Health Profile [p. 128], and Katz Index of Activities of Daily Living [p. 130]) are included in Chapter 9, "General Health Status, Functioning, and Disabilities Measures." Although the scales in Chapter 9 are similar to those in this chapter in that they measure the impact of illness on the patient's functioning, they are more broadly constructed and take into account the negative impact of physical symptoms. In contrast, several of the scales in this chapter (e.g., the GAS) either ignore physical symptoms or specifically instruct the user to exclude the impact of physical symptoms on functioning.

Scales that were designed to measure mental health status, functioning, and disability in specific age groups (e.g., childhood disorders) are covered in various other sections of this volume. For example, the CGAS (a children's version of the GAS) is reviewed in Chapter 19.

USING MEASURES IN THIS DOMAIN

The instruments reviewed here are used to provide valid and reliable measures of mental health status, functioning, and disability for clinical and research purposes. None is meant to substitute for a comprehensive clinical evaluation; rather, most are to be completed after such an evaluation. Several of these scales are used to select patients for clinical trials, to track change over time in response to therapeutic interventions, and to measure outcome for clinical trials. The MCAS is also used to evaluate program needs.

Some of the instruments described in this chapter are designed for use in special populations. For instance, the LSP is intended for use with adults with schizophrenia, and the MCAS was developed for use with chronically mentally ill adults living in the community. Although the HoNOS, a new instrument, was developed for and tested on adults with severe mental illness, it may be found useful for people with less severe disorders as well. Use of some of the instruments is problematic for some groups (e.g., the work ratings of the Sheehan Disability Scale do not apply well to retired subjects).

GUIDE TO THE SELECTION OF MEASURES

Selection of one of the measures described here for a particular use often depends on the resources available. If funding is scarce, a self-report measure may have to be used. However, if clinicians are available, one might consider a clinician-administered instrument. The sophistication of the subject pool may also dictate whether it is better to use a self-report or a clinician-administered instrument. Finally, in some cases, the material to be covered or the rating judgments to be made may be so complex that a clinician-administered instrument would be most effective.

Other considerations in choosing the most appropriate instrument include the population being studied and the specific focus of interest. For example, for patients with serious chronic mental illnesses, the MCAS or the LSP may be preferable. To focus on aspects of functioning in subjects who are less severely ill, the HoNOS, the SAS, or the Sheehan Disability Scale may be most appropriate. Overall summary ratings can be obtained for all types of subjects from the GAS, the GAF, and the SOFAS. The CGI should be considered if change over time and medication side effects are of interest.

CURRENT STATUS AND FUTURE RESEARCH NEEDS FOR ASSESSMENT

Interest in measures that assess life functioning appears to be increasing. Several of the measures covered in this chapter have been developed recently, so it will take some time for them to be tested fully across different samples.

Of note is the World Health Organization's (WHO's) effort to develop the *International Classification of Impairments, Activities, and Participation: A Manual of Dimensions of Disablement and Functioning* (ICIDH-2). The ICIDH-2 provides a conceptual model of functioning (and its negative components, disablement) and an accompanying taxonomy of functioning associated with mental and physical health conditions. This classification contains three dimensions: impairments of function and structure, activities (formerly disabilities), and participation (formerly handicaps). ICIDH-2 also contains a new classification of environmental factors that affect functioning and disablement.

The ICIDH-2 Checklist has been developed for such clinical applications as referral to rehabilitation and provision of medical evidence for disability benefits. A health care worker completes the checklist by use of any one or a combination of sources of information, including written records, informants, or direct observation. The first two sections contain personal information and a brief documentation of health information. This section is followed by a set of 17 probe questions to help the examiner in interviewing the respondent about problems in functioning, specifically in terms of participation in society and daily activities. The narrative section that follows is designed to give a thumbnail sketch of the contextual factors—both personal and environmental—that might influence the person's functioning. Four checklists follow this contextual information: participation restrictions, activity limitations, impairments of function, and impairments of structure.

For research purposes, the WHO Disablement Assessment Schedule II (WHO DAS II), also based on ICIDH-2, is designed to assess disablement and is currently being tested internationally for its psychometric properties. It is being calibrated to assess disablements associated with mental and physical conditions. The WHO DAS II contains six domains: understanding and communication, getting around, self-care, getting along with people, life activities (work and household activities), and participation in society. A short five-item version is being developed for use in epidemiological surveys, and midlength and long versions are being developed for use in clinical research. The short and midlength instruments were expected to be complete—including the testing of their psychometric properties—by the end of 1999.

Global Assessment Scale (GAS), Global Assessment of Functioning (GAF) Scale, Social and Occupational Functioning Assessment Scale (SOFAS)

R. L. Spitzer, M. Gibbon, and J. Endicott

GOALS

The Global Assessment Scale (GAS) (Endicott et al. 1976) is a 100-point single-item rating scale to indicate overall psychosocial functioning (psychological symptoms and social and occupational functioning) during a specified period on a continuum from psychological sickness to health. The primary goal of the GAS is to provide a summary score that reflects the level of a patient's overall functioning. In assigning a rating, the clinician takes into account the patient's psychological, social, and occupational functioning; however, the clinician does not include impairment in functioning due to physical (or environmental) limitations.

The GAS is a revision of the Health Sickness Rating Scale (Luborsky 1962). Two derivatives of the GAS have also been developed: the Global Assessment of Functioning (GAF) Scale and the Social and Occupational Functioning Assessment Scale (SOFAS). The GAF Scale is a revision of the GAS and the CGAS (Shaffer et al. 1983) (p. 96), a version of the GAS developed for use with children. It comprises Axis V of the DSM-IV multiaxial system.

The SOFAS, also derived from the GAS, is included in Appendix B of DSM-IV, "Criteria Sets and Axes Provided for Further Study"; its development is described by Goldman et al. (1992). It differs from the GAF Scale in that it focuses exclusively on the individual's level of social and occupational functioning and is not directly influenced by psychological symptoms. Also, in contrast to the GAF Scale, impairment in social and occupational functioning due to general medical conditions is considered in making the SOFAS rating.

These scales can be used to plan treatment, measure the impact of treatment, follow a patient's change in level of functioning over time, evaluate quality of life, and predict outcome. Because the scales cover the entire range of severity, they can be used in any situation or study in which an overall assessment of the severity of illness is needed.

DESCRIPTION

The GAS, the GAF Scale, and the SOFAS are each 100-point single-item scales that rate functioning on a hypothetical continuum of mental health to mental illness. The scale values range from 1, which represents the hypothetically most impaired individual, to 100, the hypothetically healthiest individual. The GAF Scale and the SOFAS also include a rating point of 0, which is used when there is inadequate information (i.e., missing data) to make a further judgment. The scales are each divided into 10 equal intervals, or deciles: 1–10, 11–20, and so on up to 91–100. The anchor point descriptions of each 10-point interval define the scale. For each scale, a single number comprises the final scale score (e.g., 24, 46, 67).

The scales are designed to be completed by a clinician, who uses information from any clinical source (e.g., clinical evaluation of the patient, a reliable informant, or a case record).

In contrast to the GAS and the GAF Scale, the SOFAS is designed to assess social and occupational disability and to track progress in rehabilitation, independent of the severity of psychological symptoms. The instructions for the SOFAS direct the clinician to

> consider social and occupational functioning on a continuum from excellent functioning to grossly impaired functioning. Include impairments in functioning due to physical limitations, as well as those due to mental impairments. To be counted, impairment must be a direct consequence of mental and physical health problems; the effects of lack of opportunity and other environmental limitations are not to be considered. (American Psychiatric Association 1994, p. 761)

In most instances, the GAS, GAF Scale, and SOFAS ratings should be used for the current period (i.e., the level of functioning during the week before the evaluation) because ratings of current functioning generally reflect the need for treatment or care. In some settings, it may be useful to note the rating at both admission and discharge. The scales may also be rated for other periods (e.g., the highest level of functioning for at least a few months during the past year, which may be prognostically useful).

In making a rating, one first selects the lowest interval that describes the subject's functioning during the preceding week. For example, a subject whose "behavior is considerably influenced by delusions" (GAS or GAF range of 21–30) should be given a rating in that range even though he or she may fit the description of a higher level as well (e.g., has "marked impairment in several areas"; range of 31–40). To select the specific scale point within the decile, the defining characteristics of the two adjacent intervals are examined to determine whether the subject is closer to one or the other. For example, a subject in the range of 21–30 who is much closer to the 11–20 range than to the 31–40 range would be given a specific rating of 21, 22, or 23. A subject who seems to be equidistant from the two adjoining ranges would be given a rating of 24, 25, 26, or 27. Example 8–1 provides a sample item from each of the three scales.

The two highest intervals on the GAS and the GAF, 81–90 and 91–100, describe individuals who not only are without significant psychopathology but who also exhibit many traits often referred to as components of positive mental health, such as superior functioning, a wide range of interests, social effectiveness, warmth, and integrity. Although some individuals rated above 70 may seek some form of assistance for psychological problems, the vast majority of individuals in treatment are rated between 1 and 70. Most outpatients are rated between 31 and 70, and most inpatients are rated between 1 and 40.

PRACTICAL ISSUES

Once the clinical information is obtained, it takes only 1–2 minutes for the clinician to assign a rating on the GAS, the GAF Scale, or the SOFAS. The clinical information may come from a variety of sources, ranging from a brief case vignette to a comprehensive 2-hour clinical interview.

The GAS is in the public domain and is available free of charge. The GAF Scale and the SOFAS are under copyright to the American Psychiatric Association, because they appear in DSM-IV. Permission to copy or reprint the GAF Scale and the SOFAS should be obtained from the American Psychiatric Press (202-682-6334). The GAS is included on the CD-ROM that accompanies this handbook.

Clinicians are encouraged to consult the major paper that introduced the GAS into the scientific literature (Endicott et al. 1976) for more details about its use. Instructions for using the GAF Scale and the SOFAS appear in DSM-IV. The Structured Clinical Interview for DSM-IV (SCID-CV) user's guide (First et al. 1995) also provides some detailed guidelines about making GAF Scale ratings.

A collection of case vignettes keyed to the GAS is available from

Department of Research Assessment and Training
New York State Psychiatric Institute, Unit 123
1051 Riverside Drive
New York, NY 10032

A decision tree version of the GAF Scale called GAFTREE has also been developed (First and the Multi-

EXAMPLE 8–1 ■ Sample item showing the 31–40 interval in the Global Assessment Scale, the Global Assessment of Functioning Scale, and the Social and Occupational Functioning Assessment Scale

The 31–40 range in the GAS

40	Major impairment in several areas, such as work, family relations, judgment, thinking, or mood (e.g., depressed woman avoids friends, neglects family, unable to do housework), OR some impairment in reality testing or communication (e.g., speech is at times obscure, illogical, or irrelevant), OR single serious suicide attempt.
31	

The 31–40 range in the GAF Scale

40	Some impairment in reality testing or communication (e.g., speech is at times illogical, obscure, or irrelevant) OR major impairment in several areas, such as work or school, family relations, judgment, thinking, or mood (e.g., depressed man avoids friends, neglects family, and is unable to work; child frequently beats up younger children, is defiant at home, and is failing at school).
31	

The 31–40 range in the SOFAS

40	Major impairment in several areas, such as work or school, family relations (e.g., depressed man avoids friends, neglects family, and is unable to work; child frequently beats up younger children, is defiant at home, and is failing at school).
31	

Health Systems Staff 1996). It takes the user through a series of questions that determine which decile of the GAF Scale best fits the patient's symptoms and impairments in functioning. Both the GAFTREE and a computerized version, called the GAF Report, are available from Multi-Health Systems (800-456-3003). Some evidence suggests that reliability of GAF Scale ratings in routine settings is unsatisfactory if the administrators are not trained in its use.

The GAF Scale and the SOFAS are available in every language into which DSM-IV has been translated. The GAS has also been translated into many languages. For information, contact the Department of Research Assessment and Training, New York State Psychiatric Institute, at the address given earlier. Several modifications of the GAF Scale have been developed; they vary from a self-report version (Bodlund et al. 1994) to one with enhanced anchor point descriptions and additional directions for assigning scores (Hall 1995).

PSYCHOMETRIC PROPERTIES

Reliability

Joint reliability (intraclass correlation coefficients [ICCs]) on the GAS and the GAF Scale across several studies (nine different samples of subjects, $N = 16$–451) ranged from 0.61 to 0.91 (indicating fair to excellent agreement); values from joint interviews ranged higher than from test-retest independent interviews, as expected. Reliability was equivalent for patients and for nonpatients (community subjects who were not currently in treatment). In one study, reliability was improved by developing more precise guidelines for the ratings.

Validity

The concurrent validity of the GAS was evaluated by comparing therapists' ratings of the severity of illness, using a simple 7-point scale that ranges from "not ill at all" to "among the most extremely ill," with GAS ratings made by research interviewers in a study of psychiatric inpatients. On admission, the correlation was 0.44; however, 6 months after admission, the correlation increased to 0.62, undoubtedly because of the greater heterogeneity of patients' severity scores at follow-up.

Prediction of rehospitalization for patients living in the community was evaluated by comparing the relationship of GAS ratings made by independent research interviewers 3 months after admission with the rate of rehospitalization at 3, 6, and 9 months. As would be expected, patients with GAS scores below 40 were much more likely to be rehospitalized than were patients with scores above 40.

The GAF Scale discriminated significantly between patients who had a personality disorder (mean GAF score of 70) and those who did not (mean GAF score of 80) in a study of community subjects who were not in psychiatric treatment (First et al. 1995).

The sensitivity of the GAS to change over time (6 months) was compared with the sensitivity of other measures of overall severity and scales of symptom dimensions. GAS ratings made by research interviewers were more sensitive to change than any of the other measures (i.e., Psychiatric Status Schedule total score and subscales, Mental Status Examination Record [MSER] total score and subscales, and Family Evaluation Form total score). For example, from admission to 6 months, a statistic that indexes sensitivity to change was 0.83 for researchers' GAS scores and 0.47 for therapists' overall severity MSER scores. The construct validity of the GAF Scale (i.e., independent from the severity of the psychopathology) may be increased by separately rating psychological and social/occupational functioning, as in the SOFAS (Patterson and Lee 1995).

CLINICAL UTILITY

The GAS has been used in hundreds of studies to select or describe subject samples, to track change over time in patients' levels of functioning, to assess treatment effects (especially in trials of psychopharmacological or psychotherapeutic interventions), to describe the natural history of various conditions, to validate other measures (such as measures of ego functioning, psychophysiological phenomena, personality traits, and social networks), and to predict outcome. The GAF Scale has also been

widely used, particularly to monitor change over time. In addition, the GAF Scale has been used as a guide for selecting suitable patients for short-term treatment (GAF score > 50) (Vaillant 1996).

The major strengths of these scales are their ease of use with minimal training, their reliability, and their sensitivity to change over time. Their disadvantage is the degree to which their validity depends on the quality of the information available to guide the clinical rating. The GAS and the GAF Scale have been criticized for confounding symptoms and functioning. Lack of a clear distinction between the two can make rating difficult when, for example, there are moderate or severe symptoms but functioning that is not very impaired or the reverse. A similar criticism could be made of the SOFAS in cases in which, for example, occupational functioning is high but social functioning is impaired.

REFERENCES AND SUGGESTED READINGS

American Psychiatric Association: Diagnostic and Statistical Manual of Mental Disorders, 4th Edition. Washington, DC, American Psychiatric Association, 1994

Bodlund O, Kullgren G, Ekselius L, et al: Axis V—Global Assessment of Functioning Scale: evaluation of a self-report version. Acta Psychiatr Scand 90:342–347, 1994

Endicott J, Spitzer RL, Fleiss JL, et al: The Global Assessment Scale: a procedure for measuring overall severity of psychiatric disturbance. Arch Gen Psychiatry 33:766–771, 1976

First MB, Multi-Health Systems Staff: GAF Report for the Global Assessment of Functioning Scale (Computer Program, Windows Version). Toronto, Canada, Multi-Health Systems, 1996

First MB, Spitzer RL, Gibbon M, et al: The Structured Clinical Interview for DSM-III-R Personality Disorders (SCID-II), II: multi-site test-retest reliability study. Journal of Personality Disorders 9:92–104, 1995

First MB, Spitzer RL, Williams JBW, et al: Structured Clinical Interview for DSM-IV (SCID-I) (User's Guide and Interview), Research Version. New York, Biometrics Research Department, New York Psychiatric Institute, 1995

Goldman HH, Skodol AE, Lave TR: Revising Axis V for DSM-IV: a review of measures of social functioning. Am J Psychiatry 149:1148–1156, 1992

Hall RC: Global assessment of functioning: a modified scale. Psychosomatics 36:267–275, 1995

Luborsky L: Clinicians' judgments of mental health. Arch Gen Psychiatry 7:407–417, 1962

Patterson DA, Lee MS: Field trial of the Global Assessment of Functioning Scale—Modified. Am J Psychiatry 152:1386–1388, 1995

Shaffer D, Gould MS, Brasic J, et al: Children's Global Assessment Scale (CGAS). Arch Gen Psychiatry 40:1228–1231, 1983

Vaillant GE, Schnurr P: What is a case? a 45-year study of psychiatric impairment within a college sample selected for mental health. Arch Gen Psychiatry 45:313–319, 1988

Vaillant LM: Changing Character: Short-Term Anxiety-Regulating Psychotherapy for Restructuring Defenses, Affects, and Attachment. New York, Basic Books, 1996

Clinical Global Impressions (CGI) Scale

W. Guy

GOALS

The Clinical Global Impressions (CGI) Scale (Guy 1976) is a standardized assessment tool. Its goal is to allow the clinician to rate the severity of illness, change over time, and efficacy of medication, taking into account the patient's clinical condition and the severity of side effects. The CGI Scale is widely used in clinical psychopharmacology trials as an outcome measure.

DESCRIPTION

The CGI Scale consists of three global subscales formatted for use with the Global Scoring Sheet. The first subscale, Severity of Illness, assesses the clinician's impression of the patient's current illness state; it is often used both before and after treatment. The next subscale, Global Improvement, assesses the patient's improvement or worsening from baseline, which is usually the begin-

ning of a clinical trial. Sometimes a global improvement rating from the patient and the clinician is recorded. The third subscale, the Efficacy Index, attempts to relate therapeutic effects and side effects by deriving a composite score that reflects both the therapeutic effect and the concomitant adverse reactions or side effects. This subscale is essentially a ratio of benefit to risk that attempts to assess the overall efficacy of the treatment in relation to its adverse reactions. If therapeutic effects are regarded as gross profit and side effects as cost, this index is analogous to net profit. Thus, the index requires the clinician to make separate judgments regarding the therapeutic effectiveness of the treatment (with anchor ratings listed in the rows) and the adverse reactions (with anchor ratings listed in the columns). A score that reflects the overall effectiveness of the medication is taken from the cell in the table at the intersection of the selected row and column. In general, this scale is completed at least once before treatment and at least once after completion of the treatment trial. More frequent ratings to follow change may be desirable. Example 8–2 provides a sample item from the CGI Efficacy Index.

Scores on the Severity of Illness subscale range from 1 = not ill at all to 7 = among the most extremely ill. The Global Improvement subscale also goes from 1 = very much improved to 7 = very much worse. As illustrated, the Efficacy Index involves locating a rating on a matrix of therapeutic versus side effects. Scores range from 0 = marked improvement and no side effects to 4 = unchanged or worse and side effects outweigh therapeutic effects.

Spearing et al. (1997) have developed a modification of the CGI Scale for use in assessing global illness severity and change in patients with bipolar disorder.

PRACTICAL ISSUES

It takes a clinician only 1–2 minutes to score the CGI Scale after a clinical interview. The CGI Scale is in the public domain. A copy of the scale and information on its administration are found in the Early Clinical Drug Evaluation Program (ECDEU) manual (Guy 1976). The CGI is included on the CD-ROM that accompanies this handbook.

The CGI Scale has been used in psychopharmacology trials worldwide and has therefore presumably been

EXAMPLE 8–2 ■ Sample item from the Clinical Global Impressions Efficacy Index

3. EFFICACY INDEX—Rate this item on the basis of DRUG EFFECT ONLY.
Select the terms which best describe the degrees of therapeutic effect and side effects and record the number in the box where the two items intersect.

EXAMPLE: Therapeutic effect is rated as "Moderate" and side effects are judged "do not significantly interfere with patient's functioning". Record on 06 form.

THERAPEUTIC EFFECTS	None	Do not significantly interfere with patient's functioning	Significantly interfere with patient's functioning
MARKED—Vast improvement. Complete or nearly complete remission of all symptoms	01	02	03
MODERATE—Decided improvement. Partial remission of symptoms	05	06	07
MINIMAL—Slight improvement which doesn't alter status of care of patient	09	10	11
UNCHANGED OR WORSE	13	14	15

Not Assessed = 00

translated into most languages. Unfortunately, there is no central coordination for these translations or their availability.

PSYCHOMETRIC PROPERTIES

Reliability

In one German study that is quite critical of the CGI Scale, the distribution of scores and normality of CGI items were examined at the first and last visits (8 weeks apart) in three clinical trials with a total of 175 patients with schizophrenia, depression, or anxiety disorders. The mean, standard deviation, skewness, and kurtosis were analyzed for each item and for each of the two visits. Scores on the Global Improvement and Therapeutic Effects subscales were highly correlated ($r \sim 0.90$). However, there was only a moderate correlation ($r \sim -0.47$ to -0.66) between changes in the Severity of Illness and Global Improvement subscales, where one would expect a high correlation. Both improvement ratings (i.e., Global Improvement and Therapeutic Effects) appear to be rather independent of the Side Effects rating. Severity

of Illness was also moderately correlated with the Side Effects rating.

Test-retest reliability values were calculated by correlating the ratings of each item at the first visit with all respective ratings at subsequent visits. These test-retest correlations were rather low: for Severity of Illness, reliability values ranged from 0.20 to 0.81; for Global Improvement, from 0.15 to 0.78; for Therapeutic Effects, from 0.21 to 0.78; and for Side Effects, from 0.32 to 0.80. Another study in Germany found relatively good reliability scores for the CGI Severity of Illness ratings (0.66 and 0.41 for physicians and nursing staff, respectively) but not for Global Improvement (i.e., change) ratings in a sample of 12 psychogeriatric patients with dementia (0.51 and 0.35 for physicians and nursing staff, respectively).

Validity

During an 8-week clinical trial involving 116 patients with panic disorder and depression (Leon et al. 1993), the Hamilton Rating Scale for Depression (Ham-D) (p. 524), anticipatory anxiety, and panic frequency each had positive significant relationships with clinician ratings of severity on the CGI Scale (concurrent validity). In addition, the scale had good sensitivity to change over time.

CLINICAL UTILITY

The CGI Scale is one of the most widely used outcome measures in psychopharmacology trials. However, most studies that use the CGI Scale have included only one or two of the global measures to assess drug response. Despite the widespread use of this instrument, there have been only a few studies of its psychometric characteristics, and these studies differ widely in their assessment of the usefulness and reliability of the scale.

It has been suggested in one article that the positive qualities of the CGI Scale could be enhanced by inter-rater training and more highly structured anchor points for each CGI item (Leon et al. 1993). Another publication maintains that the CGI Scale is unreliable, contains redundant information, and includes items that have extremely abnormal distribution properties in clinical trials. In addition, it claims that some of the CGI items are inappropriately constructed and are of doubtful clinical significance (Beneke and Rasmus 1992).

It has been suggested that the Global Improvement subscale not be used at regular intervals but instead be used only as a single measure of the rater's general impression at the end of a study or course of treatment. The instruction to measure improvement by comparing the patient's present condition with that at admission to the study is not recommended because of two major difficulties. First, it is difficult to indicate a worsening of the patient's condition later in the course of the trial (i.e., to judge a patient "much worse" at week 3 when he or she was rated "much improved" at week 2). Second, the rating becomes partly a memory test with an intrinsic loss function (i.e., as time goes by, the rater's memory of the first visit worsens).

The Efficacy Index has also been criticized. Parametric statistics (e.g., standard deviation) are inappropriate for use with this scale because of the abnormal distribution of scores. In addition, the instructions for the Efficacy Index state that it is to be rated "on the basis of drug effect only." However, the ability of a clinician to distinguish between drug-related improvement and total improvement is questionable. The anchor point descrip-

tions on the subscale of Therapeutic Effects are also unclear and undoubtedly lead to unreliable judgments.

REFERENCES AND SUGGESTED READINGS

Beneke M, Rasmus W: "Clinical Global Impressions" (ECDEU): some critical comments. Pharmacopsychiatry 25:171–176, 1992

Dahlke F, Lohaus A, Gutzmann H: Reliability and clinical concepts underlying global judgments in dementia: implications for clinical research. Psychopharmacol Bull 28:425–432, 1992

Guy W: ECDEU Assessment Manual for Psychopharmacology—Revised (DHEW Publ No ADM 76-338). Rockville, MD, U.S. Department of Health, Education, and Welfare, Public Health Service, Alcohol, Drug Abuse, and Mental Health Administration, NIMH Psychopharmacology Research Branch, Division of Extramural Research Programs, 1976, pp 218–222

Leon AC, Shear MK, Klerman GL, et al: A comparison of symptom determinants of patient and clinician global ratings in patients with panic disorder and depression. J Clin Psychopharmacol 13:327–331, 1993

Spearing MK, Post RM, Leverich GS, et al: Modification of the Clinical Global Impressions (CGI) scale for use in bipolar illness (BP): the CGI-BP. Psychiatry Res 73:159–171, 1997

Multnomah Community Ability Scale (MCAS)

S. Barker, N. Barron, B. McFarland, and D. Bigelow

GOALS

The Multnomah Community Ability Scale (MCAS) (Barker et al. 1993) is a standardized tool that was developed to measure the degree of psychiatric disability in four major areas of functioning in individuals with chronic mental illness who are living in the community.

DESCRIPTION

The MCAS is a 17-item instrument used to assess the functioning of people with severe and persistent mental illness. Designed to be completed by case managers, it assesses patients' functioning during the past 3 months, with the exception of a section on behavioral problems, which reflects the level of functioning during the past year. Items are worded to measure patients' ability levels, without requiring knowledge of their use of inpatient or outpatient mental health services.

The MCAS is intended for use by clinicians who work with patients consistently over time and who have a broad knowledge of the patients' functioning. It is recommended that the scale be administered at intake and at treatment plan review for all patients; it may be filled out every 3–6 months to track change over time (the minimum recommendation is once a year).

The MCAS is divided into four sections, each of which contains three to five items:

Section One: Interference With Functioning (physical health, intellectual functioning, thought processes, mood abnormality, and response to stress and anxiety)

Section Two: Adjustment to Living (ability to manage money, independence in daily life, and acceptance of illness)

Section Three: Social Competence (social acceptability, social interest, social effectiveness, social network, and meaningful activity)

Section Four: Behavioral Problems (medical compliance, cooperation with treatment providers, alcohol or drug abuse, and impulse control)

A sample item is provided in Example 8–3.

Items on the MCAS are rated on 5-point (1–5) severity or frequency scales. Each of the four sections receives a summed score of the items in that section; an overall total scale score is also calculated. The range for the total scale score is 17–85 if all items are completed.

Total scale scores are grouped into three categories: low functioning (17–47 = severe disability), medium functioning (48–62), and high functioning (63–85 = little disability). Norms are available for several age groups on the basis of samples of patients enrolled in community support units of community mental health centers.

EXAMPLE 8–3 ■ Sample item from the Multnomah Community Ability Scale

Independence in Daily Life: How well does the client perform independently in day-to-day living?

NOTE: Performance includes personal hygiene, dressing appropriately, obtaining regular nutrition, and housekeeping.

1. Almost never performs independently
2. Often does not perform independently
3. Sometimes performs independently
4. Often performs independently
5. Almost always performs independently
? Don't know

PRACTICAL ISSUES

It takes only a few minutes for a clinician to complete the MCAS. This scale is currently in the public domain. The MCAS may be obtained from

Sela Barker, M.S.W.
Director of Quality Assurance and Staff Development
Network Behavioral Healthcare
5415 SE Milwaukee Avenue, Suite 3
Portland, OR 97202

The user's manual (Barker et al. 1993) may be photocopied. The manual reviews the background and purpose of the scale and provides guidelines for rating each item, as well as scale score norms for patients of different ages. An up-to-date manual, single-sheet version of the scale, and training video can also be ordered at minimal cost from Sela Barker.

The MCAS is included on the CD-ROM that accompanies this handbook.

PSYCHOMETRIC PROPERTIES

Reliability

Test-retest (same day) reliability by two different raters for the total score was 0.85 across 43 patients; half of the items were 0.60 or greater. The four subscales each had intraclass reliability coefficients of 0.70–0.78. When these ratings were repeated on 40 of the patients after 2–4 weeks, stability over time was found to be good; the total score intraclass correlation coefficient was 0.827.

Validity

Clinicians chose a global rating (from a 4-point scale) for 33 patients in the reliability study before they completed the MCAS. The global rating had a correlation of –0.78 with the total MCAS score. In a longitudinal study of 240 patients of a local community mental health agency's community support program, all MCAS items (except social interest and intellectual functioning) correlated with criterion variables, such as subsequent admission to a state or local hospital. There were also high correlations between a 10-point clinician global rating and all the scale items. Factor analysis confirmed the four subscales.

CLINICAL UTILITY

The MCAS can be used to track patient progress and to develop treatment plans. Because it can describe an agency's case mix, it can also be used to balance workload assignments for clinical staff and to evaluate community programs. The anchor points are currently being improved, and a consumer report version is being pilot tested. Because the MCAS requires only a few minutes to complete, it is a low-cost, unobtrusive measure. It provides a common language for assessing patient care and program planning, and its use facilitates treatment planning and tracking of a patient's progress.

The MCAS was developed for use on a fairly restricted range of patients: adults with chronic mental illness. There is also no information about its use with culturally diverse populations, so it may or may not be culturally sensitive. Finally, because the MCAS is a fairly new instrument, no translations are available yet.

REFERENCES AND SUGGESTED READINGS

Barker S, Barron N, McFarland B, et al: Multnomah Community Ability Scale: User's Manual. Portland, OR, Western Mental Health Research Center, Oregon Health Sciences University, 1993

Barker S, Barron N, McFarland B, et al: A community ability scale for chronically mentally ill consumers, I: reliability and validity. Community Ment Health J 30:363–383, 1994a

Barker S, Barron N, McFarland B, et al: A community ability scale for chronically mentally ill consumers, II: applications. Community Ment Health J 30:459–472, 1994b

Health of the Nation Outcome Scales (HoNOS)

J. K. Wing, R. H. Curtis, and A. S. Beevor

GOALS

The Health of the Nation Outcome Scales (HoNOS) (Wing et al. 1996a) is a set of 12 5-point scales that are designed to be used routinely by health practitioners to measure and record problems in personal mental health and social functioning in adults and to track change over time.

DESCRIPTION

The HoNOS consists of 12 severity rating scales, each scored 0–4. The 12 types of problems rated fall into four problem areas: behavioral problems that have an impact on the user and/or others (e.g., self-harm and violence), deficits in basic functions (e.g., psychomotor slowness and cognitive and physical impairments and their direct effects on personal functioning), distressing or limiting subjective mental experiences (e.g., depression, anxiety, hallucinations, and worry), and environmental problems (housing, occupational, financial, interpersonal, and social support network) that limit the potential functional autonomy of the individual.

The severity of each item is rated from "no problem" to "severe or very severe problem," on the basis of the worst type of problem covered by that item that occurred during the period being rated. Functioning is assessed at first contact for the period extending over the prior 2 weeks. The period rated at second and subsequent assessments depends on the setting. For example, in an acute setting it could be only a few days, whereas in a long-term setting it could remain 2 weeks. HoNOS ratings are usually made at the beginning and end of periods of care (e.g., admission and discharge).

Each of the 12 scales are rated in order so that problems rated in earlier items are not included in later ratings. For the period being considered, the rating should reflect the most severe problem that occurred during that time. All scales follow the format 0 = no problem, 1 = minor problem requiring no action, 2 = mild problem but definitely present, 3 = moderately severe problem, 4 = severe to very severe problem, and 9 = not known. Example 8–4 provides a sample item for rating problems with depressed mood.

The range of scores on each of the 12 items is 0–4. An item score of 1 represents a subclinical problem, and 4 represents a very severe problem. The total score, which represents overall severity, ranges between 0 and 48. Items can also be aggregated into four section scores: behavioral problems (aggression and overactivity, self-harm, and substance use), impairment (cognition and physical health), symptomatic problems (hallucinations and delusions, depression, and other symptoms), and social problems (social relations, general functioning, housing, and activities).

In acute patient settings or other settings in which patients are resident for only a short period, the domestic situation is often not known to the staff, so items 11 and 12 cannot be rated. In this situation, items 1–10 can be used without items 11 and 12, giving a total score range of 1–40. (This total score cannot, of course, be directly compared with the 1–48 total.) In general, if more than one item cannot be scored, then it is preferable to leave HoNOS ratings until all aspects of the patient's situation are known.

PRACTICAL ISSUES

The HoNOS is completed directly after a routine interview with or assessment of the patient. It takes 15–30 minutes to complete the HoNOS the first time through; however, it takes less time with repeated administrations. A version of the HoNOS designed for self-completion was piloted but has not been fully developed and tested. It simply presents the individual patient's view of the information the clinician records. This version is available as a photocopy but is not recommended for large-scale data collection.

The HoNOS includes a glossary, chart, and score sheet. The glossary provides principles for rating each item. The chart is used to collect basic background information about the patient to put the HoNOS ratings in perspective. The score sheet records the actual item scores and can become part of the case record.

A training manual (Wing et al. 1996b) is available specifically for those responsible for training and supervising raters. Apart from a detailed description of the purpose, structure, and principles of HoNOS, the manual provides advice on rating items (illustrated by examples), suggestions for running a training course, and a discussion of the uses of the data (whether for a single patient or aggregated from a series of patients). A summary of the results from field and reliability trials is provided as an appendix, and a copy of the Raters' Pack is also included.

The Raters' Pack includes a short statement on the construction, testing, and applications of the HoNOS, answers to a list of common questions, and copies of the glossary, chart, and score sheet. The Raters' Pack alone is not intended to provide sufficient training to qualify a rater; live training and subsequent supervision are essential for the highest interrater reliability in rating the HoNOS. Training is provided in a 4-hour session, after which clinicians will have experience rating the HoNOS; skill in rating the HoNOS is relatively easy to acquire. To maintain levels of interrater reliability (or prevent drift), supervision should be arranged at regular intervals, and a supervisor should be available to offer help and answer queries during the start-up weeks.

EXAMPLE 8–4 ■ Sample item from the Health of the Nations Outcome Scales

> 7. Problems with depressed mood
>
> Do not include over-activity or agitation, rated at Scale 1.
> Do not include suicidal ideation or attempts, rated at Scale 2.
> Do not include delusions or hallucinations, rated at Scale 6.
>
> 0 No problem associated with depressed mood during the period rated.
> 1 Gloomy; or minor changes in mood.
> 2 Mild but definite depression and distress (e.g. feelings of guilt; loss of self-esteem).
> 3 Depression with inappropriate self-blame; preoccupied with feelings of guilt.
> 4 Severe or very severe depression, with guilt or self-accusation.

Reprinted with permission from the World Health Organization.

A program for computerized entry of scale scores, called HoNOSoft, has been developed. It allows data to be entered rapidly, simple analyses to be done right away, and the results to be printed out or exported for more complex analyses by use of statistical packages.

Materials, manuals, and a full report on the research can be ordered from the Research Unit for a cost of about $20.00:

> Royal College of Psychiatrists' Research Unit (CRU)
> 11 Grosvenor Crescent
> London, England SW1X 8PG

The HoNOS is Crown copyright and is owned by the Department of Health in England. Permission for reprinting or other use of the scale may be obtained from CRU. The HoNOS is included on the CD-ROM that accompanies this handbook.

Translations are available in Danish, Italian, and Spanish.

PSYCHOMETRIC PROPERTIES

Reliability

The reliability of the HoNOS items, sections, and total score is generally very good. Most item reliability values (joint reliability) ranged from 0.80 to 0.99 (intraclass correlation coefficients) in tests across two sites ($N = 100$ and $N = 97$).

The four section scores and the total score are quite reliable. In one test (the Nottingham Trial), 100 patients were jointly rated by the trainer and by each patient's caseworker or the person most knowledgeable about the patient's clinical condition. In another test (in Manchester), nine consultants and a nurse-trainer jointly evaluated 97 patients. The results are shown in Table 8–2.

Test-retest reliability (same rater) for patients rated retrospectively as not having changed over an average of 35.3 days ($N = 212$) was high (e.g., the intraclass correlation coefficient for the total score was 0.83).

Validity

When compared with the Brief Psychiatric Rating Scale (BPRS) (p. 490) and the Role Functioning Scale (RFS) (Green and Gracely 1987), agreement was found where expected on clinical grounds. In addition to the item

TABLE 8–2 ■ **Reliability results for the HoNOS**

	NOTTINGHAM STUDY ($N = 100$)	MANCHESTER STUDY ($N = 97$)
HoNOS Subscores		
A: 1–3 Behavior	0.89	0.74
B: 4–5 Impairment	0.87	0.95
C: 6–8 Symptoms	0.88	0.81
D: 9–12 Social	0.82	0.68
HoNOS Total scores		
E: Items 1–12	0.86	0.77
F: Items 1–10	0.86	0.86

analyses, the correlations between total scores were all good to very good (i.e., 0.65 with the RFS and 0.84 with the BPRS).

Scores on HoNOS items also differ predictably among diagnostic groups. For example, people with dementias scored highest on cognitive problems and physical disability, whereas people with mood disorders scored highly on depression. In addition, people who have been in the hospital for less than 3 months had high mean scores on almost every item compared with people not in hospital care, except for the item that reflects anxiety and phobic conditions. Scores on items for aggression and substance use were higher in men than in women.

The HoNOS can record a steady state, improvement, and deterioration. Scores on the four clinical sections, when ranked according to the extent to which they change from time 1 to time 2, show change in the clinically expected order: symptoms, behavioral, social, and impairment. In addition, a retrospective clinical judgment of overall change was significantly associated with the outcome as measured by HoNOS, whether the rater at time 2 was the same or different from the rater at time 1.

CLINICAL UTILITY

The HoNOS is a new instrument and is therefore not yet in widespread use. Thus far it has been used mainly in

England and Australia, although tests are now being conducted in Denmark, Italy, and Spain.

The HoNOS has been used mainly in settings in which people with or recovering from severe mental illness were evaluated. Further trials are needed to assess people with less severe disorders. The instrument is simple to use and generally clinically acceptable; it covers a broad range of clinical problems and social dysfunctions. The HoNOS appears to be sensitive to change over time or to the lack of it. It has acceptable reliability and is compatible with longer and more well-established instruments.

Training raters is simple, although a brief one-time training course may not be sufficient to guarantee comparability between individual raters or between groups of raters. Local supervision should be used to ensure adequate training and to prevent drift.

The HoNOS was not constructed to measure mental health problems in the general population or in general practice (although modification for such use deserves testing). Versions of the HoNOS for children and adolescents and for psychogeriatric patients have been completed. Learning disabilities and forensic versions are in development.

The HoNOS measures health and not health care outcomes. It deals with symptoms and dysfunctions, not diagnoses. This focus could conceivably be a disadvantage unless the instrument was used in conjunction with a diagnostic tool.

REFERENCES AND SUGGESTED READINGS

Green RS, Gracely EJ: Selecting a rating scale for evaluating services to the chronically mentally ill. Community Ment Health J 23:91–102, 1987

Wing JK, Beevor AS, Curtis RH, et al: Health of the Nation Outcome Scales (HoNOS): research and development. Br J Psychiatry 172:11–18, 1998

Wing JK, Curtis RH, Beevor AS: HoNOS: Health of the Nation Outcome Scales. Report on Research and Development, July 1993–December 1995. London, College Research Unit, Royal College of Psychiatrists, 1996a

Wing JK, Curtis RH, Beevor AS: HoNOS: Health of the Nation Outcome Scales—Trainers' Guide. London, College Research Unit, Royal College of Psychiatrists, 1996b

Life Skills Profile (LSP)

G. Parker, D. Hadzi-Pavlovic, and A. Rosen

GOALS

The Life Skills Profile (LSP) (Rosen et al. 1989) is a rater-administered questionnaire that measures functioning and disability in adults with schizophrenia. It is also used to chart general functioning over time in this population.

The LSP is designed to rate five areas of disability (self-neglect, turbulence, limited social skills, impaired communication, and irresponsibility), independent of symptom status. The five areas constitute subscales. They focus on aspects of functioning that affect survival and adaptation in the community; therefore, the scale may be useful to professionals in charge of rehabilitation programs.

DESCRIPTION

The LSP is a 39-item rating scale that may be completed by a professional or a nonprofessional rater. The 39 items are grouped into five subscales that measure self-care, nonturbulence, social contact, communication, and responsibility. None of the ratings involve clinical interpretation by the rater. Instead, the items are scored on the basis of distinct, observed behaviors. Example 8–5 provides sample items.

All items are scored 1–4, with 4 = least disability and 1 = greatest disability, thus emphasizing adaptive functioning. The total LSP score and subscale scores are summed item scores; greater disability is indicated by lower LSP scores. Total scores range from 39 to 156. Subscale scores range from 5 to 12, depending on the number of items in the subscale.

PRACTICAL ISSUES

It takes about 5 minutes to administer the LSP when it is completed by a respondent who knows the patient well

EXAMPLE 8–5 ■ Sample items from the Life Skills Profile

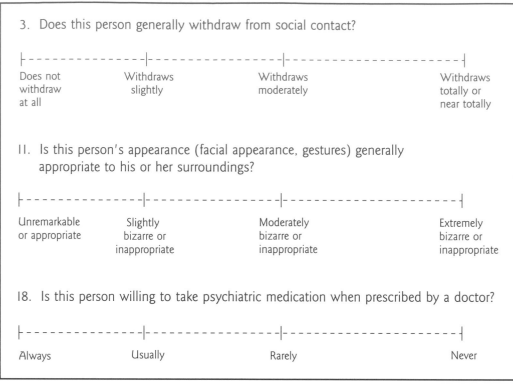

3. Does this person generally withdraw from social contact?

Does not withdraw at all	Withdraws slightly	Withdraws moderately	Withdraws totally or near totally

11. Is this person's appearance (facial appearance, gestures) generally appropriate to his or her surroundings?

Unremarkable or appropriate	Slightly bizarre or inappropriate	Moderately bizarre or inappropriate	Extremely bizarre or inappropriate

18. Is this person willing to take psychiatric medication when prescribed by a doctor?

Always	Usually	Rarely	Never

Reprinted with permission from Gordon Parker, M.D.

or up to 20 minutes if the rater is required to interview the patient or a knowledgeable informant. The item stems, created on the basis of observed behaviors, allow the LSP to be completed by anyone who knows the patient well, including family members and nonprofessionals.

Requests for forms and permission should be sent to

Gordon Parker, M.D.,
　FRANZCP, Professor and Head
School of Psychiatry
University of South Wales
Prince of Wales Hospital
High Street
Randwick, NSW 2031 Australia
Phone: 02-399-4372
Fax: 02-398-7783

The measure is under copyright to two of the authors (Parker and Rosen). The cost is $1.00 per form and $0.50 for photocopied forms; a one-page scoring instruction sheet is also provided. Costs may be waived in certain circumstances. Computerized versions have been developed to allow subscale and total scores to be calculated readily; however, rating and scoring of the paper and pencil version can also be completed rapidly. The LSP is included on the CD-ROM that accompanies this handbook.

Translations are available in French, German, Japanese, and Spanish.

PSYCHOMETRIC PROPERTIES

Reliability

On the basis of testing with 252 raters completing forms on 128 individuals with schizophrenia, the internal consistency of each of the subscales was high; Cronbach's alpha values ranged from 0.67 to 0.88.

Test-retest reliability has been quite good; parents, residential care workers, and caseworkers as raters generated a mean intraclass correlation coefficient of 0.89 for total scores with a retest interval of 4 weeks. For agreement among three other groups (health professionals, boardinghouse managers, and family members, $N = 98$

subjects), the mean total correlation coefficient was 0.68, suggesting moderately high agreement.

Validity

Overall, validity is good, as demonstrated by the association of LSP scores and different loci of care (i.e., community or hospital) to Brief Psychiatric Rating Scale (BPRS) (p. 490) ratings and to ratings on the Katz Adjustment Scale (KAS) (Katz and Lyerly 1963). For example, the total KAS and LSP scale scores had a correlation of 0.65. This correlation suggests that the LSP assesses functioning and disability, as intended, rather than symptom severity. Factor analyses and comparisons with other instruments such as the KAS indicated relative independence among the five factors in general.

Predictive validity was demonstrated in a study of 118 subjects who were followed after discharge. The baseline score was a significant predictor of readmission; discriminant function analyses indicated that the total LSP score predicted 60% of the readmissions and 75% of those not readmitted.

One study demonstrated significant improvements on all LSP subscale scores and on the total score (i.e., sensitivity to change) in a sample of persons with chronic mental illness who were treated by an assertive community mental health service.

CLINICAL UTILITY

The LSP should be helpful in defining and assessing clinical services, because it provides useful information on social impairment in those with schizophrenia. The measure is brief and simple, facilitating its use by both non-professional and professional raters. The items describe distinct behaviors, thus reducing or eliminating variability from raters' value judgments. It is expected that the LSP may be used effectively to assess social impairment in patients with chronic mental illnesses other than schizophrenia that are likely to affect the areas of disability covered in this instrument; however, psychometric data have thus far been collected only on patients with schizophrenia.

Caution should be exercised in comparing scale scores, because certain LSP scale scores (e.g., communication) have been found to vary with how well and how long the rater has known the patient.

REFERENCES AND SUGGESTED READINGS

Hambridge JA, Rosen A: Assertive community treatment for the seriously mentally ill in suburban Sydney: a programme description and evaluation. Aust N Z J Psychiatry 28:438–445, 1994

Katz MM, Lyerly SB: Methods for measuring adjustment and social behavior in the community, I: rationale, description, discriminative validity, and scale development. Psychol Rep 13:503–535, 1963

Parker G, Hadzi-Pavlovic D: The capacity of a measure of disability (the LSP) to predict hospital readmission in those with schizophrenia. Psychol Med 25:157–163, 1995

Parker G, Rosen A, Emdur N, et al: The Life Skills Profile: psychometric properties of a measure assessing function and disability in schizophrenia. Acta Psychiatr Scand 83:145–152, 1991

Rosen A, Hadzi-Pavlovic D, Parker G: The Life Skills Profile: a measure assessing function and disability in schizophrenia. Schizophr Bull 15:325–337, 1989

Trauer T, Duckmanton RA, Chiu E: The Life Skills Profile: a study of its psychometric properties. Aust N Z J Psychiatry 29:492–499, 1995

Social Adjustment Scale (SAS)

M. M. *Weissman*

GOALS

The Social Adjustment Scale (SAS) (Weissman and Bothwell 1976) is an interview (and self-report version, SAS-SR) used to assess social functioning. The SAS-SR differs from the SAS in method of administration and period covered. Both versions are discussed here. An interview version for patients with schizophrenia is also available. Some content of the SAS interview is derived from the Structured and Scaled Interview to Assess Maladjustment (SSIAM) (Gurland et al. 1972). The items have been modified considerably, the anchor points for scoring have been changed, and new items and areas have been added.

DESCRIPTION

The SAS interview covers social functioning over a 2-month (8-week) period, and the SAS-SR covers a 2-week period. The SAS and SAS-SR measure either instrumental role (i.e., performance on expected tasks) or expressive role (i.e., interpersonal relations or satisfactions) in six major areas of functioning: work (as a worker, housewife, or student), social and leisure activities, relationships with extended family, marital role as a spouse (sexual functioning), role as a parent, and role as a member of the family unit. The questions in each area generally fall into four major categories: the patient's performance at expected tasks, the amount of friction with people, interpersonal behavior (e.g., hypersensitivity, domineering behavior, withdrawal, family attachments, and submissiveness), and feelings and satisfactions. (The first three categories relate to the patient's actual behavior, and the fourth deals with inner feelings and satisfactions.) The rater also makes global evaluations in each of the areas and a rating of economic inadequacies; an overall adjustment score is assigned as well.

Each area is measured as a continuous variable. The scale for individual items ranges from 1 to 5; for global items, it ranges from 1 to 7. In all cases, higher scores reflect poorer adjustment. The interview is administered in a semistructured format that relies on open-ended (rather than yes-no) questions. The initial questions should follow the general outline but may be suitably modified. In general, the first questions should be followed up by further questioning to enable the rater to make an exact assignment to the scale point. Suggested probe questions are provided after each question. The SAS-SR uses exclusively closed-ended questions. Example 8–6 provides sample SAS interview items for assessing parent role (impaired communication and friction).

The SAS-SR is ideally completed in the presence of a research assistant who can instruct the patient about format, answer questions, and check for completeness of responses.

Two scoring systems for the SAS-SR are in use. In one, the scores of items within each role area are summed, and a mean for each area is obtained. An overall score is obtained by summing the scores of all items and dividing by the number of items actually scored. An alternative scoring system uses a dimension derived from factor analysis.

Norms for the SAS-SR are available for nonpatient community sample populations, acutely ill and recovered depressed outpatients, patients with schizophrenia, alcoholic patients, and patients with opiate addictions in methadone maintenance treatment (Newberry et al. 1979; Pottenger et al. 1978; Weissman et al. 1978).

PRACTICAL ISSUES

It takes 45–60 minutes to administer the SAS and 15–20 minutes to complete the SAS-SR. It is expected that the scale will be administered by a clinician with a clinical background; however, a research technician with a degree in a social science and some exposure to research techniques may be trained to administer the SAS.

Both the SAS and the SAS-SR are under copyright. Permission to use the SAS may be obtained from the author:

> Myrna M. Weissman, Ph.D.
> College of Physicians and Surgeons
> Columbia University and School of Public Health
> Division of Clinical and Genetic Epidemiology
> New York State Psychiatric Institute, Unit 24
> 1051 Riverside Drive
> New York, NY 10032
> Phone: 212-543-5880
> Fax: 212-568-3534
> E-mail: mmw@child.cpmc.columbia.edu

The SAS-SR can be obtained from

> Multi-Health Systems, Inc.
> 908 Niagara Falls Boulevard
> North Tonawanda, NY 14120-2060
> Phone: 800-456-3003
> Internet: www.mhs.com

SAS translations are available in Finnish, French, German, Italian, Portuguese, Spanish, and Swedish. The SAS-SR has been translated into Afrikaans, Cantonese, Czech, Danish, Dutch, Finnish, French (European), French (Canadian), German, Greek, Hebrew, Hungarian, Italian, Japanese, Mandarin, Norwegian, Portuguese,

EXAMPLE 8–6 ■ Sample items from the Social Adjustment Scale

Impaired Communication

"Have you been able to talk with your children during the last two months?" Starting with (name)."

"Does he/she come to you with problems?"

"Could you give me an example from the last two months?"

Rate each child and average

Consider what is appropriate communication for the child's age

Do not rate for children under two years of age

By communication is meant discussion of feelings and problems and other overt forms of

    communication, not just the relating of activities

DO NOT RATE FEELINGS

Communicates easily	1
Most times can communicate	2
Fair communication	3
Rarely able to talk	4
Never able to talk	5

Friction

"During the past two months how much friction has there been between you and the children?"

"Have you had to discipline them much in the last two months?"

"Do you tend to snap at them when you are tired or upset?"

Rate friction by the actual incidents, amounts of friction and amount or severity of discipline.

Include coolness or tension. Do not rate feelings, rate actual behavior.

Smooth relationships	1
A little friction or tension	2
Moderate friction	3
Marked friction	4
Constant state of friction or children are intimidated and avoid parent totally	5

Reprinted with permission from Myrna M. Weissman, M.D.

Russian, Spanish (European), Spanish (South American), and Swedish.

PSYCHOMETRIC PROPERTIES

Reliability

High internal consistency (mean Cronbach's alpha, $r = 0.74$) and test-retest stability across 2-week periods (Edwards et al. 1978) (mean coefficient, $r = 0.80$) were demonstrated for the SAS-SR. Joint reliability on the 42 individual items ranged from 0.55 to 0.97; reliability on the six global judgments ranged from 0.59 to 0.89. The overall corrected mean correlation was 0.83.

Validity

In one study, SAS and SAS-SR scores were compared in 76 consecutive depressed outpatients presenting for psychopharmacologic treatment as part of a 4-week clinical trial. Correlations between the interview and the self-report items were significant, ranging from 0.40 for family unit to 0.76 for marital role. In all roles except marital role, the patients on average rated themselves as significantly more impaired than the interviewer had rated them. This variation may be an artifact of the different periods covered by the two instruments. The correlation for the overall adjustment was 0.72, indicating very good agreement. There were no significant differences between means of the self-report and interview for marital roles. However, in all other roles and in overall adjustment, patients, on the average, rated themselves as significantly more impaired than the interviewer had rated them.

In a separate study, the validity of the SAS was tested by examining the scale's ability to discriminate between impaired and unimpaired groups. SAS scores of 40 depressed patients admitted to a drug maintenance study while acutely ill were compared with a sample of 40 control subjects from the city directory, comparable in age, sex, social class, religion, race, and marital status. Subjects with overt psychiatric disturbance at the time of the interview, previous psychiatric treatment of any kind, or current medical illness were excluded from the control population. The instrument was highly discriminative between groups on most items, except those referring solely to unmarried subjects (e.g., diminished dating), where the sample sizes were very low. The differences between groups were particularly striking in the work area.

The sensitivity of the SAS to change was tested by comparing the social adjustment scores of the same 40 depressed patients when they began psychiatric treatment and were acutely symptomatic with their scores 2 months later when considerable symptomatic improvement had occurred. These clinically improved patients were also compared with the 40 control subjects from the population sample. Patients changed in the expected direction of less impairment after 2 months of psychiatric treatment, and many scores reached statistical significance. Improvement in work performance after 2 months of treatment was highly significant. In general, when there is improvement in symptomatology, patients usually return to work, but their interpersonal relationships and personal fulfillment may not improve as consistently or as rapidly.

The SAS-SR is also sensitive to change in depressed patients. This sensitivity was demonstrated by comparing self-reported adjustment scores before treatment and at the height of the illness with those after 4 weeks of treatment. Improvement in the patients' social adjustment was concomitant with clinical recovery.

CLINICAL UTILITY

Both the SAS and the SAS-SR are widely used and cited in the literature. The SAS has been used with depressed patients; patients undergoing drug treatment and psychotherapy; patients who have attempted suicide; patients in methadone maintenance treatment; patients with schizophrenia, eating disorders, or anxiety disorders; and community-based populations without mental disorders.

The SAS-SR has been found useful in many settings and types of populations, including in community health surveys of the general population; in the evaluation of psychiatric outpatient groups receiving psychotherapy and/or psychopharmacological treatment; in patients who have bipolar disorder, substance use disorders, or schizophrenia; in heterogeneous samples of hospitalized psychiatric patients; and in a college population. The scale has limitations for use with chronically ill patients such as those with schizophrenia and with the elderly and the young, because these patients may not be functioning in many of the roles assessed (e.g., current work, marital, and parental roles).

The SAS and SAS-SR are useful for assessing social adjustment in a wide range of populations, including psychiatric patients and nonpatients in the community. The SAS-SR obviously takes less clinician time. It should be noted that the two instruments cover different periods (2 months for the SAS and 2 weeks for the SAS-SR).

There might well be confounding of some of the items. For example, subjects who rate high in the area of social discomfort might also score highly in the area of diminished social interactions for the same reason.

REFERENCES AND SUGGESTED READINGS

Edwards DW, Yarvis RM, Mueller DP, et al: Test-taking and the stability of adjustment scales: can we assess patient deterioration? Evaluation Quarterly 2:275–292, 1978

Gurland B, Yorkston NJ, Stone AR, et al: The Structured and Scaled Interview to Assess Maladjustment (SSIAM), I: description, rationale, and development; II: factor analysis, reliability, and validity. Arch Gen Psychiatry 27:259–264, 1972

Kocsis JH, Zisook S, Davidson J, et al: Double-blind comparison of sertraline, imipramine, and placebo in the treatment of dysthymia: psychosocial outcomes. Am J Psychiatry 154:390–395, 1997

Newberry P, Weissman MM, Myers JK: Working wives and housewives: do they differ in mental status and social adjustment? Am J Orthopsychiatry 49:282–291, 1979

Pottenger M, McKernon J, Patrie LE, et al: The frequency and persistence of depressive symptoms in the alcohol abuser. J Nerv Ment Dis 166:562–570, 1978

Weissman M: Social Adjustment Scale Handbook: May 1995. (For a complete list of references, contact Dr. Weissman.)

Weissman MM, Bothwell S: Assessment of social adjustment by patient self-report. Arch Gen Psychiatry 33:1111–1115, 1976

Weissman MM, Paykel ES: The Depressed Woman: A Study of Social Relationships. Chicago, IL, University of Chicago Press, 1974

Weissman MM, Prusoff BA, Thompson WD, et al: Social adjustment by self-report in a community sample and in psychiatric outpatients. J Nerv Ment Dis 166:317–326, 1978

Sheehan Disability Scale

D. V. Sheehan

GOALS

The Sheehan Disability Scale (Sheehan 1983) is a composite of three self-rated items designed to measure the extent to which three major sectors in the patient's life are impaired by panic, anxiety, phobic, or depressive symptoms. This scale has been used widely in psychopharmacology randomized controlled trials, particularly for panic disorder.

This anchored visual analog scale uses spatiovisual, numeric, and verbal descriptive anchors simultaneously to assess disability across three domains: work, social life, and family life. The scale was thus designed because some people rate numerically ("he was 1.9 m tall"), others use verbal descriptive anchors ("he was very tall"), and still others communicate their rating spatiovisually (using their hands to point while commenting "he was this tall"). Some choose a combination of two or all three methods.

The Sheehan Disability Scale was developed for use in treatment outcome studies and may also be useful for identifying primary care patients with mental health–related functional impairment. It is not intended to substitute for a comprehensive diagnostic procedure but rather to supplement symptom assessments.

DESCRIPTION

The patient rates the extent to which his or her 1) work, 2) social life or leisure activities, and 3) home life or family responsibilities are impaired by his or her symptoms on a 10-point visual analog scale. There are verbal descriptors for the points on the scale as well as numerical scores that provide more precise levels of the verbal descriptors. (Consequently, there are more numerical points than there are verbal descriptor anchors.) The Sheehan Disability Scale also provides a spatiovisual layout to accommodate those with spatial rating preferences. Example 8–7 provides items from the scale.

EXAMPLE 8–7 ■ Sample items from the Sheehan Disability Scale

Disability Scales

Work   0 not applicable

The symptoms have disrupted your work:

| Not at all | Mildly | | Moderately | | Markedly | | Extremely |

| I | | I | I | | I | I | | I | | I |

| 0 | I | 2 | 3 | 4 | 5 | 6 | 7 | 8 | 9 | 10 |

Social life

The symptoms have disrupted your social life:

| Not at all | Mildly | | Moderately | | Markedly | | Extremely |

| I | | I | I | | I | I | | I | | I |

| 0 | I | 2 | 3 | 4 | 5 | 6 | 7 | 8 | 9 | 10 |

Family life

The symptoms have disrupted your family life/home responsibilities:

| Not at all | Mildly | | Moderately | | Markedly | | Extremely |

| I | | I | I | | I | I | | I | | I |

| 0 | I | 2 | 3 | 4 | 5 | 6 | 7 | 8 | 9 | 10 |

Reprinted with permission from Dr. David V. Sheehan.

The numerical ratings of 0–10 can be translated into a percentage if desired. The three items may be summed into a single dimensional measure of global functional impairment that ranges from 0 (unimpaired) to 30 (highly impaired). It is recommended that clinicians pay special attention to patients who score ≥5 on any of the three scales, because such high scores are associated with significant functional impairment.

PRACTICAL ISSUES

The scale may be used as a self-report, administered by a clinician, or rated by both independently. Because of this flexibility of administration, it is useful with both outpatients and inpatients. The scale is quite straightforward, and no scoring manual is necessary. It takes only 1–2 minutes to rate the scale.

Dr. Sheehan holds the copyright to the Sheehan Disability Scale; permission to use it may be obtained from

> Dr. David V. Sheehan
> Institute for Research in Psychiatry
> University of South Florida
> 3515 E. Fletcher
> Tampa, FL 33613
> Phone: 813-974-4544
> Fax: 813-974-4575

Translations are available in Danish, Dutch, French, German, Italian, Portuguese, Spanish, and Swedish.

The Sheehan Disability Scale is included on the CD-ROM that accompanies this handbook.

PSYCHOMETRIC PROPERTIES

Reliability

In a study of 1,001 primary care patients, the interitem correlations of the three Sheehan Disability Scale items were fairly high (0.70 for work and family impairment, 0.72 for work and social impairment, and 0.79 for family and social impairment). As a consequence of the strong relationships among the items, the internal consistency was also high (alpha = 0.89 for the three-item scale).

Validity

In the study of 1,001 patients mentioned in the preceding section, the construct validity was substantiated in two ways. Overall, more than 80% of the patients with mental disorder diagnoses had an elevated Sheehan Disability Scale score, and nearly 50% of those with elevated scale scores had at least one disorder. Also, patients with any of six mental disorders (alcohol dependence, drug dependence, generalized anxiety disorder, major depressive disorder, obsessive-compulsive disorder, and panic disorder) had significantly higher impairment scores than those who did not have the disorders.

Validity was also indicated by the fact that the scores of subjects who reported "problems getting along with partner" were higher on both the family impairment item and the total score than the scores of subjects who denied having this type of problem. Likewise, those who reported "missing work in the past month due to emotional problems" had significantly higher scores on both the work impairment item and the total score.

An elevated Sheehan Disability Scale score (≥5) was also found to be associated with increased risk of mental disorder. Using any of the six mental disorders listed earlier as the standard, the sensitivity (0.83), specificity (0.69), positive predictive value (0.47), and negative predictive value (0.92) were respectable for helping to identify psychiatrically impaired patients with the three-item scale.

The Sheehan Disability Scale appears to reflect change over time with effective treatment. In addition, it has been shown to discriminate between active drug and placebo and even between two active treatments.

CLINICAL UTILITY

The Sheehan Disability Scale is a short, simple, and cost-effective measure of disability and functional impairment that can be quickly administered and scored without disrupting the flow of routine care. It appears to be sensitive to change with treatment.

The Sheehan Disability Scale is not intended to be used for diagnostic purposes; however, it may usefully supplement a diagnostic mental health assessment by providing a non-diagnostic-specific summary of functional impairment. In primary care practices that do not routinely screen for the major mental disorders, elevations in the Sheehan Disability Scale score may serve as a warning to indicate the need for a detailed, diagnostically oriented mental health assessment.

A significant disadvantage of this scale is that the three aspects of functioning measured are highly intercorrelated (all ≥0.70). Therefore, the value of the scale as a comprehensive global measure may be limited. Another possible disadvantage is that for some nonworking subjects (e.g., retired individuals), the work item is not applicable.

REFERENCES AND SUGGESTED READINGS

Leon AC, Shear MK, Portera L, et al: Assessing impairment in patients with panic disorder: the Sheehan Disability Scale. Soc Psychiatry Psychiatr Epidemiol 27:78–82, 1992

Leon AC, Olfson M, Portera L, et al: Assessing impairment in primary care: a psychometric analysis of the Sheehan Disability Scale. Int J Psychiatry Med 27:93–105, 1997

Sheehan DV: The Anxiety Disease. New York, Scribner's, 1983

Sheehan DV, Ballenger JC, Jacobson G: Treatment of endogenous anxiety with phobic, hysterical, and hypochondriacal symptoms. Arch Gen Psychiatry 37:51–59, 1980

Sheehan DV, Harnett-Sheehan K, Raj BA: The measurement of disability. Int Clin Psychopharmacol 11(suppl 3):89–95, 1996

CHAPTER 9

General Health Status, Functioning, and Disabilities Measures

Anthony F. Lehman, M.D., M.S.P.H.
Susan T. Azrin, M.A.
Richard W. Goldberg, Ph.D.

INTRODUCTION

Major Domains

The domain of general health status refers to the overall state of an individual's health, taking into consideration the accumulated impact of all the person's health problems and treatments. It must be distinguished from mental health status, which focuses more narrowly on the individual's mental health, from disease-specific health status, such as the level of symptoms attributable to a given illness, and from quality of life, which refers more globally and subjectively to a person's life circumstances and well-being. General health status reflects the person's overall level of functioning and perceived health. Hence, both objective (functional status) and subjective (perceived health) components are included in the concept. *General health status* is related to *quality of life* but differs in that the former emphasizes functioning and perceived health, whereas the latter emphasizes perceptions of well-being and typically covers aspects of a person's life that are not necessarily directly affected by health status, such as housing. Quality of life measures are reviewed in Chapter 10. *General health status* is also related to *mental health status* and *disease-specific health status*, but the former takes a broader view of the person's health, whereas the latter two look more narrowly on the aspects of health that are directly related to mental functioning or that are attrib-

utable to a given disease. Mental health status measures are covered in Chapter 8, and disease-specific measures are distributed throughout this book.

Organization

Six measures are included in this chapter (Table 9–1). They have been chosen from a large pool of candidates because they are the most rigorously developed and widely used measures and because they provide a representative spectrum of the types of measures available in this domain. Four of these instruments, the Dartmouth COOP Functional Assessment Charts (COOP), the Duke Health Profile (DUKE), the Sickness Impact Profile (SIP), and the SF-36 Health Survey, measure general health status across a broad array of physical, psychosocial, and role-functioning domains. The other two instruments, the Katz Index of Activities of Daily Living (Katz ADL) and the Lawton Instrumental Activities of Daily Living Scale (Lawton IADL), assess general health status in terms of functioning, ability to care for basic needs, and performance of everyday tasks. The first four measures are particularly useful as screens for overall levels of health problems in individuals and groups and for tracking progress over time. The last two measures are more useful for assessing and tracking changes in levels of health-related functional impairments among persons identified as having significant functional limitations due to health problems.

TABLE 9–1 ■ General health status, functioning, and disabilities measures

NAME OF MEASURE	DISORDER OR CONSTRUCT ASSESSED	FORMAT	PAGES
Dartmouth COOP Functional Assessment Charts (COOP)*	Functional status in adolescents and adults; designed for routine screening in busy primary care settings	Self-report or staff administered; 9 charts with questions on patient's status	121–123
Duke Health Profile (DUKE)	Functional health as an outcome of medical intervention and health promotion; designed for use in primary care settings by ambulatory adults	Self-report; 17 items	123–126
Sickness Impact Profile (SIP)	Perceived health status; can be used to assess differences between groups and change over time	Self-report; 136 items	126–128
SF-36 Health Survey (SF-36)*	Perceived health status	Self-report; 36 items	128–129
Katz Index of Activities of Daily Living (Katz ADL)	Self-care functions (bathing, dressing, going to the toilet, transfer, continence, and feeding) in chronically ill and aging populations	Observer rated; functioning in sex areas is classified as dependent or independent	130–131
Lawton Instrumental Activities of Daily Living Scale (Lawton IADL)*	Performance on everyday tasks instrumental to independent living for elderly persons (using the telephone, shopping, preparing food, housekeeping, laundering, mode of transportation, responsibility for one's own medications, and handling one's own finances)	Clinician rated on the basis of the best available sources of information; 8 items	131–133

*Measure is included on the CD-ROM that accompanies this handbook.

USING MEASURES IN THIS DOMAIN

The four measures of general health status included in this chapter (the COOP, the DUKE, the SIP, and the SF-36) are all relatively brief and easy to administer. They emphasize the centrality of the patient's point of view in monitoring the quality of general medical care outcomes. These measures are commonly used to compare the health of groups of patients with different illnesses, to provide a general assessment of an individual's level of need for care, and to track global health status changes for individuals and groups. For example, these measures can be used as a quick screen for the overall level of health-related problems among individuals presenting for care. They can provide the clinician with a quick assessment of the magnitude of the patient's

health problems and the associated need for therapeutic action. Such screening does not provide information about what health problems exist but identifies persons who are having major health-related difficulties. It may then lead to more detailed efforts to identify what problems account for the impaired general health status.

The two functional status measures (the Katz ADL and the Lawton IADL) evaluate performance of various activities of daily functioning that might be adversely affected by general medical illness and provide descriptive ratings of functional independence. These scales may be used as screens in identifying needs, as aids in formulating and implementing treatment plans, and as guides in selecting optimum levels of care. Such measures are more useful for assessing and tracking the overall functional status of impaired individuals than of general patient populations. They contrast with the first four measures in that they focus more specifically on the ability to perform various common tasks and emphasize the ability to execute these tasks rather than the patient's perceptions of health status. An example of the application of these measures is to evaluate the progress of functionally impaired persons in rehabilitation or therapy programs that are designed to enhance functioning.

The four general health status measures are designed as self-assessments that can be completed by patients. They can be easily used as questionnaires that the patient can complete in the waiting room, at home, or in some other convenient setting. The major implementation issues that arise with such measures relate to the relatively small marginal costs of having patients complete them and the more significant costs of scoring and producing summaries that are useful to the clinician. Marginal costs of administration include the cost of purchasing or copying the instrument and the small amount of staff time involved in having the patient complete the form (e.g., either mailing the form or handing the form to the patient and collecting it later). Such costs increase for more impaired patients, who may need staff assistance to complete the measures, perhaps in an interview format. A clear plan for how the data will be summarized and used is essential. In a clinic setting, the plan should include procedures to score each measure (either by hand or electronically) and to produce summary reports for the treating clinician.

The two measures of functional status involve more extensive implementation issues because they require completion by an examiner. They therefore require considerably more staff time than the first four measures. Consequently, their use is more focused and limited in most clinical settings. As with the first four measures, procedures must be in place to report results to the treating clinician.

All four general health status measures are standardized, and extensive normative data are available for each. For example, norms are available across instruments for the general population and for various demographic and patient subgroups. Some of the instruments (e.g., the SIP), however, lack documentation of use with psychiatric populations. Ample reliability data are available for the general health status measures. Most estimates of internal consistency, test-retest reliability, and joint reliability meet or exceed the acceptable standards for measures used in group comparisons.

However, some of the measures (e.g., the COOP) may be less precise when used to monitor individual patients. This distinction is often not sufficiently considered in the evaluation of measures; that is, less precision is needed when comparing groups of patients than when assessing an individual because averages across patients in a group will tend to compensate for modest errors in measurement at the individual level. More precision is needed if a measure is to be used to assess only an individual, because the measurement errors that are tolerable for group comparisons may be unacceptable for assessing and planning services for the individual. A clinician who uses any given assessment should be aware of its level of measurement imprecision and evaluate the information it yields accordingly. Less precise measures can still be quite useful in screening for problems but require good follow-up assessment to ensure the accuracy of the information.

With regard to the validity of the general health status measures, all four instruments discriminate among mutually exclusive groups of patients who have a variety of physical and mental health problems. Some of the measures demonstrate sensitivity to severity of illness (e.g., the DUKE) and to the presence or absence of chronic illness (e.g., the COOP). Some of the measures (e.g., the COOP) also have proven validity for predicting health status change.

The measures generally compare favorably with each other and with longer gold standard measures of general health and functioning. Many of these measures have been shown to be predictive of a variety of clinically and socially relevant outcomes, including cost of care, ability to work, and utilization of health services.

The two measures of functional status have supporting reliability data. Both the Katz ADL and the Lawton IADL demonstrate sound internal consistency, as evidenced by high coefficients of reproducibility. However, test-retest reliability results have not been published for either measure. Validity data are also limited for these two measures. The Katz ADL correlates well with the degree of actual assistance required by the patient, and the Lawton IADL correlates well with separate measures of physical and mental functioning. In a recent review of functional disability scales, Spector (1996) encouraged researchers to publish additional reliability and validity studies for the Katz ADL, the Lawton IADL, and similar measures to help further our understanding of the usefulness of these instruments.

GUIDE TO THE SELECTION
OF MEASURES

The four self-report general health status measures can be used to obtain global assessments of a patient's health status and treatment impact. In most applications, the investigator or clinician will want to follow up these general assessment measures with more disease-specific, focused measures or clinical assessments that will then guide care planning. These general health status measures have the advantage of providing a quick screen and a glimpse of the patient's overall state of health. Their disadvantage is that they lack specificity to guide actions. They are nonetheless valuable as part of assessments because disease-specific and other focused scales may miss the relevance of specific health problems to the patient's overall health status (i.e., the forest and trees dilemma). The general health status measures can guide the clinician in assessing the overall severity of a patient's health problems and the need to act to improve health status. The disease-specific measures are more useful in determining what can be done to address the specific health problems present.

The four general health status measures appear relevant and feasible for use in assessing patients' perceptions of their health status in a wide variety of settings. However, each measure has its weaknesses. The COOP, for example, has limited sensitivity for detecting meaningful changes in individuals. In addition, because the COOP represents health as an absence of limitations, ceiling effects (i.e., inability of the scale to differentiate among individuals who score at the high ends of the scales) are often substantial. Hence, the COOP is not useful in distinguishing among patients who do not have significant health status limitations. Similarly, data on the DUKE's sensitivity to change in monitoring individual treatment outcomes are inadequate. Because the DUKE was designed specifically for ambulatory primary care patients, floor effects are likely when it is used with severely ill or very impaired patients (i.e., very impaired patients are likely to score so low on the measure that it will fail to detect differences among patients with low functioning or modest changes in their health status). Given the imperfect state of the measurement of general health status, such caveats are not intended to discourage the use of these measures. Rather, the clinician should be well versed in their limitations when interpreting the results.

A scale that lacks sensitivity to change at the extreme ends may still be very useful in identifying which patients have the poorest health status and hence warrant special attention. Scales with limited precision at the individual patient level may nonetheless be helpful in monitoring the overall progress of groups of patients and can still provide guidance in identifying patients in need of further assessment and treatment.

Regarding the selection of a general functional status measure, both the Katz ADL and the Lawton IADL merit consideration. Selection should be on the basis of the scale's intended purpose and the target population. *Activities of daily living* (ADL) refer to basic self-care functioning, such as bathing, dressing, and feeding. *Instrumental activities of daily living* (IADL) refer to higher-level tasks such as cooking, use of transportation, and money management. Thus, the Katz scale is more useful for patients with more serious impairment, and the Lawton scale is more useful for patients with less serious impairment.

CURRENT STATUS AND FUTURE
RESEARCH NEEDS FOR ASSESSMENT

Given the increased attention being paid to patients' self-assessment of general health status and well-being, it behooves researchers and clinicians alike to continue refining the psychometric properties associated with the various general health status measures currently in use. The identification of additional domains of functioning relevant to the monitoring of medical outcomes is also warranted. Researchers should continue to publish results from applications of these measures in various settings and with various groups of patients to help further our understanding of the usefulness of these instruments and to provide relevant normative data. It is also important that future research focus on issues of cultural sensitivity in the administration of these instruments and in the interpretation of the data they produce.

Given the growing number of elderly patients and the demands they place on physical and mental health care services, it is important that efforts to refine existing self-care measures relevant to the elderly population continue. Clinicians and researchers need reliable and validated measures of functional disability to measure clinical progress and evaluate treatment programs.

REFERENCES AND SUGGESTED READINGS

Spector WD: Functional disability scales, in Quality of Life and Pharmacoeconomics in Clinical Trials, 2nd Edition. Edited by Spilker B. Philadelphia, PA, Lippincott-Raven, 1996, pp 133–144

Spilker B: Quality of life and pharmacoeconomics, in Clinical Trials, 2nd Edition. Edited by Spilker B. Philadelphia, PA, Lippincott-Raven, 1996

Dartmouth COOP Functional Assessment Charts (COOP)

E. C. Nelson, J. H. Wasson, D. J. Johnson, and R. D. Hays

GOALS

The Dartmouth COOP Functional Assessment Charts (COOP) (Nelson et al. 1987) was developed to measure functional status in adolescents and adults. It was designed for routine screening in busy primary care settings. A separate set of charts is available for adolescents. Functional status dimensions involve physical, mental, and role functions. The COOP's nine measured dimensions include physical function, change in health, emotional function, overall health, role function, social support, social function, quality of life, and pain.

DESCRIPTION

There are a total of nine COOP Charts; each consists of a title, a question referring to the patient's status over the past 2–4 weeks, and five response choices. Drawings, each depicting a level of functioning or well-being along a 5-point Likert scale, illustrate each response choice. The drawings generally involve simple stick figures. The

COOP may be self-administered or administered by office staff. A sample item is provided in Example 9–1.

Each COOP Chart is self-scoring. Scores range from 1 to 5 for each chart; lower numbers represent better functional status or less impairment and higher numbers represent worse functional status or more impairment. Norms for 15 countries including the United States are available.

PRACTICAL ISSUES

Administration time for the COOP is brief, approximately 30–45 seconds per chart. Although the COOP's authors reported that it took 1–2 minutes to administer per patient in their initial study, later studies have reported 2–3 minutes per patient to administer only four charts—the entire set consists of 9 charts—and 6 minutes on average for the whole set. Minimal training is required.

EXAMPLE 9–1 ■ Sample item from the Dartmouth COOP Functional Assessment Charts

OVERALL HEALTH

During the past four weeks...
how would you rate your health in general?

Excellent	😊	1
Very good	🙂	2
Good	😐	3
Fair	🙁	4
Poor	☹️	5

Reprinted with permission from the Dartmouth COOP Project.

Users of the COOP Charts are required to submit a brief description of their intended use of the charts, but they are not required to return data. The COOP may be obtained from

> Dartmouth COOP Project
> Hinman Box 7625
> Dartmouth Medical School
> Hanover, NH 03755-3862
> Phone: 603-650-1220
> Fax: 603-650-1331

The COOP Charts are copyrighted. The charts and introductory and administration materials cost $20.00. A computerized version (Macintosh or MS Windows) for administration and scoring is available from

> FNX Corp.
> 1 Dorrset Lane
> Lebanon, NH 03766
> Phone: 603-448-2224

Reusable questionnaires are completed with dry-erase markers; then bar-coded answers are electronically scanned. These data can generate a patient letter and a patient flow sheet detailing the patient's condition, needs, and opinion of the care received.

Translations of the COOP Charts are available in Chinese, Danish, Dutch, Finnish, French, German, Hebrew, Italian, Japanese, Norwegian, Portuguese, Slovak, Spanish (Callego), Spanish (Castilian), Spanish (Catalan), Swedish, and Urdu. The COOP Charts are available on the CD-ROM that accompanies this handbook.

PSYCHOMETRIC PROPERTIES

Reliability

In estimates of the COOP Charts' alternate-form reliability, a measure of the instrument's consistency when items are presented in different order across administrations, correlations range from 0.24 to 0.54. These correlations are in the modest range, depending on the particular chart. The resulting 95% confidence intervals are quite large, suggesting that the COOP's precision may not be adequate for monitoring individual patients. The COOP Charts demonstrated adequate test-retest reliability in a small sample of older adults in primary care and in rural private practices when the COOP was ad-

ministered by both a nurse and a physician (average intraclass correlation coefficient of 0.77 and a range of 0.50–0.98, $N = 41$). In two samples of mostly older adults in outpatient clinics, test-retest reliability studies with 1 hour between administrations found average intraclass correlation coefficients of 0.93 ($N = 231$) and 0.88 ($N = 51$); the range was 0.73–0.98 for both studies. A test-retest reliability study using the same sample as in the second study referred to earlier ($N = 51$), with 2 weeks between administrations (usually by telephone, with a take-home copy of the charts available), found an average intraclass correlation coefficient of 0.67; the range was 0.42–0.88.

Validity

The COOP Charts demonstrated high validity in several studies. Over most dimensions, the charts performed comparably with the longer RAND Scales (Nelson et al. 1990), which may be considered a gold standard measure of general health and functioning. The largest study ($N = 1,007$) comparing the RAND Scales to the COOP examined a sample of male and female patients with chronic disease, average age 58, and found correlations (r) ranging from 0.45 to 0.70. A smaller study ($N = 231$) of elderly men, who had mostly low incomes and chronic health problems, reported very similar results.

The former study ($N = 1,007$) also found that, in their sensitivity to the presence or absence of chronic illness, the RAND Scales and the COOP performed similarly along the dimensions of physical function, role function, and overall health, but the COOP did not perform as well as the RAND Scales in the dimension of emotional status. The latter study ($N = 231$) found that the presence or absence of chronic disease was significantly associated with physical function and role function but was less strongly related to emotional, social support, and health change, supporting the construct validity of the COOP. Correlations between chronic disease symptoms and the COOP range from 0.25 (health change) to 0.51 (overall health).

The COOP's ability to assess change in health status in men presenting with inguinal hernia and undergoing treatment ($N = 129$) was examined. Differences in effect sizes at baseline preoperation versus postoperation at 10 days and at 6 weeks further support the COOP's validity. The size and direction of health status change generally matched expected surgical outcomes. For example, the COOP indicated less pain and better physical and social functioning 6 weeks after operation as compared with baseline preoperation findings.

CLINICAL UTILITY

Compared with other measures of general health and functioning, the COOP Charts stand out for their practicality. They are among the shortest in length, briefest to complete, and easiest to score and interpret. Thus, the COOP Charts are most useful as a brief and practical routine screen of functional status in adults and adolescents. Their brevity and self-administration format make them particularly appropriate for use in busy primary care settings. They may also be useful as a routine screen of general functioning in psychiatric settings and with hospitalized and nursing home residents as a fast, accurate way to assess function.

However, the substantial measurement error associated with the COOP is so large (as is the case for many health status surveys) that it has relatively low sensitivity to detect meaningful change in functional status. Consequently, the COOP is inadequate for use in tracking clinical outcomes or in longitudinal monitoring of change in health status in patients with chronic disease. Additionally, because the COOP represents health as an absence of limitations (as do most health status measures), all individuals with unimpaired functioning on a dimension receive the same score. Thus, changes in functioning from very high to lower but still unimpaired levels may not be detected.

REFERENCES AND SUGGESTED READINGS

Jenkinson C, Lawrence K, McWhinnie D, et al: Sensitivity to change of health status measures in a randomized controlled trial: comparison of the COOP Charts and the SF-36. Qual Life Res 4:47–52, 1995

McHorney CA, Tarlov AR: Individual-patient monitoring in clinical practice: are available health status surveys adequate? Qual Life Res 4:293–307, 1995

Nelson E, Wasson J, Kirk J, et al: Assessment of function in routine clinical practice: description of the COOP Chart method and preliminary findings. Journal of Chronic Diseases 40(suppl 1):55S–63S, 1987

Nelson EC, Landgraf JM, Hays RD, et al: The functional status of patients: how can it be measured in physicians' offices? Med Care 28(12):1111–1126, 1990

Duke Health Profile (DUKE)

G. R. Parkerson Jr., W. E. Broadhead, and C-K. J. Tse

GOALS

The Duke Health Profile (DUKE) (Parkerson et al. 1990) is a 17-item self-report measure of functional health status. It is intended as a brief measure of health as an outcome of medical intervention and health promotion for use in primary care settings with ambulatory adult patients. The DUKE was formulated as a reconceptualized and abbreviated version of its predecessor, the well-validated 63-item Duke-UNC Health Profile (DUHP) (Parkerson et al. 1981), without loss of reliability or validity.

DESCRIPTION

The DUKE is a 17-item, self-administered questionnaire that broadly assesses health status using five mutually exclusive health scales. The Physical Health scale has five items (walking up a flight of stairs, running the length of a football field, hurting or aching, tiring easily, and trouble sleeping), the Mental Health scale has five items (like who I am, give up too easily, difficulty concentrating, feeling depressed or sad, and nervousness), the Social Health scale has five items (not an easy person to get along with, happy with family relationships, comfortable around people, socialize with other people, take part in social activities), the Perceived Health scale has one item, and the Disability scale has one item. Several additional scales are derived from combinations of these 17 items: the General

Health scale, which includes the initial 15 items of physical, mental, and social health, and Dysfunction measures of anxiety, depression, anxiety-depression, pain, and disability. Each item uses a 3-point Likert scale for which the response options depend on the item (e.g., "none," "some," or "a lot" for some items; "yes, describes me exactly," "somewhat describes me," or "no, does not describe me at all" for other items). All items are administered. Example 9–2 provides a sample item from the Social Health dimension.

Weighted scores on the DUKE range from 0 to 100. High scores for the health dimensions (Physical Health, Mental Health, Social Health, Perceived Health, Self-Esteem, and General Health) indicate good health, whereas high scores for the dysfunction dimensions (Anxiety, Depression, Pain, and Disability) indicate poor health.

PRACTICAL ISSUES

It takes about 5 minutes to administer the DUKE. It is copyrighted by the Department of Community and Family Medicine, Duke University Medical Center, Durham, North Carolina, and can be obtained at no cost from

> George R. Parkerson, M.D.
> Department of Community and Family Medicine
> Duke University Medical Center
> P.O. Box 3886
> Durham, NC 27710
> Phone: 919-681-3043
> Fax: 919-681-6560

The user's guide is available from the same source and costs $30.00. It also includes three other DUKE measures, the Severity of Illness Checklist, the Duke Case-Mix System, and the Social Support and Stress Scale. The au-

thors of the DUKE report telephone administration of the measure.

PSYCHOMETRIC PROPERTIES

Reliability

The DUKE offers ample reliability data of internal consistency. In two different samples of 683 and 314 ambulatory adult primary care patients of all ages, three-fourths female, Cronbach's alphas ranged from 0.49 for the Self-Esteem scale to 0.78 for the General Health scale (Parkerson et al. 1990, 1992).

Temporal stability with two similar samples of 55 and 54 patients ranged from 0.30 for Disability to 0.78 for both General Health and Self-Esteem; time between first and second administrations varied from 1 week to more than 10 weeks later (Parkerson et al. 1990, 1992). The DUKE's authors note that test-retest reliability may be an inappropriate standard for health measures used in a primary care setting because fluctuations over a brief period are expected in response to interventions and disease course.

Validity

The DUKE's validity compares favorably with the DUHP, its longer parent version, as well as with other established instruments, including the Sickness Impact Profile (SIP) (p. 126), a 136-item measure of the impact of sickness and disability on daily life activities, the Tennessee Self-Concept Scale (Fitts 1972), a 100-item self-esteem measure, and the Zung Self-Rating Depression Scale (p. 534), a 20-item measure of depression.

In the sample of 683 ambulatory primary care patients described earlier, correlations between the DUKE's and the DUHP's Physical Health, Mental Health, and Social Health scales were 0.72, 0.70, and 0.61, respectively. Correlations between the DUHP's symptom-status dimension and the DUKE's Physical Health, Mental Health, and Social Health scales were 0.74, 0.54, and 0.30, respectively. When a total score was generated for the DUHP as a mean of scores on its four dimensions (DUHP lacks a general health scale), its correlation with the DUKE's General Health scale was 0.86. In a sample of 43 primary care patients, the DUKE's 5-item Self-Esteem scale was compared with the DUHP's 23-item Emotional Function scale as part of a 10-week randomized clinical trial. The DUKE Self-Esteem scale demon-

EXAMPLE 9–2 ■ Sample item from the Duke Health Profile

During the past week, how often did you socialize with other people (talk or visit with friends or relatives)?

Response options: none, some, or a lot

Reprinted with permission from G. R. Parkerson Jr.

strated sensitivity to change and a greater combined effect size for change (*delta* = 1.32) than did the DUHP's Emotional Function scale (*delta* = 0.77). In a multisite study of 1,073 men with erectile dysfunction (Parkerson 1999) the DUKE Mental Health scale showed improvement in all sites 14 months after the onset of treatment with alprostadil, whereas the Physical Health and Social Health scales showed mixed results (some improved, some unchanged, and some worsened).

Correlations between similar components of the SIP and the DUKE (*N* = 103) ranged from 0.40 for the DUKE Disability scale and the SIP Mobility scale to –0.70 for the DUKE General Health scale and the SIP overall score (high scores on the SIP indicate poorer health).

Correlations between similar components of the Tennessee Self-Concept Scale and the DUKE (*N* = 101) ranged from 0.28 for the Physical Health scale to 0.80 for the Self-Esteem scale. Finally, correlations between the Zung Self-Rating Depression Scale and the DUKE were –0.70 for the DUKE Mental Health scale, –0.58 for the DUKE Self-Esteem scale, 0.63 for the DUKE Depression scale, and 0.63 for the DUKE Anxiety scale (*N* = 111; lower scores on Zung Self-Esteem and Mental Health scales represent better health).

Parkerson et al. (1995) found that the DUKE demonstrated modest predictive validity in predicting outcomes of follow-up utilization, severity of illness, and cost in the primary care setting. Scores on the DUKE Physical Health and Perceived Health scales at baseline independently predicted the following five outcome measures at 18 months: need for follow-up, number of follow-up visits, need for referral or hospitalization, severity of illness at follow-up, and cost of follow-up care.

The DUKE demonstrates validity in differentiating among patients with different clinical problems: painful physical health problems, mental health problems, and health maintenance problems (Parkerson et al. 1990). Mean Physical Health scores were higher for persons with painful physical problems than for persons with only health maintenance problems, whereas mean Mental Health scores for persons with mental health problems were lower than for persons with painful physical problems or persons with only health maintenance problems. Likewise, mean Pain scores were higher for persons with painful physical problems than for persons with mental health problems or persons with only health maintenance problems.

CLINICAL UTILITY

The major strengths of the DUKE are its brevity (it takes only about 5 minutes to administer), its broad conceptualizations of health and functioning, and the substantial validity and reliability data. Despite having only 17 items, the DUKE produces 11 scale scores, including a general health measure, and covers several important health domains. Thus, the DUKE represents a substantial improvement over the DUHP, its predecessor, in that it is substantially shorter, includes dimensions of physical, mental, and social health, and provides broader measures of both emotional and social functioning while retaining high validity and reliability standards.

The DUKE appears most useful as a brief screening measure of functional health for ambulatory patients, particularly in primary care settings. Validity findings support the DUKE's high sensitivity in detecting the impact of sickness and disability across all the DUKE's dimensions.

Preliminary evidence suggests the DUKE's validity as a modest predictor of various primary care health outcomes. However, with the exception of the Self-Esteem and Mental Health scales, there are inadequate data on the DUKE's sensitivity to change to support its use as a means of monitoring treatment outcomes, as the authors had intended. The Self-Esteem and Mental Health scales demonstrate high sensitivity to change, making these scales appropriate for monitoring the emotional impact of sickness and disability.

An advantage of the DUKE is that normative data, including means and standard deviations for the DUKE scales and individual items, are available in Parkerson et al. (1990).

Because the DUKE was designed specifically for ambulatory primary care patients, the scale is less likely to differentiate among severely ill or very impaired patients, all of whom would tend to share the same maximum score (i.e., floor effects).

REFERENCES AND SUGGESTED READINGS

Fitts WH: The self-concept and psychopathology (U.S. Department of Commerce, National Technical Information

Service, PB 235620). Springfield, VA, U.S. Department of Commerce, 1972

Parkerson GR Jr, Gehlbach SH, Wagner EH, et al: The Duke-UNC Health Profile: an adult health status instrument for primary care. Med Care 19(8):806–828, 1981

Parkerson GR Jr, Broadhead WE, Tse C-KJ: The Duke Health Profile: a 17-item measure of health and dysfunction. Med Care 28:1056–1072, 1990

Parkerson GR Jr, Broadhead WE, Tse C-KJ: Development of the 17-item Duke Health Profile. Fam Pract 8:396–401, 1991

Parkerson GR Jr, Broadhead WE, Tse C-KJ: Quality of life and functional health of primary care patients. J Clin Epidemiol 45(11):1303–1313, 1992

Parkerson GR Jr, Connis RT, Broadhead WE, et al: Disease-specific versus generic measurement of health-related quality of life in insulin-dependent diabetic patients. Med Care 31(7):629–639, 1993

Parkerson GR Jr, Broadhead WE, Tse C-KJ: Health status and severity of illness as predictors of outcomes in primary care. Med Care 33:53–66, 1995

Parkerson GR Jr, Michener JL, Yarnall KS, et al: Duke Case-Mix System (DUMIX) for ambulatory health care. J Clin Epidemiol 50:1385–1394, 1997

Parkerson GR, Willke RJ, Hays RD: An international comparison of the reliability and responsiveness of the Duke Health Profile for measuring health-related quality of life of patients treated with alprostadil for erectile dysfunction. Med Care 37:56–67, 1999

Willke RJ, Yen W, Parkerson GR Jr, et al: Quality of life effects of alprostadil therapy for erectile dysfunction: results of a trial in Europe and South Africa. Int J Impot Res 10:239–246, 1998.

Sickness Impact Profile (SIP)

M. Bergner

GOALS

The Sickness Impact Profile (SIP) (Bergner et al. 1981), designed to measure perceived health status, can be used across a wide range of clinical settings. It assesses differences among groups of patients and change over time to aid evaluation, program planning, and policy formulation. The author's implicit definition of the construct measured is the patient's perception of the degree of impact health status and illness have on his or her physical, psychosocial, and role functioning.

DESCRIPTION

The SIP is a self-administered questionnaire completed by the patient. An interviewer-administered form is also available and can be administered by a minimally trained rater. The SIP consists of 136 items with yes-no responses that are combined to yield 12 dimensional scores (Sleep and Rest, Eating, Work, Home Management, Recreation and Pastimes, Ambulation, Mobility, Body Care and Movement, Social Interactions, Alertness Behavior, Emotional Behavior, and Communication). The first five dimensions are independent, meaning they are considered separately. The next three can be combined to form the Physical dimension, and the last four can be combined into a Psychosocial dimension. All 12 dimensions can be combined into a total SIP score. The SIP must be used in its entirety. Sample items are provided in Example 9–3.

The overall score and the scores for individual dimensions range from 0 to 100. These scores reflect the percentage of the relevant items that are endorsed (answered with yes) multiplied by 100.

EXAMPLE 9–3 ■ Sample items from the Sickness Impact Profile

I sit around half asleep.
I act nervous or restless.
I get sudden frights.
I use a bedpan with assistance.
I am very clumsy in body movements.
I am not doing heavy work around the house.

The Sickness Impact Profile (SIP) is copyrighted by The Johns Hopkins University. Reprinted with permission.

PRACTICAL ISSUES

It takes about 20–30 minutes to complete the SIP. Permission for use must be obtained from the copyright holder, Johns Hopkins University; however, there is no charge to use the SIP. The manual (Damiano 1996) provides information about psychometric properties, norms (mean SIP scores) for populations with a wide range of medical conditions as well as for the general population (although no mental illnesses are included in these tables), and a bibliography by disease. The SIP and manual can be obtained from

> Health Services Research and Development Center
> Department of Health Policy and Management
> Johns Hopkins School of Public Health
> 624 North Broadway
> Baltimore, MD 21205

Training to use the SIP involves reading the manual and minimal practice. The SIP has been translated into Dutch, Spanish, and Swedish.

PSYCHOMETRIC PROPERTIES

Reliability

Internal consistency of the individual SIP category scores and the total score have been assessed among the general population and among patients in the United States, Sweden, Spain, and the Netherlands. Sample sizes in these studies ranged from 250 to more than 3,500. Alpha coefficients ranged from 0.81 to 0.97 and were similar for category and overall scores. Test-retest correlations over a 2-week interval for the category and overall scores ranged from 0.79 to 0.97.

Validity

The validity of the SIP has been assessed in a random sample ($N = 696$) of medical patients and with a variety of other samples of patients. The SIP score was moderately correlated with other health and functional status measures, including self-assessment of dysfunction, self-assessment of illness, clinician ratings of sickness, and clinician ratings of dysfunction. These correlations were generally in the range of 0.4–0.7. The authors note that the validity of the SIP is much better compared with other measures of general health status than with narrower, disease-specific measures. Few studies have assessed sensitivity to change; however, existing data suggest that the SIP is not sensitive to day-to-day change (i.e., cannot detect meaningful score changes day to day) but can detect changes over weeks or months.

CLINICAL UTILITY

Studies of the SIP report a high rate of patient acceptance. The SIP appears relevant and feasible for assessing patients' perceptions of their health status in a wide variety of settings. This acceptance enhances the clinical utility of the measure because it can be applied with confidence in a wide range of clinical circumstances and because it permits comparisons across patient groups. The latter application is certainly useful from a research perspective, but it can also be important for clinical and administrative usage. Use of the same health status measure across subgroups of patients permits the clinician to become familiar with the measure and its relative meaning. The clinician can develop a feel for the degree of health impairment experienced by various patients by using the same measure across disorders. Use of the same measure across disorders also permits aggregation of intake and outcome health status data for large numbers of patients, a function that has considerable value in the development of quality assurance and other administrative summaries. Evidence of sensitivity to change over weeks to months appears adequate. Therefore, the measure should be useful for comparing different patient populations (e.g., across treatment programs or locations within a larger provider network) or a single patient population versus the many reference populations in the manual. It may also be useful for assessing changes in groups of patients over time. Such change data can be used to assess the overall effectiveness of clinical interventions. One concern in the application of the SIP in mental health settings is the lack of documentation of its use with psychiatric patients.

REFERENCES AND SUGGESTED READINGS

Andresen EM, Patrick DL, Carter WB, et al: Comparing the performance of health status measures for healthy older adults. J Am Geriatr Soc 43:1030–1034, 1995

Bergner M, Bobbitt RA, Carter WB, et al: The Sickness Impact Profile: development and final revision of a health status measure. Med Care 19:787–805, 1981

Damiano AM: The Sickness Impact Profile: User's Manual and Interpretation Guide. Baltimore, MD, Johns Hopkins University, 1996

De Bruin AF, De Witte LP, Stevens F, et al: Sickness Impact Profile: the state of the art of a generic functional status measure. Soc Sci Med 35:1003–1014, 1992

SF-36 Health Survey (SF-36)

J. E. Ware

GOALS

The SF-36 Health Survey (Ware et al. 1993) was developed as a generic measure of perceived health status. Used across a wide range of clinical settings, it provides self-reports of behavioral functioning and perceived psychological well-being without being age, disease, or treatment specific. The self-reports of behavioral functioning in the SF-36 are used to measure observable and tangible limitations due to poor health and/or bodily pain in physical, social, and role activities. The measure also includes self-reports of the frequency and intensity of feeling states, including general mental health, bodily pain, and energy and fatigue. The SF-36 emphasizes the centrality of the patient point of view in assessing current health status, susceptibility to illness, and general health outlook.

DESCRIPTION

The SF-36 is generally self-administered by patients ages 14 and older at the time of a doctor or clinic visit. It can also be administered by telephone or an in-person interview. The measure contains 36 items that are combined to form eight scales to measure the following health concepts: Physical Functioning, Physical Role Functioning, Bodily Pain, General Health, Vitality (energy vs. fatigue), Social Functioning, Emotional Role Functioning, and Mental Health. Most items are scored as yes-no or on 5- or 6-point scales. The standard version of the SF-36 uses a 4-week recall period. Sample items are provided in Example 9–4.

The eight SF-36 scale scores range from 0 to 100; higher scores indicate better health status. Extensive normative data from rigorous sampling and survey methodologies are available for the general population of the United States and across various demographic subgroups (including norms for people between the ages of 65 and 74 years and over age 75). The manual (Ware et al. 1993) also provides normative SF-36 data across a wide variety of medical conditions (e.g., hypertension, clinical depression, diabetes, and congestive heart failure) and lists norms for the Mental Health scale among a representative sample of patients recruited from both medical practices and mental health providers.

PRACTICAL ISSUES

It takes approximately 10–12 minutes to administer the SF-36. The SF-36 is copyrighted. Permission to reproduce the measure should be requested from

> Medical Outcomes Trust
> P.O. Box 1917
> Boston, MA 02205

Permission to use the SF-36 Health Survey is routinely granted by the Medical Outcomes Trust on a royalty-free basis on receipt of a request. A copy of *SF-36 Health Survey: Manual and Interpretation Guide* (Ware et al. 1993) is also available from the Medical Outcomes Trust

EXAMPLE 9–4 ■ Sample items from the SF-36 Health Survey

> During the past 4 weeks, to what extent have your physical health or emotional problems interfered with your normal social activities with family, friends, neighbors, or groups?
>
> How much bodily pain have you had during the past 4 weeks?
>
> Does your health now limit you in lifting or carrying groceries?

Reprinted with permission from John E. Ware Jr.

and costs $53.00. In addition to the standard version, an acute version of the SF-36 that uses a 1-week recall is available. (Methodological studies that use this version are expected in the near future.) The manual also reports the existence of a British adaptation of the SF-36. The International Quality of Life Assessment (IQOLA) Project is currently translating and adapting the SF-36 for use in 15 countries, including a Spanish version for Spanish-speaking Americans.

The SF-36 is included on the CD-ROM that accompanies this handbook.

PSYCHOMETRIC PROPERTIES

Reliability

Estimates of reliability for the SF-36 scales have been reported in 14 studies representing a range of patient populations (including general population studies in the United Kingdom and the United States), diagnoses (e.g., AIDS, renal disease, and diabetes), and situations (e.g., clinic visits). Sample sizes in these studies (all summarized in the manual) ranged from 39 to 9,385. Estimates of internal consistency (alpha coefficients) ranged from 0.62 to 0.94; the majority of scores equaled or exceeded 0.80. Test-retest coefficients ranged from 0.43 to 0.90 for a 6-month interval and from 0.60 to 0.81 for a 2-week interval.

Validity

The SF-36 has been shown to correlate moderately well with other well-known health measures, including the Sickness Impact Profile (p. 126) and the Duke Health Profile (p. 123). The level of medical and psychiatric severity as measured by the SF-36 has also been shown to correlate, in expected ways, with clinical outcome criteria such as burden of care. The instrument has also been proven useful in predicting clinically and socially relevant outcomes such as ability to work and utilization of health care services. Studies have shown that the SF-36 can be used to collect valid and accurate self-reports of change in general health status over a 1-year period.

Factor and principal components analyses have been used to provide empirical tests of the validity of the SF-36. Results indicate empirical verification of the hypothesized two-dimensional structure of the instrument. More specifically, results indicate the presence of two distinct factors labeled as physical and mental health that account for 82% of the measure's reliable variance.

CLINICAL UTILITY

The SF-36 assesses health concepts that represent basic human values relevant to general functional status and well-being. The SF-36 thus has the potential to serve an important function in everyday medical practice. More specifically, information collected on the SF-36 can be used by individual practitioners and clinicians to 1) detect, assess, and explain decreased functional capacity and well-being across a wide variety of medical and psychiatric conditions; 2) keep track of changes in functioning over time; and 3) make use of standardized assessments of functioning in choosing and evaluating treatment options. According to the user's manual, the emphasis of the SF-36 on functional status and well-being will also assist policy analysts who compare the costs and benefits of competing ways of organizing and financing health care services and managers of health care organizations who seek to produce the best value for each health care dollar.

REFERENCES AND SUGGESTED READINGS

McHorney CA, Ware JE, Raczek AE: The MOS 36-Item Short-Form Health Survey (SF-36), II: psychometric and clinical tests of validity in measuring physical and mental health constructs. Med Care 31(3):247–263, 1993

McHorney CA, Kosinski M, Ware JE: Comparisons of the costs and quality of norms for the SF-36 Health Survey collected by mail versus telephone interview: results from a national survey. Med Care 32(6):551–567, 1994a

McHorney CA, Ware JE, Lu JFR, et al: The MOS SF-36 Short-Form Health Survey (SF-36), III: tests of data quality, scaling assumptions, and reliability across diverse patient groups. Med Care 32(1):40–66, 1994b

Ware JE, Sherbourne CD: The MOS 36-Item Short-Form Health Survey (SF-36), I: conceptual framework and item selection. Med Care 30(6):473–483, 1992

Ware JE, Snow KK, Kosinski M, et al: SF-36 Health Survey: Manual and Interpretation Guide. Boston, MA, Health Institute, New England Medical Center, 1993

Katz Index of Activities of Daily Living (Katz ADL)

S. Katz, A. Ford, R. Moskowitz, B. Jackson, and M. Jaffe

GOALS

The Katz Index of Activities of Daily Living (Katz ADL) (Katz et al. 1963) is intended to assess meaningful self-care functions (activities of daily living [ADL]) in chronically ill and aging populations. It defines ADL as functioning in six areas: bathing, dressing, going to the toilet, transfer (moving in and out of bed or chair), continence, and feeding. It was designed to evaluate treatment and prognosis in elderly and chronically ill patients in settings that include rehabilitation, home care, hospital (inpatient or outpatient), and custodial institutions.

DESCRIPTION

A rater asks the subject to perform tasks that allow for direct observation of some of the measured ADL domains. Specifically, the observer asks the subject to show him or her 1) the bathroom and 2) medications in another room (or a meaningful substitute object). These requests allow for direct observation of transfer, locomotion, and communication. The observer then elicits information from the subject to evaluate the remaining ADL domains. Six domains or items (as mentioned earlier) are evaluated. The evaluation sheet offers three possible response options for each item: "performs activity without assistance," "performs activity with some assistance," or "does not perform activity or performs activity with much assistance." On the basis of the ratings, the subject is then classified as dependent or independent on each of the six items, according to explicit criteria provided for each of the domains. A sample item is provided in Example 9–5.

Classifications A through G represent possible scores that reflect increasing levels of functional impairment; there is also an "other" category. The categories are defined as follows:

EXAMPLE 9–5 ■ Sample item from the Katz Index of Activities of Daily Living

> Transfer
>
> ___ Moves in and out of bed as well as in and out of chair without assistance (may be using object for support such as cane or walker)
> ___ Moves in and out of bed or chair with assistance
> ___ Doesn't get out of bed
>
> Independent: moves in and out of bed independently and moves in and out of chair independently (may or may not be using mechanic supports)
>
> Dependent: assistance in moving in or out of bed and/or chair; does not perform one or more transfers

Reprinted with permission from Katz S, Ford AB, Moskowitz RW, et al.: "Studies of Illness in the Aged: The Index of ADL, a Standardized Measure of Biological and Social Function." JAMA 185:914–919, 1963. Copyright 1963, American Medical Association.

- A. independent in feeding, continence, transferring, going to toilet, dressing, bathing
- B. independent in all but one of these functions
- C. independent in all but bathing and one additional function
- D. independent in all but bathing, dressing, and one additional function
- E. independent in all but bathing, dressing, going to toilet, and one additional function
- F. independent in all but bathing, dressing, going to toilet, transferring, and one additional function
- G. dependent in all six functions

The "other" category means that the subject is dependent in at least two functions but is not classifiable as C, D, E, or F.

PRACTICAL ISSUES

The amount of time required to administer the Katz ADL is not indicated. No specific training is required to administer, score, and interpret the results of this instrument, and no training manual is available.

PSYCHOMETRIC PROPERTIES

Reliability

The Katz ADL utilizes Guttman scaling, a method of scale construction in which items are ordered so that respondents endorsing one item of the scale (e.g., takes care of all food preparation) will likely endorse subsequent items (e.g., shops independently for small purchases or shops when accompanied by others). Guttman scale construction is used less often today because more useful measurement models that better fit actual psychological data have been developed. The Katz ADL's coefficient of reproducibility (a measure of how well items form the necessary ordered pattern) has been reported as 0.95 and higher. Joint reliability, after training, is reported as 0.95 or higher by at least two sources.

Validity

Katz et al. (1963) reported validation for the ordered arrangement of the index, from more to less dependent. They found that functioning in one or more activities indicated the subject's overall level of performance across activities ($N = 149$). In a sample of patients admitted to the hospital who were dependent in all or all but one activity ($N = 100$), they found that recovering patients passed through three stages of recovery that coincide with the ordered arrangement of the index.

The Katz ADL correlates with the degree of actual assistance required by the patient. In a sample of 154 patients with hip fractures, patients categorized as more dependent on the Katz ADL received more nonfamily attendant care (Katz et al. 1963). The Katz ADL predicted the longitudinal course of function, measured by mobility and house confinement, 2 years after discharge from the hospital (Katz et al. 1970). In a study ($N = 194$) comparing an intervention targeted at acutely ill, indigent elderly individuals at risk for hospital readmission with a control group receiving usual care, Katz ADL scores did not differ between the two groups at 1-year follow-up. However, using another ADL measure, the Older Americans Resources and Services (OARS) ADL (Fillenbaum 1975), the experimental group showed greater improvement and less decline on ADLs from baseline to 1 year.

CLINICAL UTILITY

Because the Katz ADL taps only the lower end of self-care functioning, it may not be sensitive to changes in ADL performance when functioning is normal, or nearly so, at baseline. It may also be insensitive to change that

occurs within the normal range of functioning or improvement from normal to above-average performance. The Katz ADL is probably most useful as a means of assessing need for care. It may also be useful in screening for chronic disease and disability in new patients, but only to detect gross physical impairment. As a measure of treatment effectiveness, its utility is questionable because it does not seem to be very sensitive and can likely detect only substantial change. Because the Katz ADL taps only lower levels of ADL performance, it may miss deterioration in ADL that is still within the normal range. Rubin et al. (1993) suggest that the measure may be more appropriately used with persons who demonstrate some initial ADL impairments.

REFERENCES AND SUGGESTED READINGS

Fillenbaum GG: The elderly: a brief instrumental activities of daily living measure. J Am Geriatr Soc 23:433–441, 1975

Katz S, Ford AB, Moskowitz RW, et al: Studies of illness in the aged: the Index of ADL, a standardized measure of biological and psychosocial function. JAMA 185:914–919, 1963

Katz S, Downs TD, Cash HR, et al: Progress in development of the Index of ADL. Gerontologist 10:20–30, 1970

Rubin CD, Sizemore MT, Loftis PA, et al: A randomized controlled trial of outpatient geriatric evaluation and management in a large public hospital. J Am Geriatr Soc 41(10):1023–1028, 1993

Lawton Instrumental Activities of Daily Living Scale (Lawton IADL)

M. P. Lawton and E. M. Brody

GOALS

The Lawton Instrumental Activities of Daily Living Scale (Lawton IADL) (Lawton and Brody 1969) is intended to assess performance on everyday tasks instrumental to independent living for elderly persons living in the community. It assesses competence in using the telephone, shopping, preparing food, housekeeping, laundering, mode of transportation, responsibility for one's own medications, and handling one's own finances.

DESCRIPTION

The Lawton IADL consists of eight items, each measuring one of the instrumental activities of daily living (IADL) listed earlier. It is completed by a clinician, who uses the best available sources of information concerning the subject's performance of IADL (e.g., the subject, family members, or care providers). Three to five response options, which indicate varying levels of independence in an activity, are provided for each item. A sample item is provided in Example 9–6.

Within each item, levels of independence are not weighted. Instead, responses indicating greater independence are scored 1, and those indicating less independence are scored 0. Thus, on the sample item in Example 9–6, an individual rated "operates telephone on own initiative" would receive the same score of 1 as the individual rated "answers telephone but does not dial." Only five of the eight items are administered to men, for whom the items concerning food preparation, housekeeping, and laundry are omitted. However, some users of the Lawton IADL have employed all eight items for men. Possible scores range from 0 to 8 for women and 0 to 5 for men.

PRACTICAL ISSUES

The amount of time required to administer the Lawton IADL is largely a function of the time it takes to gather the necessary data from available sources. There are no copyright restrictions on the Lawton IADL. No specific training is required to administer, score, and interpret the results of this instrument, and no training manual is available. The measure may be obtained from the original article (Lawton and Brody 1969). The Lawton IADL is included on the CD-ROM that accompanies this handbook.

PSYCHOMETRIC PROPERTIES

Reliability

Lawton and Brody (1969) report joint reliability correlations ranging from 0.85 to 0.91 for various patient populations. Like the Katz ADL (p. 129), the Lawton IADL is constructed by means of Guttman scaling, a scale construction method in which items are ordered so that respondents endorsing one item on the scale (e.g., independent in feeding, continence, transferring, going to the toilet, dressing, and bathing) will likely endorse subsequent items (e.g., independence in each category separately) as well. This scaling method is employed less often today, in favor of other measurement models that better fit psychological data. With a sample of men and women at least age 65 ($N = 265$, 168 women and 97 men), more than half of whom were applicants to or residents of an institution, Lawton and Brody (1969) reported a reproducibility coefficient (a measure of how well items form the required ordered response pattern) of 0.96 for men and 0.93 for women.

Validity

A study of 180 applicants to a geriatric institution (age and gender not specified) found moderate Pearson correlations between the Lawton IADL and four measures of physical and mental functioning: Waldsman and Fryman's Physical Classification (Waldsman and Fryman 1964), $r = 0.40$; Lowenthal's Physical Self Maintenance Scale (Lowenthal 1964), $r = 0.61$; Kahn et al.'s Mental Status Questionnaire (Kahn et al. 1960), $r = 0.48$; and Lawton and Brody's revised version of the Physical Classification (Lawton and Brody 1969), $r = 0.36$. In a sample of retirement community dwellers who ranged from being psychiatrically healthy to having moderate dementia ($N = 178$, ages 61–91 years, gender not specified), Pfeffer et al. (1982) found the following correlations:

EXAMPLE 9–6 ■ Sample item from the Lawton Instrumental Activities of Daily Living Scale

Ability to use telephone:

1. Operates telephone on own initiative—looks up and dials numbers, etc.: 1
2. Dials a few well-known numbers: 1
3. Answers telephone, but does not dial: 1
4. Does not use telephone at all: 0

1) persons categorized by a neurologist as more functionally impaired were also consistently rated as more functionally impaired on the Lawton IADL; 2) bivariate correlations between the Lawton IADL and measures of mental functioning ranged from 0.42 to 0.68; 3) bivariate correlation between the Lawton IADL and self-assessment of social function was 0.75; and 4) the Lawton IADL discriminated among the diagnostic categories of groups with and without dementia, but so did subjects' self-assessments.

CLINICAL UTILITY

The Lawton IADL appears to have adequate sensitivity to detect the presence of major impairment in the elderly person's performance of everyday tasks instrumental to independent living in the community. However, lesser degrees of impairment may go undetected because most items do not differentiate among levels of independence. For example, on the housekeeping item, the responses "Maintains house alone or with occasional assistance" and "Needs help with all home maintenance tasks" both receive scores of 1 point; only the response "Does not participate in any housekeeping tasks" receives a score of 0, indicating impairment. Thus, individuals receiving the same scores on each item may actually vary greatly in their performance of IADL and overall independent functioning.

The authors intended that the Lawton IADL be used primarily as a guide for identifying the optimum living situation for an elderly person. Although the measure provides some useful data for this purpose, no guidelines are offered on how to formulate decisions about living situations on the basis of the Lawton IADL assessment. The Lawton IADL is inappropriate for use in evaluating response to treatment or functional change over time, given the lack of evidence supporting these applications and the insensitivity of the individual item scores to improvements beyond the initial change from 0 to 1. It should also be noted that the Lawton IADL measures actual performance as opposed to ability. Finally, although the Lawton IADL produces a summary score, without appropriate comparison norms it is unclear how that score should be interpreted.

REFERENCES AND SUGGESTED READINGS

Kahn RL, Goldfarb AI, Pollack M, et al: The relationship of mental and physical status in institutionalizing aged persons. Am J Psychiatry 117:120–124, 1960

Lawton MP, Brody EM: Assessment of older people: self-maintaining and instrumental activities of daily living. Gerontologist 9:179–186, 1969

Lowenthal MF: Lives in Distress. New York, Basic Books, 1964

Pfeffer RI, Kurosaki TT, Harrah CH Jr, et al: Measurement of functional activities in older adults in the community. J Gerontol 37:323–329, 1982

Waldsman A, Fryman E: Classification in homes for the aged, in Geriatric Institutional Management. Edited by Shore H, Leeds M. New York, Putnam, 1964

CHAPTER 10

Quality of Life Measures

Judith Rabkin, Ph.D.
Glenn Wagner, Ph.D.
Kenneth W. Griffin, Ph.D.

INTRODUCTION

Major Domains

The quality of life (QOL) scales reviewed in this chapter and listed in Table 10–1 are organized into three groups:

1. Disease-specific measures intended for the severely and persistently mentally ill, including patients with dual diagnoses
2. Generic measures suitable for any patient group
3. Health-related QOL measures that assume the presence of a medical condition

The last two categories are considered generic because they are applicable to patients with any medical or psychiatric condition or combination of conditions.

ORGANIZATION

Relevant Measures Included Elsewhere in the Handbook

Because of the unclear boundaries between physical functioning and quality of life, some of the most widely used QOL measures (such as the Medical Outcomes Trust SF-36 [p. 128] and related scales) are reviewed in Chapter 9 ("General Health Status, Functioning, and Disabilities Measures"), and the reader is urged to consider them as strong candidates for health-related QOL measures.

USING MEASURES IN THIS DOMAIN

Although notions of the good life and the nature of health have been considered by philosophers, theologians, and scientists for centuries, the concept of *quality of life* is a fairly recent one. It was introduced in 1975 as a key term in medical indexes, and systematic study largely dates from the 1970s. Since then, efforts to define and measure this construct have accelerated. In the 1990s, QOL has taken its place among the ranks of bandwagon constructs of earlier decades of psychiatric inquiry, such as *instinct* in the 1950s, *anxiety* in the 1960s, *stressful life events* in the 1970s, and *social support* in the 1980s.

QOL measures are either disease specific or generic, are either global or multidimensional, and may or may not permit the respondent to assign subjective weights to the different domains being assessed. This last feature appears to be theoretically correct but may be misleading in the sense that "most individuals are not aware of the importance of something until it is no longer there" (Bernheim 1996–1997). Because no single design is clearly superior to the others, the choice should be determined by the clinical issue or research question under consideration.

TABLE 10–1 ■ Quality of life measures

NAME OF MEASURE	DISORDER OR CONSTRUCT ASSESSED	FORMAT	PAGES
Quality of Life Interview (QOLI)*	Quality of life of individuals with severe and persistent mental illness	Structured interview; full version, 158 items; brief version, 78 items	138–140
Quality of Life Scale (QLS)*	Quality of life of individuals with schizophrenia; emphasizes the deficit symptoms	Semistructured interview; 21 items	140–141
Wisconsin Quality of Life Index (W-QLI)*	Quality of life of individuals with severe and persistent mental illness	Self-administered; 42-item client version, 68-item provider version, and 28-item version for family members	141–142
Quality of Life Enjoyment & Satisfaction Questionnaire (Q-LES-Q)	Degree of enjoyment and satisfaction in various areas of daily life	Self-administered; 60-item long form (with an additional 33 optional items); 16-item short form	143–144
Quality of Life Index (QLI)*	Quality of life based on satisfaction with specific life domains and the individual importance placed on those domains	Self-report or structured interview; 35 items	144–145
Quality of Life Inventory (QOLI)	Life satisfaction as the sum of satisfaction in particular areas deemed important	Self-administered questionnaire; 16 items	146–147
Psychosocial Adjustment to Illness Scale (PAIS), interview version Self-report version (PAIS-SR)	Quality of patients' psychosocial adjustment to current or past medical illness	Interview or self-report; 46 items	147–149
Spitzer Quality of Life Index (Spitzer QL-Index)	Quality of life in patients with chronic illness to help physicians assess treatment	Clinician-rated scale; 5 items	149–150

*Measure is included on the CD-ROM that accompanies this handbook.

QOL measures are most often used to evaluate therapeutic interventions, to predict patient outcomes, and to assess the relative value of treatments that may be toxic or of uncertain therapeutic effect. Other proposed applications include circumstances in which lifelong therapy is prescribed to prevent complications of a relatively asymptomatic disease (e.g., multiple antiretroviral medications with significant adverse side effects prescribed to suppress viral activity in asymptomatic HIV-positive patients) and when there are several equally effective therapies for a given disorder that differ in their side effect profiles (MacKeigan and Pathak 1992). In addition, QOL measures are used to assess the outcomes of health and mental health services as part of program eval-

uation research. Additional questions arise concerning the consequences of managed care and caps on psychiatric services in terms of identifying potentially offsetting "costs" to the patient in quality of life when services are limited (Testa and Simonson 1996).

From the outset, investigators recognized that QOL is multidimensional. The domains usually included are physical, psychological, and social functioning, in varying combinations and definitions. Some investigators' measures inquire about jobs and housing as well as specifically health-related attributes, whereas other investigators argue for a more limited definition (Ware 1987). Most scales focus on subjective perceptions, although some that are intended for the severely mentally ill emphasize objective factors such as living conditions as reported by the patient. Some measures weigh all items equally, whereas others permit the respondent to assign weights to the domains on the basis of their perceived importance. Some measures produce an aggregated single score, whereas others generate separate scores for different domains to produce a profile of elements or subscales. Single ratings such as the query "all things considered, how would you rate your current life satisfaction and enjoyment?" may be added as a separate measure that is not included in either aggregate or profile scores. Endicott's Quality of Life Enjoyment & Satisfaction Questionnaire (Q-LES-Q) provides ratings of 13 separate domains, whereas the Spitzer Quality of Life Index (Spitzer QL-Index) yields a single score that incorporates 5 equally weighted domains.

The patient is typically the informant, whether the ratings are generated by clinical interview, self-report, or clinician observation. The measures reviewed in this chapter were all designed for and validated with adults, although they can probably be used with adolescents as well. They can be used to measure changes across the course of illness, to evaluate changes after treatment, or to characterize study samples with psychiatric or medical conditions.

GUIDE TO THE SELECTION OF MEASURES

The choice of instrument depends on several factors. A number of QOL instruments have been designed with a particular patient population in mind. When trying to determine quality of life in patients with severe and persistent mental illness, the Quality of Life Interview (QOLI), the Quality of Life Scale (QLS), and the Wisconsin Quality of Life Index (W-QLI) may be most appropriate. More specifically, for patients with schizophrenia whose negative symptoms are having a significantly adverse effect on their lives, the QLS scale may be the most sensitive. For patients with medical illnesses, the Psychosocial Adjustment to Illness Scale (PAIS) and the Spitzer QL-Index may be the most appropriate. The QOL scales with the broadest applicability are the Q-LES-Q, the Quality of Life Index (QLI), and the Quality of Life Inventory. Other important issues that determine the choice of scale include clinical feasibility, usually defined

in terms of the time and staffing needed to administer the measure. More labor-intensive instruments include the Quality of Life Interview (QOLI) and the QLS, which require an interview to collect the necessary information. The remaining self-report scales have the advantage of requiring only minimal staff time for administration and scoring.

CURRENT STATUS AND FUTURE RESEARCH NEEDS FOR ASSESSMENT

Despite the limitations noted for virtually all the scales described here, this is a field that needs fewer rather than more assessment candidates. As Gill and Feinstein (1994) recently observed, "despite the proliferation of instruments and the burgeoning theoretical literature devoted to the measurement of quality of life, no unified approach has been devised for its measurement, and little agreement has been attained on what it means" (p. 619). They selected 75 publications with the words *quality of life* in their titles and found that 159 different instruments were used, including 136 that were used only in a single study.

Gill and Feinstein noted that the term *quality of life* is often used to constitute an index of health status, whereas they conceptualize the term as referring to patients' perceptions of and reactions to their health status. In fact, QOL measures are almost always used for populations or samples whose health status is medically or psychiatrically deficient and therefore subject to treatment or palliative interventions. The implicit question seems to be "Given X circumstances, what is the person's quality of life?" It is necessarily a subjective appraisal, and, although studies have shown convergence of ratings between patients and family members and care providers, the gold standard is the patient's opinion. As such, QOL is neither an objective nor a static concept, and it is not directly correlated with health. For example, during terminal phases of illness, patients may continue to find their lives worthwhile, retaining meaningful quality even when they develop a complication that they themselves earlier had declared would be intolerable.

Unless there is a compelling reason (and sometimes there is), investigators and clinicians are urged not to construct yet another measure but rather to select one that has some psychometric respectability so that their efforts can add to (or detract from) its credibility.

REFERENCES AND SUGGESTED READINGS

Bernheim JL: Quality of life as an emergent concept. Quality of Life Newsletter 16:18–19, 1996–1997

Gill T, Feinstein A: A critical appraisal of quality-of-life measurements. JAMA 272:619–626, 1994

MacKeigan LD, Pathak DS: Overview of health-related quality-of-life measures. American Journal of Hospital Pharmacy 49:2236–2245, 1992

Testa M, Simonson DC: Assessment of quality-of-life outcomes. N Engl J Med 334:835–840, 1996

Ware JE: Standards for validating health measures: definition and content. Journal of Chronic Diseases 40:473–480, 1987

Quality of Life Interview (QOLI)

A. F. Lehman

GOALS

The Quality of Life Interview (QOLI) (Lehman 1988) was designed to assess the quality of life of individuals with severe and persistent mental illness. *Quality of life* is defined as the individual's experience of general well-being, which is a product of personal characteristics, objective life conditions, and subjective satisfaction with life. The scale was developed to assist in planning and evaluating medical and mental health services.

DESCRIPTION

There are two versions of the QOLI: the full version, which contains 158 items, and the brief version, which contains 78 items. Both are highly structured interviews to minimize interviewer effect and to permit their use by nonclinical interviewers. The interview is oriented mainly to current and recent feelings of satisfaction, functional status, and access to resources. Eight life domains, including living situation, family relations, social relations, leisure, finances, work and school, legal and safety issues, and health, are covered.

The score for the subjective component of each domain consists of the mean of the scores on the items in that domain. Items are answered on the basis of the "delighted-terrible" scale, in which 1 = terrible and 7 = delighted, given a possible range of scores of 1–7. Sample items are provided in Example 10–1.

Normative data for the full version of QOLI have been reported by the author of the scale. Mean subscale scores in a sample of individuals with chronic mental illness (N = 1,805) ranged from 3.87 to 4.97 for men, from 3.73 to 5.05 for women, from 3.84 to 4.97 for Caucasians, and from 3.76 to 5.05 for non-Caucasians. Norms across several age groups by gender are also provided by Lehman et al. (1995).

PRACTICAL ISSUES

It takes approximately 45 minutes to administer the full version of QOLI and about 16 minutes to administer the brief version. The QOLI is copyrighted, and permission to use the scale can be obtained from

Anthony F. Lehman, M.D.
Department of Psychiatry

EXAMPLE 10–1 ■ Sample items from the Quality of Life Interview

> (satisfaction with leisure activities, with 1 = terrible and 7 = delighted):
>
> How do you feel about:
>
> 1) The way you spend your spare time?
> 2) The amount of time you have to do the things you want to do?
> 3) The chance you have to enjoy pleasant or beautiful things?
> 4) The amount of fun you have?
> 5) The amount of relaxation in your life?
> 6) The pleasure you get from TV or radio?

Reprinted with permission from Anthony F. Lehman, M.D.

University of Maryland
645 West Redwood Street
Baltimore, MD 21201
Phone: 410-706-2490

The Quality of Life Toolkit (Lehman 1995), which consists of the full and brief versions of the QOLI and an interviewer manual, can be obtained at no cost from

The Evaluation Center
Health Services Research Institute (HSRI)
2336 Massachusetts Avenue
Cambridge, MA 02140
Phone: 617-876-0426

The interviewer manual provides information on administration and training. The QOLI can be administered by lay interviewers after a brief training period of supervised interviewing. The QOLI should be administered in person; administration by telephone is not recommended. The QOLI is included on the CD-ROM that accompanies this handbook.

PSYCHOMETRIC PROPERTIES

Reliability

Internal consistency of the QOLI has been demonstrated in a combined sample of individuals with chronic mental illness ($N = 1,805$) from four independent studies. Cronbach's alpha coefficients were computed for each subscale in the full and brief versions. For the full version subjective scales, alphas ranged from 0.82 to 0.89; for the objective scales, the range was 0.61–0.80. For the brief version subjective scales, alphas ranged from 0.70 to 0.87; for the objective scales, the range was 0.60–0.82. For the full version, test-retest reliability over a 1-week period showed median correlations of $r = 0.72$ for the subjective scales and $r = 0.65$ for the objective scales. Over a 2-month interval, test-retest correlations were $r = 0.57$ for the General Life Satisfaction scale, $r = 0.75$ for the Family Contact scale, and $r = 0.55$ for the Social Contact scale. Alternate form reliability was evaluated in a sample of 50 individuals, and the correlations of subscale scores between the full and brief versions ranged from 0.64 to 0.85, all highly statistically significant.

Validity

In studies that compared the full version of QOLI subscale scores with other measures, it has been reported that the General Life Satisfaction scale score is negatively correlated with depression (range of r is –0.17 to –0.56) and anxiety (range of r is –0.25 to –0.33) across several populations. The scores for the full version of QOLI were also compared with similar subscales on Heinrichs's Quality of Life Scale (p. 140); comparable constructs were significantly correlated in the low to moderate range when measured at the same time (range of r is 0.34–0.75) and over a 2-month period (range of r is 0.14–0.52).

Russo et al. (1997) conducted a study of the reliability, validity, and responsiveness of the QOLI as an outcome measure on 981 acutely ill psychiatric inpatients assessed at admission and discharge (an average of 2 weeks later). The investigators found that longitudinal changes in satisfaction "indicated that the QOLI is responsive to changes" in this interval, and they conclude that their data support its use as an outcome measure to assess quality of life in acutely ill hospitalized psychiatric patients.

CLINICAL UTILITY

The primary purpose of the QOLI is to assess quality of life in those with chronic mental illness. The scale can also be used to ascertain patient perspectives and priorities to guide service plans and revise ongoing therapeutic goals, given its sensitivity to treatment outcomes.

REFERENCES AND SUGGESTED READINGS

Lehman AF: The well-being of chronic mental patients: assessing their quality of life. Arch Gen Psychiatry 40:369–373, 1983

Lehman AF: A Quality of Life Interview for the chronically mentally ill. Evaluation and Program Planning 11:51–62, 1988

Lehman AF: Toolkit for Evaluating Quality of Life for Persons With Severe Mental Illness. Cambridge, MA, Evaluation Center at Human Services Research Institute (HSRI), 1995

Lehman AF, Postrado LT, Rachuba LT: Convergent validation of quality of life assessments for persons with severe mental illness. Qual Life Res 2:327–333, 1993

Lehman AF, Rachuba LT, Postrado LT: Demographic influences on quality of life among persons with chronic mental illness. Evaluation and Program Planning 18:155–164, 1995

Russo J, Roy-Byrne P, Reeder D, et al: Longitudinal assessment of quality of life in acute psychiatric inpatients: reliability and validity. J Nerv Ment Dis 185:166–175, 1997

Quality of Life Scale (QLS)

D. W. Heinrichs

GOALS

The Quality of Life Scale (QLS) (Heinrichs et al. 1984) was developed to assess the quality of life of individuals with schizophrenia. It emphasizes measurement of the deficit symptoms of schizophrenia (e.g., affective flattening, avolition, and anhedonia) in terms of both internal state and impaired role functioning.

DESCRIPTION

The QLS is a semistructured interview with 21 items, each of which is rated on a 7-point scale with descriptive anchors for every other point. Interviewers are encouraged to continue to ask additional probe questions until enough information has been obtained to make a rating. The instrument is designed to be used with outpatients, not patients in institutions.

The QLS has four subscales: Interpersonal Relations (eight items), Instrumental Role (four items), Intrapsychic Foundations (seven items), and Common Objects and Activities (two items). For each of the four subscales, scores from 0 to 6 are calculated by taking the mean of the relevant items. A total score is also computed by taking the mean of all 21 items. Higher scores represent better functioning (i.e., scores of 0–1 reflect severe impairment of functioning and scores of 5–6 reflect normal or unimpaired functioning). Items are rated based on the past 4 weeks. Examples of items rated include level of

activity, intimate relationships with household members, and extent of occupational role functioning.

PRACTICAL ISSUES

It takes approximately 45 minutes to administer the QLS. The scale is designed to be administered by clinicians and trained interviewers. The scale, and permission to use it, can be obtained at no cost by contacting

> William T. Carpenter Jr., Ph.D.
> Maryland Psychiatric Research Center
> P.O. Box 21247
> Baltimore, MD 21228

The QLS is included on the CD-ROM that accompanies this handbook.

PSYCHOMETRIC PROPERTIES

Reliability

To assess joint reliability, pairs of experienced interviewers (the authors of the scale) rated 24 outpatients with schizophrenia after a 30- to 45-minute joint interview. The intraclass correlation coefficient (ICC) for the total QLS score was 0.94, and the ICC for the subscales ranged from 0.91 to 0.97. ICCs for individual items ranged from 0.58 to 0.98. When 5 newly trained interviewers rated 10 patients, ICCs were 0.84–0.94 for the subscales and 0.53–0.94 for individual items.

Validity

A study with 59 subjects (Lehman et al. 1993) that compared QLS subscale scores with subscales of similar content from Lehman's Quality of Life Interview (QOLI) (p. 138) showed that scores of general well-being were correlated ($r = 0.38$), as were scores of interpersonal contacts ($r = 0.34–0.75$) and daily activities ($r = 0.63$). Correlations were considerably weaker when there was a 2-month gap between assessments.

A factor analytic study (Heinrichs et al. 1984) examined a sample of 111 patients with schizophrenia and found a four-factor structure: interpersonal relations, instrumental role, intrapsychic foundations, and common objects and activities. These four factors, which are the four subscales of the QLS, explain 73% of the variance of the scale's total score. Three of the four subscales formed distinct clusters, and one subscale—intrapsychic foundations—loaded on all factors, as expected given the variety of items. Similar factor structures were found for men and women.

Heinrichs et al. (1984) provided mean scores and standard deviations for the 21 QLS items for a sample of 111 schizophrenic patients, with scores ranging from 2.10 (SD = 1.96) for work satisfaction to 3.97 (SD = 1.67) for commonplace objects.

CLINICAL UTILITY

The QLS can be used for the direct clinical assessment of deficit symptoms in outpatients with schizophrenia, including measurement of internal state and role performance. The scale can also be used to assess deficit symptoms at the time of hospitalization. The QLS taps dimensions of interest in other diagnostic groups, such as those with chronic affective or personality disorders, and may be useful in clinical assessments of these groups. The QLS is applicable in a wide range of clinical settings in which access to other information is limited. The scale can be used to monitor change and assess outcomes as well. It can be and has been used as a supervisory tool in training psychiatric residents in the long-term management of patients with schizophrenia.

REFERENCES AND SUGGESTED READINGS

Heinrichs DW, Hanlon TE, Carpenter WT: The Quality of Life Scale: an instrument for rating the schizophrenic deficit syndrome. Schizophr Bull 10:388–397, 1984

Lehman AF, Postrado LT, Rachuba LT: Convergent validation of quality of life assessments for persons with severe mental illness. Qual Life Res 2:327–333, 1993

Wisconsin Quality of Life Index (W-QLI)

M. Becker and R. Diamond

GOALS

The Wisconsin Quality of Life Index (W-QLI) (Becker et al. 1993), formerly the Quality of Life Index for Mental Health (QLI-MH), was designed to assess the quality of life of individuals with severe and persistent mental illness. *Quality of life* is defined as a person's sense of well-being, which stems from the degree of satisfaction with areas of life perceived as important.

DESCRIPTION

The W-QLI client version is a 42-item, self-administered questionnaire that assesses nine quality of life domains: satisfaction level, occupational activity, psychological well-being, physical health, social relations, economics, activities of daily living, psychiatric symptoms, and goal attainment. Several of these domains are assessed by using preexisting validated scales, such as the Bradburn Affect Balance Scale (Bradburn 1976) to assess psychological well-being and the Brief Psychiatric Rating Scale (p. 488) to assess psychiatric symptoms.

Two additional versions of the W-QLI are available: a 68-item scale designed to be completed by providers and a 28-item scale designed to be completed by family members.

Each of the nine domains is scored separately. For existing scales, the scoring methods described by the developers of those scales are used. Sample items are provided in Example 10–2.

PRACTICAL ISSUES

It takes 20–30 minutes to complete the W-QLI client version, 10–20 minutes to complete the provider version, and about 10 minutes to complete the family member

EXAMPLE 10–2 ■ Sample items from the Wisconsin Quality of Life Index

How satisfied or dissatisfied are you with the main activity you do?

How do you feel about your physical health?

Reprinted with permission from Marion Becker, Ph.D. The instrument or any translation thereof may not be used by any other entity or group without written permission from the principal investigator.

version. The W-QLI is copyrighted, and permission to use the scale can be obtained by contacting

Marion Becker, Ph.D.
University of South Florida
Department of Community Mental Health
13301 Bruce B Downs Blvd—MHC 1423
Tampa, FL 33612-3899
Phone: 813-974-7188

The instrument and a detailed scoring manual are available from the authors at no cost, provided the user agrees to share data about the scale with the authors of the instrument. The W-QLI is probably not feasible for telephone use because of its length and differing response categories. Cultural adaptations include Afrikaans, Austrian, Dutch, English—Canadian, English—United Kingdom, Finnish, French, French—Canadian, German, Hebrew, and Spanish. The W-QLI is included on the CD-ROM that accompanies this handbook.

PSYCHOMETRIC PROPERTIES

Reliability

Test-retest reliability (r) in 10 schizophrenic outpatients ranged from 0.82 to 0.87 for subscales over a 3- to 10-day period.

Validity

Patients and providers rated quality of life domains in 37 patients with severe, chronic schizophrenia; measures of agreement ranged from 42% to 66%, and weighted kappa coefficients ranged from 0.10 (slight agreement for the social relations domain) to 0.60 (moderate agreement for the activities of daily living domain). Total scale scores of patients and providers were also compared with a

1-item uniscale of overall quality of life (scale of 1–10) completed by patients and providers. The patient W-QLI total scale score was significantly correlated $(r = 0.68)$ with the patient uniscale rating. The provider W-QLI total scale score was significantly correlated $(r = 0.80)$ with the provider uniscale rating.

CLINICAL UTILITY

The W-QLI can be used as a needs-assessment instrument to enable clinicians to identify problem areas in which patients have important needs that are not being satisfied. It is also useful for monitoring a patient's progress and response to intervention. The W-QLI can also be used to evaluate the effectiveness of treatment programs for those with chronic mental illness and for cost-containment analysis, because it is a self-report instrument that covers many domains of quality of life, each of which can be individually weighted to account for its importance to the patient.

REFERENCES AND SUGGESTED READINGS

Becker M: Quality of life instruments for severe chronic mental illness: implications for pharmacotherapy. Pharmacoeconomics 7:229–237, 1995

Becker M, Diamond R, Sainfort F: A new patient focused index for measuring quality of life in persons with severe and persistent mental illness. Qual Life Res 2:239–251, 1993

Bradburn NM: The Structure of Psychological Well Being. Chicago, IL, Aldine, 1976

Sainford F, Becker M, Diamond R: Judgements of quality of life of individuals with severe mental disorders: patient self-report versus provider perspectives. Am J Psychiatry 153:497–502, 1996

Quality of Life Enjoyment & Satisfaction Questionnaire (Q-LES-Q)

J. Endicott

GOALS

The Quality of Life Enjoyment & Satisfaction Questionnaire (Q-LES-Q) (Endicott et al. 1993) was developed as a measure of the degree of enjoyment and satisfaction experienced by respondents in various areas of daily life. The measure is intended to detect differences among groups of subjects as well as within a single subject over time.

DESCRIPTION

The Q-LES-Q is self-administered. The long form consists of 60 items and 5 subscales (Physical Health, Subjective Feelings, Leisure Time Activities, Social Relationships, and General Activities) that are administered to all respondents. Three optional subscales (Work, School, and Household Duties) with 33 items are administered when applicable. A sample item is provided in Example 10–3.

A short form, 16-item scale is also available and is a useful measure in itself. The first 14 items ask respondents to assess discrete domains such as social relationships, living or housing situation, and physical health. Item 15 concerns respondents' satisfaction with the medication they are taking. Respondents who are not taking medication are instructed to indicate this (with a check mark) and to leave the item blank. Item 16 is a global rating in

EXAMPLE 10–3 ■ Sample item from the Quality of Life Enjoyment & Satisfaction Questionnaire

When you had time, how often did you use that time for leisure activities?

(Response format: not at all; rarely; sometimes; often or most of the time; frequently or all the time)

Reprinted with permission from Jean Endicott, Ph.D.

which respondents are asked to rate their "overall life satisfaction and contentment." Each item is scored on a 5-point Likert scale that indicates the degree of enjoyment or satisfaction achieved during the past week (1 = very poor, 5 = very good).

Raw scores for subscales and total score are converted to a percentage of the maximum total score. Higher scores represent greater life enjoyment and satisfaction. Scores have not been classified to provide cutoffs for high, average, or low quality of life, nor are any cutoff scores or norms provided. In the short form, items 1–14 can be summed and used as a total score, and item 16 can be used as a single item measure.

PRACTICAL ISSUES

On average, it takes 15 minutes to complete the long form of the Q-LES-Q and less than 5 minutes to complete the short form. The scale has not been published, and copyright is pending by Jean Endicott, Ph.D. Copies of the measure may be obtained from the author:

Jean Endicott, Ph.D.
Department of Research Assessment and Training
New York State Psychiatric Institute, Unit 123
1051 Riverside Drive
New York, NY 10032
Phone: 212-543-5536

A description of the scoring system and a paper that describes the psychometric properties of the measure are available. The Q-LES-Q has been translated into a number of foreign languages, including German, Greek, Hebrew, Hindi, Russian, Spanish, and Swedish.

PSYCHOMETRIC PROPERTIES

Reliability

Internal consistency has been established; Cronbach's alphas range from 0.90 to 0.96 for subscales, and the score for the summary scale is 0.90 (in samples of depressed outpatients and psychiatric inpatients, N = 83). Test-retest reliability coefficients in the depressed sample range from 0.63 to 0.89 for subscales, and the score for the summary scale is 0.74 (N = 54). The time interval for the test-retest reliability was not specified, but both assessments were done before the onset of treatment and with patients who remained depressed.

Validity

The validity of the Q-LES-Q is supported by significant negative correlations with the Clinical Global Impression (CGI) (p. 100) severity score before the onset of depression treatment (range of r is –0.34 to –0.68 for subscales, and r is –0.62 for the summary scale). Correlation coefficients with the Hamilton Rating Scale for Depression (Ham-D) (p. 143) before treatment range from –0.33 to –0.69 for subscales and r is –0.64 for the summary scale. In a sample of depressed outpatients, intercorrelations between subscales ranged from 0.41 to 0.77, indicating a moderate level of construct validity.

The Q-LES-Q has been shown to be sensitive to change following treatment for depression. Significant negative correlations were found between the Q-LES-Q subscales and summary scale and CGI improvement ratings (range of r is –0.30 to –0.54) and change in Ham-D scores (range of r is –0.34 to –0.50). An increase in all but two (Social Relationships and Leisure Activities) of the Q-LES-Q subscales from admission to discharge has been reported with a sample of psychiatric inpatients.

CLINICAL UTILITY

The Q-LES-Q is a new quality of life instrument that is potentially useful in a wide spectrum of populations as a screening tool, an outcome measure, and a measure to detect problematic areas worthy of intervention. The questionnaire is relatively short and sensitive to change following treatment. An alternative summary scale is also available. Much more research is needed with the instrument to bolster the scale's psychometric quality. The scale needs to be studied with more varied populations and by other research teams and needs to be compared directly with other QOL scales. Normative data are needed.

REFERENCES AND SUGGESTED READINGS

Dott SG, Walling DP, Bishop SL, et al: The efficacy of short-term treatment for improving quality of life: a pilot study. J Nerv Ment Dis 184(8):507–509, 1996

Endicott J, Nee J, Harrison W, et al: Quality of Life Enjoyment & Satisfaction Questionnaire: a new scale. Psychopharmacol Bull 29:321–326, 1993

Gelfin Y, Gorfine M, Lerer B: Effect of clinical doses of fluoxetine on psychological variables in healthy volunteers. Am J Psychiatry 155:290–292, 1998

Kocsis J, Zisook S, Davidson J, et al: Double-blind comparison of sertraline, imipramine, and placebo in the treatment of dysthymia: psychosocial outcomes. Am J Psychiatry 154:390–395, 1997

Lydiard RB, Stahl S, Hertzmann M, et al: A double-blind, placebo-controlled study comparing the effects of sertraline vs amitriptyline in the treatment of major depression. J Clin Psychiatry 58:484–489, 1997

Quality of Life Index (QLI)

C. Ferrans and M. Powers

GOALS

The Quality of Life Index (QLI) (Ferrans and Powers 1985) was developed to measure quality of life in various domains on the basis of satisfaction and the importance the individual places on specific life domains. The scale, which was originally developed for use with cancer patients, is intended for use in identifying problem areas and evaluating the success of treatment.

DESCRIPTION

The QLI is primarily administered as a self-report measure, but the scale is also available in a structured interview format. The scale has two sections, each of which includes 35 items that fall into four domains: health and functioning, socioeconomic, psychological or spiritual, and family. One section measures satisfaction with various domains; the other measures the importance of the domain in the respondent's life. Examples of items include health care, marriage, occupation, and peace of mind. Each item is scored using a 6-point Likert scale.

Scores are calculated by weighting each satisfaction response with its paired importance response. Satisfaction responses are recoded and centered at 0 by subtracting 3.5 from each score, so that 0 represents the midpoint response on the 6-point (1–6) scale. The responses are then multiplied by importance responses to produce adjusted, weighted scores. Adjusted item scores are then summed to produce domain subscale scores and a total score. The range of possible scores is 0–30; higher scores represent greater life satisfaction. Cutoff scores and norms are not available.

PRACTICAL ISSUES

The average amount of time needed to complete the QLI has not been reported. The questionnaire has not been published but can be obtained from the author:

> Carol Ferrans
> University of Illinois
> College of Nursing
> Department of Medical and Surgical Nursing
> 845 South Damen Avenue
> Chicago, IL 60612-7350

Computerized scoring software is available from the author. The cost of the instrument is not indicated. Neither a manual nor foreign language translations are available. The QLI is included on the CD-ROM that accompanies this handbook.

PSYCHOMETRIC PROPERTIES

Reliability

Internal consistency has been established; coefficients range from 0.66 to 0.93 for the subscales and from 0.90 to 0.95 for the total score (in samples of cancer patients, dialysis patients, and students; N ranged from 37 to 111). Test-retest reliability has also been shown, with a coefficient of 0.87 after a 2-week interval (student sample, $N = 88$) and 0.81 after a 1-month interval (dialysis sample, $N = 37$).

Validity

Validity of the scale is supported by its correlation with a life satisfaction scale (range of r is 0.65–0.80) (Campbell et al. 1976). Significantly higher QLI scores have been found to be associated with lower levels of pain, low levels of depression, and greater success in coping with stress (when patients were divided into groups based on self-reported levels of these attributes). In a sample of patients with breast cancer, patients who were more depressed and in more pain had mean QLI scores of 18.4 and 18.8, respectively, whereas patients who were less depressed or in less pain had mean scores of 23.0 in both groups.

CLINICAL UTILITY

The QLI is a subjective measure of quality of life, with an emphasis on perceived life satisfaction. The major strength of the QLI is that it takes into account individual differences in the importance of specific life domains when assessing quality of life and life satisfaction (much like the Quality of Life Inventory). The weaknesses of the scale include the lack of normative data, the lack of published studies with diverse populations (including psychiatric populations), and the lack of data concerning its utility in detecting change following treatment.

REFERENCES AND SUGGESTED READINGS

Campbell A, Converse P, Rogers W: The Quality of American Life. New York, Russell Sage Foundation, 1976

Ferrans CE, Ferrell BR: Development of a Quality of Life Index for patients with cancer. Oncol Nurs Forum 17:15–21, 1990

Ferrans CE, Powers MJ: Quality of Life Index: development and psychometric properties. ANS Adv Nurs Sci 8:15–24, 1985

Quality of Life Inventory (QOLI)

M. Frisch

GOALS

The Quality of Life Inventory (QOLI) (Frisch 1994; Frisch et al. 1992) is a measure of life satisfaction based on the theory that one's overall life satisfaction consists of the sum of satisfaction in particular areas of life deemed important. The QOLI was developed to complement symptom-oriented measures of psychological and medical functioning for use in planning treatment, evaluating the outcome of interventions, and identifying those at high risk for health problems and relapse.

DESCRIPTION

The QOLI is a 16-item, self-administered questionnaire in which each item represents a life domain, such as health, work, recreation, friendships, love relationship, home, self-esteem, and standard of living. Each item is rated according to both its importance in the respondent's life and the level of satisfaction perceived by the respondent in that area of life. Responses for importance are rated as 0 = not at all important, 1 = important, and 2 = extremely important. Ratings of responses for satisfaction range from –3 = very dissatisfied to +3 = very satisfied. Patients are also asked to list problems that interfere with their satisfaction in each area. A sample item is provided in Example 10–4.

For each item, the importance and satisfaction ratings are multiplied to produce a weighted satisfaction score that ranges from –6 to +6 for each item. The total QOLI score is the average of all weighted satisfaction ratings that have nonzero importance ratings. Recommended cutoffs to be used when interpreting scores are provided in the manual (Frisch 1994). For raw scores, high QOL would be in the range 3.6 to 6.0, average QOL in the range 1.6 to 3.5, low QOL in the range 0.9 to 1.5, and very low QOL in the range –6 to 0.8. In general, ratings above the 20th percentile (average or high QOL) indicate that the patient is relatively free from psycho-

EXAMPLE 10–4 ■ Sample item from the Quality of Life Inventory

> Health is being physically fit, not sick, and without pain or disability.
>
> How important is health to your happiness?
>
> How satisfied are you with your health?

Items reprinted with permission from National Computer Systems (NCS), Minneapolis, MN.

logical distress and is happy and satisfied; ratings below the 20th percentile (low or very low QOL) indicate that the person is relatively unhappy and at risk for health and psychological problems. The 20th percentile distinguishes between clinical and nonclinical samples.

Nationwide adult norms, which are based on a sample of 798 individuals who approximate the 1990 U.S. Census by ethnicity, can be found in the manual. Adult norms range from the 25th to the 75th percentile and represent scores ranging from 2.0 to 3.75; student norms range from 2.0 to 3.5.

PRACTICAL ISSUES

On average, it takes 5–10 minutes to complete the questionnaire. The QOLI was published in 1994 by NCS Assessments and is copyrighted. Information can be obtained from

> National Computer Systems (NCS)
> P.O. Box 1416
> Minneapolis, MN 55440
> Phone: 800-431-1421
> Internet: www.ncs.com

A manual and treatment guide for using the scale and computerized scoring software are available. No foreign language translations are available.

PSYCHOMETRIC PROPERTIES

Reliability

Internal consistency was computed in a nationwide normative study ($N = 798$) using the sum of the weighted satisfaction ratings as a substitute for the total raw score. (These scores have been found to have a correlation of 0.99.) Cronbach's alpha in this study was 0.79. Test-retest reliability in the normative sample (subsample of $n = 55$), with a 2-week interval, indicated a correlation of 0.73.

Validity

The QOLI is positively correlated with seven measures of subjective well-being and life satisfaction, including peer-rated and clinician-rated measures, with correlations from 0.35 to 0.64. The QOLI was negatively correlated with measures of psychological distress, including the Symptom Checklist—90 (SCL-90) (p. 81), the Beck Depression Inventory (p. 517), and the Millon Clinical Multiaxial Inventory—II (MCMI-II) (p. 734); correlations ranged from -0.39 to 0.51. The construct validity of the QOLI is further supported by findings indicating that individuals who have recovered from substance abuse problems score higher than inpatients who are undergoing treatment for substance abuse problems, and general undergraduates score higher than students who are receiving counseling services. In a small study of depressed patients ($N = 16$), it was shown that QOLI scores increased significantly following treatment (mean of -0.2 at baseline and 2.1 following treatment).

CLINICAL UTILITY

The QOLI is a new scale, but it has had a fairly thorough psychometric evaluation, with the exception of a factor analytic study. The primary advantages of the QOLI are the availability of a manual and norms, the scale's brevity, its sixth-grade reading level, and the relative ease of completion, scoring, and interpretation. The instrument has been shown to be useful with different populations, both clinical and nonclinical, and change with treatment has been demonstrated. Research teams other than the authors need to do further work with the QOLI to show that the scale's reliability and validity can be replicated.

REFERENCES AND SUGGESTED READINGS

Beck AT, Steer R, Garbin MG: Psychometric properties for the Beck Depression Inventory: twenty-five years of evaluation. Clin Psychol Rev 8:77–100, 1988

Derogatis LR: SCL-90R: Administration, Scoring and Procedures Manual for the Revised Version. Towson, MD, Clinical Psychometric Research, 1983

Frisch MB: Manual and Treatment Guide for the Quality of Life Inventory. Minneapolis, MN, National Computer Systems, 1994

Frisch MB, Cornell J, Villaneuva M: Clinical validation of the Quality of Life Inventory: a measure of life satisfaction for use in treatment planning and outcome assessment. Psychological Assessment 4:92–101, 1992

Millon T: Manual for the MCMI-II. Minneapolis, MN, National Computer Systems, 1987

Psychosocial Adjustment to Illness Scale (PAIS)

L. R. Derogatis

GOALS

The Psychosocial Adjustment to Illness Scale (PAIS) (Derogatis 1986) was developed to assess the quality of the patient's psychosocial adjustment to a current medical illness or the sequelae of a previous illness. The PAIS and PAIS-SR (self-report version) were designed to measure the patient's adjustment to his or her medical condition at any given point during the course of the illness.

DESCRIPTION

The PAIS-SR is a 46-item, self-report questionnaire that assesses seven primary domains of psychosocial adjustment to illness: health care orientation, vocational environment, domestic environment, sexual relationships, extended family relationships, social environment, and psychological distress. Each item is rated on a 4-point scale (0–3); higher scores indicate poorer adjustment. An additional interview version that covers the same content areas as the self-report scale is available. A sample item is provided in Example 10–5.

Raw scores for each domain are calculated by reverse scoring relevant items and summing. The range of possible raw scores is 0–138. Next, a T-score is derived for each domain; these seven T-scores are then summed to arrive at a total PAIS-SR score. The range of possible T-scores is 0–100, and total T-scores ≥ 62 represent clinically significant levels of problematic psychosocial adjustment. PAIS-SR norms have been completed for patients with cancer (mixed sites), cardiomyopathies, diabetes, and multiple sclerosis.

PRACTICAL ISSUES

It takes about 20–25 minutes to administer the PAIS-SR. The PAIS and the PAIS-SR are copyrighted by Leonard R. Derogatis, Ph.D., and can be obtained from

> Clinical Psychometric Research
> Suite 302
> 100 W. Pennsylvania Avenue
> Towson, MD 21204
> Phone: 800-245-0277 or 410-321-6165

A detailed administration, scoring, and procedures manual (Derogatis and Derogatis 1990) for the PAIS and PAIS-SR and a computerized version are also available from Clinical Psychometric Research. Training requirements are minimal. Translations are available in Chinese, Danish, French, Hebrew, Hungarian, Icelandic, Italian, Japanese, Korean, Norwegian, Portuguese, Spanish, Swedish, and Taiwanese.

PSYCHOMETRIC PROPERTIES

Reliability

Internal consistency estimates for the domain scores of the PAIS-SR ranged from 0.47 to 0.85 in a study of 61 cardiac patients and from 0.63 to 0.87 for 269 renal dialysis patients. Joint reliability estimates are not available for the PAIS-SR; however, the joint reliability estimates for the PAIS were 0.86 and 0.83 for samples of 17 breast cancer and 37 Hodgkin's disease patients, respectively. Test-retest scores are not available.

Validity

Criterion validity data are not available for the PAIS-SR; however, it has been reported that total scores on the PAIS correlate with the Global Adjustment to Illness Scale ($r = 0.81$), the Symptom Checklist 90 Revised (SCL-90-R) Global Severity Index score (p. 81) ($r = 0.60$), and the Affect Balance Scale (Graney and Graney 1973) score ($r = 0.69$).

In a study of 120 patients with lung cancer, a factor analysis revealed seven factors that explained 63% of the variance in scores; these factors comprise the seven domains of the PAIS-SR.

CLINICAL UTILITY

The PAIS-SR is useful in assessing psychosocial adjustment in medically ill patients for research and clinical purposes. This assessment may be accomplished at a single point in time or over time with repeated measurements to document trends in psychosocial functioning. The global total score of the PAIS (in reference to normative data) can provide an indication of overall adjustment to the illness. Domain subscale scores highlight the patient's strengths and vulnerabilities, and discrete item scores provide specific information about coping and unique aspects of the patient's adjustment. Studies that demonstrate the utility of the PAIS and PAIS-SR as measures of change in adjustment following treatment need to be undertaken.

REFERENCES AND SUGGESTED READINGS

Derogatis LR: The Psychosocial Adjustment to Illness Scale (PAIS). J Psychosom Res 30:77–91, 1986

Derogatis LR: PAIS/PAIS-SR: A Bibliography of Research Reports 1975–1994. Baltimore, MD, Clinical Psychometric Research, 1990

Derogatis LR, Derogatis MA: PAIS and PAIS-SR: Administration, Scoring, and Procedures Manual II. Baltimore, MD, Clinical Psychometric Research, 1990

Derogatis LR, Fleming MP: The Psychosocial Adjustment to Illness Scale, in Quality of Life and Pharmacoeconomics in Clinical Trials, 2nd Edition. Edited by Spilker B. New York, Raven, 1996

Graney MJ, Graney EJ: Affect Balance Scale. Int J Aging Hum Dev 4:351–359, 1973

Spitzer Quality of Life Index (Spitzer QL-Index)

W. O. Spitzer

GOALS

The Spitzer Quality of Life Index (Spitzer QL-Index) (Spitzer et al. 1981) was developed as a multidimensional assessment of quality of life for patients with chronic illnesses. The goal of the measure is to help physicians assess the relative benefits and risks of various treatments and supportive services. It was designed to be brief and easily administered.

DESCRIPTION

The scale is a set of five ratings made by the clinician based on information from the patient (or the caregiver if the patient is unable to provide information). It was designed for use with medically ill patients by the attending physician (who knows a particular patient well) based on a routine clinical assessment. In psychiatric settings, ratings should be made after the clinical interview and other assessment instruments (including information about current psychosocial functioning) have been completed.

The scale assesses quality of life in five domains, each represented by a single item. The five domains include activity level and degree of independence, activities of daily living, health, social support, and emotional state

or outlook. Each domain is rated on a 3-point scale (0–2), so that the total score may range from 0 to 10. Only the total score is used. A higher score represents higher or better quality of life. A sample item is provided in Example 10–6.

PRACTICAL ISSUES

Studies have shown that the Spitzer QL-Index can be used effectively not only by physicians but also by other health providers, relatives, and patients themselves. It usually takes physicians about 1 minute to complete the scale. It was published in the *Journal of Chronic Diseases* (Spitzer et al. 1981), and permission has been granted by the journal to reproduce the items. No manual is available.

PSYCHOMETRIC PROPERTIES

Reliability

The internal consistency of the Spitzer QL-Index reported in the original publication was Cronbach's alpha = 0.77 ($N = 91$). In subsequent studies of patients with early-, intermediate-, and late-stage cancers, internal consistency coefficients ranged from 0.66 to 0.80. Joint reliability between two physicians rating the same patients on consecutive days was 0.81 and 0.74 (Spear-

EXAMPLE 10–6 ■ Sample item from the Spitzer Quality of Life Index

During the past week: [Choose one]

the subject has been having good relationships with others and receiving strong support from at least one family member and/or friend (Rating = 2)

support received or perceived has been limited from family and/or friends (Rating = 1)

support from family or friends occurred infrequently or only when absolutely necessary (Rating = 0)

Reprinted from *The Journal of Chronic Diseases*, Volume 34; Spitzer WO, Dobson AJ, Hall GI: "Measuring the Quality of Life of Cancer Patients: A Concise QL-Index for Use by Physicians," pp. 585–597, 1987, with permission from Elsevier Science.

man rank correlation) in studies of 64 English-speaking and 24 French-speaking Canadian patients. When patient and doctor ratings for 161 Australian patients were compared, Spearman's rho was 0.61.

Validity

Convergent validity has been studied by correlating total scores with established measures of physical functioning (Karnofsky Performance Index; Karnofsky et al. 1948) and emotional distress (Profile of Mood States [POMS] depression subscale [McNair et al. 1973], the Beck Depression Inventory [p. 517], the Hamilton Rating Scales for Anxiety and Depression [pp. 554 and 524], Dohrenwend's Demoralization Scale from the Psychiatric Epidemiology Research Interview (PERI) [Dohrenwend et al. 1985], and the Beck Hopelessness Scale [p. 268]). The correlation of individual items on the Spitzer QL-Index (excluding social support) with the Karnofsky Performance Index ranged from 0.39 for outlook to 0.57 for activities. Social support scores showed little variation, suggesting that the calibration is inadequate for this item.

The Spitzer QL-Index total score and the measures of emotional distress were all significantly correlated inversely in a sample of HIV-positive men; correlation coefficients exceeded –0.55 for all comparisons except the Beck Hopelessness Scale, for which the correlation was –0.43.

CLINICAL UTILITY

The Spitzer QL-Index is highly recommended as an adjunctive measure of quality of life for use in clinical trials or natural history studies of patients with chronic illnesses (e.g., in primary care settings). It is not intended for use with ostensibly medically healthy populations. The Spitzer QL-Index successfully discriminates between healthy and diseased subjects and between patients with early or moderate versus advanced disease. Two great advantages of the QLI are 1) its feasibility and acceptance by clinicians, because the average administration time is 1 minute, and 2) its inclusion of both physical and psychosocial components. When interpreting scores, the clinician should be aware that patients tend to give themselves higher scores than do their doctors, relatives, friends, or other health professionals.

REFERENCES AND SUGGESTED READINGS

Dohrenwend B, Krasnoff L, Askenasy A, et al: The Psychiatric Epidemiology Research Interview. New York, Columbia University Department of Psychiatry, 1985

Guy W: ECDEU Assessment Manual for Psychopharmacology—Revised (DHEW Publ No ADM 76-338). Rockville, MD, U.S. Department of Health, Education, and Welfare, Public Health Service, Alcohol, Drug Abuse, and Mental Health Administration, NIMH Psychopharmacology Research Branch, Division of Extramural Research Programs, 1976

Karnofsky DA et al: The use of nitrogen mustards in the palliative treatment of carcinoma. Cancer 1:634–656, 1948

McNair DM, Lorr M, Droppleman L: Manual for the Profile of Mood States. San Diego, CA, Educational and Testing Services, 1973

Mor V: Cancer patients' quality of life over the disease course: lessons from the real world. Journal of Chronic Diseases 40:535–544, 1987

Spitzer WO, Dobson AJ, Hall J, et al: Measuring the quality of life of cancer patients: a concise QL-Index for use by physicians. Journal of Chronic Diseases 34:585–597, 1981

Williams JBW, Rabkin JG: The concurrent validity of the Quality of Life Index in a cohort of HIV spectrum gay men. Control Clin Trials 12:129S–141S, 1991

CHAPTER 11

Adverse Effects Measures

Nina R. Schooler, Ph.D.
K. N. R. Chengappa, M.D.

INTRODUCTION

Major Domains

In this chapter, several tools that may help clinicians assess adverse effects of somatic treatment are reviewed. The measures selected for review are those that we judge to be feasible for use in clinical settings. Consequently, they may not provide the level of detail required by research investigators.

Assessing adverse treatment effects differs from assessing outcome. Outcome assessment focuses on a limited range of symptoms and signs that treatment is expected to reduce or remove, whereas adverse effects can occur in any organ or body system. Adverse effects may also be confounded with characteristics of the illness itself or the medication (e.g., the illness may present with insomnia, but medication may also cause insomnia). Thus, adverse events include an extremely wide domain of complaints that must be disentangled, when possible, from the signs and symptoms of the disorder. Patients may not recognize that certain signs and symptoms are actually caused by the medications (i.e., are adverse effects). Conversely, they may erroneously attribute signs and symptoms of the illness to the medication. For example, in many clinical trials, headache is reported as the most frequent adverse event; however, it is reported with similar frequency across treatments that include a placebo.

Formal measures of adverse effects can be important in clinical practice. Symptoms that occur in a temporal relation to the receipt of a new medication may influence the patient's willingness to take the medicine, particularly if the symptom is unexpected, frightening, or functionally impairing. Some symptoms (e.g., problems in sexual functioning) may be embarrassing for patients, and patients may thus be reluctant to report the symptoms spontaneously. Furthermore, questioning patients about some symptoms (e.g., sexual functioning) may also be difficult for clinicians.

Organization

The measures included in this chapter are listed in Table 11–1. Two measurement approaches—general and problem specific—can be used to assess adverse events. General measures either allow reporting of any medical event that may occur or systematically cover the full range of body systems. They can serve as a guide to documenting and reporting adverse events or they can provide a framework, through a checklist or an interview guide, to facilitate the eliciting of events. The following general measures are reviewed in this chapter: Systematic Assessment for Treatment Emergent Events—General Inquiry (SAFTEE—GI), Udvalg for Kliniske Undersogelser (UKU) Side Effect Rating Scale, and MEDWatch.

Several specific measures have also been developed to assess important adverse events associated with the use of psychotropic medications. Specific measures have been developed most extensively for the assessment of acute and late-developing extrapyramidal side effects of anti-

TABLE 11–1 ■ Adverse effects measures

Name of measure	Disorder or construct assessed	Format	Pages
Systematic Assessment for Treatment Emergent Events—General Inquiry (SAFTEE-GI)*	Treatment-emergent adverse events in the context of clinical drug trials	Open-ended inquiry using three general questions	155–159
Udvalg for Kliniske Undersogelser (UKU) Side Effect Rating Scale	Comprehensive side effect rating scale for psychotropic drugs for use in clinical trials and routine clinical practice	Three components: 48 items in 4 categories, global assessment of interference in daily performance, and consequences (actions taken by physician)	159–161
MEDWatch*	Voluntary reporting of medication adverse effects by physicians, health care professionals, and others to meet the FDA mandate	One-page reporting form for the physician	161–162
Rating Scale for Extrapyramidal Side Effects (Simpson-Angus EPS Scale)*	Extrapyramidal side effects of antipsychotic medications	Ten anchored items	163–164
Barnes Akathisia Rating Scale (BARS)*	Drug-induced akathisia associated with antipsychotic agents	Four anchored items	165–166
Abnormal Involuntary Movement Scale (AIMS)*	Dyskinetic movements associated with antipsychotic medications	Twelve anchored items	166–168

*Measure is included on the CD-ROM that accompanies this handbook.

psychotic medications. The first scale for extrapyramidal side effects was published in 1970, and several other scales have followed. The following specific measures are reviewed in this chapter: the Rating Scale for Extrapyramidal Side Effects (Simpson-Angus EPS Scale), the Barnes Akathisia Rating Scale (BARS), and the Abnormal Involuntary Movement Scale (AIMS).

USING MEASURES IN THIS DOMAIN

In this section, several issues that are highly relevant for assessing adverse effects in clinical practice are discussed:

■ Monitoring for known adverse events with a particular medication, as opposed to detecting unexpected events
■ Methods of elicitation, in particular the distinctions among spontaneous reporting, cued elicitation, and specific questioning regarding particular adverse events

■ What information should be recorded regarding an event
■ Determining whether an event is really medication related

Knowledge of the side effects expected to occur with a particular medication can be used to focus the clinical assessment on specific adverse events. When shared with patients before prescribing the medication, this information may also help prepare them for such adverse effects, thereby minimizing patients' premature medication discontinuation because of adverse events that were not explicitly anticipated. However, even the most common adverse events occur only in a small percentage of patients, so general warnings should be placed in this context to avoid raising alarm unnecessarily. In the final analysis, how best or how much to alert an individual is a clinical decision.

Much of the same reasoning applies to the decision of whether to conduct a full review of systems before initiating a new medication. Such a review serves to uncover areas that may be problematic for a given patient and therefore provides a basis for subsequent determination of whether adverse medical events that occur after medication administration are indeed medication related.

Adverse events may be monitored in several ways. The first is to simply wait until patients report adverse experiences. However, patients may not recognize that an adverse event has occurred or may be reluctant to report it. Sometimes an adverse experience may cause a patient to discontinue medication without reporting either the event or the discontinuation to the treating physician. A second strategy involves inquiring generally about adverse events that have occurred "since the last visit." This strategy is expected to elicit events that are important or salient to the patient and may provide the best signal-to-noise ratio. A third option is to conduct a review of systems, to be sure of complete coverage. Levine and Schooler (1992), who developed the SAFTEE-GI, have noted that, in the context of clinical trials, a systematic review of systems may elicit an additional 50% of events that clinicians deemed important enough to lead to a change in clinical management. A fourth option is to use a limited checklist created by the practitioner. A fifth option is to inquire generally about any medical events that have occurred and then to query the patient specifically about target events that may be relevant to the particular medication being prescribed or to the particular patient.

There are several options for determining what information should be recorded regarding an event. The severity of the event must always be recorded. Additional information might include a judgment of whether the event is causally related to the medication and whether the event interferes with daily functioning, as well as the clinical action taken in response to the event. Other information might include the onset, duration, and course of the event. The instruments for general monitoring of adverse events reviewed in this chapter include different strategies. The SAFTEE-GI uses an open-ended strategy, whereas the UKU Side Effect Rating Scale uses a checklist of specific symptoms.

Determining whether an event is truly related to medication is often difficult in routine clinical care. However, several algorithms explore the logic inherent in determining that an event is related to the administration of a drug (see, for example, Karch and Lasagna [1977]). Many of these principles are embodied in the U.S. Food and Drug Administration MEDWatch form (p. 161). In brief, critical elements in the determination are temporal relationship to drug administration, dose dependence of the event, disappearance when the drug is discontinued, and reoccurrence on rechallenge. Although all of these elements are rarely present in a given clinical situation, reviewing the list can be useful for understanding the meaning of a particular adverse event in a particular case.

On the basis of the considerations discussed, we recommend the following strategies for detecting and assessing adverse events that may be associated with the administration of psychotropic medications:

1. Assess psychiatric and general medical signs and symptoms immediately before starting new medication to help distinguish treatment-emergent events from preexisting conditions. The American Psychiatric Association (APA), in its guidelines for several disorders, also recommends that certain laboratory tests be done before initiating treatment with psychotropic drugs for several disorders. These recommendations merit implementation.

2. Inform patients about known medication side effects that are expected and common and assess specifically for the presence of those signs and symptoms.

3. Assess side effects using one of two approaches: a) a broad, open-ended assessment supplemented by detailed questioning for the known side effects of a medication or side effects that may be a problem for the particular patient (e.g., the SAFTEE-GI) or b) review of a checklist that incorporates a limited range of events that have been found useful in psychopharmacologic treatment (e.g., the UKU Side Effects Rating Scale).

4. Monitor laboratory measures (e.g., periodic lithium and anticonvulsant levels and weekly or biweekly complete blood counts for patients who take clozapine), on the basis of APA guidelines for certain classes of drugs and disorders. APA guidelines emphasize known effects of medication. Obvious examples include monitoring of thyroid and renal function in patients receiving lithium and monitoring of liver functions, blood counts, and coagulation factors for patients receiving valproate.

GUIDE TO THE SELECTION OF MEASURES

General Measures

There is a relative paucity of rating scales that assess for adverse events. A major reason for this dearth has been the belief—particularly among pharmaceutical industry sponsors of clinical trials—that the "signal" of important adverse events will be revealed without formal rating scales and that rating scales only add "noise" that makes the signal more difficult to detect. However, many investigators have developed idiosyncratic checklists for use in medication trials.

Perhaps the most elaborate system that has been developed for assessing adverse events is the Systematic Assessment for Treatment Emergent Events (SAFTEE). The SAFTEE includes two alternate standardized inquiry procedures: a general inquiry regarding health problems (SAFTEE-GI) and a detailed inquiry organized as a physician's review of systems (SAFTEE-SI). Both versions record all health-related events regardless of whether they are judged to be related to treatment. They record detailed, comprehensive information about each elicited event. The level of detail, even in the SAFTEE-GI, is well beyond what is practical in routine clinical care. However, several characteristics of the SAFTEE-GI are very attractive, and, in this review of it, recommendations for modifications to make it more user-friendly for clinical use are presented.

The second instrument reviewed here is the UKU Side Effect Rating Scale. Although this scale is widely used in Europe, it is less familiar to investigators and clinicians in the United States.

Finally, attention is drawn to the general problem of the postmarketing surveillance of adverse drug experiences and the possibility and importance of contributing to the efforts of the U.S. Food and Drug Administration to identify adverse events that may be related to medication; these efforts have become increasingly sophisticated in recent years. The MEDWatch form, which is used for postmarketing surveillance, is included in this chapter.

One well-known research scale not included in this chapter is the Dosage and Treatment Emergent Symptoms Scale (DOTES) (Guy 1976). Although the content validity and structure of this checklist have been evaluated to some degree, there have been no studies (to our knowledge) of its reliability. Among the problems with this checklist are that it includes signs and symptoms (e.g., drowsiness and dry mouth), syndromes and diagnoses (e.g., anorexia and tardive dyskinesia), and laboratory findings (e.g., electrocardiogram and hematology). Definitions are provided for many but not all items. The author makes recommendations regarding assessment.

Specific Measures

Discussed next are two important areas of specific event monitoring: extrapyramidal side effects and sexual dysfunction.

Monitoring for extrapyramidal side effects is probably the most thoroughly developed area of adverse event measurement in psychiatry. Rating scales that tap the broad range of extrapyramidal side effects are available; specialized scales are also available for akathisia and tardive dyskinesia (see de Leon and Simpson [1992] for a review). Because extensive data are available regarding many of these instruments, one extrapyramidal side effects scale from each of these areas is presented in this chapter for illustrative purposes.

Although drug-induced problems in sexual functioning are well recognized, sexual problems themselves are often ignored or minimized in clinical settings because of embarrassment on the part of patients and/or clinicians. Possibly for this reason, fewer instruments are available in this area, and they are less well developed and studied. Recently, several instruments have been developed to assess sexual functioning, particularly in the context of antidepressant medication treatment. All of these scales have separate versions for men and women. Extensive psychometric evaluation is available for the Changes in Sexual Functioning Questionnaire (Clayton et al. 1995), but it is too detailed for general clinical use. The UKU Side Effect Rating Scale, a general instrument, also includes items regarding sexual functioning. Chapter 28, "Sexual Disorders," provides information for those interested in sexual dysfunction as a target of treatment, and clinicians particularly concerned about sexual dysfunction as a medication side effect may find useful suggestions there. In general, regardless of whether a rating scale is used, direct questioning of patients is essential when sexual function is a clinical concern because evidence strongly indicates that spontaneous reporting alone grossly underestimates the prevalence and severity of sexual dysfunction.

CURRENT STATUS AND FUTURE RESEARCH NEEDS FOR ASSESSMENT

More work is needed to develop assessment instruments that are practical to use and display information in a way that enables clinicians and researchers to better monitor change over time. For example, instruments designed for research are often formatted specifically to prevent easy examination of the last rating before completing the current one. Although this approach has research utility, this format is inconvenient and less useful for clinical purposes. An improved instrument for monitoring adverse effects in a clinical environment should have the following characteristics: 1) brevity, 2) suggested standardized inquiry procedure, 3) the ability to incorporate specific adverse events of concern, 4) assessment of severity and functional disability, 5) inclusion of information to allow determination of possible relationship to treatment (e.g., change with dose reduction or increase and reappearance on rechallenge), and 6) a format that allows for tracking and reviewing of adverse events over time.

REFERENCES AND SUGGESTED READINGS

Clayton AH, Owens JE, McGarvey EL: Assessment of paroxetine-induced sexual dysfunction using the Changes in Sexual Functioning Questionnaire. Psychopharmacol Bull 31:397–406, 1995

de Leon J, Simpson GM: Assessment of neuroleptic-induced extrapyramidal symptoms, in Adverse Effects of Psychotropic Drugs. Edited by Kane JM, Lieberman JA. New York, Guilford, 1992, pp 218–234

Guy W: Dosage Record and Treatment Emergent Symptoms Scale (DOTES), in ECDEU Assessment Manual for Psychopharmacology—Revised (DHEW Publ No ADM 76-338). Rockville, MD, U.S. Department of Health, Education, and Welfare, Public Health Service, Alcohol, Drug Abuse, and Mental Health Administration, NIMH Psychopharmacology Research Branch, Division of Extramural Research Programs, 1976, pp 223–244

Karch FE, Lasagna L: Toward the operational identification of adverse drug reactions. Clin Pharmacol Ther 21:247–254, 1977

Kessler DA: Introducing MedWatch: a new approach to reporting medication and device adverse effects and product problems. JAMA 269:2765–2768, 1993

Levine J, Schooler NR: SAFTEE: a technique for the systematic assessment of side effects in clinical trials. Psychopharmacol Bull 22:343–381, 1986

Levine J, Schooler NR: General versus specific inquiry with SAFTEE (letter). J Clin Psychopharmacol 12:448, 1992

Lingjaerde O, Ahlfors UG, Bech P, et al: The UKU side effect rating scale: a new comprehensive rating scale for psychotropic drugs, and a cross sectional study of side effects in neuroleptic-treated patients. Acta Psychiatr Scand Suppl 76:1–100, 1987

Systematic Assessment for Treatment Emergent Events—General Inquiry (SAFTEE-GI)

J. Levine and N. R. Schooler

GOALS

The goal of the Systematic Assessment for Treatment Emergent Events (SAFTEE) (Levine and Schooler 1986) is to provide a strategy or technique for eliciting treatment-emergent adverse events in the context of clinical drug trials. The authors and others were dissatisfied with the postmarketing surveillance reporting of adverse drug reactions because it is a spontaneous or voluntary method of data collection and is therefore more likely to overreport life-threatening drug reactions. Methods commonly used in clinical trials also rely on spontaneous reporting on the grounds that systematic inquiry would elicit trivial complaints.

DESCRIPTION

There are two versions of the SAFTEE: the SAFTEE—General Inquiry (GI) and the SAFTEE—Specific Inquiry

(SI). The SAFTEE-SI incorporates a review of systems and inquires about specific signs and symptoms in each area. It provides a valuable and comprehensive review but is far too time-consuming and cumbersome for use in clinical practice. The SAFTEE-GI uses a general, open-ended inquiry method to elicit adverse events. Once an event has been elicited through the use of either the SAFTEE-SI or the SAFTEE-GI, the interviewer leads the patient through a series of questions designed to obtain information about the event. The interviewer asks questions regarding severity, duration, impairment, and other characteristics of the event. The SAFTEE-GI is described here.

Three basic questions are asked, all referenced to the past week (see Example 11–1). These questions represent the starting point for the inquiry. Follow-up questions are left to the interviewer's discretion. After all events that are elicited in response to direct questioning and details about them have been recorded, the interviewer may remind the patient about specific health problems. Suggested language for this inquiry is as follows:

- I notice that _____ seems to be bothering you.
- Last time you said that _____ was bothering you.

The SAFTEE-GI includes preferred terms for recording events. These terms are listed in alphabetical order and by body system.

By eliciting and recording all events (regardless of whether they are judged to be drug related) possible patient and rater biases are diminished. Onset, duration (in days), pattern (isolated, intermittent, or continuous), current status (e.g., continuing or recovered), severity (minimal to very severe), and functional impairment (minimal to very severe) are recorded for all reported adverse events. A line of questioning is suggested for each of the characteristics of an event to be recorded. The interviewer is free to modify the questions or to ask follow-up questions. For example, to elicit information regarding severity, the following opening questions are suggested: "How bad is it? Does it bother you a lot?" Additional characteristics include possible contributory factors, the relationship of the drug to the event, and the action taken.

After completing the examination, the clinician enters concluding information. This closing inquiry includes the examiner's judgment of patient reliability, any formal diagnoses that can be made, remarks on whether the U.S. Food and Drug Administration Adverse Drug Experience Report Form (MEDWatch) (p. 161) is to be filled out, and whether a consultation was needed. Space for recording dosage information and laboratory, radiological, electrocardiogram, electroencephalogram, and physical findings is also provided.

In the original version of the SAFTEE (Levine and Schooler 1986), the rater recorded the action taken (e.g., reduce dosage or suspend medication) for each adverse event identified. This approach proved cumbersome. A modification of the instrument used in the National Institute of Mental Health Treatment Strategies in Schizophrenia Study records actions taken by the clinician at the end of the instrument rather than for each adverse event elicited.

Summary scores such as number of events elicited, average severity, and functional impairment can be calculated; however, such summary scores for a clinical tool are less valuable than an inspection of the completed form. The SAFTEE-GI is recommended to clinicians as a tool for eliciting and tracking adverse events to ensure that they are monitored appropriately.

PRACTICAL ISSUES

Depending on the patient's status and the rater's familiarity and experience with the scale, it can take 5–10 minutes to complete the SAFTEE-GI. An additional 5–10 minutes may be needed to fill in the laboratory, radiological, electrocardiogram, electroencephalogram, and physical findings. The SAFTEE-GI can be used by various health care professionals (e.g., psychiatrists, psychologists, and nurses). In addition to a baseline assessment, it can provide weekly (or less frequent) evaluations at clinic visits, although no data on reliability and valid-

EXAMPLE 11–1 ■ Systematic Assessment for Treatment Emergent Events— General Inquiry

Have you had any physical or health problems?

Have you noticed any change in your physical appearance?

Have you cut down on the things you usually do because of not feeling well physically?

ity are available concerning use of the SAFTEE at less than weekly intervals.

A four-page document called SAFTEE TIPS accompanies the Levine and Schooler article (1986) and provides guidance on the use of the two forms. Both versions of the scale are in the public domain.

The Treatment Strategies in Schizophrenia version of the SAFTEE-GI is included on the CD-ROM that accompanies this handbook.

PSYCHOMETRIC PROPERTIES

Reliability

The SAFTEE-GI has been used by various health care investigators with fairly good reliability. In an early study of inpatients with schizophrenic or major depressive disorders with psychotic features and outpatients with anxiety, depression, or insomnia, good joint reliability was found when the raters were present together and used the same version of the SAFTEE (Jacobson et al. 1986). The raters were doctor-nurse pairs. Kappa coefficients of agreement for the number of adverse events detected were excellent (0.95 for the SAFTEE-GI and 0.88 for the SAFTEE-SI). Agreement on severity and functional impairment was less satisfactory (0.21 and 0.30 for the SAFTEE-GI and 0.40 and 0.31 for the SAFTEE-SI, respectively). However, a detailed examination of reliability is more encouraging. For example, using the SAFTEE-GI, the kappa coefficient for detection of drowsiness was 1.00 and the kappa coefficients for duration, severity, and functional impairment were 0.99, 0.91, and 0.92, respectively. For muscle, bone, or joint pain, the kappa coefficient for detection was 1.00 and the kappa coefficients for duration, severity, and functional impairment were 0.21, 0.75, and 0.70, respectively. Reliability was lower for ratings made on the basis of independent interviews. This study also revealed that the SAFTEE-SI elicited up to six times as many events as the SAFTEE-GI. Events elicited by the SAFTEE-GI had a higher mean severity than those elicited by the SAFTEE-SI.

A reliability study of the SAFTEE (Guy et al. 1986) among a cohort of multidisciplinary ratings used both videotaped interviews and assessments from clinical trials. In the clinical trials section of the study, the percentage of agreement between a psychiatrist and two nurses was 89.4 on number of symptoms present. An intraclass correlation coefficient of 0.73 was found on the severity of symptom ratings. The psychiatrist rated more subjects as having moderately severe symptoms than did the nurses. Agreement by two nurses regarding the presence or absence of symptoms was 84.5%; the intraclass correlation coefficient for the severity rating was 0.791.

In the videotape portion of the study, six registered nurses and six licensed practical nurses each viewed four videotapes of a registered nurse completing both the SAFTEE-GI and the SAFTEE-SI procedures on two separate occasions to evaluate both joint and test-retest reliability. The overall kappa coefficients (joint reliability) for the presence and severity of symptoms were 0.49 and 0.21, respectively, for registered nurses and 0.65 and 0.23, respectively, for licensed practical nurses. Test-retest reliability for presence of symptoms was 0.50 for registered nurses and 0.59 for licensed practical nurses.

The internal consistency of the SAFTEE-GI and the SAFTEE-SI was evaluated with a series of outpatients with anxiety, bulimia, or depressive disorders (Rabkin and Markowitz 1986). Because each event is rated on several parameters (e.g., severity, functional impairment, duration, and presence at the time of interview), these investigators used the relationship among these parameters to assess internal consistency. Severity and functional impairment were significantly correlated ($r = 0.53-0.67$) depending on the timing of the assessment and version of the SAFTEE used. Although these correlations are all statistically significant, they account for, as best, 45% of the variance. Thus, each measure contributes unique information. Internal consistency is supported by the fact that subjective distress (severity) was generally rated higher than functional impairment; that is, subjective distress may occur in the absence of functional impairment, but the converse is seldom true. The status of an event at the time of assessment is rated as continuing, recovered, or indeterminate. Both severity and functional impairment were related to this variable: continuing events were more likely to be rated as severe or very severe (22%), and 80% of events rated as causing severe or very severe functional impairment were rated as continuing. Assessors judged 43% of the events elicited by the

SAFTEE-GI as side effects of medication. This point is considered further in the discussion of the validity of the SAFTEE-GI. Results indicated good internal consistency in the capacity of the SAFTEE to distinguish between side effects and symptoms.

Validity

In the study by Guy and colleagues (1986), the SAFTEE was also compared with the Association for Methodology and Documentation in Psychiatry—Somatic Signs (AMDP-SS) (Guy and Ban 1982), a European tool developed, before the publication of the SAFTEE, to elicit side effects. The AMDP-SS was designed to be used in conjunction with efficacy instruments and thus, unlike the SAFTEE, does not include items that are thought to be related to psychopathology. It was found that the amount of information obtained on any given symptom is much greater with use of the SAFTEE than with use of the AMDP-SS. Percentage of agreement between psychologists' ratings of the AMDP-SS and nurses' ratings of the SAFTEE was 77.4%. When the items on the SAFTEE-SI considered to be related to psychopathology were dropped, almost 90% agreement was attained; the kappa coefficient for severity was 0.81.

Rabkin and Markowitz (1986) examined the validity of the SAFTEE by reviewing events that occurred 4 weeks after starting treatment with either active medication (imipramine, phenelzine, or alprazolam) or a placebo. Only 1 of 52 events that are known side effects of the medications was experienced by a patient treated with a placebo. In contrast, anxiety and depression, the treatment target in these studies, were distributed evenly across treatment conditions.

In a study to evaluate whether the SAFTEE-SI provides clinically useful information over and above the SAFTEE-GI, Rabkin et al. (1992) evaluated 226 outpatients with anxiety, eating disorders, and depressive disorders. The SAFTEE-SI did not provide additional information, and Rabkin et al. recommended that the SAFTEE-SI not be used routinely in clinical trials because of the time and effort required. In a reply, Levine and Schooler (1992) pointed out that 46% of the events meeting the authors' stringent definition of an adverse event would have been missed if the specific inquiry had not been made. Additionally, of the events rated as causing severe or very severe functional impairment, 65%

were detected by the SAFTEE-SI and 35% by the SAFTEE-GI, suggesting that the SAFTEE-SI provided additional information over and above that provided by the SAFTEE-GI.

CLINICAL UTILITY

Both forms of the SAFTEE seem to have face validity and internal consistency. It appears that multiple practitioners (psychiatrists, psychologists, and nurses) can complete the SAFTEE in a valid and reliable manner. The SAFTEE is able to identify treatment-emergent adverse events in the context of clinical trials and in outpatients with a variety of psychiatric diagnoses who are receiving different psychotropic medications.

Although there is evidence of the value of the SAFTEE-SI, we believe it is too cumbersome for routine clinical use. We therefore recommend using the SAFTEE-GI and supplementing it with an inquiry regarding specific body systems on the basis of clinical knowledge of the patient and the medication or medications administered. Although the SAFTEE-GI is the preferred instrument for clinical use, on the basis of the studies discussed, the SAFTEE-SI is preferable for use in clinical drug trials.

REFERENCES AND SUGGESTED READINGS

Guy W: Dosage Record and Treatment Emergent Symptoms Scale (DOTES), in ECDEU Assessment Manual for Psychopharmacology—Revised (DHEW Publ No ADM 76-338). Rockville, MD, U.S. Department of Health, Education, and Welfare, Public Health Service, Alcohol, Drug Abuse, and Mental Health Administration, NIMH Psychopharmacology Research Branch, Division of Extramural Research Programs, 1976, pp 223–244

Guy W, Ban TA: The AMDP System: A Manual for Assessment and Documentation in Psychopathology. Heidelberg, Springer-Verlag, 1982

Guy W, Wilson WH, Brooking B, et al: Reliability and validity of SAFTEE: preliminary analyses. Psychopharmacol Bull 22:397–401, 1986

Jacobson AF, Goldstein BJ, Dominguez RA, et al: Interrater agreement and intraclass reliability measures of SAFTEE in psychopharmacologic clinical trials. Psychopharmacol Bull 22:382–388, 1986

Levine J, Schooler NR: SAFTEE: a technique for the systematic assessment of side effects in clinical trials. Psychopharmacol Bull 22:343–381, 1986

Levine J, Schooler NR: General versus specific inquiry with SAFTEE (letter). J Clin Psychopharmacol 12:448, 1992

Rabkin JG, Markowitz JS: Side effect assessment with SAFTEE: pilot study of the instrument. Psychopharmacol Bull 22:389–396, 1986

Rabkin JG, Markowitz JS, Ocepek-Welikson K, et al: General versus systematic inquiry about emergent clinical events with SAFTEE: implications for clinical research. J Clin Psychopharmacol 12:3–10, 1992

Udvalg for Kliniske Undersogelser (UKU) Side Effect Rating Scale

O. Lingjaerde, U. G. Ahlfors, P. Bech, S. J. Dencker, and K. Elgen

GOALS

The Udvalg for Kliniske Undersogelser (UKU) Side Effect Rating Scale (Lingjaerde et al. 1987) was developed to provide a comprehensive side effect rating scale with defined and operationalized items to capture the side effects of psychotropic medications. It was designed for use in both clinical trials and routine clinical practice.

DESCRIPTION

The UKU Side Effect Rating Scale was designed to be completed by a physician or other health care professional on the basis of an interview with the patient and other relevant information from collateral sources. The UKU Side Effect Rating Scale has three components. The first component includes 48 single items that are grouped into four categories—Psychic, Neurological, Autonomic, and Other. The second component is a global assessment of the presence or absence of interference in the patient's daily performance due to side effects as assessed by the examiner and patient. The last component is for indicating consequences in terms of whether the physician took any action to address the side effect or side effects rated.

The Psychic subscale includes 9 items, some of which may be related to the illness rather than being a side effect of medication. These items are included, however, because medications could also induce these difficulties. Hence, it is particularly important to make a judgment about their association (or lack of association) with the drug in question. The Neurological subscale contains several items found in the Rating Scale for Extrapyramidal Side Effects (Simpson-Angus EPS) (p. 163), but it also has items for paresthesia and epileptic seizures (total of 8 items). The Autonomic subscale has 11 items, including anticholinergic effects, as well as polydipsia and polyuria to cover lithium-related side effects. The 19 items in the Other subscale comprise dermatological problems, sexual and reproductive functions, headache, and physical and psychological dependence.

The UKU Side Effect Rating Scale form lists the 48 items (e.g., sleepiness/sedation, tremor, and constipation) without definitions. Thus, the scale fits nicely on a single two-sided form. Each item is scored on a 4-point scale. In general, 0 = none or doubtful, 1 = present to a mild degree, 2 = present to a moderate degree, and 3 = present to a severe degree. The user is referred to a detailed manual (Lingjaerde et al. 1987) that defines each item and provides a detailed definition of each anchor point. For example, sleepiness/sedation is defined as "diminished ability to stay awake during the day. The assessment is based on clinical signs during the interview." The anchor points are 0 = no or doubtful sleepiness; 1 = slightly sleepy/drowsy as regards facial expression and speech; 2 = more markedly sleepy/drowsy. The patient yawns and tends to fall asleep when there is a pause in the conversion; and 3 = difficult to keep the patient awake and to wake the patient. Headache is defined (and noted on the scoring sheet as) tension headache, migraine, or other form of headache. The anchor points are 0 = no or doubtful headache, 1 = slight headache, 2 = moderate hampering headache which does not interfere with the patient's daily life, and 3 = pronounced headache interfering with the patient's daily life.

Each item is scored, regardless of whether it is judged to be related to the medication treatment. In general, the inquiry is made on the basis of the here and now; however, in some cases, it is more appropriate to make the assessment on the basis of the past 3 days. For certain items (e.g., menstrual function, weight changes, seizures, and drug dependence) the reference period may be longer. In most cases, the observation period is defined in the manual. All available sources of information (e.g., patient and/or family reports, physician observations, and reports from ward personnel) can be used. When there are discrepancies among the reports, the physician's observations are given more weight than patient reports.

A judgment is then made about the causal relationship (or lack of it) of each item to the medication in question, using the terms *impossible*, *possible*, or *probable*. Lingjaerde et al. (1987) suggest that the appropriate regulatory body in each country be notified when potentially dangerous, previously unknown side effects or uncommonly severe side effects are detected (see the section on the MEDWatch, p. 161).

PRACTICAL ISSUES

Once the clinician becomes familiar with the UKU Side Effect Rating Scale, it takes about 10–30 minutes to complete it, depending on the patient's condition. It is reasonably easy to use the scale in clinical practice and clinical trials.

There are no copyright restrictions on the UKU Side Effect Rating Scale. The scale is available in Danish, English, Finnish, French, German, Icelandic, Norwegian, and Swedish from

> Symposium International
> Karlebogard
> Karlebovej 91
> DK-3400
> Hillerod, Denmark

PSYCHOMETRIC PROPERTIES

Reliability

Three sites in Denmark, Sweden, and Norway carried out a joint reliability study that included 16 patients who mainly had schizophrenia, all of whom were receiving antipsychotic medications. The intraclass correlation coefficients for the total scores of the four main categories revealed moderate to high reliability (range of 0.37–0.96). Intraclass correlation coefficients for the 12 most frequent individual items were variable and less reliable across sites (range of 0.20–1.00).

Validity

Pilot studies of the UKU Side Effect Rating Scale were followed by a large cross-sectional study of 2,391 patients from 50 hospitals in the five Nordic countries—Denmark, Finland, Iceland, Norway, and Sweden—who were being treated with neuroleptic medication. Face and content validity for clinical side effects commonly associated with conventional antipsychotic medications and other psychotropic drugs were determined.

A higher frequency of most individual side effects was seen in inpatients compared with outpatients; the face validity of the scale was thus supported. The largest differences were in hypokinesia, 25% to 10%; increased sexual desire, 24% to 9%; decreased dream activity, 20% to 9%; disturbance of accommodation, 19% to 9%; increased salivation, 25% to 15%; and weight loss, 16% to 5%. A higher frequency was seen in outpatients for only 10 of the 48 individual side effects, and the largest difference was only 5%; nausea or vomiting was seen in 16% of outpatients compared with 11% of inpatients, and akathisia was seen in 32% of outpatients compared with 28% of inpatients.

Concurrent validity of the scale was also demonstrated by its ability to show differences in groups of patients on the basis of the known side effect profiles of the medications used. For example, neuroleptic medications were classified as high dose (e.g., chlorpromazine) or low dose (e.g., haloperidol). Extrapyramidal side effects, particularly akathisia and rigidity, were seen more frequently with the low-dose medications; the concurrent and face validity of the UKU Side Effect Rating Scale was thus supported. Anticholinergic and autonomic side effects (e.g., failing memory, reduced salivation, constipation, and orthostatic dizziness) were seen more frequently with the high-dose neuroleptic medications. The largest difference was in akathisia, which was seen in 35.0% of patients taking low-dose medications compared with 22.5% of patients taking high-dose medications. Use of antiparkinsonian medications was associated with a higher incidence of almost all side effects. Again, as expected, parkinsonian symptoms and akathisia were higher in the patients who received these medications.

Clinical trials conducted in Europe have used the UKU Side Effect Rating Scale, as have recent multicenter clinical trials (e.g., Marder and Meibach 1994).

CLINICAL UTILITY

The UKU Side Effect Rating Scale is fairly comprehensive, but with only 48 items, it is relatively easy to use. The manual includes definitions of all items and all anchor points for rating severity. In addition, judgments regarding causality make it useful for determining subsequent actions that need to be taken. The subscales can be useful in assessing differential side effect profiles (e.g., anticholinergic side effects, neurological side effects, and polyuria). The ability to follow individual items or subscales (e.g., the Neurological subscale) over time is useful for both clinical and research purposes.

The UKU Side Effect Rating Scale is recommended for routine clinical use and for use in clinical trials. In clinical use, it provides the advantages of a checklist to ensure that neither the clinician and assessor nor the patient overlooks important areas. Its disadvantages are that the checklist uses sophisticated medical terms that need to be translated into lay language for the patient; because everyday language for the terms is not provided, clinicians must determine appropriate word substitutions for themselves. The development of a simple checklist in lay language would be of great benefit to the field.

REFERENCES AND SUGGESTED READINGS

Guy W: Dosage Record and Treatment Emergent Symptoms Scale (DOTES), in ECDEU Assessment Manual for Psychopharmacology—Revised (DHEW Publ No ADM 76-338). Rockville, MD, U.S. Department of Health, Education, and Welfare, Public Health Service, Alcohol, Drug Abuse, and Mental Health Administration, NIMH Psychopharmacology Research Branch, Division of Extramural Research Programs, 1976, pp 223–244

Guy W: Subject's Treatment Emergent Symptom Scale (STESS), in ECDEU Assessment Manual for Psychopharmacology—Revised (DHEW Publ No ADM 76-338). Rockville, MD, U.S. Department of Health, Education, and Welfare, Public Health Service, Alcohol, Drug Abuse, and Mental Health Administration, NIMH Psychopharmacology Research Branch, Division of Extramural Research Programs, 1976, pp 347–350

Lingjaerde O, Ahlfors UG, Bech P, et al: The UKU Side Effect Rating Scale: a new comprehensive rating scale for psychotropic drugs, and a cross-sectional study of side effects in neuroleptic-treated patients. Acta Psychiatr Scand Suppl 76:1–100, 1987

Marder SR, Meibach RC: Risperidone in the treatment of schizophrenia. Am J Psychiatry 151:825–835, 1994

Simpson GM, Angus JWS: A rating scale for extrapyramidal side effects. Acta Psychiatr Scand Suppl 46:11–19, 1970

MEDWatch

D. A. Kessler

GOALS

The MEDWatch (Kessler 1993) was developed by the U.S. Food and Drug Administration (FDA) to increase voluntary reporting of medication adverse effects and product device problems by physicians, health care professionals, and others to meet the FDA mandate of protecting public safety at large. The form is designed to simplify such reporting to encourage physicians to report even "suspicions that the drug or device is related to a serious adverse effect; they are not expected to establish the connection or even wait until evidence seems compelling" (Kessler 1993).

DESCRIPTION

The MEDWatch is a one-page reporting form. It is not a rating scale. According to Kessler (1993), it is designed for "cases in which the physician suspects that an FDA regulated product was associated with a serious outcome—death, a life-threatening condition, initial or prolonged hospitalization, disability, or congenital anomaly, or when intervention was required to prevent permanent impairment or damage." The reporter provides the following information on the MEDWatch form: patient demographics, a description of the adverse event or product problem, suspected medication(s) or medical device, whether the event abated after reduction or discontinuation or reappeared on reintroduction, and the reporter's name, address, and phone number. The report form is user-friendly in that the request for information is in a format that is familiar to physicians. The major burden (a light one) in completing the form is to provide a brief narrative describing the event or problem, information regarding laboratory and other tests, and available history that may help in interpreting the event.

The individual reporting form is not scored in any traditional sense, but the FDA reviews and summarizes reports through its Medical Products Reporting Program.

PRACTICAL ISSUES

The MEDWatch form is simple and easy to use. It takes only minutes to complete, depending on the situation and the available information. The MEDWatch form (FDA Form #3500, 6/93) is in the public domain. It is reproduced in the *Physicians' Desk Reference* (Medical Economics Company 1999), the *FDA Medical Evaluations*, and the *American Medical Association Drug Evaluations*. Copies are also available by calling a toll-free number (800-FDA-1088 [800-332-1088]) 24 hours a day, 7 days a week. Callers can also obtain the *FDA Desk Guide to Adverse Event and Product Problem Reporting*. Finally, the form may be accessed electronically via the Internet (www.fda.gov/medwatch). The MEDWatch form includes a self-mailer. Alternatively, completed forms may be faxed to the FDA (800-FDA-1078 [800-332-1078]).

MEDWatch is included on the CD-ROM that accompanies this handbook.

PSYCHOMETRIC PROPERTIES

MEDWatch is a reporting form and therefore does not have any psychometric properties.

CLINICAL UTILITY

The MEDWatch is an easy-to-use form for spontaneous reporting of adverse effects associated with drugs or problems with medical devices. By increasing physician surveillance and reporting, the FDA hopes to detect serious drug- and device-related adverse events sooner and thereby take needed actions "swiftly and effectively" (Kessler 1993).

REFERENCES AND SUGGESTED READINGS

Faich GA: Adverse-drug reaction monitoring. N Engl J Med 314:1589–1592, 1986

Kessler DA: Introducing MEDWatch: a new approach to reporting medication and device adverse effects and product problems. JAMA 269:2765–2768, 1993

Medical Economics Company: Physicians' Desk Reference, 53rd Edition. Montvale, NJ, Medical Economics Company, 1999

Rossi AC, Knapp DE: Discovery of new adverse drug reactions: a review of the Food and Drug Administration's spontaneous reporting system. JAMA 252:1030–1033, 1984

Rossi AC, Knapp DE, Anello C, et al: Discovery of adverse drug reactions: a comparison of selected Phase IV studies with spontaneous reporting methods. JAMA 249:2226–2228, 1983

Strom BL, Melmon KL: Can postmarketing surveillance help or effect optimal drug therapy? JAMA 242:2420–2423, 1979

Rating Scale for Extrapyramidal Side Effects or Simpson-Angus Extrapyramidal Side Effects (EPS) Scale

G. M. Simpson and J. W. S. Angus

GOALS

The Rating Scale for Extrapyramidal Side Effects (commonly referred to as the Simpson-Angus Extrapyramidal Side Effects [EPS] Scale) (Simpson and Angus 1970) was initially developed in the 1960s to distinguish the emerging conventional neuroleptic medications in terms of the extrapyramidal side effects associated with them. It was hoped that quantifying side effects might allow for a better comparison of those agents and make it easier to separate psychopathology from side effects. The authors have subsequently modified the scale for use in ambulatory settings by deleting or changing items that required an examining table or bed.

DESCRIPTION

The Simpson-Angus EPS Scale contains 10 items for assessing parkinsonian and related extrapyramidal side effects. The scale was originally developed from clinical assessments for Parkinson's disease modified for conventional antipsychotic medications (Simpson et al. 1964). The 10 original items in the often-cited published version (Simpson and Angus 1970) were gait, arm dropping, shoulder shaking, elbow rigidity, wrist rigidity, leg pendulousness, head dropping, glabella tap, tremor, and salivation. Seven of the ten items in the 1970 version of the scale measure parkinsonian rigidity. In subsequent modifications, leg pendulousness was deleted, head rotation replaced head dropping, and akathisia was added. Each item is rated on a fully anchored 5-point scale, with 0 = the absence of the condition or normal and 4 = the most extreme form of the condition. For instance, for the gait item, a score of 4 indicates a "stooped shuffling gait with propulsion and retropulsion." After each item is rated from 0 to 4, a mean score is obtained by adding all of the scores and dividing by 10. In the 1970 publication, a mean total score of 0.3 was cited as the upper limit for patients without parkinsonian or related extrapyramidal side effects.

PRACTICAL ISSUES

It takes experienced examiners approximately 10 minutes to administer the Simpson-Angus EPS Scale. Although the Simpson-Angus EPS Scale was originally designed to be rated by physicians, subsequent studies successfully used trained nonphysicians to rate extrapyramidal side effects with the scale. As with any scale, experience using it and training help to increase joint reliability. Instructions are provided for assessing each item, and the scores are anchored for increasing severity.

The scale is in the public domain, and, consequently, there are many versions in circulation. The version of the scale on the CD-ROM included with this handbook represents a modest modification of the original version that was made by the National Institute of Mental Health in collaboration with George Simpson, the senior developer of the scale, for use in a multicenter clinical trial sponsored by the National Institute of Mental Health (Schooler et al. 1997). It has not been published elsewhere.

PSYCHOMETRIC PROPERTIES

Reliability

Correlation coefficients determined on the basis of independent examinations on the same day between two raters were reported by Simpson and Angus (1970). Correlations were high for the total score (0.87, with a mean range of 0.71–0.96 for individual items). A principal components analysis revealed four factors—rigidity, salivation, glabella tap, and tremor—that accounted for 69% of the variance.

Validity

In the original study (Simpson and Angus 1970), the Simpson-Angus EPS Scale distinguished a placebo from a low-dose haloperidol group and a low-dose from a high-dose haloperidol group. Individuals who received placebo had scores that were below the upper limit of the normal range (0.3). Individuals who received a lower haloperidol dose (6 mg/day) had scores ranging from 0.3 at the beginning of the fixed-dose phase of the study to a maximum of around 0.8 during the 8th week; the scores slowly decreased to the normal range as the drug was withdrawn. The high-dose haloperidol group (30 mg/day) scored around 0.45 at the start of the fixed-dose phase; scores increased to around 1.2 during the 5th week and then decreased toward normal on withdrawal (Simpson and Angus 1970).

The Simpson-Angus EPS Scale has been widely used in recent studies of the newer antipsychotic agents. Because these medications were hypothesized to have fewer extrapyramidal side effects than do conventional agents, studies of these medications provide opportunities to assess the validity of the Simpson-Angus EPS Scale. For example, in a study ($N = 286$) that compared two doses of quetiapine with a placebo, Small and colleagues (1997) found no statistically significant differences between placebo and quetiapine. During the 6-week trial period, 5% of patients in all groups had increases in Simpson-Angus EPS Scale scores. In studies that included haloperidol, the Simpson-Angus EPS Scale discriminated newer antipsychotic medications from haloperidol (e.g., Beasley et al. 1996; Zimbroff et al. 1997) in a dose-dependent fashion, providing robust evidence of its validity. Beasley and colleagues (1996) compared placebo, three dose ranges of olanzapine, and haloperidol (modal dose of 16.4 mg/day) in 275 subjects. Patients switched from a typical antipsychotic medication to either olanzapine or placebo showed declines in Simpson-Angus EPS Scale scores ranging from 0.3 to 0.6, whereas patients treated with haloperidol showed a mean increase of 1.0. The Simpson-Angus EPS Scale discriminated haloperidol from placebo and from the two lower doses of olanzapine. Zimbroff and colleagues (1997) compared three doses of sertindole with placebo and three doses of haloperidol (4, 8, and 16 mg/day) in 497 patients. Patients switched from a typical antipsychotic medication to either sertindole or placebo showed declines in Simpson-Angus EPS Scale scores ranging from 0.3 to 1.0, whereas patients treated with haloperidol showed increases ranging from 0.5 to 1.3. These increases were paralleled by greater use of anticholinergic medication in patients treated with haloperidol.

CLINICAL UTILITY

The Simpson-Angus EPS Scale has been used as a research tool in clinical trials of antipsychotic agents to assess extrapyramidal symptoms. It can also be readily applied in clinical practice when antipsychotic drugs are initiated, titrated, and monitored for dose-limiting side effects, and it has been used in some routine clinical practice settings, although not as frequently as the Abnormal Involuntary Movement Scale (AIMS) (p. 166). It is easy to use in inpatient, ambulatory, and nursing home settings. The scale can also be used to test the effectiveness of anticholinergic or other agents in the treatment of extrapyramidal side effects. One possible limitation is that examination for head dropping requires a padded examination table. As noted, the modified version of the scale that substitutes head rotation for head dropping addresses this difficulty.

REFERENCES AND SUGGESTED READINGS

Beasley CM Jr, Tollefson G, Tran P, et al: Olanzapine versus placebo and haloperidol: acute phase results of the North American double-blind olanzapine trial. Neuropsychopharmacology 14:111–123, 1996

Schooler NR, Keith SJ, Severe JM, et al: Relapse and rehospitalization during maintenance treatment of schizophrenia: the effects of dose reduction and family treatment. Arch Gen Psychiatry 54:453–463, 1997

Simpson GM, Angus JWS: A rating scale for extrapyramidal side effects. Acta Psychiatr Scand 212:11–19, 1970

Simpson GM, Amuso D, Blair JH, et al: Aspects of phenothiazine-produced extrapyramidal symptoms. Arch Gen Psychiatry 10:199–208, 1964

Small GS, Hirsch SR, Arvanitis LS, et al: Quetiapine in patients with schizophrenia: a high- and low-dose double-blind comparison with placebo. Arch Gen Psychiatry 54:549–557, 1997

Zimbroff DL, Kane JM, Tamminga CA, et al: Controlled dose-response study of sertindole and haloperidol in the treatment of schizophrenia. Am J Psychiatry 154:782–791, 1997

Barnes Akathisia Rating Scale (BARS)

T. R. E. Barnes

GOALS

The Barnes Akathisia Rating Scale (BARS) (Barnes 1989) was designed to measure drug-induced akathisia that occurred specifically with use of neuroleptic agents. However, it may be useful with other agents that may be associated with akathisia, such as serotonin reuptake inhibitors. It was developed on the basis of the assumption that akathisia includes both objective restless behavior and the subjective experience of restless feelings and accompanying distress.

DESCRIPTION

The BARS is a four-item fully anchored scale. Three items (i.e., objective akathisia, subjective awareness of restlessness, and subjective distress related to restlessness) are rated on a 4-point scale (0–3), and the global clinical assessment of akathisia uses a 5-point scale (0–4). For example, a rating of 1 on the objective akathisia item signifies the "presence of characteristic restless movements: shuffling or tramping movements of the legs/feet, or swinging of one leg, while sitting, and/or rocking from foot to foot or 'walking on the spot' when standing, but movements present for less than half the time observed."

Brief instructions are provided on the form regarding administration, but specific questions to be used in assessing subjective akathisia are not included.

The three items that rate objective and subjective akathisia can be summed to yield a total score ranging from 0 to 12. The global rating is distinct and ranges from 0 to 5. According to the author, a diagnosis of akathisia requires both observer-rated akathisia and a rating of at least 1 on either of the subjective items. If there is a positive score on objective akathisia but a 0 rating on the subjective items, a rating of 0 is given on the global item (this condition is called pseudoakathisia). In a small reliability study, pseudoakathisia was found to be relatively common (21%).

If only the global item is used, clinicians may wish to distinguish pseudoakathisia from a global rating of 0 that follows ratings of 0 on the objective akathisia items.

PRACTICAL ISSUES

It takes approximately 10 minutes to administer the BARS. The instructions suggest that the rater also incorporate observation outside the formal rating situation.

The scale can be reproduced freely. The scale and the brief instructions can be printed on one page and are reproduced in the Barnes (1989) publication. The BARS is included on the CD-ROM that accompanies this handbook.

The BARS has been translated into Italian, Japanese, and Spanish.

PSYCHOMETRIC PROPERTIES

Reliability

Joint reliability for two raters (one of whom is the author) was reported using Cohen's kappa (linearly weighted). Kappa values were 0.74 for the objective rating, 0.83 for subjective awareness, 0.90 for subjective distress, and 0.96 for the rater's global judgment.

Validity

The scale has been widely used in recent Phase III trials of new antipsychotic medications (e.g., Beasley et al. 1996; Small et al. 1997; Zimbroff et al. 1997). Because these medications are hypothesized to reduce akathisia in comparison with conventional agents, the studies provide opportunities to assess the validity of the BARS. For example, in a study ($N = 286$) that compared two doses of quetiapine with a placebo, Small and colleagues (1997) found no statistically significant differences between placebo and quetiapine. Between 25% and 28% of patients improved in all three groups. In studies that included haloperidol, the BARS showed differences between haloperidol and placebo as well as dose-dependent effects of some of the new antipsychotic medications (e.g., Beasley et al. 1996; Zimbroff et al. 1997). Beasley and colleagues (1996) compared placebo, three dose ranges of olanzapine, and haloperidol (modal dose of 16.4

mg/day) in 275 subjects. All three olanzapine groups showed significant reduction (ranging from 0.2 to 0.3) in BARS scores compared with baseline; in contrast, patients treated with haloperidol showed a significant increase of 0.4. Zimbroff and colleagues (1997) compared three doses of sertindole with placebo and three doses of haloperidol (4, 8, and 16 mg/day) in 497 patients. All doses of sertindole showed a reduction in the BARS score ranging from 0.2 to 1.1. The latter reduction was significantly greater than that seen with placebo. In contrast, all haloperidol groups showed increases in BARS global scores, ranging from 0.6 to 0.9, which is significantly different from the results with use of sertindole.

CLINICAL UTILITY

The BARS is useful for identifying patients who may be experiencing akathisia. In particular, it may help clarify patient descriptions that could be interpreted as anxiety or agitation from the subjective restlessness that is the hallmark of the patient experience. The scale itself does not include the kinds of terms that patients may use to describe akathisia (e.g., jittery, jumpy, or feels like bugs crawling). Clinical probing and judgment may therefore be necessary to determine whether the patient is describing akathisia. Although both the subjective and objective components of akathisia must be present for a positive global rating, the validity of this requirement is unknown.

The BARS may also be valuable for tracking change over time, particularly if patients are being treated with one of the newer antipsychotic agents, when a reduction in akathisia may be an important benefit that can be overlooked if it is not documented systematically.

The absence of reliability studies using raters who are not as familiar with the scale as the author and a colleague represents a distinct limitation.

REFERENCES AND SUGGESTED READINGS

Barnes TRE: A rating scale for drug-induced akathisia. Br J Psychiatry 154:672–676, 1989

Beasley CM Jr, Tollefson G, Tran P, et al: Olanzapine versus placebo and haloperidol: acute phase results of the North American double-blind olanzapine trial. Neuropsychopharmacology 14:111–123, 1996

Small GS, Hirsch SR, Arvanitis LS, et al: Quetiapine in patients with schizophrenia: a high- and low-dose double-blind comparison with placebo. Arch Gen Psychiatry 54:549–557, 1997

Zimbroff DL, Kane JM, Tamminga CA, et al: Controlled dose-response study of sertindole and haloperidol in the treatment of schizophrenia. Am J Psychiatry 154:782–791, 1997

Abnormal Involuntary Movement Scale (AIMS)

W. Guy

GOALS

The Abnormal Involuntary Movement Scale (AIMS) (Guy 1976) is designed to record in detail the occurrence of dyskinesias in patients receiving neuroleptic medications. It was developed by the Psychopharmacology Research Branch of the National Institute of Mental Health in consultation with several clinicians and scientists trying to develop similar scales. The AIMS is by far the most widely used scale for rating tardive dyskinesia.

DESCRIPTION

The AIMS is a 12-item anchored scale. Items 1–10 are rated on a 5-point anchored severity scale. Items 1–4 assess orofacial movements, and items 5–7 deal with extremity and truncal dyskinesias (also called limb-truncal dyskinesias). Items 8–10 deal with global severity as judged by the examiner, incapacitation due to the movements as judged by the examiner, and the patient's awareness of the movements and the distress associated with them. Items 11 and 12 are yes-no items concerning problems with teeth and/or dentures, because such problems can lead to a mistaken diagnosis of dyskinesia.

Rated items on the AIMS are scored from 0 to 4. The seven specific items and the global severity and incapacity items are rated as follows: 0 = none, 1 = minimal, may be extreme normal, 2 = mild, 3 = moderate, and 4 = severe. For the global ratings of severity and incapacity, the modifier "may be extreme normal" is omitted from the description of the minimal rating. Several scoring methods are used with the AIMS. A total score (items 1–7) can be calculated. Item 8 (severity of abnormal movements) can be used as an overall severity index. For many clinical purposes this global rating of severity, which integrates the individual item ratings, provides adequate information for ongoing clinical assessment. In other cases, clinicians may wish to track the total movement severity score (sum of items 1–7) or even, in some situations, individual body area scores. Items 9 (incapacitation) and 10 (awareness) provide additional information that may be useful in clinical decision making. Items 11 (dental status) and 12 (dentures) provide information that may be useful in interpreting lip, jaw, and tongue movements. In judging severity, the frequency, amplitude, and quality of the movement observed should be considered. Ratings are generally made regardless of presumptive etiology. Thus, an AIMS score alone does not signify a diagnosis of tardive dyskinesia.

Although specific instructions are provided in the scale for asking the patient certain questions and having him or her perform certain maneuvers, there are no guidelines on how to score the movements as mild, moderate, or severe. Score assignment is addressed fairly well in an article by Munetz and Benjamin (1988). The instructions for the original scale suggest that involuntary movements noted on "activation" be scored "one less"; however, most investigators and clinicians do not follow this suggestion but rather score the noted movement or movements at the higher rating regardless of whether they are observed spontaneously or on activation.

For research and clinical purposes, Schooler and Kane (1982) suggested the following research criteria for diagnosing tardive dyskinesia: 1) at least 3 months of cumulative exposure to neuroleptic medication, 2) the absence of other conditions that might cause the abnormal involuntary movements, and 3) movements of mild severity (score of 2 on the AIMS) in at least two discrete body parts or movements of moderate severity (score of 3 or more) in one body area. If these criteria are fulfilled, a diagnosis of probable tardive dyskinesia is made.

PRACTICAL ISSUES

The AIMS is easy to use and can be completed in 5–10 minutes in clinical practice. It has been adapted for routine clinical practice in mental health office settings and is used to evaluate dyskinesia in clinical trials of antipsychotic medications. Munetz and Benjamin (1988) describe a useful training and implementation model for use of the AIMS in clinical settings. It includes an elaboration of the instructions that are part of the AIMS itself and procedures for integrating AIMS examinations into clinical practice.

The AIMS is in the public domain. The scale is reproduced by Guy (1976) and Munetz and Benjamin (1988) and may be freely copied.

The modification of the scale developed by the National Institute of Mental Health in 1985 is provided on the CD-ROM included with this handbook.

PSYCHOMETRIC PROPERTIES

Reliability

The reliability of the AIMS has been studied by several groups (e.g., Lane et al. 1985; Smith et al. 1979a, 1979b). Smith and colleagues (1979b) assessed joint reliability using four raters in six two-person teams that rated 377 psychiatric inpatients, all of whom were receiving antipsychotic medications. To assess test-retest reliability, 35 patients rated by one team were rated 6–8 weeks later. Joint reliability (Pearson correlation coefficients) ranged from 0.66 to 0.82 for individual body area items. The correlation for the total of items 1–7 was 0.87. The correlation for overall severity was 0.75. Test-retest reliability ranged from 0.40 to 0.82 for the individual items; it was 0.81 for the sum of items 1–7 and 0.71 for overall severity.

Validity

In terms of content validity, the AIMS seems to cover the commonly observed clinical features that accompany tardive dyskinesia (i.e., facial, oral, buccal, lingual, jaw, and extremity movements) and the less common truncal movements. It does not cover rare or more severe movements, such as pharyngeal and respiratory movements or tardive dystonias. Other measures of tardive dyskinesia often use videotapes to evaluate the new measure simultaneously with an older measure such as the AIMS, although the consensual validity reasoning could be construed as circular thinking. Use of a threshold, such as the Schooler and Kane (1982) criteria, permits construct validity to establish a probable diagnosis of tardive dyskinesia associated with antipsychotic drugs and can be used in a predictive manner when drug trials are conducted to evaluate treatment response. The AIMS has been used to assess tardive dyskinesia in trials of the newer antipsychotic drugs (e.g., Tollefson et al. 1997). Given the lower acute extrapyramidal liability of the newer antipsychotic medications, the ability of a new medication to produce lower AIMS scores provides evidence of the validity of the scale. Tollefson and colleagues (1997) compared 707 patients treated with olanzapine for a median of 237 days with 197 patients treated with haloperidol for a median of 203 days. Using the total of AIMS items 1–7 as their dependent variable, they found that scores were reduced by 0.13 scale points in the olanzapine group and increased by 0.36 scale points in the haloperidol group, a statistically significant difference. At the same time point, 2.3% of patients treated with olanzapine met diagnostic criteria for tardive dyskinesia compared with 7.6% of patients treated with haloperidol (Schooler and Kane 1982); the scale was thus further validated.

CLINICAL UTILITY

The AIMS can be used to monitor for the absence or presence of tardive dyskinesia, especially before the initiation of an antipsychotic agent. It has been adapted for routine use in mental health settings such as long-stay hospitals, community mental health centers, and partial hospital programs. It may be useful in geriatric settings, where the use of these medications is extensive, especially because the incidence of tardive dyskinesia is significantly higher in the elderly. The AIMS has been used in clinical trials of both the newer and older medications that are used to treat psychoses. The AIMS can also be used to monitor response to specific treatments for tardive dyskinesia.

REFERENCES AND SUGGESTED READINGS

Guy W: ECDEU Assessment Manual for Psychopharmacology—Revised (DHEW Publ No ADM 76-338). Rockville, MD, U.S. Department of Health, Education, and Welfare, Public Health Service, Alcohol, Drug Abuse, and Mental Health Administration, NIMH Psychopharmacology Research Branch, Division of Extramural Research Programs, 1976, pp 534–537

Lane RD, Glazer WM, Hansen TE, et al: Assessment of tardive dyskinesia using the Abnormal Involuntary Movement Scale. J Nerv Ment Dis 173:353–357, 1985

Munetz MR, Benjamin S: How to examine patients using the Abnormal Involuntary Movement Scale. Hospital and Community Psychiatry 39:1172–1177, 1988

Schooler NR, Kane JM: Research diagnoses for tardive dyskinesia (RD-TD). Arch Gen Psychiatry 39:386–387, 1982

Smith JM, Kucharski LT, Eblen C, et al: An assessment of tardive dyskinesia in schizophrenic outpatients. Psychopharmacology 64:99–104, 1979a

Smith JM, Kucharski LT, Oswald WT, et al: A systematic investigation of tardive dyskinesia in inpatients. Am J Psychiatry 136:918–922, 1979b

Tollefson GD, Beasley CM, Tamura RN, et al: Blind, controlled, long-term study of the comparative incidence of treatment-emergent tardive dyskinesia with olanzapine or haloperidol. Am J Psychiatry 154:1248–1254, 1997

Patient Perceptions of Care Measures

Gregory B. Teague, Ph.D.

INTRODUCTION

Major Domains

This chapter includes measures of patient perceptions of care. As a group, these measures all generally tap patient judgment about services; however, they cover a range of definitions of satisfaction and contexts of care. Concepts underlying these measures include satisfaction with services in general or with particular services, as well as global and specific judgments about quality of care. Although theoretical distinctions can be made between patient satisfaction and patient judgments of service quality, measures based on both sets of concepts are included here. In selecting measures for inclusion in this chapter, the wide range of possible treatment settings, including small practices, hospitals, health plans, and other systems of care, was taken into account. Because much important work in the measurement of patient satisfaction has taken place in general medical practice, some measures that were originally developed in those settings are detailed here; however, all measures included in this chapter have at least been adapted and used with psychiatric patients.

Organization

The measures included in this chapter are listed in Table 12–1. The organization of the chapter reflects movement from more general to more specific applications with selected combinations of treatment populations and settings. The measures described early in the chapter are based on more generalized assumptions about satisfaction, and the measures described later are more focused and were developed for more specific settings or populations. The first measure described, the SERVQUAL, is based on a general theoretical model of perception of quality of services in general (i.e., it is not limited to health care services). The Patient Satisfaction Questionnaire (PSQ) is a survey instrument designed to measure satisfaction with medical care in general but not with specific services. The Patient Judgment System (PJS) is a multidimensional scale that assesses patients' views of several aspects of hospital care. It has been adapted for use in psychiatric hospitals. The Client Satisfaction Questionnaire—8 (CSQ-8) is a unidimensional scale that assesses satisfaction with health or mental health services. The Service Satisfaction Scale—30 (SSS-30) is a multidimensional scale that also assesses satisfaction with health or mental health services, with variants for particular types of service settings. The Youth Satisfaction Questionnaire (YSQ) measures children's and adolescents' satisfaction with a wide range of wraparound services for youth with severe emotional disturbance.

The domain of patient satisfaction detailed in this chapter does not include the related issue of the satisfaction of family members with the treatment of their relatives. However, this introductory section includes references to some measures that address this aspect of satisfaction.

TABLE 12–1 ■ Patient perceptions of care measures

Name of measure	Disorder or construct assessed	Format	Pages
SERVQUAL	Perceived service quality across a wide range of service types not limited to health care; a somewhat shorter version modified for assessing hospital services is also available	Structured, self-administered; 44 items	176–179
Patient Satisfaction Questionnaire (PSQ-II; PSQ-III)*	Aspects of satisfaction with medical care in general	Fully structured, self-administered; 55 items (PSQ-II) and 50 items (PSQ-III)	179–183
Patient Judgment System (PJS) Brief version: Patient Comment Card (PCC)	Patients' views of the quality of hospital care	Self-administered; 68 items	183–186
Client Satisfaction Questionnaire—8 (CSQ-8)	General satisfaction with health or mental health services	Fully structured, self-administered; 8 questions	186–188
Service Satisfaction Scale—30 (SSS-30)* Case management version (SSS-CM) Residential settings version (SSS-RES)	Satisfaction of groups of consumers with a range of health and human services	Self-administered questionnaire; 30 items	188–191
Youth Satisfaction Questionnaire (YSQ)	Children's and adolescents' satisfaction with wraparound services (community-based mental health and related services for youth with severe emotional disturbance and their families)	Brief, structured interview; 16 questions	191–194

*Measure is included on the CD-ROM that accompanies this handbook.

USING MEASURES IN THIS DOMAIN

Goals of Assessment

The general purpose of patient satisfaction measurement is administrative (i.e., to assess one or more aspects of performance of one or more components of a health care delivery system from the patient's perspective). Specific goals of assessment typically fall within one of two general categories. The most widely reported uses are for quality improvement and have their basis in the assumption that customer satisfaction is an indicator of quality of service. Multidimensional scales also provide independent measurement of selected aspects of service. The SERVQUAL, for example, is specifically intended as a method of uncovering broad areas of shortfalls and strengths in an organization's service quality. The PJS is designed to monitor long-term trends in quality and to identify critical areas for improvement in services. The YSQ measures satisfaction with each of several different kinds of service. With overall or unidimensional scales, summary scores can be compared across organizational entities or scores for a single organization can be used to monitor performance over time, to compare performance with different patient population groups, or to evaluate performance relative to published norms. Viewed in combination with other measurements or organizational characteristics, satisfaction data can help pinpoint both areas and strategies for quality improvement.

A second general goal of assessment of patient satisfaction is to provide information to guide choices and decision making. Summary data on patient judgments about quality or satisfaction with services can be used to inform both institutional purchasers of services and other patients in their own decisions about care. Because more objective approaches to assessment of service effectiveness can be quite complex and burdensome, satisfaction measures are often used as a convenient and face-valid alternative indicator of program quality for evaluation and marketing purposes.

Patient satisfaction may be conceptualized as an aspect of both the process and outcome of care. Insofar as satisfaction measures assess features of the interaction of providers and consumers, they are process measures; insofar as they call for summary judgments by patients of an overall episode of care, they are measures of outcome. Although the specific aspects of care assessed vary across measures, there is much similarity in the content included in specific items. Areas assessed by multidimensional scales typically include two or more of the following types of issues: technical quality of care, outcomes of care, interpersonal manner of practitioners and other staff, availability of services and access to them, physical aspects of the service environment, and financial issues. Unidimensional scales such as the CSQ-8 include items that tap multiple aspects of service.

Implementation Issues

The principal issues in implementing satisfaction measures are related to the fact that these instruments are designed to produce aggregated data from groups of respondents rather than individual data for immediate clinical purposes. Although satisfaction data may be used in conjunction with other data when the unit of analysis is the individual patient, the intended purpose of the analysis is to determine the performance of the entity providing services for groups of patients. Patients may have reason to be concerned about the possible implications of their responses for the way they are treated individually, so anonymity or confidentiality must be ensured. These two necessary features—management and analysis of aggregated data and privacy for respondents—are critical for implementation of satisfaction measures. A service provider, however small or large, must have procedures in place for distributing and recovering forms—or in some instances interviewing patients—in such a way that patients may validly believe that their responses will not be individually identifiable to their own clinicians. For example, forms should be returned to a location separated from that of the clinician. In order to draw reliable and valid inferences about the satisfaction of groups of respondents, mechanisms must be established to ensure either appropriate sampling or full inclusion of the group of interest, as well as adequate

return rates from those from whom responses are solicited. A range of techniques may be used for increasing return rates, including personal and organizational appeals and on-site distribution of self-report forms. When data are anonymous and it is not possible to link satisfaction responses to other data concerning the characteristics of the respondents, additional items must typically be included with the satisfaction items or very careful sampling must be done to restrict the variability of the responding group. Use of third-party organizations or separate organizational components may allow non-anonymous, confidential data collection; in this case, individual follow-up can be done to ensure higher response rates, and satisfaction data can be pooled with a wider range of other information. Finally, an important implementation issue is the required capacity to analyze the data and use the results.

Issues in Interpreting Psychometric Data

The principal issues in interpretation are related to theoretical assumptions about the concept of satisfaction, to the content of the measures (e.g., variation in the definition of satisfaction as operationalized in particular measures), and to the methods used to measure that content.

Several models for satisfaction have been proposed (see Pascoe [1983] for a review), and most measures of satisfaction have their basis either implicitly or explicitly in one or more of these models. Value-expectancy models define satisfaction as the sum of respective products of beliefs about the importance of particular aspects of care and evaluations of those aspects. Discrepancy theories define satisfaction as the proportion of expectations experienced. Fulfillment theories define satisfaction as the difference between what is desired and what actually occurs. Equity theories allow for social comparisons of one's own balance of inputs and outputs with that of others. Attempts to validate these models have so far suggested that very little variance in satisfaction data can be explained strictly in terms of the proposed models. Although expectations, for example, play a role in satisfaction ratings, prior expectations do not appear to contribute as theorized. Nelson and Larson (1993) offered a possible explanation for the high proportion of apparently satisfied patients—what is frequently termed a *halo effect*. These researchers showed that a majority of people who simply had not been confronted with a "bad surprise" that violated typical social values and norms were satisfied, regardless of whether they had experienced a "good surprise" of service exceeding normally expected levels. To some extent, defining a measure as a patient judgment about service quality avoids the problem of defining satisfaction per se, but questions about the basis for judgment remain. The gender and age differences in satisfaction levels that are typically noted, as well as research into the social pathways to care (Pescosolido et al. 1995), suggest that social and cultural contexts play a very important role in defining what might constitute good and bad surprises.

A second set of interpretation issues is raised by the content of the measures. To facilitate interpretation, results are typically grouped in subscales with common-sense labels, such as Access, Practitioner Manner, and so forth. Most scales are validated through standard instrument construction techniques, including factor analysis, regardless of whether items have been theoretically generated. Developers of measures usually attempt, with varying success, first to base content in the actual concerns of patients and second to validate factor structures across diverse populations. In practice, these scales have their basis in analyses of the performance of particular items using particular response options with particular populations in particular settings. Ultimately, valid interpretation of results in new settings is a function of the generalizability of the original work of scale construction.

A third set of interpretation issues involves the methodological features of both instrument and implementation. First, the response options have a strong influence on the overall distribution of scores, which has important implications for the utility of results. Typically, mean satisfaction scores are relatively high on the scale of possible values, and there is a long tail on the lower end of the distribution (i.e., distributions are highly negatively skewed), indicating little endorsement of low satisfaction. For reasons already indicated, such data should not necessarily be interpreted as showing that most people are wholeheartedly enthusiastic about their service experiences. The resulting ceiling effect makes it difficult to discriminate among levels of positive satisfaction.

Clearly, scales with more symmetrical distributions closer to the center of the range are advantageous in discriminating among programs. Careful attempts in scale construction to achieve more or less symmetrical distributions can be successful, as is the case with the PSQ. Ware and Hays (1988) showed that using a 5-point quality-rating scale (excellent–poor) rather than a 6-point satisfaction–dissatisfaction scale could improve both the distribution and the ability to discriminate among programs. The explicit anchors in the 5-point scale allocated a greater proportion of the total response range to higher quality (e.g., the midpoint anchor was "good") and resulted in greater overall variance than was produced by using the 6-point scale with only implicit anchors. Similarly, the SSS-30 uses an extreme upper anchor (i.e., "delighted"), resulting in distributions that, although high on the scale, are relatively symmetrical. Stratmann et al. (1994) proposed the use of another format to capture first the summary rating of satisfaction or quality for specific dimensions and second the infrequent but important negative experiences leading to dissatisfaction within that dimension that should spur quality improvement efforts. Continuous variables for each dimension are rated on standard scales, and a multiple-choice list of negative experiences is provided for endorsement as appropriate. Another approach to improving the distributions of ratings from long-term patients was used by Corrigan and Jakus (1993), who asked respondents to rate the focal program relative to others in which they had participated.

A second general methodological issue in interpretation involves possible bias or systematic differences in scores resulting from the characteristics of respondents. One potential source of bias is the tendency of some people to indicate disingenuous agreement with questioners. This "acquiescent response set" is more prevalent among respondents with lower income and educational levels (Ware 1978). Unless a measure controls for this phenomenon (e.g., through balanced positive and negative items), interpretation of scores should take into account this possibility. Demographic, clinical, and service context characteristics may also affect scores; for example, it is typically reported that older female respondents give more positive ratings. In addition, although Corrigan and Jakus (1993) showed that the reliability of responses from patients with severe mental disorders was unrelated to symptoms, reliability was positively associated with intelligence. Unless respondent characteristics that may be related to scores are measured and adjusted for statistically, interpretation of apparent group differences in satisfaction, particularly across nominally different program types, should include attention to the risk of bias from these sources.

A third methodological issue is response rate. Most methodologists are very cautious about interpreting data on the basis of rates much lower than 70% because of the elevated risk of significant self-selection bias, in which those who choose to respond differ in their opinions from those who do not. Typical rates for single mailed satisfaction surveys are between 20% and 40%; clearly, generalization of findings from these small returns to larger populations is risky. Inferences from low-response-rate survey data can be strengthened, although not unequivocally substantiated, by adjusting scores using data on respondent characteristics relative to those of the target population. For anonymous surveys, questions that tap these dimensions would have to be included as additional items.

GUIDE TO THE SELECTION OF MEASURES

The theory and practice of the measurement of satisfaction are continuing to develop and to grow in perceived importance, and many measures are in use in the field. Some measures that are not described in this chapter have purposes that are very similar to those included here; some have not gone through the necessary peer-reviewed validation necessary for inclusion in this manual. However, the following discussion of factors to consider in selecting a measure for a particular application includes references to some of these additional measures.

The selection of a measure of satisfaction is aided by careful consideration of costs and benefits in relation to intended uses of the data. Benefits include the likely improvements in the quality of care and/or the level of service activity. These benefits are supported by both the psychometric strengths of the measure used and an appropriate match between content and necessary procedures, on the one hand, and between population and service context, on the other. Costs include the burden on respondents and on the provider group or organization in distributing, collecting, and analyzing data and may include fees for use of proprietary instruments. Many organizations choose to minimize costs by using very brief, unidimensional measures; however, those who are ready to use multidimensional evaluations for quality improvement purposes may find the marginal increase in costs a worthwhile investment. For example, multidimensional measures may be able to detect program differences in specific areas that would be overlooked by a global scale.

The relative strengths of alternative instruments should be considered. The instruments described in this chapter are quite diverse. The SERVQUAL elicits information about characteristics of the organization as a whole and allows comparison with other types of service organizations. Because the PSQ measures satisfaction with health care in general, it may be most useful in either research studies or situations such as evaluating health plans, when a single organization is responsible for the respondents' full care. The PJS was designed for quality evaluation and improvement in general hospitals. Its exemplary construction, beginning with careful grounding in the concerns of hospital patients, may enhance its applicability even to psychiatric settings, although reports of its adaptation to psychiatric hospitals are not yet available. A tool related to the PJS, the Patient Comment Card (PCC), offers a promising, low-burden model. The CSQ-8 is brief and applicable to a wide range of settings, although its usefulness is limited by its unidimensionality and skewed scores. The SSS-30 has been designed for and used with a wide range of psychiatric patients and has more normal distributions. Both the CSQ-8 and the SSS-30 are proprietary instruments with ongoing fees for use. The YSQ is intended to measure children's perspectives on a multiorganizational service system for children.

Many other patient satisfaction measures in addition to those described in this chapter are available. Recent work especially has used qualitative methods in the initial stages of development so that the resulting measures will have a basis in patient perspectives. Measures have been developed for use with patients in a U.S. public psychiatric hospital (Holcomb et al. 1989), in a Swedish psychiatric hospital (Wilde et al. 1994), in a long-stay British hospital (MacDonald et al. 1988), and in a U.S. private psychiatric hospital (Glass 1995). Hardy et al. (1996) developed a satisfaction measure for use in a British general hospital, and Grogan et al. (1995) developed one to report satisfaction with general practitioners' services. All these measures were grounded in patients' experiences and concerns.

Structured interviews have been used to determine patient satisfaction with partial hospitalization programs (Corrigan and Jakus 1993) and to determine patient satisfaction with hospital and community residential settings (Thornicroft et al. 1993). Tanner and Stacy (1985) developed a measure of satisfaction with mental health services that was supplemented by a validity scale to correct inflated scores.

There are also measures designed for parents to rate their satisfaction with children's services. The Parent Satisfaction Scale (Brannan et al. 1996) is a long questionnaire that was used in the Fort Bragg research study (Bickman 1996). The Family Satisfaction Questionnaire (Rouse et al. 1994) is being used in state-funded programs in Texas, and psychometric refinement of this measure continues (M. Toprac, personal communication, December 1997). The Family-Centered Behavior Scale (Allen and Petr 1995) is a 26-item scale that allows parents to rate programs on the degree to which they are family centered.

Other instruments are in wide use but have not yet been reviewed in the professional literature. The consumer survey component of the Mental Health Statistics Improvement Program (MHSIP) Consumer-Oriented Mental Health Report Card (Center for Mental Health Services 1996; Teague et al. 1997) taps dimensions of access, quality or appropriateness, outcome, and general satisfaction. It was developed in collaboration with consumers and is coming into widespread use as a component in the monitoring of publicly funded mental health services in several states. A 21-item version of the MHSIP consumer survey is being evaluated for inclusion in the Health Plan Employer Data and Information Set (HEDIS) (Sennett 1996), a managed-care industry report card. Another measure, the Behavioral Healthcare Rating of Satisfaction (Dow and Ward 1996), is a multidimensional scale that was also developed in collaboration with mental health service consumers. It is in statewide use in Florida and in occasional use elsewhere. This scale uses scannable forms and direct interactive computer data collection methods. A more general measure, the Consumer Assessment of Health Plans (CAHPS), is currently in pilot testing (Cleary and Edgman-Levitan 1997). Designed to help consumers select among alternative health plans, the CAHPS has its basis in reports of events rather than ratings of satisfaction and displays results in an easily interpreted report card format.

Information to aid in the selection of patient satisfaction measures is available in several extensive reviews of the literature and comparisons of instruments. Anderson et al. (1997) and Young et al. (1995) reviewed measures for children's services. Lebow (1982), Perreault et al. (1993), Ruggeri (1994), and Wilde et al. (1993) reviewed and compared adult psychiatric measures. Several reviews of satisfaction measurement in general medical services provide good discussions of theoretical and methodological issues that are equally pertinent to psychiatric services. The reviews include those by Aharony and Strassor (1993), Lewis (1994), Pascoe (1983), and several companion articles that address related topics in the same issue by Ross et al. (1995), Rubin (1990), van Campen et al. (1995), and Wensing et al. (1994).

CURRENT STATUS AND FUTURE RESEARCH NEEDS FOR ASSESSMENT

Several authors have highlighted the challenges and directions for measurement of patient satisfaction (Aharony and Strassor 1993; Avis et al. 1995; Cleary and Edgman-Levitan 1997; Ware 1995; Williams 1994). They and many others have noted the need for additional efforts to ground the concept more thoroughly in the experience and views of patients. Recent work with consumers has suggested that satisfaction measures in general have historically underemphasized concerns such as respect, involvement in treatment, and attention to outcomes including well-being, notwithstanding the presence of items that address such issues in extant measures, including some reviewed here. This need arises in part because the way in which patient concerns are experienced and expressed changes over time along with changes in the structure and strategies of the treatment system. Appropriate use of qualitative techniques in the construction and revision of measures may help to keep content relevant. That the concept of satisfaction is itself in question is at the heart of the issue. Patient experiences are not necessarily couched in terms of satisfaction per se. At the same time, it should be noted that unvalidated ad hoc measures cannot stand on face validity alone; they, too, will need to be subject to the careful psychometric work done on most of the measures detailed in this chapter. Regarding other conceptual issues, theoretical work is needed on the issue of expectation and fulfillment—because the basic models have received little empirical support—and on the relationship of satisfaction and dissatisfaction.

At the methodological level, there is room for further improvement in measurement techniques, such as approaches to achieve better distributions and to develop items that are focused on the reporting of events rather than on judgments. Progress in the systematic integration of qualitative and quantitative approaches to measurement may result in a better overall understanding of patients' views of the processes and outcomes of care, in part by providing a more effective vehicle for identifying sources of dissatisfaction (Perreault et al. 1993). As with other patient-based, health-related measures, identification of appropriate control variables to allow for risk adjustment may enhance the reliability and validity of results. Finally, a conceptual and empirical issue is the relationship of satisfaction to other outcomes. Investigation of this set of relationships by use of brief, global measures has produced few clear results; research with more recent multidimensional measures that take into account more carefully the treatment and cultural contexts of patients may address this issue more effectively. Given the salience of patient satisfaction—or patient perceptions of care—for both consumers and providers, there is a need for better understanding of the role patient perceptions play in relation to the primary purposes of treatment, both in general and with respect to particular cultural contexts.

REFERENCES AND SUGGESTED READINGS

Aharony L, Strassor S: Patient satisfaction: what we know about and what we still need to explore. Medical Care Review 50(1):49–79, 1993

Allen RI, Petr CG: Family-Centered Behavior Scale and User's Manual. Beach Center on Families and Disability, University of Kansas, 1995

Anderson JA, Rivera VR, Kutash K: Measuring consumer satisfaction with children's mental health services, in Community-Based Programming for Children With Serious Emotional Disturbances and Their Families: Research and Evaluation. Edited by Epstein MH, Kutash K, Duchnowski AJ. Austin, TX, Pro-Ed, 1997

Avis M, Bond M, Arthur A: Satisfying solutions? a review of some unresolved issues in the measurement of patient satisfaction. J Adv Nurs 22:316–322, 1995

Bickman L: The evaluation of a children's mental health managed care demonstration. Journal of Mental Health Administration 23(1):7–15, 1996

Brannan AM, Sonnichsen SE, Heflinger CA: Measuring satisfaction with children's mental health services: validity and reliability of the satisfaction scales. Evaluation and Program Planning 19(2):131–141, 1996

Center for Mental Health Services: The MHSIP Consumer-Oriented Mental Health Report Card: Final Report of the Phase II Task Force. Rockville, MD, Substance Abuse and Mental Health Services Administration, 1996

Cleary PD, Edgman-Levitan S: Health care quality: incorporating consumer perspectives. JAMA 278(19):1608–1612, 1997

Corrigan PW, Jakus MR: The patient satisfaction interview for partial hospitalization programs. Psychol Rep 72:387–390, 1993

Dow M, Ward J: Outcomes Project: Year Three Report. Tampa, FL, Florida Mental Health Institute, 1996

Glass AP: Identifying issues important to patients on a hospital satisfaction questionnaire. Psychiatr Serv 46(1):83–85, 1995

Grogan S, Conner M, Willits D, et al: Development of a questionnaire to measure patients' satisfaction with general practitioners' services. Br J Gen Pract 45:525–529, 1995

Hardy GE, West MA, Hill F: Components and predictors of patient satisfaction. British Journal of Health Psychology 1:65–85, 1996

Holcomb WR, Adams NA, Ponder HM, et al: The development and construct validation of a consumer satisfaction questionnaire for psychiatric inpatients. Evaluation and Program Planning 12:189–194, 1989

Lebow J: Consumer satisfaction with mental health treatment. Psychol Bull 91(2):244–259, 1982

Leff HS, Mulkern V, Woocher L, et al (eds): Toolkit on Performance Measurement Using the MHSIP Consumer-Oriented Report Card, Version 1.0. Cambridge, MA, Evaluation Center, Health Services Research Institute, November 1998

Lewis JR: Patient views on quality care in general practice: literature review. Soc Sci Med 39(5):655–670, 1994

MacDonald L, Sibbald B, Hoare C: Measuring patient satisfaction with life in a long-stay psychiatric hospital. Int J Soc Psychiatry 34(4):292–304, 1988

Nelson EC, Larson C: Patients' good and bad surprises: how do they relate to overall patient satisfaction? QRB Qual Rev Bull 3:89–94, 1993

Pascoe GC: Patient satisfaction in primary health care: a literature review and analysis. Evaluation and Program Planning 6:185–210, 1983

Perreault M, Leichner P, Sabourin S, et al: Patient satisfaction with outpatient psychiatric services: qualitative and quantitative assessments. Evaluation and Program Planning 16:109–118, 1993

Pescosolido BA, Wright ER, Sullivan WP: Communities of care: a theoretical perspective on case management models in mental health. Advances in Medical Sociology 6:37–39, 1995

Ross CK, Steward CA, Sinacore JM: A comparative study of seven measures of patient satisfaction. Med Care 33(4):392–406, 1995

Rouse LW, MacCabe N, Toprac MG: Measuring satisfaction with community-based services for children with severe emotional disturbances: a comparison of questionnaires for children and parents. Paper presented at the 7th Annual Research Conference for a System of Care for Children's Mental Health: Expanding the Research Base, Tampa, FL, 1994

Rubin HR: Patient evaluations of hospital care: a review of the literature. Med Care 28(suppl 9):S3–S9, 1990

Ruggeri M: Patients' and relatives' satisfaction with psychiatric services: the state of the art and its measurement. Soc Psychiatry Psychiatr Epidemiol 29:212–227, 1994

Sennett C: An introduction to HEDIS—the Health Plan Employer Data and Information Set. Journal of Clinical Outcomes Management 32:59–61, 1996

Stratmann WC, Zastowny TR, Bayer LR, et al: Patient satisfaction surveys and multicollinearity. Quality Management in Health Care 2(2):1–12, 1994

Tanner BA, Stacy W Jr: A validity scale for the Sharp consumer satisfaction scales. Evaluation and Program Planning 8:147–153, 1985

Teague GB, Hornik J, Ganju V, et al: The MHSIP Mental Health Report Card: a consumer-oriented approach to monitoring the quality of health plans. Evaluation Review 21(3):330–341, 1997

Thornicroft G, Gooch C, O'Driscoll C, et al: The TAPS project 9: the reliability of the patient attitude questionnaire. Br J Psychiatry 162(suppl 19):S25–S29, 1993

van Campen C, Sixma H, Friele RD, et al: Quality of care and patient satisfaction: a review of measuring instruments. Medical Care Research and Review 52(1):109–133, 1995

Ware JE Jr: Effects of acquiescent response set on patient satisfaction ratings. Med Care 16(4):327–336, 1978

Ware JE Jr: What information do consumers want and how will they use it? Med Care 33(suppl 1):JS25–JS30, 1995

Ware JE, Hays RD: Methods for measuring patient satisfaction with specific medical encounters. Med Care 26:393–402, 1988

Wensing M, Grol R, Smits A: Quality judgements by patients on general practice care: a literature analysis. Soc Sci Med 38(1):45–53, 1994

Wilde B, Starrin B, Larsson G, et al: Quality of care from a patient perspective: a grounded theory study. Scandinavian Journal of Caring Sciences 7:113–120, 1993

Wilde B, Larsson G, Larsson M, et al: Quality of care: development of a patient-centered questionnaire based on a grounded theory model. Scandinavian Journal of Caring Sciences 8:39–48, 1994

Williams B: Patient satisfaction: a valid concept? Soc Sci Med 38(4):509–516, 1994

Young SC, Nicholson J, Davis M: An overview of issues in research on consumer satisfaction with child and adolescent mental health services. Journal of Child and Family Studies 4(2):219–238, 1995

SERVQUAL

A. Parasuraman, V. A. Zeithamel, and L. L. Berry

GOALS

The SERVQUAL (Parasuraman et al. 1988, 1991) is a measure designed to assess perceived service quality across a wide range of service types and is not limited to health care services. The developers distinguish service quality from customer satisfaction in that the former is defined as a global judgment about the superiority of the service, whereas the latter is related to a specific transaction between the organization and the customer. Perceived service quality stems from a comparison of expectations (i.e., what consumers feel ought to be provided and consumer perceptions of actual performance). The authors of a modification of the SERVQUAL for assessing hospital services (Babakus and Mangold 1992) specify that the instrument measures functional quality, or the manner in which health care is delivered, as opposed to technical quality.

DESCRIPTION

The SERVQUAL is designed for self-administration. The generic version, applicable to any service organization, consists of 44 items arranged in two sets: 22 items assess expectations, and 22 matched items assess perceptions of service performance. Expectation items are presented first, followed by Perception items. Each set of 22 items taps five dimensions of service quality:

1. Tangibles: the physical characteristics of the service (4 items)
2. Reliability: the ability to perform the service dependably and accurately (5 items)
3. Responsiveness: the willingness to help and provide prompt service (4 items)
4. Assurance: the display of knowledge and courtesy and the ability to inspire trust and confidence (4 items)
5. Empathy: the demonstration of caring and individual attention (5 items)

Items are rated on a 7-point Likert scale ranging from 1 = strongly disagree to 7 = strongly agree. All items are worded positively. An additional optional section for measuring relative importance asks respondents to assign a total of 100 points among the five dimensions, which are identified and described for the respondent as features of quality. Importance scores are used to produce a weighted mean service quality score. Samples of Perception of Responsiveness items and Expectation items are provided in Example 12–1.

Although the generic version of the SERVQUAL was designed for use with any type of service, the developers recommend adaptation as needed for closer correspondence to particular services. Accordingly, the measure was modified to evaluate hospital services (Babakus and Mangold 1992). Several generic items were dropped, some because variations in respondents' illnesses would result in different interpretations and some because of perceived redundancy. The resulting 15-item hospital SERVQUAL covers the same five dimensions as the original. Three items are included in each of the Tangibles, Reliability, and Responsiveness scales, four in the Assurance scale, and two in the Empathy scale. The Responsiveness scale is 5 points rather than 7 points. The Perception item given in Example 12–1 as a sample of the generic instrument was modified in the hospital instrument to read "XYZ's employees are always willing to help patients," and the corresponding Expectation item is "Hospital employees should always be willing to help patients."

Usual use of the SERVQUAL entails computing the mean of all items in each of the five scales for Expectation and Perception. Each Expectation mean is then subtracted from its corresponding Perception mean to yield a total of five Gap, or service quality, scores (one each for the Tangibles, Reliability, Responsiveness, Assurance, and Empathy scales). On the generic version, which uses a 7-point response scale, Expectation and Perception scores can theoretically range from 1 to 7. Reported item ranges in a variety of non-health-care service industries were Expectation scores for Tangibles, 5.1–5.3; all other Expectation scores, 6.2–6.6; and all Perception scores, 4.8–5.8. The reported range of Gap scores (which can theoretically range from –6 to +6; negative scores indicate that perceptions fall short of expectations) was –1.6 to 0.7. For the hospital version, Expectation and Perception scores can theoretically range from 1 to 5; reported item ranges in a regional chain of hospitals were 4.2–4.9 for Expectation items and 3.9–4.5 for Perception items. Linear combinations (i.e., either sums or means) of either individual items or the five scales can also be generated to produce single overall scores for Expectations, Perceptions, and Gap, if desired. If the optional section for measuring relative importance of dimensions has been used, a weighted mean Gap score representing overall service quality can be derived as the sum of the products of Gap scores and the respective relative importance weights. If respondents differentiate dimensions in terms of relative importance, the weighted mean Gap score can differ from the unweighted mean. Evidence suggests that respondents make such discriminations. In one example, the weights assigned by respondents in five non-health-care service companies were generally stable across companies and reflected a consistent view that tangibles were less important, and reliability more important, than the other dimensions. Mean weights, rounded to whole numbers, were 11, 32, 23, 19, and 17 for the Tangibles, Reliability, Responsiveness, Assurance, and Empathy scales, respectively.

EXAMPLE 12–1 ■ Sample items from the SERVQUAL

Perception of Responsiveness Item
Employees of XYZ are always willing to help you.

Corresponding Expectation Item
Employees of excellent (*type of organization, plural*) will always be willing to help customers.

Reprinted with permission from the author.

PRACTICAL ISSUES

Complete information about the general SERVQUAL, including directions, items for each scale and dimension, the importance scale, and guidelines for use are found in Parasuraman et al. (1991). Items for the hospital SERVQUAL are provided in Babakus and Mangold (1992). Both instruments may be used without permission.

PSYCHOMETRIC PROPERTIES

Reliability

The internal consistency of both the generic SERVQUAL and the hospital version has been assessed. In one study, questionnaires were mailed to approximately 9,000 customers of five separate service companies, including one telephone company, two insurance companies, and two banks; 1,936 were returned. Values of Cronbach's alpha for the Perception-minus-Expectation Gap scores on the generic instrument were between 0.80 and 0.93. In another study that used the hospital instrument, mailed questionnaires were analyzed from 443 respondents out of 1,999 patients discharged from several hospitals managed by a single multihospital corporation. Cronbach's alphas for Expectation scores ranged from 0.50 to 0.80, and those for Perception scores ranged from 0.76 to 0.90. Overall internal consistency was assessed through a linear combination of the five subscales. Alpha values were 0.90 and 0.96 for Expectation and Perception scores, respectively.

Validity

Studies have addressed the overall validity of the SERVQUAL as a measure of perceived quality, the validity of the separate dimensions, and the theoretical and empirical validity of the Perception-minus-Expectation Gap score. Evidence for overall validity is good. The initial generic instrument was developed by using 200 customers each from four nationally known companies: a bank, a credit card company, an appliance repair and maintenance company, and a telephone company. Gap scores were compared with single ratings of overall quality, with customer history of problems with the company, and with willingness to recommend the service to a friend. In all cases, scale scores significantly discriminated

among or between scores on other variables in the appropriate direction. Similarly, summated difference (Gap) scores on the hospital measure were highly correlated both with an overall single-item measure of quality and with intentions to return for needed hospital services in the future.

Evidence for the validity of the five features of quality as separate dimensions is generally positive but mixed. Dimensions reported in the initial study ($N = 800$, described earlier) were derived from oblique factor rotation and were correlated (mean between-scale $r = 0.35$). The developers' subsequent, also multiindustry, study ($N = 1,936$, described earlier), which was conducted to refine and validate the instrument, essentially replicated the earlier factor structure. However, several other studies have not done so. For example, in the hospital study, the Expectation and Perception scores were each found to have a single-factor structure; the five pairs of scales had the appropriate significant loadings. The SERVQUAL developers have suggested that this pattern of findings results from variation within a given organization or industry type as opposed to across industries, and they recommend use of the five scales for both continued research on the issue and practical purposes.

Evidence for the validity of the gap between expectations and perceptions as a measure of service quality is also mixed. In several studies, the Perception scales by themselves account for greater variance in the overall ratings of quality. In the hospital instrument, overall Perception and Gap scores were equally correlated with both overall quality ratings and intentions to return. Again, the developers recommend the difference concept for its utility.

CLINICAL UTILITY

The SERVQUAL is offered as an instrument with established reliability and validity that can serve a primarily administrative function as a diagnostic method for uncovering broad areas of a company's service quality shortfalls and strengths. The instrument assesses functional quality (i.e., the quality of services as perceived by the consumer or health care patient). The generic items and components of the instrument represent core evaluation criteria that cut across specific types of service settings and that can be modified and supplemented for particular settings. The hospital instrument illustrates this process, although the developers do not recommend dropping items, as was done in the reported hospital version.

The focus of the SERVQUAL is on the consumer's view of the company or organization rather than on interactions with particular staff. As a result, it may be most relevant in the health care industry for assessing perceived service quality at the level of hospitals, health plans, and so forth rather than in smaller practices. As is typical of instruments that measure consumer perceptions, data are used in the aggregate. The structure of the instrument offers the opportunity to assess and possibly address unmet expectations in specific areas, regardless of whether the validity of the definition of this gap as service quality per se can be fully established. Use of a common structure allows comparison across types of services.

Although use of the SERVQUAL in anything but a mailed survey format has not been reported, the type and level of questions about expectations and perceptions are similar to those used in interviews with psychiatric patients. However, the original method used to measure relative importance of service features (i.e., in which respondents allocate a total of 100 points among Responsiveness, Empathy, and the other scales in proportion to their perceived importance) was not used in the hospital study and might be difficult for some psychiatric patients. No evidence is yet available to assess whether importance weights found in other industries would apply to mental health care settings.

REFERENCES AND SUGGESTED READINGS

Babakus E, Mangold WG: Adapting the SERVQUAL scale to hospital services: an empirical investigation. Health Serv Res 26:767–786, 1992

Parasuraman A, Zeithaml VA, Berry LL: A conceptual model of service quality and its implications for future research. Journal of Marketing 49:41–50, 1985

Parasuraman A, Zeithaml VA, Berry LL: SERVQUAL: a multi-item scale for measuring consumer perceptions of service quality. Journal of Retailing 64:12–39, 1988

Parasuraman A, Berry LL, Zeithaml VA: Refinement and reassessment of the SERVQUAL scale. Journal of Retailing 67:420–450, 1991

Parasuraman A, Zeithaml VA, Berry LL: Reassessment of expectations as a comparison standard in measuring service quality: implications for further research. Journal of Marketing 58:111–124, 1994

Patient Satisfaction Questionnaire (PSQ)

J. E. Ware Jr., M. K. Snyder, W. R. Wright, and A. R. Davies (PSQ-II)
G. N. Marshall, R. D. Hays, C. D. Sherbourne, and K. B. Wells (PSQ-III)

GOALS

The Patient Satisfaction Questionnaire (PSQ) (Ware et al. 1976a, 1976b) is a patient satisfaction survey instrument that was designed for use in general population studies to measure aspects of satisfaction with medical care in general. The authors note that differences in levels of satisfaction reflect personal preferences and expectations, in addition to mirroring the realities of care. Nonetheless, the instrument was designed to measure patient satisfaction as an outcome of care, and the rating of satisfaction is viewed as a measure of care more than as a measure of the patient's preferences and expectations.

DESCRIPTION

The PSQ is a self-administered survey instrument that assesses patient satisfaction with medical care in general, with both overall care and specific features of care. Respondents are asked to rate medical care in general, without reference to particular time frames or instances of care. Two versions of the PSQ, the PSQ-II (Ware et al. 1976a, 1976b, 1984) and the PSQ-III (Marshall et al. 1993), have been developed. The PSQ-II consists of 55 items that are combined to form 18 subscales. One subscale is a four-item general satisfaction scale; the other 17 subscales can be combined to form 6 global scales.

The global scales (and their constituent subscales) are Non-Financial Access (Emergency Care, Convenience of Services, Access to Care), Financial Access (Cost of Care, Insurance Coverage, Payment Mechanisms), Availability of Resources (Family Doctors, Specialists, Hospitals), Continuity of Care (Family, Self), Interpersonal Manner (Explanations, Consideration), and Technical Quality (Doctor's Facilities, Prudence—Risks, Quality/Competence, Prudence—Expenses). Two pairs of the global scales are further combined to create two higher-order global scales: Access Total (Non-Financial Access and Financial Access) and Doctor Conduct Total or Quality of Care (Interpersonal Manner and Technical Quality). These two global scales are coupled with Availability of Resources and Continuity of Care to yield a total of four higher-order global scales.

Most subscales on the PSQ-II contain two to four items; however, the Consideration subscale has five items, and the Quality/Competence subscale has nine. All items are statements that are rated by respondents on a 5-point Likert scale with anchors specified as 1 = strongly agree, 2 = agree, 3 = not sure, 4 = disagree, and 5 = strongly disagree. Approximately equal numbers of statements are favorable and unfavorable. Items for each subscale are widely distributed throughout the instrument. The recommended format places statements to the left and responses to the right, with both descriptors and scores explicitly shown. Sample items from the Access to Care and Explanations subscales are provided in Example 12–2. A 43-item short form of the PSQ-II was also developed and has been used in several studies.

A derivation of the PSQ-II, the PSQ-III is a structured 50-item instrument that was used in the Medical Outcomes Study (MOS) (Tarlov et al. 1989). In developing the PSQ-III, several PSQ-II items were deleted, and some new items were added. Scales corresponding to

the level of global scales on the PSQ-II were each constructed from 2 or 3 of 17 multiitem indexes, which were derived largely from the items and scales of the earlier version. The PSQ-III scales tap general satisfaction and six specific aspects of satisfaction with care: Interpersonal Manner (7 items), Communication (5 items), Technical Competence (10 items), Time Spent With Doctor (2 items), Financial Aspects (8 items), Access to Care (12 items), and General Satisfaction (6 items).

Responses for all PSQ items are initially coded by the patient from 1 to 5, with 1 = strongly agree and 5 = strongly disagree, as described earlier. Responses for favorably worded statements are recoded in the reverse, so that the direction of a positive rating is the same for both favorable and unfavorable statements, and higher scores are associated with greater satisfaction. Each subscale or global scale consists of a linear combination of all included items. The measure was initially designed for use in general population studies, in which absolute scores would be of less interest than the association of satisfaction scales with other variables. In describing the development and use of the final PSQ-II in several studies, the authors simply reported means and standard deviations for each scale as the sum of the items. Thus, the General Satisfaction scale of the PSQ-II, with four items, has a range of 4–20, whereas the Quality/Competence scale, with nine items, has a range of 9–45. Because items were designed to have similar distributions, scale means could alternatively be used to allow more easily interpretable comparisons.

PRACTICAL ISSUES

The PSQ is self-administered. It takes an average of 11–13 seconds to complete each item; thus, the 55-item PSQ-II takes an average of 11 minutes to complete, and the 50-item PSQ-III takes about 10 minutes. Administration times are longer for subjects with lower incomes and less education. The instruments are copyrighted but may be used without permission or cost. All information about item wording, format, instructions to respondents, and the scoring of the PSQ-II is found in Ware et al. (1984). Information about the 43-item short form is available from

John E. Ware Jr.
Health Assessment Laboratory

EXAMPLE 12–2 ■ Sample items from the Patient Satisfaction Questionnaire

> Access to Care Subscale
>   If I have a medical question, I can reach someone for help without any problem.
>
> Explanations Subscale
>   Doctors hardly ever explain the patient's medical problem to him.

Reprinted with permission from John E. Ware Jr.

Health Institute
750 Washington Street
Box 345
Boston, MA 02111
Phone: 616-636-8645

PSQ-III items and scale composition are included in Marshall et al. (1993).

The PSQ is included on the CD-ROM that accompanies this handbook.

PSYCHOMETRIC PROPERTIES

Reliability

Estimates of internal consistency and test-retest reliability of the PSQ-II were derived from three household surveys and one family practice study; sample sizes ranged from 323 to 640. Internal consistency was estimated for each of the 18 subscales in each of the four studies using Cronbach's alpha. Of the possible 72 coefficients, 68 exceeded a recommended standard of 0.50; values ranged up to 0.93. Of the other 4 coefficients, 3 were between 0.46 and 0.50, and only 1 was significantly lower. Test-retest reliability was estimated by computing product-moment correlations between 17 subscale scores for the same respondents on two administrations in two sites approximately 6 weeks apart. Of the possible 34 coefficients, 28 exceeded the 0.50 level. Global scales, with more variables, were more reliable. Only one of the global alpha and none of the test-retest coefficients were below 0.50. The Doctor Conduct Total global scale, with 23 variables, was most reliable; alpha values were 0.88–0.94, and test-retest correlation coefficients were 0.78–0.82. Reliability values for Availability of Resources and Access global scales were lower than those of other global scales in some sites. Reliability values were generally lower for persons reporting lower levels of income or education.

Reliability for the PSQ-III was reported on the basis of its use in the MOS, which studied outcomes of patients with chronic medical illnesses. The sample included 2,226 subjects in the longitudinal panel for whom complete data were available. Internal consistency of the seven scales was estimated using Cronbach's alpha. Coefficients were Time, 0.87; Technical, 0.85; Interpersonal, 0.82; Communication, 0.82; Financial, 0.89; Access, 0.86; and General Satisfaction, 0.88.

Validity

Several approaches were used to evaluate the validity of the PSQ-II. First, the content of the scales showed a good match with a taxonomy of characteristics of services and providers developed by the authors from a variety of sources. Second, the empirical structure of the instrument, intended to reflect the multidimensional features of the medical care environment, was found to be stable across independent studies in diverse populations. Thus, the four higher-order global scales were observed and replicated across the four field studies described earlier. Third, satisfaction subscale ratings were compared with scores from other measures that address related content. Two of the studies included open-ended questions about satisfaction with care. In one study, complaints were made in sufficient numbers for analysis in four content areas: Technical Quality, Access, Finances, and Interpersonal Manner. Respondents who complained about these specific features of service tended to score lower on corresponding scales than those without complaints about the features; among those who complained, scores for scales corresponding to complaints were lower than scores for the other scales evaluated. Results in the other study were similar. In a separate study of medical outcomes, the Availability of Resources subscales were related to independent measures of medical resources per capita. Fourth, in two of the sites in the reliability studies reported earlier, reported satisfaction on the PSQ-II was related to patient behavior, including intentions to seek care, decisions to change providers, and decisions to cancel enrollment in health plans.

The validity of the PSQ-III was evaluated by its developers in three ways in the MOS (Tarlov et al. 1989). First, confirmatory factor analysis was used to test whether the six scales represented the best model for patient satisfaction. Although correlation among the scales was very high (7 of 15 correlations exceeded 0.80, and 4 equaled or exceeded 0.90), the six-factor model explained the greatest variance. However, the data also supported a hierarchical model in which the six specific aspects of satisfaction were represented as stemming from a single broad domain of satisfaction with care. Second, the indirect measure of general satisfaction, derived in the previous analyses from the six factors, was highly correlated with the direct measure of general satisfaction built into the scale ($r = 0.93$). Third, both direct and indirect measures of global satisfaction with medical care in general were equally and significantly but moderately related to a measure of visit-specific satisfaction ($r =$ 0.35, $P < 0.001$), indicating that satisfaction with medical care in general is related to but distinct from satisfaction with specific services.

An earlier study, conducted by authors of two different measures, also found empirical support for the distinction between general and specific satisfaction with health care. In this study, the 43-item short form was compared with two other scales of satisfaction, each designed to measure satisfaction with specific services received rather than medical services in general. The study used a sample of 300 patients in a public health clinic that offered general preventive services and chronic-disease-prevention programs. Complete data were provided by 147 individuals. Each subject responded to two measures as well as a single-item global criterion measure of overall satisfaction with services received. Measures were evaluated in pairs in regression analyses, with the global item as the dependent measure. In tandem with either of the service-specific measures, the PSQ accounted for only a small, nonsignificant proportion of the variance in the criterion measure of satisfaction with specific services. Thus, satisfaction with specific services is distinct from general satisfaction with medical services, and measures of one do not account well for the other.

a subset of this population was included in the development and validation studies. For more inclusive psychiatric patient populations, the length of the full scale may be a problem, because administration times were longer for people with lower incomes and less education. However, the six-item General Satisfaction scale of the PSQ-III correlates very highly with the latent variable derived from the scale as a whole and could thus serve well if specific aspects of care are not being evaluated.

A major strength of the PSQ is that its items were designed to have balanced distributions, so that scores are substantially less skewed than those of most satisfaction instruments (i.e., means are close to the midpoint of the scale). As a result, the PSQ yields good discrimination among upper ranges of satisfaction and thus allows potentially more interpretable results than are typical for satisfaction data. For example, the relationship between satisfaction and cancellation of enrollment in health plans was a constant 3% per point across the range of general satisfaction scores. Because the PSQ is designed to measure satisfaction with medical services in general rather than satisfaction with specific services, it may have limited administrative use in smaller service entities that do not account for most or all of the services received by respondents.

CLINICAL UTILITY

The PSQ has been shown to be a reliable and well-validated measure of satisfaction with medical services in general. Results of several studies confirm that the PSQ is tapping both a general, overarching domain of satisfaction and a set of discrete dimensions of satisfaction that reflect important aspects of care. As a consequence, the PSQ may be used in broad comparisons of providers, as well as for purposes of quality improvement of specific aspects of care. Some evidence suggests that differential satisfaction with separate dimensions of care may operate differently in different populations. Although the structure of separate scales shows a good fit with patient satisfaction with medical care in general, several pairs of scales are highly correlated, especially those that represent technical and interpersonal aspects of care. Nonetheless, this latter correlation especially appears to be a valid reflection of patient experience. Separate results for recipients of psychiatric services were not reported, but

REFERENCES AND SUGGESTED READINGS

Marshall GN, Hays RD, Sherbourne CD, et al: The structure of patient satisfaction with outpatient medical care. Psychological Assessment 5:477–483, 1993

Pascoe GC, Attkisson CC, Roberts RE: Comparison of indirect and direct approaches to measuring patient satisfaction. Evaluation and Program Planning 6:359–371, 1983

Tarlov A, Ware JE Jr, Greenfield S, et al: The Medical Outcomes Study: an application of the methods for monitoring the outcomes of medical care. JAMA 262:925–930, 1989

Ware JE, Snyder MK, Wright WR: Development and validation of scales to measure patient satisfaction with health care services. Volume 1 of a final report part A: review of literature, overview of methods, and results regarding construction of scales (NTIS Publ No PB 288–329). Springfield, VA, National Technical Information Service, 1976a

Ware JE, Snyder MK, Wright WR: Development and validation of scales to measure patient satisfaction with health care services. Volume 1 of a final report part B: results regarding scales constructed from the Patient Satisfaction Questionnaire and measures of other health care perceptions (NTIS Publ No PB 288–330). Springfield, VA, National Technical Information Service, 1976b

Ware JE, Snyder MK, Wright WR, et al: Defining and measuring patient satisfaction with medical care. Evaluation and Program Planning 6:247–263, 1984

Patient Judgment System (PJS)

E. C. Nelson, R. D. Hays, C. Larson, and P. B. Batalden

GOALS

The Patient Judgment System (PJS) (Nelson et al. 1989) is an instrument designed primarily to assess patients' views of the quality of hospital care. It is a self-administered questionnaire for use in the general health care sector and could support the monitoring of long-term trends in quality as well as the identification of critical areas for improvement. The core of the instrument is a fully structured section consisting of items that measure specific processes of care. The content of the scales was derived from earlier work on the dimensions of greatest concern to patients.

DESCRIPTION

The PJS is a 68-item, self-administered questionnaire designed for mail distribution to samples of patients discharged from general hospital care. All items, except three open-ended questions, use a fixed-response choice format. The 41 core items on specific processes of care (the PJS-41) produce 10 scales, including 1 scale that consists of all items and measures the total process of care. The 9 specific scales measure Admission, Daily Care, Information, Nursing Care, Physician Care, Auxiliary Staff, Living Arrangements, Discharge, and Billing. Each item

in this section consists of a signpost and a descriptor. A sample item from the Nursing Care scale is provided in Example 12–3.

All of the questions use the same 5-point response scale: excellent, very good, good, fair, and poor. An 11th three-item scale, Allegiance, taps behavioral intentions (i.e., whether the patient would recommend the hospital, brag about it, or return to it). Additional items beyond the core 41 included in the 10 scales tap background information on the hospital stay (11 items); overall satisfaction, intentions to recommend the hospital, and suggestions for improvement (8 items); and demographic and descriptive information (5 items).

The PJS is a second-generation instrument, significantly abbreviated from the original. The parent instrument (Meterko et al. 1989) had a total of 108 items, including a core battery of 46, the PJS-46. However, the authors believed that, for some applications, both the 41- and 68-item instruments might still be too long; they therefore derived the PJS-20 and the PJS-10 (Hays et al. 1991), 20- and 10-item subsets of the 41 items that can be used as good measures of the total process of care. To improve content coverage of physician and nursing care, the authors recommend adding 4 items, yielding optional 24- and 14-item versions. A third-generation instrument, the Patient Comment Card (PCC; Nelson et al. 1991), has one item for each of the nine dimensions corresponding to specific scales of the PJS, and much of the content of the larger PJS scales is bundled into the nine item descriptors. In addition, the PCC elicits patient comments for each area and supplements the same verbally anchored response scale with corresponding facial pictographs.

Individual items in the core section of the PJS are scored 1–5. They are summed for each scale, and the resulting scale score is transformed linearly to the range 0–100, in which 100 would correspond to all items rated as excellent and 0 to all items rated as poor. In the primary report of the PJS, the mean score for the 41-item Total Process scale across 32 hospitals was 71.7 (SD,

EXAMPLE 12–3 ■ Sample item from the Patient Judgment System

> Attention of nurses to your condition: How often nurses checked on you to keep track of how you were doing.

Reprinted with permission from Eugene Nelson, D.Sc.

18.8). Means for eight of the nine individual scale scores ranged from 70.4 (Admissions; SD, 24.7) to 78.5 (Doctor Care; SD, 22.8); the mean for the Billing scale was 60.9 (SD, 29.7). Because the PJS was intended to support quality improvement efforts in the hospitals that use it, extensive efforts have been made to enhance the valid interpretation and utilization of results. As implemented in the for-profit hospital system that participated in its development, results are compiled biennially into a comprehensive report that covers overall trends, department-specific trends, marketing data, patients' verbatim comments, and detailed tables of findings. The report is distributed to hospital managers, who are also trained in its appropriate use by local quality measurement staff.

PRACTICAL ISSUES

The PJS was designed for self-administration, with distribution by mail to a sample of discharged patients. The authors used and recommend a series of assertive follow-up steps to raise the response rate, which is typically low with mailed questionnaires. The initial questionnaire was accompanied by a signed letter from the hospital CEO. After 10 days, nonrespondents were mailed a reminder postcard. Two weeks later, remaining nonrespondents were mailed a second questionnaire with an encouraging cover letter and a pen. The resulting net response rate was 66%. The process of data collection was administered by an independent research firm to ensure patient confidentiality.

Although the PJS was developed in cooperation with a for-profit hospital system, it may be used without charge. The original 108-item instrument, including the PJS-46, is reproduced as an appendix in Meterko et al. (1989). Although the 68-item PJS has not been formally published as such, scale items can be inferred from Nelson et al. (1989). The PJS-20 and PJS-10 are detailed in full in Hays et al. (1991). The PCC is reproduced as an appendix in Nelson et al. (1991). Further information about the PJS is available from

Eugene Nelson, D.Sc.
Dartmouth Hitchcock Medical Center
1 Medical Center Drive
Lebanon, NH 03756

PSYCHOMETRIC PROPERTIES

Reliability

Reliability for the 68-item PJS was assessed using a random sample of 8,581 patients discharged from 32 urban and rural hospitals in five states, stratified by time since discharge over one quarter (Nelson et al. 1989). All patients ages 1–80 years were included except for those with mental, brain, or substance abuse disorders and those discharged against medical advice. The follow-up methods described earlier resulted in the return of 5,625 completed questionnaires, for a response rate of 66%. Scale scores were well distributed, and patient-level internal consistencies were uniformly high; Cronbach's alphas ranged from 0.86 (Allegiance) to 0.97 (Total Process). The reliability of measurement at the hospital level—relevant when organizations are the unit of analysis—was somewhat lower but still generally good in this sample; it ranged from 0.70 (Billing) to 0.89 (Living Arrangements). However, hospital-level reliability depends on within-hospital sample size. The authors provide power calculations for each scale to show the sample size required for reliability levels of 0.80 and 0.90; these sample sizes range from 84 to 261 and 184 to 572, respectively.

Test-retest reliability was estimated by comparing each hospital's ratings across two time points, covering an interval that was short compared with changes in hospital practices. The average difference from one period to the next was approximately 2 points on a 0–100 scale, or one-tenth of a standard deviation, supporting the reliability of the PJS scales.

Reliabilities for the PJS-20 and PJS-10 were also estimated using Cronbach's alpha for patient-level internal consistency; alphas were 0.56–0.92 and 0.49–0.83, respectively (single-item values for the PJS-10 were estimated by using the PJS-41 scales). Alphas for the Supplemental Nursing and Doctor scales were 0.92. Sample sizes required for given levels of power in the short forms were similar to those for the PJS-41, except that requisite sizes tended to be slightly larger for the PJS-10. Likewise, test-retest reliability values were similar.

Validity

The methods used to develop the PJS lend initial support for the validity of its content. Through an extensive literature review, focus groups, and content analysis of patients' answers to questions about hospital quality, the authors developed a comprehensive taxonomy. The dimensions and key variables of this taxonomy guided the generation of the initial item pool, which was subsequently reduced and refined in a large-scale pilot study (Meterko et al. 1989). In the 32-hospital study (Nelson et al. 1989), the validity of the PJS was assessed in four ways. First, high hospital-level reliability estimates indicate that the PJS is able to detect differences between hospitals; thus, between-hospital variance is greater than within-hospital variance. Second, patient evaluations were consistent with another source of information about similar content. Ratings of five areas of hospital quality by hospital employees (most of whom were nurses) correlated significantly and well with PJS scores; correlations ranged from 0.52 to 0.87. Third, ratings of the processes of care correlated well with two validity indicators. In addition to the three-item Allegiance scale, the PJS includes a single-item Global Quality scale that encompasses care and services. All correlations of the process scales with these indicators were significant and ranged from 0.42 to 0.69 for the Allegiance scale and from 0.52 to 0.83 for the Global Quality scale. Fourth, item-to-scale correlations, corrected for the presence of items within their own scales, were significantly higher within scales than across scales, indicating that each item measures the aspect of quality it was designed to measure rather than other aspects.

The validity of the short forms was evaluated by comparing patient and employee ratings of similar items related to doctor care and overall quality. Spearman and Pearson correlation coefficients for doctor care were moderate, with coefficents of 0.35 and 0.30, respectively, for the PJS-10 and 0.52 and 0.48, respectively, for the PJS-20; correlations for overall quality were high, ranging from 0.83 to 0.88. Associations between patient quality and validity indicators were very similar for both long and short form scales.

CLINICAL UTILITY

The PJS is a reliable, well-validated instrument for measuring patients' judgments about key dimensions of the quality of hospital services they received. It was carefully developed by a multidisciplinary team that grounded the instrument in extensive qualitative investigation to ensure that it would reflect the domains of greatest impor-

tance to patients. The PJS scales are quite reliable and, with appropriate sample sizes, can distinguish among hospitals of varying quality. Given the prevalence and attractiveness of mailed surveys for evaluating patient satisfaction, it is encouraging that the procedures developed for the PJS can achieve acceptable response rates, despite the length of the overall instrument. Shorter forms of the instrument remain psychometrically strong. The reduction in burden might further improve response rates and thus the overall validity of conclusions, but such rates have not been reported. Inclusion of the term *system* in the name of the measure is an apt reminder that maximizing the utility of this kind of instrument depends on embedding it in a system of procedures for data collection, analysis, and interpretation.

An important limitation of the PJS in the context of this volume is that patients receiving psychiatric services were not included in its development and validation. The instrument was validated on a universe of generally acute care hospitalization experiences that was comprehensive except for those involving treatment for behavioral and brain disorders. It is not certain, therefore, that the PJS validly reflects concerns that are salient for psychiatric patients; similar instrument development approaches with this population might generate a different factorial structure. It is possible, however, that the PJS omits dimensions particular to psychiatric hospitalization rather than that its dimensions are not relevant, at least for patients experiencing relatively short-term hospital treatment. If that proves to be the case, then the PJS may provide a helpful supplement to other measures that focus more specifically on psychiatric care. For more disabled populations, one of the shorter and less burdensome instruments, especially the PCC, might be most suitable.

REFERENCES AND SUGGESTED READINGS

Hays RD, Larson C, Nelson EC, et al: Hospital quality trends: a short-form patient-based measure. Med Care 29:661–668, 1991

Meterko M, Nelson EC, Rubin HR (eds): Patient judgments of hospital quality: report of a pilot study. Med Care 28(suppl):10–14, 1989

Nelson EC, Hays RD, Larson C, et al: The Patient Judgment System: reliability and validity. QRB Qual Rev Bull 15:185–191, 1989

Nelson EC, Larson CO, Davies AR, et al: The Patient Comment Card: a system to gather customer feedback. QRB Qual Rev Bull 17:278–286, 1991

Nelson EC, Larson CO, Hays RD, et al: The physician and employee judgment system: reliability and validity of a hospital quality measurement method. QRB Qual Rev Bull 18:284–292, 1992

Client Satisfaction Questionnaire—8 (CSQ-8)

C. C. Attkisson and D. L. Larsen in collaboration with W. A. Hargreaves, M. LeVois, T. D. Nguyen, R. E. Roberts, and B. Stegner

GOALS

The Client Satisfaction Questionnaire—8 (CSQ-8) (Larsen et al. 1979) is designed to assess satisfaction with health or mental health services. The authors view satisfaction as an outcome of service. The measure yields a continuous score on a single factor of general satisfaction, derived from a broad range of program performance dimensions. The primary use of the scales is to assess the aggregate satisfaction of groups of respondents.

DESCRIPTION

The CSQ-8 is designed for self-administration, although it has also been included in interviews with people with serious mental illness. Respondents answer eight questions on 4-point response scales with individually specified anchors. Items on the CSQ-8 specifically address the domains of quality of service, kind of service, outcome, and general satisfaction. These questions were selected from an earlier, more comprehensive CSQ-31, which was itself derived from a large item pool designed to tap nine conceptual domains: physical surroundings; procedures; support staff; kind or type of service; treatment staff; quality of service; amount, length, or quantity of service; outcome of service; and general satisfaction. The CSQ-8,

which consists of the items that load most heavily on the first, unrotated factor of the CSQ-31, substitutes very well for the original instrument. A sample item is provided in Example 12–4. The following versions of the CSQ are also available: two forms of the CSQ-18, one of which includes the CSQ-8 items; a CSQ-4; and a CSQ-3. All versions of the CSQ include three open-ended questions that solicit comments about what respondents liked most and least and what they would change about the service.

The CSQ-8, as with other CSQ scales, is scored by summing the scores for each item after correcting for direction, then calculating measures such as the mean, the standard deviation for individual items, and the total score for specific groups of respondents. Scores for the CSQ-8 can therefore range from 8 to 32. The mean score in the primary normative sample (Nguyen et al. 1983) was 27.09, reflecting a mean item score of 3.39 on a 4-point scale. Interpretation entails comparison of results either across specific service settings or populations or with reported norms for comparable groups. Women and respondents at extremes of age report somewhat higher levels of satisfaction.

PRACTICAL ISSUES

As a self-report instrument, the CSQ-8 can be used in a mail survey, but typically low response rates with possible problems of interpretation may result. The authors suggest that the survey be administered at the point of service or in waiting rooms by staff trained in systematically soliciting voluntary participation, an approach that yields high completion rates from designated samples.

EXAMPLE 12–4 ■ Sample item from the Client Satisfaction Questionnaire—8

Have the services helped you to deal more effectively with your problems?

4) Yes, they helped a great deal.
3) Yes, they helped somewhat.
2) No, they didn't really help.
1) No, they seemed to make things worse.

Respondents are given a standard set of instructions. It typically takes 5–8 minutes for clients to complete the closed-ended questions and the one open-ended question. The CSQ scales are copyrighted, and use of the scales is strictly limited to individuals and institutions that formally request permission directly from the authors by mail or by fax (no voice requests). The cost, which is subject to change, is currently $0.50 per use for the minimum order of 500, with subsequent orders of 250 or more at $0.30 per use; the fee includes copies of the scale. Requests should be addressed to

> Dr. C. Clifford Attkisson
> Professor of Medical Psychology
> University of California–San Francisco
> 200 Millberry Union West
> 500 Parnassus Avenue
> San Francisco, CA 94143-0244
> Fax: 415-476-9690

Supplemental materials include copies of articles and a concise guide for users that draws on published work. Permission is never granted to modify the wording of items. Several of the CSQ scales have been translated into Dutch, French, and Spanish by using culturally sensitive methods; the most extensive cross-cultural work has been done in Spanish. Translations of the CSQ-8 are also available in Cambodian, Chinese, Korean, Tagalog, and Vietnamese, and a Japanese version was expected to be available in 1999.

PSYCHOMETRIC PROPERTIES

Reliability

The CSQ-8 has demonstrated high internal consistency across a large number of studies; Cronbach's alpha ranged from 0.83 to 0.93. In the largest study, which was the primary source of mental health norms, data were obtained from 3,120 patients in 76 collaborating clinical facilities across the United States, including mental health centers, public health centers, and freestanding mental health clinics; these facilities incorporated the full range of levels of care (Nguyen et al. 1983). Cronbach's alpha for the CSQ-8 was 0.87. The mean item-total correlation was 0.65, and the mean interitem correlation was 0.47. Similar results were obtained from 1,464 participants in a court-mandated drinking driver

treatment program, in which Cronbach's alpha was 0.86, the mean item-total correlation was 0.62, and the mean interitem correlation was 0.44. In a study of 34 clients of a day treatment program in an urban community mental health center, the two forms of the CSQ-18 were highly correlated ($r = 0.82$).

Validity

The high item-total correlations demonstrated by the CSQ-8 support the authors' claim that it measures global satisfaction. Further support is provided by the high correlation (0.6–0.8) of this measure with other methods and instruments used to measure global satisfaction. On the other hand, the authors point out that the relatively lower interitem correlations suggest the presence of other factors that are not adequately explained by the global factor. Mean scores are typically very high, with negatively skewed distributions; sensitivity at higher levels of satisfaction is thus reduced. Relatively little variance is explained by demographic variables, life satisfaction, satisfaction with health care in general, or attitudes about health care providers, suggesting that satisfaction is not merely a proxy for these other patient characteristics. However, women and people at extremes of age tend to report somewhat higher levels of satisfaction. Further support for the CSQ-8 as a global measure of satisfaction comes from studies that examine reported satisfaction in relation to both measured service utilization and self-reported improvement. In a study of 49 patients receiving psychotherapy at a community mental health center, those who dropped out within the first month had significantly lower satisfaction scores ($r = 0.37$); self-ratings of global improvement also correlated significantly with satisfaction ($r = 0.53$). Therapist ratings of global improvement were not significantly related to patient-reported satisfaction. A subsequent study had similar findings.

CLINICAL UTILITY

The CSQ-8 is a brief, self-administered instrument with well-documented reliability and validity that measures a single dimension of global satisfaction with services. As is typical of service satisfaction measures, the CSQ-8 is designed to assess the aggregate level of satisfaction of selected groups of respondents, although data can be analyzed with other variables at the level of the individual respondent. Its brevity and general acceptability to patients, as well as the simplicity of its scoring and interpretation, make it easy to use in a variety of service settings. The CSQ-8 has been used extensively in mental health care, primary health care, and other human service settings, and norms are available for various populations and settings. The CSQ-8 can also be administered by interview.

Users of the CSQ must also recognize some potential limitations. Mean scores are typically quite high and negatively skewed; approximately 10% of respondents report dissatisfaction. It is consequently difficult to discriminate among the majority of respondents who report high levels of satisfaction. Although there is substantial support for the dimension of global satisfaction and its valid and reliable measurement by the CSQ-8, some evidence suggests the presence of other factors that contribute to the satisfaction of service recipients in given settings but that are not appropriately tapped by the CSQ-8 or its variants. Although demographic and other variables such as life satisfaction have not been shown to account for high amounts of variance in global satisfaction, the authors caution that in any specific application it may be important to measure and adjust for these variables. Finally, close attention to standardization of data collection procedures and use of techniques to optimize response rates will enhance the validity of interpretation of scores.

REFERENCES AND SUGGESTED READINGS

Attkisson CC, Greenfield TK: The Client Satisfaction Questionnaire (CSQ) Scales and the Service Satisfaction Scale—30, in Outcomes Assessment in Clinical Practice. Edited by Sederer LI, Dickey B. Baltimore, MD, Williams & Wilkins, 1996, pp 120–127

Attkisson CC, Greenfield TK: The UCSF Client Satisfaction Scales: the Client Satisfaction Questionnaire-8, in Psychological Testing: Treatment Planning and Outcome Assessment, 2nd Edition. Edited by Maruish ME. Hillsdale, NJ, Erlbaum, 1999

Larsen DL, Attkisson CC, Hargreaves WA, et al: Assessment of client/patient satisfaction: development of a general scale. Evaluation and Program Planning 2:197–207, 1979

Nguyen TD, Attkisson CC, Stegner BL: Assessment of patient satisfaction: development and refinement of a service evaluation questionnaire. Evaluation and Program Planning 6:299–313, 1983

Service Satisfaction Scale—30 (SSS-30)

T. K. Greenfield and C. C. Attkisson

GOALS

The Service Satisfaction Scale—30 (SSS-30) (Greenfield and Attkisson 1989) is designed to assess the satisfaction of groups of consumers with a range of health and human services. The authors' concept of satisfaction has evolved out of earlier work by their research group and is defined as a person's reaction to the context, process, and result of his or her service experience. This measure taps multiple factors of service provision that have been identified as most salient by consumers.

DESCRIPTION

Although the SSS-30 is designed for self-administration, respondents can be given assistance or items can be administered in an interview format. The 30-item instrument produces an overall score as well as scores from two to four subscales. Two subscales apply across the full range of service settings for which the measure is designed: Practitioner Manner and Skill (nine items) and Perceived Outcome (eight items). In addition, two less robust subscales are not consistently identified across service settings: Office Procedures (five items) and Service Accessibility (four items). Subscale items are distributed throughout the instrument. Remaining items assess issues such as cost and waiting time; responses to these and all other items are included in the overall score. Each item identifies one aspect of the context, process, or outcome of service and is worded as a completion of the common stem "What is your overall feeling about the . . . ?" Sample items from the Practitioner Skill and Manner and the Perceived Outcome subscales are provided in Example 12–5.

Response options for all items use the same 5-point scale: 5 = delighted, 4 = mostly satisfied, 3 = mixed, 2 = mostly dissatisfied, and 1 = terrible. The direction of the response scale is reversed for even-numbered items.

The authors recommend and provide additional questions to be asked along with the scale. These questions include an optional group item, a demographics section, one item each for rating quality of life and health status on a 7-point "delighted-terrible" scale, and three open-ended questions that solicit comments about what respondents liked most and least and what they would change about the service. Derivative forms of the instrument have been developed by the authors for use with particular services (i.e., case management [SSS-CM] and residential settings [SSS-RES]) (Greenfield et al. 1996). The SSS-RES also has a form for family members.

Item response values are first corrected for directionality, so that higher scores indicate greater satisfaction. Subscale scores are then obtained by summing items for each scale and all items for overall satisfaction. Up to two missing items per scale are allowed; totals for the remaining items are prorated. Interpretation is on the basis of the direct comparison of subscale scores either across groups of respondents or with available norms. Because items are rated on a 5-point scale, the range for scores is from one to five times the number of items (e.g., 30–150 for the overall scale). In the four reported norm samples, mean scores for the nine-item Practitioner Manner and Skill subscale were 38.35–39.15 (in a possible range of 9–45); mean scores for the eight-item Perceived Outcome subscale were 30.26–32.87 (in a possible range

of 8–40). Subscale scores can be converted to the one-to-five-item response scale for convenient comparison among subscales. This approach also allows direct reference to literal item anchors (e.g., a mean score of 4.0 indicates an average rating of mostly satisfied). The authors and their associates have reported norms from six different settings: health clinics, university mental health services, an employee assistance program, a drinking driver program, a county mental health program, and a methadone maintenance program (Greenfield and Attkisson 1999).

PRACTICAL ISSUES

Items on the SSS-30 are preceded by a standard set of instructions. As a self-report instrument, the SSS-30 can be used in a mail survey, but typically low response rates obtained through this method may present problems in interpretation. The authors suggest that the survey be administered at the point of service or in waiting rooms by staff trained in systematically soliciting voluntary participation, an approach that yields high completion rates from designated samples. The SSS-30 is copyrighted, and its use is strictly limited to those who formally request permission directly from the authors by mail, fax, or e-mail (no voice requests). The cost, subject to change, is currently $0.50 per use for the minimum initial order of 500, with subsequent orders of 250 or more at $0.30 per use; the fee includes a camera-ready master form with authorization to copy per paid use. Requests should be addressed to

Dr. Thomas K. Greenfield
Public Health Institute
200 Hearst Avenue
Suite 300
Berkeley, CA 94709-2176
Fax: 510-642-7175
E-mail: tgreenfield@arg.org

The SSS-30 is included on the CD-ROM that accompanies this handbook.

Supplemental materials include copies of articles and a concise guide for users that draws on published work. Permission is never granted to modify the wording of items. Translations are available in Italian and Spanish. In addition, 29 items from the SSS-30 have been trans-

---

EXAMPLE 12–5 ■ Sample items from the Service Satisfaction Scale—30

> Practitioner Skill and Manner Subscale
> What is your overall feeling about the ability of your practitioner(s) to listen to and understand your problems?
>
> Perceived Outcome Subscale
> What is your overall feeling about the effect of services in helping you deal with your problems?

Sample item of the Service Satisfaction Scale is reproduced with written permission. Reproduction in whole or in part is forbidden without the authors' written permission.

lated and adapted to an Italian service setting by another researcher in cooperation with the authors. These items, regarded as the Italian version of the SSS-30, were a subset of the 82-item Verona Service Satisfaction Scale (VSSS) (Ruggeri and Greenfield 1995), a larger instrument designed to include items specifically relevant to community-based psychiatric settings in Italy.

PSYCHOMETRIC PROPERTIES

Reliability

Primary information about psychometric performance of the SSS-30 comes from six studies. The general health care sample consisted of 280 patients who were served in a group of private, nonprofit medical clinics (Greenfield and Attkisson 1989). The mental health service sample consisted of 147 students who were given free psychological services in a large northwestern state university (Greenfield and Attkisson 1989). The majority received brief psychotherapy services; the modal length was 6–10 sessions. The employee assistance program sample consisted of 132 clients of a hospital-based program who were surveyed by mail (Carroll 1991). The modal number of visits was 2–3. The drinking driver program sample consisted of 1,442 clients, primarily male, who completed a court-mandated program in Delaware (Greenfield 1989). The standard program of 25 contact hours included individual and group counseling and education; participants paid $495.00 to attend. The sample of 234 individuals from a county mental health service in Texas had severe mental disorders; 68% had been receiving services for 12 weeks or more. The methadone maintenance clinic sample consisted of 60 clients in Queensland, Australia. The two main subscales of the SSS-30 showed good internal consistency across these six studies. Cronbach's alpha ranged from 0.85 to 0.93 (average of 0.88) for the Practitioner Manner and Skill subscale and from 0.80 to 0.90 (average of 0.85) for the Perceived Outcome subscale. The reliability of the smaller subscales was lower: 0.69–0.83 (average of 0.74) for Office Procedures and 0.60–0.76 (average of 0.67) for Access. The SSS-30 total score, representing composite satisfaction, had high internal consistency; alpha values ranged from 0.93 to 0.96. In the Italian study, 76 patients with severe and persistent mental disabilities, most of whom were living with their families, were interviewed by use of the 82-item VSSS (Ruggeri and Greenfield 1995). Two subscales derived from the subset of 29 items adapted from the SSS-30 corresponded closely to the primary subscales of the original instrument. The Outcome/Efficacy subscale had an alpha value of 0.89, and the Doctor-Patient Transactions subscale had an alpha value of 0.80. Results of readministration of the VSSS to 23 patients after 1–2 weeks indicated good stability within dimensions.

Validity

Primary support for the validity of the SSS-30 is provided through comparison with data on satisfaction from alternative sources and through examination of factor stability across multiple settings. Because the instrument provides a measure of overall satisfaction, the authors were able to compare the SSS-30 overall score with that of the Client Satisfaction Questionnaire—8 (CSQ-8; p. 186), a well-accepted unidimensional measure that was also developed by their research group. In their drinking driver study, total raw scores of the respective instruments correlated well ($r = 0.70$). By design, the SSS-30 provides at least two additional factors within a more comprehensive, multifactorial measure of satisfaction, for which there is both empirical and theoretical support in the literature. The subscales Perceived Outcome and Practitioner Skill and Manner are confirmed across a range of different service types. By using a statistic to measure the stability of these two factors across the six studies, the authors found that the coefficient of congruence ranged from 0.88 to 0.97 (in a possible range of –1 to +1), indicating high congruence. The Access and Office Procedures subscales are less stable across research study sites. Some support for subscale content is provided by comparisons of scale scores with responses to open-ended questions about best and worst features of service. Correlations were modest, between 0.15 and 0.30, for features such as emergency access, waiting, kind of service, and practitioner manner, but the methods used in this study may have substantially limited the results. Through the use of the 5-point "delighted-terrible" response scale, with more extreme endpoint anchors than the usual Likert format, the SSS-30 produces more symmetrical distributions without the strong ceiling effects that are sometimes found with satisfaction data. Thus, skewness for the SSS-30 data in the drinking driver study was –0.30, whereas the figure for the CSQ-8 (p. 186) in the same study was –1.03. Better distributions at higher levels of satisfaction permit finer discriminations among groups of respondents.

CLINICAL UTILITY

The SSS-30 is a multifactorial measure of satisfaction designed for self-administration in populations receiving health care or social services. There are both norms and good evidence of reliability and validity. As is the case for most service satisfaction measures, the SSS-30 is designed to assess the aggregate level of satisfaction of selected groups of respondents, although data can be analyzed with other variables at the level of the individual respondent. Because the SSS-30 is multifactorial, it can be used to compare programs or groups of patients along several separate dimensions. The Overall Satisfaction scale and the Perceived Outcome and Practitioner Skill and Manner subscales have been validated across all intended settings. The Access and Office Procedures subscales are less stable and should be used with greater caution; they may best be limited to comparisons among organizationally similar settings.

The SSS-30 has demonstrated applicability to a variety of psychiatric settings and populations, including community-based populations of people with serious mental illness, with whom interview methods have typically been used. The authors have created versions that are specifically modified for residential settings and case management programs; studies of these versions are in progress. The length of the instrument is mandated in part by its assessment of multiple factors. The authors do not report administration times. An important advantage of the SSS-30 is that many items are explicitly couched in terms of identified consumer concerns, including respect, involvement in treatment planning, and consumer-identified outcomes. Another important advantage of this instrument is the distribution of scores. With more symmetrical, less skewed (albeit still generally high) scores than those produced by many satisfaction scales, the SSS-30 has the potential to effectively discriminate among groups of generally satisfied respondents.

REFERENCES AND SUGGESTED READINGS

Attkisson CC, Greenfield TK: The Client Satisfaction Questionnaire (CSQ) Scales and the Service Satisfaction Scale—30, in Outcomes Assessment in Clinical Practice. Edited by Sederer LI, Dickey B. Baltimore, MD, Williams & Wilkins, 1996, pp 120–127

Carroll IG: Effects of referral source and subject variables on client satisfaction with employee assistance program services. Master's thesis, Wakeforest University, Winston-Salem, NC, 1991

Greenfield TK: Consumer satisfaction with the Delaware Drinking Driver Program in 1987–1988. Report to the Delaware Drinking Driver Program. University of California–San Francisco, Department of Psychiatry, 1989

Greenfield TK, Attkisson CC: Steps toward a multifactorial satisfaction scale for primary care and mental health services. Evaluation and Program Planning 12:271–278, 1989

Greenfield TK, Attkisson CC: The UCSF Client Satisfaction Scales, II: the Service Satisfaction Scale—30, in Psychological Testing: Treatment Planning and Outcome Assessment, 2nd Edition. Edited by Maruish ME. Hillsdale, NJ, Erlbaum, 1999

Greenfield TK, Stoneking BC, Sundby E: Two community support program research demonstrations in Sacramento: experiences of consumer staff as service providers. Community Psychologist 29:17–21, 1996

Ruggeri M, Greenfield TK: The Italian version of the Service Satisfaction Scale (SSS-30) adapted for community based psychiatric patients: development, factor analysis, and application. Evaluation and Program Planning 18:191–202, 1995

Youth Satisfaction Questionnaire (YSQ)

J. D. Burchard

GOALS

The Youth Satisfaction Questionnaire (YSQ) (Rosen et al. 1994) is designed to measure children's and adolescents' satisfaction with wraparound services, an integrated and individualized array of community-based mental health and related services designed to serve children with severe emotional disturbance and their families

(VanDenBerg and Grealish 1996). The YSQ assesses satisfaction with services from the respondent's point of view: the amount of contact and degree of satisfaction with each of eight specific services and with services in general, the degree of satisfaction with his or her own progress, the degree of perceived involvement in treatment, and the extent to which care is perceived as unconditional (i.e., that services will be provided no matter what happens). Data are not used at the level of the individual service recipient; instead, responses are aggregated for the purpose of evaluating particular features of a service system.

DESCRIPTION

The YSQ is a brief, structured interview administered in person or by telephone to the child or adolescent consumer by a third party (e.g., by a researcher-evaluator or administrative staff member) rather than by a service provider. It contains a total of 16 questions in two sections. First, for each of eight specific wraparound services (treatment team, caseworker, case manager, therapist, school, vocational training, respite care, and residential placement), respondents indicate amounts of both contact and satisfaction with each service. Satisfaction ratings are made by using 5-point Likert scales, on which the lower and upper anchors are extremely dissatisfied and extremely satisfied, respectively. Using the same scale, respondents then rate their satisfaction with services in general and with their own progress. A sample question in this section is provided in Example 12–6.

The second section of the scale assesses the degree to which respondents feel involvement in services (e.g., with regard to choices and decisions about their treatment). Five questions are answered on 5-point Likert scales with anchors specific to each question. A sample item is provided in Example 12–6. One final item, also assessed on a 5-point Likert scale, assesses perceived unconditional care: respondents are asked about the extent to which they believe their service providers will "stick with them no matter what." The developers explicitly distinguish satisfaction with services from both involvement in and perception of unconditional care, although aspects of the latter components have been incorporated elsewhere within a more broadly defined construct of satisfaction. The instrument can be used repeatedly to assess ongoing services, and the two sections can be administered at different time intervals (e.g., to obtain ratings of specific service contracts and satisfaction more frequently than ratings about global judgments of involvement and unconditional care).

All YSQ rating items have 1–5 response ranges; scale scores are means, also in a 1–5 range. The Service Satisfaction scale produces single ratings for eight separate service types and for services in general; the mean of all service ratings is the overall satisfaction score. The Perceived Involvement scale is the mean of five items. Satisfaction With Own Progress and Unconditional Care scales have only one item each. As expected for satisfaction measures, scores are typically in the high end of the range. In the initial study of a statewide wraparound service system ($N = 20$), the developers reported an Overall Satisfaction score of 4.13 ± 0.64 (mean $\pm$ SD), with a range of 2.5–5.0. The Satisfaction With Services in General score was higher, 4.34 ± 0.62. Scores for satisfaction with specific services ranged from 3.47 (caseworkers) to 4.37 (case managers); standard deviations ranged from 0.83 to 1.00. Respondents were significantly more satisfied with case managers than with caseworkers.

PRACTICAL ISSUES

The YSQ can be administered in 15 minutes by persons without professional training. No additional special training is required. The interview can be administered by telephone. The YSQ has been used successfully with children as young as age 11. The measure is copyrighted but may be used without cost or permission. Further information is available from

John D. Burchard
Psychology Department

EXAMPLE 12–6 ■ Sample questions from the Youth Satisfaction Questionnaire

> Satisfaction With Own Progress
> How satisfied are you with your own progress in the last 2 weeks?
>
> Involvement in Services
> How often do members of your treatment team ask for your ideas and opinions?

Reprinted with permission.

University of Vermont
Burlington, VT 05405

PSYCHOMETRIC PROPERTIES

Reliability

Reports of reliability are on the basis of one study of children and adolescents (ages 11–19, mean age 16.2 years, 60% male, $N = 20$) receiving community-based and family-based wraparound services in the community. An evaluation of the internal consistency of the satisfaction ratings yielded a Cronbach's alpha of 0.83 across individual satisfaction ratings and 0.88 for the Overall Satisfaction scale. The Overall Satisfaction scale score was correlated with that of each of the other scales: $r = 0.62$ with Unconditional Care, $r = 0.70$ with Satisfaction With Own Progress, and $r = 0.73$ with Involvement. When the level of restrictiveness of living placement was controlled, the Involvement scale score was still highly correlated ($r = 0.62$).

Validity

Establishing the validity of a satisfaction measure using a gold standard is not feasible because of the essentially subjective nature of satisfaction. The authors of the YSQ used the alternative of analyzing scores in relation to two existing measures. In this approach, scale scores of a test measure should relate to established measures in expected amounts and directions. First, scale scores were analyzed in relation to the Restrictiveness of Living Environment Scale (ROLES) (Hawkins et al. 1992). The ROLES was negatively correlated with both Overall Satisfaction (–0.48) and Involvement (–0.62) scales, but the correlation between placement restrictiveness and satisfaction was negligible when scores were adjusted for the Involvement scale score. More restrictive settings necessarily reduce patient involvement in treatment decisions and would thus also be expected to reduce satisfaction, as was found in this study. In the second analysis, YSQ scores were compared with scores from the Quarterly Adjustment Indicator Checklists (QAIC) (Burchard and Schaefer 1992), a measure of acting-out behaviors. The QAIC provides case manager ratings of 18 acting-out behaviors. It has two externalizing subscales and one internalizing subscale. Scores on the Internalizing Behavior subscale (including self-injury, anxiety, sadness, and sui-

cide attempt) were significantly and negatively related to those on the Satisfaction With Caseworker ($r = -0.64$) and Perceived Unconditional Care ($r = -0.53$) scales; relationships to the Involvement ($r = -0.40$) and Satisfaction With Own Progress ($r = -0.39$) scales were weaker. Thus, as would be expected from other reports of satisfaction, children who exhibited more depressive or self-abusive behaviors reported lower satisfaction. The Perceived Unconditional Care scale score was also negatively related to the Moderate Externalizing Behavior subscale score (including property damage, physical aggression, verbal abuse, fire setting, and cruelty to animals; $r = -0.56$) and to the Total Negative Behaviors subscale score ($r = -0.46$); however, the Overall Satisfaction score was not related to these acting-out behaviors. Thus, respondents with poorer behavioral adjustment were less likely to believe that caregivers would really "stick with them no matter what," but this belief did not influence their overall satisfaction, suggesting that the YSQ may be used to represent satisfaction independent of externalizing behavioral adjustment. Finally, the difference in reported satisfaction with caseworkers and case managers has face validity, given the difference in roles of these two categories of care providers in the wraparound service context studied.

CLINICAL UTILITY

The YSQ is useful for the specific administrative purpose for which it was designed (i.e., assessing consumer satisfaction with the performance of wraparound services). The interview is brief and easy to administer in person or by telephone. The YSQ has face validity and covers the wide range of services included in an extensive and individualized model of care for children and adolescents age 11 or older with high service needs. Data are aggregated across multiple respondents and providers and are not intended for use in individual clinical assessment. As is typical for satisfaction measures, the validity of responses depends on credible assurance of confidentiality. Use of the YSQ to investigate relationships between satisfaction and other variables has shown some consistency with other reports. Thus, narrowly defined recipient satisfaction is apparently not related to behavioral outcome as defined by providers; nonetheless, it is considered an important dimension to monitor in this service context.

Other components of satisfaction that are more broadly defined, including involvement in treatment and perception by service recipients that their care is unconditional, are related to other service and outcome variables and may be used to represent recipients' perspectives on these aspects of care. The results of the validation study suggest that the YSQ may be used to compare satisfaction across settings that differ in restrictiveness by taking into account differences in involvement.

Several psychometric limitations of the PSQ should be considered. General concerns about response set and social desirability bias apply. Conclusions about validity are on the basis of a very small sample. Two of the dimensions, Unconditional Care and Satisfaction With Own Progress, are measured with only a single item, a practice that reduces reliability in measuring a dimension. Finally, the behavioral outcome measure used in evaluating validity had only moderate internal consistency, a shortcoming that would weaken confidence in the conclusions.

REFERENCES AND SUGGESTED READINGS

Burchard JD, Schaefer M: Improving accountability in a service delivery system in children's mental health. Clinical Psychology Review 12:867–882, 1992

Hawkins RP, Almeida MC, Fabry B, et al: A scale to measure restrictiveness of living environments for troubled children and youths. Hospital and Community Psychiatry 43:54–58, 1992

Rosen LD, Heckman T, Carro MG, et al: Satisfaction, involvement, and unconditional care: the perceptions of children and adolescents receiving wraparound services. Journal of Child and Family Studies 3:55–67, 1994

VanDenBerg JE, Grealish EM: Individualized services and supports through the wraparound process: philosophy and procedures. Journal of Child and Family Studies 5:7–21, 1996

CHAPTER 13

Practitioner and System Evaluation

Richard R. Owen, M.D.
Carol R. N. Thrush, M.A.

INTRODUCTION

Major Domains

In this chapter measures that can be used to examine various elements of the quality of health care are presented. The assessment of the quality of health care typically involves measuring the structure, process, and outcomes of care (Donabedian 1980). Traditionally, quality assessment has focused on measuring processes of care, such as whether important tests were performed or treatments were prescribed for patients. More recently, however, the focus of quality assessment has shifted to patient outcomes. Instruments have been developed to measure outcomes directly or to measure key processes of care that are known to predict patient outcomes. Several of these instruments are described in this chapter. Most of these instruments collect data directly from patients. These data can then be aggregated for groups of patients to evaluate various aspects of the quality of care provided by practitioners and systems.

Organization

The measures included in this chapter are listed in Table 13–1. The instruments are described in terms of the sources of data they use, the types of data collected, and the level at which the results can be interpreted (individual patient versus system level). The measures covered in this chapter can generally be divided into three broad categories:

- Service utilization measurement instruments: the Health Plan Employer Data and Information Set, Version 3.0 (HEDIS); the Child and Adolescent Services Assessment (CASA); and the Treatment Services Review (TSR)
- Generic outcomes assessment instrument: the COMPASS OP
- Disease-specific outcomes assessment instruments: the Alcohol Outcomes Module (AOM), the Depression Outcomes Module (DOM), the Panic Outcomes Module (POM), and the Schizophrenia Outcomes Module (SCHIZOM)

The instruments within each category share similar goals and common issues of data analysis and interpretation. Service utilization instruments assess selected aspects of the process of care and are primarily used to assess the performance of practitioners or health care systems. Both generic outcomes instruments and disease-specific outcomes instruments collect patient-specific data that can be aggregated to examine outcomes at the practitioner or system level or that can inform treatment decisions for individual patients. These outcomes assessment instruments are designed for use in continuous quality improvement programs called outcomes management systems.

Relevant Measures Included Elsewhere in the Handbook

Any symptom measure that is sensitive to change with treatment can function as an outcome measure. Thus,

TABLE 13–1 ■ Measures for practitioner and system evaluation

NAME OF MEASURE	DISORDER OR CONSTRUCT ASSESSED	FORMAT	PAGES
Health Plan Employer Data and Information Set (HEDIS), Version 3.0	Health plan performance for data about the process of care	More than 100 performance measures	201–203
Child and Adolescent Services Assessment (CASA)	Information about service utilization by children ages 8–18 with mental health or substance abuse problems	Semistructured, face-to-face interview; includes child and parent components	204–206
Treatment Services Review (TSR)*	Quantitative profile of the number and types of treatment services in alcohol and drug abuse rehabilitation, designed to be used in conjunction with the Addiction Severity Index (ASI) (p. 472)	Structured technician-administered interview; 4 sections, 46 items	206–207
COMPASS OP*	General mental health status, patient characteristics, outcomes of care, and some elements of the process of care for individuals receiving outpatient mental health treatment	Structured self-administered questionnaire for patient and clinician plus follow-up assessments	207–210
Alcohol Outcomes Module (AOM)*	Process of care, patient characteristics, and outcomes of care for patients with alcohol dependence in inpatient and outpatient substance abuse treatment programs	Four components: Patient and Clinician Baseline Assessments, Patient Follow-Up Assessment, and Medical Record Review Form	210–213
Depression Outcomes Module (DOM)*	Process of care, patient characteristics, and outcomes of care for patients with major depressive disorder in mental health or primary care settings	Five components: Patient Screener for Major Depressive Disorder, Patient and Clinician Baseline Assessments, Patient Follow-Up Assessment, and Medical Record Review Form	213–215
Panic Outcomes Module (POM)	Process of care, patient characteristics, and outcomes of care for patients with panic disorder in primary care settings and in inpatient and outpatient specialty mental health care settings	Four components: Patient and Clinician Baseline Assessments, Patient Follow-Up Assessment, and Medical Record Review Form	216–218
Schizophrenia Outcomes Module (SCHIZOM)*	Process of care, patient characteristics, and outcomes of care for patients with schizophrenia in mental health care settings	Five components: Patient and Informant Baseline Assessments, Patient and Informant Follow-Up Assessments (fully structured interviews), and Medical Record Review Form	218–220

*Measure is included on the CD-ROM that accompanies this handbook.

measures of psychiatric symptom and functional status (Chapter 7, "General Psychiatric Symptoms Measures," and Chapter 8, "Mental Health Status, Functioning, and Disabilities Measures") could serve as generic psychiatric outcome measures, and disease-specific symptom measures (Section III, "Measures Related to DSM-IV Diagnostic Categories") could be used to assess disease-specific outcomes. However, these measures do not capture information about patient characteristics and processes of care that are crucial for allowing case mix to be factored into the apparent differences in outcome among different health care systems. Measures of patients' perceptions of quality of care, which may also be used to assess important aspects of practitioner and health care system performance, are covered in Chapter 12, "Patient Perceptions of Care Measures."

USING MEASURES IN THIS DOMAIN

Goals of Assessment

The goal of the instruments described in this chapter is to measure important processes and outcomes of care for patients with psychiatric and substance-related disorders. Regardless of whether these measurement systems collect data from individual patients during health care visits, from surveys of large numbers of patients, or from health system databases, they provide results that can be reported and interpreted at the level of individual providers, clinics, or entire health care systems. As noted in Tables 13–2, 13–3, and 13–4, access to care and satisfaction with care should be measured to fully assess the performance of practitioners and systems. However, these measurement domains are not specifically covered in this handbook.

As illustrated in Table 13–2, service utilization measurement instruments focus exclusively on the process of

care across disorder categories, measuring both the types (e.g., medication management and psychotherapy) and quantity (frequency and duration) of services received by patients. These instruments obtain service utilization data at either the patient level (via self-report or medical record review) or the system level (via administrative or clinical databases). Although most of these instruments collect data that can be attributed to specific patients, the measurements are generally interpreted for groups of patients to provide an indicator of practitioner or system performance. The instruments described in this chapter concentrate on service utilization issues, while also evaluating some aspects of patient characteristics, outcomes, or satisfaction.

Generic outcomes assessment instruments measure patient outcomes but do not focus on any one disorder (Table 13–3). Rather, these instruments assess general psychological symptoms, social functioning, and health status. They also measure patient characteristics to adjust for important differences in patient case mix (e.g., clinical severity). Some of these instruments quantify processes of care, such as number of psychotherapy sessions. These instruments collect data from patients and sometimes from clinicians. They are useful in measuring outcomes across diagnoses (e.g., in an entire clinic population) and can also be used to assess outcomes for disorders in which disease-specific measures have yet to be developed. Generic outcomes instruments can be used to examine outcomes of care for individual patients and also to provide an indication of the performance of practi-

TABLE 13–2 ■ Service utilization measures

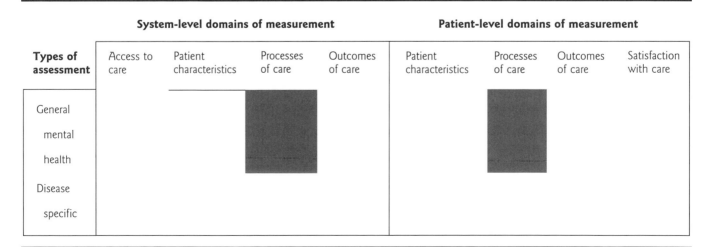

Types of assessment	System-level domains of measurement				Patient-level domains of measurement			
	Access to care	Patient characteristics	Processes of care	Outcomes of care	Patient characteristics	Processes of care	Outcomes of care	Satisfaction with care
General mental health			■			■		
Disease specific								

TABLE 13–3 ■ Generic outcomes assessment systems

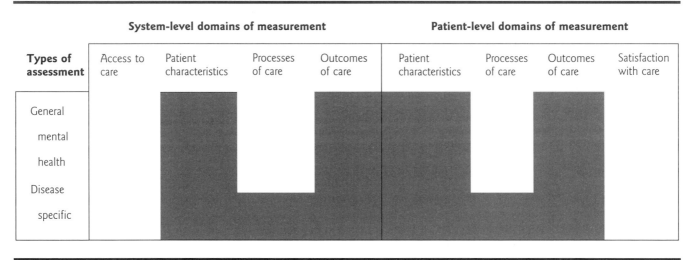

	System-level domains of measurement				Patient-level domains of measurement			
Types of assessment	Access to care	Patient characteristics	Processes of care	Outcomes of care	Patient characteristics	Processes of care	Outcomes of care	Satisfaction with care
General mental health								
Disease specific								

TABLE 13–4 ■ Disease-specific outcomes assessment systems

	System-level domains of measurement				Patient-level domains of measurement			
Types of assessment	Access to care	Patient characteristics	Processes of care	Outcomes of care	Patient characteristics	Processes of care	Outcomes of care	Satisfaction with care
General mental health								
Disease specific								

tioners and health care delivery systems. Sometimes health systems use a single rating scale to assess changes in general mental health status over time (for examples of such measures, see Chapter 8). Although these assessments can provide outcomes data for groups of patients, they are less useful than the instruments described in this chapter because they do not allow for case mix adjustment.

Disease-specific outcomes assessment instruments measure the processes and outcomes of care for specific disorders, as well as patient case mix characteristics associated with outcomes. Some of the disease-specific instruments described in this chapter include screening tools to identify patients who are likely to have the disorder, followed by questions with a basis in the corresponding DSM-IV diagnostic criteria to confirm the diagnosis. These instruments assess clinical and functional outcomes that are particularly relevant for the disorder of interest. The primary uses of disease-specific outcomes assessment instruments are to measure the performance of practitioners and health care delivery systems and, for individual patients, to monitor beneficial and adverse effects of treatment for specific disorders.

Although the generic and disease-specific outcomes assessment instruments have similar clinical uses, their approaches are fundamentally different. Generic outcomes assessment has its basis in theoretical models of patient response to treatment in general, without regard to diagnosis or disease-specific therapies. Thus, this approach could be used to monitor patients receiving treatment (regardless of diagnosis) when the similarities among patients in terms of both symptoms and treatment responses could outweigh differences in diagnosis. In contrast, the premise of disease-specific outcomes assessment is that many disorders have specific functional deficits and require specific treatments. Thus, selected elements of the process of care and disease-specific outcomes must be assessed.

Implementation Issues

In choosing a measure to assess various aspects of the quality of care, several factors must be considered, including the patient population of interest, the treatment setting(s), and the nature and extent of quality assessment to be undertaken. For example, the implementation of an outcomes management system to measure practitioner and system performance can impose burdens on patients, staff, and clinicians, depending on the measurement system employed and whether it can be integrated into the routine activities of the health care system. To reduce these burdens, many measurement systems attempt to minimize administration time for patients, practitioners, and the system as a whole. Some measures require a technician to interview patients, whereas others rely on patients and clinicians to complete self-administered questionnaires. In addition, some measures collect data from medical records or computerized information systems. The various data sources used entail different implementation strategies and resource requirements.

One important consideration in implementing an outcomes assessment system is when to begin measurement for a patient or group of patients. Patients are often enrolled in a measurement system when they first enter treatment. For a condition that usually consists of discrete episodes, such as major depressive disorder, such an approach is reasonable. However, for more chronic disorders such as schizophrenia, the appropriate trigger for initiating outcomes assessment is less clear. This consideration is particularly important when comparing the outcomes between different practitioners or systems be-

cause systematic differences in enrollment procedures can affect the validity of comparisons.

Issues in Interpreting Psychometric Data

Measurements of the process of care, including service utilization measures, may not adequately reflect the quality of the service being delivered. For example, service utilization measures typically count the number of mental health visits but do not assess the quality of the patient-provider interaction during each visit. Moreover, in comparing different systems of care or facilities, it is important to keep in mind that observed differences in service utilization may be the result of unequal patient access to that service rather than a real difference in the quality of care.

For some of the practitioner and system performance measures, data interpretation is complicated by the use of multiple informants (e.g., a patient and a clinician) to collect similar data. For example, in the DOM, both the patient and the clinician report the patient's depressive symptoms, and a symptom is rated as present if either informant reports it. For other measures, such as the SCHIZOM, this issue has not been fully resolved, and further research is under way to guide interpretation of data from multiple informants.

When interpreting service utilization and outcomes data, especially when comparing the performance of practitioners or systems, clinicians and administrators must consider at least two factors that contribute to variation in these data: random variation and differences in patient characteristics or prognosis (case mix). Because of the potential for random variation to affect outcomes measurements, a relatively large number of patients must be assessed to make meaningful comparisons of the performance of individual practitioners or systems. Comparisons must also account for any differences in patient case mix between two groups (see Chapter 4, "Considerations in Choosing, Using, and Interpreting Measures for Health Care Systems"). Some of the instruments described in this chapter collect case mix variables and provide guidance to users; consultation with experts in this area may also be useful when clinicians and administrators seek to evaluate the performance of practitioners or health care systems. Additionally, as with any assessment approach, measurement error and missing data can complicate interpretation of outcomes measures.

GUIDE TO THE SELECTION OF MEASURES

Several measures are available to assess service utilization. The HEDIS 3.0 measures mental health and chemical dependency service utilization, as well as some aspects of general medical and preventive care. Other scales in the HEDIS 3.0 assess health status (using the SF-36 Health Survey [p. 128]), access, patient satisfaction, and costs of care. The HEDIS measures are used to evaluate practitioner or system performance and do not generally assess individual patient change or outcome.

Two instruments described in this chapter quantify service utilization related to mental health and substance abuse problems and are used in conjunction with other outcomes assessment instruments. The CASA, designed to be administered with the Child and Adolescent Psychiatric Assessment (CAPA) (p. 301), provides patient and parent report of utilization from several service systems. The TSR, a companion instrument to the Addiction Severity Index (ASI) (p. 472), collects reports from adult patients regarding substance-related treatment and other services received during the course of care. The disease-specific outcomes modules also collect service utilization data.

Generic outcomes assessments can provide information on general symptoms and functioning for a large number of patients, without regard to psychiatric diagnosis. These assessments can be employed to inform treatment selection, to monitor beneficial and adverse effects of treatment, and to assess health care delivery system performance.

Disease-specific outcomes instruments, such as the DOM, POM, AOM, and SCHIZOM, can be used to monitor beneficial and adverse effects of treatment for specific disorders and to assess health care delivery system performance. Although these instruments assess general symptoms, they also assess the quality of care for one disorder or tracer condition. An organization's quality improvement efforts for patients with that disorder may also improve care of patients with other disorders in that facility or setting. Also, because these outcomes assessment instruments collect disease-specific data on both processes of care and outcomes of care, they are ideal for measuring compliance with disease-specific practice guidelines (Rost et al. 1995).

CURRENT STATUS AND FUTURE RESEARCH NEEDS FOR ASSESSMENT

The strengths of the existing instruments in this domain include their measurement of important aspects of the process of care and/or patient outcomes of care and their inclusion of both functional and symptom outcomes measures. The patient outcomes assessment instruments, whether generic or disease specific, can be used to monitor treatments and outcomes for individual patients and the performance of practitioners and health care delivery systems.

Instruments designed to assess the quality of health care have several limitations. Of particular concern is how closely a measure of a process or outcome represents the true quality of care being delivered. For instance, a service utilization measure that simply counts the number of mental health visits does nothing to assess the quality of care during each visit. Similarly, patients who did not have a follow-up outpatient visit within 30 days of hospital discharge may have received high-quality follow-up services by telephone or in another setting. Patients who receive follow-up services on the 31st day after discharge are probably not actually receiving lower-quality care than their counterparts who receive follow-up services on the 29th day after discharge. For outcomes measures to be related to the true quality of care, they must measure important constructs (i.e., clinical severity, functioning, and quality of life) reliably and validly.

Limitations of these instruments include the potential burden that their implementation can impose on busy providers or systems, the lack of documented cost-effectiveness of implementing these systems, and the need for guidance in the interpretation of data collected in routine clinical settings. Users of these measures must be aware that relatively new methods such as case mix adjustment have not been fully developed and require more research; those who use the measures must therefore exercise caution in interpreting the data they collect. Most of the measures in this chapter have been studied in relatively small patient samples, and more research is needed to identify strengths and weaknesses of the measures in different populations and settings. Also, rather than using the results generated by these instruments to penalize practitioners whose performance is outside the norm, the observations should be viewed as descriptive in nature and used to explore possible changes in health care delivery (Berwick 1989). Other future research needs in this area include clarification of the use of data provided by collateral informants, especially in areas in which patients' cognitive functioning may be compromised. In addition, further research is needed to better understand how to adjust for differences in case mix between practitioners or systems and also to what degree differences in practitioner or system performance are judged to be statistically significant and clinically meaningful.

REFERENCES AND SUGGESTED READINGS

Berwick DM: Continuous improvement as an ideal in health care. N Engl J Med 320:53–56, 1989

Donabedian A: Explorations in Quality Assessment and Monitoring. Ann Arbor, MI, Health Administration Press, 1980

Rost K, Wherry J, Williams C, et al: The process and outcomes of care for major depression in rural family practice settings. Journal of Rural Health 11:114–121, 1995

Smith GR, Rost K, Fischer EP, et al: Assessing the effectiveness of mental health care in routine clinical practice: critical components, administration, and application of outcomes modules. Evaluation and the Health Professions 20:65–80, 1997

Health Plan Employer Data and Information Set (HEDIS), Version 3.0

Committee on Performance Measurement, National Committee for Quality Assurance

GOALS

The Health Plan Employer Data and Information Set (HEDIS), version 3.0 (National Committee for Quality Assurance 1996), is used primarily to provide data about the process of care by assessing health plan performance rather than individual patient change or outcome. The

HEDIS 3.0, developed by the National Committee for Quality Assurance, is a set of standardized performance measures designed to provide information needed by purchasers and consumers to compare the performance of managed-care organizations and to provide health plans with the information needed for quality monitoring and improvement. This version, the most recent, includes a broad spectrum of clinical effectiveness measures, assesses health plan performance for acute and chronic disease, and includes measures for medical, psychiatric, and substance-related disorders. The measure also provides some information about a health plan's ability to maintain or improve the physical and mental health functioning outcomes of its Medicare beneficiaries. Specific measures within each of the eight major areas of performance were selected on the basis of three criteria:

1. Relevance and value to purchasers and consumers
2. Reasonable ability of health plans to develop and provide the requested data in the specified manner
3. Potential impact on improving the process of care delivery

DESCRIPTION

The HEDIS 3.0 is a collection of more than 100 performance measures that standardize health plan measurement in the following eight areas:

1. Effectiveness of Care
2. Access to and Availability of Care
3. Satisfaction With the Experience of Care
4. Health Plan Stability
5. Service Utilization
6. Cost of Care
7. Informed Health Care Choices
8. Health Plan Descriptive Information

The HEDIS 3.0 measures are designed so that data can be obtained from computer databases or medical records. Measures are expressed as percentages, as presence or absence of specific services, and as readmission rates for a specified provider or set of providers.

The performance measures published in the HEDIS 3.0 are divided into two categories: reporting set measures and testing set measures. Health plans were expected to begin using the reporting set measures in 1997. The testing set contains new measures that require more validation before they can become part of the reporting set.

Several of the HEDIS 3.0 reporting set measures intended for current use are specifically relevant to mental health care. The Effectiveness of Care domain is measured by the percentage of plan members hospitalized for treatment of specified mental health disorders who were seen for follow-up within 30 days of discharge. The psychiatric disorders of interest assessed by the HEDIS 3.0 include major depressive disorder, bipolar disorder, schizophrenia, several child and adolescent disorders, and personality disorders. Previous versions of the HEDIS limited this measure to the diagnosis of major depressive disorder. The Medicare Health Outcomes Survey measure (formerly the Health of Seniors Survey), also in the Effectiveness of Care domain, monitors changes in mental and physical health status over a 2-year period. This measure, in contrast to the other reporting set measures, collects individual patient reports of functioning through use of the SF-36 Health Survey (p. 128).

Within the Access to and Availability of Care domain, the availability of mental health and chemical dependency providers for each plan is reported as the number and percentage of such providers in the health plan, with categories for open, restricted, and closed panel types.

Service Utilization measures are reported separately for mental health and chemical dependency services. These measures include the percentage of plan members receiving inpatient services, day or night services, and ambulatory services; the number of inpatient discharges and average length of stay; and readmission rates.

Several categories of measures are of interest to all health plans, including mental health plans. For example, the domain of Satisfaction With the Experience of Care is measured using the Annual Member Health Care Survey of the National Committee for Quality Assurance. In future versions of the HEDIS, this survey will be adapted for use with Medicaid and Medicare populations. The Health Plan Stability measures provide information on member disenrollment, provider turnover, and financial stability. High-occurrence and high-cost diagnosis-related groups and rate trends are reported in the Cost of Care domain. The Informed Health Care Choices domain includes information on language translation services and new member orientation and education. Finally, Health Plan Descriptive Information covers a wide range of issues concerning the plan's providers and programs, including chemical dependency services and descriptions of pediatric mental health networks.

The testing set measures, which are still being evaluated and refined, include several measures relevant to mental health and substance-related disorders and mental health plans. These measures assess the availability of medication management and psychotherapy services for patients with schizophrenia, appropriate use of psychiatric medications, continuation of treatment for depression, family visits for children undergoing treatment, patient satisfaction with mental health care, continuity of care for substance abuse patients, substance abuse counseling for adolescents, failure of substance abuse treatment, and screening for chemical dependency. Other measures of interest in the testing set deal with problems obtaining care, health plan cost per member per month, and use of behavioral services. A member disenrollment survey is also included in the testing set measures.

Specific instructions are provided for calculating each HEDIS 3.0 measure using data obtained from administrative databases or medical records. However, the authors do not provide specific guidance for interpreting the results. The HEDIS 3.0 was designed to provide information to consumers, providers, and purchasers to help them compare health plan performance; thus, these measures are interpreted from several different perspectives. The authors state that no single statistic should be interpreted in isolation; rather, patterns of performance should be examined to identify areas of strength and weakness. The authors suggest that the measures might be grouped to identify important patterns of performance by domain, type of care, population, and clinical condition. In addition, because there is no absolute standard of performance, interpretation of these measures is only meaningful relative to previous performance or to the performance of other plans.

PRACTICAL ISSUES

The HEDIS 3.0 can be purchased from

National Committee for Quality Assurance
1350 New York Avenue, N.W., Suite 700
Washington, DC 20005
Phone: 800-839-6487

The HEDIS 3.0 is copyrighted by the National Committee for Quality Assurance. Four volumes that contain instructions for collecting and scoring performance measures are available:

1. *HEDIS 3.0 Narrative: What's in It and Why It Matters*
2. *Technical Specifications*
3. *HEDIS 3.0 Member Satisfaction Survey*
4. *A Road Map for Information Systems: Evolving Systems to Support Performance Measurement*

These volumes may be purchased separately or in several combinations; the entire four-volume set costs $375.00. Volumes 2 and 3 are available for $250.00; however, the authors recommend purchasing at least one copy of Volume 1. No specific training is specified to use the HEDIS 3.0, although compiling information for all elements generally requires the input of administrators, data managers, and providers.

PSYCHOMETRIC PROPERTIES

The SF-36 Health Survey (p. 128), included in the Medicare Health Outcomes Survey, has extensive psychometric data available. Because the other components of the HEDIS 3.0 are derived from data collected from medical records or databases, they do not have psychometric properties. Accuracy and completeness of available data should thus be considered when interpreting the measures.

CLINICAL UTILITY

The primary use of the HEDIS 3.0 is to assess health insurance plans or health care organization performance rather than to assess performance at the level of patients, practitioners, or individual clinics. The authors note that use of the HEDIS 3.0 enables purchasers (both private and public) to compare health plans and to monitor plan performance. In addition, regulators may use HEDIS 3.0 data as part of their oversight process. Finally, consumers can use HEDIS 3.0 data to make informed choices about health plans. The principal advantage of the HEDIS 3.0 in comparing the performance of health plans is its standardization of measurement and potential for automated data collection and reporting. However, interpretation of scores on many of the measures is a complex process. Observers must consider how differences in plan membership (i.e., case mix), health care delivery systems, and benefit plans will affect the measures. For instance, a mental health plan designed for consumers with severe psychiatric disorders would be expected to have a different pattern of effectiveness and utilization than a mental health plan designed for the general population. Another limitation is that measures derived largely from administrative data sources generally are imperfect indicators of the actual quality of health care. For example, the only Effectiveness of Care measure in the reporting set specific to mental health applies only to hospitalized patients and only to specified diagnoses. Although follow-up after hospital discharge for these patients is an important indicator of quality, other critical aspects of mental health treatment are not captured in the measures. Finally, any measurement system that relies on clinical or administrative data is only as good as the quality of these data. Variations in data collection and management procedures among health plans could result in varying validity of the measures, thus further complicating comparisons among plans.

REFERENCES AND SUGGESTED READINGS

Corrigan JM, Nielsen DM: Toward the development of uniform reporting standards for managed care organizations: the Health Plan Employer Data and Information Set (Version 2.0). Journal on Quality Improvement 19:566–575, 1993

National Committee for Quality Assurance: The Health Plan Employer Data and Information Set (Version 3.0). Washington, DC, National Committee for Quality Assurance, 1996

Child and Adolescent Services Assessment (CASA)

B. J. Burns, A. Angold, K. Magruder-Habib, E. J. Costello, and M. K. S. Patrick

GOALS

The primary goal of the Child and Adolescent Services Assessment (CASA) (Burns et al. 1994) is to collect information about service utilization by children ages 8–18 for mental health or substance abuse problems. The CASA also collects data about attitudes toward treatment and barriers to service use. The CASA was developed to aid researchers interested in children's mental health issues. It is designed to be used in conjunction with the Child and Adolescent Psychiatric Assessment (CAPA) (p. 301) or other assessments of psychiatric symptoms. The CASA interview links service use to specific mental health or behavior problems reported during the psychiatric interview. Services measured include those offered by a variety of public-sector providers (e.g., health, mental health, substance abuse, social service, education, and juvenile justice), by private providers, and by informal, personal, and community resources. Services are defined to include efforts to identify, diagnose, or treat emotional, behavioral, or substance-related problems.

DESCRIPTION

The CASA is a rater-administered, semistructured, face-to-face interview with child-report and informant-report (parent) components. It includes four sections: the Child Health Services Screen, the Detailed Child Health Services Form, Attitudes Toward Services for Children and Adolescents, and Family Demographic and Financial Information (in the parent version). A short version of the CASA has also been developed for telephone administration. The CASA covers 31 settings, including inpatient, outpatient, and informal services, and a variety of providers and sectors. It includes sections covering the following kinds of care: inpatient, out of home (e.g., residential care), and outpatient treatment; crisis services;

services from non–mental health professionals (including social services and general medical services); school services; nonprofessional help (e.g., peers, clergy, and self-help groups); and juvenile justice services. The CASA begins by screening for lifetime service use in each of these settings, as well as any service use within the past 3 months. If services have been used in one of these settings or sectors within 3 months, more detailed questions are asked about these services. The CASA also includes questions about attitudes toward treatment, out-of-pocket costs for treatment, and perceived barriers to seeking treatment. A sample question is provided in Example 13–1. The child and parent versions are essentially the same, although the parent version also includes questions about family finances and demographics.

The CASA provides a wealth of specific data about service use. The authors have analyzed service utilization data in the following categories:

- Total count of services used in each of 31 categories
- Dichotomous indicator of any service use in each category (lifetime or past 3 months)
- Assessment of satisfaction with selected services (inpatient, outpatient, and physician)

PRACTICAL ISSUES

It takes approximately 20 minutes for a child who has used a substantial amount of services to complete the CASA interview. A shorter telephone version has been developed for follow-up interviews. The CASA is available from

> Developmental Epidemiology Program
> CASA Requests
> Duke University Medical Center
> Box 3454

EXAMPLE 13–1 ■ Sample item from the Child and Adolescent Services Assessment

> Have you gotten private professional help from a psychiatrist or psychologist?

Reprinted with permission.

Durham, NC 27710

Phone: 919-687-4686, ext. 222

The CASA is copyrighted. Parent and child interviews cost $25.00. A package that includes the interviews, scoring instructions, a glossary, training materials, and additional information is available for $35.00. A 1-day training course given by the authors is recommended. Audiotapes and videotapes of model interviews are available to supplement the didactic material and practice sessions.

PSYCHOMETRIC PROPERTIES

Reliability

Test-retest reliability for the total number of services reported at time 1 and time 2 (a 1-week interval) showed a high correlation among a clinical sample of children who were newly admitted to either an outpatient clinic or an inpatient facility. Agreement varied substantially across the service categories. In general, highest reliability was associated with the most restrictive types of services, and lowest reliability was noted for assessments of services that occurred within the child's natural environment. Specifically, high test-retest reliability was found for both the past 3 months and lifetime reports of inpatient services, out-of-home placements, and juvenile justice services (kappa of 0.79–1.0 for child reports and 0.61–1.0 for parent reports; $n = 7$–34 children reporting services out of a total of 77). For services provided within the child's natural environment (nonprofessional and school categories), kappa values were in the range of 0.36–0.48 for children ($n = 29$–51) and 0.57–0.62 for parents. For services with a midlevel of restrictiveness (outpatient, crisis, and non–mental health professional services), kappa values fell between 0.51 and 0.62 for children ($n = 11$–55) and between 0.47 and 0.81 for parents.

Validity

Validity was assessed by comparing CASA data with data from a mental health center's management information system. When children had received a given service according to these records, the CASA interviews elicited this information 80%–100% of the time ($n = 56$ children, 50 parents), with the exception of case manager services, which showed agreement 58% of the time. The highest agreement reported was for therapeutic foster care (100%).

CLINICAL UTILITY

The CASA was designed to be used to gather information about service utilization by children and adolescents with mental health and substance abuse problems. The CASA can be used to complement the CAPA or similarly structured psychiatric interviews. The CASA interview is relatively short and easy to administer; it provides information on services in multiple sectors, including informal services. Although this instrument was developed for use in mental health services research, it could also be used to help clinicians better understand the range of services received by children and adolescents, as well as attitudes toward and perceived barriers to treatment. The authors state that the primary limitation of the CASA is the lower reliability of reports of use of school and informal services than of inpatient, outpatient, and other services. Nevertheless, the CASA overcomes the limitations of other data collection methods (e.g., chart review) in obtaining data concerning use of services from all sources of care in multiple settings and sectors.

REFERENCES AND SUGGESTED READINGS

Ascher BH, Farmer EMZ, Burns BJ, et al: The Child and Adolescent Services Assessment (CASA): description and psychometrics. Journal of Emotional and Behavioral Disorders 4:12–20, 1996

Burns BJ, Angold A, Magruder-Habib K, et al: The Child and Adolescent Services Assessment (CASA), Parent Interview and Child Interview. Durham, NC, Developmental Epidemiology Program, Department of Psychiatry, Duke University Medical Center, 1994

Burns BJ, Costello EJ, Angold A, et al: Children's mental health service use across service sectors. Health Aff (Millwood) 14:147–159, 1995

Burns BJ, Farmer EMZ, Angold A, et al: A randomized trial of case management for youths with serious emotional disturbance. Journal of Clinical Child Psychology 25:476–486, 1996

Farmer EMZ, Angold A, Burns BJ, et al: Reliability of self-reported service use: test-retest consistency of children's responses to the child and adolescent services assessment (CASA). Journal of Child and Family Studies 3:307–325, 1994

Treatment Services Review (TSR)

A. T. McLellan, D. Zanis, R. Incmikoski, G. Parikh, G. Stevens, and M. Brock

GOALS

The goal of the Treatment Services Review (TSR) (McLellan et al. 1989) is to provide a quantitative profile of the number and types of treatment services received by patients during alcohol and drug abuse rehabilitation. It is designed to be used in conjunction with the Addiction Severity Index (ASI) (p. 472) and focuses on the same seven problem areas as the ASI. These areas are typically affected by substance-related disorders: medical, employment, alcohol, drug, legal, family or social, and psychiatric.

DESCRIPTION

The TSR is a brief interview designed to provide information on the type, amount, and efficacy of services provided, directly or indirectly, to a substance abuse patient by his or her treatment program. The TSR was designed as a structured, technician-administered interview. Each of the seven problem areas is divided into four sections. The first section requests the patient to report the number of days that a target behavior or problem occurred during the past 2 weeks. The second section asks about the number of times during the past 2 weeks that a professional or specialist provided services. The third section records the significant group or individual discussions that were pertinent to the particular problem area during the previous week. Finally, in both the professional ser-

vices and the discussion sections of each TSR problem area, the patient is asked to report whether the services, sessions, or discussions received were from a separate agency, organization, or individual provider (out program) or from the actual treatment program (in program). The TSR contains 46 items; a sample question is provided in Example 13–2.

For each of the seven problem areas, summary or composite scores are calculated as the sum of the number of professional or specialist services (service composite score) and the number of significant group or individual discussions (discussion composite score) received by each patient during treatment. At the program or practitioner level, these composite scores can be averaged across the number of patients sampled to provide summary measures of the treatment program or practitioner under study.

PRACTICAL ISSUES

Administration of the TSR takes approximately 10 minutes, on average. The TSR is designed for administration by a trained technician in person or by telephone. Technicians are trained in administering the TSR by reading the manual and practicing the interview. The TSR and an administration manual are available without charge from

> A. Thomas McLellan, Ph.D.
> Building 7
> Philadelphia VA Medical Center
> University Avenue
> Philadelphia, PA 19104
> Phone: 215-823-5809

The TSR is included on the CD-ROM that accompanies this handbook.

EXAMPLE 13–2 ■ **Sample item from the Treatment Services Review**

> How many times did you see a nurse, nurse-practitioner, or physician's assistant in the past 2 weeks?

Reprinted with permission.

PSYCHOMETRIC PROPERTIES

Reliability

Test-retest reliability was high for in-person interviews spaced 1 day apart. Kappa coefficients were 0.62 or higher in each of the seven TSR problem areas; exact agreement averaged 88% among the problem areas ($n = 80$). In addition, agreement was high between in-person interviews and telephone administration; the average percentage of agreement across all seven problem areas was 94% ($n = 80$).

Validity

When patient self-report of services using the TSR was compared with information in medical records, no significant differences were found; correlations between measures from these two sources ranged from 0.52 to 0.91 ($n = 80$). The TSR discriminated between groups of patients receiving different levels of care ($n - 18-22$ in each group), finding significant differences in the overall amount of services provided to patients assigned to different levels. Subsequent analysis found significant between-level differences for four of the seven problem areas. Need for treatment in three problem areas (medical, drug, and psychiatric), as determined using the ASI (p. 472), was significantly correlated with the TSR measure of services received in these areas ($r = 0.45-0.77$).

CLINICAL UTILITY

The TSR is useful for assessing the performance of clinics or programs that provide substance abuse treatment services. Specifically, data from the TSR can be used to compare service delivery patterns among different treatment programs and among different patients within the same program. Ultimately, this information is useful in understanding relationships between patient outcomes and the nature and amount of treatment delivered. Advantages of this measure include its brevity and its compatibility with the ASI (p. 472). The authors have performed a series of studies demonstrating the reliability and validity of the TSR in different settings. However, a limitation is that the TSR measures only the nature and quantity of services, not the quality of care delivered.

REFERENCES AND SUGGESTED READINGS

McLellan AT, Zanis D, Incmikoski R, et al: Administration Manual for the Treatment Services Review, "TSR," Version 5. Philadelphia, PA, 1989 [Phone: 215-823-5809]

McLellan AT, Alterman AI, Cacciola J, et al: A new measure of substance abuse treatment: initial studies of the Treatment Services Review. J Nerv Ment Dis 180:101–110, 1992

McLellan AT, Grissom GR, Zanis D, et al: Improved outcomes from treatment matching in substance abuse patients. Arch Gen Psychiatry 54:730–735, 1997

COMPASS OP

K. I. Howard, P. L. Brill, and G. Grissom

GOALS

The COMPASS OP (outpatient) (Howard et al. 1995) is used primarily to assess general mental health status, patient characteristics, outcomes of care, and some elements of the process of care for individuals receiving outpatient treatment for any mental disorder. Although the COMPASS OP could be used to address research questions, it is primarily designed to provide a general and standardized measure of the severity of a patient's condition and to monitor the patient's condition over time. Changes in the COMPASS OP outcomes measures are used to monitor progress, detect unsuccessful treatment, and help providers adjust treatment as indicated. Data collected with the COMPASS OP can also be aggregated to establish norms and benchmarks and to demonstrate trends on a systemwide site and provider basis. The COMPASS OP also measures a client's satisfaction with care.

DESCRIPTION

The COMPASS OP is a questionnaire for the assessment of outpatients with any diagnosis of mental disorder. The primary outcome assessed by the COMPASS OP is a composite measure of mental health status, including an evaluation of well-being, symptoms, and functioning. At the initial clinic visit, the patient completes a self-administered questionnaire containing 109 items, and the clinician completes an 11-item questionnaire about a patient's symptoms and functioning at baseline. Follow-up assessments contain fewer items. All items are always administered and are in the form of multiple-choice, 5- or 6-point Likert scale, and yes-no questions. A sample item is provided in Example 13–3. Items are organized into three subscales (Well-being, Symptom, and Functioning) on the basis of patient self-reported well-being, symptoms, and functioning. These three subscales make up what is called the Mental Health Index, which is also used as the progress score. In the most current version, there are 33 items on the Symptom subscale, 17 items on the Functioning subscale, and 6 items on the Well-Being subscale. The authors recommend that the COMPASS OP questionnaires be completed at the first session, after the fourth session, and every six sessions thereafter.

In an effort to more widely distribute the COMPASS OP, Integra has assembled the COMPASS Suite, which includes instruments for outpatient, inpatient, chemical dependency, and primary care physician use. Further information on the COMPASS Suite can be found on Integra's Web site (www.Integra-ease.com). Because psychometric data are not yet available for these measures, this section focuses on the COMPASS OP.

The COMPASS Mental Health Index (MHI) is the overall aggregate score from the COMPASS OP and is computed by summing the three subscales. Outcome is operationally defined in the COMPASS system as the change in the patient's MHI score over the course of treatment. These outcome scores are then compared with predicted outcomes using a weighted formula derived from multiple regression techniques to adjust for patient characteristics and treatment experience. These severity-adjusted calculations indicate, for every case, the degree of patient improvement that would be expected after case mix adjustment for duration of treatment (number of sessions), initial severity (MHI score at intake), and patient characteristics that have been shown to affect outcomes. Outcomes scores are standardized by conversion to T-scores. An MHI score of ≥ 83 means that the person's responses closely resemble those of someone who is not in need of therapy.

Outcomes data for programs or providers can be adjusted by computing the difference between each patient's expected and actual outcomes and aggregating these adjusted scores across all patients treated by the program or provider. These difference scores can be used to compare program or provider performance, taking into account patient case mix differences.

PRACTICAL ISSUES

It takes about 25 minutes for patients and 5 minutes for clinicians to complete the COMPASS OP at the initial visit. It takes patients about 15 minutes to complete each follow-up assessment, and clinicians can complete the follow-up questionnaire in 3 minutes. The COMPASS OP is copyrighted. Information and a manual may be obtained from

> Integra, Inc.
> 1060 First Avenue, Suite 400
> King of Prussia, PA 19406-1336
> Phone: 610-992-7000

The cost of using the COMPASS OP is determined by the vendor, depending on the customer's needs. For example, pricing may be determined on a subscription basis that ranges from $1.00 or less per administration if purchased in bulk. Project pricing is available for those seeking an outcomes management system. Software is available to allow on-site scanning and scoring of data, and data forms can also be faxed to the COMPASS Fax Service Bureau for automated scoring and report generation. Forms can also be mailed to Integra, Inc., for standard data entry. Training in use of the COMPASS OP is recommended, and an on-site training course for staff and

EXAMPLE 13–3 ■ Sample item from the COMPASS OP

> How often during the past 2 weeks have you had the following experiences: . . . Feeling hopeless about the future?

Reprinted with permission.

clinical managers is available. Other training materials are also available. The COMPASS OP has been translated into French and Spanish.

The COMPASS OP is included on the CD-ROM that accompanies this handbook.

PSYCHOMETRIC PROPERTIES

Reliability

The internal consistency (alpha) of the COMPASS OP MHI and its subscales ranges from $r = 0.79$ to 0.94 ($n = 70–197$). The internal consistency of the Therapeutic Bond scale is 0.88, on the basis of $1,256$ observations. The clinician-rated scales (Life Functioning and Clinical Assessment Index) also have adequate internal consistency of $r = 0.84–0.86$ ($n = 1,237–1,459$). Test-retest reliability of the COMPASS OP MHI and its subscales was high, with intraclass correlation coefficients of 0.82 for administration of the Subjective Well-Being scale at a 1-week interval ($n = 93$) and $0.76–0.85$ for the other scales when administered 3–4 weeks apart ($n = 48–213$). Test-retest reliability of the Therapeutic Bond scale administered at the first and third psychotherapy sessions was $r = 0.62$ ($n = 157$). For the clinician scales, test-retest reliability ranged from $r = 0.68$ to 0.77 ($n = 81$).

Validity

The Subjective Well-Being scale correlated with the General Well-Being scale ($r = 0.79$) and with the SF-36 Health Survey scales (p. 128) ($r = 0.73–0.76$), including the SF-36 Mental Health Index ($n = 108$). In 249 patients, the Current Symptoms scale correlated with the Symptom Checklist–90—Revised (SCL-90-R, 47-item version) (p. 81) ($r = 0.91$). The Depression subscale of the Current Symptoms scale also correlated with scores from the Center for Epidemiologic Studies Depression Scale (CES-D) (p. 523) ($r = 0.68$, $n = 272$) and the Beck Depression Inventory (BDI) (p. 519) ($r = 0.87$). Moreover, patients with a diagnosis of major depressive disorder according to the Structured Clinical Interview for DSM Axis I Disorders (SCID-I) (p. 49) had significantly higher scores on the Depression subscale than other patients ($n = 44$). The clinician scales for Life Functioning correlated with the Global Assessment Scale (GAS) (p. 96) ($r = 0.74$, $n = 1,459$).

Normative longitudinal data are available on nearly 6,000 patients, and the authors state that the availability of these data allows those using the COMPASS OP to judge whether improvement is occurring at the expected rate in an individual. This normative information also allows judgments to be made in the aggregate concerning whether a program or provider is achieving expected levels of treatment effectiveness.

CLINICAL UTILITY

The primary clinical uses of the COMPASS systems include assessing clinical features to inform treatment selection and monitoring beneficial and adverse effects of treatment. The primary administrative use of the COMPASS OP is to assess the performance of health care delivery systems.

According to the authors, the initial COMPASS OP assessment provides useful information about the need for treatment by comparing the patient's score with standardized scores from the population not in need of mental health treatment (i.e., an MHI score of ≥ 83). The COMPASS OP reports also note critical signs such as substance abuse, suicidality, and severe depression. Advantages of the COMPASS system include standardization of clinical information collection and display and comparison with norms from patient and nonpatient populations. This information system can supplement the clinical interview but cannot replace it or provide diagnostic classification.

The COMPASS OP has also been used to monitor progress in therapy and to compare a patient's status with that of a large group of patients. With a system such as the COMPASS OP, the therapist (or an administrator) can monitor a patient's clinical status over time and compare it with the patient's prior status (improvement) and with clinical norms. The COMPASS OP was originally developed for patients with any mental disorder diagnosis in outpatient psychotherapy and thus does not collect case mix or outcomes data that may be important for more severe conditions. Although the COMPASS INT (Intensive) was developed for a more severely ill population, its value in monitoring outcomes may be limited by its broad scope and lack of condition-specific information.

The COMPASS systems can be used to assess the performance of mental health care systems by aggregating data; the adjustment for case mix differences is particularly important in this regard. Limitations in this use are that available case mix variables may not capture enough of the true case differences and that relatively large samples of patients and clinicians are needed to avoid making incorrect inferences on the basis of random variations in care and resulting outcomes.

REFERENCES AND SUGGESTED READINGS

Howard KI, Kopta SM, Krause MS, et al: The dose-effect relationship in psychotherapy. Am Psychol 41:159–164, 1986

Howard KI, Lueger RJ, Maling MS, et al: A phase model of psychotherapy outcome: causal mediation of change. J Consult Clin Psychol 61:678–685, 1993

Howard KI, Brill PL, Lueger RJ, et al: COMPASS OP: Psychometric Properties. King of Prussia, PA, Compass Information Services, 1995

Howard KI, Moras K, Brill PL, et al: Evaluation of psychotherapy: efficacy, effectiveness, and patient progress. Am Psychol 51:1059–1064, 1996

Sperry L: Psychopharmacology and Psychotherapy: Strategies for Maximizing Treatment Outcomes. New York, Brunner/Mazel, 1995

Alcohol Outcomes Module (AOM)

G. R. Smith Jr., T. Babor, M. A. Burnam, B. J. Burns, K. Kelleher, and K. Rost

GOALS

The Alcohol Outcomes Module (AOM) (Smith et al. 1994a) is used primarily to assess the process of care, patient characteristics, and outcomes of care for patients with alcohol dependence in inpatient and outpatient substance abuse treatment programs. Although the data collected by the AOM can be used to address research questions or to inform treatment decisions for individual patients, the AOM was primarily designed to be used as part of an outcomes management system in which data are aggregated at the provider or system level to monitor and improve patient outcomes. The AOM verifies that the individual being assessed has a diagnosis of alcohol dependence according to DSM-III-R criteria, provides data about patient outcomes (including severity and disease-specific and general functional status), assesses case mix variables to permit adjustment for comparisons across patient or practitioner groups, and quantifies the type and extent of treatment services patients receive for alcohol abuse or dependence. This information provides a framework that enables clinicians and quality managers to study how the care provided affects outcomes for patients with alcohol abuse or dependence.

DESCRIPTION

Patients with clinician-determined alcohol abuse or dependence diagnoses are appropriate for assessment according to the AOM protocol. The AOM has four components that elicit data about individual patients from a variety of sources, including the patients themselves, clinicians, and administrative records. The four components are as follows:

1. Patient Baseline Assessment
2. Clinician Baseline Assessment
3. Patient Follow-Up Assessment
4. Medical Record Review Form

The Patient Baseline Assessment includes 113 items and is completed by the patient at the initial visit for alcohol dependence treatment. The similar Patient Follow-Up Assessment (89 items) is performed at the 5-month follow-up. The Patient Baseline and Follow-Up Assessments contain questions about the severity of drinking (quantity and frequency) and physical, emotional, and social consequences. The three outcome measures of physical, social, and emotional consequences are composed of questions sorted into these domains from existing instruments. Items that scored $r = 0.30$ or higher on item-to-scale correlations were retained. Comorbid substance abuse is also assessed. Functional status measures include bed and disability days, lost work days, and an assessment of functional status using the SF-36 Health Survey (p. 128). The Clinician Baseline Assessment is a brief instrument (20 items) that the clinician completes at baseline to provide information on diagnosis of alcohol abuse or dependence, physical symptoms of alcoholism, and the type and extent of treatment at intake. Most questions on the Patient Baseline and Follow-Up Assessments and Clinician Baseline Assessment are multiple choice, although a few write-in questions are included on the Patient Baseline and Follow-Up Assessments and the Medical Record Review. The Medical Record Review contains 6 yes-no items that may be retrieved from written or computerized medical records. Sample items from the Patient Baseline Assessment, Clinician Baseline Assessment, and Medical Record Review are provided in Example 13–4.

The assessments generate several scores. The DSM-III-R diagnosis of alcohol dependence is best determined according to criterion-based questions in the Patient Baseline Assessment. Outcomes variables are calculated as the difference between baseline and follow-up measures for the following variables: alcohol consumption in the month before the assessment (quantity times frequency), physical consequences (mean of 6 items, range of 1–5), emotional consequences (mean of 5 items, range of 1–6), and social consequences (mean of 5 items, range of 1–2). Drug use at follow-up is scored as present or absent. The SF-36 health status scales are scored in the usual manner (range of 0–100). Although the change scores for these variables serve as

a measure of outcome, patient (case mix) characteristics must be controlled for when making comparisons across providers or across different systems of care. The AOM collects data about these characteristics, including baseline severity, previous treatments, age at onset, parental alcoholism, social support, support for sobriety, psychiatric comorbidities, alcohol-related physical problems, and parenting responsibilities. Complex statistical issues arise in performing these analyses, and relatively large sample sizes are needed to meaningfully compare the performance of different providers or systems.

PRACTICAL ISSUES

It takes about 20 minutes to complete the Patient Baseline Assessment and about 14 minutes to complete the Patient Follow-Up Assessment. The Clinician Baseline Assessment requires up to 5 minutes to complete. The Medical Record Review takes approximately 25 minutes to complete by hand and less time if computerized records are available. The AOM is available for $35.00, or for $25.00 per module if two or more modules (e.g., the Depression Outcomes Module [DOM], the Panic Outcomes Module [POM], or the Schizophrenia Outcomes Module [SCHIZOM]) are ordered simultaneously, from

Centers for Outcomes Research and Effectiveness
University of Arkansas for Medical Sciences
5800 West 10th Street, Suite 605
Little Rock, AR 72204
Phone: 501-660-7550

The AOM is copyrighted, but it is available for unlimited free use if it is used in clinical care or research without charge to patients. A user's manual with scoring instructions is included with each order (Smith et al. 1994b). No specific training is required to administer the AOM.

The AOM is included on the CD-ROM that accompanies this handbook.

PSYCHOMETRIC PROPERTIES

Reliability

The reliability and validity of the AOM were established in a sample of 78 inpatients beginning treatment for al-

---

EXAMPLE 13–4 ■ Sample items from the Alcohol Outcomes Module

Patient Baseline and Follow-Up Assessments
Has either your mother or father had drinking problems?

Clinician Baseline Assessment
Has the patient reported any of the following symptoms during the past 6 months? (e.g., drinking alcohol to relieve or avoid withdrawal symptoms)

Medical Record Review
Please complete the following information about the chemical dependency program the patient participated in at the time of baseline assessment (e.g., outpatient program (yes/no) number of days ____).

Reprinted with permission.

cohol dependence; follow-up assessments were performed on 85% of these patients 5 months after the baseline assessments to examine cross-sectional and longitudinal relationships with gold standard assessments. The three outcome scales from the Patient Baseline and Follow-Up Assessments (physical, emotional, and social consequences) have demonstrated good to excellent internal consistency, with Cronbach's alpha coefficients of 0.72–0.88 ($n = 78$). The test-retest reliability of case mix variables and the measure of alcohol consumption have been established; intraclass correlation coefficients range from 0.56 to 0.94. The test-retest interval was 3 days.

Validity

There was good concordance between the diagnosis derived from the Patient Baseline Assessment and the Structured Clinical Interview for DSM Axis I Disorders (SCID-I) (p. 49) diagnosis of alcohol dependence (kappa = 0.81, $n = 78$). The AOM diagnoses exhibited 100% sensitivity and 76% specificity for alcohol dependence. The measure of alcohol consumption reported on the Patient Baseline and Follow-Up Assessments correlated with the estimate obtained using the Alcohol Timeline Followback (TLFB) Method (p. 477) as a validation standard ($r = 0.74$). The module's measure of drug use during the month before follow-up had a sensitivity of 61.5%, a specificity of 96.9%, and a positive predictive value of 80% (kappa = 0.64), compared with either a SCID diagnosis of current drug use disorder or a positive urine drug screen at follow-up. Patient reports about alcohol use at follow-up showed excellent agreement; a clinical interviewer's independent rating demonstrated 87.9% sensitivity, 96.3% specificity, and 96.7% positive predictive value (kappa = 0.83). AOM measures correlated significantly with the Addiction Severity Index (ASI) (p. 472) Severity Measure ($r = 0.26$–0.44). Compared with relevant gold standard measures (e.g., SCID Onset of Drinking and ASI Family History scales), many of the case mix variables measured by the AOM (e.g., age at onset and parental alcoholism) were also found to have adequate validity (with correlations or kappa values ranging from 0.48 to 0.77), although social support and psychiatric comorbidity measures did not. The case mix measures were shown to predict change in alcohol consumption, change in disability days, and change in seven of the eight SF-36 scales. Case mix variables also discriminated between high- and low-risk groups with regard to change in alcohol consumption and social consequences. The AOM outcome variables for physical, emotional, and social consequences were also shown to be sensitive to clinically relevant change (e.g., change in level of severity of alcohol dependence as rated on the SCID between baseline and follow-up assessments, with significant correlations [$r = 0.68$–0.87]).

CLINICAL UTILITY

The AOM is useful as a comprehensive instrument for outcomes monitoring and outcomes management in routine clinical settings, particularly substance abuse treatment settings. It was designed to measure outcome in multiple domains, while being relatively brief, and to be acceptable to both clinicians and patients. Specific components of the AOM can be used to confirm the diagnosis of alcohol dependence according to DSM-III-R criteria, monitor beneficial and adverse effects of treatment, assess clinical features beyond diagnosis (e.g., case mix characteristics), and assess the performance of health care delivery systems.

The AOM identifies patients with alcohol dependence with high sensitivity and good specificity. It can be used for patients with alcohol dependence to longitudinally examine process and outcomes of care and to determine the effects of quality improvement interventions (e.g., guideline implementation).

Outcomes, adjusted for patient case mix, can be compared for groups of patients to measure the performance of practitioners or health care systems. More research is needed to understand how best to adjust for differences in patient case mix when comparing two samples and what sample sizes are needed when comparing the performance of practitioners or systems.

The module's most apparent weakness (according to the authors) is its exclusive focus on drinking and drinking-related consequences, given the high prevalence of multiple drug abuse in many chemical dependency programs. To address this limitation, the authors have developed the Substance Abuse Outcomes Module (Smith et al. 1996) to monitor the outcomes of care for patients who use multiple drugs.

REFERENCES AND SUGGESTED READINGS

Rost K, Ross R, Humphrey J, et al: Does this treatment work? validation of an outcomes module for alcohol dependence. Med Care 34:283–294, 1996

Smith GR Jr, Babor T, Burnam MA, et al: Alcohol Outcomes Module. Little Rock, AR, University of Arkansas for Medical Sciences, 1994a

Smith GR Jr, Babor T, Burnam MA, et al: Alcohol Outcomes Module: User's Manual. Little Rock, AR, University of Arkansas for Medical Sciences, 1994b

Smith GRS, Babor T, Burnam A, et al: Substance Abuse Outcomes Module. Little Rock, AR, University of Arkansas for Medical Sciences, 1996

Depression Outcomes Module (DOM)

G. R. Smith Jr., A. Burnam, B. J. Burns, P. Cleary, and K. M. Rost

GOALS

The Depression Outcomes Module (DOM) (Smith et al. 1994) is used primarily to assess the process of care, patient characteristics, and outcomes of care for patients with major depressive disorder in primary care settings and in both inpatient and outpatient specialty care settings. Although data collected by the DOM can be used to address research questions or to inform treatment decisions for individual patients, the DOM was primarily designed to be used as part of an outcomes management system in which data are aggregated at the provider or system level to monitor and improve patient outcomes. The DOM verifies that the individual being assessed has a diagnosis of major depressive disorder according to DSM-IV criteria, provides valid and reliable data about patient outcomes (including symptom severity and disease-specific and general functional status), assesses case mix variables to permit adjustment for comparisons across patient or practitioner groups, and quantifies the type and extent of treatment services patients receive for major depressive disorder. This information provides a framework that enables clinicians and quality managers to study how the care provided affects outcomes for patients with major depressive disorder.

DESCRIPTION

The DOM has five components that elicit data about individual patients from a variety of sources, including the patients themselves, clinicians, and administrative records. The five components are as follows:

1. Patient Screener for Major Depressive Disorder
2. Patient Baseline Assessment
3. Clinician Baseline Assessment
4. Patient Follow-Up Assessment
5. Medical Record Review Form

The 3-item Patient Screener is optional and can be used to identify patients who are likely to have major depressive disorder and should thus complete the full DOM assessment. If the screener is not used, the DOM can be administered to patients with a clinical diagnosis of major depressive disorder. In this case, it must be recognized that major depressive disorder may go undetected by the clinician in some patients.

The Patient Baseline Assessment includes 80 items and is completed by the patient at the initial visit for major depressive disorder. The similar Patient Follow-Up Assessment (83 items) is performed every 4–6 months until the patient is in remission from the disorder. The patient assessments contain the Depression-Arkansas (D-ARK) Scale (Smith et al., submitted 1999), which assesses severity of depressive symptoms as well as whether the patient meets DSM-IV criteria for major depressive disorder. A sample item, rated on a 4-point scale, is provided in Example 13–5. SF-36 Health Survey questions (p. 128) are included in the DOM to assess functioning. Additional questions address the comorbid conditions of drug and alcohol abuse and medical illnesses.

The Clinician Baseline Assessment is a brief instrument (20 items) that the clinician completes at baseline to provide information on diagnostic criteria for major depressive disorder, exclusion criteria such as uncomplicated bereavement or bipolar disorder, comorbid medical

EXAMPLE 13–5 ■ **Sample item from the Depression Outcomes Module**

How often in the last 4 weeks have you felt worthless or been bothered by feelings of guilt?

Reprinted with permission.

disorders and substance abuse, and initial treatment for major depressive disorder. Most questions on the Patient Baseline and Follow-Up Assessments and the Clinician Baseline Assessment are multiple choice, although several write-in questions are also included. The Medical Record Review contains 11 yes-no, multiple-choice, and write-in items that may be retrieved from written or computerized medical records.

The assessments generate several scores. For the DSM-IV diagnosis of major depressive disorder, the DOM uses both the D-ARK Scale for patient self-report and a clinician checklist of DSM-IV criteria. If either the patient or the clinician reports the appropriate symptom pattern as present, the diagnosis is considered to be positive. Outcomes variables are calculated as the difference between baseline and follow-up measures for the following variables: depressive symptom severity (the D-ARK Scale, range of 11–42), health status scales (from the SF-36, range of 0–100), social functioning (range of 1–5), bed days (in the past 28 days), disability days (in the past 28 days), and work disability (number of days absent from work in the past 28 days). Although the change scores for these variables serve as a measure of outcome, patient (case mix) characteristics must be controlled for when making comparisons among providers or across different systems of care. The DOM collects data about these characteristics, including baseline severity, psychiatric and medical comorbidities, family history, history of illness (number of episodes or hospitalization), social support, and age at onset. Complex statistical issues arise in performing these analyses, and relatively large sample sizes are needed to meaningfully compare the performance of different providers or systems.

PRACTICAL ISSUES

The Patient Baseline Assessment and the Patient Follow-Up Assessment each take about 25 minutes to complete.

The Clinician Baseline Assessment requires up to 3 minutes to complete. The Medical Record Review takes 10 minutes to complete by hand and less time if computerized records are available. The DOM is available for $35.00, or for $25.00 per module if two or more modules (e.g., the Alcohol Outcomes Module [AOM], the Panic Outcomes Module [POM], or the Schizophrenia Outcomes Module [SCHIZOM]) are ordered simultaneously, from

> Center for Outcomes Research and Effectiveness
> University of Arkansas for Medical Sciences
> 5800 West 10th Street, Suite 605
> Little Rock, AR 72204
> Phone: 501-660-7550

The DOM is copyrighted, but it is available for unlimited free use if it is used in clinical care or research without charge to patients. The DOM is available on-line (www.netoutcomes.net). A user's manual with scoring instructions (Smith et al. 1994) is included with each order. No specific training is required to administer the DOM.

The DOM is included on the CD-ROM that accompanies this handbook.

PSYCHOMETRIC PROPERTIES

Reliability

For the Depression Severity scale (D-ARK), studies of three different patient samples found internal consistency (Cronbach's alpha) of 0.90–0.92 ($n = 41$–54). There was 100% agreement between two research assistants in completing the Medical Record Review. When the Patient Follow-Up Assessment was repeated 1 week later, patients demonstrated good agreement (78%–100%) in reports of health service utilization during the follow-up interval.

Validity

The D-ARK Scale demonstrated high agreement with diagnoses of major depressive disorder derived from the Inventory to Diagnose Depression (IDD) (Zimmerman and Coryell 1987) and the Structured Clinical Interview for DSM Axis I Disorders (SCID-I) (p. 49) (kappa = 0.70–0.89, $n = 29$–54). In these studies, sensitivity and specificity of major depressive disorder diagnoses derived from the D-ARK Scale ranged from 91% to 100% and

81% to 96%, respectively. At follow-up, remission of major depressive disorder derived from patient reports of current depressive symptoms on the DOM demonstrated 67% sensitivity and 73% specificity when compared with SCID judgments of remission of major depressive disorder.

The D-ARK Scale measure of depression severity was significantly correlated with the IDD measure of severity ($r = 0.89$–0.94, $n = 24$–38). The DOM also measured treatment variables, case mix characteristics, and disease severity accurately enough to discriminate between those who received and those who did not receive effective pharmacological treatment. For example, depressive symptoms decreased only in the group receiving effective pharmacological treatment. Changes in depression symptoms correlated strongly with three general measures of health: change in number of bed days ($r = 0.56$), change in social functioning ($r = -0.52$), and change in emotional functioning ($r = -0.47$).

CLINICAL UTILITY

The DOM is useful as a comprehensive set of instruments for outcomes monitoring and outcomes management for major depressive disorder in routine clinical settings, including general medical and specialty mental health settings. It was designed to measure outcome in multiple domains, while being relatively brief, and to be acceptable to both clinicians and patients. Specific components of the DOM can be used to screen patients for depressive disorders and assess diagnosis according to DSM-IV criteria, monitor beneficial and adverse effects of treatment, assess clinical features beyond diagnosis (e.g., case mix characteristics), and assess performance of health care delivery systems. The Foundation for Accountability, an organization of public and private payers and consumer groups, has endorsed a version of the disease-specific DOM to measure performance in mental health care.

The DOM makes the diagnosis of major depressive disorder with very high sensitivity and high specificity. In practice, few false-negative results (patients with major depressive disorder missed by the DOM) and some false-positive results (patients without major depressive disorder who are classified as having the disorder on the basis of DOM score) are likely. In settings with a relatively high prevalence of major depressive disorder (e.g.,

mental health clinics), the predictive value of a DOM diagnosis of major depressive disorder would be relatively high, whereas it would be lower in primary care clinics. The DOM is useful for selecting a group of patients who are likely to have major depressive disorder and then measuring the process and outcomes of care for this patient group. Thus, this measurement system can be used to longitudinally examine the effects of quality improvement interventions (e.g., guideline implementation) on the process and outcomes of care for major depressive disorder.

Using the DOM, depression outcomes (adjusted for patient case mix) can be compared for groups of patients to measure the performance of practitioners or health care systems. More research is needed to understand how best to adjust for differences in patient case mix when comparing two samples and what sample sizes are needed when comparing the performance of practitioners or systems.

REFERENCES AND SUGGESTED READINGS

Rost K, Smith GR, Burnam MA, et al: Measuring the outcomes of care for mental health problems: the case of depressive disorders. Med Care 30:MS266–MS273, 1992

Rost K, Williams C, Wherry J, et al: The process and outcomes of care for major depression in rural family practice settings. Journal of Rural Health 11:114–121, 1995

Smith GR, Burnam MA, Burns BJ, et al: Outcomes Module for Major Depression. Little Rock, AR, University of Arkansas for Medical Sciences, 1994

Smith GR, Mosley CL, Booth BM: Measuring health care quality: major depressive disorder (AHCPR Publ No 96–N023). Rockville, MD, Agency for Health Care Policy and Research, 1996a

Smith GR, Rost K, Ross R: Psychiatric Outcomes Module: the DOM, in Outcomes Assessment in Clinical Practice. Edited by Sederer L, Dickey BJ. Baltimore, MD, Williams & Wilkins, 1996b

Smith GRS, Kramer TL, Hollenberg JA, et al: Validity of the Depression-Arkansas (D-ARK) Scale: a tool for primary and specialty care. Manuscript submitted for publication, 1999

Zimmerman M, Coryell W: The Inventory to Diagnose Depression (IDD): a self-report scale to diagnose major depressive disorder. J Consult Clin Psychol 55:55–59, 1987

Panic Outcomes Module (POM)

K. M. Rost, G. R. Smith Jr., W. Katon, J. Jones,
B. Burns, F. A. Luscombe, A. Burnam, and D. Barlow

GOALS

The Panic Outcomes Module (POM) (Rost et al. 1994a) is used primarily to assess the process of care, patient characteristics, and outcomes of care for patients with panic disorder in primary care settings and in both inpatient and outpatient specialty mental health care settings. Although the data collected by the POM can be used to address research questions or to inform treatment decisions for individual patients, the POM was primarily designed to be used as part of an outcomes management system in which data are aggregated at the provider or system level to monitor and improve patient outcomes. The POM verifies that the individual being assessed has a diagnosis of panic disorder according to DSM-III-R criteria, provides valid and reliable data about patient outcomes (including symptom severity and disease-specific and general functional status), assesses case mix variables to permit adjustment for comparisons across patient or practitioner groups, and quantifies the type and extent of treatment services patients receive for panic disorder. This information provides a framework that enables clinicians and quality managers to study how the care provided affects outcomes for patients with panic disorder.

DESCRIPTION

The POM has four components that elicit data about individual patients from a variety of sources, including the patients themselves, clinicians, and administrative records. The four components are as follows:

1. Patient Baseline Assessment
2. Clinician Baseline Assessment
3. Patient Follow-Up Assessment
4. Medical Record Review Form

The Patient Baseline Assessment includes 82 self-report items and is completed by the patient at the initial visit for panic disorder. It includes questions about impairment from panic disorder, panic symptoms, the number of panic attacks, and avoidance. The similar Patient Follow-Up Assessment (83 items) is performed every 4 months until the condition has resolved. SF-36 Health Survey (p. 128) questions are included in these patient assessments to assess functioning. Additional questions address the comorbid conditions of drug and alcohol abuse and medical illnesses. The Clinician Baseline Assessment is a brief instrument (8 items) that the clinician completes at baseline to provide information on diagnostic criteria for panic disorder. Most questions on the Patient Baseline Assessment and the Clinician Baseline Assessment are multiple choice, although there are two write-in questions. A sample question from the Patient Baseline Assessment is provided in Example 13–6. The Medical Record Review contains 10 yes-no, multiple-choice, and write-in items that may be retrieved from written or computerized medical records.

The assessments generate several scores. The diagnosis of panic disorder according to DSM-III-R criteria is determined from responses on the Clinician Baseline Assessment. Outcomes variables are calculated as the difference between baseline and follow-up measures for the following variables: frequency of panic attacks (number in past 4 weeks), number of symptoms during a panic attack (range of 0–13), sensitivity to anxiety (range of 0–4), anticipatory anxiety (range of 1–4), avoidance and distress (range of 0–4), suicidality (yes or no), occupational functioning (range of 0–28), and social support (range of 1–5). Scores are also obtained on the subscales of the SF-36 (p. 128). Although the change scores for these variables serve as a measure of outcome, prognostic or case mix variables must be controlled for when making comparisons among providers or across different systems of care. The POM collects data about these characteristics, including the severity and duration of panic disorder and psychiatric and medical comorbidities.

PRACTICAL ISSUES

The Patient Baseline Assessment and the Patient Follow-Up Assessment each require 25 minutes to complete. The Clinician Baseline Assessment requires up to 5 minutes. The Medical Record Review takes 15 minutes to complete by hand and less time if computerized records are available. The POM is available for $35.00, or for $25.00 per module if two or more modules (e.g., the De-

EXAMPLE 13–6 ■ Sample item from the Panic Outcomes Module

During the past 4 months, did you receive psychotherapy/counseling for panic attacks?

Reprinted with permission.

pression Outcomes Module [DOM], the Alcohol Outcomes Module [AOM], or the Schizophrenia Outcomes Module [SCHIZOM]) are ordered simultaneously, from

Center for Outcomes Research and Effectiveness
University of Arkansas for Medical Sciences
5800 West 10th Street, Suite 605
Little Rock, AR 72204
Phone: 501-660-7550

The POM is copyrighted, but it is available for unlimited free use if it is used in clinical care or research without charge to patients. A user's manual with scoring instructions (Rost et al. 1994b) is included with each order. No specific training is required to administer the POM.

PSYCHOMETRIC PROPERTIES

Reliability

The sample for establishing POM reliability and validity was drawn from outpatient managed mental health care programs. The internal consistency for the outcome measures by scales was high: sensitivity to anxiety (Cronbach's alpha = 0.82), distress and avoidance (alpha = 0.86), and marital functioning (alpha = 0.82–0.89, n = 73 for all analyses). Strong test-retest reliability was demonstrated for almost all of the outcome measures administered at a 3-day interval; correlations ranged from 0.78 to 0.97. The only exception was for the outcome measures of sensitivity to anxiety and self-medication of alcohol and drugs: both had significantly higher scores on the initial administration of the test.

Validity

The diagnosis of panic disorder derived from the Clinician Baseline Assessment of the POM exhibited good agreement (kappa = 0.61) with the diagnosis derived from the Anxiety Disorder Interview Schedule (ADIS) (DiNardo et al. 1993). However, the agreement of the POM patient-derived diagnosis with the ADIS diagnosis was not acceptable (kappa = 0.32) and therefore is not

used. The POM clinician diagnosis has 79% sensitivity and 92% specificity.

Most of the outcome measures in the POM were compared with multiple gold standard instruments because a single gold standard that measured the exact construct does not exist for these outcome measures. All POM measures demonstrated statistically significant positive correlations with the gold standard scales ($r = 0.22$ to 0.76). For example, relevant scales from the ADIS correlated with POM measures of frequency of panic attacks ($r = 0.71$), number of symptoms during a panic attack ($r = 0.60$), anticipatory anxiety ($r = 0.61$), and avoidance and distress ($r = 0.62$). Sensitivity to anxiety was correlated with the Acute Panic Inventory (Dillon et al. 1987) ($r = 0.72$). The POM measure of avoidance and distress was correlated with Agoraphobic subscales of the Mobility Index Inventory (Chambless et al. 1984) ($r = 0.74$–0.76). The weaker correlations represented constructs for which an ideal gold standard did not exist (e.g., severity of panic on the ADIS was weakly correlated with the POM measure of bed days [$r = 0.22$]).

Patient self-report about current agoraphobia showed good agreement with the ADIS measure of severity of agoraphobia (kappa = 0.57). Similarly, the POM measure of lifetime depression or dysthymic disorder exhibited good agreement with the assessment of these constructs by the Diagnostic Interview Schedule (DIS) (p. 61) (kappa = 0.55).

Case mix measures in the POM that had gold standard measures available exhibited strong relationships with these gold standards. Specifically, POM measures of psychiatric comorbidity exhibited good agreement (kappa = 0.55–0.62) with corresponding gold standard measures (e.g., the DIS [p. 61]).

The extent of change between baseline and follow-up in the POM self-report measures of frequency of panic attacks, anticipatory anxiety, and avoidance and distress correlated with changes in related ADIS scales as assessed by a clinical interviewer ($r = 0.44$–0.59).

CLINICAL UTILITY

The POM is useful as a comprehensive set of instruments for outcomes monitoring and outcomes management for panic disorder in routine clinical settings. To date, it has been tested only in specialty mental health outpatient settings. It was designed to measure outcomes in multiple domains, while being relatively brief, and to be acceptable to both clinicians and patients. Specific components of the POM can be used to assess diagnosis according to DSM-III-R criteria, to monitor beneficial and adverse effects of treatment, to assess clinical features beyond diagnosis (e.g., case mix characteristics), and to assess performance of health care delivery systems.

The POM clinician-derived diagnosis has good sensitivity and high specificity in specialty mental health outpatient settings. Although there are likely to be some false-negative results (patients with panic disorder missed by the POM), the high specificity means that patients without panic disorder are relatively unlikely to be selected for outcomes monitoring with this instrument. The POM is useful for selecting a group of patients who are likely to have panic disorder and then measuring the occurrence and the outcomes of care. Thus, this measurement system can be used to examine longitudinal effects of quality improvement interventions (e.g., guideline implementation) on the process and outcomes of care for panic disorder.

Using the POM, panic disorder outcomes, adjusted for patient case mix, can be compared for groups of patients to measure the performance of practitioners or health care systems. More research is needed to understand how best to adjust for differences in patient case mix when comparing two samples and what sample sizes are needed when comparing the performance of practitioners or systems.

REFERENCES AND SUGGESTED READINGS

Chambless DL, Caputo GC, Bright P, et al: Assessment of fear in agoraphobics: the body sensations questionnaire and the agoraphobic cognitions questionnaire. J Consult Clin Psychol 52:1090–1097, 1984

Dillon DJ, Lorman JM, Leibowitz MR, et al: Measurement of lactate-induced panic and anxiety. Psychiatry Res 20:97–105, 1987

DiNardo PA, Moras K, Barlow DH, et al: Reliability of DSM-III-R anxiety disorder categories using Anxiety Disorders Interview Schedule—Revised (ADIS-R). Arch Gen Psychiatry 50:251–256, 1993

Hollenberg J, Rost K, Humphrey J, et al: Validation of the Panic Outcomes Module. Evaluation and the Health Professions 20:81–95, 1997

Owen RR, Rost K, Hollenberg J, et al: Effectiveness of care and improvement in quality of life in patients with panic disorder. Evaluation Review 21:405–416, 1997

Rost KM, Smith GR Jr, Katon W, et al: Panic Outcomes Module. Little Rock, AR, University of Arkansas for Medical Sciences, 1994a

Rost K, Smith GR Jr, Katon W, et al: Panic Outcomes Module: User's Manual. Little Rock, AR, University of Arkansas for Medical Sciences, 1994b

Schizophrenia Outcomes Module (SCHIZOM)

E. P. Fischer, B. J. Cuffel, R. R. Owen, B. J. Burns, W. Hargreaves, C. Karson, A. Lehman, D. Shern, G. R. Smith Jr., and G. Sullivan

GOALS

The Schizophrenia Outcomes Module (SCHIZOM) (Fischer et al. 1996a) is primarily used to assess the process of care, patient characteristics, and outcomes of care for patients with schizophrenia in mental health care settings. Although the data collected by the SCHIZOM can be used to address research questions or to inform treatment decisions for individual patients, the SCHIZOM was primarily designed to be used as part of an outcomes management system in which data are aggregated at the provider or system level to monitor and improve patient outcomes. The SCHIZOM provides valid and reliable data about patient outcomes (including symptom severity and disease-specific and general functional status), assesses case mix variables to permit adjustment for comparisons across patient or practitioner groups, and quantifies the type and extent of treatment services patients receive for schizophrenia. This information provides a framework that enables clinicians and quality managers to study how the care provided affects outcomes for patients with schizophrenia.

DESCRIPTION

Patients with a DSM-IV diagnosis of schizophrenia are appropriate for assessment with the SCHIZOM. The SCHIZOM has five components that elicit data about individual patients from a variety of sources, including the patients themselves, informants, and administrative records. The five components are as follows:

1. Patient Baseline Assessment
2. Informant Baseline Interview
3. Patient Follow-Up Assessment
4. Informant Follow-Up Interview
5. Medical Record Review Form

The SCHIZOM baseline and follow-up assessments for both patients and informants are fully structured interviews designed to be administered by a lay interviewer to the patient and an informant (family, friend, or mental health care provider) separately. The Patient Baseline Assessment begins with questions about demographic characteristics, life satisfaction, premorbid adjustment, family history, and recent symptoms. Subsequent sections include questions about leisure activities, instrumental activities of daily living (IADLs), housing, legal problems, educational activity, work activity, alcohol and drug use, violence and suicide, medication adherence and side effects, and service use. A sample question, rated on a 4-point scale, is provided in Example 13–7. SF-36 Health Survey (p. 128) questions are also included in these interviews. Most questions are multiple-choice or 4- to 7-point ordinal scale questions with anchors. All items of the SCHIZOM are always administered by an interviewer. Patient and informant assessments are completed at baseline (93 items and 84 items, respectively, not including the SF-36 items) and at follow-up (93 items and 76 items, respectively) every 6 months. There are approximately 29 yes-no, multiple-choice, and write-in items on the Medical Record Review, some of which may be retrieved from written or computerized medical records.

The assessments generate several scores. Outcomes variables are calculated as the difference between baseline and follow-up variables. Symptom severity is scored as the average of self-ratings, elicited by the reviewer, on 11 symptom items (range of 1–4). Scores are generated for other domains, including suicide (range of 0–3), IADLs (average of 11 items, range of 1–5), productive

EXAMPLE 13–7 ■ Sample item from the Schizophrenia Outcomes Module

During the past week, how much were you bothered by: feeling that you are watched or talked about by others?

Reprinted with permission.

activity (range of 0–3), social activities (average of 5 items, range of 1–5), housing independence (range of 0–4), legal problems (range of 0–1), leisure activities (range of 0–16), and satisfaction (life, housing, and social satisfaction, each with a range of 1–7). The scales of the SF-36 are scored in the usual manner (p. 128). Outcomes variables are calculated in a similar fashion for the informant assessments. Further work is ongoing to resolve the issue of combining multiple informants' scores; however, for certain assessment domains, such as suicidal behavior, violence, and substance abuse, the assessment is positive if any respondent reports them.

Although the change scores are measures of outcome, patient (case mix) characteristics must be controlled for when comparing outcomes of different patient groups, of patients treated by different providers, or of patients treated in different clinics or health care systems. The SCHIZOM collects data on known prognostic characteristics, including baseline severity, age at onset, premorbid adjustment, substance use, family history, and family attitudes and support.

PRACTICAL ISSUES

The Patient Baseline Assessment (exclusive of the SF-36) takes an average of 25 minutes to complete, and the Patient Follow-Up Assessment takes 21 minutes. The Informant Baseline Interview takes an average of 28 minutes, and the Informant Follow-Up Interview takes 20 minutes. The SCHIZOM is available for $35.00, or for $25.00 per module if two or more modules (e.g., the Depression Outcomes Module [DOM], the Panic Outcomes Module [POM], or the Alcohol Outcomes Module [AOM]) are ordered simultaneously, from

Center for Outcomes Research and Effectiveness
University of Arkansas for Medical Sciences
5800 West 10th Street, Suite 605
Little Rock, AR 72204
Phone: 501-660-7550

The SCHIZOM is copyrighted, but it is available for unlimited free use if it is used in clinical care or research without charge to patients. The SCHIZOM is available on-line (www.netoutcomes.net). A user's manual with scoring instructions (Fischer et al. 1996b) is included with each order. No specific training is required to administer the SCHIZOM.

The SCHIZOM is included on the CD-ROM that accompanies this handbook.

PSYCHOMETRIC PROPERTIES

Reliability

The reliability and validity of the SCHIZOM were established in a sample of 100 inpatients with a diagnosis of schizophrenia confirmed by the Structured Clinical Interview for DSM Axis I Disorders (SCID-I) (p. 49); the patients were recruited from short-term psychiatry units at two public-sector hospitals. Follow-up assessments were performed 6 months after the baseline assessments. Internal consistency (Cronbach's alpha) was adequate for the measures of symptom severity (alpha > 0.70), IADLs (alpha > 0.70), and social activities (alpha = 0.59), (n = 100 for all analyses). Test-retest reliability was good, with intraclass correlation coefficients (ICCs) greater than 0.70 for all scales except suicidal behavior (ICC = 0.42), violent behavior (ICC = 0.58), and premorbid adjustment (kappa = 0.27).

Validity

The validity of the scales for the outcomes domains was generally in the acceptable to good range; significant correlations (ranging from 0.21 to 0.78) were found between SCHIZOM measures and gold standard instruments (such as the Brief Psychiatric Rating Scale [BPRS] [p. 490], the Addiction Severity Index [ASI] [p. 472], the Neurobehavioral Cognitive Status Examination [p. 434], and the Personal Profile [W. A. Hargreaves, personal communication]) for all domains except IADLs. It should be noted that the IADL items had been included primarily as a potential proxy measure for assessing negative symptoms. The lack of correlation between IADL scores and the Negative Symptoms and Anergia subscales of the BPRS (p. 490) suggest that the IADL measure is not a useful proxy for negative symptoms. For all domains measured, the SCHIZOM generally detected change between baseline and 6-month follow-up assessments in the same areas, and in the same directions, as did the gold standard instruments.

CLINICAL UTILITY

The SCHIZOM is useful as a comprehensive set of instruments for outcomes monitoring and outcomes management for patients with schizophrenia in routine mental health care settings. It was designed to measure outcome in multiple domains, while being relatively brief, and to be acceptable to both clinicians and patients. The module can be employed to monitor beneficial and adverse effects of treatment, to assess clinical features beyond diagnosis (e.g., case mix characteristics), and to assess the performance of health care delivery systems. The SCHIZOM is designed to be used with patients who meet DSM-IV criteria for schizophrenia; it is not designed to verify the diagnosis of schizophrenia.

Another important consideration in the use of the SCHIZOM is when to assess patients: during an exacerbation of schizophrenia or during a period of stability or remission. To interpret the outcomes data, practitioners and administrators must consider whether the period during which outcomes are measured represents an episode of care that is clinically meaningful and whether patients are expected to improve or remain the same during the period of monitoring.

The SCHIZOM can be used to assess clinical features, including symptom severity, functioning, and case mix characteristics. When these measures are repeated over time, they serve to monitor beneficial and adverse effects of treatment (i.e., outcomes). Outcomes of care for schizophrenia, adjusted for patient case mix, can then be compared for groups of patients to measure the performance of practitioners or health care systems. In addition, outcomes data can be tracked over time as part of quality improvement efforts.

REFERENCES AND SUGGESTED READINGS

Cuffel BJ, Fischer EP, Owen RR Jr, et al: An instrument for measurement of care for schizophrenia: issues in development and implementation. Evaluation and the Health Professions 20:96–108, 1997

Fischer EP, Cuffel BJ, Owen RR, et al: Schizophrenia Outcomes Module. Little Rock, AR, University of Arkansas for Medical Sciences, 1996a

Fischer EP, Cuffel BJ, Owen RR, et al: Schizophrenia Outcomes Module User's Manual. Little Rock, AR, University of Arkansas for Medical Sciences, 1996b

CHAPTER 14

Stress and Life Events Measures

William S. Shaw, Ph.D.
Joel E. Dimsdale, M.D.
Thomas L. Patterson, Ph.D.

INTRODUCTION

Major Domains

In this chapter self-report measures for assessing stressful life events among patients and in general population screening are described. The topic of life stress and its influence on mental and physical health has spanned many areas of medical inquiry, including epidemiology, psychosomatic medicine, and most recently psychoneuroimmunology. Measures of life stress are useful in both research and clinical applications.

Organization

Six scales are presented in this chapter: the Daily Hassles Scale, the Derogatis Stress Profile (DSP), the Life Events Scales for Children and Adolescents, the Life Experiences Survey (LES), the Perceived Stress Scale (PSS), and the Recent Life Changes Questionnaire (RLCQ; previously known as the Schedule of Recent Experience [SRE]). These six scales are easy to administer, well documented, and representative of the types of assessment tools available for clinical assessment of life stress (see Table 14–1).

All the scales reviewed in this chapter reflect subtle differences in how the measurement of stressful life events is conceptualized. Several other important scales could not be reviewed here due to space limitations. In some instances, these scales are discussed elsewhere in this volume when they pertain more closely to other areas of assessment. Some of the more extensive interview approaches to assessing life events that have been used in research applications (e.g., the Bedford College Life Events and Difficulties scale) are not practical for use in clinical settings and therefore are not presented here. Many scales are domain or population specific (e.g., Texas Inventory of Grief [Faschingbauer et al. 1977] and Caregiver Strain Index). Although such measures may be particularly useful in specialized treatment clinics, they are not included in this chapter.

Relevant Measures Included Elsewhere in the Handbook

Some measures presented elsewhere in this book are also pertinent to life events. Because stressful life events are frequently found in association with anxiety and posttraumatic stress disorders and with dissociative disorders, the chapters that cover these disorders (Chapter 25 and Chapter 27) include specialized scales pertinent to the effects of severe trauma. Some other scales for assessing stressful life events are also included in Chapter 8, "Mental Health Status, Functioning, and Disabilities Measures," Chapter 9, "General Health Status, Functioning, and Disabilities Measures," Chapter 17, "Child and Adolescent Measures for Diagnosis and Screening," Chapter 18, "Symptom-Specific Measures for Disorders Usually First Diagnosed in Infancy, Childhood, or Adolesence,"

TABLE 14–1 ■ Stress and life events measures

NAME OF MEASURE	DISORDER OR CONSTRUCT ASSESSED	FORMAT	PAGES
Daily Hassles Scale	Impact of everyday encounters with environmental stressors on mental and physical health	Self-report questionnaire; 117 items	224–227
Derogatis Stress Profile (DSP)	Stress measure with multidimensional stress profile approach; includes stressors, stress responses, and stress outcomes	Self-report questionnaire; 77 items	227–229
Life Events Scales for Children and Adolescents	Occurrence and impact or severity of both positive and negative life events	Self-report questionnaire; 30–42 items depending on age of child	229–230
Life Experiences Survey (LES)	Impact of life events; generates positive life change score, negative life change score, and total change score	Self-report questionnaire; 47 specified items and 3 open-ended items	231–232
Perceived Stress Scale (PSS)	Subjective interpretation (perceived stress) associated with life events; assesses domains of unpredictability, lack of control, burden overload, and stressful life circumstances	Self-report questionnaire; 14 items (shorter 10- and 4-item versions also available)	232–235
Recent Life Changes Questionnaire (RLCQ)*	Most frequently cited and widely recognized life events checklist	Self-report questionnaire; 87 items	235–237

*Measure is included on the CD-ROM that accompanies this handbook.

and Chapter 19, "Child and Adolescent Measures of Functional Status."

USING MEASURES IN THIS DOMAIN

Goals of Assessment

Psychiatrists routinely assess the number and severity of the stressful life events their patients confront. Formal assessment of life stress may be used to provide a foundation for history taking, to highlight life circumstances that may affect treatment planning, and to develop hypotheses for understanding the origins of stress-related disorders. A careful inquiry about major life stressors should be part of any patient evaluation, and some of the scales reviewed in this chapter can be useful adjuncts to conventional interview techniques.

In specialized research, such scales have been used to predict consequences such as the onset of medical illness, poor management of chronic health symptoms, medical noncompliance, vulnerability to substance abuse and other negative health behaviors, risk of experiencing accidents, onset of psychological disturbance, and poor school or job performance. There is an enormous body of literature on such research applications, and *stress* is one of the most common indexing terms used in *Index Medicus*.

Implementation Issues

It is not easy to measure stressful life events, in part because of different operationalizations of the concept. Some measurement procedures have been criticized because they blur the distinction between stressful life events (stressors) and the resultant strain or adaptational pressure such events may exert on the individual (stress response or distress). In addition, opinions differ as to whether inventories of stressful events should assess only negative events or whether positive events should also be considered. Some investigators believe that inventories of stressful events should count only major challenges to the individual, whereas others believe that it is valuable to tally the accumulation of the more common microstressors that individuals encounter frequently. Some measures apply a universal weighting to stressful events, whereas others allow individuals to apply their own idiosyncratic assessment of the stressfulness or emotional travail elicited by events. The latter approach has been criticized for confounding stressors and distress. Furthermore, some scales are totally self-administered, whereas others rely on highly skilled interviewers. Finally, some investigators believe that changes in stressor exposure are more relevant to health than the exposure itself. Despite some major philosophical differences among investigators, life stress has continued to be an important background variable in both research studies and clinical assessment batteries.

Issues in Interpreting Psychometric Data

Several interpretive issues separate measures of stress and life events from self-report measures of psychiatric symptoms. These scales do not assist clinicians in making differential diagnoses. There is no gold standard for assessing stressful life events. Neither is there a clear cutoff point at which the number or severity of life stressors deserves clinical attention. Furthermore, memory is fallible: when people are asked to assess the occurrence of stressful life events retrospectively, the accuracy of their recall diminishes with longer periods of assessment, so that some events may be unreported, forgotten, or denied. The recall problem, however, can cut both ways. If a patient believes that stress causes myocardial infarction or depression, he or she will be more likely to retrospectively report a stressful event before these health outcomes. This "search for meaning" can result in a spuriously high level of retrospectively identified stressful life events. To a certain extent, such problems with distortion can be mitigated either by prospective scale administration or by corroborative administration of the scale to the patient's spouse or other family member.

The reliability of life events measures is typically supported by test-retest correlations, not internal consistency estimates, because stressful events are presumably unrelated to individual dispositions. Some argue, however, that consistent response sets (either across time or between items) suggest dispositional factors (i.e., a person's tendency to remember stressful events or be bothered by them) rather than reliable reporting. Thus, establishing the reliability of stress and life events has not

been as straightforward as for many other psychological constructs.

GUIDE TO THE SELECTION OF MEASURES

The choice of which specific scale to use for a particular application depends on the age of the individuals being assessed, the desired level of detail, and whether a more or less subjective report of life stressors is needed. Of all the scales reviewed in this chapter, only the Life Events Scales for Children and Adolescents was developed specifically in a child population and includes items pertaining to family, school, and social activities. Using the other scales with children would entail modifying the items to make them applicable to youths, a process that would invalidate the applicability of the scales' psychometric data. The Life Events Scale for Children and Adolescents appears to be a useful adjunct to history taking with children and adolescents and their parents.

The five adult measures vary in their level of detail and reporting subjectivity. Although the PSS is brief (14 items) and does not ask that respondents endorse specific stressful events, it may be practical for screening patients with a high probability of having stress-related symptoms. The other four adult measures are longer (from 50 to 117 items) and include more detail about specific stressors (or frequent obstacles and frustrations in the case of the Daily Hassles Scale). If comparisons with normative data or alternate patient populations are critical, then the RLCQ might be the best choice because of the many studies that have used this measure.

When it is already known that stressful events have occurred and the focus of the assessment is instead on stress perceptions and interpretations, then the PSS, the DSP, or the Daily Hassles Scale may be more useful. The PSS assesses the experience of stress in a global rather than event-specific fashion. The DSP uses a multidimensional stress profile approach that includes stressors, stress response, and stress outcomes. The Daily Hassles Scale assesses the degree of upset related to everyday events, which may be an important measure of irritability or discontent. If an individual is experiencing symptoms that suggest the likelihood of life adversity but stress exposure is unknown, the RLCQ or the LES may be more applicable.

CURRENT STATUS AND FUTURE RESEARCH NEEDS FOR ASSESSMENT

Since the introduction of the Survey of Recent Experience in 1967 (Holmes and Rahe 1967), dozens of scales and checklists have been developed to assess the stressful life circumstances that create adversity and distress among vulnerable patient populations. The six scales presented here are some of the most comprehensive and well-recognized measures; they have respectable reliability, and their validity has been demonstrated through associations with a variety of psychological and somatic health outcomes. A strength in this area of clinical assessment has been the active cross-pollination of concepts and techniques between measures. A weakness of the existing array of available measures is their frequent lack of underlying theoretical orientations and paucity of normative data from non-college-student samples.

In developing and testing life stress measures in the future, several important issues require additional study. First, life stress scales could be better designed for use in clinical interviewing (e.g., prompting for additional details surrounding events). Second, theories linking environmental factors to health outcomes could be used to better define constructs of stress and generate more specific hypotheses. Third, the relationships between scale scores and more objective, biological measures of health (e.g., immune function) could be pursued. Finally, the validity of life events scales could be established on the basis of prospective, rather than concurrent or retrospective, reports. The six scales included in this chapter provide a valuable foundation for future studies.

REFERENCES AND SUGGESTED READINGS

Cohen S, Kessler RC, Gordon LU: Strategies for measuring stress in studies of psychiatric and physical disorders, in Measuring Stress: A Guide for Health and Social Scientists. Edited by Cohen S, Kessler RC, Gordon LU. New York, Oxford University Press, 1995, pp 3–28

Faschingbauer TR, Devaul RA, Zisook S: Development of the Texas Inventory of Grief. Am J Psychiatry 134:696–698, 1977

Holmes TH, Rahe RH: The Social Readjustment Rating Scale. J Psychosom Res 11:213–218, 1967

Monroe SM, Roberts JE: Conceptualizing and measuring life stress: problems, principles, procedures, progress. Stress Medicine 6:209–216, 1990

Rahe RH: Life change, stress responsivity, and captivity research. Psychosom Med 52:373–396, 1990

Sandler IN, Guenther RT: Assessment of life stress events, in Measurement Strategies in Health Psychology. Edited by Karoly P. New York, Wiley, 1985, pp 555–599

Skodol AE, Dohrenwend BP, Link BG, et al: The nature of stress: problems of measurement, in Stressors and the Adjustment Disorders. Edited by Noshpitz JD, Coddington RD. New York, Wiley, 1990, pp 3–20

Zimmerman M: Methodological issues in the assessment of life events: a review of issues and research. Clinical Psychology Review 3:339–370, 1983

Daily Hassles Scale

R. S. Lazarus and S. Folkman

GOALS

Unlike other life events scales that focus only on major life circumstances, the Daily Hassles Scale (DeLongis et al. 1988) was designed around the notion that everyday encounters with environmental stressors may also negatively influence mental and physical health. The domain of daily hassles includes any transactions between an individual and his or her environment, whether they appear catastrophic or tedious to others, that might be judged by the individual to be potentially threatening or challenging. The creators' theoretical orientation for this measure is described as a cognitive-phenomenological conceptualization of psychological stress in which subjective appraisals of stressful events interact with an individual's ability to mobilize coping strategies to determine outcomes.

Although developed primarily as a research instrument, the scale may have clinical applications for both interindividual and intraindividual comparisons. Its creators hoped that the Daily Hassles Scale would show stronger correlations with physical health than earlier measures of life events. The original Daily Hassles Scale was later combined with a parallel measure of positive everyday events and shortened to produce the Combined Hassles and Uplifts Scale (Lazarus and Folkman 1989). This consolidation was based on the theory that positive experiences throughout the day may help to attenuate the effects of daily hassles.

DESCRIPTION

The Daily Hassles Scale is a 117-item self-report questionnaire. All items represent frequently reported daily hassles that were originally piloted in a survey of health maintenance organization subscribers. Respondents specify the current occurrence and severity of hassles on a 4-point Likert scale of 0 (none or did not occur) to 3 (extremely severe). The written instructions on the cover sheet of the questionnaire allow the clinician or researcher to select the designated recall period (today, yesterday, past week, past month, or other); however, most normative data have been on the basis of a monthlong recall period. Sample items are provided in Example 14–1.

All 117 items of the Daily Hassles Scale are administered. Although not specified in the test manual (Laz-

EXAMPLE 14–1 ■ Sample items from the Daily Hassles Scale

The Daily Hassles Scale: 117 items used to measure the frequency and severity of a person's transactions with the environment that are considered by the person to be stressful events.

Example: How much of a hassle was this for you?

0 = None or did not occur   1 = Somewhat Severe
2 = Moderately Severe   3 = Extremely Severe

A. Misplacing or losing things 0 1 2 3
B. Troublesome neighbors 0 1 2 3
C. Concerns about money for emergencies 0 1 2 3
D. Not enough time for family 0 1 2 3

arus and Folkman 1989), the questionnaire appears to be worded at a 10th-grade reading level. The Combined Hassles and Uplifts Scale is identical in format to the Daily Hassles Scale but includes both positive and negative events in a condensed list of 53 items; respondents may report events as being either a hassle, an uplift, or both.

The Daily Hassles Scale produces both a frequency score, which represents the number of items endorsed (items receiving a rating of 1 or higher; possible range 0–117), and a severity score, which is computed on the basis of the average rating of all items endorsed (possible range 1–3). Among white, middle-class adults, ages 45–64, mean scores were 20.5 (SD = 17.7) for frequency and 1.47 (SD = 0.39) for severity. In a college student sample, mean scores were 27.6 (SD = 14.3) for frequency and 1.65 (SD = 0.38) for severity. Although not described in the manual, a single score that represents the sum of all severity ratings (possible range 0–351) has been reported in several research applications. No clinical cutoff scores have been established for designating hazardous levels of daily stress.

PRACTICAL ISSUES

It takes 5–10 minutes to administer the Daily Hassles Scale in a written format. The publisher and copyright holder of the scale is

> Mind Garden, Inc.
> 1690 Woodside Road, #202
> Redwood City, CA 94061
> Phone: 650-261-3500

Permission to use the scale and 1-year reproduction rights can be obtained for $90.00 by contacting the publisher. A sampler set is available for $25.00. A 30-page manual that includes a copy of the scale, information about administration and scoring, normative data, and reliability and validity summaries is also included with the sampler set. Administration of the scale requires no special training. The scale has been administered by telephone in several research studies, but in these cases the scale was reduced to only the 30 or 40 most frequently endorsed items.

PSYCHOMETRIC PROPERTIES

Reliability

As is the case for many life events questionnaires, internal consistency is not a useful parameter for assessing reliability of the Daily Hassles Scale. This parameter is not useful because the accumulation of endorsed items, rather than the patterns of individual ratings themselves, is intended to measure the underlying construct of daily hassles. The presence of many unendorsed items from the full scale (117 items) would also invalidate estimates of internal consistency. Nevertheless, at least one reliability study of a shortened form of the Daily Hassles Scale (using the 46 most frequently endorsed items) has produced estimates of internal consistency (Cronbach's alpha) ranging from 0.80 to 0.93 for factor scores in a young adult sample and from 0.53 to 0.90 in an older adult sample.

A better parameter for assessing reliability of the Daily Hassles Scale has been test-retest comparisons. Using a 1-month recall period in a sample of white, middle-class adult volunteers, test-retest correlations in consecutive months were high for the frequency score (mean $r = 0.79$) and moderate for the severity score (mean $r = 0.48$). In another study, test-retest correlations for frequency scores were 0.77 on consecutive days (using a single day recall) and 0.82 in consecutive months. These estimates of test-retest reliability appear sufficient given that one might expect substantial true variation in consecutive recall periods. No studies have addressed consistency between consecutive self-reports for the identical recall period. The severity score appears to fluctuate more (or is less reliable) than the frequency of daily hassles.

Validity

The Daily Hassles Scale has shown small to nonexistent correlations with earlier measures of life events. One study found Daily Hassles Scale to be correlated 0.36 with life event scores from the Social Readjustment Rating Scale (Holmes and Rahe 1967) for female participants and to be uncorrelated with life events scores for male participants. Other studies have found correlations with life events measured by other scales to be of similar magnitude. The Daily Hassles Scale has shown higher correlations with measures of burnout ($r = 0.50$) and low morale ($r = 0.56$). However, some of the larger research studies that have addressed the shared variability between life events measures have failed to include the Daily Hassles Scale, either because these studies predated the scale or because daily hassles were not expected to overlap substantially with life events. In either case, there is only limited evidence of concurrent validity for the Daily Hassles Scale with other more well-established measures of life stress.

In several studies, scores on the Daily Hassles Scale have been shown to correlate with mental and physical health outcomes. For example, a study of university retirees found hassles to be correlated 0.58 with depression symptoms and 0.64 with psychosomatic symptoms. Another study of osteoarthritis patients found hassles to be correlated 0.38 with arthritis pain and 0.37 with arthritis disability. In each of these studies, the correlation of life events with outcome measures was substantially smaller, and these relationships were nonexistent after controlling for daily hassles. Similar results have been shown for outcome measures of general health status, negative affect, and physical health symptoms in children. Daily hassles appear to be more highly related to health outcomes than are life events, at least in cross-sectional analyses, although critics argue that these higher correlations are due to the spurious influence of negativity or depressed mood. However, at least one study ($N = 50$) comparing the Daily Hassles Scale with the Recent Life Changes Questionnaire (RLCQ) (p. 235), a life events measure, has shown similar correlations with physical health. Only one study has demonstrated the ability of daily hassles to predict health symptoms in a prospective design; however, the daily diary method used in this study precluded comparison with life events measures that usually span several months' recall.

The closer association between the Daily Hassles Scale scores and psychiatric symptoms compared with more conventional life events measures has also been criticized. Some have suggested that the tendency to report more frequent and severe daily hassles is simply a manifestation of, and not a precursor to, negative affect. Unfortunately, sufficient longitudinal studies have not been conducted to rule out either possibility. Therefore, the potential confounding of daily hassles with symptoms remains a subject of contention among life events researchers. A 53-item version of the Daily Hassles Scale that excludes many of the potentially confounded items is available.

CLINICAL UTILITY

Although the Daily Hassles Scale appears to have high face validity, the selection of items for the questionnaire were on the basis of the clinical and research experience of the authors without regard to construct definition or coverage of specific subdomains. Therefore, important items may have been omitted and some insignificant items included. The Daily Hassles Scale is rather lengthy, and several researchers (including the original creators of the measure) have attempted to reduce the number of items in subsequent versions. These attempts suggest that fewer items would perhaps be adequate to assess the construct of daily stress.

Despite criticisms that daily hassles are confounded with psychiatric symptoms, the Daily Hassles Scale may be more clinically useful than life events checklists because of its stronger association with mental and physical health symptoms in both adults and adolescents. The scale may be used clinically to assess the degree of upset related to everyday events, which may be an important measure of irritability or discontent. In further interviewing, items from the Daily Hassles Scale might be used to prompt more in-depth discussion of daily coping skills.

REFERENCES AND SUGGESTED READINGS

DeLongis A, Folkman S, Lazarus RS: The impact of daily stress on health and mood: psychological and social resources as mediators. J Pers Soc Psychol 54:486 495, 1988

Holmes TH, Rahe RH: The Social Readjustment Rating Scale. J Psychosom Res 11:213–218, 1967

Kanner AD, Coyne JC, Schaefer C, et al: Comparison of two modes of stress measurement: daily hassles and uplifts versus major life events. J Behav Med 4:1–39, 1981

Lazarus RS, Folkman S: Manual: Hassles and Uplifts Scale, Research Edition. Palo Alto, CA, Mind Garden, 1989

Derogatis Stress Profile (DSP)

L. R. Derogatis

GOALS

The Derogatis Stress Profile (DSP) (Derogatis 1987) is a relatively new stress measure that incorporates a multidimensional stress profile approach. Items were selected on the basis of an interactional model of stress that includes three principal domains (i.e., Environmental Factors, Personality Mediators, and Emotional Responses) and 11 primary dimensions that fall within one of the three principal domains. The DSP was designed to try to resolve past conceptual differences in stress measurement by including stressors, stress responses, and stress outcomes in a single instrument.

DESCRIPTION

The DSP is a 77-item self-administered questionnaire. As mentioned, the 11 primary dimensions included in the measure fall within one of three principal domains. The Environmental Factors domain includes domestic, vocational, and health-related dimensions. The Personality Mediators domain includes time pressure, driven attitude posture, role, and relaxation dimensions. The Emotional Responses domain includes depression, anxiety, and hostility dimensions. Each dimension is composed of seven items. Items related to emotional stress responses are duplicated from the Brief Symptom Inventory (BSI), a well-known research instrument used to screen for psychiatric symptomatology (p. 84).

The individual responds to all items on the DSP by indicating degree of endorsement on a 5-point Likert scale. The measure also includes a single item that permits respondents to rate their overall subjective stress level on a visual analog scale from 0 to 100. All 77 items are always administered. Sample items from the three subscales are provided in Example 14–2.

The DSP can be scored on several hierarchical levels. First, raw scores for each of the 11 primary stress dimensions can be computed by simply adding scores for the

EXAMPLE 14–2 ■ Sample items from the Derogatis Stress Profile

> Environmental Factors Subscale
> I have a good relationship with my husband.
> Doing my job gives me a good feeling about myself.
>
> Emotional Responses Subscale
> I feel no interest in things.
> I get easily annoyed or irritated.
>
> Personality Mediators Subscale
> The more things I achieve in life, the less I seem to enjoy them.
> I feel there is never enough time to get things done.

Reproduced with permission from Leonard R. Derogatis, Ph.D.

seven items in each dimension. Second, a clinical profile can be generated by translating raw scores to T-scores on the basis of available normative data. T-scores for the three principal stress domains can also be computed. Finally, a total stress score (TSS) can be obtained by summing the T-scores for the three principal stress domains and subjecting this score to an additional T-score transformation. The visual analog rating of stress is referred to as the subjective stress score (SSS), and a cutoff point of 60 has been used to discriminate high-stress individuals (approximately 14% of normative samples). The normative data available for the DSP were drawn from samples of midlevel managers from the insurance, commerce, and airline industries and are stratified by age (ages 18–70).

PRACTICAL ISSUES

It takes 12–15 minutes to complete the DSP. The measure is valid for adults and older adolescents with at least a 10th-grade reading level. The scale is copyrighted. Information may be obtained from

> Leonard R. Derogatis, Ph.D.
> Clinical Psychometric Research, Inc.
> 100 W. Pennsylvania Avenue, Suite 302
> Towson, MD 21204

The cost is $55.00 for a package of 50 forms. Score profiling forms are also available at $25.00 for a package of 50. A manual including scoring instructions and psychometric data is under development. A PC-based computer scoring program is available from the publisher at an additional cost of $200.00. Translations of the scale are currently available in Arabic, Dutch, French, Greek, Italian, and Spanish. The scale was designed to be self-administered.

PSYCHOMETRIC PROPERTIES

Reliability

Reliability studies of the DSP have generated good internal consistency and test-retest correlations. For the principal domains, internal consistency (Cronbach's alpha) is 0.83 for Emotional Responses, 0.85 for Environmental Factors, and 0.88 for Personality Mediators. For the 11 primary dimensions, internal consistency ranges from 0.79 (vocational environment) to 0.93 (time pressure). These estimates of internal consistency are on the basis of the sample ($N = 847$) of midlevel corporate managers used to compile population norms.

Test-retest correlations (1-week lapse) have been studied for a much smaller sample ($N = 34$) of medical outpatients presenting with stress-related disorders. For the TSS and the SSS (visual analog), test-retest correlations were 0.90 and 0.81, respectively. For the principal stress domains, test-retest correlations were 0.82 (Emotional Responses), 0.83 (Environmental Factors), and 0.89 (Personality Mediators). Test-retest correlations varied from 0.72 (hostility) to 0.92 (time pressure) for the 11 primary stress dimensions.

Validity

The validity of the DSP has been evaluated by comparison with more established scales, factor analytic studies, correspondence with other clinical criteria, and the ability of the scale to reflect stress intervention effects. Although correlations with traditional life events checklists have been weak (e.g., 0.32 with the Daily Hassles Scale [p. 224] and 0.48 with the Life Experiences Survey [p. 231]), correlations with more subjective measures of stress have been stronger (e.g., 0.58 with a measure of the occupational stress of teachers and 0.56 with the Occupational Stress Inventory). When correlated with staff ratings of overall clinical prognosis in a cardiac rehabilitation center, several of the primary stress components of the DSP were significantly related to staff ratings.

The TSS has been used to discriminate diabetic patients with poorly controlled blood sugar levels from those with well-controlled levels and to discriminate U.S. Marine Corps officers on the basis of rank. The scale has also been correlated with self-reported use of coping strategies and heart rate reactivity. In a 12-week stress reduction program, the scale was effective in demonstrating a treatment effect (effect size = 1.0) versus a comparable control group. One factor analytic study of the scale has supported the three original conceptual domains of the scale and suggested a fourth potential domain, somatic health.

CLINICAL UTILITY

The DSP can be used for populations vulnerable to particular illnesses, for population screening, for assessing the benefits of interventions, and for other applications in behavioral medicine. The broad, multidimensional design of the scale should make it useful as a clinical instrument, although clinical uses have yet to be documented. The scale may also be useful for monitoring the success of stress interventions. The specificity of scoring options provides a useful tool for treatment planning and further history taking with adults.

REFERENCES AND SUGGESTED READINGS

Derogatis LR: The Derogatis Stress Profile (DSP): quantification of psychological stress. Adv Psychosom Med 17:30–54, 1987

Derogatis LR, Fleming MP: The Derogatis Stress Profile (DSP): a theory-driven approach to stress measurement, in Evaluating Stress: A Book of Resources. Edited by Zalaquett CP, Woods RJ. Lanham, MD, Scarecrow Press, 1997

Dobkin PL, Pihl RO, Breault C: Validation of the Derogatis Stress Profile using laboratory and real world data. Psychother Psychosom 56:185–196, 1991

Life Events Scales for Children and Adolescents

R. D. Coddington

GOALS

The Life Events Scales for Children and Adolescents (Coddington 1972a, 1972b) was developed to assess the occurrence of specific life events and assign a weighting for the impact or severity of such events. The domains of such events include items pertaining to family, school, and social activities. Both positive and negative events are tallied. The underlying assumption is that events are stressful whenever they require some adaptation of the individual. Therefore, both positive and negative events are considered in the total score.

DESCRIPTION

The Life Events Scales for Children and Adolescents is a self-administered questionnaire that includes 30–42 items, depending on the age of the child. Older children respond to more items (e.g., breaking up with a boyfriend or girlfriend) than younger children. Sample items include birth of a brother or sister, mother beginning to work outside the home, and moving to a new school district. The child is asked to indicate whether any of the events occurred in the past summer, fall, winter, or spring. The parents of a young child complete the questionnaire for their child. An optional space is provided for the child to write in additional life events that are not listed on the questionnaire.

The questionnaire can be scored categorically by totaling the number of accumulated life events (0–42) or by considering the weighting of accumulated events (0–2,143). Scores for events that occurred more than 3 months before the administration of the questionnaire require a complex weighting to allow for attenuation of memory (i.e., it is assumed that individuals will not clearly remember life events that occurred more than 3 months before testing).

Extensive age-, ethnicity-, and gender-specific norms are available for comparison with diverse patient groups.

However, no data are available concerning scores or thresholds that define impairment or psychopathology. The 75th percentile for scores of events assessed in the prior 3 months is 50 for children ages 8–10, 60 for ages 11–13, 75 for ages 14–16, and 90 for ages 17–19.

PRACTICAL ISSUES

Although the time required to complete the Life Events Scales for Children and Adolescents is not specified, it appears to take about 5 minutes. The scale is copyrighted and owned and published by Multi-Health Systems, Inc. For further information please contact

> Multi-Health Systems, Inc.
> 908 Niagara Falls Boulevard
> North Tonawanda, NY 14120-2060
> Phone: 800-456-3003
> Internet: www.mhs.com

The cost is $55.00 for a complete testing kit, including a manual and 25 quick-score test forms. The questionnaire can be administered in person or by telephone.

PSYCHOMETRIC PROPERTIES

Reliability

The reliability of the Life Events Scales for Children and Adolescents has been assessed in several different contexts. For instance, there was good agreement between parents and fourth-grade children on life events ratings (N = 33 boys and their parents), with a correlation of r = 0.45 for 7 months and r = 0.37 for 11–23 months. Test-retest reliability was studied in junior high students. The 3-, 7-, and 11-month reliability coefficients (r) were 0.69, 0.67, and 0.56, respectively.

Validity

The Life Events Scales for Children and Adolescents has good content validity. For instance, in a study of 88 middle-class fourth-grade students, 97% of the life events reported by the children were on the scale and 87% of the life events reported by parents as applying to their children were on the scale. However, validity of the scale may be lower for inner-city populations of schoolchil-

dren. There is good joint reliability among teachers, pediatricians, and child mental health workers on the subjective weightings attached to the life events.

Both the number of negative life events and the subjective weightings of such events are associated with children's depressive symptoms (r = 0.47 and 0.49, respectively). Adolescents who score in the highest quartile of events have been shown to be at higher risk for accidents in the following 5 months. Youths who abuse drugs have also been shown to have a higher incidence of stressful life events.

CLINICAL UTILITY

The Life Events Scales for Children and Adolescents appears to be a useful adjunct to history taking with children and adolescents and with their parents. It may also be an effective screening tool to identify individuals who need special monitoring because they may be at increased risk for psychiatric symptoms and/or other adverse effects (e.g., accidents).

REFERENCES AND SUGGESTED READINGS

Coddington RD: The significance of life events as etiologic factors in the diseases of children, I: a survey of professional workers. J Psychosom Res 16:7–18, 1972a

Coddington RD: The significance of life events as etiologic factors in the diseases of children, II: a survey of a normal population. J Psychosom Res 16:205–213, 1972b

Garrison CZ, Schoenbach VJ, Schlucter MD, et al: Life events in early adolescence. J Am Acad Child Adolesc Psychiatry 26:865–872, 1987

Johnson JH, Bradlyn AS: Assessing stressful life events in childhood and adolescence, in Handbook of Child Health Assessment: Biopsychosocial Perspectives. Edited by Karoly P. New York, Wiley, 1988, pp 303–331

Mullins LL, Siegel LJ, Hodges K: Cognitive problem-solving and life event correlates of depressive symptoms in children. J Abnorm Child Psychol 13:305–314, 1985

Life Experiences Survey (LES)

I. G. Sarason

GOALS

The Life Experiences Survey (LES) (Sarason et al. 1978) was constructed from the theoretical perspective that subjective ratings of life change are critical in determining the impact of life events. The authors argue that events vary in terms of their desirability depending on the circumstances and perceptions of the respondent. Because undesirable events may have more detrimental effects on an individual than desirable events, the LES allows subjects to rate the desirability or undesirability of the types of events reported to occur relatively frequently in the general population.

DESCRIPTION

The LES is a self-report questionnaire that includes 47 specified items and 3 additional open-ended items on which subjects indicate and rate other recent experiences that may have affected their lives. Respondents indicate their ratings on a 7-point scale that ranges from extremely negative (–3), through no impact (0), to extremely positive (+3). Subjects also indicate whether each event occurred during the past 6 months or during the past 7–12 months. Although the LES provides information on these two 6-month periods, most publications on the use of this scale, including those on the development of the scale, have reported change scores on the basis of the entire preceding 12-month period.

Three scores are derived from the LES scale. A positive change score is obtained by summing impact ratings for items respondents rate as having been slightly (+1), moderately (+2), or extremely (+3) positive, yielding total scores ranging from 1 to 150. A negative change score is obtained by summing items rated by the respondent as being slightly (–1), moderately (–2), or extremely (–3) negative, resulting in scores ranging from –1 to –150. Items rated as having no impact (0) do not contribute to either positive or negative change scores. As

noted by the authors, negative change is more likely to predict health-related variables. A total change score can be obtained by adding the positive and negative change scores, yielding scores that range from –150 to +150. Norms (means and standard deviations) are available only for male and female college students.

PRACTICAL ISSUES

It takes approximately 10 minutes to complete the LES. The scale can be reproduced, at no cost, from the appendix of the original article describing its development (Sarason et al. 1978). No special permission or training is required for its administration.

PSYCHOMETRIC PROPERTIES

Reliability

Reliability studies include test-retest studies of 345 undergraduate university students (174 male, 171 female) with a 5- to 6-week lapse between three administrations. Test-retest correlations for the positive change score were 0.19 between the first and second administrations and 0.53 between the second and third administrations. Test-retest correlations for the negative change score were 0.56 between the first and second administrations and 0.88 between the second and third administrations. Finally, test-retest correlations for the total change score were 0.63 between the first and second administrations and 0.64 between the second and third administrations. These findings suggest that the LES yields moderately reliable scores, particularly for negative change scores. As the authors discuss, the potential for subjects to experience new events, and adjustments made to previously reported events during the 5- to 6-week interval between assessments, may be reflected in changes in respondents' ratings and reliability coefficients and should not be considered simply a response error.

Validity

The validity of the scale has been evaluated by comparing relationships between LES scores and a variety of outcomes. For example, negative change scores were significantly related to both trait ($r = 0.29$) and state ($r =$

0.46) anxiety from the Spielberger State-Trait Anxiety Inventory (Spielberger et al. 1970), as well as to grade point average ($r = -0.38$) among 100 undergraduate students. Not surprisingly, the positive change score was unrelated to these outcomes, and correlations with the total change score were attenuated, although still significant. A similar pattern of findings was reported between negative change scores and Beck Depression Inventory (p. 519) scores (0.24) and Rotter's Internal-External Locus of Control Scale (0.32) for the sample of 100 undergraduate students. In the latter study, more stressful life experiences were associated with a more external locus of control.

To determine whether the LES represented a methodological improvement over earlier scales that focus on simple event counts or stress ratings of events on the basis of group ratings, the LES was compared with the life change score from the Recent Life Changes Questionnaire (RLCQ) (p. 235). The RLCQ is the most frequently used life events scale in the literature and was considered to be the gold standard for this study. Findings suggested that the LES negative change scores were more strongly related to depression scores on the Beck Depression Inventory (BDI) (p. 519) (0.37), social nonconformity scores on the Marlowe-Crowne Social Desirability Scale (Crowne and Marlowe 1960) ($r = 0.26$), and discomfort scores on the Psychological Screening Inventory ($r = 0.25$) than the RLCQ score, which was not significantly related to these outcomes ($N = 100$ undergraduate students).

CLINICAL UTILITY

The LES is relatively short and easy to administer. It may be useful for characterizing the potential impact of stressful environments on adult patients who suffer from stress-related disorders. Rather than rely on a simple count of stressful events, this instrument takes advantage of the patient's subjective evaluation of the amount of life change required to adapt to particular situations. Because individuals are affected differently by events, it may more accurately reflect the impact of events on a specific individual than do scales based on values derived from group ratings such as the RLCQ. Furthermore, the relative contributions made by both positive and negative life change may be studied with this instrument.

REFERENCES AND SUGGESTED READINGS

Crowne DP, Marlowe D: A new scale of social desirability independent of social psychopathology. J Consult Psychol 24:349–354, 1960

Johnson JH, Sarason IG, Siegel JM: Arousal seeking as a moderator of life stress. Percept Mot Skills 49:665–666, 1979

Sarason IG, Johnson JH, Siegel JM: Assessing the impact of life changes: development of the Life Experiences Survey. J Consult Clin Psychol 46(5):932–946, 1978

Siegel JM, Johnson JH, Sarason IG: Life change and menstrual discomfort. J Human Stress 5:41–46, 1979

Smith RE, Johnson JH, Sarason IG: Life change, the sensation seeking motive, and psychological distress. J Consult Clin Psychol 46(2):348–349, 1978

Spielberger CD, Gorsuch RR, Luchene RE: State-Trait Anxiety Inventory. Palo Alto, CA, Consulting Psychologists Press, 1970

Perceived Stress Scale (PSS)

S. Cohen

GOALS

Like the Daily Hassles Scale, the Perceived Stress Scale (PSS) (Cohen et al. 1983) emphasizes the importance of the subjective interpretation of life events. The experience of stress is assessed in a global, rather than event-specific, fashion. The creators of the PSS sought to design a measure that included items defining a single global construct, *perceived stress*, rather than including items from a list of subdomains in which stressful events may occur. Perceived stress is "the degree to which respondents perceive their life situations to be stressful (unpredictable, uncontrollable, and overloading)" (Cohen et al. 1983). Its creators hoped that the PSS would be an improvement over more objectively rated life events checklists by emphasizing stress appraisal and by broadening the conceptualization of stress, which had previously been used only in reference to discrete life events.

DESCRIPTION

The PSS is a 14-item self-report questionnaire that has been administered in both written and oral (telephone) formats. Items were developed to assess the stress domains of unpredictability, lack of control, burden overload, and stressful life circumstances. This choice of domains was shaped by the creators' assumptions that negative health consequences of life events depend on whether these events exceed an individual's perceived ability to cope. For all items, respondents specify the frequency of the feelings, thoughts, or circumstances described on a 5-point Likert scale ranging from 0 (never) to 4 (very often).

The written instructions for the questionnaire specify a recall period of 1 month; longer recall periods are not recommended because predictive validity for the onset of physical health symptoms is expected to fall off after 4–8 weeks. All 14 items are administered. Of the 14 items, 7 are reverse coded; that is, endorsements represent lack of stress (e.g., "How often have you felt that you were on top of things?"). The scale was designed for use with patient and general populations with at least a junior high school level of reading comprehension.

The PSS yields a single score that is the summed total of item responses (after reversing the scores on the seven positive items). Scores fall within a possible range of 0–56; higher scores reflect greater perceived stress. Typical scores in community samples range from 10 to 35. College student samples have produced mean scores of 23.2 (SD = 7.3) and 23.7 (SD = 7.8). Normative data from a U.S. probability sample resulted in a mean of 19.6 (SD = 7.5). Higher perceived stress ratings have been reported for psychiatric outpatients (mean = 29.1, SD = 8.8), adolescent psychiatric inpatients (mean = 33.8, SD = 10.2), and women with postpartum depression (mean = 31.5, SD = 8.5). Women have scored, on average, 1–3 points higher than men in several investigations, but these differences were statistically significant in only one study (mean of 32.9 for women vs. 26.5 for men). No clinical cutoff scores have been established for designating hazardous levels of perceived stress.

Use of the shortened 10-item version of the scale is recommended because its reliability and validity are consistent with those of the 14-item version. A further reduced 4-item scale has been developed as a very brief screening instrument, but this truncation appears to compromise the measure's psychometric properties.

PRACTICAL ISSUES

The PSS usually takes less than 3 minutes to administer in a written format and slightly longer when administered orally. The copyright holder is Sheldon Cohen, Ph.D. (1994, all rights reserved). The publisher of the scale is

> Mind Garden, Inc.
> 1690 Woodside Road, #202
> Redwood City, CA 94061
> Phone: 650-261-3500

The PSS can be obtained from the publisher and reproduced at no additional charge. No comprehensive test manual is currently available, although information concerning the administration, scoring, and psychometric properties of the scale are provided by its creators in their introductory publication (Cohen et al. 1983). No special training is required to administer the scale. Dutch and Japanese versions have been developed and tested, with somewhat reduced estimates of reliability and validity in comparison with the English version. The PSS has also been translated into Arabic, Chinese, Greek, Korean, Spanish (Mexico), Spanish (Spain), Swedish, and Vietnamese. Because the PSS has only 14 items, it can be adapted easily for inclusion in telephone screening batteries and assessments.

PSYCHOMETRIC PROPERTIES

Reliability

The reliability of the PSS has been determined from both estimates of internal consistency and test-retest correlations. Cronbach's alphas reported for the first administration of the 14-item full version of the PSS were 0.84 and 0.85 in two college student samples (N = 332 and 114) and 0.86 among working adults who were volunteers for a smoking cessation intervention (N = 64). Two more recent applications have shown similar consistency among college students (alpha = 0.83) and among U.S. corporate managers (alpha = 0.85). Estimates of internal consistency among psychiatric outpatients (alpha = 0.80) and in the general population (alpha = 0.75) have also been within acceptable limits. The general population study also demonstrated comparable reliability for the 10-item version (alpha = 0.78) and reduced reliability for the 4-item version (alpha = 0.60).

A Japanese translation of the PSS was not very reliable when administered to Japanese corporate managers (alpha = 0.50). Even among English-speaking individuals, the reliability of the scale may vary with cultural background. The scale was less reliable among English-speaking Indian corporate managers (alpha = 0.75) than among U.S. corporate managers (alpha = 0.85). Test-retest reliability appears to diminish rapidly with increased time between ratings. Among college students, the test-retest correlation was 0.85 for a 2-day lapse and 0.55 for a 6-week lapse. A 10-item Dutch version of the scale administered to white-collar workers at intervals of several weeks produced a correlation coefficient (r, on the basis of repeated scores falling within the same low, medium, or high thirds of the baseline distribution) of 0.73. Therefore, the global stress construct measured by the PSS appears to vary substantially across weeks or even days.

Validity

The PSS is intended to be far more subjective and experiential than life events checklists, which were developed to provide an objective accounting of real events and circumstances. Correlations between the PSS and life events checklists have thus been low (r = 0.25–0.35). Evidence for concurrent validity has come instead from positive correlations with measures of burnout (Maslach Burnout Inventory) (r = 0.65) among a sample of 234 male highway patrol officers. Therefore, the construct of perceived stress appears to overlap more with the related constructs of emotional and physical burden than with actual severity of life circumstances.

Studies have shown moderate and reproducible correlations between perceived stress and psychosomatic symptoms. In a Dutch study of male laborers, the most distressed workers (top third on the basis of the PSS) reported a mean of 27.5 psychosomatic symptoms versus 6.1 symptoms for undistressed workers (bottom third). Correlations with physical symptoms have ranged from

0.23 to 0.54, and these relationships generally remain statistically significant after controlling for personality and mood factors. Other validity studies have linked perceived stress to health care utilization, salivary cortisol levels on workdays, success at smoking cessation, respiratory infection, and arthritis self-efficacy. The PSS has failed to discriminate between distressed and non-distressed married couples, to predict the onset of post-partum depression, or to predict treatment outcomes for cognitive-behavioral treatments for arthritis pain and disability.

Critics of the PSS contend that its global, subjective nature creates a measure of stress that is confounded with psychiatric symptoms of neuroticism, depression, and anxiety. This criticism originates from efforts to demonstrate the negative somatic effects of real-life stressors through naturalistic investigation. This research issue has elicited several written commentaries and responses among researchers arguing for and against subjective assessments of life stress. On a cross-sectional basis, the PSS is routinely correlated with depression and anxiety (range of correlation coefficients from 0.50 to 0.80). Critics have used this evidence to suggest that the PSS (and similar measures) are merely surrogate measures of underlying psychopathology and therefore cannot be used to demonstrate convincing relationships between life stressors and psychosomatic illness. In response to these criticisms, the creators of the PSS have shown that it prospectively predicts several behavioral and psychiatric outcomes independent of depression, anxiety, and anger at the point of prediction.

CLINICAL UTILITY

Although developed primarily as a research instrument to demonstrate the consequences of stress on disease processes, the PSS, which is short, easily administered, and global in nature, also has potential clinical utility, although this application has not been documented. Proponents of subjective stress measures such as the PSS argue that, even after controlling for personality factors, relationships between perceived stress and psychosomatic illness persist. In addition, perceived stress is more strongly correlated with physical health outcomes than are life events; in multiple regression analyses, perceived stress shares a larger proportion of unique variance with health outcomes than does the sum or rating of life events. Critics of the PSS argue that these high correlations reflect poor discriminant validity for the construct of perceived stress. Therefore, although the PSS may provide a measure of stress response rather than of life circumstances, its consistent and unique association with physical and mental health outcomes makes it an important measure to consider for the screening of perceived stress in clinical settings. At least one study has demonstrated the feasibility and validity of administering the PSS to adolescent children (psychiatry inpatients, ages 12–17).

REFERENCES AND SUGGESTED READINGS

Cohen S, Williamson GH: Perceived stress in a probability sample of the United States, in The Social Psychology of Health. Edited by Spacapan S, Oskamp S. Newbury Park, CA, Sage, 1988, pp 31–67

Cohen S, Kamarck T, Mermelstein R: A global measure of perceived stress. J Health Soc Behav 24:385–396, 1983

Hewitt PL, Flett GL, Mosher SW: The Perceived Stress Scale: factor structure and relation to depression symptoms in a psychiatric sample. Journal of Psychopathology and Behavioral Assessment 14:247–257, 1992

Recent Life Changes Questionnaire (RLCQ)

T. H. Holmes and R. H. Rahe

GOALS

The Recent Life Changes Questionnaire (RLCQ) (Miller and Rahe 1997), along with its earlier versions and accompanying readjustment rating scales and weighting schemes, is the most frequently cited and most widely recognized life events checklist. Underlying the scale's early development was the clinical observation that stressful social circumstances appeared to precede a decline in physical and/or mental health in a variety of vulnerable patient populations. Since the introduction of the RLCQ (originally titled the Schedule of Recent Experiences [SRE]) in 1967, the evolution of this questionnaire has been instrumental in testing several important research questions relevant to psychosomatic research. Versions of the scale have incorporated the summing of life events; the weighting of events on the basis of population norms, group norms, or individual ratings; and the introduction of life change units. The goal of the scale was to provide a standardized measure for assessing major changes in life circumstances that could be used to investigate relationships among life changes, coping behaviors, physiological changes, and disease processes. When subjective ratings of adjustment are included in the administration, the scale is presumed to incorporate individual coping abilities in the total score.

DESCRIPTION

The RLCQ is a self-administered questionnaire that has grown from 43 to 87 items in a series of periodic updates. The original 43 items encompassed the domains of family constellation, marriage, occupation, economics, residence, group and peer relationships, education, religion, recreation, and health. Sample items are provided in Example 14–3. The 44 newer items address similar domains. Items were chosen to represent life events that would tend to result in changes in accustomed life patterns, not necessarily items that would be rated as stressful or negative. In completing the questionnaire, respondents merely indicate whether any of the events listed in the questionnaire have occurred in the past 2 years (usually stratified within four consecutive 6-month intervals). Occurrence of some events more than once during the recall period can also be recorded. All items are always administered.

EXAMPLE 14–3 ■ Sample items from the Recent Life Changes Questionnaire

Mortgage foreclosure
Trouble with boss
Change in health of a family member

Reprinted with permission from Richard Rahe, M.D.

The questionnaire can be scored in several ways. A summed total of the number of life events endorsed is the most basic scoring option. This score can range from 0 to 87, although typical scores are more likely to range from 5 to 20.

Standardized ratings of life events can also be used in scoring the questionnaire. These ratings have been developed by asking respondents in control samples to rate the relative severity of adjustment for all items using an arbitrary set point of 50 for marriage. In a recent standardization sample, these ratings varied from 18 (taking a correspondence course) to 123 (death of child). Similar rating schemes can be applied to develop group-specific norms or to obtain individualized ratings of events.

A scaled score (referred to as *life change units* [LCUs]) can then be computed by applying standardized (population- or group-based) weights to the specific items endorsed and then summing the weighted scores. If an individually based scaling is preferred, then *subjective life change units* (SLCUs) can be computed by weighting endorsed items by individual item ratings and summing the weighted scores. Mean LCU and SLCU scores in general population surveys have ranged from 500 to 800; however, within-group scores vary substantially. The normative data for item weightings were developed from surveys of senior U.S. Navy enlisted men, and similar adjustment ratings have been published for various other special groups. When administered for the purposes of tabulating item weights for a specific group, the scale is referred to as the Social Readjustment Rating Questionnaire (SRRQ). In past administrations of the SRRQ, life events have been rated as requiring more adjustment by women than by men, by unmarried than by married adults, by younger than by older adults, and by adults with less than a college education than by those with a college degree or more education. Substantial sociocultural variation in adjustment ratings has also been demonstrated. Available normative weighting schemes that have been published do not appear to be stratified by gender, age, or other factors.

PRACTICAL ISSUES

It takes 10–15 minutes to complete the questionnaire, which is valid for adults and older adolescents with at least a 10th-grade reading level. The scale is copyrighted. Information may be obtained from

> Richard H. Rahe, M.D.
> Sierra Biomedical Research Corporation
> Veterans Affairs Medical Center
> 1000 Locust Street
> Reno, NV 89520
> Phone: 702-328-1440

Copies of the RLCQ are available from Dr. Rahe at no cost. There is no manual, and no special training is necessary to administer the scale. Weights for computing LCU scores from individual items have been published for the 1965, 1977, and 1995 standardization samples. A Spanish translation of the original 43-item scale is currently available.

The RLCQ is included on the CD-ROM that accompanies this handbook.

PSYCHOMETRIC PROPERTIES

Reliability

Reliability studies have demonstrated good test-retest correlations. For the item count, reported test-retest correlations have been 0.82 for a 2-week lapse between administrations, 0.85 for a 3-week lapse, and 0.83 for a 1-month lapse. Item agreement has been greater than 90% for similar test-retest periods. When individual weights are applied to endorsed items by the respondent, the sum of SLCUs is no more or less reliable than the simple item count. This finding has led the creators of the scale and others to suggest that a simple item count may be the most valid estimate of environmental stress and that item weights and item counts are equivalent scoring methods.

Validity

The validity of the scale has been demonstrated by a large accumulation of research studies relating LCUs and item counts from the scale to various health indicators. Although these correlations have ranged from 0.3 to 0.4 in most studies, correlations have been small in large-scale ($N > 1,000$) investigations. In Rahe's most recent study of 1,917 subjects, the correlation found between magnitude of recent life change and physical and psychological symptoms was 0.45. Thirty years of accumulated studies with the RLCQ have shown small but statistically significant correlations with measures of general psychological distress, hospitalization, medical care utilization, report of physical health symptoms, depression, myocardial infarction, diabetic control, onset of narcolepsy, mortality after spinal cord injury, risk of suicide, medical compliance, and rehabilitation after surgery.

An important research issue has been the choice of alternative methods of scoring life events (item counts vs. population-based weighting schemes vs. subjective weighting schemes). Item counts are criticized for ignoring individual differences in coping strengths. Weighted scores on the basis of population-standardized weights may fail to address cultural and individual differences in adjustment ratings. Weighted scores on the basis of respondent ratings may be confounded with outcome measures. Although the philosophical differences between these approaches appear great, empirical studies comparing the validity of these scores have demonstrated them to be roughly equivalent. For this reason, and because item counts represent the "purest" and perhaps most objective measure of life circumstances, the item count method of scoring has received the most support.

Because the RLCQ (or its predecessor, the SRE) preceded all competing life events checklists, it is often used as a gold standard to establish the concurrent validity of newer measures. Therefore, it is not surprising that correlations between the RLCQ and other life event checklists are high. In contrast, correlations of the RLCQ with more subjective assessments of stress (e.g., the Perceived Stress Scale, p. 232) are small or nonexistent, and this finding has spawned debate over the choice between objective and subjective assessments of life stress. More objective measures such as the RLCQ provide more defensible research findings, whereas more subjective measures provide more information about an individual's response to stress.

CLINICAL UTILITY

The RLCQ is easy to administer and useful for describing the environmental context in which clinical symptoms may appear. The measure can be used in vulnerable illness populations and for other applications in behavioral medicine in which life stressors are a concern. Administration of the RLCQ as part of a standard intake assessment may reassure patients that no life circumstances will be overlooked, and endorsed items on the RLCQ can serve as a basis for further history taking. Subjective ratings of events can also be used to recognize life circumstances that have led to adjustment difficulties and increased use of coping behaviors.

REFERENCES AND SUGGESTED READINGS

Holmes TH, Rahe RH: The social readjustment rating scale. J Psychosom Res 11:213–218, 1967

Miller MA, Rahe RH: Life changes scaling for the 1990s. J Psychosom Res 43:279–292, 1997

Rahe RH: Epidemiological studies of life change and illness. Int J Psychiatry Med 6:133–146, 1975

Rahe RH: Life change measurement clarification. Psychosom Med 40:95–98, 1978

CHAPTER 15

Family and Relational Issues Measures

Stephen C. Messer, Ph.D.
David Reiss, M.D.

INTRODUCTION

In this chapter measures of family relationships—including the many ways family members interact, think, and feel about each other and their potential problems—are presented. The assessment of family relationship subsystems (i.e., family, partner-partner, and parent-child) and the adaptiveness of their functioning (e.g., family organization, communication, and emotional climate) are the central aims of family evaluation.

Organization

The measures included in this chapter are summarized in Table 15–1. First, measures of family functioning—the Family Assessment Device (FAD) and the Family Assessment Measure (FAM-III)—are described. Measures for assessing dyadic relationships (marital, dating, and cohabiting) are presented next: the Dyadic Adjustment Scale (DAS) and the Conflict Tactics Scales (CTS). The final measures are designed to assess relationships between parents and children or parents and adolescents: the Parenting Stress Index (PSI) and the Conflict Behavior Questionnaire (CBQ).

USING MEASURES IN THIS DOMAIN

Goals of Assessment

Three major goals of family relationship assessment are delineated: 1) initial appraisal, 2) treatment selection and planning, and 3) treatment implementation, monitoring, and outcome evaluation. First, for many disorders it is crucial to have family relationship data to assess severity and prognosis. For example, there is a well-documented relationship between major depressive disorder, marital discord, and prognosis; marital problems serve as a potent risk factor for onset and relapse. Because severe marital discord makes recovery from depression less likely in many cases, the clinical evaluation of the depressed individual should be complemented by an assessment of the person's marriage. Interventions informed by family measurement can directly influence both initial treatment success and rates of relapse and recovery.

Second, family relationship assessment helps a clinician decide whether family intervention is important and may suggest particular avenues for intervention. For example, a comprehensive clinical evaluation supplemented with a brief family measure can inform treatment planning for an adolescent presenting with anorexia

TABLE 15–1 ■ Family and relational issues measures

NAME OF MEASURE	DISORDER OR CONSTRUCT ASSESSED	FORMAT	PAGES
Family Assessment Device (FAD)*	Quality of multiple clinically relevant dimensions of family functioning to identify problem areas and operationalize the McMaster Model of Family Functioning (MMFF); quick screening	Self-report; 60 statements, with a 10-item short form	245–247
Family Assessment Measure (FAM-III) Brief FAM	Operationalizes the Process Model of family functioning for use as a screening instrument, research tool, and measure of therapy outcome	Self-report; 134 items, with a 42-item short version	247–249
Dyadic Adjustment Scale (DAS) Revised DAS (RDAS)	Adjustment of partners in committed, couple relationships	Self-report questionnaire; 32 items; RDAS has 14 items	249–251
Conflict Tactics Scales (CTS) Revised and expanded version (CTS2) Version for older children and adolescents (CTSPC)	Strategies for dealing with conflict in marital, dating, or cohabiting relationships; CTS2 includes Physical Injury and Sexual Coercion subscales; CTSPC assesses violence in relations between parents and children	Self-report questionnaire or part of a more extensive interview; 19 items	251–254
Parenting Stress Index (PSI) Short form (PSI/SF)	Child and parental characteristics and parent-child relationship dimensions associated with the presence of parenting stress and troubled relationships	Self-report; 101 items, with a 36-item short form	254–257
Conflict Behavior Questionnaire (CBQ) Revised shortened versions (CBQ-20 and CBQ-44) Issues Checklist (IC)	Perceived communication conflict between parents and adolescents; IC is a companion measure of specific areas of disagreement or dispute for treatment planning	Self-report, true-false format; 75 items (parent) and 73 items (adolescent); shortened versions have 20 and 44 items	257–260

*Measure is included on the CD-ROM that accompanies this handbook.

nervosa. When clinical evaluation and testing are consistent in pointing to the presence of family dysfunction, a family-based intervention with the patient may be a crucial component of a treatment plan that includes an intensive dietary and weight gain regimen and behavior modification program.

Third, treatment implementation and monitoring are enhanced with the use of family measures. For example, these data can assess gains after family treatment. Family relationship assessments can also be useful in monitoring the course of the illness. For example, an older adolescent with conduct disorder presents with significant impairment at school and home; he desires to quit school and take employment at a local garage. The

family feels strongly that he must graduate, and their discussions soon turn into bouts of argumentativeness, hostility, and threatening behavior. Initial and ongoing assessments of parent-adolescent conflict and negative communication, particularly between the patient and his stepfather, suggest a treatment plan to address these concerns in a problem-solving, communication-training approach. Monitoring the patient's antisocial behaviors by using family conflict measures confirms initial formulations and demonstrates a clear dimunition in the patient's and family's negative communications after sessions in which successful negotiation of a particular issue occurs. Such treatment gains can be readily assessed with available family instruments. Furthermore, assessment of the family's history of violence, current patterns of domestic aggression, and ongoing monitoring of such potentially dangerous behavior can help the clinician identify a new series of treatment targets and plans and monitor the progress of intervention for both the patient and other family members.

Implementation Issues

In the clinical evaluation of patients and their families, the gold standard for family assessment is clearly the clinical interview. Family assessment instruments can facilitate this process in many cases through the use of standardized questions that can serve to confirm, reject, or refine information obtained through the clinical interview. These instruments can function to further refine clinical data, highlight possible disagreement, and possibly reveal undiscovered family issues. To facilitate the implementation of the family assessment process, several attempts have been made to develop structured or semistructured interviews that would standardize and enhance the reliability and validity of clinically relevant information. At this time, no standardized interviews have met the two key criteria for day-to-day use in the provision of high-quality clinical care: practicality and psychometric adequacy. Therefore, family instruments should be used in an informed fashion to generate data that can supplement and complement interview-based information regarding a patient's status.

The process of the initial interview offers an opportunity to forge an alliance with the patient and/or family and to build the rapport and trust that are prerequisites for any valid information gathering or testing. In many cases, the clinician meets first with an identified patient, unaccompanied by family members. After a thorough direct clinical interview, the clinician must decide whether to seek family members' assistance through an interview and/or testing. Several considerations are of obvious importance. First, if the patient is a minor, information from other family members is critical, but it would likely help rapport if the patient was made aware of the extent, use, and benefits of the family assessment process. Second, symptomatology defining the disorder may demonstrate direct functional relationships or linkages with other family relationships. This linkage justifies including family members in assessment procedures. The previously noted example of depression with marital discord is a case in which the individual's presenting symptoms often become inextricably linked with the partner's behavior.

Failure to involve family members in the treatment plan, with the evaluation supplemented with family relationship assessments, might lead to treatment failures. Finally, the severity of the disorder and accompanying risk factors (e.g., suicide risk in patients with bipolar disorder) are important criteria to consider for family involvement. The clinician must remain highly sensitive to issues of confidentiality, alliance building, initial therapeutic stance, family comfort level, and optimizing the context for the valid provision of information when deciding on the inclusion and sequencing of family (and nonfamily) informants in a clinical family interview or evaluation.

When a clinician decides that family evaluation is essential, he or she must determine which family member should be asked to complete the instruments. Obviously, for child and adolescent patients who live at home, the parent(s) or legal guardian(s) can provide both observations about the presenting problem and important reports about the impact of the child's disturbance on their relationship. The parent or guardian is also a critical informant when adult patients continue to reside at home and are cared for by their parents (e.g., a patient with chronic schizophrenia). In some situations, a family member may not meet traditional definitions of biological or legal relatedness (e.g., homosexual partner or nonbiologically related "aunt").

Regardless of which family members or significant others participate in assessment, their responses must be interpreted with some degree of caution. Various factors may influence their reports, including attributional styles, response biases or distortions, psychopathology, or simply a lack of objectivity. Collecting useful clinical data from the patient's family members is significantly enhanced through sensitive and empathic interviews that convey expertise, trust, a nonblaming perspective, and reassurances of confidentiality. Engaging the family members as collaborators in gathering data to help the patient while selecting and using appropriate and relevant relationship measures can facilitate accurate diagnosis and treatment planning.

In trying to integrate disparate reports, the clinician should keep the following simple recommendations in mind. A similarity of reports across multiple informants suggests consensus, whereas disparate reports from various family members should probably all be viewed as valid but context or respondent specific, taking into consideration the differing contexts in which family members interact and the different perceptual filters some members may use in appraising the patient's behavior. In some contexts the most positive report may be the most informative (e.g., when considering strengths and resources of the family, such as communication skills or coping ability), whereas in other contexts the most negative report may be the most informative (e.g., when obtaining reports of relationship problems such as family violence). Consensus of family members' reports regarding problems in family functioning can be a useful basis for planning the intervention. Disparate reports can be equally informative in that they may suggest a lack of agreement concerning the role of family processes in the patient's problems. Both sets of information provide valuable input for diagnostic formulation and treatment planning. On the other hand, disparate reports may indicate that the patient's and family members' views of relationships within the family reflect marginalization of the patient. This not uncommon situation poses a problem for family intervention in terms of joining with the family on a shared mission or treatment plan. However, the clinical assessment and revelation of such factors may open the door to engagement of the family in the treatment and testing process.

A key implementation issue in the assessment of family relationships is the degree and impact of cultural and ethnic variations on reports. First, research shows that members of different cultural or ethnic groups may perceive particular aspects of families differently, including variations in perceptions of who is a member of the family (e.g., the inclusion or exclusion of fictive kin, i.e., persons recognized as family without biological or legal ties) and perceived norms of family behavior (e.g., the degree and acceptability of egalitarian role expectations or behaviors). For example, Hispanic family members providing care for their seriously mentally ill adult children report less burden or negative impact on the family than Caucasian family members. Psychiatrically disturbed children of African American heritage are more likely than Caucasian children to report that their primary caregivers are grandmothers or aunts. Unfortunately, as in most assessment domains, available data regarding the appropriateness, representativeness, validity, and clinical utility of these family relationship measures with diverse ethnic populations are limited. Nonetheless, because cultural factors appear to be important in help seeking and in the care of disturbed persons, the informed clinician uses and interprets family measures with caution.

Issues in Interpreting Psychometric Data

Some family relationship measures provide limited but important specificity in their norms. For example, the FAM-III lists norms for both adolescents and adults. However, for many family measures, additional research is needed to provide more discrete breakdowns, such as separate normative data for families with no children, preschoolers, teens, and so on. Interpretation of scores in relation to available norms, like other psychosocial measures, is desirable where possible.

Most family assessment measures are intended to be completed by children who are at least about 12 years old. This age consideration is important because many patients and their families who seek services present with younger children who are incapable of reliable responding. Therefore, in some circumstances, the parents' reports are the only reliable test information about the family. A further issue is whether the family relationship measure is sensitive to developmental changes in the family life cycle. If not, for example, the clinician may obtain a test score that suggests inadequate parental control if the family has an infant and the measure's norms were derived on the basis of families with predominantly adolescents, who require less and a different type of behavioral oversight. Gender differences among family members might also influence the interpretation of family relationship scores. For example, women often report more marital problems than men.

Finally, family relationship measures, like other types of measures, are personal and therefore often lead to defensive or distorted responses. Respondents may provide socially desirable responses, exaggerate problems to suggest that it is too early to terminate treatment, or mute reports of real problems in an effort to communicate that clinical services are not needed or to prevent release of information that they believe may lead to legal consequences.

Not surprisingly, given some of the limitations noted, most family relationship measures are not specific or sensitive enough to measure the nuances of change in family relationships. However, these limitations do not suggest that the instruments have no clinical utility as outcome measures; for example, the DAS has demonstrated such useful properties in several studies. Rather, given the state of the art in the development of family relationship measures, these instruments, particularly single instruments or scores, require further development to become highly sensitive and reliable indexes of subtle, yet clinically meaningful, change.

GUIDE TO THE SELECTION OF MEASURES

Here we briefly present our recommendations for the clinical use of several family relationship measures, organized by family subsystem (i.e., family, marital or couple, and parent-child functioning). We identified six instruments that met three critical inclusion criteria: 1) psychometric adequacy, 2) user-friendliness and administrative practicality, and 3) clinical utility and sensitivity. The many measures of family functioning available for review varied widely in the quality of their development, the frequency of their use, and the soundness of their psychometric properties. For example, many instruments have been developed exclusively for research purposes and were created and used in a study-specific manner in only a few investigations. Some clinically derived measures have seen extensive use but cannot meet rigorous methodological requirements. Therefore, although some of the many family relationship measures available appear to hold promise as clinically useful assessment tools, given the inclusion criteria and space constraints, they could not be reviewed here. (For extensive references and review texts see, for example, Grotevant and Carlson [1988] and Touliatos et al. [1989].)

Two instruments are recommended for the assessment of whole family functioning, with the entire family as the unit of analysis (as compared with dyadic relationships). The FAD and the FAM-III are well-developed and widely used instruments that tap similar dimensions of whole family functioning with somewhat different formats. Both the FAD and the FAM-III are well-designed instruments with demonstrated reliability and validity, including evidence of clinical utility. In addition, they are both undergoing continued investigation and refinement (e.g., the FAD is being used in a long-term research program that is studying family factors in the course of depressive disorders, and the FAM development group is testing a clinician-administered family-rating scale and a structured family interview).

The DAS is very likely the most widely used measure of marital or couple adjustment and satisfaction in both research and clinical settings. It has been rigorously studied in a variety of populations and has demonstrated sensitivity to interventions that address marital dissatisfaction and discord. The CTS was developed to measure strategies for dealing with conflict in marital, dating, or cohabiting relationships and is probably the most widely used instrument for detecting violence in couples' relationships. A recently revised and expanded version (CTS2) is available, as is a form that was developed explicitly for completion by older children and adolescents regarding violence in their relations with parents or siblings (CTSPC). Although the CTS appears to be a useful indicator of violence in a family relationship, the results must be interpreted carefully and cannot serve as the sole measure of family function. Family members may conceal violent incidents or minimize their severity. The danger of family violence may be clearly indicated even when a completed CTS suggests otherwise. For clinical evaluation, the CTS provides an important complement to the DAS. The sensitive use of both provides a broader and potentially more clinically useful assessment of marital and parent-child functioning.

Measures that purportedly assess several parent-child or parent-adolescent relationship domains have been constructed and used in a wide variety of research projects. Two major problems are encountered when attempting to identify a useful measure of parent-child relationships: 1) the majority of instruments, again mostly research based, have generally been used in a single study with limited samples, and 2) relatively few instruments that focus on clinically relevant aspects of parent-child relationships and functioning have been explicitly developed, consistently used, and empirically tested. These problems are quite striking given the high rates of childhood disturbance and mental health service use focusing on parent-child relationship difficulties. Even taking into account the serious problems encountered in designing instruments capable of eliciting valid responses from younger children, the yield of sound measures is meager. Nonetheless, we identified two instruments, the PSI and the CBQ, that may be clinically useful.

The PSI is a measure of parent, child, and parent-child relationship dimensions associated with the presence of parenting stress and troubled relationships. The PSI was designed in response to pediatricians' requests for a relatively brief screening test battery that would facilitate the identification of parents and parent-child relationships under severe stress and in need of mental health intervention. The PSI has been used with many clinically relevant conditions and populations in a variety of settings. It has demonstrated reliability and validity, including strong correlations with observed parent-child interactions, and sensitivity to treatment.

The major goal of the CBQ is to assess the area of perceived communication conflict between parents and older children or adolescents. The measure aims to provide a broad-based estimate of how much conflict and negative communication parents and adolescents experience in their relationships. A companion instrument, the Issues Checklist (IC), has proven useful in specifying areas of disagreement or dispute for treatment planning and has also shown sensitivity to intervention efforts.

To complement the CBQ's (and IC's) information regarding negative communication between parent and adolescent and conflictual relations, the Dyadic subscale of the FAM-III is often used for additional data on qualitative aspects of the relationship, and the CTS may be used to assess the extent to which violence and aggression factor into the parent-adolescent relationship.

CURRENT STATUS AND FUTURE RESEARCH NEEDS FOR ASSESSMENT

Several family relationship measures demonstrate adequate psychometric and clinical standards to offer the clinician a solid battery of basic family assessment tools. These instruments are useful for evaluation, monitoring, and outcome assessment purposes and are user-friendly in terms of administration, scoring, and interpretation. However, optimal effectiveness of these instruments will require further study in several critical areas.

First and foremost is the need for more normative data, both in terms of sheer numbers and in relation to breakdowns of key subgroups (e.g., age, gender, ethnicity, family composition, and clinical status). Second, the clinical utility of family measures demands explicit attention. Studies providing clinical cutoff scores with associated operating characteristics (e.g., sensitivity and specificity) would be particularly helpful. At the same time, further validation studies are critical, again with an emphasis on clinical samples (including relevant subgroup data), refinement of the instrument's ability to detect clinically significant change, and investigation of the extent of influence of social desirability, other response sets

(e.g., acquiescence), and multicultural or ethnic appropriateness. Third, major gaps in several areas of family measurement must be filled with new instruments. For example, virtually no parent-child relationship instruments have been extensively validated or developed explicitly for use by the practicing clinician. There is also a great need for instruments that can be validly completed by children and adolescents of varying ethnicities and family structures. Finally, other methods of assessment, such as interview- or clinician-based ratings (e.g., the FAD's clinical interview and rating scale) need to be developed and rigorously tested. For example, the Global Assessment of Relational Functioning (GARF) scale (American Psychiatric Association 1994, pp. 758–759) is a promising clinical rating scale modeled after the Global Assessment of Functioning Scale (Axis V) (p. 96). A preliminary report supports the psychometric integrity of the GARF, and ongoing research will clarify the research and clinical utility of this potentially valuable rating scale. Finally, more behaviorally specific family relationship instruments (similar to the CBQ and IC) that tap clinically relevant cognitions and behaviors would dovetail nicely with specific intervention targets identified on the treatment plan and would likely serve to facilitate treatment monitoring and the assessment of family relationship outcomes associated with psychiatric disorders.

REFERENCES AND SUGGESTED READINGS

American Psychiatric Association: Diagnostic and Statistical Manual of Mental Disorders, 4th Edition. Washington, DC, American Psychiatric Association, 1994

Grotevant HD, Carlson CI: Family Assessment: A Guide to Methods and Measures. New York, Guilford, 1988

Touliatos J, Perlmutter BF, Straus MA: Family Measurement Techniques. Newbury Park, CA, Sage, 1989

Family Assessment Device (FAD)

N. B. Epstein, L. M. Baldwin, and D. S. Bishop

GOALS

The Family Assessment Device (FAD) (Epstein et al. 1983) was designed as a screening instrument to 1) provide clinicians and researchers with reliable family functioning information on the basis of clinically relevant family dimensions, 2) identify problem areas in a simple and efficient self-report format, and 3) operationalize the McMaster Model of Family Functioning (MMFF) (Epstein et al. 1983). This instrument assesses the quality of multiple dimensions of family functioning. The dimensions of the FAD follow from the MMFF's postulate that the family's primary function is to facilitate the development and maintenance of family members by successfully accomplishing basic tasks (e.g., obtaining food, shelter, and nurturance), developmental tasks (e.g., managing crises that arise from life cycle changes), and hazardous tasks (e.g., crisis resolution provoked by illness, accidents, or life events).

DESCRIPTION

The FAD consists of 60 self-report statements about a person's family and can be successfully completed by children over age 12. Each statement is scaled with a 4-point Likert format (1 = strongly agree, 2 = agree, 3 = disagree, and 4 = strongly disagree). Sample items from the six dimensions or scales are provided in Example 15–1. The 12-item General Functioning scale is derived from the full scale.

The FAD generates scores on the six scales and the General Functioning scale. Each item is assigned 1 to 4 points. Items that describe healthy functioning are reversed scored. Thus, higher scores indicate more family relationship difficulties.

EXAMPLE 15–1 ■ Sample items from the Family Assessment Device

> Problem Solving
> We resolve most everyday problems around the house.
>
> Communication
> When someone is upset the others know why.
>
> Roles
> We make sure members meet their family responsibilities.
>
> Affective Responsiveness
> We express tenderness.
>
> Affective Involvement
> If someone is in trouble, the others become too involved.
>
> Behavior Control
> We have rules about hitting people.

Reprinted with permission from Dr. I. Miller.

PRACTICAL ISSUES

It takes approximately 15–20 minutes to complete the FAD. The copyrighted instrument can be obtained from

> Dr. I. Miller
> Brown University Family Research Program
> Rhode Island Hospital
> 593 Eddy Street
> Providence, RI 02903

Packets of the FAD for copying, papers on the psychometric properties, and a bibliography are provided on request. Scoring sheets and keys are available and user-friendly. There is no cost for the instrument, scoring key, or supportive documents. No manual is currently available. Specialized training is not required to administer the measure. A computer assessment and scoring program that provide clinical cut points on the basis of their normative sample are available.

The FAD has been translated into French, Spanish, and several other languages.

The FAD is included on the CD-ROM that accompanies this handbook.

PSYCHOMETRIC PROPERTIES

Reliability

The FAD demonstrates fairly good internal consistency; Cronbach's alpha ranges from 0.72 to 0.92 for the subscales on the basis of the normative sample. Alpha values were highest for the General Functioning scale (0.83–0.86) and lowest for the Roles scale (0.57–0.69). Another psychometric investigation studied three groups (see the section titled "Validity") and reported test-retest reliabilities over 1 week that ranged from 0.66 (Problem Solving scale) to 0.76 (Affective Responsiveness scale).

Validity

Normative data on the FAD have been obtained for 627 individuals who were not in a clinical setting. However, FAD scores should be interpreted in relation to ratings from both clinical and nonclinical interviews. This interview sample consisted of 503 individuals. Of these, 294 came from a group of 112 families, most of whom had one adult member who was receiving care in a psychiatric hospital. The remaining 209 persons were college students.

The FAD demonstrates a significant degree of validity. For example, the measure has shown significant correlations with other family instruments, including the Family Adaptability and Cohesion Evaluation Scales (FACES) (Miller et al. 1985). Another psychometric investigation that studied three groups (nonclinical, $n = 627$; clinical psychiatric, $n = 1,138$; and medical disability, $n = 298$) reported successful discrimination between groups. Families with an ill member (psychiatrically or medically) showed more family dysfunction than the nonclinical families. In a large general population study of the prevalence and correlates of child psychiatric disorders (i.e., the Ontario Child Health Study), the FAD General Functioning scale was one of the most powerful correlates of child disorder. The FAD has demonstrated minimal social desirability response bias; correlations range from –0.06 to –0.19 with the Marlowe-Crowne Social Desirability Scale (Miller et al. 1985). Finally, a recent confirmatory factor analysis of the six FAD scales found that 92% of the items loaded highest on their hypothesized factor. The General Functioning scale correlated highly with the principal component of the other 48 items, supporting its use as a global index of family relationship functioning.

CLINICAL UTILITY

The FAD has several potential clinical uses. First, because psychiatric disorders can carry with them the risk of family role impairment, perceived family conflict, and caregiver or spouse burden, an individual presenting with a psychiatric disorder should be screened for potential associated family dysfunction as tapped by the FAD. However, given the lack of meaningful indexes of the FAD's sensitivity and specificity in identifying family dysfunction, significant family relationship problems should be further explored through a clinical family interview.

Second, the magnitude of family dysfunction offers a context in which to judge the severity of the patient's disorder and provides indicators of sources of family support and conflict that affect prognosis and course. Although some evidence suggests that the quality of family functioning (as measured by the FAD) and improvements in family functioning are predictive of improvements in depressive symptomatology (Keitner et al. 1995), more research is necessary to investigate the validity of the claims.

Third, the FAD provides both new and consistent information that, properly interpreted, can highlight areas of treatment focus for the identified patient, other family members, and family relational units.

Fourth, as a standard of sound clinical practice, the quantification of family functioning can be useful as a clinically relevant baseline marker while also allowing for monitoring over the course of intervention. For example, several studies (Keitner et al. 1995) have demonstrated the FAD's sensitivity to clinical status and illness course. Thus, FAD scores at baseline have been found to consistently predict the subsequent course of illness for patients with depressive disorders (Keitner et al. 1995). More research is needed on the FAD's sensitivity to treatment for disorders of individuals and global family relational problems.

Fifth, although not designed for use with multicultural populations, the FAD has been used in research with samples from several countries other than the United States and Canada, and, as mentioned earlier, has been translated into French, Spanish, and several other languages. However, further work is necessary to determine its validity in these groups.

In summary, more research is needed, particularly with respect to norms for various clinical and nonclinical samples; however, the FAD has been used in studies with more than 3,000 individuals and should be useful for the multidimensional evaluation of family functioning associated with a patient's mental (or medical) disorder. The availability of the short, 12-item General Functioning scale score may be especially useful for mental health professionals in settings such as general hospital psychiatric, primary care, and emergency or trauma units. The McMaster Clinical Rating Scale (MCRS) (Miller et al. 1994) and the McMaster Structured Interview of Family Functioning (McSIFF) (Bishop et al. 1987) have been developed as complementary instruments with different assessment methods (i.e., clinical ratings and structured interview) to provide a multimethod assessment package. There is preliminary evidence for these promising instruments, but more research needs to be conducted.

REFERENCES AND SUGGESTED READINGS

Bishop D, Epstein K, Keitner G, et al: The McMaster Structured Interview for Family Functioning. Providence, RI, Brown University, Butler Family Research Program, 1987

Epstein NB, Baldwin LM, Bishop DS: The McMaster Family Assessment Device. Journal of Marital and Family Therapy 9:171–180, 1983

Keitner GI, Ryan CE, Miller IW, et al: Role of the family in recovery and major depression. Am J Psychiatry 152:1002–1008, 1995

Miller IW, Epstein NB, Bishop DS, et al: The McMaster Family Assessment Device: reliability and validity. Journal of Marital and Family Therapy 11:345–356, 1985

Miller IW, Kabacoff RI, Epstein NB, et al: The development of a clinical rating scale for the McMaster Model of Family Functioning. Fam Process 33:53–69, 1994

Family Assessment Measure (FAM-III)

H. A. Skinner, P. D. Steinhauer, and J. Santa-Barbara

GOALS

The Family Assessment Measure (FAM-III) (Skinner et al. 1995) attempts to operationalize the Process Model of family functioning, a concept that evolved from the Fam-

ily Categories Schema developed a decade earlier by Nathan Epstein and his colleagues in Montreal (Epstein et al. 1983). Central to the Process Model is the assumption that the family's ultimate goal is to successfully achieve several basic, developmental, and crisis tasks. To complete the necessary tasks to meet the ultimate common goals within families (i.e., task accomplishment), success in six process dimensions are deemed necessary: Role Performance, Communication, Affective Expression, Affective Involvement, Control, and Values/Norms. The FAM-III is used as a clinical diagnostic screening instrument, a measure of therapy outcome, and a research tool.

DESCRIPTION

The FAM-III was developed from an original pool of 800 items rated according to content saturation, clarity, and clinical relevance. Several revisions of the scale resulted in the current version. The present version of the FAM consists of 134 items, keyed to a 4-point Likert scale, that assess the family at three different levels. The General scale (50 items) focuses on the entire family system. The Dyadic Relationship scale (42 items) examines relationships between specific family member pairs or dyads, such as parent-child or brother-sister. The Self-Rating scale (42 items) measures an individual family member's perception of his or her functioning within the family. Sample items are provided in Example 15–2. In addition to providing an overall scale index for each of the three scales, the FAM-III includes a measure for each of the seven dimensions that comprise the constructs of the

EXAMPLE 15–2 ■ Sample items from the Family Assessment Measure

General Scale
We spend too much time arguing what our problems are.

Dyadic Relationship Scale
This person worries too much about me.

Self-Rating Scale
I often don't understand what other family members are saying.

Process Model. Two response bias scales are embedded within the General scale: Social Desirability and Defensiveness. The FAM-III is designed for respondents at least 10 years old.

PRACTICAL ISSUES

It takes about 30–45 minutes to complete the full FAM-III. However, the three scales can be used independently to conserve time (with the trade-off of comprehensiveness of assessment). It is possible to use only the General scale, or some combination, to conserve time. A 14-item short form, the Brief FAM-III, has also been developed (Skinner et al. 1995).

Easy-scoring templates are available with profiling and T-scores. A computer administration and scoring program is also available. The instrument and manual (Skinner et al. 1995) can be obtained from

> Multi-Health Systems, Inc.
> 908 Niagara Falls Boulevard
> North Tonawanda, NY 14120-2060
> Phone: 800-456-3003
> Internet: www.mhs.com

The FAM-III Specimen Set, which includes a manual, QuikScore forms for the General scale, the Dyadic Relationship scale, and the Self-Rating scale, and color plots, costs $45.00. Specialized training is not required to administer the FAM-III.

PSYCHOMETRIC PROPERTIES

Reliability

The FAM-III demonstrates good internal consistency; Cronbach's alphas are ≥0.90 for the General, Dyadic Relationship, and Self-Rating scales. Median Cronbach's alpha values computed across the three scales were 0.73, 0.72, and 0.53, respectively.

Validity

In the manual, the authors report normative data for adults ($n = 247$) and adolescents ($n = 65$) from psychiatrically healthy families (Skinner et al. 1995). Data

have also been obtained from various families in clinical settings (more than 2,000 individuals) that included families with a major medical disorder, families involved in therapy, and families with a psychiatrically unhealthy member.

The FAM-III significantly discriminated between clinical and nonclinical families in a sample of 475 families, approximately one-third of which were designated as having significant problems (i.e., a family with a member seeking treatment and the family scoring in a dysfunctional range on the Family Assessment Device [p. 244]). The discriminatory power of each item was demonstrated, and the influence of the response bias scales (i.e., Social Desirability and Defensiveness scales) was demonstrated in a sample of 433 persons representing 182 clinical and nonclinical families. High scores on the response bias scales successfully identified patients with independently rated clinical disorders who minimized family dysfunction from patients who acknowledged family problems. To date, no other family functioning measure has succeeded in identifying response bias to the extent of the FAM-III.

CLINICAL UTILITY

The FAM-III can be useful as a screen for the degree of family dysfunction associated with the patient's condition. For example, the FAM-III has discriminated families with school-phobic children and patients with anorexia nervosa from control subjects. As with other self-report family functioning measures, significant family relationship problems can be further explored by using a follow-up clinical family interview. In addition, the magnitude of family dysfunction provides indicators of sources of support, conflict, and control that can inform treatment planning. The FAM-III provides a unique assessment method of general, dyadic, and self-rated perceptions of family relational functioning. Data from these different perspectives may indicate areas of family consensus or estrangement that deserve clinical attention. However, more research is needed on the sensitivity of the FAM-III to treatment outcomes, whether for disorders of individuals or more global family relational problems.

REFERENCES AND SUGGESTED READINGS

Epstein NB, Baldwin LM, Bishop DS: The McMaster Family Assessment Device. Journal of Marital and Family Therapy 9:171–180, 1983

Skinner HA: Self-report instruments for family assessment, in Family Interaction and Psychopathology: Theories, Methods, and Findings. Edited by Jacob T. New York, Plenum, 1987

Skinner HA, Steinhauer PD, Santa-Barbara J: Family Assessment Measure-III (FAM-III). North Tonawanda, NY, Multi-Health Systems, 1995

Dyadic Adjustment Scale (DAS)

G. B. *Spanier*

GOALS

The Dyadic Adjustment Scale (DAS) (Spanier 1976) was developed as a rapid measure of the adjustment of partners "in any committed couple relationship." Accordingly, the DAS has been used in a large number and variety of studies and has rapidly become the standard measure of its kind in the field. The scale purportedly taps basic, multiple dimensions of couples' adjustment, which, together with the total score, can be a clinically useful instrument in the assessment, treatment, and outcome evaluation of dyadic intervention. Although it has been used predominantly in marital research, the DAS has also demonstrated applicability to all cohabiting couples.

DESCRIPTION

The DAS is a 32-item self-report questionnaire that provides a measure of overall dyadic adjustment. In addition, each of the four subscales generates useful and specific information concerning the major components that comprise dyadic adjustment. There are four empirically validated dimensions:

1. Dyadic Consensus: 13 items
2. Dyadic Satisfaction: 10 items
3. Dyadic Cohesion: 5 items
4. Affectional Expression: 4 items

Sample items from the measure are provided in Example 15–3. The Marital Adjustment scale is simply the total score and is interpreted as reflecting the overall level of marital adjustment. DAS items are worded so that they are applicable to married or cohabiting dyads. The response format varies across the 32 items and includes 5-, 6-, or 7-point Likert-scaled questions and two yes-no items. The total score ranges from 0 to 151.

The DAS can be rapidly and easily scored, either manually, with scoring sheets available from the publisher, or by using the computer administration and scoring software. Lower scores indicate poorer dyadic adjustment.

Scores are interpreted in relation to the several small normative samples and the descriptive data generated from several additional relatively small samples of couples. The appropriateness of the reference scores derived from the normative group is compromised by its lack of representativeness (i.e., 109 white, married, lower-middle-class couples from a mostly rural county). The divorced group from the development study had similar characteristics and consisted of only 90 individuals. Sev-

EXAMPLE 15–3 ■ **Sample items from the Dyadic Adjustment Scale**

> Dyadic Consensus Scale
> Aims, goals, and things believed important
>
> Dyadic Satisfaction Scale
> Frequency of quarreling
>
> Dyadic Cohesion Scale
> Calmly discuss issues
>
> Affectional Expression Scale
> Demonstrations of affection

eral additional studies have reported normative DAS data with various samples, but unfortunately these data have not been incorporated into the manual to facilitate and expand interpretation. Scores are presented in standardized format; however, these T-scores and the author's clinical cutoff suggestions (typically below 30) are based on psychometric tradition rather than detailed analysis of sensitivity and specificity. At the same time, users of the DAS typically assume that total scores below 100 suggest problems in dyadic adjustment. However, the author acknowledges that this figure is somewhat arbitrary (although based in part on the normative data).

PRACTICAL ISSUES

It takes approximately 5–10 minutes to complete the DAS and another 5 minutes to score it. A well-written manual is available. QuikScore questionnaire scoring sheets, computer scoring software, and the manual can be obtained from

> Multi-Health Systems, Inc.
> 908 Niagara Falls Boulevard
> North Tonawanda, NY 14120-2060
> Phone: 800-456-3003
> Internet: www.mhs.com

Specialized training is not required for administration. The manual provides appropriate cautions that the DAS is subject to response biases and is not intended to be the only instrument used for clinical diagnosis or treatment planning.

PSYCHOMETRIC PROPERTIES

Reliability

Item analysis indicates that the total score is reliable. High Cronbach's alpha values have been obtained in dozens of studies; the alphas for the total score range between 0.91 and 0.96. Cronbach's alpha values for two of the four subscales (Dyadic Consensus and Dyadic Satisfaction) have been reported as high, but the alpha coefficients for the two shorter subscales have shown only adequate homogeneity (range for all four subscales of 0.73–0.94). The DAS has a high test-retest reliability of 0.96 over an 11-week interval.

Validity

Validity studies indicate that the DAS correlates significantly with other criteria of marital or dyadic adjustment and satisfaction. Differences have been demonstrated between married and divorced persons on the DAS. Lower scorers have a higher probability of being associated with domestic violence and more family dysfunction. Other research has reported positive correlations with measures of marital communication and self-esteem and negative relationships with measures such as social anxiety and depression. Finally, use of the DAS with married versus cohabiting couples, heterosexual versus gay dyads, and men versus women tentatively supports the findings of validity and potential utility of the DAS with various types of intimate partnerships.

Several attempts have been made to replicate the four-factor structure of the DAS. In one study, the factor composition was successfully replicated; however, several other investigations indicated that a single dimension may most parsimoniously represent the items. These discrepant findings are likely due, at least in part, to sample differences (e.g., sample size and composition). Thus, as currently defined and constructed, the DAS subscales should be interpreted with caution. However, the Marital Adjustment score seems relatively robust, so that, at this point, the clinician can relatively safely regard the DAS total score as a reasonably sound measure of relationship adjustment. A good empirical report that deals with the issue of clinical cutoff scores for the DAS (Crane et al. 1990) is recommended for users of the scale.

CLINICAL UTILITY

Since its development, the DAS has been used in a multitude of basic and clinical research studies. At the most basic level, this scale has successfully discriminated well-adjusted from distressed, separated, and divorced couples. Therefore, the DAS can provide a reasonably sound measure of marital adjustment, which can be of use with a variety of presentations and in various settings. For couples who present with primarily relationship distress, the DAS has been used successfully to document changes that occur over the course of marital treatment. Another demonstrated clinical use of the DAS is with individuals with depressive disorder. The strong correlation (concurrent and prospective) between marital discord and depression has led several investigators to examine the utility of couples therapy as a treatment for depression in situations in which there is a discordant relationship. In these studies, the DAS showed utility in the identification of troubled relationships and treatment sensitivity as an outcome measure for the successful treatment of depression plus marital discord with couples therapy (e.g., as compared with cognitive therapy).

A potentially valuable revision, the Revised DAS (RDAS), has recently been developed (Busby et al. 1995). Through a rigorous instrument development process, the authors identified three second-order scale dimensions—Consensus, Satisfaction, and Cohesion. After a series of confirmatory factor analyses, the RDAS, which consists of 14 of the original 32 items, was created. Independent replications of the psychometric properties of the RDAS are under way but still in their early stages. Clinicians may want to stay apprised of the ongoing development of this revision of the classic measure, particularly because it shortens and simplifies the assessment task, thus adding to the clinical utility of dyadic assessment.

REFERENCES AND SUGGESTED READINGS

Belsky J, Spanier GB, Rovine M: Stability and change in marriage across the transition to parenthood. Journal of Marriage and the Family 45:567–577, 1983

Busby DM, Christensen C, Crane CR, et al: A revision of the Dyadic Adjustment Scale for use with distressed and nondistressed couples: construct hierarchy and multidimensional scales. Journal of Marital and Family Therapy 21:289–303, 1995

Crane DR, Allgood SM, Larson JH, et al: Assessing marital quality with distressed and nondistressed couples. Journal of Marriage and the Family 52:87–93, 1990

Spanier GB: Measuring dyadic adjustment: new scales for assessing the quality of marriage and similar dyads. Journal of Marriage and the Family 38:15–28, 1976

Conflict Tactics Scales (CTS)

M. A. *Straus*

GOALS

The Conflict Tactics Scales (CTS) (Straus 1995) was developed to measure strategies for dealing with conflict in marital, dating, or cohabiting relationships. More specifically, the CTS is probably the most widely used instrument for detecting violence in couples' relationships. It has been used in three studies of nationally representative samples of couples in the United States. The theoretical basis for the CTS is conflict theory, which posits that conflict is an inevitable part of human interaction but that violence as a tactic for dealing with conflict is not. The CTS measures concrete acts and events; it is not intended to assess attitudes about conflict or violence or the causes or consequences of violence. The measure assesses three key domains of coping with conflict: violence or physical aggression, verbal or symbolic aggression, and reasoning. A recently revised and expanded version is available, as is a form for older children and adolescents regarding violence in their relations with parents or siblings.

DESCRIPTION

The introduction to the CTS requests that respondents recall situations in which they had a disagreement or were angry with their partners. The respondents are asked to indicate how often they engaged in each of the acts in the past 12 months. The CTS is a 19-item Likert-type questionnaire. The seven response categories are once, twice, 3–5 times, 6–10 times, 11–20 times, more than 20 times, and never. Each item is scored both for what the respondent did and for what the other individual did. These pairs of questions can be asked for any family role relationship, such as spousal, parent-child, and sibling. Items are also presented sequentially in an order from nonviolent to severely violent acts or events. The CTS consists of three subscales:

1. Violence: 9 items
2. Verbal Aggression: 7 items
3. Reasoning: 3 items

Sample items from the CTS are provided in Example 15–4. Notably, the overall Violence subscale does not distinguish the life-threatening nature of its constituent

events. Two procedures can be used to take severity into account: the computation of the Minor and Severe Violence Indexes and the Violence Level Typology (see manual for details). The CTS can be administered as a self-report questionnaire or as part of a more extensive personal interview; it was originally developed as an interview.

EXAMPLE 15–4 ■ Sample items from the Revised Conflict Tactics Scales (CTS2—Form A)

RELATIONSHIP BEHAVIOR

No matter how well a couple gets along, there are times when they disagree, get annoyed with the other person, want different things from each other, or just have spats or fights because they are in a bad mood, are tired, or for some other reason. Couples also have many different ways of trying to settle their differences. If you or your partner did not do one of these things in the past year, but it happened before that, circle "7".

How often did this happen?
  1 = Once in the past year
    2 = Twice in the past year
      3 = 3–5 times in the past year
        4 = 6–10 times in the past year
          5 = 11–20 times in the past year
            6 = More than 20 times in the past year

              7 = Not in the past year, but it did happen before
              0 = This has never happened

Negotiation
I explained my side of a disagreement to my partner   1   2   3   4   5   6   7   0
My partner explained his or her side of a disagreement to me   1   2   3   4   5   6   7   0

Psychological Agression
I insulted or swore at my partner   1   2   3   4   5   6   7   0
My partner did this to me   1   2   3   4   5   6   7   0

Physical Assault
I twisted my partner's arm or hair   1   2   3   4   5   6   7   0
My partner did this to me   1   2   3   4   5   6   7   0

Injury
I had a sprain, bruise, or small cut because of a fight with my partner   1   2   3   4   5   6   7   0
My partner had a sprain, bruise, or small cut because of a fight with me   1   2   3   4   5   6   7   0

Sexual Coercion
I used threats to make my partner have sex   1   2   3   4   5   6   7   0
My partner did this to me   1   2   3   4   5   6   7   0

Three basic scores are derived from the CTS, reflecting the sums of responses for each of the three subscales (i.e., Reasoning, Verbal Aggression, and Violence); they range from 0 to 3, 0 to 7, and 0 to 9, respectively. The nine violent acts that constitute the Violence subscale can also be scored to provide additional useful indexes. First, they can be used to obtain an overall measure of violence, the Overall Violence Index, which is scored by summing the respective scores for each event across the entire CTS. This score can range from 0 to more than 180 incidents over the past year. The author refers to this score as a measure of "chronicity," because severity is not taken into consideration. Minor (items K, L, and M) and Severe (items N through S) Violence scores can be obtained by summing their respective endorsements. In addition, a Violence Level Typology score, which permits clinicians to identify couples whose violence is expressed only in "minor" assaults, can be obtained. It is created by classifying couples on the basis of the most severe level of violence that occurred during the year: none, minor violence only (items K, L, or M but no severe violence items), and severe violence (any occurrence of items N through S).

Extensive normative data are available on more than 8,000 individuals generally representative of the U.S. population in the early 1980s (Strauss 1995). These tables are particularly valuable in terms of gender and age breakdowns, and associated standard scores representing the prevalence of such scores by respondent, and by respondents' reports of their partners.

Because of the highly sensitive nature of the CTS items, the evaluator must remain cognizant of the possibility of social desirability response sets. In the assessment of marital violence, the clinician may consider having another informant (e.g., an older child) complete the CTS, with the focus on parent-to-parent events. (This approach was the original administration method in developing the CTS with college students.) The clinician must remain alert and responsive to any indications of violence (and its effects), regardless of the informant or focus.

PRACTICAL ISSUES

The CTS is administered in a paper and pencil format. It requires less than 10 minutes to complete and less than 5 minutes to score. Similar time should be allowed if the respondent is asked to complete the CTS for another relationship (e.g., parent-child). The reading level appears appropriate for children approximately 12 years or older, though children as young as 10 may complete the CTS in a valid manner.

A test manual (Straus 1995) with simple scoring instructions, extensive normative tables, and references is available from the author:

M. A. Straus, Ph.D.
University of New Hampshire
Family Research Laboratory
33 Mill Pond Road
Durham, NH 03824
Phone: 603-868-1495

Specialized training is not required for administering or scoring the CTS. Interpretation of scores and supplementation with other assessments where necessary demand appropriate clinical judgment and practice. Minimal charges to cover the costs of reproduction and shipping may be charged.

PSYCHOMETRIC PROPERTIES

Reliability

The CTS demonstrates adequate internal consistency; Cronbach's alphas range from 0.42 for the three-item Reasoning subscale to 0.80–0.89 for the other two subscales.

Validity

The CTS has been used in many studies since 1972. These studies involved more than 70,000 participants, including persons from diverse cultural backgrounds (e.g., African Americans and Hispanic Americans). The CTS has been successfully used in more than 20 countries. It is increasingly being used as a diagnostic aid in family therapy. Approximately 400 papers have been written on the basis of data generated from the CTS.

As detailed in the manual (Strauss 1995), extensive validity data have been established, including supportive findings from longitudinal studies of marital violence, clinical studies of violent men, studies of battered women, and several marital therapy trials (thus documenting the instrument's sensitivity to clinical interventions). Factor analyses by several investigators using diverse populations have consistently indicated a reasoning factor, a verbal aggression factor, and either a single violence factor or two violence factors, with the second tapping life-threatening events.

CLINICAL UTILITY

First and foremost, the CTS can be useful as a screen for the presence, extent, and severity of aggression and violence in any pair of family relationships. Domestic violence is unfortunately a ubiquitous dimension of family relationships, serving as symptom and/or sign of the high degrees of stressful experiences many families confront on a daily basis. Clearly, such a measure has a strategic place in the clinician's assessment battery, whether the presenting problem is a child's somatic complaints, a young adult's florid psychotic symptoms, a couple's reports of marital distress, or an elderly patient's complaints of depression. The CTS offers important advantages for clinical work: brevity in administration and scoring; concreteness of target items; the availability of extensive, representative norms; utility in multiple relational systems (e.g., spouse-spouse and child-parent); and information concerning both the occurrence and severity of violence. The CTS should be considered for inclusion in nearly any intake assessment and for use in a range of settings (e.g., specialty mental health, child and adult primary care, school health clinics, and women's shelters). Despite the strengths of the CTS, more research is needed on its operating characteristics and clinical utility in various settings.

The CTS has recently been revised; the CTS2 was published in 1996 (Straus 1996) and the Parent-Child CTS (CTSPC) in 1995 (Straus 1995). According to the author, the CTS2 offers several refinements, including additional items to enhance reliability, improved wording to increase clarity and specificity, better differentiation between minor and severe levels of each scale, new scales to measure sexual coercion and physical injury, and a new format to simplify administration and reduce response sets. Preliminary psychometric findings on the revised scale appear promising. In addition, the development of a standardized interview to supplement and complement the CTS in the assessment of contextual factors related to family violence might facilitate diagnosis, treatment planning, and outcome monitoring.

The CTS does not measure either the issues underlying the disagreement or the extent of such disagreements. Hence, there may have been conflicts over a variety of issues and there could have been violence and hostility without reference to the specific conflictual event. The author responds to the criticism that the CTS does not take into account context and meaning by referring to this complaint as analogous to criticizing a reading ability test for not identifying the reasons a child reads poorly and for not measuring the harmful effects of a reading difficulty. These issues are acknowledged as critical, but the author asserts that context must be evaluated with additional measures and approaches, such as a sensitive clinical family interview.

REFERENCES AND SUGGESTED READINGS

Aldarondo E, Straus MA: Screening for physical violence in couple therapy: methodological, practical, and ethical considerations. Fam Process 33:425–439, 1994

Straus MA: Manual for the Conflict Tactics Scales. Durham, NH, Family Research Laboratory, University of New Hampshire, 1995

Straus MA, Hamby SL, Boney-McCoy S, et al: The Revised Conflict Tactics Scales (CTS2): development and preliminary psychometric data. Journal of Family Issues 17:283–316, 1996

Parenting Stress Index (PSI)

R. R. Abidin

GOALS

The Parenting Stress Index (PSI) (Abidin 1995) was developed as a measure of child characteristics, parent characteristics, and parent-child relationship dimensions associated with the presence of parenting stress and troubled relationships. The PSI was designed in response to pediatricians' requests for a relatively brief screening test battery that would facilitate the identification of parents under severe stress and in need of mental health services. The PSI was developed by using the following assumptions: stressful life events and circumstances are additive in their effects, stressors are multifactorial as to source and multidimensional as to kind, and the parent's appraisal and coping attempts are critical. The PSI includes items that tap the literature on extensive parenting stress, difficult child temperament, and family dysfunction (i.e., poor parent-child "fit").

DESCRIPTION

The PSI consists of 101 items keyed to a 5-point Likert scale (strongly agree to strongly disagree) and an optional 19-item Stressful Life Events scale with yes-no response options. Parents are asked to respond to questions pertaining to themselves and to their children ages 1–12 years.

The 101 items are organized into two domains with the following subscales:

1. Child Characteristics Domain: Adaptability, Demandingness, Mood, Distractibility/Hyperactivity, Acceptability of Child to Parent, Child's Reinforcement of Parent
2. Parent Characteristics Domain: Depression, Attachment to Child, Social Isolation, Sense of Competence in the Parenting Role, Relationship With Spouse/Parenting Partner, Role Restrictions, Parental Health

A Validity subscale aimed at identifying defensive responding (i.e., "faking good") is also included.

The full PSI provides the full complement of subscales. As a measure of parent-child relationships, the Acceptability of Child to Parent, Child's Reinforcement of Parent, and Attachment to Child subscales are critical for the assessment of the quality of relational functioning. In addition, the PSI provides Child and Parent total domain scores, as well as a total Parenting Stress score that includes all items except the stand-alone life events checklist. Raw scores are converted into norm-based percentile scores; high scores represent disturbance. Normal

scores are considered to be in the 15th to 85th percentile range. High scores are considered to be above the 85th percentile.

In some settings, the full PSI may be too long for practical use. Therefore, in response to requests from clinicians for a briefer version of the PSI for use in a variety of settings (e.g., primary care, mental health, and school settings), a 36-item short form (PSI/SF) was developed and is currently available (Abidin 1995). Administration and scoring instructions for the PSI and the PSI/SF are very similar. However, the vast majority of validity data apply to the full PSI, not the short form.

The PSI/SF was developed through a cross-validation factor analysis study of the PSI items forced to a three-factor solution (Sample I, $n = 530$, mothers presenting at 1-year well-baby visit; Sample II, $n = 270$, mothers from the same practice attending a well-child check-up for preschool or first grade). The short form thus consists of a subset of identical items from the full version, organized into three 12-item subscales: 1) Difficult Child Temperament, 2) Dysfunctional Parent-Child Interaction, and 3) Parental Distress. The three-subscale structure reflects several factor analytic studies that suggested a three-factor solution might adequately represent the data. A Total Stress score (i.e., the overall level of parenting stress experienced by an individual [Total Parenting Stress scale]) can also be generated from the short form. This score includes stresses reported in the areas of personal parental distress, stresses derived from the parent's interaction with the child, and stresses resulting from the child's behavioral characteristics but not stresses associated with life roles and events. The Defensive Responding subscale is also included, but items are not scored with those in the other domains. Raw scores for each scale are summed and transferred to the response profile, which provides percentile scores.

PRACTICAL ISSUES

The PSI may be administered either in paper and pencil format or by computer administration. Easy-to-use manual scoring sheets are available; administration and scoring is accomplished by using a perforated two-page sheet that has been prepared to facilitate scoring. The computer scoring option includes an unlimited-use disk with a rather extensive interpretive report program with graphics output.

It takes approximately 20 minutes to complete the full 120-item PSI and about 10 minutes to score it by hand and plot the results. Computer administration may go somewhat more quickly, depending on reading level and computer familiarity. The PSI/SF takes approximately 5–10 minutes to complete.

A recently revised, well-written manual (Abidin 1995) is available from several sources, including Psychological Assessment Resources, Inc., and Multi-Health Systems, Inc.:

Psychological Assessment Resources, Inc.
PO Box 998
Odessa, FL 33556
Phone: 813-918-3003

Multi-Health Systems, Inc.
908 Niagara Falls Boulevard
North Tonawanda, NY 14120-2060
Phone: 800-456-3003
Internet: www.mhs.com

A packet on the PSI includes the manual, questionnaire booklets, scoring rules, and profile forms. The manual provides details concerning instrument development, psychometric results, and interpretation, including case studies. It also describes the development of the PSI/SF and presents initial psychometric data on the short form of the scale.

The PSI has been translated into eight languages, and separate norms are available for several ethnic groups.

PSYCHOMETRIC PROPERTIES

Psychometric properties are reported on the basis of 2,633 mothers in the normative sample, who were recruited primarily from well-child pediatric visits (41% of sample); the remainder of the sample was recruited from public day care centers, a health maintenance organization, and other public and private pediatric clinics.

Reliability

The PSI demonstrates adequate internal consistency for each of the 13 subscales, ranging from 0.70 to 0.83, on the basis of the normative sample of 2,633 parents drawn from public and private pediatric settings. For the two domain scales, Cronbach's alpha was 0.90 (Child) and 0.93 (Parent), with a Total Parenting Stress scale alpha of 0.95. The manual reports test-retest reliability findings from four different studies. Time intervals ranged from 3 weeks to 12 months or more. The test-retest reliability coefficients were as follows: Child Domain (0.57–0.82), Parent Domain (0.70–0.91), and Total Parenting Stress (0.65–0.96); higher coefficients were associated with the shorter retest intervals and larger sample sizes.

As mentioned earlier, initial psychometric data for the PSI/SF are presented in the PSI manual (Abidin 1995, see Chapter 6). Initial estimates of test-retest reliability were assessed from Sample I over a 6-month interval, yielding stability coefficients of 0.84 (Total Stress), 0.85 (Parental Distress), 0.68 (Parent-Child Dysfunctional Interaction), and 0.78 (Difficult Child). Internal consistency coefficients were computed from both samples, yielding Cronbach's alphas of 0.91, 0.87, 0.80, and 0.85, respectively.

Validity

In addition to the normative sample noted earlier (2,633 parents and their children), several independent normative samples are available from the responses of Hispanic and African American parents. The validity research on these samples is comparable with that of the larger group. This research on the PSI indicates a robust measure capable of sustaining its validity despite the translation process and between- and within-nation cultural differences. The factor structure, for example, has been validated on a variety of U.S. samples and also in several transcultural populations, including Chinese, Italian, Portuguese, Latino American, and French Canadian populations.

The manual for the PSI presents more than 250 abstracts supporting the validity of the instrument. Studies document that the PSI discriminates between levels of parental distress, predicts dysfunctional parenting behavior, and predicts deviant development and functioning in a wide range of populations. Differential levels and patterns of distress have been identified in relation to parents of children who display varying degrees of psychopathology and developmental disabilities. The PSI has been used in more than 50 program evaluation studies and has been shown to be clinically sensitive to changes in levels of parental stress as a function of the interventions. Particularly impressive are several studies demonstrating the

PSI's correspondence with observed parent-child interactional dimensions such as child and parent positive and negative affect, child compliance, maternal control and responsiveness, and infants' attachment security.

As the author cautions, some preliminary data support the validity of the PSI/SF, but more work is necessary.

CLINICAL UTILITY

As noted, the primary motive for the development of the PSI and the PSI/SF was the need for a reasonably comprehensive and brief screening instrument for the detection of stress associated with the parenting role as seen by primary care providers. Over the past 15 years or so, the PSI has demonstrated its clinical utility in three basic tasks. First, the PSI can successfully and early on identify parents who are experiencing significant and impairing parenting stress. Second, the PSI is a useful tool for detecting individual and, more importantly in this context, parent-child relationship distress, dysfunction, and possibly disorder. Third, the PSI has shown its utility as an outcome measure in several evaluation studies. Thus, the ability of the PSI to screen for and detect parenting stress and relationship dysfunction and to provide intervention-sensitive data make it a strong tool for clinical use. Its inclusion in an intake assessment packet seems warranted, and the computerized scoring and interpretive report can provide almost immediate clinical feedback that can be incorporated into referral and/or treatment planning.

Nonetheless, like any instrument, the PSI has several limitations that must moderate the clinician's use of the measure. First, there are questions concerning the validity of the component subscales, because their sensitivity and specificity for detecting clinically significant parenting role difficulties have not been established. Although traditional psychometric rules of thumb are suggested for interpreting scores as deviant, further empirical work is the only means possible by which established clinical cutoff scores can be developed. Established cutoff scores are particularly important when the clinician is relying on the measure as an indicator of parent-child relational functioning. Second, although the normative sample is impressive by several standards, the clinician must remain aware that the population on which the scores are based is not truly a general population sample, and there are restrictions (or unknown factors) regarding the clinical, previous treatment, and outcome characteristics of the normative sample for both parent (all mothers, though a small sample of paternal norms are provided) and child. Third, the PSI/SF is attractive in terms of brevity, coverage, and preliminary psychometric findings. However, much work remains to be done to establish its validity to the degree of that of the full PSI. Finally, although several studies have clearly documented the PSI's sensitivity to clinical change, more work is needed to better define the contexts in which the PSI performs optimally.

REFERENCES AND SUGGESTED READINGS

Abidin RR: Parenting Stress Index (Third Edition): Professional Manual. Odessa, FL, Psychological Assessment Resources, Inc., 1995

Abidin RR, Wilfong E: Parenting stress and its relationship to child health care. Children's Health Care 18:114–117, 1989

Kazdin AE: Premature termination from treatment among children referred for antisocial behavior. J Child Psychol Psychiatry 31:415–425, 1990

Conflict Behavior Questionnaire (CBQ)

R. J. Prinz, S. L. Foster, R. N. Kent, and K. D. O'Leary

GOALS

The major goal of the Conflict Behavior Questionnaire (CBQ) (Prinz et al. 1979) is to assess the domain of "perceived communication-conflict between parents and adolescents. The measure aims to provide a broad-based estimate of how much conflict and negative communication parents and adolescents" experience in their relationship (Robin and Foster 1989). The CBQ was designed by Prinz and coworkers as part of an assessment package for the measurement of conflict in parent-adolescent dyads. This package included the Issues Checklist (IC), a useful companion measure designed to elicit specific areas of disagreement or dispute from a list of 44 issues. An objective of the CBQ was to include clinically relevant, behaviorally specific items to measure perceptions of general arguments, misunderstandings, difficulty resolving disputes, and specific verbal and nonverbal communication deficits. The CBQ thus represents an attempt to assist the clinician in identifying focused treatment targets and in monitoring those targets over the course of therapy and their response to intervention.

DESCRIPTION

The CBQ, originally labeled the Interaction Behavior Questionnaire, comes in parallel versions for the parent and adolescent and covers a recall period of 2–3 weeks. A true-false response format is used. "The parent version contains 75 items, 53 of which concern the parent's appraisal of the adolescent child's behavior (e.g., 'My child sulks after an argument') and 22 of which are related to the parent's perceptions of interactions with the adolescent (e.g., 'We joke around often'). The adolescent version consists of 73 items, 51 items relating to the adolescent's appraisal of the parent's behavior (e.g., 'My mom doesn't understand me') and 22 items identical to those in the parent form, assessing the adolescent's perception of interactions with the parent. Item content reflects positive and negative interactive behaviors that occur in nonconflictual discussions as well as in argumentative exchanges" (Robin and Foster 1989, p. 78).

"The CBQ yields two scores (subscales) for each family member completing the measure: 1) the family member's appraisal of the other's behavior, and 2) the member's appraisal of dyadic" interaction with the other (Robin and Foster 1989). Approximately one-third of the items must first be recoded in the direction of positive appraisals. To derive a score in which high scores reflect more negative appraisals of communication conflict behavior, these items are reverse scored. Then a simple tally of the items, scored 1 or 0 (true or false), gives the score for the appropriate subscale.

Conversions of raw scores to T-scores for the CBQ, on a normative sample of 205 distressed and nondistressed families, are published in Appendix A of Robin and Foster's book (1989) (also see the later section "Validity"). These tables allow the clinician to roughly evaluate how distressed the family is in comparison with the normative sample.

Two short form versions of the CBQ have been developed. Prinz et al. (1979) developed the 44-item form known as the CBQ-44. Two subscales (i.e., Appraisal of Other and Appraisal of Dyad) from the original version are also included in the CBQ-44. However, the items that correlated best with the two subscale totals (using data from the CBQ development samples) were removed to shorten the CBQ-44. A 20-item short form (CBQ-20) has been developed on the basis of a different sample by Robin and Foster (1989). The CBQ-20 retained the items that best discriminated distressed and nondistressed families in a larger sample (i.e., the normative sample) that included fathers.

The short forms are scored somewhat differently from the full CBQ, reflecting the different normative groups on which they were based (see Appendix A of Robin and Foster 1989). Because the CBQ-44 was developed on the basis of adolescent and maternal data only, paternal ratings should be used with caution. The CBQ-20 is scored by summing the items (after reverse scoring of the positive items), providing one overall measure of negative communication conflict. The descriptive statistics of the CBQ-20 are based on the aggregated, normative sample. Means and standard deviations by distressed versus nondistressed group status are provided in Robin and Foster (1989, Appendix A, Table A-3).

A useful companion measure, the IC, was developed and norms were derived on the same samples by the same groups of investigators. The 44 issues of the IC provide three scores (Frequency, Anger Intensity, and a weighted cross-product score) that assess both conflictual issues and the perceived anger intensity of disputes over these issues (Robin and Foster 1989). Like the CBQ, parallel parent and adolescent dyad forms are available. "For each topic, the respondent indicates whether the issue has occurred during the previous 4 weeks, and for each issue endorsed, a rating of anger intensity (on a 5-point scale) is assigned" (Robin and Foster 1989, p. 80). Thus, the IC is an easily administered, brief instrument that should be considered as a companion measure for use with the CBQ.

PRACTICAL ISSUES

It takes approximately 15 minutes to administer the original CBQ to one dyad per respondent; additional dyads (e.g., adolescent-mother, adolescent-father) lengthen completion time. Because of the length of the original CBQ, the use of one of the short forms, particularly the brief CBQ-20, is appealing. It takes approximately 5 minutes to complete the CBQ-20, which correlates well (0.94–0.96) with the full CBQ. Unfortunately, no commercially available manual or scoring forms are available for any version of the CBQ. However, the instruments, administration and scoring procedures, and normative or reference group data are available in Robin and Foster (1989).

PSYCHOMETRIC PROPERTIES

Reliability

Internal consistency estimates on the basis of the Prinz et al. (1979) samples were 0.90 or above for mother and teenager reports on each subscale. Combined data from the wait list control groups in the Robin and Foster intervention studies (1989) provide an initial estimate of stability over a 6- to 8-week interval. Test-retest coefficients ranged from 0.37 to 0.85, depending on informant, with approximate mean test-retest correlations for the two subscales of 0.60 (mothers), 0.70 (fathers), and 0.70 (adolescents). Joint reliability of the CBQ has been assessed by computing the percentage of agreement between parents and adolescents on the 22 identical items. The agreement averaged 67% for distressed and 84% for nondistressed dyads (a significant difference). The reliability of the short forms, on the basis of independent samples, has not been reported. Regarding the IC, Robin and Foster (1989, p. 87, Table 5–4) report adequate test-retest reliabilities for the three scores, although the adolescents' responses showed somewhat lower levels of stability than the parents'.

Validity

Three validity studies contrasted scores on the original CBQ from responses of parents and adolescents referred for treatment of family relationship problems with scores from families with self-reports of satisfactory relationships and/or no history of treatment for relational problems. Significant differences were found on both subscales for all three studies. Robin and Foster (1989, p. 85, Table 5–2) pooled intake assessment data from two studies with the three investigations noted earlier (resulting in 205 mother-adolescent and 79 father-adolescent reports) and reported the number of members, mean, and standard deviation for the combined groups by distressed versus nondistressed status. In this aggregated sample, adolescents ranged in age from 10 to 18, were male and female, and came from lower-middle-class to upper-middle-class families.

In addition, in several studies, the CBQ has shown significant decreases in parent and adolescent scores after both behavioral and nonbehavioral family interventions (i.e., treatment sensitivity). Also, the CBQ correlates moderately (0.52) with problem-solving communication behavior coded from audiotaped interaction family tasks and with parent-reported dissatisfaction with child rearing, yielding evidence of the construct validity of the CBQ. Unfortunately, validity data for the CBQ short forms, based on new independent samples, have not been reported. Validity data regarding the IC are available in Robin and Foster (1989); the IC, too, has been shown to discriminate distressed from nondistressed groups and to be sensitive to treatment effects.

CLINICAL UTILITY

The CBQ can supplement the clinical interview and other family assessments to provide measures of the degree of perceived conflict and negative communication in parent-adolescent relationships. Therefore, it can provide an indirect, yet solid, measure of general family distress through the evaluation of a key dimension of parent-adolescent relationships—appraisals of dysfunctional communication patterns and conflict. It is easily administered, completed, and scored and is appropriate for children and young adults ages 10–19. The CBQ (or one of its short forms) is useful as a screening or intake instrument to assist in diagnosis and evaluation of associated features. "The CBQ-20 is particularly useful since it can be completed in about 5 minutes which enhances the feasibility of its use as a 'waiting-room' assessment measure and an 'end-of-session' (or intervention) evaluation instrument" (Robin and Foster 1989, p. 79).

The clinician can estimate the severity of conflict by utilizing the full CBQ normative data and the conversions of raw scores to T-scores provided by Robin and Foster (1989). Because the CBQ has parallel forms for mothers, fathers, and adolescents, information from the multiple informants can help localize relationship and appraisal problems. At the same time, the behavioral specificity of the CBQ's items is useful in developing and formulating the treatment plan and specific intervention targets. The CBQ has been documented to effectively capture treatment effects, making it a valuable assessment, monitoring, and outcome measure. The IC can be a valuable companion instrument that assists in the detailed specification of conflictual issues and the intensity of anger associated with each, thereby facilitating treatment planning.

Several limitations of the CBQ should be noted. Interpretation of scores should be approached with some caution because of the relatively small normative sample and the limitations of its representativeness (i.e., the data are the product of pooling results from five validity and treatment studies with mostly white families from the lower-middle to upper-middle social classes). As with other measures, the development of local norms, combining clinic data with general population or community data, would be wise. The CBQ has been used primarily to screen and quantify overt conflict, disagreements, and negative interactions in families with adolescents with diagnoses of a disruptive behavior disorder (e.g., conduct disorder or attention-deficit disorder). The CBQ was not designed for, and has not been validated with, adolescents who have emotional disorders (e.g., depression or anxiety), psychotic disorders, or mental retardation or developmental disorder.

The short forms also have several limitations. The CBQ-44 was developed from the original CBQ instru-

ment development sample, which is more restricted in representativeness than that of the published CBQ norms described previously. The CBQ-20 was developed from this more extensive normative data pool and thus had a larger and somewhat more heterogeneous sample for comparison purposes; descriptive statistics, by respondent, were published on the basis of these norms (Robin and Foster 1989). However, neither of the short forms has yet accumulated adequate reliability or validity data. Clearly, the CBQ should be supplemented by other clinical information sources such as personal and family interviews, as well as reports of investigations that use other instruments and informants (e.g., other parent-child interaction checklists, clinician global ratings, ratings by other members of the household, and observations if possible).

REFERENCES AND SUGGESTED READINGS

Foster SL, Prinz RJ, O'Leary KD: Impact of problem-solving communication training and generalization procedures on family conflict. Child and Family Behavior Therapy 5:1–23, 1983

Prinz RJ, Foster SL, Kent RN, et al: Multivariate assessment of conflict in distressed and nondistressed mother-adolescent dyads. J Appl Behav Anal 12:691–700, 1979

Robin AL, Foster SL: Negotiating Parent-Adolescent Conflict: A Behavioral-Family Systems Approach. New York, Guilford, 1989

Robin AL, Weiss J: Criterion-related validity of behavioral and self-report measures of problem-solving communication skills in distressed and nondistressed parent-adolescent dyads. Behavioral Assessment 2:339–352, 1980

CHAPTER 16

Suicide Risk Measures

Kenneth J. Tardiff, M.D., M.P.H.
Andrew C. Leon, Ph.D.
Peter Marzuk, M.D.

INTRODUCTION

Major Domains

Suicide attempts are complex acts for which no single set of clinical features assessed at a single point in time can be expected to be a good predictor (Clark et al. 1989). The domain of suicidal behavior is multidimensional. Factors that affect the likelihood of an attempted or completed suicide include demographic parameters (e.g., age, gender, and ethnicity), diagnostic issues (e.g., presence of concurrent disorder such as substance abuse or anxiety disorders), psychological factors (e.g., hopelessness), situational factors (e.g., living alone and lack of social support), and historical and familial factors (e.g., prior suicide attempts and family history of completed suicides). Most predictive of future suicide is a past attempt; the more previous suicide attempts there have been, the more likely there will be another attempt and that it will occur soon. It is not possible in a single chapter to adequately cover all of the diverse elements that contribute to suicide risks or to include all of the scales that could be used to quantify these parameters. Because no one scale or clinical tool of the 16 scales reviewed can substitute for a clinical interview and the complex act of weighing and integrating these diverse factors, the scope of this chapter was very much limited. Therefore a description of selected tools, each of which attempts to measure a different, but clinically salient, factor involved in the complex clinical act of evaluating suicide risk in the shorter and longer term is provided.

All of the scales reviewed in this chapter were developed for research purposes and are not routinely used in clinical practice; however, comments on their potential clinical utility are given. The inclusion of a section on tools for assessing suicide risk does not endorse or argue against the use of such tools in clinical care. However, given the complexity of judging suicide risk, no single scale will likely suffice now or in the foreseeable future.

Organization

In this chapter, three measures are reviewed that were developed to shed light on suicide risk: the Beck Scale for Suicide Ideation (BSS), which assesses the degree of suicidal ideation (thoughts, plans, and wishes); the Suicide Intent Scale (SIS), which measures the intensity of the patient's desire to die after a suicide attempt; and the Beck Hopelessness Scale (BHS), which evaluates an established risk factor, hopelessness. These measures are listed in Table 16–1.

Relevant Measures Included Elsewhere in the Handbook

As noted, a variety of factors must be weighed into the equation in judging suicide risk. Other measures included elsewhere in the handbook may be helpful in the assessment of these risk factors. Concurrent substance or al-

TABLE 16–1 ■ Suicide risk measures

Name of measure	Disorder or construct assessed	Format	Pages
Beck Scale for Suicide Ideation (BSS; self-administered version) Scale for Suicide Ideation (SSI; clinician-administered version)	Intensity, pervasiveness, and characteristics of suicidal ideation	Fully structured, self- or clinician-administered scale; 20 items	264–266
Suicide Intent Scale (SIS)	Intensity of the wish of the individual who attempts suicide to die at the time of the attempt	Fully structured, clinician-administered scale; 20 items	266–268
Beck Hopelessness Scale (BHS)	Extent of negative attitudes about the future (pessimism) in adolescents and adults	Fully structured, self-administered scale; 20 true-false items	268–270

cohol abuse or dependence increases the risk of suicide attempts severalfold. Measures that can be used to screen for substance use disorders are discussed in Chapter 22, "Substance Use Disorders Measures." Other comorbid psychiatric conditions also increase the risk of attempting suicide. Tools for assessing for psychotic symptomatology (e.g., in schizophrenia, psychotic depression, or mania) are discussed in Chapter 23, "Psychotic Disorders Measures," and measures of anxiety symptoms and disorders are reviewed in Chapter 25, "Anxiety Disorders Measures." Acute or severe chronic environmental stresses also increase the risk of suicide attempts. Measures for assessing stress are discussed in Chapter 14, "Stress and Life Events Measures."

Finally, several clinical rating scales (e.g., measures of depressive symptom severity such as the Hamilton Rating Scale for Depression [Ham-D] [p. 526], the Beck Depression Inventory [BDI] [p. 519], and the Inventory of Depressive Symptomatology [p. 529]) include items that are designed to evaluate the degree of suicidal ideation or planning, which can help clinicians appraise the current level of suicidal ideation or recent attempts on a cross-sectional basis. These measures of depression are discussed in Chapter 24, "Mood Disorders Measures."

USING MEASURES IN THIS DOMAIN

The clinical goals of assessment in this domain are 1) to identify individuals at high risk for attempting suicide in the short term (i.e., in days to weeks), 2) to determine if treatment has reduced the likelihood of a suicide attempt

in the near future, and 3) to identify those who continue to be at risk (over the longer term) of ultimately attempting or completing suicide (i.e., a public health or epidemiological perspective).

In this chapter, the focus is on evaluating whether one can predict the seriousness of the next attempt by evaluating features of the last attempt and whether one can predict short-term risk of suicide by evaluating either suicidal ideation or hopelessness (a construct that is theoretically related to suicidal ideation and risk).

Each measure included in this chapter is designed to assess suicide risk from different perspectives (i.e., different levels of conceptualization). None was initially developed to serve the immediate clinical function of determining that a particular individual is at high or low risk of imminently attempting suicide, and none is designed to stand alone. Each may add information to assist in the clinical judgment as to imminent risk. For example, the BHS has been administered to depressed and nondepressed patients to assess their future potential for suicide attempts over months to years.

Clinicians are often required to assess the risk of suicide in the course of treatment (e.g., in determining the need for hospitalization and type of pharmacological treatment). Some items included in each of the three measures discussed in this chapter represent information that most clinicians gather in deciding about the potential for suicide. For example, the BSS measures the wish to live or die, the desire to make an attempt, the duration and frequency of suicidal ideation, the sense of self-control, the deterrents to suicide (e.g., family and religion), the specificity of ideas or plans for suicide, the availability of methods, and the preparation for an attempt. The SIS measures the likelihood of rescue from a suicide attempt, the degree of planning, the patient's concept of the lethality of the attempt, and the medical seriousness of the attempt. The BHS measures pessimism about the future.

The clinical prediction of suicide, however, involves more than adding up items and using a total or subscale score to determine whether someone is at significant risk of committing suicide. In making a decision about the risk of suicide, the clinician must assess for the presence of suicidal thoughts and the degree of planning; presence of psychosis; severity of depression; impulsivity; anger; alcohol and drug use; frequency, nature, and severity of past suicide attempts; family history of suicide; medical problems; loss of loved ones, jobs, or the like; resources available to protect against suicide; access to treatment; and history of compliance with treatment.

When using these scales, it is important to recognize that predictive validity has been established only for groups of patients using diverse measures over substantial time periods. For example, hopelessness is predictive of subsequent suicide completions (Beck et al. 1990). Similarly, the SIS has differentiated between those who attempt and those who complete suicide. However, the clinician makes predictions for one patient at a time and wants to make those predictions in the short term (days to weeks) rather than in the long term (months to years). Thus, although thresholds can be set (e.g., on the BHS) to include nearly all patients who ultimately complete suicide over the ensuing several years, the vast majority of individuals above the threshold do not ultimately complete suicide. Interestingly, then, the several scales that evaluate this domain (both those included and those not included in this chapter) may be of greater interest to system administrators (who are trying to identify groups of patients) than to clinicians who must evaluate individual patients.

GUIDE TO THE SELECTION OF MEASURES

The three instruments described in this chapter are brief, can be self-administered, and have moderate reliability and construct validity. These qualities have made them popular for use in research. However, their performance in routine clinical care has not been directly evaluated

to determine whether they add to routinely executed clinical judgments. On the other hand, because the responses to several items on these scales are often sought by clinicians making judgments about immediate suicide risk, these scales (or items) have a potential clinical benefit.

The BSS, SIS, and BHS may serve as brief screening measures to identify persons who may be at risk of suicide and who warrant further clinical assessment. The BSS and SIS measure aspects of suicidality that may be of research interest (i.e., defining the phenomenology of suicide) or of clinical interest (e.g., determining whether an intervention reduced a parameter that contributes to risk of suicide). The BSS has been administered to patients who have thoughts, plans, or wishes to commit suicide but who have not made any recent attempts. The SIS has been used with patients who have recently attempted suicide to gauge the degree to which they wished to live or die; subsequent research suggests that a greater degree of intent makes future attempts more likely.

The three measures in this chapter have been selected because they were the most frequently used measures in the research literature and because they had the most documentation. Thirteen other instruments were reviewed that are not included in this chapter: the Clinical Instrument to Estimate Suicidal Risk (Motto et al. 1985), the Index of Potential Suicide (Zung 1974), the Reasons for Living Inventory (Linehan et al. 1983), the SAD PERSONS scale (Patterson et al. 1983), the Scale for Assessing Suicidal Risk (Tuckman and Youngman 1968), the Scale for Predicting Subsequent Suicidal Behavior (Buglass and Horton 1974), the Short Scale (Pallis et al. 1984), the Suicidal Death Prediction Scale (Lettieri 1974), the Suicidal Intent in Self Injury (Pierce 1981), the Suicide Potential Scale (Dean et al. 1967), the Suicide Prediction Scale (Farberow and MacKinnon 1974), the Suicide Probability Scale (Cull and Gill 1982), and the Suicide Risk Measure (Plutchik et al. 1989).

CURRENT STATUS AND FUTURE RESEARCH NEEDS FOR ASSESSMENT

Most of the research on these instruments was conducted in clinics in the northeastern United States. It is not clear how these instruments would perform in other clinical settings with a wider range of patients. The internal consistency and reliability of the scales appear adequate. However, more appropriate evaluations of joint and test-retest reliability are needed.

The BSS and SIS have not been shown to have predictive validity about who will attempt suicide. The BHS has moderate predictive validity with regard to who will attempt suicide 5–10 years after its administration. However, future evaluations of predictive validity should use much shorter follow-up periods. Clinically, the prediction of suicide is relevant for the next few days or week—that is, from one appointment to another, for a day pass from the hospital, or from discharge from the hospital to an appointment a week later in the aftercare clinic. Beyond this short period, many intervening factors may change the clinical picture from the time the decision about suicide potential was made. Furthermore, even if one could predict that someone would commit suicide 10 years later, the clinician would have little recourse to prevent the suicide. It is not feasible to hospitalize someone for years to prevent suicide after recovery from an acute disorder. Identifying patients who are at risk for suicide over a long period may reduce the risk of suicide if intervention is made early and persists over the following years.

REFERENCES AND SUGGESTED READINGS

Beck AT, Brown G, Berchick RJ, et al: Relationship between hopelessness and ultimate suicide: a replication with psychiatric outpatients. Am J Psychiatry 147:190–195, 1990

Buglass D, Horton J: A scale for predicting subsequent suicidal behaviour. Br J Psychiatry 124:573–578, 1974

Clark DG, Gibbons RD, Fawcett J, et al: What is the mechanism by which suicide attempts predispose to later suicide attempts? a mathematical model. J Abnorm Psychol 98:42–49, 1989

Cull JG, Gill WS: Suicide Probability Scale (SPS) Manual. Los Angeles, CA, Western Psychological Services, 1982

Dean RA, Miskimins W, DeCook R, et al: Prediction of suicide in a psychiatric hospital. J Clin Psychol 23:296–301, 1967

Farberow NL, MacKinnon D: A suicide prediction schedule for neuropsychiatric hospital patients. J Nerv Ment Dis 158:408–419, 1974

Lettieri DJ: Research issues in developing prediction scales, in The Psychological Assessment of Suicidal Risk. Edited by Neuringer C. Springfield, IL, Charles C Thomas, 1974

Linehan MM, Goodstein JL, Nielsen SL, et al: Reasons for staying alive when you are thinking of killing yourself: the Reasons for Living Inventory. J Consult Clin Psychol 51:276–286, 1983

Motto JA, Heilbron DC, Juster RP: Development of a clinical instrument to estimate suicide risk. Am J Psychiatry 142:680–686, 1985

Pallis DJ, Gibbons JS, Pierce DW: Estimating suicide risk among attempted suicides, II: efficiency of predictive scales after the attempt. Br J Psychiatry 144:139–148, 1984

Patterson WM, Dohn HH, Bird J, et al: Evaluation of suicidal patients: the SAD PERSONS scale. Psychosomatics 24:343–349, 1983

Pierce DW: The predictive validation of a suicide intent scale: a five year follow-up. Br J Psychiatry 139:391–396, 1981

Plutchik R, Van Praag HM, Conte HR, et al: Correlates of suicide and violence risk, I: the Suicide Risk Measure. Compr Psychiatry 30:296–302, 1989

Range LM, Knott EC: Twenty suicide assessment instruments: evaluation and recommendations. Death Studies 21:25–58, 1997

Tuckman J, Youngman WA: A scale for assessing suicide risk of attempted suicides. J Clin Psychol 24:17–19, 1968

Zung WW: Index of Potential Suicide (IPS): a rating scale for suicide prevention, in The Prevention of Suicide. Edited by Beck AT, Resnik HLP, Lettieri DJ. Bowie, MD, Charles Press, 1974

Beck Scale for Suicide Ideation (BSS)

A. Beck, M. Kovacs, and A. Weissman

GOALS

The Beck Scale for Suicide Ideation (BSS) (Beck and Steer 1991; Beck et al. 1979) was designed to measure the intensity, pervasiveness, and characteristics of suicidal ideation in adults and adolescents. It also attempts to assess the risk of a later suicide attempt in individuals who have thoughts, plans, and wishes to commit suicide. The BSS can be used in inpatient, outpatient, emergency psychiatric, and general medical settings.

DESCRIPTION

The BSS is a fully structured instrument that is self-administered by paper and pencil or on computer. An earlier version, the Scale for Suicide Ideation (SSI) (Beck et al. 1979), was designed to be administered by a clinician and comes in two forms: the SSI-C for current suicidal ideation and the SSI-W for suicidal ideation at its worst point in the patient's life. Both the BSS and the SSI contain the same 21 items scored on a 3-point Likert scale from 0 = not present to 2 = maximum severity of suicidal ideation. Sample items from the SSI are provided in Example 16–1. If either item 4 or item 5 is rated 1 or 2, the respondent then rates the rest of the items (e.g., item 6 in Example 16–1). If items 4 and 5 are rated 0, the respondent then skips to item 20 (see Example 16–1). If item 20 is rated positive, the subject then rates item 21 (see Example 16–1).

The severity of suicidal ideation is calculated by summing the ratings for the first 19 items. The range of scores is 0–38. There is no dichotomous cutoff score defining high risk, but increasing scores reflect increasing suicidal ideation and risk. It is recommended that the clinician examine a patient's responses to specific items over time for an indication of changing risk of a suicide attempt.

PRACTICAL ISSUES

It takes 5–10 minutes to self-administer the scale, and verbal administration by a clinician takes about 10 minutes. The BSS is copyrighted and was published in 1991 by

> The Psychological Corporation
> 555 Academic Court
> San Antonio, TX 78204-2498
> Phone: 800-211-8378
> Internet: www.psychcorp.com

EXAMPLE 16–1 ■ Sample item from the Beck Scale for Suicidal Ideation

> 4. Desire to make active suicide attempt

The manual (Beck and Steer 1991) costs $24.00 and includes instructions regarding administration and scoring of the scale and information on its development, interpretation, and psychometric characteristics. Training for raters is minimal. A computerized version is also available from the Psychological Corporation.

PSYCHOMETRIC PROPERTIES

Reliability

In four studies of psychiatric inpatients and outpatients ($N = 2{,}137$), internal consistency coefficients (Cronbach's alpha) for the BSS and the SSI ranged from 0.89 to 0.96, with no differences between the self-administered and clinician-administered versions. In one study of psychiatric inpatients ($N = 25$), patients were seen by two clinicians who alternated interviewing successive patients. Joint reliability was estimated to have a correlation of 0.83 between raters.

Validity

Beck and his colleagues have shown that the BSS was significantly correlated with the Beck Hopelessness Scale (BHS) ($r = 0.47$–0.62) (p. 268), the Beck Depression Inventory (BDI) ($r = 0.25$–0.75) (p. 519), and the Hamilton Rating Scale for Depression (Ham-D) ($r = 0.30$) (p. 526).

Beck et al. (1985) found that the clinician-administered version administered for the current period (SSI-C) did not significantly distinguish between those who completed suicide (mean = 11.71, SD = 7.58, $N = 14$) and those who attempted suicide (mean = 12.81, SD = 8.72, $N = 191$) in a sample of inpatients in a 10-year prospective study ($t = 0.43$, $df = 203$).

Beck et al. (1979) compared inpatients hospitalized for suicidal ideation ($n = 90$) and outpatients seeking treatment for depression ($n = 50$) using the SSI. Inpatients (mean $= 9.43$, SD $= 8.44$) had significantly higher ideation scores than outpatients (mean $= 4.42$, SD $= 5.77$, $t = 4.14$).

CLINICAL UTILITY

Although the self-administered BSS has the same internal consistency and reliability as the clinician-administered SSI, Beck does not recommend that the BSS replace clinical interviewing as a method of evaluating a patient's plans and thoughts of suicide. The SSI provides a reliable, valid, and rapid method of systematically estimating suicide ideation in psychiatric patients.

The SSI did not predict ultimate suicide among those with suicidal ideation when they were followed for a 10-year period. This result is not surprising because many factors could have intervened between the assessment of suicidal ideation and eventual suicide years later, and the behavior has an extremely low base rate. Future research should attempt to predict a suicide attempt within a shorter period (e.g., 1–2 weeks) to evaluate the predictive validity of the SSI.

It is logical to believe that the greater the degree of current preoccupation with suicidal thinking (i.e., the higher the BSS or SSI scores), the greater the immediate risk of a suicide attempt. However, this prediction has not been tested in routine practice. Further, given the low base rate of the behavior (i.e., many patients with high degrees of ideation will not attempt suicide in the short term), it is unlikely that any scale would be both highly sensitive and highly specific. On the other hand, the clinician may find that the BSS or SSI provides a quick glimpse of the patient's current ideation. If scores on the BSS or the SSI are high, the clinician might, for example, institute a formal discussion of suicidal impulses and how to manage them. Again, how much value the routine use of either scale adds to clinical care is not known.

REFERENCES AND SUGGESTED READINGS

Beck AT, Steer RA: Beck Scale for Suicide Ideation Manual. San Antonio, TX, Harcourt Brace, 1991

Beck AT, Kovacs M, Weissman A: Assessment of suicidal ideation: the Scale for Suicide Ideation. J Consult Clin Psychol 47:343–352, 1979

Beck AT, Steer RA, Kovacs M, et al: Hopelessness and eventual suicide: a 10-year prospective study of patients hospitalized with suicidal ideation. Am J Psychiatry 142:559–563, 1985

Beck AT, Steer RA, Ranieri WF: Scale for Suicide Ideation: psychometric properties of a self-report version. J Clin Psychol 44:499–505, 1988

Beck AT, Brown GK, Steer RA: Psychometric characteristics of the Scale for Suicide Ideation with psychiatric outpatients. Behav Res Ther 35:1039–1046, 1997

Steer RA, Kumar G, Beck AT: Self-reported suicidal ideation in adolescent inpatients. J Consult Clin Psychol 61:1096–1099, 1993

Suicide Intent Scale (SIS)

A. Beck, D. Schuyler, and I. Herman

GOALS

The Suicide Intent Scale (SIS) (Beck et al. 1974) was designed to record information regarding the intensity of the suicide attempter's wish to die at the time of the attempt, which the authors consider to be one component of suicide risk. Other components include access to lethal methods and the possibility of rescue. The SIS can be used in inpatient, outpatient, and emergency psychiatric settings.

DESCRIPTION

The SIS is a fully structured instrument that is administered to patients by a trained clinician. The scale contains 20 items scored on a 3-point Likert scale from $0 =$ least severe to $2 =$ most severe. Sample items are provided in Example 16–2. All items are always given for patients who have attempted suicide. The first 9 items deal with circumstances related to the suicide attempts.

EXAMPLE 16–2 ■ Sample items from the Suicide Intent Scale

3. Precautions against Discovery and/or Intervention

12. Seriousness of the Attempt

Reprinted with permission from Aaron T. Beck.

Items 10–15 assess patient reports of thoughts and feelings at the time of the attempt. Items 16–20 describe other aspects of the suicide attempt (such as the person's reaction to the attempt, number of previous attempts, and consumption of alcohol or drugs at the time of the attempt) but are not included in determining the total score.

The first 15 items are used to derive a score that ranges from 0 to 30. Although there are no established cutoff scores, the following data (on the basis of items 1–8 only) illustrate differences in mean scores between those who attempted and those who completed suicides. In people who attempted suicide twice ($N = 15$, the first a nonlethal attempt, the second a completion), the mean score plus or minus the standard deviation for the first eight items at the time of the first attempt was 5.3 ± 3.4 compared with 7.3 ± 2.3 at the time of the eventual completion (Lester et al. 1978). When 194 individuals who committed suicide were compared with 231 individuals who attempted suicide, the mean scores (for the first eight items) were 7.68 for those who committed suicide compared with 5.73 for those who attempted suicide (no standard deviation figure provided). Of the 231 individuals who attempted suicide, 19 reattempted suicide in 1 year; these 19 subjects had significantly higher total scores on the 15 items (mean of 15.58) than the 212 who did not reattempt suicide (mean of 12.45).

PRACTICAL ISSUES

It takes approximately 10 minutes to administer the scale. The SIS is copyrighted and published by

> The Psychological Corporation
> 555 Academic Court
> San Antonio, TX 78204-2498
> Phone: 800-211-8378
> Internet: www.psychcorp.com

The training required for raters is minimal. The manual costs $24.00.

PSYCHOMETRIC PROPERTIES

Reliability

One study showed that the internal consistency for the total score was acceptable (0.81) (Miezkowski et al. 1993); however, if items are used, Cronbach's alphas for two of those subscales are moderate (0.61–0.89). No studies have been undertaken to replicate these findings. The Beck study (Beck and Steer 1989) reported a correlation coefficient (r) of 0.95 in a joint clinician interview.

Validity

Three studies of the criterion validity of the scale have been done. Levy et al. (1995) reported a multiple linear regression model in which family dysfunction, socioeconomic status, and hopelessness explained only about 9% of the variance in SIS in a sample of 76 adolescents who attempted suicide. Beck et al. (1974) found that the SIS had low correlation with the Beck Depression Inventory (BDI) ($r = 0.26$) (p. 519) and moderate correlation with the Beck Hopelessness Scale (BHS) ($r = 0.47$) (p. 268) in a sample of 73 patients. DeMaso et al. (1994) found that the medical seriousness of the attempt was not significantly correlated with the SIS score in a sample of 47 adolescents.

Beck and Steer (1989) studied 413 inpatients who had been hospitalized for suicide attempts for a follow-up period ranging from 5 to 10 years. In logistic regression analysis of eventual suicide (the dependent variable), the SIS precaution item was associated with an elevated risk of eventual suicide (odds ratio 1.67; 95% confidence interval of 1.15–2.02), controlling for employment status and alcoholism.

CLINICAL UTILITY

The SIS is fairly short and simple to administer. The scale may be useful for systematically describing and quantifying the intensity of an attempter's wish to die around the time of the attempt. In practice, it is administered retrospectively, sometimes with an extended period since the attempt. Thus, it is vulnerable to the problems inherent in retrospective assessment such as recall bias.

Although it is clear that the SIS is a reliable and valid measure of the degree of intent—especially of a recent suicide attempt—questions remain about the clinical utility of that information in the management of individual patients. SIS scores have differentiated between those who completed and those who attempted suicide (SIS score obtained at the time of the prior attempt) and those who reattempted from those who did not, information that may be useful at the group level. However, the utility of such information in the care of individual patients is yet to be documented. In theory, such an appraisal (using the SIS) might provide emergency room clinicians with important information that would help them to decide whether to admit a patient who has just attempted suicide. However, whether this scaled information adds to that acquired in routine emergency room practice has again not been evaluated.

No firm data suggest that the SIS is useful prognostically. Except for one item ("Precautions against Discovery and/or Intervention"), the SIS did not predict ultimate suicide among individuals who attempted suicide when they were followed for a 10-year period. This finding is not surprising because many factors could have intervened between assessment of the suicide attempt and eventual suicide years later. Future research should use a shorter follow-up period (e.g., 1–2 weeks) in the evaluation of the predictive validity of the SIS.

REFERENCES AND SUGGESTED READINGS

Beck AT, Steer RA: Clinical predictors of eventual suicide: a 5 to 10 year prospective study of suicide attempters. J Affect Disord 17:203–209, 1989

Beck AT, Schuyler D, Herman I: Development of suicidal intent scales, in The Prevention of Suicide. Edited by Beck AT, Resnik HP, Lettieri DJ. Bowie, MD, Charles Press, 1974

DeMaso DR, Ross L, Beardslee WR: Depressive disorders and suicide intent in adolescent suicide attempters. Developmental and Behavioral Pediatrics 15:74–77, 1994

Lester D, Beck AT, Narrett S: Suicidal intent in successive suicidal actions. Psychol Rep 43:110, 1978

Levy SR, Jurkovic GL, Spirito A: A multisystems analysis of adolescent suicide attempters. J Abnorm Child Psychol 23:221–234, 1995

Miezkowski TA, Sweeney JA, Haas GL, et al: Factor composition of the Suicide Intent Scale. Suicide Life Threat Behav 23:37–45, 1993

Beck Hopelessness Scale (BHS)

A. T. Beck, A. Weissman, D. Lester, and L. Trexler

GOALS

The Beck Hopelessness Scale (BHS) (Beck et al. 1974) is designed to measure hopelessness. It adheres closely to Stotland's (1969) conception of hopelessness as a cognitive schemata of negative expectancy about the short- and long-term future. It is designed to measure the extent of negative attitudes about the future (pessimism) as perceived by adolescents and adults. Although the scale was not designed as a screening test, it has nevertheless been used as an indirect indicator of suicide risk in depressed individuals who have made suicide attempts and for detection of hopelessness in adolescent and adult populations.

DESCRIPTION

The BHS is a fully structured instrument that is self-administered by the subject using paper and pencil (or verbally administered by a clinician). It can be used in inpatient, outpatient, and emergency psychiatric settings. The BHS contains 20 true-false items. Sample items are provided in Example 16–3.

The severity of hopelessness is calculated by summing scores for the 20 items (each item being scored 0 or 1 on the basis of the accompanying response key), the total score ranging from 0 = no hopelessness to 20 = maximum hopelessness. In the manual (Beck and Steer 1993), Beck's Center for Cognitive Therapy recommends

EXAMPLE 16–3 ■ **Sample item from the Beck Hopelessness Scale**

7. My future seems dark to me.

the following classification of scores: 0–3 minimal, 4–8 mild, 9–14 moderate, and 15–20 severe.

PRACTICAL ISSUES

It takes 5–10 minutes to self-administer the scale, and verbal administration by a clinician takes 10 minutes. The BHS is copyrighted and was originally published in 1988 by

> The Psychological Corporation
> 555 Academic Court
> San Antonio, TX 78204-2498
> Phone: 800-211-8378
> Internet: www.psychcorp.com

The manual (Beck and Steer 1993) costs $24.00 and covers the administration and scoring of the scale and interpretation of the results. The training required for raters is minimal; however, the manual recommends that the scale be used and interpreted by professionals with appropriate clinical training and experience according to the guidelines established by the American Psychological Association's 1985 Standard for Educational and Psychological Testing. A computerized version for administration and scoring is also available.

PSYCHOMETRIC PROPERTIES

Reliability

In one study of results from individuals with suicidal ideation, patients who had attempted suicide, patients with alcohol dependence, patients with heroin dependence, and depressed patients, internal consistency was estimated to range from 0.82 to 0.93 (Kuder-Richardson–20

coefficients). Test-retest reliability for a sample of 21 outpatients with mixed disorders was 0.69 (1-week interval) and 0.66 (6-week interval) for a different sample of 99 outpatients.

Validity

The validity of the BHS has been evaluated in a wide range of samples. Each of these studies limited the analyses to bivariate correlations with the Beck Depression Inventory (BDI) (p. 519) or a clinical rating of hopelessness. The correlations with the BDI, minus the pessimism item, reported by Beck and Steer (1993) ranged from 0.44 to 0.74 in separate samples of individuals with suicidal ideation ($r = 0.59$, $N = 165$), individuals who had attempted suicide ($r = 0.68$, $N = 437$), patients with alcohol dependence ($r = 0.74$, $N = 105$), patients with heroin dependence ($r = 0.44$, $N = 211$), patients with a single episode of major depressive disorder ($r = 0.62$, $N = 134$), and patients with dysthymic disorder ($r = 0.62$, $N = 177$). Nekanda-Trepka et al. (1983) reported a similar correlation between the BHS and the BDI ($r = 0.47$) in a sample of depressed outpatients ($N = 140$). Keller and Wolfersdorf (1993) reported a somewhat stronger correlation between the BHS and the BDI at discharge ($r = 0.63$, $N = 61$) than at admission ($r = 0.49$, $N = 61$) among depressed inpatients. That hopelessness correlates with the overall severity of depression in diverse samples provides evidence of concurrent validity because most experts view hopelessness (view of the future) as a key element in the syndrome of depression. Beck et al. (1974) evaluated the correlation of the BHS with a clinical rating of hopelessness and found correlation coefficients (r) of 0.74 in 23 general medical outpatients and 0.62 in 62 inpatients who had recently attempted suicide. The BHS has been shown to discriminate among outpatients with major depressive disorder ($n = 199$, mean = 11.3, SD = 5.2), those with generalized anxiety disorder ($n = 48$, mean = 7.9, SD = 4.9), and a mixed group of psychiatric patients with nonaffective, nonanxiety disorders ($n = 76$, mean = 6.6, SD = 5.0).

BHS scores have been found to be reduced as depressive symptoms improve in the course of treatment (Beck et al. 1985). Young et al. (1996) described substantial change in items between depressive episodes and periods of wellness and found that stable high levels of hopelessness were more predictive of suicide attempts than high levels at only one point in time. In a prospective study of 61 depressed inpatients, Keller and Wolfersdorf (1993) found that a BHS score of (8 correctly identified 90% of the 10 patients who carried out suicidal acts during the following year.

Administration of the scale in a general population sample in Dublin, Ireland ($N = 400$), produced a mean of 4.45 (SD = 3.09) (Greene 1981). The generalizability of these results to other settings is unknown.

Beck et al. (1985), using a BHS total score of ≥10, found that the false-positive rate was 88.4% and the false-negative rate was 9.1% in predicting suicide 5–10 years later among persons who were previously inpatients. The mean BHS score was significantly higher in the group of patients who committed suicide (mean = 13.27, SD = 4.43) than in the group of patients who did not commit suicide (mean = 8.94, SD = 6.05). Beck et al. (1990) used a BHS total score of ≥9 to predict completed suicides over 10 years in outpatients with mixed diagnoses ($N = 1,958$). The false-positive rate (percentage of patients who did not commit suicide but had a score of ≥9) was 59%, and the false-negative rate (percentage of patients who committed suicide but had a score of <9) was 5.9%.

CLINICAL UTILITY

The BHS is positively associated with elevated risk of an eventual suicide attempt or suicide completion. A high score indicates that the treatment of the patient must be rigorous and constant. It is clear that for groups of depressed patients, when symptomatic, those who score ≥9 on the BHS, as a group, are at extreme risk (compared with those who score ≤8) of ultimately (over 10 years) completing suicide (11 times more likely), but the incidence of suicide in those with higher BHS scores is very low (i.e., most do not complete suicide). Beck et al. (1990) suggest that although some individuals with depression have a potential for suicide, others do not. They suggest that those with high BHS scores have a higher

potential for committing suicide, just as smoking is a risk factor for heart disease. This view would suggest that a BHS score for any individual does not have clinical utility in predicting immediate risk of suicide attempt. Rather, one might wish to monitor patients with this potential (i.e., those with a high score on the BHS) more closely in hopes of intervening early to reduce eventual suicide attempts or completions or to target this patient group with a special suicide prevention program. Whether either of these interventions have clinical value has not been studied. Thus, to date, the BHS has not been demonstrated to have immediate clinical utility for individuals.

REFERENCES AND SUGGESTED READINGS

Beck AT, Steer RA: Beck Hopelessness Scale Manual. San Antonio, TX, Harcourt Brace, 1993

Beck AT, Weissman A, Lester D, et al: The measurement of pessimism: the hopelessness case. J Clin Psychol 42:861–865, 1974

Beck AT, Steer RA, Kovacs M, et al: Hopelessness and eventual suicide: a 10-year prospective study of patients hospitalized with suicidal ideation. Am J Psychiatry 142:559–563, 1985

Beck AT, Brown G, Berchick RJ, et al: Relationship between hopelessness and ultimate suicide: a replication with psychiatric outpatients. Am J Psychiatry 147:190–195, 1990

Greene SM: Levels of measured hopelessness in the general population. Br J Clin Psychol 20:11–14, 1981

Keller F, Wolfersdorf M: Hopelessness and the tendency to commit suicide in the course of depressive disorder. Crisis 14:173–177, 1993

Nekanda-Trepka CJS, Bishop S, Blackburn IM: Hopelessness and depression. Br J Clin Psychol 22:49–60, 1983

Stotland E: The Psychology of Hope. San Francisco, CA, Jossey-Bass, 1969

Young MA, Fogg LF, Scheftner W, et al: Stable trait component of hopelessness: baseline and sensitivity to depression. J Abnorm Psychol 105:155–165, 1996

Measures Related to DSM-IV Diagnostic Categories

Measures Primarily Designed for Use With Children and Adolescents: An Overview

Deborah A. Zarin, M.D.
Neal D. Ryan, M.D.

ORGANIZATION OF THE CHILD AND ADOLESCENT MEASURES

The next three chapters deal specifically with measures for children and adolescents.

Chapter 17: Child and Adolescent Measures for Diagnosis and Screening

The instruments in Chapter 17 were designed to facilitate a broad assessment of symptoms and disorders from infancy through adolescence. These instruments are meant to be used during screening to identify children who require further evaluation, or, once children are identified, to help the clinician make a DSM-IV diagnosis during a more thorough evaluation. The chapter includes three infant and preschool diagnostic screening instruments and seven measures for school-age children and adolescents. Some of the measures are checklists that assess the severity of clusters of symptoms on a continuous scale. Other measures are designed to classify children's symptoms into diagnostic categories on the basis of the DSM-IV criteria for mental disorders.

Chapter 18: Symptom-Specific Measures for Disorders Usually First Diagnosed in Infancy, Childhood, or Adolescence

The measures in Chapter 18 were developed to assess specific disorders in children and adolescents. The mea-

sures include rating scales and diagnostic instruments that focus on the following disorders in children and adolescents:

- Attention-deficit/hyperactivity disorder
- Oppositional defiant disorder
- Conduct disorder
- Anxiety disorders (with the exception of obsessive-compulsive disorder and posttraumatic stress disorder)
- Mood disorders
- Pervasive developmental disorders
- Tic disorders

Measures of posttraumatic stress disorder and obsessive-compulsive disorder appropriate for children and adolescents are included in Chapter 25, "Anxiety Disorders Measures." Other measures for depression and anxiety disorders that may also be used with children are reviewed in Chapter 24, "Mood Disorders Measures," and Chapter 25, "Anxiety Disorders Measures." Measures for substance use disorders that are appropriate for use in children are reviewed in Chapter 22, "Substance Use Disorders Measures." Some instruments that assess antisocial symptomatology can be found in Chapter 31, "Impulse Control Disorders Measures."

Chapter 19: Child and Adolescent Measures of Functional Status

Chapter 19 presents a variety of functional status measures for children and adolescents; the measures were de-

Assessment measures appropriate for children and adolescents included elsewhere in this handbook

CHAPTER	MEASURE
Chapter 8, "Mental Health Status, Functioning, and Disabilities Measures"	Global Assessment Scale (GAS) (p. 96): child version (CGAS) (p. 96) Health of the Nation Outcome Scales (HoNOS): child version (p. 104)
Chapter 12, "Patient Perceptions of Care Measures"	Youth Satisfaction Questionnaire (YSQ) (p. 191)
Chapter 13, "Practitioner and System Evaluation"	Child and Adolescent Services Assessment (CASA) (p. 204)
Chapter 14, "Stress and Life Events Measures"	Life Events Scales for Children and Adolescents (p. 229)
Chapter 15, "Family and Relational Issues Measures"	Family Assessment Device (FAD), which can be completed by children over age 12 (p. 245) Family Assessment Measure (FAM-III), which is designed for respondents at least age 10 years (p. 247) Conflict Tactics Scales (CTS): version for older children and adolescents (CTSPC) (p. 251) Conflict Behavior Questionnaire (CBQ): adolescent version (p. 257)
Chapter 16, "Suicide Risk Measures"	Beck Hopelessness Scale (BHS): appropriate for use with adolescents (p. 268)
Chapter 21, "Neuropsychiatric Measures for Cognitive Disorders"	Galveston Orientation and Amnesia Test (GOAT): Child's Orientation and Amnesia Test (COAT) (p. 443)
Chapter 23, "Psychotic Disorders Measures"	Brief Psychiatric Rating Scale for Children (BPRS-C), a 21-item child version of the Brief Psychiatric Rating Scale (p. 490) (not reviewed in detail) Positive and Negative Syndrome Scale (PANSS): child and adolescent version (Kiddie-PANSS) (p. 494)
Chapter 25, "Anxiety Disorders Measures"	Social Phobia and Anxiety Inventory (SPAI): child version (SPAI-C) (p. 567) Yale-Brown Obsessive Compulsive Scale (Y-BOCS): child version (CY-BOCS) (p. 572) Impact of Event Scale (IES) (p. 579), which has been used in children and adolescents
Chapter 26, "Somatoform and Factitious Disorders and Malingering Measures"	Visual analog scales, which can be used in children ages 5 years and up (p. 601)
Chapter 27, "Dissociative Disorders Measures"	Child Dissociative Checklist (CDC) (p. 619) Dissociative Experiences Scale (DES): Adolescent Dissociative Experiences Scale (A-DES) (p. 621)
Chapter 29, "Eating Disorders Measures"	Eating Disorder Inventory (EDI): child version, which requires second-grade reading level (KEDS) (p. 651) Eating Disorder Examination (EDE): version for children and adolescents ages 8–15 years (ChEDE) (p. 668)
Chapter 31, "Impulse-Control Disorders Measures"	Massachusetts General Hospital (MGH) Hairpulling Scale (p. 708)

signed to assess functioning across an array of dimensions at home, at school, and in the community. These measures are not diagnosis specific but are applicable to the range of clinical conditions that children present with for treatment. The domains of functioning measured include cognitive, social, self-care or independence, self-concept or self-esteem, and general health status.

Child Measures Included in Other Chapters

Some measures that are appropriate for assessing children and adolescents are included in other chapters of this handbook, as shown in the table on the previous page.

ISSUES IN IMPLEMENTATION AND INTERPRETATION COMMON TO CHILD MEASURES

Multiple Informants

It is often essential to gather data from multiple informants (e.g., child, family, teacher, and other agencies) to adequately assess a child or adolescent. Some of the measures in Chapter 17, Chapter 18, and Chapter 19 have different versions for different informants. However, informants frequently disagree about the presence or severity of different symptoms or clinical findings. The implications of different strategies for using data from multiple informants are discussed in the descriptions of some of the specific measures in these chapters. Nevertheless, the optimum method of combining the frequently disparate data from multiple informants remains an open research question, and the definitive solution to this problem is not yet known.

Broad Age or Developmental Range

Many of the measures reviewed in Chapter 17, Chapter 18, and Chapter 19 cover broad age ranges (e.g., from young school age through adolescence) that are associated with significant changes in cognitive, emotional, and social abilities. This wide variation affects the appropriateness of the measure, because the way in which the questions are asked, the content of the questions, and the significance of the resulting information vary with developmental stage. It is therefore important for clinicians who are considering using these measures to carefully take into account the age and developmental status of the patients on whom the measure was evaluated before determining its appropriateness for a given clinical situation. In addition, the applicability of published norms and suggested cutoff scores depends, in part, on the age range of the tested population as compared with the age range of the clinical population in which the measure is to be used.

Child and Adolescent Measures for Diagnosis and Screening

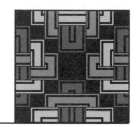

Laurence L. Greenhill, M.D.
Joan Malcolm, Ph.D.

INTRODUCTION

Major Domains

Clinicians rely on interviews with children and their parents to determine the presence and severity of childhood disorders. In response to a need for standardization, structured diagnostic and screening interview schedules have been developed for use with children and adolescents. These instruments facilitate a systematic diagnostic assessment in accordance with specific criteria for psychiatric disorders and also standardize methods for gathering information on a broad range of behaviors and problems.

These measures have advantages and disadvantages that depend on the instrument, the population, and the user. They were often not developed in clinical programs but rather in research projects—either epidemiological surveys (e.g., the National Institute of Mental Health Diagnostic Interview Schedule for Children [NIMH-DISC]) or treatment or biological research (e.g., the Schedule for Affective Disorders and Schizophrenia for School-Age Children: Present and Lifetime Version [K-SADS-PL]). Whether the goal is designing a research project or running a clinic, each professional must decide if these structured instruments will be helpful in making standardized assessments of children and adolescents in the particular program. Use of these measures has not been included in any practice standards; consequently, clinicians who adopt these measures will need specialized

training to use them effectively. In this chapter the relative strengths and weaknesses of these instruments for clinical populations are reviewed, so that both clinicians and researchers can determine which instrument or instruments may be most appropriate for a particular purpose.

Organization

The 10 interview instruments included in this chapter are listed in Table 17–1. There are three infant and preschool diagnostic screening instruments:

- Bayley Scales of Infant Development—Second Edition (BSID II)
- Denver Developmental Screening Test II (Denver II)
- Preschool Behavioral Questionnaire (PBQ)

These instruments are followed by seven measures for school-age children and adolescents:

- Schedule for Affective Disorders and Schizophrenia for School-Age Children: Present and Lifetime Version (K-SADS-PL)
- Child and Adolescent Psychiatric Assessment (CAPA)
- National Institute of Mental Health Diagnostic Interview Schedule for Children (NIMH-DISC 2.3)
- Child Behavior Checklists (CBCL/2–3 and CBCL/4–18), Teacher Report Form (TRF), and Youth Self Report (YSR)

TABLE 17–1 ■ Child diagnostic and screening measures

Name of measure	Disorder or construct assessed	Format	Pages
Bayley Scales of Infant Development—Second Edition (BSID II)	Current developmental functioning of infants and children (ages 1–42 months) within the domains of cognitive, language, personal and social, and fine and gross motor skills	Mental, Motor, and Behavior Rating Scales; 178, 111, and 30 items, respectively	288–291
Denver Developmental Screening Test II (Denver II)	General developmental screening of children from birth to age 6.5 years to identify delays in personal and social, fine motor, gross motor, and language skills	Clinician-administered test; 125 items in 4 domains	291–294
Preschool Behavior Questionnaire (PBQ)	Identify preschoolers (ages 3–6) who show symptoms of emotional problems	Completed by a teacher or teacher's aide; 36 items	294–296
Schedule for Affective Disorders and Schizophrenia for School-Age Children: Present and Lifetime Version (K-SADS-PL)*	Episodes of psychopathology to make categorical (DSM-IV) diagnoses of mood, psychotic, anxiety, behavioral, and substance abuse and other disorders	Interviewer-based, semistructured measure; includes Screening Interview with 82 items and 5 diagnostic supplement modules	296–301
Child and Adolescent Psychiatric Assessment (CAPA)	Information about psychiatric symptoms; allows interviewer to code their presence or absence and their frequency, duration, and onset; to be used with children ages 8 years and older and their parents	Standardized, interviewer-based assessment; 1,401 emphasized probes and 2,571 discretionary probes	301–305
National Institute of Mental Health Diagnostic Interview Schedule for Children (NIMH-DISC 2.3) Parent version (NIMH-DISC-P) Youth version (NIMH-DISC-C) Teacher version (NIMH-DISC-T)	DSM Axis I diagnoses of a child or adolescent; covers 33 mental disorders in 6 groups: anxiety, mood, disruptive, substance abuse, schizophrenia, and miscellaneous disorders	Completely structured, respondent-based interview; 2,930 questions (not all are always used)	305–310
Child Behavior Checklists (CBCL/2–3 and CBCL/4–18) Teacher Report Form (TRF) Youth Self Report (YSR)	Parent-scored symptom checklists on competencies and behavioral and emotional problems in preschool to adolescent children, ages 2–3 and 4–18; Youth Self Report for ages 11–18	CBCL/2–3: 100 problem items and 3 global questions; CBCL/4–18 and YSR: 112 items; TRF: 126 items	310–314
Diagnostic Interview for Children and Adolescents (DICA) Child version (DICA-C) Adolescent version (DICA-A) Parent version (DICA-P)	Psychopathology and more than 20 psychiatric diagnoses for clinical and epidemiological research; versions for children ages 6–12, adolescents ages 13-18, and parents of both age groups	Semistructured rater- or self-administered interview	314–318
Child Assessment Schedule (CAS) Parent version (P-CAS)	DSM-III diagnosis in clinical assessments and clinical research, organized around thematic topics (e.g., school, friends, and family)	Interviewer-based, semistructured assessment; 3 parts	318–321
Personality Inventory for Children (PIC)	Profile of personality characteristics of individual children (ages 3–18) that taps into behavior, affect, ability, and family function	Clinician-rated inventory; 420 items	321–324

*Measure is included on the CD-ROM that accompanies this handbook.

- Diagnostic Interview for Children and Adolescents (DICA)
- Child Assessment Schedule (CAS)
- Personality Inventory for Children (PIC)

Five of these measures do not yield formal DSM-IV diagnoses: the BSID II, the Denver II, the PBQ, the PIC, and the CBCL, which serves as a broad-band symptom checklist that covers two age ranges (2–3 years and 4–18 years) and has versions for multiple informants. The remaining measures described in this chapter are diagnostic.

The semistructured diagnostic instruments can be further subdivided into those that are interviewer based and those that are respondent based. The respondent-based interviews (e.g., the NIMH-DISC 2.3) contain a fixed set of questions that organize the responses of the patient. Because of the fixed nature of the questions and the instructions to deliver the questions exactly as written, these instruments are described as structured. In contrast, interviewer-based diagnostic interviews (e.g., the K-SADS-PL, the DICA, and the CAS) attempt to organize the approach of the interviewer by including a flexible list of questions or diagnostic probes; their use depends on the judgment of the interviewer (Angold et al. 1995). Because of their use of optional probes, these types of interviews are characterized as semistructured. The DICA allows more flexibility than the NIMH-DISC 2.3 because the interviewer is allowed to ask additional clarifying questions. Some diagnostic measures (e.g., the CAPA) combine both respondent-based approaches and interviewer-based techniques; they provide sets of required questions and extensive glossaries that define terms such as *often* that are used to inquire about the frequency of symptoms (Angold and Costello 1996).

In this chapter we describe only one cognitive measure, the BSID, which is applicable only to preschool children. The issue of cognitive impairment is equally relevant during the school-age period, but space limitations did not allow the inclusion of school-age cognitive measures. Space limitations also prevented the inclusion of an assessment of specific language delay, which is a common presenting feature among preschool children referred for child psychiatric assessment.

Relevant Measures Included Elsewhere in the Handbook

Symptom- and diagnostic-specific measures (e.g., symptom checklists) for use with children (e.g., the Conners'

Rating Scales—Revised [CRS-R] [p. 329], the Children's Depression Inventory [CDI] [p. 344], the Multidimensional Anxiety Scale for Children [MASC] [p. 341], and the Revised Children's Manifest Anxiety Scale [RCMAS] [p. 336]) are described in Chapter 18, "Symptom-Specific Measures for Disorders Usually First Diagnosed in Infancy, Childhood, or Adolescence." Functional measures for use with children (e.g., tests of adaptive skills) are described in Chapter 19, "Child and Adolescent Measures of Functional Status." Clinicians should also refer to the introduction of Chapter 6, "Diagnostic Interviews for Adults," which serves as an important point of reference, particularly for child measures that have been adapted from adult measures, such as the K-SADS-PL from the Schedule for Affective Disorders and Schizophrenia (SADS) (p. 58) and the DICA from the Diagnostic Interview Schedule (DIS) (p. 61). In addition, diagnostic instruments that represent only minimal revisions of adult measures applied to children are covered in the chapters on adult measures.

USING MEASURES IN THIS DOMAIN

Goals of Assessment

The primary goal of the measures in this domain is to respond to the need for broad-based clinician-administered tools to screen and identify psychiatric disorders in children and adolescents. Research programs, service delivery systems, and managed-care organizations have sought to overcome the lack of reliability often found in office practice diagnostic evaluations. These variations in diagnosis are a result of shifting diagnostic standards, variable training approaches, and a myriad of biases that creep into and distort the office practice diagnostic process.

What biases affect diagnosis? First, clinical training standards vary from program to program, and even professionals in the same program often do not make the same diagnosis for the same patient, even when given the same material. Angold (in press) has commented that structured interviews were created to address information collection biases that affect clinicians, including the tendency to assign diagnoses without collecting all necessary information, selectively collecting information that conforms to initial diagnostic impression while ignoring exclusionary information, or seeing correlations where none exist.

Diagnostic instruments have been designed to provide a standard organization for covering the same information. They also establish rules for the manner in which information is gathered. Using standard diagnostic nosology, these instruments yield diagnoses only after all inclusionary and exclusionary information is collected. Finally, the instruments can standardize systems for combining the information gathered, resolving discrepant information from different informants, and automating the diagnostic decision-making process.

Developing diagnostic interviews for children involves additional challenges. Standardized information gathering requires that the developers of diagnostic interviews create separate versions for parents and for children. Low levels of agreement have been found between parents' and children's ratings because the different informants provide information that produces different sets of correlations and therefore gives rise to different inferences. This difference in perspective creates an opportunity for disagreement between the two informants. Some clinicians prefer to obtain the main diagnostic information from the parent and may ignore the information from the child when discrepant. Some diagnostic instruments, such as the K-SADS-PL, include an algorithm for handling discrepant data from parent and child before a diagnosis can be obtained. Information quality also depends on the cognitive development of the child. Therefore, most structured diagnostic interviews are limited to children over a minimum age (e.g., children must be at least age 9 to participate in an NIMH-DISC 2.3 interview).

Implementation Issues

Two types of structured instruments are described in this chapter. The first are checklists of symptoms developed to measure clusters of symptoms on continuous scales, such as infant and preschool diagnostic instruments (e.g., the CBCL and the PIC). The second are diagnostic measures aimed at classifying children into DSM diagnostic categories and also have some utility in assessing changes in symptom presence or severity (e.g., the K-SADS-PL).

The instruments that inquire about lists of symptoms are also of two types. The first type, such as the NIMH-DISC 2.3 and the CAPA, elicits information. Therefore, the interviewer does not need to know the child first. The second type, such as the CBCL, codifies

information that is already in the respondent's head (E. J. Costello, personal communication). The time required for administration may thus vary; structured interviews are long because they are designed to collect information on a child who may be unknown to the interviewer before the interview, whereas questionnaires are short because they assume the informant (parent or teacher) knows the child.

The wide range of ages covered by these instruments—from infancy to older adolescence—means that the instruments must include measures of developmental achievement for infants and preschoolers and measures of psychopathology for school-age children and adolescents.

Measures can also be distinguished on the basis of whether the dimensions of child behavior they assess, derived through factor analysis, are characterized as narrow or broad band (Achenbach and Edelbrock 1978). Narrow-band symptoms concentrate on the symptoms of one disorder and can be measured by a behavior rating scale whose content is specific to that disorder. For example, the Conners' Rating Scales—Revised (p. 329) focus mainly on symptoms of one disorder, attention-deficit/hyperactivity disorder (ADHD). Such scales identify individuals who statistically deviate from the mean. Scales that measure narrow-band symptoms are more appropriate for treatment monitoring and repeated measurements during the course of a research protocol (Abikoff et al. 1993). Narrow-band symptom rating scales, such as the CDI (p. 344), the MASC (p. 341), and the RCMAS (p. 336), are covered in Chapter 18.

In contrast, the broad-band dimensions include groups of symptoms that may occur in several disorders, including those that are internalizing and externalizing. For example, the symptom of inattention is found in both ADHD and major depressive disorder. The checklists and diagnostic instruments reviewed in this chapter address broad-band symptoms (i.e., they increase understanding of the general symptoms) by organizing the history of the illness before any treatment intervention. These measures are designed to obtain information on symptom duration, onset and offset, and related functional impairment. They have been designed to classify children into specific diagnostic categories; they do not measure children's deviance from a statistical norm (as do the narrow-band instruments).

All of the instruments described in this chapter have a format that is readily usable in office practice (e.g., paper and pencil format or computer-based system). Self-administered symptom checklists (e.g., the CBCL and the PIC) are written at a sixth-grade reading level unless otherwise specified.

Issues in Interpreting Psychometric Data

Because developmental processes are rapidly changing and involve multiple domains, establishing the reliability and validity of standardized measures is especially difficult. Establishing psychometric properties is particularly difficult for the assessment tools used with infants and toddlers, because the measures are often developed in research environments for the study of normal development. Specialized training in infant and toddler assessment is necessary for standardized administration of these measures.

Although intensive office assessment by a clinician may be considered one standard for diagnostic assessment for school-age children, it is probably not the best, because office procedures have not been clearly defined or described in a standardized manner in treatment manuals. For example, most agree that both child and parent informants are necessary to make a valid diagnosis. Yet there is no universal standardization of the order of these interviews or a universal algorithm for resolving disparate parent and child responses. The developers of some instruments have also recommended extensive training, which adds to the cost of implementation.

Evaluating the validity of a diagnostic assessment instrument for a child psychiatric disorder is particularly challenging. No simple laboratory measure (e.g., a biological marker such as a positive culture for pneumococcus in the sputum of a patient with a cough and fever) can serve as the definitive test of whether a diagnosis is actually present. There is no best or gold standard. However, Spitzer's (1983) "LEAD" standard has been suggested as sufficient to establish whether a child has a particular disorder (Kraemer et al. 1987). LEAD is an acronym for Longitudinal (i.e., data collected over time about the disorder), Expert (i.e., advice attained from those most knowledgeable about the best available measures), and All Data (i.e., utilizing all available data, when necessary, including information pertaining to families). Those who use the LEAD diagnostic approach do not achieve high reliability, however (Zimmerman 1994). Even so, the LEAD diagnostic approach is roughly comparable with the best estimate diagnosis and incorporates a mix of dimensional and categorical data that

Jensen (1995) believes a sensitive and knowledgeable clinician might gather.

Another option for evaluating the validity of a diagnostic assessment instrument for a child psychiatric disorder is to reinterview the same subject with a different diagnostic instrument. If the diagnoses are the same, then the validity of both the diagnosis and the first instrument is supported.

These issues have made it difficult to calibrate sensitivity for child psychiatric diagnostic measures, resulting in overdiagnosis. As a result, some diagnostic measures may detect large numbers of comorbid diagnoses that can seem excessive to clinicians. Publications on the psychometric properties of diagnostic instruments do not always report the numbers of symptoms endorsed or the total number of diagnoses generated. Comparisons between the validity studies of the various diagnostic instruments are further complicated by procedural and criterion standard differences used in different studies (Hodges 1993; Shaffer 1994). In addition, instruments can be self-administered or administered by computer or an interviewer. Except for the CBCL, psychometric data in this chapter are derived on the basis of the paper version, given by an interviewer.

Determining the psychometric properties of these diagnostic instruments is also often hampered by variability in informants (e.g., a lack of agreement among parent, child, and teacher). These issues have not been studied in as much detail for the diagnostic instruments as for the shorter symptom checklists and are therefore covered in more detail in Chapter 18, "Symptom-Specific Measures for Disorders Usually First Diagnosed in Infancy, Childhood, or Adolescence."

Furthermore, there is relatively poor agreement between diagnoses derived on structured interviews and those obtained from clinicians doing free-form diagnostic interviews, as shown by studies of the K-SADS-PL (Kaufman et al. 1997).

Test-retest reliability, an important test of the stability of a diagnostic instrument, has been problematic because of attenuation of initial scores when the instrument is readministered 2 weeks later. This attenuation effect has been studied most thoroughly for the NIMH-DISC 2.3, which requires that questions be read exactly the same way each time they are asked, although it is undoubtedly present for most instruments, even symptom checklists, when they are repeated. Various explanations have been put forth for attenuation effects, including the patient learning that giving no answers shortens the interview, variability in symptom state, or the patient changing his or her perspective when asked the same question several times within a month. When these attenuation effects are studied, it is important to compensate for diagnostic instruments that are branching and include skip options. Interviewed children or parents fail to report symptoms on retesting that they reported at the first interview. Attenuation or reliability problems can lead to baseline shifts in treatment studies (i.e., the second symptom rating always being lower). These attenuation problems can lead to a Type I error in a clinical trial—finding a difference in populations when there is none—that could lead the investigator to attribute lack of a diagnosis on a particular scale to the treatment being used when it is just an artifact of repeated measurement. According to Lucas et al. (1997), the greatest problems with reliability have been found in the following areas: child informants, community samples, high sensitivity–low specificity (stem) questions, diagnoses placed at the beginning of highly structured interviews, and detailed questions that inquire about important concepts of symptom frequency or timing. One study estimated that more than 80% of the variance in test-retest reliability kappa scores—a statistic that is the coefficient of agreement between repeated ratings of the same patient over time—of the NIMH-DISC 2.1 could be accounted for by attenuation (Jensen et al. 1995). Lucas et al. (1997) reported that most of the diagnostic interview schedules for children suffer from attenuation problems in test-retest reliability, so that most diagnoses fall below a kappa of 0.6 and some below 0.4.

The high levels of comorbidity derived from all diagnostic instruments create problems. Mixed clinical pictures are the rule in childhood (e.g., the majority of children with ADHD are shown via diagnostic measures to have at least one additional DSM Axis I disorder that causes impairment). Although some of this comorbidity is artifactual and some real, as Rutter and Tuma note (1988), it has implications for measurement either way.

As described previously, there may be many theoretical reasons for the lack of agreement among the measures described in this chapter, including the situation specificity of childhood psychiatric symptoms, rater divergence, attenuation of ratings over time, lack of a gold standard for making a child psychiatric diagnosis, and lack of calibration among raters using interviewer-based diagnostic interviews. The effects of development and our lack of understanding of the progression of many of the childhood diagnoses constantly interact. In addition, the diagnosis of internalizing disorders relies heavily on the child's use of sophisticated language skills and his or her insight and ability to report on internal mood states that are often extremely difficult to describe even for adult patients with the same disorder.

GUIDE TO THE SELECTION OF MEASURES

Various factors can be taken into account in selecting measures, including the child's age, the purpose of the assessment, the practical aspect of using the instrument, and the disorder of interest (see Table 17–2). The first factor is the child's age. The youngest children (infants, toddlers, and preschool children) do not have the language or cognitive skills to respond to elaborate diagnostic questionnaires. Furthermore, the DSM-IV diagnostic system specifies many childhood disorders that begin in school-age children with impairments involving problems in standard classrooms. Thus, interviews with preschool children do not involve formal psychiatric interviews with the patients. Instead, a clinician generally observes and rates the child's behavior or questions the parents about the child's behavior. Very young children are screened for abnormal behaviors and their neurodevelopmental stage rather than being diagnosed. For infants, the BSID II provides an estimate of the neurodevelopmental stage. For toddlers and preschoolers, the Denver II provides a good estimate of motor and cognitive development relative to samples of normally developing children. Both these assessments require training, and the Denver II requires the purchase of a kit. Neither measure provides an opportunity to inquire about behavior, however. For that purpose, the CBCL/2–3 yields broad-band ratings of internalizing and externalizing symptoms and behaviors with norms that cover many ethnic groups and different countries. The PBQ also covers the domains of behavior in this age group but does not have the base of normative data and stability in various samples of the CBCL/2–3. However, these two scales do not provide diagnoses in either preschoolers or older children. For disorders that present in the preschool and early school-age period, such as ADHD, one would use measures that have been validated for preschool (the CAS) or for the early school-age period (the NIMH-DISC 2.3, the K-SADS-PL, or the DICA).

The second selection factor in choosing one of the instruments described in this chapter is the purpose for its use (i.e., whether one wants to screen for the presence of abnormality or make a formal diagnosis). The screening instruments (e.g., the PIC, the PBQ, the Denver II, the BDIS II, and the CBCL) play an important role in identifying patients and establishing caseness and the need for further evaluation and eventual intervention but do not provide a diagnosis. These instruments (with the exception of the BDIS II) use brief checklists, thus minimizing rater and informant burden. Screening instruments are used more often for the youngest children, whereas structured diagnostic instruments are more appropriate for school-age children and adolescents.

Use of one of the structured diagnostic instruments (e.g., the K-SADS-PL, the NIMH-DISC 2.3, the DICA, the CAPA, or the CAS) is recommended to ascertain a diagnosis. The clinician is best served by instruments that are brief and reliable for both internalizing and externalizing disorders. Instruments that are available in computer-based format (the DICA and the NIMH-DISC) are very convenient because they include prompts for the interviewer. These programs automatically provide the branching logic and skip-out questions. They also include a scoring algorithm and print a report. Their diagnostic algorithms mean that the interviewer does not have to rely on memory to correctly collect diagnostic criteria.

A clinical researcher who is carrying out a treatment study may administer an entire interviewer-based instrument (e.g., the K-SADS-PL) at baseline and use the instrument's much shorter specific symptom module (e.g., the Affective Disorders module) for subsequent weekly visits. The epidemiologist may select a respondent-based interview (e.g., the NIMH-DISC-IV) that can be administered by lay interviewers or an interviewer-based interview with glossary and required probes (e.g., the CAPA). Of course, use of the CAPA and the DICA requires extensive training periods (see later sections).

The three revisions of the DSM over the past 16 years have necessitated frequent upgrades in these diagnostic measures; consequently, the most current version may be so new that psychometric properties have not yet been published. Nevertheless, it is recommended that clinicians use the latest versions of the measures. For ex-

ample, the DSM-IV K-SADS-PL was chosen over the other K-SADS interviews not only because of its quick screening module but also because it has the most recently published, detailed psychometric properties using DSM-IV standards of any of the K-SADS interviews. However, the merits of published psychometric properties are not necessarily sufficient to endorse an instrument, and another version of the K-SADS—perhaps one with longer scales—may prove more suitable for a particular setting or project. Reported reliability also does not indicate that reliable diagnoses can be expected for everyone who uses the instrument (R. Klein, personal communication).

The third factor to be considered in selecting an instrument is the practical aspect of using the instrument: amount of training required to learn the diagnostic instrument, length of interview time, whether separate time is needed to score the interview, the cost of the interview, and the support available. Community pediatricians and psychiatrists should review these factors carefully, weighing the costs and time required for proper training in the use of these instruments. Although the publishers of screening instruments sometimes provide technical support to office practitioners who purchase the instrument (e.g., for the BSID II, the Denver II, the PBQ, and the PIC), this support is much rarer for the structured diagnostic instruments, which often do not have commercial publishers. As shown in Table 17–2, the most detailed of the structured interviews take more than an hour and are thus unlikely to find their way into clinical settings guided by managed care. In addition, the instruments may not yield the information needed to make clinical decisions.

The fourth factor to consider in selecting an instrument is the disorder of interest. Does the instrument allow one to track symptoms over time? For example, the K-SADS-PL adequately identifies mood disorders. To track depressive symptoms over time, the clinician or researcher can administer the 17 K-SADS-PL items devoted to depression. The NIMH-DISC-IV has a more extensive battery of items for substance abuse disorders. The DICA has been reported to more accurately diagnose depression and externalizing disorders than juvenile mania or substance use disorders (Carlson, personal communication). To diagnose pervasive developmental disorders, clinicians may need to use measures beyond those described in this chapter, such as the Childhood Autism Rating Scale (CARS) or the Autism Diagnostic Interview—Revised (ADI-R) (p. 351).

TABLE 17–2 ■ Features influencing ease of administration of child psychiatric diagnostic interview instruments

Measure	Number of items	Type; number of diagnoses	Patient age	Respondent	Maximum test time (minutes)	Time frame	Training time	Cost; computer version available?	Strengths	Weaknesses
Scales for infants, toddlers, and preschoolers										
BSID II	319	Developmental evaluation; N/A	1–42 months	Infant	60	Current exam	1 day	$760; no	Best "infant IQ"	Kit too elaborate
Denver II	125	Screen; N/A	1–78 months	Infant Parent	20	Current exam	1 day	$70; no	Quickest developmental screen	Too many false-positive diagnoses
PBQ	36	Screen; N/A	3–6 years	Teacher	10	6 months	1 day	$20; no	Easy to use and score	Cannot make diagnoses
CBCL/2–3 and CBCL/4–18	138	Screen; N/A	2–18 years	Parent Teacher Adolescent	20	6 months	N/A	$20–295; yes	Good symptom checklist for screening	Cannot make diagnoses
PIC	420	Screen; N/A	3–18 years	Parent	60	1 month	N/A	$225; yes		

Scales for other children

K-SADS-PL	>300	Diagnostic; 32	6–18 years	Child Parent	90–150	Lifetime; episode	2 days	N/A; under development	Good interview for mood, anxiety, and behavioral disorders	Scoring not automated
CAPA	1,401	Diagnostic; 30	9–18 years; 6–18 years	Child Parent	220	3 months	14 days	N/A; no	Most detailed interview for patients	Training expensive; 25% fail to meet certification requirements
NIMH-DISC	2,930	Diagnostic; 33	6–17 years; 9–17 years	Child Parent	140	1 year; 4 weeks	1 day computer; 4 days paper form	$900 (computer), $50 (paper); yes	Most often used for epidemiological studies; good computer version	Boring for clinician; too many false-positive diagnoses
DICA	>300	Diagnostic; 25	Three versions: 6–12 years, 13–18 years, and parents	Child Adolescent Parent	180–240	Lifetime; some disorders current	10 days	$895; yes	Good computer version that is user-friendly	Scoring of paper version not explained
CAS	>300	Diagnostic; 20	4–18 years	Child Parent	150	Lifetime	10 days	N/A; no	Very good for diagnosis of preschool child	Not all criteria needed to make a diagnosis are listed

Time considerations and utility should guide the choice of tools for clinical practice. Symptom checklists such as the CBCL can be self-administered by parents and have a very low false-negative rate for symptoms of child psychiatric disorder. Limitations imposed by managed care, such as 17-minute diagnoses and treatment-planning sessions, mean that only the quickest and simplest measure (e.g., the CBCL) can be employed in such situations.

However, more sophisticated instruments are finding a role in a variety of settings. Large-scale programs, such as Boys Town USA near Omaha, Nebraska, are now using the NIMH-DISC-IV for screening, diagnostic, and service assignment purposes. This form can be administered by a lay interviewer or by computer or it can be self-administered. Built-in diagnostic algorithms and thorough symptom assessment are its strengths.

Only two of the instruments included in this chapter obtain information from teachers—the PBQ and the TRF. Teacher information is crucial for the office practice of child psychiatry, because school function represents at least two domains of potential impairment, academic and social. The DSM-IV diagnosis of ADHD requires evidence of symptoms or impairment across a minimum of two situations (typically school and home). Ideally, all of the diagnostic instruments should include a teacher interview module. The NIMH has developed an NIMH-DISC interview for teachers, but space limitations prevent its inclusion here (Lahey et al. 1994). Similarly, it was not possible to include the Teacher Telephone Interview (Tannock et al. 1995), a telephone-based, semistructured teacher interview that covers all DSM-IV symptoms for ADHD, conduct disorder, and oppositional defiant disorder and screen questions for anxiety, depression, and obsessive-compulsive disorder. There is also a parallel semistructured interview for parents, the Parent Interview for Child Symptoms (PICS), which covers all DSM-III-R and DSM-IV items.

Structured diagnostic interviews can serve as a valuable tool for the clinician or researcher but not as an all-purpose interface between the clinician and the family. For example, the interviews do not carry out the important functions of ascertaining the chief complaint at first contact, and they do not always follow the natural sequence of questions used by the clinician in obtaining a description of the present illness. Rather, the structured diagnostic and screening interviews have been likened to a psychiatric review of symptoms (Carlson, personal communication). Consequently, the structured interview inquiry must be brought into the clinical interview at an appropriate time, not during the first 5 minutes of patient contact. Furthermore, these instruments can only address the specific disorders for which they were designed and thus cannot be used to study new or different phenomenology that is not already described in the structured interview's manual. For example, the interviews generally do not give the clinician the option of asking about nonspecific symptoms in a child with a specific disorder (e.g., emotional lability in a child with ADHD) or provide a standardized method for inquiring about delayed developmental milestones associated with significant medical illnesses. However, these factors can significantly affect the level of the child's impairment and can be a major factor in driving the parents to seek help for the child.

CURRENT STATUS AND FUTURE RESEARCH NEEDS FOR ASSESSMENT

The field of child and adolescent psychiatry has developed a group of instruments that gather information on symptoms found in children and adolescents using checklists and rating forms that can be quickly completed by adults. Psychometric data and normative samples are available for several of these instruments. More detailed diagnostic instruments require much more interview time, and analytic tools must be used to interpret the results. These structured diagnostic interviews, which have been used in a variety of research applications, are a great improvement over free-form clinical interviews. However, they still need to be improved to overcome problems with attenuation errors and with the lack of reliability when parents and children are asked to recall symptom onset for problems that last longer than 3 months. This unchangeability in recall is an obvious problem in determining DSM-IV diagnoses, which have a minimum duration criterion of 6 months (Angold, in press).

Many factors have prevented the widespread use of structured diagnostic interviews in the regular office practice of child and adolescent psychiatry, including the amount of training required, the multiplicity of versions available, the time required for their use, the complexities of scoring, and the previous lack of readily available computer-based versions, complete with scoring algorithms and automatic skip-out questions. The recent development of CD-ROM–based diagnostic measures and the growing presence of computer-based versions may change this situation for the better.

Although not perfect, diagnostic instruments have been steadily improving in their test-retest reliability and validity. Computer-based instruments that produce reports that are useful to the clinician, the parent, and the insurance company would be most appropriate for a busy office practice. None of the instruments described in this chapter has reached that stage, although a few (the CBCL, the DICA, and the NIMH-DISC 2.3) may reach that goal soon.

REFERENCES AND SUGGESTED READINGS

Abikoff H, Courtney M, Pelham W, et al: Teachers' ratings of disruptive behaviors: the influence of halo effects. J Abnorm Child Psychol 21:519–533, 1993

Achenbach T, Edelbrock C: The classification of child psychopathology: a review and analysis of empirical efforts. Psychol Bull 85:1275–1301, 1978

Angold A: Interviewer-based interviews, in Assessment Instruments in Child Psychiatry Research. Edited by Shaffer D, Richters J. Philadelphia, PA, WB Saunders, in press

Angold A, Costello EJ: Toward establishing an empirical basis for the diagnosis of oppositional defiant disorder. J Am Acad Child Adolesc Psychiatry 35:1205–1212, 1996

Angold A, Prendergast M, Cox A, et al: The Child and Adolescent Psychiatric Assessment (CAPA). Psychol Med 25:739–754, 1995

Boyle M, Offord D, Racine Y, et al: Adequacy of interviews and checklists for classifying childhood psychiatric disorder based on parent reports. Arch Gen Psychiatry 54:793–799, 1997

Chambers WJ, Puig-Antich J, Hirsch M, et al: The assessment of affective disorders in children and adolescents by semistructured interview. Arch Gen Psychiatry 42:696–702, 1985

Edelbrock C, Costello A: Structured psychiatric interviews for children, in Assessment and Diagnosis in Child Psychopathology. Edited by Rutter M, Tuma AH, Lann I. New York, Guilford, 1988

Gutterman E, O'Brien J, Young J: Structured diagnostic interviews for children and adolescents: current status and future directions. J Am Acad Child Adolesc Psychiatry 26:621–630, 1987

Hodges K: Structured interviews for assessing children. J Child Psychol Psychiatry 34:49–68, 1993

Jensen P: Scales versus categories? never play against a stacked deck. J Am Acad Child Adolesc Psychiatry 34:485–487, 1995

Jensen P, Roper M, Fisher P, et al: Test-retest reliability of the Diagnostic Interview Schedule for Children (DISC 2.1): parent, child, and combined algorithms. Arch Gen Psychiatry 52:61–71, 1995

Kaufman J, Birmaher B, Brent D, et al: Schedule for Affective Disorders and Schizophrenia for School-Age Children: Present and Lifetime Version (K-SADS-PL): initial reliability and validity data. J Am Acad Child Adolesc Psychiatry 36:980–989, 1997

Kraemer H, Pruyn J, Gibbons R, et al: Methodology in psychiatric research. Arch Gen Psychiatry 44:1100–1106, 1987

Lahey B, Appelgate B, McBurnett K, et al: DSM-IV field trials for attention deficit hyperactivity disorder. Am J Psychiatry 151:1673–1685, 1994

Lucas C, Fisher P, Piacentini J, et al: Features of interview questions associated with attenuation of symptom reports. J Abnorm Child Psychol 7:22–29, 1997

Rutter M, Tuma A: Diagnosis and classification: some outstanding issues, in Assessment and Diagnosis in Child Psychopathology. Edited by Rutter M, Tuma AH, Lann I. New York, Guilford, 1988, pp 438–440

Shaffer D: Debate and argument: structured interviews for assessing children. J Child Psychol Psychiatry 35:783–784, 1994

Spitzer R: Psychiatric diagnosis: are clinicians still necessary? Compr Psychiatry 24:399–411, 1983

Tannock R, Schachar R, Logan GD: Methylphenidate and cognitive flexibility: dissociated dose effects in hyperactive children. J Abnorm Child Psychol 23:235–267, 1995

Zimmerman M: Diagnosing personality disorders: a review of issues and research methods. Arch Gen Psychiatry 51:225–245, 1994

Bayley Scales of Infant Development—Second Edition (BSID II)

N. Bayley

GOALS

The Bayley Scales of Infant Development (BSID) (Bayley 1969) were developed to measure current developmental functioning of infants and children within the domains of cognitive, language, personal and social, and fine and gross motor skills. The BSID was designed to provide infants and young children with a set of tasks that would enable a clinician to assess their current level of developmental functioning by comparison with age peers. The BSID is also able to determine whether the child is likely to be mentally retarded. Although it is the best indicator for assessing very low functioning in infants and toddlers, the BSID is unable to specify the diagnosis or cause, such as pervasive developmental disorder or language disorder.

The content of the BSID was derived from research findings and several scales of infant development existing at the time. Bayley (1969) stated that tests of infant development in the first 2 years measured various simple cognitive functions but not intelligence. As the infant brain develops, more stable cognitive processes, such as those underlying intelligence, emerge. The constructs measured by the BSID become stable with age and are better able to predict future cognitive ability. Even so, the predictive validity of infant intelligence measures, particularly those such as the BSID that feature habituation and novelty paradigms, has been widely debated (S. Hinshaw, personal communication, 1996).

Bayley (1993) cites evidence that certain aspects of cognitive ability observed in infancy are related to cognitive ability in later childhood. Specifically, BSID scores for developmentally delayed infants who received no intervention were predictive of performance on school-age intellectual measures such as the Wechsler Intelligence Scale for Children—Revised (Wechsler 1974). Although the BSID remains limited in its ability to predict later intelligence in children with normal development, very low scores are quite predictive of later intelligence. IQ is better predicted from infant scores as one moves from early infancy (6 months) to the toddler period (24 months).

The BSID was in use for more than 20 years before it was revised and updated. Although certain essential features were retained, several important changes were made, resulting in the publication of the BSID II (Bayley 1993; Nellis and Gridley 1994). The age range was extended from 2–30 months to 1–42 months. Content coverage was improved to include changes in developmental theory and research. The stimulus materials were redesigned in color to reflect advances in graphic arts. In addition, the norms were updated using a sample that was representative of the current U.S. population by race and ethnicity, gender, parent education, and geographic location. Extensive studies were conducted to explore the reliability, validity, factor analysis, and clinical utility of the BSID II scales.

The BSID has been used primarily to identify developmental delays in infants. The BSID II can be used as a diagnostic tool when included in a developmental assessment battery. It can help teach parents of developmentally at-risk infants how to assess their infants' strengths and weaknesses. Intervention studies have employed the BSID II to assess developmental functioning in infants with delayed development before and after intervention has been introduced (Bayley 1993).

DESCRIPTION

The BSID II consists of a Mental Scale, a Motor Scale, and a Behavior Rating Scale. The Mental Scale contains 178 items that assess abilities such as memory, habituation, problem solving, number concepts, language, and social skills. The Motor Scale has 111 items that assess coordination and control of gross and fine motor skills. Items from the Mental and Motor Scales are organized into four facets—cognitive, language, motor, and personal and social development (Bayley 1993). The Behavior Rating Scale has 30 items that assess the infant's behavior during the evaluation; it is used to interpret findings on the Mental and Motor Scales. The infant's caregiver is asked to comment on to what extent the current test performance reflects his or her child's abilities. Each item is scored according to whether the infant responds appropriately.

The BSID II has a standardized format but still allows for flexibility in administration. Although each item is to be administered in the manner described by the manual, the order and speed of administration can be adjusted according to the infant's age and successful performance on previous items. Items to be administered are determined by the child's age. However, items to which the infant does not respond or responds inappropriately can be readministered later in the testing session (Bayley 1993).

The results of the Mental and Motor Scales are reported as standard scores with a mean of 100 and a standard deviation of 15 and are referred to as the Mental Development Index (MDI) and Psychomotor Development Index (PDI), respectively (Bayley 1993). The manual provides qualitative interpretation of the global scores for the MDI and the PDI (Bayley 1993). The classifications are as follows:

- Accelerated performance: 115 and above
- Within normal limits: 85–114
- Mildly delayed performance: 70–84
- Significantly delayed performance: 69 and below

Developmental ages can be calculated for the Mental and Motor Scales. The manual suggests that scores for the four facets—cognitive, language, motor, and personal and social—be obtained and compared (Bayley 1993). However, Nellis and Gridley (1994) found little empirical support for the evaluation of facet scores and pointed out that current research suggests that development is a global construct.

The Behavior Rating Scale can be interpreted in terms of total scores, factor scores, and item analysis and by comparison with the MDI and PDI (Nellis and Gridley 1994). The total score compares a child with his or her age peers. The factors assessed include attention or arousal and emotional regulation. Factor scores vary according to the child's age. The manual also provides case studies to help clinicians interpret the BSID II and to develop diagnostic impressions (Bayley 1993).

The normative data for the BSID II were obtained from 1,700 subjects in a stratified, random sample representative of the U.S. population of infants ages 1–42 months (Bayley 1993). There were 17 age groups with 50 boys and 50 girls in each group. The sample was also representative with respect to race and ethnicity, parent education, and geographic region.

PRACTICAL ISSUES

The time required for administration varies with the age and ability of the child. Nellis and Gridley (1994) suggested 25–35 minutes for children under 15 months and 60 minutes for older children.

The BSID II was designed to be used by a clinician with at least master's-level training in individual assessment and child development. Those who use this instrument need to spend 1 day in training.

The BSID II is copyrighted by and can be obtained from

> The Psychological Corporation
> 555 Academic Court
> San Antonio, TX 78204-2498
> Phone: 800-211-8378
> Internet: www.psychcorp.com

The complete test kit, manual, and record forms cost $760.00. The BSID II is available only in English.

PSYCHOMETRIC PROPERTIES

Reliability

The internal consistency of the BSID II scales was estimated with Cronbach's alpha. For the Mental Scale, alpha coefficients ranged from 0.78 at 10 months to 0.93 at 27 months, with a mean of 0.88. Alpha values reported for the Motor Scale ranged from 0.81 at 21 months to 0.87 at 36 months, with a mean of 0.84. For the total score of the Behavior Rating Scale, alpha values ranged from 0.82 at 2 months to 0.92 at 42 months, with a mean of 0.88 (Nellis and Gridley 1994).

Joint reliability was assessed using an examiner and a rater who observed the administration of the BSID II. Correlation coefficients (r) were 0.96 for the Mental Scale, 0.75 for the Motor Scale, and 0.88 for the Behavior Rating Scale total score (Bayley 1993).

Test-retest stability of the BSID II was measured using a subsample of 175 children from the standardization sample (Bayley 1993). The interval for retesting ranged from 1 to 16 days, with a median of 4 days. The stability coefficient was 0.83 for the Mental Scale, 0.77 for the Motor Scale, and 0.55 (1 month) and 0.90 (12 months) for the Behavior Rating Scale total score.

Validity

Face and content validity were assessed by a panel of experts who reviewed the BSID during the revision that resulted in the BSID II. These experts determined which domains were relevant to early development and ensured that they were adequately covered by the BSID II.

Several independent validity studies have been conducted on the BSID (Bayley 1993). The BSID has identified preschoolers (over age 2) with developmental delay, findings that were confirmed at school age with intellectual measures such as the Wechsler Intelligence Scale for Children—Revised (Wechsler 1974) and the Stanford-Binet Test of Mental Aptitude (Binet 1985). Bayley (1993) suggested that the older the infant, the more BSID scores are able to predict later intellectual functioning. The BSID has also been shown to differentiate among low-birth-weight, premature, and neurologically impaired infants and to correspond with clinicians' classifications of normal and at-risk developmental functioning (Bayley 1993).

Nellis and Gridley (1994) caution against making generalizations from the BSID to the BSID II because the correlation between the MDI and PDI scores of both scales were reported by Bayley (1993) as 0.62 and 0.63, respectively. In another study, correlations between the MDI and PDI scores on the BSID and the BSID II were 0.95 (Goldstein et al. 1995). Nellis and Gridley (1994) note that lower MDI and PDI scores on the BSID II are to be expected because the scale was revised more than 20 years after the original test was published. This problem with limited correlation between new and older versions is not specific to the BSID scales but is common to the process of renorming after 20 years (the same thing happened with scores on the Stanford-Binet Intelligence Scales). Future validity studies for the BSID II should ultimately be used to determine the ability of the newer measure.

Bayley (1993) reported correlations between the MDI and other measures of mental development in the preschool range (e.g., the Verbal Scale of the McCarthy Scales of Children's Abilities [McCarthy et al. 1974] [$r = 0.77$]). Similarly, the BSID PDI and the motor scales of these preschool measures were correlated. The correlation of the Stanford-Binet Test of Mental Aptitude (Binet 1985) with the BSID was significant ($r = 0.57$ for children ages 24–30 months). Similarly, the BSID PDI correlated ($r = 0.59$) with the McCarthy Motor subscale ($N = 30$). Correlation coefficients for the General Cognitive Index of the McCarthy Scales and the MDI and PDI were 0.79 and 0.45, respectively. The BSID showed correlation coefficients of 0.73 between the MDI and the Wechsler Preschool and Primary Scale of Intelligence— Revised (WPPSI-R) (Wechsler 1983) Verbal IQ. Correlations between the Full Scale IQ of the WPPSI and the MDI and PDI were 0.73 and 0.41, respectively. No measure seems better able to predict the later IQ of a toddler than the BSID.

The relationship between the BSID II and the Differential Ability Scale (DAS) has also been studied (Bayley 1993). Correlation between the BSID II MDI score and the DAS General Conceptual Ability Score was 0.49. The BSID II PDI score correlated ($r = 0.24$) with the DAS Nonverbal Composite Score. The correlation between the MDI score and the Total Language Score of the Preschool Language Scale—3 was 0.49 (Bayley 1993).

Overall, moderately high correlations have been reported for the BSID MDI with other tests of mental ability. On the other hand, lower correlations have been consistently reported for the BSID PDI, suggesting that it provides information not measured by traditional intelligence tests (Nellis and Gridley 1994).

To facilitate clinical interpretation of the Behavior Rating Scale, factor analyses were conducted using the standardization sample and clinical samples (Bayley 1993). These analyses showed three factors: Orientation/ Engagement, Motor Quality, and Emotional Regulation (Bayley 1993). Orientation/Engagement included arousal, affect, and interest, and Motor Quality included motor control and gross and fine motor movement. Emotional Regulation was only identified for those ages 13–42 months. Bayley (1993) reported that these factors change with age, possibly because of the maturation of the brain.

CLINICAL UTILITY

The BSID II has many strengths. It has been used in the diagnostic evaluation of developmental delay and, like the original BSID, appears to be one of the most valuable measures of infant development (Nellis and Gridley 1994). It can be used for early intervention programs to document progress in children being treated for developmental delays (Bayley 1993). The BSID II can also be used to teach the parents of premature and other infants at risk for developmental delay about their children's strengths and weaknesses (Bayley 1993). It has numerous applications in clinical, educational, and research settings, where it can be used in the assessment of various groups. The BSID II has been demonstrated to be sensitive to difference in the performance of infants with a variety of conditions, including autism, HIV infection, and Down's syndrome (Bayley 1993). The BSID II is psychometrically sound (Nellis and Gridley 1994). However, because it is a recently published test, more validity studies are expected over time. It can provide the clinician with information about an infant's developmental functioning. It is also able to distinguish average, low average, borderline, and mentally retarded ranges of functioning (Nellis and Gridley 1994). The BSID II has been commended for the improvement in the materials, including the use of colored pictures, from the first edition. The test is appealing and able to maintain even the interest of infants with developmental delays (Nellis and Gridley 1994).

The BSID II also has several weaknesses. Nellis and Gridley (1994) question whether the BSID II has an adequate floor for infants with significant developmental delays. They argue that the BSID II is not optimized for preschool children with developmental delays because it has a relatively high threshold of 50 (mean = 100) for identifying children with impairment and too few scale points below that cutoff score. Another problem is that the test kit is large and difficult to move around. Practitioners have also reported that putting the materials back in the box after use is challenging (Nellis and Gridley 1994). Like all early developmental measures used with preschool children, the BSID II has poorer predictive validity for later academic success than do measures for older, school-age children such as the Wechsler Intelligence Test for Children—Revised (Wechsler 1974).

REFERENCES AND SUGGESTED READINGS

Bayley N: Manual for the Bayley Scales of Infant Development. San Antonio, TX, Psychological Corporation, 1969

Bayley N: Bayley Scales of Infant Development, Second Edition (BSID II). San Antonio, TX, Psychological Corporation, 1993

Binet Q: The Stanford-Binet Test of Mental Aptitude. New York, Psychological Corporation, 1985

Flanagan D, Alfonso V: A critical review of the technical characteristics of new and recently revised intelligence tests for preschool children. Journal of Psychoeducational Assessment 13:66–90, 1995

Goldstein D, Fogle E, Wieber J, et al: Comparison of the Bayley Scales of Infant Development—Second Edition and the Bayley Scales of Infant Development with premature infants. Journal of Psychoeducational Assessment 13:391–396, 1995

McCarthy et al: McCarthy Scales of Children's Abilities. New York, Psychological Corporation, 1974

Nellis L, Gridley B: Review of the Bayley Scales of Infant Development—Second Edition. Journal of School Psychology 32:212–219, 1994

Wechsler J: Manual for the Wechsler Intelligence Scale for Children—Revised. New York, Psychological Corporation, 1974

Wechsler D: Wechsler Preschool and Primary Scale of Intelligence—Revised. New York, Psychological Corporation, Harcourt Brace Jovanovich, 1983

Denver Developmental Screening Test II (Denver II)

W. K. Frankenburg, J. Dodds, P. Archer, H. Shapiro, and B. Bresnick

GOALS

The Denver Developmental Screening Test (DDST) was first published in 1967 (Frankenburg et al. 1967) to assist health care providers in detecting developmental problems among infants and young children. It has been standardized in the United States and 15 other countries and is widely used in 54 others (Frankenburg et al. 1990b). Concerns were raised about outdated norms, the need for additional language items, the appropriateness of the test for various ethnic groups and children from diverse geographic areas, and the ability of the test to predict future functioning such as school performance (Frankenburg et al. 1992). To address these issues, the developers revised and restandardized the DDST, and the Denver II was published in 1990 (Frankenburg et al. 1990a, 1990b). After reviewing the content of the 105 items of the DDST, a group of experts, including the authors, eliminated 2 items, revised 21 items, and retained all other items. A normative sample of 2,096 subjects was obtained from Denver and other counties in Colorado.

The Denver II is a general developmental screening test for children from birth to age 6.5 years. It is designed to identify delays in the following domains: personal and social, fine motor, gross motor, and language skills. Frankenburg (1994) suggests that, in a fashion similar to the growth curve used by pediatricians, the Denver II indicates the normative age at which preschool children are able to perform a variety of tasks related to four general areas of development. It can be used to identify children who need further assessment and referral to remedial services. The Denver II can provide rough estimates of speech intelligibility, hearing, and vision. However, the authors recommend more specific tests to rule out vision and hearing problems.

DESCRIPTION

The Denver II has 125 items divided into four domains: Personal and Social (25 items), Fine Motor–Adaptive (29 items), Language (39 items), and Gross Motor (32 items). Five additional items enable the interviewer to evaluate the speech intelligibility and behavior of the child, including compliance with requests, alertness, fearfulness, and attention span. Within each domain, items are listed in chronological order according to the age at which most children could be expected to perform them. Items are listed with an age code letter to guide the examiner. Each item is rated pass or fail by the interviewer.

The Denver II is to be used by a clinician with graduate training in child development. Test administration is aided by good observational skills and the ability to relate to young children and their parents. Although the manual claims that a research assistant can administer the test, it is best carried out by a clinician.

The Denver II can be used as a one- or two-stage screening process. The first stage is the Prescreening Developmental Questionnaire answered by the parent about the child's developmental status. The authors suggest that children identified as more likely to have abnormal scores undergo the longer Denver II.

Scoring is as follows for verbal and performance items: 1 = pass, observed by examiner; 2 = pass, reported by parent; 3 = fail, observed by examiner; and 4 = fail, reported by parent.

Scores are interpreted in relation to the child's age and categorized in terms of developmental progress as caution, delay, no opportunity, normal, or advanced performance (Glascoe et al. 1992). Caution means the child failed or refused an item passed by 75% of children younger than him or her in the normative group. Delay means the child failed or refused an item passed by 90% of the children at a younger age. One delay and/or two or more cautions indicate a questionable score. Two or more delays result in an abnormal test score. No opportunity means that the child may not have had the opportunity to practice the developmental task.

PRACTICAL ISSUES

According to Frankenburg et al. (1990a, 1990b), it takes 10–15 minutes to administer the Prescreening Developmental Questionnaire and 20 minutes to administer the Denver II. The Denver II requires 1 day of training for reliable administration. It was copyrighted in 1990 by William K. Frankenburg and Josiah Dodds and is available from

Denver Developmental Materials, Inc.
P.O. Box 6919
Denver, CO 80206-0919
Phone: 303-355-4729

A packet containing the test kit, the *Denver II—Screening Manual*, the *Denver II—Technical Manual*, and record forms costs $70.00. The *Denver II—Screening Manual* (Frankenburg et al. 1990a) gives details on administration and scoring, and the *Denver II—Technical Manual* (Frankenburg et al. 1990b) provides information on the standardization and administration of the test, as well as training information for screeners.

The Denver II is available in English and Spanish.

PSYCHOMETRIC PROPERTIES

Reliability

Frankenburg et al. (1990b, 1992) reported a reliability study with a small sample size ($N = 34$). For 7- to 10-day intervals between testing and retesting, the mean percentage of agreement was 89.0 with use of the same testers and 87.5 with use of different testers (Frankenburg et al. 1990b).

Validity

Frankenburg (1994) suggests that the Denver II has predictive validity conceptualized as relative risk (using smoking and lung cancer as an example). The authors conceptualized relative risk as a likelihood ratio that can be obtained using abnormal scores on the Denver II. The Denver II provides an algorithm, rather than a strict cutoff score, for determining whether a preschool child may be delayed (a caution) or is definitely delayed developmentally. Children with abnormal scores on the Denver II are considered more likely to have later developmental problems, and the more deviant the score, the greater the likelihood of these future problems (Frankenburg 1994). Therefore, the validity of the Denver II is determined by how sensitive and specific it is in identifying children in need of further diagnostic assessment (Frankenburg et al. 1990b). However, no empirically derived sensitivity and specificity data were provided to support this argument; no validity studies appear in the *Denver II—Technical Manual* (Frankenburg et al. 1990b).

Frankenburg (1994) further argues that, similar to the growth curve, the validity of the Denver II is not determined by the extent to which it agrees with other measures but by the precision of the norming process. Glascoe et al. (1992) disagree, finding that the Denver II may identify too many false-positive cases. Using a sample of 104 children in Tennessee, the authors compared the Denver II with a diagnostic test battery containing widely used measures such as the Bayley Scales of Infant Development (BSID) (p. 288), the Stanford-Binet Test of Mental Aptitude (Binet 1985), and the Fluharty Preschool Speech and Language Screening Test (Fluharty 1974). The Denver II correctly identified 83% of children with developmental disabilities. However, more than half of the children identified by the other diagnostic test batteries as developmentally normal received questionable or abnormal scores on the Denver II.

This high false-positive rate led to a recommendation that more validity studies be carried out on the Denver II (Glascoe et al. 1992).

CLINICAL UTILITY

Frankenburg et al. (1992) suggest that the Denver II be used for the early detection and referral for treatment of developmental problems in children. Because no one test could adequately measure all of the domains covered by the Denver II with precision, the developers further state that it is important that the Denver II be used only as a screen. Therefore, clinical evaluation and the use of other measures such as intelligence tests and speech or language assessments should precede referral or treatment recommendations. The Denver II can also be used to track children's development over time through rescreening at periodic intervals.

The Denver II measures development among a broad range of developmental skills. It has high sensitivity (Glascoe et al. 1992) and is therefore able to detect development delays in several domains. It enjoys wide acceptance among health care providers and developmental specialists in the United States and other countries. It is also well tolerated by parents and their children. Finally, the Denver II is brief and easy to administer.

However, Glascoe et al. (1992) demonstrated a high false-positive rate using the Denver II, which could result in the overreferral of children for treatment of developmental problems. The Denver II has a low specificity rate and, as the test developers suggest, should not be used as a diagnostic instrument (Frankenburg et al. 1990b). The Denver II was standardized on the basis of a sample of 2,096 children in Colorado, stratified by age, race, maternal education, and area of residence (Frankenburg et al. 1992). The *Denver II—Technical Manual* reported additional data from small samples in Oklahoma, Tennessee, and Michigan. Standardization of the Denver II on the basis of only Colorado residents is a serious problem, because the Denver II is expected to be used nationally and internationally, as was its predecessor, the DDST. The developers' failure to conduct validity studies is also problematic. Frankenburg (1994) contends that the Denver II gives norms for the development of specific skills and hence does not need agreement with other measures such as intelligence tests. However, many measures in use today, including intelligence tests, have normative data as well as demonstrated concurrent validity with other measures. The Denver II does not base its reliability measures on comparisons with other measures such as intelligence tests.

REFERENCES AND SUGGESTED READINGS

Binet Q: The Stanford-Binet Test of Mental Aptitude. New York, Psychological Corporation, 1985

Fluharty NB: The design and standardization of a speech and language screening test for use with preschool children. J Speech Hear Disord 39:75–88, 1974

Frankenburg W: Preventing developmental delays: is developmental screening sufficient? Pediatrics 93:586–593, 1994

Frankenburg WK, Dodds J, Archer P, et al: The Denver Developmental Test-Technical Manual. Denver, CO, Denver Developmental Materials, 1967

Frankenburg WK, Dodds J, Archer P, et al: Denver II—Screening Manual. Denver, CO, Denver Developmental Materials, 1990a

Frankenburg WK, Dodds J, Archer P, et al: Denver II—Technical Manual. Denver, CO, Denver Developmental Materials, 1990b

Frankenburg WK, Dodds J, Archer P, et al: The Denver II: a major revision of the Denver Developmental Screening Test. Pediatrics 89:91–97, 1992

Glascoe F, Byrne K, Ashford L, et al: Accuracy of the Denver-II in developmental screening. Pediatrics 89:1221–1225, 1992

Preschool Behavior Questionnaire (PBQ)

L. Behar and S. Stringfield

GOALS

The Preschool Behavior Questionnaire (PBQ) (Behar and Stringfield 1974a, 1974b) was developed as a rating scale for use by mental health professionals as a first step in identifying preschoolers, ages 3–6 years, who show symptoms or constellations of symptoms that suggest the emergence of emotional problems. The underlying conceptualization of the PBQ is that behavior occurs along a continuum and that the PBQ is thus able to discriminate between psychiatrically healthy and unhealthy children. The PBQ is a modification of the Children's Behavior Questionnaire (Rutter 1967), which was standardized in England for use with school-age boys. The test developers sought additional questions from teachers in regular preschools and preschools for children with emotional problems (Behar and Stringfield 1974b). The PBQ can also be used as a measure of change before and after an educational or therapeutic intervention with preschoolers.

DESCRIPTION

The PBQ is a rater-administered scale, and all 36 items must be given. A sample item is provided in Example 17–1.

The PBQ is designed to be completed by a preschool teacher or teacher's aide. A parental version (Elander and Rutter 1996) that includes social relationship items, which has increased the acceptability of the scale, has also been developed (M. Rutter, personal communication).

Each item in the PBQ is scored as follows: 0 = does not apply, 1 = applies sometimes, and 2 = certainly applies. The total for each subject is obtained by adding the scores for the individual items. A total score of ≥17 suggests that the child's overall behavior is outside the normal range; however, rather than indicating which behavior may be causing the problem, it merely suggests

EXAMPLE 17–1 ■ Sample item from the Preschool Behavioral Questionnaire

	Doesn't Apply	Applies Sometimes	Certainly Applies
1. Restless. Runs around or jumps up and down. Doesn't keep still.	_____	_____	_____

Reprinted with permission from Lenore Behar, Ph.D.

that the child should be further evaluated (Behar and Stringfield 1974a). This score represents an increase from the norm of 1 standard deviation, which is not very stringent.

Normative data were collected from a sample of 496 psychiatrically healthy preschoolers and 102 preschoolers enrolled in early intervention programs for children with behavioral problems; the sample population was recruited from five preschools in North Carolina and Oregon. For the psychiatrically healthy preschoolers, the mean score was 9.12 (SD = 7.67); for the psychiatrically unhealthy preschoolers, the mean score was 23.36 (SD = 7.3) (Behar and Stringfield 1974a).

PRACTICAL ISSUES

It takes 10 minutes to administer the PBQ. It is a copyrighted instrument and can be obtained from

> Lenore Behar, Ph.D.
> 1821 Woodburn Road
> Durham, NC 27705
> Phone: 919-489-1888
> E-mail: Lbehar@psych.mc.duke.edu

A package that includes the manual (Behar and Stringfield 1974b), 50 answer sheets, and 50 score sheets costs $20.00. The included manual contains information on the instrument's psychometric properties and instructions about scoring.

PSYCHOMETRIC PROPERTIES

Reliability

Joint reliability was measured in a sample of 80 psychiatrically healthy preschoolers and 9 preschoolers with emotional problems. The PBQ was rated by both the teacher and the teacher's aide for the classrooms and yielded a mean joint reliability of 0.84 (Behar and Stringfield 1974a). Test-retest reliability for a 3- to 4-month interval was reported as $r = 0.87$ for the total PBQ score (Behar and Stringfield 1974a).

Validity

The developers reported that when the PBQ was given to teachers with psychiatrically healthy and unhealthy

preschoolers, it was able to accurately classify 73.4% of the individuals using a discriminant function analysis (Behar and Stringfield 1974a).

Three factors were identified by the test developers: 1) Hostile-Aggressive, 2) Anxious-Fearful, and 3) Hyperactive-Distractible (Behar and Stringfield 1974b). However, Tremblay et al. (1987) presented evidence from principal component analysis to suggest that a two-factor structure fits the PBQ better than the three factors reported by the test authors. Their data, derived from a large French-Canadian sample, indicated that the two components are Aggressive-Hyperactive and Anxious-Withdrawn. Tremblay et al. (1987) found these factors to be stable across age, sex, and socioeconomic status. The authors' explanation for the disparity between their analysis and that of Behar and Stringfield (1974b) was that the normative sample had a substantial minority of psychiatrically unhealthy preschoolers whose scores skewed the data.

CLINICAL UTILITY

Behar and Stringfield (1974b) recommend that the PBQ be used as a screen for behavioral and emotional problems and as a test before and after intervention to measure improvement. They also indicate that teachers are more valid and reliable raters than teacher's aides and that teachers should be present in the child's classroom for at least 6 weeks before using the PBQ. The authors caution against the diagnostic use of the PBQ.

The PBQ is easy to use and very easy to score. However, the PBQ literature provides minimal information about norms, standardized data, or the validity of the reported factor scores. The PBQ has not been used extensively in research settings.

REFERENCES AND SUGGESTED READINGS

Behar L, Stringfield S: A behavior rating scale for the preschool child. Developmental Psychology 10:601–610, 1974a

Behar L, Stringfield S: Manual for the Preschool Behavior Questionnaire. Durham, NC, 1974b

Elander J, Rutter M: Use and development of the Rutter Parents' and Teachers' Scales. International Journal of Methods in Psychiatric Research 6:63–78, 1996

Rutter M: A Children's Behavior Questionnaire for completion by teachers: preliminary findings. J Child Psychol Psychiatry 8:1–11, 1967

Tremblay RE, Desmarais-Gervais L, Gagnon C, et al: The Preschool Behavior Questionnaire: stability of its factor structure between cultures, sexes, ages, and socioeconomic classes. International Journal of Behavioral Development 10:467–484, 1987

Schedule for Affective Disorders and Schizophrenia for School-Age Children: Present and Lifetime Version (K-SADS-PL)

·J. Kaufman, B. Birmaher, D. Brent, U. Rao, C. Flynn, P. Moreci, D. Williamson, and N. Ryan

GOALS

The Schedule for Affective Disorders and Schizophrenia for School-Age Children (K-SADS) was originally developed in 1977 by Chambers et al. (1985) on the basis of Endicott and Spitzer's Schedule for Affective Disorders and Schizophrenia (SADS) (p. 58) for adults. The K-SADS is an interviewer-based, semistructured interview for children ages 6–18. Its primary goals are to assess episodes of psychopathology and to make categorical diagnoses by directly interviewing children and adolescents and their parents, according to DSM-III-R and DSM-IV criteria. For research studies, a single diagnostic module of the K-SADS (e.g., depression) may be used for multiple interviews of a patient during treatment to assess symptom change.

The K-SADS is currently available in several DSM-IV format versions: the K-SADS-IVR (Ambrosini and Dixon 1996), the K-SADS Present and Lifetime Version (K-SADS-PL) (Kaufman et al. 1997),

the KIDDIE-SADS-LIFETIME (K-SADS-L), and the K-SADS Epidemiological, Fourth Version (K-SADS-E-IV).

The K-SADS-E-IV is intended for epidemiological studies. It is the most widely used K-SADS in current research and has excellent psychometric properties. However, its narrow 3-point scales do not allow as wide a range of symptom scores to be given as the more often used 7-point K-SADS scale. It also employs fewer clinical probes. The K-SADS-E-IV is not evaluated in detail in this chapter. Although the remaining three versions of the K-SADS follow the basic interviewer-based, semistructured format of the original K-SADS, they differ in length, number of clinical probes per interviewer item, ease of scoring, and availability of psychometric data.

Researchers and clinicians may prefer the K-SADS-PL over the K-SADS-IVR because of its very convenient and user-friendly screening section (particularly useful for assessing psychiatrically healthy control subjects). Because of these potential advantages and because its published psychometric data are determined on the basis of DSM-IV criteria, the K-SADS-PL was selected for detailed description in this chapter.

DESCRIPTION

The K-SADS-PL is an interviewer-based diagnostic instrument with a semistructured format. The K-SADS-PL interview guides the clinician during the interview of the child and parent in preparation for scoring the items and selecting a diagnosis. The K-SADS-PL is administered separately to the child and to the parent. If the child is prepubertal, the parent is interviewed first; if the patient is an adolescent, he or she is interviewed first.

The K-SADS-PL is designed to be used by a clinical interviewer, primarily by a clinically trained therapist (physician, psychologist, or social worker). The earliest versions were used by child psychiatrists (Chambers et al. 1985). Current training courses are taught by clinicians. The K-SADS-PL has been used by lay interviewers in highly regarded research programs, but extensive training in interviewing, psychopathology, and the DSM criteria is required. Use of lay interviewers for the K-SADS-PL may involve so much supervision that it may be better to use a diagnostic instrument designed for lay interviewers (e.g., the National Institute of Mental Health Diagnostic Interview Schedule for Children [NIMH-DISC 2.3] [p. 305]) under such circumstances.

The K-SADS-PL uses a 3-point scale, whereas other K-SADS scales (the K-SADS-L and the K-SADS-IVR) have retained the original K-SADS 6-point symptom severity scale, except for a few items (e.g., psychotic symptoms), for which a 3-point scale is used. Scores of 0 indicate that no information is available, scores of 1 suggest that the symptom is not present, scores of 2 indicate subthreshold levels of symptomatology, and scores of 3 represent threshold criteria. Each item receives a parent score, a child score, and a summary score. The scores are noted by circling the correct number in each column.

The diagnostic Screening Interview (82 items) of the K-SADS-PL sets it apart from all other versions of the K-SADS. It provides a diagnostic overview of lifetime psychopathology. The screen points to more detailed questions, contained in the five Supplement Completion Checklists. For all disorders surveyed, a threshold score on any (and only one) item necessitates completion of the supplement for that disorder. The screen instructs the clinicians when a supplement is to be used on the basis of the score. The Screening Interview's gate questions identify which symptom groups to investigate and which to skip. Symptoms rated in the Screening Interview are surveyed for current (CE) and most severe past (MSP) episodes. The five diagnostic supplement modules are Affective Disorders, Psychotic Disorders, Anxiety Disorders, Behavioral Disorders, and Substance Abuse and Other Disorders.

After the interview, the clinician synthesizes all of the information and fills out the Summary Lifetime Diagnoses Checklist and the Children's Global Assessment Scale (CGAS) (p. 363) ratings. The K-SADS-PL Affective Disorders Supplement contains 28 distinct mood symptom items, 14 diagnostic items for depression, and 14 diagnostic items for mania. In Example 17–2, the rater gives scores for the parent (P), child (C), and his or her own summary (S) score. A sample item from the K-SADS-PL, the Irritability item from the Screening Interview, is provided in Example 17–2.

The K-SADS-PL covers lifetime and current episodes. In rating individual items for current disorders, the interviewer is instructed to rate symptoms "for the time when they were the most severe during the episode." The interviewer is also instructed to write in the margins if the particular symptom improved or disappeared. This documentation helps to determine if the child ever met criteria for a given disorder, if he or she still meets criteria, or if symptoms are in partial remission.

All versions provide detailed clinical symptom probes that illustrate ways to elicit the information necessary to score each symptom rating. The interviewer does not read all of the probes verbatim but simply uses as many as necessary to arrive at a well-documented rating. Clinicians are also free to adjust the probes to the developmental level of the child and to use language supplied by parent and child when querying about specific symptoms. Clinicians are asked to use their best judgment to resolve discrepancies between informants.

Scores on each item range from 0 to 3, but the number of items surveyed for each patient varies because of skip options. The K-SADS-PL requires that the parent's, the child's, and the clinician's summary scores be entered for each item on a common answer sheet. In addition, symptom scores are applied to two time frames for each symptom: the present (or past 2 weeks) and the past (or most severe episode in lifetime). Therefore, it is possible to generate six different scores for each item on the K-SADS-PL. The K-SADS-PL score sheets make it possible to sum the criteria to make diagnoses, and instructions are provided at the end of each supplement for doing so. Similar score sheets and five pages of instruction on administration and scoring are included in the K-SADS-IVR.

PRACTICAL ISSUES

The authors of the K-SADS-PL report that administration time for psychiatrically healthy control subjects (child plus parent) is estimated to be 35–45 minutes each (total up to 90 minutes) and approximately 75 minutes each for psychiatric patients (total 150 minutes).

The K-SADS is not formally published as a commercial product, and there is no editorial board controlling its format. Both the K-SADS-PL and the K-SADS-E-IV are copyrighted. All versions except the K-SADS-E-IV are available free of charge. Investigators generally reformat and revise the instrument, tailoring it for their specific research projects. Those interested in using the instrument should contact the authors of the various forms of the K-SADS.

EXAMPLE 17–2 ■ **Sample item from the Schedule for Affective Disorders and Schizophrenia for School-Age Children: Present and Lifetime Version**

Example of the Irritability item in the K-SADS-PL screening module

	P	C	S	No Information
Irritability and Anger	0	0	0	
Subjective feeling of irritability, anger, crankiness, bad temper, short tempered, resentment or annoyance, whether expressed overtly or not.				Not at all
Rate the *intensity and duration* of such feelings	I	I	I	
Was there ever a time when you got annoyed, irritated, or cranky at little things?	2	2	2	SubThreshold: Feels definitely more angry or irritable than called for by the situation, at least three times a week for more than 3 hours each time. Or often argumentative, quick to express annoyance
Did you ever have a time when you lost your temper a lot? When was that? Are you like that now?				
Was there another time you felt _____?				
What kinds of things made you _____?				
Were you feeling mad or angry also (even if you didn't show it?)	3	3	3	Threshold: Feels irritable/angry daily, or almost daily, at least 50% of the time. Or often shouts, loses temper
How angry?				
More than before?				

PAST:

	P̄	C̄	S̄

What kinds of things made you feel angry?
Did you sometimes feel angry and/or irritable and/or cranky and didn't know why?
Did this happen often?
Did you lose your temper?
  With your family?
  Your friends?
  Who else?
  At school?
What did you do?
Did anybody say anything about it?
How much of the time did you feel angry, irritable, and/or cranky?
  All of the time?
  Lots of the time?
  Just now and then?
  None of the time?
When you got mad, what did you think about?
Did you think about killing others or hurting yourself? Or about hurting them or torturing them? Did you have a plan? How?
If irritability occurs in discrete episodes within a depressive state, especially if unprovoked, rater should keep this in mind when asking about mania/hypomania

Duration of Irritable Mood:

_____

Reprinted with permission from Joan Kaufman, M.D.

The K-SADS-IV has been revised by Paul Ambrosini, and copies may be obtained from him:

> Paul Ambrosini, M.D
> 3200 Henry Avenue
> Philadelphia, PA 19129-1137
> Phone: 215-842-4402

The K-SADS-L is copyrighted by SmithKline Beecham Pharmaceuticals; interested readers should contact

> Rachel Klein, Ph.D.
> New York University Child Study Center

> 550 First Avenue
> New York, NY 10016
> Phone: 212-263-8389

Copies of the copyrighted K-SADS-E-IV may be obtained for $75.00 from

> Helen Orvaschel, Ph.D.
> Center for Psychological Studies
> Nova Southeastern University
> 3301 College Avenue

Fort Lauderdale, FL 33314

E-mail: orvasche@cps.acast.nova.edu

The K-SADS-PL was developed by

Joan Kaufman, M.D.

Department of Psychology

Yale University

P.O. Box 208205

New Haven, CT 06520

Phone: 203-432-2353

Readers can access copies of the K-SADS-PL on the Internet (www.wpic.pitt.edu/ksads).

Each version of the K-SADS includes explanatory material to guide the interviewer in administering and scoring the instrument. However, no instructions for managing the scoring sheets or interpreting the results are available for any version discussed here. Instructions are brief: two pages for the K-SADS-L, four pages for the K-SADS-IV, and five pages for the K-SADS-PL.

For training in the use of the K-SADS-PL, it is best to contact the author, Joan Kaufman. In the past, training had been available for the K-SADS-IV ($1,000.00 for 2 days at the facility) and for the K-SADS-PL ($200.00 plus expenses per day at the facility). Training arrangements must now be made individually with Dr. Kaufman.

The K-SADS-PL is available in English, Hebrew, and Spanish, and future versions in Dutch, Italian, and Russian are planned. The K-SADS-E is available in Hebrew. The K-SADS-IV is available in English, Italian, Portuguese, and Spanish. The K-SADS-L is available in English and French.

The K-SADS-PL is included on the CD-ROM that accompanies this handbook.

PSYCHOMETRIC PROPERTIES

Reliability

In the first K-SADS-P version (Present Episode Version) developed by Chambers et al. (1985), the internal consistency using Cronbach's alpha was 0.65–0.84 for eight depression scales, 0.39 for anxiety disorder scales, and 0.86 for conduct disorder scales. In the videotape study of the later K-SADS-IIIR version by Ambrosini et al. (1989), Cronbach's alphas ranged from 0.73 to 0.95 for distinct alpha scores for diagnoses of major depression, overanxious disorder, separation anxiety disorder, oppositional defiant disorder, and attention-deficit disorder.

Test-retest reliability of the most recent K-SADS-PL version ranged from $r = 0.78$ for anxiety disorders to $r = 0.9$ for attention-deficit/hyperactivity disorder (ADHD). These K-SADS-PL test-retest reliabilities are improved over the reliabilities obtained with previous versions of the K-SADS (Chambers et al. 1985). However, scores for anxiety disorders show lower reliability than those for externalizing disorders, such as ADHD, in most K-SADS versions. The K-SADS-PL reliability data are grouped and are not differentiated by the type of anxiety disorder. For example, one cannot determine the reliability of the instrument for simple phobia or separation anxiety disorder.

Test-retest reliability was established for intervals from 2 to 38 days. Test-retest agreement, which was reported only for present episode illnesses, ranged from 93% to 100%.

Validity

Several standards have been used to assess the validity of the K-SADS. Validity tests of the original K-SADS-P included inpatient unit consensual data (percentage of agreement, $r = 0.70$, kappa = 0.64) (Apter et al. 1989) and best estimate diagnoses of the two child psychiatrists (kappa ranged from 0.11 for oppositional defiant disorder to 0.69 for conduct disorder) (Carlson et al. 1987). Agreement between diagnoses generated using K-SADS interviews and chart diagnoses and diagnoses derived from clinical interviews has been fair to poor (Kaufman et al. 1997). Fair to poor agreement with clinical or chart diagnosis is not necessarily a sign of limitations of the K-SADS, because clinical and chart diagnoses are notorious for their unreliability and questionable validity. Best estimate diagnosis has been regarded as a gold standard. Using the more modern K-SADS-PL methodology, the validity results were better. Children who scored high enough on the K-SADS-PL screen to justify using the specific disorder module scored higher on the following relevant concurrently administered rating scales: the Children's Depression Inventory (CDI) (p. 344) and the Beck Depression Inventory (BDI) (p. 519), the Child Behavior Checklist (CBCL) (p. 310) internalizing scores, and the Conners Rating Scales for ADHD (p. 329) (Kaufman 1997).

There are no published reports concerning tests of the K-SADS-PL against external validators, including prospective prediction of specific outcome, family history, or longitudinal follow-up data to validate diagnoses.

However, the long-term predictive validity of the K-SADS-PL, as shown in follow-up assessments of adults with diagnoses of depression when children, has been good (Pine, personal communication). In one study, the K-SADS-IIIR was shown to be sensitive to antidepressant medication response when compared with clinicians' global ratings. These measures included both changes in the categorical diagnosis of depression and changes in depressive symptoms, as shown on a 17-item depression scale extracted from that version of the K-SADS.

Carlson et al. (1987) determined that neither the K-SADS nor the Diagnostic Interview for Children and Adolescents (DICA) (p. 315) yielded stable diagnoses for inpatients when used at admission. Children and parents tended to endorse many more symptoms and gave higher scores related to the general stress at admission.

CLINICAL UTILITY

Kaufman et al. (1997) suggest that the K-SADS be used as part of a comprehensive battery with information gathered from all sources (i.e., parents, teachers, and children). They indicate that its strength remains in diagnosis of affective and anxiety disorders. It has also been demonstrated to have good joint reliability for ADHD. Carlson et al. (1987) caution about the use of semistructured diagnostic instruments for inpatients, especially if the diagnostic interview is given at admission. A few days to a week are necessary for the stress associated with admission to decrease in parents and children to avoid a high false-positive rate for diagnoses using the instrument.

The K-SADS-PL has several strengths. It has strong content validity because it was designed to tap prespecified diagnostic criteria, and it may be especially good at selecting children who meet criteria for major affective disorders. It has been designed to lead the clinician or therapist to make a DSM-IV diagnosis during interviews of the child patient and parent. It includes detailed probes useful in eliciting clinically meaningful information and has a scale for estimating the severity of each symptom. One strength of the K-SADS-PL is its high degree of precision and detail in assessing child symptoms and their onset, severity, duration, and associated impairments. As such, the K-SADS, in any of its current versions, has become the accepted standard for determining diagnoses for patients in clinical research protocols.

The K-SADS-PL provides a clinician-friendly, front-end screening examination, which may result in a more efficient, shorter interview. Skip decisions seem reliable and have been validated by comparison with other symptom measures (e.g., the CBCL) (Kaufman et al. 1997).

The K-SADS-PL also has several weaknesses. The strongest reliability and validity data on the K-SADS-PL center on externalizing and affective disorders, whereas the instrument shows poorer reliability for diagnosing anxiety disorders. These findings are not unique to the K-SADS-PL (they are also complications of the NIMH-DISC 2.3 [p. 305]), which suggests that the problem may lie more in the nature of anxiety than with any specific instrument.

Use of the K-SADS-PL requires extensive clinical experience and instrument-specific training. Diagnostic algorithms have not been automated, so diagnoses are formulated by expert judgment.

The scoring of this semistructured interview is not described in a manual and can be inconvenient and complicated; complex grids are needed to place the answers. All versions of the K-SADS generate huge amounts of data, because of the need to record three scores (child, parent, and summary) for two time frames for each item, potentially generating six numbers each for more than 300 items. There are no widely marketed computer-based versions (as there are for the NIMH-DISC 2.3) that automate the skip options and diagnostic algorithms to simplify the management of paper and scores.

The clinical version of the K-SADS has no centralized editorial control, and thus many different versions are in use, even at the same institution. Consequently, it is difficult to know if a citation of the K-SADS in the literature refers to a particular clinical version that has known psychometric properties, such as the ones described earlier.

The copyrighted K-SADS-E-IV is carefully controlled by its author, Helen Orvaschel, Ph.D., and it remains a stable, known, well-tested semistructured diagnostic scale. It therefore has excellent psychometric properties and has not been modified. However, it has been adapted for epidemiologic use with a greatly restricted scale length and fewer diagnostic probes than are found in other versions. That the K-SADS-E-IV was designed to be used by trained raters, including college graduates, may explain why it differs in format from the clinician-rated K-SADS instruments.

The K-SADS-PL shows some irregularity in its screening probes. For example, if a child says he or she mutilated himself or herself without suicidal intent, the interviewer still has to administer the depression module, even if the patient denies mood problems. The thresholds are also set very high; for example, to use the Oppositional Defiant Disorder module, the child must have displayed symptoms (e.g., tantrums or disobedience) daily or nearly daily.

The K-SADS-PL uses a scoring scale of 0–3, which is relatively narrow for purposes of measuring symptom severity, compared with the K-SADS-L, which uses a scale of 0–6 and many more specific symptom probes. Thus, the K-SADS-PL is not as useful for determining initial symptom severity or for monitoring clinical change during treatment.

The K-SADS-PL does not include instructions to the interviewer on how best to integrate information from multiple sources or flag items in the body of the interview itself—as opposed to the summary sheet—that are diagnostic criteria; administration is thus relatively inefficient. The distinction between threshold and subthreshold symptoms is not defined, nor are there specifications of the duration of episodes. The screen includes a limited number of gating questions for some disorders and full sets of questions for others (e.g., enuresis). Some of the gating questions (e.g., engaging in dangerous activities for ADHD) are from DSM-III-R, not DSM-IV. Finally, the pattern of organization of the items is not clear, so the interview sometimes fails to flow smoothly.

REFERENCES AND SUGGESTED READINGS

Ambrosini P, Dixon M: The Schedule for Affective Disorders and Schizophrenia, Childhood Version, Fourth Edition. 1996

Ambrosini P, Metz C, Prabucki K, et al: Videotape reliability of the third edition of the K-SADS. J Am Acad Child Adolesc Psychiatry 28:723–728, 1989

Apter A, Orvaschel H, Laseg M, et al: Psychometric properties of the K-SADS-P in an Israeli adolescent inpatient population. J Am Acad Child Adolesc Psychiatry 28:61–65, 1989

Carlson C, Kashani J, Thomas M, et al: Comparison of two structured interviews on a psychiatrically hospitalized population of children. J Am Acad Child Adolesc Psychiatry 26:645–648, 1987

Chambers WJ, Puig-Antich J, Hirsch M, et al: The assessment of affective disorders in children and adolescents by semi-structured interview. Arch Gen Psychiatry 42:696–702, 1985

Kaufman J, Birmaher B, Brent D, et al: Schedule for Affective Disorders and Schizophrenia for School-Age Children: Present and Lifetime Version (K-SADS-PL): initial reliability and validity data. J Am Acad Child Adolesc Psychiatry 36:980–989, 1997

Child and Adolescent Psychiatric Assessment (CAPA)

A. Angold, A. Cox, M. Prendergast, M. Rutter, and E. Simonoff

GOALS

The Child and Adolescent Psychiatric Assessment (CAPA) (Angold et al. 1995) is a standardized, interviewer-based instrument developed for gathering information about psychiatric symptoms, as defined in a detailed glossary, and for coding their presence or absence, frequency, duration, and onset (Angold and Costello 1996) for the purpose of making a diagnostic assessment using DSM-III, DSM-III-R, DSM-IV, and ICD-10 criteria.

The interview was developed from earlier Isle of Wight interviews (Rutter et al. 1970), the Schedule for Affective Disorders and Schizophrenia for School-Age Children (K-SADS) (p. 296), and the Present State Examination (p. 53).

DESCRIPTION

The CAPA schedule contains 1,401 emphasized probes (bold, italicized, starred, and must be asked) and 2,571 discretionary probes (nonbold and may be asked for further clarification). Items are scored on several dimensions (symptom presence, duration, and number of episodes over past year) that depend on knowledge of an extensive glossary. The CAPA assesses for 30 different categorical diagnoses (e.g., disruptive behavior disorders, anxiety disorders, depressive disorders, and psychotic disorders).

A sample item from the CAPA is provided in Example 17–3. The CAPA is designed to be used by an interviewer who may range from a bachelor's-level interviewer to a clinician (physician or social worker); all interviewers must be trained for reliability in a 1-month course. This diagnostic interview is administered separately to the child and the parent. The child must be at least age 8 to be interviewed. It is best for the clinician to also gather information from teachers to supplement information gathered during the detailed interviews of the parents and children. The CAPA covers the previous 3 months.

The CAPA uses extensive symptom probes and a symptom glossary to score each symptom and impairment rating. The sequencing of items follows the clinical practice of taking a history of the present condition and then determining the mental status. There are three levels of probes: screening questions, starred probes that must be asked, and unstarred probes to be selected by the interviewer. The interviewer begins by asking screening questions about general areas of function (home and family life, school, and peer groups). When a possible symptom arises, the interviewer is cued to ask the starred probe questions about psychopathology. For each symptom, the interviewer obtains information about the context in which it occurred, aggravating and ameliorating factors and consequences, and an example. The interviewer rates the intensity, duration, onset, and confidence in the onset for each symptom. To be clinically significant, symptoms of internalizing disorders "are required to be unpleasant to the subject, to be intrusive into other activities or thoughts, and to occur during more than one activity" (Costello et al. 1996b).

There are 16 symptom domains and 17 incapacity areas. Most items are either not scored or are given a score on a 2-point scale (e.g., 2 = symptom present in at least two activities and 3 = symptom present in most activities). A total of 3,222 variables result from the child interview, and 3,287 are coded in the parent interview.

The data from the CAPA questionnaire are processed by a personal computer–based data entry and scoring application written by the instrument's authors in the PARADOX database system. This application contains logical and range checks to aid data entry. The resulting database generates files that are scored by a series of diagnostic algorithms (CAPA Originated Diagnostic Algorithms [CODA]), written by the authors of the CAPA in SAS. The CODA generates DSM-III, DSM-III-R, DSM-IV, and ICD-10 diagnoses, plus a range of symptom duration requirements mentioned in DSM-III-R. For DSM-III-R diagnoses, algorithms for combining parent and child data at the symptom level are available. See Angold et al. (1995) for examples of either-or rule algorithms about how the parent and child data are combined.

PRACTICAL ISSUES

The CAPA requires 1–2.5 hours per informant. Thus, it may take 5 hours to interview both child and parent. Breaks are allowed. Coding after the interview requires an additional 15–30 minutes. Coding is done after the interview, so the interviewer's time will extend past the time spent with the family. Shorter versions of the interview may be used, because the instrument is modular. For example, clinicians dealing with school-age children may omit the sections on psychotic phenomena or drug use problems.

The CAPA materials include the "omnibus" interview schedules for parent and child and copies of the relevant journal articles by the authors. Supplies, information, and software for data entry and analysis may be requested from

> Vermal White
> CAPA Requests
> Duke University Medical Center
> Box 3454
> Durham, NC 27710
> Phone: 919-687-4686, ext. 237
> Fax: 919-687-4737

The CAPA is copyrighted by Angold, Cox, Prendergast, Rutter, and Simonoff. Permission for copying the interview schedules may be obtained from

> Adrian Angold, M.R.C.Psych.
> Developmental Epidemiology Program
> Department of Psychiatry

EXAMPLE 17–3 ■ Sample item from the Child and Adolescent Psychiatric Assessment

Child and Adolescent Psychiatric Assessment

Codes

Definitions and questions

Coding rules

IRRITABILITY

Increased ease of precipitation of externally directed feelings of anger, bad temper, short temper, resentment, or annoyance; total daily duration of at least 1 hour. (Change may predate the primary period and continue into at least part of the primary period.)

N.B. INFORMATION OBTAINED HERE MAY ALSO BE RELEVANT TO LOSING TEMPER (PAGE 190) AND TEMPER TANTRUMS (PAGE 190)

Have you been more irritable than usual in the last 3 months?
Or made angry more easily?

What have you been "touchy" about?
Is that more than usual?
What do you do when you feel like that?
Do you keep it to yourself?
How long does it last when you feel like that?

Have you been snappy with friends or family members?

Have you gotten into arguments lately?
What has happened?
What did you say?
What did you do?

Have you hit or broken anything when you were angry?

When did you start to get "irritable" like that?

IF PRESENT, ASK:
Was there a week when you felt "irritable" most days?
Were there two weeks when you were "irritable" on at least 8 days?

Has there been a period of at least 2 months in the last year when you didn't feel like that?

IF PRESENT AT LEAST 4 HOURS A DAY, ASK:
In the last 3 months has there been a week when you were irritable like that every day?

IF IRRITABLE 4 HOURS A DAY FOR A WEEK (7 CONSECUTIVE DAYS), REMEMBER TO COMPLETE MANIA SECTION (PAGE 121)

IRRITABILITY

2 = Irritable mood present in at least 2 activities manifested by at least one instance of snappiness, shouting, quarrelsomeness and at least sometimes uncontrollable by subject

3 = Irritable mood present in most activities, accompanied by snappiness, shouting, quarrelsomeness, and nearly always uncontrollable by subject

EPISODE OF IRRITABLE MOOD

2 = At least 1 week with 4 days with irritable mood

3 = Period of 2 consecutive weeks where irritable mood present on at least 8 days

PERIOD OF 2 CONTINUOUS MONTHS WITHOUT IRRITABLE MOOD IN LAST YEAR?

0 = Yes
2 = No

CDA8I01
Intensity

CDA8F0I
Frequency

CDA8D0I
Duration

CDA8O0I
Onset

CDA8I02
Intensity

CDA8I03
Intensity

Reprinted with permission from Dr. Adrian Angold.

Duke University
Durham, NC 27710-3454

An information package containing copies of the CAPA (parent and child versions), the glossary, and psycho-metric information about the instrument may be purchased for $75.00. Training in the CAPA is required for interviewers.

The CAPA includes explanatory material to guide the interviewer in administering the instrument. However, training is required to administer the CAPA in a reliable manner. Two weeks of on-site training and an additional two weeks of practice at home are required. Training for six raters costs $7,000.00 for 1–6 raters and consists of a four-phase course (observation, practice, interviewer technique consolidation, and interviewer technique reliability assessment to 95% agreement with CAPA trainers' item ratings). Lodging for the 1-month training course and travel are additional costs. Approximately 75% of those trained at Duke University pass all requirements (i.e., a 95% reliability criterion) to be considered a competent CAPA interviewer.

PSYCHOMETRIC PROPERTIES

Reliability

Joint reliability of the CAPA ranged from $r = 0.61$ for oppositional defiant disorder to $r = 0.82$ for major depressive disorder. A diagnostic test-retest 1-week reliability study of a clinical sample of 77 children, ages 10–17, found kappa $= 0.52$ for oppositional defiant disorder, 0.61 for conduct disorder, 0.52 for separation anxiety disorder, 0.77 for overanxious disorder, 0.65 for dysthymia, 0.85 for major depressive disorder, and 1.0 for substance abuse or dependence (Angold and Costello 1995). Test-retest reliabilities for symptom severity scores yielded intraclass correlation coefficients that ranged from 0.37 for oppositional defiant disorder to 0.89 for overanxious disorder.

Validity

As with all of the structured interviews, there is no gold standard against which to validate the CAPA. However, the construct validity of the CAPA is supported by several findings: 1) prevalence rates and patterns of diagnoses for common child psychiatric disorders were comparable with those reported in other studies using respondent-based structured interviews, 2) CAPA-determined diagnoses have been associated with psychosocial impairment, 3) parent and child reports of psychopathology on the CAPA are related to parent and teacher reports of problems on well-established scales for detecting psychopathology, 4) children with CAPA-identified disorders use more mental health services than children without diagnoses, 5) CAPA-diagnosed children tend to come from families with a history of mental illness,

6) there is genetic loading for several CAPA scores and diagnoses, 7) CAPA diagnoses show consistency over time, and 8) CAPA diagnoses predict negative life outcome.

Normative data have been collected on a rural community sample (Costello et al. 1996a, 1996b).

CLINICAL UTILITY

Angold and Costello (1996) suggest that the CAPA be used by clinicians to obtain a detailed and thorough history and diagnosis. Published reports on the use of the CAPA in clinical settings have shown its utility in the management of children and adolescents with asthma (Wamboldt and Wamboldt 1995; Wamboldt et al. 1995, 1996). Because of its built-in impairment scales, the CAPA can be used to determine whether children meet criteria for serious emotional disturbance and are therefore eligible for federal funds for provision of community mental health services.

The CAPA has several strengths. It provides the most detailed glossary of symptom definitions of any standardized diagnostic instrument for children and adolescents. Use of the glossary has particular advantages for increasing the reliability of diagnoses with children who manifest internalizing and psychotic symptoms. Some other structured instruments are less reliable in this regard.

The CAPA anchors and defines incapacity ratings, which helps avoid confusion between symptom severity and degree of impairment. The CAPA has a built-in distinction between distress and impairment, which is useful for defining severe emotional disturbance. It is also possible to use the CAPA to compare diagnostic systems. The CAPA enables the interviewer to record detailed ratings of individual symptom frequencies and durations. Family and life events inquiries are also integrated into its sections.

The format of the CAPA matches that of the gold standard clinical interview and was designed to combine the thoroughness of a respondent-based interview with the flexibility of a clinician's inquiry. This approach may appeal to clinicians who find the respondent-based procedures too constricting. The CAPA has also been found to be a reliable instrument in epidemiological studies (Simonoff et al. 1997), as has the National Institute of Mental Health Diagnostic Interview Schedule for Children (NIMH-DISC 2.3) (p. 305).

The CAPA also has several weaknesses. It is a lengthy interview that takes an average of 45 minutes to 1 hour to complete, but with a highly symptomatic child, it may take up to 3 hours to complete. A newer version of the CAPA uses the same screening (or gateway) front-end section to enable skips of modules if the subject has no disorder. Where no skips occur, use of more detailed modules is triggered; preliminary testing indicates that it reduces the length of the interview to 30 minutes per subject (60 minutes total). A lengthy 4-week training course is needed to master the instrument; travel, lodging, cost of the course, and time away from practice can make use of this instrument very expensive. Even with this effort, 25% of interviewers do not reach the 95% reliability criterion necessary to obtain CAPA certification. The joint reliability data reported ($r = 0.61–0.81$) are disappointing, considering the time and cost of the training. The CAPA does not collect information for diagnoses that require a physical or psychological examination as part of the diagnostic process, such as autism and other pervasive developmental disorders, organic mental disorders, and somatoform disorders. However, the same is true of all other diagnostic and screening instruments for school-age children and adolescents described in this chapter. Finally, the CAPA cannot be used with children younger than age 8. Because the modal age at onset for attention-deficit/hyperactivity disorder is 7, the CAPA may not be used early in the course of attention-deficit/hyperactivity disorder.

REFERENCES AND SUGGESTED READINGS

Angold A, Costello E: A test-retest reliability study of child-reported psychiatric symptoms and diagnoses using the Child and Adolescent Psychiatric Assessment. Psychol Med 25:755–762, 1995

Angold A, Costello EJ: Toward establishing an empirical basis for the diagnosis of oppositional defiant disorder. J Am Acad Child Adolesc Psychiatry 35:1205–1212, 1996

Angold A, Cox A, Prendergast M, et al: The Child and Adolescent Psychiatric Assessment. Psychol Med 25:739–753, 1995

Costello E, Angold A, Burns B, et al: The Great Smoky Mountains Study of Youth: goals, design, methods, and the prevalence of DSM-III-R disorders. Arch Gen Psychiatry 53:1129–1136, 1996a

Costello E, Angold A, Burns B, et al: The Great Smoky Mountains Study of Youth: functional impairment and serious emotional disturbance. Arch Gen Psychiatry 53:1137–1143, 1996b

Rutter M, Tizard J, Whitmore K: Education, Health, and Behavior: Psychological and Medical Study of Childhood Development. London, John Wiley, 1970

Simonoff J, Pickles A, Meyer J, et al: The Virginia Twin Study of Adolescent Behavioral Development: influences of age, sex, and impairment on rates of disorder. Arch Gen Psychiatry 54:801–808, 1997

Wamboldt M, Wamboldt F: Psychological aspects of severe asthma in children, in Severe Asthma: Pathogenesis and Clinical Management. Edited by Szefler SJ, Leung DYM. New York, Marcel Dekker, 1995, pp 465–495

Wamboldt F, Wamboldt M, Gavin L, et al: Parental criticism and treatment outcome in adolescents hospitalized for asthma. J Psychiatr Res 39:995–1005, 1995

Wamboldt M, Weintraub P, Krafchick D, et al: Psychiatric family history in adolescents with severe asthma. J Am Acad Child Adolesc Psychiatry 35:1042–1049, 1996

National Institute of Mental Health Diagnostic Interview Schedule for Children (NIMH-DISC)

Edited by D. Shaffer, P. Fisher, C. Lucas, and the NIMH-DISC Editorial Board

GOALS

The National Institute of Mental Health Diagnostic Interview Schedule for Children (NIMH-DISC) (Shaffer et al. 1993) is a respondent-based diagnostic instrument developed for use by trained lay interviewers in large-scale epidemiological studies to obtain diagnoses defined by the DSM system. The NIMH-DISC grew out of a series of studies by Herjanic, Conners, and Puig-Antich that led to field trials by Costello and colleagues (Shaffer et al. 1993). Second-generation versions (NIMH-DISC 2.1 and 2.3) underwent methodological and psychometric testing as part of the Cooperative Agreement for Methodologic Research for Multi-Site Epidemiologic Surveys of Mental Disorders in Child and Adolescent Populations (MECA Study) (Lahey et al. 1996). The energetic NIMH-DISC Editorial Board updates the instrument regularly to keep it current with the most recent version of DSM. The NIMH-DISC-IV, which corresponds to the DSM-IV diagnostic criteria, is not yet available. The DISC 2.3 is the most recent version for which published reliability and validity data are available and is therefore the version reviewed here.

The NIMH-DISC 2.3, which is based on DSM-III-R, determines the DSM Axis I diagnoses of a child or adolescent during an interview of the patient and parent. It was designed to be administered by clinically untrained (lay) interviewers. Use of such entry-level interviewers is far more economical in large-scale surveys of children.

DESCRIPTION

The NIMH-DISC 2.3 is a completely structured, respondent-based interview. All symptom questions are meant to be read exactly as written. There is little or no room for independent probing, which experienced clinicians may find restricting. Response options in the NIMH-DISC 2.3 are generally limited to yes, no, and sometimes or somewhat. There are thus very few open-ended questions, and the interviewer is not able to inquire further using ad-lib probes.

The NIMH-DISC is available in parallel parent (NIMH-DISC-P), youth (NIMH-DISC-C), and partial teacher (NIMH-DISC-T) versions. The NIMH-DISC-P is for parents of children ages 6–16, and the NIMH-DISC-C is for direct administration to children ages 9–17. The NIMH-DISC-T is recommended for administration to the primary teacher for children in elementary school.

The interview covers 33 child and adolescent mental disorders that do not depend on specialized tests or observational procedures for diagnosis. The interview is organized into 19 diagnostic sections. Related diagnoses are grouped into six diagnostic modules: Anxiety Disorders, Mood Disorders, Disruptive Disorders, Substance Abuse Disorders, Schizophrenia, and Miscellaneous Disorders (Eating, Elimination, etc.). Each diagnostic module is independent of the others, so information from other modules is not necessary to make a diagnosis. Each diagnostic module contains an impairment section, so that impairment related to each diagnosis attained can be evaluated. A short introductory module includes a brief script read to the informant to establish the time frame for most symptoms and to gather basic demographic information.

The NIMH-DISC uses a hierarchical question structure. Of the 2,930 questions in the NIMH-DISC-C, 358 are stem questions (broad questions that address the most salient aspect of a symptom and must be asked), and 1,341 are contingent questions (asked only after a positive reply to a stem question). Contingent questions typically collect information on symptom frequency, duration, and intensity. If a clinically significant number of symptoms for a given diagnosis is endorsed, 732 questions (in addition to the 1,341) can be asked about age and context at onset, impairment attributable to symptoms, and treatment. Otherwise, there are very few skip options in the NIMH-DISC. Thus data are collected about all symptoms for a diagnosis, regardless of whether the child has the diagnosis, allowing the investigator to derive symptom and criteria scales from the interview that can be used as continuous measures of psychopathology.

An irritability item for major depressive disorder from the NIMH-DISC is provided in Example 17–4.

The NIMH-DISC covers the past year and the past 4 weeks (current). The computer version includes algorithms that use NIMH-DISC scores to arrive at 31 DSM diagnoses. Using a computer-assisted version of the NIMH-DISC greatly minimizes interviewer and editor error, reduces training time, and eliminates data entry costs but does not usually reduce administration time. Both the parent and youth versions of the NIMH-DISC are scored using SAS computer algorithms, according to symptom criteria listed in DSM. A third combined set integrates information from the parent and the youth versions. Symptom scales (which consist of questions inquiring about the symptoms) and criteria scales (which are counts of the number of diagnostic criteria met) have been prepared for most diagnoses. Computer algorithms are available for obtaining diagnoses, criterion scales, and symptom scale scores.

The NIMH-DISC is primarily used to generate categorical diagnoses. However, dimensional symptom

EXAMPLE 17–4 ■ Sample item from the National Institute of Mental Health Diagnostic Interview Schedule for Children

0=NO	1=SOMETIMES/SOMEWHAT	2=YES	7, 77=REFUSE TO ANSWER	8, 88=NOT APPLICABLE	9,99=DON'T KNOW

3. In the last year (*that is, since [NAME CURRENT MONTH] of last year*), was there a time when you often felt grouchy or irritable and often in a bad mood, when even little things would make you mad?

     0   2   7   9   [27]

IF YES, A. Was there a time in the last year when you felt grouchy or irritable for a long time each day?

     0   2   7   9   [28]

IF NO, GO TO NOTE 1

   B. Would you say that you felt that way for <u>most of the day</u>?

     0   2   7   9   [29]

   C. Was there a time when you felt grouchy or irritable <u>almost every day</u>?

     0   2   7   9   [30]

IF NO, GO TO NOTE 1

IF YES, D. In the last year, were there two weeks in a row when you felt grouchy or irritable almost every day?

     0   2*   7   9   [31]

IF NO, GO TO NOTE 1

   E. Now, what about the <u>last four weeks</u>? (*Since [[NAME EVENT]//the beginning of/the middle of/the end of [LAST MONTH]]*), have you often felt grouchy or irritable and in a bad mood?

     0   2   7   9   [32]

---

scores can be generated by summing the scores from selected items (Jensen et al. 1995). Published validity data (see later section) address the suitability of its output for clinical practice.

PRACTICAL ISSUES

The authors estimate that the NIMH-DISC should average 70 minutes for the child and 57 minutes for the parent, for an average of about 130 minutes (2 hours, 10 minutes) of interview time. As with other interviews, administration time varies greatly depending on the number of symptoms endorsed.

To obtain information about whether the NIMH-DISC might address specific research and/or clinical needs, please contact

     Prudence Fisher, M.S.
     NIMH-DISC Training Center
       at Columbia University
     Division of Child and Adolescent Psychiatry

     New York State Psychiatric Institute
     1051 Riverside Drive
     New York, NY 10032
     Phone: 212-543-5357 or 212-543-5424
     Fax: 212-568-8856
     E-mail: nimhdisc@child.cpmc.columbia.edu

The NIMH-DISC interview schedule must be purchased from the NIMH-DISC Training Center. For information about ordering a copy, contact

     Lynn Lucas
     NIMH-DISC Training Center
       at Columbia University
     Division of Child and Adolescent Psychiatry
     New York State Psychiatric Institute
     1051 Riverside Drive
     New York, NY 10032
     Phone: 888-814-DISC or 888-814-3472
     E-mail: disc@worldnet.att.com

The current version (NIMH-DISC-IV) costs $50.00 each for single-sided copies of the parent and child forms or $35.00 for double-sided versions of parent and child forms. The computerized NIMH-DISC-IV (the C-DISC-4.0) can be purchased by practitioners for $900.00 (installation diskettes and 2-year support contract included); by investigators funded by the U.S. Department of Health and Human Services or the National Institutes of Health for a licensing fee of $2,000.00 for support during the duration of funding; and by other research or nonprofit groups for costs that range from $300.00 for each installation (for a group of 21 or more installations) to $700.00 for each installation (for a group of 4 installations).

The NIMH-DISC was designed to be administered by lay interviewers. Training is the optimal method for learning to administer the NIMH-DISC. Training time runs 1–5 days, depending on whether computer-assisted versions will be used and how many modules in the interview need to be administered. Personnel at the NIMH-DISC Training Center can provide information about the cost and schedule for regular training sessions.

The NIMH-DISC interview is in the public domain and is not subject to copyright limitations. However, the name *NIMH-DISC* can be used to describe only instruments reviewed and approved by the DISC Editorial Board. Users are advised against modifying the NIMH-DISC because structured interviews are known to be sensitive to context, order, and length. The DISC Editorial Board warns that changes may affect the sensitivity and specificity of the NIMH-DISC to the extent that published psychometric reliability and validity data may no longer be applicable.

The computerized NIMH-DISC interview for DSM-IV (called the C-DISC-4.0) was developed in 1997 by Lucas, Fisher, and Shaffer for both English- and Spanish-speaking patients. It differs from the earlier C-DISC-2.3 in that its diagnostic algorithms can yield diagnoses for both the past year and current (past 4 weeks) for the single-informant (parent or child) interviews.

A CD-ROM–based version of an abbreviated NIMH-DISC, which addresses only current symptoms (past 4 weeks) and is useful for screening purposes, is under development. It will be called the NIMH-DISC-IV-Voice, or DISC-V. It features an interviewer's voice reading the questions, so an adolescent can self-administer it. It requires a computer with headphones or speakers.

The NIMH-DISC is available in Dutch, English, German, Icelandic, and Spanish and is being translated into Chinese. The instrument is expected to become the World Health Organization's official diagnostic instrument for children.

PSYCHOMETRIC PROPERTIES

Reliability

Test-retest reliability for the NIMH-DISC 2.1 in a clinical sample (87 outpatients and 10 inpatients) ranged from kappa = 0.40 (anxiety disorder) to 0.66 (conduct disorder) for parents, from kappa = 0.2 (major depressive disorder) to 0.60 (conduct disorder) for youth, and from kappa = 0.5 (anxiety disorder) to 0.7 (conduct disorder) for combined parent and youth (Jensen et al. 1995). Roberts et al. (1996) obtained test-retest data in youths, ages 12–17 ($N = 101$), and found a range of kappa values from 0.47 (any anxiety disorder) to 0.66 (oppositional defiant disorder). Test-retest NIMH-DISC performance is reduced by attenuation effects (Jensen et al. 1995), in which symptoms reported during the first NIMH-DISC interview are denied during the second interview, particularly by the child.

Validity

Schwab-Stone et al. (1996), working with a community sample ($N = 247$), reported on the agreement between NIMH-DISC 2.3 and clinicians' criterion ratings combined into diagnoses using a computer algorithm. These clinician ratings served as the gold standard diagnoses. Parent interviews ranged from kappa = 0.29 (separation anxiety disorder) to 0.74 (conduct disorder). Youth interviews ranged from kappa = 0.27 (attention-deficit/hyperactivity disorder) to 0.77 (conduct disorder). Combined youth and parent validity ranged from kappa = 0.4 (overanxious disorder) to 0.80 (conduct disorder). Scores for anxiety disorders and dysthymia showed relatively lower reliability and validity. The validity of the NIMH-DISC varies depending on the informant; diagnoses on the basis of the child's report have lower levels of validity than the parent report or the combined parent-child report.

The NIMH-DISC 2.3 generates prevalence data for children with psychiatric diagnoses similar to those generated by other respondent-based instruments, such as the Child and Adolescent Psychiatric Assessment (CAPA) (p. 301). When the NIMH-DISC 2.3 diagnoses are used along with impairment measures, the prevalence rates of disorders in the community (from the MECA Study) are equal to those determined by applying the Children's Global Assessment Scale (CGAS) (p. 363) (Shaffer et al. 1996). The reliability of the instrument compares favorably with that of clinicians using a semistructured interview (Piacentini 1993).

With regard to patient acceptability, respondent-opinion questions were asked of all subjects at the end of the MECA Study NIMH-DISC 2.3 interview, which took 2 hours, 20 minutes. The interview was found to be interesting by 83% of parents and 77% of children. The length of the interview was judged to be "about right" by two-thirds of both the parents and the children. Approximately three-fourths of the parents and children reported that they felt no more upset during the NIMH-DISC interview than before the interview. Approximately 95% of parents and children stated that they would advise a friend to participate in the study. More than 80% of parents and more than 62% of children were comfortable with use of the computer version, and approximately half the parent and child respondents preferred that they be asked the questions with a computer.

CLINICAL UTILITY

The NIMH-DISC has potential uses in clinical practice. One option for the clinician is to use the NIMH-DISC 2.3 to supplement his or her own clinical interview. Doing so would force the clinician to focus on DSM-IV criteria for making a diagnosis rather than making a snap diagnosis on the basis of a few salient features (Shaffer et al. 1996).

The automated generation of DSM diagnoses and symptom scales by the NIMH-DISC 2.3 make it suitable for admission evaluations to clinic programs or inpatient units and particularly useful for justification with health management organizations. It has also been used to assess diagnoses in large groups for administrative purposes, such as in a school system or for children at Boys Town USA near Omaha, Nebraska.

The NIMH-DISC 2.3 has also proven itself in a wide range of research applications, particularly for community studies. The NIMH-DISC 2.3 has been used in numerous large epidemiological research programs and stud-

ies of service delivery and has been selected as a diagnostic instrument by the World Health Organization.

Because the NIMH-DISC 2.3 uses a 6-month time frame to ascertain categorical diagnoses, its diagnostic algorithms are not appropriate for determining short-term changes such as would be needed to assess treatment response. Although it is possible to use symptom score totals from a single module, no major treatment studies have used the NIMH-DISC 2.3 in this manner.

The NIMH-DISC has several strengths. It is a very structured respondent-based interview, which makes it usable by nonclinicians with little or no training. Minimal coding is required after the interview. A computer-assisted version of the most recent interview is available, and algorithms that automate the generation of diagnoses and symptom scale scores are provided in the computerized version. The wording of the questions adheres closely to DSM and its criteria. The newest version, the NIMH-DISC-IV, provides coverage of DSM-III-R, DSM-IV, and ICD-10 diagnoses. The NIMH-DISC has been tested in both community and clinic samples and is available in English and Spanish.

The NIMH-DISC also has several weaknesses. It can be lengthy for children who have symptoms. The strict wording makes its use boring for clinicians, if not for respondents. The NIMH-DISC is prone to overdiagnosis, unless impairment criteria are explicitly used. Finally, there is difficulty with criterion or concurrent validity with younger informants in some diagnostic categories, such as major depressive disorder (King et al. 1997).

REFERENCES AND SUGGESTED READINGS

Jensen P, Roper M, Fisher P, et al: Test-retest reliability of the Diagnostic Interview Schedule for Children (Version 2.1): parent, child, and combined algorithms. Arch Gen Psychiatry 52:61–67, 1995

King C, Katz S, Ghaziuddin N, et al: Diagnosis and assessment of depression and suicidality using the NIMH Diagnostic Interview Schedule for Children (DISC-2.3). J Abnorm Child Psychol 25:173–181, 1997

Lahey B, Flagg E, Bird H, et al: The NIMH Methods for the Epidemiology of Child and Adolescent Mental Disorders (MECA) Study: background and methodology. J Am Acad Child Adolesc Psychiatry 35:855–864, 1996

Piacentini J, Shaffer D, Fisher P, et al: The Diagnostic Interview Schedule for Children—Revised Version, III: concurrent criterion validity. J Am Acad Child Adolesc Psychiatry 32:658–665, 1993

Roberts R, Solovitz B, Chen Y-W, et al: Retest stability of DSM-III-R diagnoses among adolescents using the Diagnostic Interview Schedule for Children (DISC-2.1). J Abnorm Child Psychol 24:349–362, 1996

Schwab-Stone M, Shaffer D, Dulcan M, et al: Criterion validity of the NIMH Diagnostic Interview Schedule for Children, Version 2.3 (DISC-2.3). J Am Acad Child Adolesc Psychiatry 35:878–888, 1996

Shaffer D, Schwab-Stone M, Fisher P, et al: The Diagnostic Interview for Children—Revised Version (DISC-R), I: preparation, field testing, interrater reliability, and acceptability. J Am Acad Child Adolesc Psychiatry 32:643–650, 1993

Shaffer D, Fisher P, Dulcan M, et al: The NIMH Diagnostic Interview Schedule for Children Version 2.3 (DISC-2.3): description, acceptability, prevalence rates, and performance in the MECA Study. J Am Acad Child Adolesc Psychiatry 35:865–877, 1996

cally derived on the basis of their demonstrated ability to discriminate between clinically referred and psychiatrically healthy samples (Jensen et al. 1996).

The CBCL is a dimensional measure of psychopathology designed to identify children at risk; it does not generate DSM-IV diagnoses, however. The CBCL/2–3 was designed to assess the behavioral and emotional problems of children ages 2–3 as observed by parental figures and other adults who interact with the children on a daily basis (Achenbach 1992). The CBCL/4–18 was designed to assess children and youth ages 4–18 (Achenbach 1991a). The TRF was designed to obtain teachers' reports of the school behavior of pupils ages 5–18 and is scored for the same syndromes as the CBCL. The YSR was developed to obtain self-reports about a wide range of behavioral and emotional problems displayed by adolescents ages 11–18 in the same eight syndromes as the CBCL/4–18 (Achenbach 1991b). Achenbach (1991c) considered adolescents to have sufficient cognitive and emotional maturity to recall and report their feelings and behavior. As with the CBCL, psychopathology is defined psychometrically as deviation from normal behavior. More information about the CBCL Competence Scale (p. 377) may be found in Chapter 19.

Child Behavior Checklists (CBCL/2–3 and CBCL/4–18), Teacher Report Form (TRF), and Youth Self Report (YSR)

T. M. Achenbach

GOALS

The Achenbach rating forms (Achenbach 1991a, 1991b, 1991c, 1992) comprise a family of self-scored symptom checklists that were developed to provide information on a broad range of competencies and behavior problems in preschoolers, school-age children, and adolescents. The forms are the Child Behavior Checklists (CBCL/2–3 and CBCL/4–18), Teacher Report Form (TRF), and Youth Self Report (YSR). The items in the CBCL are empiri-

DESCRIPTION

The CBCL/2–3, the CBCL/4–18, the TRF, and the YSR are forms on which a parent, teacher, or adolescent self-scores judgments of recent behavioral and emotional functioning of a child or self, plus information about competencies. In the rest of this section, these four different measures are referred to as the CBCL measures. Where differences exist, they are described.

The CBCL items are formatted at a fifth-grade reading level. The YSR can be administered orally if the adolescent scoring the measure does not read at a fifth-grade level. With the exception of the CBCL/2–3, the other CBCL measures ask the rater to describe school problems and other concerns, as well as to describe the strengths and competencies of the child or adolescent being rated. The CBCL/2–3 form is a single sheet with 100 problem items and 3 global questions about the child's physical health, the parent's greatest concern, and the child's strengths for the past 2 months. The CBCL/4–18 and the YSR are divided into 118 problem and 7 competence scales that use a 3-point Likert scale: less than average, average, or more than average. The TRF has 126 items, which are divided into 112 problem items and 14 competence scales.

Each of the measures, except the CBCL/2–3, opens with questions regarding competency, including socially desirable characteristics. The first seven questions are scales that ask for a rating of the child's or adolescent's interests and activities, comparing their participation with that of peers using a 3-point Likert scale: less than average, average, or more than average. These questions tap domains of competency (sports, hobbies, clubs, jobs, chores, friends, peer relationships, and academic performance), plus open-ended questions about illnesses, general concerns, and an item that requests the youth to describe the best things about himself or herself.

These questions are followed by 118 problem scale items describing the youth's behavior during the past 6 months. Each question is scaled on a 3-point Likert scale, with 0 = not true, 1 = somewhat/sometimes true, and 2 = very true/often true. A sample item from the CBCL/4–18 is provided in Example 17–5.

The CBCL measures are completed by parent, teacher, or adolescent. A research assistant or a master's-level clinician can provide help if needed. The clinical worker can score the instrument and graph the results or use a computer program to complete the report.

The problem items yield a total summed score that ranges from 0 to 236. These summed syndrome scales (ranging from 0 to 39, depending on the syndrome scale) are assigned normalized T-scores on the basis of percentiles of normative samples separately for each sex at ages 4–11 and 12–18 (Achenbach 1991a). The versions of the core syndrome derived from the 89 common items were compared with analogous core syndromes derived from the YSR and the TRF. Items found in analogous core syndromes from two of three instruments were used to form a cross-informant syndrome construct. The eight syndromes displayed on the 1991 CBCL hand-scored profile—withdrawn, somatic complaints, anxious/depressed, social problems, thought problems, attention problems, delinquent behavior, and aggressive behavior—can be plotted graphically. For total problem score, a T-score of 64 is considered the cutoff score for the clinical range (Achenbach 1992); T-scores of 60–63 fall in the borderline range (Achenbach 1991a). These cutoff scores were determined statistically from psychiatrically healthy and clinical samples. Normative data were determined on the basis of 2,368 children of various ages tested for the CBCL/4–18, 657 boys and 678 girls tested for the YSR, and 1,391 youth ages 5–18 tested for the TRF. These children were not receiving mental health or special education services and were representative of the U.S. population with respect to ethnicity; socioeconomic status; urban, suburban, or rural residence; and geographic region (Achenbach 1991a). A T-score of 55 was applied to all raw scores at or below the 69th percentile. A T-score of 70 was cho-

EXAMPLE 17–5 ■ Sample item from the CBCL/4–18

Below is a list of items that describe children and youth. For each item that describes your child now or within the past 6 months, please circle the 2 if the item is very true of your child. Circle the 1 if the item is somewhat or sometimes true of your child. If the item is not true of your child, circle the 0. Please answer all items as well as you can, even if some do not seem to apply to your child.

0 = Not True (as far as you know)   1 = Somewhat or Sometimes True   2 = Very True or Often True

0 1 2 1. Acts too young for his/her age
0 1 2 2. Allergy (describe) _____
_____
0 1 2 3. Argues a lot
0 1 2 4. Asthma
0 1 2 5. Behaves like opposite sex
0 1 2 6. Bowel movements outside toilet
0 1 2 7. Bragging, boasting
0 1 2 8. Can't concentrate, can't pay attention for long
0 1 2 9. Can't get his/her mind off certain thoughts; obsessions (describe): _____

0 1 2 10. Can't sit still, restless, or hyperactive

0 1 2 31. Fears he/she might think or do something bad
0 1 2 32. Feels he/she has to be perfect
0 1 2 33. Feels or complains that no one loves him/her
0 1 2 34. Feels others are out to get him/her
0 1 2 35. Feels worthless or inferior
0 1 2 36. Gets hurt a lot, accident-prone
0 1 2 37. Gets in many fights
0 1 2 38. Gets teased a lot
0 1 2 39. Hangs around with others who get in trouble
0 1 2 40. Hears sounds or voices that aren't there (describe): _____

Reprinted with permission from Thomas Achenbach, Ph.D.

sen as the cutoff score to discriminate best between referred and nonreferred children and adolescents.

PRACTICAL ISSUES

It takes 15–20 minutes to administer each of the CBCL measures, except for the CBCL/2–3, which parents can complete in 10 minutes (Achenbach 1992).

All the CBCL measures are copyrighted. Inquiries should be sent to the author:

Thomas Achenbach, Ph.D.
Department of Psychiatry
University of Vermont College of Medicine
1 South Prospect Street
Burlington, VT 05401
Phone: 802-656-2602
Fax: 802-656-8313

Interactive computer entry of all CBCL forms by respondents, scoring of machine-readable forms by optical scanners, and computer software for scoring are available. A client entry program enables parents, youths, or teachers to enter data in response to user-friendly computer screens. Data can be scored immediately using the CBCL/4–18, YSR, TRF, or Cross-Informant program.

A complete cost list is available for the CBCL measures and related materials. These materials include audiocassettes ($20.00), sample packets ($20.00), a bibliography of published studies ($45.00), checklist paper forms ($10.00 for 25 copies), computer scoring programs ($135.00 for CBCL/2–3), scanning software packages ($220.00), client entry software package ($220.00), and the Cross-Informant program to score the CBCL/4–18, TRF, and YSR ($295.00).

Although training is recommended for those scoring and interpreting the YSR forms, the CBCL is very easy to score. Detailed manuals for each of the four CBCL measures (Achenbach 1991a, 1991b, 1991c, 1992), which give specific information about the administration, scoring, and psychometrics of the instruments, are available from the author for $25.00 each and can be used for self-instruction. The author also maintains an extensive running bibliography of publications and citations.

Translations are available in Chinese, Dutch, French, German, Italian, Japanese, Portuguese, Spanish, and many other languages.

PSYCHOMETRIC PROPERTIES

Reliability

Internal consistency for the CBCL measures has been determined in different studies. For the CBCL/2–3 ($N = 321$), Cronbach's alpha was 0.96. In one study ($N = 1,201$), the CBCL/4–18 had a Cronbach's alpha of 0.96 for children ages 4–11 and for adolescents ages 12–18. The YSR was evaluated in a general population sample ($N = 1,054$), for which a Cronbach's alpha of 0.47 was reported for the competence items; in the same sample, Cronbach's alpha was 0.95 for the problem items (Achenbach 1991c). The TRF had a Cronbach's alpha of 0.97 for total problem scores in a sample of 1,275.

Data on joint reliability are available for the CBCL/2–3, the CBCL/4–18, and the TRF. Teachers seeing students under different conditions showed a mean correlation (r) of 0.55 for adaptive and academic scores and 0.54 for problem scores (Achenbach 1991b). The 1991 manual for the CBCL (Achenbach 1991a, p. 71) reports intraclass correlation coefficients (ICCs) for joint reliability, with overall ICCs of 0.927 for the 20 competence items and 0.959 for the 118 specific problem items. Teachers versus teacher's aides seeing students under similar circumstances showed a mean correlation (r) of 0.60 for academic and adaptive scores and 0.55 for problem scores (Achenbach 1991b). Parents (mother and father rating child) showed a mean agreement (r) of 0.62 for total problems on the CBCL/2–3 and 0.76 on the CBCL/4–18. Reliability is thus moderately good.

Achenbach (1991a) reported excellent test-retest reliability for the CBCL/4–18 for a 1-week interval ($N = 72$) for competence ($r = 0.97$) and problems ($r = 0.95$), which fell to $r = 0.56$ and 0.85, respectively, by 1 year ($N = 70$). Similar excellent test-retest reliability was reported for the TRF ($r = 0.90$ for academic and adaptive, and $r = 0.92$ for problem item scores) during a 15-day testing interval ($N = 44$). Test-retest reliability of the YSR has been reported in a general population sample ($N = 50$) over a 7-day period. Both the competency and problem scales showed good reliability ($r = 0.79$–0.80).

Test-retest reliability for toddlers was equally impressive. These results came from a general population sample and from a longitudinal study ($N = 20$) of toddlers with normal and low birth weights. Here the 1-week test-retest reliability ($N = 61$) was $r = 0.91$ for total problems, and the 1-year test-retest reliability ($N = 75$) was $r = 0.78$ for total problems.

Validity

The CBCL/2–3 was compared with the Behavior Problem Checklist developed for use with the same age group. Achenbach (1992) reported a correlation (r) of 0.58 ($N = 65$). The correlation between the subscales of the CBCL/4–18 total problem scores and closest counterpart scales of the Conners' Rating Scales—Revised (CRS-R) (p. 329) total scores was good ($r = 0.82$, $N = 50$). Correlation (r) between TRF subscales and the Conners' Teacher Rating Scale—Revised ranged from 0.80 to 0.83 for conduct problems, inattention, and total problem scores ($N = 38$).

For the CBCL/4–18, a demographically matched referred ($n = 4,455$) and nonreferred ($n = 2,368$) sample of boys and girls showed significantly lower problem scale scores for the nonreferred children (Achenbach 1991a). Referral status accounted for 21%–39% of the variance in adaptive functioning scores. For the TRF, in a study of 1,275 subjects in each of two demographically matched groups (clinically referred and nonreferred students), similar results were seen. The referred students showed significantly lower scores on all competency scales and higher scores on all problem scales except somatic complaints (Achenbach 1991b). Four demographically matched samples ($N = 642$) of toddlers were used to measure associations among age, socioeconomic status, and referral status. All problem scales on the CBCL/2–3 showed significantly lower scores for the nonreferred children.

Stability correlations for 1- and 2-year periods ranged from 0.70 to 0.74 for problem scales and from 0.56 to 0.63 for competence scales (Achenbach 1991a). Ethnicity in boys ages 4 and 5 accounted for 1% of the variance in social competence scores.

Using referral status as a standard of criterion validity, Achenbach reported low false-positive rates (8.4%) and higher false-negative rates (21.8%) on the CBCL/4–18, from a sample of 778 matched referred and nonreferred children. For the TRF, there were 16% false-negative results and 29% false-positive results from a sample of 2,550 referred and nonreferred children. The YSR had a 33% false-positive and a 30% false-negative rate. The YSR may have a high rate of misclassification of clinical status, underscoring the recommendation that the YSR score be used along with other clinical information.

In other studies, the CBCL has shown itself to be sensitive to treatment effects (Kazdin et al. 1987, 1992).

CLINICAL UTILITY

With the exception of the self-scored YSR, the potential uses of the CBCL measures include quick assessment of a patient by a familiar adult, in which comparison to national norms is helpful. The CBCL measures are also useful in treatment planning, clinical intervention research, and evaluation of children in medical and forensic settings (Achenbach 1991a). Patient responses suggest that the CBCL measures are easy to understand.

The TRF complements the other measures in this group. It can be used to describe students' functioning to make referrals, compare students' functioning in different classes, determine eligibility for special education services, and reevaluate after intervention (Achenbach 1991b).

The YSR is the only measure scored by patients themselves. The results of the YSR can be used to make initial assessments and reassessments and for intake evaluations, special education evaluations, treatment planning, clinical intervention research, and evaluation of adolescents in medical and forensic settings (Achenbach 1991c).

The CBCL instruments have several strengths. They serve as multifaceted symptom rating scales to screen children and adolescents for the presence of psychiatric symptoms. The initial 10 questions give global ratings of impairment and competency. These self-scored checklists are portable, easy to administer, and easy to collect and to score, so they can be used in a wide variety of clinical and research situations. All the Achenbach measures are self-scored, which means that responses will not include the bias of the interviewer. The forms and scoring program are explicit, and they allow for comparing information from informants. Parallel versions for completion by the parent, child, and teacher and versions that span a large age range are valuable.

These measures have strong and well-documented psychometric properties, including derivation of normative data in large community and clinic samples. They have become standard components of most research programs on children and adolescents and give salient information on patient characteristics in a research sample. The CBCL measures are widely used in most clinical research programs, including the most recent pediatric psychopharmacology studies involving new medications for children. The CBCL also is useful and efficient in identifying groups at risk within community settings (Jensen et al. 1996). In other studies, the CBCL has shown itself to be sensitive to treatment effects (Kazdin et al. 1987, 1992).

The CBCL measures also have several problems, however. These symptom checklists do not match the symptom criteria in standard diagnostic systems, so they cannot be used to make a diagnosis. For low-frequency disorders, such as autism, the CBCL items are particularly irrelevant.

Each of these symptom checklists represents the global impressions of its single rater; they may thus be subject to unknown biases less evident in multiinformant and multidimensional rating instruments. The CBCL is only as accurate as the information provided by the adult who completes it; thus, a misinformed adult may give erroneous information. Different adults in the child's life may show high rates of disagreement (G. Canino and E. J. Costello, personal communication). There are also high false-positive and false-negative rates for the YSR.

The CBCL measures are based on national norms and are not designed to record extremes of function. Thus the scores may not represent the degree of severity of dysfunction or pathology. The CBCL will also not work for a child with mental retardation, for whom norms of children the same age may not be a relevant comparison (G. Canino and E. J. Costello, personal communication).

Finally, parents and teachers find the measures too long. It has also been shown that the CBCL instruments provide no better discrimination than substantially shorter questionnaires (M. Rutter, personal communication).

REFERENCES AND SUGGESTED READINGS

Achenbach TM: Manual for the Child Behavior Checklist/4–18 and 1991 Profile. Burlington, VT, University of Vermont, 1991a

Achenbach TM: Manual for the Teacher's Report Form and 1991 Profile. Burlington, VT, University of Vermont, 1991b

Achenbach TM: Manual for the Youth Self-Report and 1991 Profile. Burlington, VT, University of Vermont, 1991c

Achenbach TM: Manual for the Child Behavior Checklist/2–3 and 1992 Profile. Burlington, VT, University of Vermont, 1992

Biederman J, Faraone S, Doyle A, et al: Convergence of the Child Behavior Checklist with structured interview-based psychiatric diagnoses with and without comorbidity. J Child Psychol Psychiatry 34:1241–1251, 1993

Canino G, Costello EJ: Measuring Functional Impairment and Adaptive Functioning for Clinical Trials: A Review of Measures. Handout presented at New Clinical Drug Evaluation Unit, Boca Raton, FL, May 1997

Jensen P, Wantanabe H, Richters J, et al: Scales, diagnoses, and child psychopathology, II: comparing the CBCL and DISC against external validators. J Abnorm Child Psychol 24:151–168, 1996

Kazdin A, Esveldt-Dawson K, French N, et al: Problem-solving skills training and relationship therapy in the treatment of antisocial child behavior. J Consult Clin Psychol 55:76–85, 1987

Kazdin A, Siegel T, Bass D: Cognitive problem-solving skills training and parent management training in the treatment of antisocial behavior in children. J Consult Clin Psychol 60:737–747, 1992

Diagnostic Interview for Children and Adolescents (DICA)

W. Reich

GOALS

The Diagnostic Interview for Children and Adolescents (DICA) began as a semistructured, respondent-based interview that was developed at Washington University in St. Louis, mainly for clinical and epidemiological research. The first version of the DICA, patterned after the Renard Diagnostic Interview, came out in 1969 (Herjanic and Campbell 1977). The diagnoses in the DICA were based on ICD-9 in combination with the Feighner criteria. A revised version of the DICA, patterned after the National Institute of Mental Health Diagnostic Interview Schedule (DIS) (p. 61) and based on DSM-III criteria, was developed in 1981 (Herjanic and Reich 1982). The DICA-R, developed in 1988, is fully interviewer based and uses the DSM-III-R categories of disorders (Ezpeleta et al. 1997). The DICA-IV computer-based interview, which is fully respondent based (self-administered), is commercially available from Multi-Health Systems, Inc. In this section, we discuss data on the DICA-R, which is identified in the section simply as the DICA. Different versions of the DICA cover the range from interview based to fully respondent based.

The primary purpose of the DICA is to ascertain the lifetime diagnosis of the subject. More than 20 lifetime diagnoses are covered. The DICA has been used in psychopharmacological, biological, and epidemiological research.

DESCRIPTION

There are three versions of the DICA: one for children ages 6–12 (DICA-C), another for adolescents ages 13–18 (DICA-A), and a third for parents of children of both age groups (DICA-P). The DICA has been used with children younger than age 6, with instructions to the interviewers to use their own words. The DICA interview is written at a fourth-grade reading level. It uses standard and specific probes to clarify positive responses. The interview begins with rapport-building questions about the child's grades, hobbies, friends, school, leisure time avocations, pets, and social activities. Later questions cover information about the child's relationships at home, at school, and with peers; school progress; and social behavior in the community. The DICA also includes a review of somatic symptoms and questions covering a range of psychiatric symptoms, including depression, anxiety, and psychosis. The three DICA versions include sections on psychosocial stressors, and the parent version has a section on prenatal, perinatal, and preschool information.

The DICA is rater administered. Most of the questions are answered with a range of multiple-choice options. Multiple skip options in each section speed up the interview if the child or adolescent does not appear to have a specific symptom or a given disorder. If skip options are used, the instrument cannot generate symptom or criterion scales. However, if skip options are omitted, so that questions about all symptoms are asked, symptom or criterion scales can be generated. The interviewer is encouraged to ask clarifying questions; the respondent is frequently asked for an example when a yes answer is given. The DICA covers a wide range of areas, including demographics, externalizing disorders, substance use and abuse disorders, mood disorders (including bipolar disorder), dysthymic disorder, anxiety disorders (separation anxiety disorder, avoidant disorders, overanxious disorder, and phobias), obsessive-compulsive disorder, posttraumatic stress disorder, eating and elimination disorders, menstruation, gender identity, somatization, psychotic symptoms, psychosocial stressors, and direct observations. A sample DICA item is provided in Example 17–6.

Parents and children are interviewed separately. In early trials of the DICA, the measure was administered to parents and children at the same time by different interviewers. No specific instructions are given about the order of interviews if there is one interviewer. The paper and pencil version comes with a detailed scoring manual for scoring by hand. The commercial DICA computer version self-scores.

PRACTICAL ISSUES

It takes up to 2 hours to administer the DICA to each respondent, depending on the amount of psychopathology exhibited by the child. Breaks are allowed.

Both the paper and pencil and computer versions have been copyrighted by Multi-Health Systems, Inc. Permission to use the instrument is available from Multi-Health Systems, Inc., which owns the copyright for all versions of the instrument. However, any questions regarding the DICA may be addressed to the chief author of the DICA:

Wendy Reich, Ph.D.
Washington University in St. Louis
Division of Child Psychiatry
School of Medicine
40 S. Kings Highway, Suite 4
St. Louis, MO 63108
Phone: 314-286-2263
Fax: 314-286-2265
E-mail: wendyr@twins.wustl.edu

EXAMPLE 17–6 ■ Sample item from the Diagnostic Interview for
                         Children and Adolescents

Sample DICA Item (Irritability)

   C.   **Irritability**

172A. **During the past two weeks, have you felt crabby,
or in a bad mood <u>a lot</u> more than usual?**   **(55)**

> IF NO, SKIP to Q. 172D.
> IF YES, CONTINUE:

   B. **Have you been feeling that way (crabby or in a
bad mood) everyday or nearly everyday for the
past two weeks?**   **(56)**

   C. **On days when you felt crabby, or in a bad mood,
were you that way for most of the day?**   **(57)**

   D. **Can you remember any (other) time in your life
when you felt crabby, or in a bad mood <u>a lot</u>
more than usual?**   **(58)**

> IF NO, SKIP TO INSTRUCTION
>   AFTER 172F.
> IF YES, CONTINUE:

   E. **When was that other time? Was it**

     within the past month?   **I**   **(59)**
     within the past 6 months? **2**
     within the past year?   **3**
     over a year ago?   **4**

> IF ANSWER IS OVER A YEAR AGO, ASK:

   F. **How old were you the other time when you felt
crabby, or in a bad mood?**   **(60-61)**

> IF NO POSITIVES IN EITHER THE
> DYSPHORIA, ANHEDONIA OR IRRITABLITY
> QS. 169-172, SKIP TO THE NEXT SECTION,
> <u>MANIC EPISODE</u>, Q. 194. IF ANY POSITIVE,
> CONTINUE:

NO   **I**
RARELY   **2**
SOMETIMES OR SOMEWHAT   **3**
YES   **4**

The computer version of the DICA can be used by a rater in a traditional interview mode or it can be self-administered. It can ascertain symptoms for 25 different DSM-IV diagnoses. This computer version, available from Multi-Health Systems, Inc., produces four diagnostic reports, including a concise summary report, a positive and negative symptoms report, a positive symptoms report, and a complete interview summary. The child and adolescent versions each take approximately 45 minutes to complete. The parent version (which includes a developmental history) takes about 1 hour. The computer version can be self-administered by the parent, adolescent, or child, and no training is required. When the computer version is self-administered, a computer assistant should be present to provide information about specific questions if necessary.

All DICA materials may be obtained from

Multi-Health Systems, Inc.
908 Niagara Falls Boulevard
North Tonawanda, NY 14120-2060
Phone: 800-456-3003
Internet: www.mhs.com

One computer installation of both parent and child versions costs $895.00. Prices for multiple installations can be negotiated for specific studies.

A 1-week training course for clinicians and 1-month training course for lay interviewers, with periodic retraining, is recommended for reliable use of the instrument. Raters must be able to interview both young children and adolescents. No training instruction period is required for the computerized version.

Both the paper and pencil and computer versions are accompanied by an extensive training manual that explains the use of the DICA in detail. The manual provides guidance for the interviewer on how to elicit symptom information and suggests additional probe questions that can be used for each symptom. Suggested probe questions are particularly important because there are different interviews for children and adolescents, each requiring specific, developmentally appropriate probe questions.

The DICA has been translated into Arabic, Finnish, Hebrew, Kanaka (a dialect of southern India), Russian, and Spanish. Multi-Health Systems, Inc., has produced a modification called the Missouri Assessment for Genetics Interview for Children (MAGIC).

PSYCHOMETRIC PROPERTIES

Reliability

Joint reliability of the DICA ranged from $r = 0.78$ for anxiety disorders to $r = 0.9$ for attention-deficit/hyperactivity disorder. This range is typical of the span of reliabilities for the other interviews; anxiety disorders show the lowest reliability, and externalizing disorders show the highest. Test-retest reliability was established for intervals from 2 to 21 days. Reliability ranged from a low kappa value of –0.1 for major depressive disorder on the DICA-R for children to 0.92 for conduct disorder on the DICA-R for parents (Boyle et al. 1993). No studies that compared the reliability of the interviewer-administered and computer-administered versions of the DICA were located.

Validity

Several standards have been used to assess the criterion validity of the DICA, including a comparison of psychiatric and pediatric patients in one study of inpatients (Herjanic and Reich 1982) that showed good discriminant validity in comparisons ($\chi^2 = 21.2$ for relationship problems and 18.1 for school problems). A clinician's best estimate diagnosis was used in another study as the gold standard, with a range of kappa values from 0.18 (attention-deficit/hyperactivity disorder) to 0.66 (conduct disorder) in 30 inpatients (Carlson 1987). The clinician's intake diagnosis was used as the gold standard in another study of Spanish-speaking outpatients; kappa values ranged from 0.07 (adolescents, overanxious disorder) to 0.7 (children, conduct disorder). Other studies used the clinician's discharge diagnosis as the gold standard in a total of 73 inpatients, finding agreement to range from kappa values of 0.03 for anxiety disorders (Welner et al. 1987) to 0.52–0.54 for major depressive disorder (Vitiello et al. 1990). A study of 251 community patients found that the agreement between the clinician's DICA diagnosis plus additional probing versus administration by a lay interviewer ranged from kappa = 0.21 (overanxious disorder) to kappa = 0.84 (conduct disorder) (Boyle et al. 1993).

There are no published reports concerning tests of the DICA against external validators, including prediction of outcome, family history, or longitudinal follow-up data to validate diagnoses. No studies comparing the validity of the rater-administered and computer versions of the DICA were located.

The DICA-R has not been tested in treatment studies, nor have any of its subsections been used as a change measure, so its sensitivity to change during treatment is unknown.

CLINICAL UTILITY

The original authors developed the DICA to obtain DSM diagnoses for children and adolescents in a reliable fashion in research and clinical settings. The DICA has several strengths. It is a semistructured interview that does not require a trained clinician and can be used for young children. It is user-friendly for clinicians and patients, and a computer version that includes diagnostic algorithms is available.

The DICA has some weaknesses beyond the problems with validity. To code and score the paper and pencil DICA-R, one must refer to explanations in a detailed scoring manual. Because the computer version automates this process, it is preferred. Extensive training is also required to use the paper and pencil version reliably.

REFERENCES AND SUGGESTED READINGS

Boyle M, Offord D, Racine Y, et al: Evaluation of the Diagnostic Interview for Children and Adolescents for use in general population samples. J Abnorm Psychol 21:663–671, 1993

Carlson G: Comparison of two structured interviews on a psychiatrically hospitalized population. J Am Acad Child Adolesc Psychiatry 26:645–648, 1987

Ezpeleta L, De la Osa N, Dominech J, et al: Diagnostic agreement between clinicians and the Diagnostic Interview for Children and Adolescents—DICA-R—in an outpatient sample. Journal of Psychology and Psychiatry 38:431–440, 1997

Herjanic B, Campbell W: Differentiating psychiatrically disturbed children on the basis of a structured interview. J Abnorm Child Psychol 5:127–134, 1977

Herjanic B, Reich W: Differentiating psychiatrically disturbed children on the basis of a structured interview. J Abnorm Child Psychol 5:127–134, 1977

Herjanic B, Reich W: Development of a structured psychiatric interview for children: agreement between child and parent on individual symptoms. J Abnorm Child Psychol 10:307–324, 1982

Reich W, Cottler L, McCallum K, et al: Computerized interviews as a method of assessing psychopathology in children. Compr Psychiatry 35:40–45, 1995

Vitiello B, Malone R, Buschle P, et al: Reliability of DSM-III diagnoses of hospitalized children. Hospital and Community Psychiatry 41:63–67, 1990

Welner Z, Reich W, Herjanic B, et al: Reliability, validity, and parent-child agreement studies of the Diagnostic Interview for Children and Adolescents (DICA). J Am Acad Child Adolesc Psychiatry 26:649–653, 1987

Child Assessment Schedule (CAS)

K. Hodges, J. Kline, L. Stern, D. McKnew, and L. Cytryn

GOALS

The Child Assessment Schedule (CAS) (Hodges et al. 1982a, 1982b) was developed to provide an interviewer-based, semistructured diagnostic questionnaire that would derive a DSM-III diagnosis in clinical assessments and in clinical research studies. The CAS is included in this chapter for historical reasons, because it is based on DSM-III, a diagnostic nosology that has been out of use since the publication of DSM-III-R in 1987. The CAS was designed to facilitate the development of good rapport with the child while providing for comprehensive and standardized collection of clinical information. It differs from other structured interviews in this chapter (the Schedule for Affective Disorders and Schizophrenia for School-Age Children: Present and Lifetime Version [K-SADS-PL] [p. 296], the Child and Adolescent Psychiatric Assessment [CAPA] [p. 301], the Diagnostic Interview for Children and Adolescents [DICA] [p. 314], and the National Institute of Mental Health Diagnostic Interview Schedule for Children (NIMH-DISC] [p. 305]) in that it was modeled after a traditional clinical interview with children. About half of the CAS inquiries ask about clinically relevant content that does not reflect directly on a diagnostic criterion. The interview is organized around thematic topics (e.g., school, friends, and family), with diagnostic items interspersed. Another difference in interview content is the inclusion of a separate section in which the interviewer records observations. The 56 observational items on the CAS can be contrasted with the 12 items on the NIMH-DISC. Like the CAPA, the DICA, and the NIMH-DISC, the CAS has algorithms for generating the diagnosis; the K-SADS-PL has clinician-determined diagnoses.

DESCRIPTION

The CAS is a semistructured diagnostic interview that is available in parallel child (CAS) and parent versions (P-CAS). The CAS consists of three parts. In the first part, the child begins by constructing a time line to cover the past 6 months. Then the child is asked 75 questions about 11 thematic topics including school, friends, activities and hobbies, family fears, worries and anxieties, self-image, mood, physical complaints, expressing anger, and reality testing. Symptom diagnostic–related items are embedded in these thematic content areas. Thus, questions are asked about symptoms that might cause impairment at school (e.g., attention-deficit/hyperactivity disorder and separation anxiety disorder), with friends (e.g., depression), during activities and hobbies (e.g., phobias and separation anxiety disorder), and with family (oppositional defiant disorder). The interviewer reads the questions (e.g., "Would you say that you have been feeling sad . . . ?") but records the score on the form on the basis of a response item that is not read to the subject. This response item is usually a positive endorsement of a symptom (e.g., "Feels Sad"). Specific questions that refer to DSM diagnostic criteria are emphasized in the text with shading.

The second part of the interview asks about onset and duration for specific disorders, such as separation anxiety disorder, oppositional defiant disorder, overanxious disorder, conduct disorder, attention-deficit/hyperactivity disorder, obsessive-compulsive disorder, elimination disorders, dysthymia, and major depressive disorder. Questions pertaining to DSM criteria are shaded.

The third part provides a format for the interviewer to record observations and judgments after the interview. It has 53 items that cover the following areas: grooming, insight, motor coordination, activity level (impulsivity and attention span), other physical behaviors, estimations of cognitive ability, quality of verbal communications (speech and logic), quality of emotional expression, and impressions about the quality of interpersonal interactions (Hodges et al. 1982a).

The scoring format has been designed so that all affirmative responses indicate problems or symptoms. For each response item, the child's response is coded as either true (presence of symptoms), false (absence of symptoms), ambiguous response (e.g., sometimes), no response from the child, or not applicable. For later reference, interviewers often supplement the scoring with comments on the content of the child's responses and notes on clinical impressions (Hodges et al. 1982a). The CAS provides a score for total pathology, scores for each of the 11 content areas, and scores for the 9 symptom complexes.

Algorithms are provided by the author for diagnoses, symptom scales, and content scales. The authors do not specify how information is combined across informants. In addition to these algorithms, the authors of the CAS suggest viewing the child's responses from two perspectives. First is the location of the child's impairment (such as school, friends, and family), which is reflected by the number of items endorsed for each of the various topic areas covered in the interview. Because impairment scores are not linked to diagnostic categories, it is very difficult to determine exactly what impairments a particular child may have. Second, DSM-III diagnoses are generated by algorithms for the past 6 months and 20 diagnoses are covered. Scores from the CAS can be used to compare groups on total pathology score, scores on content area scales, and symptom complex scores. These scores have been used in studies designed to assess the reliability and validity of the CAS.

PRACTICAL ISSUES

It takes 45–75 minutes per informant to administer the CAS, for a total administration time of approximately 2.5 hours. The CAS should be administered by an individual with a doctorate (M.D. or Ph.D.) and clinical training. Training time ranges from 5 to 10 days, depending on clinical experience.

The CAS, which is copyrighted, is available from the author:

> Dr. Kay Hodges
> Eastern Michigan University
> Department of Psychology
> Ypsilanti, MI 48197

A fee may be charged to cover the costs of copying the instrument. No manual or computer version is available for the CAS.

PSYCHOMETRIC PROPERTIES

Reliability

A study examined the internal consistency of the content scales of the CAS in patients ($N = 116$) and parents ($N = 92$) (Hodges and Saunders 1989). Alpha values ranged from 0.09 (activities) to 0.88 (fears) for children. Parents showed similar ranges; activity had the lowest alpha (0.27), and mood symptoms had the highest (0.87).

Test-retest reliability of the CAS ranged from kappa $= 0.38$ for overanxious disorder to kappa $= 1.0$ for major depressive disorder (Hodges et al. 1989). The instrument's author and colleagues report high joint reliability between raters of different disciplines and training (Hodges et al. 1982b), but this agreement is based on broad diagnostic groups, not individual diagnoses (Shaffer 1994). Joint reliability (r) between psychiatrists and graduate students ranged from 0.7 to 0.9, but the values were obtained on the basis of general items, such as total score on the CAS or symptom complex, not individual diagnosis (Hodges et al. 1982b).

Validity

Validity was examined by determining diagnostic concordance of the CAS with that of the gold standard, the K-SADS (p. 296), as administered by lay interviewers (Hodges et al. 1987). Both interviews were given within 32 hours. It should be noted that the use of this procedure as a gold standard is highly questionable, because the K-SADS was designed to be administered by experienced clinicians (Shaffer 1994). Agreement for attention-deficit disorder ranged from kappa $= 0.36$ for the child

interview to kappa $= 0.65$ when both parent and child interviews were used.

Validity of the CAS has been explored with tests of construct validity. However, as for all diagnostic interviews for children, no gold standard or laboratory test is available to accurately determine validity.

CLINICAL UTILITY

The CAS has several strengths. It uses easily understood language and is grouped in a naturally flowing format that moves like a conversation, touching on school, friends, and home. Because it seems more like a conversation than a list of symptoms, its use can help build rapport with the child. The instrument provides a subtle, indirect exploration of some of the more threatening issues for children (Hodges et al. 1982a). The interviewer is free to add probe questions, a natural tendency of clinicians. The CAS covers problems that are not addressed by DSM (e.g., worries about parental divorce) but that are of clinical interest.

The CAS also has several weaknesses. It is based on DSM-III, a diagnostic system that has been out of use for more than a decade. The validity data, using diagnostic concordance, are weak. For a given disorder, not all criteria are always listed (e.g., only two general questions are included for obsessive-compulsive disorder and the measure does not ask about the necessary 2-week period for persistence of separation anxiety disorder symptoms). The interviewer may find it awkward to use the second section because he or she must look back through the first section and then ask about symptoms as a group, which can result in mistakes.

REFERENCES AND SUGGESTED READINGS

Hodges K: Depression and anxiety in children: a comparison of self-report questionnaires to clinical interview. J Consult Clin Psychol 2:376–381, 1990

Hodges K: Structured interviews for assessing children. J Child Psychol Psychiatry 34:49–68, 1993

Hodges K, Saunders W: Internal consistency of a diagnostic interview for children: the Child Assessment Schedule. J Abnorm Child Psychol 17:691–701, 1989

Hodges K, Kline J, Stern L, et al: The development of a child assessment interview for research and clinical use. J Abnorm Child Psychol 10:173–189, 1982a

Hodges K, McKnew D, Cytryn L, et al: The Child Assessment (CAS) Diagnostic Interview: a report on reliability and validity. Journal of the American Academy of Child Psychiatry 21:468–473, 1982b

Hodges K, McKnew D, Burbach D, et al: Diagnostic concordance between the Child Assessment Schedule (CAS) and the Schedule for Affective Disorders and Schizophrenia for School-Age Children (K-SADS) in an outpatient sample using lay interviewers. J Am Acad Child Adolesc Psychiatry 26:654–661, 1987

Hodges K, Cools J, McKnew D: Test-retest reliability of a clinical research interview for children: the Child Assessment Schedule (CAS). Psychological Assessment. J Consult Clin Psychol 1:317–322, 1989

Shaffer D: Debate and argument: structured interviews for assessing children. J Child Psychol Psychiatry 35:783–784, 1994

Personality Inventory for Children (PIC)

D. Lachar and C. L. Gdowski

GOALS

The Personality Inventory for Children (PIC) (Lachar et al. 1986) is a clinician-rated profile of personality characteristics of individual children that taps into domains of behavior, affect, ability, and family function. The PIC is used to assess children from preschool through adolescence (ages 3–18). The scales measure cognitive ability, behavioral and emotional functioning, and family characteristics. The PIC scales also measure the validity of the inventory itself, as the Minnesota Multiphasic Personality Inventory (MMPI) (p. 89) does. Family socioeconomic status and cultural background are said to have minimal influence on the interpretation of PIC scores (Wirt et al. 1984).

The items on the PIC were chosen by experts on the basis of how well they discriminated groups of children

in terms of dysfunction. The dimensions represented by the scales selected for the PIC profile do not reflect a specific theoretical perspective in regard to personality, psychopathology, or child development but rather reflect dimensions routinely assessed by clinicians regardless of theoretical preference or bias (Lachar et al. 1986). The PIC does not generate scores that are clearly related to the DSM notion of personality disorder.

The PIC is used to screen children for behavioral and emotional problems. The PIC computer software yields an interpretive report that includes differential diagnosis and suggested educational placement. A unique characteristic of the PIC is the availability of actuarially based interpretive systems for individual scales, scale patterns, and profile types, which are available in the latest revision of the PIC manual (Lachar and Christian 1995). A revised version of the PIC, the PIC-2, is currently being developed by Western Psychological Services (see Practical Issues section).

DESCRIPTION

The most recent version of the PIC has 420 items. (The original PIC, published in the 1970s, included 600 items.) The PIC items are scored true or false by the parent. A sample item is provided in Example 17–7.

The PIC has four broad-band, factor-derived scales that reflect the major content dimensions of the PIC item pool: Undisciplined/Poor Self-Control, Social Incompetence, Internalization/Somatic Symptoms, and Cognitive/Development. It has four validity/screening scales: Lie (14 items), Frequency (42 items), Defensiveness (23 items), and Adjustment (75 items). Finally, there are 12 clinical scales: Intellectual Screening (34 items), Social Skills (30 items), Delinquency (47 items), Family Relations (35 items), Achievement (31 items), Withdrawal (25 items), Hyperactivity (36 items), Development (25 items), Psychosis (40 items), Somatic Concern (40 items), Depression (46 items), and Anxiety (30 items). Each item is located in one of the three sections of the administration booklet.

The PIC can be administered in three ways. In the standard administration, the parent completes the first 280 items, and the administrator scores the four factor scales, the Lie Scale, the Development Scale, and 14 shortened-format profile scales. However, if a longer criti-

EXAMPLE 17–7 ■ Sample item from the Personality Inventory for Children

Example of PIC Undisciplined/Poor Self-Control Factor (Explains 16.2% of variance) taken from the Revised Format Manual Supplement (Lachar 1995, pp 6±7):

Factor Scale I: UNDISCIPLINED/POOR SELF-CONTROL

Factor Component	Item
I. Ineffective Discipline (68.9%)	54. My child tends to see how much he (she) can get away with.
II. Impulsivity	42. My child jumps from one thing to another.
III. Problematic Anger (7.8%)	46. When my child gets mad, watch out.
IV. Poor Peer Relationships (5.7%)	90. Usually my child gets along well with others.
V. Limited Conscience Development	31. My child often cheats other children in deals.
VI. Poor School Behavior (3.4%)	109. Recently the school has sent home notes about my child's bad behavior.

cal item analysis on the computer report is desired, the parent can complete all 420 items. If only a brief screening profile is needed, the parent can complete only the first 131 items, which provides a measure of the informant's defensiveness (the Lie Scale) and the four broadband, factor-derived scales. Researchers may use the first 131 items of the PIC as a broad-band measure of functioning, and clinicians may use this section for screening. Of course, the most conservative approach is to have the parent score all 420 items.

Scoring can be summarized graphically on a Western Psychological Services (WPS) Revised Profile Form, which results in a profile similar to that obtained from the Child Behavior Checklists (CBCL). This profile includes the four validity/screening scales and the 16 clinical scales.

Possible raw scores vary across the 16 profile scales from 0 to a maximum of 41. The 16 profile T-scores range from 30 to 120. The scores from the four factor scales have a range of 0–30, with T-scores that extend from 20 to 120.

Each PIC scale uses T-scores, with a mean of 50 and a standard deviation of 10. Increased deviation from the mean on a given scale suggests the increased probability of psychopathology. All T-scores are set so that those over 70 (worst 2% of sample) have impairments in a variety of areas, including at school, at home, and with peers.

Four normative samples (for ages 6–16, $n = 1,187$ boys and 1,203 girls; for ages 3–5, $n = 102$ boys and 90 girls) from the original PIC manual (Wirt et al. 1984) were used to generate the four factor scores. This factor

analysis forms the basis of the PIC's scale construction and scoring template.

PRACTICAL ISSUES

On average, it takes 1 hour for parents to complete the 420-item set. The length raises concerns about poorly educated parents with problematic reading skills who might not tolerate such a long instrument. However, the PIC can be used in modular fashion, without administration of all of the sections, which reduces administration time.

The PIC is copyrighted and published by Western Psychological Services. Test materials, profile forms, hand-scored answer sheets, scoring keys, manuals, and computer disks can be obtained under product number W-152R from

> Western Psychological Services
> 12301 Wilshire Boulevard
> Los Angeles, CA 90025-1251
> Phone: 800-648-8851
> Internet: www.wpspublish.com

The cost for a package with 100 profile forms, 25 hand-scored answer sheets, and a reusable administration booklet is $225.00. Computer scoring software costs $299.50 (if purchasing two or more disks, $270.00 per disk) for 25 interviews per disk (order number W-1026).

The PIC is straightforward to administer, because it is a self-administered instrument. However, interpretation of the scales requires experience with psychometric data and computer usage. Scoring materials, computer format (recommended), manuals, and telephone support are available from Western Psychological Services.

PSYCHOMETRIC PROPERTIES

Reliability

Internal consistency was calculated for the four factor scales of the PIC in a heterogeneous clinic sample (N = 1,226). Alpha coefficients ranged from 0.57 (Intellectual Screening) to 0.86 (Depression), with a mean alpha of 0.74. Interparent agreement across four different studies, drawn on clinical and psychiatrically healthy populations, ranged from 0.38 to 0.66, somewhat lower than reported for test-retest reliability for the same parent.

Test-retest coefficients for 34 test-retest pairs from a clinic over a 15-day interval ranged from 0.46 to 0.94 (mean 0.86) across the 16 profile scales of the PIC (Lachar and Christian 1995). A second study of psychiatrically healthy control subjects (N = 46; test-retest interval of 51 days) found a test-retest reliability on 16 scales of r = 0.61, and a third mail-in study of 55 test-retest pairs polled 2 weeks apart found a test-retest reliability on 16 scales of r = 0.89.

Validity

Concordance between obtaining a clinical diagnosis from the child interview of the Diagnostic Interview for Children and Adolescents (DICA) (p. 314) and reading a T-score greater than 70 on the parent report of the PIC reached 70%–77%, with a kappa that ranged between 0.11 and 0.48 for anxiety and depression combined (Sylvester et al. 1987). Several of the clinical scales correlated well with parental ratings of children's adjustment to divorce (Kurdek 1981). Some of the PIC scales correlated satisfactorily with parent, teacher, and clinician ratings of child deviance (Lachar and Christian 1995), with the Conners Rating Scales—Revised (p. 329) (Leon et al. 1980), and with response to stimulant medication in hyperactive children (Voelker et al. 1983).

The PIC predicted the correct academic placement of children with learning disabilities, mental retardation, and emotional disturbance 79.7% of the time (Lachar et al. 1986).

The PIC scales differentiate children with attention-deficit/hyperactivity disorder only from children with learning disabilities only and psychiatrically healthy children (Breen and Barkley 1983) in a statistically significant manner, correctly identifying 75% of the children with attention-deficit/hyperactivity disorder.

CLINICAL UTILITY

The PIC discriminates well between child disorders. The measure is particularly apt at identifying children with attention-deficit/hyperactivity disorder and providing detailed profiles on their comorbid states. It is more attractive to clinicians who need an MMPI-like screening tool that highlights clinical characteristics of individual children than to most investigators, who seek shorter, more empirically developed scales for screening for specific DSM-IV diagnoses. The dimensions assessed by the PIC appear appropriate for the evaluation of children and adolescents by professionals working in pediatrics, special education, juvenile justice populations, or child psychiatry.

One weakness of the PIC is that the true-false scoring procedure does not yield any specific information on the frequency or severity of the behavior problem or characteristic described in the item.

REFERENCES AND SUGGESTED READINGS

Barkley R: Child behavior rating scales and checklists, in Assessment and Diagnosis in Child Psychopathology. Edited by Rutter M, Tuma AH, Lann I. New York, Guilford, 1988, pp 113–155

Breen M, Barkley R: The Personality Inventory for Children: its clinical utility with hyperactive children. J Pediatr Psychol 13:232–235, 1983

Kurdek LA: An integrative perspective on children's divorce adjustment. Am Psychol 36:856–866, 1981

Lachar D, Christian G: Personality Inventory for Youth (PIC) Manual, Revised Formal Manual Supplement. Los Angeles, CA, Western Psychological Services, 1995

Lachar D, Klein R, Boersma D: Personality Inventory for Children: approaches to actuarial interpretation in clinic and school settings, in The Assessment of Child and Adolescent Personality. Edited by Knoff H. New York, Guilford, 1986, pp 273–308

Leon G, Kendall P, Garber J: Depression in children: parent, teacher, and child perspectives. J Abnorm Child Psychol 8:221–235, 1980

Sylvester C, Hyde T, Reichler R: The Diagnostic Interview for Children and Personality Inventory for Children in studies of children for anxiety disorders or depression. J Am Acad Child Adolesc Psychiatry 26:668–675, 1987

Voelker S, Lachar D, Gdowski C: The Personality Inventory for Children and response to methylphenidate: preliminary evidence for predictive utility. J Pediatr Psychol 8:161–169, 1983

Wirt R, Lachar D, Kleinedinst J, et al: Multidimensional Description of Child Personality: A Manual for the Personality Inventory for Children. Los Angeles, CA, Western Psychological Services, 1984

Symptom-Specific Measures for Disorders Usually First Diagnosed in Infancy, Childhood, or Adolescence

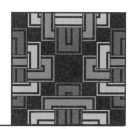

Laurie S. Miller, Ph.D.
Dimitra Kamboukos, M.A.

INTRODUCTION

Major Domains

This chapter includes measures that assess specific disorders in children and adolescents. The measures include rating scales and diagnostic instruments and rely on a variety of informants (e.g., parent, teacher, and child). Several of the instruments include versions for more than one informant.

The following disorders are covered in this chapter: attention-deficit/hyperactivity disorder, oppositional defiant disorder, conduct disorder, anxiety disorders (with the exception of posttraumatic stress disorder and obsessive-compulsive disorder), mood disorders, autistic disorder, and tic disorders.

Organization

The measures included in this chapter are listed in Table 18–1. The chapter is organized by disorder, as follows:

- For attention-deficit/hyperactivity disorder: the Conners' Rating Scales—Revised (CRS-R)
- For oppositional defiant disorder and conduct disorder: the New York Teacher Rating Scale (NYTRS)
- For anxiety disorders: the Revised Children's Manifest Anxiety Scale (RCMAS), the Anxiety Disorders Interview Schedule for DSM-IV—Child Version

(ADIS-IV-C), and the Multidimensional Anxiety Scale for Children (MASC)
- For mood disorders: the Children's Depression Inventory (CDI), the Reynolds Adolescent Depression Scale (RADS), and the Short Mood and Feelings Questionnaire (SMFQ)
- For autistic disorder: the Autism Diagnostic Interview—Revised (ADI-R)
- For tic disorders: the Yale Global Tic Severity Scale (YGTSS)

Relevant Measures Included Elsewhere in the Handbook

General and diagnostic measures for children are presented in Chapter 17, "Child and Adolescent Measures for Diagnosis and Screening," and functional measures for children are presented in Chapter 19, "Child and Adolescent Measures of Functional Status." Note that the Child Behavior Checklist (CBCL) (p. 309) and the Preschool Behavior Questionnaire (PBQ) (p. 294), which are included in Chapter 17, have subscales relevant to the assessment of oppositional defiant disorder and conduct disorder. Although the CRS-R covers a broad range of disorders, it is included in this chapter for its coverage of attention-deficit/hyperactivity disorder.

Measures of posttraumatic stress disorder and obsessive-compulsive disorder appropriate for children and adolescents can be found in Chapter 25, "Anxiety

TABLE 18–1 ■ Child symptom measures

Name of measure	Disorder or construct assessed	Format	Pages
Conners' Rating Scales—Revised (CRS-R)	Symptoms of attention-deficit/hyperactivity disorder and other psychopathology in youths ages 3–17	Six distinct rating scales for parents, teachers, and youth self-report; 27–87 items	329–332
New York Teacher Rating Scale (NYTRS)	Disruptive and antisocial behavior in the classroom	Rating scale for youth's teacher; 36 items	333–335
Revised Children's Manifest Anxiety Scale (RCMAS)	Level and nature of anxiety in children and adolescents ages 6–19	Self-report for individual child or groups of children; 37 items	336–339
Anxiety Disorders Interview Schedule for DSM-IV—Child Version (ADIS-IV-C)	DSM-IV anxiety disorders in children ages 6–17	Semistructured interview with screen or gate questions that determine total number of questions	339–341
Multidimensional Anxiety Scale for Children (MASC)	Wide range of anxiety symptoms in youth ages 8–19; based on DSM-IV criteria	Self-report; 39 items	341–344
Children's Depression Inventory (CDI)	Symptoms of depression in children and adolescents ages 7–17	Self-report; 27 items	344–347
Reynolds Adolescent Depression Scale (RADS)	Depressive symptomatology in adolescents	Self-report; 30 items	347–349
Short Mood and Feelings Questionnaire (SMFQ)	Core depressive symptoms in children and adolescents ages 8–16	Brief self-report; 13 items	349–351
Autism Diagnostic Interview—Revised (ADI-R)	Clinical diagnostic instrument for assessing autism in children and adults as defined by ICD-10 and DSM-IV criteria	Standardized, semistructured clinical interview for caregivers; 111 items	351–354
Yale Global Tic Severity Scale (YGTSS)*	Tic severity and degree of impairment in individuals with Tourette's syndrome and other tic disorders	Semistructured interview for patients and parents; symptom checklist and 10 scale scores, plus totals	354–356

*Measure is included on the CD-ROM that accompanies this handbook.

Disorders Measures." Other instruments for assessing depression and anxiety can be found in Chapter 24, "Mood Disorders Measures," and Chapter 25, respectively. Instruments for assessing substance use disorders can be found in Chapter 22, "Substance Use Disorders Measures." Some relevant instruments that assess antisocial symptomatology can be found in Chapter 31, "Impulse Control Disorders Measures." Measures for assessing attention-deficit/hyperactivity disorder in adults are not included in this chapter.

Some of the measures reviewed in this chapter have adult counterparts covered in the respective adult chapter. For example, the CDI, a child measure reviewed in this chapter, is related to the Beck Depression Inventory (BDI) (p. 519), which is covered in Chapter 24. In some cases, when the youth version is similar to the adult version of the measure, it is covered along with the adult version (e.g., the Center for Epidemiologic Studies Depression Scale [CES-D] [p. 523] and the Hamilton Rating Scale for Depression [Ham-D] [p. 526]).

Several self-report measures for assessing antisocial behavior in youth (e.g., the Self-Reported Delinquency Scale [Elliott et al. 1985] and the Antisocial Behavior Scale [Loeber et al. 1989]) were not included in this chapter because they have been used primarily in epidemiological surveys and not with clinical populations.

USING MEASURES IN THIS DOMAIN

Goals of Assessment

As outlined by Mash and Terdal (1997), there are four primary goals in assessing child behavioral functioning: 1) diagnosis, or evaluation that focuses on identifying the causes of a presenting problem; 2) prognosis, or the gathering of information that will facilitate the prediction of future behavior under certain conditions; 3) treatment design, or the collection of data that will assist the clinician in the planning and implementation of treatment; and 4) evaluation, or the assessment of the efficacy or the effectiveness of treatment. Measures presented in this chapter can serve these purposes.

Some of the instruments can be used for diagnostic purposes, and others, although not appropriate for deriving clinical diagnoses, can be used to gather important information that can contribute to a comprehensive diagnostic assessment. The appropriateness of using a particular instrument for deriving a diagnosis is noted throughout the chapter. With regard to diagnostic status, the selection of one of the measures reviewed in this chapter over an omnibus or broad-band measure reviewed in Chapter 17 presumes that the clinician has some a priori knowledge about diagnostic status or the specific symptom domain of impairment. That is, the diagnostic measures in this chapter can be used to confirm a diagnosis or can be used in conjunction with one of the screening instruments described in Chapter 17. Given the high level of comorbidity in children and adolescents, in most circumstances it would be most prudent for the clinician to use a broad-based instrument first, followed by a domain-specific instrument.

Most of the instruments provide some index of impairment or severity that can be used to inform predictions about future behavior. Furthermore, when more than one informant version of the measure is available, information about child behavior in more than one context (e.g., home and school) can often be used for prognostic purposes. For example, a child who receives clinically elevated scores on both parent and teacher versions of a measure of externalizing behavior is likely to have a poorer prognosis than a child rated as impaired only by his or her parent.

Many of the measures in this chapter can be used to facilitate treatment design, planning, and implementation. Although the measures reviewed here focus on a single symptom or disorder (e.g., anxiety or depression), in contrast to the measures reviewed in Chapter 17, many of these measures have subscales that provide important information with regard to clinical presentation. Some measures (e.g., the ADIS-IV-C and the CRS-R) also provide additional information about other possible comorbid disorders or symptoms. For example, although the ADIS-IV-C is presented here for its comprehensive coverage of anxiety disorders, it can also be used to screen out other comorbidities (e.g., externalizing disorders).

Finally, most of the instruments presented in this chapter, especially those that provide relatively quick ratings of symptom severity, can be used as repeated measures to track treatment response and to evaluate treatment efficacy and effectiveness.

Implementation Issues

As described in Chapter 17, many of the rating scales can be completed quickly by parents and teachers and rely on information that is already available to the rater. Rating scales included in this chapter, whether completed by the child, parent, or teacher, require no prior training and place little burden on the clinician. Some additional clinical time is required, however, to integrate information from multiple sources and to derive norm-based scores. In contrast, the diagnostic instruments require that the practitioner receive training, and they involve clinical time and expertise in their implementation.

Issues in Interpreting Psychometric Data

As noted in Chapter 17, rapid developmental changes across multiple domains of functioning complicate issues of establishing the reliability and validity of standardized measures. Furthermore, discrepancies between different informants and ratings of child behavior in different contexts often complicate interpretation. These issues are discussed when applicable. For some measures, psychometric data specific to age group, gender, and ethnic group are available. These data are provided when available.

GUIDE TO THE SELECTION OF MEASURES

As described in detail in Chapter 17, the selection of measures depends on various factors, including the age of the child, the purpose for which the measure is intended (e.g., to evaluate treatment response or to ascertain diagnostic information), practical issues with regard to implementation (e.g., time or training requirements), and the disorder or symptom domain of interest. Typically, the selection of a measure that is domain or disorder specific depends on what other information has already been obtained. In addition, depending on the purpose, the practitioner might choose a measure that has multiple versions (teacher, parent, and child) so that parallel information from multiple informants can be obtained and integrated. For some of the norm-based measures, data are available across a wide age range. Such an age range is desirable if the measure is to be employed at multiple time points as the child moves from one developmental period to another. Some measures in this section have not been updated to reflect DSM-IV criteria. This information is noted throughout this chapter and might influence decisions about measure selection. Information on treatment sensitivity is available for only a limited number of measures. If the measure is to be used to track treatment response or to evaluate long-term treatment outcome, this information is highly relevant.

CURRENT STATUS AND FUTURE RESEARCH NEEDS FOR ASSESSMENT

Several of the measures described in this chapter have been employed by clinicians in standard clinical practice (e.g., the CRS-R and the CDI). Use in clinical practice is especially common for the rating scales that rely on other informants (e.g., parents, teachers, and children) and do not require clinical training. However, most of these measures cannot be used to make diagnostic decisions. Diagnostic measures that require clinical time and training are less likely to be used in standard clinical practice. Currently, instruments are often selected on the basis of familiarity and not on the availability of psychometric data. Most of the measures presented in this chapter have satisfactory reliability, but the availability of data on scale validity varies widely. Information on

specificity and treatment sensitivity seems to be most lacking.

REFERENCES AND SUGGESTED READINGS

Abikoff H, Klein RG: Attention-deficit hyperactivity and conduct disorder: comorbidity and implications for treatment. J Consult Clin Psychol 60:881–892, 1992

Achenbach TM: Diagnosis, assessment, and comorbidity in psychosocial research. J Abnorm Psychol 23:45–65, 1995

Barkley RA: A review of child behavior rating scales and checklists for research in child psychopathology, in Assessment and Diagnosis in Child Psychopathology. Edited by Rutter M, Tuma H, Lann I. New York, Guilford, 1988, pp 113–155

Costello JA: Assessment and diagnosis of affective disorders in children. J Child Psychol Psychiatry 27:565–574, 1986

Elliot SN, Busse RT, Gresham FM: Behavior rating scales: issues of use and development. School Psychology Review 22:313–321, 1993

Elliott DS, Huizinga D, Ageton SS: Explaining Delinquency and Drug Use. Beverly Hills, CA, Sage, 1985

Kamphaus RW, Frick PJ: Clinical Assessment of Child and Adolescent Personality and Behavior. Needham Heights, MA, Allyn & Bacon, 1996

Kendall PC, Cantwell DP, Kazdin AE: Depression in children and adolescents: assessment issues and recommendations. Cognitive Therapy and Research 13:109–146, 1989

Klein RG, Last CG: Anxiety Disorders in Children. Newbury Park, CA, Sage, 1989

Lewis M, Miller SM (eds): Handbook of Developmental Psychopathology. New York, Plenum, 1990

Loeber R, Stouthamer-Loever M, van Kammen WB, et al: Development of a new measure of self-reported antisocial behavior for young children: prevalence and reliability, in Cross-National Research in Self-Reported Crime and Delinquency. Edited by Klein M. Dordrecht, The Netherlands, Kluwer-Nijhof, 1989, pp 203–225

Loeber R, Green SM, Lahey BB, et al: Differences and similarities between children, mothers, and teachers as informants on disruptive child behavior. J Abnorm Child Psychol 19:75–95, 1991

Lord C: Methods and measures of behavior in the diagnosis of autism and related disorders. Psychiatr Clin North Am 14:69–80, 1991

March JS, Albano AM: New developments in assessing pediatric anxiety disorders. Advances in Clinical Child Psychology. 20:213–241, 1998

Mash EJ, Terdal LG (eds): Assessment of Childhood Disorders, 3rd Edition. New York, Guilford, 1997

Ollendick TH, Heresen M (eds): Child Behavioral Assessment: Principles and Procedures. Elmsford, NY, Pergamon, 1984

Reynolds CR, Kamphaus RW (eds): Handbook of Psychological and Educational Assessment of Children: Personality, Behavior, and Context. New York, Guilford, 1990

Reynolds WM, Johnston HF (eds): Handbook of Depression in Children and Adolescents. New York, Plenum, 1994

Conners' Rating Scales— Revised (CRS-R)

C. K. Conners

GOALS

The Conners' Rating Scales—Revised (CRS-R) (Conners 1997) assess symptoms of attention-deficit/ hyperactivity disorder and other psychopathology and problem behavior in youths ages 3–17 years. The scales characterize the behaviors of a child and compare them with levels of appropriate normative groups. The scales also categorically assess symptoms, suggesting when DSM-IV criteria may be met. Although the CRS-R cover a broad range of diagnostic categories (e.g., anxiety, depression, and somatization), they are reviewed in this chapter primarily for their coverage of attention-deficit/ hyperactivity disorder symptoms.

Several investigators have developed their own versions of the CRS. The most commonly used variant is the IOWA Conners Teacher Rating Scale, a 10-item scale developed by Loney and Milich (1982). They identified the items from the original Conners Teacher Rating Scale (CTRS) (Conners 1969) that correlated with external measures of hyperactivity (inattention or overactivity) but not with measures of aggression, and items related to measures of aggression (aggression or defiance) but not to measures of hyperactivity. Although related to

the CRS, this measure is not part of the family of instruments developed by Conners and colleagues and is not reviewed here.

Conners et al. recently developed a scale for assessing attention-deficit/hyperactivity disorder in adults, the Conners' Adult ADHD Rating Scale, which is not reviewed in this chapter. Normative data and data on the scale's factor structure, reliability, and diagnostic sensitivity are available from the authors.

DESCRIPTION

The CRS-R include six distinct instruments:

- The Conners' Parent Rating Scale—Revised: Long Form (CPRS-R:L)
- The Conners' Parent Rating Scale—Revised: Short Form (CPRS-R:S)
- The Conners' Teacher Rating Scale—Revised: Long Form (CTRS-R:L)
- The Conners' Teacher Rating Scale—Revised: Short Form (CTRS-R:S)
- The Conners-Wells Adolescent Self-Report Scale: Long Form (CASS:L)
- The Conners-Wells Adolescent Self-Report Scale: Short Form (CASS:S)

Five brief auxiliary scales are also included:

- The Conners' Global Index—Parent (CGI-P)
- The Conners' Global Index—Teacher (CGI-T)
- The Conners' ADHD/DSM-IV Scales—Parent (CADS-P)
- The Conners' ADHD/DSM-IV Scales—Teacher (CADS-T)
- The Conners' ADHD/DSM-IV Scales—Adolescent (CADS-A)

The CGI is incorporated into the long-form versions and is also available separately. The CADS scales appear on both long and short form versions and are also available separately.

The CPRS-R:L contains 80 items and 14 subscales: Oppositional (10 items), Cognitive Problems/Inattention (12 items), Hyperactivity (9 items), Anxious-Shy

(8 items), Perfectionism (7 items), Social Problems (5 items), Psychosomatic (6 items), Conners' Global Index (10 items) (includes 2 empirically derived factors: Restless-Impulsive [7 items] and Emotional Lability [3 items]), ADHD Index (12 items), and DSM-IV Symptoms subscale (18 items) (includes 2 subscales: DSM-IV Inattentive [9 items] and DSM-IV Hyperactive-Impulsive [9 items]). The CPRS-R:S contains 27 items and 4 subscales: Oppositional (6 items), Cognitive Problems/Inattention (6 items), Hyperactivity (6 items), and ADHD Index (12 items). For both the short and long forms, parents are asked to consider the child's behavior during the past month. The scales use a 4-point Likert format. Each item is rated with one of four responses: 0 = not at all true (never, seldom), 1 = just a little true (occasionally), 2 = pretty much true (often, quite a bit), or 3 = very much true (very often, very frequently). Sample items are provided in Example 18–1.

The CTRS-R:L contains 59 items and includes the same subscales as the CPRS-R:L, with the exception of the Psychosomatic subscale, which is only included on the CPRS-R:L. The CTRS-R:S contains 28 items and 4 subscales. The 4 subscales and scoring procedures are the same as those on the CPRS-R:S. Teachers are asked to consider the child's behavior during the past month. Sample items are provided in Example 18–1.

The CASS:L contains 87 items and can be used with youth ages 12–17 years. There are 10 subscales: Family

Problems (12 items), Emotional Problems (12 items), Conduct Problems (12 items), Cognitive Problems/Inattention (12 items), Anger Control Problems (8 items), Hyperactivity (8 items), ADHD Index (12 items), and DSM-IV Symptom Scales (18 items) (includes 2 subscales: DSM-IV Inattentive [9 items] and DSM-IV Hyperactive-Impulsive [9 items]). The CASS:S contains 27 items and 4 subscales. The subscales parallel the subscales of the CPRS-R:S and the CTRS-R:S. Sample items are provided in Example 18–1.

The CGI-P and the CGI-T are 10-item scales that cover items known previously as the Hyperactivity Index. Although the scales contain the same items, the norms have changed and analysis indicates that both the CGI-P and the CGI-T contain two factors: emotional lability and restless-impulsive behavior.

There are three versions of the CADS: parent, teacher, and adolescent. Each version has two subcomponents, with the option of administering one or both: the ADHD Index (12 items) and the DSM-IV Symptoms subscale (18 items). The DSM-IV Symptoms subscale contains two scales: Inattentive (9 items) and Hyperactive-Impulsive (9 items).

Scores range from 0 to the number of items on the scale multiplied by 3. Individual scale scores are compared with norms for appropriate groups of children (by age and sex of the child). There are five age categories for the CRS-R: 3–5 years, 6–8 years, 9–11 years, 12–14 years, and 15–17 years. Raw scores are converted to T-scores, allowing all scales to have the same mean and standard deviation (i.e., mean = 50 and SD = 10). Therefore, T-scores can be compared across all CRS-R versions. High scale scores are indicative of problem behavior, whereas low scale scores indicate the absence of problem behavior. T-scores ≥65 are usually taken to indicate clinically significant problems.

The standardization sample included approximately 8,000 youth from regular classrooms. Data were collected on youth from 95% of the states and provinces in North America, with adequate representation from minority group samples (i.e., African American, Asian, Hispanic, and Native American). The normative sample used for the CPRS-R consisted of the parents or guardians of more than 2,400 children and adolescents ages 3–17 years. The sample used for the CTRS-R included the teachers of nearly 2,000 youth, ages 3–17. The normative sample used for the CASS:L included more than 3,400 adolescents ages 12–17 years.

EXAMPLE 18–1 ■ Sample items from the Conners' Rating Scales—Revised

CPRS-R
Restless in the "squirmy" sense
Short attention span
Irritable

CTRS-R
Defiant
Cannot remain still
Excitable, impulsive

CASS
I bend the rules whenever I can.
I have too much energy to sit still for long.
I have trouble concentrating on one thing at a time.

PRACTICAL ISSUES

In general, all forms take less than 20 minutes to complete. The short versions take approximately 5–10 minutes, and the long versions take approximately 15–20 minutes. Scales can be hand scored or scored using the CRS-R Computer Program. Scoring and profiling of each paper and pencil form take less than 10 minutes. Although raw scores and T-scores can be calculated by untrained persons, the scores must be interpreted by an experienced mental health professional.

All versions of the CRS-R are copyrighted by Multi-Health Systems, Inc. Questionnaires, manuals, scoring materials, and software support for the computerized version can be obtained from

> Multi-Health Systems, Inc.
> 908 Niagara Falls Boulevard
> North Tonawanda, NY 14120-2060
> Phone: 800-456-3003
> Internet: www.mhs.com

The costs for the long forms of the CRS-R are $26.00 for 25 forms and $95.00 for 100 forms. The short forms are available in packages of 25 ($24.00) and 100 ($92.00). The CRS-R have been translated into Spanish.

PSYCHOMETRIC PROPERTIES

Reliability

Internal consistency coefficients for all CRS-R forms have been calculated using the normative samples described. For the CPRS-R and the CTRS-R, separate Cronbach's alphas have been calculated for five different age groups. For the CASS, coefficients have been calculated for two age groups. Ranges across age groups were as follows: CPRS-R:L, 0.73–0.94; CPRS-R:S, 0.86–0.94; CTRS-R:L, 0.77–0.96; CTRS-R:S, 0.88–0.95; CASS:L, 0.75–0.92; and CASS:S, 0.75–0.85.

Internal consistency coefficients for the subscales of the CTRS-R and the CPRS-R are also high. For the CPRS-R, Cronbach's alphas for children ages 3–17 years for the DSM-IV Hyperactive-Impulsive subscale were 0.91 for boys and 0.87 for girls. For the Oppositional subscale, alphas were 0.91 for boys and 0.90 for girls. For the CTRS-R, Cronbach's alphas for children ages 3–17 years

for the DSM-IV Hyperactive-Impulsive subscale were 0.94 for boys and 0.90 for girls. For the Oppositional subscale, alphas were 0.92 for boys and 0.91 for girls.

In a 6-week test-retest reliability study of the CTRS-R:L with 50 students, Pearson product moment correlations were 0.86 for the Oppositional subscale and 0.72 for the Hyperactivity subscale. Test-retest reliabilities ($N = 49$) of the CPRS-R:L over a 6-week interval were 0.57 for the Oppositional subscale and 0.85 for the Hyperactivity subscale. Test-retest reliabilities for the four scales of the short forms ranged from 0.62 (Oppositional) to 0.85 (Hyperactivity) for the CPRS-R:S and from 0.722 (Hyperactivity) to 0.92 (Cognitive Problems/Inattention) for the CTRS-R:S.

Low to moderate correlations between parent and teacher ratings were reported for men and women: Oppositional subscale, 0.34 and 0.22; Hyperactivity subscale, 0.37 and 0.36; ADHD Index, 0.49 and 0.49; and DSM-IV Symptoms subscale, 0.46 and 0.49.

Validity

In a study of 160 adolescents with attention-deficit/hyperactivity disorder and 160 matched (on age, sex, and ethnicity) control subjects without attention-deficit/hyperactivity disorder, the CTRS-R was shown to discriminate significantly between the two groups. The mean scores (and standard deviations) for the groups with and without attention-deficit/hyperactivity disorder were 4.47 (4.94) and 0.63 (1.53), respectively, for the Oppositional subscale and 11.48 (5.62) and 2.42 (3.60), respectively, for the DSM-IV Hyperactive-Impulsive subscale. The following statistics were calculated: sensitivity, 78%; specificity, 91%; positive predictive power, 90%; and negative predictive power, 81%. The kappa coefficient was 0.69, and the overall correct classification rate was 85%; the chance classification rate was 50%.

Similar results were obtained with the CPRS-R in a study of 91 adolescents with attention-deficit/hyperactivity disorder and 91 matched control subjects without attention-deficit/hyperactivity disorder. The mean scores (and standard deviations) for the groups with and without attention-deficit/hyperactivity disorder were 10.74 (6.91) and 4.26 (3.99), respectively, for the Oppositional subscale and 10.43 (6.84) and 1.97 (3.43), respectively, for the DSM-IV Hyperactive-Impulsive subscale. The following statistics were calculated: sensitivity, 92%; specificity, 95%; positive predictive power, 94%; and negative predictive power, 93%. The kappa coefficient was 0.87, and the overall correct classification rate was 93%.

The new indexes have also been shown to discriminate between youth clinically diagnosed with attention-deficit/hyperactivity disorder and those without the disorder. In a cross-validation study of 206 children and adolescents, the ADHD Index from the CTRS-R was found to yield the following: sensitivity, 97%; specificity, 82%; positive predictive power, 84%; and negative predictive power, 97%. The kappa coefficient was 0.79, and the overall correct classification rate was 89%. The ADHD Index from the CPRS-R was found to possess the following discriminatory abilities in a cross-validation study with 80 youth: sensitivity, 100%; specificity, 93%; positive predictive power, 93%; and negative predictive power, 100%. The kappa coefficient was 0.93, and the overall correct classification rate was 96%.

Little is known about the ability of the revised scales to differentiate attention-deficit/hyperactivity disorder from oppositional defiant disorder and conduct disorder. The confounding of attention-deficit/hyperactivity disorder, oppositional defiant disorder, and conduct disorder is a notable criticism of the older versions of the scales.

CLINICAL UTILITY

The CRS-R provide a systematic way for teachers and parents to rate children's disruptive behavior, especially symptoms of attention-deficit/hyperactivity disorder. The older versions (CRS) are the most widely used and empirically supported rating scales for assessing symptoms related to attention-deficit/hyperactivity disorder. The different versions of the CRS-R have been shown to be effective screening devices for identifying children with attention-deficit/hyperactivity disorder.

Adequate sensitivity and specificity suggest that the measure is useful in discriminating youth with attention-deficit/hyperactivity disorder from youth without the disorder. Further research is needed to determine the discriminative ability of the revised scales with regard to children with attention-deficit/hyperactivity disorder versus other disorders (e.g., conduct disorder, learning disabilities, and anxiety disorders). Although the scales can be helpful in making a diagnosis, they are not intended for use as diagnostic instruments.

Users are cautioned to pay careful attention to which version of the scales they select. The many different versions of the earlier forms of the scales have led to considerable confusion in the field. Use of the copyrighted computerized scoring programs for the newly revised scales should promote proper usage. The specific version of the scale used in research studies should be indicated in any publication of study results.

The original and first revisions of the scales have been demonstrated to be sensitive to treatment effects. Such properties need to be demonstrated with the newer scales, although it is likely, given the similarities of the versions, as well as the extensive normative data and the highly satisfactory psychometric properties of the earlier versions, that the newer versions will also possess these attributes.

REFERENCES AND SUGGESTED READINGS

Conners CK: A teacher rating scale for use in drug studies with children. Am J Psychiatry 126:884–888, 1969

Conners CK: Conners' Rating Scales—Revised: Technical Manual. New York, Multi-Health Systems, 1997

Conners CK, Wells KC, Parker JDA, et al: A new self-report scale for assessment of adolescent psychopathology: factor structure, reliability, validity, and diagnostic sensitivity. J Abnorm Child Psychol 25:487–497, 1997

Conners CK, Parker JDA, Sitarenios G, et al: The revised Conners' Parent Rating Scale (CPRS-R): factor structure, reliability, and criterion validity. J Abnorm Child Psychol 26:257–268, 1998

Conners CK, Sitarenios G, Parker JDA, et al: Revision and restandardization of the Conners Teacher Rating Scale (CTRS-R): factor structure, reliability, and criterion validity. J Abnorm Child Psychol 26:279–291, 1998

Loney J, Milich R: Hyperactivity, inattention, and aggression in clinical practice, in Advances in Developmental and Behavioral Pediatrics, Vol 3. Edited by Wolraich M, Routh DK. Greenwich, CT, AJI, 1982, pp 113–147

Rowe KS, Rowe KJ: Norms for parental ratings on Conners' Abbreviated Parent-Teacher Questionnaire: implications for the design of behavioral rating inventories and analyses of data derived from them. J Abnorm Child Psychol 25:425–451, 1997

New York Teacher Rating Scale (NYTRS)

L. S. Miller, R. G. Klein, J. Piacentinni, and H. Abikoff

GOALS

The New York Teacher Rating Scale (NYTRS) (Miller et al. 1995) is a teacher rating scale that was developed to assess disruptive and antisocial behavior in the classroom. The NYTRS assesses symptoms relevant to DSM-IV diagnoses of oppositional defiant disorder and conduct disorder in children in 1st through 10th grades. Two broad-band composite scales assess antisocial behavior and disruptive behavior.

DESCRIPTION

The NYTRS is a 36-item rating scale to be completed by the youth's teacher. The scale includes three empirically derived subscales relevant to oppositional defiant disorder and conduct disorder: Defiance (14 items), Physical Aggression (5 items), and Delinquent Aggression (4 items). A fourth subscale is Peer Relations (7 items). The teacher is asked to indicate the degree to which the child has displayed certain behaviors in the classroom within the past month. The items are rated, using a 4-point Likert-type scale, from 0 = not at all to 3 = very much. Parent report and adolescent self-report versions that parallel the teacher questionnaire are also available. These companion versions are not reviewed in this chapter.

Sample items from the Defiance, Physical Aggression, Delinquent Aggression, and Peer Relations subscales are provided in Example 18–2.

Two composite scales can also be derived from the NYTRS: the Antisocial Behavior Scale (13 items) and the Disruptive Behavior Scale (27 items). The Antisocial Behavior Scale roughly corresponds to the DSM-IV symptom criteria for conduct disorder. This scale includes all items from the Physical Aggression and the Delinquent Aggression subscales, plus the following four items: "steals on the sly," "shakes down others for money or other belongings," "late for school or class," and "tru-

ants." The Disruptive Behavior Scale includes all 27 items of problem behavior (the 13 items from the Antisocial Behavior Scale plus the 14 items from the Defiance subscale).

The NYTRS also includes two Global Impairment Ratings: "How much of a conduct problem is this child at this time?" and "How much of an academic problem is this child at this time?" These items are not included in any of the scale scores.

The scores for the four factor subscales (Defiance, Physical Aggression, Delinquent Aggression, and Peer Relations) and the composite scales (the Antisocial Behavior Scale and the Disruptive Behavior Scale) are obtained by averaging the items for each scale. The range of scores for each scale is 0–3. For all of the problem behavior scales, a higher score indicates greater problems. The Peer Relations subscale is worded positively (e.g., "is liked by peers"), so that a higher score reflects better functioning.

Normative data are available on 1,258 children in 1st through 10th grades in the public schools in Westchester County, New York (N = 793), or the parochial schools in Staten Island, New York (N = 465). The standardization sample was 51% male, 71% Caucasian, 15% African American, 8% Hispanic, and 6% other. Normative data are presented for the total sample at the item and subscale level and by gender for the subscales. Normative data are not presented by grade because no clin-

---

EXAMPLE 18–2 ■ Sample items from the New York Teacher Rating Scale

> Defiance Subscale
>   Defiant
>   Breaks school rules
>   Loses temper
>
> Physical Aggression Subscale
>   Acts violently to other children or adults
>   Starts physical fights
>   Assaults others
>
> Delinquent Aggression Subscale
>   Carries a knife or other weapon
>   Has mugged someone
>   Has used a knife or other weapon in a fight
>
> Peer Relations Subscale
>   Shows remorse when does something wrong
>   Helpful to others
>   Has at least one good friend

ically meaningful grade effects were observed in the standardization sample.

PRACTICAL ISSUES

It takes approximately 15 minutes to complete and 5 minutes to score the NYTRS. The measure and scoring instructions can be obtained from

> Dr. Laurie S. Miller
> Institute for Children at Risk
> New York University Child Study Center
> 550 First Avenue
> New York, NY 10016
> Phone: 212-263-8673
> E-mail: laurie.miller.2@med.nyu.edu

PSYCHOMETRIC PROPERTIES

Reliability

In the standardization sample, Cronbach's alphas for the four subscales and the composite scales were as follows: Defiance, 0.96; Physical Aggression, 0.88; Delinquent Aggression, 0.73; Peer Relations, 0.90; Antisocial Behavior, 0.80; and Disruptive Behavior, 0.95. In a sample of 81 children in 1st through 9th grades with diagnoses of conduct disorder on the basis of DSM-III-R criteria, Cronbach's alphas were Defiance, 0.93; Physical Aggression, 0.93; Delinquent Aggression, 0.49; Peer Relations, 0.84; Antisocial Behavior, 0.78; and Disruptive Behavior, 0.92.

Test-retest reliability over a 5-week interval was determined using ratings from teachers of 21 children with diagnoses of conduct disorder. The test-retest reliabilities for the scales were Physical Aggression, 0.62; Delinquent Aggression, 0.67; Antisocial Behavior, 0.70; Defiance, 0.83; Disruptive Behavior, 0.83; and Peer Relations, 0.87.

Joint reliability was assessed using teacher ratings for 33 children with conduct disorder. Of the 33 children, 17 were rated by 4 teachers, 10 were rated by 3 teachers, and 6 were rated by 2 teachers. Intraclass correlation coefficients for the subscales and the composite scores were Defiance, 0.43; Physical Aggression, 0.59; Delinquent Aggression, 0.27; Peer Relations, 0.27; Antisocial Behavior, 0.60; and Disruptive Behavior, 0.57.

Validity

Within the standardization sample, 33 of the 36 items were significantly higher for boys than for girls. The three items for which no significant differences were observed were "late to school or class," "shakes down others for money," and "has mugged someone."

All 36 items of the NYTRS subscales and composite scales were found to be significantly different for a school-based sample compared with a sample of children with diagnoses of conduct disorder. Group differences were observed for both boys and girls. For boys, mean scores and standard deviations for the Antisocial Behavior Scale in the population and conduct disorder samples were as follows: population mean, 0.12 (0.2), and conduct disorder sample mean, 0.65 (0.5). Only 3 symptoms of 13 are required for diagnosis. A child with a diagnosis of conduct disorder likely exhibits "very much" of some symptoms and "not at all" of the majority of symptoms on the list. For girls, the population mean was 0.04 (0.1) and the conduct disorder sample mean was 0.91 (0.7). For boys, mean scores and standard deviations for the Disruptive Behavior Scale in the population and conduct disorder samples were as follows: population mean, 0.33 (0.4), and conduct disorder sample mean, 1.50 (0.6). For girls, the population mean was 0.14 (0.3) and the conduct disorder sample mean was 1.77 (0.7). Sensitivity and specificity were estimated using group status (conduct disorder sample vs. school-based sample) as the criterion. For the total samples, specificity was 95% and sensitivity was 86% for the Disruptive Behavior Scale, and specificity was 94% and sensitivity was 70% for the Antisocial Behavior Scale. Specificity and sensitivity estimates for the subscales were highest for the Physical Aggression subscale (specificity, 90%; sensitivity, 90%) and lowest for the Delinquent Aggression subscale (specificity, 69%; sensitivity, 57%).

In a study that examined the ability of the NYTRS to predict group status (children with diagnosed conduct disorder vs. a school-based sample of nonreferred children), the NYTRS was shown to have predictive utility above and beyond the conduct disorder factor of the Revised Behavior Problem Checklist (RBPC) (Quay 1983) and the Aggression Factor of the IOWA Conners Teacher Rating Scale (Loney and Milich 1982).

In a school-based sample, children's scores on the problem behavior scales were significantly related to global impairment ratings of conduct problems (ranging from $r = 0.21$ for the Delinquent Aggression subscale to

$r = 0.81$ for the Defiance subscale) and academic performance (ranging from $r = 0.14$ for the Delinquent Aggression subscale to $r = 0.48$ for the Defiance subscale). In a clinically referred sample of children with conduct disorder, similar relations were found between the scales and the teacher global impairment ratings of conduct problems (ranging from $r = -0.28$ for the Peer Relations subscale to $r = 0.72$ for the Defiance subscale) but not for academic problems.

In two placebo-controlled double-blind studies of methylphenidate in outpatient children and young adolescents (ages 6–15 years) with diagnoses of conduct disorder (DSM-III or DSM-III-R), the NYTRS was shown to be sensitive to treatment effects. Changes were observed on the symptom scales at the individual item level (e.g., obscene language, destroys property, deliberately cruel, and attacks others) and for the overall impairment rating of conduct problems. For example, in one study, posttreatment means (adjusted for pretreatment values) on the overall ratings of conduct problems for the placebo group ($n = 35$, mean = 2.3, SD = 0.1) and the medication group ($n = 36$, mean = 1.3, SD = 0.1) were significantly different. Changes on the NYTRS were paralleled by changes in blind observations of antisocial behavior in the school setting.

CLINICAL UTILITY

The NYTRS can be used to screen a general population of school-age children for conduct disorder. Both the 27-item Disruptive Behavior Scale and the 5-item Physical Aggression subscale have high sensitivity and high specificity.

The NYTRS is not a diagnostic instrument. It can, however, be used as part of a comprehensive diagnostic assessment. The scale covers all of the symptoms of conduct disorder that are observable by teachers, has acceptable test-retest and joint reliability, and has high specificity and sensitivity for differentiating both boys and girls with diagnoses of conduct disorder from a school-based sample. No data are available on the utility of the scale for distinguishing conduct disorder from other disorders in children.

The high test-retest reliability of the NYTRS over a 5-week period and its ability to detect meaningful medication-induced changes in antisocial behavior suggest that it can be used to monitor response to treatment.

The NYTRS includes an empirically derived factor to assess peer relations. This scale has high internal consistency, test-retest reliability, and joint reliability. Although not part of the criteria for conduct disorder, poor peer relations often accompany the disorder and are predictive of negative outcome. Thus, the scale is a reliable measure for assessing an important associated feature of conduct disorder that might inform the treatment plan.

REFERENCES AND SUGGESTED READINGS

Klein RG, Klass E, Abikoff H, et al: Controlled trial of methylphenidate, lithium, and placebo in children and adolescents with conduct disorders. Paper presented at the meeting of the Society for Research in Child and Adolescent Psychopathology, London, June 1994

Klein RG, Abikoff H, Klass E, et al: Clinical efficacy of methylphenidate in conduct disorder with and without attention deficit hyperactivity disorder. Arch Gen Psychiatry 54:1073–1080, 1997

Loney J, Milich R: Hyperactivity, inattention, and aggression in clinical practice, in Advances in Developmental and Behavioral Pediatrics, Vol 3. Edited by Wolraich M, Routh DK. Greenwich, CT, AJI, 1982, pp 113–147

Miller LS, Klein R, Piacentinni J, et al: The New York Teacher Rating Scale for disruptive and antisocial behavior. J Am Acad Child Adolesc Psychiatry 34:359–370, 1995

Quay HC: A dimensional approach to behavior disorder: The Revised Behavior Problem Checklist. School Psychology Review 12:244–249, 1983

Revised Children's Manifest Anxiety Scale (RCMAS)

C. R. Reynolds and B. O. Richmond

GOALS

The Revised Children's Manifest Anxiety Scale (RCMAS) (Reynolds and Richmond 1978) is a child-report instrument designed to assess the level and nature of anxiety in children and adolescents ages 6–19 years. The scale covers three anxiety symptom dimensions: physiological anxiety, worry/oversensitivity, and social concerns/concentration. The RCMAS also includes a Lie subscale to assess social desirability bias. The measure is a revision of the original Children's Manifest Anxiety Scale (Castenada et al. 1956), which was based on the Manifest Anxiety Scale (Taylor 1951), a measure of anxiety symptoms in adults. The measure was developed to require minimal administration time and to be suitable for group administration to children in elementary school.

DESCRIPTION

The RCMAS is a 37-item self-report instrument that can be administered either individually or to groups of children. The child responds to each item by circling *yes* or *no*. *Yes* indicates that the item is descriptive of the child's feelings or actions. The RCMAS yields a Total Anxiety score and four subscale scores. The four subscales are Physiological Anxiety (10 items), Worry/Oversensitivity (11 items), Social Concerns/Concentration (7 items), and Lie (9 items). Sample items are provided in Example 18–3.

Yes responses to the 28 anxiety items are summed to determine the Total Anxiety score. Scores range from 0 to 28; a high score indicates a high level of anxiety. Similarly, the raw score on each subscale is the number of items circled *yes* for that subscale. A scoring key is available for scoring responses. Raw scores are converted to scaled scores and percentiles. The Total Anxiety score is converted to a T-score, with a mean of 50 and a standard deviation of 10. The subscale scores have a mean of 10

EXAMPLE 18–3 ■ Sample items from the Revised Children's Manifest Anxiety Scale

Physiological Anxiety Subscale
  I have bad dreams.

Worry/Oversensitivity Subscale
  I worry about what is going to happen.

Social Concerns/Concentration Subscale
  I feel that others do not like the way I do things.

Lie Subscale
  I tell the truth every single time.

Items from the Revised Children's Manifest Anxiety Scale (RCMAS, "What I Think and Feel"), Western Psychological Services. Reprinted by permission of the publisher, Western Psychological Services, 12031 Wilshire Boulevard, Los Angeles, CA, 90025, U.S.A., not to be reprinted in whole or in part for any additional purpose without the expressed, written permission of the publisher. All rights reserved.

and a standard deviation of 3. Norms are provided at 1-year intervals for the total normative sample. Norms are also provided for African American boys and girls and Caucasian boys and girls. The scale was standardized on nearly 5,000 children (ages 6–19 years) who represented 13 states and more than 80 school districts from all major geographic regions of the United States. A Lie scale standard score of 13 (one standard deviation above the normative mean) is used to indicate that the Total Anxiety score should be interpreted with caution.

PRACTICAL ISSUES

It takes approximately 10–15 minutes to complete the RCMAS. It is published by

> Western Psychological Services
> 12031 Wilshire Boulevard
> Los Angeles, CA 90025-1251
> Phone: 310-478-2061 or 800-648-8851
> Internet: www.wpspublish.com

The measure was copyrighted by Western Psychological Services in 1985. It is printed on one page, with a cover page and written instructions on one side and the 37 items on the other. The manual for the RCMAS (Reynolds and Richmond 1985) is also available from Western Psychological Services. The cost for the RCMAS kit, which includes the manual and 50 answer forms, is

$92.00. The measure requires approximately a third-grade reading level. It is easily administered to groups of children ages 9.5 years or older. Individual administration is recommended for children in grades K–2. The RCMAS is available in Spanish. The cost for the Spanish kit, including 15 answer forms, is $55.00.

PSYCHOMETRIC PROPERTIES

Reliability

Internal consistencies of 0.83 and 0.85 for the Total Anxiety score were reported in two community samples of 329 and 167 children, respectively. For the entire age range, reliability coefficients were 0.84 for Caucasian boys, 0.85 for African American boys, 0.85 for Caucasian girls, and 0.78 for African American girls. In general, these coefficients are equal across groups, with the exception of African American girls. For several age groups (i.e., ages 6, 8, 10, and 11 years), the internal consistencies of the Total Anxiety scale are significantly lower for African American girls than for Caucasian girls. Internal consistency estimates for 97 kindergarten children were high (0.82). High internal consistency reliability was also reported for children with learning disabilities, for children with IQ scores of 130 or above, and for community samples of children from other countries (e.g., China).

Moderate to high internal consistency reliability was also reported for the subscales. Using the national standardization sample of nearly 5,000 Caucasian and African American children ages 6–19 years, the Physiological Anxiety subscale reliability estimates were in the 0.60s and 0.70s (with the exception of those for children ages 15 and older). Estimates for the Worry/Oversensitivity subscale were in the 0.70s and 0.80s, and estimates for the Social Concerns/Concentration subscale were generally in the 0.60s. The Lie subscale had reliability estimates in the 0.70s and 0.80s. It should be noted that the scale is considerably less reliable for younger children (especially ages 6 and 7) than for older children.

Test-retest reliabilities (over 1- and 5-week intervals) of the Total Anxiety scale were calculated in a school-based sample of boys and girls from regular sixth-, seventh-, and eighth-grade parochial school classrooms; 80 students were retested after 1 week, and 81 different students were retested after 5 weeks. Pearson correlation coefficients were 0.88 and 0.77 for the 1-week and

5-week intervals, respectively. The 1-week reliability coefficients for the three anxiety scales ranged from 0.75 to 0.85. The 5-week reliability coefficients ranged from 0.60 to 0.78. The 1-week and 5-week test-retest reliability coefficients for the Lie subscale were 0.63 and 0.75, respectively. A 3-week reliability coefficient of 0.98 (0.97 for boys and 0.98 for girls) was reported for the Total Anxiety scale in a sample of 99 children sixth grade and younger. Nine-month test-retest reliability coefficients of 0.68 and 0.58 were reported for the Total Anxiety scale and the Lie subscale using a sample of 534 children in elementary school.

Validity

The RCMAS has been shown to correlate significantly with other measures of childhood anxiety (e.g., the State-Trait Anxiety Inventory for Children (STAIC) [Spielberger 1973] and the Fear Survey Schedule for Children—Revised [Ollendick 1983]) but not with measures of intelligence.

Several studies provide information on the diagnostic utility of the RCMAS. A study of 139 children ages 8–12 years with diagnoses of either a DSM-III anxiety disorder ($n = 44$) or another type of disorder ($n = 95$) examined the ability of the RCMAS scales to differentiate between these two broadly defined diagnostic groups. Of the 44 children with an anxiety disorder, 80% had overanxious disorder, 14% had separation anxiety disorder, 4% had obsessive-compulsive disorder, and 2% had avoidant disorder. Of the 95 children with other types of disorders, 35% had attention-deficit disorder, 31% had minor diagnoses such as adjustment disorder, 26% had depressive disorders, 4% had conduct disorders, and 4% had pervasive developmental disorders or schizophrenic disorders. Diagnoses were made on the basis of interviews with the child and parent(s) using the Schedule for Affective Disorders and Schizophrenia for School-Age Children—Epidemiological (K-SADS-E) (p. 296), independent of information obtained using the RCMAS. Children with anxiety disorders scored significantly higher than those with other disorders on the Worry/Oversensitivity subscale. Although their scores on the Total Anxiety scale and the Physiological Anxiety subscale were higher than the scores of the children in the other group, differences between the two groups were not significant. The sensitivity and specificity of the Worry/Oversensitivity subscale were examined using three different cutoff levels. The greatest accuracy was produced using a T-score of 60. Using this method, the sensitivity was 41% and the specificity was 80%, with an overall correct classification rate of 68%. Six of the eight children with false-negative diagnoses had a principal diagnosis of attention-deficit disorder. No specific pattern emerged for the children with false-positive diagnoses.

In a study of 213 boys, ages 5–17 years, scores on the RCMAS and the Trait scale of the STAIC (Spielberger 1973) were compared across three groups: those with attention-deficit/hyperactivity disorder, those with anxiety disorders, and those with no history of psychiatric disorders. The 105 children in the anxiety disorders group included 22 with separation anxiety disorder, 22 with social phobia, 22 with simple phobia, 17 with overanxious disorder, 8 with obsessive-compulsive disorder, 7 with panic disorder, 4 with avoidant disorder, 1 with posttraumatic stress disorder, and 2 with anxiety disorder not otherwise specified. Groups were formed on the basis of intake interviews with the child and at least one parent using a modified K-SADS (p. 296). Rating scales were administered before the diagnostic interviews. Both the RCMAS and the STAIC scores were significantly higher for the anxious group than for those with no history of psychiatric disorders. However, neither scale differentiated the anxiety disorders group from the attention-deficit/hyperactivity disorder group.

The factor structure of the RCMAS has been supported by several studies, including one conducted with the 4,972 children in the standardization study. The factor structure has been relatively consistent across many variables, including sex, ethnicity, IQ, and some handicapping conditions. Although the Lie subscale items tend to be associated with two separate factors, they have been combined into one scale.

CLINICAL UTILITY

The RCMAS has been demonstrated to be a reliable instrument for assessing symptoms of anxiety in children. The scale appears to be less internally reliable for children ages 6 and 7 years and for African American girls in several different age groups. The instrument is simple and quick to complete, and it can be administered in a group setting for children ages 9 and older. Given the relatively good internal and test-retest reliability and ease of administration of the RCMAS, the scale has potential

as a school-based screening tool for identifying children who might have anxiety disorders. Data suggesting that mean scores are higher in children with anxiety disorders compared with psychiatrically healthy children are available; however, more comprehensive data on sensitivity and specificity are lacking to support use of the RCMAS as a screening measure.

The item content of the RCMAS and lack of empirical data regarding diagnostic group differentiation call into question its utility for informing diagnostic decisions. First, the instrument is not clearly tied to DSM-IV anxiety disorder categories. Second, the presence of mood, attentional, and impulsivity items clearly confounds its discriminatory abilities. Third, limited data are available on the scale's ability to distinguish between broadly defined diagnostic groups (anxiety disorders vs. other disorders). Only the Worry/Oversensitivity subscale has been shown to have some utility in distinguishing between those with anxiety disorders and those with other diagnoses. However, the sensitivity of the measure for this purpose is relatively low. Furthermore, several studies using the RCMAS suggest that the distinction between symptoms of anxiety and symptoms of attention-deficit/hyperactivity disorder appears to be particularly problematic. Finally, data on sensitivity to treatment effects are also lacking.

REFERENCES AND SUGGESTED READINGS

Castenada A, McCandless BR, Palermo DS: The children's form of the manifest anxiety scale. Child Dev 27:317–326, 1956

Mattison R, Bagnato S, Brubaker B: Diagnostic utility of the Revised Children's Manifest Anxiety Scale in children with DSM-III anxiety disorders. Journal of Anxiety Disorders 2:147–155, 1988

Ollendick TH: Reliability and validity of the Revised Fear Survey Schedule for Children (FSSC-R). Behav Res Ther 21:685–692, 1983

Perrin S, Last CG: Do childhood anxiety measures measure anxiety? J Abnorm Child Psychol 20:567–578, 1992

Reynolds CR: Concurrent validity of What I Think and Feel: the Revised Children's Manifest Anxiety Scale. J Consult Clin Psychol 78:774–775, 1980

Reynolds CR: Convergent and divergent validity of the Revised Children's Manifest Anxiety Scale. Educational and Psychological Measurement 42:1205–1212, 1982

Reynolds CR, Richmond B: What I Think and Feel: a revised measure of children's manifest anxiety. J Abnorm Child Psychol 6:271–280, 1978

Reynolds CR, Richmond B: Revised Children's Manifest Anxiety Scale (RCMAS) Manual. Los Angeles, CA, Western Psychological Services, 1985

Spielberger C: Manual for the State-Trait Inventory for Children. Palo Alto, CA, Consulting Psychologists Press, 1973

Taylor JA: The relationship of anxiety to the conditioned eyelid response. Journal of Experimental Psychology 41:81–92, 1951

Anxiety Disorders Interview Schedule for DSM-IV—Child Version (ADIS-IV-C)

W. K. Silverman and A. M. Albano

GOALS

The Anxiety Disorders Interview Schedule for DSM-IV—Child Version (ADIS-IV-C) (Silverman and Albano 1996) is a diagnostic interview that assesses DSM-IV anxiety disorders in children ages 6–17 years. It is a revision of the original ADIS—Child Version (Silverman and Nelles 1988), which was a modification of the Anxiety Disorders Interview Schedule (ADIS) for adults (DiNardo et al. 1983). The parent and child interviews cover the following anxiety disorders: separation anxiety disorder, social phobia, specific phobia, panic disorder, agoraphobia, generalized anxiety disorder, obsessive-compulsive disorder, posttraumatic stress disorder, and acute stress disorder.

The ADIS-IV-C also assesses situational and cognitive cues for anxiety, intensity of anxiety, extent of avoidance, precipitating events, and the history of the problem. Information is also obtained for assessing school refusal behavior, a common complication of anxiety disorders in children. Furthermore, the instrument allows the clinician to assess mood and externalizing disorders (e.g., dysthymic disorder, major depressive disorder, attention-deficit/hyperactivity disorder, and oppositional defiant disorder) and provides screening questions for substance abuse, psychosis, selective mutism, eating disorders, somatoform disorders, and learning disorders.

DESCRIPTION

The ADIS-IV-C is a semistructured interview that the clinician administers separately to the child and the child's parent(s). Both the parent and child interviews are organized around the different diagnostic categories. Questions are answered in a yes-no format. After a positive response, the interviewer often probes for further elaboration. Screen or gate questions allow the interviewer to skip over the rest of a section if a certain number of questions are not endorsed.

The child and parent interviews are very similar; both have sections on school history, school refusal behavior, interpersonal relationships and involvement in social activities, and psychosocial stressors, as well as the detailed diagnostic sections. The parent interview also includes demographic and family information and more detailed questions about the history of the problem, consequences of the problematic behavior, and treatment and medication history. The parent interview also includes additional questions about externalizing disorders, enuresis, sleep terror disorder, developmental disorders, and learning disorders. The child interview includes the optional use of a "feelings thermometer" to assist the child with the anchoring of ratings of interference in normal functioning.

Using a diagnostic summary sheet and clinical severity rating form, the interviewer derives separate diagnoses from the parent and child interviews. Clinical judgment is required to determine the principal diagnoses, as well as additional diagnoses, on the basis of the information obtained from both parent and child. In addition to determining a diagnosis on the basis of the presence or absence of symptoms, the interviewer makes a clinician severity rating on a scale ranging from 0 to 8 for each diagnosis.

When both the child and parent interviews are given (which is recommended by the authors and by research studies), composite diagnoses are derived according to fixed criteria by comparing responses to presence or absence of symptoms on the two versions. When a symptom is endorsed on one version but not on the other, both severity ratings and level of interference with functioning are considered.

PRACTICAL ISSUES

Each version of the interview takes approximately 1 hour to administer. Clinical judgment is required to establish the presence or absence of certain criteria and to distinguish primary and secondary diagnoses; the highest severity rating indicates the diagnosis that is most interfering and disabling. The scoring system allows for coprincipal diagnoses when two or more diagnoses are rated as equally severe. In studies by the developers of the scale, interviews were conducted by Ph.D.-level clinicians and doctoral students in clinical psychology with extensive training in the administration of the interview. First, interviewers observed at least five pairs of parent-child interviews. The interviewers then conducted child and parent interviews while an observer sat in and followed along. Interviewers were considered trained once diagnoses matched between trainee and observer on five separate occasions.

The ADIS-IV-C is copyrighted by Graywind Publications, Inc. The interviews and a clinician manual (Albano and Silverman 1996) can be obtained from

> The Psychological Corporation
> 555 Academic Court
> San Antonio, TX 78204-2498
> Phone: 800-211-8378
> Internet: www.psychcorp.com

Training is necessary and available from the scale developers. Dr. Wendy Silverman can be contacted at

> Florida International University
> Department of Psychology
> University Park
> Miami, FL 33199
> Phone: 305-348-2064

Dr. Anne Marie Albano can be contacted at

> NYU Child Study Center
> New York University Medical Center

> 550 First Avenue
> New York, NY 10016
> Phone: 212-263-8661
> E-mail: annemarie.albano@med.nyu.edu

PSYCHOMETRIC PROPERTIES

Reliability

All published reports on the instrument refer to the DSM-III-R version. Joint reliability was calculated in children referred for outpatient services. Using the interviewer-observer paradigm in a sample of 51 children (mean age 11 years, 7 months) presenting to a childhood anxiety specialty clinic, the following overall kappa coefficients were found for the child, parent, and combined versions: 0.84, 0.83, and 0.78, respectively. Kappa coefficients for specific diagnostic categories have also been reported; they range from 0.64 for overanxious disorder to 1.00 for simple phobia. In a sample of 50 children ages 6–17, test-retest reliability (over a 10- to 14-day interval) was reported to be 0.76 for the overall child version and 0.67 for the overall parent version. Moderate to high kappa coefficients were reported for overanxious disorder, simple phobia, and social phobia for both versions; they ranged from a low of 0.46 for social phobia using the child version to a high of 0.85 for overanxious disorder reported by the child. Composite scores derived from both the parent and child versions were found to have the following kappa coefficients: 0.84 for simple phobia, 0.73 for social phobia, and 0.64 for overanxious disorder. The overall reliability of child reports, on the basis of both symptom scores and diagnostic agreement, was found to be somewhat higher than that of parent reports.

A separate study focused on the test-retest reliability of the specific symptoms comprising DSM-III-R separation anxiety disorder, avoidant disorder, and overanxious disorder in a sample of subjects ages 6–17 years referred for outpatient services. Using the child interview, 8 of 10 symptoms of separation anxiety disorder were found to have good to excellent reliability. Using the parent interview, 8 symptoms had good reliability. The reliability of parent reports of the symptoms of overanxious disorder and avoidant disorder was also generally satisfactory; however, the reliability of child reports of these symptoms was poor.

In a study of 161 outpatients presenting to an anxiety clinic in Australia, kappa coefficients ranged from 0.59 to 0.82 using a joint reliability paradigm involving live interviews with the child and video interviews with the parent.

Validity

No published reports are available on the validity of the scale.

CLINICAL UTILITY

The ADIS-IV-C yields both categorical and dimensional information. In general, it has been shown to have satisfactory reliability in terms of diagnostic categories, as well as symptom scales. This instrument is well suited for clinicians or investigators who are specifically interested in deriving anxiety disorder diagnoses while considering the possibility of comorbid disorders. The instrument also allows clinicians to obtain important information on functional and contextual factors and the degree to which symptoms interfere with functioning; this information is essential for adequate case conceptualization and treatment planning. However, information on the scale's validity is needed to evaluate the instrument's clinical utility.

REFERENCES AND SUGGESTED READINGS

Albano AM, Silverman WK: The Anxiety Disorders Interview Schedule for DSM-IV-Child and Parent Versions: Clinician Manual. San Antonio, TX, Graywind, 1996

DiNardo PA, O'Brien GT, Barlow DH, et al: Reliability of the DSM-III anxiety disorder categories using a new structured interview. Arch Gen Psychiatry 40:1070–1074, 1983

Rapee RM, Barrett PM, Dadds M, et al: Reliability of the DSM-III-R childhood anxiety disorders using structured interview: interrater and parent-child agreement. J Am Acad Child Adolesc Psychiatry 33:984–992, 1994

Silverman WK, Albano AM: The Anxiety Disorders Interview Schedule for DSM-IV-Child and Parent Versions. San Antonio, TX, Graywind, 1996

Silverman WK, Eisen AR: Age differences in the reliability of parent and child reports of child anxious symptomatology using a structured interview. J Am Acad Child Adolesc Psychiatry 31:117–124, 1992

Silverman WK, Nelles WB: The Anxiety Disorders Interview Schedule for Children. J Am Acad Child Adolesc Psychiatry 27:772–778, 1988

Silverman WK, Rabian B: Test-retest reliability of the DSM-III-R childhood anxiety disorders symptoms using the Anxiety Disorders Interview Schedule for Children. Journal of Anxiety Disorders 9:139–150, 1995

Multidimensional Anxiety Scale for Children (MASC)

J. S. March

GOALS

The Multidimensional Anxiety Scale for Children (MASC) (March 1997) is a self-report scale designed to assess a wide spectrum of anxiety symptoms in youth ages 8–19 years. The MASC covers the range of anxiety symptoms described in DSM-IV (with the exception of those for obsessive-compulsive disorder) and corresponds with the diagnostic criteria for social phobia, selective mutism, separation anxiety, and generalized anxiety disorder. The MASC assesses four main domains: physical symptoms, social anxiety, harm avoidance, and separation/panic. It also assesses six subdomains: tense/restless symptoms, somatic/autonomic symptoms, perfectionism, anxious coping, humiliation/rejection fears, and performance fears. Domains and subdomains were derived from factor analysis. The MASC also provides a Total Anxiety scale, an Anxiety Disorders Index, and an Inconsistency Index.

DESCRIPTION

The MASC is a 39-item self-report rating scale. The child is asked to rate each item on a Likert-type 4-point scale ranging from never to often. The respondent is asked to rate "how often the statement is true for you."

Instructions inform the youth that the form is "about how you have been thinking, feeling, or acting recently."

A separate version, the MASC-10, is also available. The MASC-10 can be used when a brief, unidimensional measure is needed and is useful for group testing situations or screening.

The MASC includes four empirically derived factors: physical symptoms (12 items), social anxiety (9 items), harm avoidance (9 items), and separation/panic (9 items). The first three scales are further divided and cover the following subdomains: tense/restless symptoms (6 items), somatic/autonomic symptoms (6 items), perfectionism (4 items), anxious coping (5 items), humiliation/ rejection fears (5 items), and performance fears (4 items). Sample items are provided in Example 18–4.

The MASC also contains a 10-item MASC Total Anxiety Index, which includes the 10 items from the instrument that best discriminate between anxious and nonanxious children.

The MASC can be scored using either the MASC Computer Program or paper and pencil QuikScore forms, which can be completed in less than 10 minutes. High scale scores are indicative of anxiety symptoms, whereas low scale scores indicate the absence of anxiety. Individual scale scores are compared with norms for appropriate groups of children (by three age groups and by gender groups).

Scale scores are calculated for the following scales: Total Score, Physical Symptoms, Social Anxiety, Harm Avoidance, Separation/Panic, Tense/Restless Symptoms, Somatic/Autonomic Symptoms, Perfectionism, Anxious Coping, Humiliation/Rejection Fears, and Performance Fears. Items are rated on a 4-point Likert scale ranging from 1 = never to 4 = often. Subscale scores range from the number of items on the scale to the number of items multiplied by four. T-scores are derived on the basis of comparisons of scale scores with normative data. T-scores >70 are thought to represent clinically significant problem behavior. For example, a girl with a T-score of 72 on the Social Anxiety factor is likely to have significant concerns about how she presents herself to others. Such a score suggests that this child may meet DSM-IV criteria for social phobia. Conversely, if a child has no subscale T-score >65, the child will likely fail to meet diagnostic criteria for the anxiety disorders covered by the scale.

The Validity or Inconsistency Index is an empirically derived scale that uses summed difference scores on items that are expected to be highly correlated. Low scores indicate a pattern consistent with valid responding. Higher scores (those above suggested cutoff scores for the specified age and gender groups) suggest that the scale should be interpreted with caution because the answers appear to be internally inconsistent.

PRACTICAL ISSUES

The MASC was copyrighted in 1997 by Multi-Health Systems, Inc. The scale and the manual (March 1997) can be obtained from

> Multi-Health Systems, Inc.
> 908 Niagara Falls Boulevard
> North Tonawanda, NY 14120-2060
> Phone: 800-456-3003
> Internet: www.mhs.com

The MASC complete kit (which includes the manual and 25 QuikScore forms) is available for $55.00. Each of the elements of the complete kit may be purchased separately.

PSYCHOMETRIC PROPERTIES

Reliability

In a school-based sample of 374 youth ages 8–17 years, internal reliability coefficients for all of the main factors

---

EXAMPLE 18–4 ■ Sample items from the Multidimensional Anxiety Scale for Children

Physical Symptoms: Tense/Restless Symptoms
  I feel tense or uptight.

Separation/Panic
  I get scared when my parents go away.

Social Anxiety: Humiliation/Rejection Fears
  I worry about doing something stupid or embarrassing.

Harm Avoidance: Anxious Coping
  I check to make sure things are safe.

The Multidimensional Anxiety Scale for Children (MASC) is copyrighted material owned and published by Multi-Health Systems, Inc. For further information on the product, or to place an order, please contact MHS at the address provided. All rights reserved. Reproduced by permission.

and for the subfactors were all satisfactory, ranging from 0.60 to 0.85. The internal reliability of the total score was 0.90, with equally high reliability for boys (0.85) and girls (0.87).

Test-retest reliability was examined in a clinical population of children and adolescents with a mixture of anxiety disorders and/or attention-deficit/hyperactivity disorder. Intraclass correlation coefficients for 3-week and 3-month test-retest reliabilities for total scores were 0.79 and 0.93, respectively. The 3-week and 3-month reliabilities for all of the subscales (except for the Harm Avoidance scale at 3 weeks) were >0.70.

Test-retest reliability was also examined in a school-based sample of students in 3rd through 12th grades. Using intraclass correlation coefficients to estimate stability over a 3-week period, satisfactory coefficients were found for the total scale, all factors, and the 10-item MASC Anxiety Index. Test-retest reliability was unaffected by age (intraclass correlation coefficients of 0.77 for children and 0.79 for adolescents) or gender (intraclass correlation coefficients of 0.81 for boys and 0.75 for girls). Reliability coefficients were lower for African American than for Caucasian students (intraclass correlation coefficients of 0.84 for Caucasians and 0.61 for African Americans).

Validity

In a study of clinically referred youth with internalizing and externalizing disorders, the MASC was correlated with other measures of anxiety (e.g., the Revised Children's Manifest Anxiety Scale [RCMAS] [p. 336]), less strongly correlated with measures of depression (e.g., the Children's Depression Inventory [CDI] [p. 344]), and not at all correlated with the Abbreviated Symptom Questionnaire, a measure of disruptive behavior (Conners 1995).

Discriminant function analysis was used to examine the ability of the MASC to discriminate between patients with anxiety disorders (DSM-IV anxiety disorders, except obsessive-compulsive disorder) and psychiatrically healthy age- and sex-matched control subjects. The sensitivity was 90%, the specificity was 84%, the kappa coefficient was 0.74, and the overall correct classification was 87%. A separate study of the 10-item MASC Anxiety Index resulted in the following statistics for differentiating children with anxiety disorders from psychiatrically healthy control subjects: sensitivity, 95%; specificity, 95%; kappa coefficient, 0.90; and overall correct classification, 95%.

The 10-item MASC Anxiety Index was also shown to be effective in distinguishing children with anxiety disorders (DSM-IV anxiety disorders, except obsessive-compulsive disorder) from age- and sex-matched children with attention-deficit/hyperactivity disorder. The following statistics were derived on the basis of the classification of 140 children: sensitivity, 75%; specificity, 67%; and kappa coefficient, 0.42.

The treatment sensitivity of the MASC was tested in a treatment study using single case across setting design. Seventeen children (mean age 12 years) with posttraumatic stress disorder participated in a trial of cognitive-behavioral psychotherapy. Repeated-measures analysis of variance revealed significant main effects of treatment on the MASC. Mean MASC scores for baseline, posttreatment, and follow-up conditions were 74.46 (21.8), 53.58 (27.96), and 44.93 (22.89), respectively.

The MASC factor structure has been shown to be invariant across gender and age. As expected, mean anxiety scores for girls are higher than for boys in community samples.

CLINICAL UTILITY

The MASC can be used to screen a general population of children and adolescents for further investigation of the potential presence of anxiety disorders. High specificity and sensitivity rates of the full measure and the 10-item MASC Anxiety Index in discriminating children with anxiety disorders from psychiatrically healthy control subjects suggest that it can be used for such screening purposes.

Although the MASC is not a diagnostic instrument, it can be used as part of a diagnostic assessment. The scale's ability to discriminate between children with anxiety disorders and children with attention-deficit/hyperactivity disorder is particularly important for diagnostic assessments. Further data on this specific use are needed.

Several aspects of the MASC make it particularly useful for informing treatment selection. The MASC factors and subfactors measure separate dimensions of anxiety, making the measure well suited for discriminating patterns of anxiety in subgroups of children with anxiety disorders. High scores on certain subfactors would suggest problem areas to be targeted as well as the types of treatment to be undertaken. Further empirical data are needed on the ability of the MASC to predict the need for specific treatments. The information provided on harm avoidance may also prove useful for treatment planning.

High test-retest reliability and initial empirical data on sensitivity to psychotherapy suggest that the MASC has potential use in monitoring treatment responses over time. Currently, all data supporting the utility of the MASC come from the scale developer. Data from independent investigations are therefore needed. The measure is currently being used in several large-scale treatment studies that include both psychosocial and pharmacological treatments. Thus, essential data on treatment sensitivity from independent investigations should be available in the near future.

REFERENCES AND SUGGESTED READINGS

Conners CK: The Conners' Parent Rating Scales. Multi-Health Systems, Toronto, CA, 1995

March JS: Manual for the Multidimensional Anxiety Scale for Children (MASC). Toronto, Multi-Health Systems, 1997

March JS, Parker JD: The Multidimensional Anxiety Scale for Children (MASC), in The Use of Psychological Testing for Treatment Planning and Outcome Assessment. Edited by Marvish ME. Mahwah, NJ, Erlbaum, 1994

March JS, Amaya-Jackson L, Murray MC, et al: Cognitive-behavioral psychotherapy for children and adolescents with posttraumatic stress disorder after a single-incident stressor. J Am Acad Child Adolesc Psychiatry 37:585–593, 1997a

March JS, Parker JD, Sullivan K, et al: The Multidimensional Anxiety Scale for Children (MASC): factor structure, reliability, and validity. J Am Acad Child Adolesc Psychiatry 36:554–565, 1997b

March JS, Sullivan K, Parker J: Test-retest reliability of the Multidimensional Anxiety Scale for Children (MASC). Journal of Anxiety Disorders (in press)

Children's Depression Inventory (CDI)

M. Kovacs

GOALS

The Children's Depression Inventory (CDI) (Kovacs 1981) is a self-report measure of symptoms of depression among children and adolescents (ages 7–17 years). The CDI assesses a range of depressive symptoms, including disturbed mood, impaired hedonic capacity, vegetative functions, self-evaluation, and interpersonal behaviors. The CDI Short Form, a scale that gives a subset of 10 of the CDI items, was developed to provide a quick measure of the extent to which the child exhibits depressive symptoms.

DESCRIPTION

The CDI has 27 items. Each item is scored from 0 to 2, with 0 = absence of symptom, 1 = mild symptom, and 2 = definite symptom. The child rates his or her own behavior or feelings by selecting one of the three statements that best describes his or her behavior within the past 2 weeks. A total score and five subscale scores are derived. The subscales are Negative Mood, Interpersonal Problems, Ineffectiveness, Anhedonia, and Negative Self-Esteem. Sample items from the Negative Mood and Anhedonia subscales are provided in Example 18–5.

EXAMPLE 18–5 ■ Sample items from the Children's Depression Inventory

Negative Mood Subscale
  I am sad once in a while (0)
  I am sad many times (1)
  I am sad all the time (2)

Anhedonia Subscale
  I have fun in many things (0)
  I have fun in some things (1)
  Nothing is fun at all (2)

Three methods of administering and scoring the CDI are available. In the first, the child marks the responses on a special Multi-Health Systems QuikScore form. The form can be used to score the test accurately and rapidly transfer the scores to a Profile form for visual display and comparison with responses obtained in an appropriate normative group. Conversion to T-scores is also automatically done by the QuikScore form. The QuikScore form is self-contained and includes all materials needed to administer, score, and profile the CDI.

Alternatively, the CDI can be administered with a paper and pencil form. A computer version that is scored using an IBM-compatible microcomputer is available. The computer scores are converted to T-scores and plotted. A listing of individual item problem responses is given in an easily used format. Computer-generated narratives interpret the meaning of the score profiles using narrative rules developed through collaboration between Multi-Health Systems, Inc., and the author of the scale. Although it is preferable to administer the CDI in an individual setting, group administration is possible.

To calculate the total CDI score, the scores for each item are added. The total score ranges from 0 to 54. The CDI Short Form is scored in a similar manner, but there are no factors or subscales on the Short Form.

Total and factor scores are compared with norms for appropriate groups of children. The normative sample included 1,266 Florida public school students (592 boys and 674 girls) in grades 2–8. Approximately 77% of the sample were Caucasian, and 23% were African American, American Indian, or Hispanic. The children came primarily from middle-class families. About 20% of the sample came from single-parent families.

Scores are interpreted using the normative data, which are divided by sex and two age groups, 7–12 years and 13–17 years. Four profile columns are provided for older and younger boys and older and younger girls. High scores indicate problem behavior. Specific items have not been designated as critical; however, item 9, which asks about suicide, may be especially important for screening children in clinical settings.

PRACTICAL ISSUES

The CDI has been judged to be readable at the first-grade level. It takes 15 minutes or less to complete the CDI.

The CDI can be scored and profiled in less than 10 minutes using the Multi-Health Systems QuikScore forms, and the CDI Short Form can be scored and profiled in less than 5 minutes. The computer versions are scored and profiled in just a few seconds. The computer administration time is similar to that required for the paper forms. The QuikScore forms include all of the necessary elements for administering, scoring, and profiling the instrument. Forms contain special aids that make scoring quick and easy and minimize the potential for keying errors. The CDI is copyrighted by Multi-Health Systems, Inc. Questionnaires, manuals (Kovacs 1992), and scoring materials, for both the CDI and the CDI Short Form, can be obtained from

Multi-Health Systems, Inc.
908 Niagara Falls Boulevard
North Tonawanda, NY 14120-2060
Phone: 800-456-3003
Internet: www.mhs.com

The CDI complete kit is available from Multi-Health Systems, Inc., for $55.00. The kit includes the manual and 25 QuikScore forms. The manual and the CDI QuikScore forms may also be purchased separately.

PSYCHOMETRIC PROPERTIES

Reliability

Cronbach's alphas for CDI total scores range from 0.71 (pediatric medical outpatients) to 0.89 (clinic-referred youth). Alphas for the factor scores range from 0.59 (Interpersonal Problems) to 0.68 (Negative Self-Esteem). The 1- to 2-week test-retest reliability coefficients range from 0.38 (psychiatrically healthy youths) to 0.87 (psychiatric inpatients). The majority of studies with psychiatrically healthy youth and psychiatric outpatients and inpatients report 1-week to 1-month test-retest reliabilities >0.60. The 1-year stability coefficient ranges from 0.41 to 0.69.

Validity

The CDI has been found to correlate with other measures of childhood depression, including the Center for Epidemiologic Studies Depression Scale for Children, the Reynolds Adolescent Depression Scale (RADS) (p. 347), the Depression scale of the Child Behavior Checklist

Youth Self Report (YSR) (p. 310), the Hamilton Rating Scale for Depression (Ham-D) (p. 526), and the Depression scale of the Child Assessment Schedule (CAS) (p. 318). The CDI has also been found to correlate with measures of other related constructs, such as anxiety (e.g., the Revised Children's Manifest Anxiety Scale [RCMAS] [p. 336] and the Fear Survey Schedule for Children—Revised [Ollendick 1983]), attributional style (e.g., the Children's Attributional Style Questionnaire [Kaslow et al. 1984]), and social competence (e.g., the Perceived Competence Scale for Children [Harter 1982] and the Matson Evaluation of Social Skills With Youngsters [Matson et al. 1983]).

Numerous studies have found that children with depressive disorders score significantly higher on the CDI than psychiatrically healthy control subjects or nondepressed children with other disorders. The CDI has been shown to distinguish between children with major depressive disorder and children with major depressive disorder in partial remission ($t = 2.17$), between children with major depressive disorder and children with adjustment disorder ($t = 2.61$), and between children with major depressive disorder and nondepressed, pathological control subjects ($t = -2.70$).

Although data suggest that depressed children can be distinguished from children with other disorders and from psychiatrically healthy control subjects on the basis of CDI scores, further information on the scale's specificity and sensitivity are needed. In one study of 50 psychiatric outpatients, there was a significant difference between the CDI scores of clinically depressed and nondepressed subjects with clinical diagnoses determined on the basis of DSM-III criteria ($t = 8.58$). Using a cut point of 12, the CDI correctly distinguished between clinical depression and nondepression in 88% of the subjects. In a study of 170 hospitalized inpatient youth ages 7–13, using a cut point of 12, sensitivity and specificity were 61.2% and 57.6%, respectively. Further research is necessary to support the discriminant validity of the scale.

Some evidence suggests that the CDI is sensitive to change. In a study of the clinical course of a group of depressed youths, CDI scores were higher in children when they met full DSM-III criteria for major depressive disorder than when the same children were clinically judged to be improved. Other studies demonstrated reductions in CDI scores from before to after intervention. In a study of 250 hospitalized patients with affective disorders (70 of whom were children), there was a trend for depression scores on the CDI to decrease more over a 21-day period in subjects receiving imipramine treatment than in those receiving placebo. Additional data from randomized clinical trials are necessary to further support the measure's sensitivity to change.

CLINICAL UTILITY

The CDI is designed to be used as a screening instrument or as a measure of symptom severity. The CDI is useful for providing the clinician with structured, age and gender norm-referenced information about the child's depressive symptomatology. The CDI has acceptable internal consistency and test-retest reliability and is sensitive to changes over time. The scale's discriminant validity is not well established. The scale has been used widely in epidemiological studies and to screen for depression in children. The utility of the measure for the screening of depressed children is compromised by the fact that this scale, like other self-rating scales for children, yields high levels of false-negative diagnoses.

REFERENCES AND SUGGESTED READINGS

Craighead WE, Curry JF, Ilardi SS: Relationship of Children's Depression Inventory factors to major depression among adolescents. Psychological Assessment 7:171–176, 1995

Harter S: The Perceived Competence Scale for Children. Child Dev 53:87–97, 1982

Kaslow N, Rehm L, Siegel A: Social-cognitive and cognitive correlates of depression in children. J Abnorm Child Psychol 12:605–620, 1984

Kovacs M: Rating scales to assess depression in school-aged children. Acta Paedopsychiatrica 46:305–315, 1981

Kovacs M: The Children's Depression Inventory Manual. Toronto, Multi-Health Systems, 1992

Matson JL, Rotatari AG, Helsel WJ: Development of a rating scale to measure social skills in children: the Matson Evaluation of Social Skills With Youngsters (MESSY). Behav Res Ther 21:335–340, 1983

Ollendick TH: Reliability and validity of the Revised Fear Survey Schedule for Children (FSSC-R). Behav Res Ther 21:685–692, 1983

Saylor CF, Finch AJ, Caskin CH, et al: Children's Depression Inventory: investigation of procedures and correlates. Journal of the American Academy of Child Psychiatry 23:626–628, 1984

Saylor CF, Finch AJ, Spirito A, et al: The Children's Depression Inventory: a systematic evaluation of psychometric properties. J Consult Clin Psychol 52:955–967, 1984

Smucker MR, Craighead WE, Craighead LW, et al: Normative and reliability data for the Children's Depression Inventory. J Abnorm Child Psychol 14:25–39, 1986

Weiss B, Weisz JR, Politano M, et al: Developmental differences in the factor structure of the Children's Depression Inventory. Psychological Assessment 3:38–45, 1991

Reynolds Adolescent Depression Scale (RADS)

W. M. Reynolds

GOALS

The Reynolds Adolescent Depression Scale (RADS) (Reynolds 1986) is a self-report measure designed to assess depressive symptomatology in adolescents. The scale covers a range of symptoms associated with depression, including cognitive, motoric-vegetative, somatic, and interpersonal symptoms. A child version of the RADS, the Reynolds Child Depression Scale (RCDS), is also available but is not reviewed here.

DESCRIPTION

The RADS is a self-report measure for assessing depressive symptoms in youth ages 13–18 years. The RADS consists of 30 items with a 4-point Likert response format. The respondent indicates whether the item has occurred almost never = 1, hardly ever = 2, sometimes = 3, or most of the time = 4. Adolescents are asked to indicate how they usually feel. Items are worded in the present tense (e.g., "I feel lonely"). Several of the domains include more than one item tapping the area. Seven items

that are inconsistent with depression are reverse scored (e.g., "I feel happy"). Items were selected on the basis of symptom criteria for major depression and dysthymic disorder delineated according to DSM-III standards.

The total possible score on the RADS ranges from 30 to 120. The higher the score, the greater the level of depressive symptomatology. As part of its construction, standardization, and validation process, the RADS was administered to more than 10,000 adolescents. In the standardization sample (N = 2,460), the mean score for the total sample was 60.18, with a standard deviation of 14.29. The mean and standard deviation were 57.51 (13.41) for boys and 62.85 (14.66) for girls. The mean item score for the total sample was 2.01 (ranging from 1 to 4). Separate sample norms for boys and girls are provided.

According to the developer of the scale, a cutoff score of 77 can be used to indicate the need for further evaluation aimed at diagnosing depressive psychopathology. In several studies, a score of 77 was shown to indicate a level of symptoms associated with clinical depression.

Several items have been identified as critical items on the basis of their ability to discriminate between clinically depressed and nondepressed adolescents: "I feel like hiding from people" (item 6), "I feel like hurting myself" (item 14), "I feel I am no good" (item 20), "I feel worried" (item 26), "I like eating meals" (item 29), and "I feel like nothing I do helps any more" (item 30). As a general rule, endorsement of four or more of these items is considered to be indicative of a serious problem, regardless of the total score.

PRACTICAL ISSUES

The RADS is published by Psychological Assessment Resources, Inc. and was copyrighted in 1986. The various versions of the RADS and the manual (Reynolds 1987) can be obtained from

Psychological Assessment Resources, Inc.
P.O. Box 998
Odessa, FL 33556
Phone: 800-331-TEST (800-331-8378)

Copies of research reports, conference presentations, and articles about the RADS can be requested from Dr. William Reynolds, through Psychological Assessment Resources, Inc. A RADS introductory kit may be purchased for $93.00 and includes the manual, 50 hand-scored answer sheets, and the scoring key.

Three forms of the RADS—Form HS, Form I, and Form G—are available, and each requires 5–10 minutes to complete. Form HS is a hand-scored version appropriate for individual and small group administration; it is identified with the heading "About Myself." A key is used for scoring. Forms I and G are optical character recognition answer sheets that are machine scored by an optical scanner. Form I is for individual or small group administration, and Form G is for administration in large groups. A mail-in scoring service is provided by the publisher. For Form I, a 4- to 5-page report with in-depth analysis of item responses is provided. For Form G, which is designed to be administered to a large group of adolescents, the following information is provided: summary data for the group; a list of adolescents with scores at or above the 95th percentile; a list of individuals with scores at or above the clinical cutoff; a list of those with invalid protocols; and total scores, means, and ranges.

PSYCHOMETRIC PROPERTIES

Reliability

Internal consistency reliability (Cronbach's alpha) has been reported to be high, ranging from 0.90 to 0.95. For the total standardization sample, split-half reliability was 0.91. In a study that examined reliability separately for African American ($n = 125$) and Caucasian ($n = 602$) students, alpha coefficients were 0.90 and 0.93, respectively.

The following test-retest reliabilities were reported: 0.80 in a study of 6-week reliability with 104 10th and 11th graders, 0.79 in a study of 3-month stability in a sample of 415 9th through 12th graders, and 0.63 over a 1-year period in a sample of 601 adolescents in 10th through 12th grades.

Validity

In a study that compared the RADS with the clinician-administered Hamilton Rating Scale for Depression (Ham-D) (p. 526) ($N = 111$ depressed and nondepressed adolescents screened in school), the correlation between measures was 0.83. In a second administration to 109 of the 111 adolescents 12 weeks later, the correlation be-

tween measures was 0.84. The RADS has also been shown to correlate highly with other self-report scales of depressive symptomatology.

Studies have shown correlations ranging from 0.68 to 0.76 (median correlation of 0.73) with the 21-item Beck Depression Inventory (BDI) (p. 519), the 20-item Center for Epidemiologic Studies Depression Scale (CES-D) (p. 523), the 20-item Zung Self-Rating Depression Scale (Zung SDS) (p. 534), and the 27-item Children's Depression Inventory (CDI) (p. 344). The RADS has also been shown to be significantly correlated (ranging from 0.50 to 0.80) with measures of depression-related constructs, including hopelessness, suicidality, learned helplessness, loneliness, and anxiety.

In a study of 111 adolescents, a score of 77 on the RADS was used to identify adolescents as depressed or nondepressed, and the Ham-D (p. 526) was used as a clinical criterion measure. A Yule's Y coefficient of 0.71 was computed from a 2×2 table in which 86 subjects were identified as nondepressed according to both measures, 13 were identified as depressed on both measures, 4 were identified as depressed on the RADS and not on the Ham-D, and 8 were identified as depressed on the Ham-D but not on the RADS.

In a study of 265 inpatients, ages 12–18 years, moderately strong correlations were found between the National Institute of Mental Health Diagnostic Interview Schedule for Children (NIMH-DISC-2.3) (p. 305) symptom counts and RADS scores. In this clinical sample, RADS scores were found to be superior to scores from the Children's Depression Scale (Ticher and Lang 1983) in identifying children with NIMH-DISC-2.3 diagnoses of depression.

Some evidence suggests that the RADS is sensitive to treatment effects. One study used the RADS to compare cognitive-behavioral and relaxation training treatment conditions with a waiting list control group. After the test, subjects in both active treatment groups demonstrated significant improvements in depressive symptomatology, as measured by the RADS ($F = 5.85$). In contrast, the wait list control group had a stable level of depressive symptoms over the 5-week treatment.

CLINICAL UTILITY

The RADS measures clinically relevant levels of depressive symptoms in adolescents. It can be used as a screening measure for the identification of depression in school-based and clinical populations, for research on depression, and for evaluation of treatment outcomes. The RADS can be administered individually or in a group setting. Numerous studies using a wide variety of samples have demonstrated that the RADS is a reliable instrument, in terms of both its internal reliability and its test-retest reliability. The RADS has been shown to be highly related to scores on the Ham-D (p. 526) during clinical interviews and to other scales of depressive symptoms and related problems. The cutoff score facilitates the identification of individuals who show a clinically significant level of symptoms. Further information is needed on the sensitivity and specificity of the RADS. There is initial evidence that the RADS is sensitive to clinical change.

The RADS has been used successfully with different populations, including mentally retarded adolescents and those with emotional and behavioral problems. It is the only measure specifically designed to measure depressive symptoms in adolescents. It should be emphasized, however, that the measure is not tied to DSM-IV diagnostic criteria.

REFERENCES AND SUGGESTED READINGS

King CA, Katz SH, Ghaziuddin N, et al: Diagnosis and assessment of depression and suicidality using the NIMH Diagnostic Interview Schedule for Children (DISC-2.3). J Abnorm Child Psychol 25:173–181, 1997

Reynolds WM: Depression in children and adolescents: phenomenology, evaluation, and treatment. School Psychology Review 13:171–182, 1984

Reynolds WM: A model for the screening and identification of depressed children and adolescents in school settings. Professional School Psychology 1:117–129, 1986

Reynolds WM: Reynolds Adolescent Depression Scale: Professional Manual. Odessa, FL, Psychological Assessment Resources, 1987

Reynolds WM, Mazza JJ: Reliability and validity of the Reynolds Adolescent Depression Scale with young adolescents. Journal of School Psychology 36:353–376,1998

Ticher M, Lang M: The Children's Depression Scale: review and further developments, in Affective Disorders in Childhood and Adolesence: An Update. Edited by Cantwell DP, Carlson GA. New York, Spectrum, 1983, pp 181–202

Short Mood and Feelings Questionnaire (SMFQ)
A. Angold and E. J. Costello

GOALS

The Short Mood and Feelings Questionnaire (SMFQ) (Angold et al. 1995; Costello and Angold 1988) is a brief self-report measure of core depressive symptoms in children and adolescents ages 8–16 years. It was designed to be used primarily as a screening instrument to identify a population to be assessed in a more intensive manner. It was also designed to assess depressive symptomatology in clinical and epidemiological studies in which depression is not the primary focus but for which some measure of depressive symptoms is required. The items focus primarily on affective and cognitive symptoms of depression but also assess symptoms of tiredness, restlessness, and poor concentration.

DESCRIPTION

The SMFQ is a 13-item self-report measure of childhood and adolescent depression derived from the 34-item Mood and Feelings Questionnaire (Costello and Angold 1988). For each item, the child is asked to respond on a 3-point scale, with 2 = true, 1 = sometimes true, and 0 = not true. The respondent is asked to report on the occurrence of certain feelings and actions in the past 2 weeks. Sample items are provided in Example 18–6. A 13-item parent-report form parallels the child self-report form and presents items identical to those in the child-report form. Parents are asked to rate their children's feelings and actions in the past week.

A total score is derived by adding the responses on the SMFQ. The range of scores on both the child self-report and the parent-report measures is 0–26. Mean

EXAMPLE 18–6 ■ **Sample items from the Short Mood and Feelings Questionnaire**

I felt miserable or unhappy.

I felt lonely.

I did everything wrong.

I found it hard to think properly or concentrate.

Reprinted with permission from E. J. Costello.

scores on the child version (SMFQ-C) were reported to be 4.68 (4.66) for the pediatric sample and 7.14 (5.19) for the psychiatric sample (ages 6–17 years). Mean scores of 2.15 (3.27) and 5.79 (4.80) for pediatric and psychiatric samples were reported for the parent version (SMFQ-P). A combined score of 13 (summing the child and parent versions) has been used as a cutoff score indicating the need for further evaluation.

PRACTICAL ISSUES

It takes less than 5 minutes to complete the SMFQ, which can then be scored immediately and easily. If necessary, the child self-report measure can be read to the child. The SMFQ (both self-report and parent-report versions) was copyrighted in 1997 and can be obtained from

> Adrian Angold, M.R.C.Psych.
> Developmental Epidemiology Program
> Duke University Medical Center
> Box 3454
> Durham, NC 27710-3454
> Phone: 919-687-4686, ext. 227

There is no published manual. The cost of the SMFQ package is $10.00.

PSYCHOMETRIC PROPERTIES

Reliability

High internal reliability (Cronbach's alpha) for the SMFQ-C (alpha = 0.87) and the SMFQ-P (alpha = 0.87) has been reported for pediatric and psychiatric sam-

ples. One study of an inpatient adolescent psychiatric sample found 1-week stability of 0.75 (intraclass correlation coefficient). Twelve-month stability coefficients were reported for a community sample of first-, fourth-, and ninth-grade boys; they ranged from 0.28 for first-grade boys to 0.48 for ninth-grade boys.

Validity

The SMFQ-C correlates with the Children's Depression Inventory (CDI) (p. 344) (r = 0.67) and the National Institute of Mental Health Diagnostic Interview Schedule for Children (NIMH-DISC) (p. 305) Depression scale (r = 0.65). The SMFQ-C and the SMFQ-P are correlated with each other (r = 0.30).

The SMFQ-C and the SMFQ-P were shown to discriminate between a psychiatric group of 48 consecutive referrals to a child psychiatric outpatient clinic and a pediatric group of 125 children. Using depression scores on the NIMH-DISC as the criterion, the SMFQ-C was found to discriminate depression status better than the SMFQ-P for the full range of potential cutoff scores (on the basis of receiver operating characteristic analyses). The combination of parent and child reports predicted group status better than either version did alone. A sensitivity of 70% and a specificity of 85% were reported using a cutoff score of ≥12 on the combined SMFQ-P and SMFQ-C. The 13 items of the SMFQ-C achieved 60% sensitivity and 85% specificity using a cutoff score of ≥8. A score of 8 has been recommended as the cutoff for calculating optimal sensitivity and specificity.

The unifactorial composition of the SMFQ and invariant factor structure across different age and race groups were supported in three large cohorts of randomly selected high-risk boys.

CLINICAL UTILITY

The SMFQ can be used as an initial screen in a general population sample to identify possible subjects to be followed up with a diagnostic interview measure. It has been shown to be usable with children and adolescents up to age 17 years; its screening properties have been demonstrated for children ages 6–11 years. The SMFQ-C has been shown to have better discriminatory abilities than the SMFQ-P, and it has high sensitivity and specificity when used alone. However, the combination of both versions of the measure achieves the highest levels of sensitivity and specificity. No data are available on treatment sensitivity; thus, the utility of the SMFQ for monitoring treatment effects is unknown.

The SMFQ can also be used as an epidemiological screening measure for depression in children and adolescents. It has been shown to be a unifactorial scale that taps an underlying construct of general depression. Moderate 1-year stability data in boys (especially older boys) and the brief nature of the questionnaire suggest that it could be used in repeated assessments. Further data on test-retest reliability, especially with girls and young children, and treatment responsiveness are necessary to support the utility of the SMFQ.

REFERENCES AND SUGGESTED READINGS

Angold A, Costello EJ, Messer SC, et al: Development of a short questionnaire for use in epidemiological studies of depression in children and adolescents. International Journal of Methods in Psychiatric Research 5:237–249, 1995

Costello EJ, Angold A: Scales to assess child and adolescent depression: checklist, screens, and nets. J Am Acad Child Adolesc Psychiatry 27:726–737, 1988

Messer SC, Angold A, Costello EJ, et al: Development of a short questionnaire for use in epidemiological studies of depression in children and adolescents: factor composition and structure across development. International Journal of Methods in Psychiatric Research 5:251–262, 1995

Autism Diagnostic Interview—Revised (ADI-R)

C. Lord, M. Rutter, and A. Le Couteur

GOALS

The Autism Diagnostic Interview—Revised (ADI-R) (Lord et al. 1994) is a clinical, diagnostic instrument that

was developed to assess autism in children and adults. The ADI-R provides a diagnostic algorithm for autism as described in both ICD-10 and DSM-IV. The ADI-R is a newly modified and shortened version of the Autism Diagnostic Interview (ADI) (Le Couteur et al. 1989). The revision was intended to improve the ability of the ADI to differentiate autism from other disorders, such as Rett's syndrome, fragile X syndrome, and disintegrative disorders, especially in very young children, and to differentiate between deviance and delay. The ADI-R is appropriate for children and adults with mental ages about 18 months and above.

DESCRIPTION

The ADI-R is a standardized, semistructured clinical interview for caregivers of children and adults. The interview contains 111 items and focuses on behaviors in three content areas: Quality of Reciprocal Social Interaction (e.g., emotional sharing, offering and seeking comfort, social smiling, and responding to other children); Communication and Language (e.g., stereotyped utterances, pronoun reversal, and social usage of language); and Repetitive, Restricted, and Stereotyped Interests and Behavior (e.g., unusual preoccupations, hand and finger mannerisms, and unusual sensory interests). The measure also includes other items relevant for treatment planning, such as self-injury and overactivity. Responses are scored by the clinician, on the basis of the caregiver's description of the patient's behavior.

Questions are organized according to content area, and definitions are provided for all behavioral items. Within the area of Communication and Language, for example, "delay or total lack of language not compensated for by gesture" is further broken down into specific behavioral items: pointing to express interest, conventional gestures, nodding head, and head shaking. Similarly, within the area of Quality of Reciprocal Social Interaction, "lack of socio-emotional reciprocity and modulation to context" includes the following behaviors: use of other's body, offers comfort, inappropriate facial expressions, quality of social overtures, and appropriateness of social response.

All questions concern current behavior, with the exception of a few behaviors that occur only during specific age periods. In these cases, specific age restrictions are given. For example, items on imaginative play and group play are coded only for behavior displayed in children ages 4–10 years. Questions about circumscribed interests are scored only for children ages 4 years and older. Questions about reciprocal friendships are scored only for children ages 5 years and older.

The interview starts with an introductory question followed by 9 questions about the subject's early development. The next 31 questions cover verbal and nonverbal communication. Questions 42–69 ask about social development and play. The next 16 questions deal with interests and behaviors. The final 26 questions ask about general behavior, including questions about memory skills, motor skills, overactivity, and fainting.

The interview generates scores in each of the three content areas (i.e., Communication and Language, Quality of Reciprocal Social Interaction, and Repetitive, Restricted, and Stereotyped Interests and Behavior). Elevated scores indicate problematic behavior. Scores are determined on the basis of the clinician's judgment following the caregiver's report of the child's behavior and development. For each item, the clinician gives a score ranging from 0 to 3. A score of 0 is given when "behavior of the type specified is/was not ever present." A score of 1 is given when "behavior of the type specified is/was present but is not sufficiently severe, frequent, or marked to meet the criteria for a score of 2." A score of 2 indicates "definite abnormal behavior." A score of 3 is reserved for "extreme severity" of the specified behavior. (The authors of the measure recode scores of 3 as 2 in computing algorithms.)

For a diagnosis of autism, a child must meet criteria in each of the three content areas, as well as exhibit some abnormality in at least one content area by age 36 months. The same algorithm is used for children from mental ages 18 months through adulthood, with three versions of the interview containing minor modifications: 1) a lifetime version, 2) a version that assesses current behavior, and 3) a version for use with children under age 4 years. The algorithm specifies a minimum score in each area to yield a diagnosis of autism as described in ICD-10 and DSM-IV. The cutoff total score for the Communication and Language content area is 8 for verbal subjects and 7 for nonverbal subjects. For all subjects, the cutoff score for Quality of Reciprocal Social Interaction is 10, and the cutoff score for Repetitive, Restricted, and Stereotyped Interests and Behavior is 3.

PRACTICAL ISSUES

This interviewer-based instrument requires substantial training in administration and scoring. It takes a highly trained clinician approximately 90 minutes to administer the ADI-R to the parent of a 3- or 4-year-old suspected of having autism. The interview may take somewhat longer when administered to parents of older children or adults. Training workshops are available annually in both the United Kingdom and North America. Training videotapes that describe the organization and purpose of the ADI-R and provide detailed examples of administration and scoring are also available. The ADI-R and related materials can be obtained from

> Catherine Lord
> Department of Psychiatry
> University of Chicago
> 5841 S. Maryland Avenue, MC 3077
> Chicago, IL 60637
> Phone: 773-702-9707

The measure is copyrighted and is available for $20.00. The ADI-R has been translated into Danish, Dutch, French, German, Korean, Norwegian, Spanish, and Swedish.

PSYCHOMETRIC PROPERTIES

Reliability

A study examined the reliability of the ADI-R in a sample of 10 children with autistic disorder (mean age 49 months) and 10 children with mental handicaps or language impairment (mean age 50 months). The autistic children had received independent clinical diagnoses on the basis of DSM-III and ICD-10 criteria by a clinical psychologist or child psychiatrist. The mentally handicapped children and language-impaired children had never received a diagnosis of autism or pervasive developmental disorder according to teachers, parents, and hospital records. All children in both groups had shown significant language delays before age 36 months. The two groups did not differ in chronological age. Clinicians completed the ADI-R with the child's caregiver. The videotaped interview was then independently scored by trained medical or graduate students who did not know the subject's diagnosis. Mothers of six of the children (four autistic and two mentally handicapped) were reinterviewed 2–3 months later by different blinded raters. The following internal consistency reliabilities (Cronbach's alphas) were reported: Repetitive, Restricted, and Stereotyped Interests and Behavior, 0.69; Communication and Language, 0.84; and Quality of Reciprocal Social Interaction, 0.95. Mean weighted kappas for six rater pairs ranged from 0.73 to 0.78 for all items. Mean percentage of agreement across all items ranged from 0.90 to 0.93 for each pair; agreement for algorithm items exceeded 0.92 for all pairs. Intraclass correlation coefficients for area scores ranged from 0.93 to 0.97. Mean joint agreement (interrater agreement and test-retest reliability) over a 2- to 3-month period was 91%.

In a study of 51 autistic and 43 nonautistic, mentally handicapped preschoolers that used procedures similar to those in the study described earlier, weighted kappa values for joint reliability (calculated using percentage of exact agreement) ranged from 0.62 to 0.96. Test-retest reliabilities using intraclass correlation coefficients were >0.90 in all domains and subdomains.

A reliability study of the German form of the ADI-R with 22 individuals ages 5–29 years (mean age 13.5 years) demonstrated high levels of joint reliabilities (intraclass correlation coefficients) for all three domains: Quality of Reciprocal Social Interaction, 0.75; Communication and Language, 0.77; and Repetitive, Restricted, and Stereotyped Interests and Behavior, 0.80.

Validity

In the study of 94 preschoolers described earlier, the ADI-R was able to discriminate between groups of autistic children and nonautistic children with mental handicaps or language impairment. Using analysis of variance (ANOVA), all 15 social behaviors comprising the algorithm for the area of Quality of Reciprocal Social Interaction showed significant diagnostic differences across the groups (F scores ranged from 7.5 for showing and directing attention to 70 for offers comfort). Other social items not included in the algorithm were also different for the two groups of children (e.g., attention to voice, social smile at age 2, joining activities, and sense of humor). Although group differences were observed on items of separation anxiety, nearly 50% of the autistic preschoolers did not score in the abnormal range (i.e., they showed normal signs of separation anxiety).

Group differences in all subdomain totals within the social realm were also significant; autistic children scored higher (mean = 20.84, SD = 4.5) than the children with mental handicaps or language impairment (mean = 7.63, SD = 6.4). All autistic children had scores of at least 10, which is the designated cutoff score for this area. It should be noted that 11 of the 43 children with mental handicaps or language impairment had scores of ≥10, and 9 of the 11 were nonverbal and had mental age equivalents of less than 18 months. Within the Communication and Language area, significant group differences were observed for gesture and play, and all items within the subdomains were significantly different across groups. Group differences were observed for groups of verbal children with autism compared with verbal children with mental handicaps or language impairment and for nonverbal children with autism compared with nonverbal children with mental handicaps or language impairment. All 14 verbal children with autism had scores above the designated cutoff score of 8; 3 of the 14 verbal children with mental handicaps or language impairment also had scores in the autistic range (≥8). All of the nonverbal children with autism and 11 of the 28 nonverbal children with mental handicaps or language impairment fell in the autistic range (≥7 for nonverbal children) in the Communication and Language domain. All seven items and the mean total algorithm scores in the Repetitive, Restricted, and Stereotyped Interests and Behavior domain were significantly different for autistic children (mean = 4.86, SD = 1.5) and children with mental handicaps or language impairment (mean = 2.12, SD = 1.83). Of the 51 autistic children, 50 scored 3 or higher in this domain (3 is the cutoff score). Of the 43 children with mental handicaps or language impairment, 16 received scores ≥3.

Overall, with the exception of the one child who scored a 2 instead of the required 3 points in the Repetitive, Restricted, and Stereotyped Interests and Behavior area, all autistic children met the suggested algorithm cutoff score for autism across the three domains. Only two children with mental handicaps or language impairment and mental ages of 18 months or older were incorrectly categorized as autistic, and both the children were 2 years old.

CLINICAL UTILITY

The ADI-R is a semistructured instrument for diagnosing autism in children and adults with mental ages of 18 months and older. The instrument has been shown to be reliable and to successfully differentiate young children with autism from those with mental handicaps and language impairments. The revised version of the instrument has been tested primarily with parents of preschoolers presenting for the first time with possible autism. In this population, the algorithms, determined on the basis of DSM-IV and ICD-10 criteria, have been shown to have high levels of sensitivity and moderate levels of specificity.

The greatest difficulty is in the overdiagnosis of autism in young, severely mentally handicapped children. In one study, nearly 60% of the nonautistic children with no speech at all met criteria for autism in each of the three diagnostic areas. All of these children had mental ages of less than 18 months. Items concerning communication do not appear to be useful in differentiating autistic preschoolers from other children with severe language delays.

Further research is required to test the ability of the ADI-R to discriminate between children with autism and children with other pervasive developmental disorders. The utility of the instrument for monitoring treatment effects is unknown.

REFERENCES AND SUGGESTED READINGS

Le Couteur A, Rutter M, Lord C, et al: Autism Diagnostic Interview: a standardized investigator-based instrument. J Autism Dev Disord 19:363–387, 1989

Lord C, Rutter M, Storochuk S, et al: Using the ADI-R to diagnose autism in preschool children. Infant Mental Health Journal 14:234–251, 1993

Lord C, Rutter M, Le Couteur A: Autism Diagnostic Interview Revised: a revised version of a diagnostic interview for caregivers of individuals with possible pervasive developmental disorders. J Autism Dev Disord 24:659–685, 1994

Poutska F, Lisch S, Ruhl D, et al: The standardized diagnosis of autism, Autism Diagnostic Interview—Revised: interrater reliability of the German form of the interview. Psychopathology 29:145–153, 1996

Yale Global Tic Severity Scale (YGTSS)

J. F. Leckman, M. A. Riddle, M. T. Hardin, S. I. Ort, K. L. Swartz, J. Stevenson, and D. J. Cohen

GOALS

The Yale Global Tic Severity Scale (YGTSS) (Leckman et al. 1988) was developed as a clinician-rated measure of tic severity and degree of impairment in individuals with Tourette's syndrome and other tic disorders. The YGTSS provides an evaluation of the number, frequency, intensity, complexity, and interference of motor and phonic tics.

DESCRIPTION

The YGTSS is a clinical instrument designed to be used by experienced clinicians for the assessment of tic severity in children, adolescents, and adults. It is a semistructured interview conducted with the patient and parents. The YGTSS supersedes the Tourette's Syndrome Global Scale (TSGS) (Harcherik et al. 1984), which was created by the same developers.

First, a Tic Symptom Checklist is completed by the clinician, on the basis of the patient and parent report as well as tics observed by the clinician during the interview. The symptom list covers a description of motor and phonic tics that were present during the week preceding the interview. The Tic Symptom Checklist consists of a list of simple and complex motor tics and simple and complex phonic tics. There are 12 items provided for simple motor tics (e.g., eye blinking, shoulder shrugs, and hand jerks) and 20 items for complex motor tics (e.g., facial movements, bending, and copropraxia). There are 2 items for simple phonic symptoms (e.g., coughing and sniffing) and 8 items for complex phonic symptoms (e.g., coprolalia, syllables, and disinhibited speech).

On completion of the semistructured interview, the clinician rates the severity of the motor and phonic tics along each of five dimensions: number, frequency, intensity, complexity, and interference. All dimensions are rated on 6-point ordinal scales, ranging from 0 = none/

absent to 5 = severe/always. Descriptive statements and examples are provided as anchor points. In addition to these 10 scale scores, the clinician rates the patient's overall level of impairment on a 6-point ordinal scale, ranging from 0 = none to 50 = severe, in increments of 10. Moderate (30) is described as "tics associated with some clear problems in self-esteem, family life, social acceptance, or school or job functioning." The clinician gives one total impairment score for overall impairment due to both motor and phonic tics.

Total Motor Tic and Total Phonic Tic scores are derived by summing the scores of the five severity dimensions of motor tics and phonic tics, respectively. Ranges in these scores are as follows: Total Motor Tic score, 0–23; Total Phonic Tic score, 0–21; and Total Tic score, 0–42. The Total Motor Tic and Total Phonic Tic scores are summed and constitute the Total Tic score. The Global Severity score is derived by summing the Total Tic score and the Impairment Rating score. The range in scores is 0–42 for the Impairment Rating score and 4–87 for the Global Severity score.

PRACTICAL ISSUES

The YGTSS was developed for use by experienced clinicians. The clinician interviews the patient with other informants (e.g., parents) present and also separately. The assessment takes between 15 and 20 minutes. The YGTSS can be obtained from the author:

> James Leckman, M.D.
> Yale University Child Study Center
> 230 South Frontage Road
> P.O. Box 207900
> New Haven, CT 06520
> Phone: 203-785-2511

The measure has been translated into Dutch, German, Hebrew, Japanese, Korean, Portuguese, and Turkish.

The YGTSS is included on the CD-ROM that accompanies this handbook.

PSYCHOMETRIC PROPERTIES

Reliability

Internal consistencies of the YGTSS were reported to be high in a study of 105 children and adults with tic dis-

orders (82 of the 105 subjects were under age 18 years). Item scores were found to be highly correlated with subscale scores, ranging from 0.78 for complexity of phonic tics to 0.90 for intensity of phonic tics. As expected, item scores were less highly correlated with the Global Severity score, ranging from 0.64 for frequency and intensity of motor tics to 0.74 for number of motor tics.

In a study that evaluated joint agreement using a subset of 20 patients, intraclass correlation coefficients for three raters of 20 subjects were 0.78 for the Total Motor Tic score, 0.91 for the Total Phonic Tic score, 0.84 for the Total Tic score, 0.80 for the Impairment Rating score, and 0.85 for the Global Severity score. Joint reliability of the YGTSS was also assessed in a separate study of 20 patients (mean age 11.8 years) with a diagnosis of Tourette's syndrome. Three raters experienced with tic disorders rated the parent and child report of clinical symptoms (history), observed behavior, and overall clinical impression. The Spearman rho correlations were 0.94, 0.81, and 0.93, respectively.

Validity

The validity of the YGTSS has been supported in studies that compared the scale with other measures of tic severity, such as the Tourette's Syndrome Global Scale (TSGS) (Harcherik et al. 1984), the Shapiro Tourette Syndrome Severity Scale (TSSS) (Shapiro and Shapiro 1984), the Tourette Syndrome—Clinical Global Impression Scale (TS-CGI) (Leckman et al. 1988), and the Hopkins Motor/Vocal Tic Scale (Singer and Rosenberg 1989). The Total Motor Tic, Total Phonic Tic, and Total Tic scales of the YGTSS correlated significantly with the respective scales of the TSGS, with correlations of 0.86 for Total Motor Tic scores, 0.91 for Total Phonic Tic scores, and 0.90 for Total Tic scores. Correlations with the total scale from the Shapiro TSSS were 0.76 for Total Motor Tic, 0.54 for Total Phonic Tic, and 0.71 for Total Tic scores. Similarly, correlations with the total scale of the TS-CGI were 0.81 for Total Motor Tic, 0.65 for Total Phonic Tic, and 0.80 for Total Tic scores. The YGTSS Impairment Rating score and Global Severity score were also significantly correlated with the total scales from these three instruments; correlations ranged from 0.59 to 0.82. In a separate study of 20 patients with Tourette's syndrome, the YGTSS score was significantly correlated with the Hopkins Motor/Vocal Tic Scale total score (r = 0.87).

A study of tic counts in 20 adult subjects using videotaped observations examined the relation between the YGTSS and independently observed tic counts. The YGTSS Total Motor Tic, Total Phonic Tic, and Total Tic scores correlated significantly with observed motor ($r = 0.53$), phonic ($r = 0.44$), and total tic counts ($r = 0.62$).

Several studies have examined the relations between the YGTSS and measures of other types of psychopathology. In a study of the YGTSS's relation to scales of attention-deficit/hyperactivity disorder symptom severity and obsessive-compulsive disorder symptom severity, no significant correlations were found with the attention-deficit/hyperactivity disorder scale, but modest, highly significant associations ($r = 0.39$ for the Global Severity scale) were found with the obsessive-compulsive disorder measure.

Findings from a double-blind controlled trial suggest that the scale may be sensitive to treatment effects. In a controlled trial of deprenyl in 24 children with Tourette's syndrome and attention-deficit/hyperactivity disorder, decreases in severity of motor and phonic tics as measured by the YGTSS were observed. Several clinical trials using this measure are in progress, and further information on treatment sensitivity should be forthcoming.

CLINICAL UTILITY

The YGTSS is useful for rating the severity of tics in several domains and for documenting resultant impairment. The measure has been tested primarily with youth and adults referred for tic disorders. The YGTSS is designed for use primarily in clinical settings. It has not been tested as a screening instrument. An appropriate use might be the monitoring of treatment effects; however, further data are needed to support this use. The YGTSS is designed to be used by trained clinicians as part of a comprehensive psychiatric interview with children with suspected tic disorders. Within this context, the measure is a reliable, comprehensive, multidomain instrument

that assesses the severity of tic symptoms as described in DSM-IV. This instrument is not designed to be used by lay interviewers.

REFERENCES AND SUGGESTED READINGS

Chappell PB, Riddle MA, Scahill L, et al: Guanfacine treatment of comorbid attention-deficit hyperactivity disorder and Tourette's syndrome: preliminary clinical experience. J Am Acad Child Adolesc Psychiatry 34:1140–1146, 1995

Chappell PB, McSwiggan-Hardin MT, Scahill L, et al: Videotape tic counts in the assessment of Tourette's syndrome: stability, reliability, and validity. J Am Acad Child Adolesc Psychiatry 33:386–393, 1994

Feigin A, Kurlan R, McDermott MP, et al: A controlled trial of deprenyl in children with Tourette's syndrome and attention deficit hyperactivity disorder. Neurology 46:965–968, 1996

Harcherik DF, Leckman JF, Detlor J, et al: A new instrument for clinical studies of Tourette's syndrome. Journal of the American Academy of Child Psychiatry 23:153–160, 1984

Leckman JF, Riddle MA, Hardin MT, et al: The Yale Global Tic Severity Scale: initial testing of a clinician-rated scale of tic severity. J Am Acad Child Adolesc Psychiatry 28:566–573, 1988

Leckman JF, Towbin KE, Ort SI, et al: Clinical assessment of tic disorder severity, in Tourette's Syndrome and Tic Disorders: Clinical Understanding and Treatment. Edited by Cohen DJ, Bruun RD. New York, John Wiley, 1988, pp 55–78

Shapiro AK, Shapiro E: Controlled study of pimozide vs. placebo in Tourette's syndrome. Journal of the American Academy of Child Psychiatry 23:161–173, 1984

Singer HS, Rosenberg LA: Development of behavioral and emotional problems in Tourette syndrome. Pediatr Neurol 5:41–44, 1989

Walkup JT, Rosenberg LA, Brown J, et al: The validity of instruments measuring tic severity in Tourette's syndrome. J Am Acad Child Adolesc Psychiatry 31:472–477, 1992

Child and Adolescent Measures of Functional Status

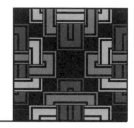

Barbara J. Burns, Ph.D.
Krista Kutash, Ph.D.

INTRODUCTION

Major Domains

In this chapter a variety of functional status measures for children and adolescents that assess an array of dimensions of functioning at home, at school, and in the community are presented. Functional status represents an individual's success or failure in coping with environmental demands. These instruments can be viewed as measures of either competence or impairment. With its emphasis on achieving tasks appropriate to a specific developmental stage, functional status has emerged as a leading indicator of the effectiveness of treatment.

Organization

The measures included in this chapter are listed in Table 19–1. Additional information on the measures is provided in Table 19–2.

Fourteen measures of functional status are presented in this chapter. First, three global measures that tap functioning across multiple domains and areas and produce a single score are described:

ACKNOWLEDGMENTS
We recognize Linda Maultsby and Anne McKee at Duke University Medical Center and Pamela Calvanese and Vestena Robbins Rivera at the University of South Florida for assistance with the organization of work and evidence-based reviews of measures for this chapter.

- Children's Global Assessment Scale (CGAS)
- Child and Adolescent Functional Assessment Scale (CAFAS)
- Columbia Impairment Scale (CIS)

Next described are 11 unidimensional measures of functioning for the following broad categories: cognitive, social, self-care or independence, self-concept or self-esteem, and health status.

Four cognitive measures that include screens for level of intellectual ability and academic achievement are presented:

- Peabody Picture Vocabulary Test—Revised (PPVT-R)
- Slosson Intelligence Test—Revised (SIT-R)
- Wide Range Achievement Test 3 (WRAT3)
- Wechsler Individual Achievement Test (WIAT)

Social functioning as a dimension of functional status has received more limited attention than cognitive functioning; however, included are three measures that address this domain:

- Social Skills Scale of the Social Skills Rating System (SSRS)
- Child Behavior Checklist (CBCL) Competence Scale
- Behavioral and Emotional Rating Scale (BERS)

TABLE 19–1 ■ Child functional measures

NAME OF MEASURE	DISORDER OR CONSTRUCT ASSESSED	FORMAT	PAGES
Children's Global Assessment Scale (CGAS)*	Overall severity of disturbance in children ages 4–16 years; unidimensional and global measure of social and psychiatric functioning	Clinician-rated scale; single scale with a range of 1–100, with 10-point anchors	363–365
Child and Adolescent Functional Assessment Scale (CAFAS)	Child and adolescent functioning and impairment	Clinician-rated or parent interview; 5 main scales plus 2 scales for caregiver	365–367
Columbia Impairment Scale (CIS)*	Global measure of impairment that taps four dimensions: interpersonal relations, psychopathology, job or schoolwork, and use of leisure time	Structured questionnaire administered by lay interviewer; parent and child versions; 13 items	367–369
Peabody Picture Vocabulary Test—Revised (PPVT-R)	Receptive vocabulary as a screen for intellectual ability in children, adolescents, and adults	Brief, structured, clinician-administered test; 175 plates (pictures)	369–370
Slosson Intelligence Test—Revised (SIT-R)	Verbal intelligence	Structured, interviewer-administered test; 187 items	370–372
Wide Range Achievement Test 3 (WRAT3)	Skills in arithmetic, decoding words, and spelling	Three subtests (Reading/Word Decoding, Spelling/Written Encoding, and Arithmetic) and two alternate forms (Blue and Tan)	372–373
Wechsler Individual Achievement Test (WIAT)	Comprehensive achievement battery: Basic Reading, Mathematics Reasoning, Spelling, Reading Comprehension, Numerical Operations, Listening Comprehension, Oral Expression, and Written Expression	Structured, individually administered test; 287 items and 4 composite scores	374–376
Social Skills Scale of the Social Skills Rating System (SSRS)	Assessment of children considered to be at risk for serious interpersonal difficulties; the SSRS contains two other scales, Academic Competence and Problem Behaviors	Fully structured, multiple-choice scale; 49 items for preschool level, 55 items for elementary level, and 40 items for secondary level	376–377
Child Behavior Checklist (CBCL) Competence Scale	Parents' report of their child's participation in diverse activities and friendships and functioning at school, at work, and alone	Self- or interviewer-administered scale; 20 items completed by parent or caregiver	377–380
Behavioral and Emotional Rating Scale (BERS)*	Emotional and behavioral strengths of children and adolescents in five dimensions: Interpersonal Strengths, Family Involvement, Intrapersonal Strengths, School Functioning, and Affective Strengths	Completed by an adult knowledgeable about the child; 52 items	380–382
Vineland Adaptive Behavior Scales—Revised, Interview Edition, Survey Form	Adaptive behavior of individuals from birth to adulthood in four domains: Communication, Daily Living Skills, Socialization, Motor Skills	Semistructured interview for administration by a trained interviewer to parent or caregiver; 297 items. Two other versions available: Interview Edition, Expanded Form (577 items) and Classroom Edition for completion by a teacher (244 items)	382–384

*Measure is included on the CD-ROM that accompanies this handbook.

TABLE 19–1 ■ Child functional measures (continued)

NAME OF MEASURE	DISORDER OR CONSTRUCT ASSESSED	FORMAT	PAGES
Self Perception Profile for Children	Children's perceptions of their competence and adequacy in the following domains: scholastic competence, social acceptance, athletic competence, physical appearance, behavioral conduct, and global self-worth	Self-report; 36 items	384–386
Child Health and Illness Profile—Adolescent Edition (CHIP-AE)	Health status of adolescents ages 11–17 years: includes satisfaction with health and self; somatic and emotional distress and limitations; physical, mental, and emotional disorders; social functioning in school and with the family; behaviors that are a risk to health; and behaviors and conditions that make a person more resilient in the face of threats to health	Self-administered, structured questionnaire; 219 questions	386–389
Child Health Questionnaire (CHQ)*	Physical, emotional, and social well-being of children and the relative burden of disease and benefits of health care	Three versions to be completed by parents (98, 50, and 28 items) and one version to be completed by child (87 items)	389–392

*Measure is included on the CD-ROM that accompanies this handbook.

The measure for self-care and independence presented in this chapter is the Vineland Adaptive Behavior Scales (Revised).

Because self-concept and self-esteem, although not a direct measure of functional status, have been moderately correlated with functioning, one measure of self-concept, the Self Perception Profile for Children, is included.

The final dimension, health status, is a measure for children with either mental disorders or comorbid mental disorders and physical illness. Within a concept of holistic health, the impact of a mental disorder or comorbidity on health is relevant to functional status. Two measures for this dimension are included:

■ Child Health and Illness Profile—Adolescent Edition (CHIP-AE)
■ Child Health Questionnaire (CHQ)

Functional status measures have been included on the basis of feasibility of administration in a clinical practice, influenced largely by time requirements for administration (with brevity as a leading factor), the level of training required for administration, and adequate psycho-metric properties. As a result, some of the measures function only as a screen, and further assessment is required. Despite the inclusion of some measures with limitations, some aspects of functioning may not be covered even if multiple strong candidates are available because of space restrictions.

Relevant Measures Included Elsewhere in the Handbook

General and diagnostic measures for children are presented in Chapter 17, "Child and Adolescent Measures for Diagnosis and Screening," and symptom-specific measures for children are presented in Chapter 18, "Symptom-Specific Measures for Disorders Usually First Diagnosed in Infancy, Childhood, or Adolescence." Scales that were designed to measure health status, functioning, and disability in adults with psychological symptoms are covered in Chapter 8, "Mental Health Status, Functioning, and Disabilities Measures." Scales that were designed to measure health status, functioning, and disability in adults primarily in general medical settings are included in Chapter 9, "General Health Status, Functioning, and Disabilities Measures."

TABLE 19–2 ■ Summary of functional status for children and adolescents

Measure	Dimension(s) covered	Age range	Administration method and time	Training requirements for administration	Informant(s)	Assessment focus
CGAS	Multiple, with global score	4–16 years	Interviewer 5 minutes	Clinician or research interviewer[a]	Clinician or parent	Level of care
CAFAS	Multiple, with global score	7–17 years	Interviewer 10 minutes (clinician) 30 minutes (lay interviewer)	Self-training manual[a]	Clinician rating or parent interview	Level of care
CIS	Multiple, with global score	7–17 years	Interviewer 5 minutes	Minimal[a]	Child or parent	Level of care
PPVT-R	Receptive vocabulary	2.5–18 years	Examiner 15 minutes	Course work in tests and measurements	Child	Intelligence screening
SIT-R	Intellectual ability	4 years and up	Examiner 10–30 minutes	Course work in tests and measurements	Child	Verbal intelligence screening
WRAT3	Achievement	5–75 years	Examiner 10–30 minutes	Course work in tests and measurements	Child	Reading, spelling, and arithmetic achievement

	Domain	Age	Format and time	Training	Respondent	Use
WIAT	Achievement	5–20 years	Examiner 15–75 minutes depending on age	Graduate degree in tests and measurements	Child	Academic achievement
SSRS	Social	4–18 years	Paper and pencil 15–20 minutes	Minimal[a]	Child, parent, or teacher	Social problems for treatment planning
CBCL (Competence Scale)	Social	4–18 years	Paper and pencil 7–10 minutes	Minimal[a]	Parent	Social competence for treatment planning
BERS	Social	School age	Paper and pencil 10 minutes	Course work in tests and measurements	Clinician, parent, or teacher	Emotional and behavioral strengths for treatment planning
Vineland (survey)	Personal and social sufficiency	0–18 years and low-functioning adults	Examiner 20–60 minutes	Graduate degree in tests and measurements	Parent	Performance of daily activities for treatment planning
Self Perception Profile for Children	Self-concept or self-esteem	8–11 years	Paper and pencil 30–60 minutes	Minimal[a]	Child	Screening for formal psychological testing
CHIP-AE	Health status	11–17 years	Paper and pencil 30–40 minutes	Minimal[a]	Child and parent	Health status for group outcomes
CHQ	Health status	5–18 years	Paper and pencil 5–10 minutes (child) 15 minutes (parent)	Minimal[a]	Child and parent	Health status for group outcomes

[a]No formal course work in tests and measurements is required.

USING MEASURES IN THIS DOMAIN

Goals of Assessment

The measures presented in this chapter can serve multiple purposes. At the individual level, they can be used for assessment and treatment planning and/or to evaluate treatment outcomes. They can also be used to assess the benefits of treatment in a given clinical practice or treatment setting (e.g., group practice, health maintenance organization, or managed-care entity) from a population perspective.

Implementation Issues

It is important to assess child functioning across multiple domains and settings and to obtain information from multiple informants. This chapter does not include single item indicators of functional status (e.g., school performance, school attendance, restrictiveness of housing, arrests, or school failure), because these and other meaningful indicators do not necessarily represent measures with psychometric properties. However, these types of indicators are important indexes of treatment benefit that clinicians may want to add to more formal measures.

The three global measures that assess multiple dimensions (the CGAS, the CAFAS, and the CIS) are administered by a clinician and/or consist of a simple parent questionnaire (for the CAFAS and the CIS); they thus require very little time in a busy practice.

The four cognitive measures included here (the PPVT-R, the SIT-R, the WRAT3, and the WIAT) are extensively used and are well established psychometrically. If a full assessment of intellectual capability is needed, then a more comprehensive measure (also requiring a higher level of training for administration) such as the Wechsler Intelligence Scale for Children (Wechsler 1974) or the Stanford-Binet Test of Mental Aptitude (Binet 1985) is indicated. The WRAT3 can be supplemented with the Gray Oral Reading Test (Wiederholt and Bryant 1989), which is not reviewed here, or another measure of reading comprehension.

Issues in Interpreting Psychometric Data

For some aspects of functional status, a gold standard for validity has not been clearly elucidated. For other aspects of functional status, measures have been developed very recently; available information about psychometric properties, although limited, is reported. Issues of discrepancies between parent and child reports are discussed when applicable under sections regarding individual measures.

GUIDE TO THE SELECTION OF MEASURES

The value of the three global measures that assess multiple dimensions (the CGAS, the CAFAS, and the CIS) is as an indicator of severity at entrance into treatment and as a single and simple index of benefit from treatment. These measures can be assessed by a clinician and are useful for treatment planning only in a fairly gross way (i.e., they offer some direction about the level of care required).

The three social functioning measures (the SSRS, the CBCL Competence Scale, and the BERS) clearly tap somewhat different aspects of social functioning. The choice of measure therefore depends on the particular interests of the clinician or investigator. The SSRS assesses cooperation, assertion, responsibility, and empathy. The CBCL Competence Scale, a widely accepted measure, focuses on a slightly different set of social behaviors, including participation in group activities, number of friends and frequency of contact, and school performance. The BERS was recently developed to assess children across the domains of interpersonal strengths, involvement with family, school functioning, and affective strengths.

The Vineland Adaptive Behavior Scales (Survey Form) can be used for the general assessment of personal and social sufficiency for all age groups, usually to assess individuals with mild to serious disabilities.

The selection of a measure of health status depends on the intended clinical or study population. The CHIP-AE was designed as a measure for children with comorbid medical conditions, whereas the CHQ was designed as a measure for the general population. Further, these are generic (not disease-specific) measures for monitoring changes in the overall health status of treated populations, integral to a health services research tradition, rather than specific measures for individual-level disease-specific assessment and treatment planning.

CURRENT STATUS AND FUTURE RESEARCH NEEDS FOR ASSESSMENT

The functional status measures included in this chapter provide a preliminary set of global and unidimensional measures for planning and assessing clinical treatment, at either the individual or the population level. Single item indicators, which are not reviewed but are embedded in the measures reviewed, may also play a role in assessing the benefits of treatment, along with other outcome measures of symptom change, family functioning measures, and system-level indicators (e.g., use of institutional care). It is clear from our review of specific measures that further measure development is indicated. However, the level of development, of both global and unidimensional measures, at both the individual and the population level is sufficient for multiple purposes, including treatment planning and determining outcomes of care for clinical monitoring or research (see Table 19–2).

Critical issues for the future development of functional status measures are 1) to standardize measures on the basis of adequate inclusion of ethnic and minority groups and 2) to consider methods for profiling functional status across multiple domains.

REFERENCES AND SUGGESTED READINGS

Binet Q: The Stanford-Binet Test of Mental Aptitude. New York, Psychological Corporation, 1985

Wechsler J: Manual for the Wechsler Intelligence Scale for Children—Revised. New York, Psychological Corporation, 1974

Wiederholdt JL, Bryant BR: Gray Oral Reading Test. Austin, TX, PRO-ED, 1989

Children's Global Assessment Scale (CGAS)

D. Shaffer, M. S. Gould, H. Bird, and P. Fisher

GOALS

The Children's Global Assessment Scale (CGAS) (Shaffer et al. 1983) is one of the most widely used measures of the overall severity of disturbance in children. It is a unidimensional (global) measure of social and psychiatric functioning for children ages 4–16 years. The CGAS is based on an adaptation of the Global Assessment Scale (GAS) for adults (p. 96) and can be used as an indicator of need for clinical services, a marker for the impact of treatment, or a single index of impairment in epidemiological studies.

DESCRIPTION

The CGAS is a single rating scale with a range of scores from 1 to 100, designed primarily to be used by clinicians who are quite knowledgeable about a child. Anchors at 10-point intervals include descriptors of functioning and psychopathology for each interval. A second version of the CGAS, designed for nonclinicians who have conducted a standardized diagnostic assessment of the child (usually in community surveys), was constructed similarly, except that the descriptors of psychopathology and functioning are written in lay terminology.

The single numerical score representing severity of disturbance ranges from 1 (most impaired) to 100 (healthiest). On the basis of the descriptors, raters are expected to synthesize their knowledge about the child's social and symptomatic functioning and condense this information into a score. For example, a score of 61–70 indicates that the child has some difficulty in a single area but is generally functioning pretty well. Scores above 70 are considered to be in the normal range, whereas scores on the low end of the continuum indicate a need for constant supervision (1–10) or considerable supervision (11–20).

PRACTICAL ISSUES

The CGAS requires no administration time because it is based on prior clinical assessment. The time to integrate knowledge of the child into a single score is estimated to be 5 minutes. No permission is required to use the CGAS. The scale is included in the *Archives of General Psychiatry* publication by Shaffer et al. (1983). However, use of training materials is highly recommended. A series of short vignettes is available from the author:

> David Shaffer, M.D.
> Department of Child Psychiatry
> College of Physicians and Surgeons
> Columbia University
> 1051 Riverside Drive
> New York, NY 10032

The CGAS is included on the CD-ROM that accompanies this handbook.

PSYCHOMETRIC PROPERTIES

Reliability

Joint reliability has been tested in research and clinical settings in a variety of ways. In research settings (whether a CGAS score is determined on the basis of case vignettes, a review of psychiatric evaluation records and test reports, or videotapes of clinical interviews), the joint reliability is quite high, ranging from 0.83 to 0.91. However, when tested in typical clinical settings, only moderate agreement has been demonstrated (0.53–0.66); three-quarters of the raters agreed within 10 points, a range that is probably reasonable for clinical use. Two test-retest reliability studies conducted using case vignettes and clinical interviews in clinical research settings found high reliability (around 0.85).

Validity

The utility of the CGAS as an indicator of caseness has been tested against measures considered to tap similar dimensions. In one study of treated youth, the CGAS was only weakly correlated with two measures of problem behavior, the Child Behavior Checklist (CBCL) (p. 310) and the Conners' Global Index—Parent (CGI-P) 10-item checklist (p. 329). These findings seem to indicate

that clinician CGAS ratings are keyed to child competence rather than to symptomatology.

In a community study in Puerto Rico, the CGAS score differentiated between children identified by diagnostic research interviews as patients and as nonpatients; in other studies the CGAS score differentiated between children in inpatient settings and those in outpatient care.

Evidence of change in CGAS scores in response to treatment has been reported for youth in outpatient treatment. For young hospitalized children (mean age 8 years, 7 months), the mean score of 38 at admission improved to 44 by discharge, but this small increment does not provide a strong indicator of validity.

CLINICAL UTILITY

The CGAS is widely used in clinical settings. When used by a well-trained clinician, it appears to be a useful measure of overall severity. It allows the rater to assimilate and synthesize knowledge about social and psychiatric functioning and to condense it into a single index. There are some indications that the CGAS may function more as an indicator of functional competence than of symptomatology. The measure is simple to use and may have potential application as a tool for evaluating clinical and functional gains as a result of treatment, but use in studies to date has not provided convincing evidence. Reliability and validity have been reasonably well established in research settings. Although reliability in clinical practice does not seem to be as high as in research settings, concordance within a 10-point range may be sufficient for most applications. The development of more formal training materials could enhance reliability in clinical practice. The CGAS appears to identify patients similarly in various geographic and ethnic samples. There are two versions of the CGAS, a clinician and a nonclinician one. Data on the psychometric properties of the nonclinician version are not yet available. The CGAS, as a single gauge, understandably does not provide information about dimensions of functioning. If a clinician is interested in specific functional domains, other measures must be used to complement the CGAS.

REFERENCES AND SUGGESTED READINGS

Bird HR, Canino G, Rubio-Stipec M, et al: Further measures of the psychometric properties of the Children's Global Assessment Scale. Arch Gen Psychiatry 44:821–824, 1987

Bird HR, Yager TJ, Staghezza B, et al: Impairment in the epidemiological measurement of childhood psychopathology in the community. J Am Acad Child Adolesc Psychiatry 29:796–803, 1990

Green B, Shirk S, Hanze D, et al: The Children's Global Assessment Scale in clinical practice: an empirical evaluation. J Am Acad Child Adolesc Psychiatry 33:1158–1164, 1994

Rey JM, Starling J, Wever C, et al: Inter-rater reliability of global assessment of functioning in a clinical setting. J Child Psychol Psychiatry 36:787–795, 1995

Shaffer D, Gould MS, Brasic J, et al: A Children's Global Assessment Scale (CGAS). Arch Gen Psychiatry 40:1228–1231, 1983

Target M, Fonagy P: Efficacy of psychoanalysis for children with emotional disorders. J Am Acad Child Adolesc Psychiatry 33:361–371, 1994

Child and Adolescent Functional Assessment Scale (CAFAS)

K. Hodges

GOALS

The Child and Adolescent Functional Assessment Scale (CAFAS) (Hodges 1996) is a multidimensional measure of child and adolescent functioning and impairment. The CAFAS assesses the degree of impairment in day-to-day functioning, secondary to behavioral, emotional, or substance use problems, for youth. It provides a snapshot of the youth's functional status at present and within the recent past (the past 3 months is the usual time period) to match needs with clinical services and to assess outcomes over time. The CAFAS covers the full age range for youth ages 7–17 years. A version for children ages 4–6 years called the Preschool and Early Childhood Functional Assessment Scale is not reviewed here but can be obtained from the author of the CAFAS (see later section).

DESCRIPTION

As the CAFAS is usually employed, a clinician rates the five main scales on the youth's functioning and the two scales about caregiver resources. The five main scale scores reflect the youth's degree of impairment in the following domains: Role Performance (School/Work, Home, and Community), Thinking, Behavior Toward Others, Moods/Self-Harm (Moods/Emotions and Self-Harmful Behavior), and Substance Use. The two additional caregiver scales assess caregiver resources in the domains of Basic Needs and Family/Social Support, thus reflecting the caregiver's resources and ability to provide for the youth. On the basis of knowledge of a child, ratings are made on each scale ranging from 0 = no impairment to 30 = severe impairment. The two-page measure contains a list of behaviorally oriented descriptors, from which the rater chooses those that best describe the patient and thus anchor the rating. For each of the domains, the rater chooses the descriptor that best describes the child's behavior during the relevant period.

A structured interview is also available for administration by a lay interviewer. The relationship between the interview and the scale is structured and is conducted with the parent. For example, a yes answer to the question "Has your child seriously hurt or beaten someone up?" corresponds to a level of 30 for severe impairment. Trained nonprofessionals can be used to rate the CAFAS without the structured interview for independent or follow-up evaluations. The raters must demonstrate reliability comparable with that attained by clinicians. The CAFAS *Self-Training Manual* contains the information and exercises needed to establish reliability (Hodges 1995).

The range of scores for each subscale related to the youth's functioning is 0–30; the range for the total score is 0–150. The following guidelines are used to interpret the scale scores:

0: Minimal or no impairment (no disruption of functioning)
1–10: Mild impairment (significant problems or distress)

11–20: Moderate impairment (major or persistent disruption)

21–30: Severe impairment (severe disruption or incapacitation)

PRACTICAL ISSUES

It takes about 10 minutes for a clinician to rate the CAFAS, and the structured lay-administered interview requires about 30 minutes. The CAFAS is copyrighted and is available from

> Kay Hodges, Ph.D.
> 2140 Old Earhart Road
> Ann Arbor, MI 48105
> Phone: 734-769-9725
> Fax: 734-769-1434

The costs for CAFAS materials are as follows: 100 CAFAS forms, $30.00; 100 CAFAS Profile forms (computer scannable), $40.00; the CAFAS Self-Training Manual, $15.00; and the CAFAS interview package, $30.00.

The manual describes administration and scoring. Training is achieved through use of the CAFAS Self-Training Manual, which contains the information and case vignettes necessary to achieve reliability. A computer program can be used to record CAFAS data and to generate patient outcome reports.

PSYCHOMETRIC PROPERTIES

Reliability

For internal consistency, Cronbach's alphas ranged from 0.63 to 0.68. Joint reliability has been assessed between lay raters and clinical staff. With both types of raters, high correlations (>0.92) have been observed for the total CAFAS score. For the individual scales, the reliability was >0.83 for Role Performance, Behavior Toward Others, and Substance Use. A test-retest study, with an interval of 2 weeks, on the 1994 version of the CAFAS also indicated acceptable reliability.

Validity

Significant and moderate correlations were observed between the CAFAS score and the total score on the Child Behavior Checklist (CBCL) (p. 310) (0.42–0.49) and the Child Assessment Schedule (CAS) (p. 318) (0.52–0.56).

Differences in the CAFAS total scores were examined by initial level of care (inpatient or residential treatment center, alternative, and outpatient) and were also examined over time (four waves—intake, 6 months, 12 months, and 18 months). There was significant variation in scores by level of care and reductions in scores over time for each level of care, an indication of discriminant validity and sensitivity to change. Predictive validity has been demonstrated through the relationship between a baseline CAFAS score and subsequent levels of service use and costs. Higher CAFAS scores were observed for youth in more restrictive settings, and CAFAS scores diminished over time for youth in all settings.

CLINICAL UTILITY

The CAFAS can be used at intake to link patient needs with available services and then with follow-up ratings to assess outcomes for youth with serious emotional disturbances. It was designed to rate impairment in children and adolescents referred for mental health services because of emotional, behavioral, substance use, psychiatric, or psychological problems. The CAFAS provides benchmarks for level of care (e.g., a total score of 20–30 indicates that a youth can be treated on an outpatient basis, whereas a score of ≥90 indicates a need for a supervised living situation).

The CAFAS offers a brief and comprehensive assessment of functioning and impairment. It is easily used by case managers or clinicians and is flexible. It can also be administered to parents. The CAFAS is sensitive to change in children and adolescents with varying levels of impairment who are referred for mental health services. It can also be used in other settings (e.g., educational, juvenile justice, social services, substance abuse programs, and general health settings).

The CAFAS is not detailed enough to explore specific areas of dysfunction. Clinician ratings could be biased toward improvement, although such evidence is not available. Two scales, Thinking and Substance Use, have been difficult to evaluate because few youth in most settings present with these problems.

REFERENCES AND SUGGESTED READINGS

Hodges K: CAFAS Self-Training Manual and Blank Scoring Forms. Ann Arbor, MI, 1995

Hodges K: Child and Adolescent Functional Assessment Scale. Ypsilanti, MI, Department of Psychology, Eastern Michigan University, 1996

Hodges K, Gust J: Measures of impairment for children and adolescents. Journal of Mental Health Administration 22:404–413, 1995

Hodges K, Wong MM: Psychometric characteristics of a multidimensional measure to assess impairment: the Child and Adolescent Functional Assessment Scale. Journal of Child and Family Studies 4:445–467, 1996

Hodges K, Wong MM: Use of the Child and Adolescent Functional Assessment Scale to predict service utilization and cost. Journal of Mental Health Administration 24:278–290, 1997

Huz S, Evans ME, McNulty TL: CAFAS as a measure of child and family functioning among children and families enrolled in intensive case management in New York State, in 8th Annual Research Conference Proceedings, A System of Care for Children's Mental Health: Expanding the Research Base. Edited by Liberton C, Kutash K, Friedman RM. Tampa, FL, University of South Florida, Florida Mental Health Institute, Research and Training Center for Children's Mental Health, 1995, pp 349–354

Columbia Impairment Scale (CIS)

H. R. Bird

GOALS

The Columbia Impairment Scale (CIS) (Bird et al. 1983) is a global measure of impairment that taps four major dimensions: interpersonal relations, psychopathology, job or schoolwork, and use of leisure time. It was developed to assess global impairment in community samples using lay interviewers. It also has potential for monitoring outcomes in clinical settings.

DESCRIPTION

The CIS is a fully structured questionnaire that can be administered by a lay interviewer and consists of 13 items that assess functioning in the four domains mentioned earlier, resulting in a single score. The scale also includes four additional items about perceived service need that are not included in the score. There are two versions of the CIS, one administered to the child and one administered to the parent. The subject responds to the questions by pointing to a card with variations of gray shading, each representing a number from 0 to 4 corresponding to the severity of the problem. One of the questions that assesses the interpersonal relations domain is provided in Example 19–1.

Responses are made on a 4-point Likert scale on which 0 = no problem and 4 = a very big problem. Responses are summed to produce a single score with a range of 0–52. The score is interpreted on the basis of the strong association in content with the Child Global Assessment Scale (CGAS) (p. 363). Information for the CIS is provided by the parent, whereas the clinician is the source for the CGAS. A cutoff score ≥15 is equivalent to a CGAS score of <61, the criterion for impairment.

PRACTICAL ISSUES

It takes less than 5 minutes to administer the CIS. The measure can be administered comfortably at home or in an office-based setting. The training required to use the CIS is minimal; there are no formal requirements for

EXAMPLE 19–1 ■ Sample item from the Columbia Impairment Scale

How much of a problem do you think he/she has with getting along with his/her mother?

training, and no training materials are available. The CIS can be obtained from

> Hector R. Bird, M.D.
> Department of Child Psychiatry
> New York State Psychiatric Institute
> 1051 Riverside Drive
> New York, NY, 10032
> Phone: 212-543-2591

The CIS can also be found in Bird et al. (1996). No permission is required to use the CIS. The CIS is included on the CD-ROM that accompanies this handbook.

PSYCHOMETRIC PROPERTIES

Reliability

Internal consistency on the basis of Cronbach's alpha was high, suggesting a single domain of impairment. The parent scale demonstrated greater internal consistency than the child scale. Internal consistency in the four domains of functioning ranged from moderate (0.43) to high (0.77). Test-retest reliability (within 30 days of first administration) was 0.89 for the parent CIS and 0.63 for the child CIS.

Validity

Validation studies were conducted with three relatively small samples: a general population survey ($N = 30$), clinic users ($N = 31$), and parents of clinic users ($N = 31$). Concurrent validity was determined on the basis of the relationship between the CIS and a clinician's CGAS score for community and clinic children. The correlation was −0.73 for the parent CIS and −0.48 for the child CIS. Concurrent validity was also assessed in a sample of chronically ill children ($N = 116$); the CIS showed moderate agreement with the Child Behavior Checklist (CBCL) (p. 310) and the Personal Adjustment and Role Skills Scale III (Ellsworth 1979) (kappa coefficients ranged from 0.58 to 0.62). Discriminant validity was established on the basis of differentiation between mean CIS scores for community (8.1) and clinic subjects (16.5) as obtained by parent report.

The main validation sample, the community sample ($N = 182$), was demographically representative of a county in New York State that was diverse with respect to ethnicity (half were nonwhite), gender (half were female), residence (urban, suburban, and rural), and socioeconomic status.

CLINICAL UTILITY

The CIS is potentially useful as a measure of impairment at entry into mental health care and at follow-up. Because the items address a range of functions applicable to all children, the CIS may also be useful for children with relatively chronic medical conditions that include physical or mental limitations. The brevity and ease of administration of the CIS and the acceptability of its items facilitate incorporation of the CIS into either pediatric or psychiatric practice settings.

The CIS can provide an important alternative to previous measures of global impairment such as the CGAS, which relies strictly on clinician assessment or interviewer ratings after a diagnostic assessment. Obtaining a parent perspective is a strength; however, the parent assessed is more likely to be a mother than a father. Because of possible discrepancies between the child score and the parent score, the clinician should consider both reports and assess the reasons for the differences.

The CIS is a new measure with relatively strong psychometric properties: reliability is high, some sensitivity to change was demonstrated, and correlation with measures of psychological dysfunction is higher for parents than for children. It offers a moderate level of discrimination among clinically different groups of children, thus making it a good candidate for use with nonreferred populations such as those with chronic medical conditions. Use with children and parents with speech impairments is also possible because of the mode of administration (responses only require pointing to a chart).

A caution is that the CIS is relatively new. It has not been tested for sensitivity to change after therapeutic intervention or differentiation among specific disorders. The CIS would benefit from further testing with larger samples and with multiple administrations over time to determine its usefulness as a measure of change. Data from a large study ($N = 579$) of children with attention-deficit/hyperactivity disorder will be available soon.

REFERENCES AND SUGGESTED READINGS

Bird HR, Shaffer D, Fisher P, et al: The Columbia Impairment Scale (CIS): pilot findings on a measure of global impairment for children and adolescents. International Journal of Methods in Psychiatric Research 3:167–176, 1983

Bird H, Schwab-Stone M, Andrews H, et al: Global measures of impairment for epidemiologic and clinical use with children and adolescents. Journal of Methods in Psychiatric Research 6:295–308, 1996

Ellsworth RG: Personal Adjustment and Role Skills Scale III. Palo Alto, CA, Consulting Psychological Press, 1979

Harris ES, Canning RD, Kelleher KJ: A comparison of measures of adjustment, symptoms, and impairment among children with chronic medical conditions. J Am Acad Child Adolesc Psychiatry 35:1025–1032, 1996

Peabody Picture Vocabulary Test—Revised (PPVT-R)

L. M. Dunn and L. M. Dunn

GOALS

The Peabody Picture Vocabulary Test—Revised (PPVT-R) (Dunn and Dunn 1981) was developed to assess receptive vocabulary as an indicator of intellectual ability in children, adolescents, and adults who have grown up in a standard English-speaking environment. Its primary use is as a screen to determine the need for further cognitive and achievement testing.

DESCRIPTION

The PPVT-R is a brief structured measure that can be administered by a clinician. Four pictures at a time are presented on a plate mounted on a carousel. In response to a word read aloud, the respondent either points to a picture relating to the word or gives the number of the picture. Although there are 175 plates, the testing is made more efficient by starting with those that correspond roughly to just below the child's chronological age (i.e., 2 = bus, 6 = parachute, and 15 = contemplating). Testing is stopped when errors in identification occur in six out of eight pictures.

The PPVT-R generates a single raw score calculated by subtracting the number of errors from the number of the ceiling items answered correctly. The raw score can be converted to an age- or grade-equivalent score or to a standard score with a mean of 100 and a standard deviation of 15. Conversion to an IQ or mental age equivalent was eliminated in the revision of the PPVT.

Norms for the PPVT-R were developed using two large samples, one for children and adolescents and one for adults. Data on a sample of 4,200 children and adolescents, ranging in age from 2.5 to 18 years, were collected May through December of 1979. This sample was stratified in accordance with the 1970 U.S. Census Bureau statistics using the stratification variables of age, gender, geographic region, occupation of parent (major wage earner for the adult sample), race, and community size. The norming program was quite sophisticated and yielded a very close match to 1970 U.S. Census Bureau statistics.

PRACTICAL ISSUES

The PPVT-R is copyrighted and is available from

American Guidance Service, Inc.
Publishers Building 1
4201 Woodland Road
Circle Pines, MN 55014
Phone: 800-328-2560

The cost for the measure, manual, and scoring material is in the range of $150.00–$200.00. It takes about 15 minutes for a clinician or a person with training in behavioral measurement to administer the PPVT-R. The PPVT-III is in development.

PSYCHOMETRIC PROPERTIES

Reliability

Split-half reliability ranges from 0.61 to 0.88, and test-retest reliability is 0.79 for immediate retest and 0.77 for delayed retest (9–31 days).

Validity

The PPVT-R correlates positively with other vocabulary tests and with vocabulary subtests of individual intelligence and psycholinguistic tests (an overall median value of 0.71 for 55 correlations). Its relationship to achievement tests is low for reading (0.29 with the Metropolitan Achievement Test) and high (0.68) for the Peabody Individual Achievement Test General Information and Total Test scores. Several investigators have reported that the PPVT-R yields slightly higher or lower scores than standard individual intelligence measures, such as the Wechsler Intelligence Scale for Children—Revised (WISCR) (Wechsler 1974) and the Stanford-Binet Test of Mental Aptitude (Binet 1985), but the PPVT-R scores are consistent with those on the McCarthy General Children's Intelligence Test.

CLINICAL UTILITY

The PPVT-R is brief and easy to administer and score and is usually not threatening to children. Despite its brevity, it is a strong measure of receptive vocabulary and functions as a useful screen for intellectual ability. As such, it offers a rough estimate of intelligence; confirmation of either mental retardation for low scores or giftedness for high scores requires further testing (e.g., a full-scale intelligence test such as the WISCR (Wechsler 1974) or the Stanford-Binet Test of Mental Apptitude [Binet 1985]). The PPVT-R is uniquely valuable for assessing children with impaired oral communications skills because response requires only pointing. The PPVT-R should not be viewed as a measure of intelligence (as it has been in the past), and it should be administered more carefully to bilingual patients, ensuring correct pronunciation. Although designed as a culture-fair test, there is anecdotal evidence that understanding of some items may be a problem for culturally deprived children.

REFERENCES AND SUGGESTED READINGS

Binet Q: The Stanford-Binet Test of Mental Apptitude. New York, Psychological Corporation, 1985

Bracken BA, Prasse DP, McCallus RS: Peabody Picture Vocabulary Test—Revised: an appraisal and review. School Psychology Review 13:49–60, 1984

Dunn LM, Dunn LM: Peabody Picture Vocabulary Test—Revised Manual for Forms L and M. Circle Pines, MN, American Guidance Service, 1981

Kamphaus RW: Clinical Assessment of Children's Intelligence. Needham Heights, MA, Allyn & Bacon, 1993

Mitchell J (ed): The Ninth Mental Measurements Yearbook, Vol 2. Lincoln, NE, Buros Institute of Mental Measurements, 1985

Robertson GJ, Eisenberg JL: Peabody Picture Vocabulary Test—Revised, Technical Supplement. Circle Pines, MN, American Guidance Service, 1981

Wechsler J: Manual for the Wechsler Intelligence Scale for Children—Revised. New York, Psychological Corporation, 1974

Slosson Intelligence Test—Revised (SIT-R)

R. L. Slosson, C. L. Nicholson (revision), and T. H. Hibpshman (revision)

GOALS

The Slosson Intelligence Test—Revised (SIT-R) (Slosson 1996a) was developed as a brief screen of verbal intelligence. It provides an estimate of IQ and mean age equivalents from age 4 years to adulthood. It is used to determine whether a more thorough assessment of cognitive ability is warranted.

DESCRIPTION

The SIT-R contains 187 items presented in increasing order of difficulty. Items produce a single score and cover the following domains: Information, Comprehension, Arithmetic, Similarities and Differences, Vocabulary, and Auditory Memory. The format is structured, and questions are read aloud by the examiner. The SIT-R is administered by an interviewer (clinician, layperson, or researcher) with basic training in and understanding of psychological testing. Although guidance is provided about the correct response to a question, judgment by the interviewer is sometimes required. Only a single form of the SIT-R has been developed.

Scoring and administration occur simultaneously. Raw scores are converted by consulting the norms tables in the Technical Manual (Slosson 1996b). The raw score is converted to a total standard score with a mean of 100 and a standard deviation of 16, which gives a score similar to an IQ. Raw scores are also converted to mean age equivalents, which give guidance about the age at which a particular score is typical. The appendix of the Technical Manual provides information for converting total standard scores to Wechsler Intelligence Scale for Children—Revised (WISCR) (Wechsler 1974) scores, College Entrance Examination Board (CEEB) scores, General Aptitude Test Battery (GATB) scores (Slosson 1996a), and T-scores.

PRACTICAL ISSUES

It takes 10–30 minutes to administer the SIT-R; the longer time is for low-ability patients and the very young. The test is not timed, and there is some flexibility in administration (e.g., a correct response to an earlier item provided at a later point counts as correct). The SIT-R is copyrighted and is available from

> Slosson Educational Publications, Inc.
> P.O. Box 280
> 538 Buffalo Road
> East Aurora, NY 14052
> Phone: 716-652-0930

The cost of a kit, which includes the manuals and 50 score sheets, is $170.00. Scoring software in Macintosh and IBM formats can be obtained for $89.00. Instructions for administration and scoring are included in the manuals. An entry-level course in tests and measurements is a requirement for administration.

PSYCHOMETRIC PROPERTIES

Reliability

Internal consistency (split-half) is very high (0.96–0.97), as is test-retest reliability (0.96 for retest after 7 days).

Validity

The SIT-R corresponds well to commonly used individual measures of intelligence such as the Wechsler Adult Intelligence Scale—Revised (Wechsler 1981) and the Wechsler Intelligence Scale for Children—Third Edition (WISC-III) (Wechsler 1991). For example, the correlation with the Full Scale WISC-III is >0.80. The SIT-R correlates more highly with the verbal than with the performance scale.

CLINICAL UTILITY

The SIT-R is easy to administer and score. It is most likely to be used when a child presents with learning problems. As a screen, it begins to differentiate between mental retardation (low score) and learning disability (high score with low achievement) and thus guides the next stage of evaluation (e.g., a comprehensive individual intelligence test for suspected mental retardation or a more extensive battery of neuropsychological tests for suspected learning disabilities). A low SIT-R score should not be equated with mental retardation. Alternatively, the SIT-R may be used to identify talented and gifted youth who may not be sufficiently challenged in school. A very high score would also suggest the need for further testing to identify strengths across cognitive domains. The SIT-R is not intended to be used as a diagnostic measure. This test can be used with blind, learning disabled, and emotionally disturbed youth. A further strength is that norms are available for young children (ages 4–5 years). The SIT-R also has some limitations: 1) the validation sample only included youth who spoke fluent English, 2) norms for individuals over age 18 are not further broken out by age groups, and 3) standardization was not done on hearing impaired or mute subjects.

REFERENCES AND SUGGESTED READINGS

Mitchell J (ed): The Twelfth Mental Measurements Yearbook, Vol 2. Lincoln, NE, Buros Institute of Mental Measurements, 1995

Slosson RL: Slosson Intelligence Test, SIT-R, for Children and Adults: Manual. Revised by Nicholson CL, Hibpshman

TL. East Aurora, NY, Slosson Educational Publications, 1996a

Slosson RL: Slosson Intelligence Test, SIT-R, for Children and Adults: Norms, Tables, and Technical Manual. Revised by Nicholson CL, Hibpshman TL. East Aurora, NY, Slosson Educational Publications, 1996b

Wechsler D: Wechsler Adult Intelligence Scale—Revised. San Antonio, TX, Psychological Corporation, 1981

Wechsler D: Manual for the Wechsler Intelligence Scale for Children—Third Edition. San Antonio, TX, Psychological Corporation, 1991

Wide Range Achievement Test 3 (WRAT3)

G. S. Wilkinson

GOALS

The Wide Range Achievement Test 3 (WRAT3) (Wilkinson 1993) was developed primarily to assess reading, spelling, and arithmetic achievement. More technically, the WRAT3 was designed to measure skills in arithmetic, decoding words, and spelling. Absolute scores, standard scores, and grade scores that can be used to compare achievement levels from kindergarten age through adulthood are provided for each of these three subtest areas. The WRAT3 can be used to identify performance on an absolute scale and in relation to age peers. It contributes to the assessment of learning disabilities in reading, spelling, and arithmetic when used in conjunction with a comprehensive test of general ability. The WRAT3 measures the development of basic academic skills over time when intervention techniques are attempted. It can also be used to study the relationships between coding aspects of reading and arithmetic and the behavioral disabilities of verbal and numerical comprehension and problem solving.

DESCRIPTION

The current version (WRAT3) provides two equivalent, alternate forms of the test, Blue and Tan, that cover the entire age range from 5 to 75 years. These two alternate forms can be used for pretesting and posttesting or combined for more comprehensive test results. A profile and analysis form can be used to compare or combine the results of the two forms.

Each form of the WRAT3 has three subtests that focus on specific coding skills. The Reading/Word Decoding subtest requires the subject to recognize and name letters and pronounce words from a given list; it is discontinued after 10 consecutive errors. The Spelling/Written Encoding subtest requires that the respondent write his or her name, write letters, and spell words from a given list; 5 seconds are allowed for each letter and 15 seconds for each word. This subtest is discontinued after 10 consecutively misspelled words. The Arithmetic subtest requires counting, reading number symbols, oral problem computations, and solving written math problems; 15 minutes are allowed to complete as many as possible.

The WRAT3 is hand scored, which yields a raw score. Tables included in the manual allow conversion of raw scores into absolute scores, standard scores, grade scores, percentiles, and normal curve equivalents. Grade scores are probably the most useful for clinical purposes, particularly for explaining test scores to parents.

The normative sample represented a mix of age, gender, and socioeconomic level determined by the 1990 U.S. Census, including 23 age groups and a total of 4,433 people.

PRACTICAL ISSUES

It takes 15–30 minutes, depending on the subject's age, to administer the WRAT3. At least a bachelor's degree in psychology or counseling or course work in the interpretation of psychological tests and measurements is required. Scoring by hand takes less than 5 minutes. The WRAT3 is copyrighted by and can be ordered from

Wide Range, Inc.
P.O. Box 3410
Wilmington, DE
Phone: 800-221-9728

The complete kit, which includes the examiner's manual (Wilkinson 1993), 25 each of the Blue and Tan test forms, 25 profile analysis forms, and plastic reading and spelling lists, costs $109.00. The spelling and arithmetic subtests may be administered to groups or individuals; the reading subtest must be administered individually. Computer software that automatically generates standard scores, percentiles, grade equivalents, absolute scores, and a score summary report is available from the publisher for $99.00.

PSYCHOMETRIC PROPERTIES

Reliability

Cronbach's alphas ranged from 0.85 to 0.95 over nine WRAT3 tests. Alternate form median correlations were 0.92 for the Reading/Word Decoding subtest, 0.93 for the Spelling/Written Encoding subtest, and 0.89 for the Arithmetic subtest. Correlated stability coefficients ranged from 0.91 to 0.98 on the nine tests, indicating strong test-retest reliability. The average interval between tests was 37.4 days, with a standard deviation of 7.2 days.

Validity

Studies of the concurrent validity of the WRAT3 with a variety of achievement tests produced the following correlations: California Test of Basic Skills, 4th Edition (sample of 46 children ages 8–16 years), 0.60–0.80; California Achievement test, form E (sample of 49 children ages 8–19 years), 0.72 for the Reading/Word Decoding subtest, 0.72 for the Spelling/Written Encoding subtest, and 0.41 for the Arithmetic subtest; and the Stanford Achievement Test (sample of 31 children ages 9–15 years), 0.87 for the Reading/Word Decoding subtest and 0.72 for the Arithmetic subtest. The relationship of intelligence and the WRAT3 is not as strong; Pearson correlations fall in the 0.20–0.60 range. Although this measure has been criticized for failure to demonstrate construct validity, given the acceptable correspondence with other achievement tests, use of the WRAT3 in office-based practice is still recommended.

CLINICAL UTILITY

In office-based practice, the WRAT3 offers a quick and reliable way to assess achievement in reading, writing, and arithmetic. In conjunction with intelligence testing, the WRAT3 can provide an initial determination of learning disabilities and confirmation of low ability. An additional use is to develop individualized instruction. The WRAT3 can be used to assess the development of basic academic skills after intervention.

As noted earlier, the two alternate forms can be used for pretesting and posttesting or can be combined for more comprehensive test results. Administration is quick, the training level for administration is minimal (bachelor's level), and a wide range of age levels can be tested. Scores are generated in a variety of ways, making the test and scores applicable for multiple purposes. Because the Reading/Word Decoding subtest does not evaluate comprehension, further assessment of reading may be required. On the basis of clinical experience, administration time may be longer than that reported.

REFERENCES AND SUGGESTED READINGS

Conoley JC, Impara JC (eds): The Twelfth Mental Measurements Yearbook. Lincoln, NE, Buros Institute of Mental Measurements, 1995, pp 1106–1111

Smith TD, Smith BL, Smithson MM: The relationship between the WISC-III and the WRAT3 in a sample of rural referred children. Psychology in the Schools 32:291–295, 1995

Vance B, Fuller GB: Relation of scores on WISC-III and WRAT3 for a sample of referred children and youth. Psychol Rep 76:371–374, 1995

Wilkinson GS: Wide Range Achievement Test 3 Administration Manual. Wilmington, DE, Wide Range, 1993

Wechsler Individual Achievement Test (WIAT)

Psychological Corporation

GOALS

The Wechsler Individual Achievement Test (WIAT) (Psychological Corporation 1992) was developed to assess a range of academic skills. This test is an individually administered, comprehensive achievement battery, co-normed with the Wechsler Intelligence Scale for Children—Third Edition (WISC-III) (Wechsler 1991). The WIAT contains eight subtests: Basic Reading, Mathematics Reasoning, Spelling, Reading Comprehension, Numerical Operations, Listening Comprehension, Oral Expression, and Written Expression. Three of these subtests (Basic Reading, Mathematics Reasoning, and Spelling) can be administered as a screen of academic skill if a brief evaluation of achievement is required.

The primary goals of this measure are 1) to provide a norm-referenced assessment of achievement levels in the eight curriculum areas underlying the WIAT subtests; 2) to provide an initial assessment of strengths and weaknesses reflected in the subtest and composite scores; 3) to provide an assessment of learning disabilities through comparison of intellectual ability (especially as measured by the Wechsler scales) with achievement levels in the seven areas in which specific learning disabilities can occur, according to Public Law 94-142; and 4) to provide an assessment of academic progress in educational programs such as those for special education and residential treatment.

DESCRIPTION

The WIAT is an individually administered assessment of academic achievement with normative data for youth from kindergarten (age 5 years) through high school. The method of administration is structured; the response required varies and includes pointing at pictures and verbal and written responses.

The Basic Reading and Reading Comprehension subtests make up the Reading Composite, Mathematics

Reasoning and Numerical Operations form the Mathematic Composite, Listening Comprehension and Oral Expression form the Language Composite, and Spelling and Written Expression form the Writing Composite. The four composite scores are combined into the total composite score.

There are 287 items on the WIAT, although no child would be given all of the items. The starting point for all tests is determined by the child's present grade level, except for the Oral Expression and the Written Expression subtests, each of which has only one starting point. Each subtest has a discontinue rule (e.g., for spelling, after six consecutive errors, the spelling test is discontinued). All of the subtests except the Oral Expression and Written Expression subtests have a reverse rule (e.g., after administering five items containing an incorrect answer, the order is reversed until five correct answers are obtained). The basal score is established by scoring 1 (1 = correct; 0 = incorrect) either on the requisite number of the first items administered or on the number of items specified in the reverse rule.

Scores are converted to a standard score with a mean of 100 and a standard deviation of 15 (a range of 40–160). Raw scores can be converted into standard scores, percentile ranks, grade equivalents, normal curve equivalents, and stanines.

The normative sample consisted of 1,000 children ages 6–16 years (median = 10.5 years) to whom the WISC-III and the WIAT were administered. The sample approximated the U.S. population for children ages 6–16 years in terms of ethnicity, gender, and parent education level, according to the U.S. Census for 1988. Each ethnic and gender group reasonably approximated the findings of the U.S. Census in terms of the percentage of children at each of the five levels of parent education.

PRACTICAL ISSUES

The WIAT Screener, which includes three subtests of the full WIAT (Basic Reading, Mathematics Reasoning, and Spelling), requires 15–20 minutes to administer to children and adolescents in grades 1–12 and about 10 minutes for children in kindergarten. According to the manual (Psychological Corporation 1992), the complete test requires 30–50 minutes for grades K–2 and 60–75 minutes for grades 3–12; however, field experience points to longer administration time. The WIAT may be taken over two sessions if necessary. This test is designed to be administered by a person with some graduate training in tests and measurements.

The WIAT is copyrighted and can be obtained from

The Psychological Corporation
555 Academic Court
San Antonio, TX 78204-2498
Phone: 800-211-8378
Internet: www.psychcorp.com

The complete kit, which includes manuals, instruments, scoring information, and norms, costs $238.00. A computerized scoring system is also available from the publisher, in Macintosh or Windows format, for $315.00. The WISC-rider software scores both the WISC-III and the WIAT.

PSYCHOMETRIC PROPERTIES

Extensive psychometric data are available for the WIAT.

Reliability

In reliability studies on internal consistency, joint and test-retest stability coefficients ranged from 0.8 to 0.9 for most subtests. Coefficients for a few subtests fell below 0.7; this finding was most common for Oral Expression and Listening Comprehension, which vary with grade level.

Validity

Validity has been established through comparisons with other achievement tests and standard tests of intelligence. Data from these studies for the WIAT, including content-, construct-, and criterion-related evidence of validity, led to the conclusion that the WIAT subtests and composites are measures of the achievement constructs that they were designed to measure. Correlations of WIAT scores with other achievement scores are substantial (in most instances correlations range from the mid 0.70s to 0.90) and are consistent across a variety of individually and group-administered tests.

CLINICAL UTILITY

The WIAT is an individually administered achievement battery developed for use in a range of settings (schools, clinics, and residential treatment settings) to make recommendations for placement, classification, diagnosis (learning disabilities), and treatment of children. It is a relatively brief but comprehensive assessment of academic achievement. Use of this measure is flexible as either a screen, a separate test of achievement in specific areas, or a comprehensive assessment. The WIAT can be used with children and adolescents from age 5 years, 0 months, to age 19 years, 11 months (kindergarten through high school). The validation sample was large and representative of the U.S. child population (in 1988) including race and ethnic groups. Later work has not shown bias related to gender or to race for African American or Hispanic children.

When used in conjunction with an individual intelligence test, the WIAT can determine eligibility for services for learning disabilities, but further testing is required to diagnose specific learning disabilities. Another limitation is that the WIAT is not adequate for measuring giftedness (i.e., higher-level mathematics such as calculus and trigonometry are not included in the measure). The WIAT may also underrepresent achievement level in children who are more difficult to test because of a handicap (e.g., blindness or deafness) or lack of fluency in the English language.

REFERENCES AND SUGGESTED READINGS

Flanagan DP, Alfonso VC: Differences required for significance between Wechsler Verbal and Performance IQs and WIAT subtests and composites: the predicted-achievement method. Psychology in the Schools 30:125–132, 1993

Glutting JJ, McDermott PA, Prifitera A, et al: Core profile types for the WISC-III and WIAT: their development and application in identifying multivariate IQ-achievement discrepancies. School Psychological Review 23:619–639, 1994

Psychological Corporation: Wechsler Individual Achievement Test Manual. San Antonio, TX, Psychological Corporation, 1992

Roid GH, Twing JS, O'Brien MS, et al: Construct validity of the Wechsler Individual Achievement Test: a multitrait-multimethod approach. Paper presented at the meeting of the National Association of School Psychologists, Nashville, TN, 1992

Wechsler D: Manual for the Wechsler Intelligence Scale for Children—Third Edition. San Antonio, TX, Psychological Corporation, 1991

Weiss LG, Prifitera A: An evaluation of differential prediction of WIAT achievement scores from WISC-III FSIQ across ethnic and gender groups. Journal of School Psychology 33:297–304, 1995

Social Skills Scale of the Social Skills Rating System (SSRS)

F. Gresham and S. Elliott

GOALS

The Social Skills Rating System (SSRS) (Gresham and Elliott 1990) is an assessment system for children considered to be at risk for serious interpersonal difficulties. Although the SSRS samples three domains of behavior (i.e., Social Skills, Problem Behaviors, and Academic Competence), the area of Social Skills is assessed most comprehensively and is the only domain reviewed here. It assists professionals in screening and classifying children suspected of having significant social behavior problems and aids in the development of appropriate interventions for the identified children. The SSRS helps in planning interventions by isolating the areas of social strengths and weaknesses that can be modified in either group or individual treatments. Further, the determination of whether social incompetencies are skill deficits or performance deficits aids in the development of appropriate treatment strategies.

DESCRIPTION

The SSRS is a fully structured self-report instrument; each item has fixed choices for the informant to endorse. The Social Skills Scale has versions for a parent, a teacher, and a child to complete. In this section, we review the Parent Form of the Social Skills Scale. The Par-

ent, Teacher, and Child Forms of the SSRS are very similar; the Teacher Form describes social behaviors at school, whereas the Parent Form describes social behaviors at home. There are also versions for preschool, elementary, and secondary school-age youth. The number of items varies, depending on the person who provides the ratings and the age of the child being rated. The Parent Form of the Social Skills Scale has 49 items for the preschool level, 55 items for the elementary level, and 40 items for the secondary level. Frequency ratings reflect how often a social behavior occurs (never, sometimes, or very often). Importance ratings (i.e., the social value placed on the behavior being assessed) may also be completed for each behavior (not important, important, or critical).

The Social Skills Scale generates a total raw score of 0–80. There are also four subscales in the Parent Form—Cooperation, Assertion, Responsibility, and Self-Control—each of which has a total raw score of 0–20. The manual (Gresham and Elliott 1990) presents raw scores, standard scores (mean = 100 and SD = 15), percentile ranks, confidence bands, and behavior levels. Behavior levels (i.e., fewer, average, and more) are descriptive methods for interpreting levels of social skills in comparison with the standardization sample.

PRACTICAL ISSUES

It takes 15–20 minutes and a third-grade reading level to complete the Social Skills Scale. The SSRS is copyrighted and was published in 1990 by

American Guidance Service, Inc.
Publishers Building 1
4201 Woodland Road
Circle Pines, MN 55014
Phone: 800-328-2560

The cost of the starter set, which includes the measures and manual, is $87.00. A computerized scoring program, the SSRS Automated System for Scoring and Interpreting Standardized Tests (SSRS-ASSIST), is available from the publisher for $150.00.

The scale can be administered and scored by many different types of personnel; however, the scores must be interpreted by trained professionals. The manual provides a user-friendly guide for professionals who want to assess and plan interventions for children with social skills deficits.

PSYCHOMETRIC PROPERTIES

Reliability

On the Parent Form across the different age levels, several studies revealed that Cronbach's alphas ranged from 0.87 to 0.90 for the total score and from 0.65 to 0.83 for the subscale scores, indicating adequate internal consistency. The test-retest reliability correlation with a 4-week interval was 0.87 for the total score on the Parent Form, elementary level; correlations for the subscales ranged from 0.77 to 0.84.

Validity

The Social Skills Scale (Parent Form, elementary level) correlates ($r = 0.58$) with the Child Behavior Checklist (CBCL) Competence Scale (this page). Numerous studies comparing the SSRS with other social competency and behavioral scales support the concurrent validity of this instrument. For example, the SSRS correlates highly with the Social Behavior Assessment (Stephens 1981) and the Harter Teacher Rating Scale. Additionally, the Teacher and Parent Forms are supported by moderate to high loadings on factor analyses using the normative sample.

CLINICAL UTILITY

The SSRS Social Skills Scale is an easy-to-administer assessment of perceived social skills in children from preschool to secondary school. The Social Skills Scale provides a better estimate of social skills deficits than social skills strengths. This instrument can be used with developmentally normal and mildly handicapped children but is not recommended for youth with more severe disabilities, such as severe developmental delay or special social skills needs associated with sensory impairment.

The standardization sample is of excellent size and fairly representative, although 11th- and 12th-grade norms were developed on the basis of a smaller sample, which limits the use of this scale with these grade levels. A further weakness of the standardization sample is an overrepresentation of whites and African Americans and an underrepresentation of Hispanic Americans and other minorities. The parent sample also contained a limited number of parents with less than a high school education, and caution should be exercised when using the SSRS with parents from low socioeconomic backgrounds. Use of the importance ratings is recommended with culturally and ethnically diverse populations, because these ratings help to assess the social validity of the skills being assessed.

REFERENCES AND SUGGESTED READINGS

Conoley JC, Impara JC (eds): The Twelfth Mental Measurements Yearbook. Lincoln, NE, Buros Institute of Mental Measurements, 1995

Demaray MK, Ruffalo SL, Carlson J, et al: Social skills assessment: a comparative evaluation of six published rating scales. School Psychology Review 24:648–671, 1995

Gresham FM, Elliott SN: Social Skills Rating System Manual. Circle Pines, MN, American Guidance Service, 1990

Stephens T: Technical Manual: Social Behavior Assessment. Columbus, OH, Cedars Press, 1981

Child Behavior Checklist (CBCL) Competence Scale

T. M. Achenbach

GOALS

The competence items of the Child Behavior Checklist (CBCL) (Achenbach 1991) elicit parents' reports of the amount and quality of their child's participation in sports, hobbies, games, activities, jobs and chores, and friendships; how well the child gets along with others and plays and works alone; and how the child functions in school. It is designed to record the competence of children ages 4–18 years. The Competence Scale contains three subscales. The Activities subscale is composed of parent ratings of the child's participation in sports, solitary activities, and chores. The Social subscale provides ratings of the child's participation in organized activities, number of friends and frequency of contact, behaviors with others, and ability to work and play independently. The School subscale is composed of ratings of the child's performance in academic subjects and the child's history of special class placement or repeated grade or school problems. More information about the CBCL (p. 310) can be found in Chapter 17, "Child and Adolescent Measures for Diagnosis and Screening."

DESCRIPTION

The 20 items on the CBCL Competence Scale are completed by a parent or caregiver. On most competence items, parents can evaluate their child as less than average = 0, average = 1, or more than average = 2 in comparison with other children of the same age. The remaining items require information about the number of close friends the child has (none or one friend = 0, two or three friends = 1, and four or more friends = 2), special education services (special education placement = 0 and none used = 1), repeat of a grade (repeated a grade = 0 and never repeated a grade = 1), and current academic, physical, and mental problems (problems present = 0 and no problems present = 1). Items can be administered by an interviewer or can be self-administered if the parent or caregiver has at least a fifth-grade reading level. A sample item is provided in Example 19–2.

The range for the raw scores is 0–10 for the Activities subscale, 0–12 for the Social subscale, and 0–6 for the School subscale. A total competence score is generated when the three subscales are added together. The responses from the individual items are transcribed onto the profile form and summed, and the total score for each subscale is circled on the graphic display. The profile provides percentiles that are displayed on the left side of the form and T-scores that are displayed on the right side. The percentiles enable the user to compare a child's raw score on each competence scale shown in the columns of the graphic display with percentiles for the normative samples of the child's sex and age range. The T-scores provide a metric unit that is similar for all scales. For the

EXAMPLE 19–2 ■ Sample item from the Child Behavior Checklist Competence Scale

Please list the sports your child most likes to take part in.

_____
_____
_____

For each sport listed, the respondent is asked the following:
  Compared to others of the same age, about how much time does he/she spend in each? (less than average, average, more than average, or don't know)
  Compared to others of the same age, how well does he/she do each one? (below average, average, above average, or don't know)

Reprinted with permission from Thomas M. Achenbach.

three subscales, T-scores <30 are considered to be in the clinical range, and scores between 30 and 33 are considered to be in the borderline clinical range. For the total competence scale, T-scores <37 are considered to be in the clinical range, and scores between 37 and 40 are considered to be in the borderline clinical range. The total competence score is not computed if any of the competence subscales scores are missing.

To score the amount and quality of participation independently of the sheer number of activities listed, one score is assigned for the number of activities, and a second score is computed for the mean of the ratings of amount and quality of participation. As a result, a child who likes only one sport, for example, gets a low score for the number of sports but can nevertheless get a high score for participating more often or more effectively in that sport than peers. Similar principles apply to scoring the child's involvement in organizations, jobs and chores, and friendships.

Normative data were drawn from a subset of nonhandicapped subjects in a national sample assessed in 1989. These subjects were chosen to be representative of the 48 contiguous states with respect to socioeconomic status; ethnicity; region; and urban, suburban, or rural residence.

PRACTICAL ISSUES

The entire CBCL can be completed in as little as 10 minutes, although 15–17 minutes is more typical. Because the scale is designed to be filled out by parents or parent surrogates, no special qualifications are needed for administration. Although the administration and scoring of the CBCL do not require special skill, proper clinical and research use require knowledge of the theory and methodology of standardized assessment procedures, as well as supervised training in working with parents and children. The CBCL competence items are copyrighted and published by

Thomas M. Achenbach
University of Vermont
Department of Psychiatry
1 South Prospect Street
Burlington, VT 05401-3456
Fax: 802-656-2602

The cost is $10.00 for a packet of 25 checklists, $7.00 for a scoring template, and $25.00 for the manual (Achenbach 1991). Computer programs are available for computer scoring and profiling. Translations are available in about 25 different languages.

PSYCHOMETRIC PROPERTIES

The majority of validity and reliability studies have been conducted by the author. These studies were conducted on demographically matched samples of referred children who had received professional attention for behavioral or emotional problems within the preceding 12 months and nonreferred children; there were approximately 2,000 children in each group.

Reliability

Internal consistency was demonstrated (Cronbach's alpha ranged from 0.42 to 0.64). The intraclass correlation coefficient for a sample of 723 children was 0.927 for the competence items. The test-retest item reliabilities were computed from ratings obtained by a single interviewer who visited mothers ($N = 72$) of children ages 4–16 at a 1-week interval. The overall intraclass correlation coefficient for this sample was 0.996. Over 1- and 2-year periods, changes in mean scores for nonreferred children (ages 6–8) did not exceed chance expectations. The average correlations over a 1-year period were 0.62 for competence scales. Over a 2-year period, the average correlation was 0.56.

Good interparent agreement was indicated by mean correlations ranging from 0.74 to 0.76 for girls and boys ranging in age from 4 to 18 years. Differences in the scale scores obtained from mothers and fathers did not exceed chance expectations. Odds ratio showed highly significant agreement between mothers' and fathers' ratings in classifying children as being in the normal versus clinical range on all CBCL scales.

Validity

In a study conducted by the author, referred children scored significantly lower (i.e., worse) than nonreferred children on all of the competence items and scale scores. The clinical cut points for the scale scores were also shown to discriminate significantly between matched referred and nonreferred children. The School subscale score and the total score discriminated between the two groups of children. The only scales that did not have large effect sizes were the School subscale for older (ages 12–18) girls and the total score for younger (ages 6–11) girls. The only difference between referred and nonreferred children that resulted in a small effect size was the Social subscale for older (age 12–18) girls. A discriminant analysis showed that both the School and Social scales were significant predictors of the referral status of the two groups. In a discriminant analysis of each item within the scale, three items were found to be strong predictors of referral: 1) an open-ended item for reporting school problems, which was the strongest predictor, 2) "gets along with others," and 3) "academic performance."

CLINICAL UTILITY

The CBCL Competence Scale is designed to record children's competence as rated by their parents or parent surrogates in a standardized format. The author of the CBCL recommends that this assessment be part of a multiaxial, empirically based assessment battery; the CBCL Competence Scale would thus reflect on the degree and quality of participation in activities, organizations, and friendships, as well as school performance. This instrument has an extensive empirical base. The Competence Scale is a useful tool for describing the social adjustment of children in comparison with a norm-referenced group of children, both with and without emotional problems.

This information may be useful when evaluating children for services and in treatment planning.

REFERENCES AND SUGGESTED READINGS

Achenbach TM: Manual for the Child Behavior Checklist/ 4–18 and 1991 Profile. Burlington, VT, University of Vermont, Department of Psychiatry, 1991

Cunningham PB, Henggeler SW, Pickrel SG: The cross-ethnic equivalence of measures commonly used in mental health services research with children. Journal of Emotional and Behavioral Disorders 4:231–239, 1996

Frankel F, Myatt R: A dimensional approach to the assessment of social competence in boys. Psychological Assessment 6:249–255, 1994

Murphy LL, Conoley JC, Impara JC (eds): Tests in Print IV, Vol 1. Lincoln, NE, University of Nebraska Press, 1994

Behavioral and Emotional Rating Scale (BERS)

M. H. Epstein and J. Sharma

GOALS

The Behavioral and Emotional Rating Scale (BERS) (Epstein and Sharma 1998) is a checklist that was developed to measure the emotional and behavioral strengths of children and adolescents. It is completed by an adult familiar with the child. The BERS assesses five dimensions: Interpersonal Strengths, Involvement With Family, Intrapersonal Strengths, School Functioning, and Affective Strengths.

DESCRIPTION

The BERS has 52 items that assess five dimensions of childhood strengths. The first dimension, Interpersonal

Strengths, measures a child's ability to control his or her emotions or behaviors in social situations. The second dimension, Family Involvement, measures a child's participation and relationship with his or her family. The third dimension, Intrapersonal Strengths, measures in a broad sense a child's outlook on his or her competence and accomplishments. The fourth dimension, School Functioning, focuses on the child's competence in school and classroom tasks. The fifth dimension, Affective Strengths, assesses a child's ability to accept affection from others and express feelings toward others. Sample items are provided in Example 19–3.

The BERS is completed by adults (e.g., clinicians, parents, and teachers) who are knowledgeable about the child. Respondents are asked to judge each of the items on a 4-point scale on which 0 = not at all like the child, 1 = not much like the child, 2 = like the child, and 3 = very much like the child. Additionally, raters are asked to complete several open-ended questions to gather further information that will form the basis for treatment planning.

A total raw score and five subscores, one for each of the dimensions assessed by the scale, are computed. Raw scores from the BERS subscores can be converted to percentile ranks and to derived standard scores with a mean of 10 and a standard deviation of 3. The sum of the subscores can be converted into the BERS Strength Quo-

EXAMPLE 19–3 ■ Sample items from the Behavioral and Emotional Rating Scale

Interpersonal Strengths
Accepts no for an answer
Reacts to disappointments in a calm manner

Family Involvement
Participates in family activities
Interacts positively with siblings

Intrapersonal Strengths
Is self-confident
Is enthusiastic about life

School Functioning
Pays attention in class
Completes school tasks on time

Affective Strengths
Accepts a hug
Asks for help

Reprinted with permission from PRO-ED.

tient with a mean of 100 and a standard deviation of 15 and its corresponding percentile rank.

Ratings in a nationally representative sample of 2,176 children without emotional and behavioral disorders and 861 children with emotional and behavioral disorders were included in the normative data. On the basis of these data, age and gender norms for children (ages 5–18 years) without emotional and behavioral disorders and clinical scores for children with emotional and behavioral disorders were established.

PRACTICAL ISSUES

It usually takes 10 minutes to administer the BERS. The BERS is copyrighted and was published in 1998 by

> PRO-ED
> 8700 Shoal Reek Boulevard
> Austin, TX 78757
> Phone: 800-897-3202

An administration, scoring, and interpretation manual (Epstein and Sharma 1998) and the BERS scales are available for $74.00 plus 10% for shipping and handling from PRO-ED.

The BERS is included on the CD-ROM that accompanies this handbook.

PSYCHOMETRIC PROPERTIES

Reliability

Two reliability studies were conducted to assess the joint and test-retest reliability of the BERS. In the joint reliability study, nine pairs of teachers rated 96 children with serious emotional disturbance. Correlation coefficients were calculated on the two groups of raters for the five subscores and for the overall scores on the BERS. Each of the correlation coefficients exceeded 0.82. In the test-retest reliability study, seven teachers rated 59 children with serious emotional disturbance twice, with ratings separated by a 2-week period, and the correlation coefficients exceeded 0.84. Cronbach's alphas measuring internal consistency also exceeded 0.80 for all subscales. The magnitude of these coefficients indicates that the BERS is a highly reliable scale.

Validity

To assess the concurrent validity of the BERS, teachers completed the BERS and either the Achenbach Teacher Report Form of the Child Behavior Checklist (p. 310) ($N = 83$), the Self Perception Profile for Children (p. 383) ($N = 78$), or the Walker-McConnell Scale of Social Competence and School Adjustment (Walker and McConnell 1995) ($N = 71$). Correlational analyses indicated that, where it would be expected, a significant relationship existed between the subscores of the BERS and the subscores on the three other measures. Another finding that supports the validity of the BERS is that children without disabilities scored significantly higher than children with emotional and behavioral disorders, as predicted by the theoretical underpinnings of the scale.

CLINICAL UTILITY

The BERS is a quickly administered and easily scored assessment of children's emotional and behavioral strengths. It can be completed by a variety of adults familiar with the child and scored by anyone familiar with the assessment manual.

The BERS is a useful tool for describing the strengths of children in comparison with norm-referenced groups of children both with and without emotional and behavioral disabilities. This information may be useful when evaluating children for services and in treatment planning. The initial psychometric properties support the validity and reliability of the scale; however, because of the recency of the BERS, sensitivity to change over time has yet to be established. Additionally, psychometric properties are derived only from studies in which teachers completed the BERS.

REFERENCES AND SUGGESTED READINGS

Epstein MH, Sharma J: Behavioral and Emotional Rating Scale: A Strength-Based Approach to Assessment. Austin, TX, PRO-ED, 1998

Harter S: Manual for the Self Perception Profile for Children. Denver, CO, University of Denver, 1985

Walker HM, McConnell SR: The Walker-McConnell Scale of Social Competence and School Adjustment—Adolescent Version. San Diego, CA, Singular Publishing Group, 1995

Vineland Adaptive Behavior Scales—Revised

S. Sparrow, D. Balla, and D. V. Cicchetti

GOALS

The Vineland Adaptive Behavior Scales—Revised (Sparrow et al. 1984) are designed to assess the adaptive behavior of individuals from birth to adulthood. Adaptive behavior is the performance of the daily activities required for personal and social sufficiency. The Vineland can be used whenever an assessment of an individual's daily functioning is required. The domains covered in the Vineland are Communication, Daily Living Skills, Socialization, and Motor Skills; the Motor Skills scale is usually given to patients under age 6 years. The scales can be used in a variety of clinical, educational, and research settings. Their primary clinical use is as a major or ancillary diagnostic tool. The Vineland can be used with all populations to determine levels of adaptive behavior and the extent to which handicaps affect daily functioning.

DESCRIPTION

There are three versions of the revised Vineland:

- Interview Edition, Survey Form
- Interview Edition, Expanded Form
- Classroom Edition

The Interview Edition, Survey Form, which is reviewed here, contains 297 items, and the Interview Edition, Expanded Form, contains 577 items. The Classroom Edition, which is completed by a teacher, contains 244 items.

The Vineland uses a semistructured interview technique for administration by a trained interviewer to a parent or caregiver. The 297 items that guide the interviewer on the Survey Form are presented in developmental sequence. These items help the interviewer begin with general questions, followed by further probes, when necessary, to obtain more specific information about the patient's activities. The interviewer begins with items that correspond to the mental or chronological age of the patient and establishes a basal and ceiling score before concluding the interview. Each item is scored to reflect whether the individual performs the activity described. A score of 2 = yes, the behavior is usually performed, 1 = sometimes or partially, and 0 = no, the behavior is never performed.

Several types of age-based norms are available for the Adaptive Behavior Composite (total score) and each domain. Standard scores (mean = 100 and standard deviation = 15) are provided, and bands of error for five levels of confidence (68%, 85%, 90%, 95%, and 99%) are available for the standard scores. National percentile ranks and stanines are also provided. Broad ranges of standard scores may be described, using the adaptive levels of high, moderately high, adequate, moderately low, and low. Age equivalents are offered for the total score and for each domain.

PRACTICAL ISSUES

It typically takes 20–60 minutes to administer the Vineland. The scales are published by

American Guidance Service, Inc.
Publishers Building 1
4201 Woodland Road
Circle Pines, MN 55014
Phone: 800-328-2560

A starter set, which consists of 10 record booklets, the manual (Sparrow et al. 1984), and one report to parents, costs $49.95. The *Survey Form Manual* provides the detailed information necessary to administer, score, and interpret the results. The manual states that the Survey Form "must be administered and scored by a psychologist, social worker, or other professional with a graduate degree and specific training and experience in individual assessment and test interpretation" (Sparrow et al. 1984). The Survey Form is also available in Spanish.

PSYCHOMETRIC PROPERTIES

Reliability

The internal consistency for 15 age groups was demonstrated in the standardization sample; split-half coefficients ranged from 0.89 to 0.98 for the total or Adaptive Behavior Composite score, from 0.73 to 0.94 for the Communication scale, from 0.83 to 0.92 for the Daily Living Skills scale, from 0.78 to 0.94 for the Socialization scale, and from 0.70 to 0.95 for the Motor Skills scale. Caregivers ($N = 160$) were interviewed twice by two different interviewers (average interval of 8 days between interviews), and the average interrater reliability coefficients for the domain scales ranged from 0.93 to 0.99. The Survey Form was also administered twice to parents ($N = 484$) by the same interviewer with a 2- to 4-week delay during the national standardization; test-retest reliability coefficients were ≥ 0.90.

Validity

Correlations between the original Vineland (Doll 1965) and the current Vineland are as follows: 0.55 for 389 individuals in the standardization sample, 0.88 for 35 children with hearing impairments in a residential facility, and 0.97 for a sample of 30 adults with developmental delays in a residential facility. Correlations between the Vineland and both the Kaufman Assessment Battery for Children (Kaufman and Kaufman 1983) ($N = 719$) and the Peabody Picture Vocabulary Test—Revised (PPVT-R) (p. 369) ($N = 2,018$ individuals participating in the standardization of the Vineland) were generally low, supporting the assumption that an adaptive behavior scale and an intelligence and achievement scale measure different areas of functioning. The progressions of mean raw scores from one age to the next provide ample support for the assumption that adaptive behavior domains, as measured by the Vineland, are age related.

A factor analysis of the Vineland was conducted for each of the age groups in the national standardization sample. Results of the analysis indicated that the Vineland is an appropriate index and, in general, confirm the organization of the subdomains into their respective domains. The developmental nature of some subdomains was apparent in the factor loadings for many ages; however, factors corresponding to the Vineland domains were confirmed.

CLINICAL UTILITY

The Vineland Adaptive Behavior Scales are applicable whenever an assessment of an individual's daily functioning is required. The major clinical use of the Vineland is as a major or ancillary diagnostic tool, particularly in the evaluation and diagnosis of individuals with mental retardation. The Vineland Adaptive Behavior Scales are also recommended for use with individuals who have other handicaps to determine levels of adaptive behavior and the extent to which the handicap affects daily functioning. Moreover, they can be used in the development and implementation of individual educational, rehabilitative, and treatment programs. The Vineland can also be used for research purposes, such as assessing treatment effects and determining the relationship of adaptive behavior to other areas of functioning and in longitudinal studies in which adaptive behavior is of interest.

Weaknesses of the Vineland include fluctuations in the means and standard deviations across age groups, which are particularly problematic in the assessment of individuals with mental retardation, and difficulties in generating questions, eliciting appropriate responses, and scoring responses. With regard to strengths of the scale, the Vineland was cited as one of only five instruments that met most of the psychometric evaluation criteria set forth in a recent review. The Vineland is also one of a few adaptive behavior scales for which a large national normative sample is available.

REFERENCES AND SUGGESTED READINGS

Bensberg GJ, Irons T: A comparison of the AAMD Adaptive Behavior Scale and the Vineland Adaptive Behavior Scale within a sample of persons classified as moderately and severely mentally retarded. Education and Training of the Mentally Retarded 21:220–228, 1986

Doll EA: Vineland Social Maturity Scale. Circle Pines, MN, American Guidance Service, 1965

Kaufman AS, Kaufman NL: Kaufman Assessment Battery for Children. Circle Pines, MN, American Guidance Service, 1983

Murphy LL, Conoley JC, Impara JC (eds): Tests in Print IV, Vol 2. Lincoln, NE, University of Nebraska Press, 1994

Sattler JM: The Tenth Mental Measurements Yearbook. Edited by Conoley JC, Kramer JJ. Lincoln, NE, University of Nebraska Press, 1989

Sparrow SS, Balla DA, Cicchetti DV: Vineland Adaptive Behavior Scales: Survey Form Manual. Circle Pines, MN, American Guidance Service, 1984

Self Perception Profile for Children

S. Harter

GOALS

The Self Perception Profile for Children (Harter 1985) is a self-report measure designed to assess children's perceptions of their competence and adequacy across specific domains, including scholastic competence, social acceptance, athletic competence, physical appearance, and behavioral conduct, as well as global self-worth. Unlike other measures of self-esteem that conceptualize global self-worth as a unidimensional construct, this instrument considers the multidimensional nature of the construct by including domain-specific judgments as well as those concerning global self-worth. The information derived is intended to facilitate the investigation of the impact of domain-specific judgment on global self-worth in children; it should be used in conjunction with other data when formulating hypotheses about a particular child.

DESCRIPTION

The instrument labeled "What I Am Like" requires children to make a judgment about their abilities on six subscales, each of which contains six items and covers a different specific area, for a total of 36 items. An additional sample item is included for practice but is not scored. Each item contains two statements referring to an identical skill. One presents a positive description, whereas the other presents a negative counterpart. A two-step response format is used, in which children must first de-

termine which of the two kinds of kids they are most like (direction) and then whether the statement is "really true" or "sort of true for me" (intensity). Consequently, there are four possible responses for each item. A sample item is provided in Example 19–4.

This instrument was initially designed for use with children in grades 3–6. It can be used with older children, but it does not provide a differentiated picture of adolescent self-concept. The author of the scale recommends that the adolescent version (Harter 1988) be used for youth in grades 9–12.

The Self Perception Profile for Children may be administered individually or in group settings by a trained examiner. Students in grade 5 or above may read the items themselves after the sample item has been explained to them. Items should be read aloud to younger children. Care must be taken to ensure that examinees endorse only one response per question.

The measure is scored by assigning a number from 1 to 4 to each item depending on the child's response; higher numbers reflect greater self-perceived competency. Scores are transferred to data coding sheets on which items are grouped according to subscale. A mean is computed for each subscale. Using the individualized pupil profile form, average scores for each subscale fall into the following categories: scores between 1 and 2 are rated as low, scores between 2 and 3 are rated as medium, and scores between 3 and 4 are rated as high. Because only raw scores are computed, norm-referenced comparisons are not possible. Thus, the raw scores cannot be compared easily with other normative evaluations of a child's abilities or social-emotional adjustment.

The scale was developed on a sample of 1,543 children in grades 3–8 from Colorado households that ranged from lower middle class to upper middle class. Approximately equal numbers of boys and girls were included. At each grade level, the sample met the minimum criterion

EXAMPLE 19–4 ■ Sample item from the Self Perception Profile for Children

> Positive Description
>   Some kids do very well at their classwork.
>
> Negative Description
>   Other kids don't do well at their classwork.

Reprinted with permission from Dr. Susan Harter.

for size; the smallest group was composed of 107 fifth-grade students. Because of the homogeneous nature of this sample, the instrument is not recommended for use with special groups of children, such as those with learning disabilities or mental retardation, and may have limited generalizability to populations that differ from the standardization sample.

PRACTICAL ISSUES

The manual (Harter 1985) does not estimate administration time, and no time limit is specified. The manual includes information about administration, scoring, and psychometric properties, a teacher rating scale, and forms for scoring and plotting the child's profile. Versions are also available for younger children, adolescents, and students with learning disabilities. Materials for administration of the instrument are available from

> Dr. Susan Harter
> University of Denver
> Department of Psychology
> 2155 South Race Street
> Denver, CO 80208-0204
> Phone: 303-871-3790

The manual, which includes a copy of the questionnaire that can be duplicated freely, costs $20.00. All orders require prepayment. The measure is copyrighted by Dr. Harter.

PSYCHOMETRIC PROPERTIES

Reliability

Studies investigating the internal consistency of the six subscales yielded reliability coefficients ranging from 0.71 to 0.86. At the subscale level, three of the six subscales possess adequate internal consistency, with median alpha coefficients of 0.83, 0.81, and 0.81; however, three scales fall slightly below the minimum criterion, with estimates of 0.79, 0.78, and 0.74.

Validity

The Self Perception Profile for Children is one of the only measures of self-concept in which the developer used factor analytic methods to select items for specific domains and global self-esteem. Factor analysis using oblique rotation yielded five specific subscales for three samples of children in grades 5–8, with no cross-loading greater than 0.18. The Global Self-Worth subscale was excluded from the factor analysis because it was thought that items loading on this scale would vary from child to child and should not emerge as a distinct factor.

CLINICAL UTILITY

Although research studies have documented a moderate relationship between self-concept and broadly defined conditions of emotional disturbance (i.e., global self-concept tends to be lower in groups with some type of disturbance), the etiological connection and/or directionality between self-concept problems and psychopathology remains unclear (Prout and Prout 1996). Some models depicting the relationship have been proposed. For example, Harter has hypothesized that global self-worth and self-esteem serve as mediators of social-emotional functioning, particularly affective and motivational states. Mediation of this sort may be particularly related to depression and suicidal ideation. Despite this lack of clarity concerning the relationship of these two constructs, lower self-concept is generally considered an indication that a full examination of the child's overall social-emotional functioning is needed. The Self Perception Profile for Children, which has undergone careful, systematic construction, has its basis in a strong theoretical model and appears to be a significant improvement over other instruments that purport to measure self-worth. To ensure its sensitivity to the dimensions of interest, the decision to use this instrument as opposed to other measures of self-esteem should be guided by consideration of the specific assessment question being asked. The results, when used in a clinical setting, should be interpreted in conjunction with other available data on the child.

Four specific limitations have been noted in the literature on this instrument. First, the use of only six items per subscale may indicate restricted content sampling in each domain. Second, the two-step response format, which requires that each item be evaluated twice, may be somewhat cumbersome for children. The first evaluation is determined mentally, whereas the second results in a mark on the answer sheet. Although this response format was designed to reduce socially desirable responding, no evidence exists to support this claim. Third, although considerable attention has been given to the research surrounding the study of children's self-esteem, very little information is provided regarding scale development or the rationale for the selection of particular domains. Finally, the normative sample, although sufficiently large, represents a narrow range of socioeconomic classes, races and ethnicities, and geographic regions. The normative sample is not representative of the population, which limits generalizability.

Some recently developed, longer instruments that meet high standards of technical adequacy have been recommended, including the Multidimensional Self-Concept Scale (Bracken 1992), a 150-item self-report inventory; the Perceptions of Ability Scale for Students (Boersma and Chapman 1992), a 70-item forced-choice questionnaire; the Self-Esteem Index (Brown and Alexander 1992), an 80-item self-report measure; and the Offer Self-Image Questionnaire—Revised (Offer et al. 1992), a 129-item objective self-report measure.

REFERENCES AND SUGGESTED READINGS

Boersma FJ, Chapman JW: Perceptions of Ability Scale for Students. Los Angeles, CA, Western Psychological Services, 1992

Bracken BA: Multidimensional Self-Concept Scale. Austin, TX, Pro-Ed, 1992

Brown L, Alexander J: Self-Esteem Index. Austin, TX, Pro-Ed, 1992

Friedman AG: Test Critiques, Vol 9. Edited by Keyser DJ, Sweetland RC. Austin, TX, PRO-ED, 1992

Harter S: Manual for the Self Perception Profile for Children. Denver, CO, University of Denver, 1985

Harter S: Manual for the Self Perception Profile for Adolescents. Denver, CO, University of Denver, 1988

Keith LK, Bracken BA: Self-concept instrumentation: a historical and evaluative review, in Handbook of Self Concept: Development, Social, and Clinical Considerations. Edited by Bracken BA. New York, Wiley, 1996

Offer D, Ostove E, Howard KI, et al: Offer Self-Image Questionnaire—Revised. Los Angeles, CA, Western Psychological Services, 1992

Prout HT, Prout SM: Global self-concept and its relationship to stressful life conditions, in Handbook of Self Concept: Development, Social, and Clinical Considerations. Edited by Bracken BA. New York, Wiley, 1996

Child Health and Illness Profile—Adolescent Edition (CHIP-AE)

B. Starfield

GOALS

The Child Health and Illness Profile—Adolescent Edition (CHIP-AE) (Starfield et al. 1995) is the first self-report measure of health status for adolescents (ages 11–17 years). The CHIP-AE describes health in a framework that includes satisfaction with health and self; somatic and emotional distress and limitations; physical, mental, and emotional disorders; social functioning in school and with the family; behaviors that are a risk to health; and behaviors and conditions that make a person more resilient in the face of threats to health. The conception of adolescent health status has its basis in a broad definition of health, clinical experience, and literature on functional status, symptom reporting, and quality of life. The specific purposes of the CHIP-AE are 1) to determine the existence of systematic differences in health among subpopulations; 2) to function as a tool for initial assessment of adolescents in public health programs such as Early Periodic Screening, Diagnosis, and Treatment; and 3) to provide a basis for assessing the impact of changes in health policies or health service interventions.

DESCRIPTION

The CHIP-AE is a self-administered, structured questionnaire with 219 questions. A fifth-grade reading level is required. The CHIP-AE assesses six broad domains of health labeled as Satisfaction, Discomfort, Resilience,

Risks, Disorders, and Achievement. Each of these broad domains has two or more subdomain scales or indexes, for a total of 20 subdomains. The responses to items on each subdomain measure are combined into a subdomain score. The subdomain scores are combined into the score for each domain, and the various domain scores thus provide a profile of the respondent's health.

The Satisfaction domain is composed of elements of satisfaction with one's health and one's self, including perceptions of well-being and self-esteem. The Discomfort domain examines physical and psychological feelings. It includes a variety of symptoms that would generally interfere with comfort or a sense of well-being, as well as positive health perceptions. The evaluation of symptoms and positive perceptions of health in children and adolescents is important because it provides a way to assess the basis for children's utilization of health services. It is also important to assess symptoms at multiple points across a person's life. The Discomfort domain of the CHIP-AE has three subdomains: Physical Discomfort, Emotional Discomfort, and Limitations of Activity. The Resilience domain includes states and behaviors known to reduce the likelihood of subsequent illness or injury, including aspects of positive health. It has four subdomains: Physical Activities, Problem-Solving, Home Safety and Health, and Family Involvement. The Risks domain is the converse of the Resilience domain and includes states and behaviors that are known to increase the likelihood of subsequent ill health or injury. The Disorders domain assesses both mental and physical illnesses, as well as injuries and impairments. It has six subdomains: Acute Minor Disorders, Acute Major Disorders, Recurrent Disorders, Long-Term Medical Disorders, Long-Term Surgical Disorders, and Psychosocial Disorders. Finally, the Achievement domain reflects the individual's state of development and has two subdomains: Academic Performance and Work Performance.

Each of the 20 subdomains has a mean of 20 and a standard deviation of 5. In scoring the CHIP-AE, the average score of the answered items is assigned to the other unanswered items in that subdomain, as long as at least 70% of the items in the subdomain are completed. The average score is determined by dividing the sum of the item scores for the answered items by the number of items answered. If fewer than 70% of the items are answered, then no subdomain score is generated and that score is considered to be missing.

The normative samples for the CHIP-AE were obtained from public junior high and high schools in both urban and rural communities. The CHIP-AE was administered to a middle school and a high school in urban northern Baltimore ($N = 865$), in four schools in rural southeast Arkansas ($N = 1,847$), and in four schools in rural southeast Maryland ($N = 350$). The latter two sites included two junior high schools and two high schools each. The mean age of the respondents among the junior high school students was 12.6 years, and the mean age of the respondents among the high school students was 15.5 years. In the combined samples, 63% were white, 34% were black, and 3% were categorized as other (Hispanics, Pacific Islanders, Asians, American Indians, and others). Half of the sample was female. Although a nationally representative sample has not been assessed to produce true normative scores, standard scores from the standardization sample provide a benchmark for evaluating the health status and health needs of new populations assessed with the CHIP-AE.

PRACTICAL ISSUES

It takes 20–30 minutes to complete the CHIP-AE, depending on age and reading ability. In a clinic setting, 45 minutes should be allowed to explain the survey, obtain consent, and complete the survey. Both parent and adolescent forms are available.

The CHIP-AE is copyrighted and can be obtained from

Dr. Barbara Starfield
Johns Hopkins University
624 North Broadway, 4th Floor
Baltimore, MD 21205

The instrument costs $25.00. The manual and computerized data entry and scoring programs cost $250.00. The manual provides instructions for administration and scoring. Telephone administration was not fully assessed in the validation process; thus telephone administration should be undertaken only under well-defined research protocols.

PSYCHOMETRIC PROPERTIES

Reliability

Internal consistency, which ranges from 0.42 to 0.93, was tested by generating Cronbach's alphas for each of the subdomain scales, with a criterion of 0.70 set for subdomains designed to measure a single construct. The single construct scales achieved an alpha of at least 0.70 in two or more of the four samples, with the exception of Academic Performance. For 8 of the 13 subdomains, an alpha of at least 0.8 was achieved in two or more samples.

Test-retest reliability was assessed with administrations on two occasions 1 week apart. A coefficient of 0.6 or higher, using either the intraclass correlation coefficient or the index pi, was considered as evidence of adequate test-retest stability by the author but may be considered only moderately acceptable evidence by others. The correlation coefficients ranged from 0.56 to 0.87 across the subdomains.

Validity

Construct validity was examined by determining whether the mean scores for each of the subdomains differed in predicted ways according to illness group, age, and gender. Existing literature was used to predict the differences that should be found when the CHIP-AE was administered to adolescents known to differ in their health status. The first stage of construct validity testing involved comparing a convenience sample of 121 adolescents belonging to four health status groups: healthy, acute illness, chronic illness, and emotional or behavioral problems. Analysis of covariance was performed to compare the scale scores across the four health status groups while controlling for differences in age and gender. Construct validity was also tested in subsequent administrations of the CHIP-AE in school sites by testing theoretical predictions regarding the differences in health that would be expected in subgroups that differed in age, gender, or socioeconomic status. The hypotheses were tested using one-way analysis of variance to compare scale scores across subgroups (i.e., male vs. female, ages 10–13 years vs. ages 14–17 years, and moderate vs. low socioeconomic status families). Correlations with school grades and parent-child agreement were also explored.

Comparison of the CHIP-AE domain and subdomain scores across the four health status groups supported the ability of the instrument to discriminate at this level. Demographic group comparisons were also consistent with predictions. The Academic Performance subdomain scores were compared with first-quarter school grades. For high school students, these correlations ranged from 0.37 to 0.43. For middle school youth, correlations with the Academic Performance scores ranged from 0.45 to 0.54.

In subdomains completed by parents, intraclass correlation coefficients ranged from 0.11 to 0.45 and kappa values ranged from 0.13 to 0.50, confirming the literature suggesting lower correlations between parent and child ratings.

The stability of responses appears adequate for a population-based measure, with the exception of Home Safety and Health in the Resilience domain. Changes over time in subdomain scores are likely to be interpretable as real changes in health status, but research evidence documenting sensitivity to interventions is not yet available.

CLINICAL UTILITY

The CHIP-AE health profiles provide a method for categorizing adolescents into 1 of 13 patterns or profiles in health on the basis of their scores on the four domains of Satisfaction, Discomfort, Risks, and Resilience. The health profiles provide an additional approach for reporting the health of populations, which should provide more information than a group's average scores. The construct validity of the profile types was supported in multiple tests in four populations ($N = 4,066$), but predictive validity has yet to be reported. Adolescents with specific psychiatric disorders were significantly more likely to have certain health profiles than their healthy peers. The profiles should be useful in planning for the health and mental health service needs of subgroups with different types of problems.

The CHIP-AE measures general health-related outcomes in children for both physical and psychosocial health. The measure is applicable irrespective of the age, gender, ethnicity, or medical condition of the adolescent. It provides a means of documenting health needs and outcomes in populations of teens with acute or chronic illness. It is suitable for evaluations of the impact of community and health services interventions with community samples or clinical groups, although these applications are not yet well documented. As a self-report, paper and pencil, and relatively brief measure, it is easy to administer in a clinical setting.

A caution is that the CHIP-AE requires a fifth-grade reading ability. The limited correspondence between parent and teen report of health status (concurrent validity) may not be problematic, because teen reports (e.g., behaviors such as smoking and alcohol use) of their health may be more valid. Other initial psychometric properties appear strong, with the exception of Home Safety and Health in the Resilience domain.

REFERENCES AND SUGGESTED READINGS

Landgraf JM, Abetz LN: Measuring health outcomes in pediatric populations: issues in psychometrics and application, in Quality of Life and Pharmacoeconomics in Clinical Trials, 2nd Edition. Edited by Spilker B. Philadelphia, PA, Lippincott-Raven, 1996, pp 793–802

Riley AW, Forrest CB, Starfield B, et al: Reliability and validity of the adolescent health profile-types. Med Care 36:1237–1248, 1998

Riley AW, Green B, Forrest CB, et al: A taxonomy of adolescent health: development of the adolescent health profile-types. Med Care 36:1228–1236, 1998

Starfield BA, Bergner M, Ensminger M, et al: The adolescent health status measurement: development of the Child Health and Illness Profile. Pediatrics 91:430–435, 1993

Starfield BA, Riley AW, Green BF, et al: The Adolescent Child Health and Illness Profile: a population-based measure of health. Med Care 33:553–566, 1995

Starfield B, Forrest CB, Ryan SA, et al: Health status of well versus ill adolescents. Arch Pediatr Adolesc Med 150:1249–1256, 1996

Child Health Questionnaire (CHQ)

J. M. Landgraf and J. E. Ware Jr.

GOALS

The Child Health Questionnaire (CHQ) (Landgraf et al. 1996) is designed to measure the physical, emotional, and social well-being of children and the relative burden of disease and benefits of health care. It is intended to measure health status in populations of interest rather than individual patients and is thus relevant for characterizing a clinic, managed-care, or general population.

DESCRIPTION

The instrument is designed to yield 14 health concepts and summary measures of physical and psychosocial functioning and well-being for children ages 5 years and older. Fourteen core health concepts are identified: Physical Functioning, Role/Social Emotional, Role/Social Behavioral, Role/Social-Physical, Bodily Pain/Discomfort, General Behavior, Mental Health, Self Esteem, General Health Perceptions, Change in Health, Parental Impact-Emotional, Parental Impact-Time, Family Activities, and Family Cohesion. There are three parent-completed CHQs—Parent Form 98, Parent Form 50, and Parent Form 28—with the short forms embedded in the fuller length forms. There is one child-completed form, Child Form 87, but no short child forms are yet available. The child form requires a third-grade reading level. A sampling of the content and response options found in the CHQ-PF50 is provided in Example 19–5.

There are two ways to score and report data for the CHQ. Overall means for the individual CHQ scales and items can be derived using a simple summated ratings approach. This method yields a profile of each of the 14 concepts standardized as 0–100. The individual scale scores can also be aggregated to derive two summary component scores of physical and psychosocial health. Scores can be compared with those of a representative sample of children in the United States; preliminary profiles for some child conditions have also been documented. The further development of scoring systems is currently being evaluated by the authors.

PRACTICAL ISSUES

Administration time ranges from 20 minutes to 1 hour depending on the length of the form used and the amount of experience with the measures and scoring approaches. The scale and a manual (Landgraf et al. 1996) cost $109.00 and can be ordered from

HealthAct
129 Newbury Street, Suite 302

EXAMPLE 19–5 ■ Sample items from the Child Health Questionnaire, Parent Form 50

List of Items[a] and Response Options[b] Found in the CHQ-PF50©

1. In general, would you say *your child's health* is:
2. Has your child been limited in any of the following activities due to *health problems*?
   a. Doing things that take a lot of energy, such as playing soccer or running?
   b. Doing things that take some energy such as riding a bike or skating?
   c. Ability (physically) to get around the neighborhood, playground, or school?
   d. Walking one block or climbing one flight of stairs?
   e. Bending, lifting, or stooping?
   f. Taking care of him/herself, that is, eating, dressing, bathing, or going to the toilet?
3. Has your child's school work or activities with friends been limited in any of the following ways due to EMOTIONAL difficulties or problems with his/her BEHAVIOR?
   a. limited in the KIND of schoolwork or activities with friends he/she could do
   b. limited in the AMOUNT of time he/she could spend on schoolwork or activities with friends
   c. limited in PERFORMING schoolwork or activities with friends (it took extra effort)
4. Has your child's school work or activities with friends been limited in any of the following ways due to problems with his/her PHYSICAL health?
   a. limited in the KIND of schoolwork or activities with friends he/she could do
   b. limited in the AMOUNT of time he/she could spend on schoolwork or activities with friends
5a. How *much* bodily pain or discomfort has your child had?
5b. How *often* has your child had bodily pain or discomfort?
6. How often did each of the following statements describe your child?
   a. argued a lot
   b. had difficulty concentrating or paying attention
   c. lied or cheated
   d. stole things inside or outside the home
   e. had tantrums or a hot temper
   f. compared to other children your child's age, in general would you say his/her behavior is:
7. *How much of the time* do you think your child:
   a. felt like crying?
   b. felt lonely?
   c. acted nervous?
   d. acted bothered or upset?
   e. acted cheerful?

8. How satisfied do you think your child has felt about:
   a. his/her school ability?
   b. his/her athletic ability?
   c. his/her friendships?
   d. his/her looks/appearance?
   e. his/her family relationships?
   f. his/her life overall?
9. How true or false is each of these statements for your child?
   a. My child seems to be less healthy than other children I know.
   b. My child has never been seriously ill.
   c. When there is something going around my child usually catches it.
   d. I expect my child will have a very healthy life.
   e. I worry more about my child's health than other people worry about their children's health.
   f. Compared to one year ago, how would you rate your child's health now:
10. How MUCH emotional worry or concern did each of the following cause YOU?
    a. Your child's physical health
    b. Your child's emotional well-being or behavior
    c. Your child's attention or learning abilities
11. Were you LIMITED in the amount of time YOU had for your own needs because of:
    a. Your child's physical health
    b. Your child's emotional well-being or behavior
    c. Your child's attention or learning abilities
12. *How often* has your child's *health or behavior*:
    a. limited the types of activities you could do as a family?
    b. interrupted various everyday family activities (eating meals, watching tv)?
    c. limited your ability as a family to "pick up and go" on a moment's notice?
    d. caused tension or conflict in your home?
    e. been a source of disagreements or arguments in your family?
    f. caused you to cancel or change plans (personal or work) at the last minute?
13. Sometimes families may have difficulty getting along with one another. They do not always agree and they may get angry. In general, how would you rate your family's ability to get along with one another?

[a]A four week recall period is used for all scales except for the Change in Health (CH) and Family Cohesion (FC) items and the General Health (GH) scale. The recall item for Change in health is "compared to last year."
[b]Options include the following: Excellent; Very good; Good; Fair; Poor • Yes, limited a lot; Yes, limited some; Yes, limited a little; No, not limited • None; Very mild; Mild; Moderate; Severe; Very severe • None of the time; Once or twice; A few times; Fairly often; Very often; Every/almost every day • Very Often; Fairly Often; Sometimes; Almost Never; Never • All of the time; Most of the time; Some of the time; A little of the time; None of the time • Very satisfied; Somewhat satisfied; Neither satisfied nor dissatisfied; Somewhat dissatisfied; Very dissatisfied • Definitely True; Mostly True; Don't Know; Mostly False; Definitely False • Much better now than 1 year ago; Somewhat better now than 1 year ago; About the same now as 1 year ago; Somewhat worse now that 1 year ago; Much worse now than 1 year ago • None at all; A little bit; Some; Quite a bit; A lot.

Reprinted with permission from Jeanne Landgraf.

Boston, MA 02116
Phone: 617-375-7800
Fax: 617-375-7801

The manual is a complete guide to administration, scoring, and interpretation. It provides tests of scaling and reliability estimates for 14 studies, results from empirical validity tests, tables of norms for the general U.S. population, preliminary benchmarks for chronic condition groups, scannable copies of the measure forms, and interviewer scripts for use when self-report is not an option. A scoring disk and test data set for use with SAS statistical software and an extensive reference list are also included. SPSS code can be obtained from the principal developer of the CHQ, Jeanne M. Landgraf, M.A., who is now affiliated with HealthAct.

More than two dozen translations are currently in different stages of development and evaluation. Contact J. Landgraf for more information.

The CHQ is included on the CD-ROM that accompanies this handbook.

PSYCHOMETRIC PROPERTIES

Reliability

The median estimate for internal consistency in 16 normative child and parent subgroups was 0.89. Among clinical samples, the median coefficient was 0.69 for the asthma sample and 0.89 for psychiatric disorders.

Validity

The measurement of general health status in children is a recent development. Because there is no gold standard for validating child health assessment measures, norms obtained for the CHQ at least provide a useful reference for interpretation. Norms were obtained for the CHQ; validity was determined on the basis of contrasting differences in CHQ scale scores, six clinical samples, and the representative U.S. sample. The CHQ was tested on 16 normative subgroups of children and parents who were representative of a normative U.S. sample, and there was extensive examination of subgroups (including gender, age, ethnicity, parent education, parent work status, and parent gender).

Data collection for the first year of a school-based study has been completed; the CHQ will be used for periodic assessment of students' health, resulting in data on the test's sensitivity to change.

CLINICAL UTILITY

The CHQ has been shown to be useful in comparing groups of children in health maintenance organizations, doctors' offices, schools, clinical trials, and large population-based studies. Although only recently developed, the CHQ is regarded by some as likely to become the standard measure of health status for children because of the level of sophistication in its development. A shorter version (in preparation) of the Child Form may increase its use. Its major use will be to monitor the health status of whole populations or subpopulations receiving health care in various types of health systems. Its use as an outcome measure will increase as studies of clinical interventions incorporate it and information about sensitivity to change becomes known.

The strengths of the CHQ include large-scale validation efforts, multiple forms of varying lengths, telephone- and self-administered options, and translation into 10 languages. A potential weakness for clinicians who lack computer access is the complicated hand scoring, particularly to arrive at the aggregate physical and psychosocial scores. Frequent changes in response formats to prevent the problem of a response set require accommodation by children and parents.

REFERENCES AND SUGGESTED READINGS

Kurtin PS, Landgraf JM, Abetz L: Patient-based health status measurements in pediatric dialysis: expanding the assessment of outcome. Am J Kidney Dis 24:376–382, 1994

Landgraf JM, Abetz LN: Measuring health outcomes in pediatric populations: issues in psychometrics and application, in Quality of Life and Pharmacoeconomics in Clinical Trials. Edited by Spilker B. Philadelphia, PA, Lippincott-Raven, 1996, pp 793–802

Landgraf JM, Abetz L: Functional status and well-being of children representing three cultural groups: initial self-reports using the CHQ-CF87. Journal of Psychology and Health 12:839–854, 1997

Landgraf JM, Abetz L: Influences of sociodemographic characteristics on parental reports of children's psychical and psychosocial well-being: early experiences with the Child Health Questionnaire (CHQ-PF50), in Quality of Life Assessment in Children. Edited by Drotar D. Mahwah, NJ, Erlbaum, 1998, pp 105–126

Landgraf JM, Abetz L, Ware JE: The CHQ User's Manual, 1st Edition. Boston, MA, Health Institute, New England Medical Center, 1996

Landgraf JM, Maunsell E, Speechley KN, et al: Canadian-French, German, and UK versions of the Child Health Questionnaire: methodology and preliminary item scaling results. Qual Life Res 7:433–445, 1998

CHAPTER 20

Behavioral Measures for Cognitive Disorders

Constantine G. Lyketsos, M.D., M.H.S.
Martin Steinberg, M.D.

INTRODUCTION

Major Domains

The DSM-IV disorders whose cardinal manifestation is an acquired disturbance in cognition include delirium, dementia, amnestic disorder, and the residual category, cognitive disorder not otherwise specified. Many measures are available for behavioral symptoms in dementia, especially Alzheimer's disease, and a few assess delirium. Few if any measures assess other cognitive disorders.

Cognitive disorders are often accompanied by a wide range of behavioral disturbances that may be a significant source of morbidity and burden and a primary focus of treatment. These disturbances include hallucinations and delusions, suspiciousness and paranoia, depression, apathy, disinhibition, restlessness, irritability, agitation, combativeness, and aggression. Although the behavioral disturbances found in cognitive disorders share many features with analogous disturbances found in other disorders, there are significant differences in phenomenology (e.g., the delusions of Alzheimer's disease typically differ from those of bipolar illness in content) and assessment (e.g., the assessment of depression in dementia requires involvement of caregivers to improve reliability and validity) that warrant the use of special instruments. Because of the disabling nature of many of these disorders, additional specialized measures have been developed in this domain to address the status of caregivers and need for care.

Organization

The measures included in this chapter are listed in Table 20–1. Four types of measures are presented:

- Two measures to assess delirium
- Three measures that cover a broad range of behavioral disturbances observed in dementia in general or in Alzheimer's disease in particular
- Two measures for specific syndromes (one for depression and one for apathy)
- Three measures that focus on caregiver burden and care requirements

Relevant Measures Included Elsewhere in the Handbook

Readers interested in assessment tools for patients with cognitive disorders may also wish to consult Chapter 21, "Neuropsychiatric Measures for Cognitive Disorders," which includes many useful cognitive tests and staging measures that cover both cognitive and functional domains (e.g., the Clinical Dementia Rating Scale [p. 446] and the Global Deterioration Scale [p. 450]). Several measures found elsewhere in this volume may also be useful. The two functional status chapters, Chapter 8, "Mental Health Status, Functioning, and Disabilities Measures," and Chapter 9, "General Health Status, Functioning, and Disabilities Measures," include several more general measures of functioning. Chapter 11, "Adverse

TABLE 20–1 ■ Behavioral measures for cognitive disorders

NAME OF MEASURE	DISORDER OR CONSTRUCT ASSESSED	FORMAT	PAGES
Confusion Assessment Method (CAM)*	Rapid and accurate diagnosis of delirium in both clinical and research settings by DSM-III-R or DSM-IV criteria	Clinician-rated, semistandardized interview; 9 items	398–399
Delirium Rating Scale (DRS)	Severity of delirium and its course and response to treatment	Clinician-rated scale; 10 items	399–401
Behavior Pathology in Alzheimer's Disease Rating Scale (BEHAVE-AD)*	Potentially remediable behavioral symptoms in patients with Alzheimer's disease	Semistructured interview of knowledgeable informant and patient observation; 25 items	401–404
Dementia Signs and Symptoms (DSS) Scale	Noncognitive symptoms associated with dementia: anxiety, mania, depression, behavior, delusions, and hallucinations or illusions	Examiner-completed scale on the basis of interviews with patient and informant; 55 items	404–405
Neuropsychiatric Inventory (NPI)	Ten domains of behavioral disturbance in dementia	Rater-administered, fully structured interview with caregiver	405–407
Cornell Scale for Depression in Dementia (CSDD)*	Quantitative ratings of depression in patients with dementia	Rater-completed scale on the basis of an unstructured interview of patient and caregiver; 19 items	407–409
Apathy Evaluation Scale (AES) Self-rated version (AES-S) Informant-rated version (AES-I) Clinician-rated version (AES-C)	Apathy in adult patients and change over time	Self-administered questionnaires to patient or informant, or clinician-rated scale after semistructured interview; 18 items	409–411
Burden Interview (BI)*	Subjective burden of serving as a caregiver	Self-administered questionnaire; 22 items	411–413
Screen for Caregiver Burden (SCB)*	Physical, psychological, emotional, social, and financial problems of caregivers of impaired older relatives, particularly those with Alzheimer's disease	Self-administered questionnaire; 25 items	413–414
Psychogeriatric Dependency Rating Scales (PGDRS)	Degree and type of dependency of elderly patients with behavioral or other psychiatric disturbances	Rater-completed assessment; 42 items	414–416

*Measure is included on the CD-ROM that accompanies this handbook.

Effects Measures," provides measures of extrapyramidal symptoms. Measures included in Chapter 6, "Diagnostic Interviews for Adults," Chapter 10, "Quality of Life Measures," and Chapter 30, "Sleep Disorders Measures," may also prove helpful in the assessment of patients with cognitive disorders, particularly when the measures have been validated for use with informants or can be easily adapted for such use.

USING MEASURES IN THIS DOMAIN

Goals of Assessment

The common goal for all the measures presented in this chapter is to assist clinical and research psychiatrists and other clinicians in assessing and treating the whole range of behavioral phenomena associated with cognitive disorders. Delirium measures assist in screening for delirium (particularly by nonspecialists), grading severity, and monitoring response to treatment. General behavioral measures are useful adjuncts for the initial and periodic evaluation of patients with dementia, because they can screen for and often grade the severity of a wide range of behavioral disturbances. In addition, both global scores and specific subscores can be used to assess any response to an intervention. Depression and apathy measures are useful in grading the severity of these symptoms in patients with dementia at baseline or in response to treatment. These measures may help to differentiate these overlapping syndromes from one another. Scales oriented toward caregivers may be used to quantify the logistical or emotional burden of caring for a patient with dementia as part of an assessment of the need for services (either respite care for the patient with dementia or direct care of the caregiver) or an assessment of an intervention and the specific care requirements of patients with dementia.

Implementation Issues

The assessment of behavioral disturbances in patients with cognitive disorders is complicated because these patients suffer from memory loss and/or other deficits that affect their ability to accurately report their mental state or their history and to appreciate time intervals. Consequently, informants, typically caregivers who know the patient well, must generally be employed. The need for a caregiver informant adds not only time but also complexity to any evaluation process. When there are two sources of information, the two may disagree, and it is not always clear which one is more accurate. Caregivers may interpret and explain away as "normal" symptoms such as depression, fear, and anxiety and thus fail to report them. Caregivers may also be eager to please doctors who are trying to help their loved ones and may thus overreport symptoms. However, they may be embarrassed to report symptoms such as hypersexuality or hallucinations. Finally, caregivers might be influenced by their own mental state (particularly if they are depressed) in a

way that causes them to overreport symptoms similar to their own in those for whom they care. The clinician who encounters a disparity between patient and informant reports should exercise caution and consider obtaining information from additional informants. Careful clinical observation over longer periods (such as through admission to the hospital, day hospital, or adult day program or through specialized video-assisted evaluation) may help to clarify the picture.

In addition, the signs and symptoms of mental and behavioral disturbances seen in patients with cognitive disturbances fluctuate over time, even within the same hour or day, and are also likely to depend on the specific context (e.g., certain behaviors may be more prominent in unfamiliar environments). Consequently, a careful interview with both the patient and the caregiver is required, particularly when examining the course of symptoms and signs over time.

Issues in Interpreting Psychometric Data

In interpreting the psychometric data reported here, several important considerations should be noted. First, although the measures presented in this chapter have all performed reasonably well in validation studies, none has been validated against a gold standard that is fully independent of clinical observation. The lack of validation against a gold standard for these measures is particularly problematic because these measures address constructs such as depression, mania, delusions, and activity disturbance that seem familiar to psychiatrists but whose precise definitions are uncertain in the context of cognitive disorders. Definitions on the basis of signs and symptoms in the context of other psychiatric disorders may not have validity in patients with cognitive disorders (e.g., sleep and appetite disturbances are common in patients with Alzheimer's disease and may therefore not be indicative of depression in such patients). There is as yet no consensus on the optimal definition of such psychiatric syndromes in persons with cognitive disorders. In addition, observed differences between measures may not reflect differences in the measures per se but rather differences in the validators used. Observed differences in psychometric properties may also reflect differences in how information from multiple sources is reconciled (e.g., a symptom being counted as endorsed if endorsed by patient or informant vs. a symptom being counted as endorsed only if endorsed by both patient and informant).

Most of the measures presented here approach their relevant construct by rating signs and symptoms along a continuum. The score they typically provide is useful clinically, particularly when it is sufficiently high to be clearly abnormal. However, when dealing with more modest scores, it is difficult to distinguish a psychiatrically healthy individual from a psychiatrically unhealthy individual, because clear cut points have generally not been established for most scales. Clear cut points have not been established partly because it is difficult to say what normative data should apply in this setting—age-matched control subjects (e.g., psychiatrically healthy elderly individuals) or dementia patients without the syndrome in question.

Finally, most of these measures have not been used extensively in settings or populations other than those in which they were developed and assessed, and thus they may have limited generalizability. For example, the delirium measures were developed in hospitalized patients, and their applicability to other settings (e.g., nursing homes, psychiatrists' offices, primary care settings, and other community settings) is not known. In contrast, the measures of behavioral disturbance in dementia were for the most part developed in outpatient settings. Many of the measures were developed primarily for patients with Alzheimer's disease and thus have limited generalizability even to other progressive demential disorders. Therefore, these measures should all be used cautiously in settings other than those in which they were developed, and, whenever possible, their use should be preceded by local assessment and validation.

GUIDE TO THE SELECTION OF MEASURES

The selection of a measure depends on the specific task. The most widely used and comprehensive measure for delirium is the Delirium Rating Scale (DRS), which psychiatrists and other clinicians can use to assist in the clinical diagnosis of delirium and to follow its course over time. It is an excellent measure of delirium; however, because it is time-consuming and must be administered by a psychiatrist, it is unsuitable for use in some settings. An alternative measure of delirium is the Confusion Assessment Method (CAM), which provides a rapid diagnosis of delirium, even in clinical settings in which psy-

chiatrists are scarce. Neither of these two measures is well validated for use in nonhospital settings, since most studies of the measures were done in settings in which the prevalence of dementia is high, such as nursing homes.

Three measures that can be used to describe and grade the severity of a whole range of behavioral disturbances in dementia are included in this chapter: the Behavior Pathology in Alzheimer's Disease Rating Scale (BEHAVE-AD), the Dementia Signs and Symptoms (DSS) Scale, and the Neuropsychiatric Inventory (NPI). All three are descriptive measures and can be used to assist in diagnosis or to assess treatment outcome in most clinical settings. The DSS Scale is the most comprehensive and includes a section on manic signs and symptoms, but it has not been extensively used. The BEHAVE-AD has been used more widely, particularly in clinical trials, but is focused specifically on Alzheimer's disease. The NPI is the briefest, because it uses gate questions and skip-out questions, and is suitable for use by lay raters. It is also widely used but does not quantify individual symptoms in depth. For those who desire more detailed coverage of these areas, several measures that could not be included here because of space constraints might be considered. The Consortium to Establish a Registry for Alzheimer's Disease (CERAD) behavior rating scale (Tariot 1996) is very comprehensive but quite lengthy. The Rating Scale for Aggressive Behavior in the Elderly (RAGE) (Patel and Hope 1992), which covers aggressive symptoms, the Columbia University Scale to Assess Psychopathology in Alzheimer's Disease (CUSPAD) (Devanand 1997), which provides in-depth coverage of psychotic phenomena in Alzheimer's disease, and the Cohen-Mansfield Agitation Scale (Cohen-Mansfield 1996), which provides extensive coverage of an undifferentiated agitation domain, might also be useful in certain clinical settings but were considered too specialized for inclusion in this handbook.

To screen for and assess the severity of depression, the widely used and well-validated Cornell Scale for Depression in Dementia (CSDD) is presented here. The Dementia Mood Assessment Scale (Sunderland et al. 1988), which could not be included here because of space limitations, is also excellent for this purpose. Finally, the Geriatric Depression Scale (GDS) (p. 544), reviewed in Chapter 24, "Mood Disorders," although not specifically developed for the population with dementia, has been used in many clinical trials of depression in patients with dementia. The Apathy Evaluation Scale (AES) screens for and assesses the severity of apathy and helps to differentiate it from depression. It is the only available scale uniquely devoted to this common and troublesome symptom; it may help clinicians and researchers learn more about apathy and how it responds to treatment.

Finally, three measures that deal with caregiver burden and care requirements are provided. The Screen for Caregiver Burden (SCB), which is widely used in clinical trials, may be preferable when the intent is to quantify both objective and subjective burden among caregivers of individuals with dementia. The Burden Interview (BI) may be preferable for assessing subjective distress associated with caregiving for patients with dementia and other chronic conditions. Because it has been validated and used more widely outside the dementia setting, it has the advantage of comparability across a range of diagnostic groups. The Psychogeriatric Dependency Rating Scales (PGDRS) focus on physical dependency, specifically the nursing time required by elderly patients. It is especially helpful for determining the levels of care necessary.

CURRENT STATUS AND FUTURE RESEARCH NEEDS FOR ASSESSMENT

Several areas require further investigation. In some, the constructs themselves need further development. For example, does delirium that develops in a cognitively disturbed individual differ from delirium in other individuals? How might the differences between these two types of delirium be measured? How can one best classify all of the noncognitive disturbances that develop in persons with cognitive disorders? Do classification schemes from other settings apply? What are the operational definitions of disturbances that are not commonly encountered in other settings, such as wandering, emotional lability, disinhibition, catastrophic reaction, frontal lobe syndrome, and noisiness? Further research is also needed in assessing a wide range of behavioral disturbances in the non-Alzheimer dementias.

In addition, new measures are needed to address areas not covered by the existing measures, such as delirium in the cognitively impaired and several other behavioral disturbances seen in patients with dementia (e.g., wandering). Measures that approach their construct categorically and not dimensionally, perhaps by exploring optimal cutoff points for specific symptoms, are also needed in some cases. Finally, further psychometric assessment in several different settings (e.g., different populations, different disorders, and other practice settings) in which these measures might be used, as well as through prospective study, is necessary if the measures discussed here are to be used more widely.

REFERENCES AND SUGGESTED READINGS

Cohen-Mansfield J: Conceptualization of agitation: results based on the Cohen-Mansfield Agitation Inventory and the Agitation Behavior Mapping Instrument. Int Psychogeriatr 8(suppl 3):309–315, 1996

Devanand DP: Use of the Columbia University Scale to assess psychopathology in Alzheimer's disease. Int Psychogeriatr 9(suppl):137–142, 1997

Ferris SH, Mackell JA: Behavioral outcomes in clinical trials for Alzheimer disease. Alzheimer Dis Assoc Disord 11(suppl 4):S10–S15, 1997

Patel V, Hope RA: A rating scale for aggressive behaviour in the elderly: the RAGE. Psychol Med 22:211–221, 1992

Smith MJ, Breitbart WS, Platt MM: A critique of instruments and methods to detect, diagnose, and rate delirium. J Pain Symptom Manage 10:35–77, 1994

Sunderland T, Alterman IS, Yount D, et al: A new scale for the assessment of depressed mood in demented patients. Am J Psychiatry 145:955–959, 1988

Tariot PN: CERAD behavior rating scale for dementia. Int Psychogeriatr 8(suppl 3):317–320, 1996

Teri L, Logsdon R, Yesavage J: Measuring behavior, mood, and psychiatric symptoms in Alzheimer disease. Alzheimer Dis Assoc Disord 11(suppl 6):50–59, 1997

Whitehouse P, Maslow K: Defining and measuring outcomes in Alzheimer disease research: introduction and overview. Alzheimer Dis Assoc Disord 11(suppl 6):1–6, 1997

Confusion Assessment Method (CAM)

S. K. Inouye, C. H. van Dyck, C. A. Alessi,
S. Balkin, A. P. Siegal, and R. I. Horwitz

GOALS

The Confusion Assessment Method (CAM) (Inouye et al. 1990) is a bedside rating scale developed to assist nonpsychiatrically trained clinicians in the rapid and accurate diagnosis of delirium in both clinical and research settings. The CAM follows DSM-III-R criteria for delirium but can be easily adapted to approximate DSM-IV criteria, which are similar.

DESCRIPTION

The CAM is a nine-item checklist to be completed by a clinician-rater after a semistructured patient interview and brief follow-up interview with a knowledgeable informant (e.g., nurse or caregiver). The two interviews are designed to assess whether the patient has exhibited an acute change and fluctuating course in his or her mental state. After the rater conducts the two interviews, he or she records answers to a series of nine questions on the CAM; a sample question is provided in Example 20–1. Each question corresponds to different, individual DSM-III-R criteria. The answers to these questions are then used to determine the absence or presence of four critical features of delirium: 1) acute onset and fluctuating course, 2) inattention, 3) disorganized thinking, and 4) altered level of consciousness. Following DSM-III-R, if features 1 and 2 and either 3 or 4 are present, the diagnosis of delirium is made.

EXAMPLE 20–1 ■ Sample item from the Confusion Assessment Method

> Is there evidence of an acute change in mental status from the patient's baseline?

Reprinted with permission from Inouye et al.: "Clarifying Confusion: The Confusion Assessment Method, A New Method for Detection of Delirium." *Annals of Internal Medicine* 113:941–948 (Appendix), 1990. Copyright 1990.

The CAM is designed to be administered by any clinician, including physicians or nurses, and may also be administered by trained lay interviewers. Data suggest that geriatricians, nurses, and trained lay interviewers perform as well as psychiatrists in rating the CAM.

PRACTICAL ISSUES

It takes an average of 20–30 minutes to administer the CAM, including both interviews and completing the checklist. The CAM is reported to be well received by both raters and patients. The CAM has been published in full, along with instructions for its use, in Inouye et al. (1990). Preliminary training for raters is needed. Raters need to understand delirium, the DSM-III-R criteria for delirium, and the structure of the CAM method. Training for physicians includes rating the CAM on 5–10 persons with or without delirium under the supervision of an experienced rater. More intensive practice in rating the CAM is necessary for nurses.

The CAM is included on the CD-ROM that accompanies this handbook.

PSYCHOMETRIC PROPERTIES

Reliability

Joint reliability was high in a single small study. Ten medical inpatients were rated independently by a geriatrician and a psychiatrist, and agreement statistics were as follows: for overall diagnosis of presence or absence of delirium, kappa = 1.0; for agreement on all nine CAM questions, kappa = 0.67; for agreement on all four features of delirium, kappa = 0.81; for agreement on individual features of delirium, kappa = 0.56 (for level of consciousness), 0.73 (for acute onset and fluctuating course), and 1.0 (for both inattention and disorganized thinking).

Validity

The CAM was compared with abnormal scores below a cutoff point on four bedside measures of cognition in 56 patients (Inouye et al. 1990). Agreement between a positive CAM rating of delirium and an abnormal score on these tests was high: kappa = 0.64 for the Mini-Mental

State Exam (p. 422), kappa = 0.59 for the story completion task, kappa = 0.82 for the Visual Analog Scale for Confusion (Inouye et al. 1990), and kappa = 0.66 for the digit span test. Medical inpatients without a psychiatric diagnosis were uniformly (100%) rated as without delirium on the CAM.

The CAM was compared against the gold standard of independent psychiatric diagnosis, using DSM-III-R criteria, in the same 56 medical inpatients at two university hospital sites (25 diagnosed with delirium by a psychiatrist and the remainder without delirium). The sensitivity of the CAM was 94% at one site and 100% at the other, and specificity scores were 90% and 95%.

CLINICAL UTILITY

The primary clinical use of the CAM is to assist nonpsychiatrists in the recognition and diagnosis of delirium in the general hospital, and its high reliability and validity (albeit demonstrated in only a single small study) suggest that it performs well. The CAM may also assist in the detection and recognition of delirium in other settings in which psychiatric patients may be found but psychiatrists are often lacking, including nursing homes, day programs, supervised housing or assisted living settings, and primary care settings. However, the method has not been assessed outside the general hospital, so it should be used with caution in these other settings. Caution is particularly indicated in nursing homes or whenever there is a suspicion of dementia, because the CAM is limited in its ability to distinguish delirium from depression or dementia.

Two other possible uses for the CAM have been suggested but not tested thus far. First, the CAM may be used as a screening measure for delirium in the general hospital or other settings, but its performance among patients when delirium is not strongly suspected has not been assessed. Second, it may be useful for following delirium over time. However, because it is a categorical measure, its utility for this purpose would be limited to assessing whether the delirium has resolved.

REFERENCES AND SUGGESTED READINGS

Inouye SK, van Dyck CH, Alessi CA, et al: Clarifying confusion: the Confusion Assessment Method, a new method for detection of delirium. Ann Intern Med 113:941–948, 1990

Delirium Rating Scale (DRS)

P. T. Trzepacz, R. W. Baker, and J. Greenhouse

GOALS

The Delirium Rating Scale (DRS) (Trzepacz et al. 1988) is designed to measure the severity of delirium, to monitor its course, and to assess its response to treatment. Delirium is defined operationally by using the DSM-III criteria, which are comparable to the DSM-IV criteria.

DESCRIPTION

The DRS consists of 10 items rated on item-specific, simple Likert scales that typically range from 0 to 3 or 4; higher numbers indicate greater likelihood and/or severity of delirium. The first item and its ratings are provided in Example 20–2. The DRS is completed using all available clinical information, including a patient interview, mental status examination, history, laboratory tests, informant (e.g., nursing) observation, and family reports. All items are always administered.

EXAMPLE 20–2 ■ Sample item from the Delirium Rating Scale

Temporal onset of symptoms

0 = no significant change from long-standing behavior
1 = gradual onset of symptoms, occurring within a 6 month period
2 = acute change in behavior or personality, over 1 month
3 = abrupt change in behavior occurring over a 1±3 day period

Total DRS scores range from 0 to 32; higher scores indicate more severe delirium. Medical inpatients without delirium and healthy persons typically score less than 2 points on the DRS, whereas patients with delirium typically score in the high teens to low twenties. Patients with dementia and secondary ("organic") mental disorders score, on average, 5–8. Patients with schizophrenia and other chronic mental disorders score, on average, 2–5, and psychogeriatric inpatients without delirium score 6–8. Thus, a cutoff score of ≥10 on the DRS has been proposed as an indicator of delirium. One week after treatment of delirium, with symptomatic improvement noted clinically, medical inpatients who have had delirium score in the range of 8–12 on the DRS.

PRACTICAL ISSUES

The DRS requires only minutes to complete, but, depending on the complexities of the case, it may take 30–45 minutes to collect all of the information needed to determine the ratings. The DRS, along with an annotated discussion of items and ratings sufficient to enable clinicians to use it, can be found in Trzepacz et al. (1988) and is copyrighted. Training for raters is recommended, but training specifications and materials are not available. Several translations, including Chinese, Dutch, French, Italian, Japanese, and Spanish, are available from

> Dr. Paula Trzepacz
> University of Mississippi
> Department of Psychiatry
> 2500 North State Street
> Jackson, MS 39216

PSYCHOMETRIC PROPERTIES

Reliability

Internal consistency is satisfactory as judged by significant item-total correlations (0.37–0.53). Several studies indicate high joint reliability, with an intraclass correlation coefficient of 0.96–0.97. In two studies of medical inpatients, the correlation was 0.81 in patients after cardiac surgery and 0.90 in patients after elective noncardiac surgery.

Validity

Using independent psychiatric diagnosis as the gold standard for the diagnosis of delirium, several studies showed excellent validity for the proposed cutoff score of ≥10. One study (Trzepacz et al. 1988) ($N = 47$) found no overlap between DRS scores for those with delirium and those without. Patients with dementia, patients with schizophrenia, and psychiatrically healthy individuals all scored ≤12, whereas medical inpatients with delirium all scored ≥12. Another study replicated these findings in patients who had undergone cardiac surgery, showing that no patients without delirium scored >11 on the DRS, although 2 of 25 patients with delirium scored <11. A third study (Rosen et al. 1994) conducted with receiver operating characteristic analysis found the overall performance of the DRS to be excellent, with an area under the curve of 0.95 (SE = 0.0095). In this study, the investigators found that a cutoff score of ≥10 maximized sensitivity at 93% and specificity at 82%.

Those defined as having delirium by a DRS score (10 had significantly lower scores on the Mini-Mental State Exam (MMSE) (p. 422) and were significantly more likely to show electroencephalographic (EEG) dysrhythmias. The DRS score was also correlated with the MMSE score ($r = -0.43$) and with the score on Part B of the Trail Making Test (Reitan 1958) ($r = 0.66$). Initial DRS score was correlated with peak dose of haloperidol administered clinically to treat delirium ($r = 0.45$). Finally, patients whose delirium resolved after 1 week had lower initial DRS scores (mean = 14, SD = 1.86) compared with those whose delirium took longer to resolve (mean = 18, SD = 2.7).

The DRS also appears to be sensitive to change. In a randomized controlled trial of haloperidol, lorazepam, and chlorpromazine for delirium in AIDS patients (Breitbart et al. 1996), the DRS was used as the outcome measure. Mean DRS scores at baseline were 20 (SD = 3.4), 18 (SD = 4.2), and 21 (SD = 3.9) for haloperidol, lorazepam, and chlorpromazine, respectively. By the end of the study, they had become 12 (SD = 6.0), 17 (SD = 5.0), and 12 (SD = 6.7), respectively.

CLINICAL UTILITY

On the basis of these psychometric data, the DRS clearly has utility for several clinical purposes, including assisting in the diagnosis of delirium (according to DSM criteria), grading the severity of delirium, and assessing response and timing of treatment response in patients with delirium. However, the relatively low specificity means that careful clinical follow-up is necessary to avoid false-positive diagnoses. In particular, persons with dementia, those of younger age, those with high rates of behavioral symptoms as indicated by high scores on the Brief Psychiatric Rating Scale (p. 490), and those with greater slowing on EEG are more likely to produce false-positives diagnoses on the DRS. When used outside the general hospital and in patients with dementia or other cognitive disorders, the DRS should be interpreted with caution, given the lack of adequate psychometric data.

Some clinicians may find the DRS too long for routine clinical use. However, given its wide use as a measure of delirium in research studies, familiarity with the DRS is critical to interpreting the results of these studies.

REFERENCES AND SUGGESTED READINGS

Breitbart W, Marotta R, Platt M, et al: A double-blind trial of haloperidol, chlorpromazine, and lorazepam in the treatment of delirium in hospitalized AIDS patients. Am J Psychiatry 153:231–237, 1996

Reitan R: Validity of the Trail Making Test as an indicator of organic brain disease. Perceptual and Psychomotor Skills 8:271–276, 1958

Rosen J, Sweet RA, Mulsant BH: The delirium rating scale in a psychogeriatric inpatient unit. J Neuropsychiatry Clin Neurosci 6:30–35, 1994

Trzepacz PT, Baker RW, Greenhouse J: A rating scale for delirium. Psychiatry Res 23:89–97, 1988

Wada Y, Yamaguchi N: Delirium in the elderly: relationship of clinical symptoms to outcome. Dementia 4:113–116, 1993

Behavior Pathology in Alzheimer's Disease Rating Scale (BEHAVE-AD)

B. Reisberg, J. Borenstein, S. P. Salob, S. H. Ferris, E. Franssen, and A. Georgotas

GOALS

The Behavior Pathology in Alzheimer's Disease Scale (BEHAVE-AD) (Reisberg et al. 1987) was developed to measure potentially remediable behavioral symptoms in patients with Alzheimer's disease. Behavioral symptoms included are those commonly seen in such patients: paranoid and delusional ideation, hallucinations, activity disturbances, aggressiveness, diurnal rhythm disturbances, affective disturbances, and anxieties and phobias. The BEHAVE-AD also attempts to provide an overall rating of the global severity of behavioral symptomatology; undesirable behaviors are conceptualized as those that are troublesome to the caregiver or dangerous to the patient.

DESCRIPTION

The BEHAVE-AD is rated after a semistructured interview of an informant (e.g., spouse or other caregiver) who is knowledgeable about the patient's behavior during the past 2 weeks and a brief period of observing the patient. The BEHAVE-AD consists of 25 items in 7 categories: Paranoid and Delusional Ideation (7 items), Hallucinations (5 items), Activity Disturbances (3 items), Aggressiveness (3 items), Diurnal Rhythm Disturbances (1 item), Affective Disturbances (2 items), and Anxieties and Phobias (4 items). Each item is rated on a scale of 0–3; higher scores indicate more pathology. Specific anchors are provided for each item. A sample item is provided in Example 20–3. Global severity ratings range from 0 = symptoms absent or not at all troubling to caregiver or dangerous to the patient to 3 = symptoms severely troubling or intolerable to the caregiver or dangerous to the patient.

The total possible score on the BEHAVE-AD ranges from 0 to 75. Scores of ≥8, with a global scale rating of

EXAMPLE 20–3 ■ Sample item from the Behavior Pathology in Alzheimer's Disease Rating Scale

People are stealing things delusion

0 = not present
1 =
2 =
3 = talking and listening to people coming into the home

Reprinted with permission from Barry Reisberg, M.D.

≥2, are typically considered indicative of clinically significant behavioral disturbance. The presence of scores other than 0 in any BEHAVE-AD category should be considered clinically significant, particularly if the global rating is ≥2 (moderately or severely troubling to the caregiver or dangerous to the patient).

The BEHAVE-AD is designed to be administered by a clinician, specifically a physician, registered nurse, or psychologist. Raters of different backgrounds produce equivalent ratings.

A companion rating scale for the BEHAVE-AD, the Empirical Behavioral Pathology in Alzheimer's Disease Rating Scale (E-BEHAVE-AD) (Auer et al. 1996), which assesses patients on the basis of direct patient observation, has also been published and shown to be reliable.

PRACTICAL ISSUES

It takes 15–20 minutes to complete the BEHAVE-AD for outpatients, including informant interview and patient observation. For hospitalized patients or those in nursing homes, as long as 30 minutes may be required. The BEHAVE-AD is available in its entirety in Reisberg et al. (1987). It is copyrighted by Dr. Barry Reisberg, who allows free use to clinicians and researchers. Specifications for scoring the BEHAVE-AD have been published in Reisberg et al. (1992). A reliability and validity study supports telephone use (Monteiro et al. 1998). Training for raters is recommended, and training videos may be obtained by contacting Dr. Reisberg at

Aging and Dementia Research Program
Department of Psychiatry
New York University Medical Center
550 First Avenue
New York, NY 10016

The BEHAVE-AD is included on the CD-ROM that accompanies this handbook.

PSYCHOMETRIC PROPERTIES

Reliability

Two studies assessed the internal consistency of the BEHAVE-AD; two raters observed the same caregiver interview and made independent ratings. Rater consistency coefficients (RCCs, analogous to alpha coefficients) for the entire scale were 0.96. For the individual scale categories, RCCs ranged from 0.65 (Anxieties and Phobias) to 0.99 (Paranoid and Delusional Ideation).

Several studies have assessed the joint reliability of the BEHAVE-AD. Rater agreement coefficients (RACs, analogous to intraclass correlation coefficients) were 0.95–0.96 for total scores. Category RACs ranged from 0.65 (Anxieties and Phobias) to 0.99 (Paranoid and Delusional Ideation). In a different study, Spearman rank correlation for both total BEHAVE-AD scores and global ratings was 1.0. In a third reliability study, kappa values for individual items were calculated by BEHAVE-AD category: Paranoid and Delusional Ideation (0.43–1.00), Hallucinations (0.64–1.00), Activity Disturbances (0.82–1.00), Aggressiveness (0.53–0.76), Diurnal Rhythm Disturbances (0.58), Affective Disturbances (0.52–0.81), and Anxieties and Phobias (0.60–0.89).

Validity

Several studies have used the BEHAVE-AD as a gold standard to validate other scales. When compared with the Dementia Signs and Symptoms (DSS) Scale (p. 404), the following correlation coefficients (r) were found: 0.83 with the BEHAVE-AD Affective Disturbances category, 0.74 with the BEHAVE-AD Activity Disturbances category, 0.62 with the BEHAVE-AD score for overall behavior, 0.92 with the BEHAVE-AD Paranoid and Delusional Ideation category, and 0.93 with the BEHAVE-AD Hallucinations category. The BEHAVE-AD was also compared with the Neuropsychiatric Inventory (NPI) (p. 405), and the following correlation coefficients (r) were reported: the total score on the BEHAVE-AD with NPI total frequency, 0.66; with NPI severity, 0.71; and with NPI frequency times severity, 0.62. There were also section-by-section correlations (of Depression with Depression categories, Anxiety with Anxiety categories, and so forth): $r = 0.54-0.78$ with NPI frequency, $r = 0.47-0.80$ with NPI severity, and $r = 0.33-0.77$ with NPI frequency times severity. The BEHAVE-AD total score is also correlated with the Brief Agitation Rating Scale (Finkel et al. 1993) ($r = 0.21-0.44$).

Scores on the BEHAVE-AD have been shown to increase with the stage or severity of Alzheimer's disease, as would be expected. Persons with mild to moderately severe Alzheimer's disease (Global Deterioration Scale [GDS] [p. 450] ratings of 4, 5, and 6) evidence higher BEHAVE-AD scores than persons with incipient or severe Alzheimer's disease and GDS scores of 3 or 7. A complete review of mean BEHAVE-AD scores, by GDS stage, in a sample of 120 outpatients of the New York University Alzheimer's Disease Research Center can be found in Reisberg et al. (1989).

BEHAVE-AD total scores and scores on the subscales for Paranoid and Delusional Ideation, Aggressiveness, and Anxieties and Phobias have been shown to change over time in response to treatment with a serotonergic agent in comparison with treatment with placebo. In a large, multicenter, double-blind study ($N = 625$) conducted with institutionalized patients with dementia (Alzheimer's disease, 73%; vascular disease, 15%; and mixed type, 12%), treatment with an antipsychotic medication produced significantly greater reductions at end point in BEHAVE-AD total scores, BEHAVE-AD psychosis subscale scores, and BEHAVE-AD Aggressiveness scores than treatment with placebo. On the other hand, although the global severity ratings on the BEHAVE-AD declined significantly during a 14-week tacrine trial, scores on individual BEHAVE-AD sections did not show any changes.

CLINICAL UTILITY

The BEHAVE-AD appears to provide a fairly brief but thorough assessment of the type and severity of behavior disturbances in patients with Alzheimer's disease across all stages of the illness. It may thus be helpful in characterizing the nature and degree of behavioral pathology and in identifying symptoms that may require specific interventions. It appears to be appropriate for use in both outpatient and nursing home settings. The domains of delusions, hallucinations, diurnal disturbances, anxiety,

activity disturbances, and aggression are particularly well covered.

The BEHAVE-AD can be used to assess the response of behavior disturbance to treatment in either clinical trials or clinical practice because it provides a quantitative assessment. Because the BEHAVE-AD is widely used in clinical trials of interventions for behavioral disturbances in patients with dementia, an appreciation of the scale will assist in interpretations of their results. The BEHAVE-AD has demonstrated sensitivity to change (i.e., significant improvement with active treatment in comparison with placebo) in both institutional and outpatient settings and in subjects with diverse dementia diagnoses.

REFERENCES AND SUGGESTED READINGS

Auer SR, Monteiro IM, Reisberg B: The Empirical Behavior Pathology in Alzheimer's Disease (E-BEHAVE-AD) Rating Scale. Int Psychogeriatr 8:247–266, 1996

Finkel SI, Lyons JS, Anderson RL: A Brief Agitation Rating Scale (BARS) for nursing home elderly. J Am Geriatr Soc 41:50–52, 1993

Levy MA, Burgio LD, Sweet R, et al: A trial of buspirone for the control of disruptive behaviors in community-dwelling patients with dementia. International Journal of Geriatric Psychiatry 9:841–848, 1994

Monteiro IM, Boksay I, Auer SR, et al: Reliability of routine clinical instruments for the assessment of Alzheimer's disease administered by telephone. J Geriatr Psychiatry Neurol 11:18–24, 1998

Reisberg B, Borenstein J, Salob SP, et al: Behavioral symptoms in Alzheimer disease: phenomenology and treatment. J Clin Psychiatry 48(suppl 5)9–15, 1987

Reisberg B, Franssen E, Sclan SG, et al: Stage specific incidence of potentially remediable behavioral symptoms in aging and Alzheimer's diseases. Bulletin of Clinical Neurosciences 54:95–112, 1989

Reisberg B, Ferris S, Torossian C, et al: Pharmacologic treatment of Alzheimer's disease: a methodologic critique based upon current knowledge of symptomatology and relevance for clinical trials. Int Psychogeriatr 1(suppl):9–42, 1992

Sclan SG, Saillon A, Franssen E, et al: The Behavior Pathology in Alzheimer's Disease Rating Scale (BEHAVE-AD): reliability and analysis of symptom category scores. International Journal of Geriatric Psychiatry 11:1–12, 1996

Dementia Signs and Symptoms (DSS) Scale

D. J. Loreck, F. W. Bylsma, and M. F. Folstein

GOALS

The Dementia Signs and Symptoms (DSS) Scale (Loreck et al. 1994) was designed to measure the noncognitive symptoms associated with dementia on a set of six ordinal scales, each pertaining to a specific domain of behavioral symptoms associated with dementia: Anxiety, Mania, Depression, Behavior, Delusions, and Hallucinations/Illusions. The DSS Scale is a comprehensive assessment of the noncognitive symptoms of dementia that can be used to track the development and progression of these symptoms or their response to an intervention.

DESCRIPTION

The DSS Scale is an examiner-completed scale rated on the basis of interviews with both the patient and a knowledgeable informant. It is modeled after the Present State Examination (PSE) (p. 53). The DSS Scale is designed to be used in its entirety, although preference may be given to individual domains (e.g., Mania Behavior) depending on the symptoms reported or observed and the purpose of the rating. The DSS Scale has a total of 55 items: the Anxiety subscale has 4 items, the Mania subscale has 6, the Depression subscale has 8, the Behavior subscale has 13, and the Delusions and Hallucinations/Illusions subscales have 12 each. Each item is rated from 0 = absent to 3 = severe or as U = unable to obtain. The scales are rated separately for patient and informant interviews; the examiner then generates a composite score. Global ratings are made by the examiner on the frequency and severity in each area. The DSS Scale is designed to be administered by psychiatrists, other clinicians, and nurses.

DSS Scale scores are best described by domain. Anxiety scores range from 0 to 12, Mania scores from 0 to 18, Depression scores from 0 to 24, Behavior scores from 0 to 39 (with three subscales: Restlessness, 0–15; Social Disruptiveness, 0–15; and Aggressiveness, 0–9), Delusions scores from 0 to 24, and Hallucinations/Illusions scores from 0 to 12. The total score ranges from 0 to 129. Elderly persons without dementia used as control subjects in the development of the DSS Scale scored on average between 0 and 2; most of the scores above 0 were accounted for by positive anxiety ratings. Thus, a score of 2 or higher on any individual DSS subscale should be considered clinically significant. Patients with dementia score as follows on the DSS Scale (mean and standard deviation): Anxiety, 2.7 and 2.1; Mania, 1.3 and 2.0; Depression, 4.2 and 3.5; Total Behavior, 7.0 and 6.1; Restlessness, 2.7 and 2.6; Social Disruptiveness, 2.8 and 2.6; Aggressiveness, 1.5 and 1.8; Delusions, 3.6 and 3.1; and Hallucinations/Illusions, 0.5 and 0.9.

PRACTICAL ISSUES

It takes 30–45 minutes to rate the DSS Scale, including interviews with the patient and an informant and completing the rating form. All items and sufficient information to complete the ratings may be found in Loreck et al. (1994). Training for raters is recommended, either in the use of the DSS Scale or in the use of the PSE (p. 53) or the Schedules for Clinical Assessment in Neuropsychiatry (SCAN) (p. 53), which have many elements in common with the DSS Scale.

PSYCHOMETRIC PROPERTIES

Reliability

In a single reliability study ($N = 15$) of outpatients, individual DSS subscales yielded Cronbach's alphas of 0.63 for Anxiety, 0.72 for Mania, 0.70 for Depression, 0.82 for Behavior (Restlessness, 0.75; Social Disruptiveness, 0.50; and Aggressiveness, 0.58), 0.57 for Delusions, and 0.37 for Hallucinations/Illusions. Joint reliability, on the basis of ratings by 2 psychiatrists viewing videotaped interviews of 15 patients with Alzheimer's disease and their informants, yielded intraclass correlation coefficients ranging from 0.92 to 0.99 across the various subscale ratings and for the total score. Reliability data are not available for populations without Alzheimer's disease.

Validity

Several standard scales were rated independently as gold standards to validate DSS subscales on 54 patients with dementia. DSS subscales had expected correlation coefficients (r) with other measures of the same domains: 0.87 for the DSS Anxiety subscale with the Hamilton Anxiety Rating Scale (p. 554); 0.94 for the DSS Mania subscale with the Young Mania Rating Scale (p. 540); 0.74 for the DSS Depression subscale with the Hamilton Rating Scale for Depression (Ham-D) (p. 526), 0.84 with the Cornell Scale for Depression in Dementia (CSDD) (p. 407), and 0.83 with the Behavior Pathology in Alzheimer's Disease Rating Scale (BEHAVE-AD) (p. 401) Depression subscale; 0.74 for the DSS Restlessness subscale with the BEHAVE-AD Restlessness subscale; 0.92 for the DSS Delusions subscale with the BEHAVE-AD Paranoid and Delusional Ideation subscale; and 0.93 for the DSS Hallucinations/Illusions subscale with the BEHAVE-AD Hallucinations subscale. The DSS Scale total score also correlated ($r = 0.62$) with the BEHAVE-AD rating of overall behavioral disturbance. DSS subscales were compared with ratings of severity of cognitive impairment on the Mini-Mental State Exam (MMSE) (p. 422) and on the Blessed-Roth Dementia Rating Scale (p. 427). As expected, all subscales correlated positively with the Blessed-Roth Dementia Rating Scale ratings ($r = 0.29$ to 0.74) and negatively with the MMSE scores ($r = -0.11$ to -0.42).

CLINICAL UTILITY

The DSS Scale may be used to characterize the nature and extent of noncognitive symptoms in patients with dementia and to track changes in these symptoms with the progression of disease or in response to interventions. Although available data are sparse, they do support the former use, with each subscale showing high reliability and generally very good validity when compared with a standard measure in that domain. The high reliability and high correlations of most subscales with dementia

severity measures found in the single small study described earlier suggest that the instrument may also prove to be a good measure of change in this population, but as yet there has been no documentation of its performance in this area.

REFERENCES AND SUGGESTED READINGS

Loreck DJ, Bylsma FW, Folstein MF: The Dementia Signs and Symptoms Scale: a new scale for comprehensive assessment of psychopathology in Alzheimer's disease. American Journal of Geriatric Psychiatry 2:60–74, 1994

Neuropsychiatric Inventory (NPI)

J. L. Cummings, M. Mega, K. Gray, S. Rosenberg-Thompson, D. A. Carusi, and J. Gornbein

GOALS

The Neuropsychiatric Inventory (NPI) (Cummings et al. 1994) was developed to assess 10 domains of behavioral disturbance that are often found in patients with dementia; assessment is made on the basis of a series of ordinal scales and a total NPI score. Each of the 10 domains is assessed in a different subsection: Delusions, Hallucinations, Dysphoria, Anxiety, Agitation/Aggression, Euphoria, Disinhibition, Irritability/Lability, Apathy, and Aberrant Motor Behavior. The primary purpose of the measure is to provide a rapid assessment of a wide variety of behaviors encountered in dementia patients, with an indicator of their frequency and severity. Other uses of the measure include assessing the response of individual behavioral disturbances to treatment and the longitudinal observation of these disturbances over the course of the demential illness.

DESCRIPTION

The NPI is a rater-administered, fully structured interview in which all questions are provided and read verbatim. The sole source of information is the interview with a caregiver who knows the patient well. A gate question is included for each of the 10 subsections If the gate question is answered in the affirmative, the interviewer then asks the seven to nine follow-up questions about the presence or absence of specific symptoms within that domain. If any one of these symptoms is endorsed, the interviewer then has the caregiver rate the whole subsection (e.g., Disinhibition) on a 4-point frequency scale (1 = occasionally, 2 = often, 3 = frequently, and 4 = very frequently) and on a 3-point severity scale (1 = mild, 2 = moderate, and 3 = severe). The total subscale score is the mathematical product of frequency and severity. The total NPI score is the sum of the subscale scores. The NPI is designed to be administered by any clinician or by a trained research assistant. Different classes of raters produce equivalent ratings on the NPI after similar training in its use.

NPI subscale scores range from 0 to 12. Total NPI scores range from 0 to 120. Psychiatrically healthy control subjects score 0 on all NPI subscales, except Dysphoria (mean of 0.25, range of 0–6), Irritability (mean of 0.05, range of 0–2), and Disinhibition (mean of 0.13, range of 0–4). The presence of any delusions or hallucinations on the NPI (i.e., a score of ≥ 1 on either subscale) should be considered clinically significant. A Dysphoria score >6, Disinhibition score >4, Irritability/Lability score >2, and scores on the Apathy, Agitation/Aggression, Euphoria, and Aberrant Motor Behavior subscales >1 were not observed in any control subjects, and thus higher scores on any of these subscales suggest the presence of psychiatric disorder. Total NPI scores across different severities of Alzheimer's disease are mild, mean = 9.8 and SD = 10; moderate, mean = 14.7 and SD = 11.3; and severe, mean = 21.9 and SD = 9.0. The overall frequency of NPI-rated behaviors were as follows in an unselected population of patients with Alzheimer's disease: delusions, 22%; hallucinations, 10%; agitation, 60%; dysphoria, 38%; anxiety, 48%; euphoria, 8%; apathy, 72%; disinhibition, 36%; irritability, 42%; and aberrant motor behavior, 38%.

PRACTICAL ISSUES

It takes 15–25 minutes to administer the NPI, depending in part on the extent of symptomatology. The NPI is well received by caregivers. The instrument can be obtained by writing to

> Dr. Jeffrey Cummings
> Reed Neurological Research Center
> University of California–Los Angeles (UCLA)
> School of Medicine
> 710 Westwood Plaza
> Los Angeles, CA 90095-1769

Although the NPI is copyrighted by Dr. Cummings, there is no cost associated with its use. There is no manual to accompany the NPI, but instructions for its use are available from Dr. Cummings. Training for raters is necessary and may be assisted by training videotapes available from Dr. Cummings at a nominal cost. Translations are available in Dutch, French, German, Greek, Hebrew, Italian, Japanese, Norwegian, Spanish, and Thai.

PSYCHOMETRIC PROPERTIES

Reliability

In a single study of the internal consistency of the NPI, a Cronbach's alpha of 0.88 was observed for the total NPI score. For individual subscales, alpha values ranged from 0.87 to 0.88. In 45 joint caregiver interviews by a psychiatrist and a nonpsychiatrist rater using the NPI, the percentage of agreement for subscales ranged from 94% to 100% for frequency ratings and from 90% to 100% for severity ratings. In follow-up interviews 2–3 weeks apart, test-retest correlation coefficients (r) ranged from 0.51 (Aggression) to 0.97 (Disinhibition) for frequency ratings and from 0.51 (Irritability) to 1.0 (Hallucinations) for severity ratings.

Validity

The NPI and its subscales correlate well with other general measures of behavioral disturbance and established measures of specific domains. When 45 patients with Alzheimer's disease were rated on the NPI, with the Behavior Pathology in Alzheimer's Disease Rating Scale (BEHAVE-AD) (p. 401) and its subscales as the gold standard, the following correlation coefficients (r) were found: total BEHAVE-AD score with NPI total frequency score, 0.66; total BEHAVE-AD score with NPI severity, 0.71; and total BEHAVE-AD score with NPI frequency times severity, 0.62. Section-by-section correlation coefficients (r) between the BEHAVE-AD subscales and corresponding NPI subscales ranged as follows: 0.54–0.78 for frequency, 0.47–0.80 for severity, and 0.33–0.77 for frequency times severity. When the Hamilton Rating Scale for Depression (Ham-D) (p. 526) was used as a gold standard for Depression section ratings, correlation coefficients (r) between the Ham-D and the NPI were 0.70 for frequency, 0.59 for severity, and 0.62 for frequency times severity.

In addition, one study suggests that the NPI is sensitive to change. In an open trial of tacrine in patients with Alzheimer's disease, with use of the NPI to rate changes in noncognitive symptoms, reductions were noted in anxiety (–40%), apathy (–33%), disinhibition (–70%), and aberrant motor behaviors (–37%). There were also significant decreases in total NPI scores at higher doses of tacrine (mean decrease of 7–8 points, SD = 8–9).

CLINICAL UTILITY

The data described suggest that the NPI may be useful in clinical settings to describe the pattern and severity of behavioral disturbances in patients with Alzheimer's disease. Psychiatrists might use the NPI information obtained by nurses or other staff members to help guide treatment decisions. In addition, because of its brevity and suitability for use by lay interviewers, the NPI appears useful for screening patients in nonpsychiatric settings (e.g., domiciliaries, nursing homes, and retirement communities) for behavioral disturbances in patients with dementia. (However, the cost of brevity is that some specific symptoms may be missed if gate questions are answered negatively.) In addition, preliminary evidence suggests that the NPI may have sufficient sensitivity to change to be used as an outcome measure in treatment trials, although this feature may not apply uniformly across the subscales.

The main limitation of the NPI is that it is fairly new and has not been subjected to widespread clinical use. Although it was developed primarily for outpatients with

Alzheimer's disease, it has now been studied in patients with a variety of disorders, including frontotemporal dementia and progressive supranuclear palsy. A nursing home version has also been developed but awaits more complete assessment.

REFERENCES AND SUGGESTED READINGS

Cummings JL, Mega M, Gray K, et al: The Neuropsychiatric Inventory: comprehensive assessment of psychopathology in dementia. Neurology 44:2308–2314, 1994

Kaufer DI, Cummings JL, Christine D: Effect of tacrine on behavioral symptoms in Alzheimer's disease: an open label study. J Geriatr Psychiatry Neurol 9:1–6, 1996

Levy ML, Miller BL, Cummings JL, et al: Alzheimer disease and frontotemporal dementias: behavioral distinctions. Arch Neurol 53:687–690, 1996

Litvan I, Mega M, Cummings JL, et al: Neuropsychiatric aspects of progressive supranuclear palsy. Neurology 47:1184–1189, 1996

Cornell Scale for Depression in Dementia (CSDD)

G. S. Alexopoulos, R. C. Abrams, R. C. Young, and C. A. Shamaian

GOALS

The Cornell Scale for Depression in Dementia (CSDD) (Alexopoulos et al. 1988a) is an ordinal scale developed to provide quantitative ratings of depression in dementia patients to describe depressive symptomatology and to assess response to treatment.

DESCRIPTION

The CSDD is a rater-completed assessment with its basis in an unstructured interview of the patient and a caregiver or other knowledgeable informant. The CSDD has a total of 19 items: 4 items to assess mood, 4 items to assess depression-associated behavior disturbance, 3 items to assess physical signs of depression, 4 items to assess cyclic (diurnal) functions, and 4 items to assess ideational disturbance. Each item is rated on a 3-point scale as 0 = absent, 1 = mild/intermittent, 2 = severe, and a = unable to evaluate. The CSDD is designed to be administered by clinicians, specifically physicians or registered nurses.

CSDD scores range from 0 to 38; higher scores indicate more depression. A cutoff score of ≥ 8 is associated with a diagnosis of major depressive disorder in patients with dementia, whereas a cutoff score of ≥ 7 may be more appropriate for elderly patients without dementia. Mean scores for patients with dementia and major depressive disorder are in the range of 12–22, whereas those without depressive disorders score about 5.

PRACTICAL ISSUES

It takes 30 minutes to administer the CSDD (20 minutes for the caregiver interview and 10 minutes for the patient interview). There is no published manual. Adequate instructions for its use can be found in Alexopoulos et al. (1988a). Training for raters is recommended. A training video is now available from the author. In the article that describes the development of the CSDD (Alexopoulos et al. 1988a), the psychiatrists who rated it had two training sessions in which they jointly rated patients with depression and dementia and then compared and discussed their ratings. The measure may be obtained by contacting the author:

> George Alexopoulos, M.D.
> New York Hospital–Cornell Medical Center
> Westchester Division
> 21 Bloomingdale Road
> White Plains, NY 10605

The CSDD is included on the CD-ROM that accompanies this handbook.

PSYCHOMETRIC PROPERTIES

Reliability

High internal consistency of the CSDD has been shown by 1) Cronbach's alpha ranging from 0.65 to 0.84 in sev-

eral studies, 2) item-to-item intercorrelations with a mean $r = 0.24$ (SE = 0.15) in one study, 3) a Kuder-Richardson split-half reliability coefficient of 0.98, and 4) correlations between item scores and scale total scores ranging from 0.64 to 0.99. In addition, joint reliability in several studies that used dual-observer paradigms showed a weighted kappa ranging from 0.67 to 0.76 for the total scale score and item kappa values from 0.56 to 1.0.

Validity

Scores on the CSDD have been shown to be correlated with scores on the Hamilton Rating Scale for Depression (Ham-D) (p. 526) ($r = 0.86$). In addition, one study compared CSDD ratings with an in-depth, semistructured psychiatric interview using Research Diagnostic Criteria for minor depression, probable major depression, and definite major depression. The CSDD was significantly associated with these diagnoses in patients with and without dementia. In a different study with a similar paradigm, the point correlation between CSDD and independent psychiatric diagnosis was high, $r = 0.8$ ($t = 5.20$, $df = 32$), and the area under the curve in receiver operating characteristic (ROC) analyses was 0.91 (SE = 0.05), indicating that the CSDD is highly informative when judged against a clinical interview. ROC analyses indicated that a CSDD cutoff score of ≥ 8 might be optimal for distinguishing depressed from nondepressed patients among those with dementia (sensitivity of 0.72 and specificity of 0.90), and a cutoff score of ≥ 7 might be best for persons without dementia (sensitivity of 0.87 and specificity of 0.92).

The CSDD has also been shown to be sensitive to change with treatment. Change in CSDD score with treatment was correlated with change in the Global Assessment Scale score (p. 96) ($r = 0.72$). After treatment for depression, CSDD scores in inpatients with dementia declined. After treatment of patients with Alzheimer's disease with L-deprenyl, CSDD scores declined in three domains: mood, behavior disturbance ($r < 0.01$), and ideational disturbance.

CLINICAL UTILITY

The CSDD may be used with a cutoff score of 8 to aid in the diagnosis of depression in elderly patients with dementia. However, a sensitivity of 0.72 against a clinical diagnosis of depression suggests that such an approach might miss a substantial fraction of cases, which is problematic given the low threshold recommended for treatment of depression in patients with dementia. A lower threshold might be used to screen for possible cases, with a follow-up clinical evaluation to rule out false-positive diagnoses, which tend to be associated with apathy and/or neurovegetative signs such as weight loss and fatigue. For patients without dementia, a cutoff score of 7 performs somewhat better, although it may be preferable to select a lower threshold to screen for possible cases.

Given its good reliability and sensitivity to change, another potential use of the CSDD is to quantify the severity of depression in patients with dementia and to assess their response to treatment.

Use of the CSDD in clinical trials is increasing, so that familiarity with the measure will assist clinicians in interpreting their results.

REFERENCES AND SUGGESTED READINGS

Alexopoulos GS, Abrams RC, Young RC, et al: Cornell Scale for Depression in Dementia. Biol Psychiatry 23:271–284, 1988a

Alexopoulos GS, Abrams RC, Young RC, et al: Use of the Cornell Scale in nondemented adults. J Am Geriatr Soc 36:230–236, 1988b

Vida S, Des Rosiers P, Carrier L, et al: Depression in Alzheimer's disease: receiver operating curve characteristic analysis of the Cornell Scale for Depression in Dementia and the Hamilton Depression Scale. J Geriatr Psychiatry Neurol 7:159–162, 1994

Apathy Evaluation Scale (AES)

R. S. Marin, R. C. Bierdzycki, and S. Firinciogullari

GOALS

The Apathy Evaluation Scale (AES) (Marin et al. 1991) was developed to quantify apathy in adult patients and to measure changes in apathy with treatment. Apathy, as conceptualized in the AES, means diminished activity due to lack of motivation. The AES operationalizes diminished motivation by evaluating (overt) behavioral (e.g., lack of productivity, lack of effort), cognitive (e.g., lack of interests or curiosity), and emotional (e.g., diminished emotional response, flat affect) aspects of goal-directed behavior.

DESCRIPTION

There are three versions of the AES: a self-rated version (AES-S), an informant-rated version (e.g., for a caregiver) (AES-I), and a clinician-rated version (AES-C). All AES ratings refer to the past 4 weeks. The AES-S and AES-I are self-administered questionnaires at a ninth-grade reading level. The AES-C covers the same items but is rated by a clinician (e.g., physician, clinician with a Ph.D. or M.S.W., or registered nurse) after a semistructured interview with the patient. Clinician raters of different professional backgrounds appear to produce comparable ratings on the AES. A rating guide instructs the clinician on how to use observations of the patient, along with specific answers to questions, to rate the AES-C.

The AES has 18 items, each describing the patient on a 4-point Likert scale from 1 = not at all characteristic to 4 = very characteristic. Four items are positively rated self-evaluations, with no examiner input allowed on the AES-C (see Example 20–4). The remaining items allow examiner judgment for the AES-C: 11 are positively rated, and 3 are negatively rated (see Example 20–4). Scores range from 18 to 72; higher scores indicate more apathy. Psychiatrically healthy subjects typically

EXAMPLE 20–4 ■ Sample items from the Apathy Evaluation Scale

Self-Evaluation
  Seeing a job through to the end is important to him/her.

Positively Rated Examiner Evaluation
  S/he is interested in things.

Negatively Rated Examiner Evaluation
  S/he puts little effort into anything.

Reprinted with permission from Dr. R. S. Marin.

score 25–35 or below, whereas patients with clinically significant apathy alone or as part of dementia or depression may score 40 or higher.

PRACTICAL ISSUES

It takes 2–10 minutes for the subject or informant to complete the AES-S or AES-I. It takes clinicians 10–20 minutes to conduct the interview and complete the AES-C. The complete AES is published, along with the semistructured interview for the AES-C and scoring instructions, in Marin et al. (1991). Practice ratings are recommended before clinicians use the AES-C formally. Detailed administration guidelines are available on request from the first author:

> Robert S. Marin, M.D.
> Western Psychiatric Institute and Clinic
> 3811 O'Hara Street
> Pittsburgh, PA 15213

PSYCHOMETRIC PROPERTIES

Reliability

In a single study of the AES ($N = 123$), Cronbach's alpha was 0.90 for the AES-C, 0.94 for the AES-I, and 0.86 for the AES-S. In joint interviewer-observer ratings, the intraclass correlation coefficient (ICC) for the AES-C overall was 0.94, and kappa values for individual items ranged from 0.35 to 0.73, with a mean of 0.58. When test-retest reliability was examined with ratings 2–3 weeks apart, ICCs were 0.88 for the AES-C, 0.94 for the AES-I, and 0.76 for the AES-S.

Validity

The AES is the first instrument designed specifically to measure apathy, so there is no gold standard against which to judge it. Therefore, efforts to validate it began by comparing ratings obtained on the three versions of the AES. The correlation coefficient (r) for the AES-C and AES-S was 0.72, for the AES-C and AES-I 0.62, and for the AES-I and AES-S 0.43. Next, AES ratings were compared with behaviors thought to express level of interest and thus to be inversely associated with apathy. When subjects were placed in a waiting room with the option of playing video games, AES ratings were inversely correlated with the percentage of time spent playing games ($r = -0.4$ for AES-C and -0.33 for AES-I) and with the average time per game ($r = -0.29$ to -0.45, depending on AES version). There was also, as would be expected, a positive correlation between AES ratings and latency between games ($r = 0.26$–0.45).

The next issue was to show that the AES could differentiate patients expected to be apathetic from psychiatrically healthy control subjects. A group of psychiatrically healthy control subjects ($n = 31$) scored about 26–28 (depending on the AES version) (SD = 6), patients with major depressive disorder scored 37–41 (SD = 11), stroke patients scored about 28–35 (SD = 9), and patients with Alzheimer's disease scored 36–45 (SD = 10). Whereas apathy is common in depressed patients, apathy as measured by the AES was, as expected on the basis of the test authors' hypothesis about apathy, partly independent of depression: the correlation between clinician-rated apathy and clinician-rated depression was only 0.39.

CLINICAL UTILITY

The most well documented use of the AES is to quantify apathy, whether occurring alone or in the context of another condition, such as dementia, major depression, or stroke or other central nervous system insult. As such, it could be used to assess response to specific treatments, such as antidepressants, stimulants, and other dopamine-augmenting agents (e.g., amantadine and L-dopa). However, it should be noted that no data regarding sensitivity to change with time are available.

Although no cutoff score has been suggested or evaluated, with further development, the AES might be used to screen for apathy in the context of dementia, depression, or stroke. Persons with moderate to severe depression and with dementia, particularly subcortical dementia, score high on all AES versions. However, work by Marin et al. (1993, 1994) shows that apathy as rated on the AES can be distinguished to some extent from depression and dementia, at least on a cross-sectional basis.

On the basis of clinical experience with the instrument, the authors of the measure suggest that it is preferable to use the AES-C under most circumstances. However, available data suggest that valid results can also be obtained from the other versions, particularly the AES-I.

REFERENCES AND SUGGESTED READINGS

Marin RS, Biedrzycki RC, Firinciogullari S: Reliability and validity of the Apathy Evaluation Scale. Psychiatry Res 38:143–162, 1991

Marin RS, Firinciogullari S, Biedrzycki RC: The sources of convergence between measures of apathy and depression. J Affect Disord 28:117–124, 1993

Marin RS, Firinciogullari S, Biedrzycki RC: Group differences in the relationship between apathy and depression. J Nerv Ment Dis 182:235–239, 1994

Marin RC, Fogel BS, Hawkins J, et al: Apathy: a treatable syndrome. J Neuropsychiatry Clin Neurosci 7:23–30, 1995

Burden Interview (BI)

S. H. Zarit and J. M. Zarit

GOALS

The Burden Interview (BI) (Zarit and Zarit 1990) was designed to assess the subjective burden of caring for an elderly or disabled person on the basis of a composite of several aspects of the caregiver's reactions to his or her experience. The primary purpose of the BI is to provide a rapid composite measure of the burden of caregiving for a wide range of elderly or disabled persons.

DESCRIPTION

The BI is a self-administered questionnaire written at an eighth-grade reading level. Each of the 22 questions asks about the impact of the patient's disabilities on the caregiver's life. Responses are scored on a 0–4 Likert scale,

indicating that the caregiver has 0 = never, 1 = rarely, 2 = sometimes, 3 = quite frequently, or 4 = nearly always had the experience in question. Sample questions are provided in Example 20–5.

BI scores range from 0 to 88. No particular cutoff score is recommended, but any score other than 0 on the BI suggests that some burden is being experienced by the caregiver. A variety of studies have reported mean scores on the BI ranging from 26 to 56 for the caregivers of elderly outpatients with dementia and for former caregivers of patients who have recently been institutionalized. The mean BI score for caregivers of elderly depressed patients recently admitted to a psychiatric unit was reported to be 27.

PRACTICAL ISSUES

It takes 10–15 minutes to complete the BI. The questionnaire is copyrighted by Steven Zarit and Judy Zarit and can be obtained from

> Dr. Steven M. Zarit
> Gerontology Center
> 105 Henderson Building South
> Pennsylvania State University
> College Park, PA 16802-6505
> Phone: 814-865-1710

A short manual for administration can be obtained at the same address. The BI has been translated into French, Japanese, and Spanish. A Spanish version is available from

> Carlos A. Mangone, M.D.
> Avenida Rivadavia 4379, Apt. 12B
> (1205) Buenos Aires, Argentina
> Fax: 54-114-982-6259

EXAMPLE 20–5 ■ Sample items from the Burden Interview

> Do you feel embarrassed over your relative's behavior?
>
> Do you feel your relative is dependent on you?

Reprinted with permission from Dr. Steven Zarit.

A French version is available from

> Rejean Hebert
> CERGG Hopital
> Youville
> 1036 Belvedere Sud
> Sherbrooke QU J1H4C4 Canada

The BI is included on the CD-ROM that accompanies this handbook.

PSYCHOMETRIC PROPERTIES

Reliability

In four studies, Cronbach's alpha ranged from 0.79 to 0.91. Test-retest scores 1 week apart yielded a correlation coefficient (r) of 0.71.

Validity

Total scores on the BI were highly correlated with the caregiver's separate global rating of burden on a 7-point Likert scale ($r = 0.71$). Total scores on the BI also correlated with the caregiver's assessment of various aspects of the caregiving relationship—communication ($r = -0.44$), affection ($r = -0.59$ to -0.61), and consensus ($r = -0.61$)—and with the estimated number of hours spent caregiving ($r = 0.38$). Total scores on the BI also correlated, as expected, with a variety of caregiver variables, including depression ($r = 0.42$), hostility ($r = 0.47$), morale ($r = -0.41$), financial impact of the patient's illness ($r = 0.67$), physical abuse of the patient by the caregiver, and respite use. In addition, BI scores correlated modestly with several relevant patient variables: physical disability ($r = 0.29$), pain ($r = 0.33$), self-efficacy expectations ($r = -0.37$), preserved cognition ($r = -0.27$), scores on the Mini-Mental State Exam (MMSE) (p. 422) ($r = 0.25$), behavior disturbance ($r = 0.53$), depression ($r = 0.36$), sleep disturbance ($r = 0.24$), impaired activities of daily living ($r = 0.29$), and paranoia ($r = 0.26$).

Finally, as would be expected, in the absence of an intervention, BI scores tend to increase over time in a progressive illness. In one intervention study of caregivers of patients with dementia conducted over an 8-month period, those who received the intervention showed more stable BI scores over time but no clear decreases. On the other hand, spouses of laryngectomy patients showed dramatic declines in BI scores from a mean of 37 immediately after surgery to a mean of 9 one year later.

CLINICAL UTILITY

The BI may be used clinically to quantify and characterize the subjective burden associated with caregiving in a wide range of caregivers, whether they or their charges are the focus of treatment. The instrument is well accepted by caregivers; some report that it helps them to clarify their emotions associated with caregiving. Although the instrument has been used as a paper and pencil questionnaire, it could in principle be read aloud as a fully structured questionnaire or even administered over the telephone. The instrument has been validated primarily for use with caregivers of dementia patients, although its focus on subjective burden may make it suitable for those caring for individuals with other illnesses.

Because the instrument has been shown to be sensitive to change over time, it may be used to assess the outcome of an intervention. However, it should be remembered that for caregivers of patients with Alzheimer's disease and other progressive illnesses, even stable scores over a period of months or longer may indicate benefit.

REFERENCES AND SUGGESTED READINGS

Anthony-Bergstone CL, Zarit SH, Gatz M: Symptoms of psychological distress among caregivers of dementia patients. Psychol Aging 3:245–248, 1988

Hebert R, Ledeclerc G, Bravo G, et al: Efficacy of a support group programme for caregivers of demented patients in the community: a randomized controlled trial. Archives of Gerontology and Geriatrics 18:1–4, 1994

Mangone CA, Sanguinetti RM, Baumann PD, et al: Influence of feelings of burden on the caregiver's perception of the patient's functioning status. Dementia 4:287–293, 1993

Quayhagen MP, Quayhagen M: Differential effects of family-based strategies on Alzheimer's disease. Gerontologist 2:150–155, 1989

Zarit SH, Zarit JM: The Memory and Behavior Problems Checklist and the Burden Interview (Pennsylvania State University, Gerontology Center Reprint Series No 189, part 3). College Park, PA, Pennsylvania State University Gerontology Center, 1990

Screen for Caregiver Burden (SCB)

P. P. Vitaliano, J. Russo, H. M. Young, J. Becker, and R. D. Maiuro

GOALS

The Screen for Caregiver Burden (SCB) (Vitaliano et al. 1991a) was designed to quantify the physical, psychological, emotional, social, and financial problems that can be experienced by those who care for impaired older relatives, particularly those with Alzheimer's disease. Several aspects of burden are incorporated into the SCB, including behaviors of the care recipient, affective responses of the caregiver, financial resources, and disruption in family and social life.

DESCRIPTION

The SCB is a self-administered questionnaire for caregivers. It is specifically worded for use with spouses but can be used with other caregivers with slight modifications in the wording. Approximately a ninth-grade reading level is required. The SCB has 25 items that cover issues about the caregiver, the care recipient, and their interactions. Each item is a statement about an experience the caregiver may or may not have had in caring for a person with dementia. Items are rated on a 5-point scale, with 0 = did not occur, 1 = occurred but caused no distress, 2 = mild distress, 3 = moderate distress, and 4 = severe distress. Sample items are provided in Example 20–6.

There are two methods for scoring the SCB. The objective burden (OB) score sums the total items rated as present (i.e., rated above 0 on the Likert scale) and ranges from 0 to 25. The subjective burden (SB) score simply adds the Likert ratings and ranges from 0 to 100.

OB scores above 4 and SB scores above 30 are probably of clinical significance. Spouses of outpatients with Alzheimer's disease scored 9–10 (SD = 4–5) on the OB score and 36–38 (SD = 8–11) on the SB score. Spouses of age- and gender-matched psychiatrically healthy control subjects had a mean OB score of 1.7 (SD = 2.4) and a mean SB score of 2.6 (SD = 3).

PRACTICAL ISSUES

It takes 2–5 minutes to complete the SCB. It is available at no cost from

> Dr. P. P. Vitaliano
> Department of Psychiatry and Behavioral Sciences
> University of Washington—Medical Center
> RP-10
> Seattle, WA 98195

There is no manual for the SCB. The key references at the end of this section provide adequate background for its use. A Spanish translation can also be obtained from Dr. Vitaliano.

The SCB is included on the CD-ROM that accompanies this handbook.

PSYCHOMETRIC PROPERTIES

Reliability

For spouses of patients with Alzheimer's disease, Cronbach's alphas were 0.84–0.85 for the OB score and 0.88–0.89 for the SB score. For spouses of psychiatrically healthy control subjects, alphas were 0.81 for the OB score and 0.82 for the SB score.

Validity

The SCB is able to discriminate between spouses of Alzheimer's disease patients and spouses of psychiatrically healthy control subjects, whether scored as OB or SB. In addition, whether scored as OB or SB, the SCB has been shown to correlate with a variety of measures of caregiver and care recipient status in spouses of outpatients with Alzheimer's disease. Consistent with the aims of the two scoring methods, the OB was more strongly correlated with care recipient functioning measures (which explained 21%–37% of OB variance at two points in time), whereas the SB was more strongly correlated with caregiver distress measures (which explained 19%–24% of SB variance). Burden as measured by the SCB, even subjective burden as embodied in SB scoring, is to some extent independent of psychiatric distress; for instance, caregiver control differences persist even after controlling for concurrent anxiety or depression in the caregiver.

When used to evaluate spouses of patients with Alzheimer's disease, the SCB has been shown to change over time, as would be expected with a progressive illness. In a study of 79 spousal caregivers of Alzheimer outpatients, OB scores were 9.0 at baseline and increased significantly after 15–18 months to 10.2. The SB scores increased similarly from 35.5 to 37.16.

CLINICAL UTILITY

The SCB may be useful for characterizing and quantifying caregiver burden when either the caregiver or the care recipient is the focus of treatment. At times, a thorough review of the possible areas of burden may help to identify the specific caregiving issues that are most distressing for the caregiver and that might be addressed through medical intervention, problem solving, or supportive psychotherapy.

Because the SCB offers a quantitative measure of burden, it might also be useful to measure changes over time, although the data demonstrating sensitivity to change are somewhat limited. On the basis of preliminary data, because the OB score correlates more with the status of the care recipient, it might be more sensitive to changes expected to decrease burden by improving the status of the care recipient (e.g., treatment of behavioral symptoms). Similarly, because the SB score correlates more with caregiver status, it might be more sensitive to interventions aimed more directly at the caregiver.

The main limitations of the SCB are that it was developed and assessed entirely on a single sample of spou-

sal caregivers of outpatients with Alzheimer's disease. Its utility as a measure of burden for adult child or other family caregivers, for professional caregivers, for caregivers of institutionalized patients, and for caregivers of patients with other types of dementia is not known but deserves further study.

REFERENCES AND SUGGESTED READINGS

Vitaliano PP, Russo J, Young HM, et al: The Screen for Caregiver Burden. Gerontologist 31:76–83, 1991a

Vitaliano PP, Young HM, Russo J: Burden: a review of measures used among caregivers of individuals with dementia. Gerontologist 31:67–75, 1991b

Psychogeriatric Dependency Rating Scales (PGDRS)

I. M. Wilkinson and J. Graham-White

GOALS

The Psychogeriatric Dependency Rating Scales (PGDRS) (Wilkinson and Graham-White 1980) were developed to describe the degree and type of dependency of elderly patients with behavioral or other psychiatric disturbances. Dependency is assessed on an ordinal scale that encompasses the three domains of orientation, behavior, and physical dependency. Dependency is defined as nursing time demanded by the patient to address impairments in orientation, behavior, and physical abilities (i.e., hearing, sight, and activities of daily living). The PGDRS was developed primarily to assist in determining an elderly patient's level of care for placement in assisted living, residential care, chronic care, or skilled nursing facilities.

DESCRIPTION

The PGDRS is a rater-completed assessment that incorporates information from a patient examination, caregiver interview, and record review. After compiling the necessary information, the clinician (generally a physician or nurse) rates all items. Three domains are systematically assessed: Orientation (10 yes-no items); Behavior (16 items rated on the basis of frequency, with 0 = never, 1 = occasionally [occurring on no more than 2 out of 5 days], and 2 = frequently [occurring on more than 2 out of 5 days]); and Physical Dependency (16 items with a variety of possible scores that address hearing, vision, speech, dressing, mobility, and personal hygiene).

In each of the three domains, which are scored separately, higher scores indicate greater dependency. Scores on the Orientation section range from 0 to 20, scores on the Behavior section range from 0 to 32, and scores on the Physical Dependency section range from 0 to 39. Typical scores are reported as follows: geriatric psychiatry outpatients without dementia score a mean of 2 (SD = 1) on the Orientation, 5 (SD = 3) on the Behavior, and 6 (SD = 2) on the Physical Dependency subscales. Dementia outpatients score 3 (SD = 2) on the Orientation, 5 (SD = 2) on the Behavior, and 5 (SD = 3) on the Physical Dependency subscales. Patients with dementia who reside in assisted living facilities score 5 (SD = 3), 12 (SD = 6), and 10 (SD = 7) and those in nursing homes score 8 (SD = 3), 14 (SD = 7), and 18 (SD = 9) on the Orientation, Behavior, and Physical Dependency subscales, respectively.

PRACTICAL ISSUES

It takes an experienced clinician 10–15 minutes to rate the PGDRS, most of which is spent reviewing information and conducting interviews with the patient and caregiver. The Psychogeriatric Dependency Rating Worksheet, which includes definitions of categories, items, and responses and instructions for assessment, is available in Wilkinson and Graham-White (1980). The PGDRS can be rated adequately by using information in the primary publication of the scale (Wilkinson and Graham-White 1980). Training, which is recommended for raters, consists of reviewing the items and their definitions and

practicing rating the scale under the guidance of an experienced rater.

PSYCHOMETRIC PROPERTIES

Reliability

In a single study of joint reliability, two independent raters concurrently rated the same patients on the PGDRS. For Orientation, the mean weighted kappa was 0.61 (item range 0.42–0.78); for Behavior, 0.48 (0.40–0.63); and for Physical Dependency, 0.58 (0.41–0.79). Correlation coefficients (r) between domain and total scores were 0.86 for Orientation, 0.71 for Behavior, and 0.87 for Physical Dependency.

Validity

Because the PGDRS is intended primarily as an assessment of care needs, PGDRS ratings were compared with actual nursing time required to care for patients on four inpatient wards. The mean correlation between total PGDRS score and nursing time was 0.72 (range of 0.47–0.97 by domain). PGDRS scores >20 were highly predictive of admission to a geriatric psychiatry ward (weighted kappa = 0.75). Total PGDRS scores were also highly predictive of mortality at follow-up (weighted kappa = 0.40–0.74). The Orientation section, with a cutoff between 1 and 2, was reportedly able to distinguish organic from functional cases, although these terms were not defined.

CLINICAL UTILITY

Because the PGDRS correlates highly with actual nursing time required, its principal use is likely to be in the determination of level of care. This determination would probably most often be made at admission to a new facility, but it could also be helpful in assessing the care needs of outpatients. Data from the PGDRS might also be aggregated and used to determine staffing ratios in hospitals and chronic care settings. In addition, because the PGDRS offers considerable detail about specific areas of patient needs, it might be used as a means to organize discussion in multidisciplinary team meetings or in meetings with families who care for patients with dementia at home.

Although few data about the PGDRS's sensitivity to change over time are yet available, the measure is sufficiently reliable and detailed that it might prove useful in monitoring a patient over time to adjust the level of care as needed.

REFERENCES AND SUGGESTED READINGS

Wilkinson IM, Graham-White J: Psychogeriatric Dependency Rating Scales (PGDRS): a method of assessment for use by nurses. Br J Psychiatry 137:558–565, 1980

Neuropsychiatric Measures for Cognitive Disorders

David P. Salmon, Ph.D.

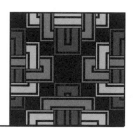

INTRODUCTION

Major Domains

Although the assessment of mental status has a long history in psychiatry and neurology (Donnelly et al. 1970), only in the last 30 years have objective, structured scales been developed and widely implemented. These scales were in many instances developed as research tools to quantify cognitive impairment so that it could be compared with physical measures of brain pathology or as clinical instruments designed as a quick and efficient means of distinguishing between organic and functional disorders in psychiatric patients. As the dementia associated with Alzheimer's disease came to be recognized as the most common cause of cognitive dysfunction in the elderly, many mental status examinations were specifically developed to assess the dementia associated with Alzheimer's disease.

Mental status examinations have generally taken two forms. First, there are structured scales or tests that are composed of a series of cognitive tasks that require relatively intact cognitive functioning for their performance. The tasks must be completed by the patient and are scored as correct or incorrect by the examiner. Second, there are staging systems for rating the presence and severity of cognitive dysfunction in an ordinal fashion on the basis of all sources of information about the patient, which may include direct mental status testing, the patient's own report of cognitive and functional status, the examiner's observations, and informants' reports of the functional competence of the patient. The staging systems provide guidelines for types of observations and cognitive testing that should be used to rate a patient, but they do not generally require a specific, structured interview. Both structured tests of mental status and dementia staging systems are reviewed in this chapter.

Organization

The measures included in this chapter are listed in Table 21–1. Structured tests of mental status are presented first, followed by dementia staging systems. The mental status tests selected for review were chosen not only because of their generally excellent reliability and validity for assessing cognitive dysfunction but also because they are relatively brief and easy to administer. The first five mental status measures presented here are currently widely used for both clinical and research purposes:

- The Mini-Mental State Exam (MMSE)
- The Information-Memory-Concentration (IMC) Test
- The Dementia Rating Scale (DRS)
- The Neurobehavioral Cognitive Status Examination (NCSE or COGNISTAT)
- The Clock Drawing Test

The next two mental status measures were developed for specialized purposes. The Alzheimer's Disease Assessment Scale (ADAS) was developed to evaluate cogni-

TABLE 21–1 ■ Neuropsychiatric measures for cognitive disorders

Name of measure	Disorder or construct assessed	Format	Pages
Mini-Mental State Exam (MMSE)*	Brief general survey of broad range of cognitive function	Fully structured scale; 30 points in 7 categories	422–427
Information-Memory-Concentration (IMC) Test	Brief survey of cognitive function with focus on orientation, concentration, and memory	Fully structured scale; 26 items	427–430
Dementia Rating Scale (DRS)	Broad, differentiated survey of cognitive function in moderate depth	Fully structured scale; 144 points in 5 subscales	430–434
Neurobehavioral Cognitive Status Examination (NCSE or COGNISTAT)*	Broad, differentiated survey of cognitive function	Fully structured scale; 11 subtests for 8 domains, with gate question in each to limit length	434–438
Clock Drawing Test	Brief assessment of cognitive function, with focus on visuospatial skills and constructional praxis	Different versions of clock drawing with quantitative and semiquantitative scoring systems	438–441
Alzheimer's Disease Assessment Scale (ADAS)*	Major cognitive and behavioral symptoms of Alzheimer's Disease	Fully structured; 21 items	441–443
Galveston Orientation and Amnesia Test (GOAT)*	Disorientation and amnesia caused by head injury	Fully structured; 10 items	443–446
Clinical Dementia Rating (CDR) Scale*	Global rating of dementia severity with focus on functional decline	Clinician rated on 5-point scale in 6 domains based on cognitive testing and semistructured interview of patient and informant	446–450
Global Deterioration Scale (GDS)* Brief Cognitive Rating Scale (BCRS) Functional Assessment Staging (FAST) Measures*: The GDS Staging System	Systematic rating system for overall (GDS), cognitive (BCRS), and functional (FAST) impairment in patients with dementia	GDS: 7-point rating scale BCRS: 7-point scale in each of 5 domains FAST: 7 major stages, with 16 successive stages and substages	450–455

*Measure is included on the CD-ROM that accompanies this handbook.

tion in clinical drug trials. The Galveston Orientation and Amnesia Test (GOAT) was developed to assess cognitive dysfunction after head injury.

Several well-known tests of cognitive ability are not reviewed here, primarily because they require extensive time and specialized training for administration (e.g., the Wechsler Adult Intelligence Scale [Wechsler 1955], the Luria-Nebraska Neuropsychological Battery [Golden et al. 1985], and the Halstead-Reitan Neuropsychological Test Battery [Reitan and Wolfson 1993]), because they are earlier versions or similar in content to other more widely used tests (e.g., the Short Portable Mental Status

Questionnaire [Pfeffer 1975]), or because they were designed primarily for use in epidemiological studies (e.g., the Cambridge Dementia Examination [CAMDEX] [Roth et al. 1986]).

Two dementia staging systems were selected for review: the Clinical Dementia Rating (CDR) Scale and the Global Deterioration Scale (GDS). Both have excellent validity and reliability and are widely used in research and clinical settings. These scales use information from both objective cognitive test results and the examiner's and an informant's observations of the patient's functional status.

Several well-known functional status scales that focus only on an informant's observations of the patient's performance are not reviewed here (e.g., the Pfeffer Outpatient Disability Scale [Pfeffer et al. 1982] and the functional portion of the Blessed-Roth Dementia Rating Scale [see IMC Test, p. 427]).

Relevant Measures Included Elsewhere in the Handbook

Readers interested in assessment tools for patients with cognitive disorders may also consult Chapter 20, "Behavioral Measures for Cognitive Disorders," which includes measures to evaluate the wide range of behavioral disturbances (e.g., hallucinations and delusions, suspiciousness and paranoia, depression, apathy, disinhibition, restlessness, irritability, agitation, combativeness, and aggression) that often accompany cognitive disorders. Measures found elsewhere in this volume may also be useful. The two functional status chapters, Chapter 8, "Mental Health Status, Functioning, and Disabilities Measures," and Chapter 9, "General Health Status, Functioning, and Disabilities Measures," include several general measures of functioning. Chapter 11, "Adverse Effects Measures," provides measures of extrapyramidal symptoms. Measures included in Chapter 6, "Diagnostic Interviews for Adults," Chapter 10, "Quality of Life Measures," and Chapter 30, "Sleep Disorders Measures," may also prove helpful in the assessment of patients with cognitive disorders, particularly when they have been validated for use with informants or can be easily adapted for such use.

USING MEASURES IN THIS DOMAIN

Goals of Assessment

The primary goals of a mental status examination are to detect and stage the degree of cognitive impairment associated with disorders of the nervous system and to track the progression of cognitive deterioration over time. These tests are also often designed and used as a means of objectively evaluating the efficacy of potential therapeutic agents that may slow, halt, or reverse the cognitive deterioration associated with various brain diseases. A final goal is to quantify the severity of cognitive dysfunction in order to discern its relationship to brain pathology. Given these goals, the optimal mental status scale

1. Is sensitive to subtle cognitive deficits that may occur after a neurological insult or that distinguish the beginning of a neurodegenerative disease such as Alzheimer's disease from normal aging

2. Assesses a wide range of cognitive functions, including verbal and nonverbal memory, language, attention, constructional and ideational praxis, conceptualization, problem solving, and judgment

3. Is sensitive to change in mental status over time and quantifies this change in an interval or ordinal manner so that remission or progression of a cognitive disorder can be measured

4. Is not so difficult as to preclude any meaningful measurement of cognitive abilities in patients with severe impairments

Implementation Issues

The structured mental status tests are conducted directly with the patient and do not require the use of an informant, except to verify the patient's answers to questions such as date of birth or occupation. Because the patient is tested directly, performance on these mental status tests can be adversely influenced by poor vision or hearing, impaired or fluctuating consciousness (e.g., delirium), or poor compliance due to concomitant behavioral or psychiatric disorders. These factors must be considered and corrected, if possible, to ensure reliable and valid cognitive assessment. Because the staging systems, in contrast, use all available information, the potentially mitigating factors described can be taken into consideration when making a global rating of the level of a patient's cognitive decline. It should be kept in mind, however, that other factors, such as the informant's observational powers or mental status and proximity to the patient, may influence the validity and reliability of the staging.

Performance on most structured cognitive tests is also clearly influenced by level of education and literacy, and these factors must be considered when interpreting test results. On the one hand, poor education or illiteracy can lead to poor test performance by individuals without cognitive impairment and a consequent false-positive classification of cognitive dysfunction. On the other hand, highly educated individuals may have a true decline in cognitive functioning but still perform within the normal range on these tests, leading to a false-negative classification of no cognitive dysfunction. This problem in interpretation can be ameliorated to some extent by the use of education-adjusted normative data and education-adjusted cutoff scores for impairment that are available for several of the mental status tests. Although race and socioeconomic status do not seem to notably affect mental status examination performance once the effect of education is accounted for, most of the tests have cultural idiosyncrasies that must be considered when the test is adapted for use with a non-English-speaking population. When dementia staging systems are used, information concerning education and literacy should be available and considered in the staging decision. In addition, measures that focus on function allow the rater to look for evidence of decline from the subject's own baseline, thus largely circumventing the problem of educational biases.

Issues in Interpreting Psychometric Data

Several factors must be considered when evaluating the effectiveness of the various measures of cognitive dysfunction. The principal factor is whether the measure is designed as an objective test of intellectual deterioration or as a subjective, global evaluation of the effects of cognitive impairment on day-to-day functioning. Although they are related, these two types of measures have different objectives, and it may not be appropriate to judge one against the other. A second factor is the choice of the gold standard against which the effectiveness of the measure is judged. The observed validity and reliability of the measure can only be as accurate as those of the gold standard. The most appropriate gold standards are cognitive dysfunction as detected by a full clinical evaluation and direct evidence of brain pathology obtained through neuroimaging, biopsy, or autopsy. A third factor that must be considered is whether the effectiveness of a measure for detecting or staging cognitive impairment was determined in a community survey that included a random selection of individuals representing a wide spectrum of normal cognition and states of health or in a more controlled comparison of patients with known cognitive impairment with carefully screened healthy individuals. In the former case, the results of the evaluation are more generalizable to the entire population but may be less accurate because of the inclusion of patients with extremely mild cognitive dysfunction that is difficult to detect and psychiatrically healthy individuals who perform poorly on the measure because of other factors such as learning disabilities, poor literacy, depression, or medical illness. In the latter case, the accuracy of the results

of the evaluation may be quite good because of the carefully screened subject samples, but the results may not generalize well to the entire population.

GUIDE TO THE SELECTION OF MEASURES

Several of the structured cognitive scales were designed specifically to detect mild cognitive dysfunction and are quite effective in this regard. The most effective tests for this purpose are the DRS, the MMSE, and the NCSE. However, the utility of the MMSE is limited in highly educated individuals, who may score perfectly (i.e., 30/30) despite evidence of functional decline. Although not initially designed to detect mild cognitive dysfunction, the Clock Drawing Test is also quite effective because normal performance on this test requires a wide variety of cognitive functions. Both the CDR Scale and the GDS effectively stage early cognitive dysfunction, but this ability relies on the thoroughness of the evaluation on which the staging is based.

In addition to being sensitive to mild cognitive deterioration, the DRS and the NCSE have subscales that provide a profile of relatively preserved and impaired cognitive abilities. These profiles have been shown to be useful for differentiating among various cognitive disorders.

The DRS, the MMSE, and the IMC Test have all been shown to effectively track the progression of cognitive deterioration in patients with Alzheimer's disease in clinical and research settings. The DRS has been found to be most effective in this regard, particularly in more severely impaired patients (Salmon et al. 1990). Unlike the other tests, the DRS was specifically designed with a step-down procedure in which a series of progressively simpler questions are asked within each cognitive domain. This step-down procedure allows the DRS to effectively measure the level of cognitive dysfunction even in patients with severe dementia. However, this benefit must be balanced against the greater length of the DRS in comparison with the IMC Test and the MMSE. The dementia staging systems were designed to track cognitive deterioration in patients with Alzheimer's disease, so it is not surprising that they are very effective for this task. In addition, they can provide a meaningful ordinal staging of cognitive and functional deterioration in end-stage dementia patients who may be mute or otherwise unable to perform even the simplest portion of a structured mental status test.

The ADAS is the most widely used measure of cognitive dysfunction in clinical pharmacological trials of antidementia drugs. Specifically designed for this purpose, the ADAS assesses a wide range of cognitive abilities that can be affected by Alzheimer's disease, using tasks that are difficult enough to detect relatively small differences in performance due to a drug's effects. The MMSE has also been used in a number of these clinical trials, but it seems to be less sensitive to the effects of pharmacological treatments than the ADAS. The IMC Test has been most widely used to quantify the severity of cognitive dysfunction for comparison with brain pathology, although the DRS and the MMSE have also been used for this purpose.

Although these dementia scales can detect and stage cognitive impairment in a global sense, they are not diagnostic for a particular disease or disorder. They also do not generally provide a detailed analysis of an individual's cognitive strengths and weaknesses that would be useful for diagnostic purposes or care planning. The dementia scales are best viewed as an initial screening device that can be used to help the clinician decide whether a more thorough cognitive evaluation is warranted. Patients may need a more thorough evaluation, including neuropsychological testing, when the diagnosis is unclear or the family needs help characterizing the patient's overall strengths and weaknesses.

For assessments in disorders other than progressive dementias, the GOAT and the NCSE both have some utility. The GOAT is specifically designed for patients with head injury; it focuses on orientation and memory and appears to provide reliable and valid information in these domains but does not assess other areas. The NCSE takes a broader approach and assesses a broad range of domains. It has been shown to detect cognitive deficits after surgery or stroke; however, its utility across a full range of conditions has not been demonstrated.

CURRENT STATUS AND FUTURE RESEARCH NEEDS FOR ASSESSMENT

Several of the currently available standardized scales of cognitive functioning and staging systems for dementia are valid, reliable, relatively brief, and easy to use in research or clinical practice. Future research on the brief measurement of cognitive disorders should focus on developing new tests that take into account innovative theoretical developments in understanding the cognitive and biological bases of dementia, head injury, and other causes of cognitive disorder. In addition, future research should endeavor to develop better methods of accurately detecting cognitive impairment in highly or poorly educated individuals and to develop measures that consider both qualitative and quantitative aspects of an individual's performance. Finally, most of the available instruments focus on progressive dementias, particularly Alzheimer's disease, and additional research is needed, for example, on the evaluation of patients with dementias of the frontal lobes or dementia related to AIDS.

REFERENCES AND SUGGESTED READINGS

Donnelly J, Rosenberg M, Fleeson WP: The evolution of the mental status: past and future. Am J Psychiatry 126:997–1002, 1970

Ferris SH, Mackell JA, Mohs R, et al: A multicenter evaluation of new treatment efficacy instruments for Alzheimer's disease clinical trials: overview and general results. The Alzheimer's Disease Cooperative Study. Alzheimer Dis Assoc Disord 11(suppl 2):S1–12, 1997

Golden CH, Purisch AD, Hammeke TA: Luria-Nebraska Neuropsychological Battery: Forms I and II. Los Angeles, CA, Western Psychological Services, 1985

Nelson A, Fogel BS, Faust D: Bedside cognitive screening instruments: a critical assessment. J Nerv Ment Dis 174:73–83, 1986

Pfeffer E: A short portable mental status questionnaire for the assessment of organic brain deficits in elderly patients. J Am Geriatr Soc 23:433–441, 1975

Pfeffer RI, Kurosaki TT, Harrah CH, et al: Measurement of functional activities in older adults in the community. J Gerontol 37:323–329, 1982

Reitan RM, Wolfson D: The Halstead-Reitan Neuropsychological Test Battery: theory and clinical interpretation. Tucson, AZ, Neuropsychology Press, 1993

Ritchie K: The screening of cognitive impairment in the elderly: a critical review of current methods. J Clin Epidemiol 41:635–643, 1988

Roth M, Tym E, Mountjoy CQ, et al: CAMDEX: a standardised instrument for the diagnosis of mental disorder in the elderly with special reference to the early detection of dementia. Br J Psychiatry 149:689–709, 1986

Salmon DP, Thal LJ, Butters N, et al: Longitudinal evaluation of dementia: a comparison of three standardized mental status examinations. Neurology 40:1225–1230, 1990

Schmitt FA, Ranseen JD, DeKosky ST: Cognitive mental status examinations. Clin Geriatr Med 5:545–564, 1989

Wechsler D: Wechsler Adult Intelligence Scale manual. New York, Psychological Corporation, 1955

Whitehouse P, Maslow K: Defining and measuring outcomes in Alzheimer disease research: introduction and overview. Alzheimer Dis Assoc Disord 11(suppl 6):1–6, 1997

Mini-Mental State Exam (MMSE)

M. F. Folstein, S. E. Folstein, and P. R. McHugh

GOALS

The Mini-Mental State Exam (MMSE) (Folstein et al. 1975) was originally designed to provide a brief, standardized assessment of mental status that would serve to differentiate between organic and functional disorders in psychiatric patients. As experience with the test has increased over the years, its major function has now become to detect and track the progression of cognitive impairment associated with neurodegenerative disorders such as Alzheimer's disease.

DESCRIPTION

The MMSE is a fully structured scale that consists of 30 points grouped into seven categories: orientation to place (state, county, town, hospital, and floor), orientation to time (year, season, month, day, and date), registration (immediately repeating three words), attention and concentration (serially subtracting 7, beginning with 100, or, alternatively, spelling the word *world* backward), recall (recalling the previously repeated three words), language (naming two items, repeating a phrase, reading aloud and understanding a sentence, writing a sentence, and following a three-step command), and visual construction (copying a design).

Several shortened forms of the MMSE have been developed on the basis of linear regression analyses that used the individual test items to predict the total score. Although these versions vary somewhat, they are generally limited to the orientation, attention and concentration, and recall items. There are also at least two telephone versions: the Telephone-Assessed Mental State (TAMS) (Lanska et al. 1993) and the Telephone Interview for Cognitive Status (TICS) (Brandt et al. 1988).

Several expanded versions of the MMSE have been developed to assess a greater range and depth of cognitive functioning or to increase the test's sensitivity to subtle cognitive deficits that may occur in specific neurological diseases such as multiple sclerosis (e.g., the Cognitive Abilities Screening Instrument [CASI] [Teng et al. 1994], the Modified Mini-Mental State [3MS] Examination [Teng and Chui 1987], and the expanded MMSE).

The MMSE is scored in terms of the number of correctly completed items; lower scores indicate poorer performance and greater cognitive impairment. The total score ranges from 0 to 30 (perfect performance). Although scoring for most MMSE items is simple and straightforward, several different scoring methods have been used for the attention and concentration item. The most commonly used procedure is to present both the serial subtraction and backward spelling items and use the higher of the two scores in calculating the MMSE total score.

Comprehensive normative data ($N = 18,056$) on the MMSE (Crum et al. 1993) collected through the Epidemiologic Catchment Area (ECA) study provide age- and education-related median, upper quartile, and lower quartile scores that can be used to identify abnormal performance. An initially recommended MMSE cutoff score of 23 or 24 provides good sensitivity and specificity for the detection of dementia; however, several recent studies suggested that this cutoff score may be too low, particularly with highly educated individuals. These studies showed that dementia can be clinically diagnosed with good accuracy in many individuals who score between 24 and 27 on the MMSE. However, these figures are focused on accuracy in community populations. For clinical purposes, even a score of 27 may be insufficiently sensitive to detect dementia in individuals with extensive education, whereas a cutoff score of 24 may be insufficiently specific in individuals with little education.

PRACTICAL ISSUES

It takes approximately 5–10 minutes to administer the MMSE. The test is designed to be easily administered by any health care professional or trained technician who has received minimal instruction in its use. The MMSE is not commercially available, but the test items, instructions for administration, and extensive normative data have been published (Crum et al. 1993; Folstein et al. 1975). The copyright for the MMSE is wholly owned by Mini Mental LLC, a Massachusetts limited liability company. For information about how to obtain permission to use or reproduce the MMSE in any written materials, contact

> John Gonsalves Jr.
> Administrator of the Mini Mental LLC
> 31 St. James Avenue, Suite 1
> Boston, MA 02116
> Phone: 617-587-4215

The MMSE is included on the CD-ROM that accompanies this handbook.

PSYCHOMETRIC PROPERTIES

Reliability

Two studies that examined the internal consistency of the MMSE obtained Cronbach's alphas of 0.82 and 0.84 in elderly patients admitted to a medical service (N = 372) and elderly nursing home residents (N = 34), respectively.

The joint reliability of the MMSE was found to be 0.827 in a study of patients with dementia (N = 19), 0.95 in a study of patients with various neurological disorders (N = 15), and 0.84–0.99 in two studies with elderly residents of nursing homes (N = 35 and 70). Intraclass correlation coefficients ranging from 0.69 to 0.78 were obtained in another study of elderly nursing home residents (N = 48). A mean kappa of 0.97 was obtained when five examiners separately scored the MMSE performance for 10 neurological patients.

The test-retest reliability of the MMSE in patients with dementia (usually of the Alzheimer's type) ranged from 0.75 to 0.94 (Pearson r) in 10 studies that employed test-retest intervals of 1 day to 9 weeks (N = 12–58). A Kendall τ of 0.65 (N = 30 neurologically impaired patients) and an intraclass correlation coefficient of 0.69 (N = 48 elderly nursing home residents) were found in two studies that examined the test-retest reliability of the MMSE over a 1-day and 2-week interval, respectively. The test-retest reliability of the MMSE was found to be 0.56 over a 1-day interval in patients with delirium (N = 7) and 0.60–0.74 over a 4- to 6-week interval in patients with schizophrenia (N = 22). A test-retest reliability of 0.88 (intraclass correlation coefficient) was obtained with a 1- or 2-year interval in geriatric patients with schizophrenia (N = 224). In elderly individuals without dementia, the test-retest reliability of the MMSE over a 1-day to 8-week interval was found to range from 0.64 to 0.85 (N = 57–481) and from 0.23 to 0.45 over a 1- to 2-year interval (N = 60–122) using various statistics.

Validity

Performance on the MMSE has been shown to be significantly correlated with a variety of other tests that measure intelligence, memory, and other aspects of cognitive functioning in a wide variety of populations. For example, scores on the MMSE significantly correlated with the full, verbal, or performance intelligence quotients from the Wechsler Adult Intelligence Scale (WAIS) (Wechsler 1958) or its revision (WAIS-R) (Wechsler 1981) in patients with dementia, stroke patients, patients with schizophrenia or depression, hospitalized and nonhospitalized developmentally delayed young adults, and psychiatrically healthy elderly individuals. MMSE performance has also been shown to be strongly correlated with the memory quotient from the Wechsler Memory Scale (Wechsler 1945) in patients with dementia and in neurologically impaired patients and with scores on the Information-Memory-Concentration (IMC) Test (p. 427) in patients with Alzheimer's disease, cognitively impaired individuals, and psychiatrically healthy control subjects.

MMSE scores were also significantly correlated with scores on the Clock Drawing Test (p. 438) in geriatric patients and patients with Alzheimer's disease, with scores on the Alzheimer's Disease Assessment Scale—Cognitive (ADAS-COG) (p. 441) in patients with Alzheimer's disease or patients referred for psychiatric evaluations, and with scores on a composite neuropsychological test battery in patients referred for dementia evaluation. In addition, significant levels of agreement were obtained between MMSE-determined impairment and impairment determined by a composite neuropsychological test battery in a study of patients evaluated after cardiac surgery ($N = 247$).

Numerous studies have shown that MMSE performance correlates with scores on scales that measure functional competence. One study found that activities of daily living (ADL) or instrumental ADL (IADL) scores were significantly worse in patients who scored ≤23 on the MMSE than in those who scored <23 on the test ($N = 244$). Two studies found that MMSE and ADL scores were significantly correlated ($r = 0.48–0.76$) in nursing home residents ($N = 70$) and in patients with Alzheimer's disease ($N = 86$), and three studies found that MMSE scores accounted for significant amounts of variance in ADL scores in individuals with dementia ($N = 59–201$; $R^2 = 0.28–0.49$) and in elderly individuals residing in the community ($N = 1,637$; $R^2 = 0.23$). Three studies showed that MMSE and Dementia Rating Scale (DRS) (p. 430) scores were correlated in patients with dementia ($N = 115$; $r = -0.71$ to -0.86), patients with Alzheimer's disease ($N = 41$; $r = -0.73$), and elderly patients referred for dementia evaluation ($N = 226$; $r = -0.86$).

MMSE scores were correlated with Brief Cognitive Rating Scale (BCRS) (p. 449) scores ($r = -0.79$) in a study of patients with dementia ($N = 82$), with Global Deterioration Scale (GDS) (p. 449) scores ($r = 0.89–0.90$) in two studies of psychiatrically healthy elderly patients ($N = 154$) or patients with Alzheimer's disease ($N = 30$), with Clinical Dementia Rating (CDR) Scale (p. 446) scores ($r = 0.78$) in a study of elderly individuals with and without dementia ($N = 668$) and in a study of patients with dementia ($N = 93$; kappa = 0.33), and with Functional Assessment Staging (FAST) (p. 450) scores ($r = 0.87$) in a study of patients with Alzheimer's disease and psychiatrically healthy control subjects ($N = 40$). MMSE scores were also found to decline significantly with FAST stages in a study of patients with Alzheimer's disease ($N = 70$). Performance on the MMSE was shown to be significantly correlated with physicians' ratings of function ($r = 0.31–0.67$; $N = 115$) and with children's ratings of level of need ($R^2 = 0.33$; $N = 201$) in two studies of dementia patients, with nursing home staff ratings of cognition ($r = 0.74$), and with nursing home staff ratings of communication ($r = 0.74$).

Three studies demonstrated a significant relationship between scores on the MMSE and quantitative measures of pathology in patients with Alzheimer's disease. MMSE scores were correlated ($r = 0.77$) with synaptic density in biopsied tissue from the frontal cortex in patients with Alzheimer's disease ($N = 8$) and with beta amyloid load ($r = -0.90$) in the cortex of patients with autopsy-proven Alzheimer's disease ($N = 20$). MMSE scores were also significantly correlated with midfrontal synaptic density ($r = 0.728$), inferior parietal synaptic density ($r = 0.645$), neurofibrillary tangles in the inferior parietal cortex ($r = -0.564$), and neurofibrillary tangles in the midfrontal cortex ($r = -0.517$) of patients with Alzheimer's disease ($N = 15$). Furthermore, a multiple regression analysis in the latter study showed that these measures and the level of choline acetyltransferase in the midfrontal cortex accounted for 86% of the variance in the MMSE scores of the patients with Alzheimer's disease.

Another study demonstrated a significant relationship between a quantitative electroencephalogram frequency measure and the MMSE scores of patients with Alzheimer's disease ($r = 0.623$; $N = 21$) and psychiatrically healthy elderly individuals ($r = 0.451$; $N = 21$). In 63 neurological patients referred for computed tomography (CT) imaging, those with a positive CT image showing atrophy or atrophy and focal abnormalities had lower MMSE scores than those with a negative CT image. The total lesion volume observed on the magnetic resonance images of the brains of patients with multiple sclerosis ($N = 56$) was correlated with their MMSE scores ($r = 0.28$), although this correlation failed to reach significance. In another study, 23% of patients with schizophrenia who scored ≤25 on the MMSE ($N = 19$) had very enlarged lateral ventricles on CT images, whereas only 5% of the patients with schizophrenia who scored >25 on the test ($N = 36$) had very enlarged ventricles.

Five studies reported that the MMSE is sensitive to dementing disorders. In one of these studies, patients with dementia ($N = 29$) scored significantly lower on the MMSE than patients with depression and cognitive impairment ($N = 10$), depressed patients without cognitive impairment ($N = 30$), and psychiatrically healthy control subjects ($N = 63$). In another study, patients with dementia ($N = 44$) scored lower on the MMSE than patients without dementia who had another psychiatric diagnosis ($N = 33$) or a neurological diagnosis ($N = 33$) or psychiatrically healthy control subjects

($N = 23$). A study that focused on elderly individuals in a residential facility ($N = 201$) found that those with dementia scored significantly lower on the MMSE than those without dementia or those with only possible dementia. Patients with moderate Alzheimer's disease ($N = 50$) in another study had lower MMSE scores than those with mild dementia ($N = 24$), who in turn had lower scores than psychiatrically healthy control subjects ($N = 74$). Finally, patients with organic mental disorder ($N = 23$) achieved significantly lower MMSE scores than patients with nonorganic mental disorders ($N = 9$) or no mental disorder at all ($N = 68$).

In other studies, MMSE scores of patients with Alzheimer's disease ($N = 141$) were significantly negatively related to estimated duration of illness ($r = -0.50$), and a significantly higher proportion of adult neurology patients with a cerebral abnormality (50%; $N = 42$) than those with only a peripheral abnormality (0%; $N = 26$) scored <24 on the MMSE; patients with schizophrenia with negative symptoms ($N = 16$) scored significantly lower on the MMSE than patients with schizophrenia with positive symptoms ($N = 18$) or mixed symptoms ($N = 18$).

A score of 23 on the MMSE was originally proposed as a cutoff score indicative of cognitive dysfunction. This score was determined on the basis of the finding that no elderly psychiatrically healthy control subject scored <21 in the initial study that introduced the MMSE ($N = 63$) and that 95% of individuals in a population-based probability sample ($N = 3,481$) scored >23 on the test, whereas no subject with a diagnosis of Alzheimer's disease scored >23. Another study found 80% agreement between MMSE scores <23 and clinically diagnosed dementia in elderly patients referred for evaluation by general practice physicians ($N = 226$).

In 13 subsequent studies that examined the effectiveness of an MMSE cutoff of ≤23 for detecting dementia, sensitivity ranged from 63% to 100% and specificity ranged from 52% to 99% when measured against an independent clinical diagnosis of dementia ($N = 23-74$ individuals with dementia and 24–2,663 individuals without dementia). Three studies that proposed higher MMSE cutoff scores of between 25 and 27 found sensitivity to range from 78% to 90% and specificity to range from 70% to 87% for the detection of clinically diagnosed dementia or cognitive impairment ($N = 50-80$ individuals with dementia and 53–93 subjects without dementia). Five studies also proposed lower MMSE cutoff

scores of between 17 and 22 and reported sensitivity for the detection of dementia that ranged from 52% to 98% and specificity that ranged from 68% to 100%. Two studies that used the MMSE to detect cognitive impairment in patients with multiple sclerosis ($N = 56-173$) found that a cutoff score of 27 resulted in sensitivity of 63%–84% and specificity of 79%–94% compared with detection by a larger battery of cognitive tests.

Five studies demonstrated that the various shortened versions of the MMSE are also sensitive to dementia. Two of these studies reported that the optimal cutoff scores on the tests provided sensitivity that ranged from 83% to 96% and specificity that ranged from 83% to 95% for the detection of dementia ($N = 72-74$ patients with dementia of the Alzheimer's type and 74–144 subjects without dementia). Another study that supplemented the shortened MMSE with verbal fluency and visual retention tests found 100% sensitivity and 90% specificity for the detection of dementia in a large epidemiological study in France ($N = 64$ patients with dementia and 2,663 without dementia). A study reported that the internal consistency of a shortened MMSE was 0.77 (Cronbach's alpha) and that the test provided 96% sensitivity and 91% specificity for detecting impairment that was defined as a score of ≤22 on the full MMSE. A correlation of $r = 0.94-0.97$ was observed between the full MMSE and a shortened version in a study that included a random sample of elderly women ($N = 783$).

The MMSE was negatively correlated with age in several community surveys of the elderly (e.g., in the ECA study, $r = -0.38$), but this relationship most likely reflects the age-related increase in the prevalence of Alzheimer's disease and other dementias. A significant correlation remains, however, when age is compared with MMSE performance in patients with diagnoses of Alzheimer's disease ($r = -0.30$ to -0.34; $N = 51-86$). MMSE performance is also related to level of education. Of 12 studies with individuals residing in the community ($N = 214-18,056$), 10 reported a significant positive relationship between level of education and MMSE scores ($r = 0.30-0.51$; multiple regression analysis $R^2 = 0.10-0.21$; or significantly lower mean MMSE scores in cohorts with low vs. high education). In contrast, four studies reported no significant correlation between education and MMSE scores in patients with dementia ($r = 0.3-0.13$; $N = 51-141$ patients with Alzheimer's disease).

Five studies that examined the sensitivity of the MMSE to cognitive decline in patients with dementia

($N = 44$–115, mostly Alzheimer's disease) found annual rates of change in scores that ranged from –1.8 to –3.2 points per year. In one of these studies, the slope in the annual change in MMSE scores of participants in an adult day care ($N = 82$, of whom 57 had dementia) was significantly correlated with the slopes in the annual change in scores on the BCRS (p. 450) ($r = -0.55$) and a measure of ADL ($r = -0.28$) (the Maryland Appraisal of Patient Progress [Porte 1986]).

CLINICAL UTILITY

The MMSE is a very brief, easily administered mental status examination that has proved to be a highly reliable and valid instrument for detecting and tracking the progression of the cognitive impairment associated with neurodegenerative diseases. Consequently, the MMSE is the most widely used mental status examination in the world. The test has been translated into many languages and has been used as the primary cognitive screening instrument in several large-scale epidemiological studies of dementia. The test is also used widely in clinical practice and is often reported in research studies as a benchmark of the severity of dementia that can be used to compare patient cohorts across studies. This prominence of the MMSE as a cognitive screening instrument is attested to by its inclusion along with the Diagnostic Interview Schedule (DIS) (p. 61), in the National Institute of Mental Health ECA study and by its listing as a recommended measure of cognitive functioning in the diagnostic criteria for Alzheimer's disease developed by the consortium of the National Institute of Neurological and Communication Disorders and Stroke and the Alzheimer's Disease and Related Disorders Association (McKhann et al. 1984).

Extensive psychometric data on the MMSE confirm that the test has very good test-retest and joint reliability and excellent validity as measured against independent clinical diagnosis of dementia and Alzheimer's disease, measures of functional impairment, or performance on other (often more rigorous) neuropsychological tests and against neuropathological features of Alzheimer's disease. Because performance on the MMSE can be adversely affected by low education in psychiatrically healthy elderly individuals, some investigators recommend the use of age- and education-adjusted cutoff scores for the detection of dementia.

The MMSE has been shown to be sensitive to cognitive decline in patients with Alzheimer's disease; scores decline an average of 1.8–3.2 points per year. This feature of the scale has led to its use as a primary or secondary outcome measure in some studies that have examined the efficacy of pharmacological agents that might slow the progression of cognitive deterioration in patients with Alzheimer's disease. The MMSE is also somewhat effective in differentiating between dementing disorders that differ in their etiology and sites of predominant neuropathology. For example, in one study, it was reported that Alzheimer's disease and Huntington's disease patients differed in the profile of deficits they produced on the individual MMSE items.

The most commonly cited limitations of the MMSE are its marginal or absent assessment of some cognitive abilities that are affected early in the course of Alzheimer's disease or other dementing disorders (e.g., limited memory and verbal fluency items and no problem solving or judgment items), its relative insensitivity to very mild cognitive decline (particularly in highly educated individuals), and its susceptibility to floor effects in tracking the progression of dementia in patients with moderate to severe cognitive impairment. Although these limitations diminish the usefulness of the MMSE to some degree, the test remains a very valuable instrument for the assessment of cognitive decline.

REFERENCES AND SUGGESTED READINGS

Anthony JC, LeResche L, Niaz U, et al: Limits of the "Mini-Mental State" as a screening test for dementia and delirium among hospital patients. Psychol Med 12:397–408, 1982

Brandt J, Spencer M, Folstein M: The Telephone Interview for Cognitive Status. Neuropsychiatry Neuropsychol Behav Neurol 1:111–117, 1988

Crum RM, Anthony JC, Bassett SS, et al: Population-based norms for the Mini-Mental State Examination by age and educational level. JAMA 269:2386–2391, 1993

Folstein MF, Folstein SE, McHugh PR: "Mini-Mental State": a practical method for grading the cognitive state of patients for the clinician. J Psychiatr Res 12:189–198, 1975

Lanska DJ, Schmitt FA, Stewart JM, et al: Telephone-Assessed Mental State. Dementia 4:117–119, 1993

McKhann G, Drachman D, Folstein M, et al: Clinical diagnosis of Alzheimer's disease: report of the NINCDS-ADRDA Work Group under the auspices of Department of Health and Human Services Task Force on Alzheimer's Disease. Neurology 34:939–944, 1984

Porte P: Severity of illness, long term care, and cost control: Maryland's approach. J Am Med Rec Assoc 57:34–35, 1986

Regier DA, Myers JK, Kramer LN, et al: The NIMH Epidemiologic Catchment Area (ECA) program: historical context, major objectives, and study population characteristics. Arch Gen Psychiatry 41:934–941, 1984

Teng EL, Chui HC: The Modified Mini-Mental State (3MS) Examination. J Clin Psychiatry 48:314–318, 1987

Teng EL, Hasegawa K, Homma A, et al: The Cognitive Abilities Screening Instrument (CASI): a practical test for cross-cultural epidemiologic studies of dementia. Int Psychogeriatr 6:45–56, 1994

Tombaugh TM, McIntyre NJ: The Mini-Mental State Examination: a comprehensive review. J Am Geriatr Soc 40:922–935, 1992

Wechsler D: A standardised memory scale for clinical use. J Psychol 19:87–95, 1945

Wechsler D: Wechsler Adult Intelligence Scale manual. New York, Psychological Corporation, 1955

Wechsler D: Wechsler Adult Intelligence Scale-revised manual. New York, Psychological Corporation, 1981

Information-Memory-Concentration (IMC) Test

G. Blessed, B. E. Tomlinson, and M. Roth

GOALS

The Information-Memory-Concentration (IMC) Test (Blessed et al. 1968, 1988) was developed to quantify intellectual deterioration in patients with dementia so that the deterioration could be related to neuropathological manifestations of the underlying disease. Although quantifying cognitive deterioration has remained a primary function of the test, the IMC Test has also been used in case-control and epidemiological studies to screen for cognitive impairment in the elderly and to track the progression of dementia in patients with probable Alzheimer's disease.

The IMC Test is the cognitive portion of the Blessed-Roth Dementia Scale (Blessed et al. 1968); the remaining portion is a functional measure used somewhat less frequently today. The term *Blessed* is sometimes used to refer to the IMC Test, sometimes to the functional portion, and sometimes to the scale as a whole. Only the IMC Test is reviewed here.

DESCRIPTION

The IMC Test originated in Great Britain as a structured scale consisting of 29 items that assess aspects of orientation, memory, and concentration. The orientation items include questions concerning personal information (i.e., name and age), time (i.e., time of day, day, date, month, season, and year), and place (i.e., name and type of place, street, and town). The memory items encompass questions about remote personal information (i.e., date and place of birth, school attended, occupation, names of employers, town of employment, recognition of two familiar people, and spouse's name) and nonpersonal information (i.e., dates of World Wars I and II and the name of the monarch and the prime minister) and also assess the ability to remember new information (i.e., a five-part name and address) over a 5-minute delay. The concentration items include counting from 1 to 20 and from 20 to 1 and saying the months of the year backward. An American adaptation of the IMC Test, developed by Paula Fuld (1978), consists of 26 items that include all of those in the original, except that 3 uninformative items (i.e., names of employers, town of employment, and recognition of two familiar people) were dropped and some items were made culturally appropriate (i.e., *monarch* and *prime minister* were changed to *president* and *vice president*). On the basis of linear regression analyses that used individual items to predict total IMC Test score, a shortened six-item version of the Fuld adaptation of the test was developed by Katzman et al. (1983). This short form of the IMC Test includes orientation (i.e., time of day, month, and year), memory (i.e., remembering a five-part name and address), and concentration (i.e., counting from 20 to 1 and saying the months backward) items.

The IMC Test is scored in terms of errors; higher scores reflect poorer performance and greater cognitive impairment. Most of the test items are scored as either correct (0 points) or incorrect (1 point). However, memory for the individual components of the five-part name and address are scored separately (for a possibility of 5 error points), and the counting and months backward items are scored on a scale of 0–2. Thus, the total score on the 29-item British version of the test ranges from 0 (perfect performance) to 37, and the total score on the 26-item Fuld adaptation ranges from 0 (perfect performance) to 33. The items on the six-item short form of the IMC Test are weighted so that the total score on this version of the test ranges from 0 (perfect performance) to 28.

PRACTICAL ISSUES

It takes approximately 10 minutes to administer the full IMC Test. It can be performed in person or over the telephone. The Spearman rank order correlation coefficient comparing in-person and telephone administration of the test was 0.96 in patients with dementia ($N = 35$). The short form of the test can be administered in approximately 5 minutes. The IMC Test can be administered by any health care professional or paraprofessional who has been trained in test administration and scoring procedures. The IMC Test is not commercially available, but the items and instructions for administration have been published (British version [Blessed et al. 1968, 1988], American version [Fuld 1978], and short version [Katzman et al. 1983]).

PSYCHOMETRIC PROPERTIES

Reliability

The test-retest reliability of the IMC Test over a 1- to 6-week interval in five studies ranged from 0.82 to 0.96 (correlation coefficients) for patients with probable Alzheimer's disease ($N = 17–41$). In one of these studies, the split-half reliability of the IMC Test was 0.89. Two

studies that used the short form of the IMC Test with patients with probable Alzheimer's disease ($N = 18–36$) found a test-retest reliability that ranged from 0.77 to 0.83 over a 1-month interval.

Validity

Three studies that compared the IMC Test with other measures of global cognitive impairment in patients with probable Alzheimer's disease ($N = 40–92$) reported correlation coefficients of –0.73 to –0.88 with the Mini-Mental State Exam (MMSE) (p. 422), –0.73 to –0.81 with the Cognitive Capacity Screening Examination (Jacobs et al. 1977), –0.79 with the Dementia Rating Scale (DRS) (p. 430), and 0.47 to 0.66 with the Sandoz Clinical Assessment—Geriatric (SCAG) (Shader et al. 1974). Four other studies that compared the short form of the IMC Test with other cognitive measures reported correlation coefficients of 0.94 with the full IMC Test ($N = 170$ nursing home residents), correlation coefficients of –0.83 to –0.93 with the MMSE ($N = 36–354$ patients with Alzheimer's disease, 89–278 psychiatrically healthy control subjects, and 110 residents of skilled nursing homes), a correlation coefficient of –0.90 with the Mental Status Questionnaire (Kahn et al. 1960) ($N = 44$ patients with dementia and 89 without dementia), and correlation coefficients of –0.46 to –0.84 with various tasks that assess specific cognitive functions (e.g., memory, reaction time, confrontation, and naming). The IMC Test was correlated (0.63) with a measure of activities of daily living in a group of patients with Alzheimer's disease ($N = 123$), and it accounted for 47% of the variance in activities of daily living scores and 33% of the variance in ratings of level of required care in 201 elderly patients with dementia.

Several studies have shown a significant correlation between scores on the IMC Test and various quantitative measures of neuropathology in patients with Alzheimer's disease. Seven studies ($N = 15–30$) reported correlations that range from 0.24 to 0.73 when comparing IMC Test scores and numbers of neuritic plaques in various neocortical and medial temporal lobe regions of patients with Alzheimer's disease. In one study, neocortical neuritic plaques were also correlated (0.54) with scores obtained on the short form of the IMC Test by patients with Alzheimer's disease ($N = 38$). In six studies, the correlation between density of neurofibrillary tangles in various neocortical regions and IMC Test scores of patients with Alzheimer's disease ($N = 15–30$) ranged from 0.52 to 0.98.

One study found that the IMC Test scores of patients with Alzheimer's disease ($N = 15$) were correlated with the density of synapses in their neocortex (from -0.57 to -0.76, depending on the region of the cortex). Two others ($N = 20–29$) showed that test scores were correlated ($0.73–0.93$) with beta amyloid load in the neocortex, and another study ($N = 18$ patients with Alzheimer's disease and 10 depressed patients) showed that IMC Test scores were correlated (0.81) with the degree of neocortical choline acetyltransferase activity.

Two studies found that patients with clinically diagnosed dementia ($N = 26–123$) score significantly worse than psychiatrically healthy elderly subjects ($N = 8–59$) on the IMC Test, and two studies found that patients with probable Alzheimer's disease ($N = 44–332$) score worse than psychiatrically healthy elderly subjects ($N = 23–278$) on the short form of the IMC Test. In another study, 97% of 54 individuals active in their communities, and presumably without dementia, between ages 68 and 93 made fewer than 9 errors on the IMC Test. On the basis of this finding, a cut point of 10 errors has been recommended for detecting cognitive impairment with the test. Using a cut point of 10, one study found that the short form of the IMC Test had 88.6% sensitivity and 94.4% specificity for differentiating between patients with dementia (probable Alzheimer's disease) ($N = 44$) and individuals without dementia ($N = 89$).

Six studies that examined the ability of the IMC Test to measure cognitive decline in patients with Alzheimer's disease ($N = 54–161$) over a 1- to 6-year period reported a generally linear decline; annual rates of change ranged from 3.0 to 4.4 points. In one of these studies, very similar annual rates of decline on the IMC Test were observed in four geographically and clinically diverse patient populations with Alzheimer's disease. An annual decline of 2.5 points on the short form of the IMC Test was reported for patients with Alzheimer's disease ($N = 52$) in a study that measured change over 1 year.

CLINICAL UTILITY

The IMC Test is an easily administered, brief mental status examination that effectively quantifies cognitive deterioration in patients with dementia. The test has been extensively validated against the neuropathological diagnosis of Alzheimer's disease, and performance on the test has been shown to correlate significantly with the severity of neuropathological changes (e.g., neuritic plaques, neurofibrillary tangles, and neocortical synapse loss) in the brains of patients with the disease. Indeed, the IMC Test was the first mental status examination with which this quantitative clinical-neuropathological relationship was demonstrated, and it remains the most widely cited test for this purpose.

The IMC Test has not been used extensively with populations of patients without Alzheimer's disease. The test is strongly weighted toward testing immediate and remote verbal memory. Other cognitive abilities that are often affected in Alzheimer's disease and non–Alzheimer's disease dementias, such as nonverbal memory, visuospatial abilities, constructional praxis, language, and "executive" functions, are not assessed by the IMC Test. Thus, caution is warranted when using the IMC Test with patients suspected of having a non–Alzheimer's disease dementing disorder (e.g., Pick's disease, progressive supranuclear palsy, or Parkinson's disease), because the test may underestimate the global level of dementia in patients who have only a mild verbal memory deficit but relatively severe deficits in other cognitive abilities.

Psychometric data indicate that the IMC Test is a reliable and valid method of quantifying cognitive deterioration over time in patients with Alzheimer's disease. Scores on the test change in a linear fashion until the more severe stages of dementia are reached, and similar annual rates of decline on the test have been reported in several studies that used independent and diverse Alzheimer's disease patient populations. In contrast, its use as a screening measure to detect dementia among elderly individuals is more controversial. Although the IMC Test has been used successfully in some research settings, and its emphasis on verbal memory may be a strength in detecting early Alzheimer's disease, there are relatively little psychometric data concerning its use as a screening measure. The sensitivity and specificity for the classification of individuals with and without dementia have not been reported for the standard IMC Test, effective cutoff scores for detecting mild dementia have not been empirically established, and the influence of gender and level of education on IMC Test performance has not been determined. Given these circumstances, the IMC Test would seem to be most effective as a means of quantifying and tracking the degree of cognitive deterioration in patients who have already received a diagnosis of Alzheimer's disease rather than as a screening instrument for the early detection of dementia.

REFERENCES AND SUGGESTED READINGS

Blessed G, Tomlinson BE, Roth M: The association between quantitative measures of dementia and of senile change in the cerebral grey matter of elderly subjects. Br J Psychiatry 114:797–811, 1968

Blessed G, Tomlinson BE, Roth M: Blessed-Roth Dementia Scale (DS). Psychopharmacol Bull 24:705–708, 1988

Fuld PA: Psychological testing in the differential diagnosis of the dementias, in Alzheimer's Disease: Senile Dementia and Related Disorders (Aging, Vol 7). Edited by Katzman R, Terry RD, Bick KL. New York, Raven, 1978, pp 185–196

Jacobs JW, Bernhard MR, Delgado A, et al: Screening for organic mental syndromes in the medically ill. Ann Intern Med 86:40–46, 1977

Kahn RL, Goldfarb AI, Pollack M, et al: Brief objective measures for the determination of mental status in the aged. Am J Psychiatry 117:326–328, 1960

Katzman R, Brown T, Fuld P, et al: Validation of a short orientation-memory-concentration test of cognitive impairment. Am J Psychiatry 140:734–739, 1983

Katzman R, Brown T, Thal LJ, et al: Comparison of rate of annual change of mental status score in four independent studies of patients with Alzheimer's disease. Ann Neurol 24:384–389, 1988

Lesher EL, Whelin WM: Reliability of mental status instruments administered to nursing home residents. J Consult Clin Psychol 54:726–727, 1986

Salmon DG, Thal LJ, Butters N, Heindel WC: Longitudinal evaluation of dementia of the Alzheimer type: a comparison of three standardized mental status examinations. Neurology 40:1225–1230, 1990

Shader WI, Harmatz JS, Salzman C: A new scale for clinical assessment in geriatric populations: Sandoz Clinical Assessment—Geriatric (SCAG). J Am Geriatr Soc 22:107–113, 1974

Thal LJ, Grundman M, Golden R: Alzheimer's disease: a correlational analysis of the Blessed Information-Memory-Concentration Test and the Mini-Mental State Exam. Neurology 36:262–264, 1986

Villardita C, Lomeo C: Alzheimer's disease: correlational analysis of three screening tests and three behavioral scales. Acta Neurol Scand 86:603–608, 1992

Dementia Rating Scale (DRS)

S. Mattis

GOALS

The Dementia Rating Scale (DRS) (Mattis 1976), sometimes referred to as the Mattis DRS or simply the Mattis, was designed to provide a brief assessment of cognitive status in patients with known cortical dysfunction arising from a neurodegenerative disorder such as Alzheimer's disease. The role of the DRS has expanded over the years and now includes the early detection of cognitive impairment in patients with suspected Alzheimer's disease and the elucidation of patterns of cognitive deficits that distinguish among dementing disorders that differ in their etiologies and sites of underlying neuropathology.

DESCRIPTION

The DRS is a standardized, fully structured mental status examination that provides a global measure of dementia derived from subscales for five cognitive capacities: Attention, Initiation and Perseveration, Construction, Conceptualization, and Memory. The Attention items include forward and backward digit span, following simple one- or two-step commands, visual search, reading a word list, and matching designs. The Initiation and Perseveration items encompass verbal fluency, verbal repetition, alternating movements, and drawing alternating designs. The Construction items consist of copying simple geometric figures. The Conceptualization items involve identifying conceptual and physical similarities and differences among items, simple inductive reasoning, and creating a sentence. The Memory items include delayed recall of sentences, questions concerning orientation (e.g., date and place) and remote memory (e.g., the president and governor), and immediate recognition of words and figures. The items that constitute each subscale span a range of difficulty to avoid floor effects with patients with severe dementia. Subscale items are presented, for the most part, in a hierarchical fashion, beginning with the most difficult item. If this initial, difficult item is performed correctly, a number of the subsequent less difficult subscale items are not administered but scored as correct. This procedure allows abilities within a given cognitive domain to be thoroughly assessed in patients with moderate and severe dementia, while significantly shortening administration time in individuals without dementia or with mild dementia.

The DRS is scored in terms of the number of correct responses; higher scores indicate better cognitive performance. The total score ranges from 0 to 144 points (perfect performance). The maximum possible scores on the subscales are 37 for Attention, 37 for Initiation and Perseveration, 6 for Construction, 39 for Conceptualization, and 25 for Memory.

PRACTICAL ISSUES

It takes approximately 30–40 minutes to administer the DRS to a patient with mild to moderate dementia. The test can be administered to an individual without dementia in about 15–20 minutes when subscales are truncated because of correct performance on the initial, most difficult items. The DRS should be administered by an examiner who is knowledgeable and has practiced the procedures presented in the DRS manual (Mattis 1988). The manual, test materials, and scoring forms are published by and commercially available from

> Psychological Assessment Resources, Inc.
> P.O. Box 998
> Odessa, FL 33556
> Phone: 800-331-TEST (800-331-8378)

The DRS introductory kit (which includes the DRS manual, 50 scoring and recording forms, and a set of stimulus cards) is available for $105.00. The kit items may also be purchased separately: DRS manual, $19.00; 50 scoring and recording forms, $74.00; and set of stimulus cards, $19.00. The DRS is copyrighted by Psychological Assessment Resources, Inc.

PSYCHOMETRIC PROPERTIES

Reliability

The test-retest reliability of the DRS total score over a 1-week period was found to be 0.97 with a group of elderly patients with dementia consistent with Alzheimer's disease ($N = 30$). The test-retest values for the individual subscales ranged from 0.61 for Attention to 0.94 for Conceptualization. The split-half reliability of the DRS total score was reported to be 0.90, as assessed in a group of nursing home residents with organic brain syndrome or senile dementia ($N = 25$). Three studies showed that the internal consistency among DRS items is 0.82–0.84 (Cronbach's alpha) in patients with dementia ($N = 221$) or patients with suspected cognitive impairment ($N = 50$) and that values for internal consistency among items in the various subscales are 0.65–0.95 for Attention, 0.44–0.87 for Initiation and Perseveration, 0.74–0.95 for Conceptualization, and 0.68–0.75 for Memory.

Validity

Five studies reported that patients with probable or possible Alzheimer's disease ($N = 22$–245) scored lower on the DRS than age- and education-matched psychiatrically healthy individuals ($N = 23$–212). Additional studies found that patients with mixed Alzheimer's and vascular disease ($N = 38$–221) performed worse on the DRS than subjects without Alzheimer's and vascular disease ($N = 15$–280), that elderly nursing home residents with organic brain syndrome ($N = 205$) scored worse than those without organic brain syndrome ($N = 205$), that patients with Parkinson's disease ($N = 130$) scored lower than individuals without Parkinson's disease ($N = 212$), that patients with minor cognitive impairment ($N = 53$) scored lower than individuals without cognitive impairment ($N = 280$), and that HIV-positive intravenous drug abusers ($N = 21$) scored lower than HIV-negative intravenous drug abusers ($N = 22$).

A DRS cutoff score of 123 was originally suggested for detecting cognitive impairment on the basis of being 2 standard deviations below the mean performance of a group of 85 psychiatrically healthy elderly individuals. More recently, a large study that examined the sensitivity and specificity of the DRS for the detection of early Alzheimer's disease reported that a cutoff score of 129 or 130 provided 97% sensitivity and 99% specificity for diagnosis ($N = 105$ psychiatrically healthy control subjects and 245 patients with Alzheimer's disease). Another study reported 95% sensitivity and 100% specificity with a cutoff score of 133 ($N = 48$ psychiatrically healthy control subjects and 22 patients with Alzheimer's disease).

Several studies have shown that performance on the DRS is correlated with other indexes of cognitive functioning. Two studies that compared DRS total score with full scale IQ in patients with dementia ($N = 15\text{--}221$) reported correlation coefficients ranging from 0.73 to 0.86. In one of these studies, DRS scores were also found to be significantly correlated with separate measures of verbal IQ ($r = 0.75$) and performance IQ ($r = 0.57$) ($N = 221$ patients with dementia). Three studies reported that the DRS scores of patients with suspected cognitive decline ($N = 50$), probable or possible Alzheimer's disease ($N = 92$), or autopsy-proven Alzheimer's disease ($N = 15$) were significantly correlated with the scores they achieved on the Mini-Mental State Exam (MMSE) (p. 422) ($r = 0.78$ to 0.90) and on the Blessed Information-Memory-Concentration (IMC) Test (p. 427) ($r = -0.79$ to -0.89). The DRS scores of patients with dementia ($N = 221$) were also found to be significantly correlated with their scores on measures of memory from the Wechsler Memory Scale—Revised (WMS-R) (Wechsler 1987), particularly those from the Attention/Concentration ($r = 0.63$) and General Memory ($r = 0.62$) subtests.

Scores achieved on the DRS by patients with dementia were shown in six studies to be related to measures of decline in their activities of daily living. One study found a correlation coefficient of -0.39 between the DRS scores of patients with dementia ($N = 221$) and their scores on the Record of Independent Living (Weintraub et al. 1982). Another study found that DRS scores, alone and in combination with a test of confrontation naming (i.e., naming an object presented visually), accounted for a significant amount of variance in functional measures of basic maintenance ($R^2 = 0.58$ and 0.62, respectively) and higher functional measures ($R^2 = 0.31$ and 0.42, respectively) obtained for patients with mild to moderate dementia ($N = 34$). One study reported that the DRS scores of patients with probable Alzheimer's disease ($N = 56$) were significantly correlated with their scores on the Independent Activities of Daily Living— Older Adult Resources Survey (IADL-OARS) (Fillenbaum and Smyer 1981) ($r = 0.38$), and that this correlation was particularly high for the DRS Memory ($r =$

0.44) and Initiation and Perseveration ($r = 0.34$) subscales. Three additional studies found that subjects judged to perform adequately on an activities of daily living (ADL) scale (Weintraub et al. 1982) ($N = 23$), or who had a classification of 0 on the Clinical Dementia Rating (CDR) Scale (p. 446) ($N = 16$), performed significantly better on the DRS than subjects classified as having mild dementia by these measures (e.g., CDR = 1, $N = 18$). The subjects with mild dementia, in turn, performed better than those classified as having moderate dementia (e.g., CDR = 2, $N = 16$). In these latter studies, there was 95% agreement between the DRS (DRS score = 103–130) and the CDR (CDR = 1) classification of mild dementia and 81% agreement between the DRS (DRS score = 40–102) and the CDR (CDR = 2) classification of moderate dementia.

Four studies showed that performance on the DRS is correlated with the degree of pathology in patients with dementia. DRS scores were found to be significantly correlated with gray matter cerebral blood flow ($r = 0.89$) in 30 patients with dementia and with cortical metabolism (as measured by fluorodeoxy glucose, positron-emission tomography [PET]) in the frontal ($r = 0.50$ left and 0.54 right), parietal ($r = 0.67$ left and 0.52 right), temporal ($r = 0.69$ left and 0.52 right), and occipital ($r = 0.67$ left and 0.51 right) cortex of patients with Alzheimer's disease ($N = 17$) and psychiatrically healthy control subjects ($N = 5$). Scores on the Initiation and Perseveration subscale of the DRS were found to be negatively correlated with the production of frontal release signs ($r = -0.43$) in patients with probable Alzheimer's disease ($N = 35$). The DRS scores of 15 patients with autopsy-proven Alzheimer's disease were found to be correlated with synaptic density in the midfrontal cortex ($r = 0.67$) and inferior parietal cortex ($r = 0.57$), with neurofibrillary tangle counts in the midfrontal cortex ($r = -0.55$) and inferior parietal cortex ($r = -0.52$), and with senile plaques in the midfrontal cortex ($r = -0.52$). A regression model that included synaptic density in the midfrontal cortex and synaptic density and plaque counts in the inferior parietal cortex accounted for 92% of the variance in the subjects' total DRS scores.

Three studies using factor analysis have provided some validity for the subscale structure of the DRS; however, the clinically established subscales do not correspond perfectly with the empirical factor structure of the scale. One study found that a three-factor solution that included factors corresponding to conceptual and organization, visuospatial and constructional, and memory and orientation abilities accounted for 64% of the variance in the performance of patients with probable Alzheimer's disease ($N = 219$). Another study reported that a four-factor solution was optimal in patients with probable or possible Alzheimer's disease ($N = 171$), with factors corresponding to attention and initiation, construction, conceptualization, and memory. These factors were found to be correlated with other putative measures of these abilities (range of r is 0.37–0.56). One study reported that a five-factor solution provided the best fit for a relatively small group of Alzheimer's disease patients ($N = 19$), patients with both Alzheimer's and vascular disease ($N = 17$), and psychiatrically healthy control subjects ($N = 49$); the factors corresponded to long-term memory and fluency, construction, memory, initiation and perseveration, and attention and the ability to follow simple commands.

Several studies have examined the ability of the DRS to track and predict cognitive decline in patients with dementia. One study reported that the DRS scores of patients with probable Alzheimer's disease ($N = 55$) declined an average of 11.4 points over a 1-year period. Another study found that the scores of 61% of 110 patients with dementia, but only 5% of psychiatrically healthy individuals, declined by more than 10 points over a little more than 1 year. This study also demonstrated that an individual with a DRS score of 100 is 2.5 times more likely to die within 1 year than an individual with a DRS score of 135. In addition, one study showed that a cutoff score of 20 on the DRS Memory subscale was 93% accurate in predicting which subjects without dementia but with memory complaints ($N = 30$) would go on to develop dementia within the next 4–6 years.

The pattern of performance on the DRS subscales has been shown to be useful in differentiating among patient groups with dementia arising from distinct diseases. In two studies, patients with Huntington's disease ($N = 10–23$) and progressive supranuclear palsy ($N = 10$) performed significantly worse than Alzheimer's disease patients ($N = 23$) on the Initiation and Perseveration subscale (and Attention subscale in one study) but better than Alzheimer's disease patients on the Memory subscale. Discriminant function analyses using these measures correctly classified 80% of patients with Alzheimer's disease ($N = 23$) and 90% of patients with Huntington's disease. A similar discriminant function analysis correctly classified 78% of Alzheimer's disease patients ($N = 50$) and 72% of Parkinson's disease patients ($N = 50$), primarily on the basis of performance on the DRS Memory and Construction subscales.

CLINICAL UTILITY

The DRS is a very effective instrument for assessing cognitive status in patients with known or suspected dementia. Almost all of the major cognitive domains that are compromised in dementing disorders are thoroughly assessed by the DRS, and the subscales for each domain contain a variety of test items that span a wide range of difficulty. This latter characteristic of the scale allows it to accurately assess cognitive status even in individuals with the most severe dementia and to effectively track the progression of dementia throughout the course of the underlying neurodegenerative disease. The DRS has some utility in differentiating among dementing disorders that vary in their etiologies and sites of predominant neuropathology. Patients with cortical dementia due to Alzheimer's disease, for example, have been shown to produce a pattern of DRS subscale scores that is distinguishable from the pattern produced by patients with equally global dementia with primarily subcortical neuropathology arising from Huntington's disease, Parkinson's disease, or progressive supranuclear palsy.

The DRS has been carefully validated against independent measures of cognitive and functional status in patients with dementia and against the neuropathological diagnosis of Alzheimer's disease. Performance on the DRS has been shown to be significantly correlated with the severity of neuropathological changes in the brains of patients with Alzheimer's disease. Extensive normative data exist for the DRS, and the test has been shown to effectively differentiate between Alzheimer's disease patients with very mild cognitive impairment and psychiatrically healthy elderly individuals. The ability of the DRS to detect cognitive impairment, like that of any cognitive test, is affected to some extent by age and education. Although a modest relationship has been observed between DRS performance and age or education level in psychiatrically healthy individuals, this relationship has not been observed in individuals with dementia.

The DRS provides a fairly thorough assessment of mental status in patients with dementia, but it is not equivalent to a full battery of neuropsychological tests.

In particular, although it includes a better evaluation of executive function than most tests of modest length, several other cognitive abilities that are often compromised relatively early in the course of Alzheimer's disease are not evaluated by the scale. For example, there are insufficient items on memory, and there is little or no naming to confrontation (i.e., naming an object presented visually). Some investigators have demonstrated that adding confrontation naming items to the DRS improves the scale's ability to detect and track the progression of Alzheimer's disease. Other investigators have proposed an extended version of the DRS (i.e., the Extended Scale for Dementia [Helmes et al. 1993; Hersch 1979]) that includes the addition of block design, orientation, simple arithmetic, counting, and paired associate learning. Although these additions may provide useful information about a patient's cognitive status, they significantly lengthen the administration time of the DRS and may not be cost-effective in terms of their additional assessment value.

REFERENCES AND SUGGESTED READINGS

Fillenbaum GG, Smyer MA: The development, validity, and reliability of the OARS multidimensional functional assessment questionnaire. J Gerontol 36:428–434, 1981

Helmes E, Mersky H, Hachinski VC, et al: An examination of psychometric properties of the Extended Scale for Dementia in three different populations. Alzheimer Dis Assoc Disord 6:236–246, 1993

Hersch EL: Development and application of the Extended Scale for Dementia. J Am Geriatr Soc 27:348–354, 1979

Mattis S: Mental status examination for organic mental syndrome in the elderly patient, in Geriatric Psychiatry: A Handbook for Psychiatrists and Primary Care Physicians. Edited by Bellak L, Karasu TB. New York, Grune & Stratton, 1976, pp 77–121

Mattis S: Dementia Rating Scale: Professional Manual. Odessa, FL, Psychological Assessment Resources, 1988

Monsch AU, Bondi MW, Salmon DP, et al: Clinical validity of the Mattis Dementia Rating Scale in detecting dementia of the Alzheimer type. Arch Neurol 52:899–904, 1995

Schmidt R, Freidl W, Fazekas F, et al: The Mattis Dementia Rating Scale: normative data from 1,001 healthy volunteers. Neurology 44:964–966, 1994

Smith GE, Ivnik RJ, Malec JF, et al: Psychometric properties of the Mattis Dementia Rating Scale. Assessment 1:123–131, 1994

Vitaliano PP, Breen AR, Russo J, et al: The clinical utility of the Dementia Rating Scale for assessing Alzheimer patients. Journal of Chronic Diseases 37:743–753, 1984

Wechsler D: Wechsler Memory Scale—Revised. New York, Psychological Corporation, 1987

Weintraub S, Barataz R, Mesulam MM: Daily living activities in the assessment of dementia, in Alzheimer's Disease: A Report of Progress in Research. Edited by Corkin S, Davis KL, Growdon JH, et al. New York, Raven, 1982, pp 189–192

Neurobehavioral Cognitive Status Examination (NCSE or COGNISTAT)

Northern California Neurobehavioral Group, Inc.

GOALS

The Neurobehavioral Cognitive Status Examination (NCSE) (Kiernan et al. 1987) was developed as a brief cognitive assessment instrument that could nonetheless provide a differentiated profile of functioning across multiple cognitive domains. The NCSE, unlike cognitive assessment scales that result in a single global score, attempts to distinguish confusional states from dementia and global dementia from isolated language, memory, or constructional deficits.

DESCRIPTION

The NCSE is a fully structured assessment instrument consisting of 11 subtests that evaluate eight major cognitive domains. The subtests are Level of Consciousness, Orientation, Attention, Language—Comprehension, Language—Repetition, Language—Naming, Visual Construction, Verbal Memory, Calculations, Verbal Reasoning—Similarities, and Verbal Reasoning—Judgment. All subtests except Level of Consciousness involve cognitive testing, and all of these except Orientation and Attention consist of a difficult screening item and a series of metric items that encompass a range of difficulty within that cognitive domain. If the screening item is passed, the cognitive domain is considered unimpaired and not tested further. When the screening item is failed, all of the metric items for that subtest are administered.

Each subtest of the NCSE is scored separately in terms of the number of items correct; lower scores reflect poorer performance and greater impairment in a given cognitive domain. If the screening item is passed, the maximum score for that subtest is credited. The maximum possible scores for each subtest are 12 for Orientation, 8 for Attention, 6 for Language—Comprehension, 12 for Language—Repetition, 8 for Language—Naming, 6 for Visual Construction, 12 for Verbal Memory, 4 for Calculations, 8 for Verbal Reasoning—Similarities, and 6 for Verbal Reasoning—Judgment. Level of Consciousness is rated as alert or impaired. Empirically derived cut points, provided in the test manual (Northern California Neurobehavioral Group 1995), are used to categorize performance as average, mildly impaired, moderately impaired, or severely impaired for each domain.

PRACTICAL ISSUES

It takes approximately 5–10 minutes to administer the NCSE to a nonimpaired individual. The administration time with an impaired individual has been estimated at 10–30 minutes, but an average of approximately 38 minutes was required in one study that involved geriatric patients with an average age of 80 years. The NCSE can be administered by any health care professional or paraprofessional who has been trained in test administration and scoring procedures. The NCSE stimulus materials, test booklets, and manual (with normative data) can be purchased under the name COGNISTAT from

Northern California Neurobehavioral Group, Inc.
P.O. Box 460
Fairfax, CA 94978
Phone: 800-922-5840

The NCSE is copyrighted by the Northern California Neurobehavioral Group, Inc. It is included on the CD-ROM that accompanies this handbook.

PSYCHOMETRIC PROPERTIES

Reliability

Because nonimpaired individuals score uniformly high on the NCSE subtests, test-retest and joint reliability have not been reported for psychiatrically healthy individuals. One study of consecutive patients admitted to a psychiatric hospital ($N = 72$) showed that the test-retest reliability of the NCSE over a 1-week period was kappa = 0.69. Another study reported test-retest reliability (calculated with Spearman rank order correlation) over a 5- to 10-day interval of 0.52 for the Verbal Memory subtest, 0.79 for the Visual Construction subtest, and 0.81 for the Calculations subtest in patients admitted to a hospital psychiatric ward or seen in a psychiatric emergency room ($N = 28$). The analyses could not be validly carried out for the other subtests because of the restricted ranges of scores. The joint reliability of scoring patients' performance on the NCSE was 0.57 (kappa coefficient) in patients admitted to a psychiatric hospital ($N = 20$).

Validity

Three studies showed that psychiatric patients with clinically diagnosed organic mental disorder ($N = 12–60$) perform significantly worse on the NCSE than psychiatric patients without organic mental disorder ($N = 58–136$). Sensitivity and specificity for the diagnosis of organic mental disorder in these studies, on the basis of a cutoff of failure on any one NCSE subtest (or on a weighted, composite subtest score of ≥ 13), ranged from 72% to 83% and from 47% to 73%, respectively. Another study found that failure on at least one NCSE subscale provided 93% sensitivity and 56% specificity for the detection of organic disturbance in nonpsychiatric patients under age 65 years ($N = 72$) but failed to detect organic disturbance in nonpsychiatric patients over age 65 ($N = 71$) or in psychiatric patients across the age range ($N = 70$). Sensitivity of 100% and specificity of 28% for distinguishing between psychiatric patients with organic mental disorder ($N = 35$) and depressed patients ($N = 18$) were obtained in another study. A study of hospitalized geriatric patients with an average age of 80 years, many with comorbid psychiatric illness, showed that failure on at least one NCSE subtest provided 100% sensitivity but only 11% specificity for differentiating between those with and without cognitive impairment, as determined by an examining psychiatrist.

A large study with more than 800 psychiatric inpatients found that young patients (ages 20–39; $N = 329$) were an average of 1.5 standard deviations below the normative value on the Orientation, Verbal Memory, and Verbal Reasoning—Judgment subtests; older patients (ages 40–60; $N = 390$) were 1.5 standard deviations below normal on the Language—Comprehension, Visual Construction, and Verbal Memory subtests; and geriatric patients (ages 67–92; $N = 128$) were 1.5 standard deviations below normal on the Orientation, Language—Comprehension, Language—Repetition, Verbal Memory, and Calculations subtests. Another study found that 32% of 73 patients with chronic musculoskeletal pain were impaired on at least one NCSE subtest and that a composite NCSE score was significantly correlated with patients' ratings of the severity of their pain ($r = 0.44$). Although these studies support the notion that the NCSE can detect cognitive impairment in psychiatric patients, neither study employed an independent measure of cognitive functioning to serve as a benchmark.

Several studies have shown that the NCSE is able to detect cognitive impairment in patients with brain damage. In one study, cognitive impairment was detected by the NCSE (i.e., a deficit on at least one subtest) in 28 of 30 candidate neurosurgical patients with brain lesions documented by magnetic resonance imaging (MRI), computed tomography (CT) imaging, or biopsy. Improvement on the NCSE was noted in one patient after surgery for a subdural hematoma and in two of three patients after removal of a brain tumor. The scores of five of seven patients who received a shunt as treatment for hydrocephalus declined on one or two NCSE subtests; these patients required a second surgery to repair the shunt. Impairment on at least one NCSE subtest was observed in 35 of 38 patients entering a stroke rehabilitation program, and NCSE subscores for Orientation, Attention, Language—Repetition, Calculations, and Verbal Reasoning—Judgment at admission accounted for 57% of the variance in improvement during the program as measured by the Barthel Index (Mahoney and Barthel 1965). Another study demonstrated that patients with left-sided cerebrovascular accidents ($N = 12$) performed worse than a group of psychiatrically healthy control subjects ($N = 12$) on the Language—Comprehension, Language—Naming, Verbal Memory, and Verbal Reasoning—Similarities subtests of the NCSE, and patients with right-sided cerebrovascular accidents ($N = 12$) performed worse than the control subjects on the NCSE Language—Naming and Visual Construction subtests. In a group of nine patients with Alzheimer's disease and seven patients with multi-infarct dementia, NCSE subtest scores for the Language Subtests, Verbal Memory, Attention, Verbal Reasoning—Judgment, and Verbal Reasoning—Similarities were correlated with cerebral blood flow in posterior brain regions as measured by single photon emission computed tomography (SPECT) imaging.

A high degree of correspondence was observed between inpatients with substance abuse ($N = 34$) who were impaired on at least one of the NCSE subtests and those who performed in the impaired range on the Luria-Nebraska Neuropsychological Battery (Golden et al. 1985) and Part B of the Trail Making Test (Reitan 1958). Significant correlation between NCSE performance and performance on a full neuropsychological test battery was observed in 54 consecutive patients referred for cognitive assessment; in particular, significant correlations were found between the Attention subtest and the Wechsler Adult Intelligence Scale—Revised (WAIS-R) (Wechsler 1981) Digit Span subtest ($r = 0.40$), between the Language—Naming subtest and the Boston Naming Test (Kaplan et al. 1983) ($r = 0.80$), between the Visual Construction subtest and the WAIS-R Block Design ($r = 0.83$) and Visual Reproduction ($r = 0.80$) tests, between the Verbal Memory subtest and the California Verbal Learning Test (Delis et al. 1987) ($r = 0.68$), between the Calculations subtest and the WAIS-R Arithmetic subtest ($r = 0.59$), between the Verbal Reasoning—Similarities subtest and the WAIS-R Similarities subtest ($r = 0.75$), between the Verbal Reasoning—Judgment subtest and the WAIS-R Comprehension subtest ($r = 0.48$), between the Language—Comprehension subtest and the Western Aphasia Battery (WAB) (Kertesz 1982) Sequential Commands item ($r = 0.55$), and between the Language—Repetition subscale and the WAB Repetition item ($r = 0.47$).

A factor analytic study with 192 patients admitted to a psychiatric hospital or seen in a psychiatric emergency room revealed that two factors accounted for more than 50% of the variance in NCSE performance. These factors corresponded to overlearned cognitive skills acquired through education and experience, as measured by the Language—Comprehension, Language—Naming, Visual Construction, and Verbal Reasoning—Similarities subtests, and functional cognitive efficiency with the environment, as represented by performance on the Verbal Memory, Calculations, and Verbal Reasoning—Judgment subtests.

CLINICAL UTILITY

The NCSE provides a brief assessment of a wide range of cognitive abilities that are often detrimentally affected in patients with neurological and psychiatric disorders. A major advantage of the test is that it allows several different cognitive functions to be evaluated independently and rated as intact or impaired relative to normative data. This characteristic of the test permits a much clearer understanding of a patient's cognitive strengths and weaknesses than can be obtained from a mental status examination that provides a single global score, and it allows identification of particular patterns of cognitive deficits that may be differentially associated with specific disorders.

Psychometric data indicate that the NCSE is reliable and that it has at least moderate validity as demonstrated against full psychiatric evaluations for organic mental disorder, evidence of brain damage from neuroimaging or neurosurgical procedures, and performance on other comprehensive neuropsychological tests. There appears to be no strong effect of age on NCSE performance in psychiatrically healthy individuals, as shown in the standardization sample, although geriatric subjects performed slightly worse than younger subjects on the Visual Construction, Verbal Memory, and Verbal Reasoning—Similarities subtests. Marginal correlations between age and performance on the Attention and Language—Repetition subtests were reported in two studies with psychiatric and neurological patients.

Performance on the NCSE, like that on most cognitive tests, is affected to some extent by education. Education has been shown to be correlated with several NCSE subtests in psychiatric and neurological patients. In addition, the originators of the NCSE caution that early loss of cognitive function may be particularly difficult to detect with the test in individuals with superior premorbid intelligence or education. Given these factors,

the possible influence of level of education on performance should be considered when interpreting the results of the NCSE.

The NCSE has been used primarily to detect cognitive dysfunction in patients with psychiatric disorders, although it has also been used to detect impairment in patients with brain disorders such as cerebrovascular disease, hydrocephalus, and other neurological maladies (e.g., tumors and subdural hematomas). Patterns of subtest performance produced by patients with suspected dementia of the Alzheimer's type are presented in the NCSE manual, but there is very limited information on the effectiveness of the NCSE for detecting and staging cognitive impairment in such patients or in patients with other progressive dementing disorders. Until such information is available, the NCSE should be used cautiously in this regard. Other limitations of the NCSE are that it may lack sensitivity for detecting frontal lobe dysfunction and it provides only cursory assessment of attentional deficits.

REFERENCES AND SUGGESTED READINGS

Delis DC, Kramer JH, Kaplan E, et al: California Verbal Learning Test: Adult Version. San Antonio, TX, Psychological Corporation, 1987

Golden CH, Purisch AD, Hammeke TA: Luria-Nebraska Neuropsychological Battery: Forms I and II. Los Angeles, CA, Western Psychological Services, 1985

Kaplan E, Goodglass H, Weintraub S: The Boston Naming Test. Philadelphia, PA, Lea & Febiger, 1983

Kertesz A: The Western Aphasia Battery. San Antonio, TX, Psychological Corporation, 1982

Kiernan RJ, Mueller J, Langston JW, et al: The Neurobehavioral Cognitive Status Examination: a brief but differentiated approach to cognitive assessment. Ann Intern Med 107:481–485, 1987

Louge PE, Tupler LA, D'Amico C, et al: The Neurobehavioral Cognitive Status Examination: psychometric properties in use with psychiatric inpatients. J Clin Psychol 49:80–89, 1993

Mahoney F, Barthel D: Functional evaluation: the Barthel Index. Md Med J 14:61–65, 1965

Marcotte TD, van Gorp W, Hinkin CH, et al: Concurrent validity of the Neurobehavioral Cognitive Status Exam subtests. J Clin Exp Neuropsychol 19:386–395, 1997

Mitrushina M, Abara J, Blumenfeld A: Aspects of validity and reliability of the Neurobehavioral Cognitive Status Examination (NCSE) in assessment of psychiatric patients. J Psychiatr Res 28:85–95, 1994

Northern California Neurobehavioral Group: Manual for COGNISTAT (The Neurobehavioral Cognitive Status Examination). Fairfax, CA, Northern California Neurobehavioral Group, 1995

Reitan R: Validity of the Trail Making Test as an indicator of organic brain disease. Perceptual and Psychomotor Skills 8:271–276, 1958

Schwamm LH, Van Dyke C, Kiernan RJ, et al: The Neurobehavioral Cognitive Status Examination: comparison with the Cognitive Capacity Screening Examination and the Mini-Mental State Examination in a neurosurgical population. Ann Intern Med 107:486–491, 1987

Wechsler D: Wechsler Adult Intelligence Scale—Revised Manual. New York, Psychological Corporation, 1981

Clock Drawing Test

H. Tuokko et al. and M. Freedman et al.

GOALS

The Clock Drawing Test (Freedman et al. 1994; Tuokko et al. 1995) is a formalization—with a variety of scoring systems—of a common bedside test involving copying a clock, putting the hands on a clock, and/or drawing a clock showing a specific time. Although originally conceived as a relatively specific test of visuospatial and constructional ability, the Clock Drawing Test has recently gained favor as a quick and easily administered screening instrument for general cognitive dysfunction. This use of the Clock Drawing Test developed from the realization that the test is sensitive to many forms of brain dysfunction. The Clock Drawing Test draws on multiple cognitive processes, including auditory comprehension of the instructions, access to the semantic representation of a clock, conceptualization and planning abilities, and visuoperceptual, visuospatial, and visuomotor skills.

DESCRIPTION

The Clock Drawing Test assesses an individual's ability to draw or copy the face of a clock, put in the correct numbers, and set the hands to indicate a specified time. Several different versions of the task have been described: requiring the clock drawing to be done on a blank sheet of paper, providing a circle and asking that the numbers and hands be drawn, providing a circle and numbers and asking only that the hands be drawn to indicate a specified time, and providing a complete clock that is to be copied. Often, both clock drawing to command on a blank sheet of paper and copying a complete clock are required so that visuospatial and visuomotor abilities required in both the command and copy conditions can be separated from the conceptual abilities that are required only in the command condition.

Several quantitative and semiquantitative scoring systems have been proposed for the various versions of the Clock Drawing Test. These systems range from simple template matching schemes, in which the target clock is compared with a series of prototypical clocks that are graded in their degree of distortion, to quantitative schemes, in which a point is awarded for the correct production of each of more than a dozen different aspects of the clock. Several of the most widely used scoring systems evaluate the presence and correctness of several critical items in the clock construction (e.g., circular contour, placement and accuracy of numbers, and placement and accuracy of hands). These scoring systems include the 3-point system of Freedman et al. (1994), the 0- to 10-point scale proposed by Sunderland et al. (1989) and its modification by Rouleau et al. (1992), the 0- to 15-point critical items scale of Freedman et al. (1994), and the 0–31 error scale proposed by Tuokko et al. (1995). The most widely used template matching scoring system is the 0 (irrelevant figures) to 10 (normal clock) ordinal scale of Wolf-Klein et al. (1989). The test may also be helpful when judged clinically to obtain an impression of specific areas in which the patient may be having difficulties.

PRACTICAL ISSUES

It takes approximately 5–10 minutes to administer the Clock Drawing Test, depending on the version of the test used. The test has been widely used at the bedside by physicians and other clinicians to obtain an overall picture of areas in which patients may have cognitive deficits. The formalized version can be administered and scored by any health care professional or paraprofessional who has reviewed the administration and scoring procedures. A version of the Clock Drawing Test, developed by Tuokko et al., is commercially available from

> Multi-Health Systems, Inc.
> 908 Niagara Falls Boulevard
> North Tonawanda, NY 14120-2060
> Phone: 800-456-3003
> Internet: www.mhs.com

In addition, administration and scoring procedures, theoretical rationale, and extensive normative data on a widely used version of the Clock Drawing Test have been published by Freedman et al. (1994). Multi-Health Systems, Inc., holds the copyright for the Tuokko version of the Clock Drawing Test. The Clock Test Kit (which includes the Clock Test manual, the Administration Tent, 25 QuikScore forms, and 25 profile sheets) costs $160.00. Each of the kit items may be purchased individually.

PSYCHOMETRIC PROPERTIES

Reliability

Ten studies that examined joint interrater reliability for the various Clock Drawing Test scoring procedures revealed correlation coefficients of 0.85–0.98 in patients with Alzheimer's disease ($N = 33$–67), 0.64–0.89 in psychiatrically healthy control subjects ($N = 83$–100), and 0.48–0.95 in groups that contained individuals with and without dementia ($N = 30$–315). In one of these studies, physicians and nurses showed similar levels of interrater reliability in scoring the test ($r = 0.93$ and 0.90, respectively). The test-retest reliability of the Clock Drawing Test was found to be $r = 0.76$ in 55 geriatric outpatients retested after a 1-week interval, $r = 0.70$ in 32 subjects retested after 4 days, and $r = 0.78$ and 0.70 in 42 patients with Alzheimer's disease retested after 12 weeks and 24 weeks, respectively.

Validity

Performance on the Clock Drawing Test is significantly correlated with performance on various tests of mental status or visuospatial function. Correlation coefficients of 0.65–0.76 were obtained between the Clock Drawing Test and the Mini-Mental State Exam (MMSE) (p. 422) in elderly medical patients ($N = 71$–75), and a correlation coefficient of 0.45 was obtained in patients with probable Alzheimer's disease ($N = 46$). Correlations with the Dementia Rating Scale (DRS) (p. 430) ranged from $r = 0.57$ to 0.70 in patients with probable Alzheimer's disease ($N = 33$–67) and from 0.24 to 0.44 in psychiatrically healthy elderly subjects ($N = 100$). The Clock Drawing Test was also significantly correlated with the Global Deterioration Scale (p. 450) ($r = 0.40$–0.56) in patients with probable Alzheimer's disease ($N = 46$–67), with a 10-item version of the Information-Memory-Concentration (IMC) Test (p. 427) in hospitalized geriatric patients (kappa = 0.63; $N = 76$) and in elderly patients attending an outpatient clinic ($r = 0.30$; $N = 431$), with the total Blessed-Roth Dementia Scale (see IMC Test, p. 427) in patients with probable Alzheimer's disease ($r = 0.51$, $N = 67$), with the Short Portable Mental Status Questionnaire (Pfeffer 1975) in elderly hospitalized patients without dementia ($r = 0.66$; $N = 75$) and patients with probable Alzheimer's disease ($r = 0.59$; $N = 67$), with the Wechsler Adult Intelligence Scale—Revised (WAIS-R) (Wechsler 1981) Block Design subtest in patients with dementia ($r = 0.57$; $N = 269$) and in psychiatrically healthy elderly subjects ($r = 0.21$–0.36; $N = 100$), and with the Rey-Osterrieth Figure Drawing Task (Osterrieth 1944) in patients with probable Alzheimer's disease ($r = 0.66$; $N = 46$) but not in psychiatrically healthy elderly subjects. Performance on the Clock Drawing Test was also shown to be correlated with performance on several other tests of cognitive function in patients with dementia ($N = 269$), including a word fluency task ($r = 0.48$); the Information ($r = 0.48$), Similarities ($r = 0.41$), and Digit Span ($r = 0.43$) subtests of the WAIS-R; and the Expressive Language ($r = 0.33$), Auditory Receptive Language ($r = 0.33$), Visual Receptive Language ($r = 0.42$), Mental Status ($r = 0.52$), and Orientation ($r = 0.55$) components of the Multifocal Assessment Scale (Coval et al. 1985).

Numerous validity studies uniformly demonstrate that patients with Alzheimer's disease ($N = 25$–121) perform significantly worse than psychiatrically healthy control subjects ($N = 49$–237) on the Clock Drawing Test, regardless of the specific administration and scoring procedures employed. In addition, one study showed that dementia patients with Huntington's disease ($N = 25$) scored significantly worse than psychiatrically healthy control subjects ($N = 25$) on the test, and another study showed that individuals who were at risk for developing Alzheimer's disease (i.e., who had demonstrated mild cognitive impairment but not functional decline; $N = 74$) scored significantly worse than psychiatrically healthy control subjects ($N = 237$).

The sensitivity and specificity for the detection of dementia of individual cutoff scores on various versions of the Clock Drawing Test were examined in 12 studies. Although the exact values depend on the administration and scoring procedures employed, the maximally effective cutoff scores provided sensitivity that ranges from 75.2% to 97% and specificity that ranges from 54% to 100% ($N = 21$–269 patients with dementia and 26–1,753 psychiatrically healthy control subjects). As for the most widely used scoring systems, a cutoff score of 6 in the Sunderland et al. (1989) system provided 78% sensitivity and 96% specificity for distinguishing between patients with Alzheimer's disease ($N = 67$) and psychiatrically healthy control subjects ($N = 83$), a cutoff score of 7 in the Rouleau et al. (1992) modification of the Sunderland system provided 88% sensitivity and 63% specificity for distinguishing between patients with Alzheimer's disease ($N = 42$) and psychiatrically healthy control subjects ($N = 237$), a cutoff score of 2 errors in the Tuokko et al. (1995) scoring system provided 80% sensitivity and 82% specificity for distinguishing between individuals with dementia ($N = 269$) and individuals without dementia ($N = 1,753$), and a rating of 7 or higher in the Wolf-Klein et al. (1989) system provided 75% sensitivity and 94% specificity in differentiating between patients with dementia ($N = 182$) and psychiatrically healthy control subjects ($N = 130$).

One study demonstrated significant decline in the Clock Drawing Test scores of patients with Alzheimer's disease ($N = 33$) over a 2-year period and further demonstrated that the production of a conceptual error on the test (e.g., writing the time rather than setting the hands) was associated with a more rapid decline, as measured by the change in the Dementia Rating Scale (DRS) (p. 430) score, than when no conceptual error was produced.

CLINICAL UTILITY

The Clock Drawing Test is a brief, easily administered task that provides a relatively effective screen for general cognitive dysfunction. Because the test simply involves drawing or copying a very familiar item, it is often perceived as a nonthreatening task by patients and is generally well tolerated. The Clock Drawing Test has been shown to have good test-retest and joint reliability, particularly when one of the proposed formalized scoring systems is employed. The test has also been shown to be sensitive to the presence of mild dementia and, in at least one study, to the cognitive decline that occurs over time in patients with Alzheimer's disease.

Performance on the Clock Drawing Test does not appear to be strongly related to age or level of education. However, Tuokko et al. (1995) found that different cutoff scores on the test provided optimal sensitivity and specificity for detecting dementia in individuals ages 65–79 years (2 error points) and individuals ages 80 years and older (5 error points).

Although the Clock Drawing Test is a relatively effective cognitive screening instrument, the test does not directly involve certain cognitive abilities that are affected in the very earliest stages of Alzheimer's disease, such as episodic memory, verbal fluency, or cognitive set shifting. Consequently, subtle but clinically significant cognitive impairment in early Alzheimer's disease may not be detected by the test.

REFERENCES AND SUGGESTED READINGS

Coval M, Crokett D, Holliday S, et al: A multifocus assessment scale for use with elderly populations. Canadian Journal of Aging 4:101–109, 1985

Freedman M, Leach L, Kaplan E, et al: Clock Drawing: A Neuropsychological Analysis. New York, Oxford University Press, 1994

Osterrieth PA: Le test de copie d'une figure complexe. Archives de Psychologie 30:206–356, 1944

Pfeffer E: A short portable mental status questionnaire for the assessment of organic brain deficits in elderly patients. J Am Geriatr Soc 23:433–441, 1975

Rouleau I, Salmon DP, Butters N, et al: Quantitative and qualitative analyses of clock drawings in Alzheimer's and Huntington's disease. Brain Cogn 18:70–87, 1992

Sunderland T, Hill JL, Mellow AM, et al: Clock drawing in Alzheimer's disease: a novel measure of dementia severity. J Am Geriatr Soc 37:725–729, 1989

Tuokko H, Hadjistavropoulos T, Miller JA, et al: The Clock Test: Administration and Scoring Manual. Toronto, Multi-Health Systems, 1995

Wechsler D: Wechsler Adult Intelligence Scale—Revised Manual. New York, Psychological Corporation, 1981

Wolf-Klein GP, Silverstone FA, Levy AP, et al: Screening for Alzheimer's disease by clock drawing. J Am Geriatr Soc 37:730–734, 1989

Alzheimer's Disease Assessment Scale (ADAS)

R. C. Mohs, W. G. Rosen, and K. L. Davis

GOALS

The Alzheimer's Disease Assessment Scale (ADAS) (Mohs et al. 1983; Rosen et al. 1984) is designed to assess all of the major cognitive and behavioral symptoms associated with Alzheimer's disease, particularly within the context of clinical trials of antidementia drugs. Toward this end, the test is devised to be sensitive to the cognitive and behavioral deterioration that occurs in patients with Alzheimer's disease in order to effectively measure the efficacy of treatments designed to reverse, halt, or slow the progression of the disease. A secondary use of the ADAS is to detect mild cognitive impairment indicative of early Alzheimer's disease.

DESCRIPTION

The ADAS is a fully structured scale consisting of 21 items that measure the severity of the major cognitive and noncognitive behavioral symptoms of Alzheimer's disease. The cognitive assessment portion of the ADAS (ADAS-COG) is administered directly to the patient and covers memory, language, and praxis with the following 11 subitems: orientation questions, a word recall task, a word recognition task, rating of ability to remember test instructions on the word recognition task, naming of ob-

jects and fingers, rating of spoken language, rating of language comprehension, rating of word finding difficulty, following commands task, ideational praxis task, and constructional praxis task. The noncognitive behavior portion of the ADAS consists of clinician ratings of depression, tearfulness, hallucinations, delusions, restlessness, pacing, concentration, tremor, and appetite on the basis of observations of the patient in the testing situation and an interview with an informant. The ADAS-COG is often scored and used separately from the total ADAS score. The noncognitive portion can also be used separately. A new version of the ADAS was recently released, but little psychometric information concerning this version is currently available. This report therefore deals with the original version.

The ADAS is scored in terms of errors; higher scores reflect poorer performance or greater disability. The total score ranges from 0 (perfect performance) to 120. Scores for the ADAS-COG portion of the test range from 0 to 70 and are determined on the basis of the following subitem scores: 0–10 for the number of errors on the word recall item, 0–12 for the number of errors on the word recognition item, 0–8 for the number of errors on the orientation item, and 0–5 on all other subitems. Scores for the noncognitive portion of the ADAS range from 0 to 50; each of the 10 subitems is scored on a scale of 0–5.

PRACTICAL ISSUES

It usually requires approximately 45 minutes to administer the ADAS; the ADAS-COG requires 35 minutes. The test should be administered by an examiner who is well versed in the procedures and conventions that are presented in the copyrighted revised administration and scoring manual. The test materials are not commercially available, but the test items and instructions for generating test materials are presented in the revised manual, which is available from the author:

Richard Mohs, Ph.D.
Psychiatry Service (116A)
Mount Sinai School of Medicine
VA Medical Center
130 W. Kingsbridge Road
Bronx, NY 10468

The ADAS is included on the CD-ROM that accompanies this handbook.

PSYCHOMETRIC PROPERTIES

Reliability

In three studies, correlations for the joint reliability of the ADAS, the ADAS-COG, and the noncognitive portion of the ADAS were shown to range from 0.92 to 0.99, 0.89 to 0.99, and 0.85 to 0.95, respectively, for patients with probable Alzheimer's disease ($N = 15-54$). Joint reliability of these three measures for psychiatrically healthy elderly subjects ($N = 27-28$) ranged from 0.89 to 0.93, 0.87 to 0.97, and 0.83 to 0.90, respectively. Three studies showed that the test-retest reliability of the ADAS over a 2-week to 2-month interval ranged from 0.84 to 0.97 for patients with probable Alzheimer's disease ($N = 15-54$) and from 0.52 to 0.57 for psychiatrically healthy elderly subjects ($N = 27-28$). The test-retest reliability of the ADAS-COG was shown in five studies ($N = 15-280$) to range from 0.86 to 0.95 over a 2-week to 2-month interval for patients with probable Alzheimer's disease and from 0.58 to 0.65 for psychiatrically healthy elderly subjects. The noncognitive portion of the ADAS was shown to have test-retest reliability that ranged from 0.59 to 0.87 for patients with probable Alzheimer's disease and from 0.47 to 0.51 for psychiatrically healthy elderly subjects.

Validity

Studies that compared the total ADAS with other measures of Alzheimer's disease severity, cognitive impairment, or behavioral change reported significant correlation coefficients of 0.52 with the Sandoz Clinical Assessment—Geriatric (SCAG) (Shader et al. 1974) ($N = 27$), 0.67 with a 20-item version of the Information-Memory-Concentration (IMC) Test (p. 427) ($N = 27$), 0.64 with the entire Blessed-Roth Dementia Scale (see IMC Test, p. 427) ($N = 27$), 0.71–0.90 with the Mini-Mental State Exam (MMSE) (p. 422) ($N = 49-61$), 0.69–0.71 with the SKT test (Erzigkeit 1989) ($N = 49-280$), and 0.77 with the Brief Cognitive Rating Scale (BCRS) (p. 450) ($N = 49$). Significant correlation coefficients were also reported between the ADAS-COG and the SCAG (0.67), the IMC Test (p. 427) (0.78), the Blessed-Roth

Dementia Rating Scale (see IMC Test, p. 427) (0.48), the MMSE (0.76–0.90), the SKT test (0.82), and the BCRS (0.80).

Several validity studies have shown that patients with clinical diagnoses of probable Alzheimer's disease ($N = 10-61$) perform significantly worse than psychiatrically healthy elderly subjects ($N = 10-52$) on the ADAS, the ADAS-COG, and the noncognitive portion of the ADAS. Although a specific cut point for detecting cognitive impairment with the ADAS or the ADAS-COG has not been recommended, one study found no overlap in the classification of patients with dementia of the Alzheimer's type ($N = 49$) and psychiatrically healthy elderly subjects ($N = 49$) using a cut point of 6 points (i.e., 2 standard deviations below the reported mean score of psychiatrically healthy elderly subjects).

Two factor analytic studies with Alzheimer's disease patients ($N = 280$ and 656) showed that, as intended, the ADAS-COG assesses three cardinal dimensions of the cognitive impairment associated with the disease: memory and orientation, language, and praxis. Test-retest reliability of the three factors ranged from 0.78 to 0.87.

Three studies that examined the sensitivity of the ADAS to cognitive decline in patients with probable Alzheimer's disease reported changes of 7.07 points ($N = 60$), 7.8 points ($N = 10$), and 9.13 points ($N = 111$) over a 12-month period. A decline of 14.0 points was reported after 24 months ($N = 25$). One study also reported 12-month declines of 5.2 and 4.0 points on the ADAS-COG and the noncognitive portion of the ADAS, respectively, in patients with probable Alzheimer's disease ($N = 10$).

CLINICAL UTILITY

The ADAS, and particularly the ADAS-COG, appears to be an effective instrument for monitoring the efficacy of antidementia drugs in clinical trials that involve patients with Alzheimer's disease. Reasonable psychometric data indicate that the ADAS is a reliable and valid means of assessing the cognitive and behavioral features of Alzheimer's disease and provides a stable and objective measure of the degree of deterioration in these features over time. Performance on the ADAS does not appear to be strongly related to the subjects' levels of education, because one study found no relationship and two others only a marginal association (limited to poorer performance in those who did not graduate from high school). Practice effects on the ADAS are also reported to be marginal for patients with Alzheimer's disease, indicating that the test can be administered repeatedly in clinical trials without strongly influencing the ability to measure treatment effects. Because of these properties, the ADAS-COG is the most widely used measure of cognitive dysfunction in clinical trials research on Alzheimer's disease, and it recently served as the primary dependent measure in trials that demonstrated the ability of cholinesterase inhibitors to slow the progression of cognitive deterioration in patients with Alzheimer's disease.

Despite its strengths, the ADAS is limited in several respects. The test does not assess attentional deficits or executive dysfunction (i.e., deficits in abstraction, set shifting, and conceptualization), even though impairment in both of these cognitive domains occurs during the course of Alzheimer's disease. Executive dysfunction is often a particularly early and prominent symptom of the disease and is potentially sensitive to the effects of antidementia drugs. A second limitation is that the ADAS was developed and has been used almost exclusively for patients with Alzheimer's disease, so its clinical utility with other dementing disorders (e.g., multi-infarct dementia and dementia of Parkinson's disease) remains unknown. Although the ADAS or the ADAS-COG may have some clinical utility as an instrument for detecting mild cognitive impairment indicative of early Alzheimer's disease, the test was not designed for this purpose and should be used cautiously in this regard. For example, the ADAS does not adequately measure some of the earliest and most salient cognitive features of the dementia associated with Alzheimer's disease, such as rapid forgetting. Research that examines the sensitivity and specificity of the ADAS for detecting true cognitive decline in patients with mild dementia is necessary before the test can be used for this purpose.

REFERENCES AND SUGGESTED READINGS

Erzigkeit H: The SKT: a short cognitive performance test as an instrument for the assessment of clinical efficacy of cognition enhancers, in Diagnosis and Treatment of Senile Dementia. Edited by Bergener M, Reisberg B. Berlin, Springer-Verlag, 1989, pp 164–174

Ihl R, Frolich L, Dierks T, et al: Differential validity of psychometric tests in dementia of the Alzheimer type. Psychiatry Res 44:93–106, 1992

Kramer-Ginsberg E, Mohs RC, Aryan M, et al: Clinical predictors of course for Alzheimer patients in a longitudinal study: a preliminary report. Psychopharmacol Bull 24:458–462, 1988

Mohs RC, Rosen WG, Davis KL: The Alzheimer's Disease Assessment Scale: an instrument for assessing treatment efficacy. Psychopharmacol Bull 19:448–450, 1983

Rosen WG, Mohs RC, Davis KL: A new rating scale for Alzheimer's disease. Am J Psychiatry 141:1356–1364, 1984

Shader WI, Harmatz JS, Salzman C: A new scale for clinical assessment in geriatric populations: Sandoz Clinical Assessment—Geriatric (SCAG). J Am Geriatr Soc 22:107–113, 1974

Zec RF, Landreth ES, Vicari SK, et al: Alzheimer Disease Assessment Scale: useful for both early detection and staging of dementia of the Alzheimer type. Alzheimer Dis Assoc Disord 6:89–102, 1992

Galveston Orientation and Amnesia Test (GOAT)

H. S. Levin, V. M. O'Donnell, and R. G. Grossman

GOALS

The Galveston Orientation and Amnesia Test (GOAT) (Levin et al. 1979) was developed to objectively measure the disorientation and amnesia that occur as a consequence of head injury to provide a means of tracking recovery throughout the posttraumatic period.

DESCRIPTION

The GOAT is a fully structured scale consisting of 10 items that provide an evaluation of orientation, an estimate of the duration of posttraumatic amnesia (i.e., loss of memory for events that occurred after injury), and an estimate of the duration of retrograde amnesia (i.e., loss of memory for events that occurred before injury). The orientation items include questions concerning person (i.e., name, date of birth, and place of residence), place (i.e., name of city and identification of hospital), and time (i.e., time of day, day of week, date, month, and year). The duration of posttraumatic amnesia is assessed by asking the patient to report and describe in detail the first event he or she can remember after the injury. The duration of retrograde amnesia is similarly assessed by asking the patient to report and describe in detail the last event he or she can recall before the injury. A pediatric version of the GOAT, the Child's Orientation and Amnesia Test (COAT) (Ewing-Cobbs et al. 1990), consists of 16 items that assess general orientation (i.e., name, age, parents' names, school, present location, and whether it is daytime or nighttime), temporal orientation (i.e., time, day of week, and date), and memory (i.e., serial numbers, counting fingers, name of examiner, and names of television characters). The temporal orientation items of the COAT are not administered to children under age 8. Questions from the GOAT concerning the duration of posttraumatic amnesia and retrograde amnesia are not included in the COAT.

The GOAT is scored in terms of error points that are subtracted from 100. The number of points to be deducted for an incorrect response is indicated for each question. The questions are weighted in value and range from 2 error points (e.g., name) to a maximum of 30 error points (e.g., missing the year by 3 or more). The number of error points assessed for an incorrect response on most temporal orientation items is graded in terms of its deviation from the correct answer (e.g., 1 point assessed for each day removed from the correct one, to a maximum of 5 points).

PRACTICAL ISSUES

The GOAT can be administered at bedside in approximately 10 minutes. Any health care professional can administer the test. The GOAT is not commercially available, but the test items, method of administration, and scoring procedures have been published (Levin et al. 1979). Similar information for the COAT has also been

published (Ewing-Cobbs et al. 1990). The GOAT may also be obtained by contacting the author:

Harvey Levin, Ph.D.
Baylor College of Medicine
Department of Physical Medicine and Rehabilitation
1333 Maursund Avenue
Houston, TX 77030

The GOAT is included on the CD-ROM that accompanies this handbook.

PSYCHOMETRIC PROPERTIES

Reliability

Joint reliability for the GOAT was found to be 0.99 (Kendall (rank correlation coefficient) in a study of patients with closed-head injury of varying severity ($N = 13$). In addition, the joint reliability coefficients for the individual items of the test consistently approximated 0.99. Two studies reported joint reliability ranging from 0.98 to 1.00 for the COAT with children with neurological injuries ($N = 11–33$) and nonneurological injuries ($N = 25$).

Validity

A standardization study showed that the median GOAT score of subjects who had recovered from mild closed-head injury ($N = 50$) was 95. No patient in this standardization group scored <65, and 8% scored between 66 and 75. On the basis of these results, the defective range of performance on the GOAT was established as <66, and scores between 66 and 75 were designated as borderline abnormal. Using these cutoff scores, the GOAT was found to significantly improve (by approximately 20%) detection of posttraumatic amnesia over simple chart review in recently hospitalized patients with closed-head injury associated with acute spinal cord injury ($N = 34$). Several studies have examined the relationship between duration of posttraumatic amnesia as measured by the GOAT and other outcomes or correlates of head injury. Duration of posttraumatic amnesia is assessed by administering the GOAT serially (e.g., once a day) from the onset of the injury or termination of coma until a score of ≥ 75 is consistently achieved (e.g., on 2 consecutive days). In one study, the duration of posttraumatic amnesia as measured by the GOAT was significantly related to indexes of best verbal response, best motor response, and degree of eye opening from the Glasgow Coma Scale (Teasdale and Jennett 1974) performed with closed-head injury patients on the day of admission to the neurosurgery ward of a hospital ($N = 52$). Furthermore, duration of posttraumatic amnesia was shown to be related to the success of long-term (i.e., 6-month) recovery from head injury in this study. Another study showed that a longer duration of posttraumatic amnesia measured by the GOAT in patients with severe head injury ($N = 314$) was significantly associated with initial total Glasgow Coma Scale score, nonreactive pupils, coma duration, and subsequent use of the anticonvulsant drug phenytoin sodium. A high degree of correspondence between the GOAT and another measure of posttraumatic amnesia, the Orientation Group Monitoring System (OGMS) (Corrigan et al. 1985), was shown in a study; 15 of 21 patients with closed-head injuries cleared posttraumatic amnesia (i.e., achieved scores in the normal range) according to both instruments within the same week.

One study reported that the duration of posttraumatic amnesia measured by the GOAT was greater for patients with head injuries with computed tomography (CT) imaging evidence of bilateral mass lesions or diffuse injury ($N = 18$) than for patients with focal mass lesions restricted to one hemisphere ($N = 14$). In another study, patients with closed-head injuries ($N = 84$) who performed poorly on a single measure of temporal disorientation from the GOAT, backward displacement of the date, were more severely impaired (as measured by the Glasgow Coma Scale) and more likely to have a focal brain injury evident on CT imaging, a longer duration of unconsciousness, and a longer duration of posttraumatic amnesia than patients who performed less poorly on that item.

A standardization study with the COAT, performed with 146 neurologically healthy children ages 3–15, established age-specific cutoff scores for impairment (2 standard deviations below the mean) that ranged from 21 for 3-year-olds (out of a total of 124 possible points) to 116 for 15-year-olds. This study also demonstrated that the duration of posttraumatic amnesia measured by the changes in serial scores on the COAT in children with traumatic brain injury ($N = 37$) was related to their initial Glasgow Coma Scale scores and their performance on both verbal and nonverbal selective reminding memory tests immediately after resolution of posttraumatic amnesia (verbal, $r = -0.37$; nonverbal, $r = -0.10$), 6 months after injury (verbal, $r = -0.45$; nonverbal, $r = -0.62$), and 1 year after injury (verbal, $r = -0.31$; nonverbal, $r = -0.55$). Another study reported a high degree of correlation ($r = 0.91$) between GOAT and COAT scores in neurologically injured children ($N = 38$).

CLINICAL UTILITY

The GOAT is a brief, easily administered test that effectively measures orientation and the duration of both posttraumatic and retrograde amnesia in patients with head injury. The instrument has been shown to have high joint reliability, and its validity has been demonstrated against several independent indexes of the effects of brain trauma such as performance on the Glasgow Coma Scale, coma duration, and the severity of brain injury indicated by CT imaging. Performance on the GOAT is not significantly related to age or education in adults, and a separate version of the test (the COAT) is available for use with children under age 16.

Serial periodic testing with the GOAT from the time of injury or recovery from coma provides an effective means of tracking the progression of recovery from posttraumatic amnesia. The duration of recovery from posttraumatic amnesia, as measured by the time it takes to achieve a GOAT score in the normal range after head injury, has been shown to indicate prospects for long-term recovery of cognitive function. The duration of recovery from posttraumatic amnesia as measured by the GOAT also provides a useful method for objectively evaluating the effects of severity of injury, age, potential drug therapies, or various other factors on short-term recovery from traumatic brain injury.

Although the GOAT is a very useful psychometric instrument for evaluating the cognitive effects of head injury, the test is heavily weighted toward assessing orientation for time, with only brief measurement of other orientation and memory abilities. This limitation might lead to an underestimation or overestimation of memory or other impairments in some patients with head injury.

REFERENCES AND SUGGESTED READINGS

Corrigan JD, Arnett JA, Houck LJ, et al: Reality orientation for brain injured patients: group treatment and monitoring of recovery. Arch Phys Med Rehabil 66:626–630, 1985

Ellenberg JH, Levin HS, Saydjari C: Posttraumatic amnesia as a predictor of outcome after severe closed head injury: prospective assessment. Arch Neurol 53:782–791, 1996

Ewing-Cobbs L, Levin HS, Fletcher JM, et al: The Child's Orientation and Amnesia Test: relationship to severity of acute head injury and to recovery of memory. Neurosurgery 27:683–691, 1990

Levin HS, O'Donnell VM, Grossman RG: The Galveston Orientation and Amnesia Test: a practical scale to assess cognition after head injury. J Nerv Ment Dis 167:675–684, 1979

Mysiw WJ, Corrigan JD, Carpenter D, et al: Prospective assessment of posttraumatic amnesia: a comparison of the GOAT and the OGMS. Journal of Head Trauma Rehabilitation 5:65–72, 1990

Teasdale G, Jennett B: Assessment of coma and impaired consciousness: a practical scale. Lancet 2:81–84, 1974

Clinical Dementia Rating (CDR) Scale

C. P. Hughes, L. Berg, W. L. Danzinger, L. A. Coben, and R. L. Martin

GOALS

The Clinical Dementia Rating (CDR) Scale (Hughes et al. 1982) is a staging system designed to provide a standardized global rating of the severity of dementia on the basis of all available information about a patient, including the results of formal cognitive testing and observational and informant-based assessment of the performance of activities of daily living. The scale was specifically developed to monitor the course of cognitive and functional deterioration in patients with Alzheimer's disease. The abbreviation *CDR* is sometimes used to refer to the CDR staging system alone but more often to staging determined on the basis of a formal assessment protocol that the test authors have developed to inform the ratings.

DESCRIPTION

The CDR Scale is a clinician-rated dementia staging system that tracks the progression of cognitive and functional deterioration throughout the course of Alzheimer's disease on a scale of 0–5, with 0 = no dementia, 0.5 = questionable dementia, 1 = mild dementia, 2 = moderate dementia, 3 = severe dementia, 4 = profound dementia, and 5 = terminal dementia. The CDR Scale stages are determined on the basis of the presumed order in which specific cognitive and functional abilities are lost during the usual natural course of Alzheimer's disease. The stages are designed to be nonoverlapping and thus to provide an ordinal scale of dementia severity.

Ratings of 0, 0.5, 1, 2, and 3 are typically made on the basis of the formal CDR Scale assessment protocol described previously, which includes a semistructured interview and set of cognitive tests (sometimes collectively referred to as the Washington University Initial Subject Protocol). Unless otherwise noted, the reliability and validity data discussed in the following sections refer to CDR Scale staging determined on the basis of the formal protocol. Although CDR Scale ratings can be made on the basis of clinical impression without the formal CDR Scale assessment protocol, the ratings are not generally as reliable. Ratings of stages 4 and 5 are assigned on the basis of clinical impression from all available data, as discussed later.

The CDR Scale assessment protocol includes separate relatively lengthy semistructured interviews with the patient and with the collateral informant, including extensive probing to pinpoint any difficulties the patient may be having and to be sure these difficulties are due to cognitive decline rather than to sensory loss or physical illness. The protocol also includes formal testing of orientation, memory, concentration, language (naming, reading comprehension, writing, and observations of verbal fluency), construction, and judgment and problem solving. On the basis of these data, the clinician rates the performance of the patient in each of six cognitive domains: Memory, Orientation, Judgment and Problem Solving, Community Affairs (e.g., job, shopping, business, and financial responsibilities), Home and Hobbies (e.g., household chores and recreational interests), and Personal Care (e.g., dressing, personal hygiene, and toileting). Each rating is made on an impairment scale consistent with the scaling of the CDR Scale stages, with

0 = none, 0.5 = questionable, 1 = mild, 2 = moderate, and 3 = severe. The ratings and interview are based on decline in comparison with the subject's own baseline level of functioning. Sample questions are provided in Example 21–1.

The overall CDR Scale stage is not simply the average of the ratings in the six cognitive domains but is determined on the basis of a weighted scoring system that gives prominence to the Memory domain. When Memory is rated 0, the overall CDR Scale score equals 0 unless two or more other domains are rated ≥0.5, in which case the overall CDR Scale stage is 0.5. When Memory is rated 0.5, the overall CDR Scale stage is 0.5 unless three other domains are rated ≥1, in which case it is 1. For Memory ratings of ≥1, the overall CDR Scale stage is equal to the Memory rating unless three or more other domains score consistently higher or lower, in which case that score is used.

In addition to the overall CDR Scale stage, the sum of the ratings for each cognitive domain is sometimes used as a global measure of dementia. This measure, which is also known as the sum of the boxes or box score (because boxes are used on some rating forms to record the score for each domain), can yield scores that range from 0 (no impairment) to 18 (severe impairment).

As noted, CDR Scale stages 4 and 5 are assigned by the clinician on the basis of only global descriptions. Stage 4 refers to profound dementia, in which language and comprehension are essentially lost, eating and walking cannot be performed without assistance, family members are not recognized, and the patient is incontinent. Stage 5 describes terminal dementia, in which the patient is totally dependent, bedridden, vegetative, incontinent, and noncommunicative.

EXAMPLE 21–1 ■ Sample items from the Clinical Dementia Rating Scale

> Home and Hobbies Domain
> Has there been any change in his/her ability to shop for things like clothes, gifts, or drug store items on his/her own?
>
> Judgment and Problem Solving Domain
> Have you noticed any change in his/her ability to cope with small sums of money, e.g., make change, leave a small tip, handle cash?

Reprinted from Morris JC: "The Clinical Dementia Rating (CDR): Current Version and Scoring Rule." *Neurology* 43:2412–2414, 1993, by permission from the author, *Neurology*, and the American Academy of Neurology.

PRACTICAL ISSUES

The CDR Scale assessment protocol, including the semistructured interview with the patient and informant and cognitive testing of the patient, is lengthy, typically requiring an hour or more to administer. CDR Scale staging independent of the formal interview generally requires less time, particularly when the clinician is already familiar with the patient. Because CDR Scale staging is determined on the basis of the synthesis of a wide range of clinical information about a patient, the staging should be performed by physicians, clinical nurse specialists, clinical psychologists, or others with extensive clinical experience with Alzheimer's disease patients. Similarly, the semistructured CDR Scale interview is best performed by an individual with clinical experience because of the need for extensive follow-up probing and assessment of a variety of factors that might be contributing to the patient's symptoms. In addition, training in use of the CDR Scale ratings and associated interview is highly recommended if reliable ratings are to be obtained. Training materials for the CDR Scale interview and ratings, including videotapes, can be obtained from

> Dr. John Morris
> Washington University School of Medicine
> 660 S. Euclid Avenue, Campus Box 8111-MDC
> St. Louis, MO 63110

The CDR Scale and updated scoring instructions have been published (Berg 1988; Heyman et al. 1987; Hughes et al. 1982). There is no cost to use the CDR Scale; however, those who wish to reprint it in a publication should obtain the necessary permission from the author and the journal *Neurology*.

The CDR is included on the CD-ROM that accompanies this handbook.

PSYCHOMETRIC PROPERTIES

Reliability

Joint reliability for the overall CDR Scale stage was 0.89 in a study of elderly individuals with and without dementia ($N = 35$). In another study of patients with Alzheimer's disease ($N = 25$), joint reliability was 0.87 (weighted kappa coefficient; 0.91 by Kendall τ) for the global CDR Scale score and 0.87 (weighted kappa; 0.90 by Kendall τ) for the sum of the boxes score. The joint reliability of the ratings for the individual cognitive domains in this study ranged from 0.75 to 0.94 (weighted kappa coefficients). In a study that included patients with Alzheimer's disease ($N = 44$) and psychiatrically healthy control subjects ($N = 58$), the joint reliability for the overall CDR Scale stage generated by three clinical nurse specialists was 0.77 (Light's K; 81% agreement), and reliability for ratings of the individual domains ranged from 0.66 (73% agreement) to 0.76 (81% agreement). The joint reliability of the overall CDR Scale stage generated by physicians and clinical nurse specialists in this study was 0.75 (80% agreement), and reliability for ratings of the individual domains ranged from 0.67 (74% agreement) to 0.77 (83% agreement).

Validity

Using a cutoff score of a CDR Scale stage of 1 to indicate dementia, 92% sensitivity and 94% specificity for the detection of clinically diagnosed dementia (using DSM-III-R criteria) were obtained in a study of a random sample of elderly individuals ($N = 656$). All of the subjects with dementia in this study had a CDR Scale stage of ≥ 0.5, and individuals without dementia who had a CDR Scale stage of ≥ 0.5 were depressed, had other psychiatric problems, had a history of stroke, or had other physical problems.

Several studies have shown that CDR Scale stage is related to other measures of functional or cognitive performance in elderly individuals. Two studies ($N = 93$–668) reported a strong correlation between ratings of dementia severity made with the CDR Scale and those based on DSM-III-R dementia staging guidelines (kappa coefficients $= 0.56$–0.60). The correlations (kappa coefficients) between the two staging methods at each CDR Scale level were 0.47 for CDR 0.5, 0.47–0.49 for CDR 1, 0.40–0.64 for CDR 2, and 0.75–0.79 for CDR 3. A study that compared CDR Scale level with performance on the functional portion of the Blessed-Roth Dementia Rating Scale (see IMC Test, p. 427) found a good correlation between decline measured on the two scales ($r = -0.64$) in patients with dementia ($N = 956$), and another study reported that the percentage of patients with Alzheimer's disease ($N = 93$) demonstrating independence in activities of daily living functions declined significantly from CDR Scale stage 0.5–1 (65%), to CDR Scale stage 2 (36%), to CDR Scale stage 3 (0%). In this latter study, a similar significant decline was observed in the ability to perform instrumental activities of daily living from CDR Scale stage 0.5–1 (31%), to CDR Scale stage 2 (10%), to CDR Scale stage 3 (0%).

Four studies reported that overall CDR Scale scores were significantly related to total scores on the Blessed-Roth Dementia Scale (see IMC Test, p. 427) in patients with dementia (Spearman $r = 0.60$; Pearson $r = 0.53$–0.59; $N = 43$–956) and in groups of individuals with and without dementia (Pearson $r = 0.74$; Kendall $\tau = 0.80$; $N = 138$–166). In two studies, the CDR Scale sum of boxes scores were also significantly correlated with total scores on the Blessed-Roth Dementia Scale in patients with Alzheimer's disease ($r = 0.42$–0.69; $N = 43$) and in a group of individuals with and without dementia ($r = 0.92$; $N = 116$) but not in psychiatrically healthy control subjects ($N = 58$). In another study, CDR Scale stages of patients with dementia ($N = 138$) were found to be correlated with ratings of quality of memory ($r = 0.87$), ratings of functional activity ($r = 0.85$), performance on memory tests (0.80), and performance on tests of abstraction and judgment (0.74). In a longitudinal study of patients with dementia ($N = 956$), CDR Scale stages were significantly correlated with subsequent nursing home placement ($r = 0.35$) or death ($r = 0.27$) during a follow-up period.

One study demonstrated that CDR Scale stages were correlated ($r = 0.78$) with Mini-Mental State Exam (MMSE) (p. 422) scores in a group of elderly individuals with and without dementia ($N = 668$), and two studies found that staging of dementia severity with the MMSE corresponded to CDR Scale stage (kappa $= 0.33$–0.45) in elderly individuals with and without dementia ($N = 93$–668). In four studies, the global CDR Scale score and the CDR Scale sum of boxes were also found to correlate significantly with scores on the Short Portable Mental Status Questionnaire (Pfeffer 1975), the Information-Memory-Concentration (IMC) Test (p. 427), the short form of the IMC Test (p. 427), and the face-hand test (Zarit et al. 1978) in patients with dementia ($r = 0.47$–0.70 for global and 0.34–0.76 for sum of boxes; $N = 43$–956) and in samples of elderly individuals both with and without dementia ($r = 0.57$–0.84 and $\tau = 0.79$–0.84 for global; $r = 0.89$–0.93 for sum of boxes; $N = 116$–138). The CDR Scale score was correlated with performance on the Boston Naming Test (Kaplan et al. 1983) ($r = 0.81$) in another study with Alzheimer's disease patients ($N = 43$) and psychiatrically healthy control subjects

(N = 43) and with performance on an aphasia battery (r = 0.32–0.71) in patients with dementia (N = 43). In one study, the percentage of aphasic patients significantly increased across CDR Scale stages 0.5 (12%), 1 (36%), and 2 (82%) (N = 150 patients with Alzheimer's disease and 58 psychiatrically healthy control subjects), and more aphasic than nonaphasic Alzheimer's disease patients converted from CDR 1 to CDR 2 over a 50-month follow-up period.

CDR Scale staging has been shown to be sensitive to the decline in cognitive functioning that occurs in dementing disorders (particularly Alzheimer's disease). In one study, subjects rated at CDR 1 (N = 89 Alzheimer's disease patients) performed significantly worse and declined more rapidly over a 4-year follow-up interval than those at CDR 0 (N = 30 psychiatrically healthy control subjects) on all tests that comprised a large neuropsychological test battery. In three studies, the global CDR Scale score or the CDR Scale sum of boxes score declined in a relatively linear fashion over approximately 4 years (N = 43–956 patients with dementia). An annual change of approximately 0.4 CDR Scale stages per year was observed in one study with Alzheimer's disease patients (N = 430), and an annual decline of approximately 2.3 sum of boxes points per year was observed in Alzheimer's disease patients (N = 43) in a second study.

CLINICAL UTILITY

The CDR Scale is an effective measure for globally staging the level of dementia severity in patients with Alzheimer's disease. The stages effectively describe the natural progression of cognitive and functional decline throughout the entire course of Alzheimer's disease and are designed to be independent and nonoverlapping. Assignment of a CDR Scale rating takes into account all available information concerning a patient's cognitive and functional status rather than just the limited amount of information that goes into staging on the basis of psychometric test performance or performance of activities of daily living alone. The clinician also takes into account information concerning a patient's health, age, educational background, and socioeconomic status when assigning a CDR Scale stage, limiting the impact of these potentially confounding factors. Moreover, the ratings are focused on the patient's own baseline level of performance, further limiting the impact of confounding due to education and related issues.

The CDR Scale appears to have excellent validity; it has been shown to be concordant with the dementia staging of other rating systems (e.g., DSM-III-R) and to correlate significantly with psychometric measures of cognitive and functional decline in patients with Alzheimer's disease. Good joint reliability has been obtained when the formal CDR Scale assessment protocol has been used by individuals trained in its use. Such reliability is not generally achieved without the formal assessment protocol or without sufficient training. In general, the reliability and the validity of the CDR Scale are only as good as the data that are gathered to stage the patient and the clinical judgment and training embodied in the ratings.

A CDR Scale rating of 0.5, or "questionable," has been used to distinguish patients who do not meet criteria for Alzheimer's disease or other dementia but who are not clearly psychiatrically healthy. This category is controversial and may represent a prodromal stage of dementia, sometimes also called "minimal cognitive impairment." However, not all such individuals progress to frank dementia, and known risk factors for Alzheimer's disease such as apolipoprotein E4 (APOE4) have been shown to predict progression to stage 1 and beyond.

Staging with the CDR Scale is clinically useful for tracking the course of Alzheimer's disease and for assessing the efficacy of pharmacological therapies that may slow the progression of dementia. Although the CDR Scale does not provide a finely graded measure of cognitive or functional performance for this purpose, a change from one CDR Scale category to another can be used as a significant clinical milestone in the progression of the disease.

REFERENCES AND SUGGESTED READINGS

Berg L: Clinical Dementia Rating (CDR). Psychopharmacol Bull 24:637–639, 1988

Berg L, Miller JP, Storandt M, et al: Mild senile dementia of the Alzheimer type, II: longitudinal assessment. Ann Neurol 23:477–484, 1988

Heyman A, Wilkinson WE, Hurwitz BJ, et al: Early onset Alzheimer's disease: clinical predictors of institutionalization and death. Neurology 37:980–984, 1987

Hughes CP, Berg L, Danzinger WL, et al: A new clinical scale for the staging of dementia. Br J Psychiatry 140:566–572, 1982

Juva K, Sulkava R, Erkinjuntti T, et al: Staging the severity of dementia: comparison of clinical (CDR, DSM-III-R), functional (ADL, IADL), and cognitive (MMSE) scales. Acta Neurol Scand 90:293–298, 1994

Kaplan E, Goodglass H, Weintraub S: The Boston Naming Test. Philadelphia, PA, Lea & Febiger, 1983

Pfeffer E: A short portable mental status questionnaire for the assessment of organic brain deficits in elderly patients. J Am Geriatr Soc 23:433–441, 1975

Zarit SH, Miller NE, Kahn RL: Brain function, intellectual impairment, and education in the aged. J Am Geriatr Soc 26:58–67, 1978

Global Deterioration Scale (GDS), Brief Cognitive Rating Scale (BCRS), and Functional Assessment Staging (FAST) Measures: The GDS Staging System

B. Reisberg, S. H. Ferris, et al.

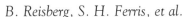

GOALS

The Global Deterioration Scale (GDS) Staging System (Reisberg et al. 1993) was designed as a systematic rating system for staging the integrity of cognitive and functional abilities in normal aging, age-related cognitive decline, and progressive dementia. Both the component scales and the comprehensive staging system have been widely used to grade and track the severity of dementia in patients with Alzheimer's disease. The GDS Staging System includes the Global Deterioration Scale (GDS) (Reisberg et al. 1982, 1988), the Brief Cognitive Rating Scale (BCRS) (Reisberg and Ferris 1988), and the Functional Assessment Staging (FAST) (Reisberg 1988) measures. Each of these measures provides ratings of cognitive and/or functional status on the same scale and can be used to inform patient staging.

DESCRIPTION

The GDS Staging System provides a 7-point rating scale designed to stage the cognitive and functional capacity of individuals from normal aging through profound dementia. The GDS per se is composed of detailed descriptions of seven clinically distinguishable stages: normal cognition and function (stage 1), subjective complaints of cognitive and/or functional deficits without clinical manifestations of these deficits (stage 2), subtle cognitive deficits that are elicited by careful clinical examination and that may be accompanied by decreased function in demanding work or social settings (stage 3), cognitive deficits that are clearly evident from a detailed clinical interview and that generally interfere with complex activities of daily living (e.g., handling finances and preparing complex meals) (stage 4), cognitive deficits that are severe enough to interfere with independent community survival (stage 5), cognitive deficits that are severe enough to interfere with basic activities of daily living (e.g., bathing and dressing) (stage 6), and deficits severe enough to require continuous assistance with basic activities of daily living (stage 7).

For each stage, the GDS provides a detailed description of both cognitive and functional deficits. A sample item for stage 2, subjective cognitive deficits, is provided in Example 21–2. GDS ratings can be made on the basis of these descriptions. GDS ratings can also be informed by the more detailed description of cognitive deficits in the BCRS and of functional deficits in the FAST.

The BCRS is a scale for grading the cognition-related capacities of individuals in different domains, and it is designed to be concordant with the GDS. Thus, each BCRS domain is rated on a 7-point fully anchored scale that ranges from normal performance to profound impairment. The domains rated on the BCRS (Part I*) are Concentration (Axis I), Recent Memory (Axis II), Past Memory (Axis III), Orientation (Axis IV), and Functioning and Self-Care (Axis V). A sample item in the Recent Memory domain is provided in Example 21–3. The BCRS also offers more detailed guidelines for scoring, including questions that might be used and advice on how to take the patient's baseline functioning and level of education into account in making the ratings.

---

* Part II of the BCRS contains six additional axes that assess speech and language abilities, motoric capacities, mood and behavior, praxis ability, calculation ability, and feeding capacity, respectively.

EXAMPLE 21–2 ■ Sample item from the Global Deterioration Scale

Subjective complaints of memory deficit, most frequently in the following areas: (a) forgetting where one has placed familiar objects; (b) forgetting names one formerly knew well. No objective evidence of memory deficit on clinical interview. No objective deficits in employment or social situations. Appropriate concern with respect to symptomatology.

Reprinted with permission from Dr. Barry Reisberg.

EXAMPLE 21–3 ■ Sample item from the Brief Cognitive Rating Scale

1 = No objective or subjective evidence of deficit in recent memory.

2 = Subjective impairment only (e.g., forgetting names more than formerly).

3 = Deficit in recall of specific events evident upon detailed questioning. No deficit in the recall of major recent events.

4 = Cannot recall major events of previous weekend or week. Scanty knowledge (not detailed) of current events, favorite TV shows, etc.

5 = Unsure of weather and/or may not know current President or current address.

6 = Occasional knowledge of some recent events. Little or no idea of current address, weather, etc.

7 = No knowledge of any recent events.

Reprinted with permission from Dr. Barry Reisberg.

The FAST is a rating scale that grades the progression of functional changes that occur with aging and dementia; like the BCRS, it is designed to be concordant with the GDS. The FAST is derived from BCRS Axis V but is more detailed and explicit than BCRS Axis V. The FAST consists of seven major stages that range from no functional difficulty (stage 1) to profound functional impairment (e.g., inability to speak, walk, or hold head up independently; stage 7). Stage 6 is subdivided into five substages, and stage 7 is subdivided into six substages. Thus, there are a total of 16 successive stages and substages in the FAST. A brief description is given for each. The five substages of stage 6 are described in Example 21–4. In addition, the FAST offers annotated guidelines for scoring that provide more detailed descriptions of each stage.

The GDS, BCRS, and FAST ratings are determined on the basis of all available information, including the results of a semistructured clinical interview of the pa-

EXAMPLE 21–4 ■ Sample item from the Functional Assessment Staging Measure

6a Difficulty putting clothing on properly
6b Unable to bathe properly without assistance
6c Inability to handle mechanics of toileting (e.g., forgets to flush, doesn't wipe properly)
6d Urinary incontinence
6e Fecal incontinence

Reprinted with permission from Dr. Barry Reisberg.

tient and reports of the patient's cognitive and functional activities from the caregiver or another knowledgeable informant.

PRACTICAL ISSUES

Clinically trained personnel such as physicians, psychologists, clinical nurses, and health care technicians can make GDS, BCRS, and FAST ratings. Because the ratings are only as accurate as the data on which they are based, interviews with the patient and a knowledgeable informant are recommended for GDS staging. Ratings for BCRS Axes I, II, and IV can be obtained from the patient directly, independently of an informant. BCRS Axis III is accurately rated with input from an informant with some knowledge of the patient's background. The FAST is primarily scored on the basis of information obtained from a knowledgeable informant. However, information on FAST stages 1 and 2 is obtained directly from the patient, and information on FAST stages 7a–7f can be obtained from either direct patient evaluation or an informant.

In a study of the GDS Staging System, which included the GDS, BCRS Axes I–IV, and the FAST, a mean interview time of approximately 15 minutes was required to obtain adequate information for staging ($N = 119$ residents of a long-term care facility). The minimum time taken in obtaining the ratings in this study was 5 minutes, and the maximum time was 53 minutes.

The GDS, BCRS, and FAST measures and guidelines for their use and scoring have been published (GDS [Reisberg et al. 1988], BCRS [Reisberg and Ferris 1988], and FAST [Reisberg 1988]). All three instruments are copyrighted by test author Dr. Barry Reisberg. Training for raters is recommended, and training videos are available from the author:

Dr. Barry Reisberg
Professor of Psychiatry
Aging and Dementia Research Center
New York University School of Medicine
550 1st Avenue
New York, NY 10016
Fax: 212-263-6991

Telephone interviews may be used to rate the GDS, the BCRS Part I (as well as most of the axes from Part II), and the FAST. A reliability and validity study supporting telephone use has been completed (Monteiro et al. 1998). The scales are also available from Dr. Reisberg in Chinese, Dutch, French, German, Polish, Portuguese, Spanish, and Swedish. There is generally no charge for noncommercial research or personal use; however, the author requests that he be informed when any of these instruments are used in published research. Charges for commercial use of the measures depend on the situation; information can be obtained from the author. The GDS and the FAST are included on the CD-ROM that accompanies this handbook.

PSYCHOMETRIC PROPERTIES

Reliability

Three studies that examined the joint reliability of the GDS reported a kappa coefficient of 1.0 for psychiatrically healthy control subjects ($N = 18$), a kappa coefficient of 0.88 for patients with dementia ($N = 18$), an intraclass correlation coefficient of 0.82 for patients with Alzheimer's disease ($N = 43$), and a Pearson product moment correlation coefficient of 0.92 for Alzheimer's disease and Parkinson's disease patients ($N = 18$).

The joint reliability for the five BCRS domains (Axes I–V) ranged from 0.92 to 0.97 (intraclass correlation coefficients) for five physicians who rated a series of psychiatric patients ($N = 20$) and from 0.76 to 0.93 for a nurse, psychologist, and psychology graduate student who rated patients at the same institution. The test-retest reliability of the BCRS over a 1-week to 4-month interval was $r = 0.96$ in a study of 38 individuals including psychiatrically healthy control subjects, patients with dementia, and patients with cerebrovascular disease. The

joint reliability for the FAST was reported as 0.87 (intraclass correlation coefficient) in a study of psychiatrically healthy elderly persons and patients with dementia ($N = 16$).

Validity

Several studies have shown a significant correspondence between the GDS stage and other measures of cognitive impairment in patients with dementia. In one study of patients with dementia ($N = 36$), the GDS stage was correlated with 13 of 19 items on the Inventory of Psychic and Somatic Complaints in the Elderly (Raskin and Rae 1981) ($r = 0.31$–0.66), and in another study ($N = 54$ patients with dementia), the GDS stage was correlated with 25 of 26 independent cognitive measures from a large battery of neuropsychological tests ($r = 0.25$–0.64). Ratings of cognitive impairment made on the basis of a battery of neuropsychological tests (e.g., the Mini-Mental State Exam [MMSE] [p. 422] and the Clock Drawing Test [p. 438]) corresponded closely (90% agreement) with GDS ratings in a study of elderly individuals ($N = 305$ individuals ages 84–90 years). In two other studies, GDS ratings were significantly correlated with scores on the MMSE ($r = 0.89$–0.90) and MMSE subscores ($r = 0.50$–0.86) in Alzheimer's disease patients ($N = 30$) and in a group of elderly individuals ($N = 154$). Ratings on the GDS were found to be significantly correlated with scores on the Alzheimer Deficit Scale (Summers et al. 1990) ($r = -0.81$ to -0.89) in a study of subjects with dementia ($n = 18$) and without dementia ($n = 18$).

Ratings for each of the five domains of the BCRS were correlated with the GDS rating ($r = 0.78$–0.88) in a study of Alzheimer's disease patients ($N = 30$). The BCRS domain scores were also correlated with relevant subscores from the MMSE ($r = 0.20$–0.84, with 22 of 25 comparisons significant) and with the subscores from the Alzheimer's Disease Assessment Scale (ADAS) (p. 441) ($r = 0.01$–0.85, with 63 of 75 comparisons significant). In one study, scores in each BCRS domain were correlated with the overall score on the Guild Memory Test (Crook et al. 1980) ($r = 0.51$–0.69; $N = 18$ elderly individuals) and, in another study, with each Guild Memory Test subscore ($r = 0.48$–0.84; $N = 50$ subjects with and without dementia).

The overall BCRS score was correlated with the MMSE scores in two studies ($r = -0.70$ to -0.79) with adult day care center participants ($N = 82$) and patients with dementia ($N = 19$). The overall BCRS score was correlated with the total score on the Guild Memory Test ($r = 0.65–0.75$) in two studies of elderly patients with and without dementia ($N = 18–50$); with each of five Guild Memory Test subscores ($r = 0.59–0.72$) and several additional neuropsychological tests ($r = 0.72–0.79$) in a study of elderly subjects with and without dementia ($N = 50$); and with the SKT test (Erzigkeit 1989) ($r = 0.66$), the ADAS total score ($r = 0.77$), and the ADAS cognitive score ($r = 0.80$) in a study of patients with dementia ($N = 49$). In another study of patients with dementia ($N = 57$), the BCRS score was correlated with scores on the Sandoz Clinical Assessment—Geriatric (SCAG) (Shader et al. 1974) ($r = 0.72–0.85$).

For the FAST, two studies demonstrated that average MMSE scores significantly declined across FAST stages in patients with severe dementia of the Alzheimer's type ($N = 70–161$). In one of these studies, a significant decline in the mean scores on the Information-Memory-Concentration (IMC) Test (p. 427) was also observed. In two other studies ($N = 40$ and 56), significant correlations were observed between FAST ratings and MMSE scores ($r = 0.83–0.87$). Correlations were also observed between FAST scores and scores on 10 independent psychometric tests ($r = 0.59–0.73$; $N = 50$ patients with Alzheimer's disease and psychiatrically healthy control subjects). A strong relationship was reported between FAST ratings and scores on the Modified Ordinal Scales of Psychological Development (M-OSPD) (Auer et al. 1994) ($r = -0.77$) and the M-OSPD subtests (Spearman $r = -0.65$ to -0.73; $N = 70$ patients with Alzheimer's disease). In a study of Alzheimer's disease patients and psychiatrically healthy control subjects ($N = 50$), FAST ratings were significantly correlated with an independent clinical assessment of functioning ($r = 0.83–0.94$); in another study ($N = 56$ patients with Alzheimer's disease), functional deficits determined by both specific query and chart review proceeded in accordance with the ordinal pattern used by the FAST in 50 out of 56 patients.

Three studies showed that GDS ratings are correlated with measures of brain pathology in patients with dementia. In one study, GDS ratings were correlated with ratings of ventricular dilation ($r = 0.62$) and sulcal enlargement ($r = 0.53$) on computed tomography (CT) scans of patients with dementia ($N = 43$). In two other studies, GDS ratings were associated with reduced ventricular size ($r = 0.37$) on CT scans, with hypometab-

olism in the right and left hemispheres and a whole brain slice on positron-emission tomography (PET) scans ($r = 0.51–0.54$), and with decreased metabolism in the caudate, thalamus, and temporal lobe regions ($r = 0.69–0.83$) of patients with dementia of the Alzheimer's type ($N = 7–23$).

A study using the BCRS found that patients with Alzheimer's disease ($N = 15$) with severe impairment had significantly lower cerebral blood flow in frontal and temporoparietal regions on single photon emission computed tomography (SPECT) scans than did those with only moderate impairment as rated by the BCRS. Two studies that examined the relationship between BCRS ratings and changes in electroencephalogram (EEG) activity ($N = 20–48$) found correlations between BCRS and EEG alpha and beta activity and peak latency ($r = 0.35–0.45$) and also that the maximal beta activity in an EEG shifted from occipito-parietotemporal to frontotemporal brain regions as BCRS severity increased.

Another study reported that the prevalence and ratings of the severity of frontal release signs and pyramidal and extrapyramidal motor signs increased across FAST levels of functional impairment in patients with Alzheimer's disease ($N = 56$), and a second study reported that the FAST level was correlated with the prevalence of joint contractures in Alzheimer's disease patients with severe dementia ($N = 161$).

Postmortem neuropathological assessments of brain change have correlated robustly with FAST stage levels. In a study of 13 patients with severe Alzheimer's disease at a severity level of stage 7 (MMSE = 0), volumetric loss in hippocampal brain regions correlated with FAST levels: $r = -0.70$ for the cornu ammonis, -0.79 for the subicular complex, and -0.62 for the entorhinal cortex (Bobinski et al. 1995). Further study of these same patients found correlations between total neuronal number in brain hippocampal subdivisions and FAST levels of $r = -0.90$ and $r = -0.79$ for the cornu ammonis and subiculum, respectively (Bobinski et al. 1997).

The GDS and the BCRS were shown to be sensitive to the progression of dementia in three studies. One study demonstrated an average annual decline of 0.46 GDS points in patients with Alzheimer's disease ($N = 30$), as well as an average annual decline on the BCRS domain scores of 0.63 for Concentration, 0.55 for Recent Memory, 0.68 for Past Memory, 0.68 for Orientation, and 0.61 for Functioning and Self-Care. A second study reported an annual BCRS decline of 0.40 stages in adult day care participants ($N = 82$) and 0.50 stages in only the patients with dementia ($N = 57$). In this latter study, the slope of the change in the BCRS score was significantly correlated with the slope of the change in the MMSE score ($r = -0.55$) and the slope of the change in a measure of activities of daily living ($r = 0.36$). In the third study, Alzheimer's disease patients ($N = 106$) who scored 4–6 on the GDS were significantly more likely than those who scored 2 or 3 to be institutionalized after approximately 4 years of follow-up.

CLINICAL UTILITY

The GDS Staging System is an effective method for staging the cognitive and functional deterioration that occurs throughout the course of Alzheimer's disease. The stages are determined on the basis of phenomenological observation of Alzheimer's disease patients' symptoms and are designed to be clinically distinguishable and ordinal in nature so that the cognitive and functional deficits that define one stage all occur before the emergence of deficits that define a subsequent stage. This goal is largely met by the GDS and the associated measures in the GDS Staging System. However, some investigators point out that this strict ordinality is not always apparent in patients with Alzheimer's disease. This finding may be as much a reflection of the heterogeneity of Alzheimer's disease and the common occurrence of comorbidity in the elderly and patients with Alzheimer's disease as a shortcoming of the GDS, but it highlights the possible limitations of using the GDS to stage severity of dementia in other dementing disorders that may not follow the same pattern of cognitive and functional progression as Alzheimer's disease.

Substantial data indicate that the GDS is a reliable and valid staging instrument. The GDS proper and the BCRS and FAST have all been shown to have excellent joint and test-retest reliability in staging individuals with and without dementia. The validity of the scales has been demonstrated by their correlation with independent measures of cognitive and functional abilities and with the presence and severity of neuropathological, structural, metabolic, and electrophysiological brain abnormalities in patients with Alzheimer's disease. The GDS, the BCRS, and the FAST have also been shown to be sensitive to the progression of dementia in longitudinal studies that follow patients with Alzheimer's disease throughout the entire course of the disease.

REFERENCES AND SUGGESTED READINGS

Auer SR, Sclan SG, Yaffee RA, et al: The neglected half of Alzheimer disease: cognitive and functional concomitants of severe dementia. J Am Geriatr Soc 42:1266–1272, 1994

Bobinski M, Wegiel J, Wisniewski HM, et al: Atrophy of hippocampal formation subdivisions correlates with stage and duration of Alzheimer disease. Dementia 6:205–210, 1995

Bobinski M, Wegiel J, Tarnawski M, et al: Relationships between regional neuronal loss and neurofibrillary changes in the hippocampal formation and duration and severity of Alzheimer disease. J Neuropathol Exp Neurol 56:414–420, 1997

Crook T, Gilbert JG, Ferris S: Operationalizing memory impairment for elderly persons: the Guild Memory Test. Psychol Rep 47:1315–1318, 1980

Erzigkeit H: The SKT: a short cognitive performance test as an instrument for the assessment of clinical efficacy of cognition enhancers, in Diagnosis and Treatment of Senile Dementia. Edited by Bergener M, Reisberg B. Berlin, Springer-Verlag, 1989, pp 164–174

Monteiro IM, Boksay I, Auer SR, et al: Reliability of routine clinical instruments for the assessment of Alzheimer's disease administered by telephone. J Geriatr Psychiatry Neurol 11:18–24, 1998

Raskin AS, Rae DS: Psychiatric symptoms in the elderly. Psychopharmacol Bull 17:96–99, 1981

Reisberg B: Functional Assessment Staging (FAST). Psychopharmacol Bull 24:653–659, 1988

Reisberg B, Ferris SH: Brief Cognitive Rating Scale (BCRS). Psychopharmacol Bull 24:629–636, 1988

Reisberg B, Ferris SH, De Leon MJ, et al: The Global Deterioration Scale for Assessment of Primary Degenerative Dementia. Am J Psychiatry 139:1136–1139, 1982

Reisberg B, Ferris S, Anand R, et al: Functional staging of dementia of the Alzheimer type. Ann N Y Acad Sci 435:481–483, 1984

Reisberg B, Ferris SH, De Leon MJ, et al: Global Deterioration Scale (GDS). Psychopharmacol Bull 24:661–663, 1988

Reisberg B, Ferris S, Torossian C, et al: Pharmacologic treatment of Alzheimer's disease: a methodologic critique based upon current knowledge of symptomatology and relevance for clinical trials. Int Psychogeriatr 4(suppl 1):9–42, 1992

Reisberg B, Sclan SG, Franssen E, et al: Clinical stages of normal aging and Alzheimer's disease: the GDS staging system. Neuroscience Research Communications 13(suppl 1):551–554, 1993

Reisberg B, Franssen E, Bobinski M, et al: Overview of methodologic issues for pharmacologic trials in mild, moderate, and severe Alzheimer's disease. Int Psychogeriatr 8:159–193, 1996

Sclan SG, Reisberg B: Functional Assessment Staging (FAST) in Alzheimer's disease: reliability, validity, and ordinality. Int Psychogeriatr 4(suppl 1):55–62, 1992

Shader WI, Harmatz JS, Salzman C: A new scale for clinical assessment in geriatric populations: Sandoz Clinical Assessment—Geriatric (SCAG). J Am Geriatr Soc 22:107–113, 1974

Summers WK, DeBoynton V, Marsh GM, et al: Comparison of seven psychometric instruments used for evaluation of treatment effect in Alzheimer's disease. Neuroepidemiology 9:193–207, 1990

Yesavage JA, Poulsen SL, Sheikh J, et al: Rates of change of common measures of impairment in senile dementia of the Alzheimer's type. Psychopharmacol Bull 24:531–534, 1988

CHAPTER 22

Substance Use Disorders Measures

Bruce J. Rounsaville, M.D.
James Poling, Ph.D.

INTRODUCTION

Major Domains

This chapter includes measures that can guide treatment of patients with substance use disorders (i.e., dependence and abuse) at several phases of the treatment process: screening, treatment planning, and monitoring progress and outcome.

Organization

The measures included in this chapter are listed in Table 22–1. The assessments are grouped according to the central functions for which they are used, with measures used for screening or case finding described first, followed by instruments that are used to develop treatment strategy and assess treatment outcome.

Relevant Measures Included Elsewhere in the Handbook

Many measures discussed elsewhere in this book are pertinent to the assessment of substance use disorders. All of the instruments included in Chapter 6 ("Diagnostic Interviews for Adults") contain sections on the diagnosis of substance use disorders. Rates of comorbidity of substance use disorders with other Axis I and Axis II conditions are high. Thus, assessments in all other sections of this manual may be useful in treatment planning, particularly if psychiatric impairment is detected in unstruc-

tured assessments or through the formal use of a problem-oriented instrument such as the Addiction Severity Index (ASI) or the Personal Experience Screening Questionnaire (PESQ).

USING MEASURES IN THIS DOMAIN

Instruments included in this chapter are designed for three general clinical functions: screening or case finding, development of a treatment strategy, and assessing treatment outcome.

Because of the covert nature of substance use disorders in nonspecialty settings, many of the scales included in this chapter are designed for use in clinical and general population settings to screen for alcohol use disorders in adults (the Michigan Alcoholism Screening Test [MAST], the Alcohol Use Disorders Identification Test [AUDIT], the CAGE Questionnaire, and the TWEAK Test), illicit drug use disorders in adults (the Drug Abuse Screening Test [DAST]), nicotine dependence (the Fagerstrom Test for Nicotine Dependence [FTND]), or drug or alcohol use disorders in adolescents (the PESQ). The principal function of all these scales is to alert clinicians to the need for more extensive assessment of substance use patterns and substance-related symptoms.

The remaining instruments are designed to guide the treatment-planning process and the monitoring of treat-

TABLE 22–1 ■ Substance use disorders measures

Name of measure	Disorder or construct assessed	Format	Pages
Alcohol Use Disorders Identification Test (AUDIT)*	Harmful or hazardous alcohol consumption in a range of clinical and nonclinical settings	Clinician-administered or self-reported core assessment of 10 questions, plus optional clinical screening procedure	460–462
CAGE Questionnaire*	Clinically significant alcohol problems	Clinician interview or self-report; 4 items	462–464
Drug Abuse Screening Test (DAST)	Abuse of or dependence on a wide range of psychoactive substances other than alcohol	Fully structured self-report or interview; 28- and 20-item versions	464–465
Fagerstrom Test for Nicotine Dependence (FTND)	Dependence on nicotine from cigarette smoking	Interview or self-report; 6 questions	465–467
Michigan Alcoholism Screening Test (MAST) Brief version (Brief MAST) Short version (SMAST) Geriatric version (MAST-G)	Alcoholism	Fully structured self-report or interview with 25 questions; 10- and 13-item shorter versions; geriatric version	467–468
Personal Experience Screening Questionnaire (PESQ)	Substance use disorders in adolescents ages 12–18	Self-report; 40 items	469–470
TWEAK Test*	Current or past heavy drinking in women	Clinician interview or self-report; 5 items	470–472
Addiction Severity Index (ASI)* Teen version (T-ASI)	Problems of patients with substance use disorders for use in treatment planning and monitoring progress	Clinician- or technician–administered semistructured interview; 142 items	472–474
Alcohol Dependence Scale (ADS)*	Severity of alcohol dependence syndrome	Fully structured, self-administered paper and pencil or computer questionnaire; 25 items	474–476
Alcohol Expectancy Questionnaire (AEQ)*	Anticipated positive effects of using alcohol in specialty clinical settings	Self-administered questionnaire; 90 statements for response	476–477
Alcohol Timeline Followback (TLFB)*	Quantity of alcohol consumption on a daily basis	Guide to enhance accuracy of drinking estimates for 30–160 days	477–479
Clinical Institute Withdrawal Assessment for Alcohol (CIWA-AD)*	Current severity of alcohol withdrawal (in clinical and research settings)	Semistructured, clinician-administered; 8 items	479–481
Obsessive Compulsive Drinking Scale (OCDS)*	Obsessive and compulsive cognitive aspects of alcohol "craving"	Self-rated; 14 items	481–482
University of Rhode Island Change Assessment (URICA)	Readiness to change to reduce problems from alcohol, nicotine, or illicit drug use	Self-report or clinician administered; 32 items for response on a 5-point scale	482–484

*Measure is included on the CD-ROM that accompanies this handbook.

ment outcome. The intensity of alcohol use measured by the Alcohol Timeline Followback (TLFB) and the severity of alcohol dependence measured by the Alcohol Dependence Scale (ADS) can be used to determine the optimal initial treatment intensity. The ASI can be used to determine which dimensions of drug- and alcohol-related problems require the most clinical attention. The Clinical Institute Withdrawal Assessment for Alcohol (CIWA-AD) measures current severity of alcohol withdrawal symptoms. The University of Rhode Island Change Assessment (URICA) measures readiness for change and provides a guide for both the content and the intensity of planned interventions. The Alcohol Expectancy Questionnaire (AEQ) is useful for identifying motivations for alcohol use and tailoring treatment to attack specific expectancy areas to foster abstinence and prevent relapse. The potential for a patient to relapse can be monitored by using the Obsessive Compulsive Drinking Scale (OCDS). Treatment outcome can be quantitatively described through use of repeated assessments with the TLFB for alcohol use disorders and the ASI for substance use disorders.

The measures included in this chapter, which represent only a tiny fraction of the scales that have been developed to assess individuals with substance use disorders, were chosen principally on the basis of their utility in clinical settings (e.g., ease of assessment and scoring), the demonstration of reliability and validity, and their relevance to clinical decision making. Assessments that were not included fall into three general categories. First, many assessments (e.g., measures of craving and withdrawal symptom severity) were not included because formal assessments were not judged to be more useful than general clinical assessments in nonresearch settings. Second, assessments were not included if they were designed to guide or provide a proximal outcome measure for a specific treatment approach. This category includes measures of medication side effects and measures of constructs linked to cognitive therapy (e.g., self-efficacy, decisional balance) or to 12-step treatments (e.g., spirituality, progress in recovery steps). Third, most content areas are represented by a single instrument; other comparable measures were not included unless they had major advantages or differences from the instrument chosen.

Nearly all the measures in this chapter have a high degree of face validity; inaccurate results may therefore be obtained from individuals motivated to deny or minimize psychoactive substance use and problems related to this use. In settings or with individuals in which denial is likely, reports from significant others or the use of biological markers may be crucial in detecting covert cases or developing a complete picture of substance use patterns. However, neither of these types of assessments can replace information provided by the individual.

Reports on substance use from significant others are limited by the covert nature of many individuals' substance use. Hence, in the face of disparate reporting from patients and informants, the greater estimate of use is the most credible.

The most sensitive and specific methods of measuring biological markers involve detecting recent use by measuring abused substances or their metabolites in breath, blood, or urine. Other indicators of subacute and chronic intake, such as liver function tests in alcoholic patients, are mainly useful only for measuring comparatively heavy and chronic levels of use but have generally low sensitivity for detecting mild to moderate use. Although detection of substances in body fluids has the great advantage of being objective, the limited time frame of biological tests makes them inadequate to serve many functions such as distinguishing use from a pattern of abuse or dependence or distinguishing a single slip from a full relapse. In addition, cost and practical considerations usually dictate a testing schedule that leaves large time gaps uncovered, allowing pathological use to go undetected.

Despite these limitations, biological detection of recent substance use is a unique tool in the broader context of mental health treatment, because no similarly specific biological indicators of symptomatology or relapse exist for any other class of mental disorders (e.g., depression, schizophrenia). Moreover, the judicious use of laboratory drug tests (e.g., setting up a random, intermittent testing schedule) can greatly enhance the validity of patients' self-reports of substance use and of substance-related problems.

GUIDE TO THE SELECTION OF MEASURES

Many of the measures described in this chapter were first used and developed in the context of research projects to provide a quantifiable measure of the domain assessed. Most are simply systematic, structured methods of assessing areas that are amenable to informal evaluation in the course of an unstructured clinical examination. However, there are several advantages in incorporating formal assessments into routine initial evaluations and in using them to monitor patient progress. First, it is often more efficient to use formal assessments than unstructured interviews. Most of the measures included in this chapter can be used as self-reports and can be administered to either groups or individuals without the presence of a trained clinician. Moreover, the use of brief screening methods to detect problematic substance use has been shown to have greater sensitivity and specificity than open-ended questioning by clinicians. Structured evaluations also avoid problems related to omission of topics. Second, norms are available for most of the assessments discussed in this chapter, providing the clinician with a comparative picture of problem severity, enhancing communication across settings, and aiding quality assurance purposes. Third, structured assessments may be useful to patients if the assessments encourage patients to consider previously unexamined dimensions of their problems. Results of formal evaluations can also enhance motivation by providing comparatively objective evidence of substance use or problem severity in comparison with the general population or other patients.

As mentioned earlier, a single measure for most content areas in this chapter was included. However, several measures that are used for screening and case finding in nonspecialty settings are included because of continued evidence that most cases of substance use disorders go undetected and untreated. Four of these screening measures are designed to detect heavy drinking or alcohol use disorders: the CAGE, the MAST, the AUDIT, and the TWEAK. Each has its strengths, and reliability and specificity levels do not differ substantially or consistently across these four measures. CAGE and TWEAK are both extremely brief and are principally useful for raising the index of suspicion for an alcohol-related diagnosis. The TWEAK may be more sensitive for case finding among women and is less specific in screening for clinically significant problems in men. The AUDIT is slightly longer than the CAGE and the TWEAK but provides more detailed assessment that corresponds to the concepts of hazardous use, harmful use, and dependence on alcohol. The MAST is the longest of the screening instruments and samples a variety of problems associated with alcohol use over a person's lifetime. As such, the MAST may be clinically useful in detecting the presence of alcohol prob-

lems across an individual's life but less useful in detecting current alcohol problems.

CURRENT STATUS AND FUTURE RESEARCH NEEDS FOR ASSESSMENT

Most of the measures included in this chapter cover alcohol-related topics. Assessments of similar domains in users of other psychoactive substances have been employed and evaluated less frequently, which in part reflects the great diversity in patterns of use and clinical features associated with other psychoactive substances. Those who are developing assessments that focus on non-alcoholic substances must choose between generalized inquiry that collapses across a range of "drugs" or more narrowly focused and/or repetitive questions that cover many drug classes individually. Either strategy limits the utility of such formal assessments for general clinical purposes. Another comparatively unstudied area is the assessment of substance-related topics in adolescents.

REFERENCES AND SUGGESTED READINGS

National Institute on Alcohol Abuse and Alcoholism: Assessing alcohol problems: a guide for clinicians and researchers (NIH Publ No 95–3745). Edited by Allen JP, Columbus M. Bethesda, MD, National Institute of Health, 1995

Alcohol Use Disorders Identification Test (AUDIT)

T. F. Babor

GOALS

The Alcohol Use Disorders Identification Test (AUDIT) (Babor et al. 1992) was designed as a screening instrument for use in a range of clinical and nonclinical settings to detect alcohol consumption that has become hazardous or harmful to health rather than alcoholism per se. It was designed to identify persons with early-stage alcohol problems and uses procedures suitable for health care workers in both developing and developed countries. It includes items that assess three domains: alcohol dependence, harmful drinking (drinking that causes direct negative consequences on mental or physical health or social or occupational functioning), and hazardous drinking (drinking that puts one at increased risk for the development of future problems). Because these three domains are included in the ICD-10 for alcohol use disorders and dependence is included in the DSM-IV, the instrument is useful for detecting more broadly and diversely defined, clinically significant alcohol misuse. A positive score on the AUDIT is meant to alert the examining clinician to engage in further inquiry about a patient's alcohol use patterns and alcohol-related problems and symptoms.

two questions about traumatic injury, five findings from a physical examination and serum gamma-glutamyltransferase (GGT), and a liver function test. Because the clinical screening items do not involve direct inquiry about alcohol use or problems, they may be useful for screening when denial is likely or suspected.

The 10 items in the core questionnaire are scored from 0 to 4 and summed to yield a total score of 0–40. The 8 clinical screening items are scored from 0 to 3 and yield a total score of 0–24. For detecting an alcohol use disorder as defined by ICD-10 criteria, a score of 8 on the core questionnaire produced the highest sensitivity, and a score of 10 or more had the highest specificity. A high score on the quantity and frequency items (1–3) indicates hazardous alcohol use, a high score on the second three items (4–6) implies alcohol dependence, and a high score on the remaining items (7–10) suggests harmful use (Babor et al. 1992).

DESCRIPTION

The AUDIT contains a core screening assessment and a more extensive, optional clinical screening procedure. The core assessment can be administered by a clinician or self-report and consists of 10 multiple-choice and yes-no questions, 3 on the quantity and frequency of alcohol consumption, 3 on harmful drinking, and 4 on hazardous drinking. All of the questions are scored using a 5-point (0–4) Likert scale. A sample item is provided in Example 22–1.

The optional clinical screening procedure requires a physical examination and a blood test and includes

EXAMPLE 22–1 ■ Sample item from the Alcohol Use Disorders Identification Test

> How often during the last year have you needed a first drink in the morning to get yourself going after a heavy drinking session?
>
> Never (scored 0)
> Less than monthly (scored 1)
> Monthly (scored 2)
> Weekly (scored 3)
> Daily or almost daily (scored 4)

Reprinted with permission from the World Health Organization.

PRACTICAL ISSUES

It takes less than 2 minutes to administer the AUDIT core questionnaire and less than 2 minutes to score it. No training is required to administer and score the core assessment. The clinical screening module is meant to be used by medically trained professionals and takes 10 minutes to complete when incorporated into other aspects of a medical evaluation.

The AUDIT core questionnaire is copyrighted but can be reproduced without permission. Scoring instructions are included in the key reference (Babor et al. 1992). The clinical screening module should be used only by trained personnel. A training module that includes a videotape and a manual is available for $75.00 and may be obtained from

> Thomas F. Babor
> Alcohol Research Center
> University of Connecticut Health Center
> Farmington, CT 06030–0410

The scale has been translated into Japanese, Norwegian, Rumanian, Slavic, Spanish, and Swahili; these versions are available from

Program on Substance Abuse
World Health Organization
1211 Geneva, Switzerland

The AUDIT is included on the CD-ROM that accompanies this handbook.

PSYCHOMETRIC PROPERTIES

Reliability

In a study of 989 undergraduate students, Cronbach's alpha was 0.80.

Validity

In a study of nonabstinent subjects in clinical and nonclinical populations, the core questionnaire of the AUDIT was especially highly correlated with other self-reports of alcohol problems, such as the MAST ($r = 0.88$), and was also significantly correlated with biological indices (e.g., with the GGT: for men a correlation of 0.31, and for women a correlation of 0.46). In the same study, construct validity was suggested by positive correlations with measures of risk factors (e.g., family history of alcoholism), drinking consequences, and drinking attitudes.

The principal measure of the utility of the AUDIT is its sensitivity and specificity in relationship to detection of individuals with clinically significant alcohol use disorder as defined by World Health Organization (WHO) or DSM criteria. In a sample of 989 undergraduate students, an AUDIT cutoff of 11 or higher (recommended by WHO) yielded sensitivity and specificity scores for a DSM-III alcohol use disorder (assessed by the Diagnostic Interview Schedule [p. 61]) of 0.84 and 0.71, respectively. A cutoff of 13 or higher yielded a sensitivity and specificity of 0.70 and 0.78, respectively, which may be better for screening purposes.

CLINICAL UTILITY

The AUDIT core questionnaire performs well as a screening instrument that can be administered quickly in a variety of clinical and nonclinical settings. Its use of items related to the three subtypes of alcohol use disorders included in the ICD-10 criteria makes it particularly pertinent for clinicians who use this system. Because the

time frame for most AUDIT questions is the present or the past year, it may be especially appropriate for detecting current problems. The face validity of the AUDIT core questionnaire (i.e., the fact that the assessment goal of each item is immediately evident to the subject) limits its utility for patients or populations who are motivated to deny problems related to alcohol use.

REFERENCES AND SUGGESTED READINGS

Allen JP, Litten RZ, Fertig JB, et al: A review of research on the Alcohol Use Disorders Identification Test (AUDIT). Alcohol Clin Exp Res 21(4):613–619, 1997

Babor TF, de la Fuente JR, Saunders J, et al: AUDIT, The Alcohol Use Disorders Identification Test: guidelines for use in primary health care (WHO Publ No PSA/92.4). Geneva, World Health Organization, 1992

Babor TF, Bohn MJ, Kranzler HR: The Alcohol Use Disorders Identification Test (AUDIT): validation of a screening instrument for use in medical settings. J Stud Alcohol 56(4):423–432, 1995

Claussen B, Aasland OG: The Alcohol Use Disorders Identification Test (AUDIT) in a routine health examination of long-term unemployed. Addiction 88:363–368, 1993

Saunders JB, Aasland OG, Babor TF, et al: Development of the Alcohol Use Disorders Identification Test (AUDIT): WHO Collaborative Project on Early Detection of Persons With Harmful Alcohol Consumption, II. Addiction 88:791–804, 1993

CAGE Questionnaire

J. A. Ewing

GOALS

The CAGE Questionnaire (Ewing 1984) was designed to briefly screen for clinically significant alcohol problems in a variety of treatment and nontreatment settings. A positive score on the CAGE is meant to alert the clinician to engage in further inquiry about a patient's alcohol use patterns and alcohol-related problems and symptoms.

DESCRIPTION

The CAGE contains four yes-no items that can be administered in a self-report or clinician-interview format. Items may be grouped together or asked separately by embedding them within the context of questionnaires that cover health and lifestyle issues. The name CAGE is a mnemonic device based on key words from the four questions (see Example 22–2). Each yes response to a CAGE question is scored as 1. A total score of 0–4 results from summing positive answers. A score of 2 or higher is considered clinically significant and should raise the clinician's index of suspicion that the individual has an alcohol-related problem or diagnosis.

PRACTICAL ISSUES

It takes less than 1 minute to administer and score the CAGE. It may be used without permission. No special training is required to administer, score, or interpret the CAGE. The CAGE has been translated into Flemish, French, Hebrew, Japanese, Polish, Portuguese, and Spanish.

The CAGE is included on the CD-ROM that accompanies this handbook.

PSYCHOMETRIC PROPERTIES

Validity

The principal measures of the utility of the CAGE have been the sensitivity and specificity of this brief measure in relationship to the detection of individuals determined to have a lifetime history of clinically significant alcohol problems (e.g., DSM-IV alcohol abuse or alcohol dependence) by more extensive assessments (e.g., using structured interviews such as the Composite International Diagnostic Interview [CIDI]). The CAGE has been included in numerous studies with large sample sizes of patients seeking treatment in general medical or psychiatric settings. In general, a cutoff score of 1 or more yields higher sensitivity and lower specificity than a score of 2 or more. From three exemplary studies, sensitivities for a cutoff score of 1 or more range from 0.86 to 0.90, with specificities ranging from 0.52 to 0.93. Sensitivities for a cutoff of 2 or more range from 0.78 to 0.81, and specificities range from 0.76 to 0.96. Studies that compare the CAGE with single items such as "How much do you drink?" or to biological measures such as liver function tests or breath tests for alcohol show greatly improved sensitivity and specificity over those screening procedures.

CLINICAL UTILITY

The CAGE is one of the most widely used methods to screen for alcohol problems. Although other instruments such as the MAST and the TWEAK have better sensitivity-to-specificity ratios, the CAGE is useful because of its brevity and ease in scoring. A cut point of 1 detects approximately 90% of those with an alcohol-related disorder, with 48% false-positive diagnoses. Although the items are worded in a nonthreatening manner, they have great face validity and are subject to falsely negative reporting.

REFERENCES AND SUGGESTED READINGS

Ewing JA: Detecting alcoholism: the CAGE Questionnaire. JAMA 252(14):1905–1907, 1984

Liskow B, Campbell J, Nickel EJ, et al: Validity of the CAGE Questionnaire in screening for alcohol dependence in a walk-in (triage) clinic. J Stud Alcohol 56:277–281, 1995

Magruder-Habib K, Stevens HA, Alling WC: Relative performance of the MAST, VAST, and CAGE versus DSM-III-R

EXAMPLE 22–2 ■ The CAGE Questionnaire

C	Have you ever felt you should Cut down on your drinking?
A	Have people Annoyed you by criticizing your drinking?
G	Have you ever felt bad or Guilty about your drinking?
E	Have you ever had a drink first thing in the morning to steady your nerves or to get rid of a hangover (Eye opener)?

criteria for alcohol dependence. J Clin Epidemiol 46(5):435–441, 1993

Mayfield D, McLeod G, Hall P: The CAGE Questionnaire: validation of a new alcoholism screening instrument. Am J Psychiatry 131:1121–1123, 1974

EXAMPLE 22–3 ■ Sample item from the Drug Abuse Screening Test

Have you ever had withdrawal symptoms as a result of heavy drug intake?

Drug Abuse Screening Test (DAST)

H. Skinner

GOALS

The Drug Abuse Screening Test (DAST) (Skinner 1982) was designed to provide a quantifiable self-report instrument for use in clinical and nonclinical settings to detect drug abuse or dependence pertaining to a range of psychoactive substances other than alcohol. It was adapted from the MAST (p. 467), which focuses solely on alcohol-related problems, and shares most of the properties of the parent instrument. Although it is primarily a screening device, its face-valid items allow a total score to serve as a lifetime measure of problem severity, because they cover a range of drug-related problems, diminished control over drug use, and neuroadaptive symptoms (i.e., tolerance, withdrawal) of drug dependence.

DESCRIPTION

The original version of the DAST contained 28 yes-no questions that were suitable for a self-report or interview format. A 20-item version of the DAST was found to have psychometric properties comparable with the 28-item version. Both versions have been referred to as the DAST in the literature; the 20-item version has occasionally been called the brief DAST, but this usage is by no means consistent. A sample item from the DAST is provided in Example 22–3. Each yes answer is scored 1, and each no answer is scored 0. The items are summed to provide a single overall score that is used to determine the likelihood that an individual has a past or present clinically significant drug-related diagnosis.

The DAST 28-item version yields an overall score ranging from 0 to 28 based on the sum of individual items. A cutoff score of 5 or more (on the 28-item DAST) indicates a probable drug use disorder.

PRACTICAL ISSUES

It takes approximately 5 minutes to administer the DAST and 2 minutes to score it. The DAST can be scored by the person who administered it or by computer. No special training is required for administration. The instrument is in the public domain and, along with scoring procedures, can be found in its entirety in Skinner (1982). The author's address is

Harvey Skinner, Ph.D.
University of Toronto
Department of Behavioural Sciences
12 Queens Park, Crescent West
McMurrich Building, 1st Floor
Toronto, Ontario M5S 1A8, Canada

PSYCHOMETRIC PROPERTIES

Skinner (1982) reports the correlation between the 28-item version of the DAST and the 20-item version as being almost perfect ($r = 0.99$), with the 20-item DAST having excellent psychometric properties that are comparable with those of the 28-item DAST. Given the correlation between the two versions, the psychometric properties of the DAST are reviewed here without reference to the specific version.

Reliability

Measures of internal consistency from a study of individuals with substance abuse disorders who sought treatment

($N = 256$) and another of general psychiatric admissions ($N = 250$) were 0.92 and 0.94 (Cronbach's alpha), respectively.

Validity

The principal measure of the validity of the DAST has been its sensitivity and specificity for detecting drug use disorders as determined by clinician interviews and case records. In an initial study of individuals with mixed substance abuse disorders who sought treatment, a cut score of 5 detected all the patients seeking treatment for drug use without alcoholism and 91% of patients with mixed current alcohol and drug use diagnoses. In another study of 256 individuals with substance abuse disorders who sought treatment (Skinner 1982), DAST scores for those with alcohol problems only were substantially lower than those for patients with drug use diagnoses (alcoholic patients, mean = 4.5; patients with drug abuse problems, mean = 17.8). In a study of 250 consecutive admissions to a hospital psychiatry department (which included inpatients, day-hospital patients, outpatients, and outpatients with substance abuse diagnoses) (Staley and El-Guebaly 1990), DAST scores significantly differed between the substance abuse sample and the other psychiatric populations. Using DSM-III-R diagnoses of a substance-related disorder determined by a psychiatrist as the standard, a cut point of 5 gave sensitivity and specificity scores of 0.96 and 0.81, whereas a cut point of 10 yielded scores of 0.82 and 0.91. Finally, in a study of 501 patients seeking treatment at an alcohol and drug treatment center (Gavin et al. 1989), receiver operating characteristic (ROC) analysis showed a cutoff of either 5 or 6 to be the best, with sensitivity and specificity scores of 0.96 and 0.79 (i.e., both 5 and 6 were equal in sensitivity and specificity).

DAST scores have been shown to be significantly correlated with frequency of drug use in the past 12 months across a host of drugs (e.g., heroin, other opiates, amphetamines, barbiturates, hallucinations, cannabis, and glue) (Skinner 1982). They are also positively correlated with a variety of psychopathology measures that assess hypochondriasis, depression, anxiety, interpersonal problems, and social deviation.

CLINICAL UTILITY

The DAST covers a wide range of consequences related to drug abuse without being specific about the drug, thus alleviating the necessity of using different instruments specific to each drug. The DAST performs well as a screening instrument to detect abuse or dependence diagnoses with a range of different drugs of abuse in a variety of clinical and nonclinical settings. It is most useful for detecting these disorders in settings in which seeking treatment for drug use problems is not the patient's stated goal (e.g., alcohol clinics or general mental health settings). In addition to its function in detecting drug abuse or dependence, it provides a general measure of lifetime problem severity that can be used to guide further inquiry into drug-related problems and to help determine treatment intensity. Because the items do not specify a time frame, the DAST does not distinguish between current and past drug-related diagnoses, nor is it useful as a change measure. The high degree of face validity for all items provides no protection from falsely negative reporting.

REFERENCES AND SUGGESTED READINGS

Gavin DR, Ross HE, Skinner HA: Diagnostic validity of the Drug Abuse Screening Test in the assessment of DSM-III drug disorders. British Journal of Addiction 84:301–307, 1989

Skinner HA: The Drug Abuse Screening Test. Addict Behav 7:363–371, 1982

Staley D, El-Guebaly N: Psychometric properties of the Drug Abuse Screening Test in a psychiatric patient population. Addict Behav 15:257–264, 1990

Fagerstrom Test for Nicotine Dependence (FTND)

K. O. Fagerstrom

GOALS

The Fagerstrom Test for Nicotine Dependence (FTND) (Fagerstrom and Schneider 1989) was designed to provide an ordinal measure of nicotine dependence related to cigarette smoking. It contains items that evaluate the quantity of cigarette consumption, the compulsion to use, and dependence. The scale is useful as a screen for nicotine dependence and as a severity rating that can be used for treatment planning and prognostic judgments.

DESCRIPTION

The FTND contains four yes-no and two multiple-choice questions and can be used in an interview or self-report format. The items on the FTND are scored 0 and 1 for yes and no items, respectively, and from 0 to 3 for multiple-choice items; the items are summed to yield a total score of 0–10. No specific cutoff points are used to yield a diagnosis of dependence. The average score in randomly selected smokers is approximately 4–4.5. In samples of cigarette smokers seeking treatment, mean scores have ranged from 5.2 to 6.3. The scale in its entirety is included in Example 22–4 because of its brevity.

EXAMPLE 22–4 ■ Fagerstrom Test for Nicotine Dependence

---

1. How many cigarettes a day do you smoke? (CPD)
   0 = ≤10
   1 = 11±20
   2 = 21±30
   3 = 31+
2. Do you smoke more in the morning than during the day?
   0 = no
   1 = yes
3. How soon after you wake up do you smoke your first cigarette? (TTF)
   0 = >60 min
   1 = 31±60 min
   2 = 6±30 min
   3 = ≤5 min
4. Which cigarette would you hate most to give up?
   0 = not first
   1 = first of day
5. Do you find it difficult to refrain from smoking in places where it is forbidden, for example, in church, at the library, in the cinema, etc?
   0 = no
   1 = yes
6. Do you smoke if you are so ill that you are in bed most of the day?
   0 = no
   1 = yes

PRACTICAL ISSUES

It takes 2 minutes or less to administer the FTND and 2 minutes or less to score it. No training is required to administer and score the instrument. The FTND is copyrighted but can be reproduced without permission and is available in the *British Journal of Addiction* (Heatherton et al. 1991). Information on the scores derived from clinical samples is available from the references at the end of this section. A French translation is available, and administration by telephone has been reported (Pomerleau et al. 1994).

PSYCHOMETRIC PROPERTIES

Reliability

Test-retest reliability from a sample first screened on the telephone and then interviewed in person was 0.88. Cronbach's alpha coefficients from three clinical samples ranged from 0.56 to 0.64.

Validity

The FTND has been shown to correlate with biochemical measures of intake (i.e., conitine and alveolar carbon monoxide), with r values of 0.25–0.40, and with number of years smoked ($r = 0.52$). In two smoking cessation studies, correlations between FTND scores at intake with success in quitting smoking were low but significant (correlations of –0.16 with patients who have quit by the end of treatment and –0.11 with patients who have continued to abstain at 16-month follow-up). Additionally, in most studies, smokers with higher FTND scores tended to have more withdrawal symptoms and to better regulate their smoking to achieve accustomed nicotine blood levels.

CLINICAL UTILITY

The FTND can be used as a screening device and as a guide for planning treatment strategy and intensity. No specific cut points exist for diagnosing nicotine dependence. Several studies indicate that smokers who score high on the FTND benefit from use of nicotine gum and nicotine nasal spray and that they need higher doses of these products. On the other hand, the nicotine patch and bupropion appear equally beneficial to smokers with high and low FTND scores. The brevity and easy scoring of the FTND make it an efficient way to obtain clinically meaningful information. The FTND can be incorporated into general health and lifestyle screening questionnaires in clinical and nonclinical settings.

REFERENCES AND SUGGESTED READINGS

Fagerstrom KO, Schneider NG: Measuring nicotine dependence: a review of the Fagerstrom Tolerance Questionnaire. J Behav Med 12(2):159–182, 1989

Heatherton TF, Kozlowski LT, Frecker RC, et al: The Fagerstrom Test for Nicotine Dependence: a revision of the Fagerstrom Tolerance Questionnaire. British Journal of Addiction 86:1119–1127, 1991

Niaura R, Goldstein MG, Abrams DB: Matching high and low dependence smokers to self-help treatment with or without nicotine replacement. International Journal of Preventative Medicine 23:1–8, 1994

Payne TJ, Smith PO, McCracken LM, et al: Assessing nicotine dependence: a comparison of the Fagerstrom Tolerance Questionnaire (FTQ) with the Fagerstrom Test For Nicotine Dependence (FTND) in a clinical sample. Addict Behav 19(3):307–317, 1994

Pomerleau CS, Carton SM, Lutzke ML, et al: Reliability of the Fagerstrom Tolerance Questionnaire and the Fagerstrom Test for Nicotine Dependence. Addict Behav 19(1):33–39, 1994

Michigan Alcoholism Screening Test (MAST)

M. L. Selzer

GOALS

The Michigan Alcoholism Screening Test (MAST) (Selzer 1971) was designed principally to provide a quanti-

fiable, self-report instrument for the detection of alcoholism. Although it is primarily a screening device, its 25 face-valid items allow the total score to serve as a lifetime problem severity measure, because they cover a range of alcohol-related problems, diminished control over drinking, and neuroadaptative symptoms (i.e., tolerance, withdrawal) of alcohol dependence. Symptoms included in the MAST are not explicitly linked to any standard diagnostic criteria for alcohol use disorders such as those set forth in DSM-IV or ICD-10.

DESCRIPTION

The MAST is a self-report instrument that can also be administered by a minimally trained interviewer. It contains 25 yes-no questions that are differentially weighted. The MAST yields an overall score ranging from 0 to 53 by summing individual items as follows: no answers get a score of 0, and yes answers get a score of 1, 2, or 5 depending on the inherent severity of the symptom covered in the item. The recommended interpretation of the total score is for 0–4 to indicate absence of alcoholism, 5–6 to suggest possible alcoholism, and 7 and up to indicate probable alcoholism.

Several briefer versions of the MAST are available. These tests include the 13-item Short MAST (SMAST) (Selzer et al. 1975), the 10-item Brief MAST (Pokorny et al. 1972), and a geriatric version called the MAST-G (Blow 1991).

PRACTICAL ISSUES

It takes approximately 5 minutes to administer the MAST and 2 minutes to score it. It can be scored by the administrator or by computer. No special training is required for administration. The instrument is in the public domain, and items and scoring instructions can be found in Selzer (1971). A packet of tests and a scoring key are also available from the author for $40.00:

Melvin L. Selzer
6967 Paseo Laredo
La Jolla, CA 92037

PSYCHOMETRIC PROPERTIES

Reliability

One study of 120 psychiatric inpatients reported test-retest reliability coefficients of 0.97 for a 1-day interval, 0.86 for a 2-day interval, and 0.85 for a 3-day interval between the initial test and retest. Another study of psychiatric patients found a test-retest reliability of 0.84 using a 4-month interval. Cronbach's alphas from nine different studies ranged from 0.83 to 0.95.

Validity

The validity of the MAST has principally been established by its ability to detect alcoholism as defined by clinician diagnosis; criteria vary across studies. Selzer's (1971) original study included 41 white men admitted to a hospital for alcoholism, 67 white male blue-collar employees, and 36 white men visiting an allergy clinic. In this study the MAST missed only 2 of the 128 subjects with diagnoses of problem drinking. Moore (1972) found 78% agreement between the MAST and a psychiatrist's opinion of whether a patient had a drinking problem in a sample of 40 adult psychiatric outpatients. Sensitivity and specificity have varied across samples and with differing cutoff points. In a representative study of 501 patients seeking general addiction treatment, Ross et al. (1990) found the best combination of sensitivity and specificity scores (0.89 and 0.79, respectively) for detecting DSM-III alcohol abuse or dependence with a cutoff score of 15; a cutoff of 5 yielded sensitivity and specificity ratings of 0.99 and 0.57. The MAST was also shown to be significantly correlated with other measures of alcohol use severity, including the Alcohol Dependence Scale (0.79), any current DSM-III alcohol diagnosis (0.65), any lifetime DSM-III alcohol diagnosis (0.58), and alcohol-related symptoms (0.72).

CLINICAL UTILITY

The MAST performs well as a screening instrument. It can be administered in a variety of clinical and nonclinical settings using either a self-report or interview format. Although not intended to be a complete measure of alcohol-related problems, it provides a gross, general measure of lifetime problem severity that can be used for choosing treatment intensity and guiding further inquiry into alcohol-related problems. Because the items do not specify a time frame, the scale does not distinguish between current and past alcohol problems and is not useful as a change measure. Furthermore, because the focus is typically on late-stage symptoms of alcoholism, it may miss less severe use or patterns of use that occur earlier in the course of the illness. Given the face-valid nature of the questions, there are no safeguards against falsely negative reporting.

REFERENCES AND SUGGESTED READINGS

Blow F: Michigan Alcoholism Screening Test—Geriatric Version (MAST-G). Ann Arbor, MI, University of Michigan Alcohol Research Center, 1991

Moore RA: The diagnosis of alcoholism in a psychiatric hospital: a trial of the Michigan Alcoholism Screening Test (MAST). Am J Psychiatry 128:1565–1569, 1972

Pokorny AD, Miller BA, Kaplan HB: The brief MAST: a shortened version of the Michigan Alcoholism Screening Test. Am J Psychiatry 129:342–345, 1972

Ross HE, Gavin DR, Skinner HA: Diagnostic validity of the MAST and the Alcohol Dependence Scale in the assessment of DSM-III alcohol disorders. J Stud Alcohol 51(6):506–513, 1990

Selzer ML: The Michigan Alcoholism Screening Test: the quest for a new diagnostic instrument. Am J Psychiatry 127(12):1653–1658, 1971

Selzer ML, Vinokur A, van Roojen L: A self-administered Michigan Alcoholism Screening Test (SMAST). J Stud Alcohol 36:117–126, 1975

Zung BJ: Psychometric properties of the MAST and two briefer versions. J Stud Alcohol 40(9):845–859, 1979

Zung BJ: Evaluation of the Michigan Alcoholism Screening Test (MAST) in assessing lifetime and recent problems. J Clin Psychol 38(2):425–439, 1982

Personal Experience Screening Questionnaire (PESQ)

K. Winters

GOALS

The Personal Experience Screening Questionnaire (PESQ) (Winters 1991) was designed to screen adolescents ages 12–18 for substance use disorders. The instrument yields scores that measure substance problem severity and indicate the need for more detailed evaluation of alcohol and drug use patterns; it is not intended to determine whether a specific diagnosis of substance use disorder is present. It also contains scales designed to tap reporting biased toward minimizing or maximizing problems. The purpose of the PESQ is to detect substance use disorders in settings in which substance use issues are not the primary focus of evaluation (e.g., general mental health or medical settings, schools, correctional institutions).

DESCRIPTION

The PESQ consists of 40 yes-no and multiple-choice Likert items intended for self-report administration. The questions cover several content areas related to frequency, patterns, and consequences of drug and alcohol use and evaluate defensiveness of reporting and overestimation of use. Sample items that assess pattern of use, defensiveness, and overestimation are provided in Example 22–5.

The PESQ may be scored with the PESQ AutoScore Form. As the examinee circles responses directly on this form, the answers are transferred to the scoring sheets on the inside pages of the form. The inside of the form, which is not accessible to the examinee, is used for scoring and includes scoring instructions. The AutoScore Form provides formal scores and supplementary information. It yields three scales that are used as indicators of a need for further assessment: Problem Severity (range 18–72, cut scores depend on age; for 12- to 15-year-olds, a score of 30 or greater indicates a need for a more de-

tailed evaluation; for 16- to 18-year-olds, a score of 35 or greater for males and 34 or greater for females indicates a need for further evaluation), Defensiveness (fake good) (range 5–10; a score of 9 or greater is a red flag for possible minimizing of substance use), and Infrequency (fake bad) (range 3–12; a score of 4 or greater is a red flag for possible overstatement of substance use frequency). Norms are provided in the manual for a school sample, a school clinic sample, a drug clinic sample, and a juvenile correctional institution sample.

EXAMPLE 22–5 ■ Sample items from the Personal Experience Screening Questionnaire

> How often have you been upset about other people talking about your using or drinking?
>   Answers: Never, Once or Twice, Sometimes, Often
>
> I am always willing to admit it when I make a mistake.
>   Answers: Yes/No
>
> How often have you lost your sense of taste for several days after using drugs?
>   Answers: Never, Once or Twice, Sometimes, Often

PRACTICAL ISSUES

It takes 10 minutes or less to administer and score the PESQ, and no special training is needed. The PESQ is written at a fourth-grade reading level. It is copyrighted by Western Psychological Services. The PESQ is offered as a kit for $75.00 and includes the manual and 25 tests. Additional forms are available in a pack of 25 for $32.50. The price for bulk purchases of forms is slightly lower.

Western Psychological Services
12031 Wilshire Boulevard
Los Angeles, CA 90025-1251
Phone: 310-478-2061 or 800-648-8851
Internet: www.wpspublish.com

PSYCHOMETRIC PROPERTIES

Reliability

Internal consistency derived from drug clinic ($n = 231$), juvenile offender ($n = 411$), and school ($n = 1,539$) samples ranged from 0.90 to 0.95.

Validity

In a sample of drug clinic patients ($n = 231$), subjects with prior drug abuse treatment had significantly higher scores on the PESQ than subjects without prior treatment (means of 50.4 vs. 41.3), subjects with an intake diagnosis of dependence had significantly higher scores than individuals with a diagnosis of abuse (48 vs. 42.5), and the entire drug clinic sample had higher scores than the juvenile offender sampler and normal school sample (44.5 vs. 35.4 vs. 27.5). In a school clinic sample, PESQ scores predicted referral for drug abuse evaluations (mean score 40.2 on the sample referred for evaluation vs. 28.3 for the nonreferred students). Discriminant function analysis showed an optimal cut point of 40 or greater, with sensitivity and specificity ratings of 0.91 and 0.84, which was replicated in a second sample (sensitivity and specificity scores of 0.88 and 0.85).

CLINICAL UTILITY

The brief self-report format and the use of items designed to assess characteristics of teenage substance use make the PESQ a useful instrument for detecting the need for referral to substance abuse clinics from other settings in which services are provided to adolescents. Although the items that pertain to substance use patterns are highly face valid, this instrument addresses the issue of biased reporting by including scales to indicate defensiveness and infrequency of reporting, which can be used to determine the need for a more detailed assessment. The PESQ is not designed to be used as a change measure or to determine a formal diagnosis of substance abuse or dependence. Thus, more extensive evaluation is required in specialty settings.

REFERENCES AND SUGGESTED READINGS

George MS, Skinner HA: Assessment, in Drug Use by Adolescents: Identification, Assessment, and Intervention. Ed-

ited by Annis HM, Davis CS. Toronto, Canada, Alcoholism and Drug Addiction Foundation, 1991, pp 85–108

Winters K: Manual for the Personal Experience Screening Questionnaire (PESQ). Los Angeles, CA, Western Psychological Services, 1991

Winters KC: Development of an adolescent alcohol and other drug abuse screening scales: Personal Experiences Screening Questionnaire. Addict Behav 17:479–490, 1992

TWEAK Test

M. *Russell*

GOALS

The TWEAK (Russell et al. 1991) briefly screens for heavy drinking and clinically significant current or past alcohol problems in both treatment and nonclinical settings. It was originally designed to screen for risky drinking behavior during pregnancy and was originally validated in that population with regard to the establishment of cutoff scores. Because the items themselves are not gender specific, the test can be used for both women and men. A positive score on the TWEAK can be used to determine the need for further assessment regarding alcohol use patterns and alcohol-related problems.

DESCRIPTION

The TWEAK is a five-item self-report measure that can also be administered in a clinician-interview format. The name *TWEAK* is an acronym derived from the five items in the measure (see Example 22–6).

The tolerance question is considered positive if the subject reports being able to "hold" five or more drinks or reports that it takes three or more drinks to feel high. All other questions are considered positive if answered yes.

The tolerance and worry items each count 2 points if positive, and the remaining items count 1 point; the

EXAMPLE 22–6 ■ The TWEAK Test

> T (*Tolerance*): How many drinks can you "hold," or how many drinks does it take before you begin to feel the first effects of alcohol?
>
> W Have close friends or relatives Worried or complained about your drinking in the past year?
>
> E (*Eye-Opener*): Do you sometimes take a drink in the morning when you first get up?
>
> A (*Amnesia, Blackouts*): Has a friend or family member ever told you about things you said or did while you were drinking that you could not remember?
>
> K (C): Could you sometimes feel the need to Cut down on your drinking?

test yields a possible total score of 7 when all items are summed. A score of 2 or higher is recommended for detecting risky drinking among pregnant women, and a score of 3 or more is recommended for identifying alcohol abuse or dependence.

PRACTICAL ISSUES

It takes less than 1 minute to administer and score the TWEAK. It may be used without permission. No special training is required to administer, score, or interpret this measure. Copies of the TWEAK may be obtained from

> Marcia Russell, Ph.D.
> Research Institute on Addiction
> 1021 Main Street
> Buffalo, NY 14203
> Phone: 716-887-2507

The TWEAK is included on the CD-ROM that accompanies this handbook.

PSYCHOMETRIC PROPERTIES

Validity

The principal method for measuring validity has been to determine the sensitivity and specificity of the TWEAK for detecting risky drinking or an alcohol use disorder as defined by DSM-III-R or ICD criteria. In one study of 4,743 African American women assessed at an inner-city prenatal clinic, a cut score of 2 or higher gave sensitivity and specificity scores of 0.79 and 0.83, and a score of 3

or higher gave scores of 0.59 and 0.94 for detecting women who drank 1 or more oz of absolute alcohol daily or 14 or more drinks weekly. A more diverse sample of 1,635 male and female subjects from clinical and nonclinical samples found sensitivity and specificity rates of 0.94 and 0.89 when a score of 3 or higher was used to detect DSM-III-R alcohol dependence in the past year. Separate analyses for men and women indicated greater specificity for women (e.g., in a clinical sample, sensitivity and specificity scores were 1.00 and 0.69 for men and 0.83 and 0.96 for women), which probably reflects greater tolerance for alcohol in men. Use in an emergency room sample with a score of 3 or higher yielded sensitivity and specificity scores of 0.87 and 0.86 for ICD-10 harmful drinking and 0.84 and 0.86 for ICD-10 alcohol dependence as determined by the CIDI (p. 61). When used to assess risky drinking during pregnancy, scores of 2 or higher on the TWEAK have been associated with significantly lower birth weight, lower Apgar scores, a smaller head circumference at birth, and cognitive deficits at age 6 (Russell et al. 1991).

CLINICAL UTILITY

The TWEAK is one of only a few screening instruments for heavy drinking and alcohol use disorders that has been specifically designed for and validated in samples of women, although it can be used with either men or women. It is brief, easily understood, and easily scored and can be used in either a self-report or interview format. Although there are no reliability data to date, as a screening instrument (sensitivity and specificity) the TWEAK outperformed the CAGE Questionnaire (p. 462) and the MAST (p. 467). Another potential advantage of the TWEAK over the CAGE and the MAST is that it is worded in the present tense; it can thus distinguish between lifetime and current alcohol problems. Although the items are worded in what is intended to be a nonthreatening format, they have high face validity and thus are subject to falsely negative reporting.

REFERENCES AND SUGGESTED READINGS

Chan AWK, Pristach EA, Welte JW, et al: Use of the TWEAK test in screening for alcoholism/heavy drinking in three populations. Alcohol Clin Exp Res 17(6):1188–1192, 1993

Cherpitel CJ: Screening for alcohol problems in the emergency department. Ann Emerg Med 26(2):158–166, 1995

Russell M, Czarnecki DM, Cowan R, et al: Measures of maternal alcohol use as predictors of development in early childhood. Alcohol Clin Exp Res 15:991–1000, 1991

Russell M, Martier SS, Sokol RJ, et al: Screening for pregnancy risk-drinking. Alcohol Clin Exp Res 18(5):1156–1161, 1994

Addiction Severity Index (ASI)

A. T. McLellan

GOALS

The Addiction Severity Index (ASI) (McLellan et al. 1980) is a semistructured interview designed to provide a multidimensional assessment of problems presented by patients with substance use disorders to guide initial treatment planning and to allow monitoring of patient progress over time. It is designed for use in inpatient and outpatient alcohol and drug abuse treatment settings.

DESCRIPTION

The ASI is a clinician- or technician-administered, semistructured interview that gathers information on seven functional areas often affected by substance abuse: medical status, employment and support, drug use, alcohol use, legal status, family or social status, and psychiatric status. The 142-item test begins with a section on general demographic information and then covers each of the seven problem areas separately, using a common format. Each section includes questions about the frequency, duration, and severity of problems over the patient's lifetime and in the past 30 days. Questions include both objective indicators of problem severity and the patient's subjective assessment of these problems. Item format varies, with yes-no, multiple-choice, and open-ended items in each section. Sample items are provided in Example 22–7. A considerably shortened follow-up version allows for measurement of change and covers only the past 30 days.

At the end of the assessment of each functional area, patients are asked to rate how troubled or bothered they have been by these problems over the past 30 days and the degree to which they feel they need treatment in addition to any current treatment they may be receiving for this problem area. These ratings are made on a 0–4 scale. For each functional area, the interviewer also makes severity ratings (0–9) that reflect the degree to which the interviewer believes the patient needs additional treatment. The patient and the interviewer severity ratings are meant to aid initial treatment planning and referral but are not intended to provide an ongoing measure of improvement with treatment. The ASI provides a composite score that may be used to evaluate problem severity currently and across time.

Normative data (composite scores and background variables) are available for numerous populations including treated male and female alcohol, opiate, and cocaine abusers. Norms are also given on the basis of the type of treatment episode (inpatient, partial hospitalization, and outpatient substance abuse) and for those with substance abuse problems who are pregnant, out of treatment, incarcerated, psychiatrically ill, coerced, or homeless (McLellan et al. 1992).

PRACTICAL ISSUES

The ASI is designed in an interview format to be used by trained individuals. Successfully trained individuals have included receptionists, college students, police officers, physicians, and research technicians. Administration of the ASI over the telephone has been reported (McLellan et al. 1985), although telephone administra-

EXAMPLE 22–7 ■ Sample items from the Addiction Severity Index

> How many times have you been treated for any psychological or emotional problems?
>
> How much have you been troubled or bothered by these psychological or emotional problems in the past 30 days?

tion is recommended for follow-up evaluations only. It requires 45–75 minutes to complete the initial assessment and 15–20 minutes to complete the follow-up version.

The ASI is in the public domain, and there is no charge for its use. For a nominal charge copies of the interview, training, and reference materials are available from

> DeltaMetrics
> One Commerce Square
> 2005 Market Street, 11th Floor
> Philadelphia, PA 19103
> Phone: 800-238-2433 or 215-665-2888

In addition, the National Institute on Drug Abuse (NIDA) has produced a set of training materials that includes two training videotapes, a training facilitator's manual, a handbook for program administrators, and a resource manual. This package costs $53.00 and is available from

> National Technical Information Service
> Phone: 703-487-4650
> Order Number: AVA19615VNB2KVS

An automated, self-scoring version, the Easy ASI, has also been developed for administration with a laptop computer. It is available for about $900.00 from

> Quickstart Computing
> 11551 Forest Central Drive, Suite 134
> Dallas, TX 72543
> Phone: 214-342-9020

Another automated, self-scoring version of the ASI for use on computers is available for $369.00 from

> Accurate Assessments
> 800-324-7966

The ASI is available in 17 different languages including Dutch, French, German, Japanese, Russian, and Spanish. The ASI is included on the CD-ROM that accompanies this handbook.

PSYCHOMETRIC PROPERTIES

Reliability

The ASI has been extensively studied regarding joint reliability, test-retest reliability, and internal consistency of composite scores, with generally excellent results. In a study of 407 methadone maintenance patients, internal consistency (Cronbach's alpha) ranged from 0.62 for the drug scale to 0.87 for the alcohol and psychiatric scales. In a study of 152 dual-diagnosis outpatients, internal consistency was lower, ranging from 0.48 for the legal scale up to 0.88 for the medical scale. Hodgins and El-Guebaly (1992) demonstrated average joint reliability scores of 0.89. Test-retest reliability calculated on a sample of 40 inpatients at time of admission (McLellan et al. 1985) showed reliability coefficients of 0.92 or above for severity ratings. The interrater reliability of the interviewer-rated severity scores is generally lower than that shown for the computer-scored composite scores (e.g., 0.30–0.96 vs. 0.57–0.94 in a study of 15 dual-diagnosis outpatients).

Validity

Concurrent, predictive, and discriminant validity have been demonstrated in a range of patient populations and treatment settings. In a study of 181 patients (McLellan et al. 1985), discriminant validity was demonstrated by correlating ASI composite scores with a variety of measures. For example, the ASI psychiatric composite score correlated 0.52 with the Beck Depression Inventory (BDI) (p. 519) and 0.47 with the Symptom Checklist—90 (SCL-90) (p. 81), and the alcohol composite score correlated 0.58 with the MAST (p. 467) and 0.87 with the Quantitative Inventory of Drinking Behavior (Hayashida 1981). Furthermore, after dividing the ASI problem severity ratings into low, medium, and high ranges, critical items in each of the ASI sections were found to be significantly different based on the severity category. In a study of 524 male veterans with substance use problems (McLellan et al. 1980), problem severity scores correlated with a variety of independent variables (e.g., total number of convictions, number of overdoses) in the expected directions, with correlations ranging from 0.43 to 0.72. The ASI is designed to be used as a change measure and has proved to be a sensitive change indicator in numerous studies.

CLINICAL UTILITY

The multidimensional ASI can be used as the principal tool to guide initial assessment and treatment planning for patients seeking inpatient or outpatient treatment for abuse of or dependence on a variety of substances. The abbreviated, follow-up version can be used to monitor patient progress and treatment outcome.

The major strength of the ASI is its efficient coverage of the multiple major problem areas for patients with a range of different abused substances, both at the initial evaluation and over the course of treatment. It is designed for use by personnel without advanced clinical training and provides data that can be easily comprehended and used at the time of the interview. It can be readily used for program evaluation or quality assurance purposes. The ASI is in the public domain and is widely used nationally and internationally. Normative data are available from numerous populations.

Limitations of the ASI include its high degree of face validity (allowing patient misrepresentation of information), its unsuitability for use in a self-report format, and the 45- to 75-minute period needed to administer it. ASI is not appropriate for use with patients with very severe, chronic mental disorders such as schizophrenia, because it makes assumptions regarding self-sufficiency. Although the ASI is not judged to be suitable for adolescent populations, a teen-focused version of the ASI (T-ASI) with good reliability and validity statistics has been developed (Kaminer et al. 1991).

REFERENCES AND SUGGESTED READINGS

Alterman AI, Brown LS, Zaballero A, et al: Interviewer severity ratings and composite scores of the ASI: a further look. Drug Alcohol Depend 34:201–209, 1994

Hayashida M: Quantitative inventory of drinking behavior scale. Paper presented at sixth annual meeting of the Coatesville Conference on Addiction, Coatesville, PA, 1981

Hodgins DC, El-Guebaly N: More data on the Addiction Severity Index: reliability and validity with the mentally ill substance abuser. J Nerv Ment Dis 180(3):197–201, 1992

Kaminer Y, Bukstein O, Tarter RE: The Teen-Addiction Severity Index: rationale and reliability. International Journal of Addiction 26:219–226, 1991

McLellan AT, Luborsky L, Woody GE, et al: An improved diagnostic evaluation instrument for substance abuse patients: the Addiction Severity Index. J Nerv Ment Dis 168(1):26–33, 1980

McLellan AT, Luborsky L, Cacciola J, et al: New data from the Addiction Severity Index: reliability and validity in three centers. J Nerv Ment Dis 173:412–423, 1985

McLellan AT, Kushner H, Metzger D, et al: The fifth edition of the Addiction Severity Index. J Subst Abuse Treat 9:199–213, 1992

Alcohol Dependence Scale (ADS)

J. L. Horn, H. A. Skinner, K. Wanberg, and F. M. Forster

GOALS

The Alcohol Dependence Scale (ADS) (Skinner and Allen 1982) was designed to yield a quantitative measure of severity of the alcohol dependence syndrome, as described by Edwards and Gross (1976). This construct focuses on a core dependence syndrome, the elements of which include impaired control over alcohol, tolerance, repeated episodes of alcohol withdrawal, and a compulsive drinking style.

DESCRIPTION

The ADS is a self-administered paper and pencil or computer-administered questionnaire with 25 yes-no and multiple-choice items that cover alcohol-related symptoms and behaviors over the past 12 months. A sample item is provided in Example 22–8. Constructs covered in the ADS include alcohol withdrawal symptoms, increased tolerance to alcohol, impaired control over drinking, awareness of a compulsion to drink, and salience of drinking.

The instrument yields a single ordinal scale of alcohol dependence severity ranging from 0 to 47. All items are arranged by order of severity to allow either computer scoring or scoring by the administrator. Scores of 9 and over are strongly related to a diagnosis of alcohol dependence according to DSM-III-R or DSM-IV criteria.

EXAMPLE 22–8 ■ Sample item from the Alcohol Dependence Scale

Have you tried to cut down on your drinking and failed?
a. No
b. Once
c. Several Times

PRACTICAL ISSUES

It takes 5 minutes to administer the ADS. Minimal training is required. The ADS is copyrighted and is available from

> Marketing Services
> Addiction Research Foundation
> Toronto, Ontario M5S 2S1, Canada
> Phone: 416-545-6000

The cost for 25 questionnaires is $6.50. A packet that contains 25 questionnaires and a scoring manual is $15.00. A version with computerized scoring and interpretation is available as part of the Computerized Lifestyle Assessment from Multi-Health Systems (United States: 800-456-3003). The instrument has been translated into French.

The ADS is included on the CD-ROM that accompanies this handbook.

PSYCHOMETRIC PROPERTIES

Reliability

Internal consistency was 0.92 in an initial study of 225 alcoholic patients seeking treatment and 0.85 in a second study of 268 patients admitted to an inpatient alcohol treatment program.

Validity

In one study of alcoholic patients seeking treatment ($N = 225$), the ADS was correlated 0.69 with the MAST (p. 467) and significantly correlated with measures of daily alcohol consumption, social consequences,

prior use of alcohol to change mood, and increased feelings of guilt. In a second study of alcoholic inpatients ($N = 268$), the ADS was positively correlated with daily alcohol consumption, previous alcohol treatment episodes, and years of drinking problems measured concurrently. It was also predictive of relapse following discharge. In a sample of medical outpatients who drank heavily, very poor agreement was shown between a DSM-III-R diagnosis of alcohol dependence and the ADS (Willenbring and Bielinski 1994). In this study even patients with a DSM-III-R diagnosis of alcohol dependence scored in the lowest range of the ADS (this is designated in the manual as indicating low or slight dependence). Although the ADS scoring manual states that a score of 14 or higher indicates moderate dependence, use of this score as a cutoff yielded poor agreement with the DSM-III-R diagnosis in this study (kappa = 0.11). Lowering the ADS cutoff score for dependence to 2 or 3 improved agreement (sensitivity and specificity scores were 0.77 and 0.69; kappa was 0.4).

CLINICAL UTILITY

The ADS is useful for screening, case finding, and treatment planning in a variety of settings. Its brief, self-administered format and ready scoring make it a widely applicable tool for use in treatment settings and other institutional settings such as schools and for general population surveys. It has been incorporated into systems for matching patients to treatments of differing intensity, including the American Society of Addiction Medicine Placement Criteria.

The instrument was originally designed to assess dependence severity in the past 12 months. However, this time window can be shortened to as few as the past 3 months to enable use of the scale as a change measure. Its clinical applicability is limited by the fact that it is designed to determine the severity of dependence according to the dimensional alcohol dependence syndrome, which is not equivalent to the categorical DSM-III-R definition of dependence.

REFERENCES AND SUGGESTED READINGS

Edwards G, Gross MM: Alcohol dependence: provisional description of a clinical syndrome. BMJ 285(1):1058–1061, 1976

Kivlahan DR, Sher KJ, Donovan DM: The Alcohol Dependence Scale: a validation study among inpatient alcoholics. J Stud Alcohol 50(2):170–175, 1989

Skinner HA, Allen BA: Alcohol dependence syndrome: measurement and validation. J Abnorm Psychol 91(3):199–209, 1982

Willenbring ML, Bielinski JB: A comparison of the Alcohol Dependence Scale and clinical diagnosis of alcohol dependence in male medical outpatients. Alcohol Clin Exp Res 18(3):715–719, 1994

Alcohol Expectancy Questionnaire (AEQ)

M. Goldman, S. Brown, and B. Christiansen

GOALS

The Alcohol Expectancy Questionnaire (AEQ) (Brown et al. 1987) was designed for specialty clinical settings to measure the degree to which individuals expect alcohol to produce a variety of general and specific positive effects. Unrealistic and unbalanced expectancies pertaining to rewarding aspects of drinking may motivate patients with alcohol dependence or abuse to continue drinking. Determining the patient's expectancies allows the clinician to challenge and test these beliefs and assumptions as part of an alcohol treatment program. Hence, detection of expectancies can guide efforts to reinforce motivation to cut down or stop pathological patterns of alcohol use.

DESCRIPTION

The AEQ is a self-administered questionnaire that contains 90 statements about the effects of drinking alcohol, to which the respondent answers agree or disagree. A sample item is provided in Example 22–9. The items cover a wide range of potential physical, mental, and interpersonal results of drinking alcohol. These items yield a total score and six subscales derived from factor anal-

EXAMPLE 22–9 ■ Sample item from the Alcohol Expectancy Questionnaire

> When I feel "high" from drinking, everything seems to feel better.

Reprinted with permission from Mark S. Goldman, Ph.D.

ysis: Positive Global Change in Experience, Sexual Enhancement, Social and Physical Pleasure, Assertiveness, Relaxation and Tension Reduction, and Arousal and Interpersonal Power.

The AEQ generates a total score and scores on the six expectancies subscales. Norms are available for a general adult and adolescent population and an adult and adolescent alcoholic population (Brown et al. 1987). Examples of AEQ norms (mean and standard deviation) in both a general adult population and a population of adult alcoholic patients in treatment are as follows: Positive Global Change in Experience, 9.85 ± 8.55 in general population versus 14.54 ± 5.38 in alcoholic population; Sexual Enhancement, 2.50 ± 2.49 in general population versus 3.13 ± 2.12 in alcoholic population; Social and Physical Pleasure, 5.50 ± 2.55 in general population versus 6.57 ± 2.01 in alcoholic population, Assertiveness, 5.44 ± 3.82 in general population versus 7.53 ± 3.05 in alcoholic population; Relaxation and Tension Reduction, 5.19 ± 2.80 in general population versus 6.15 ± 2.19 in alcoholic population; Arousal and Interpersonal Power, 0.88 ± 0.75 in general population versus 1.10 ± 0.72 in alcoholic population.

PRACTICAL ISSUES

It takes 20–30 minutes to administer the AEQ in a self-report or interview format. No special training is required to administer or score the instrument. The AEQ is copyrighted but may be used free of charge, as long as it is not altered. Items and scoring are available in Brown et al. (1987) or from

> Mark S. Goldman, Ph.D.
> Department of Psychology
> University of South Florida
> Tampa, FL 33620

The AEQ is included on the CD-ROM that accompanies this handbook.

PSYCHOMETRIC PROPERTIES

Reliability

Internal consistency in a population of adults without drinking problems ($N = 176$) ranged from 0.72 to 0.92 for the subscales and 0.84 overall. A study of 465 college students showed 4-week test-retest reliability coefficients ranging from 0.47 to 0.76 for the subscales, with a mean of 0.66, and 8-week agreement levels ranging from 0.48 to 0.72, with a mean of 0.64.

Validity

In a study of 580 subjects including college students, medical patients, and alcohol treatment program participants, Brown et al. (1985) showed that increased AEQ expectancies were significantly associated with increased levels of alcohol consumption. These investigators also found that specific expectancies discriminate excessive drinkers and alcoholic patients from nonexcessive drinkers. For example, alcoholic patients and medical patients who drink excessively expected more global positive changes, social assertiveness, and social and physical pleasure from alcohol than did medical patients without drinking problems. A study of 324 college students (Brown et al. 1987) showed AEQ scores to be independent of the Marlowe-Crowne Social Desirability Scale (Crowne and Marlowe 1960).

CLINICAL UTILITY

The AEQ can be used to guide the clinician's psychosocial interventions by detecting alcoholic patients' unrealistic or unbalanced positive thoughts about continuing to drink or reinitiating drinking after a period of abstinence. These unrealistically positive expectations have been shown to be predictive of current and future drinking practices, persistence and participation in therapy, and relapse following treatment. Thus, treatment interventions aimed at challenging unrealistically positive expectancies or focusing on counterbalancing them with negative alcohol expectancies may be useful for enhancing and sustaining motivation to continue efforts at recovery and avoid relapse. Clinicians should be aware that the efficacy of treatments targeted in this manner are largely untested, although the approach is closely related

to proven cognitive-behavioral treatments. The AEQ is most likely to be useful in assessing individuals who are contemplating or seeking treatment for alcohol use disorders.

REFERENCES AND SUGGESTED READINGS

Brown SA: Tension reduction and social interactions: alcohol versus expectancy effects. Pharmacol Biochem Behav 20:988, 1984

Brown SA, Goldman MS, Inn A, et al: Expectations of reinforcement from alcohol: their domain and relation to drinking patterns. J Consult Clin Psychol 48(4):419–426, 1980

Brown SA, Goldman MS, Christiansen BA: Do alcohol expectancies mediate drinking patterns of adults? J Consult Clin Psychol 53(4):512–519, 1985

Brown SA, Christiansen BA, Goldman MS: The Alcohol Expectancy Questionnaire: an instrument for the assessment of adolescent and adult alcohol expectancies. J Stud Alcohol 48(5):483–491, 1987

Crowne DP, Marlowe D: A new scale of social desirability independent of social psychopathology. J Consult Psychol 24:349–354, 1960

Alcohol Timeline Followback (TLFB)

L. C. Sobell and M. B. Sobell

GOALS

The Alcohol Timeline Followback (TLFB) (Sobell and Sobell 1992) is a method for assessing the quantity of alcohol consumption on a daily basis. With a calendar as a guide, the interviewee provides a retrospective estimate of daily drinking over a specified period of as long as the previous year. The goal is to provide a detailed record of patterns of alcohol use that can be used to guide treatment and to assess treatment outcome.

DESCRIPTION

The TLFB provides a calendar of the targeted period for recording the number of standard drinks consumed on each day. A standard drink is equivalent to 12 oz of regular beer, 5 oz of regular wine, or 1.5 oz of distilled spirits (e.g., whiskey, vodka). The time frame can vary from 30 to 360 days, and the subject is given detailed instructions designed to enhance the accuracy of recall and reporting of drinking behavior. The TLFB has recently been extended for use with other drugs and with cigarettes.

The TLFB can be used to obtain the following scores: daily drinking summary, monthly drinking summary, amount of money spent on drinking, total number of drinks in the past year, cost of drinking at home, cost of drinking at a bar, calories consumed, number of days on which drinking occurred, number of drinks per ordinary day, number of calories per day, maximum number of drinks in one day, maximum number of continuous abstinent days, maximum number of continuous drinking days, average drinks consumed per week, percentage of days in which drinking occurred, and others. Norms for both Canadian and American samples are available in the manual by age and sex groups for many derived variables such as number of drinks consumed per day.

PRACTICAL ISSUES

The TLFB can be administered in various formats, including interview, paper and pencil, and computer. It takes 10–15 minutes to complete the TLFB for a 90-day period and about 30 minutes for a 12-month period. Interviewers require no clinical expertise but some training, for which a training video and an instruction manual are available (Sobell and Sobell 1996). The instrument is copyrighted, but the paper and pencil version is available free of charge from the author:

> Linda C. Sobell, Ph.D.
> Center for Psychological Studies
> Nova Southwestern University
> 3301 College Avenue
> Fort Lauderdale, FL 33314
> Phone: 954-262-5811
> Fax: 954-262-3895
> E-mail: sobelll@cps.nova.edu

A manual, training video, computer-administration version, and scoring program are available separately or in a package (at a cost of $199.95) from

> Marketing Department
> Addiction Research Foundation
> 33 Russell Street
> Toronto, Ontario M5S 2S1, Canada
> Phone: 800-661-1111

The TLFB is also available in French. The TLFB is included on the CD-ROM that accompanies this handbook.

PSYCHOMETRIC PROPERTIES

Reliability

Test-retest reliability has been studied in numerous populations, including outpatients with alcohol dependence ($N = 12$), college students ($N = 80$), and "normal drinkers" ($N = 62$). At 30- and 90-day follow-up periods, correlations from 0.79 to 0.96 have been reported for a wide range of variables derived from the TLFB, including frequency and intensity of drinking.

Validity

Several studies have compared TLFB reports with verifiable events and found correlations of 0.94–0.99 for days spent in jail and 0.97–0.98 for days spent in the hospital. Correlations with informant reports range from 0.79 to 0.92 for days abstinent and from 0.41 to 0.95 for reports that distinguish between heavy and light drinking days. TLFB-derived variables have been shown to be significantly related to biochemical laboratory tests including serum glutamic-oxaloacetic transaminase (SGOT), GGT, and mean corpuscular volume (MCV); the highest correlations were seen between drinking patterns and SGOT (e.g., for number of days drinking, 0.52; for number of drinks per drinking day, 0.51). Higher scores on the ADS (p. 474) were significantly and positively correlated with three TLFB variables: number of standard drinks consumed, mean number of drinks per drinking day, and number of days on which 10 or more standard drinks were consumed.

CLINICAL UTILITY

The TLFB has several clinical uses. It can be used early in treatment to enhance motivation to change by providing the patient with detailed, individualized feedback about drinking patterns in comparison with population norms and about drinking consequences, including financial and health issues. It can be used in the course of treatment to plan coping strategies by helping the patient focus on periods of high and low risk in an attempt to identify factors related to relapse or the ability to abstain. Detailed measures of improvement can be generated throughout the course of treatment and at treatment termination. The detailed level of information provided by this instrument and the comparison with norms can be more convincing than more global estimates of drinking patterns derived from less structured clinical interviewing. Because of its length, the TLFB is somewhat impractical when time is at a premium or little detailed information regarding alcohol use is needed.

REFERENCES AND SUGGESTED READINGS

Sobell LC, Sobell MB: Timeline Follow-Back: a technique for assessing self-reported alcohol consumption, in Measuring Alcohol Consumption: Psychosocial and Biological Methods. Edited by Litten RZ, Allen J. Towota, NJ, Humana Press, 1992, pp 41–72

Sobell LC, Sobell MB: Timeline Followback Users Manual. Toronto, Canada, Addiction Research Foundation, 1996

Sobell LC, Sobell MB, Leo GI, et al: Reliability of a timeline method: assessing normal drinkers' reports of recent drinking and a comparative evaluation across several populations. British Journal of Addiction 83:393–402, 1988

Sobell LC, Brown J, Leo GI, et al: The reliability of the Alcohol Timeline Followback when administered by telephone and by computer. Drug Alcohol Depend 42:49–54, 1996

Sobell MB, Sobell LC, Klajner F, et al: The reliability of a timeline method for assessing normal drinker college students' recent drinking history: utility for alcohol research. Addict Behav 11:149–162, 1986

Clinical Institute Withdrawal Assessment for Alcohol (CIWA-AD)

E. M. Sellers

GOALS

The Clinical Institute Withdrawal Assessment for Alcohol (CIWA-AD) (Sellers et al. 1991) was designed to allow clinicians to quantify the current severity of alcohol withdrawal in clinical and research settings in which detection of alcohol withdrawal is important and in which the severity of withdrawal symptoms needs to be closely monitored. It can be repeated as often as necessary to measure progression of withdrawal.

DESCRIPTION

The CIWA-AD is a semistructured, clinician-administered instrument that contains eight items rated on ordinal scales of 0–7 on the basis of clinical observations and patients' answers to probing questions. All items include observable anchors. Four items (pulse rate, sweating, hand tremor, and agitation) are rated on the basis of observation, and four (anxiety, sensory disturbances, nausea or vomiting, and headache) are rated on the basis of answers to semistructured questions. All items except headache correspond to DSM-IV criteria for alcohol withdrawal and are rated at the time of the interview. (The DSM-IV grand mal seizures item is the only symptom from the DSM-IV criteria for withdrawal that is not included in the CIWA-AD.) A sample observational item is pulse rate, which is translated into a score of 0–7. Another set of questions pertains to nausea or vomiting (see Example 22–10).

The current version is abbreviated from earlier ones, the CIWA-A (Shaw et al. 1981), which contained 15 items, and the CIWA-AR (Sullivan et al. 1989), which contained 10 items.

The eight items are each scored from 0 to 7 and are summed to create an overall withdrawal score that ranges between 0 and 56; a higher score indicates greater severity. Sellers et al. (1991) present a scoring method in

EXAMPLE 22–10 ■ **Sample item from the Clinical Institute Withdrawal Assessment for Alcohol**

Do you feel sick to your stomach? Have you vomited?
Rated 0 (no nausea and no vomiting) to 7 (constant nausea, frequent dry heaves, and vomiting)

---

which symptoms with scores greater than 2 are considered positive. They then recommend that one positive symptom be considered very mild withdrawal, two positive symptoms indicate mild withdrawal, three positive symptoms indicate moderate withdrawal, and four positive symptoms indicate severe withdrawal.

PRACTICAL ISSUES

The CIWA-AD is designed to be administered in an interview and clinical observation format by trained clinical observers. It takes 5 minutes to complete and score; the total score is obtained by simply summing scores on the eight items. Minimal training is required to facilitate accurate observations (e.g., taking pulse) and to use anchored ratings consistently. The scale can be obtained in its entirety from Sellers et al. (1991), and permission is not required for its use. The scale has been translated into German.

The CIWA-AD is included on the CD-ROM that accompanies this handbook.

PSYCHOMETRIC PROPERTIES

Reliability

Reliability has been established with earlier versions of the instrument. In one study in which seven observers rated videotapes, joint reliability was 0.94 for the total score. In a later study with 100 alcoholic patients undergoing detoxification, joint reliability was at the 0.9 level or higher for the total score and for all of the individual items included in the current version.

Validity

The instrument has been used as a standard measure in numerous clinical trials that evaluated methods of alco-

hol detoxification. It is sensitive to change over time and discriminates improved from standard withdrawal protocols. In a study of 38 patients with alcohol withdrawal, the original 15-item version was shown to correspond well with independent expert clinician ratings of alcohol withdrawal severity. In a heterogeneous sample of 137 alcoholic patients in alcohol withdrawal, Sellers et al. (1991) found that if an item score of 2 is used to indicate a positive symptom, then very mild, mild, moderate, and severe alcohol withdrawal correspond to two, three, four, and five positive items, respectively. This scoring system accurately classified 97.5% of alcohol withdrawal patients. Raising the threshold to 3 to indicate a positive symptom excludes 10.9% of mild withdrawal patients and 2.2% of moderate withdrawal patients.

CLINICAL UTILITY

The CIWA-AD provides an efficient, reliable method of quantifying current alcohol withdrawal severity in clinical settings. It has become a standard measure for research aimed at improving detoxification treatments. In general clinical settings, it can be used to determine when pharmacologically assisted detoxification treatments are needed and the degree to which such treatments are successful in maintaining mild or acceptable symptom levels. Untreated alcohol withdrawal can lead to progressively more severe symptoms at subsequent episodes. Success in detecting and treating clinically significant alcohol withdrawal symptoms can be efficiently documented with this scale.

REFERENCES AND SUGGESTED READINGS

Sellers EM, Sullivan JT, Somer G, et al: Characterization of DSM-III-R criteria for uncomplicated alcohol withdrawal provides an empirical basis for DSM-IV. Arch Gen Psychiatry 48:442–447, 1991

Sellers EM, Sullivan JT, Somer G, et al: Characterization of DSM-III-R criteria for uncomplicated alcohol withdrawal: proposal for a diagnostic inventory and revised withdrawal scale, in Novel Pharmacological Interventions for Alcoholism. Edited by Naranjo CA, Sellers RM. New York, Springer-Verlag, 1992, pp 369–371

Shaw JM, Kolesar GS, Sellers EM, et al: Development of optimal treatment tactics for alcohol withdrawal, I: assessment and effectiveness of supportive care. J Clin Psychopharmacol 1:382–388, 1981

Sullivan JT, Sykora K, Schneiderman J, et al: Assessment of alcohol withdrawal: the revised Clinical Institute Withdrawal Assessment for Alcohol Scale (CIWA-Ar). British Journal of Addiction 84:1353–1357, 1989

Obsessive Compulsive Drinking Scale (OCDS)

R. F. Anton

GOALS

The Obsessive Compulsive Drinking Scale (OCDS) (Anton et al. 1995) was designed to measure the obsessive and compulsive cognitive aspects of alcohol craving. The scale was constructed on the basis of the observation that many aspects of craving for alcohol in the dependent individual are similar to the thought patterns and behaviors of patients with obsessive-compulsive disorder. The OCDS is a modification of the Yale-Brown Obsessive Compulsive Scale (Y-BOCS) (p. 572) and is designed to measure these thought patterns and behaviors in heavy drinkers.

DESCRIPTION

The OCDS is a 14-item, self-rated instrument. Each question has five possible answers scored on a scale of

EXAMPLE 22–11 ■ Sample item from the Obsessive Compulsive Drinking Scale

> How much of your time when you're not drinking is occupied by ideas, thoughts, impulses, or images related to drinking?

0–4. A sample item is provided in Example 22–11. The OCDS items are summed to produce a total score, an Obsessive Thoughts subscale score, and a Compulsive Drinking subscale score. The cognitive dimension measured by these scales is more a measure of the state of illness than an indicator of actual drinking behavior. The OCDS has been shown to discriminate between abstinent patients and patients who have slipped or relapsed.

The OCDS is scored in a manner consistent with the scoring of the Y-BOCS. In scoring the OCDS, the 14 items are reduced to 10 items by using only the higher score of items 1 and 2, 7 and 8, 9 and 10, and 13 and 14. After this adjustment is made, the 10 remaining scores are summed to create a total score. The Obsessive Thoughts subscale is calculated by adding the scores on items 1–6 (adjusted as described earlier). The compulsive drinking subscale total is calculated by summing items 7–14 (again adjusted as described earlier). In an inpatient population the average score ranged from 20 to 22, and among outpatients the average scores ranged from 16 to 18.

PRACTICAL ISSUES

It takes approximately 5 minutes to complete the OCDS. It is easily scored by hand, and no training is required for administration. The instrument is in the public domain and can be copied. Scoring and test items are included in Anton et al. (1995). The instrument has been translated into German and Swedish and is currently being translated into Dutch, Flemish, French, Hebrew, Italian, Japanese, and Spanish.

The OCDS is included on the CD-ROM that accompanies this handbook.

PSYCHOMETRIC PROPERTIES

Reliability

In one study of 60 individuals with alcohol dependence who had recently been admitted to a detoxification program, the OCDS was shown to have an internal consistency of 0.86. The Obsessive Thoughts subscale had an alpha of 0.85, and the Compulsive Drinking subscale had an alpha of 0.73. Test-retest reliability statistics for a subsample ($n = 18$) indicate correlations of 0.96 for the total score, 0.94 for the Obsessive Thoughts subscale, and 0.86 for the Compulsive Drinking subscale.

Validity

In a heterogeneous sample of 41 subjects who met criteria for alcohol dependence, the OCDS was shown to correlate 0.48 with the alcohol composite score from the ASI (p. 472) and 0.42 with the ADS (p. 474). Longitudinal data for the OCDS indicate that total and subscale scores fall during the initial stages of sobriety and remain low in abstinent patients. Patients who drink alcohol but do not relapse have higher OCDS scores than those who remain abstinent. Patients who eventually relapse have even higher OCDS scores that remain elevated. The total scores of abstaining patients exhibit about a 75% drop during the first 2 weeks of treatment. Patients who drink at least some alcohol have less than a 50% drop in the total score.

CLINICAL UTILITY

The OCDS appears to have predictive value for future alcohol consumption and can be used to monitor patients as an early predictor of relapse. Because it appears that the OCDS score drops in relation to the time since the last drinking episode, scores that will be used as baseline measures should be obtained within the first week of abstinence. Alternatively, scores may be obtained on abstinent patients; deviations upward from this abstinent level indicate a potential for relapse.

REFERENCES AND SUGGESTED READINGS

Anton RF, Moak DH, Latham P: The Obsessive Compulsive Drinking Scale: a self-rated instrument for the quantification of thoughts about alcohol and drinking behavior. Alcohol Clin Exp Res 19(1):92–99, 1995

Anton RF, Moak DH, Latham PK: The Obsessive Compulsive Drinking Scale: a new method of assessing outcome in alcoholism treatment studies. Arch Gen Psychiatry 53:225–231, 1996

Bohn MJ, Barton BA, Barron KE: Psychometric properties and validity of the obsessive-compulsive drinking scale. Alcohol Clin Exp Res 20(5):817–823, 1996

University of Rhode Island Change Assessment (URICA)

J. O. Prochaska

GOALS

The University of Rhode Island Change Assessment (URICA) (McConnaughy et al. 1983) is designed to assess an individual's readiness to change to reduce problems related to alcohol, nicotine, or illicit drug use. The URICA yields factor scores corresponding to a stage model of readiness to change proposed by Prochaska et al. (1992). According to this formulation, behavioral change is associated with a sequence of decisions and motivational states that can be usefully divided into a sequential array of stages. The URICA is used to operationally define four stages of change, which are also the subscales: Precontemplation, Contemplation, Action, and Maintenance. The stages of change model actually postulates five stages of change. The additional stage (which follows Contemplation) has been variously called Decision Making, Preparation, and Determination. For the purposes of the URICA, this stage has been dropped because its items have a high loading on adjacent stages (Contemplation and Action).

On the basis of the individual patient's stage of readiness to change, the intensity and content of treatment recommendations or interventions can be chosen. Although no empirical evidence currently exists to support the effectiveness of targeting interventions in this manner, the stages of change model is growing in popularity, and many clinical resources are available to guide interested clinicians (e.g., Miller and Rollnick 1991).

DESCRIPTION

The URICA consists of 32 items with which the respondent registers agreement or disagreement on a 5-point, Likert-type scale in which a score of 1 indicates strong disagreement and a score of 5 shows strong agreement. The URICA items do not specify problems but are general in nature, which makes them applicable to a wide variety of patient problems. The scale consists of eight items used to rate attitudes and behaviors for each of the four stages of change.

The URICA yields four scores (each ranging from 5 to 40) corresponding to four stages of change: Precontemplation, Contemplation, Action, and Maintenance. The profile of these scores can be used to classify an individual's most prominent stage of change and to identify attitudes indicative of other stages. Normative data are available on treatment-seeking psychiatric patients (McConnaughy et al. 1983, 1989) and alcoholic patients (DiClemente and Hughes 1990). The scores of the URICA are typically plotted by stage (with the stage on the horizontal axis and the stage score on the vertical axis). This plotting allows for the creation of a stage of change profile. These profiles can be compared with cluster profiles published in McConnaughy et al. (1983, 1989). These clusters include distinct profiles such as decision making, maintenance, participation, and uninvolved.

PRACTICAL ISSUES

It takes 10–15 minutes to administer the URICA in either a self-report or interview format. The URICA can be scored by the individual who administers it. This scale is often scored by "eyeballing" a profile rather than going by ranges of means. No special training is required to administer or score the URICA. The URICA is copyrighted by the University of Rhode Island and Dr. James Prochaska. The measure is available in McConnaughy et al. (1989) or from

Jan Prochaska
Department of Psychology
University of Rhode Island
Kingston, RI 02881
Phone: 401-874-2830

PSYCHOMETRIC PROPERTIES

Reliability

The internal consistency of the four subscales was determined in three samples (N = 155, 327, and 224) and ranged from 0.69 to 0.89.

Validity

Factor analysis to support the stages of change model has been reported from two separate samples of psychiatric patients. Cluster analysis of the URICA stages from an alcoholic outpatient sample yielded five somewhat different patient profiles: precontemplation, ambivalence, participation, uninvolved, and contemplation. In two samples of patients with alcoholism who were seeking treatment, these profiles differed on measures of alcohol use patterns, drinking expectancies, and alcohol-related consequences.

CLINICAL UTILITY

The URICA can hypothetically be used to guide the content and intensity of treatments recommended and delivered to individuals with substance use disorders who present to specialty clinical settings, although the effectiveness of this use has not been empirically evaluated. Clinicians interested in the concept of motivational interviewing may find it a useful tool to evaluate a patient's stage of change. For voluntary patients at early stages of change, interventions focused on problem awareness or motivational enhancement are most likely to be accepted. More extensive and demanding treatment and self-help recommendations can be reserved for patients at the action stage. Because the scale is written in the present tense without a specific time frame, it can be used to assess changes in motivational stage over the course of treatment.

The URICA as yet lacks test-retest reliability and more in-depth validity data. The factors seem robust, however, and the preliminary validity work with patients with alcohol dependence appears promising.

REFERENCES AND SUGGESTED READINGS

DiClemente CC, Hughes SO: Stages of change profiles in outpatient alcoholism treatment. J Subst Abuse 2:217–235, 1990

McConnaughy EA, Prochaska JO, Velicer WF: Stages of change in psychotherapy: measurement and sample profiles. Psychotherapy: Theory, Research, and Practice 20(3):368–375, 1983

McConnaughy EA, DiClemente CC, Prochaska JO, et al: Stages of change in psychotherapy: a follow up report. Psychotherapy 26(4):494–503, 1989

Miller WR, Rollnick S: Motivational Interviewing. New York, Guilford, 1991

Prochaska JO, DiClemente CC, Norcross JC: In search of how people change: applications to addictive behaviors. Am Psychol 47:1102–1114, 1992

Psychotic Disorders Measures

Diana O. Perkins, M.D., M.P.H.
T. Scott Stroup, M.D., M.P.H.
Jeffrey A. Lieberman, M.D.

INTRODUCTION

Major Domains

In this chapter discussion is focused on tools that measure the key constructs related to the assessment of the DSM-IV psychotic disorders, including schizophrenia, schizoaffective disorder, schizophreniform disorder, brief psychotic disorder, and delusional disorder. The instruments chosen cover the broad range of psychopathology found in patients with these psychotic disorders. Important psychopathological domains covered by these measures include positive (e.g., hallucinations and delusions), negative (e.g., avolition and blunted affect), disorganization (e.g., disorganized speech), mood (e.g., depression, hostility, and excitement), and comorbid substance use symptoms. In addition, two instruments that evaluate areas important to treatment compliance—insight into illness and subjective response to pharmacotherapy—are reviewed.

Organization

The measures included in the chapter are listed in Table 23–1. General psychopathology measures review the broad range of clinically important symptoms that commonly occur in patients with schizophrenia and other psychotic disorders. Although numerous excellent measures of general psychopathology exist, the four instruments reviewed in this chapter were chosen because they

are widely used and have demonstrated reliability and validity. The general psychopathology instruments reviewed here are the Brief Psychiatric Rating Scale (BPRS), the Positive and Negative Syndrome Scale (PANSS), the Scale for the Assessment of Positive Symptoms (SAPS), and the Scale for the Assessment of Negative Symptoms (SANS). Also included is the Schedule for the Deficit Syndrome (SDS), which can help clinicians assess primary negative symptoms in patients with schizophrenia.

Symptoms of comorbid major depressive and substance use disorders are common in patients with schizophrenia and other psychotic disorders. Instruments designed to assess major depressive and substance use disorders in nonpsychotic patients may be less than adequate for patients with schizophrenia (see Chapter 22 and Chapter 24 for a review of these instruments). For example, some symptoms of major depressive disorder, including poor concentration, anhedonia, insomnia, and social withdrawal, are also common symptoms of schizophrenia. In this chapter, we review the Calgary Depression Scale for Schizophrenia (CDSS) and the Clinical Alcohol Use Scale (AUS) and Drug Use Scale (DUS), instruments designed to assess comorbid disorders in patients with schizophrenia and other psychotic disorders.

Many patients with schizophrenia are ambivalent about participating in treatment. Patients' willingness to follow through with a treatment plan is often related to their perception and understanding of the illness and

TABLE 23–1 ■ Psychotic disorders measures

NAME OF MEASURE	DISORDER OR CONSTRUCT ASSESSED	FORMAT	PAGES
Brief Psychiatric Rating Scale (BPRS)*	Severity of general psychopathology, including positive, negative, mood, and behavioral symptoms in patients with moderate to severe mental disorders	Clinician-rated scale; 18 items	490–494
Positive and Negative Syndrome Scale (PANSS) Children's (ages 6–11) version (Kiddie-PANSS)	Severity of positive, negative, and mood symptoms and general psychopathology in patients with schizophrenia and other psychotic disorders	Clinical interview by trained rater or semistructured interview; 30 items	494–497
Scale for the Assessment of Positive Symptoms (SAPS)* Scale for the Assessment of Negative Symptoms (SANS)*	Complementary instruments used to assess the severity of positive, negative, and disorganization symptoms in patients with schizophrenia and other psychotic disorders	Clinical interview by trained rater; the SAPS has 30 items and 4 global domain ratings, and the SANS has 20 items and 5 global domain ratings	498–502
Schedule for the Deficit Syndrome (SDS)	Presence of the deficit syndrome in patients with schizophrenia	Clinician-administered interview; 4 criteria	502–504
Calgary Depression Scale for Schizophrenia (CDSS)*	Symptoms of major depressive episode in patients with schizophrenia	Clinician-administered interview; 9 items	504–507
Clinician Alcohol Use Scale (AUS)* Clinician Drug Use Scale (DUS)*	Severity of substance use disorder in patients with severe mental illness, especially psychotic disorders	Clinician-rated scale; 1 item	507–509
Drug Attitude Inventory (DAI)*	Patient's subjective response to medications	Self-report inventory; 10 items	509–512
Insight and Treatment Attitudes Questionnaire (ITAQ)	Awareness of illness and insight into need for treatment in patients with schizophrenia	Clinician-administered questionnaire; 11 items	512–513

*Measure is included on the CD-ROM that accompanies this handbook.

to their individual assessment of the costs and benefits of treatment. Assessment of insight and treatment attitudes provides the clinician with information that helps identify patients who are likely to comply poorly with treatment. Systematic review of a patient's understanding of his or her illness and appraisal of the risks and benefits of treatment can influence both pharmacological and psychotherapeutic interventions. The two instruments reviewed in this chapter that address issues of insight and treatment attitudes are the Drug Attitude Inventory (DAI) and the Insight and Treatment Attitudes Questionnaire (ITAQ). The DAI elicits patients' subjective assessment of medication helpfulness and side effects. The ITAQ assesses patients' level of knowledge of psychiatric illness and perceived need for treatment.

Relevant Measures Included Elsewhere in the Handbook

Many areas important for the clinical management of schizophrenia and other psychotic disorders are reviewed in detail elsewhere in this book. Schizophrenia often results in significant functional impairment, which has an impact on many areas important to quality of life. The disability associated with schizophrenia may affect work, social relationships, and general life satisfaction. From the patient's (and his or her family's) perspective, improved functional ability and quality of life may be the most important outcomes of treatment. Numerous instruments that have been developed to assess quality of life are appropriate for patients with schizophrenia. In particular, the Quality of Life Interview (QOLI) (p. 138) has been developed specifically for patients with schizophrenia and is relatively easy to administer. Instruments that assess adequacy of housing, economic resources, social relationships, and related quality of life issues, including the QOLI, are reviewed in Chapter 10, "Quality of Life Measures."

The diverse symptoms that occur in patients with schizophrenia and other psychotic disorders result in functional impairment that can range from mild to very severe. For many patients with schizophrenia and other psychotic disorders, symptoms are chronic, and impairment in functioning crosses all aspects of life—work, friendships, family, and management of day-to-day activities. Similar types of functional impairment occur in most chronic, disabling illnesses. Assessing functioning in schizophrenia, as well as in other chronic, disabling psychiatric illnesses, is an important aspect of treatment planning and evaluation. The Multnomah Community Abilities Scale (MCAS) (p. 102) and the Life Skills Profile (LSP) (p. 107) provide assessments of daily functioning that are relevant for persons with psychotic disorders. Measures that assess functional abilities in relation to mental health status, including the MCAS and the LSP, are reviewed in detail in Chapter 8, "Mental Health Status, Functioning, and Disabilities Measures."

Many of the medications used to treat psychotic disorders have adverse effects that are difficult to tolerate and that impair ability to function, quality of life, and willingness to comply with treatment. The conventional antipsychotic medications often cause extrapyramidal side effects (e.g., parkinsonian syndrome and akathisia). Tardive dyskinesia is a potentially irreversible adverse effect associated with treatment with antipsychotic medications. Antipsychotic medications affect several neurotransmitter systems, which can result in various adverse effects, including dry mouth and constipation (due to antagonism at cholinergic receptors), sedation (due to antagonism at histaminic receptors), weight gain (due to antagonism at serotonin receptors), and orthostatic hypotension (due to antagonism at alpha-adrenergic receptors). Instruments to assess adverse effects are reviewed in Chapter 11, "Adverse Effects Measures." Instruments of particular relevance include the Simpson-Angus Rating Scale for Extrapyramidal Side Effects (p. 163), which

assesses parkinsonian side effects, the Barnes Akathisia Rating Scale (BARS) (p. 165), which assesses akathisia, and the Abnormal Involuntary Movement Scale (AIMS) (p. 166), which assesses dyskinetic movement disorders including tardive dyskinesia.

Psychotic symptoms occur in a variety of Axis I disorders, including brief psychotic disorder, schizophreniform disorder, schizophrenia, schizoaffective disorder, delusional disorder, bipolar disorder, major depressive disorder, dementia, delirium, psychotic disorder due to a general medical condition, and substance-induced psychotic disorder. Semistructured interviews such as the Schedule for Affective Disorders and Schizophrenia (SADS) (p. 58), the Structured Clinical Interview for DSM-IV Axis I Disorders (SCID) (p. 49), and the Schedules for Clinical Assessment in Neuropsychiatry (SCAN) (p. 53) (see Chapter 6, "Diagnostic Interviews for Adults") may be useful tools to guide clinicians through the often difficult differential diagnoses of psychotic symptomatology.

Recent studies suggest that as many as 90% of patients with schizophrenia have comorbid conditions. The presence of a comorbid condition usually has important implications for treatment. Comorbid conditions often require separate therapeutic interventions from the primary psychotic illness and sometimes may be the primary clinical focus. A systematic psychiatric review of systems is often essential in detecting comorbid conditions, because patients often do not spontaneously volunteer information about such symptoms. The structured and semistructured diagnostic interviews reviewed in Chapter 6 are also useful tools in screening for comorbid conditions.

USING MEASURES IN THIS DOMAIN

Goals of Assessment

The measures reviewed in this chapter have the common goal of systematically evaluating symptoms that are important for the treatment of patients with schizophrenia and other psychotic disorders. Accurate assessment of clinical symptoms is essential for the appropriate selection of pharmacological, psychotherapeutic, and psychosocial rehabilitative interventions. Appropriate measures of psychopathology help the clinician systematically review potential problem areas in a patient. These tools are also useful for systematically monitoring response to treatment.

Implementation Issues

Many patients with schizophrenia and other psychotic disorders experience a fluctuation of symptoms over time, independent of treatment interventions. Monitoring symptom response to treatment interventions may require sequentially repeated evaluations to detect true symptom improvement over and above random fluctuations in symptom severity.

The items included in many of the measures cover related, but not identical, symptom constructs. Both the descriptions of the symptom and the anchors used to guide severity assessment may differ in important ways. Symptoms that sound similar across instruments may in fact not be interchangeable from one instrument to another. Consequently, use of different tools to longitudinally evaluate symptom severity in a particular patient over multiple points in time is not recommended. For example, using a more detailed tool to assess symptoms initially and a briefer tool for follow-up evaluation is not recommended because of questionable comparability of the results.

The ability of a patient to participate in clinical evaluations often depends on the severity of symptoms at the time of evaluation. Participation may be particularly difficult during the early phases of hospitalization for an acute symptom exacerbation or for more severely ill patients. In particular, severe disorganization, paranoia, and poverty of speech may impair a patient's ability to communicate symptoms. When symptoms are severe, the clinician must often depend on collateral informants to supply relevant clinical information to establish a diagnosis and to assess severity of symptoms. The use of information from family members, close friends, and other health care providers often contributes to the validity of the assessment and, when feasible, is recommended as part of the evaluation process.

Information obtained from informants may contradict information obtained from the patient. For example, the patient may deny hallucinations, but others may describe the patient responding verbally as if to hallucinations. Careful clinical evaluation is required to assess discrepant information from multiple sources. Although there is no consensus, clinicians often rely on the source that provides the most detailed information. Some scales provide specific guidance on how to handle discrepant information.

Negative symptoms (e.g., decreased experience of emotions, decreased expression of emotions, decreased initiation of activities, decreased motivation, and decreased interest in social contact), although clearly of major clinical importance, require a careful differential diagnosis. Negative symptoms that may be primary to schizophrenia have been called the deficit syndrome. Negative symptoms may also occur secondary to major depressive disorder, and the anhedonia that is a hallmark symptom of major depressive disorder may be clinically indistinguishable from the negative symptom of decreased motivation. Social withdrawal and decreased motivation are both common in patients with major depression and are also negative symptoms of schizophrenia. Demoralization and institutionalization are other potential causes of negative symptoms if patients give up seeking employment or attempting to socialize because of repeated failures. The adverse effects of antipsychotic medications may include decreased motivation, decreased experience of emotions, and decreased facial expression, which are very difficult to distinguish from the negative symptoms associated with the disorder itself. Finally, negative symptoms can also occur as a consequence of the patient's positive symptoms. For example, command hallucinations instructing the patient not to move or overwhelming persecutory delusions of danger lurking around every corner can result in withdrawal and decreased initiation of other activities. Most measures of negative symptoms, including all but one measure in this chapter, do not attempt to differentiate primary from secondary negative symptoms, despite the profound treatment implications. The SDS addresses the issue of differentiating primary from secondary negative symptoms and allows the clinician to diagnose the deficit syndrome, which is characterized by primary, enduring negative symptoms.

Issues in Interpreting Psychometric Data

Although there is substantial agreement among the instruments about the symptom domains that should be assessed in patients with schizophrenia and other psychotic disorders, there are important differences concerning the conceptualization of how to group symptoms into particular constructs. For example, studies generally agree that hallucinations and delusions belong to the symptom construct of positive symptoms. However, studies give differing interpretations of positive thought disorder (e.g., looseness of associations); some investigators consider thought disorder a positive symptom, others a negative symptom, and others part of the domain of disorganization. Thus, instruments may differ in the exact items that are included in summary scale scores. Recent carefully designed studies, however, have lent support to the notion that symptoms of behavioral disorganization are not related to either positive or negative symptoms and should therefore be assessed and monitored as an independent domain.

Although the construct of a negative syndrome in schizophrenia and the symptoms that contribute to this construct remain controversial, negative symptoms are clearly an important feature of schizophrenia. Fenton and McGlashan (1992) compared eight scales that purported to measure negative symptoms and found high concordances among the symptoms but little agreement between the variously defined negative syndromes.

GUIDE TO THE SELECTION OF MEASURES

The selection of instruments depends primarily on the clinical need for symptom detection and monitoring. Instruments appropriate for general symptom detection and monitoring include the BPRS, the PANSS, the SAPS, and the SANS. These instruments include items that assess positive, negative, and disorganization symptoms. The BPRS and the PANSS have additional items that assess mood and other general symptoms. In choosing measures of general psychopathology, clinicians need to weigh the time required to administer the assessment tool with the level of detail obtained. It takes more time to get more detailed information about symptoms. Depending on the clinical situation, briefer or more detailed instruments may be appropriate. The BPRS has the fewest items and is less detailed in coverage of each domain but takes the least time to administer. The PANSS is somewhat more detailed and thus takes somewhat longer to administer. The SAPS and the SANS provide comprehensive and detailed assessments of the domains of positive, negative, and disorganization symptoms but take longer to administer. For most tools, however, the time required to review the necessary items decreases over time as they are used with an individual patient (i.e., as

the patient's understanding of the target symptoms increases, he or she often becomes a more efficient informant). Cost may also be a factor in choosing an instrument, because some but not all instruments are available at no cost.

In contrast to measuring the severity of negative symptoms offered by the BPRS, the PANSS, and the SANS, the SDS is designed to differentiate primary from secondary causes of negative symptoms, potentially helping the development of appropriately targeted treatment interventions. The CDSS is best suited for monitoring the severity of depressive symptoms in patients for whom a comorbid major depressive disorder is the focus of treatment. The AUS and the DUS assist in the systematic evaluation of comorbid substance use disorders. The DAI and the ITAQ may be useful early in treatment to evaluate the patient's perceptions of illness and treatment, which may affect his or her compliance with interventions.

CURRENT STATUS AND FUTURE RESEARCH NEEDS FOR ASSESSMENT

The symptom domains that comprise schizophrenia and related psychotic disorders require further clarification and are likely to be modified from their present form over time. Symptom domains are particularly important areas in schizophrenia research, because the available evidence suggests that the various domains of psychopathology may differ in their responsiveness to pharmacological interventions. Also, until recently, the focus has been on the more obvious psychopathology seen in patients with schizophrenia, especially the flamboyant positive symptoms and more disturbing negative symptoms that affect patients' ability to interact socially. Studies have suggested, however, that the less obvious symptoms that affect cognitive abilities, such as impaired concentration and distractibility, impaired working memory, and problems in executive function (e.g., planning), may be very important predictors of functional outcome, but further research is needed concerning the exact nature of the cognitive deficits in patients with schizophrenia and related psychotic disorders. Unfortunately, the instruments available for evaluating cognitive deficits in patients with schizophrenia are designed to be interpreted by a neuropsychologist, require highly specialized training, and are not suitable for use by the general clinician. Instruments to assess cognitive deficits suitable for clinician administration are therefore needed. An instrument that can reliably detect prodromal symptoms of schizophrenia is also needed. Such an instrument could help clinicians plan early interventions that could prevent severe relapses or minimize their consequences. One possible instrument for this purpose, the Early Signs Questionnaire (ESQ) (Herz and Melville 1980), was carefully examined for inclusion in this volume. Although the ESQ has face validity, published data do not support its predictive validity. At this time, no instrument appears to have better clinical utility than a careful clinical interview in detecting the symptoms that signal early relapse.

Except for the PANSS, all of the tools reviewed in this chapter still require paper and pencil administration, and no computerized versions are generally available. In addition, most tools must be administered by a clinician. The development of reliable and valid self-report measures of psychopathology would improve time efficiency when more lengthy interviews are impractical.

REFERENCES AND SUGGESTED READINGS

Andreasen NC: Symptoms, signs, and diagnosis of schizophrenia. Lancet 346:477–481, 1995

Fenton WS, McGlashan TH: Testing systems for assessment of negative symptoms in schizophrenia. Arch Gen Psychiatry 49:179–184, 1992

Herz MI, Melville C: Relapse in schizophrenia. Am J Psychiatry 137:801–805, 1980

Brief Psychiatric Rating Scale (BPRS)

J. E. Overall and D. R. Gorham

GOALS

The Brief Psychiatric Rating Scale (BPRS) (Overall and Gorham 1988) is a clinician-rated tool designed to assess change in severity of psychopathology. The BPRS was initially designed to measure symptom change in patients with psychotic illness. Thus, the items on the BPRS focus on symptoms that are common in patients with psychotic disorders, including schizophrenia and other psychotic disorders, as well as those found in patients with severe mood disorders, especially those with psychotic features. The items cover the broad range of symptoms that are commonly seen in psychotic relapse, including hallucinations, delusions, and disorganization, as well as the mood disturbances that may also accompany relapse (e.g., hostility, anxiety, and depression). The BPRS was not designed to comprehensively measure theoretical domains of psychopathology.

The BPRS provides a continuous total score that is most often used to assess the effectiveness of treatment interventions. The BPRS is also used to classify patients into subgroups to summarize patient characteristics that may predict treatment response.

The BPRS was developed in hospitalized patients with functional psychotic disorders from the longer Lorr Multidimensional Scale for Rating Psychiatric Patients (MSRPP) (Lorr 1953) and the Inpatient Multidimensional Psychiatric Scale (IMPS) (Lorr et al. 1962). Multivariate analytic techniques were used to identify items that were sensitive to change on the basis of change scores before and after pharmacological treatment. Thus, the authors did not attempt to use statistical techniques to identify independent dimensions of psychopathology.

DESCRIPTION

The BPRS includes 18 items that address somatic concern, anxiety, emotional withdrawal, conceptual disorganization, guilt feelings, tension, mannerisms and posturing, grandiosity, depressive mood, hostility, suspiciousness, hallucinatory behaviors, motor retardation, uncooperativeness, unusual thought content, blunted affect, excitement, and disorientation. The scale originally published in 1962 contained only the first 16 items; 2 additional items (excitement and disorientation) were added in 1972. The 18-item BPRS is the most commonly used version.

The BPRS is designed to be administered by experienced clinicians on the basis of information obtained during a clinical interview and from patient observation.

The BPRS has been successfully used to evaluate both inpatients and outpatients. It is less useful for patients with low levels of psychopathology (e.g., adjustment disorders).

Items on the BPRS are rated on a 7-point scale anchored as follows: not present, very mild, mild, moderate, moderately severe, severe, and extremely severe. The total score is the simple sum of the items. Some scoring systems use anchor values with a range of 0–6 and have a total score range of 0–108. Alternative methods use anchors with a range of 1–7 and have a total score range of 18–126.

Although the BPRS is most commonly used without descriptors for each of the anchors, some investigators have developed versions that include explanations for each of the ratings. These more detailed anchors can improve the ease with which reliable or consistent ratings are achieved by both a single clinician over time and especially between raters. Detailed anchor descriptors are also useful in minimizing the gradual changes that occur over time in ratings (i.e., interviewer drift). Many research sites have found use of the more detailed anchor descriptors useful and necessary to obtain reliable ratings among multiple raters. However, the authors of the BPRS argue against the use of detailed explanations for each anchor, because such descriptors could alter the psychometric properties of the BPRS. In addition, they believe that the constructs measured are multidimensional and that detailed anchor descriptions would unnecessarily restrict the meaning of each item.

The time frame used for symptom assessment is typically the week before the current evaluation, although time frames of greater length are also used.

Various factor analytic studies have identified subscales of the BPRS that have descriptive utility. A four-factor solution has been replicated in many studies in different countries. The score for each subscale is obtained by summing the individual items. The four subscales are 1) Thinking Disturbance (sum of scores for conceptual disorganization, hallucinatory behaviors, and unusual thought content), 2) Withdrawal/Retardation (sum of scores for emotional withdrawal and motor retardation), 3) Hostile/Suspiciousness (sum of scores for hostility, suspiciousness, and uncooperativeness), and 4) Anxious/Depression (sum of scores for anxiety, guilt feelings, and depressive mood) (Hedlund and Vieweg 1980). An additional factor, activation (sum of scores for tension, mannerisms and posturing, and excitement), has

also been described (Hedlund and Vieweg 1980). An alternative scoring system groups items as 1) specific to schizophrenia (sum of scores for emotional withdrawal, conceptual disorganization, mannerisms and posturing, grandiosity, suspiciousness, hallucinatory behaviors, unusual thought content, and blunted affect) and 2) general symptoms (sum of scores for somatic concern, anxiety, guilt feelings, tension, depressive mood, hostility, motor retardation, uncooperativeness, excitement, and disorientation) (Gur et al. 1991).

Many systems have been proposed for grouping the items from the BPRS into positive and negative symptom subscales (Nicholson et al. 1995); this approach is driven by the phenomenological distinction and differential treatment response of positive and negative symptoms to treatment interventions. The simplest definitions of positive symptoms (sum of scores on conceptual disorganization, hallucinatory behaviors, and unusual thought content) and negative symptoms (sum of scores on blunted affect, emotional withdrawal, and motor retardation) have demonstrated good reliability and validity (see later section). Other, less widely used subscales for the BPRS have been proposed (Hedlund and Vieweg 1980).

The 21-item BPRS-C has been developed for use with children. The BPRS-C is not related in development or in item structure to the original BPRS (Overall and Pfefferbaum 1982). Thus, the tool shares a common name but is otherwise unrelated to the original BPRS. In addition, the reliability and validity of the BPRS-C have not been investigated, and thus the clinical or research usefulness of the tool is unknown. The BPRS-C is thus not reviewed in detail here; interested readers may refer to Overall and Pfefferbaum (1982).

PRACTICAL ISSUES

It usually takes 20–30 minutes to administer the BPRS, depending on familiarity with the patient and on patient cooperation.

The original 18-item BPRS is available in Overall and Gorham (1988). Commonly used anchors for the BPRS are included in Woerner et al. (1988) and McGorry et al. (1988). Other anchors have also been proposed in the medical literature. The BPRS is in the public domain and is available without cost.

Several semistructured interview guides are available for the BPRS, including one developed by Rhoades and Overall (1988), one from Hillside Hospital (Woerner et al. 1988), and one designed for nurses who work with inpatients (McGorry et al. 1988). The interviews are semistructured and briefly review the domains that depend on patient self-report. The BPRS is to be rated after the interview has been completed, consolidating information gained during the interview.

The BPRS is designed for use by clinicians experienced in the evaluation and treatment of psychotic disorders. Clinicians should review the administration instructions provided in Overall and Gorham (1988) and Rhoades and Overall (1988). If anchored versions are used, the clinician should become familiar with the individual item descriptions and anchors.

The BPRS has been translated into many languages, including Czechoslovakian, Danish, Dutch, French, German, Italian, Spanish, and Turkish.

The BPRS is included on the CD-ROM that accompanies this handbook.

PSYCHOMETRIC PROPERTIES

Reliability

The joint reliability of the BPRS varies with the training and experience of the clinicians performing the ratings and the extent to which the results of joint rating sessions are discussed with the goal of improving reliability over time. Good joint reliability can be achieved on the BPRS, but it often requires substantial time and effort. For example, in a review of published research studies of the BPRS that reported interrater reliability (Hedlund and Vieweg 1980), the Pearson correlations (which tend to overestimate reliability compared with the intraclass correlation coefficient [ICC] in common use today) for the total pathology score were 0.80 or greater for 10 out of 13 studies. The median reported Pearson correlation for individual items ranged from 0.63 to 0.83 in 5 studies. In a Danish study of the psychometric properties of the BPRS, the investigators described needing more than 30 joint rating sessions to achieve consistently reliable scoring among seven psychiatrists (ICC > 0.80). In general, it is more difficult to achieve reliable ratings of the observational items (e.g., blunted affect) than of the items

that use the patient's verbal report of symptomatology (e.g., hallucinatory behaviors).

The effort often required to achieve acceptable joint reliability has prompted several study sites to develop and use versions of the BPRS with detailed anchor descriptors. For example, an inpatient treatment unit for patients with functional psychosis was able to achieve good joint reliability by nursing staff using a version of the BPRS with detailed anchor descriptors. Staff training was minimal and consisted of an overview of the instrument and routine joint ratings of patients. The weighted kappa coefficient ranged from 0.52 to 0.90 for individual items; the mean value for all items was 0.72. Another research group found improvement in reliability for 15 of the 18 items when moving from original anchors to anchors with detailed descriptors (Gabbard et al. 1987).

Assessments of internal consistency have not been reported for most subscales. The simplest definition of positive symptoms and negative symptoms has demonstrated good internal consistency (Cronbach's alpha of 0.81 and 0.91, respectively) (Nicholson et al. 1995).

Validity

Numerous studies have compared BPRS results with results from other scales (Hedlund and Vieweg 1980). The reported validity of the BPRS is generally high when compared with that of other measures of general psychopathology. Items from the BPRS that are components of the diagnostic criteria for schizophrenia (i.e., emotional withdrawal, conceptual disorganization, mannerisms and posturing, grandiosity, suspiciousness, hallucinatory behaviors, unusual thought content, and blunted affect) have been found to be correlated ($r = 0.63$) with scores on two scales designed to measure the severity of positive symptoms (the Scale for the Assessment of Positive Symptoms [SAPS] [p. 498]) and negative symptoms (the Scale for the Assessment of Negative Symptoms [SANS] [p. 498]) in a study of 47 patients with schizophrenia or schizoaffective disorder (Gur et al. 1991). In addition, in a study of 56 patients with schizophrenia or schizoaffective disorder (Bell et al. 1992), the positive and negative symptom scales of the BPRS were highly correlated with the same scales from the Positive and Negative Syndrome Scale (PANSS) (p. 494) ($r = 0.92$ and 0.82, respectively). Total scores from the PANSS and the BPRS were also highly correlated ($r = 0.84$), although the general scale scores were only moderately correlated ($r = 0.61$). In this same study, individual items from the BPRS were modestly related to similar items from the PANSS. Three items on the BPRS were in excellent agreement (kappa > 0.75 for hallucinatory behaviors, grandiosity, and blunted affect), and eight other items had good agreement (kappa = 0.60–0.74 for unusual thought content, conceptual disorganization, suspiciousness, somatic concern, guilt feelings, depressive mood, motor retardation, and disorientation). Agreement was only fair to poor (kappa < 0.60) for the remaining seven BPRS items (excitement, hostility, anxiety, tension, mannerisms and posturing, uncooperativeness, and emotional withdrawal).

Several hundred studies have successfully used the BPRS to measure change in pharmacological and non-pharmacological treatment trials (see Hedlund and Vieweg 1980), including recent trials with the atypical antipsychotic medications (e.g., Tollefson et al. 1997). Concurrent validity in these studies is demonstrated by similar changes as measured by other tools, including the Clinical Global Impressions (CGI) Scale (p. 100), the Hamilton Rating Scale for Depression (Ham-D) (p. 526), and the Nursing Observation Scale for Inpatient Evaluation (Faustman 1994; Hedlund and Vieweg 1980; McGorry et al. 1988).

CLINICAL UTILITY

The BPRS has been in widespread use for more than 30 years and remains popular for research studies that assess patient change in response to treatment interventions. In the clinical setting, the BPRS is most appropriately used as a global measure of response to treatment interventions in patients with moderate to severe psychotic disorders.

The primary advantage of the BPRS is that it provides a simple and efficient review and summary of a broad range of clinically relevant psychopathology. The BPRS is brief, taking about 20–30 minutes (or less) to administer. The items of the BPRS are consistent with domains routinely covered in typical clinical assessments in patients with psychotic disorders and include the clinically relevant domains of positive and negative symptoms.

The usefulness of the BPRS in clinical settings has not been empirically demonstrated. Clinicians may have to expend much effort to rate the items consistently, par-

ticularly in the original version without detailed descriptions to accompany the anchors. Use of versions with detailed anchor descriptors and semistructured interviews usually reduces the time it takes to achieve acceptable reliability of ratings and increases the ultimate level of reliability achieved. In addition, although the items are broad and reflect important common target symptoms for treatment interventions, the tool does not cover all areas of potential interest to the clinician. The BPRS is not diagnostic of a particular disorder. Finally, the tool is less able to assess change in patients with relatively mild levels of psychopathology (Overall and Gorham 1988).

REFERENCES AND SUGGESTED READINGS

Bell M, Milstein R, Beam-Goulet J, et al: The Positive and Negative Syndrome Scale and the Brief Psychiatric Rating Scale: reliability, comparability, and predictive validity. J Nerv Ment Dis 180:723–728, 1992

Faustman WO: Brief Psychiatric Rating Scale, in The Use of Psychological Testing for Treatment Planning and Outcome Assessment. Edited by Maruish ME. Hillsdale, NJ, Erlbaum, 1994, pp 371–401

Gabbard GO, Kennedy LL, Deering CD, et al: Interrater reliability in the use of the Brief Psychiatric Rating Scale. Bull Menninger Clin 51:519–531, 1987

Gur RE, Mozley PD, Resnick SM, et al: Relations among clinical scales in schizophrenia. Am J Psychiatry 148:472–478, 1991

Hedlund JL, Vieweg BW: The Brief Psychiatric Rating Scale (BPRS): a comprehensive review. Journal of Operational Psychiatry 11:48–65, 1980

Lorr M: Multidimensional Scale for Rating Psychiatric Patients. Veteran's Administration Technical Bulletin 10-507:1–44, 1953

Lorr M, Klett CJ, McNair DM, et al: Inpatient Multidimensional Psychiatric Scale Manual. Palo Alto, CA, Consulting Psychologists Press, 1962

McGorry PD, Goodwin RJ, Stuart GW: The development, use, and reliability of the Brief Psychiatric Rating Scale (Nursing Modification): an assessment procedure for the nursing team in clinical and research settings. Compr Psychiatry 29:575–587, 1988

Nicholson IR, Chapman JE, Neufeld RWJ: Variability in BPRS definitions of positive and negative symptoms. Schizophr Res 17:177–185, 1995

Overall JE, Gorham DR: The Brief Psychiatric Rating Scale (BPRS): recent developments in ascertainment and scaling. Psychopharmacol Bull 24:97–99, 1988

Overall JE, Pfefferbaum B: The Brief Psychiatric Rating Scale for Children. Psychopharmacol Bull 18:10–16, 1982

Rhoades HM, Overall JE: The semistructured BPRS Interview and Rating Guide. Schizophr Bull 24:101–104, 1988

Tollefson GD, Beasley CM Jr, Tron PV, et al: Olanzapine versus haloperidol in the treatment of schizophrenia and schizoaffective and schizophreniform disorders: results of an instructional collaborative trial. Am J Psychiatry 154:457–465, 1997

Woerner MG, Mannuzza S, Kane JM: Anchoring the BPRS: an aid to improved reliability. Psychopharmacol Bull 24:112–117, 1988

Positive and Negative Syndrome Scale (PANSS)

S. R. Kay, L. A. Opler, and A. Fiszbein

GOALS

The Positive and Negative Syndrome Scale (PANSS) (Kay et al. 1987a), designed to measure severity of psychopathology in adult patients with schizophrenia, schizoaffective disorder, and other psychotic disorders, emphasizes positive and negative symptom dimensions. The Positive and Negative scales are intended to measure the theoretical constructs of positive and negative symptoms in patients with schizophrenia. The General Psychopathology scale is meant to measure nonspecific symptoms and does not have a basis in a theoretical construct.

Items from the PANSS include those of the Brief Psychiatric Rating Scale (BPRS) (p. 490) and additional items from the Psychopathology Rating Schedule (Singh and Kay 1987). The goal of the authors was to develop a rating scale that improved on the BPRS by including additional symptoms that are clinically important in schizophrenia, including mood symptoms and additional negative symptom items. In addition, the PANSS was

developed with an expanded and well-described anchor system to improve the reliability of ratings. The Kiddie-PANSS (Fields et al. 1994) is an adaptation of the PANSS for children and adolescents ages 6–16 with severe psychiatric illness (e.g., schizophrenia, schizoaffective disorder, and pervasive developmental disorders). The definitions of 10 of the 30 PANSS items have been modified, and most of the anchors are modified to account for developmental differences in symptom expression in children and adolescents. The Kiddie-PANSS is still in development.

DESCRIPTION

The PANSS includes 3 scales and 30 items: 7 items make up the Positive scale (examples are delusions, conceptual disorganization, and hallucinatory behavior), 7 items make up the Negative scale (examples are blunted affect, emotional withdrawal, poor rapport, and passive/apathetic social withdrawal), and 16 items make up the General Psychopathology scale (examples are somatic concern, anxiety, guilt feelings, mannerisms and posturing, motor retardation, uncooperativeness, disorientation, poor impulse control, and preoccupation). PANSS ratings are made after the completion of a semistructured interview and using additional reports of daily function from caregivers or family members and a review of available clinical material.

The recommended interview begins with asking the patient to discuss his or her illness and life circumstances generally. This part of the interview should last several minutes and be nondirective so that observer-rated items can be evaluated. The interviewer then explores possible symptoms that have been volunteered. Next, the interviewer asks specific questions to elicit information about the presence and severity of other symptoms evaluated on the PANSS. The final portion of the interview focuses as needed on areas in which the patient was defensive, ambivalent, or guarded to clarify specific symptoms. The interviewer may be more confrontational in this portion of the interview and assess the impact of this stress on the patient's conceptual organization. The time frame for rating the PANSS must be specified and is usually the week before rating. A semistructured interview, the Structured Clinical Interview for the Positive and Negative Syndrome Scale (SCI-PANSS) (Opler et al. 1992), is also available from the publisher.

Administration of the Kiddie-PANSS requires a primary caregiver interview and a structured play interview designed to specifically evaluate symptoms in children with major psychiatric illness.

Individual items are scored on an anchored Likert scale; values range from 1 to 7. Scores above 1 indicate that a clinical symptom is present, and ratings of 2–7 indicate increasing severity. Detailed anchors are provided for severity ratings.

The items from the PANSS are summed to determine scores on the Positive, Negative, and General Psychopathology scales and total PANSS scores. The potential range for the Positive and Negative scales is 7–49, and the range for the General Psychopathology scale is 16–112. Normative data for the PANSS is available from a study of 240 adult patients (61 women, 179 men, 106 blacks, 60 whites, and 74 Hispanics) who met DSM-III criteria for schizophrenia and were taking antipsychotic medication (Kay and Sevy 1990). The mean age of these patients was 33 years, and the mean duration of illness was 11 years. In this study, the 50th percentile corresponded to a raw score of 20 on the Positive, 22 on the Negative, and 40 on the General Psychopathology scales. Raw scores on the PANSS scales may be converted to T-scores by using the profile form, which is available from the publisher.

The PANSS may also be scored to indicate predominantly positive or negative symptom typology by using the Composite scale score, which is derived by taking the difference of the Negative from the Positive scale score. The Composite scale scores may range from –42 (when only negative symptoms are present) to +42 (when only positive symptoms are present). A patient may be considered to have the positive subtype when the valence of the Composite scale score is positive, and the negative subtype when the valence is negative.

PRACTICAL ISSUES

It takes 30–40 minutes to administer and score the PANSS interview. The PANSS is designed to be administered by trained mental health professionals (e.g., psychiatrists, psychologists, clinical social workers, and psychiatric nurses). Users of the PANSS should have

training in psychiatric interview techniques and clinical experience working with patients with schizophrenia and related psychotic disorders.

The PANSS, the SCI-PANSS, and the Kiddie-PANSS are copyrighted by the authors and Multi-Health Systems, Inc. The PANSS, a manual that describes the PANSS and provides basic information on administration and scoring (Kay et al. 1994), the SCI-PANSS, administration instructions, scoring manuals, and score sheets are all available from the publisher:

Multi-Health Systems, Inc.
908 Niagara Falls Boulevard
North Tonawanda, New York 14120-2060
Phone: 800-456-3003
Internet: www.mhs.com

A computerized form of the PANSS that can be used to administer, score, and produce scale results is in development.

The Kiddie-PANSS is currently available from the authors, but a published version including a manual is in development and will be available in the future from Multi-Health Systems, Inc.

The cost of the PANSS manual, 25 SCI-PANSS interviews, and 25 QuikScore forms is $95.00. Additional SCI-PANSS interviews are available at a cost of $50.00 for 25 and $180.00 for 100. Cost for the Kiddie-PANSS has not yet been established by Multi-Health Systems, Inc.

The PANSS has been translated into numerous languages, including Chinese, Danish, Dutch, Finnish, French, German, Italian, Norwegian, Polish, Spanish, and Swedish. Psychometric data are available for the French, German, Italian, Spanish, and Swedish versions.

PSYCHOMETRIC PROPERTIES

Reliability

Numerous investigators have been able to establish good to excellent joint reliability with the PANSS; intraclass correlation coefficients (ICCs) above 0.80 for the Positive, Negative, and General Psychopathology scales are readily obtainable (Kay 1990). In most cases, clinicians are able to reliably rate the PANSS items after corating and discussing 8–10 patient interviews.

Good internal consistency of the Positive, Negative, and General Psychopathology scales has been demonstrated in several studies (Kay et al. 1994). For example, in a study of 101 patients with chronic, stable, severe schizophrenia, internal consistency as measured by Cronbach's alpha was 0.73 for the Positive scale, 0.83 for the Negative scale, and 0.87 for the General Psychopathology scale (Kay et al. 1987b).

The reliability of the Kiddie-PANSS has similarly been demonstrated in a study of 34 children, ages 6–16, who were hospitalized with schizophrenia and other severe mental illnesses (Fields et al. 1994). The joint reliability was high (ICC = 0.76, 0.78, 0.81, and 0.86 for the Positive, Negative, General Psychopathology, and Total scales, respectively). Internal consistency of the Positive, Negative, and General Psychopathology scales was moderate to good (Cronbach's alpha = 0.61, 0.82, and 0.78, respectively).

Validity

Studies comparing the Positive and Negative subscales of the PANSS with similar scales from the BPRS (p. 488), the Scale for the Assessment of Positive Symptoms (SAPS) (p. 498), and the Scale for the Assessment of Negative Symptoms (SANS) (p. 498) have consistently demonstrated good concurrent validity. For example, concurrent ratings were made during joint interviews with the PANSS and BPRS in 56 hospitalized patients with schizophrenia or schizoaffective disorder. There was moderate agreement of the individual items in the PANSS shared with the BPRS, with ICC > 0.70 for 14 corresponding items, and even lower agreement for the corresponding items rating anxiety (ICC = 0.57), uncooperativeness (ICC = 0.51), mannerism and posturing (ICC = 0.68), and emotional withdrawal (ICC = 0.43) (Bell et al. 1992). Thus it appears that the PANSS item definitions and severity anchors significantly alter the meaning of the corresponding items from the BPRS.

In another study, concurrent ratings of 51 patients with schizophrenia showed high correlation (r) between the PANSS Positive subscale and the SAPS (0.77) and between the PANSS Negative subscale and the SANS (0.77) (Kay et al. 1987b). Furthermore, the correlation (r) between the PANSS General Psychopathology subscale and the Clinical Global Impression (CGI) Scale (p. 100) was 0.52 (Kay et al. 1987b).

Comparisons of ratings on the Kiddie-PANSS Positive scale with simultaneous ratings on unmodified versions of the SAPS, the SANS, and the Child Behavior Checklist (CBCL) (p. 309) demonstrated good concurrent validity (r = 0.69, 0.89, and 0.52, respectively) (Fields et al. 1994).

A factor analytic study done by the PANSS authors with 240 inpatients with schizophrenia lends partial support to the assessment of valid syndromes by the Positive and Negative scales (Kay et al. 1994). Five PANSS negative symptom items loaded on a Negative factor (emotional withdrawal, passive/apathetic social withdrawal, lack of spontaneity and flow of conversation, blunted affect, and poor rapport). The remaining negative symptoms (abstract thinking and stereotyped thinking) loaded on a Cognitive and Other factor. Three PANSS positive symptoms loaded on a Positive factor (delusions, hallucinatory behavior, and grandiosity), two others (hostility and excitement) loaded on an Excited factor, and the remaining two (conceptual disorganization and suspiciousness/persecution) loaded on a Cognitive and Other factor. The Cognitive and Other factor contains items that appear to reflect disorganization, as characterized by Andreasen and others (see discussion of SAPS [p. 498], including conceptual disorganization, difficulty in abstract thinking, stereotyped thinking, and disorientation). The two other factors, Excited and Depressive, appear to reflect mood symptoms and impassivity, symptoms frequently described in patients with schizophrenia.

Similar factors have been obtained by other investigators, including Positive, Negative, Cognitive, Hostility (corresponding to Excited), and Emotional Discomfort (corresponding to Depressive) factors. In a study of 147 patients with schizophrenia diagnosed on the basis of DSM-III-R criteria (Bell et al. 1994), scores on the Cognitive factor (difficulty in abstract thinking, stereotyped thinking, cognitive disorganization, lack of judgment and insight, poor attention, and mannerisms and posturing) were significantly correlated with cognitive impairment as measured by neuropsychological test performance, especially on a test that assesses higher cortical function. Neuropsychological function was not significantly related to severity of illness. In addition, in a subgroup of 61 of these patients, PANSS Cognitive and Negative factor scores significantly predicted successful work performance after 13 weeks in a rehabilitative work program (Bell and Lysaker 1995).

The PANSS has been successfully used to monitor treatment response in numerous studies. In addition, studies of the PANSS have shown differential treatment response of positive and negative symptoms to pharmacological treatment interventions.

CLINICAL UTILITY

The PANSS provides an objective and reliable assessment of common symptoms in patients with schizophrenia and other psychotic disorders. The PANSS may be used in clinical settings to assess severity of symptoms, to delineate and describe target symptoms, and to quantify severity of relapse. In particular, the PANSS is potentially useful as a quantified monitor of response to treatment interventions.

The advantage of the PANSS is that it provides a comprehensive review of symptoms that are clinically important in the treatment of schizophrenia and other psychotic disorders. Positive, negative, and disorganization symptoms, as well as associated disturbances in mood, are covered. The PANSS may be administered as part of a routine clinical interview and usually requires at least a 30- to 40-minute interview to achieve adequate ratings. The PANSS items are well described and carefully anchored, making the instrument relatively easy to use reliably. A version appropriate for children and adolescents is also available.

The usefulness of the PANSS in clinical settings has not been empirically demonstrated. The validity of the symptom constructs, including the positive, negative, and disorganization domains, is an active, evolving area of phenomenological study in schizophrenia. The clinical usefulness of these constructs is probably limited to differential treatment effects on positive, negative, mood, and disorganization symptoms. Future studies may provide the clinician with better information about how specific symptoms and symptom constructs respond differentially to pharmacological and other treatment interventions and relate to the prognosis and etiology of psychotic diseases.

The PANSS is sensitive to symptom change and thus is a useful tool to assess symptom response to treatment interventions. The PANSS may also be used as a prognostic indicator, with patients who have predominately negative symptoms as having a poorer prognosis (Kay et al. 1994).

REFERENCES AND SUGGESTED READINGS

Bell MD, Lysaker PH: Psychiatric symptoms and work performance among persons with severe mental illness. Psychiatr Serv 46:508–510, 1995

Bell M, Milstein R, Beam-Goulet J, et al: The Positive and Negative Syndrome Scale and the Brief Psychiatric Rating Scale: reliability, comparability, and predictive validity. J Nerv Ment Dis 180:723–728, 1992

Bell MD, Lysaker PH, Milstein RM, et al: Concurrent validity of the cognitive component of schizophrenia: relationship of PANSS scores to neuropsychological assessments. Psychiatry Res 54:51–58, 1994

Fields JF, Kay SR, Grosz D, et al: Assessing positive and negative symptoms in children and adolescents. Am J Psychiatry 151:249–253, 1994

Kay SR: Positive-negative symptom assessment in schizophrenia: psychometric issues and scale comparison. Psychiatr Q 61:163–178, 1990

Kay SR, Sevy S: Pyramidical model of schizophrenia. Schizophr Bull 16:537–545, 1990

Kay SR, Fiszbein A, Opler LA: The Positive and Negative Syndrome Scale (PANSS) for schizophrenia. Schizophr Bull 13:261–276, 1987a

Kay SR, Opler LA, Lindenmayer JP: Reliability and validity of the Positive and Negative Syndrome Scale for schizophrenics. Psychiatry Res 23:99–110, 1987b

Kay SR, Opler LA, Fiszbein A: Positive and Negative Syndrome Scale Manual. North Tonawanda, NY, Multi-Health Systems, 1994

Opler LA, Kay SR, Lindenmayer JP, et al: Structured Clinical Interview for the Positive and Negative Syndrome Scale (SCI-PANSS). Toronto, Multi-Health Systems, 1992

Singh MM, Kay SR: Anticholinergic-neuroleptic antagonism in terms of positive and negative symptoms of schizophrenia: implications for psychobiological subtyping. Psychol Med 17:39–48, 1987

Scale for the Assessment of Positive Symptoms (SAPS) and Scale for the Assessment of Negative Symptoms (SANS)

N. Andreasen

GOALS

The Scale for the Assessment of Positive Symptoms (SAPS) (Andreasen 1984) and the Scale for the Assessment of Negative Symptoms (SANS) (Andreasen 1982, 1983) are complementary instruments used to assess the severity of symptoms in patients with schizophrenia or other psychotic disorders. The primary goal of the SAPS is to assess positive and disorganization symptom psychopathology, including hallucinations, delusions, bizarre behaviors, and formal thought disorder. The SANS is designed to rate the presence and severity of negative symptoms, including affective flattening, social withdrawal, and avolition.

The SAPS and the SANS have been used primarily as research tools to explore the phenomenology of schizophrenia and to evaluate treatment response. The SAPS provides detailed documentation of positive and disorganization symptoms that are clinically important and are commonly responsive to antipsychotic medications. The negative symptoms measured by the SANS are hypothesized to be associated with poorer prognosis and poorer response to typical antipsychotic medications.

DESCRIPTION

The SAPS contains 30 items and the SANS contains 20 items that are organized into domains. The SAPS domains include Hallucinations, Delusions, Bizarre Behavior, and Formal Thought Disorder. The SANS domains include Affective Flattening and Blunting, Alogia, Avolition-Apathy, Anhedonia-Asociality, and Attentional Impairment. The number of items varies according to the domain. Each domain includes assessment of specific symptoms and a global item representing the rater's determination of the overall severity of the symptoms in that domain.

The SAPS domains contain the following individual items:

1. Hallucinations: auditory hallucinations, voices commenting, voices conversing, somatic or tactile hallucinations, olfactory hallucinations, and visual hallucinations
2. Delusions: persecutory, of jealousy, of sin or guilt, grandiose, religious, somatic, reference, controlled, mind reading, thought broadcasting, thought insertion, and thought withdrawal
3. Bizarre Behavior: clothing and appearance, social and sexual behavior, aggressive and agitated behavior, and repetitive behavior
4. Formal Thought Disorder: derailment, tangentially, incoherence, illogicality, circumstantially, pressure of speech, distractible speech, and clanging

In addition to the 30 individual items, a global severity rating is made for each of the 4 SAPS domains (Hallucinations, Delusions, Bizarre Behavior, and Formal Thought Disorder).

The SANS domains contain the following individual items:

1. Affective Flattening and Blunting: unchanging facial expression, decreased spontaneous movements, paucity of expressive gestures, poor eye contact, affective nonresponsivity, inappropriate affect, and lack of vocal inflections
2. Alogia: poverty of speech, poverty of content of speech, blocking, and increased latency of response
3. Avolition-Apathy: grooming and hygiene, impersistence at work or school, and physical anergia
4. Anhedonia-Asociality: recreational interests and activities, sexual interest and activity, ability to feel intimacy and closeness, and relationships with friends and peers
5. Attentional Impairment: social inattentiveness and inattentiveness during mental status testing

In addition to the 20 individual items, a global severity rating is made for each of the 5 SANS domains (Affective Flattening and Blunting, Alogia, Avolition-Apathy, Anhedonia—Asociality, and Attentional Impairment).

Ratings are made by trained raters on the basis of a standard clinical interview, observed behaviors during the interview, review of clinical material, and collateral information from the subject's family and caregivers.

A relevant time frame should be specified by the clinician; in reported studies the time frame has varied from the past week for patients in treatment for an acute episode to the past 6 months for patients with chronic, clinically stable illness.

Each of the SANS and SAPS items are scored on a 6-point Likert-type scale (0–5). A score of 0 means that the symptom (or symptom complex) is absent, and a score of 5 means that the symptom (or symptom complex) is present in a severe form. A subscale score for each domain is the sum of the scores for each item in that domain, including the global rating. The range of scores for each subscale depends on the number of items in that domain. For example, the Affective Flattening and Blunting subscale contains eight items, so the range of scores is 0–40, whereas the Attentional Impairment subscale contains three items, so the range of scores is 0–15. For the SAPS, the sum of the 4 global domain scores produces a summary score (ranging from 0 to 20), and the sum of the 30 individual items provides a composite score (ranging from 0 to 150). For the SANS the sum of the 5 global domain scores produces a summary score (ranging from 0 to 25), and the sum of the 20 individual items provides a composite score (ranging from 0 to 100). The author of the scale recommends using the summary score as a measure of overall severity of positive and negative symptom severity. Higher scores represent more severe impairment than lower scores.

PRACTICAL ISSUES

The SAPS and the SANS each take approximately 30 minutes to administer. Raters are expected to be psychiatric clinicians, and training specific to the scales is required to achieve reliable ratings. Valid administration of the scales requires clinical experience working with patients with schizophrenia and related psychotic disorders, as well as training and experience in psychiatric interview techniques. The instrument and the training manuals provide basic information needed for administration and scoring.

The scales are copyrighted and are available from the author without cost. Manuals describing the SAPS (Andreasen 1984) and the SANS (Andreasen 1983) and the Comprehensive Assessment of Symptoms and History (CASH) (Andreasen et al. 1992), in which a semistructured diagnostic interview for the SAPS and the SANS is embedded, are available from the authors. Permission to use the SAPS and the SANS should be sought from the author:

> Nancy P. Andreasen, M.D., Ph.D.
> 200 Hawkins Drive
> Room 2911 JPP
> Iowa City, IA 52242
> Phone: 319-356-1553

The SANS has been translated into Chinese, Dutch, French, German, Italian, Japanese, Polish, Spanish, and Swedish. The psychometric properties of the SANS have been explored for the Chinese, French, Italian, and Spanish versions. The SAPS has been translated into Chinese, French, German, Italian, Japanese, Polish, and Spanish, and psychometric properties have been evaluated for the Chinese, French, Italian, Japanese, and Spanish versions, as well as a version used in India (Moscarelli et al. 1987; Phillips et al. 1991).

The SAPS and the SANS are included on the CD-ROM that accompanies this handbook.

PSYCHOMETRIC PROPERTIES

Reliability

Several published studies examine the reliability of the SAPS and the SANS, and numerous research groups report reliable use of the tools in diverse studies of treatment, phenomenology, and neurobiology of psychotic disorders. A study designed to compare the interrater reliability of the SAPS and the SANS with the PANSS involved joint interviews of 85 patients with schizophrenia (Norman et al. 1996). Raters were random pairs of four experienced clinicians who were trained on all instruments. The interrater reliability for the SAPS summary score was good and for the SANS summary score was fair (0.84 and 0.60, respectively). For the SAPS global domain scores the intraclass correlation coefficients (ICCs) were fair to excellent (Hallucinations, 0.91; Delusions, 0.86; Bizarre Behavior, 0.50; and Formal Thought Disorder, 0.75). For the SANS global domain scores the ICCs were mostly fair (Affective Flattening and Blunting, 0.35; Alogia, 0.57; Avolition-Apathy, 0.53; Anhedonia-Asociality, 0.64; and Attentional Impairment, 0.46). Other investigators have reported generally acceptable levels of interrater reliability with the SAPS and the SANS, however. For example, in a study of the test-retest reliability of the SAPS and the SANS (Malla et al. 1993), interrater reliability on the basis of 15 joint interviews was excellent, with an ICC of 0.94 for the SAPS summary score and 0.84 for the SANS summary score. For the global ratings of each domain the ICCs ranged from 0.61 to 0.98. The author of the SANS has reported that the ICCs for individual items on the SANS ranged from 0.70 to 0.92 (Andreasen 1982). In addition, the summary score ICC was 0.92, and the ICC for the five domains ranged from 0.86 to 0.93. As with these studies, most published studies using the SAPS and the SANS report establishing good to excellent levels of interrater reliability.

In addition, moderate test-retest reliability for the SAPS and the SANS is demonstrated in a study of 59 stable patients with schizophrenia tested initially and 1 year later (Malla et al. 1993). Here ICCs were 0.64 for the SAPS total score and 0.45 for the SANS total score. For the SAPS domains the test-retest ICCs ranged from 0.25 to 0.55, and for the SANS domains test-retest ICCs ranged from 0.13 to 0.40. Test-retest reliability of the Chinese version of the SANS has also been evaluated (Phillips et al. 1991). The range of values among the subscales was 0.66–0.87, and the composite ICC value was 0.82. The modest levels of test-retest reliability most likely reflect the fluctuations of symptom severity commonly seen in patients with psychotic disorders in addition to the variability inherent in the SAPS and the SANS.

The internal consistency of the SAPS and the SANS is high. For example, in a study of 117 patients with schizophrenia (Andreasen and Grove 1986), Cronbach's alpha values for the four SAPS domains were 0.75 for Hallucinations, 0.66 for Delusions, 0.74 for Formal Thought Disorder, and 0.79 for Bizarre Behavior. Cronbach's alpha values for the five SANS domains were 0.63 for Alogia, 0.83 for Affective Flattening and Blunting, 0.74 for Avolition-Apathy, 0.77 for Anhedonia-Asociality, and 0.75 for Attentional Impairment. The internal consistency of the overall SAPS assessed by examining the four global domains is relatively low (Cronbach's alpha of 0.48), reflecting the two distinct constructs (positive and disorganization symptoms) measured by the SAPS. The internal consistency of the overall SANS assessed by examining the five global domains is high (Cronbach's alpha of 0.86),

suggesting that the SANS is assessing an internally consistent construct. Other studies have reported similar results for internal consistency of the SAPS and the SANS (e.g., Andreasen 1982; Mueser et al. 1994; Phillips et al. 1991).

Validity

Concurrent ratings of patients with the SAPS and the SANS and other commonly used scales that assess positive and negative symptoms in schizophrenia, including the Positive and Negative Syndrome Scale (PANSS) (p. 494) and the Brief Psychiatric Rating Scale (BPRS) (p. 490), have consistently shown high correlations between scales, suggesting that these scales measure similar constructs. For example, correlations were generally high in a comparison of the SAPS and the SANS with the corresponding scales on the PANSS on the basis of concurrent joint ratings of 85 patients with schizophrenia (Norman et al. 1996). In this study the correlation of SAPS summary scores with PANSS Positive subscale scores was 0.91 and that of SANS summary scores with PANSS Negative subscale scores was 0.88. A study using joint interviews of 100 patients with schizophrenia compared ratings on the BPRS with those on the SAPS and the SANS (Nicholson et al. 1995). Various definitions of BPRS negative symptoms demonstrated high correlations with the SANS composite score ($r > 0.85$). Similarly high correlations were found when comparing various definitions of the BPRS positive symptoms with the SAPS composite score ($r > 0.89$).

The commonly described factors from the BPRS may assess overlapping but somewhat different constructs from those assessed by the SAPS and the SANS. A study using concurrent ratings of the BPRS, SAPS, and SANS in 47 patients with schizophrenia found modest correlations of the severity of BPRS schizophrenia items with the SANS (0.38) and SAPS (0.61) summary scores (Gur et al. 1991). Correlations of the SAPS and SANS domain scores with the BPRS factors of anxiety-depression, activity, and hostility were generally low, suggesting that these BPRS factors reflect different constructs than those measured by the SAPS and the SANS. The SAPS domains of Hallucinations, Delusions, and Formal Thought Disorder were modestly correlated with the BPRS thought disorder factor ($r = 0.53$–058), suggesting that the scales are assessing related but not identical constructs. Similarly, the SANS domains were modestly correlated with the BPRS anergic factor ($r = 0.43$–0.69).

The Schedule for the Deficit Syndrome (SDS) (p. 502) may also evaluate an overlapping but not identical construct to that assessed with the SANS. Individual patients classified as having the deficit syndrome had higher mean scores on the SANS domain scales but did not differ from patients without the deficit disorder on the SAPS domain scales (deficit-nondeficit by negative-positive interaction, $F = 12.13$, $P < 0.0001$) (Gur et al. 1991). Thus the SANS, BPRS anergia factor, and deficit syndrome assessments appear to be measuring related but not identical constructs.

The predictive validity of the SAPS and the SANS has been demonstrated by the numerous studies in which these scales have been successfully used to monitor treatment response (e.g., Shiloh et al. 1997; Tollefson et al. 1997).

The authors have systematically and carefully investigated the validity of the psychopathological constructs measured by the SAPS when it has been administered in conjunction with the SANS (see Andreasen et al. 1995a, 1995b for a review). Although the symptoms measured by the SAPS were originally conceived of as a single domain, numerous cross-sectional and one longitudinal factor analysis indicated that the SAPS actually measures two separate domains, Psychoticism and Disorganization. The Psychoticism factor consists of the Hallucinations and Delusions items, and the Disorganization factor contains the Formal Thought Disorder and Bizarre Behavior items from the SAPS and the Affective Flattening and Blunting item from the SANS (Andreasen et al. 1995a, 1995b).

Factor analyses of the SANS have yielded conflicting results. Mueser et al. (1994) found a three-factor model (affective blunting, avolition and anhedonia, and alogia-inattention) to be most parsimonious. Factor analyses using all items from both the SAPS and the SANS (Moscarelli et al. 1987; Phillips et al. 1991) found the negative symptom complex to be very cohesive. Thus, there is considerable support for a negative syndrome, but the usefulness of the SANS subscales is less clear.

CLINICAL UTILITY

The SANS and the SAPS used together comprehensively describe symptoms in patients with schizophrenia and other psychotic disorders. They have been success-fully used together to monitor treatment response in numerous studies. The SAPS and the SANS may be used to quantify the severity of psychotic, disorganization, and negative symptoms in patients with schizophrenia and other psychotic disorders reliably and objectively. They can delineate and provide detailed documentation of the severity of specific target symptoms (e.g., thought broadcasting, visual hallucinations, and derailment). In particular, the SAPS and the SANS are potentially useful in monitoring and quantifying response to treatment interventions and in quantifying the severity of relapse.

The SAPS and the SANS may be administered as part of a routine clinical interview. The items are well described and carefully anchored, making the instruments relatively easy to use reliably. A potential advantage of the SAPS and the SANS in clinical settings is that the global rating includes the impact of the symptom on patient functioning. The SAPS and the SANS collect highly detailed information about positive, negative, and disorganization symptoms.

The validity of the psychopathological constructs that underlie these tools continues to evolve. The authors have reported that they are developing revisions of scaling that should further improve on the validity and clinical usefulness of the SAPS (Andreasen et al. 1995b). Neither the SAPS nor the SANS includes items to assess the mood symptoms (e.g., depression and excitement) that often occur in patients with psychotic disorders, especially at times of symptom exacerbation.

As research tools, the SAPS and the SANS have proven their utility in numerous studies of phenomenology and in clinical trials. Their usefulness in clinical settings has not been empirically demonstrated. The training required to achieve reliable ratings, in addition to the time required to complete the scale, are practical limitations of utility in many clinical settings. The SAPS and the SANS are probably more difficult to learn and take longer to administer than either the PANSS or the BPRS.

REFERENCES AND SUGGESTED READINGS

Andreasen NC: Negative symptoms in schizophrenia: definition and reliability. Arch Gen Psychiatry 39:784–788, 1982

Andreasen NC: Scale for the Assessment of Negative Symptoms (SANS). Iowa City, IA, University of Iowa, 1983

Andreasen NC: Scale for the Assessment of Positive Symptoms (SAPS). Iowa City, IA, University of Iowa, 1984

Andreasen NC, Grove WM: Evaluation of positive and negative symptoms in schizophrenia. Psychiatry and Psychobiology 1:108–121, 1986

Andreasen NC, Flaum M, Swayze VW, et al: Positive and negative symptoms in schizophrenia: a critical reappraisal. Arch Gen Psychiatry 47:615–621, 1990

Andreasen NC, Flaum M, Arndt S: The Comprehensive Assessment of Symptoms and History (CASH): an instrument for assessing psychopathology and diagnosis. Arch Gen Psychiatry 49:615–623, 1992

Andreasen NC, Arndt S, Miller D, et al: Correlational studies of the Scale for the Assessment of Negative Symptoms and the Scale for the Assessment of Positive Symptoms: an overview and update. Psychopathology 28:7–17, 1995a

Andreasen NC, Arndt S, Alliger R, et al: Symptoms of schizophrenia: methods, meanings, and mechanisms. Arch Gen Psychiatry 52:341–351, 1995b

Gur RE, Mozley PD, Resnick SM, et al: Relations among clinical scales in schizophrenia. Am J Psychiatry 148:472–478, 1991

Malla K, Norman RM, Williamson P: Stability of positive and negative symptoms in schizophrenia. Can J Psychiatry 38:617–621, 1993

Minas IH, Klimidis S, Stuart GW, et al: Positive and negative symptoms in the psychoses: principal components analysis of items from the Scale for the Assessment of Positive Symptoms and the Scale for the Assessment of Negative Symptoms. Compr Psychiatry 35:135–144, 1994

Moscarelli M, Maffei C, Cesana BM, et al: An international perspective on assessment of negative and positive symptoms in schizophrenia. Am J Psychiatry 144:1595–1598, 1987

Mueser KT, Sayers SL, Schooler NR, et al: A multisite investigation of the reliability of the Scale for the Assessment of Negative Symptoms. Am J Psychiatry 151:1453–1462, 1994

Nicholson IR, Chapman JE, Neufeld RWJ: Variability in BPRS definitions of positive and negative symptoms. Schizophr Res 17:177–185, 1995

Norman RM, Malla AK, Cortese L, et al: A study of the interrelationship between and comparative interrater reliability of the SAPS, SANS, and PANSS. Schizophr Res 19:73–85, 1996

Phillips MR, Xiong W, Wang RW, et al: Reliability and validity of the Chinese versions of the Scales for Assessment of Positive and Negative Symptoms. Acta Psychiatr Scand 84:364–370, 1991

Shiloh R, Zemishlany Z, Aizenberg D, et al: Sulpiride augmentation in people with schizophrenia partially responsive to clozapine: a double-blind, placebo-controlled study. Br J Psychiatry 171:569–573, 1997

Tollefson GD, Beasley CM, Tran PV, et al: Olanzapine versus haloperidol in the treatment of schizophrenia and schizoaffective disorders: results of an international collaborative trial. Am J Psychiatry 154:457–465, 1997

Schedule for the Deficit Syndrome (SDS)

B. Kirkpatrick, R. W. Buchanan, P. D. McKenney, L. D. Alphs, and W. T. Carpenter Jr.

GOALS

The Schedule for the Deficit Syndrome (SDS) (Kirkpatrick et al. 1989) is designed to assess the deficit syndrome in patients with schizophrenia. The deficit syndrome is defined as enduring negative symptoms that are part of the schizophrenic illness. The SDS assesses for the presence of the deficit syndrome versus secondary causes of negative symptoms (see the introduction to this chapter [p. 485] for a more complete discussion).

The SDS is an operationalized version of the deficit syndrome defined by Carpenter et al. (1988). The information required for the schedule is obtained from an open-ended interview and from collateral sources, including clinicians and family members. The SDS yields a categorical classification of either deficit or nondeficit. It also includes a global rating scale that rates the severity of the deficit syndrome.

DESCRIPTION

The presence or absence of the deficit syndrome is defined by four criteria. Criterion 1 evaluates six negative symptoms: restricted affect, diminished emotional range, poverty of speech, curbing of interests, diminished sense of purpose, and diminished social drive. At least two of the symptoms must be rated as present in at least moderate form for criterion 1 to be met. Criterion 2 is that at least two of the six negative symptoms in the first criterion must have been present for the 12 months preceding the rating. Criterion 3 is that the negative symptoms rated in the first two criteria are judged to be primary manifestations of schizophrenia rather than secondary (e.g., due to anxiety or depression, adverse drug effects, psychotic symptoms, mental retardation, or demoralization). Thus, each of the six negative symptoms rated as present (in criterion 1) and enduring (in criterion 2) are judged to be either primary to schizophrenia or secondary to other causes. To meet criterion 3, at least two of the negative symptoms must be rated as primary. Criterion 4 is that the current DSM criteria of schizophrenia are met. If all four criteria are met, then the patient is judged to have the deficit syndrome. A global severity rating is then made by use of an anchored scale.

The SDS can be administered by clinicians experienced in evaluating and treating patients with schizophrenia. Longitudinal knowledge of a patient's symptoms and behaviors during a time of clinical stability is needed to rate the SDS. This information is obtained from responses to an interview, from observations made during the interview, and from other sources of information as needed. Family members and other clinicians are suggested as collateral informants.

Each of the six negative symptoms in criterion 1 is rated on a scale from 0 = normal to 4 = severe. The first deficit syndrome criterion requires a score of at least 2 (moderate) on two or more of the six symptoms. On the basis of criteria 2, 3, and 4, a global deficit or nondeficit categorization is made. Additionally, patients are given a global score (0–4) rating the severity of the deficit syndrome; a score of 2 or more indicates the definite presence of the syndrome.

PRACTICAL ISSUES

An interview to obtain the information required to complete the SDS takes approximately 30 minutes. Additional time is required to obtain information from collateral sources. The SDS is designed to be used by clinicians experienced in the evaluation and treatment of psychotic disorders. Clinicians should review administration instructions before using the SDS.

The authors' permission is not required to use the SDS. The SDS can be obtained without cost from

Brian Kirkpatrick, M.D., M.S.P.H.
Maryland Psychiatric Research Center
P.O. Box 21247
Baltimore, MD 21228
Phone: 410-455-7662

Administration instructions and a scoring manual are available from the authors and in Kirkpatrick et al. (1989).

PSYCHOMETRIC PROPERTIES

Reliability

Internal consistency of the SDS has been assessed using rank order correlation of each symptom item with each of the other five, using Spearman's rho (Kirkpatrick et al. 1989). The correlations are considered good (range of 0.47–0.84) and suggest that the items are addressing a unitary concept.

Reliable use of the SDS requires a thorough understanding of the concepts of the deficit syndrome and primary and secondary negative symptoms. In addition, the SDS cannot be reliably administered without knowledge of the longitudinal course of negative symptoms. With these caveats, the joint reliability of the global categorization and global severity score is very good (kappa of 0.73 and 0.72, respectively) (Kirkpatrick et al. 1989).

Validity

The items included in the SDS are derived from the earlier work of Carpenter et al. (1988) and are well-accepted negative symptoms. A study that used the SDS to examine psychiatric patients with a variety of diagnoses (Gerbaldo and Philipp 1995) found the deficit syndrome to be most common in patients with psychotic disorders, but the study also found it in 9%–30% of patients with other diagnoses. These authors questioned the specificity of the construct for psychotic disorders, because the SDS had low predictive value for schizophrenia.

The instrument's authors noted that the high correlation ($r = 0.77$) between the item diminished social drive and the other five symptom items indicates that this item is a reasonable proxy for the entire scale.

The validity of the deficit syndrome as measured by the SDS has been demonstrated in several studies. Ribeyre et al. (1994) found significant differences in plasma homovanillic acid concentrations at certain times of the day between patients categorized as either having or not having the deficit syndrome. In addition, patients with the deficit syndrome as defined by the SDS have been shown to have poorer performance on neurocognitive tests of attentional performance (Buchanan et al. 1997) and greater abnormalities in smooth pursuit eye movements (Ross et al. 1996).

CLINICAL UTILITY

As specific interventions for deficit forms of schizophrenia are developed or recognized, the SDS has potential use in guiding treatment decisions. For example, Kopelowicz et al. (1997) report that negative symptoms respond well to social skills training in patients without the deficit syndrome, whereas patients with the deficit syndrome show little improvement. In addition, some clinicians have found the SDS to be helpful in making the differential diagnosis of negative symptoms, with potential impact on treatment planning aimed at reducing negative symptoms. For example, negative symptoms that are secondary to a major depressive episode improve when the major depressive episode is identified and treated. Negative symptoms that are secondary to medication side effects improve with interventions that reduce side effects (dose reduction or switching to alternative medication).

Once the concepts of primary and secondary negative symptoms are understood, the SDS is relatively easy to learn and simple to administer, making it user-friendly in clinical settings; however, the usefulness of the SDS in clinical settings must still be empirically demonstrated.

REFERENCES AND SUGGESTED READINGS

Buchanan RW, Strauss ME, Breier A, et al: Attentional impairments in deficit and nondeficit forms of schizophrenia. Am J Psychiatry 154:363–370, 1997

Carpenter WT, Heinrichs DW, Wagman AMI: Deficit and nondeficit forms of schizophrenia: the concept. Am J Psychiatry 145:578–583, 1988

Gerbaldo H, Philipp M: The deficit syndrome in schizophrenic and nonschizophrenic patients: preliminary studies. Psychopathology 28:55–63, 1995

Kirkpatrick B, Buchanan RW, Mckenney PD, et al: The Schedule for the Deficit Syndrome: an instrument for research in schizophrenia. Psychiatry Res 30:119–123, 1989

Kopelowicz A, Liberman RP, Mintz J, et al: Comparison of efficacy of social skills training for deficit and nondeficit negative symptoms in schizophrenia. Am J Psychiatry 154:424–425, 1997

Ribeyre JM, Lesier P, Vaoquaux O, et al: A comparison of plasma homovanillic acid in deficit and nondeficit subtypes of schizophrenia. Biol Psychiatry 36:230–236, 1994

Ross DE, Thaker GK, Buchanan RW, et al: Association of abnormal smooth pursuit eye movements with the deficit syndrome in schizophrenic patients. Am J Psychiatry 153:1158–1165, 1996

Calgary Depression Scale for Schizophrenia (CDSS)

D. Addington, J. Addington, and B. Schissel

GOALS

The Calgary Depression Scale for Schizophrenia (CDSS) (Addington et al. 1990) was developed to assess symptoms of major depressive disorder in patients with schizophrenia. Rating scales developed to assess depressive symptoms in patients without comorbid schizophrenia, such as the Hamilton Rating Scale for Depression (Ham-D) (p. 526), have questionable validity in patients with schizophrenia. In particular, the symptoms rated by the Ham-D may overlap with the negative symptoms of schizophrenia. The CDSS proposes to address these problems.

The CDSS was originally developed from the 17-item Ham-D and the depressive items from the Present State Examination (PSE) using factor analytic techniques. Items that were best able to assess depression were chosen for the 11-item CDSS, including 4 items from the Ham-D. Two items, delusions of guilt and weight loss, were later omitted because of low variance in subsequent samples, leaving nine items in the final scale (Addington et al. 1992). The CDSS was specifically designed to assess comorbid depressive symptoms in patients with schizophrenia; its use in other patient populations has not been tested.

DESCRIPTION

The CDSS consists of nine items: depressed mood, hopelessness, self-deprecation, guilty ideas of reference, pathological guilt, depression worse in the morning, early wakening, suicide, and observed depression. The items on the CDSS are all typical depressive symptoms and do not appear to overlap with the negative symptoms of schizophrenia (e.g., anhedonia is not included as a CDSS item).

The time frame is typically the 2 weeks before the interview, although the authors stipulate that the time frame may be varied depending on the needs of the user. Although the original version contained 11 items, most data about the scale are based on the 9-item version. Thus, use of the 11-item version of the scale is not recommended.

Each item includes interview questions and descriptive anchors for scoring. For example, the Depression domain is rated on the basis of the questions provided in Example 23 1.

Severity of depression is based on the following anchors:

Mild: Expresses some sadness or discouragement on questioning

EXAMPLE 23–1 ■ Sample item from the Calgary Depression Scale for Schizophrenia

> How would you describe your mood over the last two weeks:
>
> Do you keep reasonably cheerful or have you been very depressed or low spirited recently?
> In the last two weeks how often have you (own words) every day? All day?

Moderate: Distinct depressed mood persisting up to half the time over last 2 weeks: present daily

Severe: Markedly depressed mood persisting daily over half the time interfering with normal motor and social functioning

Items are scored 0 = absent, 1 = mild, 2 = moderate, and 3 = severe. Total scores may range from 0 to 27. A total score of 5 may identify individuals at high risk for major depressive disorder (Addington et al. 1992, 1993a,b).

PRACTICAL ISSUES

It takes 15–20 minutes to administer the CDSS. The CDSS is designed for use by clinicians with prior experience evaluating and treating patients with schizophrenia. Joint reliability is usually achieved with the rating of 5–10 interviews. The CDSS is designed to be used by clinicians experienced in the evaluation and treatment of patients with psychotic disorders. Clinicians should review administration instructions provided in Addington et al. (1990).

The scale and interview guide are contained in the appendix of Addington et al. (1990). No formal permission is needed to use the CDSS; however, it should be properly cited in all publications. There is no charge for use of the CDSS. Information about the CDSS may be obtained from

> Donald Addington, M.D.
> Department of Psychiatry
> Foothills Hospital
> 1403 29th Street, N.W.
> Calgary, Alberta T2N 2T9, Canada
> Phone: 403-670-1296
> Fax: 403-270-3451

Translations of the CDSS are available in Chinese, Danish, Dutch, French, Greek, Italian, Polish, Spanish, and Swedish.

The CDSS is included on the CD-ROM that accompanies this handbook.

PSYCHOMETRIC PROPERTIES

Reliability

Reliability of the CDSS has been reported in several studies. The internal consistency was good in both inpatients and outpatients (Cronbach's alphas range from 0.7 to 0.9) (Addington et al. 1990). High internal consistency has been found in several different studies. In one study of 50 inpatients and 100 outpatients who met the DSM-III criteria for schizophrenia, Cronbach's alpha was 0.79 (alpha of 0.78 for inpatients and 0.71 for outpatients) (Addington et al. 1992). Two later studies similarly demonstrated high internal consistency in patients with schizophrenia. Cronbach's alpha was 0.84 in a group of 50 inpatients and 100 outpatients (Addington et al. 1994) and was 0.82 in another group of 112 inpatients (Addington et al. 1996). In these studies high interrater reliability was demonstrated by joint interview of 10 subjects, with intraclass correlation coefficients (ICCs) of 0.90 (Addington et al. 1992), 0.96 (Addington et al. 1994), and 0.89 (Addington et al. 1996). The authors report that experienced clinicians should be able to reliably use the CDSS after review of the tool and 5–10 joint practice interviews (Addington et al. 1993).

Validity

The CDSS has demonstrated good validity for measuring the severity of depressive symptoms, as assessed by comparisons with other standard measures of depression. A study of 100 inpatients and 50 outpatients compared CDSS scores with clinical diagnoses of DSM-III-R major depression. Using discriminative function analysis, the CDSS correctly classified 93% of the patients with major depression. In this study, the CDSS was also highly correlated with other measures of depression, including the Ham-D (p. 526) (ICC = 0.8), the Beck Depression Inventory (BDI) (p. 519) (ICC = 0.8), and the Brief Psychiatric Rating Scale (BPRS) (p. 490) Depressive Mood subscale (ICC = 0.9). Similar results were obtained in a smaller study of 31 patients with chronic schizophrenia. A score of 13 on the CDSS correctly identified all patients with major depression but incorrectly identified 46% of the nondepressed patients as depressed. A score of 5 on the CDSS did not misidentify any nondepressed patients as having major depression but did fail to identify 26% of the patients with major depression.

The CDSS is able to assess symptoms that are distinct from the negative symptoms of schizophrenia and extrapyramidal side effects. In a study of patients with schizophrenia, both at admission (n = 112) and 3 months after discharge (n = 89), the correlation of the CDSS with a rating scale for negative symptoms (Positive and Negative Syndrome Scale [PANSS] Negative sub-

scale [p. 494]) was low and not statistically significant. In contrast, correlations between Ham-D scores and negative symptoms were moderate and statistically significant at both admission and 3 months after discharge. Similarly, in a group of 31 patients with chronic schizophrenia, the CDSS assessed symptoms distinct from extrapyramidal symptoms (as measured by the Simpson-Angus Rating Scale for Extrapyramidal Side Effects [p. 163]) (r = 0.16). In contrast, an earlier study of 50 acutely ill inpatients and 100 outpatients with schizophrenia found that the CDSS score was significantly correlated (r = 0.33) with negative symptoms (as determined by the PANSS) in the inpatients but that there was no significant correlation between the CDSS score and negative symptoms in the outpatients (r = 0.18). The authors suggest that the correlation between negative symptoms and the CDSS score in the inpatients and not in the outpatients is confounded by a general increase in psychopathology associated with relapse and does not support the idea that the CDSS is assessing negative symptoms. This interpretation is upheld by a confirmatory factor analysis of CDSS depression symptoms and PANSS negative symptoms in this study that strongly supported the hypothesis that the instruments are assessing separate constructs.

In addition, one study suggests that the CDSS is sensitive to change. The mean score in 89 patients with schizophrenia during acute hospitalization was 6.5. Three months after discharge, the mean score had decreased to 4.7 (t = 3.3).

CLINICAL UTILITY

The CDSS is a reliable and valid measure of the severity of depressive symptoms in patients with schizophrenia. It is currently being used successfully in both clinical and research settings. The instrument is potentially useful in screening patients with schizophrenia to identify those with possible major depressive disorder. The CDSS is also potentially useful in monitoring the response of depressive symptoms to treatment.

Data from one study suggest that scores of 5 or higher identify patients who are at high risk for comorbid major depressive disorder; however, the diagnosis of major depressive disorder needs to be confirmed by a clinical examination. Unlike other available measures of depressive symptoms, the CDSS appears to differentially assess depressive symptoms that are distinct from other symptoms of schizophrenia, including primary negative symptoms and negative symptoms that are secondary to the extrapyramidal side effects of antipsychotic medications.

The CDSS is limited by the newness of the scale and the need for further studies demonstrating the scale's ability to assess major depression, the sensitivity and specificity of various cutoff scores in inpatient and outpatient settings, and the scale's sensitivity to change with treatments targeting depressive symptoms. In addition, the reliability and validity of the scale need to be confirmed by others besides the developers of the CDSS. Fortunately, such studies are ongoing.

REFERENCES AND SUGGESTED READINGS

Addington D, Addington J, Schissel B: A depression rating scale for schizophrenics. Schizophr Res 3:247–251, 1990

Addington D, Addington J, Maticka-Tyndale E, et al: Reliability and validity of a depression rating scale for schizophrenics. Schizophr Res 6:201–208, 1992

Addington D, Addington J, Maticka-Tyndale E: Assessing depression in schizophrenia: the Calgary Depression Scale. Br J Psychiatry Suppl 22:39–44, 1993a

Addington D, Addington J, Maticka-Tyndale E: Rating depression in schizophrenia: a comparison of a self-report and an observer report scale. J Nerv Ment Dis 181:561–565, 1993b

Addington D, Addington J, Maticka-Tyndale E: Specificity of the Calgary Depression Scale for Schizophrenics. Schizophr Res 11:239–244, 1994

Addington D, Addington J, Atkinson M: A psychometric comparison of the Calgary Depression Scale for Schizophrenia and the Hamilton Depression Rating Scale. Schizophr Res 19:205–212, 1996

Wing JK, Cooper JE, Sartorius N: The Measurement and Classification of Psychiatric Symptoms. London, Cambridge University Press, 1974

Clinician Alcohol Use Scale (AUS) and Clinician Drug Use Scale (DUS)

R. E. Drake, K. T. Mueser, and G. J. McHugo

GOALS

The Clinician Alcohol Use Scale (AUS) and Drug Use Scale (DUS) (Drake et al. 1996) are designed to rate the substance use of persons with severe mental illness, especially psychotic disorders. The instruments use clinicians' ratings to classify patient substance use according to DSM-III-R criteria. The scales do not currently incorporate changes in the diagnostic criteria for substance use disorders made in DSM-IV.

The authors developed the scales because existing instruments, including the Alcohol Dependence Scale (ADS) (p. 474), the CAGE Questionnaire (p. 462), and the Michigan Alcoholism Screening Test (MAST) (p. 467), have questionable validity and reliability for patients with comorbid psychotic disorders.

DESCRIPTION

The AUS and the DUS each consist of a single item that asks the clinician to "rate your client's use of [drugs or alcohol] over the past 6 months according to the following scale." The clinician is instructed to draw on the patient's self-reported behavior and clinical observations, interviews, and collateral requests from family members, friends, and other clinicians.

The ratings are scored from 1 to 5 on the basis of the following descriptions:

1. Abstinent: Client has not used alcohol (drugs) during this time interval.
2. Use Without Impairment: Client has used alcohol (drugs) during this time interval, but there is no evidence of persistent or recurrent social; occupational, psychological, or physical problems related to use and no evidence of recurrent dangerous use.
3. Abuse: Client has used alcohol (drugs) during this time interval and there is evidence of persistent or recurrent

social, occupational, psychological, or physical problems related to use and no evidence of recurrent dangerous use. For example, recurrent alcohol (drug) use leads to disruptive behavior and housing problems. Problems have persisted for at least 1 month.

4. Dependence: Meets criteria for use without impairment, plus at least three of the following: greater amounts or intervals of use than intended, much of time used obtaining or using substance, frequent intoxication or withdrawal interferes with other activities, important activities given up because of alcohol (drug) use, continued use despite knowledge of substance-related problems, marked tolerance, characteristic withdrawal symptoms, alcohol (drugs) taken to relieve or avoid withdrawal symptoms. For example, binges and preoccupation with alcohol (drugs) have caused client to drop out of job training and nonalcohol (nondrug) social activities.

5. Dependence With Institutionalization: Meets criteria for dependence plus related problems are so severe that they make non-institutional living difficult. For example, constant drinking (drug use) leads to disruptive behavior and inability to pay rent so that client is frequently reported to police and seeking hospitalization.

Because the ratings use common clinical language, the meaning of the nominal categories is easy to interpret. The clinicians are given specific instructions about how to interpret these criteria in patients with severe mental illness. For example, clinicians are instructed to include substance-related interference with ability to manage their mental illness and to comply with treatment as "persistent problems" related to substance use. In addition, the authors emphasize that dependence may have more serious consequences for individuals with comorbid psychotic disorders, leading to institutionalization or homelessness at earlier stages of addiction.

PRACTICAL ISSUES

The AUS and the DUS can each be completed in 5 minutes by a clinician with longitudinal knowledge about a patient's substance use. However, the validity of the ratings depends on the acquisition of information from multiple sources. If used as intended—by clinicians rating their own patients—acquiring information from

others will require little additional effort. In the administration toolkit, the authors describe a five-step training process: an introduction to the concepts of substance use disorders, a description of the instruments, practice sessions and discussions, reliability checks, and validity checks. Clinicians familiar with substance use disorders are expected to be able to learn to use the AUS and the DUS with less than 1 hour of training.

The AUS and the DUS are in the public domain, no formal permission is needed to use them, and there is no charge for their use. Information may be obtained from

Human Services Research Institute
2336 Massachusetts Avenue
Cambridge, MA 02140

The instructions appear on the instrument itself, so no scoring manual is necessary. To assist clinicians in interpreting the scale, a toolkit (Mueser et al. 1995a) that provides detailed information about the AUS and the DUS is available from Human Services Research Institute.

The AUS and DUS are included on the CD-ROM that accompanies this handbook.

PSYCHOMETRIC PROPERTIES

Reliability

In two studies of the reliability of the AUS and the DUS (Drake et al. 1989, 1990), the instruments' authors found excellent joint reliability between scores obtained by a psychiatrist and those obtained by a clinical case manager. For current diagnoses, the kappa coefficient on the AUS was 0.95 and 0.80 on the DUS. For lifetime diagnosis of alcohol use disorders, the kappa coefficient was 0.72. An additional study also found high interrater reliability, with intraclass correlation coefficients between 0.58 and 0.85 (Mueser et al. 1995b).

Validity

Because the AUS and the DUS have their basis in DSM-III-R criteria and definitions of substance use disorders, they have high face validity. When compared with a consensus diagnosis by a team of experienced psychiatrists, the AUS achieved a sensitivity of 84% for a lifetime diagnosis and a sensitivity of 95% for a current diagnosis. The specificity was 100% for both lifetime and current alcohol use disorders.

CLINICAL UTILITY

The instruments are brief, and their format is simple. The AUS and the DUS are potentially useful in the assessment and monitoring of substance use disorders in individual clients. They may also be useful to program administrators when making case assignment and resource allocation decisions. When used together, the rating scales may be useful as outcome measures in judging the success of treatment programs and in research studies. The scale does not provide a comprehensive assessment of substance-related symptoms or impact of substance use on functioning, limiting its utility for comprehensive evaluations and for treatment planning.

REFERENCES AND SUGGESTED READINGS

Drake RE, Osher FC, Wallach MA: Alcohol use and abuse in schizophrenia: a prospective community study. J Nerv Ment Dis 177:408–414, 1989

Drake RE, Osher FC, Norrdsy DL, et al: Diagnosis of alcohol use disorders in schizophrenia. Schizophr Bull 16:57–66, 1990

Drake RE, Mueser KT, McHugo GJ: Clinician rating scales: Alcohol Use Scale (AUS), Drug Use Scale (DUS), and Substance Abuse Treatment Scale (SATS), in Outcomes Assessment in Clinical Practice. Edited by Sederer L, Dickey B. Baltimore, MD, Williams & Wilkins, 1996

Mueser KT, Drake RE, Clark RE, et al: Toolkit for Evaluating Substance Abuse in Persons With Severe Mental Illness. Cambridge, MA, Human Services Research Institute, 1995a

Mueser KT, Nishith P, Tracey JI, et al: Expectations and motives for substance use in schizophrenia. Schizophr Bull 21(3):367–378, 1995b

Drug Attitude Inventory (DAI)

T. P. Hogan and A. G. Awad

GOALS

The Drug Attitude Inventory (DAI) (Hogan et al. 1983) assesses the patient's subjective response to medications. The instrument focuses on unpleasant and negative subjective responses that are common adverse effects of antipsychotic medications.

DESCRIPTION

The DAI consists of 10 self-report items (derived from the original 30-item scale). Patients read each short statement and indicate if the item is true or false for them. Three items refer to how the medications make them feel: "weird, like a 'zombie'," "more relaxed," and "tired and sluggish." Other items reflect attitudes and beliefs about medication effects (see Example 23–2).

The DAI is designed to be a self-report instrument; however, persons with low literacy or an inability to complete the form independently may complete the form by responding orally to the questions. The time frame for the DAI is how the patient feels currently.

The nondysphoric response to six items is true (items 1, 3, 4, 7, 9, and 10) and to four items is false (items 2, 5, 6, and 8). Nondysphoric responses are given a score of 1; dysphoric responses are given a score of –1. The DAI scale score is the sum of scores and ranges from –10 to 10. The results may be dichotomized to positive subjective response (scores > 0) or a negative (dysphoric) subjective response (scores < 0).

EXAMPLE 23–2 ■ Sample item from the Drug Attitude Inventory

> For me, the good things about medication outweigh the bad.

PRACTICAL ISSUES

The DAI is brief and takes less than 10 minutes for patients to complete. Patients with low literacy or severe psychotic symptoms may need assistance from the staff to complete the DAI. Such assistance typically involves reading questions aloud and asking the patient to respond true or false. No training is required to read the items to patients who are unable to read the items themselves.

The DAI has been published in Hogan et al. (1983). Copies may also be obtained from the author:

> A. George Awad, M.D.
> Clarke Institute of Psychiatry
> 250 College Street, Suite 724
> Toronto, Ontario M5T 1R8, Canada
> Phone: 416-979-6865
> Fax: 416-979-6936

No formal permission is needed to use the DAI; however, it should be properly cited in all publications. The DAI is available without cost. A scoring manual is included in Awad (1993) or may be obtained from the author.

The DAI has been translated into Chinese, Finnish, French, German, Greek, Italian, Japanese, Polish, and Spanish.

The DAI is included on the CD-ROM that accompanies this handbook.

PSYCHOMETRIC PROPERTIES

Reliability

The reliability of the DAI was assessed in a study of 150 outpatients with a clinical diagnosis of schizophrenia (Hogan et al. 1983). In this study, the internal consistency of the DAI was good (Cronbach's alpha of 0.81). In addition, the test-retest reliability in a random sample of 27 of the original 150 study subjects was also good (intraclass correlation coefficient of 0.82).

Validity

Items on the DAI reflect aspects of subjective responses to medication (e.g., "I feel weird, like a 'zombie', on medication"), attitudes about medications (e.g., "For me, the good things about medications outweigh the bad"), and

beliefs about medication (e.g., "By staying on medications I can prevent getting sick"). Although these items may appear to reflect somewhat different constructs, the high internal consistency of the scale indicates that the items reflect a homogeneous construct.

The DAI has been compared with the Rating of Medication Influences (ROMI) (Weiden et al. 1994), a comprehensive interview-based measure that assesses seven domains that are theoretically linked to antipsychotic medication compliance in patients with schizophrenia. In a group of 33 patients with schizophrenia, correlations between the DAI and the ROMI 1 month after hospital discharge were good: 0.56 with the ROMI Reasons for Compliance scale and –0.47 with the ROMI Reasons for Non-Compliance scale. In a group of 42 hospitalized patients with schizophrenia, the DAI was compared with the older Neuroleptic Dysphoria (ND) scale (a 4-item interview-based scale that assesses subject response) (Hogan and Awad 1992). Correlations between the DAI and the ND were also good: 0.76 at 24 hours after beginning antipsychotic medication treatment and 0.74 at 48 hours after beginning antipsychotic medication treatment. Both the DAI and the ND can be scored as a dichotomous variable (i.e., dysphoric vs. nondysphoric response). There is good agreement between the DAI and the ND using this scoring system, with agreement in the classification of 39 out of 42 inpatients with schizophrenia at 24 hours and 34 out of 41 patients at 48 hours after initiation of antipsychotic medication treatment. Discrepancies in classification as dysphoric versus nondysphoric responder were mainly due to the ND scale classifying patients as dysphoric when the DAI classified them as nondysphoric. In this study, after 3 weeks of treatment with antipsychotic medication, a significantly greater percentage (55%) of the inpatients who were classified as dysphoric on the DAI also had motor rigidity (a symptom of parkinsonism induced by antipsychotic medication), as compared with 9% of patients classified as nondysphoric. Thus, dysphoric medication responses were correlated with an increased likelihood of extrapyramidal side effects and may represent an emotional component of parkinsonism induced by antipsychotic medication.

The ability of the 10-item DAI to predict medication compliance in patients with schizophrenia has been studied retrospectively in 150 outpatients with a clinical diagnosis of schizophrenia (Hogan et al. 1983). The outpatient psychiatrist treating the patient classified the patient as either a "habitual or occasional medication refuser" or as "no drug reluctance/overreliant" on antipsychotic medications, without knowledge of the DAI responses. In the preliminary validation study, the usefulness of each of the original 30 items of the DAI to predict compliant versus noncompliant was determined. The 10 items that best predicted compliance became the 10-item DAI. In this preliminary analysis, of the 69 patients who were considered compliant by their outpatient psychiatrist, 66 were classified as nondysphoric and 3 as dysphoric on the DAI. Of the 81 patients who were considered noncompliant by their outpatient psychiatrist, 67 had dysphoric and 14 had nondysphoric scores on the DAI. Thus, preliminary data suggest that the DAI may predict a history of antipsychotic medication compliance (96% accuracy) and noncompliance (83% accuracy). Similar results were found in a second group of 19 hospitalized inpatients. Here, 8 of 11 patients (73%) with a history of medication compliance and 5 of 8 patients (63%) with a history of noncompliance were correctly categorized by the DAI. Interestingly, in both studies a positive score on the DAI proved better at predicting compliance than a negative score did at predicting noncompliance. Perhaps this finding is explained by the presence of dysphoric medication response as one of several factors that predict noncompliance; these other factors (e.g., insight into illness, ability to adhere to medication regimen, and alcohol and drug abuse) influence noncompliance regardless of whether the patient has a dysphoric or nondysphoric medication response. However, a positive subjective response to medication is highly predictive of continued medication compliance.

In one study (Hogan and Awad 1992), the DAI predicted short-term antipsychotic medication treatment response as measured by the Brief Psychiatric Rating Scale (BPRS) (p. 490) in 55 acutely hospitalized patients who met at least five of the World Health Organization discriminating criteria for schizophrenia. After 3 weeks of treatment with antipsychotic medication, a significantly greater percentage (82%) of patients classified as nondysphoric on the DAI showed >10 points improvement on the BPRS, compared with 27% of patients classified as dysphoric. In this study, the DAI score after 24 hours of treatment was significantly associated with the total BPRS score (partial $r = -0.75$) and the Global Assessment of Functioning (GAF) Scale (p. 96) score (partial $r = 0.68$).

CLINICAL UTILITY

In clinical settings, the DAI may be used to identify patients at highest risk for poor compliance with prescribed medication(s) related to subjective medication response. Such patients may benefit from a medication change that may decrease dysphoric adverse effects. Other psychotherapeutic interventions to decrease the risk of noncompliance may also be appropriate.

The DAI is a brief, easy-to-use self-report instrument. Most outpatients and many inpatients can independently complete the form. The DAI provides a reliable and valid assessment of dysphoric response to antipsychotic medication. The DAI may be useful in identifying patients at high risk for noncompliance with antipsychotic medication treatment. In addition, the DAI may be useful in predicting the likelihood of short-term improvement in psychosis with use antipsychotic medication.

The DAI does not attempt to comprehensively assess all domains associated with antipsychotic medication noncompliance. A more comprehensive instrument, the ROMI, is available, but it is lengthy and requires substantial training to administer (Weiden et al. 1994).

There are no prospective studies demonstrating the ability of the DAI to predict the likelihood of medication compliance; therefore, the clinical usefulness of the DAI has not been empirically demonstrated. Few published studies report on the DAI; those that do have been conducted by the author of the instrument. However, the DAI is currently being used by others in both research studies and clinical settings. Thus, there is a need to obtain further information about the psychometric properties of the DAI, particularly its predictive validity.

REFERENCES AND SUGGESTED READINGS

Awad AD: Subjective response to neuroleptics in schizophrenia. Schizophr Bull 19:609–618, 1993

Hogan TP, Awad AG: Subjective response to neuroleptics and outcome in schizophrenia: a re-examination comparing two measures. Psychol Med 22:347–352, 1992

Hogan TP, Awad AG, Eastwood R: A self-report scale predictive of drug compliance in schizophrenics: reliability and discriminative validity. Psychol Med 13:177–183, 1983

Weiden P, Rapkin B, Mott T, et al: Rating of Medication Influences (ROMI) scale in schizophrenia. Schizophr Bull
20:297–310, 1994

Insight and Treatment Attitudes Questionnaire (ITAQ)

*J. P. McEvoy, L. J. Apperson, P. S. Appelbaum,
P. Ortlip, J. Brecosky, K. Hammill, J. L. Geller,
and L. Roth*

GOALS

The Insight and Treatment Attitudes Questionnaire
(ITAQ) (McEvoy et al. 1989) was designed to measure
awareness of illness and insight into need for treatment
in patients with schizophrenia. The ITAQ was developed
as a research instrument to enable investigators to examine the relationship between insight and psychopathology, treatment compliance, and the course of the
illness.

The authors define *insight* as an awareness that some
perceptions, thoughts, emotions, or behaviors represent
an illness that requires mental health treatment. Poor
insight is common in patients with schizophrenia, and
studies have demonstrated associations between lack of
insight and poorer treatment compliance (see McEvoy et
al. 1989 for a review). Thus, determination of a patient's
insight into his or her illness may help in treatment planning.

DESCRIPTION

The ITAQ is a single scale consisting of 11 items that
are phrased as questions to elicit open-ended responses
from patients. Results are reported as a summary score.
Sample items are provided in Example 23–3. Six of the
items refer to the need for inpatient treatment; thus, the
scale is designed for use with hospitalized patients.

**EXAMPLE 23–3 ■ Sample items from the Insight and
Treatment Attitudes Questionnaire**

> 1. At the time of admission to this hospital, did you have
>   mental (nerve, worry) problems that were different from
>   most other people?
>
> 9. After you are discharged, will you need to take
>   medications for mental (nerve or worry) problems?
>
> 11. Do the medications do you any good?

Responses to each of the 11 questions are scored 0 =
no insight, 1 = partial insight, or 2 = good insight.
Descriptive anchors are provided for scoring. Total scores
range from 0 to 22. Patients with total scores of 15 or
higher are defined as having good insight, those with
scores of 8–14 as having fair insight, and those with scores
of 7 or lower as having poor insight.

PRACTICAL ISSUES

It takes 15–20 minutes to administer the ITAQ, including the time needed to rate patient responses. The ITAQ
is designed to be used by clinicians who are experienced
in evaluating and treating patients with schizophrenia
and other psychotic disorders. Clinicians should review
administration instructions before using the ITAQ.

The ITAQ is available without cost. Information
about the ITAQ is available from

> Joseph P. McEvoy, M.D.
> John Umsted Hospital
> 1003 12th Street
> Butner, NC 27509

Brief scoring instructions that provide anchors for rating
the open-ended responses are available from the authors.

PSYCHOMETRIC PROPERTIES

Reliability

Test-retest reliability has been assessed in one study of 22
patients at baseline and 1-year follow-up (McEvoy et al.
1993). The reliability of the ITAQ in this study was good
($r = 0.70$), suggesting that the level of insight is stable

over a 1-year period and that it can be consistently rated at two different time points by different raters.

Validity

The validity of the ITAQ has been assessed by comparisons with experienced psychiatrists' judgment of insight and by examining correlations with psychopathology measures and measures of noncompliance (McEvoy et al. 1989). Psychiatrists' ratings of insight on the basis of an independent interview were highly and significantly correlated with the ITAQ total score ($r = 0.85$). Medication compliance and ITAQ scores were inversely correlated at initial ($r = -0.35$) and subsequent assessments 14 days later ($r = -0.36$). As measured by total scores on the Brief Psychiatric Rating Scale (BPRS) (p. 490) and the Clinical Global Impressions (CGI) Scale (p. 100) Severity of Illness scores, more severely ill patients demonstrated poorer insight, although not all of these correlations were statistically significant.

Predictive validity was determined by comparing the level of insight during hospitalization with treatment compliance after discharge and readmission rates in 22 patients with schizophrenia (McEvoy et al. 1993). Although the associations were in the expected direction, they did not reach statistical significance at the 0.05 level, possibly because of the small number of patients studied.

CLINICAL UTILITY

The ITAQ was included in this chapter despite the limited amount of psychometric data because of the clinical relevance of the concept of *insight*. There is good empiric evidence that a patient's degree of insight affects willingness to comply with treatment and clinical outcome. The ITAQ represents an early attempt to systematically evaluate insight in psychiatric patients; thus, the clinical value of the ITAQ has not yet been empirically assessed. Conceivably, determination of a patient's level of insight into illness may help in treatment planning. For example, patients with little insight may benefit from intensive outreach services such as assertive community treatment (ACT) or greater family involvement in outpatient treatment or they may require depot antipsychotic medication to improve medication compliance.

The ITAQ is brief and easy to administer. It is a straightforward instrument that has quantified a clinically relevant domain.

The ITAQ does not assess all of the theoretical dimensions of insight. For example, the ITAQ does not assess awareness of social consequences of the symptoms or beliefs about causes of symptoms (Ghaemi et al. 1995). Because it was designed for hospitalized patients, the existing version of the ITAQ may have limited utility in outpatient settings.

A few published studies report on the ITAQ, but these studies have been conducted by the author of the instrument. Thus, further information must be obtained about the psychometric properties of the ITAQ, particularly its predictive validity and reliability.

REFERENCES AND SUGGESTED READINGS

Ghaemi SN, Stoll AL, Pope HG: Lack of insight in bipolar disorder: the acute manic episode. J Nerv Ment Dis 183:464–467, 1995

McEvoy JP, Apperson LJ, Appelbaum PS, et al: Insight in schizophrenia: its relationship to acute psychopathology. J Nerv Ment Dis 177:43–47, 1989

McEvoy JP, Freter S, Everett G, et al: Insight about psychosis among outpatients with schizophrenia. Hospital and Community Psychiatry 44:883–884, 1993

CHAPTER 24

Mood Disorders Measures

Kimberly A. Yonkers, M.D.
Jacqueline Samson, Ph.D.

INTRODUCTION

Major Domains

This chapter covers 13 scales that may help the clinician in the assessment and management of mood disorders. Although only one of the included measures has been specifically designed to assist the clinician in making a DSM-IV diagnosis of mood disorder, the scales measure symptoms that are characteristic of the various mood disorders contained in DSM-IV. Like DSM-IV, the scales are divided into those that measure depressive symptoms and those that measure manic symptoms. Because hypomania is defined in DSM-IV as a less severe form of mania in terms of duration and consequent impairment, the so-called mania scales may be relevant in measuring hypomania as well.

Organization

This chapter is divided into three sections (see Table 24–1). The first section presents seven depression rating scales that were developed for a general psychiatric population (inpatient or outpatient). The second section contains three scales that measure mania or hypomania. The final section contains three depression scales that were developed for use in special populations, specifically one scale each for use in postpartum women, elderly people, and the medically ill.

Relevant Measures Included Elsewhere in the Handbook

Measures relating to the diagnosis of mood disorders in conjunction with other psychiatric disorders are included elsewhere in this manual. See, for example, the mood disorders section of the Structured Clinical Interview for DSM-IV (SCID) (p. 49) and the Schedule for Affective Disorders and Schizophrenia (SADS) (p. 58). Scales for evaluating mood disorders in children are included in Chapter 18, "Symptom-Specific Measures for Disorders Usually First Diagnosed in Infancy, Childhood, or Adolescence." Chapter 23, "Psychotic Disorders Measures," includes the Calgary Depression Scale for Schizophrenia (CDSS) (p. 504), which was designed expressly for the assessment of symptoms of major depressive episode in patients with a diagnosis of schizophrenia.

Symptom measures that evaluate multiple emotional or behavioral states (e.g., vitality and anxiety), such as the Profile of Mood States (POMS) (McNair et al. 1971), are not included in this section because we are reviewing specialized scales that detect or rate the severity of depression and manic episodes. Finally, instruments that require administration by an inpatient team, such as the Beigel Mania Rating Scale (BMRS) (Beigel et al. 1971), are not included in this chapter because they are not intended for use in an office-based setting.

TABLE 24–1 ■ Mood disorders measures

Name of measure	Disorder or construct assessed	Format	Pages
Depression rating scales for general psychiatric or community populations			
Beck Depression Inventory (BDI) First revision (BDI-IA) Second revision (BDI-II)	Severity of depressive symptoms	Self-report; 21 items	519–523
Center for Epidemiologic Studies Depression Scale (CES-D)*	Severity of depressive symptoms in community populations	Self-report; 20 items	523–526
Hamilton Rating Scale for Depression (Ham-D)	Severity of depressive symptoms in patients with primary depressive illness	Interviewer-administered scale; 17 items	526–529
Inventory of Depressive Symptomatology (IDS)* Self-report version (IDS-SR) Clinician-administered version (IDS-C)	Severity of signs and symptoms of depression (includes all DSM criteria items)	Self-report (IDS-SR) or clinician-administered semistructured interview (IDS-C); 28- and 30-item versions	529–531
Montgomery-Asberg Depression Rating Scale (MADRS)	Severity of depressive symptoms	Interviewer-administered checklist; 10 items	531–533
Raskin Scale (Three-Area Severity of Depression Scale)*	Severity of depression in three areas: subjective experience, behavioral manifestations, and secondary signs of depression	Interviewer-rated scale; 3 items	533–534
Zung Self-Rating Depression Scale (Zung SDS)*	Severity of depressive symptoms	Self-report; 20 items	534–537
Mania rating scales			
Clinician Administered Rating Scale for Mania (CARS-M)*	Severity of manic and psychotic symptoms	Clinician-administered scale; 15 items with question prompts	537–538
Internal State Scale (ISS)*	Severity of manic symptoms (conceptualized as activation, perceived conflict, and well-being) and depressive symptoms in patients with bipolar disorder	Self-report; 17 items	539–540
Young Mania Rating Scale (YMRS)*	Severity of manic symptoms; relapse or recurrence of manic symptoms	Clinician-administered checklist; 11 items	540–542
Depression rating scales for use in special populations			
Edinburgh Postnatal Depression Scale (EPDS)	Screening test for postpartum depression	Self-report; 10 items	542–544
Geriatric Depression Scale (GDS)*	Screening test for depression in elderly people	Self-report; 30 items	544–547
Hospital Anxiety and Depression Scale (HADS)	Severity of depression and anxiety in medically ill patients	Self-report; 14 items	547–548

*Measure is included on the CD-ROM that accompanies this handbook.

USING MEASURES IN THIS DOMAIN

Goals of Assessment

The most common goal of assessment is to measure the severity of depressive or manic symptoms, in terms of both the severity of individual symptoms and the total number of mood-related symptoms that have been present. Measuring severity is particularly useful in setting a baseline so that repeated administration during the course of treatment may be used to document improvement.

Recent changes in medical care service provision have resulted in larger numbers of patients with mood disorders being treated in nonpsychiatric settings, such as primary care and nursing home facilities, so that instruments specifically developed to screen for mood disorders in such settings are needed. Unfortunately, generic depression symptom severity indexes may have less than optimal performance in populations such as patients with general medical illness, postpartum women, and elderly individuals. In particular, most depressive scales include items for rating the presence of somatic symptoms, such as insomnia or fatigue. In these populations, the high incidence of somatic symptoms unrelated to depression may lead to an overdiagnosis of depression by inappropriately counting these symptoms as being due to a depressive syndrome. Hence, special scales validated specifically in these populations have been developed: the Geriatric Depression Scale (GDS) for use with elderly people in nursing home settings, the Hospital Anxiety and Depression Scale (HADS) for use in primary care or hospital settings, and the Edinburgh Postnatal Depression Scale (EPDS) for use with postpartum patients in primary care settings.

Three of the depressive symptom severity scales included in this chapter (the Beck Depression Inventory [BDI], the Center for Epidemiologic Studies Depression Scale [CES-D], and the Zung Self-Rating Depression Scale [Zung SDS]) are also used to screen for depressive illness in the community or in general medical populations. This application requires a two-stage approach; the first-stage screen selects persons likely to have a mood disorder, and these patients then go on to a second-stage clinical diagnostic interview. This strategy is cost-effective because paper and pencil questionnaires may be used to identify a smaller number of persons for a clinician-administered diagnostic interview.

Implementation Issues

The self-report instruments reviewed in this chapter require that individuals be able to read at a minimal reading level and that they speak the language used in one of the translations of the instrument. The use of these instruments is also limited in patients who have cognitive impairment. Some experts believe that self-report instruments perform less well in patients with severe illness.

The clinician-administered scales range from checklists to structured interviews, and all but the Montgomery-Asberg Depression Rating Scale (MADRS) recommend that clinicians administering the scale be trained. For some scales (e.g., the Hamilton Rating Scale for Depression [Ham-D]), it is also suggested that the clinician using the scale have training in psychiatry or psychology. Most of the clinician-administered scales do not rely on the use of additional information obtained outside the clinical interview; however, in some instances (e.g., in patients with poor insight), such information may be beneficial.

All of the depressive rating scales have been used as screens and can indicate the presence of depressive symptoms. However, unless the screen were used in a patient with an earlier determined diagnosis of depressive disorder, the clinician would still need to completely assess the patient before diagnosing depressive disorder (i.e., the measures cannot be used to diagnose depression).

None of the depression scales included in this chapter provides good coverage of psychotic symptoms in depression, although the Ham-D includes some hints at psychotic symptoms in the severity anchors.

Issues in Interpreting Psychometric Data

There is no gold standard for determining whether an individual has a mood disorder. In many instances, the construct of *depression* or *mania* used by the authors was defined by diagnostic criteria in DSM-IV (e.g., the Inventory of Depressive Symptomatology [IDS]) and by standardized diagnostic instruments such as the SADS (p. 58) (e.g., the Clinician Administered Rating Scale for Mania [CARS-M]). In some instances, however, the author's clinical experience was used to select items pertaining to the construct (e.g., the Ham-D, the MADRS, and the Young Mania Rating Scale [YMRS]). In depression scales developed before 1980, this method of selecting items resulted in an overemphasis on symptoms of endogenous depression and less inclusion of atypical symptoms such as hyperphagia and hypersomnia. This overemphasis on endogenous symptoms may thus have implications for identifying subpopulations of individuals with mood disorders (i.e., those with atypical or melancholic depression) and also for the comprehensiveness with which the instrument covers the construct. For example, the Ham-D is less comprehensive than newer scales such as the IDS in its rating of the severity of atypical depressive illnesses.

In several scales, we note problems in distinguishing depressive symptoms from anxiety symptoms. The relationship between depression and anxiety is reflected by large correlations between the depression symptom severity measure and measures of anxiety. This relationship may contribute to the low specificity and poor positive predictive values found in studies of screening instruments. It is a complicated problem because research data suggest that approximately 60% of depressed individuals show comorbid anxiety symptoms. Other studies suggest that a subgroup of patients may cycle between anxiety and depression or may show a baseline of anxiety symptoms that periodically escalate and show comorbidity with superimposed depressive episodes. Thus, the distinction between these two disorders is not clinically clear. Data on this problem are included, when available, in discussions of the specific measures.

Studies have found a range of estimates of sensitivity and specificity, depending on the base rates of depression in the sample screened and the comorbid medical and psychiatric conditions that are present. Again, further work is needed to maximize the screening efficiency of these measures, but we include examples of the best available.

GUIDE TO THE SELECTION OF MEASURES

The selection of a specific measure depends on when the measure is to be used, the type of scale to be used, and the application. Clinicians should consider three factors in selecting measures: 1) cost, 2) time, and 3) coverage. One might consider doing a cost-benefit analysis of the measure to determine whether the output of the instrument (i.e., whether the measure captures what the clinician wishes to capture) is worth the time and effort involved in its administration. Relative cost versus coverage and validity should also be weighed when choosing between self-report and clinician-administered questionnaires. Advantages of self-report formats include time savings and the ability of clinicians to routinely track a symptom without asking about it specifically (e.g., suicidal ideation).

The screening instruments reviewed in this chapter were developed either for use in nonpsychiatric populations (the CES-D, the EPDS, the HADS, and the GDS) or for measuring illness severity in previously diagnosed populations (the Ham-D, the Raskin Scale, the BDI, the MADRS, the Zung SDS, the CARS-M, and the Internal State Scale [ISS]). A problem with some screening measures, such as the CES-D and the EPDS, is that rather than specifically selecting for depression, they identify persons who show general distress. For example, followup interviews suggest that individuals with other conditions, such as anxiety disorders, may also screen positive with the CES-D and the EPDS. Data representative of these problems are covered in the sections on three instruments (the CES-D, the BDI, and the Zung SDS). Furthermore, scales such as the HAD, the BDI, the MADRS, the GDS, and the EPDS rely less on somatic symptoms to screen for or rate mood and are more appropriate for postpartum or geriatric populations or those who have general medical illnesses.

All of the scales in this chapter that assess symptom severity show good reliability and validity when used in populations of patients with diagnosed mood disorders. Thus, most instruments are good indicators of symptom change over time and are highly useful for monitoring the comparative efficacy of treatments over time or for documenting outcomes in populations of patients treated in a group practice or other outpatient settings. Different measures cover different sets of depressive symptoms. For example, atypical symptoms are not assessed effectively with the standard 17-item Ham-D, the BDI, the Zung SDS, or the MADRS. The IDS, which queries about atypical symptoms, may be more helpful for measuring the severity of atypical symptoms. On the other hand, endogenous symptoms are adequately addressed by all of the depressive symptom scales evaluated. The BDI (version II), the IDS, and the CARS-M include all DSM-III-R and DSM-IV criteria and thus provide complete data regarding change in individual DSM symptoms. Measures that include DSM criteria may be helpful in managed-care settings in which information on improvement in DSM-IV symptoms is often required.

Although the screening and measuring tools reviewed in this chapter can be helpful in identifying mood disorders, they cannot establish a diagnosis. Clinical interview and structured clinical diagnostic instruments should also be employed to obtain accurate diagnoses for these patients

CURRENT STATUS AND FUTURE RESEARCH NEEDS FOR ASSESSMENT

Although there are a plethora of instruments for measuring the severity and existence of depressive disorders, relatively few validated instruments identify and evaluate mania and hypomania. Further, relatively small populations have been used to validate the existing instruments. Thus, future research should focus on developing instruments and techniques to evaluate mood states in patients with mania and hypomania. Inclusion of questions regarding the depressed phase and the manic phase of illness would also enhance the utility of instruments for patients with bipolar disorder.

REFERENCES AND SUGGESTED READINGS

Beckham EE, Leber WR (eds): Handbook of Depression: Treatment, Assessment, and Research. IL, Dorsey Press, 1985

Beigel A, Murphy DZ, Bunney WF: The Manic State Rating Scale. Arch Gen Psychiatry 25:256–261, 1971

Dunn G, Sham P, Hand D: Statistics and the nature of depression. Psychol Med 23:871–889, 1993

Faravelli C, Albanesi G, Poli E: Assessment of depression: a comparison of rating scales. J Affect Disord 11:245–253, 1986

Fischer J, Corcoran M: Measures for Clinical Practice: A Sourcebook, 2nd Edition. New York, Free Press, 1994

McNair DM, Kerr M, Droppleman LF: Profile of Mood States Manual. San Diego, CA, Educational and Industrial Testing, 1971

Meakin CJ: Screening for depression in the medically ill: the future of paper and pencil tests. Br J Psychiatry 160:212–216, 1992

Moran PW, Lambert MJ: A review of current assessment tools for monitoring changes in depression, in The Assessment of Psychotherapy and Outcomes. Edited by Lamber MD,

Christiensen ER, Dejolie SS. New York, Wiley, 1983, pp 263–303

Naughton MJ, Wiklund I: A critical review of dimension-specific measures of health-related quality of life in cross-cultural research. Qual Life Resh 2:397–432, 1993

Snaith P: What do depression rating scales measure? Br J Psychiatry 163:293–298, 1993

Thompson C: Affective disorders, in The Instruments of Psychiatric Research. Edited by Thompson C. New York, Wiley, 1989

Beck Depression Inventory (BDI)

A. T. Beck and R. A. Steer

GOALS

The Beck Depression Inventory (BDI) (Beck et al 1961) was developed to measure the behavioral manifestations of depression in adolescents and adults. It was designed to standardize the assessment of depression severity in order to monitor change over time or to simply describe the illness. The items of the BDI were originally derived from observations of depressed patients made during the course of psychoanalytic psychotherapy. Attitudes and symptoms that appeared to be specific to this group of patients were described by a series of statements, and a numerical value was assigned to each statement.

In its original form, 21 behavioral manifestations were covered, each area represented by four or five statements describing symptom severity from low to high. Subjects were asked to identify the statement that best described their feelings "right now." Items were then scored and summed to obtain a total score for depressive symptom severity. An abbreviated version containing 13 items was published in the Early Clinical Drug Evaluation Program (ECDEU) assessment manual (Guy 1976). In 1978, the full scale was revised (BDI-IA) to eliminate duplicate severity descriptors and to reword certain items. In addition, the time frame for assessment was lengthened to the "last week, including today." In 1993, the guidelines for scoring were modified to reflect data collected at the Center for Cognitive Therapy. In 1996, a new version of the BDI (BDI-II) with a modification of items to reflect DSM-IV criteria and to simplify wording was published. The time frame was extended to include the "last 2 weeks."

Although psychometric data presented in the manual for the new BDI-II look promising, the time frame extension to 2 weeks makes this instrument less useful for assessing patterns of change over time. Further studies are needed from a variety of centers to validate its use. Thus, in this section we focus on properties of the BDI-IA.

DESCRIPTION

The BDI-IA contains 21 item sets, each with a series of four statements. Statements describe symptom severity along an ordinal continuum from absent or mild (a score of 0) to severe (a score of 3). The item set for sad mood is provided in Example 24–1.

Although the original instrument (BDI-I) was meant to be read aloud by an interviewer who would record subject choices, the scale has subsequently been used primarily as a self-report questionnaire. Depression severity scores are created by summing the scores of the items endorsed from each item set. The most recent guidelines suggest the following interpretation of severity scores: 0–9, minimal; 10–16, mild; 17–29, moderate; and 30–63, severe. Subscale scores may be calculated for a cognitive-affective factor and a somatic-performance factor.

PRACTICAL ISSUES

It takes 5–10 minutes to complete the BDI-IA. Oral administration may require 15 minutes. In some severely

EXAMPLE 24–1 ■ Sample item from the Beck Depression Inventory (BDI-IA)

0 = I do not feel sad
1 = I feel sad
2 = I am sad all the time and can't snap out of it
3 = I am so sad or unhappy that I can't stand it

obsessional patients, administration time may be somewhat longer.

The scale is copyrighted and may be obtained from

> The Psychological Corporation
> 555 Academic Court
> San Antonio, TX 78204-2498
> Phone: 800-211-8378
> Internet: www.psychcorp.com

A manual (Beck and Steer 1993) that documents the development of the questionnaire and its psychometric properties and provides scoring and interpretation guidelines is included. Computer software is available from the Psychological Corporation for on-screen administration, for use with paper and pencil administration, or for input of data from a desktop scanner. The program may be used to administer a single questionnaire or to integrate the results of sequential administrations of the questionnaire.

The BDI has been translated into several languages, including Chinese, Dutch, Finnish, French (Canadian), German, Korean, Swedish, and Turkish (Naughton and Wiklund 1993).

PSYCHOMETRIC PROPERTIES

Reliability

The BDI shows high internal consistency. In a review of 25 years of research on the BDI, Beck et al. (1988) found 25 studies of internal consistency. For psychiatric populations in nine studies, with a range of $N = 63–248$ subjects per study, Cronbach's alphas ranged from 0.76 to 0.95. For student populations in nine studies, with a range of $N = 91–568$ subjects per study, alphas ranged from 0.82 to 0.92. For nonpsychiatric, nonstudent samples in five studies, with a range of $N = 65–214$, alphas ranged from 0.73 to 0.90. Internal consistency reported for 248 consecutive admissions to the Center for Cognitive Therapy in 1978–1979 was an alpha value of 0.86. Consistency ratings achieved by various patient diagnostic groupings were as follows: major depressive disorder, single episode, alpha = 0.80; major depressive disorder, recurrent episode, alpha = 0.86; dysthymic disorder, alpha = 0.79; alcohol abuse or dependence, alpha = 0.90; and heroin abuse or dependence, alpha = 0.88. Across studies, the lowest item-total correlation was obtained for the item measuring weight loss.

Assessments of BDI test-retest reliability are problematic because repeated testing has often involved comparing questionnaires repeated outside the time frame mandated by the first administration of the questionnaire. To assess the stability of 1-week assessments, repeated measurements must be made using the same unit of observation but varying the time of administration (e.g., morning and afternoon). Measurements taken after longer intervals may be expected to change in a population undergoing treatment for depression. Studies using the original version (BDI-I), with a time frame of "right now" and retesting 1–6 hours later, showed $r = 0.83$ for retesting after 1–6 hours and $r = 0.81$ for retesting after 4–6 hours in a student population.

Validity

Correlations between the BDI and other standard measures of depressive symptom severity show high, but not complete, concordance across measures. Correlations between clinical ratings of depression and the BDI for psychiatric patients range from 0.55 to 0.96, with a mean of 0.72. For nonpsychiatric subjects, correlations range from 0.55 to 0.73, with a mean of 0.60. Studies of correlations between BDI severity scores and scores from the Hamilton Rating Scale for Depression (Ham-D) (p. 526) in psychiatric patients show coefficients that range from 0.61 to 0.86, with a mean of 0.73. The test manual (Beck and Steer 1993) reports the following correlations between BDI and Ham-D scores calculated by diagnostic group: mixed sample, $r = 0.66$; major depressive disorder, single episode, $r = 0.40$; major depressive disorder, recurrent episode, $r = 0.56$; dysthymic disorder, $r = 0.56$; alcohol dependence, $r = 0.87$; and heroin dependence, $r = 0.69$. In two nonpsychiatric samples, correlations between BDI and Ham-D scores were 0.73 and 0.80. Eight psychiatric studies that examined the correlation between the BDI and the Zung SDS showed a range of coefficients from 0.57 to 0.83, with a mean of 0.76. In nonpsychiatric samples, the range was 0.66 to 0.86, with a mean of 0.71. Finally, the test manual reports correlations (r) of 0.76 with the Symptom Checklist–90 (SCL-90) Depression subscale (p. 81), 0.60 with the Minnesota Multiphasic Personality Inventory Depression Scale (MMPI-D) (p. 89), and 0.60 with the Beck Hopelessness Scale (BHS) (p. 268).

Although no statistics are given, the test manual reports that several studies have indicated that the BDI can discriminate psychiatric patients from psychiatrically healthy control subjects, dysthymic patients from those with major depressive disorder, and patients with generalized anxiety disorder from those with major depressive disorder. In a review of this literature, Beck et al. (1986) reported that the dysthymic and depression samples showed poor discrimination (although the mean score was higher in the group with major depressive disorder) and that mean ratings of 18 BDI items, with the exception of sense of failure, punishment, and crying, were comparable in patients with recurrent depression and patients with dysthymia. Although item scores for nonsomatic symptoms were higher in patients with dysthymic disorder and major depressive disorder than in those with generalized anxiety disorder, scores cannot be used to determine diagnosis. Thus, within psychiatric samples, the discriminative ability of the BDI is poor.

In a study of 307 young adults (outpatients ages 18–37 years), Rudd and Rajab (1995) found BDI sensitivity for the presence of a DSM-III-R mood disorder maximized at the following score levels: 83.77% at BDI = 9 (the lowest score obtained in the study), 76.62% at BDI = 14, 66.88% at BDI = 18, and 58.4% at BDI = 20. Specificity rates were highest (88.36%) at BDI = 30 (the highest score obtained in the study) and dropped to 61.64% at BDI = 20, to 58.90% at BDI = 18, and to 44.52% at BDI = 14. The authors recommend the use of a cutoff score of 18 for maximal efficiency. Higher sensitivity scores have been reported in nonpatient populations. Rudd and Rajab (1995) also found that comorbid conditions affect specificity at both the high and low ends of severity ratings. Elevated BDI scores were indicative of prominent anxiety and comorbid disorders. Low BDI scores were common among subjects with psychoactive substance abuse. These findings indicate that, especially in populations with comorbid psychiatric conditions, the BDI should not be used in the absence of other clinical information as a screen for the presence of mood disorders. Other investigations using the BDI in patients with comorbid alcoholism showed mixed results; some studies support its use as a screening instrument. Clark et al. (1993) identified a subscale of 13 items that defined a distinct depressive syndrome in this population. Several medical conditions show correlations with BDI severity scores, most likely because of shared symptom expression, leading the authors of the scale to recommend that assessments of depression in the medically ill be made using only cognitive-affective factor scores (Beck et al. 1988). Clark and Steer (1994) found that the Cognitive-

Affective subscale of the BDI differentiates depressed patients from those with chronic medical illness (Wilks lambda = 0.59) and correlates highly with severity scores for the Depression subscale of the Hospital Anxiety and Depression Scale (HADS) (p. 547) (r = 0.73).

Some evidence suggests reporting biases (e.g., that higher scores are obtained from women, adolescents, and elderly people, as well as from certain minorities and individuals with lower levels of education). It is not clear whether these trends are the result of differences in the rates of depression across these groups (epidemiological reports suggest that depression is more common in these groups) or of a problem of reporting bias. Lyness et al. (1995) found that older psychiatric inpatients underreport symptom severity on the Psychological-Affective subscale of the BDI but not on the Somatic-Neurovegetative subscale. Allen-Burge et al. (1994) note that the BDI is more likely to miss cases of depression in geriatric men than in geriatric women. Beck et al. (1988) report a relationship between BDI scores and social desirability but note that endorsement of socially undesirable items is also associated with a negative view of self and measures of low self-esteem.

In a review of eight studies of comparative sensitivity to change, Moran and Lambert (1983) found that the BDI was sensitive to statistically significant change in both psychotherapy and drug therapy outcome studies.

chomotor retardation are not included. The revised version of the BDI (BDI-II), which extends the time frame to 2 weeks, has been developed to address this problem, but it is less useful for repeated measures in treatment response studies. However, with further use, the BDI-II may prove to provide broader coverage for the full spectrum of depressive symptoms and could be used with a shortened time frame as needed.

A second use of the BDI is to screen patients who may have depressive illness and may require intervention. When used as a screening device, the BDI should be followed up with a diagnostic instrument or a clinical interview. The advantages of the BDI are that it is easy to use (self-administered), uses simple language, and is easy to score. A shortened version that is limited to the cognitive-affective items is appropriate for use in a general medical population. Disadvantages are that biases have been noted (e.g., women, the less educated, adolescents, elderly people, and individuals with certain comorbid psychiatric diagnoses tend to show higher scores). It is not clear whether these biases are the result of true differences in symptom distribution, reporting biases that are found in many self-report symptom inventories, or specific properties of the BDI scale. If followed by a diagnostic interview, the BDI, with cutoff scores at the low end of the severity scale, appears to be a good choice for a screening device.

CLINICAL UTILITY

The primary clinical use of the BDI is to assess severity of depressive symptoms in patients with previously diagnosed depressive illness. Repeated assessments may be used to monitor the beneficial or adverse effects of treatment. There is good evidence for the internal consistency of the scale in both clinical and nonclinical populations. The scale has been widely used in treatment studies to assess symptom change over time and shows high concurrent validity with other measures of depressive symptom severity, such as the Ham-D (p. 526) and the Zung SDS (p. 534).

One drawback of the BDI-IA is that it was developed primarily to reflect symptoms found in severe depressions and does not provide complete coverage of the symptoms used in the DSM-IV criteria. Specifically, items reflecting increase in appetite, increase in sleep, agitation, and psy-

REFERENCES AND SUGGESTED READINGS

Allen-Burge R, Storandt M, Kinscherf DA, et al: Sex differences in the sensitivity of two self-report depression scales in older depressed inpatients. Psychol Aging 9:443–445, 1994

Beck AT, Steer RA: Beck Depression Inventory Manual. San Antonio, TX, Psychological Corporation, Harcourt, Brace, 1993

Beck AT, Ward CH, Mendelson M, et al: An inventory of measuring depression. Arch Gen Psychiatry 4:53–63, 1961

Beck AT, Steer RA, Brown GK: Beck Depression Inventory—Second Edition Manual. San Antonio, TX, Psychological Corporation, Harcourt, Brace, 1986

Beck AT, Steer RA, Garbin MG: Psychometric properties of the Beck Depression Inventory: twenty-five years of evaluation. Clinical Psychology Review 8:77–100, 1988

Clark DA, Steer RA: Use of nonsomatic symptoms to differentiate clinically depressed and nondepressed hospitalized patients with chronic medical illnesses. Psychol Rep 75:1089–1090, 1994

Clark DC, Gibbons RD, Haviland MG, et al: Assessing the severity of depressive states in recently detoxified alcoholics. J Stud Alcohol 54:107–114, 1993

Guy W: ECDEU Assessment Manual for Psychopharmacology—Revised (DHEW Publ No ADM 76-338). Rockville, MD, U.S. Department of Health, Education, and Welfare, Public Health Service, Alcohol, Drug Abuse, and Mental Health Administration, NIMH Psychopharmacology Research Branch, Division of Extramural Research Programs, 1976

Lyness JM, Cox C, Curry J, et al: Older age and underreporting of depressive symptoms. J Am Geriatr Soc 43:216–221, 1995

Moran PW, Lambert MJ: A review of current assessment tools for monitoring changes in depression, in The Assessment of Psychotherapy and Outcomes. Edited by Lamber MD, Christiensen ER, Dejolie SS. New York, Wiley, 1983, pp 263–303

Naughton MJ, Wiklund I: A critical review of dimension-specific measures of health-related quality of life in cross-cultural research. Qual Life Res 2:397–432, 1993

Rudd MD, Rajab MH: Specificity of the Beck Depression Inventory and the confounding role of comorbid disorders in a clinical sample. Cognitive Therapy and Research 19:51–68, 1995

Center for Epidemiologic Studies Depression Scale (CES-D)

L. S. Radloff and B. Z. Locke

GOALS

The Center for Epidemiologic Studies Depression Scale (CES-D) (Radloff 1977) was developed to measure symptoms of depression in community populations. At the time of its development, researchers were interested in the health correlates of depressive symptoms and in tracking changes in severity of symptoms over time. The scale has also been used in many studies as a screen for the presence of depressive illness. Items were selected to represent the major components of depression on the basis of the clinical literature and factor analytic studies. Components include depressed mood, feelings of worthlessness, feelings of hopelessness, loss of appetite, poor concentration, and sleep disturbance. The scale does not include items for increased appetite or sleep, anhedonia, psychomotor agitation or retardation, guilt, or suicidal thoughts.

DESCRIPTION

The scale is a composite of 20 items selected mainly from the following sources: the Zung Self-Rating Depression Scale (Zung SDS) (p. 534), the Beck Depression Inventory (BDI) (p. 519), the Raskin Scale (p. 533), a depression checklist developed by E. A. Gardner (unpublished manuscript, 1968), and the Minnesota Multiphasic Personality Inventory Depression Scale (MMPI-D) (p. 89). Four of the items are worded in a positive direction to control for response bias. Subjects are asked to rate each item on a scale from 0 to 3 on the basis of "how often you have felt this way during the past week": 0 = rarely or none of the time (less than 1 day), 1 = some or a little of the time (1–2 days), 2 = occasionally or a moderate amount of time (3–4 days), and 4 = most or all of the time (5–7 days). Sample items are provided in Example 24–2.

CES-D scores range from 0 to 60; higher scores indicate more severe depressive symptoms. Total severity is calculated by reversing scores for items 4, 8, 12, and 16 (the items that control for response bias), then summing all of the scores. A score of 16 or higher was identified

EXAMPLE 24–2 ■ Sample items from the Center for Epidemiologic Studies Depression Scale

I felt depressed.
People were unfriendly.
I thought my life had been a failure.

in early studies as identifying subjects with depressive illness.

PRACTICAL ISSUES

It takes approximately 5 minutes to complete the CES-D. The scale appears in several publications, including Weissman et al. (1977). The scale has been published in its entirety in Radloff (1977) and is available from

National Institutes of Health
Epidemiology Branch
5600 Fishers Lane
Rockville, MD 20857

The reliability and validity of the CES-D have been tested in African American, Asian American, French, Greek, Hispanic, Japanese, and Yugoslavian populations (Naughton and Wiklund 1993). The CES-D has been translated into several languages, including Chinese (Cantonese and Mandarin), French, Greek, Japanese, and Spanish. The CES-D is included on the CD-ROM that accompanies this handbook.

PSYCHOMETRIC PROPERTIES

Reliability

Internal consistency as measured by Cronbach's alpha is high across a variety of populations (generally around 0.85 in community samples and 0.90 in psychiatric samples). Split-half reliability is also high, ranging from 0.77 to 0.92. Test-retest reliability studies ranging over 2–8 weeks show moderate correlations (r = 0.51–0.67), which is desirable for a test of symptoms that are expected to show change over time. Studies of African American versus Anglo-American versus Mexican American respondents showed no differences in measures of internal consistency reliability (Roberts 1980).

Validity

In samples of outpatients with depression, alcoholism, drug addiction, or schizophrenia, correlation coefficients (r) between CES-D scores and Symptom Checklist–90 (SCL-90) (p. 81) Depression subscale scores were high, ranging from 0.73 to 0.89. Correlations with the Ham-ilton Rating Scale for Depression (Ham-D) (p. 526) scores were variable and ranged from 0.49 for patients with acute depression to 0.85 for patients with schizophrenia. Correlations with the Raskin Scale (p. 533) were also variable, ranging from 0.28 for patients with acute depression to 0.79 for patients with schizophrenia (Weissman et al. 1977).

Studies of elderly patients report only fair agreement between scores on the CES-D and the short form of the Geriatric Depression Scale (GDS) (p. 544) (Gerety et al. 1994) and a correlation (r) of 0.69 between the CES-D and the Zung SDS (p. 534) (DeForge and Sobal 1988).

In a sample of 406 psychiatric outpatients, CES-D scores were higher in currently depressed patients than in other patient groups (Weissman et al. 1977). Mean CES-D scores for various patient groups were 38.10 for acute depression (n = 148 and SD = 9.01), 14.85 for depression in remission (n = 87 and SD = 10.06), 22.97 for alcohol dependence (n = 61 and SD = 13.58), 17.05 for drug dependence (n = 60 and SD = 10.69), and 12.98 for schizophrenia (n = 50 and SD = 12.94)

In a primary care sample (N = 53), Fechner-Bates et al. (1994) reported that a chi-square test that compared DSM-III-R categories of mild, moderate, and severe depression with and without psychotic features against CES-D scores above or below a cutoff score of 16 was not significant. Analysis of variance (ANOVA) tests for overall differences in severity of CES-D scores across the three DSM groups showed a significant difference between the mild and severe depression groups but not between moderate and mild or between moderate and severe groups.

In a sample of 35 acutely depressed patients treated with medication, patients who were judged to be recovered by clinicians at the end of the study showed a mean decrease in CES-D scores of 20 points, whereas nonresponders or partial responders showed a decrease of 12 points (Weissman et al. 1977).

In a study of the utility of the CES-D in discriminating depression in 406 psychiatric outpatients with a range of psychiatric diagnoses, Weissman et al. (1977) used a CES-D cutoff score of 16 to define case status. As expected, the CES-D showed a high sensitivity (99%) for acute primary depression and for depression in patients with alcohol dependence (94%) and schizophrenia (93%). Sensitivity was lower in patients with drug dependence (74%). Specificity, however, was low in patients whose depression had remitted (56%) and in those with drug dependence (59%) and somewhat higher in those with alcohol dependence (84%) and schizophrenia (86%). The authors concluded that the scale's performance in differentiating primary depressions from those that occur in association with other disorders was less than optimal.

In a community study of 720 subjects, Boyd et al. (1982) found that sensitivity for major depression as determined by Research Diagnostic Criteria (RDC) was low (64%) but specificity was high (94%) at a cutoff score of 16. However, the positive predictive value for major depressive disorder was only 33%. False-negative results were attributed to subjects who answered positively in the Schedule for Affective Disorders and Schizophrenia (SADS) (p. 58) interview but negatively on the questionnaire. False-positive diagnoses were produced in subjects who showed CES-D symptoms associated with anxiety, drug abuse, phobias, panic, or somatization disorder.

The results from a large follow-up study of 310 mothers of handicapped children are consistent with these findings. In examining the diagnoses obtained from the Diagnostic Interview Schedule (DIS) (p. 61) of those who scored ≥16 on the CES-D, Breslau (1985) found sensitivity of 87.5% and specificity of 73% for current major depression but also found that the sensitivity was 80% and the specificity was 73% when the target diagnosis was changed to generalized anxiety disorder. When subjects qualifying for both diagnoses were removed, sensitivity was 75% for major depression and 67% for generalized anxiety disorder.

In 528 community subjects, Roberts and Vernon (1983) found that the CES-D yielded a false-positive rate of 16.6% and a false-negative rate of 40% for major depression as determined by RDC. The efficacy of the scale was not improved substantially when diagnosis was expanded to include minor depression or the depressive personality. Similarly, Myers and Weissman (1980) found a false-positive rate of 6.1% and a false-negative rate of 36.4% in a sample of 515 community respondents. Thus, the major community studies performed do not support the use of the CES-D alone as a screen for clinical depressions.

In a sample of 425 primary medical care patients, Fechner-Bates et al. (1994) compared CES-D scores at or above 16 with DSM-III-R diagnoses obtained from the Structured Clinical Interview for DSM-III-R Axis I Disorders (SCID-I) (p. 49). The CES-D was significantly related to a diagnosis of major depression but also to other Axis I diagnoses. For major depression, sensitivity was 79.5% and specificity was 71.1%. The positive predictive value was 27.9%. Adding subjects with bipolar disorder increased the positive predictive value to 31.3%. Of the subjects with elevated CES-D scores, 72.1% did not meet criteria for major depression, and a fifth of the depressed subjects scored below the CES-D cut point. The authors conclude that the CES-D should be considered a measure of general distress.

CLINICAL UTILITY

Although the CES-D was developed to measure the severity of depressive symptoms in community samples and shows internal and test-retest reliability, validity studies suggest that the measure is not specific for depression. In this way, the CES-D is similar to several other self-report depression scales used as first-stage screening devices in general community or primary care studies. Indeed, validity data obtained with the CES-D are comparable to those obtained with the BDI (p. 519) and the Zung SDS (p. 534) when they are used as first-stage screening devices. Thus, although the scale was developed to assess depression in community surveys, studies do not support its use in undiagnosed populations without a follow-up interview.

REFERENCES AND SUGGESTED READINGS

Boyd JH, Weissman MM, Thompson WD, et al: Screening for depression in a community sample: understanding the discrepancies between depression symptom and diagnostic scales. Arch Gen Psychiatry 39:1195–1200, 1982

Breslau N: Depressive symptoms, major depression, and generalized anxiety: a comparison of self-reports on CES-D and results from diagnostic interviews. Psychiatry Res 15:219–229, 1985

Craig TJ, Van Natta PA: Influence of demographic characteristics on two measures of depressive symptoms. Arch Gen Psychiatry 36:149–154, 1979

DeForge BR, Sobal J: Self-report depression scales in the elderly: the relationship between the CES-D and the Zung. Int J Psychiatry Med 18:325–328, 1988

Fechner-Bates S, Coyne JC, Schwenk TL: The relationship of self-reported distress to depressive disorders and other psychopthology. J Consult Clin Psychol 62:550–559, 1994

Gerety MB, Williams JW Jr, Mulrow CD, et al: Performance of case-finding tools for depression in the nursing home: influence of clinical and functional characteristics and selection of optimal threshold scores. J Am Geriatr Soc 42:1103–1109, 1994

Husaini BA, Neff JA, Harrington JB, et al: Depression in rural communities: validating the CES-D scale. Journal of Community Psychology 8:20–27, 1980

Myers JK, Weissman MM: Use of a self-report symptom scale to detect depression in a community sample. Am J Psychiatry 137:1081–1084, 1980

Naughton MJ, Wiklund I: A critical review of dimension-specific measures of health-related quality of life in cross-cultural research. Qual Life Res 2:397–432, 1993

Radloff LS: The CES-D Scale: a self-report depression scale for research in the general population. Applied Psychological Measurement 1:385–401, 1977

Roberts RE: Reliability of the CES-D in different ethnic contexts. Psychiatry Res 2:125–134, 1980

Roberts RE, Vernon SW: The Center for Epidemiologic Studies Depression Scale: its use in a community sample. Am J Psychiatry 140:41–46, 1983

Weissman MM, Sholomskas D, Pottenger M, et al: Assessing depressive symptoms in five psychiatric populations: a validation study. Am J Epidemiol 106:203–214, 1977

Hamilton Rating Scale for Depression (Ham-D)

M. *Hamilton*

GOALS

The Hamilton Rating Scale for Depression (Ham-D) (Hamilton 1960) was designed to measure the severity of depressive symptoms in patients with primary depressive illness. The quantification of symptom severity may be used to 1) estimate symptom severity before treatment, 2) gauge the effect of treatment on symptoms, or 3) detect a return of symptoms (e.g., relapse or recurrence).

The Ham-D is perhaps the most commonly used observer-rated depressive symptom rating scale. Although it was designed for use in patients with major depressive disorder, it has been used to measure depressive symptoms in other populations. This use is potentially problematic because the majority of validity studies have been conducted on populations with major depressive disorder. Although the original scale had 21 items, Hamilton suggested scoring only the initial 17 items because the last 4 items either occurred infrequently (e.g., depersonalization) or described aspects of the illness rather than its severity (e.g., diurnal variation). A difficulty with interpreting Ham-D scores in research studies is that many investigators have modified the instrument and added additional items without appropriate psychometric evaluations of these revisions. This review focuses on the properties of the 17-item Ham-D (i.e., the first 17 items of the original 21-item version).

DESCRIPTION

The Ham-D is a checklist of items that are ranked on a scale of 0–4 or 0–2. Items with quantifiable severity are scored 0–4; 4 indicates the greatest severity. Hamilton believed some symptoms were more difficult to quantify reliably, and these items have a range of 0–2. Sample items are provided in Example 24–3.

The Ham-D was designed to be administered by clinicians such as physicians, psychologists, and social workers who have experience with psychiatric patients. In clinical research, it is also administered by nonclinicians trained in its use.

The scale was originally designed to be administered by two interviewers corating the same subject. The two

EXAMPLE 24–3 ■ Sample items from the Hamilton Rating Scale for Depression

Depressed Mood: Gloomy attitude, pessimism about the future, feeling of sadness, tendency to weep

0 = symptoms not present
1 = sadness
2 = occasional weeping
3 = frequent weeping
4 = extreme symptoms

scores were to be tallied for a total possible score of 100, because the range for the 17-item scale is 0–50. In practice, this technique is rarely used, but raters are trained to administer the scale in a way that yields scores similar (within 2 points) to those obtained by others at the same research center.

In one study, scores on the Ham-D were compared with a global measure of depression severity; the following thresholds resulted: very severe, >23; severe, 19–22; moderate, 14–18; mild, 8–13; and normal, ≤7 (Kearns et al. 1982). Similar thresholds have been reported by others (Endicott et al. 1981).

PRACTICAL ISSUES

It takes about 15–20 minutes to administer the Ham-D. It was originally published by Hamilton in 1960, but no guidelines were included with that publication. Hamilton subsequently published recommendations for rating each item (Hamilton 1967, 1980). A modification of the scale's structure with anchor points was published in the Early Clinical Drug Evaluation Program (ECDEU) assessment manual (Guy 1976). For example, the ECDEU rendition of the item in Example 24–3 is "Depressed Mood (Sadness, hopeless, helpless, worthless): 0 = absent; 1 = these feeling states indicated only on questioning; 2 = these feeling states spontaneously reported verbally; 3 = communicates feeling state nonverbally; 4 = Patient reports VIRTUALLY ONLY these feeling states in his spontaneous verbal and nonverbal communication." This version of the scale is the one most commonly used (Zitman et al. 1990). Several investigators (Potts et al. 1990; Whisman et al. 1989; Williams 1988) have published structured clinical interviews that may enhance the reliability of the instrument. Several self-report modifications (Carroll et al. 1981; Reynolds and Kobak 1995) and computerized versions (Ancill et al. 1985; Kobak et al. 1990) of the Ham-D have also been published. Translations are available in Chinese, Dutch, French, German, Italian, Japanese, Russian, Spanish, and Yugoslavian.

PSYCHOMETRIC PROPERTIES

Reliability

The reliability of the Ham-D varies with conditions but is generally acceptable. An international study that in-cluded more than 120 patients found that the internal consistency as measured by Cronbach's alpha was 0.48 before treatment and 0.85 after treatment (Gastpar and Gilsdorf 1990). Internal consistency (Cronbach's alpha) was 0.76 in a study of 141 subjects (Rehm and O'Hara 1985) and 0.92 in a study of more than 300 patients (Reynolds and Kobak 1995). The internal consistency tends to be higher (≥0.8) with the structured than with the unstructured interview (Potts et al. 1990).

As mentioned, use of structured clinical interviews based on the Ham-D (Potts et al. 1990; Whisman et al. 1989; Williams 1988) may enhance the reliability of the instrument. For example, in a structured interview designed by Potts et al. (1990), the severity of symptoms was operationalized, wording for an explicit time frame was added, and instructions for symptoms possibly affected by concurrent medical problems or medication were also added. When 10 raters administered this instrument to 989 subjects, 75% in a current episode and 25% with a past episode of major depressive disorder, the intraclass correlation coefficient was 0.92. Potts et al. (1990) found similar reliability and validity with phone administration of a structured interview version compared with in-person administration.

Hamilton found excellent correlation (0.9) between raters in his original paper (Hamilton 1960). Since then, others have continued to find high degrees of joint reliability, ranging from 0.65 (Maier et al. 1988a) to 0.9 for the total score (Rehm and O'Hara 1985). This reliability holds for raters who corate using a videotaped interview.

Validity

The validity of the scale has been evaluated by several groups. The Ham-D has correlations with global measures of depressive severity that range between 0.65 and 0.90. Results from the Ham-D are also highly correlated with the results from other observer-rated instruments such as the Montgomery-Asberg Depression Rating Scale (MADRS) (p. 531), the Inventory of Depressive Symptomatology (IDS) (p. 529), and the Bech Melancholia Scale (BMS) (Bech et al. 1975). Correlations between the Ham-D and these clinician-rated instruments range between 0.80 and 0.90.

Validity is not high in all populations. The depressive symptoms of older patients, who are more likely to have general medical illnesses, may be overrated because of the reliance of the Ham-D on somatic symptoms. In a study of more than 500 patients with depression and general medical illness who were 70 years and older, eight items from the Ham-D were probably elevated by the concurrent somatic disorder (Linden et al. 1995). These items included somatic anxiety, gastrointestinal symptoms, general somatic symptoms, hypochondriasis, weight loss, middle insomnia, and work.

In addition, some of the items perform less well than others. Scores on loss of insight, gastrointestinal symptoms, and loss of libido correlated less well with scores on other measures of depression (Rehm and O'Hara 1985). One study found that a subset of six items (depressed mood, guilt, work and interests, psychomotor retardation, anxiety, and somatic symptoms) had better validity than the entire scale (Knesevich et al. 1977).

Change over time in total scores was strongly correlated (0.68) with a global depression rating in one study (Knesevich et al. 1977). However, another group found that change on the Ham-D correlated more highly with global changes in anxiety than with global changes in depression (Maier et al. 1988b). Loss of insight, obsessive symptoms, agitation, and hypochondriasis may be less sensitive to changes in overall severity than the remaining items (when compared with global measures of severity, such as the Raskin Scale [p. 533] [Maier et al. 1988b]).

CLINICAL UTILITY

Ham-D severity (total score) is a useful gauge of the degree of symptom severity in depressed cohorts. The Ham-D is also useful for monitoring changes in depressive symptoms with treatment and in comparing the efficacy of various interventions if the patient requires more than one type of treatment. Several investigations into its reliability and validity have been conducted, and the results are generally favorable.

In using the Ham-D, several caveats must be kept in mind. The Ham-D is best used by individuals who have been trained in its use. For those who have not received training, a structured format may be easier to use and produce more reliable results. The Ham-D was designed for patients with major depressive disorder, although one of the structured formats, the Hamilton Depression Index, includes items germane to dysthymic disorder (e.g., poor self-esteem and pessimism about the future) and has been validated in this population. The validity and reli-

ability appear to be less in some subgroups, such as older people and individuals with general medical illness. Several modifications have been made to the instrument, many of which have not been evaluated psychometrically.

Several design considerations may limit the clinical utility of the Ham-D. Because the Ham-D was developed before the Research Diagnostic Criteria or the DSM-III, it does not include several symptoms that are part of the criteria for depression as defined by these diagnostic systems (e.g., anhedonia). It gives more weight to somatic signs and symptoms (e.g., fatigue and decreased appetite) than to cognitive symptoms (e.g., guilt). It does not include reverse neurovegetative symptoms (e.g., oversleeping and overeating) and may underestimate depressive severity in patients with atypical features. It also includes several noncriterion symptom items on anxiety that may reduce its specificity as a measure for depressive symptoms.

REFERENCES AND SUGGESTED READINGS

Ancill RJ, Rogers D, Carr AC: Comparison of computerized self-rating scales for depression with conventional observer ratings. Acta Psychiatr Scand 71:315–317, 1985

Bech PI, Gram LF, Dein E, et al: Quantitative rating of depressive states: correlation between clinical assessment, Beck's self-rating scale, and Hamilton's objective rating scale. Acta Psychiatr Scand 51:161–170, 1975

Carroll BJ, Feinburg M, Smouse PE, et al: The Carroll Rating Scale for Depression: development, reliability, and validation. Br J Psychiatry 138:194–200, 1981

Endicott J, Cohen J, Nee J, et al: Hamilton Depression Rating Scale: extracted from regular and change versions of the Schedule for Affective Disorders and Schizophrenia. Arch Gen Psychiatry 38:98–103, 1981

Gastpar M, Gilsdorf U: The Hamilton Depression Rating Scale in a WHO collaborative program, in The Hamilton Scales (Psychopharmacology Series 9). Edited by Bech P, Coppen A. Berlin, Springer-Verlag, 1990

Guy W: ECDEU Assessment Manual of Psychopharmacology—Revised (DHEW Publ No ADM 76-338). Rockville, MD, U.S. Department of Health, Education, and Welfare, Public Health Service, Alcohol, Drug Abuse, and Mental Health Administration, NIMH Psychopharmacology Research Branch, Division of Extramural Research Programs, 1976

Hamilton M: A rating scale for depression. J Neurol Neurosurg Psychiatry 23:56–62, 1960

Hamilton M: Development of a rating scale for primary depressive illness. Br J Soc Clin Psychol 6:278–296, 1967

Hamilton M: Rating depressive patients. J Clin Psychiatry 41(12):21–24, 1980

Kearns NP, Cruickshank CA, McGuigan KJ, et al: A comparison of depression rating scales. Br J Psychiatry 141:45–49, 1982

Knesevich JW, Biggs JT, Clayton PH, et al: Validity of the Hamilton Rating Scale for Depression. Br J Psychiatry 131:49–52, 1977

Kobak KA, Reynolds WM, Rosenfeld R, et al: Development and validation of a computer-administered version of the Hamilton Depression Rating Scale. Psychological Assessment 2:56–63, 1990

Linden M, Borchelt M, Barnow S, et al: The impact of somatic morbidity on the Hamilton Depression Rating Scale in the very old. Acta Psychiatr Scand 92:150–154, 1995

Maier W, Phillip M, Heuser I, et al: Improving depression severity assessment, I: content, concurrent, and external validity of three observer depression scales. J Psychiatr Res 22:3–12 1988a

Maier W, Heuser I, Philipp M, et al: Improving depression severity assessment, II: content, concurrent, and external validity of three observer scales. J Psychiatr Res 22(1):13–19, 1988b

Potts MK, Daniels M, Burnam A, et al: A structured interview version of the Hamilton Depression Rating Scale: evidence of reliability and versatility of administration. J Psychiatr Res 24:335–350, 1990

Rehm L, O'Hara M: Item characteristics of the Hamilton Rating Scale for Depression. J Psychiatr Res 19:31–41, 1985

Reynolds WM, Kobak KA: Reliability and validity of the Hamilton Depression Inventory: a paper-and-pencil version of the Hamilton Rating Scale Clinical Interview. Psychological Assessment 7:472–483, 1995

Whisman MA, Strosahl K, Fruzzetti AE, et al: A structured interview version of the Hamilton Rating Scale for Depression: reliability and validity. Psychological Assessment 1(3):238–241, 1989

Williams JBW: A structured interview guide for the Hamilton Depression Rating Scale. Arch Gen Psychiatry 45:742–747, 1988

Zitman FG, Mennen MFG, Griez E, et al: The different versions of the Hamilton Depression Rating Scale, in The Hamilton Scales (Psychopharmacology Series 9). Edited by Bech P, Coppen A. Berlin, Springer-Verlag, 1990, pp 28–34

Inventory of Depressive Symptomatology (IDS)

A. J. Rush, D. E. Giles, M. A. Schlesser, and C. L. Fulton

GOALS

The Inventory of Depressive Symptomatology (IDS) (Rush et al. 1985) was designed to measure the signs and symptoms of depression in both inpatients and outpatients. The instrument includes all items for major depressive disorder found in DSM-III-R and DSM-IV. However, the instrument was validated on a wider range of patients, including patients with euthymia at the time of administration and patients with dysthymic disorder.

The IDS is unique among depression rating scales in that a self-report form (IDS-SR) and a clinician-administered form (IDS-C) were developed simultaneously. The authors attempted to add several features to this instrument, including a comprehensive coverage of depression and DSM criteria and questions regarding subtypes of depression such as atypical and melancholic features. They also attempted to consider both somatic and cognitive features of depression. Finally, they designed the scale so that all items are weighted equally.

DESCRIPTION

There are 28- and 30-item versions for both the self-report and the clinician-administered instrument. The 30-item version of the IDS includes 2 additional items, interpersonal sensitivity and leaden paralysis or lack of physical energy. The sequence of items is the same in both versions.

The IDS-SR contains multiple-choice questions. Most items are scaled 0–3; 0 is the least severe and 3 is the most severe. A sample item from the IDS-SR is provided in Example 24–4. For items 11 and 12, which cover increased or decreased appetite, and items 13 and 14, which cover weight loss and gain, the subject is instructed to choose one or the other.

The IDS-C is similar in structure, and each item is scored on the same 4-point anchored scales as the IDS-SR. The clinician administering this scale is instructed to circle the descriptor that best describes the patient over the course of the previous 7 days. Just as in the IDS-SR, the clinician is instructed to score either item 11 or item 12, which refer to appetite changes, and either item 13 or item 14, which refer to weight changes. A sample item from the IDS-C is provided in Example 24–4.

The IDS-C is designed to be administered by a trained clinician. A semistructured interview guide aids clinicians in its administration. For example, the semistructured interview guide provides several prompts for the clinician under item 1:

- How have you been sleeping in the past week?
- Have you had trouble falling asleep when you go to bed?
- Right after you go to bed, how long does it take you to fall asleep?
- How many days in the past week have you had trouble falling asleep?

EXAMPLE 24–4 ■ Sample items from the Inventory of Depressive Symptomatology

IDS-SR
Falling asleep
0 = I never take longer than 30 minutes to fall asleep
1 = I take at least 30 minutes to fall asleep, less than half the time
2 = I take at least 30 minutes to fall asleep, more than half the time
3 = I take more than 60 minutes to fall asleep, more than half the time.

IDS-C
Sleep onset insomnia
0 = never takes longer than 30 minutes to fall asleep
1 = takes at least 30 minutes to fall asleep, less than half the time
2 = takes at least 30 minutes to fall asleep, more than half the time
3 = takes more than 60 minutes to fall asleep, more than half the time

Reprinted with permission from A. John Rush Jr., M.D.

The scale and the descriptors are the same as those mentioned.

The range of possible scores for the 28-item IDS-SR or IDS-C is 0–78, and the range for these two instruments using the 30-item version is 0–84. On the basis of a study of nearly 300 patients (Rush et al. 1985), the authors have provided the following guide for the 28-item IDS scores: severely ill, ≥39; moderately to severely ill, 30–38; moderately ill, 22–30; mildly ill, 14–22; and normal, ≤13.

PRACTICAL ISSUES

It takes 15–20 minutes to complete the IDS-SR and approximately 30 minutes to administer the IDS-C. The copyright for the 28- and 30-item instruments is held by A. John Rush, M.D., and there is no fee for its use. Copies of the measure and permission to use it can be obtained by writing

A. John Rush, M.D.
University of Texas Southwestern Medical Center
5323 Harry Hines Boulevard
Dallas, TX 75235-9101

Training in the use of the IDS is recommended, and training videos are available from the author. No training courses are available. The instrument has been translated into Dutch, French, German (IDS-C only), Italian, Japanese, Romanian, and Spanish.

The IDS is included on the CD-ROM that accompanies this handbook.

PSYCHOMETRIC PROPERTIES

Reliability

Both the IDS-SR and the IDS-C have been validated in large patient groups of more than 400 symptomatic patients and more than 500 patients in a mixed population of symptomatic patients and patients with disorder in remission. Cronbach's alpha was 0.92 for the 28-item IDS-C and 0.94 for the 30-item IDS-C among all subjects. Internal consistency was lower only among symptomatic patients (0.67 for the 28-item IDS-C and 0.67 for the 30-item IDS-C). Joint reliability was 0.96 for the IDS-C.

The internal consistency was similar for the IDS-SR, with 0.93 for the 28-item version and 0.94 for the 30-item version in all subjects. Consistency was higher for the self-report version among symptomatic patients than among mixed populations: for the 28- and 30-item versions, Cronbach's alpha was 0.77 in symptomatic patients.

Validity

The IDS is highly correlated with other depression rating scales. Total score correlations between the 17-item Hamilton Rating Scale for Depression (Ham-D) (p. 526) and the 28-item IDS-C and the 30-item IDS-C were 0.94 and 0.95, respectively. The correlation between the IDS-SR and the Beck Depression Inventory (BDI) (p. 519) was 0.92 for the 28-item version and 0.93 for the 30-item version. Finally, correlations between the clinician- and self-administered scales were 0.88 for the 28-item version and 0.91 for the 30-item version. Not surprisingly, the correlation of the Ham-D with the 28-item IDS-C is higher (0.94) than with the 28-item IDS-SR (0.85). Similarly, the correlation of the BDI with the 28-item IDS-SR is higher (0.92) than with the 28-item IDS-C (0.83) (Rush et al. 1996). In patients with major depressive disorder, the self-report score is an average of 2 points higher than the clinician-rated score (Rush et al. 1996).

The IDS has been used to classify patients with endogenous and nonendogenous depression. The IDS-C correctly classified 78% of endogenous and 90% of nonendogenous depressions, whereas the IDS-SR correctly classified only 57% of endogenous and 70% of nonendogenous depressions. The finding provides evidence for the validity of the items in the scale aimed at these two subtypes.

CLINICAL UTILITY

The IDS-C has been used effectively in both biological and psychopharmacological studies to evaluate the severity of depressive illness and the change in illness severity with treatment. The IDS has a wider range in total score than other clinician-administered and self-report instruments and can thus be used to detect depressive illness in less severely ill populations. Like the Montgomery-Asberg Depression Rating Scale (MADRS)

(p. 531), the IDS is less dependent on somatic factors than is the Ham-D. It has the additional benefit of being able to detect differences between endogenous and nonendogenous depressive subtypes; some practitioners believe that endogenous depression is more clearly responsive to tricyclic antidepressant medications. The scoring of the individual items is 0–3 for all items, which leads to more consistent weighting of symptoms in order to obtain a total score gauging overall severity. Both the IDS-SR and the IDS-C perform well in terms of concurrent validity with other depression measures. The IDS-SR total score is slightly (2–4 points) higher than that of the IDS-C. The IDS is also evaluated using a well-established time frame (i.e., 1 week), so that duration of symptom expression can be considered in the overall severity score.

The main disadvantage of the IDS is that it has not been as widely used as scales such as the Ham-D (p. 526) and therefore provides less of a framework for clinicians and researchers when attempting to intuit the patient's stress severity.

REFERENCES AND SUGGESTED READINGS

Rush AJ, Giles DE, Schlesser MA, et al: The Inventory for Depressive Symptomatology (IDS): preliminary findings. Psychiatry Res 18:65–87, 1985

Rush AJ, Gullion BM, Basco MR, et al: The Inventory of Depressive Symptomatology (IDS): psychometric properties. Psychol Med 26:477–486, 1996

Montgomery-Asberg Depression Rating Scale (MADRS)

S. A. Montgomery and M. Asberg

GOALS

The Montgomery-Asberg Depression Rating Scale (MADRS) (Montgomery and Asberg 1979) was designed to be used in patients with major depressive disorder to measure the overall severity of depressive symptoms. The authors' first goal was to design a scale that would assess treatment-sensitive change. A second goal was to construct an instrument that could be used by both psychiatrists and professionals without specific psychiatric training (e.g., nonpsychiatric nurses).

The MADRS has often been used in psychopharmacology research (Montgomery and Asberg 1979). The items are taken from the 65-item Comprehensive Psychopathological Rating Scale (CPRS) (Asberg et al. 1978) and were selected because of their association with major depressive disorder and their sensitivity to change.

DESCRIPTION

The MADRS is a 10-item checklist. Items are rated on a scale of 0–6 with anchors at 2-point intervals. The rater is encouraged to use his or her observations of the patient's mental status as an additional source of information. For example, item 1, Apparent Sadness, is defined as "representing despondency, gloom, and despair, more than just ordinary transient low spirits reflected in speech, facial expression, and posture. Rate by depth and inability to brighten up." A sample item is provided in Example 24–5. Scores on the MADRS range from 0 to 60.

PRACTICAL ISSUES

It takes approximately 15 minutes to administer the MADRS. It is copyrighted by the *British Journal of Psychiatry*, in which the scale was published in 1979. No manuals describing its use are available. According to the authors of the scale, the training needed to use the

EXAMPLE 24–5 ■ Sample item from the Montgomery-Asberg Depression Rating Scale

> Apparent Sadness
> 0 = no sadness
> 2 = looks dispirited, but does brighten up with difficulty
> 4 = appears sad and unhappy most of the time
> 6 = looks miserable all the time, extremely despondent

MADRS should be minimal, and it can be used by those who are not mental health professionals (e.g., general practitioners) and by mental health professionals without doctoral medical degrees (e.g., psychiatric nurses). In the original study by Montgomery and Asberg (1979), the correlation in ratings on the total score between a psychiatrist and a general practitioner was 0.97.

PSYCHOMETRIC PROPERTIES

Reliability

The reliability of the MADRS is acceptable and comparable to those of other observer-rated depression scales. In the only study on internal consistency, correlations between each item and the remaining items ranged between 0.12 (reduced appetite) and 0.84 (apparent sadness). Joint reliability for the total score in several studies ranged from 0.76 to 0.95 (Davidson et al. 1986; Montgomery and Asberg 1979).

In a study of hospitalized patients meeting Research Diagnostic Criteria for major depressive disorder, scores on the MADRS before treatment with antidepressant medication showed a correlation of 0.45–0.47 with the Hamilton Rating Scale for Depression (Ham-D) (p. 526). Lower correlations were achieved when a subgroup of patients with an endogenous subtype of depression were evaluated (0.22–0.54).

In one study, change scores on the MADRS and the Ham-D were compared with global expert ratings (Montgomery and Asberg 1979). The MADRS had a correlation of 0.70 with the change on global ratings, and the Ham-D had a correlation of 0.59 with these same global ratings. Patients in this study included 106 patients with depression defined by Feighner Criteria who varied in the severity of illness at baseline (Feighner et al. 1972). The high correlation between change in the MADRS and global measures supports the developers' contention that the instrument is sensitive to change.

Validity

In one study, all symptoms of the MADRS were present in 70% of depressed patients who met Research Diagnostic Criteria for major depressive disorder (Davidson et al. 1986). In a study by Kearns et al. (1982), the following mean scores correlated with global severity measures: very severe, 44; severe, 31; moderate, 25; mild, 15; and recovered, 7.

CLINICAL UTILITY

The MADRS is a useful gauge of the degree of symptom severity in depressed patients. As mentioned, its particular utility is in evaluating changes in symptom severity, such as those occurring with treatment. Because of its reliance on cognitive features of major depression, it is less likely to misdiagnose depression in patients with general medical illness. The scale is easy to administer and does not require any special training. It is short and not burdensome in terms of time for administration. Another advantage of the scale is that it provides easy-to-follow anchors for various intervals in each item. One problem with the MADRS is that it does not specify a time frame during which the patient should be rated, yet time frame is a domain that many clinicians use in establishing the severity of an item (e.g., 7 days of reduced sleep indicates greater sleep disturbance than 2 days of reduced sleep).

REFERENCES AND SUGGESTED READINGS

Asberg M, Montgomery S, Perris C, et al: A comprehensive psychopathological rating scale. Acta Psychiatr Scand S271:24–28, 1978

Davidson J, Turnbull CD, Strickland R, et al: The Montgomery-Asberg Depression Scale: reliability and validity. Acta Psychiatr Scand 74:544–548, 1986

Feighner JP, Robins E, Guze SB, et al: Diagnostic criteria for use in psychiatric research. Arch Gen Psychiatry 26:57–63, 1972

Kearns P, Cruiskshank CA, McGuigan KJ, et al: A comparison of depression rating scales. Br J Psychiatry 141:45–49, 1982

Montgomery SA, Asberg M: A new depression scale designed to be sensitive to change. Br J Psychiatry 134:382–389, 1979

Raskin Scale or Three-Area Severity of Depression Scale

A. Raskin

GOALS

The Three-Area Severity of Depression Scale (Raskin 1988), known as the Raskin Scale after its originator, was developed to assess severity of depression in subjects screened for participation in a large, multicenter drug treatment study. A parallel scale to measure severity of anxiety was developed by Dr. Lino Covi. Together, the two scales are known as the Raskin-Covi Scales (Raskin 1988).

DESCRIPTION

The Raskin Scale contains three items that assess 1) subjective experience of depression (verbal report), 2) primary behavioral indicators of depression, and 3) secondary signs of depression, such as sleep, appetite, or cognitive changes. A brief description accompanies each item to assist rating. Ratings are made on a 5-point Likert scale. The subjective experience item is provided in Example 24–6. The total depression severity score consists of the sum of the three item scores and may range from 3 to 15. In the original study, a total severity score of at least 9 was used as a criterion for treatment. Subsequent studies have used the lower criterion of a total severity score of 7.

EXAMPLE 24–6 ■ Sample item from the Raskin Scale

VERBAL REPORT: feels blue, helpless, hopeless, worthless, complains of loss of interest, may wish to be dead, reports crying spells

1 = not at all
2 = somewhat
3 = moderately
4 = considerably
5 = very much

PRACTICAL ISSUES

Ratings are made by clinical interview and observation. The ratings themselves take only a few minutes to complete but must be determined on the basis of sufficient interaction with the patient to complete the assessment accurately. Raters have typically been mental health professionals. No manual or training guide is available. There are no copyright restrictions on use of the Raskin Scale. It is included on the CD-ROM that accompanies this handbook.

PSYCHOMETRIC PROPERTIES

Reliability

No measures of internal consistency have been reported. Cicchetti and Prusoff (1983) studied test-retest joint reliability in a sample of male and female outpatients, ages 18 to 55 years, who met Research Diagnostic Criteria for nonpsychotic, unipolar major depressive disorder. Patients were evaluated (usually on the same day at different times) by two types of independent assessors (a psychiatrist and a nonpsychiatrist master's- or doctoral-level clinical evaluator) at two time periods: at intake for the study ($N = 86$) and after completion of a drug treatment trial ($N = 81$). At intake, intraclass correlation coefficients (ICCs) were 0.34 for verbal report, 0.57 for behavior, and 0.45 for secondary signs. At end point, the ICCs were 0.74 for verbal report, 0.69 for behavior, and 0.66 for secondary signs. The test author reports intraclass reliability coefficients of around 0.88.

Validity

Although its sensitivity to change has not been examined in psychometric studies, the Raskin Scale has demonstrated sensitivity to change in clinical state over time in many treatment trials (see Cicchetti and Prusoff [1983] and Raskin et al. [1970]).

CLINICAL UTILITY

The Raskin Scale was developed as a brief rating scale to provide an empirical estimate of the severity of depressive symptoms to identify individuals sufficiently depressed to warrant treatment with medication. However, no studies have been done to determine whether those who are identified by the scale are actually more likely to benefit from treatment than those who are not. The scale is intended for use in populations of patients with diagnosed depressive illnesses. It has also been used to assess changes in depression severity over time in treatment outcome studies. Although the Raskin Scale is useful for this purpose, it offers only a global assessment and no clear documentation of changes in specific symptoms. Finally, although the Raskin Scale is brief and has high face validity, there are limited psychometric data available to support its use.

REFERENCES AND SUGGESTED READINGS

Cicchetti DV, Prusoff BA: Reliability of depression and associated clinical symptoms. Arch Gen Psychiatry 40:987–990, 1983

Raskin A: Three-Area Severity of Depression Scale, in Dictionary of Behavioral Assessment Techniques. Edited by Bellack AS, Herson M. New York, Pergamon, 1988

Raskin A, Schulterbrandt JG, Reatig N, et al: Differential response to chlorpromazine, imipramine, and placebo: a study of subgroups of hospitalized depressed patients. Arch Gen Psychiatry 23:164–173, 1970

Zung Self-Rating Depression Scale (Zung SDS)

W. W. K. Zung

GOALS

The Zung Self-Rating Depression Scale (Zung SDS) (Zung 1965) was developed as a self-administered measure of depression severity. The author intended the scale to be all-inclusive with respect to symptoms of the illness but also short, simple, and quantitative. Items were selected to tap affective, cognitive, behavioral, and physiological aspects of depression. Items were selected on the basis of the diagnostic criteria for depression and factor analytic studies available at the time the scale was developed. Although there is coverage for most DSM-IV symptom criteria, no items clearly cover psychomotor retardation or symptoms that are more common in atypical depressions, such as increased appetite, weight gain, or hypersomnia.

DESCRIPTION

The original form of the Zung SDS (Zung 1965) contains 20 items, with 10 items keyed negatively and 10 positively. For each item, the subject rates whether the item occurred 1 = a little of the time, 2 = some of the time, 3 = a good part of the time, or 4 = most of the time. The time frame is the present. Sample items are provided in Example 24–7.

A revised version that appears in the Early Clinical Drug Evaluation Program (ECDEU) manual (Guy 1976) changes the wording of two items, adds a rating of 0 = none of the time, and extends the time frame to the past week. A companion interview version of the Zung SDS, called the Depression Status Inventory, is also given in the ECDEU manual.

To obtain a total severity score, positive items are reversed, and then all items are summed. Zung SDS scores are interpreted as follows: <50, within normal range; 50–59, minimal to mild depression; 60–69, moderate to severe depression; >70, severe depression. A severity index may be calculated by dividing the total score by 80 (the total possible).

EXAMPLE 24–7 ■ **Sample items from the Zung Self-Rating Depression Scale**

I feel down-hearted and blue.
I have trouble sleeping at night.
I find it easy to do the things I used to do.

Reprinted from Zung WK: "A Self-Rating Depression Scale." *Arch Gen Psychiatry* 12:63–70. Copyright 1965 American Medical Association.

PRACTICAL ISSUES

The Zung SDS can be completed in 5 minutes by higher-functioning patients, although it may take up to 30 minutes to complete, depending on patient pathology. The instrument and instructions for scoring it appear in the original article (Zung 1965). Later versions are included in the ECDEU manual (Guy 1976). There are no training requirements. The Zung SDS has been used in a variety of other countries. Cross-cultural validation studies are available from Dutch, Finnish, Hmong, and Japanese investigations. Other translations have been used in studies in Austria, Czechoslovakia, France, Germany, Iran, Italy, Poland, Sweden, and Venezuela (Naughton and Wiklund 1993). The Zung SDS is included on the CD-ROM that accompanies this handbook.

PSYCHOMETRIC PROPERTIES

Reliability

Split-half reliability studies in a psychiatric population found a correlation (r) of 0.73 (Zung 1972). In a community survey of 1,173 subjects, Cronbach's alpha was satisfactory at 0.79 (Knight et al. 1983).

Validity

In sample of 159 outpatients, there were no significant correlations between Zung SDS total score and age, sex, marital status, educational level, financial status, or intelligence level (Zung 1967). A significant correlation was found with the Minnesota Multiphasic Personality Inventory Depression Scale (MMPI-D) (p. 89) $(r = 0.65)$. In a study of 41 depressed outpatients (Biggs et al. 1978), there were strong correlations between the Zung SDS and the Hamilton Rating Scale for Depression (Ham-D) (p. 526) (range of r is 0.68–0.76) during treatment weeks 2, 4, and 6 but not at study intake $(r = 0.45)$. Correlations were higher when Ham-D scores were below 10 $(r = 0.63)$ and lowest when Ham-D scores were above 20 $(r = 0.45)$.

As an indicator of sensitivity to change, Zung (1965) reported that the mean Zung SDS index scores in depressed patients before and after treatment were 0.73 and 0.39, respectively. Biggs et al. (1978) reported a correlation (r) of 0.63 between change on the Ham-D and change on the Zung SDS in a 6-week treatment trial. However, in a review of drug treatment studies, Moran and Lambert (1983) identified five studies that used the Zung SDS in comparison with another symptom measure; the Zung SDS was not found to be more sensitive to change than the comparison tool in any of these studies. Thus, sensitivity to change over time is low compared with other available measures (including the Beck Depression Inventory [BDI] [p. 519] and the Ham-D [p. 524]).

Zung (1965) reported a range of Zung SDS index scores from 0.63 to 0.90 with a mean of 0.74 (total score equivalent of 59) in depressed outpatients, whereas hospital staff control subjects showed a range of 0.25–0.43 with a mean of 0.33 (total score equivalent of 26). Thus, Zung SDS scores discriminated depressed from nondepressed samples. In a study of depression subgroups, Maes et al. (1988) found that patients with minor depression according to the DSM-III criteria showed lower Zung SDS scores than those with major depressive disorder, and those with major depressive disorder with melancholic or psychotic features showed higher Zung SDS scores than either of the other two groups. Mean total scores for five diagnostic groups were as follows (Guy 1976): 65 for depressive disorders ($n = 96$), 53 for anxiety disorders ($n = 22$), 48 for transient situational disorder ($n = 12$), 52 for schizophrenia ($n = 25$), and 56 for personality disorders ($n = 54$). Thus the Zung SDS is a non–diagnostically specific indicator of depressive symptomatology.

CLINICAL UTILITY

The Zung SDS is a popular tool used to rate the severity of depressive symptoms in patients with diagnosed depressive illnesses. Psychometric data documenting the reliability of the measure are sparse, but those that exist show good internal consistency. Validity studies show that the Zung SDS is sensitive to differences in severity of symptoms across subgroups of patients with diagnosed unipolar depression but is less sensitive to change in symptoms over time than other measures. Difficulties in sensitivity appear more often in the upper ranges of the scale; better results are obtained at mild or moderate severity levels. Although developed for use in patient populations, the Zung SDS has also been used in primary

care and community settings and as a screen for depression (Meakin 1992). As a screening tool, the performance of the Zung SDS is similar to that of the BDI, the Hospital Anxiety and Depression Scale (HADS) (p. 547), and the General Health Questionnaire (GHQ) (p. 75); none are ideal for this purpose (Meakin 1992).

The advantages of the Zung SDS are that it is simple and easy to use and that it has been widely used. The disadvantages are that it lacks coverage of the symptoms common in atypical depressions, such as hyperphagia and hypersomnia, and that it may be less sensitive to change than other available scales.

REFERENCES AND SUGGESTED READINGS

Biggs JT, Wylie LT, Ziegler VE: Validity of the Zung Self-Rating Depression Scale. Br J Psychiatry 132:381–385, 1978

Guy W: ECDEU Assessment Manual of Psychopharmacology—Revised (DHEW Publ No ADM 76-338). Rockville, MD, U.S. Department of Health, Education, and Welfare, Public Health Service, Alcohol, Drug Abuse, and Mental Health Administration, NIMH Psychopharmacology Research Branch, Division of Extramural Research Programs, 1976

Knight RG, Waal-Manning J, Spears GF: Some norms and reliability data for the State-Trait Anxiety Inventory and the Zung Self-Rating Depression Scale. Br J Clin Psychol 22:245–249, 1983

Maes M, DeRuyter M, Suy E: Self-rated depression in relation to DSM-III classification: a statistical isolinear multiple components analysis. Acta Psychiatr Scand 77:27–31, 1988

Meakin C: Screening for depression in the medically ill. Br J Psychiatry 160:212–216, 1992

Moran PW, Lambert MJ: A review of current assessment tools for monitoring changes in depression, in The Assessment of Psychotherapy and Outcomes. Edited by Lamber MD, Christiensen ER, Dejolie SS. New York, Wiley, 1983, pp 263–303

Naughton MJ, Wiklund I: A critical review of dimension-specific measures of health-related quality of life in cross-cultural research. Qual Life Res 2:397–432, 1993

Zung WWK: A self-rating depression scale. Arch Gen Psychiatry 12:63–70, 1965

Zung WWK: Factors influencing the Self-Rated Depression Scale. Arch Gen Psychiatry 16:543–547, 1967

Zung WWK: The depression status inventory: an adjunct to the Self-Rating Depression Scale. J Clin Psychol 28:539–543, 1972

Clinician Administered Rating Scale for Mania (CARS-M)

E. G. Altman, D. R. Hedeker, P. G. Janicak, J. L. Peterson, and J. M. Davis

GOALS

The Clinician Administered Rating Scale for Mania (CARS-M) (Altman et al. 1994) was designed to evaluate the severity of core features of mania and to illustrate changes in manic symptoms over time or with treatment. It was also designed to evaluate the severity of both mania and psychotic symptoms and includes subscales for each of these domains. Of note, the construct of mania measured by the scale is defined by Research Diagnostic Criteria. The CARS-M was primarily derived from the Schedule for Affective Disorders and Schizophrenia (SADS) (p. 58). Items were selected from the SADS for their ability to characterize manic behavior. All items that are used to define mania according to the DSM-III-R criteria are included; the items were modified and refined for clarity and reliability.

DESCRIPTION

The scale contains 15 items that are rated from 0 to 5 on a 6-point Likert scale, except for one item, insight, which is scored 0–4. Each item has anchors, and the scale also includes prompt questions to assist the clinician in making a rating. A sample item is provided in Example 24–8.

Prompt questions follow the item from Example 24–8:

EXAMPLE 24–8 ■ Sample item from the Clinician Administered Rating Scale for Mania

> Elevated/euphoric mood (inappropriate optimism about the present or future which lasted at least several hours and was out of proportion to the circumstances)
>
> 0 = absent
> 1 = slight (e.g., good spirits, more cheerful than others, of questionable clinical significance)
> 2 = mild, but definitely elevated or expansive mood, overly optimistic and somewhat out of proportion to one's circumstances
> 3 = moderate, mood and outlook clearly out of proportion to circumstances
> 4 = severe, clear quality of euphoric mood
> 5 = extreme, clearly exhausted, extreme feelings of well-being, inappropriate laughter and/or singing

Reprinted with permission from Dr. Edward Altman.

- Have there been times in the past week/month when you felt unusually good, cheerful, or happy?
- Did you feel like everything turned out just the way you wanted?
- Is this different from your normal mood?
- How long did it last?

In making the ratings, clinicians are encouraged to use other information, such as nursing and family reports. The authors of the scale recommend that scoring be determined on the basis of the previous 7-day period.

The CARS-M contains two subscales, each of which is scored individually. The Mania subscale includes items 1–10, and scores range from 0 to 50. The second subscale measures psychotic symptoms and disorganization and includes items 11–15. The range of scores for this subscale is 0–24. The scores from both scales may be totaled to yield a global measure with a range of 0–74. Guidelines available from the authors give the following interpretation of scores on the Mania subscale:

- 0–7 = none, or questionable mania
- 8–15 = mild mania
- 16–25 = moderate mania
- ≥26 = severe symptomatology

No interpretation was provided for scores on the second subscale.

PRACTICAL ISSUES

It takes approximately 30 minutes to administer the CARS-M. It is designed to be administered by clinicians trained in its use. The CARS-M is available from the authors. Videotapes for training purposes and translations in Spanish are also available:

> Edward Altman, Psy.D.
> Department of Psychiatry
> Psychiatric Institute (M-C912)
> 1601 West Taylor Street
> Chicago, IL 60612

The authors recommend that joint reliability be established across a sample of 7–10 patients. Because scoring depends on clinician observation, the CARS-M is not appropriate for telephone use. The CARS-M is included on the CD-ROM that accompanies this handbook.

PSYCHOMETRIC PROPERTIES

Reliability

Psychometric data are available from a study of 96 patients with the following disorders: bipolar disorder ($n = 32$), schizoaffective disorder ($n = 14$), major depressive disorder ($n = 26$), and schizophrenia ($n = 24$) (Altman et al. 1994). Internal consistency (Cronbach's alpha) was 0.88 for the manic factor and 0.63 for the psychosis factor. Intraclass correlation coefficients among five raters of 14 videotaped patients (inpatients with various diagnoses who had recently been admitted) had a mean of 0.81 and ranged from 0.54 to 0.99. Joint reliability for the 15 CARS-M items ranged from 0.66 to 0.94, with an average of 0.83. As mentioned, the scale has two factors or subscales (for mania and psychotic symptoms) that evaluate two components of bipolar disorder, because not all patients with bipolar disorder exhibit florid psychosis. In the patients with bipolar disorder ($n = 32$), test-retest reliability was 0.78 for the manic factor and 0.95 for the psychosis factor. In the group of patients without bipolar disorder ($n = 64$), test-retest reliability was 0.88 for the manic factor and 0.94 for the psychosis factor.

Validity

The validity of the CARS-M was evaluated by comparing it with the Young Mania Rating Scale (YMRS) (p. 538)

in the sample of 96 patients described earlier (Altman et al. 1994). The correlation was 0.94. The CARS-M was able to distinguish the manic subgroup from other patients reliably using the Manic subscale. When the cutoff scores listed previously were used in the patients with bipolar disorder ($n = 32$), 9.4% were classified as mild, 62.5% as moderate, and 28.1% as severe. Applying the same cutoff scores to the 64 patients without mania, 81% were classified as mild, 15.6% as moderate, and 1.6% as severe.

CLINICAL UTILITY

The CARS-M is useful in evaluating the severity of mania in patients with bipolar disorder. It is also able to detect the DSM-III-R symptoms of mania. It is easy to administer and has well-constructed anchors with appropriate prompt questions. Training is available from the developers. Given the paucity of well-validated mania scales, the CARS-M provides a useful option because a well-designed and fairly extensive validity study has been done. A problem with the scale in patients with bipolar disorder is that it does not measure depression, so another scale must be administered to evaluate depressive symptoms.

REFERENCES AND SUGGESTED READINGS

Altman EG, Hedeker DR, Janicak PG, et al: The Clinician Administered Rating Scale for Mania (CARS-M): development, reliability, and validity. Biol Psychiatry 36:124–134, 1994

Internal State Scale (ISS)

M. S. Bauer, P. Crits-Christoph, W. A. Ball,
E. Dewees, T. McAllister, P. Alahi, J. Cacciola,
and P. C. Whybrow

GOALS

The Internal State Scale (ISS) was developed by Bauer and colleagues (1991) as a self-report rating scale of manic and depressive symptoms for patients with bipolar disorder. The authors' intent was to develop an instrument that would be helpful in the prospective assessment of various bipolar conditions, including rapid cycling, cyclothymia, and mixed states. On the basis of the literature (Goodwin and Jamison 1990) and consultation with experts and patients, the authors hypothesized that a heightened sense of activation would be a core characteristic of mania. The ISS is designed to assess this putative core feature, as well as either depressed (or dysphoric) mood or euphoric mood. Another goal of the authors was to design an instrument that would be sensitive to changing mood state.

DESCRIPTION

The ISS is a 17-item self-report form. Each item constitutes a visual analog scale; subjects are instructed to mark an X at some point along the line that ranges from 0 to 100. Each end point of the line has an anchor—0 = not at all, rarely, and 100 = very much so, much of the time—with the exception of the last item, which scores mood with 0 = depressed and down and 100 = manic and high. The subject is instructed to score these items on the basis of the way he or she has felt during the previous 24 hours. An example is provided in Example 24–9.

The range of scores for the entire scale is 0–1,700, but the full scale is not generally used. The authors have defined four subscales that were originally identified by factor analysis. The subscales are Activation, Perceived Conflict, Well-Being, and Depression. The Activation and Perceived Conflict subscales have five items each

EXAMPLE 24–9 ■ Sample item from the Internal State Scale

> Today my mood is changeable.

Reprinted with permission from Mark S. Bauer, M.D.

(range of 0–500 for each). The Well-Being subscale has three items (range of 0–300), and the Depression subscale has two items (range of 0–200). No information regarding interpretation of these scores was provided in the original article.

PRACTICAL ISSUES

It takes 10–15 minutes to complete the ISS. The scale, a manual, and a scoring key are available from the author:

Mark S. Bauer, M.D.
Chief
Mental Healthcare and Behavioral Sciences Services
Department of Veterans Affairs Medical Center
830 Chalkstone Avenue
Providence, RI 02908-4799

Training is not required because the ISS is a self-report instrument. There are no published data regarding telephone administration. The ISS is included on the CD-ROM that accompanies this handbook.

PSYCHOMETRIC PROPERTIES

Reliability

Psychometric information is available on the basis of a study of 89 patients, including patients with recurrent major depressive disorder or bipolar disorder, and 24 psychiatrically healthy control subjects (Bauer et al. 1991). Measures of internal consistency (Cronbach's alpha) are available for each of the subscale factors: 0.92 for the Depression subscale, 0.87 for the Well-Being subscale, 0.84 for the Activation subscale, and 0.81 for the Perceived Conflict subscale. Test-retest reliability was shown to be good in psychiatrically healthy control subjects, but significant change occurred in subscale scores among patients with mood disorders who switched mood state and filled out the ISS a second time when there was change in mood state (no time interval specified).

Validity

In a discriminant function analysis using the Activation and Well-Being subscales, the ISS correctly classified 89% of patients (96% depressed, 80% manic, and 92% control subjects). The Activation subscale of the ISS had a correlation of 0.6 with the Young Mania Rating Scale (YMRS) (p. 540); it was the only subscale to correlate with the YMRS. The Depression subscale had a correlation of 0.84 with the Hamilton Rating Scale for Depression (Ham-D) (p. 526). The Well-Being subscale also correlated with the Ham-D ($r = 0.73$), except in the subgroup of depressed subjects.

Various subscales of the ISS were compared with either the Ham-D or the YMRS at two time points to evaluate sensitivity to change. The correlation between the Ham-D and the Depression subscale of the ISS was 0.83. The correlation between the Activation subscale and the YMRS was 0.42.

CLINICAL UTILITY

The ISS has clinical utility in that it is an easy-to-complete form for patients who have bipolar disorder or bipolar spectrum disease. The Activation subscale appears to be the best scale for discriminating between manic patients and patients with other illnesses, because it has shown the ability to differentiate manic patients from "normal" control subjects. The various subscales have good concurrent validity with depression and mania clinical ratings. The ISS can thus be used to measure the severity of both poles of the illness. It has the ability to detect change with treatment or improvement.

Limitations of the ISS are that it is a self-report form and that it may be influenced by patients' self-perceptions and reliability. It was not dependably completed by patients with a thought disorder, although modest levels of psychosis did not preclude completion. It also does not include the DSM-IV criteria for bipolar disorder, so it is not appropriate as a diagnostic instrument. It evaluates a short time frame, which is both advantageous and disadvantageous. It is advantageous in that it can detect changes in clinical state, but it is disadvantageous in that it offers only a snapshot of how the patient is doing dur-

ing that 24-hour period. However, by using a booklet available from the author, the ISS can be used as a monthlong log. Finally, its use is supported by only one validity and reliability study, and thus further exploration of its psychometric properties is warranted.

REFERENCES AND SUGGESTED READINGS

Bauer MS, Crits-Christoph P, Ball WA, et al: Independent assessment of manic and depressive symptoms by self-rating: scales characteristics and implications for the study of mania. Arch Gen Psychiatry 48:807–812, 1991

Goodwin FK, Jamison KR: Manic Depressive Illness. New York, Oxford University Press, 1990

Young Mania Rating Scale (YMRS)

R. C. Young, J. T. Biggs, V. E. Ziegler, and D. A. Meyer

GOALS

The Young Mania Rating Scale (YMRS) was published in 1978 (Young et al. 1978). The authors note that at the time there were very few rating scales for mania compared with the number of rating scales for depression. Their intent in developing the YMRS was to construct a scale that was broader in scope than several of the available scales yet shorter and simpler to use than the Beigel Mania Rating Scale (BMRS) (Beigel et al. 1971), which was developed for administration by nurses during inpatient hospitalization.

The YMRS was designed to measure the severity of manic symptoms and to gauge the effect of treatment on mania severity. It can also be used to detect a return of manic symptoms (e.g., relapse or recurrence). The items were selected on the basis of published descriptions of the core symptoms of mania and were intended to reflect symptoms occurring in both mild and severe illness. It was developed to follow the style of the Hamilton Rating Scale for Depression (Ham-D) (p. 524).

DESCRIPTION

The YMRS is a checklist of 11 items that are ranked on a scale of 0–4 or 0–8. Seven items are ranked 0–4 and have descriptors associated with each severity level. Four items (irritability, speech, content, and disruptive-aggressive behavior) are scored 0–8 and have descriptors for every other increment. These items are given twice the range to compensate for the poor cooperation seen in severely ill patients. Sample 4-point (elevated mood) and 8-point (irritability) items are provided in Example 24–10.

The YMRS is designed to be administered by clinicians such as psychiatrists and nurses. The training required is minimal (joint reliability assessment), and, in one study, psychiatric residents who had not been previously exposed to this scale scored similarly to trained psychiatrists.

The range of scores for the YMRS is 0–60. In the original work by Young et al. (1978), the YMRS was compared with a global mania scale and two commonly used scales, the Petterson Mania Scale (Petterson et al. 1973) and the BMRS (Beigel et al. 1971). The average scores

EXAMPLE 24–10 ■ Sample items from the Young Mania Rating Scale

Elevated Mood
0 = absent
1 = mildly or possibly increased on questioning
2 = definite subjective elevation; optimistic, self confident; cheerful; appropriate to content
3 = elevated, inappropriate to content; humorous
4 = euphoric; inappropriate laughter; singing

Irritability
0 = absent
2 = subjectively increased
4 = irritable at times during the interview; reveals episodes of anger or annoyance on ward
6 = frequently irritable during the interview; is curt throughout
8 = hostile, uncooperative; interview impossible

Reprinted from Young RC, Biggs JT, Ziegler VE, et al.: "A Rating Scale for Mania: Reliability, Validity, and Sensitivity." *British Journal of Psychiatry*, Volume 133, pp. 429–435. Copyright 1978, by permission.

on the YMRS were 13 for minimal severity, 20 for mild, 26 for moderate, and 38 for severe. These averages need to be viewed cautiously, however, because only 20 patients were rated and 15 of those 20 were rated on two occasions.

PRACTICAL ISSUES

It takes 15–30 minutes to administer the YMRS, depending on the severity of the patient's illness. The copyright is held by the *British Journal of Psychiatry*. No scoring materials are available. Those who administer this scale would benefit from training in joint reliability, as previously stated. Telephone use is not appropriate for this scale because several items depend on rater observation.

The YMRS is included on the CD-ROM that accompanies this handbook.

PSYCHOMETRIC PROPERTIES

Reliability

The reliability of the instrument was evaluated by comparing each individual item with the total YMRS score. Correlations ranged from 0.41 (appearance) to 0.85 (language and thought disorder) (Young et al. 1978). In this same study, the joint reliability for total scores was 0.93, and the correlation between raters for individual items ranged from 0.66 (disruptive-aggressive behavior) to 0.95 (sleep). A second study found joint reliability of 0.84 (Altman et al. 1994). In this study, the intraclass correlation coefficient among raters for 14 videotaped patients and across all items ranged from 0.36 to 0.96.

Validity

The validity of the YMRS was evaluated by comparing its performance with that of the Petterson Mania Scale (Petterson et al. 1973), the BMRS (Beigel et al. 1971), and a global measure of mania (Young et al. 1978). The correlation was 0.88 between the YMRS and a global mania rating scale, 0.71 between the YMRS and the BMRS, and 0.89 between the YMRS and the Petterson Rating Scale.

The YMRS appears to be sensitive to change. Treated manic patients showed significantly different scores than manic patients before treatment (Young et al. 1978).

CLINICAL UTILITY

The YMRS is a useful instrument for evaluating the severity of mania. It can also be employed for evaluating changes in manic symptoms with treatment or over time. Although the available information suggests its reliability and validity are acceptable, it should be emphasized that very few studies have evaluated these parameters and that the study populations have been small.

The instrument is easy to administer and has anchors for the severity for each item. However, the inclusion of four items with scores ranging from 0 to 8 rather than 0 to 4 leads to some confusion, and it is unclear that this varied scoring adds to the use of the scale. There is no time frame on which to score the patients, so the dimension of duration cannot be included in the scale.

REFERENCES AND SUGGESTED READINGS

Altman EG, Hedeker DR, Janicak PG, et al: The Clinician Administered Rating Scale for Mania (CARS-M): development, reliability, and validity. Biol Psychiatry 36:124–134, 1994

Beigel A, Murphy DL, Bunney WEJ: The manic-state rating scale: scale construction, reliability, and validity. Arch Gen Psychiatry 25:256–262, 1971

Double DB: The factor structure of manic rating scales. J Affect Disord 18:113–119, 1990

Petterson V, Fyro B, Sedval G: A new scale for the longitudinal rating of manic states. Acta Psychiatr Scand 49:248–256, 1973

Young RC, Biggs JT, Ziegler VE, et al: A rating scale for mania: reliability, validity, and sensitivity. Br J Psychiatry 133:429–435, 1978

Young RC, Nysewander RW, Schreiber MT: Mania scale scores, signs, and symptoms in forty inpatients. J Clin Psychiatry 44:98–100, 1983

Edinburgh Postnatal Depression Scale (EPDS)

J. L. Cox, J. M. Holden, and R. Sagovsky

GOALS

The developers' goal in constructing the Edinburgh Postnatal Depression Scale (EPDS) (Cox et al. 1987) was to design a brief self-report scale that would identify patients with postpartum depression. The use of standard depression rating scales to detect depression in postpartum patients has limitations. For example, many scales measure disturbances in somatic symptoms that may not be valid in postpartum patients who commonly lose sleep because of childbearing needs and may be tired and lethargic secondary to anemia. The items from the EPDS are derived in part from other scales such as the Hospital Anxiety and Depression Scale (HADS) (p. 547). The developers also constructed several other items that reflected problems commonly seen in women with postpartum depression.

DESCRIPTION

The EPDS is a 10-item self-report questionnaire. Each item has four possible responses ranging from 0 to 3, indicating the severity of the symptom. Some items have the most severe answer first, and other items have the most severe response last. Sample items are provided in Example 24–11.

Possible scores range from 0 to 30. The authors find that a score above 12 is indicative of probable major or minor depression on the basis of Research Diagnostic Criteria (RDC). When the threshold is reduced to 9 or 10, the EPDS fails to diagnose fewer than 10% of women with postpartum depression.

PRACTICAL ISSUES

It takes 10 minutes or less to complete the EPDS. The copyright is held by the *British Journal of Psychiatry*, and permission to reprint the scale can be obtained from

Mr. David Jago
Business Manager

EXAMPLE 24–11 ■ Sample items from the Edinburgh Postnatal Depression Scale

I have been able to laugh and see the funny side of things.
   0 = as much as I always could
   1 = not quite so much now
   2 = definitely not so much now
   3 = not at all

I have felt sad or miserable.
   3 = yes, most of the time
   2 = yes, quite often
   1 = not very often
   0 = no not at all

Reprinted from Cox JL, Holden JM, Sagorsky R: "Detection of Postnatal Depression: Development of the 10-Item Edinburgh Postnatal Depression Scale." *British Journal of Psychiatry*, Volume 150, pp. 782–786. Copyright 1987, by permission.

British Journal of Psychiatry
17 Belgrave Square
London SW1X8PG
United Kingdom

Although there is no specific manual for the EPDS, a book on the scale (Cox and Holden 1994) includes several articles describing its use in various populations. This book also includes numerous translations of the scale, including Chinese, Czech, Dutch, French, German, Greek, Hindi, Japanese, Portuguese, Spanish, Swedish, and Urdu versions. There is also a computerized version of the scale.

PSYCHOMETRIC PROPERTIES

Reliability

In a community study of 60 postpartum women with major or minor depression (average age of mother, 26 years; average age of baby, 3 months), the internal consistency (Cronbach's alpha) was 0.87 (Cox et al. 1987).

Validity

In a larger cohort of 84 mothers, which included women with depressive illness and control subjects, using a threshold of 12 or 13, the sensitivity of the EPDS for identifying women with major or minor depression (diagnosed by RDC) was 86%. In this same group, the specificity was 78%, and the positive predictive value of iden-

tifying women who met RDC for major or minor depression was 73% (Cox et al. 1987). In a second study of 676 women 6 weeks postpartum (depressed and nondepressed), depressive illness was diagnosed by Goldberg's Standardized Psychiatric Interview (SPI) (Goldberg 1972), augmented with additional questions to make a diagnosis according to RDC. The sensitivity was 52% for minor depression, 81% for major depression, and 68% for either when using a cutoff score of 12.5. The specificity was 95.7% (Murray and Carothers 1990). A third study of 142 postpartum women (depressed and nondepressed) who were screened 6–8 weeks after giving birth found sensitivity and specificity of 95% and 93%, respectively (Harris et al. 1989). Again, the gold standard used to diagnose a depressive disorder was application of RDC.

In a study comparing the EPDS with the Beck Depression Inventory (BDI) (p. 519), postpartum women (depressed and nondepressed) were administered the EPDS and the BDI at 2 and 6 months after giving birth (Lussier et al. 1996). The correlation (*r*) for these scales was 0.67 at 2 months and 0.79 at 6 months. Applying standard cutoff scores (7/8 on the BDI and 12/13 on the EPDS), 8% and 12% were categorized as depressed according to the BDI and 8% and 13% were characterized as depressed according to the EPDS, at 2 and 6 months after giving birth, respectively (Lussier et al. 1996). A second study comparing the BDI with the EPDS (Harris et al. 1989) found that the EPDS correlated more highly with the Raskin Scale (p. 533) (0.80) and the Montgomery-Asberg Depression Rating Scale (MADRS) (p. 531) (0.79) than with the BDI (0.68). When the DSM-III criteria for major depressive disorder were applied to this mixed cohort of more than 120 women, the EPDS had greater sensitivity (95%) than the BDI (68%) and was about equivalent to the MADRS (91%) and the Raskin Scale (100%) in identifying major depressive disorder (Harris et al. 1989).

The EPDS shows sensitivity to change. In one study (the original validation study by Cox et al. [1987]), the women who improved were evaluated with the EPDS and Goldberg's SPI, and the changes in scores on the two scales were significantly associated.

CLINICAL UTILITY

The EPDS appears to be very well accepted. Compliance with its use was excellent, and patients found it unobtrusive. It appears to be helpful in aiding general practitioners who work in large clinical settings in detecting major and minor depressive disorder occurring in the postpartum period. It has the advantage that many normative somatic features in postpartum women, including changes in sleep and energy, are not scored as pathological.

One disadvantage of the EPDS is that, in some instances, it may detect severe personality disorder rather than major and minor depression, as shown by several high-scoring patients in the clinical validation studies (Cox et al. 1987). In addition to performing as a screening tool, the EPDS measures the severity of depression. However, the psychometric properties of its use as a severity measure have not been well characterized.

REFERENCES AND SUGGESTED READINGS

Cox J, Holden J (eds): Perinatal Psychiatry: Use and Misuse of the Edinburgh Postnatal Depression Scale. London, Gaskell, 1994

Cox JL, Holden JM, Sagovsky R: Detection of postnatal depression: development of the 10-item Edinburgh Postnatal Depression Scale. Br J Psychiatry 150:782–786, 1987

Glaze R, Cox JL: Validation of a computerised version of the 10-item (self-rating) Edinburgh Postnatal Depression Scale. J Affect Disord 22:73–77, 1991

Goldberg DP: The Detection of Psychiatric Illness by Questionnaire (Maudsley Monograph, 21). Oxford, Oxford University Press, 1972

Harris B, Huckle P, Thomas R, et al: The use of rating scales to identify postnatal depression. Br J Psychiatry 154:813–817, 1989

Lussier V, David H, Saulier J-F, et al: Self-rating assessment of postnatal depression: a comparison of the Beck Depression Inventory and the EPDS. Pre- & Peri-natal Psychology Journal 11:81–91, 1996

Murray L, Carothers AD: The validation of the Edinburgh Post-natal Depression Scale on a community sample. Br J Psychiatry 157:288–290, 1990

Geriatric Depression Scale (GDS)

J. A. Yesavage and T. L. Brink

GOALS

The Geriatric Depression Scale (GDS) (Yesavage and Brink 1983) was developed to assess depression in geriatric populations. The identification of depressive symptoms in geriatric populations presents several challenges. Most of the currently available symptom scales were developed and validated in samples of medically healthy younger adults. However, depressive symptoms such as sleep difficulties, decreased energy, and decreased libido are commonly found in nondepressed elderly persons. Thoughts of death and hopelessness about the future have a different meaning for those in the last phase of life. In addition, chronic medical conditions are more common in the geriatric population and may be associated with motor retardation or decreased activity levels. Finally, comorbid dementia may affect concentration and cognitive processing. Thus, there is a need to use a different set of symptom descriptors when assessing depression in geriatric populations.

Beyond content, the format of rating scales may need to be altered for use in geriatric populations. Likert-style items with multiple choices and scales that require respondents to look across several statements and choose the one that best describes them may be confusing to rate. Simpler formats, with easy-to-read items and responses, are best for geriatric populations.

The GDS was designed to provide a reliable screening test for depression that would be easy to score and simple to administer. The items, which were empirically derived to maximize discrimination of depressed from nondepressed elderly people, reflect a variety of symptoms relevant to depression, including lowered mood, poor self-image, poor motivation, past versus future orientation, cognitive problems, obsessive traits, and agitation.

Sheikh and Yesavage (1986) subsequently created a shorter version that consists of the 15 items from the original scale that showed the highest correlation with depression. Items were reordered to maximize acceptance of the questionnaire. The short form shows a high correlation ($r = 0.84$) with the original scale and takes 5–7 minutes to complete. More recently, Jamison and Scogin (1992) created an interview-based version of the GDS, with 29 of the original GDS items and 6 additional items (early, middle, and late insomnia, weight loss, change in appetite, and somatic anxiety symptoms). This rating scale correlates highly with the original GDS ($r = 0.85$) and also with ratings obtained using the Hamilton Rating Scale for Depression (Ham-D) (p. 526) ($r = 0.83$). In this review, we focus on the psychometric properties of the original version of the GDS. Additional comments on the use of the Beck Depression Inventory (BDI) (p. 519) and the Zung Self-Rating Depression Scale (Zung SDS) (p. 534) in elderly people are found in the sections that cover those scales.

DESCRIPTION

The GDS is a self-report scale that consists of 30 questions, each answered by circling yes or no. Sample questions are provided in Example 24–12. Of the 30 items, 10 are negatively keyed and 20 are positively keyed. Questions are arranged with more acceptable items first and are presented on a single page. Subjects are asked to choose the best answer for "how you felt over the past week." Scores are calculated by counting the number of depressive responses endorsed, with a total possible score of 30.

PRACTICAL ISSUES

The GDS is published in the Yesavage and Brink (1983) article in the *Journal of Psychiatric Research*. Directions for administration and scoring as well as information

EXAMPLE 24–12 ■ Sample items from the Geriatric Depression Scale

> Do you often feel downhearted and blue?
>
> Do you feel pretty useless the way you are now?
>
> Are you basically satisfied with your life?

Reprinted with permission from Jerome Yesavage.

about the development of the scale and psychometric studies are detailed in the article. A telephone version tested by Burke et al. (1995) showed good agreement with the self-report questionnaire. The GDS is included on the CD-ROM that accompanies this handbook.

PSYCHOMETRIC PROPERTIES

Reliability

The GDS was constructed using a two-stage design. An initial sample of 47 subjects (both men and women over age 55 years) was used to identify the 30 items out of an initial list of 100 that best discriminated depressed from nondepressed subjects. The resulting 30-item scale was then tested in a second sample of 40 nondepressed and 60 depressed subjects. Using the entire second sample of 100, the mean intercorrelation (r) among GDS items was 0.36 and Cronbach's alpha was 0.94. Split-half reliability (r), tested using the Spearman-Brown formula, was 0.94. Internal consistency values were higher than those obtained when the Zung SDS was administered to the same subjects and about equal to those obtained using the Ham-D. Test-retest reliability studies found a correlation (r) of 0.85 in 20 subjects repeating the questionnaire after 1 week.

Validity

The GDS shows high concurrent validity with scores on the Zung SDS ($r = 0.84$) and the Ham-D ($r = 0.83$) (Yesavage and Brink 1983).

Yesavage and Brink (1983) also conducted a one-way analysis of variance (ANOVA) to compare GDS scores in 40 nondepressed and 60 depressed subjects. Depressed subjects were subdivided into mild or severe depression groups on the basis of whether they met Research Diagnostic Criteria (RDC) for major depressive disorder. GDS scores in nondepressed subjects were lower than in depressed subjects and were highest in the subjects with severe depression. ANOVA studies were repeated using the Ham-D and Zung SDS scores. These results showed that the GDS and the Ham-D are equally able to discriminate among depression severity groups, and both did so better than the Zung SDS.

Comparing 20 elderly subjects with no reported depression and 51 elderly subjects hospitalized for depression, Brink et al. (1982) found a sensitivity of 90% and specificity of 80% using a GDS cutoff score of 9. Sensitivity was slightly lower using a Ham-D cutoff score of 11 (86% sensitivity and 80% specificity). Both of these scales performed better than the Zung SDS (with a cutoff score of 37, 86% sensitivity and 70% specificity).

The GDS has been shown to differentiate depressed from nondepressed elderly people in samples of patients with arthritis (Yesavage and Brink 1983), stroke (Agrell and Dehlin 1989), and mild to moderate dementia (Feher et al. 1992; Harper et al. 1990). McGivney et al. (1994) suggest using a two-step procedure in nursing home residents, in which patients are first tested using the Mini-Mental State Exam (MMSE) (p. 422), and then those with a total score of ≥ 15 are selected for further screening with the GDS. This procedure resulted in a sensitivity of 84% and a specificity of 91% in a sample of 66 subjects, using a GDS cutoff score of 10.

One study reported a bias in GDS scores (i.e., that geriatric medical patients who are more elderly or who have higher verbal intelligence scores underreport symptoms) (Harper et al. 1990), and another reported that geriatric men score lower than geriatric women (Allen-Burge et al. 1994). Underreporting of symptoms in men has also been noted with use of the BDI.

CLINICAL UTILITY

The GDS can be used to screen for depressive illness in geriatric patients. Its advantages are that it was specifically created for use in the elderly population, that it eliminates somatic items likely to be shared by those with medical disorders or elderly people, and that it is simple to read and is in an easy-response format. Psychometric studies show that the GDS is highly reliable and valid, with good sensitivity and specificity for depression. Good results have been obtained when using the scale in community and nursing home populations, as well as in certain populations of the elderly who are medically ill. Biases have been noted (i.e., underreporting of symptoms in men, older individuals, and those with high verbal intelligence), but it is not clear whether these biases are specific to the GDS or would also be seen with other self-report measures.

A second use of the GDS is to assess the severity of depression for monitoring change over time or with treatment. Use of the scale for this purpose has been limited and awaits further validation studies.

REFERENCES AND SUGGESTED READINGS

Agrell G, Dehlin O: Comparison of six depression rating scales in geriatric stroke patients. Stroke 20:1190–1194, 1989

Allen-Burge R, Storandt M, Kinscherf DA, et al: Sex differences in the sensitivity of two self-report depression scales in older depressed inpatients. Psychol Aging 9(3):443–445, 1994

Brink TL, Yesavage JA, Lum O, et al: Screening tests for geriatric depression. Clinical Gerontologist 1:37–43, 1982

Burke WJ, Roccaforte WH, Wengel SP, et al: The reliability and validity of the Geriatric Depression Rating Scale administered by telephone. J Am Geriatr Soc 43:674–679, 1995

Feher EP, Larrabee GJ, Crook TH: Factors attenuating the validity of the Geriatric Depression Scale in a dementia population. J Am Geriatr Soc 40:906–909, 1992

Harper RG, Kotik-Harper D, Kirby H: Psychometric assessment of depression in an elderly general medical population: over- or underassessment? J Nerv Ment Dis 178:113–119, 1990

Jamison C, Scogin F: Development of an interview-based geriatric depression rating scale. Int J Aging Hum Dev 35:193–204, 1992

McGivney SA, Mulvihill M, Taylor B: Validating the GDS depression screen in the nursing home. J Am Geriatr Soc 42:490–492, 1994

Sheikh JI, Yesavage JA: Geriatric Depression Scale (GDS): recent evidence and development of a shorter version. Clinical Gerontologist 5:165–173, 1986

Yesavage JA, Brink TL: Development and validation of a geriatric depression screening scale: a preliminary report. J Psychiatr Res 17:37–49, 1983

Hospital Anxiety and Depression Scale (HADS)

R. P. Snaith and A. S. Zigmond

GOALS

The Hospital Anxiety and Depression Scale (HADS) (Zigmond and Snaith 1983) was designed to screen for the presence of a mood disorder in medically ill patients. It is appropriate for use in either community or hospital settings. To distinguish psychiatric presentations from physical illness, items focus on subjective disturbance of mood rather than physical signs. The Depression subscale is oriented toward the core symptom of anhedonia rather than sadness. Although the HADS does not reflect the full range of depressive symptoms as defined in DSM-IV, there is good evidence that anhedonic symptoms are a sensitive indicator of depression in the medically ill. Items on suicidal ideation, guilt, and hopelessness are not included.

DESCRIPTION

The HADS is a self-report scale and contains 14 items rated on 4-point Likert-type scales. Two subscales assess depression and anxiety. A typical item is provided in Example 24–13.

The seven-item Depression subscale yields a score of 0–21 that is interpreted with the following cut points: 0–7, normal; 8–10, mild mood disturbance; 11–14, moderate mood disturbance; and 12–21, severe mood disturbance.

EXAMPLE 24–13 ■ Sample item from the Hospital Anxiety and Depression Scale

> I look forward with enjoyment to things:
>
> As much as I ever did 0
> Rather less than I used to 1
> Definitely less than I used to 2
> Hardly at all 3

Reprinted with permission from Nfer-Nelson.

PRACTICAL ISSUES

It takes only a few minutes to complete the HADS. It is copyrighted and available from

> Nfer-Nelson
> Darville House
> 2 Oxford Road East
> Windsor, Berkshire
> SL4 IDF, England

A test manual (Snaith and Zigmond 1994) accompanies the scale and describes administrative and scoring procedures as well as some psychometric properties of the scale. Translations are available in Arabic, Chinese, Dutch, French, German, Hebrew, Italian, Japanese, Spanish, and Urdu.

PSYCHOMETRIC PROPERTIES

Reliability

Moorey et al. (1991) found high internal consistency (Cronbach's alpha of 0.90) using the Depression subscale in a population of 575 patients with recently diagnosed cancer. Zigmond and Snaith (1983) found item–total correlations (r) ranging from 0.30 to 0.60 in 50 patients in a general outpatient clinic. The test manual reports Depression subscale test-retest reliability (r) in healthy respondents to be 0.92.

Validity

Although the subscale content was derived on the basis of clinical judgment, subsequent correlational studies were used to refine the construct. Factor analytic studies performed by Moorey et al. (1991) confirmed the presence of two factors that accounted for 53% of scale variance. Anxiety and depression items loaded on separate factors with the exception of item 7 ("I can sit at ease and feel relaxed"). Factor analytic results were replicated in a split-sample design and were also shown to be consistent for both the male and female cancer patients. Difficulties obtaining the two-factor structure were reported in one study (Razavi et al. 1990) that used the French translation.

Correlations (r) between HADS Depression subscale scores and Montgomery-Asberg Depression Rating Scale

(MADRS) (p. 531) scores were at least 0.70 in a sample of 133 inpatients treated in cancer or internal medicine units (Razavi et al. 1990) and 0.77 in 41 primary care outpatients diagnosed with mood disorders (Aylard et al. 1987). Zigmond and Snaith (1983) reported a correlation of 0.79 between the HADS Depression subscale and concurrent ratings on a 5-point clinical rating scale for depression constructed specifically for this study.

In studies that compared HADS Depression subscale scores with gold standard clinical assessments in medically ill patients (Goldberg 1985; Silverstone 1994), sensitivity estimates ranged from 56% to 100%, and specificity estimates ranged from 73% to 94%. The best sensitivity estimates are found when using the lower bound for identification of a case (Depression subscale score of 8, or borderline case), and the best specificity estimates are found when using the upper bound (Depression subscale score of 11, or definite case). Positive predictive values range from 19% to 70%. Higher positive predictive values are found in studies with higher base rates for major depression (at least 30%), and lower values are found in studies with lower base rates for major depression (5.9%). These estimates are comparable to those obtained in other studies using the Beck Depression Inventory (BDI) (p. 519), the Center for Epidemiologic Studies Depression Scale (CES-D) (p. 523), and the General Health Questionnaire (GHQ) (p. 75).

In psychiatric sample populations without medical illness, sensitivity is high (80% with a cutoff score of 8 and 58% with a cutoff score of 11), but the specificity of the subscale is inadequate (28% with a cutoff score of 8 and 51% with a cutoff score of 11).

CLINICAL UTILITY

The HADS is a short, easy-to-use screen for the presence of depressive disorder in nonpsychiatric populations. The brevity of the measure and use of simple and nonthreat- ening questions (i.e., they do not ask about severe symptoms that are clearly indicative of a psychiatric disturbance) suggests that it would be useful in a primary care setting as a screening device. Once depression is identified, other measures with more complete coverage of depressive symptomatology should be administered. Use is not indicated for non–medically ill psychiatric populations. The scale may also be useful for monitoring changes in depressive mood over time. Other validity studies have not been performed yet to examine the relationship between scores on the HADS Depression subscale and response to antidepressant treatment or to evaluate whether patients with high HADS Depression subscale scores show worse outcome.

REFERENCES AND SUGGESTED READINGS

Aylard PR, Gooding JH, McKenna PJ, et al: A validation study of three anxiety and depression self-assessment scales. J Psychosom Res 31:261–268, 1987

Goldberg D: Identifying psychiatric illness among general medical patients. BMJ 291:161–162, 1985

Moorey S, Greer S, Watson M, et al: The factor structure and factor stability of the Hospital Anxiety and Depression Scale in patients with cancer. Br J Psychiatry 158:255–259, 1991

Razavi D, Delvaux N, Farvacques C, et al: Screening for adjustment disorders and major depressive disorders in cancer in-patients. Br J Psychiatry 156:79–83, 1990

Silverstone PH: Poor efficacy of the Hospital and Anxiety Depression Scale in the diagnosis of major depressive disorder in both medical and psychiatric patients. J Psychosom Res 38:441–450, 1994

Snaith RP, Zigmond AS: The Hospital Anxiety and Depression Scale Manual. Windsor, Berkshire, England: Nfer-Nelson, 1994

Zigmond AS, Snaith RP: The Hospital Anxiety and Depression Scale. Acta Psychiatr Scand 67:361–370, 1983

CHAPTER 25

Anxiety Disorders Measures

M. Katherine Shear, M.D., Ulrike Feske, Ph.D.,
Charlotte Brown, Ph.D., Duncan B. Clark, M.D., Ph.D.,
Oommen Mammen, M.D., Joseph Scotti, Ph.D.

INTRODUCTION

Major Domains

This chapter covers measures that assess the key constructs related to the assessment of anxiety and DSM-IV anxiety disorders (i.e., panic disorder and agoraphobia, social phobia, generalized anxiety disorder, obsessive-compulsive disorder, and posttraumatic stress disorder), as well as several general measures of anxiety symptoms. A group of measures that provide broad coverage of anxiety symptomatology are also included for use in situations in which a clinician cannot identify a particular DSM-IV anxiety disorder diagnosis. For example, some patients have a mixed picture that meets criteria for multiple anxiety disorders. Other patients have clinically significant anxiety that falls below the minimum threshold set by the anxiety disorder criteria and would have a DSM-IV diagnosis of anxiety disorder not otherwise specified. In some situations, the clinician may not have sufficient time to complete a full diagnostic assessment. These broader measures should not be confused, as they often are, with measures for generalized anxiety disorder, which is a specific DSM diagnosis.

Organization

This chapter is divided into six sections, as shown in Table 25–1. The first section covers overall measures of anxiety. These measures assess the severity of symptoms that occur in each of the anxiety disorders and do not discriminate between the different DSM-IV disorders. Consequently, the scales are useful when more than one anxiety disorder is present and when no specific diagnosis has been made. The remaining sections each focus on a particular DSM-IV anxiety disorder: panic disorder with agoraphobia, social phobia, obsessive-compulsive disorder, posttraumatic stress disorder, and generalized anxiety disorder. One of the types of specific phobia (i.e., blood-injury phobia) is covered in the Fear Questionnaire (FQ) (p. 558), which is included in the first section because of its broad coverage (i.e., it measures agoraphobia, social phobia, and anxiety and depression as well).

Relevant Measures Included Elsewhere in the Handbook

Diagnostic instruments and procedures and overall measures of functional impairment are not included here but are covered in Chapter 8, "Mental Health Status, Functioning, and Disabilities Measures," with the exception of measures of phobic avoidance (e.g., the FQ) which are, de facto, measures of interference in behavior. Instead, the focus of this chapter is instruments that measure the severity of different types of symptomatic anxiety, specific to each of the DSM-IV anxiety disorders.

TABLE 25-1 ■ Anxiety disorders measures

Name of measure	Disorder or construct assessed	Format	Pages
General anxiety and mixed anxiety disorder measures			
Hamilton Anxiety Rating Scale (HARS) Clinical Anxiety Scale (CAS)	Overall measure of anxiety with a focus on somatic and psychic symptoms; the CAS is a shortened form of the HARS	Semistructured clinician-administered scale; 14 items (HARS) Explicit scoring instructions; 6 items (CAS)	554–557
Beck Anxiety Inventory (BAI)	General measure of anxiety with a focus on somatic symptoms	Self-report questionnaire; 21 items	557–558
Fear Questionnaire (FQ)*	Severity of common phobias (e.g., agoraphobia, blood-injury phobia, and social phobia) and associated anxiety and depression	Self-report questionnaire with five scales: three phobia scales, Anxiety/Depression scale, and Global-Phobia scale	558–561
Panic disorder and agoraphobia			
Anxiety Sensitivity Index (ASI)	Fear of anxiety symptoms or consequences	Self-report questionnaire; 16 items	561–562
Mobility Inventory for Agoraphobia (MI)* Version for accompanied situations (MI-AAC) Version for patient alone (MI-AAL)	Severity of agoraphobic avoidance behavior	Respondents rate 26 situations	562–564
Mastery of Your Anxiety and Panic II (Panic Attack Record)	Method for recording panic attacks	Self-monitoring record for at least 2 weeks on a 10-point scale	564–565
Panic Disorder Severity Scale (PDSS)*	Severity of DSM-IV panic disorder symptoms	Clinician-administered rating; 7 items	565–567
Social phobia			
Social Phobia and Anxiety Inventory (SPAI) Child version (SPAI-C)	Social phobia as defined in DSM: somatic, cognitive, and avoidance and escape symptoms	Self-report questionnaire; two subscales (Social Phobia, 32 items, and Agoraphobia, 13 items)	567–569
Brief Social Phobia Scale (BSPS)*	Severity and treatment response in social phobia as defined by DSM criteria	Semistructured interview; 11 items	569–570
Liebowitz Social Anxiety Scale (LSAS)	DSM social phobia through the evaluation of fear and avoidance in social situations	Semistructured clinician-administered interview; 24 items	570–572

*Measure is included on the CD-ROM that accompanies this handbook.

TABLE 25—1 ■ Anxiety disorders measures (continued)

NAME OF MEASURE	DISORDER OR CONSTRUCT ASSESSED	FORMAT	PAGES
Obsessive-compulsive disorder			
Yale-Brown Obsessive Compulsive Scale (Y-BOCS)* Child version (CY-BOCS)	Severity of obsessive-compulsive symptoms	Clinician-administered semistructured interview; 10 items (self-report version also available)	572–574
Padua Inventory (PI)* Revised version (PI-R)	Obsessive-compulsive symptoms in clinical and nonclinical populations and response to treatment	Self-report questionnaire; 60, 39, and 41 items	575–576
Posttraumatic stress disorder			
Clinician-Administered PTSD Scale (CAPS)	Type and severity of DSM-III-R posttraumatic stress disorder symptoms with scoring that can be modified for DSM-IV criteria	Clinician-administered structured interview; 17 items and 5 global rating scales	577–579
Impact of Event Scale (IES)* Version with arousal symptoms (IES-R)	Psychological response to traumatic stressors or stressful life events (Intrusion and Avoidance subscales)	Self-report questionnaire; 15 items, with 6 additional items for the IES-R	579–581
Posttraumatic Stress Diagnostic Scale (PDS)	Diagnosis of DSM-IV posttraumatic stress disorder and quantification of symptom severity	Self-report; 49 items	581–583
Mississippi Scale (MSS)* Civilian version (Civilian MSS)	Severity of trauma-related symptoms in Vietnam combat veterans	Self-report questionnaire; 35 items	583–584
Minnesota Multiphasic Personality Inventory PTSD Scale (MMPI-PTSD) Revised, shortened version (MMPI-2 PTSD)	Discriminate patients with posttraumatic stress disorder from those without	Interview-based, 49-item subset of the MMPI; 46 items	585–587
Generalized anxiety disorder			
Penn State Worry Questionnaire (PSWQ)*	Trait symptoms of pathological worry	Self-report questionnaire; 16 items	587–589

*Measure is included on the CD-ROM that accompanies this handbook.

USING MEASURES IN THIS DOMAIN

Goals of Assessment

The goals of the measures presented in this chapter include the following:

1. Detecting anxiety symptomatology in at-risk populations

2. Identifying the prevalence of clinically significant anxiety in a chosen sample of interest for administrative purposes

3. Calibrating the severity of symptoms in patients with diagnoses of a specific DSM-IV anxiety disorder

4. Identifying the presence and type of symptoms of anxiety in patients with other DSM or medical diagnoses

5. Evaluating the outcome of anxiety disorder treatment

6. Detecting relapse in treated patients

Anxiety disorders are the most prevalent mental disorders in the community, and symptomatic anxiety occurs even more commonly; thus assessment of anxiety is of importance in most clinical work. Anxiety that accompanies depression usually heralds a poorer outcome. Anxiety that occurs with medical illness may influence the course or treatment of the medical problem. Thus, it is important to recognize and treat anxiety in a variety of clinical settings. To do so, clinicians can use screening questionnaires, structured interviews to aid in diagnosis, and rating scales to calibrate and monitor symptom severity. This chapter covers a wide range of instruments that may be used for screening or for calibrating and monitoring symptoms.

Implementation Issues

For the most part, instruments included in this domain can be implemented in a standard clinical setting without modification. Although obtaining information from multiple informants is always valuable, it is not essential, except with children. Such a strategy might also be useful in assessing anxiety in patients with cognitive impairment or substance abuse problems. However, because anxiety is an internalizing symptom, the reports of other informants may be relatively inaccurate. Moreover, to our knowledge, psychometric data are not available for any of the instruments presented here when administered to an informant.

Virtually all of the measures presented were developed for use in patients with a previously diagnosed DSM anxiety disorder, although some were developed before publication of DSM-III. When using these scales in other situations, clinicians should be aware that anxiety symptoms may be confused with symptoms of medical or other psychiatric illness. For example, an individual with hyperthyroidism could have tremulousness, tachycardia, and other manifestations of autonomic arousal that are also seen with anxiety. Patients with depression may be unwilling or unable to leave their homes but may not be truly phobic. Thus, interpretation of these scales in patients who meet criteria for other illnesses should be modified appropriately.

Few of the rating scales presented here have been evaluated to determine whether there are consistent gender or ethnic differences in response rates or patterns. Such differences are possible, but most of the scales have now been administered to a wide range of subjects, including those from different ethnic backgrounds.

GUIDE TO THE SELECTION OF MEASURES

In conducting assessments of anxiety it is important to specify the goals of the assessment in advance. Broad goals are presented here, but clinicians should be aware that there may be subgoals within each broad goal that are related to the specific type of anxiety the clinician wishes to capture. For example, although several instruments are appropriate for the broad goal of screening for anxiety, only one is recommended for screening for obsessive-compulsive disorder.

To detect anxiety symptomatology in at-risk populations, suggested are the Beck Anxiety Inventory (BAI) for somatic anxiety; the FQ for agoraphobia, social phobia, and blood-injury phobia; the Brief Panic Disorder Screen of the Anxiety Sensitivity Index (ASI) for panic vulnerability; the Penn State Worry Questionnaire (PSWQ) for worry; the Yale-Brown Obsessive Compulsive Scale (Y-BOCS) for obsessive-compulsive symptoms; and the Impact of Event Scale (IES), the Posttraumatic Stress Diagnostic Scale (PDS), or the Minnesota Multiphasic Personality Inventory PTSD Scale (MMPI-PTSD) for symptoms of posttraumatic stress disorder.

To identify the prevalence of clinically significant anxiety in a chosen sample of interest for administrative purposes, the BAI, the PSWQ, and the FQ are suggested because together they target the three main domains of anxiety symptomatology: somatic, cognitive, and behavioral, respectively. Any of the scales suggested for screening purposes can be used administratively if a specific anxiety disorder is the target condition.

Several measures are available to calibrate severity of symptoms in patients with diagnoses of a specific DSM-IV anxiety disorder. For social phobia, suggested are a self-report measure, the Social Phobia and Anxiety Inventory (SPAI), and one of two clinician-interview measures, the Brief Social Phobia Scale (BSPS) or the Liebowitz Social Anxiety Scale (LSAS). For generalized anxiety disorder, the self-report PSWQ is suggested. The Hamilton Anxiety Rating Scale (HARS) has frequently been used for calibrating generalized anxiety symptoms, although it is not recommended as a specific measure for this purpose. For obsessive-compulsive disorder, the best interview measure is the Y-BOCS, and self-report choices for obsessive-compulsive disorder are the Padua Inventory (PI) and the self-report version of the Y-BOCS. For panic disorder, the ASI is recommended as a self-report measure and Mastery of Your Anxiety and Panic II (Panic Attack Record)—a diary measure of panic—and the Panic Disorder Severity Scale (PDSS) as interview rating scales. For agoraphobia, the Mobility Inventory (MI) is recommended. For posttraumatic stress disorder, the Clinician-Administered PTSD Scale (CAPS) and one of several possible self-report measures listed previously are suggested.

Any of the scales that are useful for screening or administrative purposes are also helpful in identifying the presence and type of symptoms of anxiety in patients with other DSM or medical diagnoses. However, the rater should be cautious about interpretation, as noted earlier.

Virtually all of the scales presented in this chapter should be useful in evaluating the outcome of anxiety disorder treatment and in detecting relapse in treated patients. However, little information is available in the literature with regard to monitoring relapse, so the scales are virtually untested for this purpose.

Several measures may be particularly helpful in the assessment of specific anxiety symptoms. In particular, the Fear Survey Schedule (FSS) (Wolpe and Lang 1964) is a very lengthy and extensive instrument for assessing phobic fears. The Social Interaction and Anxiety Scale (R. P. Mattick and J. C. Clarke, unpublished manuscript, 1989), and the Social Phobia Scale (R. P. Mattick and J. C. Clarke, unpublished manuscript, 1989) may be useful and broad measures of social anxiety. The brief version of the Fear of Negative Evaluation Scale (Leary 1983) can be used to assess the cognitive aspects of social anxiety. The Agoraphobic Cognitions Questionnaire (ACQ) and the Body Sensations Questionnaire (BSQ) (Chambless et al. 1984) are excellent measures of fear of bodily sensations but are somewhat longer and more cumbersome than the recommended ASI. The State-Trait Inventory (Spielberger et al. 1970) and the Maudsley Obsessional Compulsive Inventory (Hodgson and Rachman 1977) have been widely used in research studies but no longer seem to be the most useful for identifying specific constructs.

The assessment of posttraumatic stress disorder in children deserves special mention. The IES has been employed with children and adolescents, and it is probably the most suitable of several measures because of its brevity and reading level. One study of high school juniors exposed to urban violence obtained good results with the MMPI-PTSD and the Mississippi Scale (MSS) (Berton and Stabb 1996). However, more generally useful in child assessments (especially in very young children) are indications of behavioral change, such as loss of previously acquired skills, increased withdrawal and clinging, sleep disturbances, phobias, and repetitive trauma-related play (Lyons 1987; McNally 1991; Peterson et al. 1991). The Child Behavior Checklist (CBCL) (p. 310), a parent-report measure, can be useful in the evaluation of such symptoms. Wolfe et al. (1989) reported that sexually abused girls scored higher than a nonabused sample on a 20-item scale of the CBCL. The following scales are also available for use with children: the Children's Impact of Traumatic Events Scale—Revised, a 78-item measure that can be completed by self-report or interview of the child (Wolfe et al. 1989), and the Post-Traumatic Stress Disorder Reaction Index for Children, a 20-item measure developed as a semistructured interview that can also be used for self-report (La Greca et al. 1996).

CURRENT STATUS AND FUTURE RESEARCH NEEDS FOR ASSESSMENT

A wide range of assessment instruments are available for measuring symptoms and syndromes of anxiety. Many of these measures are psychometrically sound but have not been administered systematically to individuals from different cultural backgrounds and have not been studied for potential gender differences. There is a need for a single overall measure of the severity of anxiety that can be used in populations with or without a diagnosed anxiety disorder as a simple way of screening for clinically significant anxiety and monitoring outcome. This measure should tap cognitive, somatic, and behavioral components of anxiety. To our knowledge no such measure exists; we therefore currently recommend the use of three separate self-report measures (the BAI, the PSWQ, and the FQ) to serve this purpose.

REFERENCES AND SUGGESTED READINGS

Berton MW, Stabb SD: Exposure to violence and post-traumatic stress disorder in urban adolescents. Adolescence 31:489–498, 1996

Briere J: Psychological Assessment of Adult Posttraumatic States. Washington, DC, American Psychological Association, 1997

Chambless DL, Caputo GC, Bright P, et al: Assessment of fear in agoraphobics: the Body Sensations Questionnaire and the Agoraphobic Cognitions Questionnaire. J Consult Clin Psychol 52:1090–1097, 1984

Cox BJ, Swinson RP: Assessment and measurement, in Social Phobia: Clinical and Research Perspectives. Edited by Stein MB. Washington, DC, American Psychiatric Press, 1995, pp 261–291

Feske U, Chambless DL: A review of assessment measures for obsessive-compulsive disorder, in Treatment Challenges in Obsessive-Compulsive Disorder. Edited by Goodman WK, Rudorfer M, Maser JD. Mahwah, NJ, Erlbaum, 1999

Fisher J, Corcoran K (eds): Measures for Clinical Practice: A Sourcebook, Vol 2: Adults. New York, Free Press, 1994

Heimberg RG, Liebowitz MR, Hope DA, et al. (eds): Social Phobia: Diagnosis, Assessment, and Treatment. New York, Guilford, 1995

Hersen M, Bellack S (eds): Dictionary of Behavioral Assessment Techniques. New York, Pergamon, 1988

Hodgson RJ, Rachman S: Obsessional-compulsive complaints. Behav Res Ther 15:389–395, 1977

La Greca AM, Silverman WK, Vernberg EM, et al: Symptoms of posttraumatic stress in children after Hurricane Andre: a prospective study. J Consult Clin Psychol 64:712–723, 1996

Leary MR: A brief version of the Fear of Negative Evaluation Scale. Personality and Social Psychology 9:371–375, 1983

Lyons JA: Posttraumatic stress disorder in children and adolescents: a review of the literature. Developmental and Behavioral Pediatrics 8:349–356, 1987

McNally RJ: Assessment of posttraumatic stress disorder in children. Psychological Assessment 3:531–537, 1991

Peterson KC, Prout MF, Schwarz RA (eds): Post-Traumatic Stress Disorder: A Clinician's Guide. New York, Plenum, 1991

Spielberger CD, Gorsuch RR, Luchene RE: State-Trait Anxiety Inventory. Palo Alto, CA, Consulting Psychologists Press, 1970

Taylor S: Assessment of obsessions and compulsions: reliability, validity, and sensitivity to treatment effects. Clinical Psychology Review 15:261–296, 1995

Wilson JP, Keane TM (eds): Assessing Psychological Trauma and PTSD. New York, Guilford, 1997

Wolfe VV, Gentile C, Wolfe DA: The impact of sexual abuse on children: a PTSD formulation. Behavior Therapy 20:215–228, 1989

Wolpe J, Lang PJA: A Fear Survey Schedule for use in behavior therapy. Behav Res Ther 2:27–30, 1964

Hamilton Anxiety Rating Scale (HARS)

M. Hamilton

GOALS

The Hamilton Anxiety Rating Scale (HARS) (Hamilton 1959) provides an overall measure of global anxiety, including psychic (cognitive) and somatic symptoms. The measure was initially designed as an indicator of severity of anxiety neurosis, a construct that is no longer part of the psychiatric lexicon. Although often used as a main outcome measure in clinical trials of generalized anxiety disorder, the scale does not focus on symptoms of generalized anxiety disorder as defined by DSM-IV. Worry, the key feature of generalized anxiety disorder, receives less emphasis than phobic symptoms, and symptoms of autonomic arousal, which are no longer part of the definition of generalized anxiety disorder, are featured prominently.

DESCRIPTION

The HARS is a clinician-administered rating scale. The measure consists of 14 items that assess anxious mood, tension, fear, insomnia, intellectual (cognitive) symptoms, depressed mood, behavior at interview, somatic (sensory) symptoms, cardiovascular symptoms, respiratory symptoms, gastrointestinal symptoms, genitourinary symptoms, autonomic symptoms, and somatic (muscular) symptoms. Component symptoms are provided for each item, but specific anchor points are not delineated. For example, the item for cardiovascular symptoms includes the following components: tachycardia, palpitations, pain in chest, throbbing of vessels, fainting feelings, and missing beat. The item for anxious mood includes worries, anticipation of the worst, fearful anticipation, and irritability. Each item is rated on a 5-point scale (from 0 = no symptoms to 4 = severe, grossly disabling symptoms).

A shortened version of the HARS, the Clinical Anxiety Scale (CAS) (Snaith et al. 1982), has also been developed. The CAS includes six elements from the anxious mood and tension items of the HARS: worrying, psychic tension, ability to relax, startle response, apprehension, and restlessness. Explicit instructions for item scoring are also added.

Total scores for the HARS range from 0 to 56. A score of ≥14 has been suggested to indicate clinically significant anxiety (Kobak et al. 1993). This guideline was established on the basis of the observation that 85% of patients with generalized anxiety disorder and none of the control subjects scored >14 on the HARS. Nonclinical subjects typically score ≤5 points. Reported scores for persons with depressive disorders range from 14.9 to 27.6. Persons with schizophrenia were found to score as high as 27.5.

PRACTICAL ISSUES

The administration time of the HARS has not been formally reported, but experience with the scale indicates that it takes approximately 15–30 minutes to administer. Although training is recommended for research applications, clinicians can use the scale without training. When used without training, it is important that the same person rate the subject before and after treatment, because the scale lends itself to idiosyncratic interpretations. There is no cost associated with use of this measure. Permission is not needed to use the scale, which can be found in the original article (Hamilton 1959). Several structured interview formats are available (Bruss et al. 1994; Williams 1996) and may increase reliability. A structured interview format of the HARS is available from

M. Katherine Shear, M.D.
Anxiety Disorders Prevention Program
Western Psychiatric Institute and Clinic
3811 O'Hara Street
Pittsburgh, PA 15213

A computer-administered version has a high correlation with the clinician-administered version ($r = 0.92$) and has good psychometric properties. Individuals interested in the computer version should contact

Kenneth A. Kobak
Dean Foundation for Health, Research, and Education
8000 Excelsior Drive, Suite 302
Madison, WI 53717-1914

Administration of the HARS by remote video appears to be reliable (Baer et al. 1995).

PSYCHOMETRIC PROPERTIES

Reliability

The HARS shows good internal consistency; Cronbach's alphas ranged from 0.79 to 0.86. With careful training, adequate joint reliability for raters using the conventional HARS ($r = 0.74–0.96$) and excellent 1-day and 1-week test-retest reliability ($r = 0.96$) have been demonstrated. For adolescents, fair stability over a 1-year period has been demonstrated ($r = 0.64$). However, because there are no operationalized anchor points for the scale, rater training is likely to be idiosyncratic and site specific. A study is currently under way to test cross-site joint reliability of the standard HARS compared with the HARS administered using the structured interview guide developed by Shear (personal communication, 1996).

Validity

The HARS total score has been found to correlate with scores on other anxiety scales, including the global rating of anxiety by Covi ($r = 0.63–0.75$) (Lipman 1982) and the Beck Anxiety Inventory (BAI) (p. 557) ($r = 0.56$). The concurrent validity correlation coefficients between the HARS and the Covi were determined on the basis of one study (Maier et al. 1988) that included two different samples. The first sample ($r = 0.63$) included 97 inpatients and outpatients with panic disorder, 45 of whom had comorbid major depression. The second sample ($r = 0.75$) included 101 inpatients with major depression, 28 of whom had comorbid panic disorder with or without agoraphobia. Correlation coefficients between the HARS and the BAI ($r = 0.56$) (Beck and Steer 1991) were determined on the basis of a sample of 367 outpatients with different types of anxiety disorders as diagnosed by the Structured Clinical

Interview for DSM-III-R Axis I Disorders (SCID-I) (p. 49). The HARS can distinguish patients with anxiety disorders from nonclinical control subjects (Kobak et al. 1993). The mean HARS score in a sample of 78 nonclinical control subjects was 2.40 (SD = 2.47), the mean score in a sample of 86 treatment-seeking subjects with anxiety disorders (without secondary depression) was 18.95 (SD = 8.43), and the mean score in a sample of 132 treatment-seeking subjects with major depression (without secondary anxiety) was 20.31 (SD = 6.03). However, HARS scores correlate highly (r = 0.62–0.73) (Clark et al. 1994; Riskind et al. 1987) with Hamilton Rating Scale for Depression (Ham-D) (p. 526) scores. Omitting items that refer to depression (e.g., depressed mood and insomnia) from the HARS and items that refer to anxiety from the Ham-D (p. 526) allows for better discrimination between patients with generalized anxiety disorder and major depressive disorder as determined by DSM-III-R criteria.

The HARS is sensitive to change with treatment, and change scores correlate significantly with change scores on other global anxiety scales, such as the Covi (r = 0.59). However, because medication side effects may be similar to HARS somatic items, it is necessary to discriminate between the two in medication outcome assessments.

CLINICAL UTILITY

Relatively few psychometric studies of the HARS have been undertaken, considering how long this instrument has been available; however, those that do exist indicate good reliability with trained raters and good validity as a measure of overall anxiety. The HARS can be used to assess the severity of overall anxiety in patients who meet criteria for anxiety or depressive disorders and to monitor the outcome of treatment. The instrument does not distinguish symptoms of a specific anxiety disorder or distinguish an anxiety disorder from an anxious depression. However, the HARS correlates with other measures of anxiety and discriminates between patients with anxiety disorders and nonclinical control subjects. The instrument is reliable and valid in adolescents as well as adults. Its main advantage is that it is the most widely used anxiety measure in pharmacotherapy studies of anxiety, so clinicians can use published results to anchor their work.

However, the scale is not appropriate as a screening or diagnostic instrument. Moreover, administration of the HARS requires valuable clinician time, and the BAI (p. 557), a brief, well-validated self-report questionnaire, also measures overall anxiety.

REFERENCES AND SUGGESTED READINGS

Baer L, Cukor P, Jenike MA, et al: Pilot studies of telemedicine for patients with obsessive compulsive disorder. Am J Psychiatry 152:1383–1385, 1995

Beck AT, Steer RA: Relationship between the Beck Anxiety Inventory and the Hamilton Anxiety Rating Scale with anxious outpatients. Journal of Anxiety Disorders 5:213–223, 1991

Bruss GS, Gruenberg AM, Goldstein RD, et al: Hamilton Anxiety Rating Scale interview guide: joint interview and test-retest methods for interrater reliability. Psychiatry Res 53:191–202, 1994

Clark DB, Donovan JE: Reliability and validity of the Hamilton Anxiety Rating Scale in an adolescent sample. J Am Acad Child Adolesc Psychiatry 33:354–360, 1994

Clark DA, Steer RA, Beck AT: Common and specific dimensions of self-reported anxiety and depression: implications for the cognitive and tripartite models. J Abnorm Psychol 103:645–654, 1994

Hamilton M: The assessment of anxiety states by rating. Br J Med Psychol 32:50–55, 1959

Kobak KA, Reynolds WM, Greist JH: Development and validation of a computer-administered version of the Hamilton Anxiety Scale. Psychological Assessment 5:487–492, 1993

Lipman RS: Differentiating anxiety and depression in anxiety disorders: use of rating scales. Psychopharmacol Bull 18:69–82, 1982

Maier W, Buller R, Philipp M, et al: The Hamilton Anxiety Scale: reliability, validity, and sensitivity to change in anxiety and depressive disorders. J Affect Disord 14:61–68, 1988

Riskind JH, Beck AT, Brown G, et al: Taking the measure of anxiety and depression: validity of the reconstructed Hamilton Scales. J Nerv Ment Dis 175:474–479, 1987

Snaith RP, Baugh SJ, Clayden AD, et al: The Clinical Anxiety Scale: an instrument derived from the Hamilton Anxiety Scale. Br J Psychiatry 141:518–523, 1982

Williams JBW: Structured Interview Guide for the Hamilton Anxiety Scale (SIGH-A). New York, New York State Psychiatric Institute, Biometrics Research Department, 1996

Beck Anxiety Inventory (BAI)

A. T. Beck, N. Epstein, G. Brown, and R. A. Steer

GOALS

The Beck Anxiety Inventory (BAI) (Beck et al. 1988a) assesses anxiety, with a focus on somatic symptoms. The BAI was specifically developed as a measure that would discriminate between anxiety and depression.

DESCRIPTION

The BAI is a 21-item self-report questionnaire. Sample items include typical symptoms of anxiety: nervousness, inability to relax, dizziness or light-headedness, and heart pounding or racing. Patients record how much they have been bothered by each symptom during the past week, including the day the questionnaire is administered. Each item is rated on a 4-point Likert scale ranging from 0 = not at all to 3 = severely: I could barely stand it.

The total score ranges from 0 to 63. The following guidelines are recommended for the interpretation of scores: 0–9, normal or no anxiety; 10–18, mild to moderate anxiety; 19–29, moderate to severe anxiety; and 30–63, severe anxiety.

PRACTICAL ISSUES

Administration time of the BAI has not been formally reported, but experience with the scale suggests that it takes approximately 5 minutes to complete. The BAI is

copyrighted by Dr. Aaron T. Beck. The measure costs $53.00 and can be obtained from

> The Psychological Corporation
> 555 Academic Court
> San Antonio, TX 78204-2498
> Phone: 800-211-8378
> Internet: www.psychcorp.com

A computer-administered version is available (Steer et al. 1993) and may be obtained from the Psychological Corporation.

PSYCHOMETRIC PROPERTIES

Reliability

The BAI has high internal consistency; Cronbach's alphas reported in five studies ranged from 0.90 to 0.94 in samples of psychiatric inpatients ($N = 250$), outpatients ($N = 40$ and 160), undergraduates ($N = 326$), and adults in the community ($N = 225$). Item-total correlations ranged from 0.30 to 0.71. The BAI has satisfactory to high test-retest reliability; correlation coefficients ranged from 0.67 to 0.93 over a 1-week interval ($N = 40$–250), and the correlation coefficient was 0.62 over a 7-week interval ($N = 326$).

Validity

The BAI has demonstrated good convergence with other measures of anxiety in adults, adolescent psychiatric patients, older psychiatric patients, and community samples. In adult clinical populations, the BAI demonstrated moderate to high correlations with the Hamilton Anxiety Rating Scale (HARS) (p. 554) ($r = 0.51$), the State-Trait Anxiety Inventory (Spielberger et al. 1970) ($r = 0.47$–0.58), and the Anxiety subscale of the Symptom Checklist–90—Revised (SCL-90-R) (p. 81) ($r = 0.81$). Despite efforts to provide a distinct measure of anxiety, correlation coefficients between the BAI and measures of depression are substantial: 0.61 for the Beck Depression Inventory (BDI) (p. 519) and 0.62 for the Depression subscale of the SCL-90-R (p. 81). Correlation coefficients between the BAI and other measures of depression ranged from 0.48 to 0.63. Still, the BAI was found to discriminate more accurately between anxiety and depression than other self-report inventories of anxiety such as the State-Trait Anxiety Inventory (Spielberger et al. 1970). Furthermore, in some studies, the BAI proved to discriminate patients with anxiety disorders from those with depression and nonclinical control subjects. The measure's sensitivity to change with treatment is well documented (Brown et al. 1997).

CLINICAL UTILITY

The BAI is a reliable and well-validated measure of somatic anxiety symptoms found across the anxiety disorders and also in depression. It is a short, self-administered scale and is simply scored. The BAI is well suited for monitoring change with treatment. Because it is easy to administer and because data on nonclinical individuals are available, the BAI may be a useful screening tool for unselected individuals in a general medical setting. Its simplicity also supports its potential as an administrative tool for documenting the performance of health care delivery systems in treating anxiety. It is important to note that the BAI does not assess worry, a key symptom of generalized anxiety disorder, nor does it focus on other DSM-IV symptoms of generalized anxiety disorder, such as difficulty concentrating, irritability, or sleep disturbance. Therefore, it cannot be considered a specific measure for generalized anxiety. It does not discriminate well among anxiety disorders or distinguish anxiety disorders from anxious depression.

REFERENCES AND SUGGESTED READINGS

Beck AT, Steer RA: Relationship between the Beck Anxiety Inventory and the Hamilton Anxiety Rating Scale with anxious outpatients. Journal of Anxiety Disorders 5:213–223, 1991

Beck AT, Epstein N, Brown G, et al: An inventory for measuring clinical anxiety: psychometric properties. J Consult Clin Psychol 56:893–897, 1988a

Beck AT, Steer RA, Garbin MS: Psychometric properties of the Beck Depression Inventory: twenty-five years of evaluation. Clinical Psychology Review 8:77–100, 1988b

Beck AT, Sokol L, Clark DA, et al: A crossover study of focused cognitive therapy for panic disorder. Am J Psychiatry 149:778–783, 1992

Brown GK, Beck AT, Newman CF, et al: A comparison of focused and standard cognitive therapy for panic disorder. Journal of Anxiety Disorders 11:329–345, 1997

Creamer M, Foran J, Bell R: The Beck Anxiety Inventory in a non-clinical sample. Behav Res Ther 33:477–485, 1995

Fydrich T, Dowdall D, Chambless DL: Reliability and validity of the Beck Anxiety Inventory. Journal of Anxiety Disorders 6:55–61, 1992

Osman A, Barrios FX, Aukes D, et al: The Beck Anxiety Inventory: psychometric properties in a community population. Journal of Psychopathology and Behavioral Assessment 15:287–297, 1993

Spielberger CD, Gorsuch RR, Luchene RE: State-Trait Anxiety Inventory. Palo Alto, CA, Consulting Psychologists Press, 1970

Steer RA, Rissmiller DJ, Ranieri WF, et al: Structure of the computer-assisted Beck Anxiety Inventory with psychiatric inpatients. J Pers Assess 60:532–542, 1993

Fear Questionnaire (FQ)

I. M. Marks and A. Mathews

GOALS

The Fear Questionnaire (FQ) (Marks and Mathews 1979) is a self-report instrument that was developed to assess the severity of common phobias (agoraphobia, social phobia, and blood-injury phobia) and associated anxiety and depression and to monitor change in these symptoms with treatment.

DESCRIPTION

The FQ consists of the 15-item Total Phobia scale, the 1-item Global Phobic Distress index, and the 5-item Anxiety/Depression scale. The Total Phobia scale includes three subscales: Agoraphobia (5 items), Blood/Injury (5 items), and Social Phobia (5 items). Sample items from the subscales are provided in Example 25–1.

Respondents rate how much they would avoid each of the situations listed in the Total Phobia scale because of fear or other unpleasant feelings. Each item included in the Total Phobia scale is rated on a 9-point Likert-type scale ranging from 0 = would not avoid it to 8 = always avoid it. The Global Phobic Distress item assesses how distressing or disabling the phobic symptoms are on a 9-point Likert-type scale ranging from 0 = no phobias present to 8 = very severe, disturbing, disabling. Items included in the Anxiety/Depression scale are also rated on a 9-point Likert-type scale ranging from 0 = hardly at all to 8 = very severely troublesome. Sample items from the Anxiety/Depression scale are provided in Example 25–1.

Scores range from 0 to 120 for the Total Phobia scale, the most commonly used FQ scale. Scores for the Agoraphobia, Blood/Injury, and Social Phobia subscales and the Anxiety/Depression scale range from 0 to 40 each.

Normative data are available from two samples: a sample of undergraduates who never received treatment (N = 251) and a community sample (N = 111) representing 72% of those contacted. Mean scores for the Total Phobia scale were 27.7 (SD = 13.3) for the undergraduates and 40.5 (SD = 16.2) for the community sample.

PRACTICAL ISSUES

Time for completion is not reported, but experience suggests that it takes less than 10 minutes to complete the FQ. The scale may be obtained from

> Issac Marks, M.D.
> Maudsley Hospital
> Institute for Psychiatry
> De Crespigny Park
> London SE4 8AF
> United Kingdom

Telephone administration of the FQ has been reported. The FQ is included on the CD-ROM that accompanies this handbook.

PSYCHOMETRIC PROPERTIES

Reliability

Internal consistency of the FQ is good; Cronbach's alphas ranged from 0.83 to 0.86 for the Total Phobia scale and

EXAMPLE 25–1 ■ Sample items from the Fear Questionnaire

Agoraphobia Subscale
Traveling alone by bus or coach

Blood/Injury Subscale
Injections or minor surgery

Social Phobia Subscale
Eating or drinking with other people

Anxiety/Depression Scale
Feeling miserable or depressed
Feeling tense or panicky

Reprinted with permission from Issac Marks, M.D.

from 0.71 to 0.83 for the three phobia subscales in large samples of patients with anxiety disorders. Investigations with nonclinical samples yielded less satisfactory results with respect to the measure's internal consistency; Cronbach's alphas ranged from 0.44 to 0.78 for the three phobia subscales. The FQ is stable over time; 1-week test-retest correlation coefficients ranged from 0.82 to 0.96 across all subscales. Good test-retest stability for the three phobia subscales was also found for longer intervals of 2–10 weeks (r = 0.73–0.86) and 3–16 weeks (r = 0.84–0.86).

Validity

In the majority of psychometric studies, researchers examined the properties of the Agoraphobia and Social Phobia subscales, the most frequently used FQ subscales. The Agoraphobia subscale showed good convergence with the avoidance indexes (for both Alone and Accompanied subscales) of the Mobility Inventory for Agoraphobia (MI) (p. 562); correlation coefficients ranged from 0.44 to 0.78. Similarly, the Social Phobia scale demonstrated good convergence with the Social Phobia and Anxiety Inventory (SPAI) (p. 567) and the Social Avoidance and Distress Scale (Watson and Friend 1969) (r = 0.42–0.65). In both clinical and nonclinical samples, the FQ Total Phobia scale and the three subscales showed moderate to large correlations (r = 0.25–0.44) with dissimilar measures of anxiety and depression, including the Beck Depression Inventory (BDI) (p. 519), the State-Trait Anxiety Inventory (Spielberger et al. 1970), and the Anxiety Sensitivity Index (ASI) (p. 561). In addition, the total scale and subscales are only moderately related ($r = -0.25$ to -0.34) to the Marlowe-Crowne Social Desirability Scale (Crowne and Marlowe 1964), indicating that the FQ is not significantly influenced by social desirability, which supports its validity.

An examination of the ability of the FQ to differentiate between outpatients with different types of anxiety disorders showed that the Agoraphobia and Social Phobia subscales differentiated patients with panic disorder with agoraphobia and social phobia from those with panic disorder without agoraphobia and without generalized anxiety disorder. The FQ total score, on the other hand, did not prove to be a good discriminator. The Agoraphobia and Social Phobia subscales accurately differentiated 82% of outpatients with DSM-III-R agoraphobia and social phobia. Both the Agoraphobia and the Social Phobia subscales proved to be sensitive to change with treatment for agoraphobia and social phobia, respectively (Gelernter et al. 1991; Mattick and Peters 1988).

CLINICAL UTILITY

The FQ Agoraphobia and Social Phobia subscales may be useful as brief screening instruments for symptoms of agoraphobia and social phobia in community samples or general medical settings given the scales' ability to discriminate patients with agoraphobia and social phobia from patients with panic and generalized anxiety disorder. Phobic symptoms are easily overlooked in clinical settings, because patients often avoid mentioning them or do not recognize them as symptoms because they have become an ingrained part of life. The FQ can be used to overcome this problem by determining whether phobic symptoms are present. This ability may be especially helpful in situations in which an anxiety disorder is present and treatment is not producing the expected improvement. The clinical utility of the Blood/Injury subscale is less well documented, but this scale should be useful as a screening device as well, particularly in medical settings. Psychometric data on the FQ Anxiety/Depression scale are satisfactory, although examination of the scale's items suggests that they capture general distress rather than specifically assessing anxiety or depression.

Taken together, the three Total Phobia subscales are brief and psychometrically sound measures of avoidance behavior related to agoraphobia, social phobia, and blood-injury fears. However, the scales are not useful for detecting avoidance symptoms related to panic disorder without agoraphobia (e.g., avoidance of physical arousal), obsessive-compulsive disorder (e.g., avoidance of cooking or driving), specific phobias (e.g., avoidance of flying), or posttraumatic stress disorder or for detecting symptoms of generalized anxiety disorder. The subscale scores yielded by the three phobia scales are more informative than the FQ total score.

REFERENCES AND SUGGESTED READINGS

Chambless DL, Caputo GC, Jasin SE, et al: The Mobility Inventory for Agoraphobia. Behav Res Ther 23:35–44, 1985

Cox BJ, Swinson, RP, Shaw BF: Value of the Fear Questionnaire in differentiating agoraphobia and social phobia. Br J Psychiatry 159:842–845, 1991

Cox BJ, Swinson RP, Parker JDA, et al: Confirmatory factor analysis of the Fear Questionnaire in panic disorder with agoraphobia. Psychological Assessment 5:235–237, 1993

Crowne DB, Marlowe D: The Approval Motive: Studies in Evaluative Dependence. New York, Wiley, 1964

Gelernter CS, Uhde TW, Cimbolic P, et al: Cognitive-behavioral and pharmacological treatments of social phobia: a controlled study. Arch Gen Psychiatry 48:938–945, 1991

Herbert JD, Bellack AS, Hope DA: Concurrent validity of the Social Phobia and Anxiety Inventory. Journal of Psychopathology and Behavioral Assessment 13:357–368, 1991

Lee HB, Oei TPS: Factor structure, validity, and reliability of the Fear Questionnaire in a Hong Kong Chinese population. Journal of Psychopathology and Behavioral Assessment 16:189–199, 1994

Marks IM, Mathews AM: Brief standard self-rating scale for phobic patients. Behav Res Ther 17:263–267, 1979

Mattick RP, Peters L: Treatment of severe social phobia: effects of guided exposure with and without cognitive restructuring. J Consult Clin Psychol 56:251–260, 1988

Michelson L, Mavissakalian M: Temporal stability of self-report measures in agoraphobia research. Behav Res Ther 21:695–698, 1983

Oei TPS, Moylan A, Evans L: Validity and clinical utility of the Fear Questionnaire for anxiety-disorder patients. Psychological Assessment 3:391–397, 1991

Osman A, Barrios FX, Osman JR, et al: Further psychometric evaluation of the Fear Questionnaire: responses of college students. Psychol Rep 73:1259–1266, 1993

Osman A, Barrios FX, Aukes D, et al: Psychometric evaluation of the Social Phobia and Anxiety Inventory in college students. J Clin Psychol 51:235–243, 1995

Spielberger CD, Gorsuch RR, Luchene RE: State-Trait Anxiety Inventory. Palo Alto, CA, Consulting Psychologists Press, 1970

Swinson RP, Cox BJ, Shulman ID, et al: Medication use and the assessment of agoraphobic avoidance. Behav Res Ther 30:563–568, 1992

Watson D, Friend R: Measurement of social-evaluative anxiety. J Consult Clin Psychol 33:448–457, 1969

Anxiety Sensitivity Index (ASI)

S. Reiss, R. A. Peterson, D. M. Gursky, and R. J. McNally

GOALS

The Anxiety Sensitivity Index (ASI) (Reiss et al. 1986) assesses fear of anxiety symptoms or consequences. It evaluates the degree to which individuals interpret symptoms of anxiety as threatening (e.g., as indicating a serious illness, a source of embarrassment, or loss of control).

DESCRIPTION

The ASI is a 16-item self-report questionnaire. Scale items are rated on a 5-point Likert scale ranging from 0 = not at all to 4 = severe. The ASI is scored as a simple sum of each item score, and the total score ranges from 0 to 64. A 4-item version of the ASI, the Brief Panic Disorder Screen (Apeldorf et al. 1994), has also been developed. The range of scores for this 4-item scale is 0–16.

The Childhood Anxiety Sensitivity Index (CASI) is an 18-item version of the ASI that measures anxiety sensitivity in children. The wording and several of the questions were changed to make the questionnaire more understandable and relevant to children.

PRACTICAL ISSUES

Information regarding administration time is not formally reported, but experience suggests that it takes about 5 minutes to complete the ASI. The measure is copyrighted and can be obtained from

IDS Publishing Corporation
P.O. Box 389
Worthington, OH 43085

Introductory orders cost $55.00 plus a 10% charge for shipping and handling.

PSYCHOMETRIC PROPERTIES

Reliability

The ASI has high internal consistency; Cronbach's alphas ranged from 0.84 for a sample of college students with arachnephobia ($N = 142$) to 0.88–0.90 for a clinical sample of patients with anxiety disorder ($N = 327$). Adequate 2-week test-retest reliability ($r = 0.75$) was found in a college student population ($N = 147$). The 4-item ASI has also shown high internal consistency ($r = 0.88$) in a sample of college students who reported tension, anxiety, or nervousness ($N = 120$).

Validity

For two samples of college students ($n = 49$ and $n = 98$), Reiss et al. (1986) reported moderate to high correlations between the ASI and the Fear Survey Schedule (Wolpe and Lang 1964) ($r = 0.59$ and 0.71, respectively), the Anxiety Frequency Checklist ($r = 0.36$ and 0.32, respectively), and the Taylor Manifest Anxiety Scale (Taylor 1953) ($r = 0.43$ and 0.50, respectively). In multiple regression analyses using Fear Survey Schedule scores as the dependent variable, the ASI accounted for 17.3% additional variance over the Anxiety Frequency Checklist alone in a college student sample and an additional 23.7% of variance in an anxiety disorder sample. Other analyses using the ASI as a dependent variable have found that the Cognitive-Somatic Anxiety Questionnaire (Schwartz et al. 1978) and the Reactions to Relaxation and Arousal Questionnaire (Heide and Borkovec 1983) as independent variables explained only 39% of the variance in the ASI. These findings point to the distinction between general anxiety and fear of anxiety-related symptoms or consequences as measured by the ASI.

The ASI differentiates college students from outpatients with agoraphobia and other anxiety disorders. In addition, anxious college students yielded higher ASI scores than nonanxious college student control subjects. Patients with panic disorder scored higher than patients with posttraumatic stress disorder on only 7 of the 16 ASI items, all of which assess reactions to bodily sensations. Thus, this scale is a valid screen for panic disorder. It is also of interest that scores on the ASI have been shown to predict development of panic disorder in college students.

Using a cutoff score of 11, the 4-item Brief Panic Disorder Screen (Apeldorf et al. 1994) demonstrated good sensitivity (78%) and specificity (73%) in a sample of 143 outpatients with a diagnosis of primary anxiety disorder as determined by the Structured Clinical Interview for DSM-III-R Axis I Disorders (SCID-I) (p. 49). The Brief Panic Disorder Screen was effective in discriminating patients with panic disorder from patients with other anxiety disorders.

somatic anxiety symptoms have been shown to be negative prognostic indicators in this group.

REFERENCES AND SUGGESTED READINGS

Apeldorf WJ, Shear MK, Leon AC, et al: A brief screen for panic disorder. Journal of Anxiety Disorders 8:71–78, 1994

Heide FJ, Borkovec TD: Relaxation induced anxiety: paradoxical anxiety enhancement due to relaxation training. J Consult Clin Psychol 51:171–182, 1983

Peterson RA, Heilbronner RL: The Anxiety Sensitivity Index: construct validity and factor analytic structure. Journal of Anxiety Disorders 1:117–121, 1987

Reiss S, Peterson RA, Gursky DM, et al: Anxiety sensitivity, anxiety frequency, and the prediction of fearfulness. Behav Res Ther 24:1–8, 1986

Schwartz GE, Davidson RJ, Goleman DJ: Patterning of cognitive and somatic processes in the self-regulation of anxiety: effects of medication versus exercise. Psychosom Med 40:321–328, 1978

Taylor JA: A personality scale of manifest anxiety. Journal of Abnormal Social Psychology 48:285–290, 1953

Taylor S, Koch WJ, McNally RJ, et al: Conceptualizations of anxiety sensitivity. Psychological Assessment 4:245–250, 1992

Wardle J, Ahmad T, Hayward P: Anxiety sensitivity in agoraphobia. Journal of Anxiety Disorders 4:325–333, 1990

Wolpe J, Lang PJA: A Fear Survey Schedule for use in behavior therapy. Behav Res Ther 2:27–30, 1964

CLINICAL UTILITY

The ASI is a brief questionnaire that can be used as a screening device, a measure of symptom type and severity at baseline, and a clinical outcome measure in patients with panic disorder. In particular, the 4-item version (the Brief Panic Disorder Screen) is potentially useful as a screening instrument in settings such as general medical clinics. Although not a diagnostic measure, the ASI can be used to distinguish patients with panic disorder from patients with other anxiety disorders, with the possible exception of posttraumatic stress disorder. The ASI could also be used as a measure of baseline fear of bodily sensations in depressed patients, because panic disorder and

Mobility Inventory for Agoraphobia (MI)

D. L. Chambless, G. C. Caputo, S. E. Jasin, E. J. Gracely, and C. Williams

GOALS

The Mobility Inventory for Agoraphobia (MI) (Chambless et al. 1985) is a self-report questionnaire designed to assess the frequency of panic attacks and the severity of agoraphobic avoidance behavior in both situations in which the patient is accompanied by a trusted companion and situations in which the patient is alone.

DESCRIPTION

In the first part of the MI, respondents rate the degree to which they avoid 26 situations because of anxiety or discomfort. Each item is rated on a 5-point Likert scale (from 1 = never avoid to 5 = always avoid), and the respondent is asked to provide two ratings for each situation: the first rating indicates the degree of avoidance while accompanied by a trusted companion, and the second rating indicates the degree of avoidance while the person is alone. Sample items are provided in Example 25–2. In addition, panic attacks are defined, and respondents are asked to report the number of attacks they experienced in the past week and in the past 3 weeks. The severity of the panic attack or attacks is rated on a 5-point Likert scale. Finally, respondents indicate whether they have a safety zone and record its location and distance from home.

Two subscale scores are calculated: the MI-AAC (ranging from 1 to 5) reflects the average degree of agoraphobic avoidance in accompanied situations, and the MI-AAL (also ranging from 1 to 5) reflects the average degree of avoidance when alone. MI-AAC and MI-AAL scores are only moderately correlated with each other, thus underscoring the importance of this distinction in measurement of the severity of agoraphobic avoidance.

PRACTICAL ISSUES

It takes about 20 minutes to complete the MI. The MI is copyrighted by Elsevier Science, the Netherlands. Permission to use the measure may be obtained from

> Dianne L. Chambless, Ph.D.
> Department of Psychology
> University of North Carolina–Chapel Hill
> CB# 3270
> Davie Hall
> Chapel Hill, NC 27599-3270
> Phone: 919-962-3979

EXAMPLE 25–2 ■ Sample items from the Mobility Inventory for Agoraphobia

Supermarkets

Riding in trains

Driving or riding in a car on expressways

Walking on the street

Reprinted with permission from Dianne Chambless, Ph.D.

The measure is available at no cost. Dutch, German, Greek, Portuguese, Spanish, and Swedish versions are available. The MI is included on the CD-ROM that accompanies this handbook.

PSYCHOMETRIC PROPERTIES

Reliability

The MI-AAL and MI-AAC subscales demonstrated excellent internal consistency; Cronbach's alphas ranged from 0.91 to 0.97. Both scales were found to be stable over time; 31-day test-retest correlation coefficients ranged from 0.75 to 0.90. Test-retest reliability for panic frequency was lower ($r = 0.56–0.62$), as would be expected given the more erratic nature of panic attacks.

Validity

The MI avoidance indexes showed good convergence with the only other widely used measure of agoraphobic avoidance, the Agoraphobia subscale of the Fear Questionnaire (FQ) (p. 558); correlation coefficients ranged from 0.44 to 0.63 for the MI-AAC and from 0.68 to 0.84 for the MI-AAL. MI-AAC and MI-AAL scores were only moderately correlated with each other ($r = 0.67$), underscoring the importance of this distinction in measurement. Both MI avoidance indexes generally showed moderate correlations with other measures of anxiety, including the State-Trait Anxiety Inventory (Spielberger et al. 1970) Trait scale ($r = 0.25$, $P = .01$; $r = 0.38$, $P = .001$) (Chambless et al. 1985), the Blood/Injury subscale of the FQ (p. 558) ($r = 0.34$ and 0.45, $P = .001$) (Arrindell et al. 1995), the Social Phobia subscale of the FQ (p. 556) ($r = 0.26$ and 0.38, $P = .001$) (Arrindell et al. 1995), and the Anxiety Sensitivity Index (ASI)

(p. 561) (r = 0.39 and 0.42, P = .001) (Arrindell et al. 1995). Substantial correlations were found between the MI-AAC and MI-AAL and the Beck Depression Inventory (BDI) (p. 519) (r = 0.44 and 0.51, P = .001) (Chambless et al. 1985). Overall, the MI is more strongly related to agoraphobic avoidance than to dissimilar symptoms, providing support for its validity. Both MI avoidance indexes were found to differentiate between patients with and without agoraphobia, patients with agoraphobia and patients with social phobia, and patients with agoraphobia and nonclinical populations. Both MI scales demonstrated good sensitivity to change with treatment.

CLINICAL UTILITY

The MI is the best available measure of agoraphobic avoidance to date. It is psychometrically sound and has proven to be sensitive to change with treatment. Because the MI assesses avoidance of a variety of places and situations, it is well suited to assist clinicians in developing a hierarchy of patients' feared situations, making it a useful tool for planning exposure-based treatments. Note that many individuals with agoraphobia are very mobile when accompanied but severely restricted when alone. The MI-AAL scale is therefore a better indicator of agoraphobic severity than is the MI-AAC. Its length limits its use as an administrative or screening tool.

REFERENCES AND SUGGESTED READINGS

Arrindell WA, Cox BJ, van der Ende J, et al: Phobic dimensions, II: cross-national confirmation of the multidimensional structure underlying the Mobility Inventory (MI). Behav Res Ther 33:711–724, 1995

Chambless DL, Caputo GC, Jasin SE, et al: The Mobility Inventory for Agoraphobia. Behav Res Ther 23:33–44, 1985

Craske MG, Rachman SJ, Tallman K: Mobility, cognitions, and panic. Journal of Psychopathology and Behavioral Assessment 8:199–210, 1986

de Beurs E, Lange A, van Dyck R: Self-monitoring of panic attacks and retrospective estimates of panic: discordant findings. Behav Res Ther 30:411–413, 1992

Kwon SM, Evans L, Oei TPS: Factor structure of the Mobility Inventory for Agoraphobia: a validational study with Australian samples of agoraphobic patients. Journal of Psychopathology and Behavioral Assessment 12:365–374, 1990

Spielberger CD, Gorsuch RR, Luchene RE: State-Trait Anxiety Inventory. Palo Alto, CA, Consulting Psychologists Press, 1970

Mastery of Your Anxiety and Panic II (Panic Attack Record)

R. M. Rapee

GOALS

The Mastery of Your Anxiety and Panic II (Panic Attack Record) (Rapee 1985) is a method for recording self-monitored panic attacks. The measure requires that any panic attacks be recorded as soon as the attacks are over, providing what is believed to be the most accurate measure of frequency, intensity, and duration of panic episodes.

DESCRIPTION

Individuals are given small cards or pieces of paper on which they record panic attacks whenever they occur. Panic frequency data can be collected over any specified period, although a minimum of 2 weeks is recommended to establish a reliable baseline for this highly variable symptom. The Panic Attack Record requires respondents to record the occurrence of panic, the time at onset and offset of each attack in minutes, and the maximum intensity of distress associated with each attack on a 10-point scale. The measure includes a checklist of individual panic symptoms. Respondents also indicate whether the attack was expected and whether it occurred while another person was present.

Use of the Panic Attack Record requires teaching patients how to identify and rate panic attacks. In particular, panic attacks must be distinguished from anticipatory anxiety (which can reach high levels) and limited-symptom episodes (panic attacks with fewer than four symptoms). Patients often have difficulty with one or both of these concepts.

Scoring is achieved by simply adding the number of records obtained over a specified period. Characteristics of the panic attacks over this period can be scored as mean intensity, duration, number of symptoms, and so forth.

PRACTICAL ISSUES

Administration time has not been reported. The measure is copyrighted and may be obtained from

> The Psychological Corporation
> 555 Academic Court
> San Antonio, TX 78204-2498
> Phone: 800-211-8378
> Internet: www.psychcorp.com

PSYCHOMETRIC PROPERTIES

Psychometric data on the Panic Attack Record are not available, as is typical for diary or continuous monitoring procedures. Because patients' ratings are individualized, the instrument is considered to be an idiographic rather than a nomothetic measure.

CLINICAL UTILITY

The Panic Attack Record and similar measures of self-monitoring (e.g., the Panic Diary [Laberge et al. 1993]) are widely used as the main outcome measure in studies of panic disorder. Such measures are considered by experts to be the most accurate measure of sporadic and variable events such as panic. The Panic Attack Record would not be useful as a screening tool because a detailed introduction to the concept of *panic attack* must be provided. The Panic Attack Record is a useful instrument for characterizing panic attacks at baseline and for monitoring treatment effects. By encouraging the patient to identify panic symptoms as part and parcel of an anxiety

disorder and promoting self-monitoring, this type of instrument has been shown to be therapeutic in and of itself and should probably be used for the treatment of most patients with panic disorder.

REFERENCES AND SUGGESTED READINGS

Barlow DH, Hayes SC, Nelson RO: Self-monitoring, in The Scientist Practitioner: Research and Accountability in Clinical and Educational Settings. New York, Pergamon, 1984, pp 95–113

Clark DM, Salkovskis PM, Chalkey AJ: Respiratory control as a treatment for panic attacks. J Behav Ther Exp Psychiatry 16:23–30, 1985

Laberge B, Gauthier JG, Cote G, et al: Cognitive-behavioral therapy of panic disorder with secondary major depression: a preliminary investigation. J Consult Clin Psychol 61:1028–1037, 1993

Rapee RM: A case of panic disorder treated with breathing retraining. J Behav Ther Exp Psychiatry 16:63–65, 1985

Panic Disorder Severity Scale (PDSS)

M. K. Shear, D. Barlow, T. Brown, R. Money, D. Sholomskas, S. Woods, J. Gorman, and L. Papp

GOALS

The Panic Disorder Severity Scale (PDSS) (Shear et al. 1997) was developed to provide a simple way of measuring the overall severity of DSM-IV panic disorder. It is a brief instrument intended to assess severity and monitor treatment outcome.

DESCRIPTION

The clinician-administered PDSS, modeled on the Yale-Brown Obsessive Compulsive Scale (Y-BOCS) (p. 572), provides operationalized ratings of DSM-IV panic disorder symptoms, using a scripted interview. The PDSS consists of seven items, each rated on a 5-point Likert scale. The items are carefully anchored and assess panic frequency, distress during panic, panic-focused anticipatory anxiety, phobic avoidance of situations, phobic avoidance of physical sensations, impairment in work functioning, and impairment in social functioning. A sample item from the PDSS that concerns the severity of anticipatory anxiety (worry about having panic attacks) is provided in Example 25–3.

A total score is calculated by summing the scores for all seven items. Individual responses are scored on a scale of 0–4, and total scores range from 0 to 28.

PRACTICAL ISSUES

Experience suggests that the scale can be administered in 5–10 minutes. Clinical training in the evaluation of panic disorder is recommended for effective use of the scale. Raters who use the scale for research purposes must be trained. The scale is copyrighted by the University of Pittsburgh and is available from

> M. Katherine Shear, M.D.
> Anxiety Disorders Prevention Program
> Western Psychiatric Institute and Clinic
> 3811 O'Hara Street
> Pittsburgh, PA 15213
> Phone: 412-624-5500

Use is freely permitted without further permission in the following situations: clinical use in a not-for-profit institution and use in a research protocol approved by an institutional review board. All other uses require written permission from the principal author, M. Katherine Shear, M.D., including but not limited to the following: redistribution of the instrument in printed, electronic, or other forms, commercial use of the instrument, or modification of the instrument. A computerized version is being developed but is not currently available. The PDSS is included on the CD-ROM that accompanies this handbook.

PSYCHOMETRIC PROPERTIES

Reliability

Evaluation of internal consistency in 198 patients with DSM-III-R panic disorder yielded a Cronbach's alpha of 0.64. Joint reliability ranged from 0.84 to 0.88 for trained raters.

Validity

The PDSS total score showed moderate correlations with both panic disorder severity ratings of the Anxiety Disorders Interview Schedule—Revised (ADIS-R) ($r = 0.54$) (DiNardo and Barlow 1988) and severity ratings of the Clinical Global Impression (CGI) Scale ($r = 0.66$) (p. 100). Individual PDSS item scores were strongly associated ($r = 0.60–0.78$) with ADIS-R items of similar content and less strongly associated ($r = 0.35–0.47$) with CGI Scale and ADIS-R severity ratings. The PDSS items most highly correlated with similar ADIS-R items were panic frequency ($r = 0.71$), anticipatory anxiety ($r = 0.78$), agoraphobic fear and avoidance ($r = 0.73$), and sensation fear and avoidance ($r = 0.69$). The PDSS total score was not significantly correlated with that of the Hamilton Rating Scale for Depression (Ham-D) (p. 526) ($r = 0.11$). The PDSS has proved to be sensitive to change with treatment.

CLINICAL UTILITY

The PDSS is a brief, clinician-administered interview rating. It is a useful way of assessing overall panic disorder severity at baseline, and it provides a profile of severity of the different panic disorder symptoms. It is a good monitoring tool because it is brief and sensitive to change. Because it is meant for use after diagnosis, it is

EXAMPLE 25–3 ■ **Sample item from the Panic Disorder Severity Scale**

> Over the past month, how much have you worried about when your next panic will occur?
>
> What worries you most about having panic attacks?
>
> Do you worry about what the panic might mean about your physical health? Your mental health? How intense is your worry?

Reprinted with permission from M. Katherine Shear, M.D.

not appropriate for screening, and it is not a diagnostic instrument. It could be used administratively to monitor the outcome of panic disorder specifically.

REFERENCES AND SUGGESTED READINGS

DiNardo PA, Barlow DH: Anxiety Disorders Interview Schedule, Revised (ADIS-R). Albany, NY, Phobia and Anxiety Disorders Clinic, State University of New York, 1988

Shear MK, Brown TA, Barlow DH, et al: Multicenter collaborative Panic Disorder Severity Scale. Am J Psychiatry 154:1571–1575, 1997

Social Phobia and Anxiety Inventory (SPAI)

S. M. Turner, D. C. Beidel, C. V. Dancu, and M. A. Stanley

GOALS

The Social Phobia and Anxiety Inventory (SPAI) (Turner et al. 1989) is a comprehensive self-report questionnaire developed specifically to assess social phobia as defined in DSM. It includes items designed to assess somatic, cognitive, and avoidance and escape behaviors.

DESCRIPTION

The SPAI is composed of two subscales, the 32-item Social Phobia Scale and the 13-item Agoraphobia Scale. Each item is scored on a 7-point Likert scale from 1 = never to 7 = always. Of the 32 social phobia items, 21 assess the degree of distress in different social settings and require separate ratings on the basis of the presence of four different audience groups (i.e., strangers, authority figures, the opposite sex, and people in general). Other social phobia items assess the degree to which respon-

dents experience somatic and cognitive symptoms in anticipation of or during social situations. Finally, the Social Phobia Scale measures the frequency with which respondents avoid or escape social situations. The Agoraphobia Scale was added to allow for preliminary determination of whether the social distress might be due to a fear of having panic attacks or being trapped rather than to a fear of negative evaluation. Sample items from the Social Phobia Scale and the Agoraphobia Scale are provided in Example 25–4.

Scores range from 0 to 192 for the Social Phobia Scale and from 0 to 78 for the Agoraphobia Scale. The SPAI difference score, also called the SPAI total score, is calculated by subtracting the Agoraphobia score from the Social Phobia score.

PRACTICAL ISSUES

Average administration time is between 20 and 30 minutes for respondents with at least sixth-grade reading skills. The SPAI is copyrighted by Multi-Health Systems, Inc. The measure may be obtained from

> Multi-Health Systems, Inc.
> 908 Niagara Falls Boulevard
> North Tonawanda, NY 14120-2060
> Phone: 800-456-3003
> Internet: www.mhs.com

The approximate cost of the SPAI is $55.00 per kit, which includes the manual and 25 quick-score sheets.

EXAMPLE 25–4 ■ Sample items from the Social Phobia and Anxiety Inventory

---

Social Phobia Scale
I feel anxious when in a small gathering with: (a) strangers, (b) authority figures, (c) opposite sex, (d) people in general.
I experience the following in a social situation: (a) sweating, (b) blushing, (c) shaking, (d) frequent urge to urinate, (e) heart palpitations.

Agoraphobia Scale
I feel anxious when I am home alone.
Being in large open spaces makes me feel anxious.

Computerized scoring and a manual are available (Turner et al. 1995). The SPAI has been translated into several languages, including Dutch, German, Portuguese, and Spanish.

PSYCHOMETRIC PROPERTIES

Reliability

The SPAI has demonstrated good to excellent internal consistency; Cronbach's alphas ranged from 0.95 to 0.96 for the Social Phobia Scale and from 0.85 to 0.95 for the Agoraphobia Scale. Two-week test-retest reliability ($N = 182$) for the SPAI difference score was good ($r = 0.86$).

Validity

Both the SPAI Distress Score and the Social Phobia Score showed moderate to high correlations ($r = 0.51–0.79$) with other questionnaire measures of social anxiety, including the Social Phobia scale of the Fear Questionnaire (FQ) (p. 558), the Fear of Negative Evaluation Scale (Leary 1983), and the Social Avoidance and Distress Scale (Watson and Friend 1969). The SPAI demonstrated weaker associations with instruments that assess dissimilar anxiety symptoms and depression. The Distress Score and Social Phobia Score generally showed low to moderate correlation with the Agoraphobia scale of the FQ (p. 558) ($r = -0.15$ to 0.42), the Trait scale of the State-Trait Anxiety Inventory (Spielberger et al. 1970) ($r = 0.36$ and 0.45), the Hamilton Anxiety Rating Scale (HARS) (p. 554) ($r = 0.27$), and the Beck Depression Inventory (BDI) (p. 519) ($r = 0.20$ and 0.33). The SPAI was found to be able to distinguish between subjects with social phobia, those with other anxiety disorders, and nonanxious control individuals in adult and adolescent samples. Overall diagnostic accuracy rates by discriminant analyses for patients with social phobia and other anxiety disorders ranged from 67% to 74.4%. In addition, the measure is sensitive to change with psychosocial and pharmacological treatment.

CLINICAL UTILITY

The SPAI demonstrated excellent psychometric properties in a series of well-conducted studies. It is a compre-

hensive measure of social phobia symptoms and is a useful tool for social phobia treatment planning and for monitoring change. The length of the SPAI precludes its use as a screening tool. It may be useful in differentiating those with social phobia from those with agoraphobia. Scores for adolescents with social phobia may be somewhat lower than those reported with adult samples. The primary weaknesses of the SPAI are its length and somewhat cumbersome scoring system, although computerized scoring is available.

A child version of the SPAI (SPAI-C) (Beidel et al. 1995) was recently developed. The SPAI-C is a 39-item empirically derived self-report measure that has excellent internal consistency and high test-retest reliability across 2-week and 10-month intervals. The instrument has also been shown to discriminate children with social anxiety from children without it.

REFERENCES AND SUGGESTED READINGS

Beidel DC, Turner SM, Stanley MA, et al: The Social Phobia and Anxiety Inventory: concurrent and external validity. Behavior Therapy 20:417–427, 1989

Beidel DC, Turner SM, Cooley MR: Assessing reliable and clinically significant change in social phobia: validity of the Social Phobia and Anxiety Inventory. Behav Res Ther 31:331–337, 1993

Beidel DC, Turner SM, Morris TL: A new inventory to assess childhood social anxiety and phobia: the Social Phobia and Anxiety Inventory for Children. Psychological Assessment 7:73–79, 1995

Clark DB, Turner S, Beidel D, et al: Reliability and validity of the Social Phobia and Anxiety Inventory for Adolescents. Psychological Assessment 6:135–140, 1994

Herbert JD, Bellack AS, Hope DA: Concurrent validity of the Social Phobia and Anxiety Inventory. Journal of Psychopathology and Behavioral Assessment 13:357–368, 1991

Leary MR: A brief version of the Fear of Negative Evaluation Scale. Personality and Social Psychology 9:371–375, 1983

Osman A, Barrios FX, Aukes A, et al: Psychometric evaluation of the Social Phobia and Anxiety Inventory in college students. J Clin Psychol 51:235–243, 1995

Spielberger CD, Gorsuch RR, Luchene RE: State-Trait Anxiety Inventory. Palo Alto, CA, Consulting Psychologists Press, 1970

Turner SM, Beidel DC, Dancu CV, et al: An empirically derived inventory to measure social fears and anxiety: the Social Phobia and Anxiety Inventory. Psychological Assessment 1:35–40, 1989

Turner SM, Beidel DC, Dancu CV: Social Phobia and Anxiety Inventory Manual. North Tonawanda, NY, Multi-Health Systems, 1995

Watson D, Friend R: Measurement of social-evaluative anxiety. J Consult Clin Psychol 33:448–457, 1969

Brief Social Phobia Scale (BSPS)

J. R. T. Davidson, N. L. S. Potts, E. A. Richichi, S. M. Ford, K. R. R. Krishnan, R. D. Smith, and W. Wilson

GOALS

The Brief Social Phobia Scale (BSPS) (Davidson et al. 1991) is a semistructured interview for assessing severity and treatment response in social phobia as defined by DSM criteria.

DESCRIPTION

The BSPS consists of 11 items. The first 7 items require respondents to provide separate ratings for the severity of fear and the severity of avoidance for each of the following situations: public speaking, talking to people in authority, talking to strangers, being embarrassed or humiliated, being criticized, social gatherings, and doing something while being watched. The second part includes 4 items that assess physiological symptoms (i.e., blushing, trembling, palpitations, and sweating) experienced while being confronted with or while anticipating social situations. The severity of each item is rated for the previous week (or any other time reference) on a 5-point Likert-type scale (from 0 = none to 4 = extreme).

Individual item scores are summed to yield three subscale scores (Fear [BSPS-F], Avoidance [BSPS-A], and Physiological [BSPS-P]) and one total score (BSPS-T = BSPS-F + BSPS-A + BSPS-P). Scores range from 0 to 72 for the BSPS-T, from 0 to 28 for the BSPS-A and the BSPS-F, and from 0 to 16 for the BSPS-P. A total score of >20 has been judged to reflect social phobia symptoms severe enough to warrant treatment.

The authors recommend that the BSPS be used after administration of a clinical interview, so that the interviewer is familiar with the patient's social phobia symptoms, and that the BSPS be administered with the patient looking at a copy of the scale. When administering the scale, the interviewer must ensure that fear and avoidance are rated along with fear of negative evaluation and that avoidance is not the result of other factors such as lack of interest. If the respondent states that he or she has not had the opportunity to be in a particular situation, the interviewer should clarify that the question also concerns the respondent's thoughts about the situation.

PRACTICAL ISSUES

Average administration time has not been reported, but experience suggests that the scale can be completed in approximately 10–15 minutes. Formal interviewer training is not necessary. The measure is copyrighted and may be obtained from

> Jonathan R. T. Davidson, M.D.
> Anxiety and Traumatic Stress Program
> Department of Psychiatry and Behavioral Sciences
> Duke University Medical Center
> Box 3812
> Durham, NC 27710
> Phone: 919-684-2880

The BSPS is included on the CD-ROM that accompanies this handbook.

PSYCHOMETRIC PROPERTIES

Reliability

Examination of the internal consistency of the BSPS in a large sample (N = 275) of treatment-seeking persons with DSM-III-R social phobia yielded acceptable Cronbach's alphas of 0.81 (BSPS-T), 0.70 (BSPS-F), 0.78 (BSPS-A), and 0.60 (BSPS-P). Internal consistency for the BSPS-P would be expected to be somewhat low given that this scale only includes four items. Joint reliability was established with multiple methods in several small samples; correlation coefficients ranged from 0.83 to 0.90 across scales. One-week test-retest reliability in a large sample ($N = 136$) of persons with DSM-III-R social phobia was good; correlation coefficients ranged from 0.77 for the BSPS-P to 0.91 for the BSPS-T.

Validity

In a large sample ($N = 275$) of treatment-seeking individuals with DSM-III-R social phobia, the BSPS-T score showed large correlations with other measures of social anxiety and phobia, including the Liebowitz Social Anxiety Scale (LSAS) (p. 570) ($r = 0.70$) and the Fear of Negative Evaluation Scale (Leary 1983) ($r = 0.45$). Correlations of the BSPS-F and the BSPS-A with the LSAS ($r = 0.45$–0.73) and Fear of Negative Evaluation Scale (Leary 1983) ($r = 0.43$ and 0.51) were also strong. However, the BSPS-P was not associated with these two measures of social anxiety ($r = -0.03$ to 0.05). As would be expected, associations between the BSPS and the Hamilton Anxiety Rating Scale (HARS) (p. 554), a measure of general as opposed to social anxiety, were notably lower ($r = 0.20$–0.34). With the exception of the BSPS-P, the BSPS was strongly related ($r = 0.49$–0.55) to interference in the domain of social life as assessed with the Sheehan Disability Scale (p. 113). The BSPS demonstrated sensitivity to change with pharmacological treatment of social phobia (Davidson et al. 1997).

CLINICAL UTILITY

The BSPS is a brief and easy-to-administer instrument that seems to tap the major feared situations associated with social phobia; one study conducted with a large sample of patients with social phobia found that the measure is psychometrically sound. However, psychometric properties of the BSPS-P are weak, raising questions about the usefulness of this scale. It is therefore recommended that clinicians rely on the BSPS-T, BSPS-F, and BSPS-A scores. The absence of operationalized definitions of items may lead to idiosyncratic application of the ratings.

The BSPS does not provide information about the duration of social phobia symptoms or the degree of distress or interference they cause in occupational, social, or other important areas of functioning. In addition, the instrument is unable to yield information about whether the symptoms are unrelated to another mental disorder (e.g., anorexia nervosa and bulimia nervosa), as required for a DSM diagnosis of social phobia. The BSPS should therefore not be used as a diagnostic instrument.

REFERENCES AND SUGGESTED READINGS

Davidson JRT, Potts NLS, Richichi EA, et al: The Brief Social Phobia Scale. J Clin Psychiatry 52:48–51, 1991

Davidson JRT, Tupler LA, Potts NLS: Treatment of social phobia with benzodiazepines. J Clin Psychiatry 55:28–32, 1994

Davidson JRT, Miner CM, De Veaugh-Geiss J, et al: The Brief Social Phobia Scale: a psychometric evaluation. Psychol Med 27:161–166, 1997

Leary MR: A brief version of the Fear of Negative Evaluation Scale. Personality and Social Psychology 9:371–375, 1983

Liebowitz Social Anxiety Scale (LSAS)

M. R. Liebowitz

GOALS

The Liebowitz Social Anxiety Scale (LSAS) (Liebowitz 1987) is a clinician-administered semistructured interview designed to assess social phobia as determined by DSM criteria through the evaluation of fear and avoidance in a wide variety of social and performance situations.

DESCRIPTION

The LSAS includes 24 items, 13 describing performance situations and 11 describing social interactional situations. Each item is rated separately for fear (on a Likert scale ranging from 0 to 3, with 0 = none and 3 = severe) and avoidance (also scored from 0 to 3, with 0 = never and 3 = usually). The LSAS yields four subscales: Fear-Social, Avoidance-Social, Fear-Performance, and Avoidance-Performance. Sample items are provided in Example 25–5. Three additional spaces are provided for individually created items.

Scale and subscale scores are obtained by summing the individual item scores. Fear and avoidance items are summed across social and performance situations to yield total fear and total avoidance scores, each of which ranges from 0 to 72.

PRACTICAL ISSUES

Average administration time has not been reported, but experience suggests that it takes approximately 15–20 minutes. The LSAS may be found in Liebowitz (1987) and Greist et al. (1995). Formal interviewer training is not required (M. Liebowitz, personal communication, July 9, 1997).

PSYCHOMETRIC PROPERTIES

Reliability

The LSAS demonstrated good internal consistency in a sample of 312 patients enrolled in various clinical trials;

EXAMPLE 25–5 ■ Sample items from the Liebowitz Social Anxiety Scale

Participating in small groups

Meeting strangers

Speaking up at a meeting

Resisting a high pressure salesperson

Cronbach's alphas ranged from 0.82 to 0.92 across the various subscales.

Validity

Limited validity data are available for the LSAS. The LSAS Avoidance and Fear scales were found to be strongly associated with social anxiety measures assessing similar constructs on the Social Interaction and Anxiety Scale (R. P. Mattick and J. C. Clarke, unpublished manuscript, 1989) (r = 0.75–0.76) and the Social Phobia Scale (R. P. Mattick and J. C. Clarke, unpublished manuscript, 1989) (r = 0.61–0.64). Correlations with the Social Avoidance and Distress Scale (Watson and Friend 1969) (r = 0.33–0.34) and the Fear of Negative Evaluation Scale (Leary 1983) (r = 0.18–0.22) were noticeably lower. The LSAS total scale was found to be highly correlated with the Social Phobia and Anxiety Inventory (SPAI) (p. 567) (r = 0.87) and the Brief Social Phobia Scale (BSPS) (p. 569) (r = 0.76).

Individuals with generalized social phobia as determined by DSM-III-R criteria were found to score higher than those with the nongeneralized subtype on the LSAS Avoidance and Fear scales. Similarly, both scales discriminated between persons with DSM-III-R generalized social phobia, plus avoidant personality disorder, generalized social phobia, or nongeneralized social phobia.

The LSAS demonstrated sensitivity to change with pharmacological and cognitive-behavioral treatment for social phobia.

CLINICAL UTILITY

The LSAS is one of two clinician-administered scales for social phobia. Although the LSAS is not a diagnostic instrument, it covers a broad range of potentially fearful situations and separates anxiety ratings from avoidance ratings. It is easy to administer and appears to be a useful tool for developing a fear hierarchy and tracking treatment progress. A disadvantage is the lack of items assessing the cognitive or physiological symptoms associated with social phobia. Thus, the LSAS might not be able to detect symptomatic improvement in a patient who has a decrease in psychological arousal symptoms while confronted with a phobic stimulus occurring in the absence of a decrease in avoidance behavior. Although the LSAS has been used in several studies with relatively large samples of patients with social phobia and has been more thoroughly evaluated than the BSPS (p. 566), published psychometric data are scarce.

REFERENCES AND SUGGESTED READINGS

Brown EJ, Heimberg RG, Juster HR: Social phobia subtype and avoidant personality disorder: effect on severity of social phobia, impairment, and outcome of cognitive-behavioral treatment. Behavior Therapy 26:467–486, 1995

Davidson JRT, Potts NLS, Richichi EA, et al: The Brief Social Phobia Scale. J Clin Psychiatry 52:48–51, 1991

Greist JH, Kobak KA, Jefferson JW, et al: The clinical interview, in Social Phobia: Diagnosis, Assessment, and Treatment. Edited by Heimberg RG, Liebowitz MR, Hope DA, et al. New York, Guilford, 1995, pp 185–201

Holt CS, Heimberg RG, Hope DA: Avoidant personality disorder and the generalized subtype of social phobia. J Abnorm Psychol 101:318–325, 1992

Horner KJ, Juster HR, Brown EJ, et al: Psychometric properties of the Liebowitz Social Anxiety Scale. Paper presented at the 16th annual meeting of the Anxiety Disorders Association of America, Orlando, FL, 1996

Johnson MR, Emmanuel N, Ware M, et al: Differentiating generalized from specific social phobia by responses on the Liebowitz Social Anxiety Scale. Paper presented at the 16th annual meeting of the Anxiety Disorders Association of America, Orlando, FL, 1996

Leary MR: A brief version of the Fear of Negative Evaluation Scale. Personality and Social Psychology 9:371–375, 1983

Liebowitz MR: Social phobia. Mod Probl Pharmacopsychiatry 22:141–173, 1987

Liebowitz MR, Schneier F, Campeas R, et al: Phenelzine vs atenolol in social phobia: a placebo-controlled comparison. Arch Gen Psychiatry 49:290–300, 1992

Watson D, Friend R: Measurement of social-evaluative anxiety. J Consult Clin Psychol 33:448–457, 1969

Yale-Brown Obsessive Compulsive Scale (Y-BOCS)

W. K. Goodman, L. H. Price, S. A. Rasmussen, C. Mazure, R. L. Fleischmann, C. L. Hill, G. R. Heninger, and D. S. Charney

GOALS

The Yale-Brown Obsessive Compulsive Scale (Y-BOCS) (Goodman et al. 1989a) was developed to measure the severity of obsessive-compulsive symptoms in patients with diagnoses of obsessive-compulsive disorder. Both obsessions and compulsions are rated in terms of time spent, interference with functioning, distress, resistance, and control, independent of the particular type of obsession or compulsion.

DESCRIPTION

The Y-BOCS is a clinician-administered semistructured interview. The interview is preceded by an optional 64-item checklist that is used to identify the content of obsessive-compulsive symptoms. Examples are provided for each item on the checklist. A sample item from the symptom checklist is provided in Example 25–6. The interviewer then asks the subject to identify the three obsessions and compulsions that are most distressing and to focus on them during the Y-BOCS interview.

The Y-BOCS scale is divided into two subscales: the Obsessions subscale and the Compulsions subscale. For each subscale, five aspects of pathology related to either the obsessions or the compulsions are rated from 0 = no symptoms to 4 = extreme symptoms. Specifically, the

EXAMPLE 25–6 ■ Sample item from the Yale-Brown Obsessive Compulsive Scale

> I have violent or horrific images in my mind (Examples: images of murders, dismembered bodies, or other disgusting scenes).

Reprinted with permission from Wayne Goodman, M.D.

obsessions and compulsions are assessed with regard to how much time they occupy, interfere with normal functioning, cause subjective distress, are actively resisted by the respondent, and can be controlled by the respondent. Detailed probes and anchor points are provided for each item. For instance, for control over compulsions, two questions are posed: "How strong is the drive to perform the compulsive behavior?" and "How much control do you have over the compulsions?" Specified anchor points range from 0 = complete control to 4 = no control, drive to perform behavior experienced as completely involuntary and overpowering, rarely able to even momentarily delay activity.

Scores of the Y-BOCS interview are summed to yield one total score and two subscale scores (Obsessions and Compulsions). Total scores range from 0 to 40; higher scores indicate greater severity. Subscale scores range from 0 to 20. In pharmaceutical trials of obsessive-compulsive disorder, total scores of ≥16 are typically used as inclusion criteria. Total scores for persons with obsessive-compulsive disorder average about 25, as compared with <8 for populations without obsessive-compulsive disorder.

An interview version for children, the CY-BOCS, is available (Riddle et al. 1992). It differs from the adult version mainly in the use of simpler language for the various item probes.

PRACTICAL ISSUES

Initial administration of the Y-BOCS interview requires approximately 30 minutes, but administration time usually decreases with repeated administrations with the same patient. Administration time for the questionnaire version ranges from 10 to 15 minutes. Self-report versions of the Y-BOCS, both paper and pencil (Steketee et al. 1996) and computer administered (Rosenfeld et al. 1992), are available. Administration and scoring manuals can be obtained from

Wayne Goodman, M.D.
University of Florida
College of Medicine
Department of Psychiatry
P.O. Box 100256
1600 S.W. Archer Road
Gainsville, FL 32610

Clinicians can use the instrument after reading this material, but raters who administer the scale in research studies should be trained. Telephone administration of the Y-BOCS using an automated system is now being used successfully, and good agreement with ratings obtained via traditional in-person administration has been demonstrated (Baer et al. 1993). The Y-BOCS is included on the CD-ROM that accompanies this handbook.

PSYCHOMETRIC PROPERTIES

Reliability

The Y-BOCS has acceptable internal consistency; Cronbach's alphas ranged from 0.69 to 0.91 for the total scale and from 0.51 to 0.85 for the two subscales. The total score has demonstrated excellent joint reliability; intraclass correlation coefficients ranged from 0.80 to 0.99. These estimates are made on the basis of two independent evaluators' ratings of the same interview. Test-retest reliability using the same rater and 1-week test-retest intervals indicated good stability; intraclass correlation coefficients ranged from 0.81 to 0.97.

Validity

The total scale and the subscales demonstrated moderate convergence (r = 0.33–0.62) with questionnaire measures of obsessive-compulsive symptoms, including the Maudsley Obsessional Compulsive Inventory (Hodgson and Rachman 1977) and the Compulsive Activity Checklist (Steketee and Freund 1993). There are also moderate associations with general anxiety (r = 0.23–0.47) and depression (r = 0.33–0.60) as assessed with the Hamilton Anxiety Rating Scale (HARS) (p. 554), the Hamilton Rating Scale for Depression (Ham-D) (p. 526), and the Anxiety and Depression scales of the Symptom Checklist–90—Revised (SCL-90-R) (p. 81). In two studies, the Y-BOCS was more strongly related to measures of depression and general anxiety than to other measures of obsessive-compulsive symptoms. The total score distinguishes between persons with obsessive-compulsive disorder and persons with other anxiety disorders and nonclinical individuals. The Y-BOCS was shown to be sensitive to change with pharmacological and psychosocial treatments for obsessive-compulsive disorder.

Correlations between the clinician-administered Y-BOCS and the self-report version were good (total scale, $r = 0.75–0.79$; Obsessions subscale, $r = 0.69–0.73$; and Compulsions subscale, $r = 0.65–0.79$). The computer-administered version was highly correlated with the clinician-administered version in two samples of patients with and without anxiety. For the clinical sample, the correlation (r) was 0.88 for the total score, 0.87 for the Obsessions subscale, and 0.86 for the Compulsions subscale; for the nonpatient sample, correlations were lower (0.77 for the total score, 0.72 for the Obsessions subscale, and 0.70 for the Compulsions subscale). In both samples, the patients rated themselves somewhat higher on the computer version than clinicians rated the patients.

CLINICAL UTILITY

The Y-BOCS has become the gold standard for assessing obsessive-compulsive symptoms. It is the best available measure of overall obsessive-compulsive disorder severity. The Y-BOCS proper does not assess the content of obsessive-compulsive symptoms. Content is captured by the Y-BOCS symptom checklist, which includes a wide spectrum of symptoms. The Y-BOCS is well suited for assessing the severity of obsessive-compulsive symptoms and for monitoring change with treatment. It can be used as a screening instrument, but it is not a diagnostic instrument, because it does not specifically assess whether the diagnostic criteria for DSM-IV obsessive-compulsive disorder have been met. The self-report, and especially the telephone-administered version, could have specialized administrative use in following performance of treatment facilities in managing obsessive-compulsive disorder. Individuals who present with either obsessions or compulsions may score spuriously low on the Y-BOCS total scale, despite severe symptoms. Use of the subscale scores prevents this problem.

REFERENCES AND SUGGESTED READINGS

Baer L, Brown-Beasley MW, Sorce J, et al: Computer-assisted telephone administration of a structured interview for obsessive-compulsive disorder. Am J Psychiatry 150:1737–1738, 1993

Frost RO, Steketee GS, Krause MS, et al: The relationship of the Yale-Brown Obsessive Compulsive Scale (YBOCS) to other measures of obsessive compulsive symptoms in a nonclinical population. J Pers Assess 65:158–168, 1995

Goodman WK, Price LH, Rasmussen SA, et al: The Yale-Brown Obsessive Compulsive Scale, I: development, use, and reliability. Arch Gen Psychiatry 46:1006–1011, 1989a

Goodman WK, Price LH, Rasmussen SA, et al: The Yale-Brown Obsessive Compulsive Scale, II: validity. Arch Gen Psychiatry 46:1012–1016, 1989b

Hodgson RJ, Rachman S: Obsessional-compulsive complaints. Behav Res Ther 15:389–395, 1977

Kim SW, Dysken MW, Kuskowski M: The Yale-Brown Obsessive-Compulsive Scale: a reliability and validity study. Psychiatry Res 34:99–106, 1990

Kim SW, Dysken MW, Kuskowski M: The Symptom Checklist–90: Obsessive-compulsive subscale: a reliability and validity study. Psychiatry Res 41:37–44, 1992

Kim SW, Dysken MW, Kuskowski M, et al: The Yale-Brown Obsessive Compulsive Scale (Y-BOCS) and the NIMH Global Obsessive Compulsive Scale (NIMH-GOCS): a reliability and validity study. International Journal of Methods in Psychiatric Research 3:37–44, 1993

Richter MA, Cox BJ, Direnfeld DM: A comparison of three assessment instruments for obsessive-compulsive symptoms. J Behav Ther Exp Psychiatry 25:143–147, 1994

Riddle MA, Scahill L, King RA, et al: Double-blind, crossover trial of fluoxetine and placebo in children and adolescents with obsessive-compulsive disorder. J Am Acad Child Adolesc Psychiatry 31:1062–1069, 1992

Rosenfeld R, Dar R, Anderson D, et al: A computer-administered version of the Yale-Brown Obsessive Compulsive Scale. Psychological Assessment 4:329–332, 1992

Steketee GS, Freund B: Compulsive Activity Checklist: further psychometric analyses and revision. Behavioral Psychotherapy 21:13–25, 1993

Steketee G, Front R, Bogart K: The Yale-Brown Obsessive Compulsive Scale: interview vs. self-report. Behav Res Ther 34:675–685, 1996

van Oppen P, Emmelkamp PMG, van Balkom AJL, et al: The sensitivity to change of measures for obsessive-compulsive disorder. Journal of Anxiety Disorders 9:241–248, 1995

Woody SR, Steketee GS, Chambless DL: Reliability and validity of the Yale-Brown Obsessive-Compulsive Scale. Behav Res Ther 33:597–605, 1995

Padua Inventory (PI)

E. Sanavio

GOALS

The Padua Inventory (PI) (Sanavio 1988) is a self-report measure of the severity of obsessive-compulsive symptoms in clinical and nonclinical populations, and it can also be used to assess response to treatment.

DESCRIPTION

The PI is a 60-item self-report questionnaire. Two revised versions of the PI are available: the 39-item and the 41-item PI-R. Whereas the 60-item PI was developed using nonclinical subjects, the 41-item PI-R was developed on the basis of the factor structure found in large samples of obsessive-compulsive patients, patients with other anxiety disorders, and nonclinical individuals. Items that were poor or impure measures of factors identified in these samples were deleted (van Oppen et al. 1995b). To improve the ability of the PI to differentiate between symptoms of obsession and worry, Burns et al. (1996) organized 39 of the 60 PI items into five categories of obsessions and compulsions (on the basis of the content of the items), excluding items they judged to reflect both worry and obsessions. The five analytically derived content dimensions were replicated in factor analytic studies on a very large sample of nonclinical subjects, prompting introduction of the 39-item PI-R. Subjects rate the degree of disturbance associated with each obsessive-compulsive symptom on a 5-point Likert-type scale from 0 = not at all to 4 = very much. Scores are summed to yield one total score and subscale scores for Contamination, Checking, Rumination, and Urges/Worries of Losing Control Over Motor Behaviors. Sample items are provided in Example 25–7.

The PI is scored by summing all items. Scores for the 60-item version range from 0 to 240; higher scores indicate greater symptomatology. In a normative Italian sample, means ranged from 46.8 to 66.6 for men across all age groups and from 55.1 to 70.1 for women (SD = 23.5–33.3). A normative American sample showed lower

EXAMPLE 25–7 ■ Sample items from the Padua Inventory

> **Contamination**
> I wash my hands more often and longer than necessary.
>
> **Checking**
> I return home to check doors, windows, drawers etc., to make sure they are properly shut.
>
> **Rumination**
> When I start thinking about things, I become obsessed with them.
>
> **Urges/Worries of Losing Control Over Motor Behaviors**
> I sometimes feel the need to break or damage things for no reason.

Reprinted with permission from G. Leonard Burns, Ph.D.

means: 42.08 for men (SD = 26.27) and 41.01 for women (SD = 25.40).

PRACTICAL ISSUES

Administration time has not been reported. However, it may take approximately 30 minutes for a person with obsessive-compulsive disorder to complete the 60-item scale. The 39-item revised version of the PI is available from

> G. Leonard Burns, Ph.D.
> Department of Psychology
> Washington State University
> P.O. Box 644820
> Pullman, WA 99164-4820

The Padua Inventory is included on the CD-ROM that accompanies this handbook.

PSYCHOMETRIC PROPERTIES

Reliability

The PI has good to excellent internal consistency; alpha coefficients ranged from 0.80 to 0.94. The measure has adequate test-retest reliability (r = 0.71–0.83) for intervals of 1 and 2 months. Satisfactory 6- to 7-month test-retest reliability (r = 0.76) was found for the 39-item PI-R as well.

Validity

The PI and the 41-item PI-R showed high correlations ($r = 0.70$–0.75) with other self-report measures of obsessive-compulsive disorder, including the Maudsley Obsessional Compulsive Inventory (Hodgson and Rachman 1977) and the Symptom scale of the Leyton Obsessional Inventory (Kazarian et al. 1977). The PI and the 41-item PI-R were shown to have low correlations with social desirability ($r = -0.01$ to -0.21) and psychoticism ($r = -0.14$ to 0.20) assessed via the Eysenck Personality Questionnaire (Eysenck and Eysenck 1993); however, they were strongly associated ($r = 0.46$–0.61) with depression and general anxiety. The 39-item PI-R proved to be more independent of worry than the original PI, as measured by the Penn State Worry Questionnaire (PSWQ) (p. 587).

Validity of the PI Contamination and Checking subscales is well established. For example, the PI Contamination subscale was found to be more strongly associated with the Maudsley Obsessional Compulsive Inventory Cleaning subscale than the Maudsley Obsessional Compulsive Inventory Checking subscale, whereas the reverse was found for the PI Checking scale. Validity of the two obsessive subscales (Rumination and Urges/Worries of Losing Control Over Motor Behaviors) requires further examination, because these scales were found to correlate more highly with depression and general anxiety than with obsessive-compulsive symptoms. The PI distinguished patients with obsessive-compulsive disorder from a mixed group of patients with other disorders, and the 41-item PI-R Washing, Checking, Rumination, and Precision subscales discriminated persons with obsessive-compulsive disorder from patients with panic disorder, patients with social phobia, and nonclinical control subjects.

The 41-item PI-R has demonstrated sensitivity to change with behavior therapy, cognitive therapy, and combined drug and psychosocial treatment, yielding large effect sizes that were in the same range as those produced by the Yale-Brown Obsessive Compulsive Scale (Y-BOCS) (p. 572).

CLINICAL UTILITY

The PI and PI-R provide a broad assessment of obsessive-compulsive symptoms. The PI is not a diagnostic instrument. The PI and PI-R are useful primarily as instruments to assess the severity of diagnosed obsessive-compulsive disorder and as a way of monitoring treatment response. These instruments are too lengthy to be useful in screening unselected populations or in monitoring treatment for administrative purposes. They are judged to be the best available self-report inventories of severity of obsessive-compulsive disorder as determined by DSM-IV criteria.

REFERENCES AND SUGGESTED READINGS

Burns GL: Padua Inventory—Washington State University Revision. Pullman, WA, Washington State University, 1995

Burns GL, Keortge SG, Formea GM, et al: Revision of the Padua Inventory of obsessive compulsive disorder symptoms: distinctions between worry, obsessions, and compulsions. Behav Res Ther 34:163–173, 1996

Eysenck HJ, Eysenck SPB: Recent advances in the cross-cultural study of personality, in Advances in Personality Assessment, Vol 2, Edited by Butcher JN, Speilberger CD. Hillsdale, NJ, Erlbaum, 1993

Hodgson RJ, Rachman S: Obsessional-compulsive complaints. Behav Res Ther 15:389–395, 1977

Kazarian SS, Evans DR, Lefave K: Modification and factorial analysis of the Leyton Obsessional Inventory. J Clin Psychol 33:422–425, 1977

Kyrios M, Bhar S, Wade D: The assessment of obsessive-compulsive phenomena: psychometric and normative data on the Padua Inventory from Australian non-clinical student samples. Behav Res Ther 34:85–95, 1996

Sanavio E: Obsessions and compulsions: the Padua Inventory. Behav Res Ther 26:169–177, 1988

Sternberger LG, Burns GL: Obsessions and compulsions: psychometric properties of the Padua Inventory with an American college population. Behav Res Ther 28:341–345, 1990

van Oppen P: Obsessions and compulsions: dimensional structure, reliability, convergent and divergent validity of the Padua Inventory. Behav Res Ther 30:631–637, 1992

van Oppen P, Emmelkamp PMG, van Balkom AJL, et al: The sensitivity to change of measures for obsessive-compulsive disorder. Journal of Anxiety Disorders 9:241–248, 1995a

van Oppen P, Hoekstra RJ, Emmelkamp PMG: The structure of obsessive compulsive symptoms. Behav Res Ther 33:15–23, 1995b

Clinician-Administered PTSD Scale (CAPS)

D. D. Blake, F. W. Weathers, L. N. Nagy,
D. G. Kaloupek, G. Klauminzer, D. S. Charney,
and T. M. Keane

GOALS

The Clinician-Administered PTSD Scale (CAPS) (Blake et al. 1990) is a structured interview scale developed to assess the type and severity of DSM-III-R posttraumatic stress disorder symptoms with scoring that can be modified for DSM-IV criteria. Although the measure was developed primarily within the Veterans Affairs Medical Center system, it is appropriate for assessing the psychological impact of both combat and civilian trauma.

DESCRIPTION

The CAPS consists of 17 interviewer-rated items that cover the core symptoms of posttraumatic stress disorder according to the DSM criteria, including reexperiencing of the traumatic event, corresponding to posttraumatic stress disorder criterion B (e.g., intrusive thoughts, flashbacks, and distressing dreams); avoidance of stimuli related to the trauma and numbing of general responsiveness, corresponding to posttraumatic stress disorder criterion C (e.g., efforts to avoid trauma-related thoughts or situations and restricted affect); and increased arousal, corresponding to posttraumatic stress disorder criterion D (e.g., sleep problems, irritability, and hypervigilance). Eight additional items are included to measure the frequency and intensity of features frequently associated with posttraumatic stress disorder (e.g., guilt over acts of commission or omission, survivor guilt, depression, and homicidality). In addition, the CAPS includes five global rating scales that reflect the impact of symptoms on social and occupational functioning, general severity, any recent changes in severity, and the assessor's evaluation of the validity of the patient's report. Sample items that assess the frequency and intensity of reexperiencing of symptoms are provided in Example 25-8.

For each of the 17 items, the interviewer rates the frequency (0 = never, 1 = once or twice, 2 = once or twice a week, 3 = several times a week, and 4 = daily or almost every day) and the intensity (0 = none, 1 = mild, 2 = moderate, 3 = severe, and 4 = extreme) of these symptoms. A total score is calculated by summing the frequency and intensity scores for each item. Thus scores can range from 0 to 8 per item or from 0 to 136 for all 17 symptoms. The CAPS can also be scored according to the DSM diagnostic criteria for posttraumatic stress disorder, rendering a dichotomous rating of the presence or absence of posttraumatic stress disorder. The recommended rule is to rate a symptom as present if the frequency rating is at least 1 and the intensity rating is at least 2. The number of symptoms per criterion area is then tallied; there must be at least one symptom of reexperiencing (criterion B), three symptoms of avoidance (criterion C), and two symptoms of arousal (criterion D), all subsequent to a traumatic event (criterion A).

PRACTICAL ISSUES

The full CAPS interview takes approximately 45–60 minutes, although administration time decreases with repeated administrations to the same individual. Because the CAPS was developed under the auspices of a governmental agency, it is in the public domain. The CAPS and its companion manual, which covers administration and scoring, are widely available for use in Veterans Affairs Medical Centers. For use outside those settings, contact

> Terence M. Keane, Ph.D.
> National Center for PTSD (116B2)
> VA Boston Healthcare System
> 150 South Huntington Avenue
> Boston, MA 02130
> Phone: 617-232-9500 ext. 4143
> E-mail: Terry.Keane@med.va.gov

EXAMPLE 25-8 ■ Sample items from the Clinician-Administered PTSD Scale

Have you ever suddenly acted or felt as if the event was happening again? How often in the past month?

At its worst, how much did it seem that the event was happening again? How long did it last? What did you do while this was happening?

The companion administration manual is sufficient for trained clinicians familiar with administering structured clinical interviews. Training workshops are available by contacting the National Center for PTSD. The CAPS has been translated into Dutch, Farsi (Dari) (for use with Afghan refugees), French, German, Hebrew, Japanese, Norwegian, Pushto (for use with Afghan refugees), Spanish, and Swedish.

PSYCHOMETRIC PROPERTIES

Reliability

The CAPS demonstrated high internal consistency; Cronbach's alphas for the individual subscales and total score ranged from 0.76 to 0.88. Joint reliability was good to excellent in a sample of individuals who had been raped or involved in a motor vehicle accident (kappa = 0.84; correlations on individual items ranged from 0.84 to 0.99) and Afghan refugees (correlations ranged from 0.86 to 1.0).

Validity

The CAPS correlates well with other self-report measures of posttraumatic stress disorder, including the Mississippi Scale (MSS) (p. 583) ($r = 0.73$), the Impact of Event Scale (IES) (p. 579) ($r = 0.62$ for total score, 0.57 for intrusion component, and 0.58 for avoidance component), and the Minnesota Multiphasic Personality Inventory PTSD Scale (MMPI-PTSD) (p. 585) ($r = 0.74$). Differential psychophysiological reactivity to trauma-relevant stimuli has been demonstrated repeatedly in Vietnam combat veterans identified as having posttraumatic stress disorder by the CAPS. Similarly, categorization of subjects with and without posttraumatic stress disorder on the basis of the CAPS yielded evidence of a differential heart rate response in individuals involved in motor vehicle accidents to audiotaped descriptions of their accident.

The CAPS appears sensitive to symptom improvement with psychological treatment (e.g., an intensive trauma management program for Vietnam veterans) and spontaneous remission (e.g., 12-month follow-up with individuals involved in motor vehicle accidents).

CLINICAL UTILITY

The CAPS interview is a psychometrically sound instrument that is closely tied to DSM-IV criteria for posttraumatic stress disorder. Although its psychometric properties were initially determined with veteran populations, the CAPS has been utilized with both civilian and refugee populations. Studies evaluating the CAPS for use with women who have been sexually assaulted, individuals who have been criminally assaulted, and other traumatized populations are lacking. The scale can be used as a diagnostic instrument, as a measure of baseline severity of posttraumatic stress disorder, and as a treatment outcome measure. Because of its length, it is not very useful as a screening measure or as an administrative monitoring tool.

REFERENCES AND SUGGESTED READINGS

Blake DD, Weathers FW, Nagy LN, et al: A clinician rating scale for assessing current and lifetime PTSD: the CAPS-1. Behavior Therapist 18:187–188, 1990

Blanchard EB, Kolb LC, Gerardi RJ, et al: Cardiac response to relevant stimuli as an adjunctive tool for diagnosing posttraumatic stress disorder in Vietnam veterans. Behavior Therapy 17:592–606, 1986

Blanchard EB, Hickling EJ, Buckley TC, et al: Psychophysiology of posttraumatic stress disorder related to motor vehicle accidents: replication and extension. J Consult Clin Psychol 64:742–751, 1996

Blanchard EB, Jones-Alexander J, Buckley TC, et al: Psychometric properties of the PTSD Checklist (PCL). Behav Res Ther 34:669–673, 1996

Frueh BC, Turner SM, Beidel DC, et al: Trauma management therapy: a preliminary evaluation of a multicomponent behavioral treatment for chronic combat-related PTSD. Behav Res Ther 34:533–543, 1996

Hovens JE, van der Ploeg HM, Klaarenbeek MTA, et al: The assessment of posttraumatic stress disorder with the Clinician Administered PTSD Scale: Dutch results. J Clin Psychol 50:325–340, 1994

Malekzai ASB, Niazi JM, Paige SR, et al: Modification of CAPS-1 for diagnosis of PTSD in Afghan refugees. J Trauma Stress 9:891–898, 1996

Malloy PF, Fairbank JA, Keane TM: Validation of a multi-method assessment of posttraumatic stress disorder in Vietnam veterans. J Consult Clin Psychol 51:488–494, 1983

Impact of Event Scale (IES)

M. J. Horowitz, N. Wilner, and W. Alvarez

GOALS

The Impact of Event Scale (IES) (Horowitz et al. 1979) was originally developed to measure the psychological response to specific traumatic stressors or stressful life events (e.g., bereavement). More precisely, it was intended to capture symptoms of intrusion and avoidance, the primary symptom domains resulting from traumatic life events, according to Horowitz (1976). Although the publication of the IES predated the adoption of posttraumatic stress disorder as a diagnostic category in DSM-III, the measure has been used widely to assess posttraumatic stress disorder symptoms after combat and civilian trauma. However, the IES can be employed with any stressful life events; the events need not be considered traumatic or result in posttraumatic stress disorder.

DESCRIPTION

The IES is a 15-item self-report questionnaire composed of two scales, the seven-item Intrusion subscale and the eight-item Avoidance subscale. Respondents rate how frequently they experienced each of the 15 IES symptoms during the prior 7 days on a 4-point scale (0 = not at all, 1 = rarely, 3 = sometimes, and 5 = often). Sample items from the Intrusion and Avoidance subscales are provided in Example 25–9.

The individual item scores are summed to yield one total score (range of 0–75) and two separate scores for the Intrusion (range of 0–35) and Avoidance (range of 0–40) subscales. Although there is no clear cutoff score that indicates posttraumatic stress disorder in any one

EXAMPLE 25–9 ■ Sample items from the Impact of Event Scale

Intrusion Subscale
  I thought about the event when I did not mean to.
  I had dreams about the event.

Avoidance Subscale
  I tried to remove thoughts of the event from my memory.
  I stayed away from reminders of the event.

Reprinted with permission from Mardi Horowitz, M.D.

population or across populations, the authors have suggested that for the IES total score, low scores are those <8.5, medium scores are 8.6–19.0, and high scores are >19.0. A general pattern for IES subscale scores at baseline is for the Intrusion scores to be higher than the Avoidance scores immediately after the traumatic event. Continuing posttraumatic stress disorder symptoms are associated with increasing Avoidance scores.

Note that the IES does not assess hyperarousal symptoms (e.g., irritability and exaggerated startle response), which are part of the DSM-IV diagnostic criteria for posttraumatic stress disorder. To address this shortcoming, investigators developed a revised version of the IES (IES-R) (Weiss and Marmar 1996) that includes six items to assess arousal symptoms.

PRACTICAL ISSUES

It takes about 5–10 minutes to administer the IES. The most common administration format employs the form presented in Zilberg et al. (1982). The IES is copyrighted and is available from

> Mardi Horowitz, M.D.
> University of California–San Francisco
> P.O. Box 0984, Box F-LPP 357
> San Francisco, CA 94143

The IES-R is copyrighted and is available free of charge from

> Daniel S. Weiss, Ph.D.
> Director of PTSD Research, SFVAMC
> Department of Psychiatry
> University of California–San Francisco
> San Francisco, CA 94143
> E-mail: dweiss@itsa.ucsf.edu

Various formats for the measure based on the form presented in Zilberg et al. (1982) have been used. The IES has been translated into Hebrew and Swedish.

The IES is included on the CD-ROM that accompanies this handbook.

PSYCHOMETRIC PROPERTIES

Reliability

The IES subscale scores have shown good to high internal consistency. Cronbach's alpha ranged from 0.79 to 0.92 for the Intrusion subscale and from 0.73 to 0.91 for the Avoidance subscale. Test-retest reliability for the total score ($N = 20$) was $r = 0.93$ over a 1-week interval. Correlations between the two subscales ranged from 0.57 to 0.78 at three different times points (before therapy, 4 months after therapy, and 12 months after therapy).

Validity

Mean scores have been found to discriminate between groups that do or do not meet posttraumatic stress disorder diagnostic criteria. Correlations are fair to moderate but statistically significant with measures such as the PTSD module of the Structured Clinical Interview for DSM Axis I Disorders (SCID-I) (p. 49) (Intrusion subscale, $r = 0.48$; Avoidance subscale, $r = 0.32$; and total score, $r = 0.48$), Mississippi Scale (MSS) (p. 583) (Intrusion subscale, $r = 0.56$; Avoidance subscale, $r = 0.29$; and total score, $r = 0.53$), and the Minnesota Multiphasic Personality Inventory PTSD Scale (MMPI-PTSD) (p. 585) (Intrusion subscale, $r = 0.33$; Avoidance subscale, $r = 0.21$; and total score, $r = 0.33$). In addition, IES scores are related to the severity of an event, the extent of injury, and the total number of events experienced. IES scores 1 week after trauma predicted posttraumatic stress disorder diagnosis 6 months later with 92.3% sensitivity (correct identification of patients with posttraumatic stress disorder) but only 34.2% specificity (correct identification of patients without posttraumatic stress disorder) in a sample of 61 Israelis who had experienced accidents, assaults, and terrorist acts. In another study of 95 women who had been raped, a combination of Rape Aftermath Symptom Test (RAST) (Kilpatrick 1988) and IES Intrusion scores (RAST >100, IES Intrusion >25) correctly identified 89.6% of those with posttraumatic stress disorder at 1

month and 61.3% of those not meeting posttraumatic stress disorder diagnostic criteria at 1 month.

The IES has demonstrated sensitivity to change with psychosocial and pharmacological treatment for posttraumatic stress disorder.

CLINICAL UTILITY

Although it is not a diagnostic instrument, the IES provides a brief, reliable assessment of intrusion and avoidance symptoms associated with posttraumatic stress disorder. Because the wording of the IES is not event specific, it can be and has been used for the assessment of a wide variety of trauma populations, including combat veterans and those who have experienced rape, sexual abuse in childhood, life-threatening medical conditions, and natural disaster. Because of its brevity and sound psychometric properties, the IES has potential for use as a screening instrument or an administrative monitoring tool. Given the high face validity of the items, caution must be used in interpreting the results in populations that might be prone to malingering. When high scores suggest a stress response, follow-up with other measures is recommended.

Of particular interest, the IES holds promise for the early identification of persons likely to meet criteria for posttraumatic stress disorder some weeks or months after the event, making it potentially useful in early identification of high-risk individuals.

REFERENCES AND SUGGESTED READINGS

Davidson JR, Kudler HS, Saunders WB, et al: Predicting the response to amitriptyline in posttraumatic stress disorder. Am J Psychiatry 150:1024–1029, 1993

Foa EB, Rothbaum B, Riggs DS, et al: Treatment of posttraumatic stress disorder in rape victims: a comparison between cognitive-behavioral procedures and counseling. J Consult Clin Psychol 59:715–723, 1991

Horowitz MJ: Stress Response Syndromes. New York, Jason Aronson, 1976

Horowitz MJ, Wilner N, Alvarez W: Impact of Event Scale: a measure of subjective distress. Psychosom Med 41:209–218, 1979

Kilpatrick DG: Rape aftermath symptom test, in Dictionary of Behavioral Assessment Techniques. Edited by Hersen M, Bellack AS. New York, Pergamon, 1988, pp 366–367

Rothbaum BO, Foa EB, Riggs DS, et al: A prospective examination of post-traumatic stress disorder in rape victims. J Trauma Stress 5:455–475, 1992

Schwarzwald J, Solomon Z, Weisenberg M, et al: Validation of the Impact of Event Scale for psychological sequelae of combat. J Consult Clin Psychol 55:251–256, 1987

Shalev AY, Peri T, Canetti L, et al: Predictors of PTSD in injured trauma survivors: a prospective study. Am J Psychiatry 153:219–225, 1996

Weiss DS, Marmar CR: The Impact of Event Scale—Revised, in Assessing Psychological Trauma and PTSD. Edited by Wilson JP, Keane TM. New York, Guilford, 1996, pp 399–411

Zilberg NJ, Weiss DS, Horowitz MJ: Impact of Event Scale: a cross validation study and some empirical evidence supporting a conceptual model of stress response syndromes. J Consult Clin Psychol 50:407–414, 1982

Posttraumatic Stress Diagnostic Scale (PDS)

E. B. Foa

GOALS

The Posttraumatic Stress Diagnostic Scale (PDS) (Foa 1995) was developed as a brief self-report instrument for obtaining a reliable diagnosis of DSM-IV posttraumatic stress disorder and for quantifying the severity of posttraumatic stress disorder symptoms. The PDS is not intended to be a replacement for a structured diagnostic interview.

DESCRIPTION

The PDS is a 49-item self-report scale with items that reflect DSM-IV diagnostic criteria. The scale has four sections. Part 1 includes a listing of different types of trauma, and respondents indicate the traumatic event or events that happened to them or that they witnessed. In part 2, respondents briefly describe the traumatic event that bothers them the most and indicate how long ago it happened. In addition, respondents state whether they were injured or whether someone else was injured during the event, whether they perceived a threat to their own or someone else's life, and whether the event caused feelings of helplessness and terror. Parts 1 and 2 thus refer to criterion A of the DSM-IV diagnostic criteria. Part 3 assesses the 17 posttraumatic stress disorder symptoms included in sections B, C, and D of the DSM-IV diagnostic criteria. Respondents rate how often each of the symptoms has bothered them during the past week: 0 = not at all or only one time, 1 = once a week or less/once in a while, 2 = 2 to 4 times a week/half the time, and 3 = 5 or more times a week/almost always. Sample items for part 3 are provided in Example 25–10. Part 4 assesses interference caused by these posttraumatic stress disorder symptoms in various areas of life (e.g., work, relationships with family, and fun and leisure activities).

Scoring provides a profile of diagnosis, symptom severity, symptom description, and level of impairment. A categorical diagnosis of posttraumatic stress disorder is obtained with an algorithm that requires that the individual's responses meet the following criteria: that the stressful event involve either the presence of physical injury or perception of life threat; that the person felt helpless or terrified during the event; endorsement (rating of 1 or higher) of at least one reexperiencing symptom, three avoidance symptoms, and two arousal symptoms; duration of at least 1 month; and impairment in at least one area of functioning. The PDS symptom severity score, which is obtained by summing the scores of the 17 symptom items, ranges from 0 to 51. Scoring can be done by hand; a computerized version is also available.

PRACTICAL ISSUES

It takes 10–15 minutes to complete the PDS, which is written at an eighth-grade reading level. The PDS is most commonly administered in the form of a paper and pencil questionnaire, but it can also be administered on-line using software available from National Computer Systems, Inc. A manual (Foa 1995) that describes the develop-

EXAMPLE 25–10 ■ **Sample items from the Posttraumatic Stress Diagnostic Scale**

Having bad dreams or nightmares about the traumatic event

Feeling distant or cut off from people around you

Items reprinted with permission from National Computer Systems, Inc., Minneapolis, MN.

ment, psychometric properties, and use of the PDS is available.

The PDS is protected by copyright and cannot be copied without permission in writing from

> National Computer Systems, Inc.
> P.O. Box 1416
> Minneapolis, MN 55440
> Phone: 800-627-7271

An interview version of the PDS is also available. The PDS on-line version requires the purchase of Microtest Q Assessment Systems Software with an annual licensing fee of $89.00. Each assessment profile costs $4.25 for the first 50 reports. Prices for the PDS paper and pencil version are $44.00 for the starter kit (which includes 1 manual, 10 answer sheets, 10 work sheets, and 1 scoring sheet) and $117.00 for the reorder kit (which includes 50 answer sheets, 50 work sheets, and 1 scoring sheet). All are available from National Computer Systems, Inc.

PSYCHOMETRIC PROPERTIES

Reliability

Psychometric properties of the PDS were examined in a sample of 248 women and men who were recruited from several posttraumatic stress disorder treatment centers, as well as from non–treatment-seeking populations at high risk for trauma (e.g., from women's shelters and fire stations). The majority of the subjects had experienced civilian trauma. Internal consistency of the 17-item PDS symptom severity scale was good; Cronbach's alphas were 0.92 for the total scale, 0.78 for the Reexperiencing subscale, 0.84 for the Avoidance subscale, and 0.84 for the Arousal subscale. Test-retest reliability of the symptom severity scale conducted over a 2- to 3-week interval

($N = 110$) was high; correlation coefficients ranged from 0.77 to 0.85 across the total scale and its three subscales. Test-retest reliability of posttraumatic stress disorder diagnoses obtained from the PDS, established across the same 2- to 3-week interval with the same sample, yielded a satisfactory kappa of 0.74 and a percentage of agreement of 87%.

Validity

Correlations between PDS symptom severity scores and the revised version of the Impact of Event Scale (IES) (p. 579) ranged from 0.49 to 0.93, indicating good convergence. However, the PDS was also strongly related to depression and general anxiety, as assessed with the Beck Depression Inventory (BDI) (p. 519) and the State-Trait Anxiety Scale (Spielberger et al. 1970); correlation coefficients ranged from 0.62 to 0.90. The strong association between PDS symptom severity and depression, as well as general anxiety, is problematic but may reflect the considerable overlap of posttraumatic stress disorder with symptoms of depression and anxiety rather than poor validity of the PDS.

Diagnostic agreement with the Structured Clinical Interview for DSM Axis I Disorders (SCID-I) (p. 49) was assessed, and a kappa of 0.65 was obtained, with an 82% agreement between the two measures. The sensitivity of the PDS was 89% and the specificity was 75% using the SCID-I.

CLINICAL UTILITY

Because the proper psychiatric diagnosis requires an evaluation by a trained clinician, the diagnosis derived from the PDS should be used for screening purposes only. Nonetheless, the current data and ease of administration support use of the PDS as a screening instrument in both clinical and at-risk populations. Furthermore, the measure provides a reliable and valid assessment of the severity of posttraumatic stress disorder symptoms according to DSM-IV criteria and may thus be used to monitor change with treatment. Given the high face validity of the items, caution must be used in interpreting the results in populations that might be prone to malingering. When high scores suggest a stress response, follow-up with other measures is recommended.

REFERENCES AND SUGGESTED READINGS

Foa EB: Posttraumatic Stress Diagnostic Scale: Manual. Minneapolis, MN, National Computer Systems, 1995

Foa EB, Cashman L, Jaycox L, et al: The validation of a self-report measure of posttraumatic stress disorder: the Posttraumatic Diagnostic Scale. Psychological Assessment 9:445–451, 1997

Spielberger CD, Gorsuch RR, Luchene RE: State-Trait Anxiety Inventory. Palo Alto, CA, Consulting Psychologists Press, 1970

Mississippi Scale (MSS)

T. M. Keane, J. M. Caddell, and K. L. Taylor

GOALS

The Mississippi Scale (MSS) (Keane et al. 1988) is a self-report questionnaire that was originally developed to assess the severity of trauma-related symptoms on the basis of the DSM-III criteria for posttraumatic stress disorder in Vietnam combat veterans. Although the original scale was developed for combat-related posttraumatic stress disorder, it has been modified for use with civilian trauma populations by substituting references to the military with other specific events or simply referring to "the event." This modified version is called the Civilian MSS.

DESCRIPTION

The 35-item self-report MSS assesses symptoms related to posttraumatic stress disorder that fall into four categories, three of which are closely related to the DSM criteria for posttraumatic stress disorder: Reexperiencing (11 items), Withdrawal and Numbing (11 items), Hyperarousal (8 items), and Self-Persecution (e.g., suicidality and survivor guilt) (5 items). Respondents rate the

presence of each symptom on similar 5-point Likert-type scales (e.g., 1 = not at all true to 5 = extremely true, 1 = never true to 5 = always true, 1 = very unlikely to 5 = extremely likely, and 1 = never to 5 = very frequently). Sample items from the Civilian MSS are provided in Example 25–11.

After reversing the scores of the 10 positively worded items (e.g., "I am able to get emotionally close to others"), individual item scores are summed to yield a total score. Thus, total scores range from 35 to 175. In addition, the total score can be dichotomized to indicate whether posttraumatic stress disorder is present. The suggested cutoff score for a diagnosis of posttraumatic stress disorder in Vietnam veterans is 107 (Keane et al. 1988). There are no clear or agreed-on cutoff scores for other trauma populations.

PRACTICAL ISSUES

It takes about 5–20 minutes for patients to complete the MSS. The original publication indicates that the measure is copyrighted, although it is used widely within the Veterans Affairs Medical Center system. Permission to use the MSS can be obtained from

> Terence M. Keane, Ph.D.
> National Center for PTSD (116B2)
> VA Boston Healthcare System
> 150 South Huntington Avenue
> Boston, MA 02130
> Phone: 617-232-9500, ext. 4143
> E-mail: Terry.Keane@med.va.gov

The MSS has been translated into Hebrew and Spanish.

The MSS is included on the CD-ROM that accompanies this handbook.

EXAMPLE 25–11 ■ Sample items from the Civilian Mississippi Scale

> When I think of some of the things that I did at the time of the event, I wish I were dead.
>
> It seems as if I have no feelings.
>
> I lose my cool and explode over minor everyday things.

Reprinted with permission from Terence M. Keane, Ph.D.

PSYCHOMETRIC PROPERTIES

Reliability

The MSS has high internal consistency (Cronbach's alphas of 0.86–0.94, including a version in Spanish); average correlations of each item with the total score were 0.58 (range of 0.23–0.73). Test-retest reliability ($N = 39$ male combat veterans) over a 1-week interval was 0.97. Alternative form reliability ($N = 55$ adults fluent in both English and Spanish at two universities) was 0.84.

Validity

Validity is supported by moderate to high correlations (0.29–0.88) with other measures of posttraumatic stress disorder, such as the number of symptoms endorsed in the PTSD module of the Structured Clinical Interview for DSM Axis I Disorders (SCID-I) (p. 49) ($r = 0.65$), the Impact of Event Scale (IES) (p. 579) (total score, $r = 0.53$; Intrusion subscale, $r = 0.56$; and Avoidance subscale, $r = 0.29$), and the Minnesota Multiphasic Personality Inventory PTSD Scale (MMPI-PTSD) (p. 585) ($r = 0.71$–0.88). There is also a moderately high relation between the MSS and measures of event severity, such as combat exposure ($r = 0.25$), dissociative symptoms ($r = 0.54$), and life threat and injury (higher scores are associated with life threat and injury combined than with either alone or neither). The MSS discriminated between veterans with and without diagnosed posttraumatic stress disorder, with a sensitivity of 93% and a specificity of 89%, using the Jackson Structured Interview for PTSD (Keane et al. 1985) as the gold standard. In a sample of civilians exposed to violence (Shalev et al. 1996) or a natural disaster (Norris and Perilla 1996), those with a diagnosis of posttraumatic stress disorder scored higher, on average, on the MSS than those not diagnosed with posttraumatic stress disorder.

The MSS has been used as a treatment outcome measure, but it may not be very sensitive to improvement. For example, a study of a treatment program for Vietnam veterans demonstrated improvements in other measures (e.g., overall functioning, hopelessness, and shame) but not MSS scores.

CLINICAL UTILITY

The MSS is a useful self-report measure of baseline posttraumatic stress disorder cardinal symptoms. It is not a diagnostic measure. Somewhat surprisingly, it appears to be less useful than other scales as a treatment outcome measure. Given the high face validity of the items, caution must be used in interpreting the results in populations that might be prone to malingering. When high scores suggest a stress response, follow-up with other measures is recommended.

REFERENCES AND SUGGESTED READINGS

Keane TM, Fairbank JA, Caddell JM, et al: A behavioral approach to assessing and treating post-traumatic stress disorder in Vietnam veterans, in Trauma and Its Wake: The Study and Treatment of Post-Traumatic Stress Disorder. Edited by Figley CR. New York, Brunner/Mazel, 1985, pp 257–294, 417–438

Keane TM, Caddell JM, Taylor KL: Mississippi Scale for Combat-Related Posttraumatic Stress Disorder: three studies in reliability and validity. J Consult Clin Psychol 56:85–90, 1988

Norris FH, Perilla JL: The Revised Civilian Mississippi Scale for PTSD: reliability, validity, and cross-language stability. J Trauma Stress 9:285–298, 1996

Norris FH, Riad JK: Standardized self-report measures of civilian trauma and posttraumatic stress disorder, in Assessing Psychological Trauma and PTSD. Edited by Wilson JP, Keane TM. New York, Guilford, 1996, pp 7–42

Ragsdale KG, Cox RD, Finn P, et al: Effectiveness of short-term specialized inpatient treatment for war-related posttraumatic stress disorder: a role for adventure-based counseling and psychodrama. J Trauma Stress 9:269–283, 1996

Shalev AY, Peri T, Canetti L, et al: Predictors of PTSD in injured trauma survivors: a prospective study. Am J Psychiatry 153:219–225, 1996

Minnesota Multiphasic Personality Inventory PTSD Scale (MMPI-PTSD)

T. M. Keane, P. F. Malloy, and J. A. Fairbank

EXAMPLE 25–12 ■ Sample item from the Minnesota Multiphasic Personality Inventory PTSD Scale

> I have nightmares every few nights.

GOALS

The Minnesota Multiphasic Personality Inventory PTSD Scale (MMPI-PTSD) (Keane et al. 1984), composed of a subset of items from the Minnesota Multiphasic Personality Inventory (MMPI), is intended to discriminate patients with interview-based diagnoses of posttraumatic stress disorder from those without posttraumatic stress disorder. The MMPI-PTSD was developed for use with Vietnam veterans, but it has since been used with other trauma groups, including those who have experienced motor vehicle accidents and violent crime.

DESCRIPTION

The MMPI-PTSD is a 49-item subset of the MMPI. The MMPI-2 PTSD (i.e., a revision of the PTSD Scale derived from the MMPI-2) contains only 46 items. (Three of the original items were represented twice on the MMPI and thus on the MMPI-PTSD. These repetitions were deleted from the MMPI-2, thus also removing them from the MMPI-2 PTSD). The items, which are answered in a true-false format, indicate general distress, but most do not match specific DSM criteria. Although the scale is typically administered as part of the full MMPI or MMPI-2, it has been shown to be useful when administered separately. A sample item from the MMPI-PTSD is provided in Example 25–12.

Scores range from 0 to 49 on the MMPI-PTSD and from 0 to 46 on the MMPI-2 PTSD (because of the deletion of the three repeated items). There is some concern about how to address the item difference in the two versions: 1) adjust the cutoff scores or 2) double count the score on the three items that were originally repeated on the scale. The item difference is more of a concern when hand scoring the MMPI-PTSD as a stand-alone instrument; within the context of the MMPI-2, a T-score

is calculated. Cutoff scores of <30 (without posttraumatic stress disorder) and ⩾30 (with posttraumatic stress disorder) apply for the identification of posttraumatic stress disorder in samples of Vietnam veterans. Scores >38 or 40 indicate possible fabrication of symptoms. For civilian trauma survivors, the suggested cut point is in the range of 15–19. The cut point is set depending on the cost versus benefit of the ratio of false-negative to false-positive diagnoses. Although the MMPI-PTSD has been used as a stand-alone instrument, it is most commonly used by administering the full MMPI to take advantage of its validity scales and configural patterns. On the full MMPI, PTSD is supported by an F test T-score in the range of 80–110 and high points on scales 2 (Depression) and 8 (Schizophrenia). Readers should refer to Litz et al. (1991) and Lyons and Keane (1992) for further discussion of the MMPI-PTSD, item and scoring considerations, and a comparison of the MMPI and MMPI-2 with regard to the identification of posttraumatic stress disorder.

PRACTICAL ISSUES

It takes about 5–15 minutes to complete the 49-item stand-alone scale, making it more useful in research settings or with distressed patients unlikely to successfully complete the full MMPI. The MMPI-2 PTSD is part of the full MMPI-2 and is discussed in the MMPI-2 manual and scored through either hand or computer scoring methods (available from National Computer Systems, Inc.). Practitioners most often use the MMPI-2 PTSD within a full MMPI-2 administration, because reproducing the scale separately requires additional copyright permission from National Computer Systems, Inc. The MMPI-PTSD may be obtained by contacting

Terence M. Keane, Ph.D.
National Center for PTSD (116B2)
VA Boston Healthcare System

150 South Huntington Avenue
Boston, MA 02130
Phone: 617-232-9500, ext. 4143
E-mail: Terry.Keane@med.va.gov

PSYCHOMETRIC PROPERTIES

Reliability

In a sample of combat veterans who were administered both versions of the scale (i.e., within the full MMPI and as a stand-alone questionnaire), test-retest reliability was high (94.3% of veterans similarly classified in both formats, with a cutoff score of 30) when comparing repeated administration of the 49 items within and outside the context of the MMPI.

Validity

Studies showed moderate to high correlations ($r = 0.21$–0.78) with other measures of posttraumatic stress disorder, such as the Mississippi Scale (MSS) (p. 583) ($r = 0.71$), the Impact of Event Scale (IES) (p. 579) (total score, $r = 0.33$; IES Intrusion, $r = 0.33$; and IES Avoidance, $r = 0.21$), and the number of symptoms endorsed on the Structured Clinical Interview for DSM Axis I Disorders (SCID-I) (p. 49) ($r = 0.46$). Validity is further supported by the relationship between MMPI-PTSD scores and measures of event severity, depression, and anxiety. The MMPI-PTSD also has the ability to differentiate those with posttraumatic stress disorder, those with subthreshold posttraumatic stress disorder, and those without posttraumatic stress disorder, using a structured diagnostic interview as the gold standard; the MMPI-PTSD correctly classified 82%–90% of those with posttraumatic stress disorder.

In one treatment study of Vietnam veterans receiving implosive or flooding therapy, the MMPI-PTSD failed to discriminate the treatment group from the wait list control group, whereas other measures such as the Beck Depression Inventory (BDI) (p. 519), and the State-Trait Anxiety Inventory (Spielberger et al. 1970) showed such differences. Thus, the MMPI-PTSD may not be sensitive to treatment gains.

CLINICAL UTILITY

The MMPI-PTSD can be administered as part of the MMPI or the MMPI-2, if one of the full tests is being used anyway, and it can also be a useful screening device when administered as a separate questionnaire. It has the advantage of being less obviously related to posttraumatic stress disorder diagnostic criteria than other measures of posttraumatic stress disorder and thus is less prone to fabrication. It has the further advantage of the existence of a specific range of scores associated with posttraumatic stress disorder. Consequently, it may help to discriminate posttraumatic stress disorder from other psychiatric problems and may be of use in disability or other compensation cases. The scale provides a baseline measure of distress due to posttraumatic stress disorder, but its usefulness as a treatment outcome measure appears to be questionable. It is not a diagnostic instrument.

REFERENCES AND SUGGESTED READINGS

Blanchard EB, Hickling EJ, Taylor AE, et al: Psychiatric morbidity associated with motor vehicle accidents. J Nerv Ment Dis 183:495–504, 1995

Fairbank JA, McCaffrey RJ, Keane TM: Psychometric detection of fabricated symptoms of posttraumatic stress disorder. Am J Psychiatry 142:501–503, 1985

Gaston L, Brunet A, Koszycki D, et al: MMPI profiles of acute and chronic PTSD in a civilian sample. J Trauma Stress 9:817–832, 1996

Keane TM, Malloy PF, Fairbank JA: Empirical development of an MMPI subscale for the assessment of combat-related posttraumatic stress disorder. J Consult Clin Psychol 52:888–891, 1984

Keane TM, Fairbank JA, Caddell JM, et al: Implosive (flooding) therapy reduces symptoms of PTSD in Vietnam combat veterans. Behavior Therapy 20:245–260, 1989

Koretzky MB, Peck AH: Validation and cross-validation of the PTSD subscale of the MMPI with civilian trauma victims. J Clin Psychol 46:296–300, 1990

Litz BT, Penk WE, Walsh S, et al: Similarities and differences between Minnesota Multiphasic Personality Inventory (MMPI) and MMPI-2 applications to the assessment of post-traumatic stress disorder. J Pers Assess 57:238–253, 1991

Lyons JA, Keane TM: Keane PTSD Scale: MMPI and MMPI-2 update. J Trauma Stress 5:111–117, 1992

Lyons JA, Scotti JR: Comparability of two administration formats of the Keane Posttraumatic Stress Disorder Scale. Psychological Assessment 6:209–211, 1994

Scotti JR, Veltum-Sturges L, Lyons JA: The Keane PTSD scale extracted from the MMPI: sensitivity and specificity with Vietnam veterans. J Trauma Stress 9:643–650, 1996

Spielberger CD, Gorsuch RR, Luchene RE: State-Trait Anxiety Inventory. Palo Alto, CA, Consulting Psychologists Press, 1970

EXAMPLE 25–13 ■ Sample items from the Penn State Worry Questionnaire

My worries overwhelm me.

Many situations make me worry.

Once I start worrying, I can't stop.

I find it easy to dismiss worrisome thoughts.

Penn State Worry Questionnaire (PSWQ)

T. J. Meyer, R. L. Miller, R. L. Metzger, and T. D. Borkovec

GOALS

The Penn State Worry Questionnaire (PSWQ) (Meyer et al. 1990) was designed to assess trait symptoms of pathological worry. It was created to evaluate the tendency of an individual to worry, the excessiveness or intensity of worry, and the tendency for the worrying to be generalized and not restricted to one or a small number of situations. Thus, the scale is relevant to the assessment of three of the DSM-IV diagnostic criteria for generalized anxiety disorder (i.e., the requirements that the worry last 6 months or longer, that it be excessive, and that it be generalized).

DESCRIPTION

The PSWQ is a 16-item self-report questionnaire that assesses the frequency and intensity of worry symptoms. Sample items are provided in Example 25–13. Each item is rated on a Likert scale from 1 = not at all typical to 5 = very typical.

The total score is a sum of item ratings and ranges from 16 to 80. Some items are reverse scored. Patients with generalized anxiety disorder typically score ≥60 points. Patients with anxiety disorders other than generalized anxiety disorder score about 10 points lower but higher than nonanxious control subjects. However, patients in a major depressive episode typically score as high as patients with generalized anxiety disorder. Normative values for the PSWQ taken from a community sample in a shopping mall ranged from 18 to 76 and are available in Gillis et al. (1995).

PRACTICAL ISSUES

The PSWQ is a brief self-report measure that can be administered in approximately 5 minutes. The measure is in the public domain and may be obtained by contacting

Thomas Borkovec
Pennsylvania State University
Department of Psychology
544 Moore Building
University Park, PA 16802

The PSWQ is included on the CD-ROM that accompanies this handbook.

PSYCHOMETRIC PROPERTIES

Reliability

The PSWQ demonstrated a high degree of internal consistency in diverse populations; Cronbach's alphas ranged from 0.86 to 0.93 for anxiety disorder patients and from 0.91 to 0.95 for community samples. Test-retest reliability proved to be good, ranging from 0.75 over a 2-week interval to 0.92 over an 8- to 10-week interval.

Validity

The PSWQ showed good convergence with other measures of worry in nonclinical student populations. The measure proved to be highly correlated with other questionnaire measures of worry, including the Worry Domains Questionnaire (Tallis et al. 1992) ($r = 0.59$) and the Student Worry Scale (Davey et al. 1992) ($r = 0.67$). Correlations with a single item reflecting the percentage of the day spent worrying were also high ($r = 0.52$).

In studies with clinical samples, the PSWQ proved to be weakly correlated with dissimilar measures of anxiety and depression. Correlation coefficients ranged from −0.02 to 0.18 for the Hamilton Anxiety Rating Scale (HARS) (p. 554), the Trait scale of the State-Trait Anxiety Inventory (Spielberger et al. 1970), and the Zung Self-Rating Depression Scale (Zung SDS) (p. 534). Correlations with the Hamilton Rating Scale for Depression (Ham-D) (p. 526) and the Beck Depression Inventory (BDI) (p. 519) ranged from −0.10 to 0.04. Tests of the measure's validity in nonclinical college samples yielded somewhat mixed results because of the strong association of the PSWQ with the Trait scale of the State-Trait Anxiety Inventory (Spielberger et al. 1970) ($r = 0.64$ and 0.74). The PSWQ was found to be less strongly related to the State scale of the State-Trait Anxiety Inventory (Spielberger et al. 1970) ($r = 0.49$), the BDI ($r = 0.36$), and social desirability as measured with the Marlowe-Crowne Social Desirability Scale (Crowne and Marlowe 1964) ($r = −0.09$). In addition, the PSWQ has been shown to reflect worry symptoms that are distinct from obsessive-compulsive symptoms measured by the Padua Inventory (PI) (p. 575).

Patients with generalized anxiety disorder as determined by DSM-III-R criteria were found to score significantly higher on the PSWQ than patients with other DSM-III-R anxiety disorders (i.e., panic disorder, social phobia, simple phobia, and obsessive-compulsive disorder) and individuals without any current or past mental disorder. Cutoff scores have not been published, but inspection of published data suggests that nonanxious, community control subjects score ≤40, patients with anxiety disorders other than generalized anxiety disorder score between 40 and 60, and patients with generalized anxiety disorder tend to score ≥60. Patients with major depression were found to score similarly to those with generalized anxiety disorder. The PSWQ is sensitive to change with treatment.

CLINICAL UTILITY

The PSWQ is a brief, psychometrically sound measure of the worry dimension of generalized anxiety disorder. It is recommended as a measure of severity of pathological worry and change. It may be useful as a screening tool to detect pathological worry, but it cannot be used to diagnose generalized anxiety disorder in nonclinical populations because worry is related to many disorders (e.g., depression, obsessive-compulsive disorder, and hypochondriasis) besides generalized anxiety disorder. Although relevant to the assessment of DSM-IV generalized anxiety disorder, it does not assess other issues that are important in determining whether the criteria are met for generalized anxiety disorder, such as the frequency, intensity, content, or degree of uncontrollability of the worry.

REFERENCES AND SUGGESTED READINGS

Borkovec TD, Costello E: Efficacy of applied relaxation and cognitive-behavioral therapy in the treatment of GAD. J Consult Clin Psychol 61:611–619, 1993

Brown TA, Antony MM, Barlow DH: Psychometric properties of the Penn State Worry Questionnaire in a clinical anxiety disorders sample. Behav Res Ther 30:33–37, 1992

Crowne DB, Marlowe D: The Approval Motive: Studies in Evaluative Dependence. New York, Wiley, 1964

Davey GCL, Hampton J, Farrell J, et al: Some characteristics of worrying: evidence for worrying and anxiety as separate constructs. Personality and Individual Differences 13:133–147, 1992

Freestone MF, Ladouceur R, Rhaume J, et al: Self-report of obsessions and worry. Behav Res Ther 32:29–36, 1994

Gillis MM, Haaga DAF, Ford G: Normative values for the Beck Anxiety Inventory, Fear Questionnaire, Penn State Worry Questionnaire, and Social Phobia and Anxiety Inventory. Psychological Assessment 7:450–455, 1995

Meyer TJ, Miller RL, Metzger R, et al: Development and validation of the Penn State Worry Questionnaire. Behav Res Ther 6:487–495, 1990

Molina S, Borkovec TD: The Penn State Worry Questionnaire: psychometric properties and associated characteristics, in Worrying: Perspectives on Theory, Assessment, and Treatment. Edited by Davey GCL, Tallis F. New York, Wiley, 1994, pp 265–283

Spielberger CD, Gorsuch RR, Luchene RE: State-Trait Anxiety Inventory. Palo Alto, CA, Consulting Psychologists Press, 1970

Starcevic V: Pathological worry in major depression: a preliminary report. Behav Res Ther 33:55–56, 1995

Tallis F, Eysenck M, Mathews A: A questionnaire for the measurement of nonpathological worry. Personality and Individual Differences 13:161–168, 1992

CHAPTER 26

Somatoform and Factitious Disorders and Malingering Measures

Katharine A. Phillips, M.D.
Brian Fallon, M.D.

INTRODUCTION

Major Domains

This chapter includes measures for the DSM-IV somatoform disorders, factitious disorder, and malingering (see Table 26–1). Measures for evaluating the severity and quality of pain are also included. The somatoform disorders are characterized by the presence of physical symptoms that suggest a general medical condition and are not fully explained by a general medical condition, by the direct effects of a substance, or by another mental disorder (such as panic disorder). Factitious disorder and malingering may also be characterized by physical symptoms that are not accounted for by a general medical condition, but they differ from the somatoform disorders in that the symptoms are intentionally produced. Factitious disorder and malingering may also be characterized by the intentional production of psychological symptoms or both physical and psychological symptoms.

Organization

The first three measures presented can be used to diagnose a wide range of somatoform disorders as defined by the ICD-10 Research Diagnostic Criteria; one of the measures (the Somatoform Disorders Schedule [SDS]) also uses DSM-IV criteria. The next measures presented each focus on a particular somatoform disorder (i.e.,

pain disorder, hypochondriasis, and body dysmorphic disorder). Finally, an instrument designed to assess psychological (but not physical or neuropsychological) symptoms due to factitious disorder or malingering is presented.

Relevant Measures Included Elsewhere in the Handbook

Chapter 6, "Diagnostic Interviews for Adults," includes some instruments that assess some or all of the somatoform disorders: the Structured Clinical Interview for DSM-IV Axis I Disorders (SCID-I) (p. 49), the Schedule for Affective Disorders and Schizophrenia (SADS) (p. 58), the Schedules for Clinical Assessment in Neuropsychiatry (SCAN) (p. 53), the Primary Care Evaluation of Mental Disorders (PRIME-MD) (p. 65), the Symptom-Driven Diagnostic System for Primary Care (SDDS-PC) (p. 68), the Diagnostic Interview Schedule (DIS) (p. 61), and the Composite International Diagnostic Interview (CIDI) (p. 61). Given that some consider the development of conversion symptoms to be a dissociative phenomenon, some of the instruments in Chapter 27, "Dissociative Disorders Measures," assess conversion symptoms. In addition, some nondiagnostic scales (e.g., the Symptom Checklist–90—Revised [SCL-90-R] [p. 81]) include subscales that assess somatic symptoms in a dimensional way.

TABLE 26–1 ■ Somatoform and factitious disorders and malingering measures

Name of measure	Disorder or construct assessed	Format	Pages
Somatoform Disorders Symptom Checklist*	Wide range of somatoform disorders (including somatization disorder, undifferentiated somatoform disorder, conversion disorder, persistent somatoform pain disorder, somatoform autonomic dysfunction, and neurasthenia), using the ICD-10 Research Diagnostic Criteria	Semistructured checklist; 65 items	596–598
Screener for Somatoform Disorders*	Wide range of somatoform disorders (including somatization disorder, undifferentiated somatoform disorder, conversion disorder, persistent somatoform pain disorder, somatoform autonomic dysfunction, and neurasthenia), using the ICD-10 Research Diagnostic Criteria	Self-report or interviewer-administered screen; 12 items	596–598
Somatoform Disorders Schedule (SDS)*	Wide range of somatoform disorders (including hypochondriasis, body dysmorphic disorder, somatization disorder, undifferentiated somatoform disorder, conversion disorder, persistent somatoform pain disorder, somatoform autonomic dysfunction, and neurasthenia), using the ICD-10 Research Diagnostic Criteria and DSM-IV criteria	Fully structured interview; 114 items	596–598
McGill Pain Questionnaire (MPQ)*	Quantitative and qualitative aspects of pain	Fully structured interview with four parts that assess location, quality, temporal properties, and intensity of pain	598–601
Visual analog scales	Dimensions of pain (e.g., intensity)	Horizontal or vertical line to be marked by patient; uses verbal descriptors, sometimes accompanied by numbers	601–603
West Haven–Yale Multidimensional Pain Inventory (WHYMPI)*	Psychosocial and behavioral aspects of chronic pain; a version for significant others assesses responses to patients' demonstrations of pain	Self-report; 52 items Version for significant others: self-report with 17 items	603–605
Whiteley Index of Hypochondriasis*	Hypochondriacal attitudes, severity of hypochondriasis, and change in response to treatment	Self-administered questionnaire; 14 items	605–607
Illness Attitude Scale (IAS)	Attitudes, fears, and beliefs associated with hypochondriasis and abnormal illness behavior; screen for disorder of hypochondriasis; and change in response to treatment	Self-report; 29 items	607–610
Body Dysmorphic Disorder Examination (BDDE)*	Body dysmorphic disorder diagnosis, severity of negative body image, and change in response to treatment	Semistructured interview; 34 items	610–612

*Measure is included on the CD-ROM that accompanies this handbook.

TABLE 26–1 ■ Somatoform and factitious disorders and malingering measures (continued)

Yale-Brown Obsessive Compulsive Scale Modified for Body Dysmorphic Disorder (BDD-YBOCS)*	Severity of DSM-IV body dysmorphic disorder and change in response to treatment	Semistructured interview; 12 items	612–614
Structured Interview of Reported Symptoms (SIRS)	Degree to which an individual deliberately exaggerates or fabricates symptoms associated with a mental disorder; assists in diagnosis of malingering and factitious disorder with predominantly psychological signs and symptoms	Fully structured interview; 172 items	614–616

*Measure is included on the CD-ROM that accompanies this handbook.

USING MEASURES IN THIS DOMAIN

Goals of Assessment

Several measures presented in this chapter are intended to determine whether a patient's presentation meets the diagnostic criteria for a somatoform disorder (the Somatoform Disorders Symptom Checklist, the SDS, the Body Dysmorphic Disorder Examination [BDDE], and the Structured Interview of Reported Symptoms [SIRS]). Several other instruments screen for the presence of somatoform disorders (i.e., a high score on the measure indicates a high likelihood of the presence of a somatoform disorder): the Screener for Somatoform Disorders, the Whiteley Index of Hypochondriasis, and the Illness Attitude Scale (IAS).

Some measures, such as the McGill Pain Questionnaire (MPQ), the visual analog scales, the Whiteley Index of Hypochondriasis, the BDDE, and the Yale-Brown Obsessive Compulsive Scale Modified for Body Dysmorphic Disorder (BDD-YBOCS), assess the severity of a condition or related constructs.

Some of the measures in this chapter assess dimensions that cut across more than one somatoform disorder. For example, the severity of pain as measured by the MPQ may also be relevant in the evaluation of somatization disorder, because pain symptoms are required for that diagnosis. Some instruments assess different aspects or dimensions of the same disorder or construct. For example, the visual analog scales are usually used to assess the physical severity of pain, whereas the West Haven–Yale Multidimensional Pain Inventory (WHYMPI) assesses psychosocial and behavioral aspects of pain.

Several instruments in this domain, including the MPQ, the visual analog scales, the Whiteley Index

of Hypochondriasis, the IAS, the BDDE, and the BDD-YBOCS, have been shown to be sensitive to change and may be used to measure change over time, usually with the purpose of documenting apparent response to treatment.

Implementation Issues

When evaluating patients who present with physical symptoms, careful review of all available medical records and a thorough medical evaluation (or verification that an adequate medical evaluation has been done in the past) is critical to rule out a general medical condition or substance use as the sole cause of the presenting symptoms. Available scales generally do not accomplish this objective. Omitting a medical evaluation (or accepting the negative results of an incomplete or cursory evaluation) may lead to the inappropriate labeling of medical symptoms as somatoform. Mislabeling medical symptoms as somatoform most often occurs when the symptoms are nonspecific, when available laboratory tests are inadequate, or when the patient has a medical syndrome that is not well understood or for which there is no effective treatment. Because many medical conditions (such as Lyme disease, multiple sclerosis, systemic lupus erythematosus, systemic parasitic infection, hypercalcemia, and hemochromatosis) may present with vague symptoms and a waxing and waning course, a careful reassessment of a negative medical workup should be considered when evaluating patients who present with multiple, stress-exacerbated, or confusing symptoms. On the other hand, many patients are unnecessarily exposed to a long series of expensive, painful, or even dangerous diagnostic procedures because the clinician has not considered the possibility that the presenting symptoms are due to a somatoform or other mental disorder (e.g., major depressive disorder or panic disorder).

When diagnosing the somatoform disorders, as well as factitious disorder and malingering when they present with physical complaints, it is important to conduct a careful and thorough psychiatric clinical interview, combined with adequate medical evaluation in collaboration with the patient's primary care physician. In addition, when evaluating factitious disorder and malingering, review of available records (including criminal records in the case of malingering) and consultation with prior health care professionals are critical for evidence of duplicitous behavior regarding past presenting symptoms.

As previously noted, the somatoform disorders have multiple dimensions (e.g., physical, affective, and cognitive). Such dimensions may in turn have multiple components (e.g., the cognitive dimension of hypochondriasis includes degree of preoccupation and insight). Most measures assess only certain aspects of these disorders, and, depending on clinical needs, it may be advantageous to use several measures that assess different aspects of the disorder or construct; however, multiple measures that appear complementary do not take the place of a thorough medical review.

Cultural factors may play an important role in the presentation and evaluation of somatic complaints. The type and frequency of somatic symptoms characteristic of a somatoform disorder may differ across cultures. For example, burning hands and feet represent a pseudoneurological symptom that is more common in Africa and South Asia than in North America. Whether it is unreasonable for a preoccupation with disease to persist despite appropriate medical evaluation and reassurance (as in hypochondriasis) must also be judged relative to the individual's cultural background. Many of the instruments presented in this chapter have not been cross-culturally validated and may therefore have limitations when used with certain ethnic populations. It is important that clinicians be familiar with the ways in which somatoform symptoms present in the patient populations they are evaluating and treating and to adjust symptom reviews accordingly.

Issues in Interpreting Psychometric Data

Most measures in this domain do not assist with differential diagnosis. Somatic symptoms are not pathognomonic of the somatoform disorders, factitious disorder, or malingering; the symptoms may instead be better ac-

counted for by a general medical condition, substance use (drugs of abuse and prescription medication), or another psychiatric disorder (e.g., major depressive disorder or panic disorder). Guidelines for differential diagnosis are presented in DSM-IV.

A major problem in determining the validity of these measures is the lack of a gold standard for either the disorders or the symptoms (e.g., pain). Typically, somatoform and malingering scales are validated against other scales that measure similar constructs or against clinical judgment, using all available medical, psychiatric, and (when relevant) forensic data. However, for many of these disorders, other scales that might be used as validators do not exist or have significant limitations. The gold standard of clinical judgment is limited by the difficulty that even expert clinicians can experience when attempting to ascertain whether a given symptom is medical or psychiatric. The absence of a diagnosis of a general medical condition is not necessarily indicative of a somatoform disorder, because some medical conditions present with vague symptoms, are difficult to diagnose definitively, or may take years to fully manifest themselves. On the other hand, the presence of a general medical condition does not preclude the presence of a somatoform disorder. In addition, it may sometimes be difficult to differentiate somatoform disorder symptoms from those caused by a general medical condition because a given symptom may reflect a combination of both psychological and physical etiologies.

GUIDE TO THE SELECTION OF MEASURES

Somatization Disorder and Undifferentiated Somatoform Disorder

Several instruments that assess somatoform disorders can be used to evaluate somatization disorder and undifferentiated somatoform disorder. The Screener for Somatoform Disorders screens for the presence of somatization disorder and undifferentiated somatoform disorder, and the Somatoform Disorders Symptom Checklist assists clinicians in diagnosing these disorders. The SDS, a fully structured diagnostic instrument, is used primarily in epidemiological surveys.

No measures that assess specifically for undifferentiated somatoform disorder have been developed. However, because the disorder constitutes a residual category for persistent somatoform conditions that do not meet full criteria for somatization disorder, a diagnosis of undifferentiated somatoform disorder can be derived from instruments that assess for somatization disorder. When considering a diagnosis of undifferentiated somatoform disorder, it is particularly important to rule out a general medical condition or another mental disorder and to carefully investigate new symptoms, because the much lowered threshold for the number of required symptoms (i.e., one or more) makes it more likely that the symptoms will eventually be accounted for by a general medical condition or another mental disorder.

Conversion Disorder

No stand-alone instruments assess conversion disorder. However, this diagnosis can be derived from three instruments published by the World Health Organization: the Somatoform Disorders Symptom Checklist, the Screener for Somatoform Disorders, and the SDS, which contain many conversion symptoms.

Pain Disorder

Three measures included in this chapter are useful for assessing pain severity. The visual analog scales are most useful when a quick assessment of pain severity or another pain dimension is needed. Advantages of the scales are their brevity and simplicity. The MPQ is useful when a more comprehensive assessment of pain, such as location, intensity, and quality, is needed. A significant advantage of this scale is its multidimensional nature and the richness and subtlety of the information obtained. The WHYMPI is preferred when information about the psychosocial and behavioral dimensions of pain (e.g., ability to perform common activities) is needed. It may be advantageous to use several of these instruments when assessing patients.

The instruments included in this chapter do not diagnose DSM-IV pain disorder per se or attempt to differentiate the different subtypes of pain disorder (i.e., pain disorder associated with psychological factors, pain disorder associated with both psychological factors and a general medical condition, and pain disorder associated with a general medical condition [which is not considered a mental disorder]) from one another. In addition, the measures have generally been studied in general medical or pain clinics but not in psychiatric settings.

Hypochondriasis

Two instruments described in this chapter have been used to assess hypochondriacal attitudes among patients with or without medical illness. The Whiteley Index of Hypochondriasis has the advantages of ease of administration and scoring and inclusion of subscores for key dimensions of hypochondriasis; it is easily used in primary care settings. The IAS expands on the Whiteley Index by eliciting information such as health habits and treatment experience. Two scales that may be used to assess hypochondriacal attitudes are not described in this section. The Somatosensory Amplification Scale (SAS), developed by Barsky and colleagues (1990), was designed to assess the degree to which a person is unduly disturbed by normal bodily sensations. The scale is not included here because it is still primarily a research instrument and its clinical usefulness is uncertain. The Hypochondriasis subscale of the Minnesota Multiphasic Personality Inventory (MMPI-2) (p. 89) primarily assesses bodily preoccupation and is of limited use in assessing the more cognitively weighted diagnosis of hypochondriasis (i.e., preoccupation with fears of having, or fear that one has, a serious illness); it may also incorrectly identify patients with real multisystemic disease as having hypochondriasis.

Body Dysmorphic Disorder

The BDDE can be used to assist in diagnosing body dysmorphic disorder and is potentially useful in assessing the severity of body dysmorphic disorder. The BDD-YBOCS assesses the severity of body dysmorphic disorder and is more useful than the BDDE in assessing symptom severity in moderately to severely ill patients.

Some of the implementation and interpretation issues discussed earlier are less relevant to body dysmorphic disorder than to the other somatoform disorders. Because the presenting symptoms of body dysmorphic disorder are predominantly cognitive and involve concerns about appearance (e.g., a preoccupation with the belief that one's nose is grotesquely large) rather than physical dysfunction, it is less often an issue to rule out a general medical condition or substance use as a cause of the presenting symptom. However, some individuals may believe that an underlying medical problem is responsible for the putative appearance problem or that the "ugly" body part is also malfunctioning, in which case a thorough medical evaluation is of greater importance.

Factitious Disorders and Malingering

The SIRS is the most comprehensive measure for diagnosing malingering, although it assesses only psychological symptoms. Although studies on the use of the SIRS in patients with factitious disorder have not been published, the measure may also be used to assess that disorder because, like malingering, factitious disorder involves conscious feigning of symptoms. Several other instruments, such as the MMPI-2 (the Infrequency subscale, the Fake Bad scale, and other scales) (p. 89), are also available for assessing malingering.

CURRENT STATUS AND FUTURE RESEARCH NEEDS FOR ASSESSMENT

Although the measures described in this chapter are potentially useful in clinical settings, more work is needed to develop additional measures in this domain. Few diagnostic or other assessment instruments are available for some of the somatoform disorders. Sensitivity to change has not been established for many of the measures in this domain and needs further study so that the measures can be used in treatment studies, an underinvestigated area. In addition, many of the instruments in this domain are not specifically designed to assess somatoform disorders as defined in DSM-IV.

Future research should focus on the development of culturally sensitive instruments and cross-cultural validation of measures. In addition, because patients with these disorders may present differently in general medical settings than they do in psychiatric settings (e.g., those presenting in psychiatric settings often have already had several unsatisfying encounters with health care professionals), research is needed on the validity and utility of these instruments in both these settings.

REFERENCES AND SUGGESTED READINGS

Barsky AJ, Wyshale G, Kresman GL: The somatosensory amplification scale and its relationship to hypochondriasis. J Psychiatr Res 24:323–334, 1990

Berry DTR, Wetter MW, Baer RA: Assessment of malingering, in Clinical Personality Assessment. Edited by Butcher JN. New York, Oxford University Press, 1995, pp 237–248

Chapman CR, Casey KL, Dubner R, et al: Pain measurement: an overview. Pain 22:1–31, 1985

Kellner R: Somatization and Hypochondriasis. New York, Praegar, 1986

Roger R (ed): Clinical Assessment of Malingering and Deception, 2nd Edition. New York, Guilford, 1997

Somatoform Disorders Symptom Checklist, Screener for Somatoform Disorders, and Somatoform Disorders Schedule (SDS)

A. Janca and World Health Organization

GOALS

The Somatoform Disorders Symptom Checklist, the Screener for Somatoform Disorders, and the Somatoform Disorders Schedule (SDS) were developed by the World Health Organization (Janca et al. 1995a, 1995b) to assess ICD-10 somatoform disorders cross-culturally. These instruments include certain culture-specific symptoms and have been field tested cross-culturally; the treatment history section in the SDS includes questions concerning traditional and religious healers and ritual cures. The Somatoform Disorders Symptom Checklist is intended to assist clinicians in diagnosing somatoform disorders, the Screener for Somatoform Disorders screens for the presence of somatoform disorders, and the SDS is a diagnostic instrument for use in epidemiological surveys.

DESCRIPTION

The Somatoform Disorders Symptom Checklist consists of 60 symptom items with yes-no responses and 5 additional items with yes-no responses. No specific interview questions are provided to assist users in the assessment of symptoms. A sample item is provided in Example 26–1.

EXAMPLE 26–1 ■ Sample items from the Somatoform Disorders Symptom Checklist, the Screener for Somatoform Disorders, and the Somatoform Disorders Schedule

Somatoform Disorders Symptom Checklist
  Double vision

Screener for Somatoform Disorders
  Headache

Somatoform Disorders Schedule
  Have you ever had pains in the joints?

Reprinted with permission from the World Health Organization.

The Somatoform Disorders Symptom Checklist lists the criteria for ICD-10 somatization disorder and also includes a scoring guide that provides general guidance on how to derive the following ICD-10 diagnoses: undifferentiated somatoform disorder, conversion disorder, persistent somatoform pain disorder, somatoform autonomic dysfunction, and neurasthenia (the latter two diagnoses are not included in DSM-IV). The Somatoform Disorders Symptom Checklist also includes questions about whether symptoms could be explained by a general medical disorder. Some additional culture-specific symptoms (e.g., loss of semen in India) are also included.

The Screener for Somatoform Disorders is a 12-item checklist with yes-no responses that screens for the presence of the same somatoform disorders as the Somatoform Disorders Symptom Checklist. A sample item is provided in Example 26–1. It can be used as a self-report instrument or administered by an interviewer; positive answers can then be further evaluated using the Somatoform Disorders Symptom Checklist. Positive responses to three or more physical symptoms that have persisted for 3 or more months warrant further evaluation with the Somatoform Disorders Symptom Checklist.

The SDS is a fully structured 114-item diagnostic instrument with a rating scale from 1 to 5, with 5 = positive and psychiatrically relevant; 4 = positive but due to physical illness, injury, or condition, or to alcohol, drug, or medication; 2 = positive but too mild to be considered clinically significant; and 1 = negative. It is based on the Composite International Diagnostic Interview (CIDI) (p. 61) and the Diagnostic Interview Schedule (DIS) (p. 61) and is intended for use by trained lay interviewers in cross-cultural epidemiological research.

A sample item is provided in Example 26–1. The SDS assesses for hypochondriasis and body dysmorphic disorder (included in ICD-10 as a type of hypochondriasis), as well as the somatoform disorders assessed for by the Somatoform Disorders Symptom Checklist. In addition to diagnosing the somatoform disorders, the SDS elicits information concerning symptom severity, treatment received, and comorbidity. A scoring algorithm is used to generate diagnoses with the SDS; both ICD-10 and DSM-IV diagnoses can be derived.

PRACTICAL ISSUES

It generally takes about 45 minutes to administer the SDS. The average administration times for the Somatoform Disorders Symptom Checklist and the Screener for Somatoform Disorders have not been reported, but the measures are briefer than the SDS. The Somatoform Disorders Symptom Checklist can be used by clinicians who are familiar with ICD-10 criteria, and the SDS is intended for administration by experienced CIDI or DIS lay interviewers. The instruments were published in 1994 by the World Health Organization and are copyrighted. The instruments, instructions for administration, and draft versions of training and reference manuals can be obtained at no cost from

> Division of Mental Health
> World Health Organization
> CH-1211
> Geneva 27, Switzerland

Translations are available in Italian, Kannada (India), Portuguese, and Shona (Zimbabwe). A computerized data entry and scoring program for the SDS that generates both ICD-10 and DSM-IV diagnoses is also available from the World Health Organization.

The measures are included on the CD-ROM that accompanies this handbook.

PSYCHOMETRIC PROPERTIES

Reliability

A reliability study of an earlier version of the SDS (N = 120) that assessed only somatization disorder yielded joint reliability of kappa = 0.87 and test-retest reliability of kappa = 0.72 (A. Janca, unpublished manuscript, 1994). Test-retest reliability of the complete SDS was assessed as part of a larger international reliability study conducted in the United States, Brazil, Italy, India, and Zimbabwe in general psychiatry, primary care, and general medical settings (N = 180) (Janca et al. 1995a). Using clinician and nonclinician raters at the first and second interviews, respectively, which were done within a 3-day interval, this study yielded an intraclass correlation coefficient of 0.76 for the total number of ratings of 5; the range of intraclass correlation coefficients across sites was 0.36–0.89. For individual SDS symptom questions, kappa values ranged from 0.16 to 0.78. Kappa values were generally in the fair to good range; one-third of the items had a kappa of 0.6 or higher. As would be expected in a setting in which the prevalence of the disorder appears to be higher, the intraclass correlation coefficients were generally higher for patients seen in primary care and general medical settings than for patients in mental health settings.

CLINICAL UTILITY

The Screener for Somatoform Disorders is potentially useful to clinicians in screening for somatoform disorders, and the Somatoform Disorders Symptom Checklist is potentially useful in diagnosis and differential diagnosis. To our knowledge, the Screener for Somatoform Disorders, the Somatoform Disorders Symptom Checklist, and the SDS are the only stand-alone instruments that assess for several somatoform disorders. The ease of administration and applicability of the Screener for Somatoform Disorders and the Somatoform Disorders Symptom Checklist in a variety of cultures, languages, and health care systems are notable strengths. However, a significant drawback of these instruments at this time is the lack of validity data. In particular, sensitivity and specificity data are needed to establish the validity and usefulness of the Screener for Somatoform Disorders in clinical settings. Another limitation is that clinicians need to derive DSM-IV diagnoses from the measures because the instruments are based on ICD-10 criteria; the SDS, however, provides both DSM-IV and ICD-10 diagnoses. Clinicians should be cautioned that the DSM-IV somatization disorder field trial, which compared the ICD-10 and DSM-IV defini-

tions of somatization disorder, showed a much lower prevalence of ICD-10 somatization disorder than DSM-IV somatization disorder; the difference was most likely due to the ICD-10 requirement for medical utilization. In addition, neither the Somatoform Disorders Symptom Checklist nor the Screener for Somatoform Disorders assesses for hypochondriasis or body dysmorphic disorder; the SDS likely underdiagnoses body dysmorphic disorder because the ICD-10 criteria require medical utilization and also because the question asks about hypochondriasis and body dysmorphic disorder in the same sentence and one or the other could be missed.

REFERENCES AND SUGGESTED READINGS

Janca A, Burke JD Jr, Isaac M, et al: The World Health Organization Somatoform Disorders Schedule: a preliminary report on design and reliability. Eur Psychiatry 10:373–378, 1995a

Janca A, Isaac M, Costa e Silva JA: World Health Organization International Study of Somatoform Disorders: background and rationale. European Journal of Psychiatry 9:100–110, 1995b

McGill Pain Questionnaire (MPQ)

R. Melzack

GOALS

The McGill Pain Questionnaire (MPQ) (Melzack 1975) is designed to assess several qualitative and quantitative aspects of pain, including location, quality, temporal properties, and intensity.

DESCRIPTION

The MPQ is a fully structured instrument. It divides the assessment of pain into several parts:

- Pain *location*, in which the patient marks the location of his or her pain on a figure drawing.
- Pain *quality*, in which the patient selects one word, or none, from each of 20 word lists (subclasses). The 20 word lists that describe pain quality are categorized according to the pain dimensions they describe: *sensory* (lists 1–10; e.g., "cramping"), *affective* (lists 11–15; e.g., "frightful"), *evaluative* (list 16; e.g., "unbearable"), and miscellaneous (lists 17–20; e.g., "numb"). The total number of words included is 78.
- *Temporal* properties of the pain, in which the patient selects words (e.g., "continuous" or "transient") from three categories.
- Present pain *intensity*, which consists of a 5-point scale (mild, discomforting, distressing, horrible, and excruciating).

The instrument also elicits additional descriptive information at the baseline assessment.

A short form of the MPQ (Melzack 1987) contains 15 of the 78 word descriptors from the sensory and affective dimensions. These descriptors are rated on a 4-point intensity scale (from 0 = none to 3 = severe). It also includes the previously noted Present Pain Intensity (PPI) scale and a visual analog scale for pain intensity anchored by "no pain" and "worst possible pain." The information provided in this section pertains to the standard (i.e., long form) version unless otherwise noted.

The scale's developer has indicated that the validity of ratings is increased if an interviewer (e.g., clinician, research assistant, or clinical assistant) administers the scale, reading the instructions, answering questions, and defining words if necessary. In a study (N = 80) that compared MPQ scores from interview administration and MPQ scores from self-administration, significantly higher scores were obtained when the MPQ was administered by an interviewer (Melzack 1975).

Three types of scores are commonly obtained:

- Present Pain Intensity (PPI), a global rating from the 5-point intensity scale (score of 1–5).
- Number of Words Chosen (NWC) from the 20 word lists that assess pain quality (range 0–20).
- Pain Rating Index (PRI), a score determined on the basis of rank values of the words chosen from the 20 word lists (range 0–78). (The words within each word list are ordered in terms of intensity and assigned a rank value; the rank values of the chosen words are then

summed to obtain the PRI.) A total PRI score and a PRI score for each pain dimension (sensory, affective, evaluative, and miscellaneous) are obtained. An alternative scoring method involves calculating the average value of the words chosen within each dimension.

The short form of the MPQ is scored by summing the intensity values for the word descriptors, from which three pain scores are derived (sensory, affective, and total). The PPI and visual analog scale are also scored.

PRACTICAL ISSUES

It initially takes an interviewer 15–20 minutes to administer the MPQ, but, with increasing experience, it can be administered in 5–10 minutes. The short form can be given in 2–5 minutes. The MPQ can be obtained from published articles (Melzack 1975, 1987). Both forms of the scale are copyrighted by Ronald Melzack, who gives permission for their use in clinical settings. Translations are available in Danish, Dutch, Finnish, French (short form), Italian, and Norwegian. The MPQ is included on the CD-ROM that accompanies this handbook.

PSYCHOMETRIC PROPERTIES

Reliability

One study (N = 297) of patients with a wide variety of pain syndromes found fair to high correlations among the scored components of the MPQ; for example, the NWC and PRI total scores had a correlation of 0.89, and correlations between the PPI and the PRI subscales (Sensory, Affective, Evaluative, and Miscellaneous) ranged from 0.18 to 0.49, with a correlation of 0.42 between the PPI and the PRI total score. In another study of cancer patients (N = 36), the NWC was positively correlated with the total PRI score, although the PPI was correlated only with the Affective (r = 0.40) and Evaluative (r = 0.36) subclasses of the PRI. Another study of oral surgery patients (N = 60) found correlations (r) among MPQ components that ranged from 0.26 to 0.78. In two studies (N = 132, 24) of patients with various types of pain, the total scores for word descriptors on the short form were also generally correlated with the visual analog scale (0.60–0.93) and with the PPI (r = 0.32–0.83).

Test-retest reliability was assessed in a study of 18 cancer patients. The scale was administered weekly for 4 weeks, yielding agreement of pain descriptor subclasses from 66% to 80%. In another study ($N = 10$) in which the MPQ was administered three times at intervals of 3–7 days, PPI scores did not vary across administrations, and the percentage of agreement in choice of word descriptor subclasses ranged from 50% to 100%, with a mean of 70.3%.

Validity

Studies of a variety of pain syndromes have assessed correlations between MPQ scores and scores on other pain measures; most yielded fair to high correlations (e.g., 0.29 [nonsignificant] to 0.88; $N = 24$–95). In one study, 32 patients with chronic pain who had high MPQ and PRI Affective scores had higher Depression, Anxiety, and Somatization scores on the Brief Symptom Inventory (BSI) (p. 84) and greater perceived physical and psychosocial disability due to pain as assessed by the Sickness Impact Profile (SIP) (p. 126). MPQ scores were also associated in several studies ($N = 60$–166) with analgesia use and with recovery time after oral surgery.

With regard to the validity of the short version of the scale, in two studies ($N = 132, 24$) of patients with various types of pain, scores on the short form of the MPQ were generally correlated with scores on the standard version for PRI ($r = 0.65$–0.94) and PPI ($r = 0.69$–0.87) scores.

Several studies found that the MPQ appears to discriminate among patient populations with different pain syndromes. For example, one study found that 91% of 53 patients and 90% of 21 patients (validation sample) with trigeminal neuralgia or atypical facial pain were correctly classified according to pain syndrome. Other studies found that 73% of 63 patients with cluster headache and 74% of 325 patients with migraine or mixed headache were correctly classified by three items from the MPQ Sensory subscale and that 77% of 95 patients with eight different pain syndromes (e.g., arthritis, toothache, and labor pain) were correctly classified by MPQ word descriptors, although validation samples were not used in these studies. However, in a study of choice of pain descriptors in 35 patients with cancer pain, the results poorly replicated those from a previous study.

In one study, an attempt to use the MPQ as a weekly summary measure of pain was not successful, suggesting that the MPQ is best used as a measure of immediate pain.

In several treatment and postoperative studies ($N = 24$–70), the MPQ (PRI, PPI, and NWC scores) was sensitive to change, although in one study Affective scores did not change significantly and in another NWC scores did not change. Correlations of change in the different MPQ components were $r = 0.82$–0.96 for PPI and PRI percentage of change scores in one study ($N = 24$) and $r = 0.36$–0.97 in another study ($N = 40$). In a study of 24 patients with various pain syndromes, the MPQ discriminated among groups of patients treated with modalities of differing effectiveness. The short form of the MPQ was also sensitive to change with different types of treatment in a study of 70 patients with various types of pain.

CLINICAL UTILITY

The MPQ has been studied extensively and is applicable to a wide variety of populations with pain. It elicits information on numerous important aspects of pain and is useful in monitoring treatment effects in patients with various pain syndromes, as shown in numerous treatment and postoperative studies. Advantages include its multidimensional nature and the richness and subtlety of the information obtained, which allows the complex experience of pain to be described both qualitatively and quantitatively. The scale weights sensory aspects of pain more heavily than affective and evaluative aspects, which may be an advantage or a disadvantage, depending on the intended use of the scale.

Although numerous studies demonstrate that the MPQ is reliable and correlates well with other established pain measures, readers should be cautioned that joint reliability was established using less stringent statistical tests. When the scale was used to discriminate among different pain syndromes, results were mixed; some studies reported good results, whereas in others some patients were misclassified, validation samples were not used, or results of previous studies were not replicated. The MPQ is generally acceptable to patients, but a potential disadvantage is that it is more time-consuming and complex than many other pain scales, which may make it less suitable for very sick patients. It also requires a relatively sophisticated vocabulary, raising the question of whether educational level might affect its use. Words such as *lancinating* and *rasping* may not be easily understood by all patients and could be problematic when the scale is used with patients with limited education or with certain cultural or subcultural groups. The short form largely avoids these problems, but it has been studied much less extensively than the standard form.

REFERENCES AND SUGGESTED READINGS

Melzack R: The McGill Pain Questionnaire: major properties and scoring methods. Pain 1:277–299, 1975

Melzack R: The short-form McGill Pain Questionnaire. Pain 30:191–197, 1987

Visual Analog Scales

E. C. Huskisson

GOALS

Visual analog scales are designed to provide a global, subjective assessment of dimensions of pain. Although the scales are most often used to measure intensity (severity), they may also be used to assess other pain dimensions, such as distress or pain relief resulting from treatment.

DESCRIPTION

Each of the visual analog scales is a straight line, either horizontal or vertical, the length of which represents the continuum of the pain experience. Typically, the visual analog scales consist of 10-cm horizontal lines, with perpendicular lines at the ends defined as the extreme limits of the pain construct being measured. Anchor points at each end are characterized by a brief, readily understood verbal expression, such as "no pain" or "none" at one end and "the worst possible pain" or "unbearable" at the other end. In some visual analog scales, verbal descriptors are accompanied by a number (e.g., "none" may be accompanied by 0 and "unbearable" by 100). The patient is asked to mark the line corresponding to the intensity of the pain construct being measured. Example 26–2 shows a typical visual analog scale for measuring the intensity of pain. Other measured constructs include pain-related distress (see Example 26–3) and pain relief (with anchors, for example, of no pain relief and complete pain relief).

The graphic rating scale is a version of the visual analog scale with numbers or descriptive terms (e.g., mild, moderate, and severe) placed at intervals along the line.

Visual analog scales are scored by measuring the distance (e.g., in millimeters) from the end of the scale indicating absence of pain (or no distress or no pain relief) to the place marked by the patient.

PRACTICAL ISSUES

It usually takes less than 30 seconds to administer a visual analog scale. Visual analog scales are generally easily understood, even by patients with little education. However, patients must be carefully instructed in how to use the scales, and the particular construct (e.g., intensity of pain or pain-related distress) being measured must be clearly defined. The scale should be completed under supervision before being done alone. It is important to be aware that photocopying may change the length of the line. Versions of the scales can be obtained from several published articles (e.g., Huskisson 1974, 1983; Scott and Huskisson 1976). In one study, a computerized visual analog scale was used to generate and continuously score (every second) pain intensity ratings.

PSYCHOMETRIC PROPERTIES

Reliability

A test-retest reliability study of a visual analog scale for pain intensity found a correlation ($r = 0.78$) between

EXAMPLE 26–2 ■ A visual analog scale for measuring intensity of pain

None	Unbearable
0	100

ratings done four times a day on days 1, 3, and 5 and ratings done on days 2, 4, and 6. In a study ($N = 33$) that compared visual analog interpretations of verbal pain intensity descriptors (e.g., mild) over successive administrations several days apart, visual analog scale scores did not differ significantly.

In two clinical studies ($N = 100$ outpatients with "painful conditions" and $N = 100$ outpatients) and in a nonclinical study ($N = 107$ healthy volunteers ages 18–60 years), scores on vertical and horizontal versions of a visual analog scale for intensity were comparable ($r = 0.91$–0.99 in the two clinical studies); however, in two of the three studies, scores on the horizontal version were slightly (but not significantly) lower. Score distributions with visual analog scales for intensity are generally fairly uniform (and generally more uniform than those with graphic rating scales), although one study ($N = 107$) found a more uniform distribution with a horizontal than with a vertical scale. A study that compared scores on visual analog scales for intensity and distress found a correlation of 0.88.

Validity

Numerous studies of patients with various types of pain generally demonstrated adequate correlation between scores on visual analog scales for intensity and other scales of pain intensity (such as numerical, verbal descriptive, adjectival, and graphic rating scales); correlations ranged from 0.30 to 0.92. Several studies found that visual analog scale intensity ratings generally correlated with ratings from the McGill Pain Questionnaire (MPQ) (p. 598). In one of these studies ($N = 40$), correlations ranged from 0.49 to 0.65 for visual analog scale intensity and distress ratings with the MPQ Present Pain Intensity (p. 598) and adjective descriptors. In another study ($N = 40$), visual analog scale ratings were correlated with sensory, affective, and evaluative scores ($r = 0.42$–0.57). In a third study ($N = 26$), correlations between a visual analog scale for intensity and the MPQ Present

Pain Intensity (p. 598) were $r = 0.29$ (nonsignificant) on day 1 after childbirth and 0.71 on day 2 after childbirth; the visual analog scale for intensity also correlated with 6 of 15 adjective descriptors from the MPQ (p. 598) rated on a 7-point scale. One of these studies ($N = 40$) also found that scores on a visual analog scale for pain intensity were correlated with analgesic use ($r = 0.58$).

In several studies (e.g., a 1-month analgesic treatment study of 74 patients with chronic pain, a 6-day study of 40 patients after cholecystectomy, and a 2-day study of 26 women undergoing episiotomy), visual analog scales for pain intensity were found to be sensitive to change when pain on different days was compared using categories of more, the same, or less (kappa of 0.47). In one of these studies, visual analog scale distress ratings also decreased. In another treatment study ($N = 86$), change scores on a visual analog scale for intensity were correlated with change scores on a verbal descriptive scale ($r = 0.6$), although in several studies a visual analog scale appeared more sensitive to change.

In a treatment study ($N = 92$) that measured pain severity over relatively long intervals (2 weeks to 3 years), patients tended to overestimate pain severity when initial ratings were not available to them; errors increased with increasing duration of treatment. However, such errors were not found in a short-term treatment study in which pain was rated daily.

CLINICAL UTILITY

The visual analog scale is a widely used measure that is easy to administer in clinical practice and is useful for assessing pain intensity (severity), change in pain intensity, and distress due to pain, although distress scales have been less studied than intensity scales.

To rate change in pain intensity, it has been recommended that a visual analog scale designed specifically to measure pain relief be used, although this issue needs

EXAMPLE 26–3 ■ A visual analog scale for measuring pain-related distress

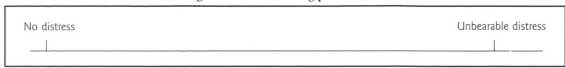

No distress   Unbearable distress

further study. The rationale for preferring a measure of pain relief is that if pain relief is measured by subtracting the pain score after treatment from the initial pain score, a relationship will always be found between pain relief and initial pain score; a small imbalance between initial values in two groups of patients may lead to a significant difference in the measure of pain relief obtained. However, when a pain relief scale is used, all patients start at the same baseline and all have the same amount of potential response.

Because patients have shown a tendency to overestimate ratings of intensity when pain is chronic, if a pain intensity scale is used to assess change over a relatively long interval (e.g., >1 year), patients should be shown their initial rating.

Although horizontal and vertical versions of the visual analog scale appear generally similar, some differences have been found. In addition, the psychometric properties of visual analog scales differ to some extent from those of graphic rating scales. Thus, the same version of the visual analog scale (e.g., horizontal vs. vertical choice of descriptors) should be used for repeated administrations with a given patient or when comparing patient groups.

Advantages of visual analog scales are their brevity, simplicity, and patient acceptability. The scales are usually readily understood with only minimal instruction, and their use is relatively independent of language skills. They can be used in all age groups, including children as young as age 5, although some elderly individuals have difficulty using the scales, perhaps because of a deterioration in abstract ability; a numeric scale or an adjectival-numeric scale is thus recommended for use with elderly patients.

A disadvantage of visual analog scales is their unidimensional nature (i.e., they assess only one aspect of pain), which oversimplifies the complexity of the pain experience. However, several visual analog scales, such as sensory (e.g., intensity) and affective (e.g., distress) scales, can be used concurrently to measure more than one dimension of pain.

REFERENCES AND SUGGESTED READINGS

Huskisson EC: Measurement of pain. Lancet 2:1127–1131, 1974

Huskisson EC: Visual analog scales, in Pain Measurement and Assessment. Edited by Melzack R. New York, Raven, 1983, pp 33–37

Scott J, Huskisson EC: Graphic representation of pain. Pain 2:175–184, 1976

Sriwatanakul K, Kelvie W, Lasagna L: Studies with different types of visual analog scales for measurement of pain. Clin Pharmacol Ther 34:234–239, 1983

West Haven–Yale Multidimensional Pain Inventory (WHYMPI)

R. D. Kerns, D. C. Turk, and T. E. Rudy

GOALS

The West Haven–Yale Multidimensional Pain Inventory (WHYMPI) (Kerns et al. 1985), also known as the Multidimensional Pain Inventory, is designed to assess psychosocial and behavioral aspects of chronic pain. It is theoretically linked to a cognitive-behavioral perspective, and it is intended for use with other measures as part of a comprehensive clinical evaluation of chronic pain. A version of the WHYMPI for patients' significant others assesses their responses to the patients' demonstrations of pain (Kerns and Rosenberg 1995).

The WHYMPI is the basis of an empirically derived classification system for chronic pain, the Multiaxial Assessment of Pain (MAP). This approach, which is based on psychosocial and behavioral data, is intended to complement more traditional taxonomies based on psychophysiological data.

DESCRIPTION

The WHYMPI is a multidimensional self-report instrument that consists of 52 questions, each scored on a 7-point Likert scale (0–6). It has three separate sections that each contain several scales (for a total of 12 scales). The three sections are 1) Pain Experience (five scales that assess perceived pain intensity and the impact of pain on various aspects of patients' lives), 2) Pain-Relevant Significant Other Responses (three scales that assess patients' perceptions of the responses of significant others to their communication of pain), and 3) Daily Activities (four scales that assess performance of common activities, such as household chores). A sample item is provided in Example 26–4.

The version of the WHYMPI for significant others is a self-report scale derived from the second section of the WHYMPI. It consists of 17 items, which are divided into three scales. It is completed by the significant other and assesses responses to the patient's demonstrations of pain. This review pertains to the patient version unless otherwise noted.

Mean scores are obtained for each scale and range from 0 to 6. A scoring algorithm is used to generate section scores and a total score, which can be compared with normative data available from the author. The patient's MAP profile can be derived from scale scores.

PRACTICAL ISSUES

It takes about 10–15 minutes to complete the WHYMPI, which is written at a fifth-grade reading level; the version

EXAMPLE 26–4 ■ Sample item from the West Haven–Yale Multidimensional Pain Inventory

Rate the level of your pain at the present moment (0 = no pain, 6 = very intense pain).

Reprinted with permission from Dr. Robert Kerns.

for significant others is even briefer. The scales, scoring procedure, and norms are available at no cost from

> Dr. Robert Kerns
> Psychology Service, 116B
> VA Connecticut Healthcare System
> 950 Campbell Avenue
> West Haven, CT 06516

A computerized scoring instrument is available for $25.00 from

> Pain Evaluation and Treatment Institute
> University of Pittsburgh School of Medicine
> Baum Boulevard at Craig Street
> Pittsburgh, PA 15213

The patient version of the WHYMPI has been translated into Dutch, Finnish, French, Italian, Portuguese, Spanish, and Swedish.

The WHYMPI is included on the CD-ROM that accompanies this handbook.

PSYCHOMETRIC PROPERTIES

Reliability

Studies of internal consistency (in orthopedic, oncology, and heterogeneous populations with chronic pain; $N = 83–194$) yielded Cronbach's alpha coefficients for scale scores ranging from 0.53 to 0.91. Alpha coefficients for the significant other version ($N = 123$) were 0.75–0.80 for scale scores. Intraclass correlation coefficients among scale scores were shown to be relatively low for both the patient and significant other versions (range of 0.39–0.72), indicating the discriminant distinctiveness of each scale. Test-retest reliability of scale scores in a heterogeneous pain population ($N = 60$) at an interval of 2 weeks ranged from 0.62 to 0.91 for individual scales.

Validity

Studies in various pain populations found that scores from the WHYMPI (including the significant other version) were generally correlated with other pain-related measures. For example, in a study of 287 patients with back pain, correlations for the WHYMPI Pain Severity and Interference subscale scores with the Pain Disability Index, a self-report scale of pain disability, were 0.48 and 0.60, respectively; in a study of 315 patients with various pain syndromes, the correlation of the Interference subscale with the Oswestry Back Pain Disability Questionnaire was 0.66. The WHYMPI was also shown to discriminate ($N = 500$) among patients with different types of pain (low back pain, headache, and temporomandibular pain).

Several studies that used cluster analysis and multivariate classification procedures in various pain populations ($N = 122–500$) suggested that the WHYMPI yields three distinct patient profiles (which are the basis of the MAP pain classification system): Dysfunctional, Interpersonally Distressed, and Adaptive Copers. These studies generally supported the uniqueness and external validity of each profile and demonstrated a high rate of accurate classification by profile.

CLINICAL UTILITY

The WHYMPI enables clinicians to obtain useful information on psychosocial and behavioral aspects of pain (the pain experience, responses of others, and participation in daily activities) in various clinical populations, which may usefully supplement psychophysiological pain-related data. Other strengths of the WHYMPI are its brevity, scope, and ease of administration and the availability of data on its psychometric properties. The version for significant others provides an easy method for obtaining valuable information that might otherwise be overlooked. However, the WHYMPI and MAP classification system require further research, particularly concerning whether the WHYMPI is sensitive to change with treatment and whether WHYMPI scores or a MAP profile predict treatment response. Although the significant other version of the scale appears promising, available data are limited.

REFERENCES AND SUGGESTED READINGS

Kerns RD, Rosenberg R: Pain-relevant responses from significant others: development of a significant-other version of the WHYMPI Scales. Pain 61:245–249, 1995

Kerns RD, Turk DC, Rudy TE: The West Haven-Yale Multidimensional Pain Inventory (WHYMPI). Pain 23:345–356, 1985

Whiteley Index of Hypochondriasis

I. Pilowsky

GOALS

The Whiteley Index of Hypochondriasis (Pilowsky 1967) is designed to screen for the disorder hypochondriasis, to assess the severity of hypochondriacal attitudes (illness fear, disease conviction, and bodily preoccupation), and to measure change in response to treatment. The Whiteley Index broadens the assessment of hypochondriasis beyond a simple report of physical symptoms by including questions that address fear of disease, response to reassurance, and reactions to reports of disease in the media.

DESCRIPTION

The Whiteley Index is a self-administered 14-item questionnaire that is scored categorically (i.e., as yes or no). Sample questions are provided in Example 26–5. On the basis of a factor analysis, three subscales that account for 10 of the 14 items were derived: Bodily Preoccupation (3 items), Disease Phobia (4 items), and Conviction of the Presence of Disease With Nonresponse to Reassurance (3 items).

A 5-point Likert scale version of the Whiteley Index is also available. Because the categorical version is the original scale and has been used most extensively, and because it is unclear whether the Likert scale version offers any advantages, in this review we focus on the categorical version unless otherwise noted.

The 14-item Whiteley Index can be used as a freestanding scale or it can be derived from the larger 62-

EXAMPLE 26–5 ■ **Sample items from the Whiteley Index of Hypochondriasis**

> Are you afraid of illness?
>
> If you feel ill and someone tells you that you are looking better, do you become annoyed?

Reprinted with permission from Issy Pilowsky.

item categorical Illness Behavior Questionnaire (IBQ) (Pilowsky and Spence 1994), which assesses a broader array of abnormal illness behaviors, including such features as psychological versus somatic focusing, affective inhibition, affective disturbance, and denial.

Each yes response is scored as 1, for a maximum possible score of 14. The only exception is the item "Is it easy for you to forget about yourself, and think about all sorts of other things?" for which a no response is given a score of 1. Subscale scores are 0–3 for Bodily Preoccupation, 0–4 for Disease Phobia, and 0–3 for Conviction of the Presence of Disease With Nonresponse to Reassurance. As a screening tool, a score of ≥8 on the Whiteley Index is considered consistent with a diagnosis of probable hypochondriasis.

PRACTICAL ISSUES

It takes approximately 5 minutes for the patient to complete the Whiteley Index. The scale and the third edition of a manual that describes the Whiteley Index and the IBQ, copyrighted in 1994 (Pilowsky and Spence 1994), are available from

> Professor Issy Pilowsky
> University of Adelaide
> Department of Psychiatry (RAH)
> Adelaide, South Australia, 5000

The manual costs $40.00, and 20 questionnaires cost $10.00. A computer-administered version of the IBQ is available from which the Whiteley Index can be derived. The IBQ has been translated into 14 languages, including Chinese, French, German, Italian, Portuguese, and Spanish. The Whiteley Index is included on the CD-ROM that accompanies this handbook.

PSYCHOMETRIC PROPERTIES

Reliability

In a study of three clinical and nonclinical populations ($N = 117–253$), Cronbach's alpha ranged from 0.76 to 0.80. Test-retest reliability was assessed in two studies; correlations of 0.81 in 71 psychiatric patients at an interval of 2–44 weeks (mean 18.4) and 0.90 in 80 general

medical outpatients at a mean interval of 4.2–4.3 weeks were found.

Validity

One study yielded fair correlations between the Whiteley Index and two factor analytically derived subscales of the Illness Attitude Scale (IAS) (p. 607) among 130 general medical outpatients, 113 general practice patients, and 245 subjects from a general practice registry. Linear regression coefficients ranged from 0.21 to 0.30 for the IAS factor Health Anxiety and from 0.31 to 0.36 for the IAS factor Illness Behavior. Another study ($N = 188$) found a correlation (r) of 0.59 between patient scores on the Whiteley Index and scores on a spouse-rated questionnaire concerning the patient's hypochondriasis.

In a study that compared item scores on the Whiteley Index for 100 psychiatric inpatients with hypochondriasis and 100 psychiatric inpatients without hypochondriasis, scores for each item were higher among the hypochondriacal patients. Similarly, a study that compared 100 hypochondriacal psychiatric patients and 47 patients with malignancy found a higher total score on the Whiteley Index among the patients with hypochondriasis. However, in a study that used the longer IBQ in a coronary care unit, there was no significant difference in the IBQ scores of 120 patients with an unequivocal diagnosis of myocardial infarction and 40 patients with chest pain who had no cardiac problem, except on the Conviction of the Presence of Disease With Nonresponse to Reassurance subscale, on which the patients with myocardial infarction scored higher.

A study that compared patients with illness phobia (a subgroup of patients with hypochondriasis who have good insight into the unreasonableness of their fears) with patients with panic disorder ($n = 14$ in each group) revealed significantly higher subscale scores on the Whiteley Index among the patients with illness phobia. However, in an earlier report by the same author, the total Whiteley Index scores for 32 patients with panic disorder more closely approximated the total Whiteley Index scores of the 14 patients with illness phobia and were considerably higher than the scores for the patients with panic disorder in the second study. It therefore remains unclear whether patients with illness phobia have more hypochondriacal attitudes than patients with panic disorder.

In an open-label medication treatment study of 14 patients with hypochondriasis as determined by

DSM-III-R criteria, the total score on the Whiteley Index decreased by 23.5% between baseline and end of treatment. In a study of 60 patients with panic disorder, 8 of the 14 items of the Whiteley Index decreased in a 6-week trial of alprazolam. The mean Whiteley Index score and the three subscale scores also decreased with treatment.

A study of 100 psychiatric patients with hypochondriasis and 100 patients without hypochondriasis demonstrated three factors that correspond to the three subscales of Bodily Preoccupation, Disease Phobia, and Conviction of the Presence of Disease With Nonresponse to Reassurance. However, these factors were not replicated in another study of three large samples ($N = 113–204$) in which only one factor was identified.

CLINICAL UTILITY

The Whiteley Index of Hypochondriasis is valuable in its ability to identify hypochondriacal attitudes, to assess the severity of such attitudes, and to measure change. Because the Whiteley Index has the advantage of brevity as well as ease of administration and scoring, mental health and primary care clinicians could easily include the scale in a patient's initial self-report assessments. A score of ≥ 8 would alert the clinician to probe further to determine whether the patient meets DSM-IV criteria for hypochondriasis. Similarly, the scale is useful in assessing whether hypochondriacal attitudes diminish with treatment.

The main limitation of the scale is that no items ask whether the patient has been given a medical diagnosis. A patient with lupus erythematosus or multiple sclerosis, for example, might score high on many of the items, not because he or she is hypochondriacal but because of legitimate concern about a serious illness with multiple manifestations. In addition, patients with medically unexplained pain, for example, may score high on the Whiteley Index simply because doctors have not been able to identify the cause or find an effective treatment. Thus, the Whiteley Index should not be used as a diagnostic tool because it cannot discriminate between patients who are justifiably worried about a medical illness and patients who are purely hypochondriacal. However, among patients who do not have an unstable or undiagnosed medical illness, it may be used to discriminate

between patients with and without hypochondriacal attitudes.

As with most somatoform assessments, the Whiteley Index should be used only in conjunction with a thorough medical evaluation. Further research is needed to determine the sensitivity and specificity of the Whiteley Index in discriminating among the DSM-IV diagnosis of hypochondriasis, stable and unstable medical illness, somatization disorder, and panic disorder.

REFERENCES AND SUGGESTED READINGS

Pilowsky I: Dimensions of hypochondriasis. Br J Psychiatry 113:89–93, 1967

Pilowsky I, Spence ND: Manual for the Illness Behavior Questionnaire (IBQ), 1994

Speckens AEM, Spinhoven P, Sloekers PPA, et al: A validation study of the Whiteley Index, the Illness Attitude Scale, and the Somatosensory Amplification Scale in general medical and general practice patients. J Psychosom Res 40:95–104, 1996

Illness Attitude Scale (IAS)

R. Kellner

GOALS

The Illness Attitude Scale (IAS) (Kellner et al. 1983–1984) is designed to measure the attitudes, fears, and beliefs associated with hypochondriasis and abnormal illness behavior. The aim was to create a scale that excludes items that occur commonly in other disorders, such as trouble sleeping, feeling depressed, or somatic symptoms. In addition to measuring aspects of hypochondriasis, the IAS is used to screen for the disorder hypochondriasis and to quantify change in response to treatment.

DESCRIPTION

The IAS is a self-report instrument with 29 questions divided into 9 scales: Worry About Illness (questions 1–3), Concern About Pain (questions 4–6), Health Habits (questions 7–9), Hypochondriacal Beliefs (questions 10–12), Thanatophobia (i.e., fear of death) (questions 13–15), Disease Phobia (questions 16–18), Bodily Pre-occupation (questions 19–21), Treatment Experience (questions 23–25), and Effects of Symptoms (questions 27–29). Each scale contains three questions; sample questions are provided in Example 26–6. Each item is rated on a 5-point frequency scale (0 = none to 4 = most of the time), with the exception of the Treatment Experience items, which use a 5-point scale with more specific time markers to indicate how often the person sees a doctor. Two additional questions (questions 15 and 26) request more descriptive information, such as whether the person has a current diagnosis of an illness.

There are three versions of the IAS: 1) the state version (feelings of the past month), 2) the trait version (feelings generally), and 3) the standard version (no time focus). Most published studies have used the standard version. A more recent version of the scale (Kellner et al. 1987), in which several questions were changed and new questions were added, is available.

Scores for the three items in each of the nine scales are summed to provide a score on that particular feature of hypochondriasis. The range for each scale is 0–12. A total score is not calculated. Certain items (15a and 26) are always excluded from scoring. For individuals with a serious physical illness (identified in question 15a), a different scoring method is used for the Disease Phobia scale; in this situation, one of the items (16, 17, or 18) is not scored. When the IAS is used as a screening measure, a score of 3 or 4 on any of the three questions on the Hypochondriacal Beliefs scale or the Disease Phobia

EXAMPLE 26–6 ■ Sample items from the Illness Attitude Scale

Are you worried that you may get a serious illness in the future?

Do you believe that you have a physical disease, but the doctors have not diagnosed it correctly?

Reprinted with permission from Robert Kellner, M.D.

scale is considered highly suggestive of clinical hypochondriasis.

PRACTICAL ISSUES

It takes about 10 minutes to complete the IAS. The scale was originally copyrighted in 1983. The manual for the 1987 edition (Kellner 1987) is available at no charge by writing to

> Department of Psychiatry
> School of Medicine
> University of New Mexico
> 2400 Tucker N.E.
> Albuquerque, NM 87131
> Phone: 505-272-2223

PSYCHOMETRIC PROPERTIES

Psychometric studies on the IAS were done only with the original version, which contained the first eight scales. The ninth scale, Effects of Symptoms, has not been psychometrically evaluated.

Reliability

A factor analytic study ($N = 447$) identified two factors, Health Anxiety and Illness Behavior, in each of three clinical and nonclinical samples. The two subscales were moderately correlated in all three groups ($r = 0.55$–0.62). Alpha coefficients ranged from 0.85 to 0.87 for the Health Anxiety factor and from 0.70 to 0.80 for the Illness Behavior factor. Test-retest reliability of these factors in 80 patients from the general medical clinic over a mean interval of 4 weeks was 0.93 for Health Anxiety and 0.87 for Illness Behavior (Cronbach's alpha). Test-retest reliability for the IAS scales was also assessed in several other populations ($N = 26$ and 20 subjects from nonclinical settings) at intervals of 1 week and 4 weeks. Correlation coefficients (r) ranged from 0.62 for Hypochondriacal Beliefs to 1.0 for Disease Phobia.

Validity

The two factor analytically derived IAS factors (Health Anxiety and Illness Behavior) were shown to correlate with the total score on the Whiteley Index of Hypochondriasis (p. 605) in 130 patients from a general medical clinic ($r = 0.30$ and 0.36), 113 patients from a general practice setting ($r = 0.20$ and 0.33), and 204 patients from a community sample ($r = 0.21$ and 0.31). In a nonclinical sample ($N = 60$) that used the Symptom Checklist–90 (SCL-90) (p. 81), IAS scores for Worry About Illness and Disease Phobia were correlated with scores on the Depression subscale of the SCL-90 ($r = 0.30$ and 0.34), and scores for Worry About Illness, Hypochondriacal Beliefs, and Disease Phobia were correlated with scores on the Anxiety subscale of the SCL-90 ($r = 0.38$, 0.26, and 0.36). However, in another nonclinical sample ($N = 60$), none of these three IAS scales were correlated with the Depression subscale, and only Worry About Illness was correlated with the Anxiety subscale ($r = 0.32$).

In a study in which 21 patients with a DSM-III diagnosis of hypochondriasis were compared with age- and sex-matched subjects from each of three groups (psychiatric patients without psychosis, family practice patients, and nonclinical control subjects; $n = 21$ in each group), the hypochondriacal patients scored higher than each of the other groups on seven of eight scales. In another study, scores on five of the first eight scales were higher among 44 psychiatric outpatients without psychosis than among 50 randomly chosen nonclinical control subjects; however, when the individuals in each group who reported having a medical illness were excluded from the analysis, the psychiatric patients no longer had significantly higher scores than the control subjects on the two IAS scales that are most representative of hypochondriasis (Hypochondriacal Beliefs and Disease Phobia).

Regarding the use of cutoff scores to classify individuals with a diagnosis of hypochondriasis, one study found that a score of 3 or 4 (often or most of the time) on any of the Hypochondriacal Beliefs or Disease Phobia items had a sensitivity of 90% (i.e., the scales correctly identified 19 of 21 individuals with clinical diagnoses of DSM-III hypochondriasis) and a specificity of 86%–100% depending on the comparison group used (incorrectly identified 3 of 21 psychiatric outpatients and 0 of 21 employee control subjects as having hypochondriasis).

In a study of 20 patients with DSM-III nonpsychotic melancholia treated with amitriptyline and 20 age- and sex-matched nonclinical control subjects, mean scores on two scales (Hypochondriacal Beliefs and Disease Phobia) were higher before treatment in the patients with melancholia than in the control subjects, whereas, after

4 weeks of treatment, a difference between the groups was no longer seen. In addition, before treatment, more than one-third of the patients with melancholia screened positive for hypochondriasis compared with 1 of 20 control subjects, whereas, after treatment, one patient in each group screened positive. There was a 40% reduction in mean score on the Hypochondriacal Beliefs subscale and a 63% decrease in mean score on the Disease Phobia subscale in the melancholic group. Although these scales did not significantly differ from baseline scores (presumably because of the small sample size), these findings suggest that the IAS can be used to measure the degree of change in hypochondriasis in melancholic individuals.

In a study in which the IAS was administered before and after open fluoxetine treatment to 100 patients with major depression as determined by DSM-III-R criteria, there was a decrease in scores over 8 weeks on four of six scales.

CLINICAL UTILITY

The IAS provides clinicians with a rapid and potentially useful assessment of hypochondriacal attitudes and behaviors, as well as a means of screening for the disorder hypochondriasis. The Treatment Experience scale provides important historical information about hypochondriacal behaviors that the busy clinician might otherwise fail to detect.

An advantage of this instrument is its ability to assess not only the presence of a symptom but also the degree to which it affects the patient's life. Another advantage is that, unlike some other somatoform disorder questionnaires, which fail to ask if the patient is physically ill, the IAS asks whether the patient has a diagnosis of some illness. A disadvantage of the IAS, however, is the scoring method, which is somewhat difficult if illness is present. Ambiguity about the definition of *serious disease* creates some confusion about how to score the IAS in patients with medical illnesses. Another disadvantage is that scores from the Health Habits scale may be difficult to interpret because an item about bodily checking confounds good health habits with compulsive bodily checking.

Using only the two scales of Hypochondriacal Beliefs and Disease Phobia, clinicians can easily screen for the disorder hypochondriasis. Nonetheless, a positive screen score does not by itself justify the diagnosis. Misleadingly high IAS scale scores may occur in certain clinical situations, such as pregnancy and painful disease. This instrument is therefore best used with patients with either no apparent physical disease or a disease that is stable and typically not associated with extreme disease worry. Because IAS cutoff scores were derived from a study with a small sample size, further research with different and larger samples is needed to adequately assess its sensitivity and specificity as a screening instrument in clinical and nonclinical populations.

Further research is also needed to assess the usefulness of the IAS in measuring change over time, because available studies indicate that the scale has some limitations in this regard. In addition, because there have been no studies of the use of the IAS in a treatment study of hypochondriasis, conclusions about the scale's sensitivity to change within this group cannot be drawn.

REFERENCES AND SUGGESTED READINGS

Kellner R: Somatization and Hypochondriasis. New York, Praeger, 1986

Kellner R: Abridged Manual of the Illness Attitude Scales, 1987 (available from the author)

Kellner R, Abbott P, Pathak D, et al: Hypochondriacal beliefs and attitudes in family practice and psychiatric patients. Int J Psychiatry Med 13:127–139, 1983–1984

Kellner R, Abbott P, Winslow WW, et al: Fears, beliefs, and attitudes in DSM-III hypochondriasis. J Nerv Ment Dis 175:20–25, 1987

Body Dysmorphic Disorder Examination (BDDE)

J. Rosen

GOALS

The Body Dysmorphic Disorder Examination (BDDE) is designed to diagnose body dysmorphic disorder, measure the severity of negative body image, and quantify change in response to treatment (Rosen and Reiter 1996). It addresses cognitive and behavioral features of body dysmorphic disorder. In addition to use in patients with body dysmorphic disorder, it can be used in other clinical populations characterized by distortions of body image, such as patients with eating disorders.

DESCRIPTION

The BDDE is a 34-item semistructured interview that addresses six areas: 1) preoccupation with and negative evaluation of body appearance; 2) self-consciousness, embarrassment, and feeling scrutinized in public; 3) excessive importance given to appearance in self-evaluation; 4) avoidance of social situations or activities in public and avoidance of physical contact with others; 5) body camouflaging; and 6) body checking behavior in the form of self-inspection, repetitive grooming, reassurance seeking, and comparing oneself with others. A sample item is provided in Example 26–7. Answers are rated on a 7-point scale (e.g., 0 = [0 days] no body checking to 6 = [22–28 days] body checking every or almost every day).

The scale is administered by a clinician, who uses a rating summary score sheet; the patient uses a separate form and discusses his or her responses with the interviewer during the assessment. The subject's self-rating is a guide for the interviewer; the interviewer's rating is considered the actual rating.

To qualify for the diagnosis of body dysmorphic disorder, a patient's scores on certain items must meet a preestablished cutoff. For example, to meet criterion A ("preoccupation with an imagined defect in appearance"), the patient must meet the cutoff score on six items that address the following areas: defect not observable or minimal, somatic complaints concern ap-

EXAMPLE 26–7 ■ Sample item from the Body Dysmorphic Disorder Examination

Over the past 4 weeks, have you inspected (e.g., looked at, felt, or measured in some way) your (*defect*) in order to check the extent of the problem?

Reprinted with permission from Dr. James Rosen.

pearance, preoccupation occurred 12 or more days in the past month, moderate worry or embarrassment about appearance in public or social situations, the concern about appearance represents one of the main aspects of self-evaluation, and the evaluation is at least moderately negative.

A total symptom severity score is calculated by adding the ratings for 28 symptom items (all of the items except 1, 2, 3, 22, 33, and 34; total score = 0–168). This score provides an overall severity index. Because patients may receive a high BDDE total score but not have body dysmorphic disorder (e.g., patients with eating disorders), the total score is not used to diagnose body dysmorphic disorder. The total score may be used to assess the severity of negative body image and change over time.

PRACTICAL ISSUES

It usually takes about 15–30 minutes to administer the BDDE. The BDDE, copyrighted in 1994, is available for $3.00 from

James C. Rosen, Ph.D.
Department of Psychology
University of Vermont
Burlington, VT 05405
E-mail: james.rosen@uvm.edu

A Spanish translation is available. The BDDE self report version is included on the CD-ROM that accompanies this handbook.

PSYCHOMETRIC PROPERTIES

Reliability

Cronbach's alphas for the 28 items were 0.81 among 82 subjects with body dysmorphic disorder, 0.88 among 177 clinical subjects without body dysmorphic disorder, 0.93 among 295 students, and 0.91 among 140 randomly selected university staff. Joint reliability (r) among 25 nonclinical subjects was 0.99 (intraclass correlation coefficient). Test-retest reliability (r) over a 2-week interval using the same rater was 0.94 among 29 consecutive students and 0.87 among 24 consecutive clinical subjects.

Over a 1-week interval and using different raters, test-retest reliability was 0.86 (intraclass correlation coefficient) among another 20 consecutive clinical subjects, with agreement on the diagnosis of body dysmorphic disorder of 0.81 (kappa).

Validity

The BDDE was shown to correlate with a variety of other instruments that measure similar constructs. In the study of all of the groups described (n = 82 subjects with body dysmorphic disorder, n = 177 clinical subjects without body dysmorphic disorder, n = 295 students, and n = 140 randomly selected university staff), the BDDE score was associated with negative body image on the Body Shape Questionnaire (BSQ) (p. 654) (r = 0.60 to 0.77), greater psychological symptoms on the Brief Symptom Inventory (BSI) (p. 84) (r = 0.37 to 0.50), and lower self-esteem on the Rosenberg Self-Esteem Scale (–0.33 to –0.50). BDDE scores were less highly correlated with scores on the Multidimensional Body-Self Relations Questionnaire (r = –0.25 to 0.58). Furthermore, those with body dysmorphic disorder reported more severe symptoms on the BDDE than the three other groups. Using a hierarchical logistic regression to test the incremental validity of the BDDE in predicting membership in the clinical (patients with and without body dysmorphic disorder) or nonclinical groups, age and BDDE score led to the greatest improvement in prediction. In contrast, none of the other body image scales or self-esteem measures contributed significantly to classifying subjects. In a study of 184 subjects, agreement on the diagnosis of body dysmorphic disorder was shown using the BDDE and an independently administered body dysmorphic disorder diagnostic module based on the Structured Clinical Interview for DSM Axis I Disorders (SCID-I) (p. 49) (kappa of 0.82).

The BDDE was also tested in patients with bulimia nervosa and was shown to contribute new information above and beyond existing eating disorder questionnaires in discriminating patients with eating disorders from clinical and nonclinical control subjects.

A 50% decrease in BDDE total score was obtained in a treatment study (N = 54) of cognitive-behavioral therapy for body dysmorphic disorder; only a 7% decrease occurred in a wait list control group. Clinically significant improvement was also demonstrated with the BDDE, if clinical improvement is defined as 1) no longer meeting criteria for body dysmorphic disorder on the

BDDE and 2) having a lower score after treatment than before treatment, minus 2 standard errors of measurement. Of the 27 patients who received active treatment in this study, 22 (81.5%) met these criteria, compared with only 2 of 27 (7.4%) wait list control subjects. Improvement on the BDDE was correlated with improvement on other outcome measures, such as the BSQ (p. 654) ($r = 0.69$), the BSI (p. 84) ($r = 0.59$), and the Rosenberg Self-Esteem Scale ($r = -0.52$).

CLINICAL UTILITY

The BDDE provides clinicians with a reliable way to diagnose body dysmorphic disorder and assess multiple aspects of its phenomenology. A significant advantage is its use of multiple questions to assess various aspects of body dysmorphic disorder and related behaviors. For example, six questions are devoted to different aspects of avoidance (public situations, social situations, physical contact, physical activity, looking at self, and allowing others to look at self). By addressing a variety of cognitive and behavioral aspects of body dysmorphic disorder over the preceding 4 weeks, it gives a detailed assessment of typical symptoms that could be targeted in treatment, making this scale particularly useful for cognitive-behavioral therapists.

The scale's main disadvantage is that it is time-consuming and must be administered by a clinician. It is probably too time-consuming to be used as a routine screening instrument. In addition, this scale does not appear able to detect differences among patients with more severe body dysmorphic disorder. For example, the most severe rating option of 6 applies to patients whose symptoms occur every day or almost every day. Most moderately or severely ill patients with body dysmorphic disorder do not have a day without symptoms, so the scale is unlikely to be able to distinguish these patients from those with less severe disorder. Another drawback is that frequency of avoidance has no clear anchors, except for subjective ones such as slight, moderate, and extreme. This scale needs to be tested in patients with body dysmorphic disorder who are more severely ill to assess its utility (in particular, its sensitivity to change) in this group. Finally, because the scale asks for the frequency of symptoms over the past 4 weeks, change over a shorter period is not determined, possibly precluding assessment

of rapidity of response when comparing different treatments.

REFERENCES AND SUGGESTED READINGS

Rosen JC, Reiter JL: Development of the Body Dysmorphic Disorder Examination. Behav Res Ther 34:755–766, 1996

Yale-Brown Obsessive Compulsive Scale Modified for Body Dysmorphic Disorder (BDD-YBOCS)

K. A. Phillips, E. Hollander, S. A. Rasmussen, B. R. Aronowitz, C. DeCaria, and W. K. Goodman

GOALS

The Yale-Brown Obsessive Compulsive Scale Modified for Body Dysmorphic Disorder (BDD-YBOCS) is designed to measure severity of DSM-IV body dysmorphic disorder and change in response to treatment (Phillips et al. 1997).

DESCRIPTION

The BDD-YBOCS, which is based on the Yale-Brown Obsessive Compulsive Scale (Y-BOCS) (p. 572), is a 12-item semistructured instrument designed to assess the severity of body dysmorphic disorder during the past week. It is administered by a clinician or research assistant. Items 1–5 assess obsessional preoccupations: time occupied, interference with functioning due to the preoccupations, subjective distress due to the preoccupations, resistance against the preoccupations, and control over the preoccupations. Items 6–10 assess compulsive behaviors, similarly addressing time spent performing the behaviors, interference due to the behaviors, distress experienced if the behaviors are prevented, attempts to resist the behaviors, and control over the behaviors. Item 11 assesses insight and item 12 assesses avoidance, both of which are experimental items on the Y-BOCS. The BDD-YBOCS also uses a different probe from the Y-BOCS for the insight question to address the conviction and fixity of the belief.

Like the Y-BOCS, the BDD-YBOCS has specific questions or probes and five anchors for each item; descriptions correspond to each anchor. The score for each of the 12 items ranges from 0 (no symptoms) to 4 (extreme symptoms). A sample item is provided in Example 26–8.

The scale is not intended for use as a diagnostic instrument. However, the instructions include a definition of body dysmorphic disorder, questions to ask in helping to make the diagnosis, and a checklist of the more commonly associated behaviors.

The total BDD-YBOCS score is the sum of items 1–12 (range of 0–48). Each item is rated as a composite of all of the patient's appearance-related obsessions and compulsive behaviors independent of their content.

PRACTICAL ISSUES

It takes approximately 10–15 minutes to administer the BDD-YBOCS. The scale and instructions are available at no cost by writing to

> Katharine Phillips, M.D.
> Butler Hospital/Brown University
> 345 Blackstone Boulevard

EXAMPLE 26–8 ■ Sample item from the Yale-Brown Obsessive Compulsive Scale Modified for Body Dysmorphic Disorder

How much of your time is occupied by THOUGHTS about a defect or flaw in your appearance?

0 = none
1 = mild (less than 1 hr/day)
2 = moderate (1–3 hrs/day)
3 = severe (greater than 3 and up to 8 hrs/day)
4 = extreme (greater than 8 hrs/day)

Reprinted with permission from Katharine Phillips, M.D.

> Providence, RI 02906
> Phone: 401-455-6490

The BDD-YBOCS is copyrighted and is included on the CD-ROM that accompanies this handbook.

PSYCHOMETRIC PROPERTIES

Reliability

In a series of 125 patients with body dysmorphic disorder, Cronbach's alpha was 0.80, and Pearsons's correlations between each item and the total score (minus that item) ranged from 0.29 to 0.58. Joint reliability was assessed by audiotaping 15 interviews that were then independently rated by three other experienced clinicians. Joint reliability for the individual items ranged from 0.79 to 1.0. Joint reliability for the total score was 0.99. Test-retest reliability was assessed in 30 subjects by the same rater at an interval of 1 week, and the correlation for the total score was 0.88.

Validity

Total body dysmorphic disorder scores were positively correlated with the Clinical Global Impressions (CGI) Scale (p. 100) ($r = 0.55$, $N = 33$) and negatively correlated with the Global Assessment of Functioning (GAF) Scale (p. 96) ($r = -0.51$, $N = 54$). The BDD-YBOCS was positively correlated with the Beck Depression Inventory (BDI) (p. 519) ($r = 0.47$, $N = 52$), probably because of the high frequency of depression among patients with body dysmorphic disorder. However, the BDD-YBOCS was not correlated with the Brief Psychiatric Rating Scale (BPRS) (p. 490) ($r = 0.19$, $N = 13$), indicating that it is not a measure of general psychopathology.

The total score decreased by 45.6% in a 16-week, open-label trial of fluvoxamine in 30 patients with body dysmorphic disorder; each scale item demonstrated a decrease between study baseline and termination. In addition, a reduction of body dysmorphic disorder scores from baseline was correlated with global response (CGI Scale [p. 100] score) of body dysmorphic disorder symptoms to medication treatment ($r = 0.79$).

Using the CGI Scale (p. 100) as a gold standard, a 30% decrease in the BDD-YBOCS best corresponded to much or very much improved on the CGI Scale. Using the BDD-YBOCS and the 30% threshold, this cutoff score produced one false-negative diagnosis (96% sensitivity) and one false-positive diagnosis (93% specificity).

CLINICAL UTILITY

The BDD-YBOCS is likely to be the main measure used in treatment studies of body dysmorphic disorder. It is also useful for assessing body dysmorphic disorder severity and change with treatment in a clinical setting. It has the advantages of ease of administration and brevity. Because the items do not depend on specific content, the scale is capable of assessing any presentation of body dysmorphic disorder obsessions and/or compulsions. Although compulsions are not part of the DSM-IV definition of body dysmorphic disorder, they are clearly part of the clinical profile and are engaged in by more than 90% of patients with the disorder. Another advantage of the scale is the inclusion of specific anchors for frequency for each day and degree of distress, as well as the ability to assess change in daily body dysmorphic disorder behaviors.

A limitation of the scale is that the items that measure resistance to obsessions and compulsions are a problematic item in the Y-BOCS, and their inclusion in the BDD-YBOCS seems to repeat that problem. Specifically, the correlation of these items with the total score was relatively low (0.29 and 0.33, respectively) as compared with the other items.

REFERENCES AND SUGGESTED READINGS

Phillips KA, Hollander E, Rasmussen SA, et al: A severity rating scale for body dysmorphic disorder: development, reliability, and validity of a modified version of the Yale-Brown Obsessive Compulsive Scale. Psychopharmacol Bull 33:17–22, 1997

Structured Interview of Reported Symptoms (SIRS)

R. Rogers

GOALS

The Structured Interview of Reported Symptoms (SIRS) (Rogers et al. 1992) is designed to assist in diagnosing malingering and other forms of dissimulation (deliberate distortions in self-reported symptoms) in clinical and forensic settings. The SIRS assesses the degree to which an individual deliberately exaggerates or fabricates symptoms associated with a mental disorder. Thus, the SIRS facilitates the detection of malingering and factitious disorder with predominantly psychological signs and symptoms.

DESCRIPTION

The SIRS is a fully structured interview that the clinician administers directly to the patient. It contains 172 items scored on a 3-point scale (some items are scored as no, yes, or yes and unbearable and others as no, qualified yes/sometimes, and definite yes). The SIRS covers a wide range of genuine psychopathology, as well as symptoms that are unlikely to be true. It consists of 13 scales, 8 of which are considered primary scales and 5 of which are supplementary scales used mainly for descriptive purposes. The 8 primary scales consist of common malingering strategies, such as rare, improbable and absurd, or blatant (i.e., obvious indicators of severe psychopathology) symptoms. The 5 supplementary scales consist of constructs such as direct appraisal of honesty.

Scores are interpreted on two levels: 1) a descriptive analysis of scale scores, which illustrates how the patient presents himself or herself (primary and supplementary scales), and 2) classification of patients as honest or feigning (primary scales only). The interview generates scores on all 13 scales; higher scale scores on the 8 primary scales signify feigning. Individuals who have elevated scores on multiple scales are more likely to be feigning. To identify feigning, the developers recommend using the following criteria for primary scales: 1) three or more scores in the probable feigning range or 2) any score in the definite range.

PRACTICAL ISSUES

It usually takes 30–45 minutes to administer the SIRS. The developers of the scale recommend that it be administered by a "mental health professional with formal training in structured interviews" who is "well versed in psychopathology" and interviewing psychiatric patients. The developers also recommend that the administrator practice the SIRS before using it clinically. The SIRS is copyrighted and was published in 1992 by

> Psychological Assessment Resources, Inc.
> P.O. Box 998
> Odessa, FL 33556
> Phone: 800-331-TEST (800-331-8378)

An administration, scoring, and interpretation manual (Rogers et al. 1992) and 25 SIRS interview booklets are available for $185.00.

PSYCHOMETRIC PROPERTIES

Reliability

In three studies (of general psychiatric outpatients, psychiatric inpatients and malingerers from a forensic unit, and correctional and community samples; $N = 217$), internal consistency was demonstrated; alpha coefficients ranged from 0.66 to 0.92 for individual scales, and item-scale correlations ranged from 0.24 to 0.55. In a study of joint reliability in a sample of malingerers and psychiatric inpatients ($N = 27$), a mean correlation of 0.96 was obtained, with a range of 0.89–1.0.

Validity

In a study that compared the SIRS with other measures of malingering ($N = 115$), 78% of the SIRS scales had correlations of 0.6 or greater with the Minnesota Multiphasic Personality Inventory (MMPI-2) (p. 89) Fake Bad indicators; mean correlations of 0.72, 0.67, and 0.65 were found with the M-test scales (another measure of malingering). Validity studies that compared SIRS results in

malingerers or simulators with results from nonmalingering groups (patients, community samples, or student volunteers) in a variety of clinical and forensic settings showed differences on most scales. One study ($N = 116$) found that when simulators were coached to avoid detection by the SIRS, their scores decreased; however, the SIRS still discriminated between coached simulators and psychiatric patients on eight of nine scales. Discriminant function analysis yielded a high rate of accurate classification (88% of a sample of simulators and malingerers vs. nonmalingerers).

A simulation design was used to test the ability of the SIRS to detect malingering in evaluations of competency to stand trial. In this study, 30 simulators were compared with 23 incompetent defendants, 25 competent defendants, 30 offender control subjects, and 7 suspected malingerers. The simulators and suspected malingerers scored significantly higher on all SIRS primary scales.

Regarding the use of cutoff scores to classify individuals as feigners versus nonfeigners, one study found that a total SIRS score of 83 yielded sensitivities of 83% (25 of 30 true-positive diagnoses) for simulators and 71% (5 of 7 true-positive diagnoses) for suspected malingerers and a specificity of 100% for several nonmalingerers ($N = 78$, all of whom were correctly identified as nonmalingerers by the SIRS). Using elevations on three or more SIRS scales as an indicator of definite feigning (as the developers recommend), the same study yielded sensitivities of 97% for simulators and 100% for suspected malingerers, with specificity of 96%–100% for three different groups; the manual, however, indicates a sensitivity of 48.5% (identifying 100 of 206 feigners) and a specificity of 99.5% (with 1 of 197 false-positive diagnoses). Thus, when the recommended cutoff scores are used, the scale tends to underdiagnose malingering but is unlikely to falsely identify an individual as malingering.

CLINICAL UTILITY

In conjunction with other clinical data, the SIRS can be helpful in diagnosing or ruling out malingering or factitious disorder with predominantly psychological symptoms in clinical and forensic settings. It is the most comprehensive measure for this purpose. Psychometric data indicate that it has greater strength in "ruling out" than in "ruling in" these diagnoses. Available studies obtained a specificity near 100% (a very low false-positive rate). However, clinicians must consider the potential negative consequences of even a rare false-positive diagnosis of malingering. The sensitivity has varied between 48.5% and 100% but is generally lower than the specificity, meaning that some individuals with malingering will be missed, depending on the prevalence in the population being tested. The implications of missing the diagnosis vary depending on the clinical or forensic context in which the SIRS is used. The relatively low sensitivity supports the developers' recommendation that the SIRS be used in conjunction with other indicators of malingering to determine the diagnosis. Coaching of simulators can decrease SIRS scores, potentially reducing the likelihood of identifying them with the SIRS; however, in available studies, the SIRS maintained its ability to discriminate coached simulators from psychiatric patients.

A strength of the SIRS is that it has been tested in diverse populations, including psychiatric patients and correctional samples. One study also found it useful in assessing feigning of incompetence to stand trial. However, relatively few subjects with actual malingering have been included in published studies, and more research incorporating malingerers is needed. Further published research is also needed on the choice of cut points. The SIRS can assist in differentiating malingering from factitious disorder in two ways: 1) malingers have been shown to have much higher scores on five scales of the SIRS than those with factitious disorder, so high eleva-

tions on those five scales may be suggestive of malingering rather than factitious disorder, and 2) the SIRS provides sample questions as a starting point for a detailed interview concerning the subject's motivation. However, malingering and factitious disorder must also be differentiated on the basis of information obtained from other sources. The SIRS also does not detect malingering characterized by neuropsychological or other physical symptoms. Another limitation is that the SIRS is somewhat lengthy, although the construct it assesses is admittedly complex.

REFERENCES AND SUGGESTED READINGS

Gothard S, Viglione DJ Jr, Meloy SR, et al: Detection of malingering in competency to stand trial evaluations. Law and Human Behavior 19:493–505, 1995

Rogers R, Gillis JR, Bagby RM: The SIRS as a measure of malingering: a validation study with a correctional sample. Behavioral Sciences and the Law 8:85–92, 1990

Rogers R, Gillis JR, Dickens SE, et al: Structured assessment of malingering: validation of the structured interview of reported symptoms. Psychological Assessment 3:89–96, 1991

Rogers R, Bagby RM, Dickens SE: Structured Interview of Reported Symptoms Professional Manual. Odessa, FL, Psychological Assessment Resources, 1992

CHAPTER 27

Dissociative Disorders Measures

Frank W. Putnam, M.D.
Jennie Noll, Ph.D.
Marlene Steinberg, M.D.

INTRODUCTION

Major Domains

This chapter covers measures for the detection of pathological dissociation and for the diagnosis of the dissociative disorders (dissociative identity disorder, dissociative amnesia, dissociative fugue, depersonalization disorder, and dissociative disorder not otherwise specified). The instruments included in this section are used to screen for pathological dissociation (e.g., the Dissociative Experiences Scale [DES]) and to diagnose dissociative disorders according to DSM criteria (e.g., the Dissociative Disorders Interview Schedule [DDIS]).

Organization

The measures included in this chapter are listed in Table 27–1. Two measures that can be used to screen for pathological dissociation—the Child Dissociative Checklist (CDC) and the DES—are presented first, followed by two diagnostic measures—the DDIS and the Structured Clinical Interview for DSM-IV Dissociative Disorders—Revised (SCID-D-R).

Relevant Measures Included Elsewhere in the Handbook

Measures for posttraumatic stress disorder may also be relevant for the evaluation of patients with possible dissociative disorders, because many patients with dissociative disorders have a history of exposure to traumatic events (e.g., sexual abuse). Posttraumatic stress disorder measures are reviewed in Chapter 25, "Anxiety Disorders Measures."

USING MEASURES IN THIS DOMAIN

The goals of the measures included in this chapter are 1) to screen for pathological dissociation in adults (the DES) and in children (the CDC) and 2) to aid in the diagnosis of dissociative disorders (the DDIS and the SCID-D-R).

As with other psychological interviews, clinicians should not rely solely on assessment measures in the evaluation process. Patients with dissociative disorders, especially dissociative identity disorder, frequently present for psychiatric care with multiple symptoms that are often thought to be manifestations of mood and anxiety disorders, personality disorders, and psychosis. When evaluating patients suspected of having a dissociative disorder, it is important to rule out other conditions, substance use, and malingering or factitious disorders.

Age is another important issue to consider. Some types of dissociative behaviors may be more common in children than in adults. The diagnostic interviews for dissociative disorders (the DDIS and the SCID-D-R) have not been standardized on children, although the SCID-

TABLE 27–1 ■ Dissociative disorders measures

NAME OF MEASURE	DISORDER OR CONSTRUCT ASSESSED	FORMAT	PAGES
Child Dissociative Checklist (CDC)*	Degree and type of dissociative behavior in children ages 5–12	Parent or adult observer report; 20 items	619–621
Dissociative Experiences Scale (DES)* and DES-II Version for adolescents (A-DES)	Type and degree of dissociative experiences; produces a dimensional measure of level of dissociation	Self-report; 28 questions (DES uses visual analog scale; DES-II uses multiple-choice format; DES-T is subset of 8 items from the DES)	621–624
Dissociative Disorders Interview Schedule (DDIS)*	DSM-III-R and DSM-IV dissociative disorders, with additional sections on child abuse, borderline personality disorder, somatization disorder, major depressive disorder, and substance abuse	Fully structured interview; 128 questions	624–626
Structured Clinical Interview for DSM-IV Dissociative Disorders—Revised (SCID-D-R)	DSM-IV dissociative disorders and acute stress disorder; assesses severity of five dissociative symptoms and distinguishes between substance-induced and primary dissociative symptoms	Semistructured interview; 276 questions	626–629

*Measure is included on the CD-ROM that accompanies this handbook.

D-R has been successfully used with older adolescents in some instances.

The scores and subscales of the screening tools (e.g., the DES) dimensional measures reviewed here can help identify patients with high levels of dissociation, but they do not establish a diagnosis. Some patients with high levels of absorption (the tendency to become deeply lost in thought and block out external stimuli) may score high on dimensional dissociation scales (i.e., the DES and the CDC) without meeting DSM-IV criteria for a dissociative disorder. These self-report measures do not have validity scales and may be subject to over- and underreporting; they should therefore be followed up with a clinical evaluation and/or a more comprehensive and diagnostic interview, such as the SCID-D or the DDIS.

GUIDE TO THE SELECTION OF MEASURES

The primary factor in selecting which measure or measures to use is whether the purpose is clinical screening for dissociative symptoms or the formal diagnosis of a dissociative disorder. Many clinicians and researchers adopt the strategy of first using the DES as a screening measure and then using a structured diagnostic interview (e.g., the SCID-D-R or the DDIS) to follow up when subjects score above a certain threshold, often set at a DES score of ≥30. The DDIS is a highly structured interview that includes yes-no response sets to questions, including questions regarding comorbid disorders. Because items on the DDIS consist of checklists of symptoms or rewordings of DSM criteria, the clinician obtains information about the presence or absence of certain experiences or symptoms. The DDIS also includes explicit questions regarding patients' abuse history, which patients may find stressful to answer.

On the other hand, the SCID-D uses open-ended questions and embeds DSM-IV criteria throughout the interview. The SCID-D allows for a systematic assessment of the severity of specific dissociative symptoms, as well as the dissociative disorders, without the use of leading questions. The open-ended nature of the SCID-D questions provides the clinician with elaborate descriptions of the patients' dissociative symptoms, as well as documentation for psychological and forensic evaluations. Although the SCID-D does not include questions regarding traumatic experiences, frequently patients give spontaneous descriptions of preexisting trauma in response to SCID-D items.

CURRENT STATUS AND FUTURE RESEARCH NEEDS FOR ASSESSMENT

Reliable screening and diagnostic instruments for the assessment of dissociative disorders in adults are now available. The SCID-D has also been successfully used to diagnose dissociative disorders in adolescents. The most serious deficit in dissociative disorders measures is the lack of a reliable and valid diagnostic interview for children and younger adolescents. Several such interviews are currently being developed, but none has achieved sufficient psychometric validation to be included in this handbook. The two adult diagnostic interviews included in this handbook, the SCID-D-R and the DDIS, have not yet been tested against each other.

REFERENCES AND SUGGESTED READINGS

Ross C: Dissociative Identity Disorder. New York, Wiley, 1997

Steinberg M: Interviewer's Guide to the Structured Clinical Interview for DSM-IV Dissociative Disorders (SCID-D), Revised. Washington, DC, American Psychiatric Press, 1994

Steinberg M: Structured Clinical Interview for DSM-IV Dissociative Disorders (SCID-D), Revised. Washington, DC, American Psychiatric Press, 1994

Steinberg M: Handbook for the Assessment of Dissociation: A Clinical-Guide. Washington, DC, American Psychiatric Press, 1995

Child Dissociative Checklist (CDC)

F. W. Putnam

GOALS

The Child Dissociative Checklist (CDC) (Putnam et al. 1993) is a parent or adult observer report scale that was developed to assess the degree and types of dissociative behavior exhibited by children ages 5–12 years. Several early versions were circulated. The current version, V 3.0–2/90, incorporates, in order, all of the items from earlier versions plus additional items. The primary goal of the CDC is to screen for pathological dissociation in children. The CDC does not necessarily indicate whether the DSM criteria for a dissociative disorder have been met; instead, it provides a score that reflects the level of dissociative psychopathology.

DESCRIPTION

The CDC contains 20 items. Each item describes a behavior that is clinically associated with pathological dissociation in children. The CDC uses a 3-point (0 = not true, 1 = somewhat or sometimes true, and 2 = very true) response format similar to that of the Child Behavioral Checklist (CBCL) (p. 310) and related parent and teacher report measures. The parent or adult respondent is asked to circle the number that best describes how true each item is for the child now or within the past 12 months. A sample CDC item is provided in Example 27–1. Scores on each item range from 0 to 2. The total score is the sum of the item scores and may range from 0 to 40.

EXAMPLE 27–1 ■ Sample item from the Child Dissociative Checklist

0 1 2 Child goes into a daze or trance-like state at times or often appears "spaced-out."

Teachers may report that he or she "daydreams" frequently in school.

Mean scores for psychiatrically healthy control children in three studies ranged from 1.6 to 2.3. The average score for inpatient children who had been sexually abused was 16.1 (SD = 9.38); the average score for outpatient girls who had been sexually abused was 6 (SD = 6.4). Children in outpatient psychiatric treatment averaged scores of 6.9 (SD = 5.5). Children with diagnoses of dissociative disorder not otherwise specified averaged scores of 16.8–19.8 in three studies, and children with diagnoses of dissociative identity disorder averaged scores of 23.6–24.5 in two studies. On the basis of the results of the three studies mentioned, scores of ≥12 are strongly associated with dissociative psychopathology.

PRACTICAL ISSUES

It typically takes 5–10 minutes to complete the CDC. The CDC is in the public domain. Copies are available from

> Sidran Foundation
> 2328 West Joppa Road, Suite 15
> Lutherville, MD 21093
> Phone: 410-825-8888

One copy of the CDC is available free of charge by request. Additional copies may be duplicated by the user without special permission. The article "Further Validation of the Child Dissociative Checklist" (Putnam and Peterson 1994) serves as a manual and summarizes psychometric information on psychiatrically healthy and clinical samples. This article also contains a reproducible copy of the CDC. A Spanish translation is available, and other translations are in progress. The CDC is included on the CD-ROM that accompanies this handbook.

PSYCHOMETRIC PROPERTIES

Reliability

Internal consistency of the CDC is adequate, as indicated by a mean Cronbach's alpha of 0.79 across nine clinical and nonclinical samples. The mean Guttman split-half reliability in seven samples was 0.80. The mean test-retest reliability over 4-week to 1-year intervals was 0.62. This correlation is in line with test-retest correlations for well-accepted child measures, which generally show more variability over time (as compared with adult measures) as a result of developmental change.

Validity

The CDC items are worded to be understandable to a wide range of individuals (Putnam et al. 1993). Scale items were developed from evaluations of children with dissociative disorder and children who had been maltreated and consultations with experts, and they have good face validity.

The CDC is significantly correlated ($r = 0.33$) with a clinician-completed child dissociative measure for children with diagnoses of dissociative identity disorder or dissociative disorder not otherwise specified (Putnam and Peterson 1994). To date, there are no comparisons of CDC scores with diagnoses derived from structured diagnostic interviews for dissociative disorders. Putnam and Peterson (1994) reported correlations between the CDC and the Clinician Dissociation Scale (CDS), a clinician's counterpart to the CDC ($r = 0.33$), and the Dissociative Disorders of Childhood (DDoC), a dissociative symptom checklist based on DSM-III-R diagnoses ($r = 0.36$). Malinosky-Rummell and Hoier (1991) reported correlations between the CDC and the Child Interview for Subjective Dissociation Experiences (CISDE) ($r = 0.51$) and the Dissociation subscale of the Child Behavior Checklist (CBCL) (p. 310) ($r = 0.63$). These levels of correlation are typical when two observers fill out two different scales that are nominally related by a common construct; in fact, correlations for two observers filling out the same scale on children are rarely higher than about 0.60.

The CDC discriminates psychiatrically healthy children from children who have been maltreated and from children with dissociative disorders as diagnosed by DSM-III-R or DSM-IV criteria. In some but not all studies, the CDC discriminates between children with diagnoses of dissociative disorder not otherwise specified and dissociative identity disorder (Hornstein and Putnam 1992; Putnam and Peterson 1994). Analyses to date have not found gender or ethnic differences. There is a small negative correlation between age and CDC scores (i.e., younger children score higher) in both psychiatrically healthy and clinical samples.

CLINICAL UTILITY

The CDC can be used to screen for pathological dissociation in children ages 5–12 years. It has been used in both routine clinical evaluations and research studies. The CDC can be completed by parents, teachers, therapists, or inpatient nursing staff. Preliminary data indicate that it can be used as an outcome measure for treatment of dissociative symptoms in children.

The CDC is a quick, reliable, and valid screening measure for pathological dissociation in children. However, it does not yield a DSM diagnosis, which must be established through a clinical evaluation. The CDC is less sensitive in diagnosing dissociative behaviors in adolescents.

REFERENCES AND SUGGESTED READINGS

Hornstein N, Putnam F: Clinical phenomenology of child and adolescent dissociative disorders. J Am Acad Child Adolesc Psychiatry 31:1077–1085, 1992

Malinosky-Rummell R, Hoier T: Validating measures of dissociation in sexually abused and nonabused children. Behavioral Assessment 13:341–357, 1991

Putnam F, Peterson G: Further validation of the Child Dissociative Checklist. Dissociation 7:204–211, 1994

Putnam F, Helmers K, Trickett P: Development, reliability, and validity of a child dissociation scale. Child Abuse Negl 17:731–741, 1993

Wherry J, Jolly J, Feldman J, et al: The Child Dissociative Checklist: preliminary findings of a screen instrument. Child Sexual Abuse 3:51–66, 1994

Dissociative Experiences Scale (DES)

E. B. Carlson and F. W. Putnam

GOALS

The Dissociative Experiences Scale (DES) (Bernstein and Putnam 1986) is a self-report scale that assesses the degree and types of dissociative experiences present. There are two authorized versions: the DES and the Dissociative Experiences Scale—II (DES-II) (Carlson and Putnam 1993).

The primary goal of the DES is to allow clinicians to quickly screen for high levels of dissociation. The DES is a self-report measure designed to assess the types and frequency of chronic dissociative symptoms experienced by a patient. Like the Child Dissociative Checklist (CDC) (p. 615), the DES cannot indicate whether the DSM criteria have been met for a dissociative disorder; instead, it provides a score that reflects the level of dissociative psychopathology.

DESCRIPTION

The DES and the DES-II contain the same 28 questions and differ only in response format. Each question describes a dissociative experience and asks how often the subject has had that experience. The DES uses a 100-mm visual analog line. Subjects make a slash on the visual analog line to indicate how often that experience occurs. The DES-II uses an 11-point, multiple-choice response format that ranges from 0% to 100%. The subject circles the percentage of time that most closely fits with his or her experience. Studies have found high correlations ($r = 0.85$–0.96) between the two versions in clinical and nonclinical samples.

An example of an amnesia item in the DES-II is provided in Example 27–2.

Scores on each item range from 0% to 100%. On the DES, each item is scored by measuring in millimeters from the 0% mark to the slash mark made by the patient on the 100-mm visual analog scale. (In practice, item scores are often rounded to the nearest 5 mm). On the

DES-II, the circled percentage is the item's score. The DES score is the sum of all item scores divided by 28 (the number of items). DES scores range from 0 to 100. Scores of ≥30 on the DES are associated with DSM diagnoses of dissociative disorder. Most psychiatrically healthy individuals and general psychiatric patients score <20 on the DES.

The sample size weighted mean score for psychiatrically healthy individuals (11 studies, $n = 1,578$) was 11.05 (van IJzendoorn and Schuengel 1996). Psychiatric samples included patients with anxiety disorders (3 studies, scores of 3.9–10.4), affective disorders (2 studies, scores of 6.0–12.7), eating disorders (4 studies, scores of 12.7–17.8), schizophrenia (4 studies, scores of 10.5–20.6), borderline personality disorder (2 studies, scores of 18.2–20.1), posttraumatic stress disorder (5 studies, scores of 27.0–41.1), dissociative disorder not otherwise specified (3 studies, scores of 29.8–40.8), and dissociative identity disorder (5 studies, scores of 40.7–57.1).

The DES-T, a subscale of the DES, was developed using the principles of taxometric analysis (Waller et al. 1996). The DES-T, which is highly specific for pathological dissociation, consists of DES items 3, 5, 7, 8, 12, 13, 22, and 27. These item scores are summed and divided by 8 (number of DES-T items) to yield the DES-T score. DES-T scores of ≥30 are highly associated with DSM diagnoses of dissociative disorder.

A modified version of the DES, the Adolescent Dissociative Experience Scale (A-DES) (Armstrong et al. 1997) has been shown to reliably measure dissociation in adolescent populations. The A-DES is a 30-item scale that uses a 0–10 response format. Questions cover the same constructs as the DES, but the language and examples have been adapted for adolescents.

PRACTICAL ISSUES

The DES and the DES-II typically take 10–20 minutes to complete. They are in the public domain. Copies are available from

> Sidran Foundation
> 2328 West Joppa Road, Suite 15
> Lutherville, MD 21093
> Phone: 410-825-8888

One copy of each version is available free of charge by request. Additional copies may be duplicated by the user

---

EXAMPLE 27–2 ■ Sample item from the Dissociative Experiences Scale—II

> Some people have the experience of finding themselves in a place and having no idea of how they got there. Circle a number to show what percentage of the time this happens to you.
>
> 0%   10   20   30   40   50   60   70   80   90   100%

---

without special permission. The article "An Update on the Dissociative Experiences Scale" (Carlson and Putnam 1993) serves as a manual and summarizes data on psychiatrically healthy and clinical samples. This article also contains a reproducible copy of the DES-II. A reprint may be obtained from the Sidran Foundation. The A-DES may also be requested from the Sidran Foundation.

The DES has been translated into more than 20 languages, including Dutch, French, German, Hebrew, Indian, Japanese, Korean, Norwegian, Russian, Spanish, and Turkish. Information about the availability of translations can be obtained from the Sidran Foundation.

The DES is included on the CD-ROM that accompanies this handbook.

PSYCHOMETRIC PROPERTIES

Reliability

Internal consistency of the DES was shown to be quite high; in 16 studies, the mean Cronbach's alpha was 0.93 (van IJzendoorn and Schuengel 1996). Mean test-retest correlation in six studies was 0.87 (van IJzendoorn and Schuengel 1996). The individual values for the six studies were 0.84 ($N = 26$, 4–8 weeks), 0.93 ($N = 78$, 2 weeks), 0.93 ($N = 30$, 4 weeks), 0.79 ($N = 46$, 6–8 weeks), 0.90 ($N = 16$, 11 weeks), and 0.78 ($N = 83$, 1 year). Joint reliability of the determination of the subject's score on the analog line scale (i.e., the correlation of two individuals independently measuring the score) was quite high (0.99) (Frischholz et al. 1990).

Validity

More than 25 studies found correlations between the DES and other dissociation scales and structured interviews; a sample size weighted mean correlation of $r = 0.67$ was found across all measures (van IJzendoorn and

Schuengel 1996). For example, correlations between the DES and similar questionnaires were 0.63 for the Perceptual Alternations Scale (Sanders 1986) (seven studies, N = 1,627), 0.54 for the Tellegen Absorption Scale (Tellegen and Atkinson 1974) (six studies, N = 1,421), 0.80 for the Questionnaire of Experiences of Dissociation (Riley 1988) (four studies, N = 1,903), and 0.53 for the Bliss Scale (M. Wogan, unpublished manuscript, 1995) (two studies, N = 355).

Several studies indicated that the DES is relatively uninfluenced by the demographic variables that one would predict to be unrelated to dissociativity. A meta-analysis of 19 studies indicated that the DES is not influenced by gender. There is consistent weak negative correlation (r ~ −0.12) with age (i.e., younger subjects score slightly higher than older subjects), but this finding fits with clinical models of a decline in dissociative symptoms with age. Five studies found no effects of education (which is often a proxy for the effect of socioeconomic status), but one study reported a significant negative correlation with IQ.

Comparisons of DES scores with structured diagnostic interviews for dissociative disorders (the Structured Clinical Interview for DSM Dissociative Disorders [SCID-D] [p. 626] and the Dissociative Disorders Interview Schedule [DDIS] [p. 624]) found good agreement in five studies, especially for the diagnosis of dissociative identity disorder. The average correlation was 0.76 with the SCID-D in two studies and 0.68 with the DDIS in three studies. The DES was used in several studies as a measure of treatment outcome for dissociative identity disorder.

Three studies used receiver operating characteristic analysis to determine the best cutoff score for identifying pathological dissociation. In the largest receiver operating characteristic study to date, a threshold score of ≥30 correctly identified 74% of subjects with dissociative identity disorder and 80% of subjects without dissociative identity disorder (Carlson et al. 1993). Of the subjects without dissociative identity disorder who scored ≥30, 61% had another dissociative disorder or posttraumatic stress disorder.

CLINICAL UTILITY

The DES and the DES-II can be used to screen patients for pathological dissociation associated with a DSM-IV diagnosis of dissociative disorder or posttraumatic stress disorder. They have been used to monitor the effectiveness of treatment in patients with dissociative identity disorder (Ellason and Ross 1997) and are widely used as a research measure of dissociation in psychiatrically healthy and clinical samples.

The DES and the DES-II are quick, reliable, and valid self-report screening measures for the detection of high levels of dissociation. The DES and the DES-II do not generate a DSM diagnosis, which must be established through a structured diagnostic interview or a clinical evaluation. The DES is not validated for adolescents younger than age 16 years, although an adolescent version of the DES, the A-DES, is available for screening adolescents.

REFERENCES AND SUGGESTED READINGS

Armstrong JG, Putnam FW, Carlson EB, et al: Development and validation of a measure of adolescent dissociation: the Adolescent Dissociative Experiences Scale (A-DES). J Nerv Ment Dis 185:491–497, 1997

Bernstein E, Putnam FW: Development, reliability, and validity of a dissociation scale. J Nerv Ment Dis 174:727–735, 1986

Carlson EB, Putnam FW: An update on the Dissociative Experiences Scale. Dissociation 6:16–27, 1993

Carlson EB, Putnam FW, Ross CA, et al: Validity of the Dissociative Experiences Scale in screening for multiple personality disorder: a multicenter study. Am J Psychiatry 150:1030–1036, 1993

Ellason JW, Ross CA: Two year follow-up of inpatients with dissociative identity disorder. Am J Psychiatry 154:832–839, 1997

Frischholz EJ, Braun BG, Sachs RG, et al: The Dissociative Experiences Scale: further replication and validation. Dissociation 3:151–153, 1990

Riley K: Measurement of dissociation. J Nerv Ment Dis 176:449–450, 1988

Sanders S: The Perceptual Alteration Scale: a scale measuring dissociation. Am J Clin Hypn 29:95–102, 1986

Tellegen A, Atkinson G: Openness to absorbing and self-altering experiences ("absorption"): a trait related to hypnotic susceptibility. J Abnorm Psychol 83:268–177, 1974

van IJzendoorn M, Schuengel C: The measurement of dissociation in normal and clinical populations: meta-analytic validation of the Dissociative Experiences Scale (DES). Clinical Psychology Review 16:365–382, 1996

Waller NG, Putnam FW, Carlson EB: Types of dissociation and dissociative types: a taxometric analysis of dissociative experiences. Psychological Methods 1:300–321, 1996

Dissociative Disorders Interview Schedule (DDIS)

C. Ross

GOALS

The Dissociative Disorders Interview Schedule (DDIS) (Ross et al. 1989b) is a fully structured diagnostic interview that was developed for the diagnosis of dissociative disorders according to DSM-III-R and DSM-IV criteria. The DDIS also contains sections with explicit questions regarding child abuse. The content of these questions often causes discomfort for the patient. The DDIS also includes yes-no questions for diagnosis of comorbid conditions such as borderline personality disorder, somatization disorder, and major depressive disorder. It is not useful for diagnosis of DSM-III-R or DSM-IV depersonalization disorder because poor interrater reliability has been found for this disorder. The measure is intended to be used as a clinical diagnostic instrument and as a screening measure to detect pathological dissociation.

DESCRIPTION

The DDIS includes 131 items consisting of 1) checklists of symptoms and psychiatric history including somatic symptoms, Schneiderian symptoms, child abuse, and extrasensory experiences; and 2) questions that reword DSM criteria and require yes-no responses. Several questions contain multiple parts. There are 16 separate sections. The final section, Concluding Items, contains one interviewer-rated item regarding the subject's thought processes. If the patient is assessed as having dissociative

identity disorder, then two additional items are included concerning the role played by the alter personality states in headaches and depressive symptoms. The interview is designed to be administered by a wide range of professional staff including psychiatrists, psychologists, social workers, and nurses.

The 16 sections of the DDIS are scored independently, and there is no total score. The first nine sections are as follows: 1) somatic complaints, 2) substance abuse history, 3) psychiatric history, 4) major depressive disorder, 5) Schneiderian first-rank symptoms, 6) trances, sleepwalking, childhood companions, 7) childhood abuse, 8) features associated with dissociative identity disorder, and 9) supernatural/possession/ESP/cults. Generally the DDIS has one question per DSM criterion item; the questions are essentially reworded versions of the criteria. The DSM disorders are thus scored according to the diagnostic algorithms provided in DSM-IV. A sample item from the DDIS Dissociative Amnesia subscale is provided in Example 27–3.

The remaining sections collect information on borderline personality disorder and the dissociative disorders. One scale covers Schneiderian first-rank symptoms (mean of 6.5 for dissociative identity disorder [$N = 20$], 2.4 for schizophrenia [$N = 20$], 0.7 for panic disorder [$N = 20$], and 1.4 for eating disorders [$N = 20$]). Another scale covers related dissociative symptoms that are not included in DSM but are commonly reported in patients with dissociative disorders. A third scale tabulates

EXAMPLE 27–3 ■ Sample items from the Dissociative Disorders Interview Schedule

Dissociative Amnesia Subscale
Have you ever experienced inability to recall important personal information, particularly of a traumatic or stressful nature, that is too extensive to be explained by ordinary forgetfulness?
Yes = 1
No = 2
Unsure = 3

Features Associated With
Dissociative Identity Disorder Subscale
Have you ever noticed that there are things present where you live, and you don't know where they came from or how they got there? e.g., clothes, jewelry, books, furniture.
Never = 1
Occasionally = 2
Fairly Often = 3
Frequently = 4
Unsure = 5

the number of DSM dissociative disorder criteria for all dissociative disorders that are positive in the patient and serves as a measure of comorbidity. A sample item from the Features Associated With Dissociative Identity Disorder subscale is provided in Example 27–3.

PRACTICAL ISSUES

It usually takes 30–60 minutes to administer the DDIS to patients with dissociative identity disorder. The DSM-IV version of the DDIS is available as a reproducible appendix in Ross (1997). A copy is available by request at no cost from

> Colin A. Ross, M.D.
> 1701 Gateway, Suite 349
> Richardson, TX 75080

Administration and scoring of the DSM-III-R version are described in the original article (Ross et al. 1989b). Administration and scoring of the DSM-IV version are described in the book by Ross (1997). The DDIS has been translated into Dutch, French, Hebrew, Italian, Japanese, Polish, Spanish, and Turkish. Information on the availability of translations can be obtained from Dr. Ross.

The DDIS is included on the CD-ROM that accompanies this handbook.

PSYCHOMETRIC PROPERTIES

Reliability

The interrater reliability (with an interval of 6 months) of the diagnosis of dissociative identity disorder using the DSM-III-R version of the DDIS was kappa = 0.68 in the original study (Ross et al. 1989a, 1989b), which included only nine patients with dissociative identity disorder.

Poor interrater reliability (r = 0.56) was reported for depersonalization disorder using the DDIS (Ross et al. 1989a). Interrater reliability for the comorbid disorders assessed with the DDIS has not been published. It is also unknown how the assessment of comorbid disorders with the DDIS compares with that of reliable tests such as the SCID.

Validity

Agreement between the DDIS and clinicians for the diagnosis of DID was kappa = 0.95 in a sample of 299 general psychiatric patients that included 80 patients with dissociative identity disorder. In another study of a mixed sample of 696 patients including 196 with dissociative identity disorder, the kappa value for clinician and DDIS agreement was 0.96 (Ross 1997). Several studies have compared DDIS diagnoses with the scores on the Dissociative Experiences Scale (DES) (p. 621). DES scores are significantly correlated (r = 0.67–0.78) with pertinent dissociative identity disorder sections on the DDIS. Patients with dissociative identity disorder as diagnosed with the DDIS scored significantly higher (mean of 41.4) on the DES than comparison groups of patients with schizophrenia, eating disorders, and panic disorder. DDIS section scores discriminated patients with dissociative identity disorder from comparison groups in several studies (Ross 1997; Ross et al. 1989a). A discriminant function analysis using DDIS scores correctly assigned 94.1% of 166 patients with dissociative identity disorder to the dissociative identity disorder diagnostic category established by clinical evaluation (Ross et al. 1992).

CLINICAL UTILITY

The DDIS can be used to screen for and diagnose dissociative disorders according to DSM criteria. It is also used as a research measure. The DDIS allows the interviewer to evaluate major depression, somatization disorder, borderline personality disorder, the dissociative disorders, and various associated features. It can be administered by professional staff and, because it is fully structured, does not depend as much on clinical judgment. The fully structured approach (in contrast to the semistructured approach utilized in the Structured Clinical Interview for DSM-IV Dissociative Disorders—Revised [SCID-D-R] [p. 626]) lacks utility in the evaluation of previously undetected, complex, and/or atypical cases.

REFERENCES AND SUGGESTED READINGS

Ross C: Dissociative Identity Disorder: Diagnosis, Clinical Features, and Treatment of Multiple Personality. New York, Wiley, 1997

Ross C, Heber S, Norton C, et al: Differences between multiple personality disorder and other diagnostic groups on structured interview. J Nerv Ment Dis 177:487–491, 1989a

Ross C, Heber S, Norton G, et al: The Dissociative Disorders Interview Schedule: a structured interview. Dissociation 2:169–189, 1989b

Ross C, Anderson G, Graser G, et al: Differentiating multiple personality disorder and dissociative disorder not otherwise specified. Dissociation 5:88–91, 1992

Structured Clinical Interview for DSM-IV Dissociative Disorders—Revised (SCID-D-R)

M. Steinberg

GOALS

The Structured Clinical Interview for DSM-IV Dissociative Disorders—Revised (SCID-D-R) is a semistructured clinician-administered interview that assesses the presence and severity of five core dissociative symptoms (amnesia, depersonalization, derealization, identity confusion, and identity alteration), thereby making DSM-IV diagnoses of the five dissociative disorders (dissociative amnesia, dissociative fugue, depersonalization disorder, dissociative identity disorder, and dissociative disorder not otherwise specified) and of acute stress disorder (Steinberg 1994b).

DESCRIPTION

The interview includes 276 questions that explore the presence and severity of five dissociative symptoms, enabling clinicians to reach a diagnosis of dissociative disorder. The SCID-D-R utilizes a semistructured interview format modeled on the Structured Clinical Interview for DSM-III-R Disorders (SCID) (Spitzer et al. 1992) and open-ended questions with DSM criteria embedded throughout the interview. Individualized follow-up items are provided for exploring endorsed symptoms. This format elicits informative descriptions of dissociative experiences rather than mere yes or no responses. In addition to providing information about dissociative symptoms, individuals frequently provide spontaneous histories of traumatic experiences. This feature of the SCID-D-R allows clinicians to document that they have obtained historical information regarding trauma without the use of leading or intrusive questions. A sample item from the Depersonalization Disorder section is provided in Example 27–4.

The format of the SCID-D-R is particularly relevant to the evaluation of individuals who abuse drugs or alcohol because it enables the interviewer to evaluate whether each reported dissociative symptom occurs only in connection with substance use (i.e., is chemically induced) or whether it occurs independent of use. If a subject endorses symptoms only in the context of drug or alcohol use, a dissociative disorder is excluded.

The complete guidelines for the administration, scoring, and interpretation of the SCID-D-R are described in *The Interviewer's Guide to the Structured Clinical Interview for DSM-IV Dissociative Disorders—Revised* (Steinberg 1994a). SCID-D-R diagnosis relies on a systematic process of 1) screening the individual symptom for the presence of key distinguishing features of the dissociative disorders, 2) rating the individual symptom for severity, and 3) comparing the overall pattern of symptoms with the pattern of symptoms enumerated in the DSM criteria for the various dissociative disorders. If the individual's symptoms meet DSM criteria for a dissociative disorder, the diagnosis is made.

In addition to determining the presence or absence of a dissociative disorder, the SCID-D-R provides an assessment of dissociative symptom severity. Severity rating definitions were developed to operationalize the assessment of these symptoms. The severity of each of the five dissociative symptoms is rated on a 4-point scale, with 1 = absent, 2 = mild, 3 = moderate, and 4 = severe. After rating each symptom, the interviewer calculates the cumulative score, which ranges from a lower limit of 5 (or 1×5) for completely asymptomatic patients to an upper limit of 20 (or 4×5) for patients experiencing the severest levels of all five symptoms.

EXAMPLE 27–4 ■ Sample item from the Structured Clinical Interview for DSM-IV Dissociative Disorders—Revised

---

38. Have you ever felt that you were watching yourself from a point outside of your body, as if you were seeing yourself from a distance (or watching a movie of yourself)?

IF YES: What is that experience like?

  DESCRIBE:

39. How often have you had that experience?

(Rate most frequent period.)

Depersonalization   ? No Yes Inconsistent Information

"An alteration in the perception or experience of the self so that one feels detached from, and as if one is an outside observer of, one's mental processes or body (e.g., feeling like one is in a dream)" (DSM-IV, p. 766)

"Patients feel that their point of conscious 'I-ness' is outside their bodies, commonly a few feet overhead, from where they actually observe themselves as if they were a totally other person" (Nemiah 1989, p. 1042)

Frequency of depersonalization

☐ unclear
☐ rarely (total of 4 isolated episodes)
☐ occasionally (up to 4 episodes per year)
☐ frequently (5 or more per year)
☑ monthly episodes (up to 3 per month)
  ☐ daily or weekly episodes (4 or more per month)

Reprinted with permission from American Psychiatric Press, Inc.

PRACTICAL ISSUES

SCID-D-R administration time is less than 30 minutes for subjects without psychiatric disorders, 45–90 minutes for subjects with nondissociative psychiatric disorders, 60–120 minutes for subjects with dissociative disorders, and up to 3 hours for subjects with complicated histories and severe dissociative symptomatology.

The SCID-D-R and the *Interviewer's Guide* (Steinberg 1994a) are available from the publisher:

American Psychiatric Publishing Group
1400 K Street, N.W.
Washington, DC 20005
Phone: 800-368-5777
Internet: www.appi.org

The SCID-D-R is available in packets of five interviews.

Guidelines for the administration, scoring, and interpretation of the SCID-D-R are described in the *Interviewer's Guide*. Recent research indicates that the SCID-D-R can be administered to adolescents (as young as age 11 years) as well as adults. Virtually identical SCID-D-R symptom profiles have been found in adolescents and adults with dissociative identity disorder (Steinberg 1995).

The SCID-D-R should be administered by trained mental health professionals experienced in conducting clinical diagnostic interviews. Training of SCID-D-R interviewers should include review of the SCID-D-R and the *Interviewer's Guide*, which includes severity rating definitions of each of the five dissociative symptoms and case examples of sample SCID-D-R interviews. Two introductory training audiotapes titled *A Clinician's Guide to Diagnosing Dissociative Symptoms and Disorders: The SCID-D* (Steinberg 1996a) and *Tips and Techniques for Assessing and Planning Treatment With Dissociative Disorder Patients: A Practical Guide to the SCID-D* (Steinberg 1996b) are available from Multi-Health Systems, Inc. (800-456-3003; www.mhs.com).

The SCID-D-R has been translated into more than 10 languages, including Dutch, German, Italian, Japanese, Norwegian, Russian, and Spanish.

PSYCHOMETRIC PROPERTIES

Reliability

Good to excellent interrater and test-retest reliability of the SCID-D for the assessment of dissociative symptom severity and the dissociative disorders has been reported in a variety of populations. The SCID-D field trials conducted by Steinberg, Rounsaville, and Cicchetti utilized a test-retest reliability design, blinded assessment, and a sample consisting of 141 psychiatric patients to examine both the interexaminer and the temporal reliability of the SCID-D over three periods (at baseline, 2 weeks, and 6 months). The range of weighted kappa values for both the presence and extent of symptomatology was very good to excellent for each period (0.77–0.86). Similarly, interexaminer agreement levels for the type of dissociative disorder also ranged between very good (0.72) and excellent (0.86). Test-retest reliability analyses indicated very good reliability for the total overall assessment of the presence of a dissociative disorder (kappa of 0.88). These results have been replicated by researchers in the United States and elsewhere.

Validity

Numerous investigators have reported that the SCID-D is effective in distinguishing between patients with clinically diagnosed dissociative disorders and other psychiatric disorders and in detecting previously undiagnosed dissociative disorders that were later confirmed over time by repeat SCID-D interview and by treating clinicians (Goff et al. 1992; Steinberg et al. 1990, 1994). SCID-D severity scores were also found to discriminate between patients with and without dissociative disorders. Researchers found that subjects with SCID-D diagnoses of dissociative disorder had significantly higher dissociative symptom severity scores and total SCID-D scores ($P \leq 0.0001$) than subjects with other psychiatric disorders. In addition, the range, severity, and nature of the five dissociative symptom areas evaluated by the SCID-D can assist clinicians in distinguishing between individuals with dissociative disorders and individuals with other psychiatric disorders (including anxiety disorder, personality disorders, substance abuse, eating disorders, and psychotic disorders). Investigators have also noted that the SCID-D is able to distinguish between patients with seizures and those with pseudoseizures (on the basis of clinician diagnosis and electroencephalogram results) (Bowman and Markand 1996).

CLINICAL UTILITY

The SCID-D-R is reliable and cost-effective in terms of its demonstrated ability to detect previously undiagnosed dissociative disorder and to confirm clinically diagnosed dissociative disorder. In addition to determining the presence of a dissociative disorder diagnosis on the basis of standardized criteria, the assessment of dissociative symptom severity has been shown to discriminate between clinically important subgroups of patients and therefore is useful for guiding treatment. Steinberg and Hall (1997) reviewed the utility of the SCID-D-R in the development of appropriate treatment plans for patients with dissociative disorder.

Among the available instruments, the SCID-D-R is unique in that it enables clinicians to distinguish between dissociative symptoms occurring with and without use of drugs or alcohol. The SCID-D-R is widely used by clinicians and researchers and provides detailed documentation of symptoms for psychological and forensic evaluations. The format of the SCID-D-R (as opposed to yes-no response sets) is particularly relevant to the evaluation of malingering because it requires subjects to provide elaborate informative descriptions in support of all endorsed dissociative experiences. Because symptoms of dissociative identity disorder are difficult to feign for extended periods, the content, consistency, and complexity of responses to SCID-D-R items, when evaluated in the context of a comprehensive psychological assessment, can assist clinicians in the evaluation of malingering.

REFERENCES AND SUGGESTED READINGS

Bowman ES, Markand O: Psychodynamic and psychiatric diagnoses of pseudoseizure subjects. Am J Psychiatry 153:57–63, 1996

Goff DC, Olin JA, Jenike MA, et al: Dissociative symptoms in patients with obsessive-compulsive disorder. J Nerv Ment Dis 180:332–337, 1992

Spitzer RL, Williams JB, Gibbon M, et al: The Structured Clinical Interview for DSM-III-R (SCID), I: history, rationale, and description. Arch Gen Psychiatry 49:624–629, 1992

Steinberg M: The Interviewer's Guide to the Structured Clinical Interview for DSM-IV Dissociative Disorders—Revised, 2nd Edition. Washington, DC, American Psychiatric Press, 1994a

Steinberg M: The Structured Clinical Interview for DSM-IV Dissociative Disorders—Revised (SCID-D), 2nd Edition. Washington, DC, American Psychiatric Press, 1994b

Steinberg M: Handbook of the Assessment of Dissociation: A Clinical Guide, 2nd Edition. Washington, DC, American Psychiatric Press, 1995

Steinberg M: A Clinician's Guide to Diagnosing Dissociative Symptoms and Disorders: The SCID-D (cassette recording and audiotape manual). Toronto, Ontario, Multi-Health Systems, 1996a

Steinberg M: Tips and Techniques for Assessing and Planning Treatment With Dissociative Disorder Patients: A Practical Guide to the SCID-D. Toronto, Ontario, Multi-Health Systems, 1996b

Steinberg M, Hall P: The SCID-D diagnostic interview and treatment planning in dissociative disorders. Bull Menninger Clin 61:108–120, 1997

Steinberg M, Rounsaville B, Cicchetti D: The Structured Clinical Interview for DSM-III-R Dissociative Disorders: preliminary report on a new diagnostic instrument. Am J Psychiatry 147:76–82, 1990

Steinberg M, Rounsaville B, Buchanan J, et al: Distinguishing between multiple personality disorder (dissociative identity disorder) and schizophrenia using the Structured Clinical Interview for DSM-IV Dissociative Disorders. J Nerv Ment Dis 182:495–502, 1994

(

Sexual Disorders Measures

Leonard R. Derogatis, Ph.D.
Peter J. Fagan, Ph.D.
Julia G. Strand, Ph.D.

INTRODUCTION

Major Domains

Although numerous aspects of human sexual functioning have been subjected to measurement, the areas of primary relevance addressed in this chapter involve the DSM-IV sexual dysfunctions. Thus, the emphasis here is on brief screening instruments that are suitable for use in office practice. In particular, measures included in this chapter assess current sexual functioning and satisfaction both from the perspective of the individual and in the context of evaluating relational functioning.

None of the instruments reviewed here is explicitly designed to assess the paraphilias. This area is excluded largely because most individuals are extremely reluctant to report paraphilic fantasies or behavior, except in the context of very secure and trusting therapeutic relationships. The highly covert and guarded nature of these conditions has seriously complicated the development of valid, effective instruments designed to assess them, because genuine cooperation of the respondent is often compromised.

This chapter also does not include any measures of gender identity disorder. Although several instruments are currently available to assess an individual's historical cross-gender behaviors and current gender dysphoria (Blanchard and Freund 1983), these measures are primarily useful in research settings and do not assist in the current diagnosis of gender identity disorder.

Organization

The measures included in this chapter are listed in Table 28–1. Inventories of sexual functioning are presented first, followed by measures that focus on the quality of a heterosexual couple's sexual functioning within the relationship.

USING MEASURES IN THIS DOMAIN

Few (if any) instruments designed to measure human sexual functioning result in explicit DSM-IV diagnostic assignments. To a large extent, this limitation simply reflects the nature of measurement in this area, which tends to evaluate different aspects of sexual functioning by comparisons of scores with relevant norms. The diagnosis of a DSM-IV disorder usually requires a more complex interview format that considers historical and temporal relationships in more detail to determine the clinical significance of the dysfunction.

The repertoire of sexual behaviors of men and women, though parallel, are nonetheless distinct. The patterns of normal sexual behavior, as well as sexual dysfunction and disorder, are sufficiently distinctive across gender to require differential evaluations of men and women. These distinctions are reflected in the assessment instruments in this area, which provide distinct versions for men and women or parallel subsections for male and

TABLE 28–1 ■ Sexual disorder measures

NAME OF MEASURE	DISORDER OR CONSTRUCT ASSESSED	FORMAT	PAGES
Brief Sexual Function Inventory (BSFI)*	Current sexual functioning in men: sex drive, erectile capacity, ejaculatory function, and satisfaction with sexual performance	Self-report; 11 items	634–635
Brief Index of Sexual Functioning for Women (BISF-W)	Current levels of female sexual functioning and satisfaction: sexual desire, quality of orgasm, sexual satisfaction, sexual anxiety, body image, and partner satisfaction	Self-report; 22 items	635–637
Sexual Arousability Inventory (SAI) (for women)* Sexual Arousability Inventory— Expanded (SAI-E) (for men)	Female and male sexual arousability	Self-report; 28 items	637–638
Derogatis Sexual Functioning Inventory (DSFI)	Quality of an individual's current sexual functioning in a multidimensional format; includes 10 scales: Information, Experiences, Drive, Attitudes, Psychological Symptoms, Affects, Gender Role Definition, Fantasy, Body Image, and Sexual Satisfaction	Self-report; 254 items	639–641
Derogatis Interview for Sexual Functioning (DISF) Self-report version (DISF-SR)	Current sexual functioning at multiple levels of interpretation; keyed to gender	Semistructured interview (DISF) or self-report (DISF-SR); 26 items	641–643
Golombok Rust Inventory of Sexual Satisfaction (GRISS)	Quality of a heterosexual relationship and of each partner's sexual function within that relationship	Self-report; 28 items	643–644
Sexual Interaction Inventory (SII)	Heterosexual couple's sexual functioning and satisfaction with respect to 17 heterosexual behaviors	Self-report; 102 items (6 questions each for the 17 behaviors)	644–646

*Measure is included on the CD-ROM that accompanies this handbook.

female respondents. Some measures are also completely gender specific (e.g., the Brief Sexual Function Inventory [BSFI] for men). Gender represents a major phenomenological distinction in sexual functioning, one that is clearly reflected in the inventories and interviews designed to evaluate sexual behavior.

Several of the instruments reviewed in this section (e.g., the Golombok Rust Inventory of Sexual Satisfaction [GRISS]) are specifically designed to elicit both partners' responses, which may be subsequently charted on comparable normative profiles. Other instruments (e.g., the Derogatis Interview for Sexual Functioning [DISF]) have distinct male and female versions, with separate gender-keyed norms. When evaluating sexual dysfunction in couples, it is always preferable to administer a test to both partners, because of the substantial prevalence of dual sexual dysfunctions among heterosexual couples.

Goals of Assessment

The principal goal of assessment within the domain of sexual dysfunctions is to quantify critical aspects of sexual behavior to determine whether the respondent currently has the capacity to perform normal sexual relations. The quality and quantity of central features of the sexual response cycle (e.g., drive, erection, lubrication, and orgasm) are assessed to facilitate judgments concerning the functional status of the individual under evaluation. The most fundamental goal of assessment in this domain is to generate a single quantitative score that characterizes the individual as either "functional" or "dysfunctional" with a high degree of confidence. Some measures go beyond this fundamental goal to profile functional areas of relative strength and weakness, and several attempt to provide functional comparison profiles of both members of a heterosexual couple. Additional goals involve the implementation of these instruments as adjuncts to the differential diagnostic process and as outcomes criteria for the evaluation of treatment efficacy.

Issues in Interpreting Psychometric Data

A major problem in assessing sexual dysfunctions is the absence of gold standards. Most of the instruments reviewed here currently have, or are in the process of developing, adequate interpretive norms. The central problem remains, however, that these actuarial tables have as yet not been closely articulated to tangible pathophysiological benchmarks. Much of the problem, particularly in the area of female sexual dysfunctions, arises from the lack of empirically determined standards for what constitutes "normal" sexual functioning (see Derogatis and Conklin-Powers 1998). Systematic efforts, through consensus conferences and other mechanisms, are currently under way to address this important issue and hopefully strengthen definitional and diagnostic rigor.

GUIDE TO THE SELECTION OF MEASURES

As mentioned, some of the instruments included here assess explicit, direct aspects of sexual functioning (e.g., arousal and orgasmic functioning), and others evaluate important related aspects that are further removed from core sexual behavior (e.g., sexual attitudes and body image). As a rule of thumb, in situations in which the focus is on the diagnosis or treatment of sexual dysfunctions, instruments that measure the fundamental aspects of sexual behavior tend to have the most clinical utility. In such clinical contexts, these more specific measures are clearly necessary and usually sufficient to address and answer the questions being asked. When quality of sexual functioning in a more general sense is being evaluated, aspects of functioning that are further removed from core

sexual behavior tend to have increased utility. Although often not feasible, an optimal assessment would include both of these aspects of functioning.

Consequently, the measures in this chapter move from brief, unidimensional scales that find their major use as screening instruments to longer, multidimensional measures that assess sexual functioning as a broader concept and cover a wider range of behaviors. Scales such as the BSFI and the Brief Index of Sexual Functioning for Women (BISF-W) are brief screening measures of current sexual functioning. The Sexual Arousability Inventory (SAI) and its expanded version (SAI-E) are unidimensional measures that function as screening devices.

The Derogatis Sexual Functioning Inventory (DSFI) is an omnibus, multidimensional measure of sexual functioning that defines and assesses the principal components of sexual behavior. The DISF and its self-report version (DISF-SR) provide the opportunity for measurement via both self-report and clinician rating and evaluate sexual functioning at multiple levels of interpretation. The GRISS profiles sexual functioning for both members of a couple, thereby helping to facilitate treatment planning. Both members of a couple may also complete the Sexual Interaction Inventory (SII), which assesses sexual interaction across multiple sexual behaviors.

CURRENT STATUS AND FUTURE RESEARCH NEEDS FOR ASSESSMENT

In 1979 a panel completing a compendium of psychological measures of human sexual functioning observed that more than 90% of the instruments under review had been developed after 1970 (Schiavi et al. 1979). The delayed development of this area of measurement relative to other areas of psychological assessment was in large measure a function of the social prohibitions of the time. Sexual behavior was a forbidden topic, even in clinics and consulting rooms. Since that time there has been a dramatic shift in society's attitudes about sexuality toward much more openness. Furthermore, the emergence of innovative and effective pharmacological treatments for sexual disorders and a growing social commitment to the public health aspects of sexual behaviors have led to the development of a substantial number of useful measures designed to assess human sexual behavior. As the pace and volume of research in these areas increase even more dramatically, the demand for valid and reliable outcome measures for related clinical trials grows apace. These forces, in conjunction with serious efforts at delineating a nosology of sexual disorders that is more strongly based on empirical data about normal sexual functioning, will result in substantial improvements in measurement in this area in the very near future.

REFERENCES AND SUGGESTED READINGS

Blanchard R, Freund K: Measuring masculine gender identity in females. J Consult Clin Psychol 51:205–214, 1983

Derogatis LR, Conklin-Powers B: Psychological assessment measures of female sexual functioning in clinical trials. Int J Impot Res 10(suppl 2):S111–S116, 1998

Schiavi RC, Derogatis LR, Kuriansky J, et al: The assessment of sexual function and marital interactions. J Sex Marital Ther 5:169–224, 1979

Brief Sexual Function Inventory (BSFI)

P. O'Leary, F. J. Fowler, W. R. Lenderking, B. Barber, P. Sagnier, H. A. Guess, and M. J. Barry

GOALS

The principal objective of the Brief Sexual Function Inventory (BSFI) (O'Leary et al. 1995) is to provide a brief self-report measure of current sexual functioning in men. The instrument covers sex drive, erectile capacity, ejaculatory function, and satisfaction with sexual performance. It was designed specifically in the context of urological treatments, particularly for patients with prostate cancer. However, the instrument is more broadly applicable across categories of biogenic and psychogenic male sexual dysfunctions. It was designed to be used as both an evaluative measure in clinical practice and an outcomes measure in clinical research trials.

DESCRIPTION

The BSFI is a very brief self-report inventory. It consists of 11 items, scored on a 5-point (0–4) Likert scale. The BSFI assigns quantitative scores to various aspects of male sexual functioning, treated conceptually as four functional domains: Sexual Drive, Erectile Function, Ejaculation, and Sexual Satisfaction. The format of the BSFI is similar to that of the American Urological Association Symptom Index for Benign Prostatic Hyperplasia (Barry et al. 1992). A sample item is provided in Example 28–1.

Scores for the four principal domains assessed are determined by simply summing the items for each scale. There is no overall, global score for the instrument, although the Sexual Drive, Erectile Function, and Ejaculation scales can be summed to obtain the Problem Index.

PRACTICAL ISSUES

Administration of the BSFI requires very little time. Copies of the BSFI can be obtained from

> Michael P. O'Leary, M.D., M.P.H.
> Division of Urology
> Brigham and Women's Hospital
> 45 Frances Street
> Boston, MA 02115

The BSFI has been translated into Afrikaans, Brazilian, Dutch, French, German, Hebrew, Italian, Norwegian, Portuguese, Spanish, and Walloon. Translated versions of the scale are available for a small handling charge from

> Dr. Catherine Acquadro
> MAPI Research Institute
> 27 Rue de la Vilette

EXAMPLE 28–1 ■ Sample item from the Brief Sexual Function Inventory

During the past 30 days, what is the most erect your penis has become at any time? (0 = no erection at all; 4 = full erection)

Lyon, France
Phone: 33-72-13-66-67

The BSFI is a relatively new instrument, and, as yet, there is no administrative or scoring manual beyond the article published in *Urology*. The BSFI is included on the CD-ROM that accompanies this handbook.

PSYCHOMETRIC PROPERTIES

The BSFI was derived from a 50-item version that was tested across a series of sequential studies. It was initially reduced to a 22-item version and then, on the basis of explicit psychometric criteria, was eventually pared down to the final 11-item version. Data have been obtained from men within general medicine clinics (e.g., $N = 60$) and from men with complaints of sexual dysfunction (e.g., $N = 74$).

Reliability

Internal consistency reliabilities (Cronbach's alpha) for the domain scores have been in the range of 0.85–0.90 for Sexual Drive, 0.90–0.95 for Erectile Function, 0.60–0.65 for Ejaculation, and 0.80–0.85 for the Problem Index. In the final 11-item version, Sexual Satisfaction is measured by a single item, thereby rendering internal consistency reliability inapplicable. Test-retest reliabilities for 1-week intervals, as measured by the intraclass correlation coefficient, have been in the range of 0.85–0.90 for Sexual Drive, 0.80–0.85 for Erectile Function, 0.75–0.80 for Ejaculation, and 0.85–0.90 for the Problem Index.

Validity

Discriminant function validation of the BSFI was reported with respect to age-adjusted contrasts of the mean scores on the five scales across groups of individuals with sexual dysfunction versus groups of individuals without sexual dysfunction. Significant differences in favor of the group without sexual dysfunction were observed for the Erectile Function, Sexual Satisfaction, and Problem Index scores. Failure to achieve significant discrimination in the case of Sexual Drive was explained on the basis of patient self-selection (i.e., men sufficiently motivated to endure a urological workup are almost certain to possess normal or near normal sex drive) and in the case of Ejaculation on the basis of its classification as a low-base-rate

sexual problem. Validation of the BSFI is in the early stages: studies to evaluate its differential sensitivity to therapeutic interventions are currently under way, and norms are under development.

CLINICAL UTILITY

The brevity, careful development, and demonstrated reliability and discriminative validity of the BSFI to date indicate that it is likely to become a useful measure. Because of its exclusive focus on male sexual functioning, application of the BSFI is limited to male populations. Within this significant constraint, however, its ease of administration and scoring make it a potentially useful measure in both clinical and research settings. It could be very useful as a screening instrument for male sexual dysfunction in general clinical populations.

REFERENCES AND SUGGESTED READINGS

Barry MJ, Fowler FJ, O'Leary MP, et al: The American Urological Association Symptom Index for Benign Prostatic Hyperplasia. J Urol 148:1549–1557, 1992

O'Leary MP, Fowler FJ, Lenderking WR, et al: A brief male sexual function inventory for urology. Urology 46:697–706, 1995

Brief Index of Sexual Functioning for Women (BISF-W)

J. F. Taylor, R. C. Rosen, and S. R. Leiblum

GOALS

The Brief Index of Sexual Functioning for Women (BISF-W) (Taylor et al. 1994) was designed to provide a brief, valid measure of current levels of female sexual functioning and satisfaction that may be used in clinical office practice, surveys of community populations, or clinical trials.

The BISF-W assesses the principal dimensions of current sexual functioning in women, such as sexual desire, quality of orgasm, and sexual satisfaction. Corollary aspects of female sexual functioning, such as sexual anxiety, body image, and partner satisfaction, are also assessed.

DESCRIPTION

The BISF-W is a brief self-report inventory. It contains 22 items, scored on a 4-point to 9-point Likert scale. Items evaluate diminished arousal or lubrication, pain during intercourse, and difficulties achieving orgasm, as well as frequencies of various sexual behaviors, including sexual fantasy, masturbation, and intercourse. Items that address the impact of health problems on sexual functioning are also included. A sample item is provided in Example 28–2. The BISF-W is straightforward to administer and score. It can be used with either heterosexual or homosexual women and with healthy individuals in the community, medical patients, and women with a diagnosable DSM-IV sexual disorder.

The total score is derived by summing the scores across all 22 items. However, three scales for Sexual Interest/Desire, Sexual Activity, and Sexual Satisfaction have been identified through factor analysis as components of the BISF-W and are scored separately as subtests. Low scores on the Sexual Interest/Desire subscale indicate dysfunction, whereas high scores on the Sexual Activity and Sexual Satisfaction subscales indicate dysfunction. No guidelines for interpreting scores or formal published norms for the derivation of cutoff scores are yet available, although they are under development.

EXAMPLE 28–2 ■ Sample item from the Brief Index of Sexual Functioning for Women

> Overall, how satisfied have you been with your sexual relationship with your partner? (0 = no partner; 1 = very satisfied; 5 = very dissatisfied)

Reprinted with permission from Raymond C. Rosen, Ph.D.

PRACTICAL ISSUES

It typically takes 15 minutes to complete the BISF-W. A copy of the test appears as an appendix to the article in which it was introduced (Taylor et al. 1994), and copies are available from

> Raymond C. Rosen, Ph.D.
> Department of Psychiatry
> Robert Wood Johnson Medical School
> 675 Hoes Lane
> Piscataway, NJ 08854

The BISF-W is a relatively new instrument, and, as yet, there is no administrative scoring manual beyond the introductory article.

PSYCHOMETRIC PROPERTIES

Initial studies on the BISF-W have been confined largely to reliability and validity within currently healthy women in the community, the majority of whom were registered for routine gynecological care at a university hospital. Their ages ranged from 20 to 75, and at least 50% were married. Samples were also limited largely to Caucasian women with at least a partial college education.

Reliability

Test-retest reliability, with a 1-month interval between baseline and retest, and internal consistency reliability (Cronbach's alpha) have been reported for the BISF-W. Reliability coefficients are given only for the three primary subscales, not for the total score. Test-retest coefficients ranged from 0.68 for Sexual Satisfaction to 0.78 for Sexual Activity. Internal consistency in the range of 0.80–0.85 was reported for Sexual Activity and 0.70–0.75 for Sexual Satisfaction but only 0.35–0.40 for Sexual Interest/Desire. The authors have indicated that further revision of the items on the last scale should improve its homogeneity.

Validity

The correlation between the BISF-W Sexual Activity subscale and the Derogatis Sexual Functioning Inventory (DSFI) (p. 639) Drive scale was 0.59, and the correlation between the BISF-W Sexual Satisfaction subscale and the DSFI Sexual Satisfaction scale was 0.67. The BISF-W Sexual Interest/Desire subscale was also correlated (negatively) with the DSFI Drive scale (–0.46), which would be expected given that low scores on the BISF-W and high scores on the DSFI are indicative of low levels of interest or desire. Analyses that evaluated the impact of age and social desirability on the BISF-W scores did not suggest that these are substantial factors in determining subtest scores.

CLINICAL UTILITY

The BISF-W is a brief, easy-to-use measure of the quality of current sexual functioning in female respondents. It may be used as a screening and treatment-planning aid in clinical practice and as an outcomes measure in clinical trials focused on female sexual functioning, as it has been used in several pharmaceutical drug trials. However, norms must be developed for specific populations; these norms promise to make the instrument even more useful in documenting not only the nature but also the degree of sexual dysfunctions within various populations. Current data limit the interpretation of the BISF-W across different populations. However, it could be useful as a screening instrument for sexual functioning in women in general clinical settings.

REFERENCES AND SUGGESTED READINGS

Taylor JF, Rosen RC, Leiblum SR: Self-report assessment of female sexual function: psychometric evaluation of the Brief Index of Sexual Functioning for Women. Arch Sex Behav 23:627–643, 1994

Sexual Arousability Inventory (SAI)

E. F. Hoon, P. W. Hoon, and J. P. Wincze

GOALS

The Sexual Arousability Inventory (SAI) (E. F. Hoon et al. 1976) is designed to assess, in general clinical settings, female sexual arousability, or, more specifically, a woman's remembered or imagined sexual arousal in response to visual or tactile contact with another, to imaginative stimuli, or to self-stimulation. An expanded version of the SAI (SAI-E) was developed to assess male sexual arousability and sexual anxiety (W. M. Hoon and Chambless 1988). Arousability is defined as a conscious physiological response to a variety of stimuli.

DESCRIPTION

The SAI is a brief, 28-item self-report inventory that assesses a single sexual arousability dimension. Endorsements are registered on a 5-point Likert scale, ranging from 1 = adversely affects arousal to 5 = extremely arousing. Sample items are provided in Example 28–3.

The SAI is scored by adding the negative and positive endorsements. To facilitate interpretation, normative data (means and standard deviations) are available for nonclinical heterosexual and homosexual women on the SAI and for heterosexual men on the SAI-E. Normative data for clinical populations are not available.

EXAMPLE 28–3 ■ Sample items from the Sexual Arousability Inventory

When you undress a loved one

When you see a pornographic movie (stag film)

When a loved one stimulates your genitals with mouth and tongue

Reprinted with permission from Dr. John Wincze.

PRACTICAL ISSUES

It takes about 15 minutes to complete the SAI. The SAI is described in the article by E. F. Hoon et al. (1976) and the SAI-E in the chapter by W. M. Hoon and Chambless (1988). Copies of the SAI can be obtained from

> Dr. John Wincze
> Brown University
> Division of Biology and Medicine
> Providence, RI 02912

The SAI is included on the CD-ROM that accompanies this handbook.

PSYCHOMETRIC PROPERTIES

Reliability

With samples of students and community volunteers, the SAI demonstrated internal consistency (Cronbach's alpha) >0.90 for the validation and the cross-validation samples and a Spearman-Brown split-half coefficient >0.90 for both samples. Retesting of a subsample after an 8-week interval produced a test-retest reliability coefficient of 0.69. The SAI-E also obtained internal consistency (Spearman-Brown) coefficients >0.90 for Arousal and 0.90 for Anxiety.

Validity

The total score on the SAI correlates at a level of 0.42 ($P < 0.01$) with another inventory of sexual experience (the Bentler Heterosexual Experiences Scale) and with self-reported satisfaction with sexual response, awareness of physiological arousal, number of sexual partners, frequency of orgasm, and frequency of intercourse.

The SAI has been shown to agree with subjective ratings of arousal in epileptic subjects and diabetic subjects, with no difference between patient groups and control subjects without epilepsy or diabetes; physiological measures did discriminate between the groups. These findings demonstrate convergent validity between the SAI and the other self-report data, both of which fail to agree with the physiological measure. Discrepancy between physiological and subjective measures of arousal is not unusual and probably reflects, among other factors, the difference between the central nervous system ex-

perience and the peripheral organ event (e.g., the difference between the subjective sense of excitement and the fact of vaginal lubrication). The SAI discriminated between the original cross-validation sample and a very small clinical sample of women with sexual dysfunction, although means and standard deviations for the clinical sample were not provided and sensitivity and specificity were not assessed. The SAI has also been shown to discriminate between heterosexual and homosexual women; the latter show higher levels of arousal.

CLINICAL UTILITY

The SAI is brief and easy to administer in general clinical settings. However, the absence of clinical norms and data concerning sensitivity and specificity limits its interpretability.

REFERENCES AND SUGGESTED READINGS

Coleman EM, Hoon PW, Hoon EF: Arousability and sexual satisfaction in lesbian and heterosexual women. Journal of Sex Research 19:58–73, 1983

Hoon EF, Hoon PW, Wincze JP: An inventory for the measurement of female sexual arousability: the SAI. Arch Sex Behav 5:291–300, 1976

Hoon WM, Chambless D: Sexual Arousability Inventory (SAI) and Sexual Arousability Inventory—Expanded (SAI-E), in Sexually-Related Measures: A Compendium. Edited by Davis C. Lake Mills, IA, Graphic, 1988, pp 21–24

Morrell MJ, Sperling ME, Stecker M, et al: Sexual dysfunction in partial epilepsy: a deficit in physiologic arousal. Neurology 44:243–247, 1994

Wincze JP, Albert A, Bansal S: Sexual arousal in diabetic females: physiological and self-report measures. Arch Sex Behav 22:587–601, 1994

Derogatis Sexual Functioning Inventory (DSFI)

L. R. Derogatis

GOALS

The Derogatis Sexual Functioning Inventory (DSFI) (Derogatis 1975) is designed to be an omnibus self-report inventory to measure the quality of an individual's current sexual functioning in a multidimensional format. The instrument measures principal components of successful sexual behavior (e.g., sex drive and sexual satisfaction), as well as aspects of functioning that are closely related to successful sexual functioning (e.g., body image and gender role definition). The DSFI also incorporates several basic indicators of general well-being via affective and symptomatic assessments.

DESCRIPTION

The DSFI contains 254 self-report items that are arranged in 10 scales that reflect the principal components of effective sexual behavior: Information, Experiences, Drive, Attitudes, Psychological Symptoms, Affects, Gender Role Definition, Fantasy, Body Image, and Sexual Satisfaction. Items are scored in different formats, from true-false endorsements to a variety of multiple-point Likert scales. Sample items are provided in Example 28–4.

Of the 10 subscales, 2 are composed of independent psychological tests. The Brief Symptom Inventory (BSI) (p. 84) serves as the Psychological Symptoms subscale; the Derogatis Affects Balance Scale (DABS) (Derogatis 1996) provides an assessment of affective status.

Raw score item values are summed and then transformed to a standardized area T-score via the published norm tables. For the DSFI Total Score, or Sexual Functioning Index, the T-scores for the 10 primary dimensions are summed, and this total score is then transformed to a T-score via a separate normative table. Norms for the DSFI were developed on the basis of a sample of 230 individuals who were attending university continuing

EXAMPLE 28–4 ■ **Sample items from the Derogatis Sexual Functioning Inventory**

> Simultaneous orgasm is not necessary for a good sexual relationship. (true or false)
>
> How often do you experience sexual fantasies? (0 = not at all to 8 = four or more times per day)
>
> I am less attractive than I would like to be. (0 = not at all to 4 = extremely true)

Reproduced with permission from Leonard R. Derogatis, Ph.D.

education classes. The majority of the subjects were white (80%) and middle-aged and had some college education. Approximately 60% of the subjects were married; the majority (75%) were from middle-class and upper-middle-class backgrounds. The author does not recommend the use of a uniform cutoff score for interpretation across different populations, because interpretations for the same cutoff score vary across populations. However, scores below a standardized score of 40 (i.e., 1 standard deviation below the mean, or in the 15th percentile of the distribution) might be considered clinically significant.

PRACTICAL ISSUES

It usually takes 30–40 minutes to complete the DSFI, although some individuals may require up to 60 minutes. The DSFI is a copyrighted inventory. The test, administration manual (Derogatis 1975), score and profile forms, and other related materials are available exclusively from

> Clinical Psychometric Research, Inc.
> 100 W. Pennsylvania Avenue
> Suite 302
> Towson, MD 21204
> Phone: 410-321-6165
> Fax: 410-321-6341

A package of 25 DSFI test booklets costs $75.00, 25 score and profile forms cost $12.00, and the preliminary DSFI manual costs $12.50. Personal computer programs for both the administration (ADMNDSFI) and scoring (SCORDSFI) of the DSFI are also available. The DSFI has been translated into Arabic, Chinese, French, French

Canadian, Indian, Korean, Norwegian, Spanish, and Turkish.

PSYCHOMETRIC PROPERTIES

Reliability

Internal consistency reliability coefficients for individual scales (with $N = 325$) ranged from 0.60 to 0.97. Test-retest coefficients across a 14-day interval ranged from 0.70 to 0.95.

Validity

The subtests of the DSFI that comprise separate multi-dimensional test instruments (e.g., the BSI and the DABS) have been repeatedly validated concurrently and with external criteria in their relevant substantive domains. Other subtests have been validated concurrently against instruments that are relevant to the constructs they measure (e.g., Information and Attitudes against Lief's SKAT (Lief and Karle 1976), Gender Role Definition against the Bem SRI (Bem 1974), and Experiences against Bentler's Heterosexual Behavioral Assessment Scale). The DSFI Total Score has been validated repeatedly against clinical judgment and diagnosis and used in discriminant function studies to successfully discriminate between community and sexually dysfunctional populations.

Several studies demonstrated the capacity of the DSFI to discriminate between male and female sexually dysfunctional patients and respective control subjects without sexual dysfunction, between gender-dysphoric men and women and gender-compatible control subjects, between medically compromised populations (e.g., those with breast cancer, testicular cancer, or diabetes) and control subjects without medical problems, and between individuals with major depressive disorder and individuals without major depressive disorder. Discriminant function analyses, conducted separately for men and women, on dysfunctional versus nondysfunctional samples indicated 77% correct classification of a diagnosis of overall sexual dysfunction in men and 75% correct assignment in women. Derogatis and Melisaratos (1979) also reported a factor analysis on the basis of 380 non-patient individuals. They derived seven interpretable factors that closely matched hypothesized dimensions of the instrument.

The DSFI was used as an outcome measure in more than 50 published studies on sexual functioning. Beutler et al. (1986) compared standard penile prostheses in biogenically impotent men with inflatable prostheses using the DSFI. Several dimensions, including Sexual Satisfaction, showed significantly greater improvement for the group with inflatable prostheses. Andersen et al. (1986) used selected subtests of the DSFI with women with gynecological cancer; they reported negative changes in sexual functioning to be one of the earliest indicators of cancer morbidity, often appearing long before a formal cancer diagnosis was made.

CLINICAL UTILITY

The DSFI is a reliable, well-validated instrument. Since its introduction in the 1970s, the DSFI has been used as an outcome measure in many published studies (Derogatis 1992). The DSFI has been used with individuals with male and female sexual dysfunctions, gender dysphorias, male erectile disorders of biogenic origins, breast cancer, testicular cancer, Hodgkin's disease, depression, and type I and type II diabetes. The majority of studies have found the DSFI to be sensitive to naturally occurring and disease-induced interference with sexual functioning and to positive effects derived from a range of therapeutic interventions. However, the DSFI scales are not keyed to specific DSM-IV sexual dysfunction categories.

The DSFI is designed to be used in a comprehensive clinical evaluation of a patient with complaints of sexual difficulties or disorder. It provides an extensive evaluation of the individual's sexual behavior and activities as a valid assessment of current psychological integration. It may be used as a stand-alone evaluation or as a complement to a clinical diagnostic workup.

The major constraint of the DSFI is its length, particularly in the case of clinical trials in which assessment inevitably involves a comprehensive battery of measures. Consequently, the DSFI is recommended for use at baseline and end-point evaluation in research protocols and clinical trials. Strengths of the instrument include the comprehensive nature of the DSFI evaluation, its reliability and validation status, and its gender-keyed norms in terms of area T-scores.

REFERENCES AND SUGGESTED READINGS

Andersen BL, Lachenbruch PA, Anderson B, et al: Sexual dysfunction and signs of gynecological cancer. Cancer 57:1880–1886, 1986

Bem SL: The measurement of psychological androgyny. J Consult Clin Psychol 42:155–162, 1974

Beutler LE, Scott FB, Roger RR, et al: Inflatable and non-inflatable penile prostheses: comparative follow-up evaluation. Urology 27:136–139, 1986

Derogatis LR: Derogatis Sexual Functioning Inventory (DSFI): Preliminary Scoring Manual. Baltimore, MD, Clinical Psychometric Research, 1975

Derogatis LR: DSFI: A Bibliography of Research Reports (1975–1992). Baltimore, MD, Clinical Psychometric Research, 1992

Derogatis LR: Brief Symptom Inventory (BSI): Administration, Scoring, and Procedures Manual, 3rd Edition. Minneapolis, MN, National Computer Systems, 1993

Derogatis LR: Derogatis Affects Balance Scale (DABS): Administration, Scoring, and Procedures Manual. Baltimore, MD, Clinical Psychometric Research, 1996

Derogatis LR, Melisaratos N: The DSFI: a multidimensional measure of sexual functioning. J Sex Marital Ther 5:244–281, 1979

Derogatis LR, Meyer JK: A psychological profile of the sexual dysfunctions. Arch Sex Behav 8:201–223, 1979

Derogatis LR, Schmidt CW, Fagan PJ, et al: Subtypes of anorgasmia via mathematical taxonomy. Psychosomatics 30:166–173, 1989

Lief H, Karle A (eds): Sex Education in Medicine. New York, Spectrum, 1976

Derogatis Interview for Sexual Functioning (DISF)

L. R. Derogatis

GOALS

The Derogatis Interview for Sexual Functioning (DISF) and the self-report version, the DISF-SR (Derogatis 1997), were developed to address a need for a set of brief, gender-keyed, multidimensional outcome measures that represent and quantify the status of an individual's current sexual functioning at multiple levels of interpretation.

DESCRIPTION

The DISF is a relatively brief semistructured interview that consists of 26 items (e.g., assessing ability to have an orgasm or the presence of a full erection on awakening). The DISF-SR is a self-report version of the DISF, with 26 items that correspond closely to the DISF items. Each instrument has separate gender-oriented formats. Items within each instrument vary in the format of their scoring. The DISF and DISF-SR represent quality of current sexual functioning in five domains that to some degree parallel phases of the sexual response cycle: 1) Sexual Cognition/Fantasy, 2) Sexual Arousal, 3) Sexual Behavior/Experience, 4) Orgasm, and 5) Sexual Drive/Relationship. Sample items are provided in Example 28–5.

The DISF and DISF-SR can be interpreted at three distinct levels: individual items, the five functional domains (e.g., Sexual Arousal), and a global summary (i.e., the DISF Total Score). The five domain scores and the Total Score are obtained by summing raw scores across respective items that are then transformed to standardized scores on the basis of published norms. Norms for

EXAMPLE 28–5 ■ Sample items from the Derogatis Interview for Sexual Functioning

Male Version
  During the past 30 days, how often did you engage in sexual intercourse, oral sex, etc.? (0 = not at all to 8 = four or more times a day)
  During the past 30 days, how satisfied have you been with your sense of control (timing) of your orgasm? (0 = not at all to 4 = extremely)

Female Version
  With the partner of your choice, what would be your ideal frequency of sexual intercourse? (0 = not at all to 8 = four or more times per day)
  During the past 30 days, how satisfied have you been with your ability to have an orgasm? (0 = not at all to 4 = extremely)

Reproduced with permission from Leonard R. Derogatis, Ph.D.

DISF and DISF-SR scores are gender keyed and were developed on the basis of several hundred nonpatient community respondents. The author does not recommend the use of a uniform cutoff score for interpretation across different populations, because interpretation for the same cutoff score varies across populations. However, a Total Score below a standardized score of 40 (i.e., 1 standard deviation below the mean, or in the 15th percentile of the distribution) would be considered clinically significant.

PRACTICAL ISSUES

It takes approximately 15–20 minutes of interviewing time to administer the DISF. Time requirements for administration can be reduced through the joint use of the DISF-SR. Both the DISF and the DISF-SR are copyrighted. The tests, administration and scoring manual, and supporting materials are available from

> Clinical Psychometric Research, Inc.
> 100 W. Pennsylvania Avenue
> Suite 302
> Towson, MD 21204
> Phone: 410-321-6165
> Fax: 410-321-6341

A package of 50 DISF or DISF-SR booklets costs $47.50, and the respective score and profile forms cost $25.00. The DISF items are relatively straightforward and can be administered by lay interviewers. The DISF and DISF-SR have been translated into Danish, Dutch, French, Italian, Spanish, and Norwegian.

PSYCHOMETRIC PROPERTIES

Reliability

DISF joint reliability coefficients (Pearson r) obtained from a multicenter trial involving the participation of 16 clinical judges ranged from a low of 0.84 for the Orgasm domain to a high of 0.92 for Sexual Cognition/Fantasy. Joint reliability for the DISF Total Score was in the range of 0.90–0.95. Internal consistency and test-retest reliabilities for the DISF-SR were obtained from community samples ranging from 120 to 170 participants. Cronbach's alpha ranged from a low of 0.74 for the Sexual Drive/Relationship domain score to a high of 0.80 for Orgasm. Test-retest coefficients (over a 1-week interval) ranged from 0.80 to 1.0 for the domain scores and from 0.85 to 0.90 for the Total Score.

Validity

Much of the clinical research done with the DISF and DISF-SR has involved corporate-sponsored, proprietary clinical trials, for which the data sets are generally unavailable. Published validation data are thus somewhat limited. In a study with prostate cancer patients about to undergo radiation treatment—with detailed clinical evaluation as the external criterion—sensitivity was 86% and specificity was 80%, and the positive predictive power was 86% with respect to overall sexual functioning. After treatment, patients were assigned to three functional categories (i.e., totally functional, marginally functional, and impotent). Domain scores were significantly different across these groups, which had total scores of 48.2, 21.5, and 14.0, respectively.

CLINICAL UTILITY

The DISF and DISF-SR are both relatively brief and easy to administer. In addition, each possesses actuarial, gender-keyed norms that were determined on the basis of representative community samples. The DISF and DISF-SR are therefore well suited to evaluate sexual dysfunction and the nature of dysregulation of normal sexual functioning. The DISF-SR might be particularly useful as a screening instrument and the DISF as a relatively brief follow-up interview. Both the DISF and the DISF-SR can be used effectively in the office with individual patients or in clinical trials with large samples of subjects.

REFERENCES AND SUGGESTED READINGS

Derogatis LR: The Derogatis Interview for Sexual Functioning (DISF/DISF-SR): an introductory report. J Sex Marital Ther 23:291–304, 1997

Zinreich E, Derogatis LR, Herpst J, et al: Pre and posttreatment evaluation of sexual function in patients with adenocarcinoma of the prostate. Int J Radiat Oncol Biol Phys 19:729–732, 1990

Zinreich E, Derogatis LR, Herpst J, et al: Pretreatment evaluation of sexual function in patients with adenocarcinoma of the prostate. Int J Radiat Oncol Biol Phys 19:1001–1004, 1990

Golombok Rust Inventory of Sexual Satisfaction (GRISS)

J. Rust and S. Golombok

GOALS

The Golombok Rust Inventory of Sexual Satisfaction (GRISS) (Rust and Golombok 1986a, 1986b) is designed to assess the quality of a heterosexual relationship and of each partner's sexual functioning within that relationship; it covers areas of functioning that a sex therapist might want to see change during the course of therapy. The GRISS provides a global score as well as 12 subscale scores that assess sexual functioning for each partner. The single profile generated for the couple may be used to supplement a clinical diagnosis or to screen for sexual dysfunction.

DESCRIPTION

The GRISS is a 28-item self-report inventory with male and female versions. Each item is scored on a 5-point Likert scale. The GRISS includes 12 subscales, 6 of which target domains specific to DSM sexual disorders: Avoidance (male and female), Anorgasmia (female only), Vaginismus (female only), Premature Ejaculation (male only), and Impotence (male only). The remaining subscales assess behaviors of both partners that may be problematic to the sexual relationship: Non-sensuality (male and female versions), Dissatisfaction (male and female versions), Infrequency (completed by men or women), and Non-communication (completed by men or women).

The GRISS produces both an overall score and subscale scores for the individual. Of the 28 items, 24 are added to determine the overall raw score, which is then transformed using a scale (ranging from 1 to 9) located on each scoring page. Any score ≥5 suggests that a clinical problem may exist. The subscale scores are obtained in a similar manner, by summing the items from each of the seven subscales for each partner (i.e., there are seven possible subscales for each sexual partner). Using the transformation scale, these scores are then converted into transformed subscale scores. As with the transformed overall score, any transformed subscale score ≥5 suggests that a clinical problem may exist in that particular domain. It is possible to plot both partners' scores on a single scale; this feature allows for a graphical description and comparison of the sexual functioning of each partner. Such a graphic representation can assist the clinician in generating hypotheses about the sexual interaction of the partners and the etiology of the dysfunction as well as possible treatment strategies.

PRACTICAL ISSUES

It takes less than 10 minutes to complete the GRISS. The GRISS is copyrighted and can be obtained from

> Psychological Assessment Resources, Inc.
> P.O. Box 998
> Odessa, FL 33556
> Phone: 800-331-TEST (800-331-8378)

The price for the professional manual (Rust and Golombok 1986a) is $29.00; a package of 25 questionnaires and profile forms is $18.00 (specify male or female). However, Psychological Assessment Resources, Inc., may not continue to publish the GRISS. The publisher in the United Kingdom is

> NFER-NELSON Publishing Company, Ltd.
> Darville House
> 2 Oxford Road East
> Windsor, Berks
> SL4 1DF, England

PSYCHOMETRIC PROPERTIES

Reliability

The GRISS was standardized on couples in sex therapy in clinics throughout the United Kingdom. The total of the male and female scales had split-half reliabilities of 0.87 and 0.94, respectively. The internal consistencies of the subscales averaged 0.74; they ranged between 0.61 for Non-communication and 0.83 for Anorgasmia. Test-retest reliabilities were calculated on the basis of the pre- and posttherapy scores of 41 couples, 20 of whom had participated in marital therapy and 21 of whom had participated in sex therapy. Even with considerable therapeutic change reported, the values obtained were 0.76 for the male scale and 0.65 for the female scale. Subscale test-retest reliabilities averaged 0.65 and ranged from 0.47 for female Dissatisfaction to 0.84 for Premature Ejaculation.

Validity

The validity of the GRISS was assessed by therapists who completed questionnaires on data from 68 men and 63 women (62 couples). The therapists rated specific sexual problems and the severity of each problem. Individuals in the sexual problem group ($n = 42$ women and 57 men) were compared with a sample from a general medical clinic ($n = 29$ men and 30 women). Therapists' ratings of the severity of the sexual problems correlated with both the male overall score ($r = 0.53$; $N = 68$) and the female overall score ($r = 0.56$; $N = 63$). The GRISS discriminated between the sexual problem group and the general clinical subjects in both the overall female score (point biserial $r = 0.63$) and the overall male score (point biserial $r = 0.37$). Of the 99 individuals in the sexual dysfunction group, 19 had lower scores than the mean of the general control group, which the authors attributed to factors mainly related to the dysfunction of the subjects' partners. On the targeted diagnostic subscales of Impotence, Premature Ejaculation, Vaginismus, and Anorgasmia (avoidance not reported), all sex clinic subjects differed significantly from the general clinic control subjects. Five of the eight other scales showed significant trends in the expected directions. Only Non-communication, male Non-sensuality, and male Avoidance did not differ between the two groups.

CLINICAL UTILITY

The GRISS is an easily interpreted instrument that both therapists and patients can use as a point of departure in designing a treatment program. At times, the subscale scores on the profile may alert the clinician to conditions that may have been unreported in the sexual histories of the partners. The overall scores may be useful for group comparisons or pre- and posttreatment comparisons. Because of the relatively small sample for the standardization of the GRISS, further validation studies are needed.

REFERENCES AND SUGGESTED READINGS

Rust J, Golombok S: The Golombok Rust Inventory of Sexual Satisfaction. Odessa, FL, Psychological Assessment Resources, 1986a

Rust J, Golombok S: The GRISS: a psychometric instrument for the assessment of sexual dysfunction. Arch Sex Behav 15:153–165, 1986b

Rust J, Golombok S: Diagnosis of sexual dysfunction: the relationship between DSM-III-R and the GRISS. Sexual and Marital Therapy 3:119–124, 1988

Sexual Interaction Inventory (SII)

J. LoPiccolo

GOALS

The Sexual Interaction Inventory (SII) (LoPiccolo and Steger 1974) is designed to assess a heterosexual couple's sexual functioning and sexual satisfaction with respect to 17 different, specific heterosexual behaviors. The measure can be used clinically to assess sexual dysfunction of the couple or in research as a therapy outcome measure.

DESCRIPTION

The SII is a self-report instrument for assessing the frequency and pleasure associated with 17 specific heterosexual behaviors, most of which are illustrated by line drawings in the test booklet. The behaviors are dyadic, including visual stimulation, manual stimulation, oral stimulation, intercourse, and orgasm (e.g., drawings of a man seeing a woman when she is nude, a woman caressing a man's genitals with her mouth, a man caressing a woman's breasts with his hands, and a man and a woman having intercourse with both having an orgasm). Each member of the couple completes the instrument separately. Six questions are posed for each of the 17 behaviors regarding 1) current frequency, 2) desired frequency, 3) how pleasant respondent finds the activity, 4) how pleasant respondent thinks mate finds the activity, 5) how pleasant respondent would like to find this activity, and 6) how pleasant respondent would like mate to find this activity. Six multiple-choice options, ranging from pleasant to unpleasant, are provided for each question. In sum, the SII includes 102 items (i.e., six questions for each of the 17 behaviors).

An 11-scale profile of standard scores is derived from the responses to respective question(s) concerning the 17 behaviors for each couple. The scales reflect satisfaction with frequency and range of sexual behavior, pleasure obtained from sexual behavior, self-acceptance, acceptance of partner, and accuracy of perception of partner's sexual preferences. Raw scores, which are derived by summation or calculation of difference scores, are then plotted on profile sheets. For example, the Frequency Dissatisfaction scale (male and female) is the total difference between question 1 (current frequency) and question 2 (desired frequency) across the 17 behaviors, the Perceptual Accuracy scale (male and female) is the total difference between question 3 (how pleasant respondent finds the activity) for one partner and question 4 (how pleasant respondent thinks mate finds the activity) for the other partner across the 17 behaviors, and the Mate Acceptance scale (male and female) is the total difference between question 5 (how pleasant respondent would like to find this activity) and question 6 (how pleasant respondent would like mate to find this activity) across the 17 behaviors. Norms were established on the basis of a sample of 124 couples who reported a satisfactory sexual relationship. The same six questions are asked after the respondent has viewed the drawing of the sexual activity. A sample question is provided in Example 28–6.

PRACTICAL ISSUES

It takes approximately 10 minutes to complete the SII. The copyright for the SII is held by Joseph LoPiccolo, Ph.D., and test booklets, a test manual, and profile sheets are available from him:

> Joseph LoPiccolo, Ph.D.
> Department of Psychology
> University of Missouri–Columbia
> 719 McAlester Hall
> Columbia, MO 65211

PSYCHOMETRIC PROPERTIES

Reliability

The 11 scales of the SII had internal consistency coefficients (Cronbach's alpha) ranging from 0.80 to 0.93 in a

EXAMPLE 28–6 ■ Sample item from the Sexual Interaction Inventory

How pleasant do you currently find this activity to be? How pleasant do you think your mate finds this activity to be?

21. I find this activity:

1) Extremely unpleasant
2) Moderately unpleasant
3) Slightly unpleasant
4) Slightly pleasant
5) Moderately pleasant
6) Extremely pleasant

22. I think my mate finds this activity:

1) Extremely unpleasant
2) Moderately unpleasant
3) Slightly unpleasant
4) Slightly pleasant
5) Moderately pleasant
6) Extremely pleasant

Reprinted with permission from Joseph LoPiccolo, Ph.D.

community sample ($N = 78$ couples). Test-retest reliability for the scales at a 2-week interval (Pearson product moment correlations) ranged from 0.50 to 0.90 in a community sample ($N = 15$ couples). In both cases, Perceptual Accuracy of Partner was the least stable scale.

Validity

The SII has been shown to discriminate between clinical and nonclinical samples and to be a sensitive measure of change. Nine of the eleven scales discriminated between sexually dysfunctional ($n = 28$ couples) and nonclinical ($n = 78$ couples) samples with a series of t tests. All 11 scales discriminated between pre- and posttreatment administration for several clinical samples. However, correlations between global ratings of couples' sexual satisfaction and the 11 scales were low, peaking at 0.35 for a community sample ($N = 70$ couples). Nevertheless, the correlations were in the predicted direction.

CLINICAL UTILITY

The SII would be most useful clinically in providing information about couples before they enter therapy and then, subsequently, as a measure of therapy progress and outcome. Because of the explicitness of the illustrations, patients may desire some privacy while completing the measure.

REFERENCES AND SUGGESTED READINGS

LoPiccolo J, Steger JD: The Sexual Interaction Inventory: a new instrument for assessment of sexual dysfunction. Arch Sex Behav 3:585–595, 1974

LoPiccolo J, Heiman JR, Hogan DR, et al: Effectiveness of single therapist versus cotherapy teams in sex therapy. J Consult Clin Psychol 53:287–294, 1985

Morokoff PJ, LoPiccolo J: A comparative evaluation of minimal therapist contact and 15-session treatment of female orgasmic dysfunction. J Consult Clin Psychol 54:294–300, 1986

CHAPTER 29

Eating Disorders Measures

Kathleen M. Pike, Ph.D.
Sara L. Wolk, M.A., Ed.M.
Marci Gluck, Ph.D.
B. Timothy Walsh, M.D.

INTRODUCTION

Major Domains

This chapter covers instruments that measure the key constructs related to the assessment of eating pathology and eating disorders. The primary eating disorder diagnoses, according to DSM-IV, are anorexia nervosa, bulimia nervosa, and binge eating disorder. Anorexia nervosa and bulimia nervosa have been recognized as distinct diagnostic entities for quite some time, and although binge eating disorder is a provisional diagnosis in DSM-IV, its apparent prevalence has generated significant clinical and research attention. The inclusion of binge eating disorder in DSM-IV as a provisional diagnosis reflects the growing awareness among professionals in the area of eating disorders that a distinct pattern of binge eating without compensatory behavior presents a serious problem for a subset of individuals. Binge eating disorder increases as weight increases; however, only a subset of obese individuals meet criteria for binge eating disorder, and the disorder represents a particular syndrome distinct from physical weight status. In addition to information on measures focused on these specific disorders, the chapter also includes instruments that provide continuous measures of the severity of behavioral and attitudinal disturbances relevant to the assessment of all the eating disorders, including eating disorder not otherwise specified.

Organization

The measures included in this chapter are listed in Table 29–1. We review six self-report measures and one interview measure in this chapter. The self-report measures that assess a wide range of attitudinal and behavioral features associated with the full range of eating disturbances are discussed first. Self-report measures that target core features specific to anorexia nervosa, bulimia nervosa, and binge eating disorder follow. The last instrument we describe is the interview-based Eating Disorder Examination (EDE), which provides descriptive and diagnostic data across the range of eating disorders.

Relevant Measures Included Elsewhere in the Handbook

In addition to the measures included in this chapter, several instruments included in Chapter 6, "Diagnostic Interviews for Adults," assess eating disorders. In particular, the Structured Clinical Interview for DSM-IV Axis I Disorders (SCID-I) (p. 49) includes all the eating disorders, and the Primary Care Evaluation of Mental Disorders (PRIME-MD) (p. 65), a screening instrument, includes an eating disorders section.

USING MEASURES IN THIS DOMAIN

Goals of Assessment

The Eating Disorder Inventory (EDI), the Body Shape Questionnaire (BSQ), and the Three Factor Eating

TABLE 29–1 ■ Eating disorders measures

Name of measure	Disorder or construct assessed	Format	Pages
Eating Disorder Inventory (EDI) Expanded version (EDI-2) Children's version (KEDS)	Multidimensional measure of attitudes, behaviors, and traits thought to be clinically relevant to the onset and maintenance of eating disorders	Self-report; 64 items (EDI), 91 items (EDI-2), and 14 items (KEDS)	651–654
Body Shape Questionnaire (BSQ)*	Concerns about body shape and weight	Self-report; 34 items	654–657
Three Factor Eating Questionnaire (TFEQ) (Eating Inventory)	Three dimensions of eating behavior important in the dysregulation of eating associated with eating disorders and obesity	Self-report; 51 items	657–659
Mizes Anorectic Cognitions (MAC) Questionnaire	Severity of cognitive distortions associated with anorexia nervosa and bulimia nervosa	Self-report; 45-, 33-, and 24-item versions	659–662
Bulimia Test—Revised (BULIT-R)	Binge eating, compensatory behavior, and weight and shape concerns consistent with core diagnostic criteria for bulimia nervosa	Self-report; 36 items	662–665
Questionnaire on Eating and Weight Patterns—Revised (QEWP-R)*	Identification and diagnosis of binge eating disorder	Self-report; 28 items	665–668
Eating Disorder Examination (EDE) Self-report version (EDE-Q) Children's version (ChEDE)	Severity of eating pathology, including key behavioral problems and associated disturbances	Semistructured, investigator-based interview, 4 or 5 subscales; self-report and children's versions, 38 items	668–671

*Measure is included on the CD-ROM that accompanies this handbook.

Questionnaire (TFEQ) assess a wide range of eating- and weight-related cognitions and attitudes relevant to all the eating disorders. The Mizes Anorectic Cognitions (MAC) Questionnaire assesses the cognitions characteristic of anorexia nervosa and bulimia nervosa. The Bulimia Test—Revised (BULIT-R) provides a continuous measure of the symptoms and severity of bulimia nervosa, and the Questionnaire on Eating and Weight Patterns—Revised (QEWP-R) is a screening instrument designed to identify probable cases of binge eating disorder. The EDE is the only interviewer-based instrument included in this chapter. It provides both continuous measures of the level of pathology and diagnostic questions for determining case status.

Implementation Issues

The vast majority of assessment measures for eating disorder pathology are self-report instruments. Administra-

tion and scoring procedures for these instruments are usually simple and therefore do not require extensive training. Thus, the measures provide a relatively economical means for gathering information. However, they are subject to certain limitations that affect interpretation. In particular, self-report is subject to significant variability in definitions of binge eating and loss of control over eating. In addition, it is often difficult for individuals to recall the frequency of binge eating episodes. Thus, these self-report data may be less reliable for the purpose of diagnosis. However, it is possible to enhance the accuracy of self-reporting by providing definitions of these phenomena and instructing individuals to record binge eating episodes on an ongoing basis.

In contrast, structured clinical interviews may have an advantage over self-report instruments because interviewers can be trained to assess clinically defined constructs. For complex constructs (e.g., the definition of a binge) or constructs for which the clinical standard differs from everyday usage (e.g., distortion of body image), the use of structured clinical interviews may be especially advantageous. However, such assessment procedures require extensive clinical training and are therefore more costly.

Regardless of whether data are collected by self-report or interview format, assessment of the critical features of eating disorders relies on the reporting of the individual because most of the behavioral and attitudinal components of the disorders cannot be directly observed. Perhaps the only feature of eating disorders that is directly observable is the severe weight loss associated with anorexia nervosa. In addition, no physical parameters provide objective measures of severity. Also, individuals binge and purge in secret; they worry about their eating and feel remorse or shame in silence. Even amenorrhea, a diagnostic criterion for anorexia nervosa, is assessed by self-disclosure.

With the exception of observational studies of binge eating and purging that are conducted in laboratory settings, symptom assessment for the most part depends on the open disclosure of the respondent. Therefore, the greatest problems with implementation in assessing eating disorders derive from the denial often associated with anorexia nervosa, the shame and secrecy associated with having an eating disorder, and the variable use of terms used to describe important clinical phenomena. As a result, it is important to collect data using a variety of procedures, and it is essential that diagnosis be made on the basis of informed clinical judgment.

Issues in Interpreting Psychometric Data

Several issues are important to consider in interpreting data related to eating disturbances and eating disorders. In particular, characteristics of study samples and normative samples affect interpretation. Additionally, the rates of normative discontent or disturbance in different segments of the population must be considered, and the methods of data collection may affect rates of reported symptomatology, including overreporting and underreporting of symptoms.

In terms of sample characteristics, it is important to consider gender, race, and developmental stage when interpreting data. The vast majority of studies have been conducted with predominantly Caucasian girls and young women in their adolescent and young adult years. This limited sampling reflects the assumption, common

until recently, that ethnic minority groups were not vulnerable to eating disorders. Especially with the recent inclusion of binge eating disorder in the psychiatric nomenclature, this assumption requires revisiting, and additional data need to be gathered to accurately interpret and put into context reported rates of eating pathology among ethnic minority groups. Rates of eating disturbance among certain segments of the male population and at different developmental stages also need to be interpreted with reference to appropriate normative groups. Rates of dieting among adolescent girls vary significantly from those among adolescent boys, and methods of weight control among adult men may be quite different from those among adult women, for example.

In addition to different rates of eating disturbances among different segments of the population, another issue in interpreting assessments of eating disturbance is the documentation of a continuum of eating pathology, particularly among girls and women, by many large-scale community studies. Mild to moderate levels of weight concern and body dissatisfaction are quite common, and it is not unusual to find very high reported rates of single, specific features such as weight concern or binge eating. Therefore, it is important to clarify whether assessment procedures identify symptoms or syndromes.

Finally, many of the constructs that are central to the diagnosis of eating disorders require clinical definitions that are more narrow and specific than the colloquial usage of terms such as *binge eating* and *dieting*. Because of the significant distress, shame, and secrecy often associated with eating disorders, some individuals may underreport the severity of their eating pathology. Underreporting severity may be a particular problem among individuals with anorexia nervosa because they commonly deny the severity of their symptoms. Consequently, it is important to carefully assess the way in which data are collected and consider the method when interpreting reported rates of eating disturbances and eating disorders or when trying to understand differences between results obtained with different measures.

GUIDE TO THE SELECTION OF MEASURES

For the purposes of general assessment of eating pathology, the EDI and the EDE are perhaps the most useful. The EDI has the practical advantage of being a self-report instrument, but that is also its greatest limitation given the tendency for eating disorder patients to under-report their symptomatology. The EDE is a clinician-administered instrument that provides descriptive assessments of the severity of eating pathology as well as diagnostic data. It has the advantage of providing detailed and comprehensive assessment tempered by clinical judgment, but it may be too time-consuming for routine clinical application.

Each eating disorder is characterized by specific features that require more tailored assessment. The BSQ is especially useful for an assessment of body shape and weight concerns in clinical and nonclinical populations. The TFEQ provides a detailed assessment of the cognitive and behavioral components of eating regulation, which may be useful in the assessment and monitoring of eating disorder symptomatology. Specifically, it evaluates cognitive restraint, susceptibility to loss of control over eating, and perceived hunger. The MAC Questionnaire also assesses cognitions related to eating pathology but focuses more on the overall distortions associated with anorexia nervosa and bulimia nervosa. The BULIT-R assesses bulimic symptomatology and is an efficient self-reporting screening instrument for bulimia nervosa. The QEWP-R provides the most complete self-report screening assessment for binge eating disorder.

The use of these instruments for self-monitoring is an important and widespread means of collecting important information regarding eating disturbances. In particular, self-monitoring procedures that entail recording eating behavior, purging and/or exercising, affective states, and related cognitions can be extremely useful during the course of treatment. Self-monitoring of binge eating and purging behaviors has been shown to be very reliable and can therefore be used quantitatively to measure behavioral change during the course of treatment. Additionally, the qualitative information garnered from the self-monitoring can inform clinical treatment.

Many individuals with eating disorders also meet criteria for other Axis I or II disorders. In particular, it is important to assess individuals with eating disorders for affective or anxiety disorders, given their high rates of concurrence. Appropriate assessment procedures are reviewed in relevant sections of this handbook (e.g., Chapter 6, "Diagnostic Interviews for Adults," Chapter 24, "Mood Disorders Measures," and Chapter 25, "Anxiety Disorders Measures"). In addition, the Yale-Brown-

Cornell Eating Disorder Scale (Mazure et al. 1994) specifically targets eating-related preoccupations and/or rituals. It has documented reliability and validity and may be especially useful in assessing these dimensions in individuals with anorexia nervosa. This instrument is an adaptation of the Yale-Brown Obsessive Compulsive Scale (Y-BOCS) (p. 572).

CURRENT STATUS AND FUTURE RESEARCH NEEDS FOR ASSESSMENT

The assessment of eating pathology and eating disorders has become increasingly complex and sophisticated as distinct disorders have been identified (e.g., binge eating disorder) and further distinctions have been made in the existing nomenclature (e.g., the distinction between the restricting subtype and the binge eating and purging subtype of anorexia nervosa). The evolving nature of the field introduces complexities into the assessment of eating disorders. As details regarding diagnosis change with different versions of DSM, instruments and norms must be revised. Such revisions present problems in comparing samples and studies.

Another issue in the study of eating disorders that warrants attention is improved procedures and instruments for identifying individuals at risk. Because of the relatively low incidence of actual cases of eating disorders, large-scale prevention studies are limited in their efficacy. However, the field has yet to develop instruments that can accurately and economically target individuals at high risk for the development of clinical eating disorders.

It will be important in the future to develop more comprehensive instruments that adopt consistent constructs. Currently, most self-report measures are insufficient to assess the full range of symptoms relevant to eating disorders. Thus, partial information is gathered from multiple sources, often resulting in redundancy and gaps in the description of an individual's eating disorder. Although the EDE provides a comprehensive picture, its use is not always practical. A well-designed self-report instrument might be able to provide a comprehensive description of an individual's eating disturbances and diagnostic status.

Another challenge to the field is the development of more culturally and developmentally sensitive instruments. Contrary to earlier assumptions, it appears that all cultural or ethnic groups are vulnerable to eating disorders, although the rates of specific disorders may vary depending on certain cultural or ethnic factors. Similarly, it would be valuable to have more information regarding the assessment of younger and older individuals with eating disorders. The age span of patients with diagnosed eating disorders continues to expand in both directions.

It will be important in the future for the field to determine whether there are accurate means of distinguishing in more detail the heterogeneous group of individuals who are classified as having eating disorder not otherwise specified. Although this group probably constitutes the largest group of individuals with eating disorders, it is also the most diverse and least studied. Assessment instruments that could assist in the further refinement of the eating disorder nosology might be of substantial benefit.

REFERENCES AND SUGGESTED READINGS

Allison DB (ed): Handbook of Assessment Methods for Eating Behaviors and Weight-Related Problems. Thousand Oaks, CA, Sage, 1995

Crowther JH, Sherwood NE: Assessment, in Handbook of Treatment for Eating Disorders. Edited by Garner DM, Garfinkel PE. New York, Guilford, 1997, pp 34–49

Mazure CM, Halmi KA, Sunday SR, et al: The Yale-Brown-Cornell Eating Disorder Scale: development, use, reliability, and validity. J Psychiatr Res 28:425–445, 1994

Thompson JK (ed): Body Image, Eating Disorders, and Obesity: An Integrative Guide for Assessment and Treatment. Washington, DC, American Psychological Association, 1996

Eating Disorder Inventory (EDI)

D. M. Garner, M. P. Olmsted, and J. Polivy

GOALS

The Eating Disorder Inventory (EDI) (Garner et al. 1983) is a multidimensional self-report measure designed to assess the attitudes, behaviors, and traits thought to be clinically relevant to the onset and maintenance of eating disorders (particularly anorexia nervosa and bulimia nervosa as determined by the DSM-IV criteria). The original EDI has 64 items that form eight subscales, three of which are designed to assess specific disturbances in eating attitudes and behaviors. The other five subscales are designed to measure more general psychological constructs thought to be important in understanding individuals with eating disorders. More recently, Garner (1991) developed the EDI-2, which includes the items from the original scale plus three additional subscales that were designed to assess three other dimensions thought to be characteristic of individuals with eating disorders.

DESCRIPTION

The EDI-2 has 91 items organized into 11 subscales. It retains the original 8 subscales (64 items) of the EDI (Drive for Thinness, Bulimia, Body Dissatisfaction, Ineffectiveness, Perfectionism, Interpersonal Distrust, Interoceptive Awareness, and Maturity Fears) and includes 3 additional subscales (27 items) that further assess the psychological characteristics of individuals with eating disorders (Asceticism, Impulse Regulation, and Social Insecurity). All possible answers are specified using a 6-point Likert scale. Respondents indicate whether the item is true about themselves always, usually, often, sometimes, rarely, or never. The EDI may be completed using paper and pencil or a computer. All items should always be completed, and respondents are instructed not to skip any items.

An easy reading version and a children's version (KEDS) of the EDI are available; both require a second-grade reading level. The KEDS is a 14-item self-report instrument on which responses are rated on a 3-point scale (yes, no, and you don't know); it also includes a set of eight figure drawings for assessing body shape concerns. Its norms were derived from a large sample of children ages 9–16 years.

Responses for each item on the EDI are weighted from 0 to 3; a score of 3 is assigned to the responses farthest in the symptomatic direction, scores of 2 and 1 for the next two responses, respectively, and a score of 0 for the three responses that are farthest in the asymptomatic direction. Subscale scores are computed by simply summing all item scores for that particular subscale; higher scores indicate a greater manifestation of that particular trait. Each EDI subscale is intended to measure a conceptually independent trait; therefore, the authors assign more importance to the subscale scores than to the total EDI score.

Normative data for individuals with anorexia nervosa, individuals with bulimia nervosa, and college-age women are reported in Table 29–2. The diagnostic groups differ from each other on six subscales; however, all means from the diagnostic groups are elevated well above the normal range (with the exception of the low scores on the Bulimia subscale for the anorexia nervosa—restricting group). The authors indicate that because of the large sample sizes, the statistical differences between diagnostic groups may not have much clinical significance. Instead, they emphasize the considerable consistency among the EDI subscale scores across the eating disorder samples.

Additional normative data are available in the EDI-2 manual (Garner 1991) for male college, high school, and junior high school students, as well as female high school and junior high school students. As would be expected, boys and men appear less symptomatic than girls and women across the range of EDI subscales. Interestingly, some data suggest that race and socioeconomic status do not significantly affect the subscales that directly tap eating disorder symptoms; however, upper-class and Caucasian girls are more likely to report lower scores on the Interpersonal Distrust subscale than lower-class and minority girls.

Two subscales warrant particular attention regarding interpretation of scores: Body Dissatisfaction and Drive for Thinness. Body dissatisfaction has consistently been

TABLE 29–2 ■ Normative data on the Eating Disorder Inventory

	Anorexia nervosa—restricting $n = 129$	Anorexia nervosa—bingeing and purging $n = 103$	Bulimia nervosa $n = 657$	Comparison group—college women $n = 205$	Combined eating disorders $n = 889$
Drive for Thinness	11.3 ± 7.0	15.0 ± 5.6	15.0 ± 5.0	5.5 ± 5.5	14.5 ± 5.5
Bulimia	1.8 ± 3.5	8.9 ± 5.8	10.8 ± 5.4	1.2 ± 1.9	10.5 ± 1.2
Body Dissatisfaction	11.9 ± 7.9	14.4 ± 8.5	17.9 ± 7.9	12.2 ± 8.3	16.6 ± 12.2
Ineffectiveness	11.4 ± 8.4	13.1 ± 8.7	11.0 ± 7.5	2.3 ± 3.6	11.3 ± 2.3
Perfectionism	8.9 ± 5.3	9.5 ± 5.1	8.8 ± 4.8	6.2 ± 3.9	8.9 ± 6.2
Interpersonal Distrust	6.9 ± 5.3	7.3 ± 4.9	5.3 ± 4.5	2.0 ± 3.1	5.8 ± 2.0
Interoceptive Awareness	9.2 ± 6.9	12.9 ± 7.5	11.1 ± 6.8	3.0 ± 3.9	11.0 ± 3.0
Maturity Fears	4.8 ± 5.1	4.6 ± 4.9	4.4 ± 4.6	2.7 ± 2.9	4.5 ± 2.7
Asceticism[a]	6.9 ± 5.3	7.3 ± 4.9	5.3 ± 4.5	2.0 ± 3.1	8.3 ± 4.7
Impulse Regulation[a]	9.2 ± 6.9	12.9 ± 7.5	11.1 ± 6.8	3.0 ± 3.9	6.0 ± 5.3
Social Insecurity[a]	4.8 ± 5.1	4.6 ± 4.9	4.4 ± 4.6	2.7 ± 2.9	8.6 ± 4.9

[a]N = 22 (anorexia nervosa—restricting), 17 (anorexia nervosa—bingeing and purging), and 68 (bulimia nervosa).

found to be a strong predictor of eating pathology. It is correlated with symptom severity, poor treatment outcome, and treatment relapse in patients with bulimia nervosa. Therefore, it may be useful to target individuals with high scores on the Body Dissatisfaction subscale for early intervention efforts. However, body dissatisfaction is also correlated with weight in both clinical and nonclinical female samples. An adjustment to the Body Dissatisfaction subscale, the Body Illusion Index, was thus devised to statistically eliminate the effects of relative body weight on Body Dissatisfaction scores. This adjustment systematically increases Body Dissatisfaction scores at lower weights. Details regarding this adjustment are available in the manual.

A cutoff score of 14 on the Drive for Thinness subscale has been identified as an appropriate threshold for screening individuals who are most likely at risk for developing an eating disorder or who currently have an eating disorder.

The questions on the EDI were not designed to elicit the kind of information necessary for determining whether the criteria are met for a DSM-IV eating disorder. An adjunct self-report instrument, the EDI— Symptom Checklist (EDI-SC), was developed by the authors and can be administered along with the EDI-2. The EDI-SC provides detailed information regarding the frequency and history of binge eating and compensatory behavior as well as menstrual functioning. The EDI-SC provides the more precise behavioral information necessary for the diagnosis of eating disorders. However, although it is designed to assist in formulating a diagnosis, it is not intended to be used as the sole basis for diagnosis.

PRACTICAL ISSUES

The EDI-2, which is copyrighted by Psychological Assessment Resources, Inc., takes 15–20 minutes to complete. The questionnaire uses language that is easily understandable and unambiguous. The manual (Garner 1991), administration information, EDI-2 and EDI-SC questionnaires, scoring instructions, and costs for the materials can be obtained from

> Psychological Assessment Resources, Inc.
> P.O. Box 998
> Odessa, FL 33556
> Phone: 800-331-8378

The EDI-2 has been translated into Arabic, Chinese, Dutch, Estonian, French, German, Hebrew, Spanish, and Swedish.

PSYCHOMETRIC PROPERTIES

Reliability

The internal consistency of the EDI subscales in clinical and nonclinical samples has been demonstrated; Cronbach's alphas ranged from 0.83 to 0.92 for the clinical samples and were >0.70 for all subscales in four nonclinical samples ($N = 271$, 268, 158, and 354), with the exception of 0.65 for Maturity Fears in one sample. Test-retest reliability was also documented in three independent studies. Pearson product moment correlation coefficients after a 1-week interval ranged from 0.79 to 0.95 ($n = 70$), with the exception of Interoceptive Awareness (0.67); after a 3-week interval, the range was 0.81–0.97 ($n = 70$), with the exception of Maturity Fears (0.65); and after a 1-year interval the range was 0.41–0.75 ($n = 282$).

Validity

The EDI subscales correlate with other related measures, as would be expected. The Drive for Thinness subscale has been shown to correlate with the Eating Attitudes Test (EAT) (Garner and Garfinkel 1979) total score ($r = 0.71$) and with the Restraint Scale (Herman and Polivy 1975) ($r = 0.61$). The Bulimia subscale has been shown to correlate with the Bulimia and Food Preoccupation subscales of the EAT ($r = 0.68$).

The EDI is able to discriminate between eating disorder patients and nonpatient samples, and self-report ratings from the EDI correlate moderately with ratings by a trained clinician ($r = 0.43$–0.68). Several clinical treatment studies have also demonstrated that the EDI is sensitive to clinical changes in patients with bulimia nervosa.

Overall, factor analytic studies have consistently supported the eight factors of the original EDI. However, the Interoceptive Awareness subscale includes three eating- or hunger-related items that tend to yield low item-total correlations on this subscale. In fact, these items have sometimes failed to show a clear pattern of providing a factor analysis. In addition, the limited factor analytic studies that have been conducted to date have not supported either the reliability or the validity of the three additional scales of the EDI-2.

CLINICAL UTILITY

The EDI is an easily administered self-report instrument designed to identify characteristics common in individuals with eating disorders. It can be used in multiple settings. The primary use of the EDI is the clinical evaluation of symptoms associated with eating disorders. In clinical settings, it can provide a measure of the severity of symptoms that may be useful in planning treatment. The EDI is also sensitive to change, and repeated assessment can provide information regarding clinical status and serve as a measure of treatment response.

The EDI is also designed to be useful in nonclinical or primary care settings as part of a screening procedure for identifying individuals at high risk for eating disorders or individuals with subclinical eating disturbances. The EDI can be used effectively in a two-part screening procedure to identify high-risk individuals (e.g., a cutoff score of 14 on the Drive for Thinness subscale has been used in some studies to target individuals who are then interviewed in the second stage of the screening).

In clinical research, the EDI may be useful as both an outcome measure and a prognostic indicator for treatment studies.

REFERENCES AND SUGGESTED READINGS

Boyadjieva S, Steinhausen H: The Eating Attitudes Test and the Eating Disorders Inventory in four Bulgarian clinical and nonclinical samples. Int J Eat Disord 19:93–93, 1996

Childress AC, Brewerton TD, Hodges EL, et al: The Kids' Eating Disorders Survey (KEDS): a study of middle school students. J Am Acad Child Adolesc Psychiatry 32:843–850, 1993

Garner DM: Eating Disorder Inventory—2 Professional Manual. Odessa, FL, Psychological Assessment Resources, 1991

Garner DM: Eating Disorder Inventory—2 (EDI-2), in Outcomes Assessment in Clinical Practice. New York, Williams & Wilkins, 1995, pp 92–96

Garner DM, Garfinkel PE: The Eating Attitudes Test: an index of the symptoms of anorexia nervosa. Psychol Med 9:273–279, 1979

Garner DM, Olmsted MP, Polivy, J: Development and validation of a multidimensional eating disorder inventory for anorexia nervosa and bulimia. Int J Eat Disord 2:15–34, 1983

Garner DM, Olmsted MP, Davis R, et al: The association between bulimic symptoms and reported psychopathology. Int J Eat Disord 9:1–15, 1990

Garner DM, Garner MV, Van Egeren LF: Body dissatisfaction adjusted for weight: the Body Illusion Index. Int J Eat Disord 12:263–271, 1992

Garner DM, Rockert W, Davis R, et al: Comparison of cognitive-behavioral and supportive-expressive therapy for bulimia nervosa. Am J Psychiatry 150:37–46, 1993

Herman CP, Polivy J: Anxiety, restraint, and eating behavior. J Pers 84:666–672, 1975

Raciti MC, Norcross JC: The EAT and EDI: screening, interrelationships, and psychometrics. Int J Eat Disord 6:579–586, 1987

Wear RW, Pratz O: Test-retest reliability for the Eating Disorder Inventory. Int J Eat Disord 6:767–769, 1987

Body Shape Questionnaire (BSQ)

P. J. Cooper, M. J. Taylor, Z. Cooper, and C. G. Fairburn

GOALS

The Body Shape Questionnaire (BSQ) (Cooper et al. 1987) is a self-report instrument designed to measure concerns about body shape and weight, particularly the experience of "feeling fat" in individuals with and without eating disorders. Body weight and shape concerns exist on a continuum in the general population; increased concerns are associated with increased risk for the development of eating pathology. Significant body image disturbance constitutes one of the diagnostic criteria for both anorexia nervosa and bulimia nervosa. The BSQ provides a comprehensive assessment of the severity of body image disturbance by assessing body shape concern and body size overestimation, the core components of body image disturbance. Thus, the BSQ is meant to provide a continuous, descriptive assessment of body image disturbance in clinical and nonclinical populations and can be used to assess the role of body image disturbance in the development, maintenance, and treatment of anorexia nervosa and bulimia nervosa.

DESCRIPTION

The BSQ is a self-administered 34-item questionnaire. Answers are specified using a 6-point frequency-based Likert scale. Consistent verbal descriptors for all 34 items are provided (i.e., never, rarely, sometimes, often, very often, and always), and subjects are asked to respond to each question on the basis of how well it describes their attitudes, feelings, or behavior over the past 4 weeks. Items on the BSQ attempt to assess feelings about body shape, as well as behavioral and emotional consequences of such feelings. Sample questions are provided in Example 29-1.

The BSQ has also been validated in a short, alternate form with a nonclinical sample. Two 16-item scales were established by dividing 32 of the 34 original questions of the BSQ. Items 26 and 32 (assessing laxative and vomiting use as means of weight and shape control) were deleted from these shortened versions because of their relatively low loading on the primary component of the BSQ and on the grounds that they represent very specific behavioral correlates of body image disparagement that are likely to be skewed in the general population (Evans

EXAMPLE 29-1 ■ Sample items from the Body Shape Questionnaire

> Have you felt ashamed of your body?
>
> Have you avoided wearing clothes which make you particularly aware of the shape of your body?
>
> Have you worried about your flesh being dimply?

Cooper PJ, Taylor MJ, Cooper Z, et al.: "The Development and Validation of the Body Shape Questionnaire." *International Journal of Eating Disorders*, Volume 6, pp. 485–494. Copyright 1987. Reprinted by permission of John Wiley & Sons, Inc.

and Dolan 1993). One 16-item version of the BSQ includes items 1, 3, 5, 7, 8, 9, 10, 11, 15, 17, 20, 21, 22, 25, 28, and 34. The other includes items 2, 4, 6, 12, 13, 14, 16, 18, 19, 23, 24, 27, 29, 30, 31, and 33. The two 16-item scales correlate highly ($r = 0.96$) with each other and also with the 34-item BSQ ($r = 0.96$–0.99). Even shorter versions of the BSQ were established by further dividing the two 16-item questionnaires into four scales with 8 items each, resulting in alpha values in the range of 0.87–0.92; however, those very short versions were not as highly correlated with one another or with the total BSQ.

The BSQ generates a single score by summation of the 34 items on the instrument. The total possible score ranges from 34 to 204. In the original validation studies, patients with bulimia nervosa ($n = 38$) reported a mean score of 136.9 (SD = 22.5) compared with a sample of women in the community ($n = 535$), who reported a mean score of 81.5 (SD = 28.5). In addition to individuals with eating disorders, several other groups, such as dieters and individuals preoccupied with their weight, have been shown to report elevated BSQ scores. Thus, unique threshold scores for the identification of individuals with probable eating disorders have not been established.

PRACTICAL ISSUES

It takes approximately 10 minutes to complete the BSQ. The entire measure is published in the article by Cooper et al. (1987), which describes the development and validation of the BSQ. Correspondence and questions regarding the BSQ should be directed to

> Dr. Peter Cooper
> University of Reading
> Department of Psychology
> White Knights Road
> Reading RG6 2AL
> United Kingdom

The BSQ is included on the CD-ROM that accompanies this handbook.

PSYCHOMETRIC PROPERTIES

Reliability

In a nonclinical sample of 342 women, a Cronbach's alpha coefficient of 0.97 was reported. Cronbach's alphas for the 16- and 8-item versions of the BSQ are only slightly lower. Cronbach's alphas of 0.93–0.96 were obtained for the 16-item versions, and Cronbach's alphas of 0.87–0.92 were obtained for the 8-item versions. One study of 33 undergraduate women provided test-retest reliability data over a 3-week interval; the Pearson product moment correlation coefficient was 0.88.

Validity

Initial construction of the BSQ included 51 items that were derived from open-ended interviews with 28 women who were expected to show some concern about their shape: 6 women with bulimia nervosa, 4 women with anorexia nervosa, 7 women on weight loss diets, 3 women who exercised regularly, and 8 university students. These women were asked to describe their experience of "feeling fat," to describe the specific circumstances that provoke such feelings, and to provide an account of the emotional and behavioral consequences of such feelings. On the basis of a series of four studies, the 51-item questionnaire was reduced to a final set of 34 questions.

The BSQ has been compared with other body image measures such as the Body Dysmorphic Disorder Examination (BDDE) (p. 610), the Body Self-Relations Questionnaire (Brown et al. 1990), and the Body Dissatisfaction subscale of the Eating Disorder Examination (EDE) (p. 668). Studies that compared the BSQ with these related measures showed significant Pearson product moment correlation coefficients ranging from 0.61 to 0.81. These correlations indicate that, for both clinical and nonclinical samples, negative body image attitudes expressed on the BSQ are related to other types of negative body image symptoms, including concerns about appearance that are not related to weight.

Validity studies that compared individuals with bulimia nervosa, with possible bulimia nervosa, and without eating disorders resulted in statistically significant mean differences on the BSQ. A study of 38 individuals with diagnoses of bulimia nervosa reported a group mean on the BSQ of 136.9, compared with 10 subthreshold or probable bulimia nervosa patients (mean = 129.3) and individuals who definitely did not have eating disorders (mean = 71.9). In a comparison of nonpatients, those who exhibited body concerns and were actively dieting had a mean score of 109, whereas the group of individuals without body concerns who were not dieting had a mean score of 55.9.

Another study indicated significant differences in BSQ scores among four groups: patients without eating disorders in therapy to address body image issues (mean score for obese subjects = 135.6 and nonobese subjects = 125.1), obese dieters (123.1), university undergraduates (96.3), and university staff (75.8). Results from these studies indicate that the BSQ can accurately distinguish clinical and nonclinical individuals as well as individuals with greater weight concerns. Higher scores on the BSQ have also been positively correlated with the degree of being overweight.

Studies of the BSQ indicate that the factorial structure of this instrument is dominated by one main construct that accounts for more than half the variance in the scale. These studies suggest that the BSQ is an effective measure of body shape and weight concerns that hold together as a unidimensional construct and that cannot be distinguished on this measure.

CLINICAL UTILITY

The BSQ is an easily administered paper and pencil questionnaire that assesses shape and weight concerns. Elevated scores on the BSQ reflect increased body image disturbance. The BSQ provides a comprehensive measure of body shape and weight concerns. It is, however, best suited to assess the degree of body shape concerns in both clinical and community samples rather than to screen for individuals with eating disorders because such concerns represent only one criterion of eating disorders and because elevated weight and shape concerns are reported by groups other than individuals with eating disorders (e.g., obese individuals and extreme dieters). However, the BSQ may be an effective measure to screen for individuals at risk for developing eating disorders, given the etiological importance of these concerns in the development of eating disorders. Because body dissatisfaction is correlated with weight, the BSQ may be less useful in discriminating among obese individuals. The BSQ is well suited for and used widely in clinical practice and treatment to assess the degree to which body shape and weight may predict response to treatment. Also, the BSQ offers a comprehensive assessment of symptom change over time or in response to treatment. The 16-item versions of the BSQ offer the advantage of brief assessments that are useful in terms of economy of time and in situations in which individuals will be assessed repeatedly. These two versions could be alternated to reduce the likelihood that respondents will recall specific responses on particular items in the past.

REFERENCES AND SUGGESTED READINGS

Brown TA, Cash TF, Mikulka P: Attitudinal body image assessment: factor analysis of the Body Self-Relations Questionnaire. J Pers Assess 35:134–144, 1990

Cooper PJ, Taylor MJ, Cooper Z, et al: The development and validation of the Body Shape Questionnaire. Int J Eat Disord 6:485–494, 1987

Evans C, Dolan B: Body Shape Questionnaire: derivation of shortened "alternate forms." Int J Eat Disord 13:315–321, 1993

Garner DM, Garfinkel PE: The Eating Attitudes Test: an index of the symptoms of anorexia nervosa. Psychol Med 9:273–279, 1979

Mumford DB, Whitehouse AM, Platts M: Sociocultural correlates of eating disorders among Asian schoolgirls in Bradford. Br J Psychiatry 158:222–228, 1991

Rosen JC, Jones A, Ramirez E, et al: Body Shape Questionnaire: studies of validity and reliability. Int J Eat Disord 20:315–319, 1996

Three Factor Eating Questionnaire (TFEQ) (Eating Inventory)

A. J. Stunkard and S. Messick

GOALS

The Three Factor Eating Questionnaire (TFEQ) was developed by Stunkard and Messick (1985) to expand on earlier efforts to assess restrained eating and its relationship to obesity and eating disorders. The TFEQ (which is marketed by the Psychological Corporation as the Eating Inventory) is a self-report questionnaire intended to assess three dimensions of eating behavior that are thought to be important in understanding the dysregulation of eating associated with eating disorders and obesity. Specifically, it aims to measure cognitive restraint in eating (defined as the tendency to restrict food intake to control body weight), susceptibility to periodic disinhibition of control over eating caused by a range of situations or states, and perceived hunger.

DESCRIPTION

The TFEQ is a 51-item self-report questionnaire composed of 36 true-false items in Part I and 15 items rated on a 4-point Likert scale in Part II. The TFEQ includes three subscales. The Cognitive Restraint subscale is composed of 12 items in Part I and 9 items in Part II. The Disinhibition subscale is composed of 13 items in Part I and 3 items in Part II. The Hunger subscale is composed of 11 items in Part I and 3 items in Part II.

The TFEQ is scored by subscale. Only 1 point is given for each item in both Part I and Part II. In Part II, if either of the most symptomatic responses is endorsed, 1 point is added to the appropriate subscale score. Scores are summed for each subscale. Details concerning scoring procedures are provided on the Ready Score Answer Sheet.

Raw scores can be compared with the following normative guidelines: Low to average scores are estimated to fall between 0 and 10, 0 and 8, and 0 and 7 for the Cognitive Restraint, Disinhibition, and Hunger subscales, respectively. High range scores are estimated to fall between 11 and 13, 9 and 11, and 8 and 10 for each subscale, respectively, and a score of 14, 12, or 11 is estimated to be in the clinical range for each respective subscale. However, these norms were determined on the basis of limited data and should be interpreted with caution.

Studies of weight loss programs for obese individuals indicate that high levels of cognitive restraint and low levels of disinhibition are associated with greater success in losing weight and maintaining weight loss. High scores on the Disinhibition subscale may be associated with binge eating. High scores on the Hunger subscale may suggest that an individual could benefit from appetite suppressant medication or behavioral programs that emphasize hunger control techniques; however, empirical trials have not yet tested the utility of these interventions in reducing scores on the Hunger subscale of the TFEQ.

Means and standard deviations for control groups, individuals who diet regularly, bulimic individuals, individuals who binge, and obese individuals are available in the *Eating Inventory Manual,* published by the Psychological Corporation (Stunkard and Messick 1988).

PRACTICAL ISSUES

It takes 10–15 minutes to complete the TFEQ, and it can be used with both adult and adolescent samples.

Although it does not require any special training to administer the TFEQ, given that it is a self-report questionnaire, it is suggested that interpretations be supervised by a professional experienced in the clinical treatment of obesity and eating disorders and in psychological testing.

The TFEQ items are presented in a reusable test booklet, and responses are recorded on the Ready Score Answer Sheet, both of which are available from the Psychological Corporation. The TFEQ is copyrighted and marketed as the Eating Inventory by

> The Psychological Corporation
> 555 Academic Court
> San Antonio, TX 78204-2498
> Phone: 800-211-8378
> Internet: www.psychcorp.com

The questionnaire, question booklet, scoring sheet, manual, and current prices are available to professionals with relevant training and experience in assessment and can be ordered from the Psychological Corporation.

PSYCHOMETRIC PROPERTIES

Reliability

A satisfactory degree of internal consistency has been demonstrated; alpha coefficients for the three subscales ranged from 0.80 to 0.93 and sample sizes from 45 to 901. For individuals who restrained their intake of food, alpha coefficients ranged from 0.79 to 0.84; for those who did not restrain their intake of food, the range was 0.84–0.92 for the three factors. Very limited test-retest reliability

data are available. One study of 17 individuals reported reliability coefficients of 0.93, 0.80, and 0.83 for the three subscales, respectively, over a test-retest interval of 1 month.

Validity

The initial pool of items for the TFEQ was derived from three sources: the Restraint Scale (Herman and Polivy 1975), the Latent Obesity Questionnaire (Pudel et al. 1975), and the clinical experience of the first author of this measure, A. J. Stunkard. Scores on the TFEQ have been found to correlate with severity of binge eating and to distinguish bulimic subjects from control subjects without bulimia. Means and standard deviations of the scores in groups of individuals who restrained and did not restrain their intake of food are consistently differentiated in the predicted direction. Binge severity, as measured by the Binge Eating Scale (Gormally et al. 1982), significantly correlated with the Disinhibition subscale ($r = 0.61$) and with the Hunger subscale ($r = 0.54$). TFEQ scores were shown to be significantly correlated with the Restraint scale of the Dutch Eating Behavior Questionnaire (Van Strien et al. 1986) ($r = 0.66$) and with the mean caloric intake of subjects as recorded in food diaries ($r = 0.46$).

The Cognitive Restraint subscale has been shown to serve a valuable function in monitoring progress in treatment for obesity and binge eating. Positive response to treatment is correlated with increases in scores on the Cognitive Restraint subscale paralleled by decreases in scores on the Disinhibition and Hunger subscales for obese individuals. At the same time, one study indicated that the combination of high restraint and low disinhibition at pretreatment predicted greater weight loss. Scores on the Disinhibition subscale are elevated in subjects with bulimia nervosa and binge eating disorder and are highly correlated with the severity of binge eating. In cases in which binge eating recurred, scores on the TFEQ returned to baseline, reflecting the sensitivity of the TFEQ to accurately describe changes in the cognitive and behavioral components of restraint, disinhibition, and hunger.

CLINICAL UTILITY

The TFEQ has both clinical and research utility. The TFEQ can be used in clinical evaluations to aid in developing treatment goals specific to the eating problems of each patient. Elevated scores on individual subscales could call for distinct interventions depending on the particular eating and weight problems of the individual. For example, for obese individuals who score low on the Cognitive Restraint subscale, successful weight loss treatment will require a focus on increasing restraint. However, for individuals of normal weight with bulimia nervosa, high scores on the Cognitive Restraint subscale are likely to be associated with high scores on the Disinhibition subscale and to be correlated with binge eating. For such individuals, treatment interventions would be aimed at reducing restraint.

The TFEQ also has important research applications. It can be used in research to assess cognitive processes and behavioral adaptation or control related to eating behavior, weight regulation, and perceived hunger. The TFEQ also provides important data regarding the links among restraint, disinhibition, and hunger in different eating and weight disorders; the links are important in understanding the interplay of these factors in the etiology and maintenance of eating and weight disturbances.

REFERENCES AND SUGGESTED READINGS

Allison DB, Kalinsky LB, Gorman BS: A comparison of the psychometric properties of three measures of dietary restraint. Psychological Assessment 4:391–398, 1992

Gormally J, Black S, Daston S, et al: The assessment of binge eating severity among obese persons. Addict Behav 7:47–55, 1982

Herman CP, Polivy J: Anxiety, restraint, and eating behavior. J Pers 84:666–672, 1975

Laessle RG, Tuschl RJ, Kotthaus BC, et al: A comparison of the validity of three scales for the assessment of dietary restraint. J Abnorm Psychol 98:504–507, 1989

Pudel VE, Metzdorff M, Oetting MX: Zur Persoehnlichkeit Adipoeser in psychologischen Tests unter Beruecksichtigung latent Fettsuechtiger. [The personality of the adipose fat person under consideration for latent obesity factors in psychological testing.] Z Psychosom Med Psychoanal 21:345–350, 1975

Stunkard AJ, Messick S: The Three-Factor Eating Questionnaire to measure dietary restraint, disinhibition, and hunger. J Psychosom Res 29:71–83, 1985

Stunkard AJ, Messick S: Eating Inventory Manual. San Antonio, TX, Psychological Corporation, Harcourt Brace, 1988

Stunkard AJ, Messick S: The Three Factor Eating Questionnaire (Eating Inventory), in Obesity Assessment: Tools, Methods, Interpretations. Edited by Sachilko T. New York, Chapman & Hall, 1997, pp 824–829

Van Strien T, Frijters JER, Bergers GPA, et al: The Dutch Eating Behavior Questionnaire (DEBQ) for assessment of restrained, emotional, and external eating behavior. Int J Eat Disord 5:295–315, 1986

Mizes Anorectic Cognitions (MAC) Questionnaire

J. S. Mizes

GOALS

The Mizes Anorectic Cognitions (MAC) Questionnaire (Mizes 1988) is designed to assess the severity of core cognitions associated with anorexia nervosa and bulimia nervosa as defined in DSM-IV. The MAC Questionnaire does not assess the core diagnostic criteria but rather is designed to provide a continuous measure of the severity of cognitive distortions thought to be specific to the etiology and maintenance of eating disturbances. The measure assesses three domains in particular: perception of weight and eating as the basis of approval from others, the belief that rigid self-control is fundamental for self-worth, and the rigidity of efforts to regulate weight and eating.

DESCRIPTION

The original MAC Questionnaire was composed of 45 items; however, the majority of the studies of the measure used a shortened, 33-item questionnaire. A 24-item version of the MAC Questionnaire with three 8-item subscales was recently developed. The studies investigating the validity and reliability of the 24-item MAC Questionnaire have not yet been published, although the authors report (Mizes et al., personal communication) that the preliminary data regarding the psychometric properties of the instrument are consistent or better than the data reported for the earlier 33-item version. The information regarding reliability and validity of the MAC Questionnaire that follows refers to the 33-item version unless otherwise indicated; information regarding the 24-item MAC Questionnaire should be sought directly from the author until it is published.

Respondents rate all items on the MAC Questionnaire using a consistent 5-point Likert scale (1 = strongly disagree to 5 = strongly agree). The questionnaire is administered using paper and pencil, and all items should always be completed. The three MAC Questionnaire subscales are derived from the domains mentioned previously: Rigid Weight Regulation; Self-Control of Eating and Self-Esteem; and Appearance, Weight, and Approval. Sample items are provided in Example 29–2.

The three subscales yield three empirically supported subscale scores. Total MAC Questionnaire and subscale scores are derived by summing the responses. The possible range for the 33-item version is 33–165 for the total MAC Questionnaire. Approximately half the items are reverse scored.

A study of 105 college men and 100 college women reported mean MAC Questionnaire scores for the 33-item instrument of 68.52 (SD = 15.88) for the men and 81.05 (SD = 20.22) for the women. Their combined mean was 74.94 (SD = 19.25). The mean score on the 33-item MAC Questionnaire for individuals with bulimia nervosa (n = 15) was 119.5 (SD = 20.5). The mean score was 115.6 (SD = 14.7) for individuals with anorexia nervosa (n = 8) and 65.1 (SD = 12.3) for individuals with other psychiatric disorders (n = 11). Another study that compared 20 women with bulimia nervosa and 20 control subjects without bulimia nervosa found that the mean score for the eating disorder group on the 45-item MAC Questionnaire was 149.6 (SD = 30.0) compared with the control group mean of 96.7 (SD = 15.19).

PRACTICAL ISSUES

It takes approximately 10 minutes to complete the questionnaire. The MAC Questionnaire uses language that is easily understandable and unambiguous. The directions for the measure are clear, and a sixth-grade reading level is required. The questionnaire and scoring instructions are available from

Multi-Health Systems, Inc.
908 Niagara Falls Boulevard
North Tonawanda, NY 14120-2060
Phone: 800-456-3003
Internet: www.mhs.com

PSYCHOMETRIC PROPERTIES

Reliability

The internal consistency of the subscales and the total score for the 33-item MAC Questionnaire were first assessed with data from a study of 105 college men and 100 college women. These data indicate that the instrument has good internal consistency. Cronbach's alphas for the three subscales were 0.89, 0.75, and 0.78. Cronbach's alpha was 0.91 for the entire instrument and 0.93 in an independent sample of 100 college women. Similar levels of internal consistency were found in a study of patients. Although the sample sizes were relatively small (15 individuals with bulimia nervosa; 8 individuals with anorexia nervosa; and 11 individuals with psychiatric disorders, predominantly affective disorders, for comparison), Cronbach's alphas ranged from 0.75 to 0.91.

EXAMPLE 29–2 ■ Sample items from the Mizes Anorectic Cognitions Questionnaire

Rigid Weight Regulation Subscale
   If I don't have a specific routine for my daily eating, I'll lose control and I'll gain weight.
   When I feel hungry, I can't give in to that hunger. If I do, I'll never stop eating and I'll soon be fat.

Self-Control of Eating and Self-Esteem Subscale
   I feel victorious over my hunger when I am able to refuse sweets.
   I am proud of myself when I can control my urge to eat.

Appearance, Weight, and Approval Subscale
   How much I weigh has little to do with how popular I am. (reverse scored)
   My friends will like me regardless of how much I weigh.

Reprinted with permission from J. Scott Mizes, Ph.D.

Test-retest reliability was also documented on a sample of 100 nonclinical college women. This study reported a correlation coefficient of 0.78 on the basis of a participation rate of 86% after a 2-month interval.

Validity

The MAC Questionnaire has been shown to correlate with related measures of eating pathology. Specifically, in a study of 100 women, the MAC Questionnaire correlated with the Bulimia Test (BULIT) (p. 662) ($r = 0.69$), the Gormally Cognitive Factors on the Binge Eating Scale (Gormally et al. 1982) ($r = 0.51$), and the Eating Attitudes Test–26 (EAT-26) (Garner and Garfinkel 1979) ($r = 0.64$). Other studies of individuals with eating disorders reported that the MAC Questionnaire is significantly correlated with the EDI (p. 651) ($r = 0.80$), the Gormally Binge Eating Scale (Gormally et al. 1982) ($r = 0.87$), and the Cognitive Factors subscale on the Gormally Binge Eating Scale ($r - 0.79$). Taken together, these data reflect strong correlations, but they are in a range that suggests that the MAC Questionnaire is measuring related but unique aspects of eating-related pathology. Finally, data from the nonclinical sample of 100 college women indicate that the MAC Questionnaire is measuring constructs specifically related to eating pathology that are not a function of social desirability, academic achievement, or personality. The MAC Questionnaire correlated with the Marlowe-Crowne Social Desirability Scale (Crowne and Marlowe 1964) ($r = -0.12$), with the Spelling portion of the Wide Range Achievement Test (WRAT-Spelling) (Jastak and Jastak 1964) ($r = 0.01$), and with the Jenkins Type A Scale (Jenkins et al. 1978) ($r - 0.08$); it did not correlate with the WRAT-Arithmetic ($r = 0.00$). The extent to which the MAC Questionnaire is associated with measures of depression and anxiety is unknown.

In a sample of 20 women with bulimia nervosa and 20 women without eating disorders, the MAC Questionnaire was able to discriminate between groups; the MAC accounted for 60% of the between-group variance. At the same time, those who scored high on the MAC Questionnaire were found to differ significantly from those who scored low in terms of weight regulation efforts, ideal weight, importance of weight, importance of appearance, methods of caloric restriction, and calorie-burning strategies.

The MAC Questionnaire has been shown to discriminate between individuals with other psychiatric disorders ($n = 11$) and individuals with eating disorders ($n = 15$ with bulimia nervosa and 8 with anorexia nervosa). However, the mean MAC Questionnaire scores for the individuals with bulimia nervosa and anorexia nervosa were not significantly different, suggesting that the MAC Questionnaire is assessing cognitions associated with the entire range of eating pathology rather than unique aspects of different eating disorders.

The three subscales of the MAC Questionnaire appear to be conceptually useful and have been empirically validated. In the initial factor analytic studies, the three factors—Rigid Weight Regulation, Self-Control of Eating and Self-Esteem, and Appearance, Weight, and Approval—accounted for approximately 50% of the variance of the measure. These factors were replicated in an independent nonclinical sample.

CLINICAL UTILITY

The MAC Questionnaire is an easily administered paper and pencil questionnaire that provides relevant clinical information that can be used to assess the dysfunctional cognitions and attitudes related to the etiology and maintenance of eating pathology. The MAC Questionnaire may aid the clinician in developing a more complete picture of the pathology before the initiation of treatment and is part of a comprehensive evaluation. It has been studied in clinical samples of individuals and community samples with consistent reliability and validity. However, the clinical samples have been relatively small, and thus more widespread use of this measure in clinical settings will be necessary to establish its clinical utility. The MAC Questionnaire could be used in clinical research studies as a continuous measure of eating disorder cognitions that may be useful in predicting response to treatment and risk of relapse associated with eating disorders. The measure has been shown to be sensitive to decreases in eating pathology resulting from successful cognitive-behavioral treatment for bulimia nervosa. Further studies reporting on its use in clinical treatment with other eating disorder samples would be useful.

Finally, the MAC Questionnaire may be useful in identifying individuals at risk for developing eating disorders, because it measures the cognitive factors that are likely to precede the actual behavioral components of developing eating disorders. Given the limited success of primary prevention programs for eating disorders, it may be useful to apply instruments such as the MAC Questionnaire to identify high-risk individuals and focus prevention efforts.

REFERENCES AND SUGGESTED READINGS

Crowne DP, Marlowe D: Approval Motive: Studies in Evaluation Dependence. Westport, CT, Greenwood, 1964

Garner DM, Garfinkel PE: The Eating Attitudes Test: an index of the symptoms of anorexia nervosa. Psychol Med 9:273–279, 1979

Gormally J, Black S, Daston S, et al: The assessment of binge eating severity among obese persons. Addict Behav 7:47–55, 1982

Jastak JF, Jastak SR: Short forms of the WAIS and WISC vocabulary sets. J Clin Psychol 20:167–199, 1964

Jenkins CD, Zyzanski SJ, Rosenman RH: Coronary-prone behavior: one pattern or several? Psychosom Med 40:25–43, 1978

Mizes JS: Personality characteristics of bulimic and non-eating-disordered female controls: a cognitive behavioral perspective. Int J Eat Disord 7:541–550, 1988

Mizes JS: Criterion-related validity of the Anorectic Cognitions Questionnaire. Addict Behav 15:153–163, 1990

Mizes JS: Construct validity and factor stability of the Anorectic Cognitions Questionnaire. Addict Behav 16:89–93, 1991

Mizes JS: Validity of the Mizes Anorectic Cognitions Scale: a comparison between anorectics, bulimics, and psychiatric controls. Addict Behav 17:283–289, 1992

Mizes JS, Christiano BA: Assessment of cognitive variables relevant to cognitive behavioral perspectives on anorexia nervosa and bulimia nervosa. Behav Res Ther 33:95–105, 1995

Mizes JS, Klesges RC: Validity, reliability, and factor structure of the Anorectic Cognitions Questionnaire. Addict Behav 14:589–594, 1989

Bulimia Test—Revised (BULIT-R)

M. C. *Smith and* M. H. *Thelen*

GOALS

The Bulimia Test—Revised (BULIT-R) (Smith and Thelen 1984) is a self-report instrument designed to assist in the identification and diagnosis of bulimia nervosa. Consistent with the core diagnostic criteria for bulimia nervosa, the BULIT-R assesses binge eating, compensatory behavior, and weight and shape concerns. The BULIT-R was revised from the original BULIT to be consistent with the diagnostic criteria of DSM-III-R and has been validated with the DSM-IV criteria for bulimia nervosa as well. In addition to screening and diagnostic assessments, the BULIT-R is designed to provide a continuous score of bulimic symptomatology and thus a descriptive measure of overall symptom change.

DESCRIPTION

The BULIT-R is a self-administered 36-item questionnaire. All possible answers are specified using an item-specific 5-point Likert scale. The questionnaire is administered using paper and pencil, and all items should always be completed. Computer response forms may also be utilized for computer scoring. A shorter, 16-item version is also available and appears quite reliable, but it has had limited assessment of validity.

The questionnaire assesses all the core criteria for bulimia nervosa and provides the necessary response choices to determine whether respondents meet criteria for bulimia nervosa according to their own self-report. One of the major criteria measured by the BULIT-R is binge eating. Assessment of this behavior is often difficult because the term has a wide range of subjective definitions in the general population. One of the strengths of this questionnaire is that the criteria for binge eating are clearly specified, so that respondents have a uniform understanding of the questions that assess this behavior. Binge eating is defined and assessed in question 9 of the BULIT-R (see Example 29–3). Other items assess both

EXAMPLE 29-3 ■ Sample items from the Bulimia Test—Revised

How long have you been binge eating (eating uncontrollably to the point of stuffing yourself)?
1 = not applicable; I don't binge eat
2 =
3 =
4 =
5 = 3 or more years

I am satisfied with the shape and size of my body.
1 = frequently or always
2 =
3 =
4 =
5 = seldom or never

Reprinted with permission from Dr. Mark Thelen.

eating attitudes and behavior both during binge episodes and while not binge eating (see Example 29–3).

Eight items provide important descriptive and clinical information regarding bulimia nervosa but are not entered into the total score. The items assess the compensatory behaviors of using laxatives, using diuretics, fasting, and exercising. These compensatory behaviors are less frequent than vomiting but are nonetheless diagnostically important criteria. Each behavior is assessed by two items that probe for the frequency with which the respondent engages in these behaviors for the purpose of controlling or losing weight (e.g., "I use laxatives or suppositories to help control my weight," with response choices ranging from 1 = once a day or more to 5 = once a month or less, or never). The BULIT-R generates a single score by summation of 28 of the 36 items on the instrument (excluding the 8 items that measure compensatory behaviors as noted earlier). Thus, the total possible score ranges from 28 to 140. Several large-scale studies provide data regarding expected means for women with and without bulimia nervosa. Mean scores on the BULIT-R for young adult women without eating pathology consistently fall between 53 and 60. In contrast, mean scores on the BULIT-R for women with diagnoses of bulimia nervosa consistently fall between 114 and 120. The mean differences between the women with bulimia nervosa and the control subjects without bulimia nervosa are significantly different both statistically and clinically. As would be expected, mean scores for women with subthreshold bulimia nervosa and other eating disturbances (eating disorder not otherwise specified) tend to

fall between 68 and 91. In a relatively small but informative study of 20 women with eating pathology, those who met criteria for subthreshold bulimia nervosa had a mean BULIT-R score of 98. Women who were classified as binge eaters (without compensatory behaviors) had a mean score of 86.5, and women who reported purging but no binge eating had a mean score of 70.5. Given this continuum of eating pathology, the BULIT-R is able to distinguish between women with bulimia nervosa and those with no eating pathology. When the BULIT-R is used as a screening instrument, the misclassification of individuals is most likely to occur with individuals who meet criteria for eating disorder not otherwise specified. On the basis of these studies, the authors of the instrument have suggested a cutoff score of 104 for maximizing the identification of individuals with probable bulimia nervosa while minimizing the rate of false-positive diagnosis.

PRACTICAL ISSUES

It takes approximately 10 minutes to complete the questionnaire. The BULIT-R uses language that is easily understandable and unambiguous. The questionnaire and scoring instructions are available from

Mark Thelen, Ph.D.
Department of Psychology
210 McAlester Hall
University of Missouri–Columbia
Columbia, MO 65211
Phone: 573-882-7410
E-mail: psymt@showme.missouri.edu

There is no manual for the BULIT-R. The cost for the instrument and scoring procedures is $70.00 for a single study and $150.00 for ongoing research or clinical use.

PSYCHOMETRIC PROPERTIES

Reliability

The internal consistency of the BULIT-R was assessed in five studies ranging in sample size from 39 to 486 and ranging in sample characteristics from community samples without eating disorders to individuals identified as having bulimia nervosa or eating disorder not otherwise specified. On the basis of these studies, the BULIT-R has consistently demonstrated high internal consistency; alpha coefficients have ranged from 0.92 to 0.98. Test-retest reliability has also been documented in three studies ($n = 39$, 69, and 98); correlations ranged from 0.83 to 0.95 with a 6- to 8-week interval between administrations.

Validity

The BULIT-R correlates highly with the earlier version of the instrument ($r = 0.99$), and therefore earlier studies of concurrent validity of the BULIT can be interpreted as supportive of the validity of the BULIT-R as well. Studies that compared the BULIT-R with other related measures of bulimic symptoms showed a correlation ranging from 0.60 to 0.93 (e.g., the Bulimic Investigatory Test—Edinburgh [BITE] [Henderson and Freeman 1987], the Eating Attitudes Test [EAT] [Garner and Garfinkel 1979], the Eating Disorder Inventory [EDI] [p. 651], and the Binge Scale [Hawkins and Clement 1980]). Two-point, biserial correlations of the BULIT-R and DSM-III-R diagnosis of bulimia nervosa as assessed by clinical interview were 0.57 and 0.62. Thus, although the BULIT-R covers all the core criteria for bulimia nervosa and appears to have acceptable reliability, it cannot replace a clinical interview in diagnosing the disorder.

Validity studies that compared individuals with bulimia nervosa and individuals without eating disorders indicated that the BULIT-R can distinguish accurately between these groups but is less able to distinguish between individuals with bulimia nervosa and those with eating disorder not otherwise specified. The authors also note that, in the initial test construction, they included items designed to distinguish between individuals with anorexia nervosa and individuals with bulimia nervosa. However, in the psychometric studies, no items proved satisfactory in distinguishing these groups.

Using the recommended cutoff score of 104 for identifying individuals with bulimia nervosa, the BULIT-R has a sensitivity of 91% and a specificity of 96% for a clinical diagnosis of DSM-IV bulimia nervosa. When used as a screening measure in a nonclinical sample of 319 women, another study recommended a cutoff score of 98 to maximize the positive predictive value of the instrument. At this cutoff point, the BULIT-R had a sensitivity of 100% and a specificity of 99%. However, it is important to note that these higher sensitivity and specificity rates were determined on the basis of DSM-III-R criteria and reflect only one false-negative and one false-positive diagnosis.

One study demonstrated greater change on the original BULIT in 27 women with DSM-III bulimia who participated in treatment than in individuals who did not undergo treatment.

Two factor analyses of the BULIT-R were conducted on independent samples of 180 and 161 subjects. These analyses revealed five factors: binge and control, radical weight loss efforts, laxative use, vomiting, and exercise. However, scoring for the BULIT-R is determined on the basis of the total score, and subscale scores are not discussed.

CLINICAL UTILITY

The BULIT-R is a widely used and easily administered paper and pencil questionnaire that covers all the DSM-IV criteria for bulimia nervosa. Researchers used the BULIT-R successfully as a screening instrument in a two-stage assessment procedure; they used the BULIT-R to identify potential cases in stage 1 and then conducted clinical interviews in stage 2. The BULIT-R is also useful in clinical practice to describe change in bulimic symptoms over time or in response to treatment. Although the BULIT-R appears to be sensitive overall to detecting eating pathology and change in eating pathology, some points of caution should be noted. The BULIT-R should be considered a measure of eating pathology, with primary focus on binge eating and compensatory behavior; as such, it is a good screening instrument for detecting probable cases of bulimia nervosa. However, it is not intended to be utilized as a diagnostic instrument. At the same time, the BULIT-R is able to distinguish between eating disorder groups and control subjects without eating disorders, but because of the continuum of eating pathology across anorexia nervosa, bulimia nervosa, and binge eating disorder, a high score on the BULIT-R may be associated with any of these diagnoses.

In the case of anorexia nervosa, it is likely that individuals with subtype II (binge eating and purging subtype) would score high on the BULIT-R, although mean scores for this group are not currently available. On the basis of the provisional criteria provided for binge eating disorder in DSM-IV, it is likely that the BULIT-R could be used to screen for the disorder; however, certain limitations in this application are important to note. The BULIT-R does not assess the frequency of days per week on which an individual binge eats, which is required for the DSM-IV proposed criteria for binge eating disorder. Also, the duration question does not offer a response choice that would clearly indicate that someone has been binge eating for a minimum of 6 months, as would be required for a diagnosis of binge eating disorder. If the BULIT-R is to be used for screening for binge eating disorder, it would be advisable to append questions that assess the number of binge days per week and the duration of illness.

Finally, the BULIT-R has demonstrated that overall it is sensitive to change in eating disturbances; however, data from the original BULIT indicate that this instrument should not be used to replace more specific reports of daily self-monitoring of binge eating and vomiting. Data that compare the BULIT-R with such self-monitoring data are not available at this time.

REFERENCES AND SUGGESTED READINGS

Brelsford TN, Hummel RM, Barrios BA: The Bulimia Test Revised: a psychometric investigation. Psychological Assessment 4:399–401, 1992

Garner DM, Garfinkel PE: The Eating Attitudes Test: an index of the symptoms of anorexia nervosa. Psychol Med 9:273–279, 1979

Hawkins RC, Clement PF: Development and construct validation of self-report measure of binge eating tendencies. Addict Behav 5:219–226, 1980

Henderson M, Freeman CPL: A self-rating scale for bulimia: the "BITE." Br J Psychiatry 150:18–24, 1987

Smith MC, Thelen MH: Development and validation of a test for bulimia. J Consult Clin Psychol 52:863–872, 1984

Thelen MH, Farmer J: A revision of the Bulimia Test: BULIT-R. Psychological Assessment 3:119–124, 1991

Thelen MH, Mintz LB, Vander Wal JS: The Bulimia Test—Revised: validation with DSM-IV criteria for bulimia nervosa. Psychological Assessment 8:219–221, 1996

Welch G, Hall A: The reliability and discriminant validity of three potential measures of bulimic behaviours. J Psychiatr Res 23:125–133, 1989

Welch G, Thompson L, Hall A: The BULIT-R: its reliability and clinical validity as a screening tool for DSM-III-R bulimia nervosa in a female tertiary education population. Int J Eat Disord 14:95–105, 1993

Wertheim EH: Analysis of the internal consistency and component parts of the Bulimia Test using both university and eating problem samples. Int J Eat Disord 8:325–334, 1989

Williamson DA, Prather RC, Bennett SM, et al: An uncontrolled evaluation of inpatient and outpatient cognitive-behavior therapy for bulimia nervosa. Behav Modif 13:340–360, 1989

Questionnaire on Eating and Weight Patterns— Revised (QEWP-R)

R. L. Spitzer, S. Z. Yanovski, and M. D. Marcus

GOALS

The Questionnaire on Eating and Weight Patterns—Revised (QEWP-R) (Spitzer et al. 1994) is a screening instrument designed to assist in the identification and diagnosis of individuals with binge eating disorder, consistent with the provisional DSM-IV diagnostic criteria. The primary purpose of the measure is to screen for individuals with binge eating disorder, offer descriptive and demographic information related to binge eating disorder symptomatology, and distinguish probable cases of binge eating disorder from purging or nonpurging bulimia nervosa. Thus, the QEWP-R assesses the nature and frequency of overeating episodes, loss of control and distress associated with overeating, behavioral correlates of binge eating (e.g., eating more rapidly than usual, eating large amounts of food when not physically hungry, and eating alone because of embarrassment), and use of compensatory behaviors to avoid the weight gain associated with binge eating.

DESCRIPTION

The QEWP-R is a self-administered 28-item questionnaire. It is well organized and provides clear directions for the respondent regarding the time frame of reference. All the questions may not be applicable to the respondent, and therefore the QEWP-R has clear directions so that the respondents can follow appropriate skip patterns. The first nine questions of the QEWP-R assess demographic information regarding age, gender, ethnicity, education, height, weight, history of highest weight, history of overweight, and weight cycling. Items 10–15 ask specific questions about overeating behavior to determine whether the respondent regularly engages in binge eating. For example, if the respondent answers no to item 10, he or she skips to questions 15; otherwise, the respondent continues with question 11 (see Example 29–4). Once it is established that an individual engages in eating episodes that include an unusually large amount of food accompanied with a loss of control, behavioral frequency and distress symptoms are assessed. Questions 16–23 assess concerns about weight and shape and compensatory behavior (see Example 29–4).

The QEWP-R has also been administered in a clinical interview format. In a weight control study of 44 obese individuals, a kappa of 0.60 was obtained for a comparison of the self-report and clinical interview formats of the QEWP-R.

Because of the structure of this instrument, it does not yield an overall total score. Instead, the QEWP-R is to be scored on the basis of the decision rules provided for diagnosing binge eating disorder. Specifically, the diagnosis of binge eating disorder requires a response of 1 to questions 10 and 11; a response of 3, 4, or 5 to question 12; three or more items marked yes from 13 a–e; and a response of either 4 or 5 to either question 15 or question

16. The scoring procedures also provide specifications for the diagnosis of purging and nonpurging bulimia nervosa. The Binge Eating Syndrome subscale is scored by summing the frequency with which an individual endorses the eight items that assess loss of control, episodic overeating, and six binge-associated symptoms. Thus, the range of scores on this scale is 0–8.

PRACTICAL ISSUES

It takes 5–15 minutes to complete the questionnaire. The questionnaire should be scored by a trained examiner who is familiar with both the decision rules and the core diagnostic criteria for bulimia nervosa and binge eating disorder. The QEWP-R can also be administered in an interview format in which the questionnaire is read to the respondent. In such situations, the interviewer's familiarity with decision rules and core diagnostic criteria enhances the utility and objectivity of the instrument because consistent interpretations of behavior and threshold can be employed. For example, item 14c asks respondents to list all food eaten during a typical binge eating episode, and the interviewer's knowledge of thresholds for defining amounts of food required to constitute a binge standardizes the self-report data.

The QEWP-R is copyrighted by the authors (Spitzer et al. 1994) and is available along with scoring procedures from

> Susan Yanovski, M.D.
> Director, Obesity and Eating Disorders Program
> Building 45, Room 6AN-18B
> 45 Center Drive MSC 6600
> National Institute of Diabetes and Digestive and
>   Kidney Diseases
> Bethesda, MD 20892-6600
> Phone: 301-594-8880
> Fax: 301-480-8300
> E-mail: hyperlinkmalto.syz9f@nih.gov

An adolescent version of the QEWP-R is available in both self-report and parent-report versions. These versions of the QEWP-R are available from

> William Johnson, Ph.D.
> University of Mississippi, School of Medicine
> 2500 N. State Street

EXAMPLE 29–4 ■ Sample items from the Questionnaire on Eating and Weight Patterns—Revised

> 10. During the past **six** months, did you often eat within any two hour period what most people would regard as an unusually large amount of food? (Yes or No)
>
> 11. During the times when you ate this way, did you often feel you couldn't stop eating or control what or how much you were eating? (Yes or No)
>
> 18. During the past **three** months did you ever make yourself vomit in order to avoid gaining weight after binge eating? (Yes or No)

Reprinted with permission from Susan Yanovski, M.D.

Jackson, MS 39216-4505
Phone: 802-984-5805

Italian, Portuguese, and Spanish versions are available. The QEWP-R is included on the CD-ROM that accompanies this handbook.

PSYCHOMETRIC PROPERTIES

Reliability

The internal consistency of the QEWP-R was assessed in the initial multisite study of more than 1,700 individuals who were participating in weight loss programs and almost 1,000 individuals drawn from the community. Cronbach's alphas of 0.75 and 0.79 were found in the weight control and community samples, respectively. The individual item-subscale correlations ranged from 0.50 to 0.66 in the weight control samples and from 0.55 to 0.71 in the community samples.

In a sample of 52 individuals with binge eating behavior and 52 individuals without eating disorders, a test-retest reliability assessment of the QEWP-R over a 3-week interval resulted in kappa coefficients that ranged from 0.57 to 0.58. Stability of assessment of binge eating behavior as measured by the QEWP-R is supported by a relatively high correlation between weeks 1 and 3 of the probability of binge eating ($r = 0.70$).

Validity

Using self-monitoring reports from 52 self-referred individuals with eating disorders, researchers assessed the ability of the QEWP-R to discriminate between those with high- and low-frequency binge eating behavior. The QEWP-R demonstrated a sensitivity of about 75% and a specificity of about 66%, resulting in an overall predictive efficiency of approximately 70%.

In a study of 100 obese women, the agreement between the QEWP-R and clinical diagnosis determined by the Structured Clinical Interview for DSM-IV Axis I Disorders (SCID-I) (p. 49) was modest; the chance-corrected kappa coefficient was 0.57. Interestingly, the differences between the QEWP-R and the SCID-I were not due to the QEWP-R overestimating the number of individuals with binge eating disorder compared with the SCID-I, which is often the case in such screening instruments. The QEWP-R identified 40 cases of binge eating disorder compared with 43 identified on the basis of ex-

pert clinical interviews. Discrepancies between the QEWP-R and the SCID-I were due to the tendency of individuals to report less frequent binge episodes, less loss of control associated with overeating, and more marked distress on their self-report than experts rated them on the basis of the SCID-I interviews.

CLINICAL UTILITY

The QEWP-R is an easily administered questionnaire that can be used to screen individuals in the general population for binge eating disorder and to distinguish between binge eating disorder and purging and nonpurging bulimia nervosa. It has also been administered as a clinical interview. It can be administered to both clinical and community samples with fair reliability and validity. One strength of the QEWP-R is that it is a criterion-based instrument that assesses the specific diagnostic variables associated with binge eating disorder. The wording of the QEWP-R regarding the frequency and duration of binge eating is consistent with the DSM-IV proposed diagnostic criteria for binge eating disorder but not for bulimia nervosa. Therefore, the QEWP-R criteria are better suited to identifying probable cases of binge eating disorder than of bulimia nervosa.

Because the concordance between the QEWP-R and clinical interview is only fair, the QEWP-R should not be the exclusive means of diagnosing binge eating disorder in community or clinical studies. As a screening instrument the QEWP-R can clearly identify probable cases of binge eating disorder, which can be confirmed by clinical interview.

The QEWP-R can also be used as a continuous measure of binge eating symptomatology on the basis of the identified Binge Eating Syndrome subscale of the QEWP-R.

REFERENCES AND SUGGESTED READINGS

Brody ML, Walsh BT, Devlin MJ: Binge eating disorder: reliability and validity of a new diagnostic category. J Consult Clin Psychol 62:381–386, 1994 de Zwaan M, Mitchell JE, Specker SM, et al: Diagnosing binge eating disorder: level of agreement between self-report and expert-rating. Int J Eat Disord 14:289–295, 1993

Nangle DW, Johnson WG, Carr-Nangle RE, et al: Binge eating disorder and the proposed DSM-IV criteria: psychometric analysis of the Questionnaire of Eating and Weight Patterns. Int J Eat Disord 16:147–157, 1994

Pike KM, Loeb K, Walsh BT: Binge eating and purging, in Handbook of Assessment Methods for Eating Behaviors and Weight-Related Problems. Edited by Allison DB. London, Sage, 1995, pp 303–346

Spitzer RL, Devlin M, Walsh BT, et al: Binge eating disorder: a multisite field trial of the diagnostic criteria. Int J Eat Disord 11:191–203, 1992

Spitzer RL, Yanovski S, Wadden T, et al: Binge eating disorder: its further validation in a multistate study. Int J Eat Disord 13:137–153, 1993

Spitzer RL, Yanovski SZ, Marcus MD: Questionnaire on Eating and Weight Patterns—Revised. Behavioral Measurement Database Services (Producer), McLean, VA, BRS Search Service (Vendor) (Hopi Record), 1994

Eating Disorder Examination (EDE)

C. G. Fairburn and Z. Cooper

GOALS

The Eating Disorder Examination (EDE) (Cooper and Fairburn 1987; Fairburn and Cooper 1993) is a semistructured interview designed to provide a comprehensive assessment of the specific psychopathology of eating disorders. A serious gap in the field of eating disorders was filled by the development of the EDE, both because of its thorough coverage of eating pathology and because it is an interviewer-based assessment rather than a self-report measure. The major clinical advantage of the EDE is that it is designed to generate operationally defined eating disorder diagnoses on the basis of the DSM-IV criteria and to assess the severity of eating pathology. The EDE is designed to cover the full range of specific eating disorder

pathology, including key behavioral problems (i.e., overeating and the use of extreme methods of weight control), associated disturbances in terms of caloric restraint and eating, shape and weight concerns, and eating disorder diagnoses. The EDE was designed primarily for use in studies of the psychopathology of eating disorders and for clinical investigations into the effects of treatment. It can be used in the assessment of eating pathology for individuals ages 16 years and older, and a children's version is available for individuals ages 8–15 years.

DESCRIPTION

The original EDE included five subscales; however, the most recent version (12.01) was shortened to include four subscales: Restraint, Eating Concern, Weight Concern, and Shape Concern. The EDE-12.01 also includes items that contribute to the assessment of two key behavioral aspects of eating disorders (overeating and extreme methods of weight control), as well as diagnostic items sufficient to determine a diagnosis of anorexia nervosa, bulimia nervosa, or eating disorder not otherwise specified. However, the diagnostic items on the EDE do not include sufficient detail to determine a diagnosis of binge eating disorder. Questions regarding loss of control, distress after overeating, and duration of binge eating need to be added to the EDE to elicit sufficient information to diagnose binge eating disorder.

The EDE distinguishes between three forms of overeating, on the basis of the presence or absence of the two basic criteria for binge eating: loss of control and consumption of what most people would consider a large amount of food. An objective bulimic episode includes both of these criteria and would be counted in terms of diagnosis. Objective overeating is defined as the consumption of a large amount of food without the associated loss of control. A subjective bulimic episode includes the experience of loss of control but the absence of an objectively large amount of food.

Each of the questions on the EDE has at least one mandatory probe question and several optional subsidiary questions. These questions are designed to help the interviewer elicit sufficient information to make adequate ratings. Ratings are determined by the interviewer, and clear instructions are given for how to make ratings. A sample item from the EDE (Restraint subscale) is provided in Example 29–5.

The EDE is concerned with the present state of the patient, and therefore most questions refer to the patient's behaviors and attitudes over the previous 4 weeks, with the exception of diagnostic questions, which require assessment of the previous 3 months (e.g., frequency and duration of objective binge episodes).

Items on the EDE are scored in terms of either their severity (0 = absence of the feature to 6 = feature present to an extreme degree) or their frequency of occurrence at a certain threshold of severity (0 = absence of the feature to 6 = present every day). Subscale scores on the EDE are calculated on the basis of the mean of the appropriate items. The EDE Global score measures the overall severity of eating pathology and is the mean score of the four subscale scores. Decision rules for determining DSM-IV diagnoses on the basis of the EDE questions are outlined by Fairburn and Cooper (1993).

A self-report version (EDE-Q) and a slightly modified version of the EDE interview for use with children (ChEDE) have been developed. The EDE-Q is a 38-item questionnaire rated on a 7-point Likert scale. The EDE-Q uses the same initial probe questions and rating scale as the interview, although frequencies of behavioral disturbances are rated on the basis of the number of days rather than the number of episodes. The ChEDE is modified slightly with simplified language to facilitate comprehension. It can be used for children ages 8–15 years. Overall, data from the questionnaire and interview versions of the EDE are highly consistent on measures of dietary restraint, eating, weight and shape concerns, self-induced vomiting, and laxative misuse. However, some data suggest that the questionnaire version results in slightly higher scores than the interview version, especially in terms of binge eating.

EXAMPLE 29–5 ■ Sample item from the Eating Disorder Examination

Over the past 4 weeks have you gone for periods of 8 or more waking hours without eating anything?

```
0 = no such days
1 =
2 =
3 =
4 =
5 =
6 = avoidance every day
```

Reprinted with permission from Dr. Christopher Fairburn.

Group means and standard deviations from the EDE are provided in Table 29–3.

PRACTICAL ISSUES

The EDE is designed to be administered by interviewers trained in the assessment of eating disorders. The time required to complete the interviews varies considerably depending on the severity of eating pathology. Most interviews can be completed within 30–60 minutes. The EDE interview, scoring description, and instructions for interviewers are copyrighted and are provided in the chapter by Fairburn and Cooper (1993). Although there is no charge for using the EDE, proper training is essential before administering the interview. Training tapes are not currently available; however, Dr. Fairburn and other senior eating disorder experts have provided on-site training for the EDE for numerous eating disorder programs. A copy of the measure may be obtained from the author:

> Dr. Christopher Fairburn
> Department of Psychiatry
> Warneford Hospital
> Oxford OX# 7JX
> England

PSYCHOMETRIC PROPERTIES

Reliability

A satisfactory degree of internal consistency on the EDE has been demonstrated; Cronbach's alphas ranged from 0.68 to 0.90 for all subscales. Joint reliability studies have also demonstrated good reliability for the EDE. The initial psychometric report of the EDE included an assessment of three trained raters—each of whom administered four interviews and rated the recorded interviews of the other interviewers. There were a total of 12 subjects, 9 of whom met criteria for bulimia nervosa and 3 of whom had no eating disorder. Subsequent studies have reported similarly high interrater reliability. Pearson product moment correlation coefficients were consistently high. There was perfect agreement among raters for 27 of the 62 items, and the coefficients of the other items ranged from 0.69 to 1.0; two of the three items whose correlation coefficients were <0.9 were dropped for the current ver-

TABLE 29–3 ■ Eating Disorder Examination means and standard deviations for the subscales

	RESTRAINT	BULIMIA[a]	EATING CONCERN	WEIGHT CONCERN	SHAPE CONCERN
Bulimia nervosa[b] n = 53	3.14 (1.22)	3.42 (0.79)	2.43 (1.30)	3.14 (1.44)	3.55 (1.35)
Bulimia nervosa[c] n = 15	3.27 (0.26)	2.61 (0.22)	2.40 (0.34)	3.96 (0.34)	3.82 (0.31)
Bulimia nervosa[d] n = 28	3.70 (1.70)	3.40 (0.90)	3.50 (1.40)	3.80 (1.70)	4.10 (1.10)
Bulimia nervosa[e] n = 125	3.45 (1.18)	2.17 (0.86)	2.63 (1.42)	3.73 (0.39)	3.90 (1.28)
Anorexia nervosa[b] n = 47	3.17 (1.47)	1.58 (1.55)	2.17 (1.62)	2.40 (1.48)	2.85 (1.22)
Anorexia nervosa[d] n = 50	3.80 (1.70)	1.90 (0.90)	2.80 (1.40)	2.90 (1.50)	3.50 (1.60)
Restrained eaters[c] n = 15	3.15 (0.33)	0.14 (0.10)	1.25 (0.23)	2.12 (0.19)	2.55 (0.20)
Dieters[e] n = 57	1.66 (1.07)		0.50 (0.84)	1.79 (0.92)	1.99 (1.13)
Overweight subjects[e] n = 15	1.69 (1.35)		0.64 (0.86)	1.92 (1.24)	1.97 (1.33)
Psychiatrically healthy control subjects[b] n = 42	0.91 (0.91)	0.41 (0.87)	0.22 (0.33)	0.52 (0.62)	0.64 (0.75)
Psychiatrically healthy control subjects[e] n = 337	0.79 (0.79)		0.20 (0.51)	1.00 (0.87)	1.14 (0.98)

[a]The Bulimia subscale is not included in the current version of the EDE (12.01).
[b]Cooper et al. (1989).
[c]Wilson and Smith (1989).
[d]Beumont et al. (1993).
[e]Fairburn and Wilson (1993). (Overweight is defined as a body mass index ≥30.)

sion of the instrument. Subsequent studies of joint reliability have reported results consistent with these data.

Validity

Both individual items and subscale scores have been shown to discriminate groups with eating disorders from control subjects without eating disorders. Furthermore, in a study that compared patients with bulimia nervosa and highly restrained eaters, the EDE yielded significant differences between the groups on all but the Restraint subscale, whereas a self-report measure of eating disorder psychopathology (the Eating Disorder Inventory [EDI] [p. 651]) did not. However, another study found that the EDE Shape Concern and Weight Concern subscales did not show any advantage over a self-report measure (the Body Shape Questionnaire [BSQ] [p. 654]) in discriminating between women with eating disorders and control subjects with restrained eating patterns.

Comparisons of daily self-monitoring and EDE data regarding the frequency of binge eating and vomiting indicate a consistently high correlation between daily self-monitoring and EDE ratings of vomiting frequency ($r = 0.90$–0.95). The correlation between daily self-monitoring and binge frequency has also been shown to be high for individuals in treatment for bulimia nervosa ($r = 0.90$ before treatment and $r = 0.91$ after treatment). In contrast, for individuals with binge eating disorder, one study reported that the correlation between the interview and self-report versions of the EDE yielded estimates of binge eating frequencies that were only slightly related to each other.

The EDE has been shown to be sensitive to changes in eating pathology in many clinical trials. For example, in a 1-year outcome study of three forms of treatment for bulimia nervosa, those who had a good outcome also had substantially decreased EDE subscale scores. These scores were within 1 standard deviation of the scores obtained from a general population sample of women of the same age.

CLINICAL UTILITY

The EDE fills a major gap in the assessment of eating disorders because it is a clinician-based interview and it provides sufficient data for both diagnosis and a comprehensive description of eating pathology. This interview is widely used for clinical treatment studies for eating disorders and has documented sensitivity to change in eating pathology.

The primary application of the EDE has been in clinical research; however, its utility may be extended to many clinical settings. It is the only standardized interview for eating disorders that provides both diagnostic data and continuous data regarding the severity of symptomatology. Thus, it can be useful in distinguishing the different eating disturbances and tailoring treatment interventions to address the specific eating symptoms identified by the interview. Furthermore, given its sensitivity to change, the EDE may be useful in documenting patient progress in treatment.

Despite these clear advantages, the EDE requires extensive training and therefore may not be practical in certain settings. It is costly to use because of the training requirements, including the significant amount of time needed to complete training. Also, one of the strengths of the EDE can be a disadvantage at times in that the level of detail assessed by the EDE requires intense concentration and recall. Some individuals find this level of detail difficult to tolerate because of either shame, difficulty concentrating, or severe disorganization or depression. In these situations, the EDE-Q may prove to be the most appropriate choice in informing clinical diagnosis and treatment planning.

REFERENCES AND SUGGESTED READINGS

Beumont PJV, Kopee Schrader EM, Talbot P, et al: Measuring the specific psychopathology of eating disorder patients. Aust N Z J Psychiatry 27(3):506–511, 1993

Black CMD, Wilson GT: Assessment of eating disorders: interview versus questionnaire. Int J Eat Disord 20:43–50, 1996

Bryant-Waugh RJ, Cooper PJ, Taylor CL, et al: The use of the Eating Disorder Examination with children: a pilot study. Int J Eat Disord 19:391–397, 1996

Cooper Z, Fairburn CG: The Eating Disorder Examination: a semi-structured interview for the assessment of the specific psychopathology of eating disorders. Int J Eat Disord 6:1–8, 1987

Cooper Z, Cooper PJ, Fairburn CG: The validity of the Eating Disorder Examination and its subscales. Br J Psychiatry 154:807–812, 1989

Fairburn CG, Beglin SJ: Assessment of eating disorders: interview or self-report questionnaire? Int J Eat Disord 16:363–370, 1994

Fairburn CG, Cooper Z (eds): The Eating Disorder Examination, 12th Edition, in Binge Eating: Nature, Assessment, and Treatment. Edited by Fairburn CG, Wilson GT. New York, Guilford, 1993, pp 317–360

Fairburn CG, Wilson GT (eds): Binge Eating: Nature, Assessment, and Treatment. New York, Guilford, 1993

Loeb KL, Pike KM, Walsh BT, et al: Assessment of diagnostic features of bulimia nervosa: interview versus self-report format. Int J Eat Disord 16:75–81, 1994

Rosen JC, Vara L, Wendt S, et al: Validity studies of the Eating Disorder Examination. Int J Eat Disord 9:519–528, 1990

Wilfley DE, Schwartz MB, Spurrell EB, et al: Assessing the specific psychopathology of binge eating disorder patients: interview or self-report? Behav Res Ther 35:1151–1159, 1997

Wilson GT, Smith D: Assessment of bulimia nervosa: an evaluation of the Eating Disorders Examination. Int J Eat Disord 8:173–179, 1989

CHAPTER 30

Sleep Disorders Measures

Ruth Benca, M.D., Ph.D.
Thomas Kwapil, Ph.D.

INTRODUCTION

Major Domains

This chapter covers selected nonlaboratory measures that provide clinically relevant information in the evaluation of sleep disorders. Included are screening questionnaires for sleep disorders as well as measures of daytime sleepiness and sleep disturbance that provide clinically relevant information about disturbances in sleep and wakefulness but do not provide specific information about clinical diagnosis. No nonlaboratory measure alone is sufficient to diagnose a specific sleep disorder.

Sleep disturbances assessed by these scales include sleep apnea, narcolepsy, periodic limb movements, idiopathic hypersomnia (comparable to the DSM-IV category primary hypersomnia), disorders that cause insomnia, and sleep disturbances related to psychiatric disorders. (Note that these domains do not correspond precisely to DSM-IV diagnostic categories.) Patients with primary sleep disorders (i.e., disorders that are not secondary to another psychiatric diagnosis, such as sleep apnea, narcolepsy, and periodic leg movements) may show abnormalities on any or all of the scales. Circadian rhythm disorders, parasomnias, and substance-induced sleep disorders are not covered in this book because they are secondary to other conditions and because separate scales for assessing these types of sleep disturbances are not available. Scales for children are not included be-

cause of space limitations and also because scales that assess sleep disturbances in children are less well developed than those for use in adults.

Many patients with psychiatric disorders other than a sleep disorder may experience sleep problems that can be assessed using these instruments. Sleep disturbance in psychiatric patients may be secondary to their psychiatric illness, its treatment, or medications taken for other general medical conditions or may indicate the presence of a primary sleep disorder.

There is a long tradition of using various sleep logs or diaries to assess sleep patterns for clinical and research purposes (Akerstedt et al. 1994; Haythornthwaite et al. 1991; Monk et al. 1994). Although these instruments generally provide useful descriptive information, it is difficult to assess their reliability and validity in a manner that allows for meaningful comparisons. Therefore, sleep diaries are not specifically reviewed in this chapter. However, sleep logs may be quite helpful in documenting sleep schedule disturbances, poor sleep hygiene, or response to treatment.

Organization

The chapter begins with scales that have the widest coverage in terms of types of sleep disturbances that are being assessed (Table 30–1). The first two scales, the Sleep Disorders Questionnaire (SDQ) and the Pittsburgh Sleep Quality Index (PSQI), are the most comprehensive in that they focus on several aspects of disturbed sleep. The

TABLE 30–1 ■ Sleep disorders measures

NAME OF MEASURE	DISORDER OR CONSTRUCT ASSESSED	FORMAT	PAGES
Sleep Disorders Questionnaire (SDQ)	Sleep disturbances during past 6 months; subscales include Narcolepsy, Sleep Apnea, Periodic Limb Movement Disturbance, Psychiatric Sleep Disorder, Posttraumatic Stress Disorder, and Total Response Validity	Self-report questionnaire; 176 items	676–678
Pittsburgh Sleep Quality Index (PSQI)*	Sleep quality during the previous month	Self-report questionnaire; 19 items	678–680
Excessive Daytime Sleepiness and Nocturnal Sleep subscales of the Sleep/Wake Activity Inventory (SWAI)*	Daytime sleepiness and sleep disturbance	Self-report questionnaire; 59 items	680–682
Epworth Sleepiness Scale (ESS)*	Overall level of daytime sleepiness	Self-report questionnaire; 8 items	682–684
Stanford Sleepiness Scale (SSS)	Changes in sleepiness over short periods	Self-report questionnaire; 1 item	684–685

*Measure is included on the CD-ROM that accompanies this handbook.

Excessive Daytime Sleepiness and Nocturnal Sleep sub-scales of the Sleep/Wake Activity Inventory (SWAI) are included next; they highlight daytime sleepiness and also briefly cover some elements of nocturnal sleep disturbance. The remaining two scales, the Epworth Sleepiness Scale (ESS) and the Stanford Sleepiness Scale (SSS), cover daytime sleepiness exclusively.

Relevant Measures Included Elsewhere in the Handbook

Patients with mood disorder with a seasonal pattern (e.g., major depressive disorder or bipolar disorder, depressed phase) usually experience excessive daytime sleepiness. Measurement of sleep disturbances in association with mood disorders is reviewed elsewhere (see Chapter 24, "Mood Disorders Measures").

USING MEASURES IN THIS DOMAIN

Goals of Assessment

The gold standard in the diagnosis of sleep-wake disorders is a laboratory evaluation—the sleep polysomnogram—combined with clinical history. The time and expense of this laboratory tool, however, suggests a

potential role for clinical screening tools that could identify those in need of polysomnographic evaluation.

Another domain of clinically relevant information is response to treatment. Clinical tools that are sensitive to change and correspond sufficiently to polysomnogram findings over time could substitute for the polysomnogram in assessment of outcome when more than a clinical evaluation is needed.

Thus, measures in this domain are primarily intended as first-line screening tools to identify significant sleep disturbance in patients in sleep clinics and in general medical and psychiatric settings. Some measures identify the nature of sleep problems and therefore suggest a range of possible clinical diagnoses. These measures may also be used to monitor longitudinal course and treatment outcome. They are not primarily designed to help clinicians develop treatment strategies.

Implementation Issues

The existence of an objective gold standard for diagnosing sleep disorders allows for direct criterion validation of paper and pencil screening measures of sleep disturbance—an option that is not available for many other psychiatric domains. As a screening measure, polysomnographic testing can be both expensive and time-consuming compared with paper and pencil measures.

Although none of the currently available screening measures replaces the combination of polysomnography and careful clinical assessment as definitive diagnostic tools, the availability of brief, inexpensive, and noninvasive measures of sleep disturbance may help to identify individuals who require further assessment for sleep disorders.

As with any measure of pathology, the possibility exists that respondents may over- or underreport their symptoms of sleep disturbance. Therefore, the measures discussed in this chapter should be used primarily as screening measures, and other sources of information (e.g., reports of family members, clinical history, and polysomnography) should be obtained whenever possible. Furthermore, individual differences in sleep needs should also be considered when interpreting the results of these measures.

It should be noted that fatigue and sleepiness are not equivalent. Sleepiness refers to an increased tendency to fall asleep, whereas fatigue may not be associated with an increased propensity to sleep. For example, individuals with insomnia often complain of fatigue but do not fall asleep quickly as measured by the multiple sleep latency test (MSLT). Some scales have been validated for sleepiness, not fatigue, but patients with fatigue (e.g., patients with chronic fatigue syndrome) may have elevated scores on these scales. Different instruments have different specificities for assessing sleepiness and fatigue. For example, the Visual Analogue Scale for Fatigue (VAS-F) (Lee et al. 1991) is sensitive to both sleepiness and fatigue.

Issues in Interpreting Psychometric Data

Instruments that assess specific symptoms (such as sleepiness) have the advantage of brevity but tend to have questionable reliability and validity. Longer, empirically derived questionnaires tend to have better psychometric characteristics.

The existence of an objective gold standard (i.e., polysomnography) largely mandates its use as a validator for measures in this domain. Although the sleep scales discussed in this chapter are inexact measures, they may help to identify patients who might benefit from further clinical evaluation and intervention. Not all patients who show abnormalities on these scales require polysomnographic studies, however.

GUIDE TO THE SELECTION OF MEASURES

Excessive daytime sleepiness is a common feature of many sleep disorders (particularly sleep apnea and narcolepsy), psychiatric illnesses (e.g., depression), and medical disorders and may occur as a side effect of medical and psychiatric treatments. Although the ESS and the SSS both provide brief assessments of daytime sleepiness, the ESS is more consistently correlated with the MSLT, the gold standard for measuring sleepiness. Other measures that include assessment of daytime sleepiness are the SWAI and the PSQI. The SWAI provides a more comprehensive measure of daytime sleepiness than either the SSS or the ESS. The PSQI is particularly useful in assessing overall sleep quality, including disturbances in falling asleep and maintaining sleep.

The SDQ was developed to provide diagnostic rather than descriptive information. It is the longest of the measures reviewed in this chapter but is also the most diagnostically specific. The PSQI and the SDQ appear to be the most useful for general screening of clinical and nonclinical populations.

CURRENT STATUS AND FUTURE RESEARCH NEEDS FOR ASSESSMENT

In general, clinical information about sleep disturbance has not been obtained in a psychometrically rigorous fashion because of the existence of objective neurophysiological measures. Recent scales represent an attempt to develop psychometrically sound instruments validated by polysomnography. Although the development of screening measures for sleep disorders is not as advanced as in other psychiatric domains, this domain has the advantage of having an objective standard that can be used for validation of psychometric instruments. However, comparisons of psychometric and laboratory measures of sleep disturbance have often produced mixed results, which suggest that either the paper and pencil measures fail to adequately tap aspects of sleep disturbance (see Johnson et al. 1990) or the screening measures assess different aspects of sleep disturbances than do measures such as the MSLT (see Chervin et al. 1997). Further validation and refinement of current instruments, as well as development of instruments for assessing the full range of sleep disorders in our nosologies (e.g., circadian rhythm disorders and parasomnias), are clearly needed. Norms should be established with reference to gender, age, and ethnicity and in psychiatric, medical, and nonpatient groups. In addition, scales or subscales that assess sleep disturbance should be incorporated into standard psychiatric screening questionnaires.

REFERENCES AND SUGGESTED READINGS

Akerstedt T, Hume K, Minors D, et al: The subjective meaning of good sleep: an intraindividual approach using the Karolinska Sleep Diary. Percept Mot Skills 79:287–296, 1994

American Sleep Disorders Association: The International Classification of Sleep Disorders. Diagnostic and Coding Manual. Lawrence, KS, Allen Press, 1990

Chervin RD, Aldrich MS, Pickett R, et al: Comparison of the results of the Epworth Sleepiness Scale and the multiple sleep latency test. J Psychosom Res 42:145–155, 1997

Haythornthwaite JA, Hegel MT, Kerns RD: Development of a sleep diary for chronic pain patients. J Pain Symptom Manage 6:65–72, 1991

Johnson LC, Spinweber CL, Gomez SA, et al: Daytime sleepiness, performance, mood, nocturnal sleep: the effects of benzodiazepine and caffeine on their relationship. Sleep 13:121–135, 1990

Kryger MH, Roth T, Dement WC: Principles and Practice of Sleep Medicine, 2nd Edition. Philadelphia, PA, WB Saunders, 1989

Lee KA, Hicks G, Nino-Murcia G: Validity and reliability of a scale to assess fatigue. Psychiatry Res 36:291–298, 1991

Monk TH, Reynolds CF, Kupfer DJ: The Pittsburgh Sleep Diary. Journal of Sleep Research 3:111–120, 1994

Sleep Disorders Questionnaire (SDQ)

A. Douglass, R. Bornstein, and G. Nino-Murcia

GOALS

The Sleep Disorders Questionnaire (SDQ) (Douglass et al. 1986) was developed to provide reliable and valid differential diagnostic information regarding sleep disorders and to assess sleep disturbances during the past 6 months. The questionnaire contains empirically derived primary subscales developed to distinguish diagnostic groups. The initial four subscales are Narcolepsy, Sleep Apnea, Periodic Limb Movement Disturbance, and Psychiatric Sleep Disorder. The items in the Psychiatric Sleep Disorder subscale include primarily anxious and dysphoric symptoms that interfere with sleep, such as "racing thoughts at bedtime" and "sad/depressed at bedtime." Three additional subscales—Chronic Fatigue Syndrome, Posttraumatic Stress Disorder, and Total Response Validity—have subsequently been derived. The items in the SDQ were refined from the Sleep Questionnaire and Assessment of Wakefulness (SQAW) (Guilleminault et al. 1982). Items selected from the SQAW had a high completion rate, differentiated among clinical groups, and described symptoms of a major sleep disorder.

DESCRIPTION

The SDQ is a self-report scale that contains 176 items that are each rated on a 5-point scale from 1 = never (strongly disagree) to 5 = always (strongly agree). The scale contains 143 items that inquire about the frequency and severity of disturbances of sleep and wakefulness over the past 6 months, 4 items for women that inquire about sleep disturbance during pregnancy and menopause, 5 items for men regarding erectile dysfunction, and 23 items that inquire about demographic characteristics. A final item, body mass, is computed by the examiner and scored on a 5-point scale. All items are written at an eighth-grade reading level.

The SDQ produces six factor-derived subscales and a Total Response Validity subscale. Douglass et al. (1995)

recommend that the total score on the SDQ be in the range of 193–527 to be considered valid. The range of scores is 12–60 on the Sleep Apnea subscale, 15–75 on the Narcolepsy subscale, 9–45 on both the Periodic Limb Movement Disturbance and the Psychiatric Sleep Disorder subscales, 10–50 on the Chronic Fatigue Syndrome subscale, and 11–55 on the Posttraumatic Stress Disorder subscale.

PRACTICAL ISSUES

It takes approximately 30 minutes for most patients to complete the full 176-item scale. Although only 45 of the 176 items are required to compute the four primary subscales, the authors recommend administration of the entire scale to create a database and to facilitate the development of new subscales. A scoring manual (Douglass 1993) is provided with the questionnaire. Scoring graphs included in the manual show percentile distributions for nonpatient and patient samples for each of the four initial factor-derived scales. Administration and scoring can be facilitated by the use of computer software (available for $25.00 from the primary author). The SDQ is copyrighted but is distributed without charge by the primary author. Dutch, French, German, Italian, Spanish, Swedish, and Turkish translations are available. Sources for translations are available from the primary author:

A. B. Douglass, M.D.
Department of Psychiatry
University of Michigan
1500 E. Medical Center Drive
Ann Arbor, MI 48109-0840

PSYCHOMETRIC PROPERTIES

Reliability

In a sample ($N = 519$) of patients from a sleep disorders clinic and psychiatrically healthy control subjects, Cronbach's alpha ranged from 0.70 to 0.86 for the four original subscales and the Posttraumatic Stress Disorder subscale. However, these values may be somewhat inflated because they were computed from the same sample used to derive the subscales on the basis of factor analysis. Values have

not been reported for the Chronic Fatigue Syndrome and Total Response Validity subscales.

Test-retest reliability (average interval of 3–4 months) with 130 patients with sleep disorders ranged from 0.75 to 0.85 for each of the four primary subscales.

Validity

The sensitivity and specificity of the primary subscales were computed separately for male and female subjects using receiver operating characteristic analysis with a sample of 519 subjects (both individuals with sleep disturbances and control subjects). Sensitivity and specificity were computed on the basis of polysomnography and clinical assessment of sleep disorders. The sensitivity and specificity of the Posttraumatic Stress Disorder subscale were computed in a sample of 367 patients with diagnoses of sleep disorders and posttraumatic stress disorder as determined by structured diagnostic interviews. Sensitivity and specificity values were not available for the Chronic Fatigue Syndrome subscale. The cut points, sensitivity, and specificity are shown in Table 30–2.

The primary subscales successfully distinguished patients with sleep apnea, narcolepsy, periodic limb movement disturbance, and psychiatric sleep disturbances as diagnosed by clinical interviews, nocturnal polysomnography, and the multiple sleep latency test (MSLT). Further information on the relation between polysomnography and scores on the SDQ is in preparation.

CLINICAL UTILITY

The SDQ was designed as a simple self-report diagnostic measure, as opposed to measures of subjective sleep quality, and as an inexpensive screening instrument. The authors note that the measure does not replace polysomnography as a means of deriving accurate diagnoses. However, the scale can be used to provide initial screening information that might not be obtained as part of a clinical interview.

Preliminary data on the SDQ have been collected from patients seeking treatment for sleep disorders. The scale may also be useful for screening other patient populations with illnesses associated with excessive sleepiness, although additional normative data are needed. The SDQ is a cost-effective method of reliably identifying individuals with excessive daytime sleepiness and is also

TABLE 30–2 ■ Cut points, sensitivity, and specificity of the Sleep Disorders Questionnaire

Subscale	Gender	Cut point	Sensitivity	Specificity
Sleep Apnea	M	36	0.85	0.76
	F	32	0.88	0.81
Narcolepsy	M	30	0.84	0.68
	F	31	0.80	0.72
Psychiatric Sleep Disorders	M	19	0.79	0.65
	F	21	0.79	0.64
Periodic Limb Movement Disturbance	M	21	0.67	0.46
	F	21	0.65	0.49
Posttraumatic Stress Disorder	M	26	0.80	0.75

appropriate for use in assessing sleepiness in groups or individually for research purposes.

The SDQ has been used primarily in sleep disorder clinics, but it may also be useful to evaluate patients with significant sleep complaints in other medical or psychiatric settings. However, the performance of the scale at sites other than that of the author has yet to be evaluated. Completion of the entire scale provides a useful database for both clinical evaluation and the derivation of additional subscales. Whether the length of the SDQ will preclude its use in screening for sleep disorders in the general population is not known. The SDQ provides important diagnostic information about sleep disorders, but the scale is not a replacement for polysomnographic assessment for sleep disorders.

REFERENCES AND SUGGESTED READINGS

Douglass AB: Sleep Disorders Questionnaire (SDQ) Scoring Manual—Version B. Ann Arbor, MI, Douglass, 1993

Douglass AB, Bornstein R, Nino-Murcia G, et al: Creation of the "ASDC Sleep Disorders Questionnaire" (abstract). Sleep Research 15:117, 1986

Douglass AB, Shipley JE, Nino-Murcia G, et al: Validation of the "Psych" scale of the Sleep Disorders Questionnaire (SDQ) (abstract). Sleep Research 21:150, 1992

Douglass AB, Bornstein R, Nino-Murcia G, et al: The Sleep Disorders Questionnaire, I: creation and multivariate structure of SDQ. Sleep 17:160–167, 1994

Douglass AB, Man G, Baran S, et al: Creation of a total-of-responses validity scale "TOT" for the Sleep Disorders Questionnaire (SDQ) (abstract). Sleep Research 24:470, 1995

Douglass AB, Liberzon I, Amdur R, et al: Creation of a PTSD scale for the Sleep Disorders Questionnaire (SDQ, unpublished data).

Guilleminault C (ed): Sleeping and Waking Disorders: Indications and Techniques. Menlo Park, CA, Addison-Wesley, 1982

Pittsburgh Sleep Quality Index (PSQI)

D. J. Buysse, C. F. Reynolds III, T. H. Monk, S. R. Berman, and D. J. Kupfer

GOALS

The Pittsburgh Sleep Quality Index (PSQI) (Buysse et al. 1989a) was developed to measure sleep quality during the previous month and to discriminate between good and poor sleepers. Sleep quality is a complex phenomenon that involves several dimensions, each of which is covered by the PSQI. The covered domains include Subjective Sleep Quality, Sleep Latency, Sleep Duration, Habitual Sleep Efficiency, Sleep Disturbances, Use of Sleep Medications, and Daytime Dysfunction.

DESCRIPTION

The PSQI is composed of 19 self-rated questions and 5 questions rated by a bed partner or roommate (only the self-rated items are used in scoring the scale). The self-administered scale contains 15 multiple-choice items that inquire about frequency of sleep disturbances and subjective sleep quality and 4 write-in items that inquire about typical bedtime, wake-up time, sleep latency, and sleep duration. The 5 bed partner questions are multiple-choice ratings of sleep disturbance. All items are brief and easy for most adolescents and adults to understand. The items have also been adapted so that they can be administered by a clinician or research assistant. Sample self-rated items are provided in Example 30–1.

The PSQI generates seven scores that correspond to the domains listed previously. Each component score ranges from 0 (no difficulty) to 3 (severe difficulty). The component scores are summed to produce a global score (range of 0–21). A PSQI global score >5 is considered to be suggestive of significant sleep disturbance. Cutoff scores are not available for component scales.

PRACTICAL ISSUES

It takes most patients 5–10 minutes to complete the PSQI. No training is needed to administer and score it.

EXAMPLE 30–1 ■ Sample items from the Pittsburgh Sleep Quality Index

During the past month, how often have you taken medicine to help you sleep?
  not during the past month
  less than once a week
  once or twice a week
  three or more times a week

During the past month, what time have you usually gone to bed at night? (Write in answer.)

Reprinted with permission from Daniel J. Buysse, M.D.

Scoring time is less than 5 minutes. The scale and scoring instructions are available in the original publication (Buysse et al. 1989a) or by request from the author:

> Daniel J. Buysse, M.D.
> Western Psychiatric Institute and Clinic
> 3811 O'Hara Street
> Pittsburgh, PA 15213

A French translation is available. The PSQI is included on the CD-ROM that accompanies this handbook.

PSYCHOMETRIC PROPERTIES

Reliability

Internal consistency was demonstrated in a sample of healthy control subjects ($n = 52$), patients with sleep disorders ($n = 62$), and depressed patients ($n = 34$); Cronbach's alpha was 0.83 for the global score. Correlations between the component scales and the total score ranged from 0.35 to 0.76. Correlations of items with the total score ranged from 0.20 to 0.66. Test-retest reliability (average interval of 28 days) with a subset of 91 of the patients and control subjects described earlier (43 control subjects, 22 depressed patients, and 26 patients with sleep disorders) was 0.85 for the global score and 0.65–0.84 for component scales. A small sample of elderly patients ($n = 19$) evaluated over an average interval of 19 days revealed similar findings (global reliability = 0.82; component scale score = 0.45–0.84).

Validity

Patients with sleep disorders ($n = 62$) or psychiatric disorders associated with sleep disturbances (e.g., depressive and anxiety disorders) ($n = 34$) scored significantly higher than healthy control subjects ($n = 52$) on global and component scales. Component scales significantly differentiated diagnostic groups. A post hoc cutoff score of 5 on the PSQI produced a sensitivity of 89.6% and a specificity of 86.5% of patients versus control subjects. This cutoff score correctly identified 84% of patients with disorders of initiating or maintaining sleep, 89% of patients with disorders of excessive sleepiness, and 97% of depressed patients. Group differences on the PSQI between patients and control subjects were substantiated by comparable group differences in polysomonographic measures for sleep latency, sleep efficiency, sleep duration, and number of arousals. However, PSQI component scale scores were not significantly correlated with corresponding polysomnographic measures (in the same sample of 148 patients and control subjects), with the exception of sleep latency ($r = 0.33$). The global PSQI score was correlated with sleep latency ($r = 0.20$) but not with any other polysomnographic measures.

In studies that compared patients with anxiety disorders with control subjects, those with panic disorder and those with social phobia exceeded the control group on global PSQI scores and on Subjective Sleep Quality, Sleep Latency, Sleep Disturbances, and Daytime Dysfunction subscales.

CLINICAL UTILITY

The PSQI was designed to provide a reliable, valid, and standardized measure of sleep quality. Preliminary results with the scale suggest that it is successful on all three counts.

Within sleep disorder treatment settings, the test should be useful in providing initial indexes of the severity and nature of sleep disturbances. Within a general psychiatric or medical setting, the PSQI appears to be useful as an initial screen to identify good and poor sleepers. Furthermore, although not as psychometrically sound as the overall score, the component scales appear to provide preliminary signs of specific types of sleep disturbance. Although in theory the PSQI should be useful in identifying patients for whom polysomnographic evaluation may be necessary, its actual performance as a screening tool has not been reported (i.e., false-positive and false-negative rates compared with results from the polysomnogram). The PSQI component scales do not, by and large, reflect corresponding polysomnographic findings. In any case, the PSQI is not sufficient to provide accurate clinical diagnoses of sleep disorders. Furthermore, there are no data establishing its sensitivity to change; thus, it is not known whether the scale is useful for monitoring treatment response.

REFERENCES AND SUGGESTED READINGS

Buysse DJ, Reynolds CF, Monk TH, et al: Pittsburgh Sleep Quality Index: a new instrument for psychiatric practice and research. Psychiatry Res 28:193–213, 1989a

Buysse DJ, Reynolds CF, Monk TH, et al: Quantification of subjective sleep quality in healthy elderly men and women using the Pittsburgh Sleep Quality Index. Sleep 14:331–338, 1989b

Gentilli A, Weiner DK, Kuchhibhatla M, et al: Test-retest reliability of the Pittsburgh Sleep Quality Index in nursing home residents (letter). J Am Geriatr Soc 43:1317–1318, 1995

Stein MB, Chartier M, Walker JR: Sleep in nondepressed patients with panic disorder, I: systematic assessment of subjective sleep quality and sleep disturbance. Sleep 16:724–726, 1993

Stein MB, Kroft CDL, Walker JR: Sleep impairment in patients with social phobia. Psychiatry Res 49:251–256, 1993

Excessive Daytime Sleepiness and Nocturnal Sleep Subscales of the Sleep/Wake Activity Inventory (SWAI)

L. Rosenthal, T. A. Roehrs, and T. Roth

GOALS

The Sleep/Wake Activity Inventory (SWAI) (Rosenthal et al. 1993) was designed as a brief, multidimensional self-report measure of daytime sleepiness and (subjective) sleep disturbance. The scale was developed as a screening measure that would correlate with the more time-consuming and expensive assessment of daytime sleepiness, the multiple sleep latency test (MSLT).

DESCRIPTION

The complete SWAI is composed of 59 self-rated items that are each scored on a 9-point Likert scale. The items inquire about excessive daytime sleepiness, nocturnal sleep, psychic distress, social desirability, energy level, and ability to relax. Although the 59 items were used in the derivation of the scale, it is only necessary to administer the 12 items that comprise the Excessive Daytime Sleepiness and Nocturnal Sleep subscales to obtain clinically useful information about sleepiness. It should be noted that the content of the Nocturnal Sleep subscale focuses on falling asleep rather than on other qualitative or quantitative parameters of nocturnal sleep. This review is limited to the shortened version of the SWAI, which consists of the Excessive Daytime Sleepiness subscale (nine items) and the Nocturnal Sleep subscale (three items). Sample items from the Excessive Daytime Sleepiness and Nocturnal Sleep subscales are provided in Example 30–2.

The rating of each item ranges from 1 = always to 9 = never. Because lower scores on either the Excessive Daytime Sleepiness or the Nocturnal Sleep subscale indicate greater levels of sleep disturbance, the 9-point scale is reversed (1 = never; 9 = always) for some items on which a higher rating would indicate greater sleep disturbance (e.g., "Even if I take a nap, I sleep well at night"). The SWAI Excessive Daytime Sleepiness subscale is calculated by adding items 1, 2, 4, 6, 8, 9, 10, 11, and 12. The Nocturnal Sleep subscale is calculated by adding items 3 (reversed), 5, and 7. The total subscale scores are the sum of the item scores and range from 9 to 81 for the Excessive Daytime Sleepiness subscale and from 3 to 27 for the Nocturnal Sleep subscale. Norms and cutoff scores are not presently available, but the mean ratings on the Excessive Daytime Sleepiness subscale for a mixed group that included patients with sleep complaints (n = 421) and individuals without sleep complaints (n = 133) were 42.1 ± 16.2 for the patients with sleep complaints and 59.1 ± 11.7 for those without sleep complaints.

PRACTICAL ISSUES

Minimal training is needed to administer and score the instrument. On average, it takes 15 minutes to complete the entire 59-item SWAI and considerably less time to complete the abbreviated version. The SWAI is available in the original publication (Rosenthal et al. 1993) or by request from the author:

Leon Rosenthal, M.D.
Medical Director
Sleep Disorders Center
Henry Ford Hospital

EXAMPLE 30–2 ■ Sample items from the Sleep/Wake Activity Inventory

Excessive Daytime Sleepiness Subscale
I can take a nap anywhere.

Nocturnal Sleep Subscale
I have difficulty with falling asleep.

Reprinted by permission of Elsevier Science from "The Sleep-Wake Activity Inventory: A Self-Report Measure of Daytime Sleepiness," by Rosenthal L, Roehrs TA, Roth T. *Biological Psychiatry*, Volume 34, pp. 810–820, Copyright 1993 by the Society of Biological Psychiatry.

1 Ford Place, Suite 1D
Detroit, MI 48202

A Spanish translation is available. The SWAI is included on the CD-ROM that accompanies this handbook.

PSYCHOMETRIC PROPERTIES

Reliability

Internal consistency was demonstrated in a sample of 421 patients with sleep disorders and 133 healthy control subjects; Cronbach's alpha was 0.89 for the Excessive Daytime Sleepiness subscale and 0.69 for the Nocturnal Sleep subscale. The lower reliability of the Nocturnal Sleep subscale is likely related to the limited number of items on the scale. These values may overestimate the actual reliability of the subscales because they were computed from the same sample used to derive the subscales.

Validity

Patients with sleep disorders (n = 421) differed significantly from individuals without sleep complaints (n = 133) on the Excessive Daytime Sleepiness subscale but not the Nocturnal Sleep subscale. The Excessive Daytime Sleepiness subscale was inversely correlated with hours of sleep during the preceding week and ease of falling asleep and positively correlated with severity of snoring and diagnoses of major depression and anxiety disorders.

Both the Excessive Daytime Sleepiness and Nocturnal Sleep subscales significantly predicted sleep latency as measured by the MSLT in a mixed group of 379 individuals with (n = 315) and without (n = 64) sleep disorders. A mean Excessive Daytime Sleepiness subscale score of 38 ± 14 and a mean Nocturnal Sleep subscale score of 11 ± 6 were reported for individuals with sleep latency means <5 minutes (a sleep latency <5 minutes indicates a pathological level of daytime sleepiness).

Sensitivity to change was demonstrated in a sample of patients with sleep apnea who showed significant improvement in Excessive Daytime Sleepiness subscale scores after a minimum of 6 weeks of treatment.

CLINICAL UTILITY

The Excessive Daytime Sleepiness and Nocturnal Sleep subscales of the SWAI provide brief screening assessments of daytime sleepiness that correlate with the gold standard measure of MSLT. The SWAI does not replace the MSLT for diagnostic purposes because it has not been adequately validated and is also a more inexact measure, but it should be a useful screening tool for detecting the excessive daytime sleepiness found in a variety of sleep and psychiatric disorders. Its performance as a screening tool in routine clinical care has not been evaluated. Thus, we do not know the preferred threshold score and the false- and true-positive and false- and true-negative rates compared with the gold standard (polysomnography). The Excessive Daytime Sleepiness subscale may have some utility in measuring change in excessive sleepiness with treatment, given its demonstrated sensitivity to change, at least in a population of patients with sleep apnea.

REFERENCES AND SELECTED READINGS

Breslau N, Roth T, Rosenthal L, et al: Daytime sleepiness: an epidemiological study of young adults. Am J Public Health 87:1649–1653, 1997

Rosenthal L, Roehrs TA, Roth T: The Sleep-Wake Activity Inventory: a self-report measure of daytime sleepiness. Biol Psychiatry 34:810–820, 1993

Epworth Sleepiness Scale (ESS)

M. W. Johns

GOALS

The Epworth Sleepiness Scale (ESS) (Johns 1991) is designed to assess the overall level of daytime sleepiness. It was developed to be a brief and inexpensive alternative to, or screening tool for identifying those needing, polysomnographic evaluation of daytime sleep complaints (e.g., the multiple sleep latency test [MSLT]).

DESCRIPTION

The ESS is a self-rated questionnaire with eight items that describe normative daily situations known to vary in their soporific qualities. Subjects rate the likelihood of dozing off or falling asleep in each of these situations. All items are brief and easy for most adolescents and adults to understand. The ESS also can be administered by a clinician. A sample item is provided in Example 30–3.

Each item is rated on a 4-point scale from 0 = would **never** doze to 3 = **high chance** of dozing. The item scores are summed to produce a total score (range of 0–24). Scoring takes less than a minute. Scores may need to be prorated if any of the situations described in the test items are not relevant to the patient. Scores >10 (95th percentile) are considered to be suggestive of significant daytime sleepiness. Scores >15 have been associated with pathological sleepiness that may be due to specific conditions such as obstructive sleep apnea or narcolepsy.

EXAMPLE 30–3 ■ Sample item from the Epworth Sleepiness Scale

Watching television

0 = would **never** doze
1 = **slight chance** of dozing
2 = **moderate chance** of dozing
3 = **high chance** of dozing

Reprinted with permission from M. W. Johns.

PRACTICAL ISSUES

It takes less than 5 minutes for most patients to complete the ESS, and minimal training is needed to administer and score it. The scale and scoring instructions are available in the original publication (John 1991). The scale is in the public domain and may be freely used provided the original source is acknowledged. The ESS has been translated into Flemish, French, and Portuguese. The ESS is included on the CD-ROM that accompanies this handbook.

PSYCHOMETRIC PROPERTIES

Reliability

Internal consistency was demonstrated in samples of medical students ($n = 104$) and patients with sleep disorders ($n = 150$); Cronbach's alphas ranged from 0.73 to 0.88. Test-retest reliability for medical students ($N = 87$) across a 5-month interval yielded a correlation of 0.82. In sleep apnea patients ($N = 45$) assessed across an average 28-day interval, the correlation was 0.91.

Joint reliability between the self-assessment of snoring patients ($n = 50$) and assessment by spouses yielded $r = 0.74$.

Validity

Mean ESS scores of patients with sleep apnea ($n = 165$) exceeded those of primary snorers ($n = 108$). The severity of obstructive sleep apnea was positively associated with ESS score ($r = 0.44$) (Johns 1993).

In patients with obstructive sleep apnea ($N = 55$) who typically report daytime sleepiness, the ESS was correlated with the respiratory disturbance index ($r = 0.55$) and inversely correlated with minimum oxygen saturation ($r = -0.46$). In patients with sleep disorders ($N = 138$), ESS scores were inversely correlated with sleep latencies determined by overnight polysomnographic studies ($r = -0.38$) and by daytime MSLT ($r = -0.51$), which is as expected given that short sleep latencies and low scores on the MSLT are laboratory indications of daytime sleepiness. The ESS was not significantly associated with frequency of periodic leg movements ($r = 0.05$), indicating that excessive daytime sleepiness and periodic leg movement disorder are separate disturbances

and supporting the divergent validity of the ESS. Patients with periodic leg movements on polysomnogram do not necessarily have daytime sleepiness.

Consistent with the measure's relatively high internal consistency, factor analysis demonstrated a single factor (daytime sleepiness).

Several studies of patients with sleep apnea who were successfully treated with continuous positive airway pressure demonstrated reductions in ESS scores with treatment response, indicating sensitivity of the ESS to change in clinical status.

CLINICAL UTILITY

The ESS is a brief self-report tool that assesses general sleep propensity and excessive daytime sleepiness, which often accompanies sleep disorders such as sleep apnea, narcolepsy, and idiopathic hypersomnia. The ESS is reliable, is valid in that it correlates well with laboratory measures of sleepiness and yields high scores in populations expected to have daytime sleepiness (e.g., those with sleep apnea), and has been shown to be sensitive to change induced by treatment. Thus, the ESS is best used as an initial measure of the severity of daytime sleepiness and may also be useful in monitoring treatment response longitudinally. Although in theory it should be useful as a screening measure to identify patients with excessive daytime sleepiness, its performance as a screening tool in routine practice and its false-positive and false-negative rates have not yet been evaluated. The ESS does not provide clinical diagnoses because the presence of excessive daytime sleepiness is not, in and of itself, sufficient to make a diagnosis of a DSM-IV sleep disorder. Additional factors such as duration, clinical significance, and etiology (e.g., associated with medication, drugs, or a general medical condition) are not evaluated by the ESS.

REFERENCES AND SUGGESTED READINGS

Chervin RD, Aldrich MS, Pickett R, et al: Comparison of the results of the Epworth Sleepiness Scale and the multiple sleep latency test. J Psychosom Res 42:145–155, 1997

Johns MW: A new method of measuring daytime sleepiness: the Epworth Sleepiness Scale. Sleep 14:540–545, 1991

Johns MW: Reliability and factor analysis of the Epworth Sleepiness Scale. Sleep 15:376–381, 1992

Johns MW: Daytime sleepiness, snoring, and obstructive sleep apnea: the Epworth Sleepiness Scale. Chest 103:30–36, 1993

Johns MW: Sleepiness in different situations measured by the Epworth Sleepiness Scale. Sleep 17:703–710, 1994

Stanford Sleepiness Scale (SSS)

E. Hoddes, V. Zarcone, H. Smythe, R. Phillips, and W. C. Dement

GOALS

The Stanford Sleepiness Scale (SSS) (Hoddes et al. 1972, 1973) was one of the first self-report measures of sleepiness. It was developed to assess discrete changes in sleepiness in periods as brief as 15 minutes.

DESCRIPTION

The SSS is a self-administered single-item scale that inquires about the individual's immediate level of sleepiness. The scale contains seven ordinal anchor points that cover the range from wakefulness to severe sleepiness.

The score is determined on the basis of the response to the one item; seven specified responses characterize increasing levels of subjective sleepiness:

1 = Feeling active and vital; alert; wide-awake
2 = Functioning at a high level, but not at peak; able to concentrate
3 = Relaxed; awake; not at full alertness; responsive
4 = A little foggy; not at peak; let down
5 = Fogginess; beginning to lose interest in remaining awake; slowed down
6 = Sleepiness; prefer to be lying down; fighting sleep; woozy
7 = Almost in a reverie; sleep onset soon; lost struggle to remain awake

The measure is generally used to assess change in sleepiness over time. Therefore, absolute scores are difficult to interpret and norms are not available.

PRACTICAL ISSUES

The scale and administration instructions are available in the article by Hoddes et al. (1973). French and Hebrew translations are available.

PSYCHOMETRIC PROPERTIES

Reliability

Reliability of single-item scales is notoriously low. However, alternate forms reliability (in which separate but equivalent versions of the SSS [i.e., with different descriptions associated with each score] were administered to the same subjects on two different occasions) yielded a reliability coefficient (r) of 0.88 ($n = 10$).

Validity

It could be hypothesized that daytime sleepiness would be accompanied by performance decrements; however, attempts to correlate SSS scores with performance decrements in individuals with sleep deprivation have yielded mixed results. It could also be hypothesized that individuals with narcolepsy would endorse more daytime sleepiness than control subjects without narcolepsy. This hypothesis was supported by research that found that patients with narcolepsy exceeded healthy control subjects on mean SSS ratings, whereas the ratings of patients with insomnia did not differ from those of control subjects.

Several studies have compared SSS scores and sleep latencies determined by the multiple sleep latency test (MSLT) in both patient and nonpatient samples. Although some studies reported significant correlations, most failed to document a significant association between SSS score and sleep latency. In a study of 14 "young, good" sleepers, the correlation between the SSS and the MSLT was $r = 0.56$. However, in three studies (of 10 narcolepsy patients and 10 matched healthy control subjects without narcolepsy; in 80 young, healthy male subjects; and in 20 subjects with insomnia and 20 without insomnia), correlations between the SSS and the MSLT were not significant. The SSS was correlated with the Visual Analogue Scale for Fatigue (VAS-F) (Lee et al. 1991) in measuring fatigue ($r = 0.52$). The VAS-F includes 18 items that assess fatigue and energy level (e.g., "not at all tired" to "extremely tired").

The SSS was primarily designed to measure change in subjective sleepiness over short periods. Significant changes in SSS scores have been associated with sleep deprivation and recovery sleep (Carskadon and Dement 1981; Herscovitch and Broughton 1981; Hoddes et al. 1973).

CLINICAL UTILITY

The SSS is one of the quickest and most easily administered assessments of sleepiness available. Despite these qualities, its clinical utility appears to be quite limited. Its exclusive focus on state sleepiness renders it virtually useless as a diagnostic or screening tool, because making the diagnosis of all sleep disorders requires establishing that the sleep symptoms are clinically significant (i.e., they interfere with functioning or cause marked distress). In this regard, a cross-sectional assessment of sleepiness would not be of much help. Furthermore, the absence of standardized norms makes it difficult to evaluate the diagnostic significance of a particular score. With regard to its potential use as an inexpensive alternative to the gold standard MSLT, results are also disappointing, given the poor correlations between SSS scores and results of the MSLT. This weak correlation may reflect differences between subjective and biobehavioral evaluations of sleepiness. For example, fatigue and sleepiness are not neces-

sarily the same thing (see "Using Measures in This Domain" in the introduction to this chapter [p. 674]). The SSS appears to be most useful in clinical laboratory settings as a measure of on-line sleepiness and for monitoring patterns of sleepiness in patients with sleep disorders.

REFERENCES AND SUGGESTED READINGS

Babkoff H, Caspy T, Mikulincer M: Subjective sleep ratings: the effects of sleep deprivation, circadian rhythmicity, and cognitive performance. Sleep 14:534–539, 1991

Billiard M: Le sommeil normal et pathologique: troubles du sommeil et de l'eveil. Paris, Masson, 1994

Carskadon MA, Dement WC: Cumulative effects of sleep restriction on daytime sleepiness. Psychophysiology 18:107–113; 1981

Herscovitch J, Broughton R: Sensitivity of the Stanford Sleepiness Scale to the effects of cumulative partial sleep deprivation and recovery oversleeping. Sleep 4:83–92, 1981

Hoddes E, Dement WC, Zarcone V: The development and use of the Stanford Sleepiness Scale (SSS) (abstract). Psychophysiology 9:150, 1972

Hoddes E, Zarcone V, Smythe H, et al: Quantification of sleepiness: a new approach. Psychophysiology 10:431–436, 1973

Lee KA, Hicks G, Nino-Murcia G: Validity and reliability of a scale to assess fatigue. Psychiatry Res 36:291–298, 1991

Lichstein KL, Wilson NM, Noe SL, et al: Daytime sleepiness in insomnia: behavioral, biological, and subjective indices. Sleep 17:693–702, 1994

CHAPTER 31

Impulse-Control Disorders Measures

Eric Hollander, M.D.
Lisa Cohen, Ph.D.
Lorraine Simon, M.A.

INTRODUCTION

Major Domains

This chapter covers tests and instruments that assess the DSM-IV category of impulse-control disorders, which is composed of the following diagnoses: intermittent explosive disorder, trichotillomania, pathological gambling, kleptomania, pyromania, and impulse-control disorder not otherwise specified. Also described are state and trait measures of anger, aggression, and impulsivity. At present there are no published tests specifically designed to measure most of the impulse-control disorders listed. Therefore, we include instruments for only two of the six diagnoses: a measure of pathological gambling (the South Oaks Gambling Screen [SOGS]) and two measures for trichotillomania (the Psychiatric Institute Trichotillomania Scale [PITS] and the Massachusetts General Hospital [MGH] Hairpulling Scale). The remaining five measures in this chapter assess general dimensions of anger, aggression, and impulsivity.

Impulsivity is generally defined as acting without thinking or as behaving recklessly without regard to consequences. Impulsivity as a dimension is measured by the Barratt Impulsiveness Scale, Version 11 (BIS-11). Anger, aggression, and hostility cover a range of constructs that encompass subjective emotional experience, quality of emotional reactivity, patterns of emotional expression, inhibition or disinhibition of anger responses, and asso-

ciated verbal and physical behaviors. In this chapter we include four anger and aggression instruments that differ considerably in their focus: the Anger, Irritability, and Assault Questionnaire (AIAQ); the Buss-Durkee Hostility Inventory (BDHI); the Overt Aggression Scale–Modified (OAS-M); and the State-Trait Anger Expression Inventory (STAXI). The relationship between the constructs of impulsivity and aggression and specific impulse-control disorders is complex. Although these dimensional scales do not measure specific diagnostic entities, they are included because of their relevance to the constructs underlying the diagnostic category of impulse-control disorder. High trait levels of impulsivity and/or aggression may dispose people to perform the behaviors associated with specific impulse-control disorders, such as pathological gambling, intermittent explosive disorder, or impulse-control disorder not otherwise specified. For example, high scores on the Motor Impulsiveness factor of the BIS-11 have been associated with a greater number of impulsive acts in inmates.

Organization

The measures included in this chapter are listed in Table 31–1. Because *impulsiveness* is a general concept that cuts across these disorders, the first measure presented is the BIS-11. We then describe four scales for assessing anger and aggression that may be relevant in the assessment of the DSM-IV category intermittent explosive disorder. Finally, we present the three scales that can be used to

TABLE 31–1 ■ Impulse-control disorders measures

NAME OF MEASURE	DISORDER OR CONSTRUCT ASSESSED	FORMAT	PAGES
Barratt Impulsiveness Scale, Version 11 (BIS-11)*	Impulsivity	Self-administered questionnaire; 30 items	691–693
Anger, Irritability, and Assault Questionnaire (AIAQ)*	Impulsive aggression	Self-report; 84 items (original), 210 items (revised)	694–697
Buss-Durkee Hostility Inventory (BDHI)*	Components of hostility	Self-report; 75 items	697–699
Overt Aggression Scale— Modified (OAS-M)*	Aggressive behavior in outpatients	Semistructured interview; 25 items	699–702
State-Trait Anger Expression Inventory (STAXI)	Components of anger	Self-administered questionnaire; 44 items	702–706
South Oaks Gambling Screen (SOGS)*	Pathological gambling	Interview or self-report; 20 items	706–708
Massachusetts General Hospital (MGH) Hairpulling Scale*	Trichotillomania	Self-report questionnaire; 7 items	708–710
Psychiatric Institute Trichotillomania Scale (PITS)*	Trichotillomania	Semistructured interview; 6 items	711–712

*Measure is included on the CD-ROM that accompanies this handbook.

assess specific DSM diagnoses, one for pathological gambling and two for trichotillomania.

Relevant Measures Included Elsewhere in the Handbook

With the exception of the OAS-M, measures of auto-aggressive or self-mutilative behavior are found in Chapter 16, "Suicide Risk Measures." Measures that primarily assess children's and adolescents' behavior are found in Chapter 17, "Child and Adolescent Measures for Diagnosis and Screening," Chapter 18, "Symptom-Specific Measures for Disorders Usually First Diagnosed in Infancy, Childhood, or Adolescence," and Chapter 19, "Child and Adolescent Measures of Functional Status."

USING MEASURES IN THIS DOMAIN

Goals of Assessment

The main goals of assessment within this domain are measuring current, recent, and remote episodes of violent or aggressive behavior; determining the severity of current anger, aggression, hostility, hair pulling, or gambling; and measuring change over time. Assessment is intended to aid in determining the patient's propensity toward impulsivity, anger, or hostility as a personality trait and thus whether a patient meets the criteria for a particular impulse-control disorder. Such information can be of use in clinical evaluation, treatment planning, and evaluation of response to treatment. All of the measures are appropriate for use in research as well.

Implementation Issues

Six of the eight measures are self-report questionnaires, although one (the SOGS) can also be administered as a semistructured interview. Two measures (the PITS and the OAS-M) are semistructured interviews.

Measures also have varying time frames; they can assess current state (e.g., the STAXI), state or trait across the past week (e.g., the AIAQ, the OAS-M, the MGH Hairpulling Scale, and the PITS), or trait across lifetime (e.g., the STAXI, the AIAQ, and the SOGS). The AIAQ offers three time frames in the initial version and five time frames in a later revision. Neither the BDHI nor the BIS-11 specifies a time frame.

Many of the measures included in this chapter have common limitations. First, all the dimensional measures assess traits that are generally considered socially undesirable and are thus sensitive to social desirability biases, because subjects may be tempted to underreport undesirable traits. Moreover, most of the dimensional instruments are self-report measures, which are vulnerable to several reporting biases. Findings may be confounded by subjects' poor insight into their own attitudes and behaviors, by desires to portray themselves favorably or to exaggerate their impairment and distress in an attempt to affect treatment, and by subjects' misunderstanding of the questions or instructions.

In addition, most self-report scales are aimed at subjects of normal intellect. Thus, many scales may not be appropriate for intellectually impaired subjects. Although none of the scales in this chapter are specifically designed for nonverbal or intellectually impaired subjects, those that focus primarily on assessment of concrete behavior, such as the OAS-M, the PITS, and the MGH Hairpulling Scale, have potential clinical utility with this population.

Of particular concern, many of the dimensional instruments appear to become less sensitive at more extreme levels, for several reasons. The oldest and most widely used measures in this domain (the BDHI and the BIS-11) were developed for research purposes and were, in large part, validated on university students, who differ considerably in age, level of education, and socioeconomic status from many clinical populations. Thus, these instruments do not always generalize well to clinical samples. Many of the self-report measures rely heavily on questions that ask subjects to make generalizations about relevant attitudes or behavioral patterns. According to a fairly large body of literature, highly impulsive and aggressive people have difficulties conceptualizing their own personal traits and, consequently, demonstrate poor insight into their own behavior.

Few of the scales focus on concrete behavioral manifestations of impulsive or aggressive traits. Such questions are of most interest to clinicians who work with these populations and are also likely to best identify high levels of impulsive and aggressive behavior. For example, many subjects may feel like slapping someone else, but the frequency with which they act on this impulse determines their true levels of impulsivity and aggression.

Therefore, additional assessment of concrete aggressive behaviors would still be needed for a complete evaluation. The scales should thus be used only with great caution for predicting future aggressive behavior and only in combination with other sources of information.

Issues in Interpreting Psychometric Data

Limitations in the psychometric properties of most of these instruments hamper the interpretation of individual test scores. Few of the scales in this domain have standardized norms or cutoff scores. The STAXI is the only trait measure for which norms have been determined, and the SOGS is the only diagnostic measure for which a cutoff score has been determined. Similarly, most of the scales were validated on samples of limited size. Hence, it is difficult to interpret the clinical significance of individual scores.

The three scales that assess diagnostic categories are, by definition, more closely geared toward clinical phenomena than the other scales. They are more oriented toward assessing specific behavioral symptoms (e.g., time spent pulling hair in the past week) and should thus maintain sensitivity at high levels of clinical severity. Because both of the trichotillomania scales are fairly new and are in the preliminary stages of validation, no standardized norms or cutoff scores are available for these scales.

Other than the SOGS, which functions as the gold standard for its domain, there is no gold standard in determining the validity of any of these scales. For example, for the trichotillomania scales covered in this chapter, each scale uses its correlation with the other as the sole evidence of validity.

GUIDE TO THE SELECTION OF MEASURES

All the instruments presented here may be of some use in clinical settings. For example, they can help provide a systematic assessment of baseline symptomatology and of change across treatment. In group settings, such as clinics, hospitals, and even large practices, these measures can be used to assess the impact of specific clinical factors (impulsivity and aggression) on a range of treatment variables, including treatment success, treatment compliance, rehospitalization, and therapeutic alliance. None of these instruments, however, should substitute for a thorough clinical evaluation, and most should be administered in conjunction with other measures. When possible, clinicians should use measures of a different format along with self-report measures. All the instruments in this chapter are especially appropriate for research purposes, for which sensitivity to variation in group means is most important.

For the purpose of measuring impulsivity as a state or trait that might cut across the diagnostic categories covered in this chapter and the entire spectrum of disorders with associated impulsive behavior (e.g., bipolar disorder, conduct disorder, borderline personality disorder, antisocial personality disorder, eating disorders, paraphilias, and substance use disorders), the only scale that might be applicable is the BIS-11. Although supporting data are currently lacking, the BIS-11 also may be useful in measuring change in an individual's impulsivity over time in response to treatment. The lack of norms and standardized scores limits its utility as a clinical assessment tool, but the BIS-11 has been shown to discriminate between impulsive and nonimpulsive groups.

Despite the lack of measures specifically designed to diagnose intermittent explosive disorder, several measures that might be helpful in the assessment of anger and aggression, two essential components of this disorder, are available. The self-report BDHI is the most widely known instrument for measuring anger and hostility, but its lack of standardized norms makes interpretation of individual scores difficult.

The STAXI, which focuses on modes of anger expression, is very well standardized and has detailed norms. It also has some utility in predicting stress-related physical conditions, such as hypertension. However, the STAXI has limited utility in populations with extreme levels of anger or aggression, such as subjects with antisocial personality disorder or prisoners, because it fails to measure the frequency of concrete, aggressive behaviors. The AIAQ, another self-report measure of anger and aggression, is more extensive and covers irritability, anger, and concrete aggressive behavior over three different time frames. However, the absence of norms, clear cutoff scores to assess diagnostic relevance, and standardized scores limits the clinical utility of both the STAXI and the AIAQ. The OAS-M is the only measure of aggression that actually assesses concrete aggressive behavior in detail; such an evaluation is generally of greatest interest to clinicians who treat aggressive patients.

For pathological gambling, the gold standard is the SOGS, although it has some significant limitations, in-

cluding that it does not correspond exactly with the DSM-IV diagnosis of pathological gambling or take into account frequency of gambling behaviors. Although the two trichotillomania scales have limited validity and reliability data, they appear to be useful in clarifying the breadth and severity of clinical features. The choice between these scales depends primarily on the intended mode of administration; the PITS is clinician administered, whereas the MGH Hairpulling Scale is a self-report measure.

None of the scales in this chapter was designed to predict the likelihood of future violence. The probability of violent behavior is notoriously difficult to predict. Perhaps the best predictor of future violence is a history of violence. As such, only the OAS-M, which assesses the frequency of various aggressive behaviors in the past week, might contribute relevant information. The 1-week time frame, however, may be overly restrictive in this case.

Instruments were selected for this chapter for their proven psychometric properties, wide use in the field, potential clinical utility, or evident promise as up-and-coming measures. Because of space limitations, several instruments that assess aggression or relevant impulsive behavior could not be included in this chapter. For those assessing long-term aggressive behavior, the Brown Goodwin Life History of Aggression (Brown et al. 1982) and the Life Time History of Aggression (Coccaro et al. 1997) may be of interest. Two trichotillomania instruments that were not included in this chapter may also be useful: the National Institute of Mental Health Trichotillomania Scale (Swedo et al. 1989) and an adaptation of the Yale-Brown Obsessive Compulsive Scale (Y-BOCS) (p. 572) (Stanley et al. 1993). The Y-BOCS has also been adapted to measure compulsive buying (Monahan et al. 1996).

CURRENT STATUS AND FUTURE RESEARCH NEEDS FOR ASSESSMENT

The instruments that assess impulse-control disorders and related dimensions are for the most part in the preliminary stages of development. In general, more scales and increased psychometric data derived from larger and more varied samples are needed. More diagnostic instruments are needed for all the impulse-control disorders, especially for pyromania and kleptomania. Both questionnaires and semistructured interviews would be useful; in both formats, items should assess concrete behavior in greater detail than do current instruments to improve sensitivity at high levels of impulsivity and aggression.

REFERENCES AND SUGGESTED READINGS

Brown GL, Goodwin FK, Ballenger JC, et al: Aggression in humans correlates with cerebrospinal fluid metabolites. Am J Psychiatry 139:741–746, 1982

Coccaro E, Berman ME, Kavoussi RJ: Assessment of life-history of aggression: development and psychometric characteristics. Psychiatry Res 73:147–157, 1997

Monahan P, Black D, Gabel J: Reliability and validity of a scale to measure change in persons with compulsive buying. Psychiatry Res 64:59–67, 1996

Stanley MA, Prather RC, Wagner AL, et al: Can the Yale-Brown Obsessive Compulsive Scale be used to assess trichotillomania? a preliminary report. Behav Res Ther 31:171–177, 1993

Swedo S, Leonard H, Rapoport JL, et al: A double-blind comparison of clomipramine and desipramine in the treatment of trichotillomania (hairpulling). N Engl J Med 321:497–501, 1989

Barratt Impulsiveness Scale, Version 11 (BIS-11)

E. Barratt

GOALS

The current version of the Barratt Impulsiveness Scale, Version 11 (BIS-11) (Barratt and Stanford 1995), and its predecessors were developed to assess impulsivity. Impulsivity is conceptualized as related to the control of thoughts and behavior and is broadly defined as acting without thinking. The BIS-11 looks at impulsivity in terms of three domains: Motor Impulsiveness, Nonplanning Impulsiveness, and Attentional Impulsiveness. This and previous versions of the BIS were designed primarily as research instruments to aid in the description of impulsivity in psychiatrically healthy individuals and to explore the role of impulsivity in psychopathology.

DESCRIPTION

The BIS-11 is a self-administered questionnaire with 30 items scored on a 4-point scale ranging from 1 = rarely/never to 4 = almost always/always. Sample items are provided in Example 31–1. Possible scores range from 30 to 120. There are no standardized norms for the BIS-11, but the total score averaged 63.8 ± 10.2 in a sample of 412 undergraduates, 69.3 ± 10.3 in a sample of 164 psychiatric inpatients with substance abuse problems, 71.4 ± 12.6 in 84 general psychiatric inpatients, and 76.3 ± 11.9 in 73 male prison inmates.

PRACTICAL ISSUES

Administration time is not specified but is estimated to be about 10–15 minutes. The test requires a fifth-grade reading level and is intended for individuals ages 13 and older. The test is printed in full in the chapter by Barratt and Stanford (1995). For additional information about the measure, the author can be contacted at the following address:

Ernest S. Barratt, Ph.D.
Professor, Department of Psychiatry and Behavioral Sciences
University of Texas Medical Branch at Galveston
205 Communications Building

EXAMPLE 31–1 ■ Sample items from the Barratt Impulsiveness Scale, Version 11

> I squirm at plays or lectures.
>
> I don't "pay attention."

Reprinted with permission from Ernest S. Barratt, Ph.D.

301 University Boulevard
Galveston, TX 77555-0443

The BIS-11 is included on the CD-ROM that accompanies this handbook.

PSYCHOMETRIC PROPERTIES

Reliability

There is good evidence of internal consistency. The BIS-11 was derived from the 34-item BIS-10 on the basis of item-total correlations (the correlation of each item with the total test score) and the ability of items to distinguish between subjects in the top and bottom quartile in a sample of 412 undergraduate students. Four items were removed according to these criteria. Cronbach's alpha for the 30-item BIS-11 in this sample was 0.82, and it ranged from 0.79 to 0.83 in large samples of undergraduates and clinical and prison populations.

Validity

Some of the findings presented in this section are from studies on the BIS-10, which has a high correlation ($r = 0.98$) with the BIS-11.

Moderate correlations have been found between the BIS-11 and other measures of impulsivity-related traits. In particular, the BIS-11 is correlated with several measures of hostility and anger. In a sample of 214 university students, the BIS-11 correlated with the Buss-Durkee Hostility Inventory (BDHI) (p. 697) Total Hostility score and with six of the subscales ($r = 0.17-0.38$) as well as with the number of aggressive incidents in the past month ($r = 0.25$). The BIS-11 correlated with the Anger Out scale of the State-Trait Anger Expression Inventory (STAXI) (p. 702) ($r = 0.51$). The Anger Out scale measures the tendency to express anger outwardly toward people and objects in the environment. In regard to related personality traits, the BIS-10 correlated with the Eysenck Personality Questionnaire (EPQ) Psychoticism scale (Eysenck and Eysenck 1975) ($r = 0.66$) but not with the Extroversion and Neuroticism scales. It also correlated with Cluster A, B, and C Personality Disorder scores on the Personality Diagnostic Questionnaire—Revised (PDQ-R) (p. 732) ($r = 0.31-0.47$).

The BIS-11 has also been shown to distinguish impulsive aggressive from nonaggressive college students, noninmate control subjects from prisoners, male college students and psychiatric patients from prisoners, and female college students from psychiatric patients. In these same studies, the BIS-11 did not distinguish impulsively from nonimpulsively aggressive inmates or male college students from psychiatric patients.

Some studies suggest a relationship between impulsivity and reduced cognitive function. Barratt, the author of the BIS, is particularly interested in this relationship, as reflected in his definition of *impulsivity* as acting without thinking. In a combined sample of prison inmates and noninmate control subjects, the BIS-11 was inversely related to several cognitive measures (e.g., the Wechsler Adult Intelligence Scale [WAIS] [Wechsler 1955], the Wechsler Memory Scale—Revised [WMS-R] [Wechsler 1987], and the Gray Oral Reading Test [GORT] [Gray 1963]) and psychophysiological measures (e.g., evoked potentials), supporting the notion that impulsivity is related to reduced cognitive efficiency ($r = -0.52$ to -0.21). In other words, subjects with elevated levels of impulsivity also demonstrate decreased performance on, and lowered electrophysiological responsivity to, various cognitive tasks.

Barratt is also interested in identifying the components of impulsivity so that it can be assessed with greater precision. A factor analysis that produced three higher-order factors—Attentional Impulsiveness, Motor Impulsiveness, and Nonplanning Impulsiveness—was therefore performed. In a study of the BIS-10 in 72 male inmates, the Motor Impulsiveness factor, but not the Attentional Impulsiveness factor or the Nonplanning Impulsiveness factor, correlated with the total number of impulse-control problems and differentiated inmates with three or more problem behaviors from those with two or fewer. Specific impulse-control problems measured included alcohol abuse, sedative dependence, other drug abuse, repeated aggression, and impulsive fire setting. Although these problem behaviors do not correspond exactly with the DSM-IV criteria for impulse-control disorders, there is some overlap (e.g., fire setting). These results also show a relationship between this trait measure of impulsivity and the presence of impulse-control disorders.

CLINICAL UTILITY

The BIS-11 is perhaps the most widely known measure of impulsivity and is easily administered and widely used.

It is comparable to self-report measures of similar domains (e.g., measures of impulsive aggression) in its ability to discriminate between impulsive and nonimpulsive groups and in its evidence of various forms of validity. There are no formal norms, however, and no standardization of scores, which limits its utility as a clinical assessment tool.

The BIS-11 is subfactored into Motor, Nonplanning, and Attentional Impulsiveness, and the test items seem relevant to these three domains (e.g., item 9, "I concentrate easily"; item 1, "I plan tasks carefully"; item 14, "I say things without thinking"; and item 17, "I act 'on impulse' "). The factors also make intuitive sense and may add to a fuller assessment of impulsive behavior. Nonetheless, factor loadings have not been reliably replicated. Moreover, because most studies provide validity data for the total score rather than for the factor scores, the scale is best suited to provide a general measure of impulsivity.

The scale items seem to be geared to a nonclinical middle-class population and have less relevance to severely impulsive populations and those of low socioeconomic status. For example, it is doubtful that most populations of low socioeconomic status will frequent plays or lectures (items 11 and 32).

Most questions assess general characteristics and depend on subjects' ability to accurately form abstract assessments of their own behavior (e.g., item 12, "I am a careful thinker," and item 8, "I am self-controlled"). However, as discussed earlier, research indicates that such high-level cognitive abilities may be compromised in highly impulsive subjects.

In addition, few questions on the BIS-11 tap severe or concrete manifestations of impulsivity, which would be expected to differentiate highly impulsive from less impulsive groups with greater sensitivity than the more general questions included on the BIS-11. Thus, the BIS-11 may have reduced sensitivity at extreme levels of impulsivity. For example, in the initial publication of the BIS-11, mean scores of male prisoners and male college students did not differ dramatically. Nonetheless, in its sensitivity to variation at extreme levels, this instrument is comparable to, and no worse than, many similar measures of related domains. Some evidence suggests that the Motor Impulsiveness factor has greater sensitivity at high levels of impulsivity than the other two factors.

The BIS-11 is probably best suited for use as a research instrument in tandem with other related measures. Given the lack of established norms and the possibility of decreased sensitivity at extreme levels, it is not strongly indicated for use in individual clinical assessment and is poorly indicated for use in the prediction of future impulsive behavior. However, although supporting literature is currently lacking, the BIS-11 may be useful as a means of measuring change over time or individuals' progress in treatment.

REFERENCES AND SUGGESTED READINGS

Barratt E: Impulsiveness and aggression, in Violence and Mental Disorder: Developments in Risk Assessment. Edited by Monahan J, Steadman HJ. Chicago, IL, University of Chicago Press, 1994, pp 61–79

Barratt ES, Stanford MS: Impulsiveness, in Personality Characteristics of the Personality Disordered Client. Edited by Costello CG. New York, Wiley, 1995, pp 91–118

Barratt ES, Stanford MS, Kent TA, et al: Neuropsychological and cognitive psychophysiological substrates of impulsive aggression. Biol Psychiatry 47:1045–1061, 1997

Eysenck HJ, Eysenck SBG: Manual of the Eysenck Personality Questionnaire. London, Hadder & Stoughton, 1975

Gray W: Gray Oral Reading Test Manual. Wilmington, DE, Jastak, 1963

Hyler SE, Reider RO, Williams JBW, et al: The Personality Diagnostic Questionnaire: development and preliminary results. J Personal Disord 2:229–237, 1988

Patton JH, Stanford MS, Barratt ES: Factor structure of the Barratt Impulsiveness Scale. J Clin Psychol 51:768–774, 1995

Stanford MS, Greve KW, Dickens TJ: Irritability and impulsiveness: relationship to self-reported impulsive aggression. Person Indiv Diff 19:757–760, 1995

Wechsler D: Wechsler Adult Intelligence Scale: Manual. New York, Psychological Corporation, 1955

Wechsler D: Wechsler Memory Scale-Revised: Manual. New York, Psychological Corporation, 1987

Anger, Irritability, and Assault Questionnaire (AIAQ)

E. F. Coccaro, P. D. Harvey, E. Kupsaw-Lawrence, J. L. Herbert, and D. P. Bernstein

GOALS

The Anger, Irritability, and Assault Questionnaire (AIAQ) (Coccaro et al. 1991) was designed to evaluate impulsive aggression. It includes three subdomains, Labile Anger, Irritability, and Assault. *Labile anger* refers to an unpredictable dysregulation of anger or to inappropriately intense anger responses in the absence of clear provocation. *Irritability* is defined as a tendency to respond with negative affect in reaction to aversive stimuli or with hypersensitivity to aversive stimuli. *Assault* refers to the tendency to actually assault when angry.

The AIAQ was primarily designed for neurobiological research, and the domains were chosen for their association with serotonin dysfunction in impulsive-aggressive patients. The scale focuses primarily on the inability to control aggression. A revised scale, however, also addresses verbal and indirect modes of expressing anger. Neither the scale nor the revision addresses the suppression of anger or the subjective experience of anger.

DESCRIPTION

The AIAQ is a self-report questionnaire composed of three continuous subscales, Labile Anger, Irritability, and Assault. In addition to the original AIAQ (Coccaro et al. 1991), there is a longer, revised version (Coccaro and Kavoussi 1997). The original AIAQ has 28 questions rated on 4-point Likert scales (1 = very uncharacteristic to 4 = very characteristic). Each question is rated on three time frames: past week, past month, and my adulthood (≥18 years). Thus, there are a total of 84 items.

Two new subscales, which include 14 new questions and two additional time frames (my adolescence [12–18 years] and my childhood [6–10 years]), were included in the revised AIAQ, for a total of 210 items. In the revised version, the five subscales are grouped into two overarching scales, Irritability, which includes the Labile Anger and Irritability subscales, and Aggression, which includes the original Assault subscale and the new Indirect Assault and Verbal Assault subscales.

The three subscales on the original AIAQ (Labile Anger, Irritability, and Assault) were adapted from two previously published instruments: the Buss-Durkee Hostility Inventory (BDHI) (p. 697) and the Affective Lability Scales (ALS) (Harvey et al. 1989). The Assault and Irritability subscales were entirely derived from the analogous BDHI scales; the original yes-no format was modified for the AIAQ's 4-point scales. The Labile Anger subscale was similarly adapted from the ALS. Sample items are provided in Example 31–2.

Scores are computed only for the subscales. Total scores are not calculated. On the original AIAQ, a maximum score of 40 can be obtained on the 10-item Assault subscale, a maximum of 44 on the 11-item Irritability subscale, and a maximum of 28 on the 7-item Labile Anger subscale. For the revised AIAQ, a maximum score of 72 is obtainable on the 18-item combined Irritability scale and a maximum of 96 on the 24-item Aggression scale.

There are no standardized norms for the AIAQ, but means for the three original subscales in 22 psychiatric outpatients and 20 control subjects were published in the original article (Coccaro et al. 1991). The means across time frames are listed in Table 31–2.

EXAMPLE 31–2 ■ Sample items from the Anger, Irritability, and Assault Questionnaire

(A = Very characteristic of me, B = Rather characteristic of me, C = Rather uncharacteristic of me, D = Very uncharacteristic of me)

1. It's very common for me to be extremely angry about something and then to suddenly feel like my normal self.
   Past Week   A B C D
   Past Month   A B C D
   My Adulthood (18 +)   A B C D

5. At times people have pushed me so far that we came to blows.
   Past Week   A B C D
   Past Month   A B C D
   My Adulthood (18 +)   A B C D

Reprinted with permission from Emil Coccaro, M.D.

TABLE 31–2 ■ Mean scores for the Anger, Irritability, and Assault Questionnaire

	PATIENTS	CONTROL SUBJECTS
Labile Anger	17.1 ± 5.1 to 16.1 ± 4.5	10.2 ± 3.7 to 10.5 ± 3.4
Irritability	29.1 ± 6.4 to 28.4 ± 5.4	20.7 ± 6.2 to 21.9 ± 6.6
Assault	21.7 ± 7.8 to 21.5 ± 6.8	13.4 ± 2.5 to 14.1 ± 3.2

On the revised AIAQ, a sample of 40 outpatients (28 of whom were men) with personality disorders had mean past week scores of 41.7 ± 12.0 for the Aggression scale and 18.4 ± 4.1 for the Irritability scale.

PRACTICAL ISSUES

Administration times are not specified but may be estimated to be about 35 minutes for the original AIAQ and about 50 minutes for the revised AIAQ. Faster readers may take less time.

The AIAQ can be obtained from the author:

> Emil Coccaro, M.D.
> Department of Psychiatry
> Medical College of Pennsylvania
> Eastern Pennsylvania Psychiatric Institute
> 3200 Henry Avenue
> Philadelphia, PA 19129

The AIAQ is included on the CD-ROM that accompanies this handbook.

PSYCHOMETRIC PROPERTIES

There are few published studies on the psychometric properties of the AIAQ. Most of the following data are drawn from the initial study (Coccaro et al. 1991) in which the original AIAQ was administered to 20 outpatient psychiatric patients and 22 nonpatient control subjects.

Reliability

Although there are no published data on internal consistency for the AIAQ, there are such data on the BDHI (p. 691) and on the ALS (Harvey et al. 1989).

Data on test-retest reliability are fairly strong. For 22 psychiatric outpatients over a 1- to 2-week period, test-retest coefficients were 0.57–0.86 for Labile Anger, 0.70–0.76 for Irritability, and 0.53–0.93 for Assault. For 20 nonpatient control subjects (hospital staff members) test-retest reliability coefficients were 0.66–0.98 for Labile Anger, 0.88–0.94 for Irritability, and 0.78–0.84 for Assault.

Validity

The Labile Anger, Irritability, and Assault subscales were correlated with their original models, ALS Anger, BDHI Irritability, and BDHI Physical Assault, respectively, over all three time frames: past week ($r = 0.55$–0.78 for patients, 0.62–0.81 for control subjects), past month ($r = 0.60$–0.83 for patients, 0.57–0.84 for control subjects), and across adulthood ($r = 0.31$–0.69 for patients, 0.69–0.86 for control subjects).

The original article also included correlations with the Overt Aggression Scale—Modified (OAS-M) (p. 699), a semistructured interview that assesses overt aggression. The OAS-M Global Irritability subscale correlated with the AIAQ Labile Anger subscale ($r = 0.50$) and with the AIAQ Irritability subscale ($r = 0.48$). The OAS-M Subjective Irritability subscale did not correlate with either scale. Four out of five items from the OAS-M Verbal Assault subscale correlated with at least one AIAQ subscale.

The AIAQ distinguished clinical from nonclinical groups: 22 outpatient psychiatric patients (primary diagnoses of major depressive disorder or personality disorder) scored significantly higher than 20 control subjects recruited from hospital staff on all three subscales for all three time frames.

Clinician rating of alcohol use, posited to reflect another form of maladaptive impulsive behavior, correlated with the AIAQ Labile Anger and Irritability subscales. The quantity of drinking in the past week also correlated with the Assault subscale ($r = 0.48$). Correlations with drug use, depressed mood, anxiety, and compulsive behavior were not significant.

The only data on sensitivity to change come from a study of the effectiveness of fluoxetine versus placebo on impulsive aggression in 40 patients (28 of whom were men) with personality disorders. There was no significant drug effect on the revised AIAQ Irritability or Aggression subscale scores, although predicted differences were demonstrated in OAS-M scores.

Intercorrelations between the three original subscales suggest that they measure related constructs. Scale intercorrelations show a relationship between the Labile Anger and Irritability subscales across all time frames ($r = 0.63$–0.83 for 22 psychiatric outpatients and 0.73–0.78 for 20 control subjects). Scores on the Irritability and Assault subscales were related for patients ($r = 0.53$–0.67) but not for control subjects. Scores on the Labile Anger and Assault subscales were related for patients ($r = 0.53$–0.67) but only in adulthood for control subjects ($r = 0.50$).

CLINICAL UTILITY

The original AIAQ is a self-report questionnaire designed to measure three aspects of impulsive aggression that are putatively related to serotonergic function. The revised AIAQ adds two new subscales that provide a fuller assessment of aggressive behavior. The items are clearly written, the self-report format allows for convenient administration, and the different time frames provide additional information. Although there are only preliminary validity data on fairly small samples, there is reasonable evidence of reliability and validity, and the items are derived from previously published instruments.

The domains of the AIAQ are of interest for both clinical and scientific purposes. Assault items address concrete aggressive behaviors (e.g., "When I really lose my temper, I am capable of slapping someone") but do not go into much detail. Greater detail may be warranted when assessing impulsive aggression in clinical settings. Moreover, the distinction between the Irritability and Labile Anger subscales is not entirely clear. *Irritability* refers to a hypersensitivity to provocation. *Labile anger* refers to readiness to anger without clear provocation. Some subjects' perceptions of provocation, however, may

be sufficiently idiosyncratic that no clear external provocation is identifiable by outside observers. The revised version appears to address this issue, however, by collapsing the Labile Anger and Irritability subscales into the larger Irritability scale.

Like many self-report instruments, there are inherent advantages and disadvantages. The format permits quick and convenient administration. However, self-report instruments are more vulnerable to social desirability biases than are clinical interviews. In addition, patients with a greater tendency toward impulsive aggression may have difficulty maintaining consistent assessments of their own behavior and mental states over time. In support of this hypothesis, in the studies mentioned previously, patients but not control subjects demonstrated slightly elevated test-retest coefficients, mean scores, and external validity on more recent time frames compared with more distant time frames.

There are few studies of validity. Although the subscales were derived from previously published tests (the BDHI and the ALS), the ALS is not widely known and the BDHI has been criticized for the psychometric properties of its subscales. Moreover, the only study that addresses sensitivity to change showed a negative response. Thus, further validity data derived from comparison with other established measures are needed.

The scale was designed for research purposes, particularly for neurobiological or psychopharmacological studies on impulsive aggression, and it is well suited for this purpose. The evidence of reliability and validity suggests adequate sensitivity to variation in group scores, the self-report format is convenient for research settings, and the constructs have been related to serotonin function in individuals with impulsive aggression.

For clinical purposes, the instrument might be of use as part of an evaluation of clinical severity or to help assess change over time. The instrument has been shown to differentiate an outpatient population from a control group. However, the absence of norms, of clear cutoff scores to assess diagnostic relevance, and of standardized scores limits the clinical utility of the measure.

REFERENCES AND SUGGESTED READINGS

Buss AH, Durkee A: An inventory for assessing different kinds of hostility. J Consult Psychol 21:343–349, 1957

Coccaro EF, Kavoussi RJ: Fluoxetine and impulsive-aggressive behavior in personality disordered subjects. Arch Gen Psychiatry 54:1081–1088, 1997

Coccaro EF, Harvey PD, Kupsaw-Lawrence E, et al: Development of neuropharmacologically based behavioral assessments of impulsive aggressive behavior. J Neuropsychiatry Clin Neurosci 3(2):S44–S51, 1991

Harvey PD, Greenberg BR, Serper MR: The Affective Lability Scales: development, reliability, and validity. J Clin Psychol 45:786–793, 1989

Buss-Durkee Hostility Inventory (BDHI)

A. H. Buss and A. Durkee

GOALS

The Buss-Durkee Hostility Inventory (BDHI) (Buss and Durkee 1957) was developed to systematically assess various components of hostility to aid in clinical assessment and in research on anger and aggression. This measure was intended to assess hostility both as an overall characteristic and as a complex trait with multiple dimensions. Although *hostility* is not defined in the original 1957 article, it appears to serve as a general term for aggression, incorporating emotional, attitudinal, and behavioral aspects of aggression. Hence, hostility includes a range of modes of expression, from negative attitudes to subtly aggressive behavior to outright violent behavior. Current studies generally employ more specific definitions of *hostility* and *aggression*.

DESCRIPTION

The BDHI is a 75-item self-report questionnaire with a yes-no (true-false) format. There are eight subscale scores and the Total Hostility score. The subscales are Assault, Indirect Hostility, Irritability, Negativity, Resentment, Suspicion, Verbal Hostility, and Guilt. The Total Hostil-

ity score includes all the subscales except Guilt. Two sample items are provided in Example 31–3.

The total maximum score is 66; the maximum subscale scores range from 5 to 13. Although no well-standardized norms have been derived from large samples, the original Buss-Durkee study (1957) included means and standard deviations for 85 male and 88 female college students. The mean Total Hostility scores were 30.87 ± 10.24 and 27.74 ± 8.75, respectively. In a study of 69 psychiatric outpatients (38 men and 31 women), the Total Hostility score for the whole sample was 35.68 ± 12.80. Because of some question about the validity of the subscales, two overarching scales, Overt Hostility and Covert Hostility, have been introduced as alternatives (see later section).

PRACTICAL ISSUES

It takes about 15–20 minutes to complete the BDHI, which is filled out by the subject with only minimal instructions. The test questions are printed in full in the original publication (Buss and Durkee 1957), which is protected by copyright. The BDHI is included on the CD-ROM that accompanies this handbook.

PSYCHOMETRIC PROPERTIES

Reliability

Studies investigating internal consistency in undergraduate populations reported Cronbach's alpha coefficients of 0.58–0.72. Good test-retest correlations were reported for the total score ($r = 0.82$ over a 2-week period and 0.92 over a 7-day period) in undergraduate and outpatient populations. Over a 5-week period test-retest correlations (r) were reported to range from 0.56 to 0.78.

EXAMPLE 31–3 ■ **Sample items from the Buss-Durkee Hostility Inventory**

> Once in a while I cannot control my urge to harm others. (T scored 1)
>
> I can think of no good reason for ever hitting anyone. (F scored 1)

Reprinted with permission from A. H. Buss.

Validity

The BDHI correlates well with other measures of similar domains. In a study of 69 outpatients, the total score correlated with the State ($r = 0.62$) and Trait ($r = 0.83$) scales of a predecessor to the State-Trait Anger Expression Inventory (STAXI) (p. 702), the State Trait Anger Scale (STAS); correlations of the BDHI subscale scores were 0.18–0.55 with the State scale and 0.47–0.68 with the Trait scale of the STAS. The total score correlated with the general scale score of the Hostility and Direction of Hostility Questionnaire (HDHQ) (Foulds et al. 1960) ($r = 0.83$) and with the Intropunitive ($r = 0.72$) and Extrapunitive ($r = 0.80$) subscales of the HDHQ. BDHI subscale correlations ranged from 0.42 to 0.82 with the General Hostility scale on the HDHQ.

The BDHI subscales were originally intended to distinguish between different components or types of hostility. Their value in this regard is questionable. First, the subscale items are not more strongly correlated with their designated scales than with nonrelated subscales. In a study of 203 undergraduates, only 14 out of 75 items had significantly higher item-scale correlations with their designated scale than with irrelevant scales. Moreover, when BDHI subscales and subscales of other anger and hostility measures, such as the Personal Incidents Record (PIR) (Biaggio et al. 1981) and the HDHQ Intropunitive and Extrapunitive scales, were examined, correlations were no greater with similar scales than with dissimilar scales.

Another indication of the validity of a hostility measure is its ability to distinguish between groups known to differ in level of hostility. In one study, both the BDHI Total Hostility score and the Irritability and Suspicion subscale scores differentiated violent from nonviolent adolescent prisoners. Another study found no differences in the BDHI scores of violent and nonviolent prisoners, although there were significant differences across different racial and ethnic groups. The BDHI differentiated violent groups from control groups in two other studies but not in a third. One possible explanation is that the BDHI has less sensitivity to variation at extreme levels of hostility and aggression (e.g., in prison populations). In comparing means from studies of undergraduate, outpatient, and prisoner populations, the prisoners had the lowest BDHI scores, and the outpatients scored higher than the undergraduates. That a prison population scored lower than college men on all subscales strongly suggests that the scale loses sensitivity at high levels of hostility and aggression.

Some evidence suggests that response to the scale may be moderately biased by the social desirability of the items. In a sample of 120 college students, the probability of item endorsement was correlated with the item's social desirability rating ($r = 0.27$–0.30). Thus, the scale suffers from the vulnerability of any self-report instrument to conscious and unconscious disclosure biases.

Interestingly, in a sample of 69 outpatients, the BDHI Total Hostility score and six of the subscale scores correlated with depression scores as measured by the Hamilton Rating Scale for Depression (Ham-D) (p. 526) and the Beck Depression Inventory (BDI) (p. 519).

The BDHI subscales were reconfigured into two overarching scales, Covert Hostility and Overt Hostility; the Covert Hostility and Overt Hostility scales correlated more strongly with related subscales than with unrelated subscales of Spielberger's Anger Expression Scale (a predecessor of the STAXI [p. 702]) and the Anger Self-Report Scale (Zelin et al. 1972), showing good discriminant validity. These overarching scales also had adequate internal consistency (alpha = 0.67 and 0.77) and higher item-scale correlations with designated scales than with irrelevant scales.

In an attempt to improve the psychometric properties of the subscales, Buss and Perry (1992) adapted the BDHI into a 29-item Likert scale, the Aggression Questionnaire, with four subscales: Physical Aggression, Verbal Aggression, Anger, and Hostility. Repeated factor analyses on data from three separate samples of undergraduates ($N = 1,253$) suggested that the subscales measured distinct constructs and thus contributed unique information.

CLINICAL UTILITY

The BDHI is the oldest and possibly best-known anger and hostility instrument. It is a practical test that is easy to administer and score. The test wording is easy to understand, although some contemporary subjects may find the colloquial language of 1957 somewhat alien.

Several significant limitations restrict this scale's clinical utility, however. There are no well-established norms, which makes interpretation of individual scores difficult. In addition, the true-false format reduces clinical sensitivity. A Likert format would allow for more gradations of response (e.g., "somewhat true" and "always true"). Moreover, the test does not appear to be sensitive to variation at extreme levels of hostility and contains no questions that address severe aggression. The scale is heavily weighted toward assessing subjects' attitudes about hostility, as opposed to the frequency of specific aggressive behaviors. This approach may undermine its sensitivity in extremely aggressive subjects, because there is substantial evidence that highly impulsive people have an impaired capacity to conceptualize their own emotional experience and behavioral patterns. Thus, subjects' capacity for self-reflection may vary as a function of their impulsive aggression. Social desirability effects may also lead some subjects to minimize their responses to avoid socially undesirable answers. The scale does not include a subscale to measure a subject's response set (e.g., a tendency to either minimize or maximize pathology). Finally, concern about test confidentiality and the effects of test results may produce biased results in some circumstances (e.g., in prison or classroom settings).

In regard to the subscales, the choice of items seems arbitrary at times. For example, several items on the Indirect Hostility subscale might be highly related to general assaultiveness or explosiveness (e.g., "When I am mad, I sometimes slam doors" and "Since the age of 10, I have never had a temper tantrum"). Because the subscales do not appear to measure separate constructs, they do not add any new information to the total score. On the other hand, the Covert Hostility and Overt Hostility scales appear promising; they have greater validity than the original subscales. The revised Aggression Questionnaire also appears promising but, at present, lacks extensive psychometric data.

The BDHI was designed to assess how aggression may relate to other behavioral traits in populations of people; in this regard, it is successful. The Total Hostility score has good internal consistency and test-retest reliability, and there are strong correlations with other similar measures. For these reasons the BDHI is likely to be most successful in research settings in nonclinical populations or in clinical settings with populations of moderate psychopathology. The scale is probably most useful as a research tool for measuring the relationship between aggression and other behavioral traits across populations. Although evidence is currently lacking, the scale may also be useful as a measure of clinical change in individual patients or in patient groups. However, the BDHI is not optimal as a baseline assessment of an individual patient's personality profile, level and pattern of aggressive tendencies, or likelihood for violence.

REFERENCES AND SUGGESTED READINGS

Biaggio MK, Supplee K, Curtis N: Reliability and validity of four anger scales. J Pers Assess 45:639–649, 1981

Buss AH, Durkee A: An inventory for assessing different kinds of hostility. J Consult Psychol 21:343–349, 1957

Buss AH, Perry M: The Aggression Questionnaire. J Pers Soc Psychol 63:453–459, 1992

Foulds GA, Caine TM, Creasy MA: Aspects of extra- and intropunitive expression in mental illness. Br J Psychiatry 106:599–610, 1960

Lothstein LM, Jones P: Discriminating violent individuals by means of various psychological tests. J Pers Assess 42:237–243, 1978

Ramanaiah NV, Conn SR, Schill T: On the content saturation of the Buss-Durkee Hostility Inventory scales. Psychol Rep 61:591–594, 1987

Schill T, Ramanaiah N, Conn SR: Development of Covert and Overt Hostility scales from the Buss-Durkee Inventory. Psychol Rep 67:671–674, 1990

Zelin ML, Adler G, Myerson PG: Anger self-report: an objective questionnaire for the measurement of aggression. J Consult Clin Psychol 39:340, 1972

Overt Aggression Scale— Modified (OAS-M)

E. Coccaro

GOALS

The Overt Aggression Scale—Modified (OAS-M) (Coccaro et al. 1991) was designed to assess various manifestations of aggressive behavior in outpatients. This measure is intended to evaluate the severity, type, and frequency of aggressive behavior and is a revised version of an earlier measure designed for inpatient populations. The scale incorporates three overall domains: Aggression, Irritability, and Suicidality.

DESCRIPTION

The OAS-M is a 25-item clinician-administered, semistructured interview with nine subscales. Three overall areas are rated: Aggression, Irritability, and Suicidality. For Aggression, there are four subscales of behavior: Verbal Aggression, Aggression Against Objects, Aggression Against Others, and Auto-Aggression (Aggression Against Self). For Irritability, there are two subscales: Global Irritability and Subjective Irritability. For Suicidality, there are three subscales: Suicidal Tendencies (Ideation and Behavior), Intent of Attempt, and Lethality of Attempt. The Aggression items were adapted from the Overt Aggression Scale (OAS), which was designed for inpatient populations (Yudofsky et al. 1986). The OAS-M should be distinguished from other modifications of the OAS, such as the Modified Overt Aggression Scale (MOAS) (Sorgi et al. 1991), which, like the original OAS, assesses aggressive behavior in residential settings. The Irritability and Suicidality items were adapted from the Schedule for Affective Disorders and Schizophrenia (SADS) (p. 58). The time frame of the OAS-M is restricted to the past week.

Although the measure is considered a semistructured interview, the authors do not provide specific interview questions or probes but include instructions on administration and suggested interview questions (e.g., "In the past week how many times did you . . . ?").

Two different formats are used in this measure. For each of the four Aggression subscales, seven characteristic behaviors are listed in order of severity and weighted accordingly. Subscale items are not mutually exclusive, and scoring involves the weighted sum of all endorsed behaviors. The Irritability and Suicidality subscales use a Likert-type format in which a single continuous scale includes up to seven mutually exclusive scale points. Sample items are provided in Example 31–4.

Final scores are rated on three scales: Aggression (subscales 1–4), Irritability (subscales 5–6), and Suicidality (subscales 7, 7a, and 7b). The two Irritability and three Suicidality subscales are rated on 6- or 7-point Likert-type scales from 0 = none or not at all to 5 = extreme or 6 = very extreme. The maximum possible score is 10 for the Irritability scale and 16 for the Suicidality scale. The Aggression scale uses a different format in which each specific behavior is scored separately by frequency and then multiplied by assigned weights.

For each Aggression subscale, seven specific behaviors are listed in order of severity, then weighted by their respective rank (see Example 31–4). The weighted frequencies are summed to form each subscale score. Subscale scores are then multiplied by their own assigned weights: Verbal Aggression by 1, Aggression Against Objects by 2, and Auto-Aggression and Aggression Against Others by 3. Weighted subscale scores are added to obtain a final scale score for Aggression.

Norms are not available, and sample means were not presented in the original publication.

PRACTICAL ISSUES

Administration time is not specified but may be estimated to be approximately 30 minutes. The test is copyrighted by Emil Coccaro, M.D.:

> Emil Coccaro, M.D.
> Department of Psychiatry
> Medical College of Pennsylvania
> Eastern Pennsylvania Psychiatric Institute
> 3200 Henry Avenue
> Philadelphia, PA 19129

The author has given permission for the test to be used without cost. The OAS is included on the CD-ROM that accompanies this handbook.

PSYCHOMETRIC PROPERTIES

There are very limited data available on psychometric properties, but preliminary results appear promising.

Reliability

The OAS-M was administered to 22 subjects (15 men and 7 women) with a primary diagnosis of either personality disorder or major depressive disorder. Joint reliability in two raters was assessed by intraclass correlation for the Aggression and Irritability total scores (intraclass correlation coefficient > 0.91). Test-retest reliability for the Aggression and Irritability scales, assessed in two administrations separated by 1–2 weeks, was less impressive (intraclass correlation coefficient = 0.46 and 0.54). However, this low reliability may reflect the inherent affective instability of the sample population.

EXAMPLE 31–4 ■ Sample item from the Overt Aggression Scale—Modified

1. Verbal assault:	0 = No events.	
Assessment of verbal outbursts or threats made at spouse, boy/girl friend, close friends, strangers.	1 = Snapped or yelled at someone. 2 = Cursed at or personally insulted someone. 3 = Engaged in a verbal argument with someone. 4 = Verbally threatened to hit someone the pt knows well. 5 = Verbally threatened to hit a stranger.	_____ _____ _____ _____ _____
	TOTAL WEIGHTED SCORE =	_____ × 1 = _____

Reprinted with permission from Emil Coccaro, M.D.

Validity

Validity data on the OAS-M are preliminary. There are no data on the Suicidality scale.

Intercorrelations between Irritability and Aggression scores suggest that they are measuring a related construct, presumably an overarching construct of aggressive behavior. Total scores for OAS-M Irritability and Aggression scales were correlated ($r = 0.53$). OAS-M Subjective Irritability and Global Irritability subscale scores were correlated with each other ($r = 0.69$) and with the total Aggression scale score ($r = 0.60$ and 0.42, respectively). The Aggression Against Objects subscale and the Verbal Aggression subscale scores were correlated with the Irritability scale score ($r = 0.59$ and 0.45, respectively).

The only external validity data come from a comparison of selected items in the OAS-M and in the Anger, Irritability, and Assault Questionnaire (AIAQ) (p. 694). The OAS-M Global Irritability subscale correlated significantly with the AIAQ Labile Anger subscale ($r = 0.50$) and the AIAQ Irritability subscale ($r = 0.48$). Correlations between the OAS-M Subjective Irritability subscale and the AIAQ subscales that assess irritability were not significant. OAS-M items on the Verbal Aggression subscale correlated with AIAQ subscales: OAS-M swearing obscenities with AIAQ Labile Anger ($r = 0.48$), OAS-M arguing with AIAQ Assault ($r = 0.44$), and OAS-M threatening violence with AIAQ Labile Anger ($r = 0.44$), Irritability ($r = 0.53$), and Assault ($r = 0.36$).

Although data are limited, some evidence suggests that the OAS-M is sensitive to change. A 12-week trial of fluoxetine versus placebo in 40 outpatients with personality disorders demonstrated significant drug-placebo differences on OAS-M Aggression and Irritability scores

and on clinician-rated Clinical Global Impressions (CGI) Scale scores (p. 100) but not on self-report AIAQ scores. Post hoc analyses revealed significant differences between the Verbal Aggression and the Aggression Against Objects subscales but not between the Aggression Against Self or Aggression Against Others subscales. Because items on these latter scales involved more severe forms of aggression, they were less frequently endorsed and thus less sensitive to change.

CLINICAL UTILITY

The OAS-M is a fairly short instrument and relatively easy to administer. Despite the paucity of psychometric data, the format of the OAS-M offers several advantages over most available anger and aggression instruments. Moreover, unlike many aggression instruments, for which the norms were derived from undergraduate students, the OAS-M emerged from work with highly aggressive clinical populations.

Specifically, the OAS-M is one of the only aggression measures that actually assesses concrete aggressive behavior, which is generally of greatest interest to clinicians treating aggressive patients. The use of weighted items in Aggression scale scores takes into account that high-severity items are both less frequent and more significant than low-severity items. Likewise, the score does not derive solely from subjects' self-reports of highly generalized evaluations of aggressive attitudes and behavior, which are vulnerable to several potential confounding factors. One such factor is variation in the subjects' verbal abilities and their capacity to form abstract conceptions of their own thoughts and behavior, because these abilities are often impaired in highly aggressive subjects. Thus, the format of the OAS-M offers advantages for assessing high levels of aggression. In addition, the interview format allows clinicians to probe vague and inconsistent answers, presumably increasing the accuracy of responses and counteracting subjects' hesitancy to disclose socially undesirable behavior.

Because of the inclusion of items that probe subjects' mental states, particularly in the Irritability and Suicidality scales, this instrument is not ideal for nonverbal or intellectually impaired subjects. The original OAS (Yudofsky et al. 1986) and its adaptation, the MOAS (Sorgi et al. 1991), rely on staff observations of subjects' aggressive behavior and thus are more appropriate for nonverbal subjects or those with low IQs, particularly in residential settings.

The lack of sufficient reliability and validity data is a shortcoming, however, and the absence of specified interview questions may reduce reliability. The absence of norms also makes it difficult to determine the significance of individual scores. Although some data are available for the Irritability and Aggression scales, there are no data on the Suicidality scale. Nonetheless, all items were modified from previously published instruments, the Aggression scales from the OAS (Yudofsky et al. 1986) and the Irritability and Suicidality items from the SADS (p. 58).

Given its focus on detailed behavioral assessment, the OAS-M would be well suited for clinical evaluations of aggressive behavior and for evaluation of change over time. There is some evidence that the OAS-M is more sensitive to change than the self-report AIAQ (p. 694). The lack of norms, however, suggests that such evaluations should be done in conjunction with other instruments. The OAS-M is also well suited as a research instrument and might complement many of the self-report measures currently in use. Further research would also contribute new psychometric data.

REFERENCES AND SUGGESTED READINGS

Coccaro EF, Kavoussi RJ: Fluoxetine and impulsive aggressive behavior in personality disordered subjects. Arch Gen Psychiatry 54:1081–1088, 1997

Coccaro EF, Harvey PD, Kupsaw-Lawerence E, et al: Development of neuropharmacologically based behavioral assessments of impulsive aggressive behavior. J Neuropsychiatry Clin Neurosci 3:S44–S51, 1991

Sorgi P, Ratey J, Knoedler DW, et al: Rating aggression in the clinical setting. A retrospective adaptation of the Overt Aggression Scale: preliminary results. J Neuropsychiatry Clin Neurosci 3:S52–S56, 1991

Spitzer R, Endicott J: Schedule for Affective Disorders and Schizophrenia. New York, New York State Psychiatric Institute, 1978

Yudofsky SC, Silver JM, Jackson W, et al: The Overt Aggression Scale for the objective rating of verbal and physical aggression. Am J Psychiatry 143:35–39, 1986

State-Trait Anger Expression Inventory (STAXI)

C. D. Spielberger

GOALS

The State-Trait Anger Expression Inventory (STAXI) (Spielberger et al. 1985) is designed to assess different components of anger in the evaluation of normal and abnormal personality. The STAXI was also developed to assess the contribution of various components of anger to the development of medical conditions such as hypertension, coronary heart disease, and cancer. *Anger* is defined here as an emotional state, varying in intensity from mild annoyance to rage, that is accompanied by arousal of the autonomic nervous system. The cognitive components of anger, such as systematic processing biases that may predispose an individual to angry reactions, are not included in this definition. The measure addresses two domains of anger: state-trait anger and the mode of anger expression. The state-trait dimensions distinguish between a general propensity to experience angry feelings (trait) and the level of anger experienced in the present moment (state). The anger expression domain is considered independent of the state-trait domain and addresses the extent to which expression of anger is directed outwardly toward the environment, directed inwardly toward the self, or consciously controlled.

DESCRIPTION

The STAXI is a 44-item self-administered questionnaire from which eight different scale (or subscale) scores can be derived. State Anger (S-Anger) is a 10-item scale that measures intensity of angry feelings at the time of testing. Trait Anger (T-Anger) is also a 10-item scale and assesses the propensity to experience anger. Two 4-item subscales can be derived from it: Angry Temperament (T-Anger/T) measures disposition to experience anger without specific provocation, and Angry Reaction (T-Anger/R) measures the tendency to express anger when criticized or treated unfairly by others.

The next four scales are Anger Expression scales. Anger In (AX/In) is an 8-item scale that measures the frequency with which angry feelings are held in or suppressed. Anger Out (AX/Out) is an 8-item scale that measures the frequency with which anger is expressed outwardly. The 8-item Anger Control (AX/CON) scale measures the frequency with which the individual attempts to control the expression of anger and calm him- or herself. The AX/CON scale can be seen as a measure of appropriate anger modulation, an adaptive trait. In contrast, the AX/In and AX/Out scales reflect failures of modulation—that is, elevated levels of anger or aggression that differ in their mode of expression. The Anger Expression (AX/EX) scale consists of the 24 items that make up the AX/In, AX/Out, and AX/CON scales and provides a general index of the frequency with which anger is expressed, regardless of direction of expression. The state-trait and anger expression components were originally published separately as the State-Trait Anger Inventory and the Anger-Expression Scales.

Items are rated on a 4-point scale assessing intensity (from 1 = not at all to 4 = very much so) on the S-Anger scale and frequency (from 1 = almost never to 4 = almost always) on all other scales.

The STAXI is scored only on individual scales. There is no total score. Scores on the S-Anger and T-Anger scales range from 10 to 40. Scores on the two subscales of the T-Anger, T-Anger/T and T-Anger/R, range from 4 to 16. On the next three Anger Expression scales (AX/In, AX/Out, and AX/CON), scores range from 8 to 32. Scores on the calculated Anger Expression scale (AX/EX) are calculated by a formula and range from 0 to 72.

The STAXI manual provides norms on male and female adults, college students, and adolescents drawn from samples of several thousand subjects. Norms for adults are also broken down into age groups: ages 18–30, 31–40, and over 40 years. Norms for select scales are also provided for special groups (e.g., medical and surgical patients, prison inmates, and military recruits). Scores on all scales decrease across age groups, with the exception of the AX/CON scale score, which increases with age. People who fall within the 25%–75% range of an age- and gender-matched population may be considered within normal limits.

PRACTICAL ISSUES

The test takes about 10–12 minutes to complete and 3–4 minutes to score and profile. It requires a fifth-grade reading level and is intended for subjects ages 13 and older. The STAXI is copyrighted by

> Psychological Assessment Resources, Inc.
> P.O. Box 998
> Odessa, FL 33556
> Phone: 800-331-TEST (800-331-8378)

Two forms of the test can be ordered from Psychological Assessment Resources, Inc. Form HS is a four-page booklet with test instructions, test items, and a scoring grid for interpreting percentiles and T-scores. Form G is designed for large group administration, and tests are mailed in for machine scoring. A comprehensive manual can be ordered along with the test (Spielberger 1996). The manual includes administration and scoring procedures, demographically stratified norms, and discussion of reliability and validity studies. Form HS can be ordered in a kit for $85.00, which includes the manual ($27.00 separately), 50 item booklets ($34.00 separately), and 50 rating sheets ($34.00 separately). Form G is available in packages of 50 for $65.00.

A Russian translation is available.

PSYCHOMETRIC PROPERTIES

Reliability

Given the small number of items per scale, internal consistency and test-retest reliability are surprisingly strong. Cronbach's alphas for the first six scales ranged from 0.70

to 0.93. In addition, 14-day test-retest correlations ranged from 0.62 to 0.81 for all scales except S-Anger ($r = 0.27$ for men and 0.21 for women), for which stability over time would not be expected.

Validity

The STAXI scales have shown strong correlations with other anger and hostility measures. In addition, the individual subscales show strong evidence of discriminant validity, in that they appropriately correlate with measures of similar traits and poorly correlate with measures of dissimilar traits.

The T-Anger scale was strongly correlated with the Total Hostility score of the Buss-Durkee Hostility Inventory (BDHI) (p. 697) ($r = 0.66$–0.73). The T-Anger scale was also correlated with the Hostility and Overt Hostility scale of the Minnesota Multiphasic Personality Inventory (MMPI) (p. 89). Ranges of correlations were 0.43–0.59 and 0.27–0.32, respectively.

The T-Anger and S-Anger scales were also correlated with the Eysenck Personality Questionnaire (EPQ) (Eysenck and Eysenck 1975) and the State and Trait Curiosity and Anxiety scales of the State Trait Personality Inventory (STPI). Neither the S-Anger nor T-Anger scale was related to extraversion ($r = -0.06$ to -0.08), but they were moderately related to the EPQ scales sensitive to negative affect, such as Neuroticism ($r = 0.27$ to 0.50) and Psychoticism ($r = 0.20$ to 0.27). Likewise, the S-Anger scale was highly related to the State Anxiety ($r = 0.63$) and moderately related to the Trait Anxiety ($r = 0.30$–0.35) scales on the STPI. The T-Anger scale was less related to the State Anxiety ($r = 0.19$–0.25) than to the Trait Anxiety scale ($r = 0.37$–0.38). Neither the S-Anger nor T-Anger scale was positively related to either the State Curiosity or Trait Curiosity scale ($r = -0.07$ to -0.20).

On the other hand, the T-Anger scale, but not the S-Anger scale, was inversely correlated with the MMPI Lie scale ($r = -0.20$ to -0.25), pointing to some degree of a social desirability bias. It is possible that the T-Anger scale is seen as reflecting a personal characteristic more than a transient state of anger and hence is more vulnerable to social desirability biases.

The STAXI Anger Expression scales were correlated with the Covert and Overt Hostility factors of the BDHI (p. 697), which measure constructs very similar to those of the AX/In and AX/Out scales. The AX/In scale correlated with the Covert Hostility scale ($r = 0.57$–0.72) and with the Overt Hostility scale ($r = 0.07$–0.22), and the AX/Out scale correlated with the Covert Hostility scale ($r = 0.28$–0.37) and with the Overt Hostility scale ($r = 0.44$–0.56). The AX/CON scale was inversely correlated with both the Covert Hostility scale ($r = -0.44$ to -0.48) and the Overt Hostility scale ($r = -0.53$ to -0.65).

Factor analyses suggest that the AX/In, AX/Out, and AX/CON scales are all measuring distinct constructs and contribute unique information. Factor analysis of the combined AX/In and AX/Out scales was conducted in a sample of 1,114 high school students. For AX/In items, factor loadings ranged from 0.58 to 0.72 on the AX/In factor and from -0.16 to -0.17 on the AX/Out factor; for AX/Out items, factor loadings ranged from 0.44 to 0.72 on the AX/Out factor and from -0.12 to -0.17 on the AX/In factor. Another factor analysis was conducted on the Anger Expression scales (24 items for AX/In, AX/Out, and AX/CON) in 409 undergraduates to demonstrate validity for the AX/CON scale. The AX/CON factor correlated inversely with the AX/Out factor ($r = -0.59$) and did not correlate with the AX/In factor.

To assess the relationship of the STAXI scales to measures of appropriate assertiveness and specific consequences of anger dysregulation, a revision of the scale with 35 new items was administered to 274 undergraduates. Items associated with the AX/In, AX/Out, and T-Anger scales all correlated with aggressive items ($r = 0.20$ to 0.69) and negative consequences ($r = 0.07$ to 0.59) but not with prosocial assertiveness ($r = -0.22$ to -0.45). In contrast, the AX/CON scale was highly correlated with appropriate assertiveness items ($r = 0.51$ to 0.77) but poorly correlated with aggressive items ($r = -0.25$ to -0.66) and negative consequences of aggression ($r = -0.03$ to -0.48).

Sensitivity to change on the STAXI was demonstrated in a treatment study of 29 undergraduates previously rated high on the T-Anger and S-Anger scales. After relaxation and coping skills training, both T-Anger and S-Anger scores were significantly reduced.

The STAXI scales were also intended to predict certain medical conditions. A significant amount of research has been conducted on the relationship of STAXI scales to various medical problems, such as hypertension, other cardiovascular disease, and chronic pain. In one study, systolic and diastolic blood pressures in 1,114 high school students were correlated with the AX/In, AX/Out, and an early three-item version of the AX/CON scale. Blood pressure was more highly correlated with AX/In for men (systolic blood pressure, $r = 0.47$; diastolic blood pressure, $r = 0.29$) and women (systolic blood pressure, $r = 0.27$; diastolic blood pressure, $r = 0.16$) than with the AX/Out or the calculated AX/EX scores ($r = -0.45$ to 0.05); these findings are consistent with the hypothesis that suppressing anger leads to raised blood pressure.

CLINICAL UTILITY

The STAXI is a well-standardized measure, with detailed norms, percentages, and T-scores. It is a short test that is easy to administer and understand, and it has unusually strong psychometric properties for a multiscaled instrument of this length. The scales show excellent discriminant validity and make clinical sense. The different scales appear to be measuring distinct constructs and to contribute unique information. The scale was designed for assessment of personality profiles and appears to be useful in distinguishing modes of anger expression. It also has some utility in predicting stress-related physical conditions, such as hypertension.

Nonetheless, there are some limitations. Although the scales appear to have strong discriminant validity psychometrically, the constructs underlying the scales are not always clear. For example, although the AX/CON scale has been correlated with measures of prosocial assertiveness, appropriate assertiveness is not assessed directly. Thus, it is not clear how the appropriate expression of anger would be scored. Moreover, although the AX/In scale is an Anger Expression scale, some of the items imply suppression of anger ("I keep things in") as opposed to its indirect expression. It is therefore not entirely clear how the AX/In scale, which measures the inward expression of anger, differs from the AX/CON scale, which measures the control of anger and the attempt to reduce anger arousal. Other authors have suggested, however, that the AX/In scale measures the suppression of angry behavior but not cognitive and affective arousal (Deffenbacher et al. 1996). Also, although the author states that cognitive components of angry experience are outside the scope of the scale, the T-Anger/R scale relies on cognitive appraisals of other people's behavior and its effect on subjects' self-esteem ("I feel annoyed when I am not given recognition for doing good work" and "It makes me furious when I am criticized in front of others"). Thus,

the scores on the T-Anger/R scale may be confounded by cognitive factors as well as the stability of subjects' self-esteem, suggesting that the scale is measuring a more complicated construct than intended.

In addition, the measure may have limited utility in populations with extreme levels of anger or aggression, such as subjects with antisocial personality disorders or prisoners. First, the inventory relies on self-report of general behavioral and psychological patterns. In populations characterized by severe problems with impulse control, there is substantial evidence of impaired conceptual ability to self-reflect. Results may therefore be biased by inaccurate self-perceptions. Second, the lack of detailed questions about behavioral manifestations of anger (e.g., slamming doors vs. forms of violence) may further reduce sensitivity at higher levels of anger and aggression, because concrete questions about forms of aggressive behavior might differentiate highly aggressive subjects with greater sensitivity than more general questions. Finally, social desirability factors may lead subjects to minimize their responses, and abstract evaluations of general tendencies may be more easily distorted than actual facts about specific behavior. Likewise, the norms for prison populations provided in the manual are not markedly higher than those for the general population. Reduced sensitivity at high levels is a common feature of most anger or hostility measurements, however.

Nonetheless, of all the anger and aggression instruments available, the STAXI is one of the best suited for individual clinical assessment, primarily because of its extensive norms. The scale may be helpful in assessing mild to moderate difficulties in anger regulation and in clarifying the focus of treatment. However, additional assessment of concrete aggressive behaviors would still be needed for a complete evaluation. Moreover, the scale should be used only with great caution for predicting future aggressive behavior and only in combination with other sources of information. The scale might also be useful as a measure of treatment response and change over time. In addition, the scale would be appropriate for use with large sample populations in studies on the effects of anger.

REFERENCES AND SUGGESTED READINGS

Deffenbacher JL, Demm PM, Brandon AK: High general anger: correlates and treatment. Behav Res Ther 24:481–489, 1986

Deffenbacher JL, Oetting ER, Lynch RS, et al: The expression of anger and its consequences. Behav Res Ther 34:575–590, 1996

Eysenck HJ, Eysenck SBG: Manual of the Eysenck Personality Questionnaire. London, Hadder & Stoughton, 1975

Jacobs GA, Latham LE, Brown MS: Test-retest reliability of the State-Trait Personality Inventory and the Anger Expression Scale. Anxiety Research 1:263–265, 1988

Schill T, Ramanaiah N, Conn SR: Development of Covert and Overt Hostility scales from the Buss-Durkee Hostility Inventory. Psychol Rep 67:671–674, 1990

Spielberger C: State-Trait Anger Expression Inventory: STAXI Professional Manual. Odessa, FL, Psychological Assessment Resources, 1996

Spielberger CD, Johnson EH, Russell SF, et al: The experience and expression of anger: construction and validation of an anger expression scale, in Anger and Hostility in Cardiovascular and Behavioral Disorders. Edited by Chesney MA, Rosenman RH. New York, Hemisphere/McGraw-Hill, 1985, pp 5–30

South Oaks Gambling Screen (SOGS)

H. R. Lesieur and S. B. Blume

GOALS

The South Oaks Gambling Screen (SOGS) (Lesieur and Blume 1987, 1993) was developed as a quantifiable, structured instrument to assess pathological gambling; it can be easily administered by professionals and nonprofessionals. Although the SOGS questions do not correspond exactly with either the DSM-III-R or the DSM-IV criteria for pathological gambling, they assess the essential features of the disorder as defined in both DSM editions. Specifically, the SOGS assesses recurrent and maladaptive gambling behavior that disrupts personal, family, and vocational pursuits. Whereas DSM-III-R and DSM-IV also address the emotional components of gambling, the SOGS does not; rather, it focuses primarily on associated maladaptive social and financial behavior.

DESCRIPTION

The SOGS is a 20-item questionnaire that can be administered in either interview or self-report format. The measure includes 26 questions that incorporate 35 actual items; however, only 20 items are scored. The first three questions (on the type and frequency of gambling activities, maximum amount gambled in one day, and parental gambling history) are intended to provide background information and to help respondents define their gambling behavior. The original version (Lesieur and Blume 1987) uses primarily a yes-no format. The revision (Lesieur and Blume 1993) incorporates more Likert-type, multiple-choice questions, allowing more gradations of response (e.g., "some of the time" and "every time"). Questions assess the degree and breadth of consequences (social, financial, and occupational) caused by gambling losses and maladaptive compensatory behaviors, such as borrowing or gambling further to recoup losses. The SOGS addresses gambling behavior across the lifetime. The SOGS may also be completed by an informant to provide a cross-check of an individual's responses. Sample items are provided in Example 31–5.

Scores are obtained by summing all positive responses. Multiple-choice responses are changed into dichotomous scores, so that all positive responses are coded yes. Although the 1993 version incorporates more Likert-type responses than the original version, the scoring does not differ across versions. For both versions, possible scores range from 0 to 20. The authors identify ≥5 as a cutoff score for probable pathological gambling, a score of 1–4 as signifying some problem, and a score of 0 as suggesting no problem.

PRACTICAL ISSUES

Administration time is not specified but may be estimated to be about 20 minutes. There is no manual for

EXAMPLE 31–5 ■ Sample items from the South Oaks Gambling Screen

> Did you ever gamble more than you intended to?
>
> Have you ever borrowed from someone and not paid them back as a result of your gambling?

Reproduced with permission from the South Oaks Foundation, Inc.

this measure, although the Lesieur and Blume (1987) article provides instructions on administration and scoring. The SOGS has been translated into many languages, including Cambodian, Dutch, French, German, Hmong, Italian, Japanese, Lao, Spanish, Swedish, Turkish, and Vietnamese. No validity studies have been conducted on any of the versions except the English version.

The items are printed in full in the original article (Lesieur and Blume 1987). The revised items are also printed in full in the later article (Lesieur and Blume 1993). The SOGS is copyrighted by the South Oaks Foundation. Individual professionals may copy and use the SOGS in their clinical work without specific permission. Organizations and institutions interested in using the SOGS should write for permission to

Sheila B. Blume, M.D.
South Oaks Foundation
400 Sunrise Highway
Amityville, NY 11701

The author may be contacted at the following address:

Henry R. Lesieur
Department of Criminal Justice Sciences
Illinois State University
Normal, IL 61790-5250

The SOGS is included on the CD-ROM that accompanies this handbook.

PSYCHOMETRIC PROPERTIES

Most reliability and validity studies were conducted with the original 1987 version of the SOGS.

Reliability

Reliability was assessed in a sample of 749 subjects, including 213 members of Gamblers Anonymous, 384 college students, and 152 hospital employees. The SOGS was found to be highly internally consistent; Cronbach's alpha was 0.97.

To evaluate test-retest reliability, 74 inpatients and 38 outpatients at South Oaks Hospital completed the SOGS at two time points 30 or more days apart. Of these subjects, 20 (18%) were identified as pathological gamblers. Using a dichotomous classification of pathological gambling, the test-retest correlation was 0.71 for all patients (1.0 for outpatients and 0.61 for inpatients). Among inpatients, scores dropped between the two testings, lowering test-retest reliability for the sample as a whole. This decline was attributed to inpatients' awareness that scores were being used for treatment-planning purposes—hence their motivation to underreport their gambling problems.

Validity

Patients' self-reported SOGS scores correlated strongly with evaluations of gambling behavior by counselors and family members. A total of 297 patients admitted for drug or alcohol abuse completed the SOGS on admission to South Oaks Hospital. Counselors also independently evaluated these patients on a 5-point scale. Patients' scores on the SOGS were highly correlated with counselors' independent assessments ($r = 0.86$). A total of 127 family members were asked to assess their relatives' gambling behavior. Family members' assessments were also correlated with patients' scores on the SOGS ($r = 0.60$).

The SOGS was assessed against the Problematic Signs Index (Lesieur and Heineman 1988), a four-factor index based on the DSM-III-R criteria for evaluating gambling-related functional impairment (family disruption, work or school problems, financial problems, and illegal behavior). In a sample of 100 inpatient adolescent and young adult substance abusers, the SOGS correlated with the total index ($r = 0.84$) and with individual factors ($r = 0.57–0.71$).

The SOGS was also found to correlate with scores on a self-report checklist of DSM-III-R criteria for pathological gambling in a sample of 213 members of Gamblers Anonymous, 384 college students, and 152 hospital employees ($r = 0.94$).

To assess the sensitivity (ability to avoid false-negative results) and specificity (ability to avoid false-positive results) of the SOGS, the SOGS and DSM-III-R checklist scores were cross-checked. Using a SOGS cutoff score of 5, only 4 (2%) of the Gamblers Anonymous members, 18 (5%) of the college students, and 1 (1%) of the hospital employees were erroneously classified. Across the three populations, false-negative results ranged from 0.5% to 1.3% and false-positive results ranged from 0.0% to 3.4%.

CLINICAL UTILITY

The SOGS is a comprehensive measure of an understudied disorder. The brevity of the measure makes it easy to administer and score. Well-standardized measures to assess symptom severity or treatment response in gambling are lacking, and this instrument serves as the gold standard for the assessment of pathological gambling. It is a reliable and valid measure with good sensitivity and specificity. Methodological strengths also include large sample sizes for validity and reliability studies. The SOGS was validated in a variety of populations, including substance abusers and members of Gamblers Anonymous, as well as in nonpsychiatric control subjects. The variety of subjects distinguishes the SOGS from many other clinical measures, which are validated primarily among university undergraduates. Finally, the formal norms and cutoff scores make the SOGS a useful measure for diagnostic purposes.

One criticism of the measure is that individuals can obtain a score of 5 independent of their gambling frequency, because none of the scored questions assess frequency of gambling behavior. There are also doubts about the stringency of the cutoff score. Scores of 3–4 indicate problem gambling, the clinical significance of which may be underestimated with a cutoff score of 5. Moreover, the scale assesses lifetime gambling behavior and thus does not differentiate those with current problems from those with problems in remission. Other authors have used different time frames, including the past month, past 6 months, past 12 months, and across the lifetime. The authors were concerned that 1 month may be too short; they believe that if a limited time frame is to be used, it should be at least 6 months.

When used only as a self-report measure, the SOGS may result in minimization or misrepresentation of symptoms because of patients' attempts to present themselves in a socially desirable light. Thus, the authors suggest that informants and clinicians also complete the SOGS to improve its validity. In fact, the South Oaks Leisure Activities Screen (SOLAS), a 13-item Likert-style questionnaire to be filled out by family members, is also published in the later article by Lesieur and Blume (1993). The SOLAS asks about the patients' interests in various gambling activities and can also serve as a cross-check of patients' responses to the SOGS.

REFERENCES AND SUGGESTED READINGS

Lesieur HR, Blume SB: The South Oaks Gambling Screen (SOGS): a new instrument for the identification of pathological gamblers. Am J Psychiatry 144:1184–1188, 1987

Lesieur HR, Blume S: Revising the South Oaks Gambling Screen in different settings. Journal of Gambling Studies 9:213–223, 1993

Lesieur HR, Heineman M: Pathological gambling among youthful multiple substance abusers in a therapeutic community. British Journal of Addiction 83:765–771, 1988

Templer DI, Kaiser G, Siscoe K: Correlates of pathological gambling propensity in prison inmates. Compr Psychiatry 34:347–351, 1993

Volberg RA, Banks SM: A review of two measures of pathological gambling in the United States. Journal of Gambling Studies 6:153–163, 1990

Massachusetts General Hospital (MGH) Hairpulling Scale

N. J. Keuthen, R. L. O'Sullivan, J. N. Ricciardi, D. Shera, C. R. Savage, A. S. Borgmann, M. A. Jenike, and L. Baer

GOALS

The Massachusetts General Hospital (MGH) Hairpulling Scale (Keuthen et al. 1995) was developed to evaluate the severity of trichotillomania, a disorder characterized by repetitive hair pulling. The measure was modeled after the Yale-Brown Obsessive Compulsive Scale (Y-BOCS) (p. 572) but differs from the Y-BOCS in that it does not include questions on obsessional ideation. This measure assesses the urge to pull hair, the actual amount of pulling, perceived control over hair pulling, and associated distress. The MGH Hairpulling Scale was designed to evaluate the baseline severity of trichotillomania and to assess change in symptom severity over time. The scale is intended for both clinical and research settings.

DESCRIPTION

The MGH Hairpulling Scale is a seven-item self-report questionnaire scored on a 5-point Likert scale ranging from 0 = no symptoms to 4 = severe symptoms.

The first three items of the scale assess frequency, intensity, and perceived control over hair pulling urges. Items 4–6 assess attempts to resist hair pulling urges and control over hair pulling behavior. Item 7 assesses distress associated with hair pulling behavior. Sample items are provided in Example 31–6.

The total score, which ranges from 0 to 28, is obtained by summing the answers to the seven individual questions. Higher scores indicate greater severity. Because the scale was developed relatively recently, there are no standardized scores. On the original study of 118 outpatients with trichotillomania, however, mean scores ranged from 1.72 ± 1.21 to 2.73 ± 1.15 across the seven questions.

PRACTICAL ISSUES

Administration time is not specified but may be estimated at about 10 minutes. The test questions are printed

EXAMPLE 31–6 ■ **Sample items from the Massachusetts General Hospital Hairpulling Scale**

On an average day, how often did you feel the urge to pull your hair?

  0 This week I felt no urges to pull my hair.
  1 This week I felt an occasional urge to pull my hair.
  2 This week I felt an urge to pull my hair often.
  3 This week I felt an urge to pull my hair very often.
  4 This week I felt near constant urges to pull my hair.

On an average day, how often did you actually pull your hair?

  0 This week I did not pull my hair.
  1 This week I pulled my hair occasionally.
  2 This week I pulled my hair often.
  3 This week I pulled my hair very often.
  4 This week I pulled my hair so often it felt like I was always doing it.

Reproduced with permission from S. Karger AG, Basel.

in full in the original journal article (Keuthen et al. 1995).

The author of the measure can be contacted at the following address:

> Nancy J. Keuthen, Ph.D.
> Obsessive-Compulsive Disorders Clinic and
>   Research Unit
> Massachusetts General Hospital—East, 9th floor
> 149 Thirteenth Street
> Charlestown, MA 02129

The MGH Hairpulling Scale is included on the CD-ROM that accompanies this handbook.

PSYCHOMETRIC PROPERTIES

Reliability

There is good evidence of internal consistency. Cronbach's alpha was 0.89 for 119 subjects with diagnoses of trichotillomania determined on the basis of DSM-IV criteria. Item-total correlations (correlations between individual items and the total score) ranged from 0.49 to 0.76, suggesting that all items measure a related construct.

Test-retest reliability of the MGH Hairpulling Scale was also assessed. Twenty-two patients with trichotillomania completed the scale before and after a regular scheduled treatment appointment; administrations were separated by about 1 hour. Scores from the two administrations were correlated ($r = 0.97$).

Validity

Validity data were derived from a study of 26 patients with trichotillomania who were in pharmacological or behavioral treatment. Although to date there has been only one study (and the sample size was small), validity data appear promising. When compared with other measures of similar domains, the MGH Hairpulling Scale yielded strong positive correlations. The MGH Hairpulling scale was highly correlated with both the Psychiatric Institute Trichotillomania Scale (PITS) (p. 711) ($r = 0.63$) and the Clinical Global Impressions—Severity of Illness Scale Subscale (p. 100) ($r = 0.75$). The MGH Hairpulling Scale did not correlate with the Beck Depression Inventory (BDI) (p. 519) ($r = 0.30$) or the Beck Anxiety Inventory (BAI) (p. 557) ($r = 0.01$). These findings suggest that the MGH Hairpulling Scale measures a specific domain and cannot be considered a nonspecific measure of general psychiatric dysfunction.

Sensitivity to change was assessed in 23 patients at two different time points separated by 2–4 weeks. Change on the MGH Hairpulling Scale was inversely correlated with change on the Clinical Global Impressions (CGI) Scale (p. 100) ($r = -0.50$) and positively correlated with change on the PITS (p. 711) ($r = 0.83$) and on the CGS Scale (p. 100) ($r = 0.74$).

CLINICAL UTILITY

The MGH Hairpulling Scale is a self-report measure of an understudied disorder. The brevity of the measure makes it easy to administer and score. The development of well-standardized trichotillomania measures is in the early stages, and the authors have made promising steps toward a reliable and valid measure appropriate in a variety of settings.

One strength of the MGH Hairpulling Scale is that, in contrast to most of the other clinical instruments reviewed in this section, it was validated on patients with clinical symptoms and not on an undergraduate population. To date, however, there are no reports of the use of the MGH Hairpulling Scale in comparison groups such as psychiatrically healthy control subjects, psychiatric control subjects, or non–treatment-seeking trichotillomania patients.

Given the early state of development, there are no formal norms and no standardization of scores, which limit this scale's utility as a clinical assessment tool. Other methodological difficulties include the small sample sizes in the validity and reliability studies and the short period (only 1–2 hours) between administrations of the scale in test-retest reliability assessments.

Although the authors state that this measure was developed to assess severity of trichotillomania, there is no mention of cut points to identify what score would indicate the presence of the disorder or would differentiate mild from severe trichotillomania.

Given the prevalence of trichotillomania in children and in mentally retarded populations, as well as the inherent limitations of self-report instruments, administration of this instrument to key informants, such as parents, siblings, or spouses, might be of use. Although there are no reports regarding administration of this measure to informants, the items that focus on direct observation (e.g., frequency of pulling) may be adapted fairly easily to such a format. For items that pertain to subjects' mental state (e.g., perceived control over symptoms), informants' responses could involve inferences drawn from their observations of subjects' behavioral patterns.

The authors also note that the MGH Hairpulling Scale addresses only the behavioral aspects of trichotillomania. They note that it does not address the negative self-image and shame that are common aspects of this disorder, nor does it address frequently associated behaviors such as social avoidance and use of head coverings and hairpieces.

The MGH Hairpulling scale is a promising scale with strong, but preliminary, reliability and validity data. This scale appears to be useful as a measure of baseline severity of trichotillomania and of sensitivity to change. Given the absence of cutoff scores and of data in nonpatient control subjects, it is not recommended as a diagnostic tool at this time.

REFERENCES AND SUGGESTED READINGS

Keuthen NJ, O'Sullivan RL, Ricciardi JN, et al: The Massachusetts General Hospital (MGH) Hairpulling Scale, I: development and factor analyses. Psychother Psychosom 64:141–145, 1995

O'Sullivan RL, Keuthen NJ, Hayday CF, et al: The Massachusetts General Hospital (MGH) Hairpulling Scale, II: reliability and validity. Psychother Psychosom 64:146–148, 1995

Psychiatric Institute Trichotillomania Scale (PITS)

R. M. Winchell, J. S. Jones, A. Molcho, B. Parsons, B. Stanley, and M. Stanley

GOALS

The Psychiatric Institute Trichotillomania Scale (PITS) (Winchel et al. 1992a) was developed to assess trichotillomania. This measure assesses the number of hair pulling sites, quantity of hair loss, time spent pulling and thinking about pulling, resistance to hair pulling urges, distress regarding hair pulling behavior and its consequences, and interference with daily activities. The PITS is designed to evaluate current symptom severity as well as change in symptom profile and severity over time.

DESCRIPTION

The PITS is a six-item semistructured interview designed to be administered by a clinician. The measure includes a seven-item hair pulling history interview, in which the interviewer asks questions about age at onset, course of illness, sites of hair pulling, and associated maladaptive behavior. The responses from this section are not included in the final score but are used to aid scoring of the following six scales. These six scales—Sites, Severity, Duration, Resistance, Interference, and Distress—form the heart of the interview. Each scale includes several structured questions (e.g., "On an average day this past week, how much time would you say you spent pulling your hair or thinking about it?"). Several scales also include optional probes ("Is it closer to a few minutes or a few hours?"). The first two questions on sites and severity are scored on the basis of both direct clinical observation and patient report. The remaining four questions, on duration, resistance, distress, and interference, rely on patient report alone. Items are rated on an 8-point scale ranging from 0 = no symptoms to 7 = severe symptoms. Subjects' responses reflect their behavior during the past week. Sample items are provided in Example 31–7.

Possible scores range from 0 to 42; higher scores reflect greater severity. Neither normative data nor cutoff scores are provided.

PRACTICAL ISSUES

Administration time is not specified but might be estimated to be approximately 20 minutes. Detailed instructions on administration and scoring are provided, and the scale is printed in full in the article by Winchel et al. (1992a). The PITS is included on the CD-ROM that accompanies this handbook.

PSYCHOMETRIC PROPERTIES

Reliability

Reliability data are not yet available.

EXAMPLE 31–7 ■ Sample items from the Psychiatric Institute Trichotillomania Scale

---

1) SITES: (The score for this item should be based on both interview and direct inspection.)
From what part or parts of your body do you pull hair? Do you ever pull hairs on your arms or legs, or other places like your torso or from pubic areas? Any other places?
(Some people pull hair from areas they find embarrassing to talk about. Do you feel that way? If YES, Which sites do you find embarrassing to discuss?)
0 = No sites
1 = 1 non-scalp site
2 = 1 scalp site
3 = 2 non-scalp sites
4 = 2 sites including scalp
5 = 3 sites
6 = 4 sites
7 = 5 sites or more

4) RESISTANCE:
When the urge to pull is present, are you ever able to resist? How much of the time can you resist the urge and not pull? Some of the time? A lot of the time? More than half the time, less than half the time?
0 No urge
1 Always able to resist
2 Almost always able to resist
3 Able to resist 3/4 of the time
4 Able to resist 1/2 to 3/4 of the time
5 Able to resist 1/4 to 1/2 of the time
6 Rarely able to resist
7 Never able to resist

Reprinted with permission from R. M. Winchel, M.D.

Validity

Twenty-six subjects with diagnoses of trichotillomania according to DSM-IV criteria completed the PITS and the Massachusetts General Hospital (MGH) Hairpulling Scale (p. 708). The PITS was strongly correlated with the MGH Hairpulling Scale ($r = 0.63$).

The PITS and the MGH Hairpulling Scale were also administered at two time points, separated by 2–4 weeks, to 22 patients in behavioral and pharmacological treatment for trichotillomania. Change on the PITS was significantly correlated with change on the MGH Hairpulling Scale ($r = 0.83$). It should be noted that the MGH Hairpulling Scale has not been validated on any specific measure of trichotillomania other than the PITS.

CLINICAL UTILITY

The PITS is a comprehensive interview-based measure that evaluates an understudied disorder. Few measures have been developed to assess trichotillomania, and this scale is an attempt to address this need.

The format of the instrument offers several potential advantages. The interview format is useful because the examiner is able to ensure that subjects understand the questions, and comprehensive information about the disorder can be obtained. The PITS assesses a range of associated feelings and behaviors and allows quantified observations of actual hair loss. It also provides detailed evaluation of symptom site and severity.

Although there is preliminary evidence of convergence with other similar measures, as well as evidence of sensitivity to change, the PITS is still in the preliminary stages of standardization. No reliability studies have been published, and only one study has addressed validity. Moreover, the measure used to assess criterion validity (the MGH Hairpulling Scale) is also in the early stages of validation. Finally, there are no formal norms or cutoff scores for this scale. Thus, interpretation of individual scores is difficult, as is determination of a formal diagnosis of trichotillomania.

The interview format may be difficult for some subjects, because much shame and embarrassment are associated with this disorder. Subjects may be reluctant to show hair pulling sites to the clinician and may underreport the extent of their symptoms. Subjects may also attempt to present themselves in a socially desirable light and may not report symptoms accurately.

Given the prevalence of childhood trichotillomania and the high comorbidity of trichotillomania and mental retardation, administration of this instrument to key informants, such as parents or other caregivers, might be of use. Although there are no reports regarding administration of this measure to informants, the items that require direct observation (e.g., number of hair pulling sites) may be adapted fairly easily to such a format. For items that pertain to subjects' mental state (e.g., distress regarding hair pulling behavior), informants could draw inferences from their observations of subjects' behavioral patterns. Items that involve systematic observation by the interviewer (e.g., amount of hair loss) would probably best remain in the original format.

The PITS is a promising and fairly comprehensive scale designed to evaluate severity and sensitivity to change in patients with trichotillomania. However, this measure requires considerable additional evaluation.

REFERENCES AND SUGGESTED READINGS

O'Sullivan RL, Keuthen NJ, Hayday CF, et al: The Massachusetts General Hospital (MGH) Hairpulling Scale, II: reliability and validity. Psychother Psychosom 64:146–148, 1995

Winchel RM, Jones JS, Molcho A, et al: The Psychiatric Institute Trichotillomania Scale (PITS). Psychopharmacol Bull 28:463–476, 1992a

Winchel RM, Jones JS, Molcho A, et al: Rating the severity of trichotillomania: methods and problems. Psychopharmacol Bull 28:457–462, 1992b

CHAPTER 32

Personality Disorders, Personality Traits, and Defense Mechanisms Measures

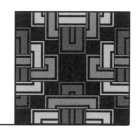

Arthur L. Kaye, Ph.D.
M. Tracie Shea, Ph.D.

INTRODUCTION

This chapter covers instruments that measure personality disorders, personality traits, and defense mechanisms. As conceptualized in DSM-IV, "*Personality traits* are enduring patterns of perceiving, relating to, and thinking about the environment and oneself *that are exhibited* [italics added] in a wide range of social and personal contexts. Only when personality traits are inflexible and maladaptive and cause significant functional impairment or subjective distress do they constitute *Personality Disorders* [italics added]" (American Psychiatric Association 1994, p. 630).

Organization

The instruments included in this chapter are listed in Table 32–1. The chapter begins with a general discussion of issues in personality assessment. This is followed by a section that describes common aspects (e.g., psychometric properties and clinical utility) of five semistructured interviews that assess all 10 of the DSM-IV personality disorders (the Diagnostic Interview for DSM-IV Personality Disorders [DIPD-IV], the International Personality Disorder Examination [IPDE], the Personality Disorder Interview—IV [PDI-IV], the Structured Clinical Interview for DSM-IV Axis II Personality Disorders [SCID-II], and the Structured Interview for DSM-IV Personality

[SIDP-IV]). Unique features of each instrument are presented.

This section is followed by reviews of two semistructured interviews designed to assess specific personality disorders: borderline personality disorder (the Diagnostic Interview for Borderline Patients [DIB]) and psychopathy (the Hare Psychopathy Checklist—Revised [PCL-R]). Three questionnaires that cover all of the personality disorders are then reviewed (the Personality Diagnostic Questionnaire—4 [PDQ-4], the Millon Clinical Multiaxial Inventory—III [MCMI-III], and the Wisconsin Personality Disorders Inventory—IV [WISPI-IV]). Next, four questionnaires that can be used to assess personality traits (the Personality Assessment Inventory [PAI], the NEO Personality Inventory—Revised [NEO-PI-R], the Inventory of Interpersonal Problems [IIP], and the Structural Analysis of Social Behavior [SASB]) are reviewed. Finally, one instrument that measures defense mechanisms (the Defense Style Questionnaire [DSQ]) is described.

Relevant Measures Included Elsewhere in the Handbook

The Minnesota Multiphasic Personality Inventory (MMPI) (p. 89), which includes some subscales for personality assessment (e.g., Social Introversion-Extroversion), is covered in Chapter 7, "General Psychiatric Symptoms Measures."

TABLE 32–1 ■ Instruments for measuring personality disorders, personality traits, and defense mechanisms

Name of measure	Disorder or construct assessed	Format	Pages
Diagnostic Interview for DSM-IV Personality Disorders (DIPD-IV)*	DSM-IV personality disorders; assessed categorically	Semistructured clinical interview; 108 question sets	720–721
International Personality Disorder Examination (IPDE)	DSM-IV and/or ICD-10 personality disorders; assessed categorically and/or dimensionally	Semistructured clinical interview; 99 question sets in DSM-IV Module, 67 question sets in ICD-10 Module	721–722
Personality Disorder Interview—IV (PDI-IV)	DSM-IV personality disorders; assessed categorically and/or dimensionally	Semistructured clinical interview; 93 question sets in thematic version, 94 question sets in disorder-by-disorder version	722–723
Structured Clinical Interview for DSM-IV Axis II Personality Disorders (SCID-II)	DSM-IV personality disorders; assessed categorically and/or dimensionally	Semistructured clinical interview; 119-item screening questionnaire, plus 119 question sets	723–724
Structured Interview for DSM-IV Personality (SIDP-IV)	DSM-IV or ICD-10 personality disorders; assessed categorically and/or dimensionally	Semistructured clinical interview; 101 question sets in thematic version, 107 question sets in disorder-by-disorder version	724–726
Diagnostic Interview for Borderline Patients (DIB)*	Categorical assessment of borderline personality disorder, as originally conceptualized by J. G. Gunderson and colleagues before DSM-III	Semistructured clinical interview; 132 units of information	727–729
Hare Psychopathy Checklist—Revised (PCL-R) Hare Psychopathy Checklist: Screening Version (PCL:SV)	Psychopathy, particularly in adult male forensic populations; assessed categorically and/or dimensionally	Checklist; 20 items in PCL-R; 12 items in PCL:SV	729–732
Personality Diagnostic Questionnaire—4 (PDQ-4)	DSM-IV personality disorders assessed categorically and with an overall index of personality disturbance	Self-administered questionnaire; 85 true-false items	732–733
Millon Clinical Multiaxial Inventory—III (MCMI-III)	Clinical personality styles, personality disorders, and major clinical syndromes as conceptualized in Millon's theory of personality and psychopathology and DSM-IV; assessed categorically and/or dimensionally	Self-administered questionnaire; 175 true-false items	734–736
Wisconsin Personality Disorders Inventory—IV (WISPI-IV)	DSM-IV Axis II personality disorders from the perspective of L. S. Benjamin's Structural Analysis of Social Behavior; assessed categorically and/or dimensionally	Self-administered questionnaire; 214 items	736–738

*Measure is included on the CD-ROM that accompanies this handbook.

TABLE 32–1 ■ Instruments for measuring personality disorders, personality traits, and defense mechanisms (continued)

Name of measure	Disorder or construct assessed	Format	Pages
Personality Assessment Inventory (PAI)	Major clinical syndromes, personality features, and potential treatment complications	Self-administered questionnaire; 344 items	738–740
NEO Personality Inventory—Revised (NEO-PI-R) NEO Five-Factor Inventory (NEO-FFI)	Five major domains of the five-factor model of personality (Neuroticism, Extraversion, Openness, Agreeableness, and Conscientiousness) and the 30 facets of these five broad domains; assessed dimensionally	Self-administered questionnaire; 240 items (NEO-PI-R), 60 items (NEO-FFI)	740–742
Inventory of Interpersonal Problems (IIP) IIP-Circumplex Scales (IIP-C) IIP-Circumplex Short Form Scales (IIP-SC)	Dysfunctional interpersonal problems (IIP); octants of the circumplex model of interpersonal dispositions (IIP-C and IIP-SC)	Self-administered questionnaire; 127 items (IIP), 64 items (IIP-C), and 32 items (IIP-SC)	743–745
Structural Analysis of Social Behavior (SASB)	Patients' views of interpersonal and intrapsychic interactions for the purpose of informing and facilitating psychotherapy; assessed from the perspectives of object relations and interpersonal theories	Series of self-administered questionnaires; 16–64 items per questionnaire	745–747
Defense Style Questionnaire (DSQ)*	Conscious derivatives of defense mechanisms; assessed dimensionally	Self-administered questionnaire; 88 items	747–749

*Measure is included on the CD-ROM that accompanies this handbook.

USING MEASURES IN THIS DOMAIN

Goals of Assessment

Personality disorders can be assessed either categorically or dimensionally (i.e., quantitatively). Dimensional scores provide more information, are more precise, and are more reliable, but they can be more complex and cumbersome. Categorical diagnoses may be overly simplistic and imprecise, but they are useful as shorthand forms of communication. The DSM-IV or alternative criteria sets can be the basis of both approaches, and clinicians may wish to use both approaches to fully assess threshold or subthreshold personality disorder symptomatology. Assessment of normal personality traits, vis-à-vis personality disorders, may be useful even when a diagnosable personality disorder is not present. Finally, evaluation of the nature and extent of typically employed defense mechanisms may be useful to clinicians.

Treatment goals may be derived from an initial assessment that covers personality psychopathology (categorically and dimensionally), extent of normal personality traits (including strengths and weaknesses), and characteristically used defense mechanisms (Strupp et al. 1997). An accompanying treatment plan may incorporate personality data into conceptualizing a case, setting treatment objectives, anticipating obstacles to successful treatment, devising means for monitoring adherence to treatment, and evaluating treatment outcome. For instance, a personality disorder assessment may reveal an Axis II disorder that could have a deleterious impact on the course or treatment of comorbid mental disorders. Furthermore, the assessment could identify personality traits that may contribute to improved treatment cooperation or responsivity. Personality assessment can also substantiate treatment plans submitted to third-party payers.

Implementation Issues

When conducting an assessment using either semistructured interviews or questionnaires, patient self-report is the principal source of information. However, patient self-report in personality assessment is problematic for several reasons. First, retrospective recall is difficult and often unreliable (i.e., patients are asked to recall, over many years, their usual patterns of behavior). Second, the social undesirability of some personality traits can make patients reluctant or unable to acknowledge them. Third, some personality traits and symptoms may be too complex to convey or assess adequately with just a few self-report questions. Fourth, personality disorders are characterized in part by impairment of self-awareness and self-description. Fifth, some patients may intentionally misrepresent their self-description (e.g., to obtain discharge from a facility, disability compensation, or a change in treatment modality). Finally, the presence of other mental disorders (e.g., depression) can significantly influence memory and self-description. Therefore, whenever possible, it is advisable to corroborate self-report findings with information from a clinical chart, behavioral observations, and interviews with persons who know the patient well (e.g., relatives or close friends). Furthermore, when another mental disorder is present, personality assessment may be of questionable validity and should be interpreted cautiously.

Issues in Interpreting Psychometric Data

The measurement of personality disorders has been considered to be among the least reliable (joint and test-retest) of the mental disorders. However, reliability has vastly improved with the advent of semistructured interviews. Personality disorder diagnoses, when assessed with semistructured interviews, can be as reliable as diagnoses of other mental disorders.

When comparing reliability data across the different instruments, one should carefully review differences in study design and implementation to ensure they are comparable as well. Several factors can serve to inflate or diminish measurement reliability, including whether the reliability is joint or test-retest (joint reliability is higher), the base rates of the personality disorder in the sample (reliability is generally lower in samples with very low rates of personality disorder), and the nature of the raters

(raters working closely together for years obtain higher reliability than raters drawn from different sites who have never met).

Adequate reliability is necessary to obtain valid clinical diagnoses. However, the validity of diagnostic instruments for personality disorders continues to be problematic, in part because of the absence of an acceptable gold standard against which to compare alternative instruments. One frequently cited standard is the LEAD (i.e., Longitudinal observation by Experts using All available Data as sources of information [Spitzer 1983]), but this standard is cumbersome, time-consuming, and has gained only limited acceptance (Perry 1992; Zimmerman 1994). Semistructured interviews may serve as an alternative gold standard because they have an inherent procedural validity (i.e., they are systematic and comprehensive) that makes findings more replicable, less prone to idiosyncratic biases, and presumably more valid (Widiger and Sanderson 1995; Zimmerman 1994). In addition, arguments have been made for developing approaches that model the more unstructured interviews often used in general clinical practice (Perry 1992; Westen 1997). The ultimate validation is the extent to which the instrument provides replicable and useful answers to questions concerning etiology, course, and treatment. Much of this information can currently be obtained with semistructured interviews.

GUIDE TO THE SELECTION OF MEASURES

The major issue in the selection of measures concerns the choice of method—that is, whether to use a semistructured interview or a self-report questionnaire.

Questionnaires

Questionnaires are useful for assessing personality traits but are often inadequate when used alone—especially for making categorical diagnostic decisions. They may have high false-positive rates, in part because of the lack of opportunity to ask follow-up questions to confirm the presence of symptoms. Therefore, when diagnosing personality disorders, it is advisable to use one of the semistructured interviews or to use a questionnaire only as a screening device (Widiger and Sanderson 1995; Zimmerman 1994).

Questionnaires often have several advantages, however, including 1) increased efficiency and reduced time required of clinicians; 2) subtle items or scales to detect symptom exaggeration, acquiescence, denial, intentional faking, and other threats to validity; and 3) normative data to guide interpretation of scores. However, sufficient normative data across different cultures have yet to be obtained for most questionnaires. Because mismatched normative comparison can invalidate interpretation, clinicians should ensure that norms employed are consistent with the ethnic, gender, or cultural backgrounds of their patients.

Semistructured Interviews

Semistructured interviews are invaluable in guiding the careful, systematic, and thorough assessment of personality characteristics. In addition, they can substantially improve the consistency and joint reliability of personality disorder diagnoses. In contrast, unstructured clinical interviews are usually unreliable. Therefore, in this chapter, we emphasize semistructured clinical interviews to encourage and facilitate more systematic, comprehensive, and replicable clinical assessments of personality disorder symptomatology.

Semistructured interviews provide explicit outlines and probes (with space for recording patient responses) for carefully assessing each diagnostic criterion. In comparison with questionnaires, they allow greater flexibility because the clinician interacts with the patient during the interview and can devise individualized follow-up queries. Semistructured interviews for personality disorders are not fully structured, because they use probes, optional requests for examples and clarifications, and follow-up inquiries in response to ambiguous responses. The successful application of these additional inquiries depends on the interviewer's skill in the administration of the interview. This task is not difficult for expert clinicians, but it can be time-consuming and requires patience and clinical judgment.

CURRENT STATUS AND FUTURE RESEARCH NEEDS FOR ASSESSMENT

Several potentially very good instruments have not been included in this chapter because they have been used primarily for research purposes or are relatively new and have inadequate data available to assess their psychometric properties or clinical utility. Instruments used extensively in research settings include the Standardized Assessment of Personality (SAP) (Mann et al. 1981) and the Personality Assessment Schedule (PAS) (Tyrer and Alexander 1979), both of which have been used in studies of the ICD-10 personality disorder nomenclature, as well as the Ways of Coping Questionnaire (WCQ) (Folkman and Lazarus 1988). The Dimensional Assessment of Personality Pathology—Basic Questionnaire (DAPP-BQ) (Lively et al. 1993) and the Temperament and Character Inventory (TCI) (Cloninger et al. 1993) are also used frequently in research settings to assess dimensions of personality functioning relevant to the diagnosis of personality disorder (e.g., affective lability, anxiousness, and callousness by the DAPP-BQ; reward dependence and self-transcendence by the TCI). This important, evolving strategy is likely to become prominent in future diagnostic classification systems. However, both instruments are still in development and are not currently ready for clinical use. For one instrument—the MMPI (p. 89)—personality scales developed by Morey et al. (1985) for the original scale are now being supplanted by the MMPI-2 personality disorder scales developed by Somwaru and Ben Porath (1995). Finally, the Schedule for Nonadaptive and Adaptive Personality (SNAP) (Clark 1993) is a relatively inexpensive 375-item true-false questionnaire that has been used primarily in research settings. The SNAP was developed to assess 3 broad temperament and 12 more specific personality trait dimensions that may be present in both clinical and nonclinical populations (e.g., mistrust, manipulativeness, exhibitionism, and workaholism). The SNAP also includes scales to assess each of the DSM-III-R personality disorders.

The instruments reviewed in this chapter represent the state of the art in personality assessment and diagnosis. Most are well established and widely accepted. Some are relative newcomers and are included because of their potential for wide clinical use in the near future. Although these instruments incorporate many advances in measurement of personality and personality disorders, innovation is needed to resolve several continuing issues that face this field of inquiry.

Future psychometric research is needed along several fronts. First, although interrater reliability for diagnosis of personality disorders has increased in recent years, there is room for additional improvement. Research is needed to systematically investigate factors (e.g., patient fatigue and extent of rater training) that may improve reliability. Second, validity of personality disorder categories continues to be elusive. Additional work is needed on construct validity, on the establishment of a widely accepted gold standard, and on the applicability of normative data to nonnormative populations. Finally, more data are needed on the operating characteristics (i.e., sensitivity, specificity, positive predictive value, and negative predictive value) of instruments that measure personality disorder.

Psychometric issues of current measurement methods aside, additional research is needed in developing innovative approaches for measuring personality disorder. For instance, the current dimensional approach to personality disorder diagnoses is rather simplistic, at least as incorporated into the semistructured clinical interviews. This approach merely involves adding up criterion scores or the number of positively endorsed criteria. Research is needed in the application of formal test development procedures to the development of dimensional approaches to measuring personality disorders. Furthermore, research is needed to investigate alternative conceptualizations to understanding personality disorders (e.g., the five-factor model). Development of innovative measurement approaches may be facilitated by research investigating the basic underlying dimensions of Axis II psychopathology and the relationship of normal personality traits to personality psychopathology.

Research also is needed on the clinical utility of personality assessment data. First, data are needed on the utility of combining categorical and dimensional diagnosis of personality disorders. Second, the specific application of personality assessment data to treatment planning and to accountability to third-party payers requires investigation. Finally, research is needed on personality feature and trait contributions to the risk for and the etiology of Axis I disorders and to understanding the mechanisms by which personality features maintain Axis I chronicity.

Semistructured Interviews for Assessing All the DSM-IV Personality Disorders

Among the instruments reviewed in this chapter are the five semistructured interviews that assess all the DSM-IV personality disorders:

- DIPD-IV
- IPDE
- PDI-IV
- SCID-II
- SIDP-IV

Because these interviews share many features, their general features, psychometric properties, and clinical utility are reviewed together first and then the instruments and their practicalities (e.g., how to obtain the instrument) are described in separate sections.

DESCRIPTION

The interviews are formatted such that items are grouped into sets organized either by personality disorder category (i.e., the DIPD-IV and the SCID-II) or into topical thematic areas, such as friendships and relationships or work (i.e., the IPDE). Some interviews provide both formats (i.e., the PDI-IV and the SIDP-IV). Items assess each criterion for each DSM-IV personality disorder, and more than one probe is usually provided for each criterion. For example, the SCID-II assessment of borderline unstable and intense relationships asks the following:

- "Do your relationships with people you really care about have lots of extreme ups and downs?"
- "Tell me about them."
- "Were there times when you thought they were everything you wanted and other times when you thought they were terrible?"
- "How many relationships were like this?"

The interviews are administered directly to the patient and include preliminary sections for priming the patient's self-report capacity by asking several open-ended questions about potential problems and issues. Many researchers also obtain useful information by administering these interviews to relatives, spouses, and other persons who are very familiar with the patient. Clinical chart data can serve as an additional source of information. The IPDE and the SCID-II include screening questionnaires to reduce interview time. For the other interviews, one of the self-report questionnaires reviewed later in this chapter could be used for this purpose.

Each criterion is scored across a short range (e.g., 0 = absent, 1 = subthreshold, and 2 = present). Then each personality disorder is scored categorically, as present or absent on the basis of the number of criteria met, or dimensionally, by adding up the points for each criterion. The IPDE and the SCID-II include computer scoring programs, and the SCID-II has a computer administration program. A computer administration and scoring program is in development for the SIDP-IV.

PRACTICAL ISSUES

Authors of the IDPE, the PDI-IV, and the SCID-II recommend administration only by experienced clinicians; the SIDP-IV and the DIPD-IV do not include this requirement. All require training before administration. Training videos are available for the SCID-II and the SIDP-IV, and training workshops are available for the IPDE, the PDI-IV, the SCID-II, and the SIDP-IV. The PDI-IV has the most detailed manual, followed by the SCID-II, the IPDE, and the SIDP-IV.

Each interview requires at least 45 minutes and up to 2 hours for administration. Administration time is a function of the number of probes (i.e., questions) within the interview, the number of affirmative responses, and the patient's style of speech. When traits are endorsed, thorough follow-up is required to obtain convincing descriptions or examples. Follow-up queries help to establish the pathological nature of the trait, the persistence over time (e.g., present since early adulthood, present for at least 5 years, frequently occurring, or currently present), and the pervasiveness across situations (e.g., work, home, and several relationships).

When interviews become lengthy, the quality of the information can erode due to fatigue. A screening questionnaire can ameliorate this problem by limiting the scope of the interview to only a subset of the personality disorders. This focus will significantly decrease the amount of time needed to administer a semistructured interview. Furthermore, when the focus of the interview concerns only a subset of the personality disorders, a disorder-by-disorder interview format (available with the DIPD-IV, the PDI-IV, the SCID-II, and the SIDP-IV) makes administration less time-consuming because it is easier to locate applicable criteria. This format also facilitates clinical judgment regarding the significance of individual criteria (i.e., the criterion's relevance to a potential diagnosis is more readily apparent). The thematic format (available with the IPDE, the PDI-IV, and the SIDP-IV) also offers advantages. This format may be less susceptible to halo effects and biased expectations regarding individual disorders and may also be more satisfying (e.g., less wearying) for patients because redundancy is decreased through the reorganization of the diagnostic criteria into common issues or themes.

PSYCHOMETRIC PROPERTIES

Empirical findings from independent research teams have been reported more frequently for the IPDE, the SCID-II, and the SIPD-IV than for the DIPD-IV or the PDI-IV.

Reliability

Joint reliability and test-retest reliability of semistructured clinical interviews are substantially better than that obtained by clinical judgment (i.e., unstructured clinical interviews). Joint reliability for the scoring of interview responses has been consistently good to excellent when categorically diagnosing the presence versus absence of any personality disorder (i.e., kappa values ranged from 0.58 to 0.93) or when assessing dimensional scores (i.e., most intraclass correlation coefficients were in the range of 0.60–0.99). When diagnosing individual disorders, some studies have found fair to poor joint reliability (i.e., kappa coefficients <0.56), even with interviews for which a substantive amount of research has been reported. For most disorders, however, joint reliability for categorical diagnoses has been good to excellent (i.e., kappa values of 0.58–1.0). Test-retest reliability for dimensional scores and for categorical diagnoses for specific personality disorders (or for the presence of any unspecified personality disorder) is roughly similar to, but slightly lower than, joint reliability for the same constructs (reported earlier).

Validity

Concurrent validity coefficients have ranged widely, from very poor to good. Statistically significant correlations with questionnaire assessments of the same personality disorders are usually obtained; they range from 0.30 to 0.70 when statistically significant. Somewhat higher coefficients have been reported among semistructured interviews (i.e., kappa values of 0.16 to 0.70 for specific personality disorders, with median kappa values of 0.36 to 0.53 in various studies) than between semistructured interviews and questionnaires (i.e., Pearson correlations of –0.32 to 0.78 for specific personality disorders, intraclass correlation coefficients of 0.05 to 0.63, and kappa coefficients of –0.05 to 0.63, with median kappa coefficients of 0.13 to 0.42 in various studies). Concurrent validity coefficients between semistructured interviews and clinical judgment have been poor (i.e., kappa values of –0.06 to 0.64 for specific personality disorders and 0.18 to 0.37 for presence vs. absence of personality disorder), but this finding may reflect the weaker reliability or validity of the latter method of assessment. Research using semistructured interviews has consistently obtained good to excellent data concerning the validity and importance of the contribution of personality disorders to the development, treatment, and course of patient symptomatology.

CLINICAL UTILITY

All five of the semistructured interviews we review in this chapter provide systematic and comprehensive assessments of the DSM-IV diagnostic criteria for personality disorders. Disability, forensic, and other professional clinical assessments are well supported when guided by one of the established semistructured interviews. Also, systematic assessments may reveal the presence of unanticipated personality disorders that may complicate the treatment of other disorders.

Only a few studies have compared the different interviews with one another. It is currently unclear which, if any, of the different semistructured interviews provides the most valid assessment. None of the interviews is considered to be clearly superior to any of the others.

Diagnostic Interview for DSM-IV Personality Disorders (DIPD-IV)

M. C. Zanarini, F. R. Frankenburg, A. E. Sickel, and L. Yong

The Diagnostic Interview for DSM-IV Personality Disorders (DIPD-IV) (Zanarini et al. 1987) is a semistructured clinical interview developed to categorically assess the DSM-IV personality disorders. Criteria are organized by personality disorder. The interview contains 108 sets of questions (yes-no and open-ended formats); each set is designed to assess a specific DSM-IV personality disorder criterion. The interview also covers passive-aggressive (negativistic) personality disorder and depressive personality disorder, both from Appendix B of DSM-IV ("Criteria Sets and Axes Provided for Further Study"). The DSM-IV criterion is provided in bold below each set of questions.

Each diagnostic criterion is scored as 2 = present and clinically significant, 1 = present but of uncertain clinical significance, 0 = absent or clinically insignificant, or NA if not applicable. Personality disorders are scored categorically, according to the number of criteria met, as 2 = yes, 1 = subthreshold (one less than required number of criteria), or 0 = no. A sample item is provided in Example 32–1.

About 90 minutes are needed to administer the DIPD-IV. The manual provides limited information on

EXAMPLE 32–1 ■ Sample item from the Diagnostic Interview for DSM-IV Personality Disorders

> During the past two years, have you . . .
>
> #81. . . .often been unsure of who you are or what you're really like?
>
> Frequently gone from feeling sort of OK about yourself to feeling that you're bad or even evil?
>
> Often felt that you had no identity?
>
> How about that you had no idea of who you are or of what you believe in?
>
> That you don't even exist?
>
> (Identity disturbance: markedly and persistently unstable self-image or sense of self: 2, 1, 0)

Reprinted with permission from Mary C. Zanarini, Ed.D.

administration and scoring (only two pages of introductory text). The instrument's developers state that the interviewer's formal educational background is not as important as clinical experience and that a person with only a bachelor's degree can administer and score the DIPD-IV if he or she has had at least a year of clinical experience. The DIPD-IV is copyrighted by the authors. Training videos and workshops are available, as is a Spanish version. The DIPD-IV costs $10.00 and may be obtained from

> Mary C. Zanarini, Ed.D.
> McLean Hospital
> 115 Mill Street
> Belmont, MA 02178
> Phone: 617-855-2660
> Fax: 617-855-3580
> E-mail: mzanarin@warren.med.harvard.edu

The DIPD-IV appears to be a well-constructed instrument. Although very good reliability data were reported for the DSM-III version in one study, none have yet been reported for the DSM-IV version. The reliability and validity of the DIPD-IV are currently being studied. Overall, very few psychometric studies have been conducted on this instrument, but it is being used in a large, multisite study on the validity and clinical utility of personality disorder diagnosis.

The DIPD-IV is included on the CD-ROM that accompanies this handbook.

International Personality Disorder Examination (IPDE)

A. W. Loranger

The International Personality Disorder Examination (IPDE) (Loranger et al. 1994) is a semistructured interview that was designed to categorically and/or dimensionally (i.e., continuously) assess DSM-IV and/or ICD-10 personality disorders. Items on the IPDE are organized thematically. Loranger developed the IPDE on the basis of worldwide field trials conducted by the World Health Organization (WHO) and the National Institutes

of Health (NIH). It is available in two versions: a DSM-IV Module that contains 99 sets of questions and an ICD-10 Module that contains 67 sets of questions. The yes-no and open-ended questions are organized into the following six areas: Work, Self, Interpersonal Relationships, Affects, Reality Testing, and Impulse Control. A 77-item true-false screening questionnaire (59 items for the ICD-10 version) may be used to reduce interview time by identifying personality disorders unlikely to be present; items associated with unlikely personality disorders may then be omitted from the interview.

Each criterion is scored 0 = absent or normal, 1 = exaggerated or accentuated, 2 = criterion level or pathological, NA = not applicable, or ? = patient refuses or is unable to answer. A positive score (i.e., 1 or 2) requires a 5-year minimum duration. Criteria may also be scored as "past" (positive in the past but not during the past 12 months) and "late onset" (not present until after age 25 years). Personality disorders are scored categorically and/ or dimensionally. Detailed scoring guidelines are provided in the manual and in the interview itself, and a separate column is provided for informant data. A sample item from the IPDE is provided in Example 32–2.

The IPDE is one of the more established Axis II semistructured clinical interviews. The manual for the IPDE is carefully constructed and covers topics such as history of the IPDE; structure, scope, and limitations; training requirements; administration and scoring; and frequently asked questions. Average administration time is 90 minutes for the interview. Administration time can be reduced by using the screening questionnaire.

The DSM-IV and ICD-10 Modules of the IPDE, including the screen, manual, scoring sheets, and an optional computer scoring program, are distributed by

> Psychological Assessment Resources, Inc.
> P.O. Box 998
> Odessa, FL 33556
> Phone: 800-331-TEST (800-331-8378)

Information about foreign language versions and training courses may be obtained from

> Armand W. Loranger, Ph.D.
> Professor Emeritus of Psychiatry (Psychology)
> Cornell University Medical College
> New York Hospital–Cornell Medical Center
> 21 Bloomingdale Road

EXAMPLE 32–2 ■ Sample item from the International Personality Disorder Examination

| 15. | 0 1 2 ? | 0 1 2 | Is overconscientious, scrupulous, and inflexible about matters of morality, ethics, or values (not accounted for by cultural or religious identification) Obsessive-Compulsive: 4 |

Are morals and ethics much more important to you than they are to most people?
If yes: Including people from your own background or religion?
 If yes: Give me some examples of what you mean.

Are you (also) very concerned about rules and regulations?
If yes: Give me some examples.

Are you so strict or conscientious, that you spend a lot of time worrying whether you might have broken any rules or done something wrong?
If yes: Give me some examples.

If no: Have people accused you of being too strict or rigid about what's right and wrong?
 If yes: Why do you think they've said that?

It is not uncommon for people to view themselves as conscientious or subscribing to a higher morality than others. This is insufficient grounds for a positive rating. There must be evidence of an excessive concern about ethics, morality, rules, or matters of right and wrong. This may express itself in extreme rigidity and inflexibility about such matters, undue concern or preoccupation with doing what is right, or excessive worrying about having broken rules or done something immoral or unethical. It is not necessary that subjects impose their scrupulosity or rigidity on others. It is particularly important to view the subjects' behavior within the context of their religious beliefs or allegiances. Religious individuals should be judged in relation to others of the same sect, and scored positively only if members of the same religion would also view them as scrupulous or inflexible. The criterion should not be scored positively if the behavior is present only during isolated episodes of depression or obsessive-compulsive disorder.

2 Usually is overconscientious, scrupulous, and inflexible about matters of morality, ethics, or values
1 Occasionally is overconscientious, scrupulous, and inflexible about matters of morality, ethics, or values
0 Denied, rare, confined to isolated episodes of depression or obsessive-compulsive disorder, or not supported by convincing examples.

Reprinted with permission from Armand W. Loranger, Ph.D.

White Plains, NY 10605
Phone: 914-997-5922

or from

Division of Mental Health and Prevention of
 Substance Abuse
World Health Organization
20 Avenue Appia
1211 Geneva 27, Switzerland

The IPDE DSM-IV Kit and the IPDE ICD-10 Kit are available for $129.00 each. Each kit includes the instruction manual and the DSM-IV and ICD-10 interviews. In addition, each kit includes 25 screening questionnaires, 50 answer sheets, and 25 scoring booklets for the module ordered. All of these items, for both the DSM-IV and ICD-10 versions, may be purchased separately.

Personality Disorder Interview—IV (PDI-IV)

T. A. Widiger, S. Mangine, E. M. Corbitt, C. G. Ellis, and G. V. Thomas

The Personality Disorder Interview—IV (PDI-IV) is a semistructured clinical interview that was developed to categorically and/or dimensionally (i.e., continuously) assess the DSM-IV personality disorders. It is available in two separate versions; the items are organized thematically in one version and by personality disorder in the other. Both versions also cover passive-aggressive (negativistic) and depressive personality disorders, from Appendix B of DSM-IV ("Criteria Sets and Axes Provided for Further Study"). The thematic version contains 93 sets of questions organized by criterion into the following nine topical areas: Attitudes Toward Self, Attitudes Toward Others, Security of Comfort With Others, Friendships and Relationships, Conflicts and Disagreements, Work and Leisure, Social Norms, Mood, and Appearance and Perception. The disorder-by-disorder version contains 94 sets of questions. Questions are of yes-no and open-ended formats. A screening questionnaire is not provided.

Each criterion is scored 0 = not present; 1 = present at a clinically significant level, according to the DSM-IV definition of the criterion; and 2 = present to a more severe or substantial degree. Personality disorders may be scored both categorically, as either present or absent, and dimensionally on the following scale: absent, traits, subthreshold, threshold (i.e., presence of the disorder), moderate, or extreme.

Perhaps the most unique strength of the PDI-IV is its manual (Widiger et al. 1995), which is a very rich source book (267 pages, hardcover) and includes extensive reviews of each personality disorder and thorough discussions of each diagnostic criterion. A weakness of the PDI-IV is that relatively few psychometric studies of the interview have been conducted by independent investigators, although joint reliability and validity data have been satisfactory at the test construction site. The PDI-IV is currently being used in a large-scale international study on cross-cultural issues in personality disorders and personality dimensions.

Administration time is about 90–120 minutes. The PDI-IV is copyrighted by Psychological Assessment Resources, Inc. The measure may be obtained from

Psychological Assessment Resources, Inc.
P.O. Box 998
Odessa, FL 33556
Phone: 800-331-TEST (800-331-8378)

The cost is $85.00 for an introductory kit (which consists of the manual, two copies of each interview booklet, and 10 profile booklets), $42.00 for the manual, $11.00 per copy for either version of the interview booklet ($10.00 each if ordering five or more), and $19.00 for a package of 10 profile booklets. Information regarding foreign language versions is available from

Thomas A. Widiger, Ph.D.
University of Kentucky
115 Kastle Hall
Lexington, KY 40506-0044
Phone: 606-257-6849
E-mail: widiger@pop.uky.edu

Structured Clinical Interview for DSM-IV Axis II Personality Disorders (SCID-II)

M. B. First, M. Gibbon, R. L. Spitzer, J. B. W. Williams, and L. S. Benjamin

The Structured Clinical Interview for DSM-IV Axis II Personality Disorders (SCID-II) (First et al. 1995) is a semistructured clinical interview that was developed to categorically and/or dimensionally assess the DSM-IV personality disorders. Items are organized by personality disorder. A 119-item yes-no screening questionnaire is available to reduce interview time by identifying personality disorders that are unlikely to be present. Paralleling the screen, the SCID-II interview contains 119 sets of questions (yes-no and open-ended format), plus several additional questions to assess antisocial personality disorder. The interview also covers passive-aggressive (negativistic) and depressive personality disorders from Appendix B of DSM-IV ("Criteria Sets and Axes Provided for Further Study").

Each criterion is scored as 1 = absent or false, 2 = subthreshold, 3 = threshold or true, or ? = inadequate information. Specific (but relatively brief) guidelines for a score of 3 are provided. Personality disorders may be scored categorically or dimensionally. A sample item from the borderline personality disorder section of the SCID-II is provided in Example 32–3.

The SCID-II has a shorter reported administration time than the other semistructured interviews for measuring all the personality disorders. The average administration time is 20 minutes for the SCID-II screening questionnaire and less than an hour for the SCID-II interview, when used in conjunction with the screen. The SCID-II manual (First et al. 1997) is published separately from that for the Structured Clinical Interview for DSM-IV Axis I Disorders (SCID-I) (p. 49). The manual is well organized and provides brief commentaries that more fully explicate each personality disorder criterion.

The interview, screen, manual, and scoring sheets are available from

American Psychiatric Publishing Group
1400 K Street, N.W.
Washington, DC 20005

EXAMPLE 32–3 ■ Sample item from the Structured Clinical Interview for DSM-IV Axis II Personality Disorders

> 94. You've said that you are [Are you] different   ? 1 2 3
>   with different people or in different
>   situations so that you sometimes don't
>   know who you really are.
>
>   Give me some examples of this.
>   (Do you feel this way a lot?)
>
>   ? = inadequate information
>   1 = absent or false
>   2 = subthreshold
>   3 = threshold or true

Reprinted with permission from American Psychiatric Press, Inc.

Phone: 800-368-5777

Internet: www.appi.org

The cost is $46.00 for a starter kit, which includes the manual and five instruments. The SCID-II is copyrighted by the authors. Further information about the SCID-II can be found on the SCID Web page (http://cpmcnet.columbia.edu/dept/scid). A computer-administered version of the screen and interview (Computer-Assisted SCID-II) is available for $450.00 (unlimited use) from

Multi-Health Systems, Inc.
908 Niagara Falls Boulevard
North Tonawanda, NY 14120-2060
Phone: 800-456-3003
Internet: www.mhs.com

A training videotape and information about training workshops and foreign language versions are available from

Biometrics Research Department
New York State Psychiatric Institute
1051 Riverside Drive, Unit 60
New York, NY 10032
Phone: 212-543-5524

The SCID-II exhibits reliability coefficients that are comparable with those of the other semistructured personality interviews; however it has been viewed as somewhat less comprehensive in terms of the number of queries.

Structured Interview for DSM-IV Personality (SIDP-IV)

B. Pfohl, N. Blum, and M. Zimmerman

The Structured Interview for DSM-IV Personality (SIDP-IV) (Pfohl et al. 1997) is a semistructured clinical interview that was developed to categorically and/or dimensionally (i.e., continuously) assess the DSM-IV and/or ICD-10 personality disorders. It is currently available in two versions: a DSM-IV version with items organized thematically and a DSM-IV version with items organized by personality disorder (i.e., modular format). A thematically organized version that combines DSM-IV, DSM-III-R, and ICD-10 criteria (i.e., the Super SIDP) is being developed. Both DSM-IV versions include passive-aggressive (negativistic) and depressive personality disorders, from Appendix B of DSM-IV ("Criteria Sets and Axes Provided for Further Study"), as well as self-defeating personality disorder. The modular version also includes criteria for sadistic personality disorder. The DSM-IV thematic version contains 101 sets of questions organized into the following 10 topical areas: Interests and Activities, Work Style, Close Relationships, Social Relationships, Emotions, Observational Criteria, Self-Perception, Perception of Others, Stress and Anger, and Social Conformity. The latest draft of the modular version contains 107 sets of questions. The questions are of yes-no and open-ended formats. A screening questionnaire is not provided.

Each criterion is scored 0 = not present or limited to rare isolated examples, 1 = subthreshold, 2 = present—criterion is clearly present, and 3 = strongly present—criterion is associated with subjective distress or functional impairment. For a positive score (i.e., 1, 2, or 3), the criterion must have been present for most of the past 5 years. Personality disorders may be scored categorically and, although not explicitly endorsed by the test authors, dimensionally. Scoring procedures emphasize that positively scored disorders must meet the DSM-IV general diagnostic criteria for all personality disorders. A sample item from the SIDP-IV on self-perception is provided in Example 32–4.

The SIDP-IV is one of the more established Axis II semistructured clinical interviews. It takes about 90 minutes to administer the DSM-IV versions of the interview,

EXAMPLE 32–4 ■ Sample item from the Structured Interview for DSM-IV Personality

1. Identify disturbance: markedly and persistently unstable self-image or sense of self   3-BORDL   0 1 2 3

Does the way you think about yourself change so often, that you don't know who you are anymore?
(IF YES): Tell me what this is like.

Do you ever feel like you're someone else, or that you're evil, or maybe that you don't even exist?
(IF PRESENT): Tell me about that.

Some people think a lot about their sexual orientation, for instance trying to decide whether or not they might be gay (or lesbian). Do you often worry about this?

Scoring guidelines:
0 = not present or limited to rare isolated examples
1 = subthreshold—some evidence of the trait but it is not sufficiently pervasive or severe to consider the criterion present
2 = present—criterion is clearly present for most of the last 5 years (i.e., present at least 50% of the time during the last 5 years)
3 = strongly present—criterion is associated with subjective distress or some impairment in social or occupational functioning, or intimate relationships

Reprinted with permission from American Psychiatric Press, Inc.

plus an additional 20 minutes if an informant is interviewed. The developers report successful administration by interviewers who have an undergraduate degree in one of the social sciences, plus 6 months of experience interviewing patients with mental disorders. Instructions are provided in three introductory pages to the interview, and there is not a separate manual. The SIDP-IV is copyrighted by the author.

The DSM-IV thematic version of the interview may be obtained from

American Psychiatric Publishing Group
1400 K Street, N.W.
Washington, DC 20005
Phone: 800-368-5777
Internet: www.appi.org

The cost is $21.95 for a package of five instruments. The modular version, foreign language versions, a computer scoring program, a computer-administered interview, a training video, and information about training courses may be obtained from

Bruce Pfohl, M.D.
Department of Psychiatry
University of Iowa College of Medicine
Iowa City, IA 52242
Phone: 319-356-1350

Fax: 319-356-2587
E-mail: bruce_p@compuserve.com

GENERAL REFERENCES AND SUGGESTED READINGS

American Psychiatric Association: Diagnostic and Statistical Manual of Mental Disorders, 4th Edition. Washington, DC, American Psychiatric Association, 1994

Clark LA: Manual for the Schedule for Nonadaptive and Adaptive Personality. Minneapolis, MN, University of Minnesota Press, 1993

Cloninger CR, Svrakic DM, Przybeck TR: A psychobiological model of temperament and character. Arch Gen Psychiatry 50:975–990, 1993

Folkman S, Lazarus RS: Coping as a mediator of emotion. J Pers Soc Psychol 54:466–475, 1988

Livesley WJ, Jang KL, Jackson DN, et al: Genetic and environmental contributions to dimensions of personality disorder. Am J Psychiatry 150:1826–1831, 1993

Mann AH, Jenkins R, Cutting JC, et al: The development and use of a standardized assessment of abnormal personality. Psychol Med 11:839–847, 1981

Morey LC, Waugh MH, Blashfield RK: MMPI scales for DSM-III personality disorders: their derivation and correlates. J Pers Assess 49:245–251, 1985

Perry JC: Problems and considerations in the valid assessment of personality disorders. Am J Psychiatry 149:1645–1653, 1992

Somwaru DP, Ben-Porath YS: Development and reliability of MMPI-2 based personality disorder scales. Paper presented at the 30th Annual Workshop and Symposium on Recent Developments in the Use of the MMPI-2 and MMPI-A. St. Petersburg Beach, FL, 1995

Spitzer RL: Psychiatric diagnosis: are clinicians still necessary? Compr Psychiatry 24:399–411, 1983

Stangl D, Pfohl B, Zimmerman M, et al: A Structured Interview for the DSM-III Personality Disorders. Arch Gen Psychiatry 42:591–596, 1985

Strupp HH, Horowitz LM, Lambert MJ (eds): Measuring Patient Changes in Mood, Anxiety, and Personality Disorders. Washington, DC, American Psychological Association, 1997

Tyrer P, Alexander J: Classification of personality disorder. Br J Psychiatry 135:163–167, 1979

Westen D: Divergences between clinical and research methods for assessing personality disorders: implications for research and the evolution of Axis II. Am J Psychiatry 154:895–903, 1997

Widiger TA, Sanderson CJ: Assessing personality disorders, in Clinical Personality Assessment: Practical Approaches. Edited by Butcher JN. New York, Oxford University Press, 1995, pp 380–394

Zimmerman M: Diagnosing personality disorders: a review of issues and research methods. Arch Gen Psychiatry 51:225–245, 1994

DIPD-IV REFERENCES AND SUGGESTED READINGS

Zanarini MC, Frankenburg FR, Chauncey DL, et al: The Diagnostic Interview for Personality Disorders: interrater and test-retest reliability. Compr Psychiatry 28:467–480, 1987

IPDE REFERENCES AND SUGGESTED READINGS

Loranger AW: International Personality Disorder Examination (IPDE): DSM-IV and ICD-10 Modules. Odessa, FL, Psychological Assessment Resources, 1999

Loranger AW, Sartorius N, Andreoli A, et al: The International Personality Disorder Examination: the World Health Organization/Alcohol, Drug Abuse, and Mental Health Administration International Pilot Study of Personality Disorders. Arch Gen Psychiatry 51:215–224, 1994

PDI-IV REFERENCES AND SUGGESTED READINGS

Widiger T, Frances A, Trull T: Interviewing for personality disorders, in Clinical and Diagnostic Interviewing. Edited by Craig R. New York, Jason Aronson, 1989, pp 221–236

Widiger TA, Mangine S, Corbitt EM, et al: Personality Disorder Interview-IV: A Semi-Structured Interview for the Assessment of Personality Disorders. Odessa, FL, Psychological Assessment Resources, 1995

SCID-II REFERENCES AND SUGGESTED READINGS

First MB, Spitzer RL, Gibbon M, et al: The Structured Clinical Interview for DSM-III-R Personality Disorders (SCID-II), I: description. Journal of Personality Disorders 9:83–91, 1995

First M, Gibbon M, Spitzer RL, et al: User's Guide for the Structured Clinical Interview for DSM-IV Axis II Personality Disorders. Washington, DC, American Psychiatric Press, 1997

SIDP-IV REFERENCES AND SUGGESTED READINGS

Pfohl B, Blum N, Zimmerman M: Structured Interview for DSM-IV Personality. Washington, DC, American Psychiatric Press, 1997

Diagnostic Interview for Borderline Patients (DIB)

J. G. Gunderson

GOALS

The Diagnostic Interview for Borderline Patients (DIB) (Gunderson et al. 1981) was developed to categorically assess borderline personality disorder as originally conceptualized by J. G. Gunderson and colleagues before publication of DSM-III. (For more information on semistructured personality disorder interviews, see the introduction to the chapter [p. 713].)

DESCRIPTION

The DIB is a semistructured clinical interview that was developed in the middle to late 1970s. Items consist of 132 units of information (e.g., questions and observations) that are used to rate 29 summary statements that in turn are used to rate 5 areas of functioning theorized to be discriminating in diagnosing borderline personality disorder. The five areas of functioning are Social Adaptation (four summary statements), Impulse Action Patterns (five summary statements), Affects (five summary statements), Psychosis (eight summary statements), and Interpersonal Relations (seven summary statements). A sample item from the Affects section and the questions used to rate functioning in that area are provided in Example 32–5.

A somewhat different version of the DIB, the Revised Diagnostic Interview for Borderlines (DIB-R), was developed in 1983 and revised in 1992. The DIB-R differs from the DIB in five main ways:

1. Adjustments in the number, structure, content, and organization of items and summary statements
2. Standardization of the time frame to the past 2 years when assessing personality features
3. Deletion of the Social Adaptation section because it was found to add little discriminating power to the interview
4. Incorporation of the Psychosis section into a Cognition section that was expanded to include various forms of disturbed but nonpsychotic thought

EXAMPLE 32–5 ■ Sample item from the Diagnostic Interview for Borderline Patients

> The patient is angry, hot tempered, or sarcastic.
>
> (a) Have you felt more angry or hostile than usual during the past three months? How much?
> (b) Have you lost your temper?
> (c) Have you been irritable?
> (d) Have you been argumentative?
> (e) Have you been sarcastic?

Reproduced with permission from John G. Gunderson, M.D.

5. Scoring adjustments, including more weight being given to the Impulse Action Patterns and Interpersonal Relations sections and a higher cutoff for positive diagnosis

As reflected in the research literature, the DIB-R has been used far less than the DIB, and its psychometric properties have been less extensively explored. It is unknown to what extent either instrument has been used for clinical purposes. J. G. Gunderson (personal communication, February 1997) does not view the DIB-R as having replaced the DIB.

The items and summary statements are scored, with few exceptions, as follows: 0 = no, 1 = probably, and 2 = yes. These scores are then summed and scaled to yield section-scaled scores ranging from 0 to 2 (0 to 3 on the DIB–R). The five scaled section scores (four in the DIB-R) are then added to yield a total score ranging from 0 to 10. A score of 7 or higher (8 or higher on the DIB-R) is considered indicative of borderline personality disorder.

PRACTICAL ISSUES

It takes about 50–90 minutes to administer the DIB. The interview is designed to be administered by experienced clinicians, although the author does not consider training necessary for strictly clinical purposes. An unpublished manual and several foreign language versions are available. The DIB and DIB-R may be obtained, free of charge for the initial copy, from

John G. Gunderson, M.D., or Mary C. Zanarini, Ed.D.
McLean Hospital

115 Mill Street
Belmont, MA 02178-9106
Phone: 617-855-2293
Fax: 617-855-3299

The DIB-R is included on the CD-ROM that accompanies this handbook.

PSYCHOMETRIC PROPERTIES

Reliability

The joint reliability of the DIB was found to be very good in numerous studies (generally, kappa coefficients >0.70 and intraclass correlation coefficient >0.80), whether reliability was examined categorically or with continuous scores. Test-retest reliability was also good (kappa = 0.71; r = 0.71) in the only such study conducted. Finally, in the only study on the internal consistency of the DIB, high reliability was found for the total instrument (Kuder-Richardson coefficient = 0.75) but only modest reliability within the separate sections (Kuder-Richardson coefficients = 0.32–0.69; median = 0.53). Reliability of the DIB-R has not been reported.

Validity

When the DIB was compared with other assessment methods for measuring borderline personality disorder, validity coefficients were modest. Kappa coefficients for DSM diagnoses ranged from –0.33 to 0.69, with most <0.50. Inconsistent findings have been reported regarding whether the DIB under- or overdiagnoses compared with number of DSM criteria for borderline personality disorder met. In two studies that examined agreement with Kernberg's Structural Interview (Kernberg 1977), kappa was 0.49 in one study, and agreement uncorrected for chance was 62.5% in the other. Correlations between continuous scores from the DIB and other measures (e.g., number of DSM-III borderline criteria met) were somewhat higher but still modest (i.e., generally 0.50–0.75).

The DIB has been shown to adequately discriminate borderline personality disorder from schizophrenia and unipolar depression. However, its ability to discriminate borderline personality disorder from other personality disorders is less certain, and preliminary evidence indicates that the DIB-R might be better able to do so.

The operating characteristics of the DIB were examined in numerous studies, most often with DSM-III as the criterion standard. In these studies sensitivity ranged from approximately 0.70 to 1.0 and specificity ranged from 0.75 to 1.0, indicating partial overlap between the two diagnostic systems. These data are somewhat inconsistent with the modest kappa coefficients reviewed earlier; the discrepancy is due in part to differences in research procedures (e.g., sample composition and interviewer training). In the only study that reports such data for the DIB-R, sensitivity was 0.82, specificity was 0.80, positive predictive power was 0.74, and negative predictive power was 0.87, with Axis II diagnosis by more than 50 therapists as the criterion standard.

CLINICAL UTILITY

The DIB and DIB-R are best used to assess borderline personality disorder as conceptualized within Gunderson's theoretical model. The DIB and DIB-R provide more information (e.g., more detail concerning aberrant cognitions and dissociative experiences) than an assessment with one of the DSM-IV–oriented semistructured interviews. However, clinicians should not rely on the DIB to make a DSM-IV diagnosis, because the DSM-IV and DIB conceptualizations of borderline personality disorder are somewhat different. Interpretation of individual DIB scale scores (e.g., the Affects scale score) should be avoided because their reliability has not been demonstrated, and the developers did not intend for these scales to be interpreted. Clinicians should also use caution in interpreting the degree of borderline features on the basis of the total DIB score, because the instrument was not developed for this purpose and the meaning of such scores has not been explored. Finally, in choosing between the DIB and the DIB-R, clinicians should be aware that they are somewhat different instruments and that the reliability and validity of the DIB have been studied more extensively.

REFERENCES AND SUGGESTED READINGS

Gunderson JG, Singer MT: Defining borderline patients: an overview. Am J Psychiatry 132:1–10, 1975

Gunderson JG, Kolb JE, Austin V: The Diagnostic Interview for Borderline Patients. Am J Psychiatry 138:896–903, 1981

Kernberg O: The structural diagnosis of borderline personality organization, in Borderline Personality Disorders: The Concept, the Syndrome, the Patient. Edited by Hartocollis P. New York, International Universities Press, 1977

Ludolph PS, Silk KR, Lohr NE, et al: Guidelines for the Administration of the Diagnostic Interview for Borderlines. Ann Arbor, MI, VA Medical Center, 1982

Zanarini MC, Gunderson JG, Frankenburg FR, et al: The Revised Diagnostic Interview for Borderlines: discriminating BPD from other Axis II disorders. Journal of Personality Disorders 3:10–18, 1989

Hare Psychopathy Checklist—Revised (PCL-R)

R. D. Hare

GOALS

The Hare Psychopathy Checklist—Revised (PCL-R) (Hare 1991) was developed to assess psychopathy categorically and dimensionally, particularly within adult male forensic populations. The PCL-R measures a concept of psychopathy originally described by Cleckley (1976) and modified somewhat by Hare. The PCL-R construct of psychopathy includes elements such as glibness and superficial charm, need for stimulation and proneness to boredom, pathological lying, lack of remorse or guilt, shallow affect, and parasitic lifestyle. Although there is substantial overlap between Hare's construct of psychopathy and DSM-IV antisocial personality disorder, the two are not synonymous. DSM-IV places relatively more emphasis on antisocial behavior and does not include glibness and charm, grandiosity, lack of empathy, or shallow affect within its diagnostic criteria.

DESCRIPTION

The PCL-R is a checklist of 20 items used to rate psychopathic personality characteristics (Factor 1) and socially deviant behaviors (Factor 2). The instrument yields separate scores in each of these areas and a combined total score. Sample items from Factors 1 and 2 are provided in Example 32–6. Items are rated on the basis of a semistructured interview and a review of collateral information.

An abbreviated, 12-item screening version of the PCL-R, the Hare Psychopathy Checklist: Screening Version (PCL:SV) (Hart et al. 1995), is available. The PCL:SV is highly correlated with the PCL-R and takes about half as long to administer. If a patient scores positively on the PCL:SV, the author recommends administering the full PCL-R.

Items are rated as follows: 2 = yes, the item does apply to the person; 1 = the item applies somewhat or in a limited sense; and 0 = no, the item definitely does not apply. Each item is rated on the degree to which the description of the item in the manual matches the individual's lifetime functioning. Items are often scored on the basis of forensic, prison, or medical records rather than on direct interview questions. Scoring for most but not all items requires substantial clinical judgment and inference. Items are summed to yield a total score ranging from 0 to 40 and two factor scores that represent, respectively, psychopathic personality characteristics (range of 0–16) and socially deviant behaviors (range of 0–18).

Raw scores may be interpreted in several ways. First, they may be viewed dimensionally (i.e., continuously) as representing the extent to which an individual matches the profile of a "prototypical psychopath." Second, they

EXAMPLE 32–6 ■ Sample items from the Hare Psychopathy Checklist—Revised

Factor 1
Glibness/Superficial Charm

Factor 2
Parasitic Lifestyle

The Hare Psychopathy Checklist—Revised is copyrighted material owned by R. D. Hare and published by Multi-Health Systems, Inc. Reproduced by permission.

may be converted to percentile ranks that permit ranking of the subject's score on the basis of normative data collected on male prison inmates or male forensic patients, as appropriate. Finally, a cutoff score ≥30 can be used to classify individuals with psychopathy. This cutoff score has been found, according to the manual, to differentiate those with psychopathy from those without psychopathy on a variety of behavioral, self-report, and experimental variables.

PRACTICAL ISSUES

The PCL-R is designed to be administered by clinicians experienced with forensic populations. Administration time is 90–120 minutes for the interview plus 60 minutes to review collateral information, thus making the assessment rather labor intensive. The manual has been carefully and thoroughly prepared. A French-Canadian version of the PCL-R is available, and several foreign language versions (German, Spanish, and Swedish) are in development. Training courses and videos are available through the publisher. The PCL-R, PCL:SV, and associated materials are copyrighted by R. D. Hare and published by Multi-Health Systems, Inc. For further information on the products, or to place an order, contact

> Multi-Health Systems, Inc.
> 908 Niagara Falls Boulevard
> North Tonawanda, NY 14120-2060
> Phone: 800-456-3003
> Internet: www.mhs.com

The PCL-R Complete Kit (which consists of the manual, reusable rating booklet, 25 QuikScore forms, and 25 interview guides) costs $250.00, and individual items can be purchased separately (e.g., $100.00 for 25 and $340.00 for 100 interview guides).

PSYCHOMETRIC PROPERTIES

Reliability

Intraclass correlation coefficients for joint reliability of the PCL-R total and factor scores ranged from 0.73 to 0.95 across numerous samples of both male prison inmates and male forensic psychiatric inpatients. Alpha co-efficients for internal consistency, across numerous samples, ranged from 0.77 to 0.91. In the few studies that examined test-retest reliability, coefficients of stability ranged from 0.78 to 0.94 for both the PCL-R total and factor scores.

Validity

The PCL-R total and factor scores were found to correlate in expected directions with other measures of social deviance. Correlations (r) with global ratings of psychopathy according to Cleckley's criteria ranged from 0.80 to 0.90 for the total score, from 0.85 to 0.89 for Factor 1, and from 0.65 to 0.74 for Factor 2. Correlations with antisocial personality disorder were somewhat lower and in most studies ranged from 0.45 to 0.63 for the total score, from 0.21 to 0.49 for Factor 1, and from 0.55 to 0.63 for Factor 2. Antisocial personality disorder was more highly correlated with Factor 2 (socially deviant behaviors) than with Factor 1 (psychopathic personality characteristics). Correlations with various self-report scales (e.g., the Millon Clinical Multiaxial Inventory—II [MCMI-II] [p. 734] Antisocial scale and the Minnesota Multiphasic Personality Inventory [MMPI] [p. 89] Scale 4) were generally ≤0.35. Perhaps, as suggested in the manual, these low correlations are the result of the impression management skills (i.e., ability to recognize questionnaire items designed to assess psychopathic features and respond in a socially appropriate direction) of inmates or lack of demonstrated reliability for most of these self-report scales in prison and forensic psychiatric populations. The two factor scores of the PCL-R (i.e., psychopathic personality characteristics and socially deviant behaviors) were consistently validated in several factor analytic studies.

The PCL-R was also shown to be related to outcome after release from prison and outcome after treatment. Among inmates with PCL-R scores of ≥25, 33%–85% failed to comply with conditional release from prison. About one-quarter to three-quarters of inmates with PCL-R scores ≥26 committed at least one violent crime after release from prison. Finally, in one study, inmates with scores ≥27 attended treatment for a shorter period, put less effort into treatment, and improved less than inmates with lower scores.

The PCL-R was shown to be related in expected ways to several clinical and demographic measures. PCL-R scores were found to be statistically significantly higher in inmates with antisocial personality disorder than in those with diagnoses of adult antisocial behavior and conduct disorder. In a sample of forensic patients, PCL-R scores were found to be more highly correlated with antisocial personality disorder than with histrionic personality disorder or nonalcohol substance use disorders. Correlations (r) between PCL or PCL-R scores and self-report instruments generally were ≤0.40 but in the expected directions. For instance, scales that represent antisocial behavior, passive-aggressive personality traits, and substance dependence had higher (i.e., generally >0.26) correlations with the PCL or PCL-R than scales that represent avoidant or histrionic personality traits (i.e., generally <0.20). At the same time, negative correlations were found with scales that represent dysthymic disorder and anxiety disorders, perhaps, as suggested in the manual, because individuals with psychopathy tend not to experience such subjective distress due to personality traits characterized by lack of remorse or guilt, lack of affect and emotional depth, and callousness. PCL and PCL-R scores were found to have correlations ranging from 0.29 to 0.37 with low social class, low occupational class, and poor quality of family background and to have a negative correlation (–0.34) with highest grade completed before incarceration; stronger relationships were demonstrated on Factor 2 (socially deviant behaviors) than on Factor 1 (psychopathic personality characteristics).

The PCL-R was also shown to be consistently associated with various types of criminal behavior (r = 0.30–0.50, or significant differences between those with and without psychopathy), such as total number of offenses, variety of offenses, number of violent offenses, number of nonviolent (i.e., property) offenses, violent offenses per year while not incarcerated, likelihood of having used a weapon, number of prison terms served, months spent in prison, number of institutional offenses, and use of aliases. Those with psychopathy who scored high on both PCL factors were found, in one study, to exhibit particularly high levels of violence. They were also found, in another study, to be less likely than those without psychopathy to have committed violent crimes during periods of extreme emotional arousal (e.g., domestic disputes) and more likely to have committed crimes that involve callous and cold-blooded violence or violence that was part of an aggressive display.

Finally, several studies investigated the association between various indexes of socially deviant behavior (e.g., violent and aggressive behavior in prison) and

PCL-R and PCL total scores, PCL-R and PCL diagnoses, or DSM antisocial personality disorder. Correlations were found to be higher for the PCL-R and PCL indexes than for antisocial personality disorder. Correlations (r) for the three measures mentioned were found to be 0.33–0.49 (mean = 0.46), 0.25–0.56 (mean = 0.44), and 0.20–0.39 (mean = 0.28), respectively.

CLINICAL UTILITY

The PCL-R is a carefully developed and well-researched instrument with an extensive history. Its reliability and validity have been shown to be good. The instrument has been found to be clinically useful, although its lengthy administration time makes it somewhat unwieldy. The manual is comprehensive and well written. Preliminary use of the PCL-R has been reported for decisions concerning placement, treatment, and conditional release of inmates and forensic patients.

The PCL-R was designed to assess psychopathy in adult male forensic populations including those from correctional facilities, forensic psychiatric hospitals, and pretrial evaluation or detention facilities. It has not been sufficiently validated for use with female forensic, juvenile correctional, substance abuse, or noncriminal populations, and clinicians should therefore proceed cautiously when using the instrument with these populations. In addition, collateral file information may not be readily available for noncriminal and nonforensic populations, and lack of such information has been shown to result in lower PCL-R scores.

The PCL-R concept of psychopathy is broader than the DSM-IV concept of antisocial personality disorder; the former places greater emphasis on additional psychopathic personality characteristics. Hare (1991) suggests that approximately 90% of criminals with psychopathy as determined by PCL-R meet criteria for antisocial personality disorder, whereas only 20%–30% of inmates with antisocial personality disorder meet criteria for PCL-R psychopathy. For clinicians primarily interested in diagnosis, an assessment of antisocial personality disorder may be strengthened by employing the PCL-R as a measure of the severity of psychopathy. For clinicians primarily concerned with treatment of forensic patients or with readiness for release from institutional care, the PCL-R will probably provide more useful information.

REFERENCES AND SUGGESTED READINGS

Cleckley H: The Mask of Sanity, 5th Edition. St. Louis, MO, Mosby, 1976

Hare RD: The Hare Psychopathy Checklist-Revised Manual. North Tonawanda, NY, Multi-Health Systems, 1991

Hart SD, Hare RD, Harpur TJ: The Psychopathy Checklist: an overview for researchers and clinicians, in Advances in Psychological Assessment, Vol 7. Edited by Rosen J, Mc-Reynolds P. New York, Plenum, 1992

Hart SD, Cox DN, Hare RD: The Hare PCL:SV Psychopathy Checklist: Screening Version Manual. North Tonawanda, NY, Multi-Health Systems, 1995

Personality Diagnostic Questionnaire—4 (PDQ-4)

S. E. Hyler

GOALS

The Personality Diagnostic Questionnaire—4 (PDQ-4) (Hyler 1994; Hyler et al. 1988) was developed to categorically assess the DSM-IV personality disorders and to provide a quantitative index of overall personality disturbance.

DESCRIPTION

The PDQ-4 is an 85-item true-false self-administered questionnaire; each item assesses a specific DSM-IV personality disorder diagnostic criterion. For each item, the person is asked to indicate how he or she has tended to feel, think, and act over the last several years. An item that assesses schizoid personality disorder is provided in Example 32-7.

Several noteworthy changes have been made from previous versions of the PDQ. First, items are no longer

EXAMPLE 32–7 ■ Sample item from the Personality Diagnostic Questionnaire—4

> Over the last several years . . . spending time with family or friends just doesn't interest me.

Reprinted with permission from Steven E. Hyler, M.D.

organized by personality disorder, thereby reducing the transparency of the instrument. Second, the PDQ-4 contains two validity scales designed to identify individuals who underreport in order to present themselves in a positive fashion and to identify individuals who are either lying, responding randomly, or not taking the questionnaire seriously. Finally, when a personality disorder is positively identified, its clinical significance can be assessed with a Clinical Significance Scale, which is a brief interview administered by a clinician or paraprofessional rater.

Two alternative versions of the PDQ-4 are available. The PDQ-4+ assesses the 10 DSM-IV personality disorders covered by the PDQ-4 as well as passive-aggressive (negativistic) and depressive personality disorders from DSM-IV's Appendix B ("Criteria Sets and Axes Provided for Further Study"). A change version is also available in the computer-administered format. The change version instructs patients to respond to items on the basis of a time interval of the past several weeks or months, rather than the past several years, and may therefore be useful for assessing response to treatment.

Individual personality disorders are scored as either present or absent, according to the number of DSM-IV criteria met. In addition, an index of overall personality disturbance is provided by the total score, which ranges from 0 to 79, with one point added for each endorsed item (excluding the validity scales). Scores ≥30 indicate that significant personality disturbance is likely, scores of 20–30 are common in psychotherapy patients without significant personality disturbance, and scores of ≤20 have been found in psychiatrically healthy control subjects. These thresholds were determined on the basis of previous versions of the instrument and initial research with the PDQ-4. They should be viewed as best approximations until additional studies can be conducted.

PRACTICAL ISSUES

It takes about 20–30 minutes to administer the PDQ-4. The manual consists of a two-page instruction sheet that covers administration, scoring, and interpretation. Versions of the PDQ-4 are available in Chinese, Dutch, French, Italian, Japanese, Korean, and several other languages. Paper and pencil copies may be obtained by mail (and duplicated as needed) for $10.00 by contacting

> AlphaLogic Ltd.
> Putman Avenue, Unit 1
> Ottawa, Ontario, Canada K1M 1Z1

Copies of the test may also be downloaded from the Internet (www.travel-net.com/~alphalog/index.html). A computer-administered and/or computer scoring version (unlimited use) may be obtained for $125.00 ($250.00 institutional use) from

> Steven E. Hyler, M.D.
> NiJo Software
> Box 126-H
> Scarsdale, NY 10583
> Phone: 914-722-9011 (evenings)

A demonstration version of the computerized PDQ-4 may also be downloaded from the Web site listed earlier.

PSYCHOMETRIC PROPERTIES

Reliability

For earlier versions of the PDQ, kappa coefficients for assessing test-retest reliability were in the range of 0.50–0.60, overall, with higher reliability for some disorders (e.g., >0.70 for antisocial and obsessive-compulsive disorders) and, in some research reports, inadequately low reliabilities for other disorders (e.g., <0.30 for narcissistic, histrionic, and passive-aggressive disorders). Internal consistency reliability coefficients were found, in two out of three studies (including one unpublished study of the PDQ-4+), to be ≥0.60 for most of the personality disorder scales.

Validity

When earlier versions of the PDQ (as well as the PDQ-4+ in one unpublished study) were compared with semistructured clinical interviews, kappa coefficients ranged from –0.03 to 0.63 for specific personality disorders, with most kappa coefficients <0.50. In addition, when compared with semistructured interviews, the PDQ exhibits a high rate of false-positive diagnoses, in that it

identifies more patients as having personality disorders and assigns more personality disorders per patient. Specificity was <0.30 for most personality disorders in the few studies that examined operating characteristics. However, the PDQ generally has been shown to be highly sensitive to most patients who have a personality disorder and to be accurate when assessing the absence of a personality disorder.

CLINICAL UTILITY

As noted by the instrument's developer, the PDQ-4 has a high false-positive rate. Although the Clinical Significance Scale was designed to address this problem, its effectiveness in reducing false-positive diagnoses has not yet been demonstrated. Accordingly, the PDQ-4 is probably best used as a screening instrument to rule out the likelihood of personality disorder and also to identify patients who might have a personality disorder. Because the instrument has a low false-negative rate, a patient is unlikely to have a personality disorder if the threshold is not met for any of the PDQ-4 diagnoses. In addition, because of its high sensitivity, patients who have personality disorders are likely to meet criteria for one or more PDQ-4 diagnoses. However, not all patients who meet PDQ-4 criteria actually have personality disorders, given the instrument's high false-positive rate. Moreover, specific personality disorders identified by the PDQ-4 may be inaccurate, because diagnostic agreement with semistructured interviews has been poor. Clinicians should follow up positive diagnoses made by the PDQ-4 with one of the semistructured clinical interviews that covers all of the DSM-IV Axis II disorders. Finally, although the reliability and validity of the PDQ-4 are likely to be similar to those found for earlier PDQ versions, research has yet to demonstrate this correspondence.

REFERENCES AND SUGGESTED READINGS

Hyler SE: Personality Diagnostic Questionnaire—4. New York, New York State Psychiatric Institute, 1994

Hyler SE, Rieder RO, Williams JBW, et al: The Personality Diagnostic Questionnaire: development and preliminary results. Journal of Personality Disorders 2:229–237, 1988

Millon Clinical Multiaxial Inventory—III (MCMI-III)

T. Millon, R. Davis, and C. Millon

GOALS

The Millon Clinical Multiaxial Inventory—III (MCMI-III) (Millon et al. 1997) was developed to assess clinical personality styles (both dimensionally and categorically), personality disorders, and major clinical syndromes in accordance with both Millon's theory of personality and psychopathology and DSM-IV. (This review focuses exclusively on the assessment of personality.) Elements of Millon's theory include a distinction between clinical personality styles and severe personality pathology. The latter is viewed as a more severe variant of the former, with less integration of personality organization, more vulnerability to everyday strains, and less effectiveness at coping.

DESCRIPTION

The MCMI-III is a 175-item true-false self-report inventory that provides scores on 24 scales, including 11 that measure clinical personality patterns (Schizoid, Avoidant, Depressive, Dependent, Histrionic, Narcissistic, Antisocial, Aggressive [Sadistic], Compulsive, Passive-Aggressive [Negativistic], and Self-Defeating) and 3 that measure severe personality patterns (Schizotypal, Paranoid, and Borderline). The MCMI-III also includes four modifying indexes (Disclosure, Desirability, Debasement, and Validity) that are used to adjust scale scores or ascertain the extent of their validity. The MCMI-III is intended for use with adults (with items written at an eighth-grade reading level) seeking mental health treatment. A sample item from the Antisocial scale is provided in Example 32–8.

Raw scale scores are converted to base rate scores (differentiated by gender) by use of a transformation table. Base rate scale scores range from 0 to 115; scores of 75–84 indicate the presence of traits, and scores ≥85 indicate disorder status. Base rate scale scores can be in-

EXAMPLE 32–8 ■ Sample item from the Millon Clinical Multiaxial Inventory—III

> I've gotten into trouble with the law a couple of times (true/false).

terpreted individually or by profile analysis. The base rates used for raw score transformations were developed from informal (unstructured) clinical interviews of 600 patients by participating clinicians. The patients did not constitute a representative sample of a clinical population but were the patients of clinicians who regularly used the earlier version of the instrument (i.e., the MCMI-II). This sample was 51% female; 86% white; 28% never married, 38% married, and 18% divorced; 63% between ages 26 and 45 years; approximately 82% with high school diplomas and 20% with college degrees; and 49% outpatients and 26% inpatients.

PRACTICAL ISSUES

The MCMI-III takes 20–30 minutes to complete. It can be scored 1) by hand, although doing so is time-consuming and complex; 2) by computer on-site; or 3) by National Computer Systems, to which completed test response sheets are mailed. The test manual notes that results should be interpreted by individuals with sufficient background in test logic, psychometric methods, and clinical practice and should generally be limited to persons with at least a master's degree in clinical or counseling psychology or psychiatric social work, psychiatric residency status, or internship status. The manual provides substantial psychometric data, as well as case studies and samples of automated computer reports.

The MCMI-III is copyrighted and is available from

> National Computer Systems
> P.O. Box 1416
> Minneapolis, MN 55440
> Phone: 800-627-7271
> E-mail: IASPP@aol.com

Costs of the MCMI-III are $225.00 for a hand scoring starter kit (including the manual; user's guide; 10 test booklets; and 50 answer sheets, worksheets, profile forms, and answer keys), $109.00 for a preview package for the mail-in service, and $109.00 for a package for on-site computer scoring.

PSYCHOMETRIC PROPERTIES

Reliability

Internal consistency coefficients reported in the manual ranged from 0.66 to 0.89 (Cronbach's alpha); test-retest coefficients (5–14 days) for dimensional scores ranged from 0.85 to 0.93. Using earlier versions of the MCMI-III, other researchers obtained test-retest coefficients ranging from 0.60 to 0.89 for dimensional scores, but test-retest reliability of categorical (diagnostic) scores was low (i.e., kappa coefficients <0.45 for all personality disorders) in the only study of this type.

Validity

Moderate validity coefficients were reported for dimensional trait scores correlated with other self-report inventory measures such as the Symptom Checklist–90—Revised (SCL-90-R) (p. 81) and the Minnesota Multiphasic Personality Inventory (MMPI) (p. 89) (most correlations >0.50 for each scale) using the current and earlier versions of the MCMI, with somewhat lower coefficients when correlated with continuous scores from semistructured interview assessments. Weak coefficients were reported for categorical scores (i.e., personality disorder diagnoses) when compared with semistructured clinical interviews (particularly for the Compulsive scale). Like most self-report inventories, the MCMI-III generates higher rates of personality disorder diagnoses than do interview methods. A recent revalidation study suggested that the operating characteristics of the MCMI-III are similar to or better than those of the earlier versions. Using clinical judgment for the presence of a personality disorder (as defined by DSM-IV and Millon), sensitivity ranged from 0.44 to 0.92 (median = 0.60), and positive predictive power ranged from 0.30 to 0.81 (median = 0.69).

CLINICAL UTILITY

The MCMI-III has a long history relative to other personality disorder measures. It has been used extensively and is reported to be clinically useful. Its relative brevity and basis in Millon's theory of personality and psychopathology are two of its strongest features. However, questions have been raised regarding scoring and interpretive aspects of the instrument.

Concerns about scoring include the considerable item overlap among the scales (i.e., single items count toward more than one scale) and the use of base rates in calculating cutoff scores for scale interpretation. The item overlap results in artificially high correlations among scales, complicating profile interpretations. Individuals often meet the DSM-IV criteria for more than one personality disorder, but a particular extent and direction of co-occurrence is compelled by the overlap among the MCMI-III scales. Regarding base rates, if the population at a local clinical site is significantly different from the standardization sample with respect to the prevalence rates of the personality disorders, the transformed scale scores and diagnostic cutoff scores may be inaccurate. Use of base rates specific to a particular clinical setting may solve this problem, but such data can be difficult to accumulate.

Several interpretive issues are worth noting. First, profile interpretations are of indeterminate validity because of insufficient accumulation of empirical data on their correlates, as acknowledged in the manual. Second, the application of findings from earlier versions of the instrument (the MCMI and the MCMI-II) to the current version of the test (the MCMI-III) is uncertain. Third, although the manual describes the process by which the 95 new items for the MCMI-III were selected, it does not describe how different they are from their predecessors. Fourth, although the manual is quite comprehensive, specific guidelines for the interpretation of test scores are hard to find and are somewhat vague. Finally, the operating characteristics should be considered with caution because unstructured (perhaps unreliable) clinical diagnoses were used in calculating them.

The MCMI-III is best used to evaluate personality and psychopathology as conceptualized in Millon's theoretical model and secondarily to identify DSM-IV personality disorder diagnoses. Earlier versions of the instrument have exhibited high false-positive rates. Although revisions have been made to address this problem, the ability of the MCMI-III to accurately diagnose DSM-IV personality disorders has yet to be demonstrated. Therefore, when diagnosing DSM-IV personality disorders, the MCMI-III may be most strategically used, at present, as a good screening instrument, perhaps to be followed by one of the semistructured interviews reviewed earlier in this chapter.

REFERENCES AND SUGGESTED READINGS

Craig RJ, Weinberg D: MCMI: review of the literature, in The Millon Clinical Multiaxial Inventory: A Clinical Research Information Synthesis. Edited by Craig RJ. Hillsdale, NJ, Erlbaum, 1993, pp 23–69

Davis RD, Wenger A: Validation of the MCMI-III, in The Millon Inventories. Edited by Millon T. New York, Guilford, 1997, pp 327–359

Millon T, Davis R, Millon C: MCMI-III Manual, 2nd Edition. Minneapolis, MN, National Computer Systems, 1997

Wisconsin Personality Disorders Inventory—IV (WISPI-IV)

M. H. Klein and L. S. Benjamin

GOALS

The Wisconsin Personality Disorders Inventory—IV (WISPI-IV) (Klein et al. 1993) was developed to assess the DSM-IV Axis II personality disorders dimensionally and categorically, from the interpersonal perspective of L. S. Benjamin's Structural Analysis of Social Behavior.

DESCRIPTION

The WISPI-IV is a 214-item self-administered questionnaire that provides dimensional (i.e., quantitative) as well as categorical scores on the 10 DSM-IV Axis II personality disorders and on passive-aggressive (negativistic) personality disorder from Appendix B of DSM-IV ("Criteria Sets and Axes Provided for Further Study"). Ten

items from the Marlowe-Crowne Social Desirability Scale (Crowne and Marlowe 1964) are also included to assess for a social desirability response set. Each item is rated on a 10-point scale anchored at either end (i.e., 1 = never, not at all to 10 = always, extremely). Subjects are asked to respond to each item on the basis of "how much or how often it has been true of you during the last five years or more."

The WISPI-IV was developed to provide quantitative assessments of the DSM personality disorders from the interpersonal perspective of Benjamin's (1996) Structural Analysis of Social Behavior. This model characterizes interpersonal behavior by making distinctions in three areas: 1) focus (on other, on self, or within self); 2) affiliation (attack vs. friendliness); and 3) interdependence (control vs. autonomy). The model was used to develop interpersonal descriptors, and then items, for each DSM-IV personality disorder diagnostic criterion. Items were also written to reflect the perspectives of patients rather than those of outside observers.

Item scores are averaged to yield dimensional scores ranging from 1 to 10 for each personality disorder. These scores are then transcribed onto a profile form that permits relative comparisons among disorders. Standardized z-scores can be calculated for comparisons within a given profile or with a normative sample. In the latter case, the z-scores may be plotted on the WISPI-IV Normative Profile form. The WISPI-IV may also be scored categorically to yield DSM-IV diagnoses.

The WISPI-IV is interpreted by examining the magnitude of each scale, by comparing relative magnitudes among scales, by comparing scale scores with those of a normative sample, and by assessing for a socially desirable response set. There are no standard cut points for interpreting scale scores. Norms were derived on the basis of 889 persons who were not currently receiving mental health treatment. The authors caution that WISPI-IV scores should be used in conjunction with other information when making diagnoses.

PRACTICAL ISSUES

It takes less than 1 hour to complete the WISPI-IV. The manual consists of a three-page introductory letter with brief guidelines for administration, scoring, and interpretation. A computer-administered and computer scoring version is available, as is an SPSS scoring program for use with personal computers. The WISPI-IV is copyrighted and is available free of charge from

Marjorie H. Klein, Ph.D.
Professor of Psychiatry
University of Wisconsin–Madison Medical School
Wisconsin Psychiatric Institute and Clinics
6001 Research Park Boulevard
Madison, WI 53719-1179
E-mail: mhklein@facstaff.wisc.edu

The instrument has been translated into Dutch, German, and Italian. The SPSS scoring program is also available free of charge; however, there is a $25.00 charge for the computer-administered and computer scoring program.

PSYCHOMETRIC PROPERTIES

Reliability

Internal consistency coefficients (i.e., alphas) from three studies ranged from 0.84 to 0.96 (Klein et al. 1993), from 0.86 to 0.97, and from 0.81 to 0.94 (Barber and Morse 1994); test-retest coefficients (i.e., correlations over 1- to 46-day intervals) generally ranged from 0.71 to 0.96 (0.71–0.94 [Klein et al. 1993] and 0.82–0.96 [Moras et al. 1991]). Test-retest correlations in a study that employed a somewhat longer interval (i.e., 3–4 months) ranged from 0.69 to 0.80. In addition, in one unpublished study with an average 17-day test-retest interval, the same scale had the highest elevation of all the scales on both test and retest in 60% of subjects and profiles appeared relatively stable (mean rank order correlation of 0.89; range of 0.48–0.99). Finally, for the individual scales, a mean item-total correlation of 0.49 was reported by the test authors (range of 0.42–0.65).

Validity

Evidence of content validity was reported by the test authors. When two pairs of clinicians sorted all the WISPI items into the 11 DSM-III-R Axis II categories, median kappa coefficients for agreement on the assignments were 0.82 and 0.89 for each pair; individual kappa coefficients ranged from 0.57 to 0.98. When correspondence was assessed between two interpersonal ratings of each item, the authors found a mean correlation of 0.68 (range of 0.43–0.97). When correspondence was assessed between

an interpersonal rating of each item and an interpersonal rating of its associated personality disorder category, a mean correlation of 0.69 was found (range of 0.41–0.93). When the concordance between the dimensional scores of the WISPI and those of other measures of personality disorders (e.g., the Millon Clinical Multiaxial Inventory [MCMI] [p. 734], the Personality Diagnostic Questionnaire [PDQ] [p. 732], the Structured Clinical Interview for DSM-IV Axis II Personality Disorders [SCID-II] [p. 723], and the International Personality Disorder Examination [IPDE] [p. 721]) and therapists' clinical ratings was measured, median scale correlations ranged from 0.39 to 0.67.

The authors also reported evidence for the discriminative ability of the WISPI. They found significantly higher scores on 8 of the 11 scales when comparing mental health patients with nonpatients and higher scores on 7 scales for patients with a personality disorder than for patients without a current personality disorder or without a history of personality disorder. High interscale correlations have been found (e.g., mean of 0.62 in one study), a finding that may be due to the overlapping nature of the DSM personality disorder diagnoses. The validity of the WISPI categorical scores has not been reported.

CLINICAL UTILITY

The WISPI-IV appears to be a promising instrument representing the dimensional (i.e., quantitative) approach to personality disorder assessment. Unique features are the inclusion of interpersonal theory and items written from the perspective of the patient. It takes relatively little time for clinicians to administer the instrument, and its cost is negligible; however, scoring is time-consuming when done by hand. Although concordance between the dimensional scores of the WISPI-IV and those of other instruments that assess the personality disorders has been moderate at best, initial reliability and validity data otherwise appear good in the psychometric studies conducted to date.

REFERENCES AND SUGGESTED READINGS

Barber JP, Morse JQ: Validation of the Wisconsin Personality Disorders Interview with the SCID-II and PDE. Journal of Personality Disorders 8:307–319, 1994

Benjamin LS: Interpersonal Diagnosis and Treatment of Personality Disorders, 2nd Edition. New York, Guilford, 1996

Crowne DP, Marlowe D: Approval Motive: Studies in Evaluation Dependence. Westport, CT, Greenwood, 1964

Klein MH, Benjamin LS, Rosenfeld R, et al: The Wisconsin Personality Disorders Interview: development, reliability, and validity. Journal of Personality Disorders 7:285–303, 1993

Personality Assessment Inventory (PAI)

L. C. Morey

GOALS

The Personality Assessment Inventory (PAI) (Morey 1991) was developed to assess major clinical syndromes, personality features, and potential treatment complications dimensionally to provide information relevant to diagnosis, treatment planning, and screening for psychopathology.

DESCRIPTION

The PAI is a 344-item self-administered questionnaire that provides continuous scores on 22 full scales (4 validity, 11 clinical, 2 interpersonal, and 5 treatment consideration); 10 of the full scales are divided into a total of 31 subscales.

In this review we focus on the four personality scales of the PAI. Among the 11 clinical scales, 2 assess personality features, the Borderline Features scale and the Antisocial Features scale. The Borderline Features scale contains four subscales that assess affective instability, identity problems, negative relationships with others, and impulsive self-harm. The Antisocial Features scale contains three subscales that assess antisocial behaviors, egocentricity and poor empathy, and stimulus seeking. Two additional interpersonal scales are based on an interpersonal circumplex model of personality; they assess the dimensions of dominating and controlling versus meekly submissive and warm and affiliative versus cold and rejecting.

Items for each scale were selected to identify components (i.e., phenomenology and symptomatology) central to the construct being measured. Items are scored on only one scale, and each item has four answer choices: 0 = false, not at all true, 1 = slightly true, 2 = mainly true, or 3 = very true.

A short form of the PAI that consists of only the first 160 items from the full PAI is available. The short form does not provide scores for any subscale and provides only estimates for the full scales. The test author recommends using the short form only when the full PAI cannot be administered.

Scales range in length from 8 to 24 items; scores range from 0 to 24 for the 8-item scales and from 0 to 72 for the 24-item scales. Subscales range in length from 6 to 8 items. Raw scores are entered on the profile form, which provides for easy identification of associated T-scores. Normative interpretation is thus possible by comparison with scores of a community group of 1,000 adults selected to match the 1995 U.S. Census projections and with those of a clinical sample of 1,246 adults consisting of inpatients, outpatients, prisoners, substance abuse patients, and general medical patients. The profile form also enables clinicians to interpret an entire profile of scores. Although guidance is provided in the manual, profiles should be interpreted cautiously because empirical work to identify correlates of specific profiles has only begun. The manual also provides norms for 117 census-matched black community subjects, 219 census-matched subjects over age 60, and 1,051 college students, thus permitting normative interpretation of scores for these specific populations.

PRACTICAL ISSUES

It takes 40–50 minutes to complete the PAI. It can be administered and scored by a technician but should be interpreted by a trained professional. The instrument was developed for use with adults, ages 18 and older, with at least a fourth-grade reading level. The PAI can be either hand or computer scored. Hand scoring is easy but perhaps a bit tedious. A mail-in service is available for computer scoring and interpretation. Personal computer–

based scoring software may also be purchased. The PAI can be computer administered, if desired. The test author cautions that the computer-generated interpretive reports should be considered as consultations and that clinicians should use these reports in combination with other data.

The manual (Morey 1991) provides detailed and comprehensive data on administration, scoring, interpretation, test construction procedures, and reliability and validity data. Those seeking an interactive forum for discussing the PAI can send the message "info pai-net" to majordomo@teleport.com (without a signature) to receive further information. An introductory workshop presented by the test's developer is available through the publisher, as is a Spanish version of the instrument. The PAI is copyrighted and may be obtained from

> Psychological Assessment Resources, Inc.
> P.O. Box 998
> Odessa, FL 33556
> Phone: 800-331-TEST (800-331-8378)

The PAI Comprehensive Kit is available for $149.00 and includes the *Personality Assessment Inventory: Professional Manual*, 2 reusable item booklets, 2 administration folios (hard surfaces for writing), 25 Form HS (hand-scorable) answer sheets, 25 adult profile forms, and 25 critical item forms. Personal computer–based software for unlimited automated scoring and interpretation costs $495.00; 25 computerized administrations may be purchased for $125.00.

PSYCHOMETRIC PROPERTIES

Reliability

Median internal consistency coefficients in various samples (i.e., community, clinical, college student, and alcohol dependent) were above 0.80 for full scales and above 0.70 for subscales, and coefficients for the four personality scales were near or above 0.80. Median test-retest reliability coefficients in various samples (i.e., community, college student, and mixed community and clinical) ranged from 0.73 to 0.85 for full scales and from 0.77 to 0.80 for subscales; coefficients for the four personality scales ranged from 0.60 to 0.90. Internal consistency and test-retest reliability were somewhat lower, however, in the one psychometric study of the Spanish

and English versions in a Mexican-American sample. Finally, high T-scores in subjects with significant elevations were found to be stable in nearly 80% of individuals in the one study that examined these data.

Validity

Because the PAI is a relatively new instrument, a substantial body of validity data has yet to emerge. However, in the several validity studies conducted to date, the PAI personality scales generally performed as expected when assessed with specific populations or when compared with scores on instruments that measure related or dissimilar constructs. For instance, patients with borderline, but not antisocial, personality disorder were found to have elevated mean scores on the Borderline Features scale. Furthermore, Morey (1991) reported that the Dominance scale, but not the Warm scale, correlated highly ($r = 0.71$) with the Assertiveness facet of the NEO Personality Inventory (NEO-PI) (p. 740). Gender, race, and age differences were also found to be negligible or small. Finally, mixed findings were reported concerning the accuracy of the validity scales and the nature of the factor structure of the PAI, although most factor analytic findings are consistent with those reported in the manual.

CLINICAL UTILITY

The PAI is a relatively new and promising instrument. The manual is well written and comprehensive, and the test is relatively easy to use and interpret. Development of the PAI was methodologically sophisticated and stressed rational test construction and quantitative scale development. Initial data on its validity, reliability, and clinical utility are very good for the personality scales. However, further psychometric studies are needed, especially with underserved populations (as is generally true for all instruments reviewed in this chapter) and on profile configurations. Clinicians who use the PAI in these latter two circumstances should proceed cautiously.

REFERENCES AND SUGGESTED READINGS

Morey LC: Personality Assessment Inventory: Professional Manual. Odessa, FL, Psychological Assessment Resources, 1991

Morey LC: An Interpretive Guide to the Personality Assessment Inventory (PAI). Odessa, FL, Psychological Assessment Resources, 1996

Morey LC, Henry W: Personality Assessment Inventory, in The Use of Psychological Testing for Treatment Planning and Outcome Assessment. Edited by Maruish ME. Hillsdale, NJ, Erlbaum, 1994, pp 185–216

NEO Personality Inventory—Revised (NEO-PI-R)

P. T. Costa Jr. and R. R. McCrae

GOALS

The goal of the NEO Personality Inventory—Revised (NEO-PI-R) (Costa and McCrae 1992) is to dimensionally assess the five major domains of the five-factor model of personality and the 30 facets of these five broad domains. The five domains are Neuroticism, Extraversion, Openness, Agreeableness, and Conscientiousness.

The five-factor model of personality has emerged from several decades of research in what has been called the lexical tradition. Trait theorists have hypothesized that by identifying groups of intercorrelated traits among a comprehensive or representative set of trait terms within the language, the basic or most important characteristics of personality could be identified. One result of this line of research has been the five-factor model of personality; the NEO-PI-R is an instrument developed to measure these five factors.

DESCRIPTION

The NEO-PI-R is a 240-item self-administered questionnaire that yields continuous scores in each domain and on the six facets within each domain. For example, the Neuroticism domain contains the facets of Anxiety, Angry Hostility, Depression, Self-Consciousness, Impulsivity, and Vulnerability. Each facet is assessed by eight

(nonoverlapping) items, and each item is rated on a 5-point scale (strongly disagree, disagree, neutral, agree, and strongly agree). Three validity items ask whether the respondent has responded honestly and accurately, has completed all items, and has marked responses in the correct spaces. Items are written at a sixth-grade reading level. Two parallel forms are available: Form S (self-report) and Form R (completed by a peer, spouse, or expert rater). A short form of the NEO-PI-R (the NEO Five-Factor Inventory [NEO-FFI]) consists of 60 items that provide scores for only the five domains.

Each item is scored from 0 = strongly disagree to 4 = strongly agree. The raw score for each facet is calculated by summing item scores; the resulting range is 0–32. Facet scores are summed for domain scores that range from 0 to 192. Facet and domain scores are transcribed onto a profile form that permits plotting of standardized T-scores. Profile forms, separated by gender, are provided for both adults (ages 21 and older) and college-age individuals (ages 17–20) for Form S (self-report) and for adults for Form R (other report). A brief report form is also available for providing written feedback to clients.

Results are interpreted by comparing domain and facet scores with an appropriate normative group and by looking at the relative magnitude of domain and facet scores for a given individual. Normative interpretation can be conducted by either analysis of T-scores as plotted on the profile sheets or examination of percentile ranks provided in the manual. Norms were developed from various studies conducted largely within the Baltimore, Maryland, community. For Form S, the adult norms were derived on the basis of samples of 500 men and 500 women; individuals were selected to provide age, gender, and racial group distributions that match the U.S. Census projections for 1995. The college student norms for Form S were derived on the basis of samples of 148 men and 241 women, with an age range of 17–20, selected from two college campuses (in Canada and the southeastern United States). Adult norms for Form R were derived on the basis of samples of 123 men and 110 women rated by either peers or spouses.

PRACTICAL ISSUES

It takes 35–40 minutes to complete the NEO-PI-R. The measure is appropriate for individuals ages 17 and older.

It takes about 10–15 minutes to complete the shorter NEO-FFI. Both versions can be administered and scored by a technician, although trained professionals should interpret the results. The NEO-PI-R can be administered and scored by computer or by hand; the NEO-FFI can be scored by computer. Hand scoring is easily accomplished, although somewhat tedious for the 30 facets. A mail-in service and personal computer software are available for computer scoring and interpretation.

The manual (Costa and McCrae 1992) provides suggestions for clinical use and data on administration, scoring, interpretation, test construction procedures, and reliability and validity. A Spanish version is available for clinical purposes, and versions in other languages are available for research purposes. The NEO-PI-R is copyrighted and may be obtained from

Psychological Assessment Resources, Inc.
P.O. Box 998
Odessa, FL 33556
Phone: 800-331-TEST (800-331-8378)

Costs are as follows: $129.00 for the NEO-PI-R Comprehensive Kit (which includes the manual, 10 reusable Form S [self-report] item booklets, 10 reusable Form R [observer report] item booklets, 25 hand-scorable answer sheets, 25 Form S and 25 Form R adult profile forms, and 25 feedback sheets), $21.00 for 25 college student profile forms, $79.00 for mail-in computer scoring and interpretation for 10 administrations, $495.00 for personal computer–based software for unlimited automated scoring and interpretation, $125.00 for 25 computerized administrations, and $85.00 for the NEO-FFI Introductory Kit.

PSYCHOMETRIC PROPERTIES

Reliability

Internal consistency coefficients (i.e., alpha coefficients) for Forms S and R ranged from approximately 0.86 to 0.95 for domain scores and from 0.56 to 0.90 for facet scores (median of 0.71 for Form S and 0.78 for Form R); internal consistency for facet scores of the Conscientiousness and Agreeableness domains was slightly lower than that for the other facet scores. Correlations for short-term test-retest reliability ranged from 0.86 to 0.91 for Neuroticism, Extraversion, and Openness and from 0.66 to 0.92 for their facets. Test-retest reliability

(over a 6- to 7-year interval) ranged from 0.63 to 0.83 for the five domains for self-report and ratings by others and from 0.51 to 0.82 for facet scores of the Neuroticism, Extraversion, and Openness domains. Internal consistency coefficients for the NEO-FFI ranged from 0.68 to 0.86; short-term test-retest reliability ranged from 0.75 to 0.83.

Validity

The test developers report high correlations between domain scores and factors extracted from the NEO-PI-R (e.g., 0.89–0.95); the facets have their highest correlations with corresponding domain scores (e.g., 0.68 between Straightforwardness and the Agreeableness domain). The five NEO-PI-R scales correlated well (e.g., 0.60–0.69) with corresponding scales from a wide variety of other five-factor measures. The NEO-PI-R scales also correlated well with comparable scales from a variety of instruments that assess different, but related, theoretical constructs, including career interests (e.g., $r = 0.56$ between the Artistic scale of the Self Directed Search [Holland 1985] and the Aesthetics facet of the Openness domain), Jungian types (e.g., $r = -0.59$ between the Introversion scale of the Myers-Briggs Type Indicator [Myers and McCaulley 1985] and the Gregariousness facet of the Extraversion domain), needs and motives (e.g., $r = 0.64$ between the Affiliation scale of the Personality Research Form [Jackson 1984] and the Warmth facet of the Extraversion domain), psychopathology (e.g., $r = 0.47$ between the Borderline Personality Disorder scale of the Minnesota Multiphasic Personality Inventory [MMPI] [p. 89] and the Angry Hostility facet of the Neuroticism facet), and multidimensional personality instruments (e.g., $r = 0.49$ between the Independence scale of the Revised California Psychological Inventory [Gough 1987] and the Competence facet of the Conscientiousness domain). In addition, relationships were found between the five factors of the NEO-PI-R and measures of less closely related constructs such as psychological well-being (e.g., unemotional individuals score low in the Neuroticism and Extraversion domains) and coping style (e.g., self-blame is related to high scores in the Neuroticism domain). However, the 12 facets of the Agreeableness and Conscientiousness domains are less internally consistent than the other facets and have demonstrated lower convergence with measures of similar constructs.

The five factors of the NEO-PI-R were found in a variety of samples (e.g., men and women, whites and nonwhites, and young adults and older adults). The five broad factors emerged in factor analytic studies of both the individual items and of the 30 facets, with Form S and Form R, although the 30 facets were not always confirmed in factor analytic studies, and confirmatory factor analysis did not always reproduce the five factors. Additional factors may be necessary to fully account for all of the important traits of personality (Tinsley 1994).

CLINICAL UTILITY

The NEO-PI-R is a prominent measure of the five-factor model of normal personality traits. In addition, substantial research over the past decade has demonstrated that its five factors are related in meaningful ways to other measures of mental, social, and occupational functioning. Clinicians may find the NEO-PI-R useful for ascertaining the nature and degree of clients' personality traits relative to those of psychiatrically healthy individuals and for conceptualizing the effect of personality attributes on clinical functioning (Widiger and Trull 1997).

The manual is well written and contains thoughtful and pragmatic explanations of psychometric terms and careful descriptions of constructs. However, information on evaluating or applying the instrument in clinical settings is at times inadequate. The adequacy of the normative sample is difficult to assess because the manual provides only sketchy descriptions of the samples and the procedures used in selecting them. The manual offers many suggestions for clinical use, including the anticipation of the course of therapy, development of rapport, aiding in diagnosis, selection of optimal treatment, vocational counseling, and industrial and organizational consulting, but explicit, specific empirical support for these applications is at times unclear. These suggestions for clinical applications are best viewed as hypotheses, as the instrument's developers acknowledge. In addition, the NEO-PI-R may not adequately assess all of the maladaptive variants of each domain of personality functioning, particularly the traits associated with the obsessive-compulsive and schizotypal personality disorders.

Short-term test-retest reliability within clinical settings has not yet been well studied. The three validity checks may also be too simplistic and rely on clients' forthrightness. The original item construction has also been criticized (Juni 1996). Important conceptual and theoretical issues are the names for the five factors and the theoretical basis of the five-factor model. It is difficult to select one word to represent a broad domain of traits, yet that word (e.g., *Agreeableness*) has implications for how the domain is understood. Finally, although the instrument has substantial empirical support and is relatively free of theory, some have suggested that both the five-factor model and the NEO-PI-R stem from an implicit theoretical base that has not been adequately conceptualized or articulated.

REFERENCES AND SUGGESTED READINGS

Costa PT, McCrae RR: NEO PI-R Professional Manual. Odessa, FL, Psychological Assessment Resources, 1992

Gough HG: California Psychological Inventory Administrator's Guide. Palo Alto, CA, Consulting Psychologists Press, 1987

Holland JL: Self-Directed Search—1985 Edition. Odessa, FL, Psychological Assessment Resources, 1985

Jackson DN: Personality Research Form Manual, 3rd Edition. Port Huron, MI, Research Psychologists Press, 1984

Juni S: Review of the revised NEO Personality Inventory, in 12th Mental Measurements Yearbook. Edited by Conoley JC, Impara JC. Lincoln, NE, University of Nebraska Press, 1996, pp 863–868

Myers IB, McCaulley MH: Manual: A Guide to the Development and Use of the Myers-Briggs Type Indicator. Palo Alto, CA, Consulting Psychologists Press, 1985

Tinsley HEA: NEO Personality Inventory—Revised, in Test Critiques, Vol 10. Edited by Keyser DJ, Sweetland RC. Austin, TX, PRO-ED, 1994, pp 443–456

Widiger TA, Trull TJ: Assessment of the five-factor model of personality. J Pers Assess 68:228–250, 1997

Inventory of Interpersonal Problems (IIP)

L. M. Horowitz

GOALS

The Inventory of Interpersonal Problems (IIP) (Horowitz et al. 1988) was developed to dimensionally assess the nature of dysfunctional interpersonal patterns that clients report as presenting complaints.

DESCRIPTION

The IIP is a self-administered questionnaire that provides an overall quantitative index of interpersonal problems as well as scores on either six or eight scales, depending on how the instrument is scored. The original instrument has 127 items scored on four scales that represent interpersonal areas that may be distressing for a person (Assertive, Sociable, Intimate, and Submissive) and two that represent interpersonal behaviors that a person may engage in too often (Responsible and Controlling). These scales consist of 10–21 items.

A subsequent and more frequently used version of the IIP (IIP-Circumplex Scales [IIP-C]) has 64 items taken from the original instrument. The IIP-C is scored on eight scales that represent the octants of the circumplex model of interpersonal dispositions (eight items per scale): Domineering, Vindictive, Cold, Socially Avoidant, Nonassertive, Exploitable, Overly Nurturant, and Intrusive. A short form of the IIP-C (IIP-Circumplex Short Form Scales [IIP-SC]) contains 32 items, with 4 items per scale. The test developer recommends using the circumplex scales.

The interpersonal model employed in the circumplex scales was originally developed by Timothy Leary in 1957. In this model, interpersonal behavior is plotted in a two-dimensional circumplex (circular) space characterized by dominance versus submission on a vertical axis and hostility versus friendliness on a horizontal axis. This interpersonal space may be divided into eight sectors (octants), each of which reflects combinations of the two personality axes.

The IIP items assess a wide range of interpersonal problems and were developed from analysis of intake interviews with psychotherapy outpatients. For each item, the respondent is instructed to indicate how distressing the problem has been on a 5-point scale: 0 = not at all, 1 = a little bit, 2 = moderately, 3 = quite a bit, and 4 = extremely.

Scores for the overall index and each scale are the average of all items included, regardless of the version used. Scores may also be ipsatized to eliminate variance caused by the subject's overall level of distress. This procedure involves expressing each score as a deviation from the subject's mean score across all items. For the original 127-item IIP, scores may be interpreted by comparing them with normative data from a psychiatric sample (N = 134) and nonpsychiatric student sample (N − 134) for the overall mean index and scale scores, as well as for ipsatized scores. For the 64-item IIP-C, the publisher has developed new norms on the basis of data from a sample of 800 adults selected to closely match the 1995 U.S. Census.

PRACTICAL ISSUES

It takes 20–30 minutes to complete the 127-item IIP. The instrument can be administered and scored by a technician, but a trained professional should interpret the results. The IIP was developed for use with adults, ages 18 and older. The 64-item IIP-C is currently being prepared for publication (to be called simply the Inventory of Interpersonal Problems [IIP]), and definitive details regarding the manual, computer administration and scoring, foreign language versions, training opportunities, and costs are unavailable at this time. It is expected, however, that the manual, when it becomes available, will provide information concerning administration, scoring, interpretation, test construction procedures, and reliability and validity. The IIP is copyrighted and will be available from

The Psychological Corporation
555 Academic Court
San Antonio, TX 78204-2498
Phone: 800-211-8378
Internet: www.psychcorp.com

PSYCHOMETRIC PROPERTIES

Reliability

In the only reliability study conducted with the 127-item IIP, internal consistency (alpha coefficient) ranged from 0.82 to 0.94 for the six scales, and 10-week test-retest reliability (r) ranged from 0.80 to 0.87. Test-retest reliability for the overall index was 0.98; an alpha coefficient was not reported for the overall index. In the only published reliability study on the 64-item IIP-C, internal consistency (alpha coefficient) ranged from 0.72 to 0.85 for the eight octant scales (alpha for five scales >0.80). In the only published reliability study on the 32-item IIP-SC, internal consistency (alpha coefficient) on three samples ranged from 0.88 to 0.89 for the overall index and from 0.68 to 0.84 (median of 0.78) for the octant scales; 2-month test-retest reliability (r) on one of the samples was 0.83 for the overall index and 0.61–0.79 (median of 0.72) for the octant scales.

Validity

Only a few validity studies have been conducted. A significant correlation (0.57–0.64) was found between the total scores of the 127-item IIP and the Symptom Checklist–90—Revised (SCL-90-R) (p. 81), indicating that both instruments assess general distress. In addition, the UCLA Loneliness Scale (Russell et al. 1980) showed the highest correlation with the IIP on the Sociable scale (r = 0.73); the short form of the Rathus Assertiveness Scale (Rathus 1973) showed the highest correlation with the IIP on the Assertiveness scale (r = 0.64), indicating that the IIP can also accurately assess more specific intended constructs.

The two factors of the circumplex model were replicated in two samples of undergraduates who completed the 127-item IIP and, in a third undergraduate sample, using items only from the IIP-C. The octant scales of the IIP-C that were developed with the first two samples were also cross-validated in the third. Some investigators, however, have not replicated the factor structure serving as the basis for the 127-item IIP scale and the two larger circumplex axes. Additional evidence for the validity of the octant circumplex scales is significant correlation (r = 0.36–0.58) with the corresponding scale of another circumplex measure, the Revised Interpersonal Adjectives Scales (IAS-R) (Wiggins et al. 1988). Furthermore, in seven of eight octants, the highest possible correlation

of each IIP-C scale was with the theoretically appropriate scale of the IAS-R, and in five of eight octants the highest negative correlations were with the theoretically opposite scales of the IAS-R. In addition, the developers of the 32-item IIP-SC found correlations >0.90 between the IIP-SC and corresponding octants of the IIP-C, providing evidence that these two circumplex versions yield similar results. Finally, the 127-item IIP was found by its developers to be sensitive to clinical change in that IIP change correlated well (i.e., r = 0.61–0.74) with improvement as assessed by patient self-reports, therapists' judgments, and assessments by independent observers. Similar sensitivity to clinical change has been found with both the IIP-C and the IIP-SC.

CLINICAL UTILITY

The IIP is a relatively new and promising instrument. It is easy to use and relatively easy to interpret. In addition, its appeal stems from its origins in the interpersonal complaints of psychotherapy outpatients, the developers' careful attention to scale development, and its theoretical connection to the circumplex model of interpersonal dispositions. Preliminary findings indicate that the IIP is able to identify specific types of interpersonal problems and their amenability to treatment and also that it is sensitive to therapeutic progress. Initial validity and reliability data are also good, but further studies are needed concerning the psychometric properties and potential clinical utility of the IIP.

REFERENCES AND SUGGESTED READINGS

Alden LE, Wiggins JS, Pincus AL: Construction of circumplex scales for the Inventory of Interpersonal Problems. J Pers Assess 55:521–536, 1990

Horowitz LM: The study of interpersonal problems: a Leary legacy. J Pers Assess 66:283–300, 1996

Horowitz LM, Rosenberg SE, Baer BA, et al: Inventory on Interpersonal Problems: psychometric properties and clinical applications. J Consult Clin Psychol 56:885–892, 1988

Rathus S: A 30-item schedule for assessing assertive behavior. Behavior Therapy 4:398–406, 1973

Russell D, Peplau LA, Cutrona CE: The Revised UCLA Loneliness Scale: concurrent and discriminant validity evidence. J Pers Soc Psychol 39:472–480, 1980

Soldz S, Budman S, Demby A, et al: A short form of the Inventory of Interpersonal Problems circumplex scales. Assessment 2:53–63, 1995

Wiggins JS, Trapnell P, Phillips N: Psychometric and geometric
characteristics of the Revised Interpersonal Adjectives
Scales (IAS-R). Multivariate Behavioral Research
23:517–530, 1988

Structural Analysis of Social Behavior (SASB)

L. S. Benjamin

GOALS

The goal of the Structural Analysis of Social Behavior
(SASB) (Benjamin 1984) is to assess, from the perspectives of object relations and interpersonal theories, patients' views of interpersonal and intrapsychic interactions for the purpose of informing and facilitating
psychotherapy

The SASB model emphasizes intrapsychic variables
and postulates principles for understanding dynamic and
adaptive behavior toward or in reaction to others and
toward oneself. The SASB has features similar to those
of the interpersonal circumplex model (described in the
section on the Inventory of Interpersonal Problems [IIP]
[p. 743]) but provides more specific information and is
thus potentially more useful although also more complex.
The SASB model retains the horizontal axis of affiliation
(i.e., friendliness vs. hostility) of the interpersonal circumplex model, but, rather than opposing dominance
with submission, the SASB opposes enmeshment (control and submission) with differentiation (emancipation,
separation, and assertiveness) on an interdependence
axis. The SASB model also codifies the affiliation and
interdependence axes in three different ways: action toward others (transitive), reaction to others (intransitive),
and action toward self (introjective). The introjective
surface is intended to measure H. S. Sullivan's (1953)
hypothesis that self-concept is a reflection of social experience.

DESCRIPTION

For clinical purposes, the SASB consists of a series of self-
administered questionnaires that assess and provide
quantitative scores on patients' present or past views of
themselves and significant others. The 13 specific questionnaires to be administered are determined collabora-
tively by the clinician and patient, with a standard series
directed toward self (introjective version), significant
other, mother, father, mother in relationship with father,
and father in relationship with mother.

The number of items per questionnaire ranges from
16 to 64 (short form). The original long form of the
SASB had 108 items, one item for each of the 36 points
on each of the three surfaces (transitive, intransitive, and
introjective); the short form items summarize the information sampled by these original 108 items. Patients are
asked to rate themselves or others at their best and at
their worst, in separate sections, to describe how apt or
true an item is or how frequently it applies. Clinicians
may substitute other frames of reference (e.g., sober and
drunk or before and after a divorce). Items are written at
a sixth-grade reading level.

Each item is rated from 0 to 100, at 10-point intervals, on a scale that is anchored at either end with 0 =
never, not at all and 100 = always, perfectly. SASB questionnaires can be scored by hand; however, computer
scoring is recommended for more complete profiles, special indexes, and interpretive reports. Separate profiles
are generated for the three surfaces of interaction, and
each profile plots patients on both the interdependence
and affiliation axes. For each profile, pattern coefficients
are generated to indicate the extent of three therapeu-
tically relevant variables: attack, control, and conflict.
For instance, the attack coefficient indicates the extent
to which endorsements centered on the horizontal (i.e.,
affiliation) axis indicate hostility (positive values) or
friendliness (negative values). Numerous other quantitative indexes are available, including a weighted
affiliation-autonomy vector that quantifies the average
thrusts on the affiliative and interdependence axes; a coefficient of internal consistency that quantifies the ex-
tents to which similar items are given similar ratings, independent items are given uncorrelated ratings, and

opposite items are given opposite ratings; average quadrant scores; and numerous others. Scoring is conducted with complex mathematical procedures that involve circumplex logic, Markov chaining, and comparison of actual scores with theoretical scores that are based on cosine curves or are defined by orthogonal polynomials. The manual (Benjamin 1988) provides norms derived on the basis of samples of college student volunteers taking abnormal psychology classes ($N = 41$ and $N = 39$ for the two versions of the short form). The average age of the volunteers was the mid-20s, and two-thirds of the sample were women.

PRACTICAL ISSUES

It takes about 1 hour to complete the SASB short form series. The manual (Benjamin 1988) provides guidelines for administration, scoring, and interpretation and several clinical illustrations. Training is required and may consist of attendance at, or videotape viewing of, a 1-day workshop. Users should also be familiar with the SASB model and with object relations theory. The SASB has been translated into approximately 12 languages. The questionnaire and software are copyrighted by the University of Utah. The initial program cost is $50.00 for software, and the royalties thereafter are $2.00 per patient for clinical applications. The SASB can be ordered from

> Intrex
> Department of Psychology
> University of Utah
> Salt Lake City, UT 84112

PSYCHOMETRIC PROPERTIES

Reliability

Average internal consistency for the long forms has been reported at about 0.90 (defined as the degree to which ratings are maximal at one point on the circumplex and progressively lower as distance from that point increases), but the developer reports that it is not possible to calculate internal consistency on the short forms because there are too few data points. Test-retest reliability coefficients (r) were generally >0.80 in several studies with few subjects (i.e., <20), but coefficients were somewhat lower (0.55–0.65) for ratings of self and others at worst.

Validity

The validity of the SASB model has been assessed in factor analytic studies, in studies of various predicted relationships among aspects of the model, and in expected differences among clinical groups. When naive undergraduates rated SASB questionnaire items on scales representing the underlying theoretical SASB dimensions, the developer found that substantial proportions of variance (i.e., 55%–69%) in their ratings could be accounted for by factors that corresponded to SASB theory. Furthermore, affiliation correlated highly with the first factor (e.g., $r = 0.92$), as did autonomy with the second (e.g., $r = 0.88$); correlations that were crossed (e.g., affiliation with the second factor) were low (e.g., $r < 0.15$). It was also found that when items were rated separately for affiliation, interdependence, and focus, the result was a reasonable facsimile of the cluster version of the SASB model. The developer reports clinically reasonable findings of differences among various groups (e.g., family relationships among individuals with anorexia nervosa, bulimia nervosa, and psychiatrically healthy control subjects). Finally, in a comparison of the SASB with the interpersonal circumplex model as operationalized by the Revised Interpersonal Adjectives Scales (Wiggins et al. 1988), correlations were small (–0.20 to –0.40) but in the expected direction, a finding that the test developer interprets as logical given the theoretical discrepancies between the two models.

CLINICAL UTILITY

The SASB has a history dating to the early 1970s, is conceptually intriguing, and has been said by adherents to facilitate psychotherapy. As described by the developer, the SASB can be used to inform construction of treatment plans, measure change during psychotherapy, define the clinical problem of differentiation failure, and characterize patient-therapist interactions. The greatest strength of the SASB might be its psychotherapy-oriented theoretical model. However, the model is complex and requires considerable investment for mastery; the relative lack of organization within the manual and the use of somewhat esoteric terminology further hamper efforts to learn the model. The manual covers the usual topics, such as administration and scoring, but administration procedures are difficult to follow and the clinical anecdotes are scattered somewhat haphazardly throughout the text. Noticeably absent is a section on test and item development. Only a few reliability studies have been conducted, and the number of subjects was low in each study. Validity studies have supported various aspects of the SASB, but more studies are needed, as acknowledged by the developer. These difficulties notwithstanding, the creativity and depth of SASB theory, as well as its psychotherapeutic relevance, make the SASB an attractive psychotherapy tool for those willing to invest themselves in learning the model.

REFERENCES AND SUGGESTED READINGS

Benjamin LS: Principles of prediction using Structural Analysis of Social Behavior, in Personality and the Prediction of Behavior. Edited by Zucker RA, Aronoff J, Rabin AI. New York, Academic Press, 1984, pp 121–174

Benjamin LS: SASB Short Form User's Manual. Salt Lake City, UT, University of Utah, 1988

Benjamin LS: Interpersonal Diagnosis and Treatment of Personality Disorders. New York, Guilford, 1993

Sullivan HS: The Interpersonal Theory of Psychiatry. New York, WW Norton, 1953

Wiggins JS, Trapnell P, Phillips N: Psychometric and geometric characteristics of the Revised Interpersonal Adjectives Scales (IAS-R). Multivariate Behavioral Research 23:517–530, 1988

Defense Style Questionnaire (DSQ)

M. *Bond*

GOALS

The goal of the Defense Style Questionnaire (DSQ) (Bond et al. 1983) is to dimensionally assess conscious derivatives of defense mechanisms. The authors conceive of defense mechanisms as reflecting a person's character-

istic style, whether conscious or unconscious, of dealing with conflict or stress. The premise underlying the DSQ is that people are sufficiently aware of these characteristic styles to provide information useful for assessing defense mechanisms.

DESCRIPTION

The DSQ is an 88-item self-administered questionnaire that provides continuous (i.e., quantitative) scores on four styles of defensive functioning: Maladaptive Action (33 items), Image-Distorting (15 items), Self-Sacrificing (8 items), and Adaptive (7 items). Each defensive style consists of particular defense mechanisms. The Maladaptive Action style includes passive aggression, projection, regression, inhibition, projective identification, acting out, somatization, withdrawal, fantasy, help rejecting, complaining, consumption, and undoing. The Image-Distorting style includes omnipotence, omnipotence and devaluation, denial, splitting, primitive idealization, projection, and isolation. The Self-Sacrificing style includes pseudoaltruism, reaction formation, and denial. The Adaptive style includes suppression, sublimation, humor, anticipation, and affiliation. Included are 25 items that do not assess any of the four styles; 10 of these are for the assessment of social desirability. Each item is rated on a 9-point scale anchored at either end with 1 = strongly disagree and 9 = strongly agree. Sample items from the Maladaptive Action and Adaptive styles are provided in Example 32–9.

The score for each of the defense styles is simply the sum of its items. An optional computer scoring program is available. The four styles are conceptualized to exist on a continuum from unhealthy to healthy defensive functioning, in the following order: Maladaptive Action,

EXAMPLE 32–9 ■ **Sample items from the Defense Style Questionnaire**

Maladaptive Action Style: Acting Out
I get openly aggressive when I feel hurt.

Adaptive Style: Suppression
I'm able to keep a problem out of my mind until I have time to deal with it.

Reprinted with permission from Michael Bond, M.D.

Image-Distorting, Self-Sacrificing, and Adaptive. Scores may be interpreted by comparison with normative data provided in the manual for nonpatients, general psychiatric patients, patients with borderline personality disorder, and patients with other personality disorders.

PRACTICAL ISSUES

It takes about 20 minutes to complete the DSQ. The manual (Bond and Wesley 1996) provides scoring guidelines, normative data, and an extensive review of the published literature on the psychometric properties and clinical utility of the DSQ. The DSQ is copyrighted and is available free of charge from

> Michael Bond, M.D.
> Department of Psychiatry
> Sir Mortimer B. Davis—Jewish General Hospital
> 4333 Chemin De La Cote Ste-Catherine
> Montreal, Quebec, Canada H3T 1E4
> Phone: 514-340-8210
> Fax: 514-340-7507

Separate fees of $20.00 are charged for the manual and for the optional computer scoring program. The DSQ has been translated into Chinese, Dutch, Egyptian Arabic, Finnish, French, German, Italian, and Norwegian.

The DSQ is included on the CD-ROM that accompanies this handbook.

PSYCHOMETRIC PROPERTIES

Reliability

Statistically significant item-total correlations have been reported. Six-month test-retest reliability ranged from 0.68 to 0.73 for the four styles.

Validity

Evidence for the validity of the DSQ is provided by studies of its relation to other approaches for measuring defense mechanisms, relation to instruments for measuring other constructs, factor structure, ability to distinguish among patients and between patients and nonpatients, and ability to predict treatment outcome.

At least half of the DSQ items have correlated significantly, but modestly (i.e., absolute value <0.30), with clinical ratings of defenses made years earlier. Modest but theoretically consistent relationships were found between DSQ defense styles and interview-based ratings of defense mechanisms (e.g., $r = 0.36$ between the Maladaptive Action style and ratings of immature defenses). Statistically significant negative correlations were found between the first three styles and measures of ego functioning, and significant positive correlations ($r = 0.19$–0.32) were found between the Adaptive style scale and measures of ego functioning. Theoretically consistent, statistically significant correlations were also found with measures of personality disorder, although not always. For instance, the more primitive styles (i.e., Maladaptive Action and Image-Distorting) were found to correlate positively (e.g., $r = 0.52$) with a composite index of personality disorder, significant correlations were found between an immature factor and eight DSM personality disorders, and a modest negative correlation (i.e., $r = -0.23$) was found between the Adaptive style and a composite index of personality disorder. Moderately positive correlations (e.g., $r = 0.45$) were found between the severity of psychosocial stressors and the Maladaptive Action and Image-Distorting styles.

Several factor analytic studies yielded factors consistent with the Maladaptive Action and Adaptive ends of a continuum of defensive functioning, but factor structure has varied across studies.

The DSQ defensive styles were found to distinguish among patient groups and between patients and nonpatients. For instance, patients with borderline personality disorder were found to use the Maladaptive Action and Image-Distorting styles significantly more often than patients without borderline personality disorder and to use the Adaptive style significantly less often. This same pattern was found in studies that compared mental health patients with nonpatients; patients more frequently used the immature defensive styles and less frequently used the Adaptive style. The manual describes numerous patient groups (e.g., patients with eating disorders and delinquents) from which the DSQ is able to differentiate psychiatrically healthy subjects. Patients with depression, anxiety disorders, and eating disorders who used more immature defensive functioning were found to be less responsive to psychotherapeutic treatment than patients who used more mature defenses.

CLINICAL UTILITY

The DSQ represents a significant attempt at standardizing the assessment of defensive functioning (an accomplishment that has been elusive for many years. The simplicity of the administration and scoring of the DSQ make it easy to use and also render the simple meaning of scores rather straightforward. However, aside from studies on high versus low scores, the relative magnitudes of scores and their meanings have not been well studied. Further complications in interpretation arise from the insufficient documentation for normative data in the manual and from the scoring system, which allows varying ranges of possible scores among the four defensive styles. Reliability reported to date has been good, but little data exist. Perhaps the greatest attribute of the DSQ is its clinical relevance for psychodynamically oriented psychotherapists: the instrument has been shown to be useful in measuring immature versus mature defensive functioning, and these styles have been shown to relate to patient response to treatment.

REFERENCES AND SUGGESTED READINGS

Bond M, Wesley S: Manual for the Defense Style Questionnaire. Montreal, Quebec, McGill University, 1996

Bond M, Gardner ST, Christian J, et al: Empirical study of self-rated defense styles. Arch Gen Psychiatry 40:333–338, 1983

Bond M, Perry JC, Gautier M, et al: Validating the self-report of defense styles. Journal of Personality Disorders 3:101–112, 1989

Advisers for the Handbook of Psychiatric Measures

Advisers for Diagnostic Interviews for Adults

Nancy Andreasen, M.D., Ph.D.
Mary C. Blehar, Ph.D.
Jonathan Borus, M.D.
Linda B. Cottler, Ph.D.
Jean Endicott, Ph.D.
Marshall Folstein, M.D.
Alexander Janca, M.D.
Charles Kaelber, M.D.
Kenneth Kendler, M.D.
John Nurnberger, M.D.
Eugene Paykel, M.D.
Lee Robins, Ph.D.
Bruce Rounsaville, M.D.
Norman Sartorius, M.D., Ph.D.
Robert Spitzer, M.D.
Myrna Weissman, Ph.D.
Janet B. W. Williams, D.S.W.
John Wing, M.D.
Hans-Ulrich Wittchen, Ph.D.
Mark Zimmerman, M.D.

Advisers for General Psychiatric Symptoms Measures

Bradley N. Axelrod, Ph.D.
Thomas McGlashan, M.D.
Jane M. Murphy, M.D.
John Oldham, M.D.
Arthur Rifkin, M.D.

Mark Russ, M.D.
Gregory Simon, M.D.
Margaret Woerner, Ph.D.

Advisers for Mental Health Status, Functioning, and Disabilities Measures

Per Bech, M.D.
Elliot Gershon, M.D.
Howard Goldman, M.D., Ph.D.
Uriel Halbreich, M.D.
Martin M. Katz, M.D.
Kenneth Kobak, Ph.D.
Andrew C. Leon, Ph.D.
Michael Liebowitz, M.D.
Jane Murphy, M.D.
Jonathan Rabinowitz, D.S.W.
Norman Sartorius, M.D., Ph.D.
Andrew E. Skodol, M.D.
Robert Spitzer, M.D.
Gary J. Tucker, M.D.
Myrna Weissman, Ph.D.
Janet B. W. Williams, D.S.W.

Advisers for General Health Status, Functioning, and Disabilities Measures

Robert Brook, M.D.
Barbara J. Burns, Ph.D.
Margaret Chesney, Ph.D.

Jaqueline Golding, Ph.D.
Howard Goldman, M.D., Ph.D.
Alan Gruenberg, M.D.
Wayne Katon, M.D.
Nicole Lurie, M.D.
Juan Mezzich, M.D., Ph.D.
Richard Owen, M.D.
Donald Patrick, Ph.D.
Kathryn Rost, Ph.D.
Norman Sartorius, M.D., Ph.D.
Anita Stewart, Ph.D.

Advisers for Quality of Life Measures

Margaret Chesney, Ph.D.
Jean Endicott, Ph.D.
Michael Frisch, Ph.D.
Uriel Halbreich, M.D.
Anthony Lehman, M.D.
R. Bruce Lydiard, M.D., Ph.D.
Mark Rapaport, M.D.
Howard Waxman, Ph.D.

Advisers for Adverse Effects Measures

Thomas R. E. Barnes, M.D.
Per Bech, M.D.
Guy Chouinard, M.D., F.R.C.P.C.
James L. Claghorn, M.D.
Jonathan R. T. Davidson, M.D., F.R.C.P.

C. Lindsay DeVane, Pharm.D.
David L. Dunner, M.D.
W. Wolfgang Fleischhacker, M.D.
Alan Gelenberg, M.D.
Robert Hirschfeld, M.D., M.A.
Jorge Juncos, M.D.
John M. Kane, M.D.
James H. Kocsis, M.D.
Irene Litvan, M.D.
Richard Owen, M.D.
Frederic M. Quitkin, M.D.
Judith G. Rabkin, Ph.D.
Barry Reisberg, M.D.
George M. Simpson, M.D.
Rege S. Stewart, M.D.
Oldrich Vinar, M.D., D.Sc.
John L. Waddington, Ph.D., D.Sc.

Advisers for Patient Perceptions of Care Measures

Jeffrey Anderson, Ph.D.
C. Clifford Attkisson, Ph.D.
Patrick Corrigan, M.D.
Mary Fristad, Ph.D.
Thomas K. Greenfield, M.D.
Krista Kutash, Ph.D.
Anthony Lehman, M.D.
Michel Perreault, Ph.D.
P. Nelson Reid, Ph.D.
Lee Rosen, Ph.D.
Mirella Ruggeri, M.D., Ph.D.
Denise Stuntzer-Gibson, Ph.D.
Barry A. Tanner, M.D.
Graham Thornicroft, M.D.
John E. Ware, Ph.D.

Advisers for Practitioner and System Evaluation

Jacque Bieber, Ph.D.
Peter Brill, M.D.
Barbara J. Burns, Ph.D.
Susan Essock, Ph.D.
Anthony Lehman, M.D.
Bentson McFarland, M.D., Ph.D.
Thomas McLellan, Ph.D.
David Shern, Ph.D.

Advisers for Stress and Life Events Measures

Andrew Baum, Ph.D.
Margaret Chesney, Ph.D.
Sheldon Cohen, Ph.D.

Jean Endicott, Ph.D.
Ellen Frank, Ph.D.
Mardi Horowitz, M.D.
Rudolph Moos, Ph.D.
Jane M. Murphy, Ph.D.
Jeffrey Newcorn, M.D.
Richard Rahe, M.D.
Lon Schneider, M.D.
James Strain, M.D.
Joel Yager, M.D.

Advisers for Family and Relational Issues Measures

Adrian Angold, M.D.
Diana Baumrind, Ph.D.
William R. Beardslee, M.D.
Duane Bishop, M.D.
Pauline Boss, Ph.D.
Robert H. Bradley, Ph.D.
Barbara J. Burns, Ph.D.
Bob Caplan, Ph.D.
James Coyne, Ph.D.
Nathan B. Epstein, M.D.
Lawrence Fisher, Ph.D.
Rex Forehand, Ph.D.
Alan S. Gurman, Ph.D.
Nadine J. Kaslow, Ph.D.
Patricia Minuchin, M.D.
Susan O'Leary, Ph.D.
Joy Osofsky, Ph.D.
Gerald Patterson, Ph.D.
Ronald J. Prinz, Ph.D.
Earl Schaefer, M.D.
Harvey Skinner, Ph.D.
Graham B. Spanier, M.D.
M. Duncan Stanton, Ph.D.
Paul Steinhauer, Ph.D.
John Touliatos, Ph.D.
Ming T. Tsuang, M.D., Ph.D.
Frederick S. Wamboldt, M.D.
Beatrice L. Wood, Ph.D.
Lyman Wynne, M.D., Ph.D.
Stephen H. Zarit, Ph.D.

Advisers for Suicide Risk Measures

Lori L. Altshuler, M.D.
Jules Angst, M.D.
Bonnie Aronowitz, Ph.D.
Ernest S. Barratt, Ph.D.
Mark S. Bauer, M.D.
Aaron Beck, M.D.

Donald W. Black, M.D.
William Bunney Jr., M.D.
Paula Clayton, M.D.
Concetta M. DeCaria, Ph.D.
Jean Endicott, Ph.D.
Dwight L. Evans, M.D.
Allen Frances, M.D.
Marc Galanter, M.D.
Paul J. Goodnick, M.D.
John Greden, M.D.
Uriel Halbreich, M.D.
Robert Hirschfeld, M.D.
Martin Kafka, M.D.
Nadine J. Kaslow, Ph.D.
Ronald Kessler, Ph.D.
Kenneth Kobak, Ph.D.
David Kupfer, M.D.
Markku Linnoila, M.D., Ph.D.
J. John Mann, M.D.
Paul Markovitz, M.D.
John Markowitz, M.D.
Antonia New, M.D.
Andrew Nierenberg, M.D.
Barbara Parry, M.D.
Robert Post, M.D.
Frederic Quitkin, M.D.
Judith G. Rabkin, Ph.D.
Mark Rapaport, M.D.
Harold Sackeim, Ph.D.
Larry J. Siever, M.D.
Daphne Simeon, M.D.
Michael Thase, M.D.
Herman Van Praag, M.D.
Myrna Weissman, Ph.D.
Sidney Zisook, M.D.

Advisers for Child and Adolescent Measures for Diagnosis and Screening

Howard Abikoff, Ph.D.
Helen Abramowicz, M.D.
Thomas M. Achenbach, Ph.D.
Paul J. Ambrosini, M.D.
L. Eugene Arnold, M.D.
Hector R. Bird, M.D.
Susan J. Bradley, M.D.
Gabrielle A. Carlson, M.D.
Donald J. Cohen, M.D.
C. Keith Conners, Ph.D.
E. Jane Costello, Ph.D.
Mina K. Dulcan, M.D.

George DuPaul, Ph.D.
Rex Forehand, Ph.D.
Linda N. Freeman, M.D.
Barry Garfinkel, M.D.
Madelyn S. Gould, Ph.D., M.P.H.
Jeffrey M. Halperin, Ph.D.
Emily Harris, M.D.
Lily Hechtman, M.D.
Scott Hennegler, Ph.D.
Stephen Hinshaw, Ph.D.
Peter Jensen, M.D.
Joan Kaufman, Ph.D.
Cheryl A. King, Ph.D.
Rachel G. Klein, Ph.D.
Markus Kruesi, M.D.
Krista Kutash, Ph.D.
Stan Kutcher, M.D.
James Leckman, M.D.
Henrietta L. Leonard, M.D.
Jan Loney, Ph.D.
John March, M.D.
Keith McBurnett, Ph.D.
Robert Milich, Ph.D.
Craig Morris, M.D.
Laura Mufson, Ph.D.
Jeffrey Newcorn, M.D.
Helen Orvaschel, Ph.D.
Rhea Paul, Ph.D.
John Piacentini, Ph.D.
Daniel S. Pine, M.D.
Judith Rapoport, M.D.
Wendy Reich, Ph.D.
Lawrence Richards, M.D.
Mary Jane Rotheram, Ph.D.
Sir Michael Rutter, M.D.
Russell Schachar, M.D.
David Shaffer, M.D.
Mark Stein, Ph.D.
Michael Strober, Ph.D.
Rosemary Tannock, Ph.D.
Fred R. Volkmar, M.D.
Gail A. Wasserman, Ph.D.
Myrna Weissman, Ph.D.
John S. Werry, M.D.
Gwendolyn Zahner, Ph.D.
Alan Zametkin, M.D.

Advisers for Symptom-Specific Measures for Disorders Usually First Diagnosed in Infancy, Childhood, or Adolescence

Richard Abidin, Ph.D.
Howard Abikoff, Ph.D.
Helen Abramowicz, M.D.
Thomas M. Achenbach, Ph.D.
Paul J. Ambrosini, M.D.
L. Eugene Arnold, M.D.
Russell Barkley, Ph.D.
Lenore Behar, Ph.D.
Hector R. Bird, M.D.
Susan J. Bradley, M.D.
Gabrielle A. Carlson, M.D.
Donald J. Cohen, M.D.
C. Keith Conners, Ph.D.
E. Jane Costello, Ph.D.
Mina K. Dulcan, M.D.
George DuPaul, Ph.D.
Prudence Fisher, Ph.D.
Linda N. Freeman, M.D.
Barry Garfinkel, M.D.
Madelyn S. Gould, Ph.D., M.P.H.
Jeffrey M. Halperin, Ph.D.
Emily Harris, M.D.
Lily Hechtman, M.D.
Scott Hennegler, Ph.D.
Stephen Hinshaw, Ph.D.
Peter Jensen, M.D.
Rachel G. Klein, Ph.D.
Maria Kovacs, M.D.
Markus Kruesi, M.D.
Stan Kutcher, M.D.
James Leckman, M.D.
Henrietta L. Leonard, M.D.
Jan Loney, Ph.D.
John March, M.D.
Keith McBurnett, Ph.D.
Richard Milich, Ph.D.
Craig Morris, M.D.
Laura Mufson, Ph.D.
Jeffrey Newcorn, M.D.
Helen Orvaschel, Ph.D.
John Piacentini, Ph.D.
Daniel S. Pine, M.D.
Judith Rapoport, M.D.
Cecil Reynolds, Ph.D.
William M. Reynolds, Ph.D.
Anne Riley, Ph.D.

Mary Jane Rotheram, Ph.D.
Sir Michael Rutter, M.D.
Russell Schachar, M.D.
Barbara Starfield, M.D., M.P.H.
Rosemary Tannock, Ph.D.
Fred R. Volkmar, M.D.
Gail A. Wasserman, Ph.D.
Myrna Weissman, Ph.D.
John S. Werry, M.D.
Gwendolyn Zahner, Ph.D.
Alan Zametkin, M.D.

Advisers for Child and Adolescent Measures of Functional Status

Richard R. Abidin, Ph.D.
Howard Abikoff, Ph.D.
Helen Abramowicz, M.D.
Thomas M. Achenbach, Ph.D.
Paul J. Ambrosini, M.D.
L. Eugene Arnold, M.D.
Hector R. Bird, M.D.
Susan J. Bradley, M.D.
Gabrielle A. Carlson, M.D.
Ana Mari Cauce, Ph.D.
Donald J. Cohen, M.D.
C. Keith Conners, Ph.D.
Ward Cromer, Ph.D.
Mina K. Dulcan, M.D.
George DuPaul, Ph.D.
Rex Forehand, Ph.D.
Linda N. Freeman, M.D.
Barry Garfinkel, M.D.
Madelyn S. Gould, M.D., M.P.H.
Jeffrey M. Halperin, Ph.D.
Emily Harris, M.D.
Lily Hechtman, M.D.
Stephen Hinshaw, M.D.
Peter Jensen, M.D.
Joan Kaufman, Ph.D.
Kelly J. Kelleher, M.D., M.P.H.
Cheryl A. King, Ph.D.
Rachel G. Klein, Ph.D.
Stan Kutcher, M.D.
James Leckman, M.D.
Henrietta L. Leonard, M.D.
Jan Loney, Ph.D.
John March, M.D.
Keith McBurnett, Ph.D.
Robert Milich, Ph.D.
Craig Morris, M.D.

Laura Mufson, Ph.D.
Jeffrey Newcorn, M.D.
Helen Orvaschel, Ph.D.
John Piacentini, Ph.D.
Daniel S. Pine, M.D.
Judith Rapoport, M.D.
Lawrence Richards, M.D.
Mary Jane Rotheram, Ph.D.
Sir Michael Rutter, M.D.
Russell Schachar, M.D.
Sara S. Sparrow, Ph.D.
Michael Strober, Ph.D.
Gail A. Wasserman, Ph.D.
Myrna Weissman, Ph.D.
John S. Werry, M.D.
Gwendolyn Zahner, Ph.D.

Advisers for Behavioral Measures for Cognitive Disorders

George Alexopoulos, M.D.
Daniel Blazer, M.D.
Kathy Christensen, Ph.D.
Munro Cullum, Ph.D.
Jeffrey L. Cummings, M.D.
Igor Grant, M.D.
Kenneth Kendler, M.D.
Elizabeth Koss, Ph.D.
Barry Lebowitz, Ph.D.
Harvey Levin, Ph.D.
Irene Litvan, M.D.
Steven Mattis, Ph.D.
Richard Mohs, Ph.D.
Peter Rabins, M.D.
Barry Reisberg, M.D.
Charles Reynolds, M.D.
Barry Rovner, M.D.
Teresa Rummans, M.D.
Lon Schneider, M.D.
Esther Strauss, Ph.D.
Gary Tucker, M.D.
Peter Whitehouse, M.D., Ph.D.
Thomas Wise, M.D.

Advisers for Neuropsychiatric Measures for Cognitive Disorders

George Alexopoulos, M.D.
Daniel Blazer, M.D.
Munro Cullum, Ph.D.
Jeffrey L. Cummings, M.D.
Igor Grant, M.D.

Suzanne Holroyd, M.D.
Elisabeth Koss, Ph.D.
Barry Lebowitz, Ph.D.
Harvey Levin, Ph.D.
Richard Mohs, Ph.D.
Peter V. Rabins, M.D.
Barry Reisberg, M.D.
Charles Reynolds, M.D.
Barry Rovner, M.D.
Teresa Rummans, M.D.
Lon Schneider, M.D.
Esther Strauss, Ph.D.
Gary J. Tucker, M.D.
Peter J. Whitehouse, M.D., Ph.D.
Thomas Wise, M.D.

Advisers for Substance Use Disorders Measures

Bryon Adinoff, M.D.
Raymond Anton, M.D.
Thomas Babor, Ph.D.
Kathleen Brady, M.D., Ph.D.
Linda B. Cottler, Ph.D.
Marc Galanter, M.D.
Shelly Greenfield, M.D.
John Helzer, M.D.
John Hughes, M.D.
Thomas Kosten, M.D.
David Lewis, M.D.
Alan Marlatt, Ph.D.
Roger Meyer, M.D.
William Miller, Ph.D.
Edgar Nace, M.D.
Peter Nathan, Ph.D.
Patricia Isbell Ordorica, M.D.
Marc Schuckit, M.D.
Harvey Skinner, Ph.D.
Linda Sobell, Ph.D.
Mark Sobell, Ph.D.
George Woody, M.D.

Advisers for Psychotic Disorders Measures

Nancy Andreasen, M.D., Ph.D.
Allan Bellack, Ph.D.
John Davis, M.D.
Wayne Fenton, M.D.
David Garver, M.D.
John Kane, M.D.
Kenneth Kendler, M.D.
Robert Paul Liberman, M.D.
Joseph McEvoy, M.D.

Thomas McGlashan, M.D.
Henry Nasrallah, M.D.
George Simpson, M.D.
Philip Veenhuis, M.D.
Glenn Wagner, Ph.D.

Advisers for Mood Disorders Measures

Lori L. Altshuler, M.D.
Jules Angst, M.D.
David Avery, M.D.
Mark S. Bauer, M.D.
Aaron Beck, M.D.
Daniel Blazer, M.D.
Paula Clayton, M.D.
Jonathan Cole, M.D.
William Coryell, M.D.
Dwight L. Evans, M.D.
Maurizio Fava, M.D.
Ellen Frank, Ph.D.
Alan Gelenberg, M.D.
J. Christian Gillin, M.D.
Paul J. Goodnick, M.D.
James I. Hudson, M.D.
Donald Klein, M.D.
Kenneth Kobak, Ph.D.
James Kocsis, M.D.
J. John Mann, M.D.
John Markowitz, M.D.
Charles Nemeroff, M.D.
Andrew Nierenberg, M.D.
Eugene Paykel, M.D.
Robert Post, M.D.
Judith Rabkin, Ph.D.
Mark Rapaport, M.D.
Jerrold F. Rosenbaum, M.D.
Harold Sackeim, Ph.D.
Patricia Suppes, M.D., Ph.D.
Michael Thase, M.D.
Myrna Weissman, Ph.D.
Peter Whybrow, M.D.
Sidney Zisook, M.D.

Advisers for Anxiety Disorders Measures

James Ballenger, M.D.
David Barlow, Ph.D.
Aaron Beck, M.D.
Diane L. Chambless, Ph.D.
Marylene Cloitre, Ph.D.
Michelle Craske, Ph.D.
Raymond Crowe, M.D.

Jonathan R. T. Davidson, M.D., F.R.C.P.
Edwin DeBuers, Ph.D.
Anke Ehlers, M.D.
Edna B. Foa, Ph.D.
Abby Fyer, M.D.
Michael Gelder, M.D.
Wayne Goodman, M.D.
Tana Grady, M.D.
Richard Heimberg, Ph.D.
Wayne Katon, M.D.
Michael R. Liebowitz, M.D.
Isaac Marks, M.D.
Jack D. Maser, Ph.D.
Richard J. McNally, Ph.D.
Russell Noyes Jr., M.D.
Laszlo Papp, M.D.
Mark Pollack, M.D.
Jerrold F. Rosenbaum, M.D.
Jerilyn Ross, L.I.C.S.W.
Sir Martin Roth, M.D.
Peter P. Roy-Byrne, M.D.
Paul Salkovskis, Ph.D.
David Sheehan, M.D.
Diane E. Sholomskas, Ph.D.
David Spiegel, M.D.
Vladan Starcevic, M.D.
Murray B. Stein, M.D.
Richard P. Swinson, M.D.

Advisers for Somatoform and Factitious Disorders and Malingering Measures

Arthur Barsky, M.D.
David Berry, Ph.D.
Edwin Cassem, M.D.
C. Robert Cloninger, M.D.
Stuart Eisendrath, M.D.
Javier Escobar, M.D.
Marc Feldman, M.D.
Jack Froom, M.D.
Rollin Gallagher, M.D.
Richard Goldberg, M.D.
Frederick Guggenheim, M.D.
Samuel Guze, M.D.
Jimmie Holland, M.D.
Eric Hollander, M.D.
Alexander Janca, M.D.
Charles Kaelber, M.D.
Roger Kathol, M.D.
Wayne Katon, M.D.

Kelly Kelleher, M.D., M.P.H.
Robert Kerns, Ph.D.
Laurence Kirmayer, M.D.
Kurt Kroenke, M.D.
James Levenson, M.D.
Mack Lipkin, M.D.
Juan Lopez-Ibor, M.D.
John Lyon, M.D.
Ronald Margolis, Ph.D.
Ronald L. Martin, M.D. (deceased)
Dale Matthews, M.D.
Juan Mezzich, M.D., Ph.D.
Issy Pilowsky, Ph.D.
Phillip Resnick, M.D.
Richard Rogers, Ph.D.
James Rosen, Ph.D.
Norman Sartorius, M.D., Ph.D.
Gregory Simon, M.D.
Robert Spitzer, M.D.
Alan Stoudemire, M.D.
James Strain, M.D.
Raymond Tait, Ph.D.
Troy Thompson, M.D.
Michael Wise, M.D.
Thomas Wise, M.D.
Sean Yutzy, M.D.

Advisers for Dissociative Disorders Measures

Judith G. Armstrong, Ph.D.
Elizabeth S. Bowman, M.D.
Etzel Cardena, Ph.D.
Eve B. Carlson, Ph.D.
James A. Chu, M.D.
C. Robert Cloninger, M.D.
Philip M. Coons, M.D.
Steven King, M.D.
Richard Kluft, M.D.
Dorothy O. Lewis, M.D.
Ronald L. Martin, M.D. (deceased)
Katharine A. Phillips, M.D.
Colin A. Ross, M.D.
David Spiegel, M.D.
Alan Stoudemire, M.D.
James Strain, M.D.

Advisers for Sexual Disorders Measures

John Bancroft, M.D.
Raymond Blanchard, Ph.D.
Clive Davis, Ph.D.
Sandra Leiblum, Ph.D.

Stephen Levine, M.D.
Raymond Rosen, Ph.D.
Chester Schmidt, M.D.
Leslie Schover, Ph.D.
R. Taylor Segraves, M.D.
John Wincze, Ph.D.
Thomas Wise, M.D.

Advisers for Eating Disorders Measures

W. Stewart Agras, M.D.
Arnold E. Andersen, M.D.
William R. Beardslee, M.D.
Pierre Beaumont, M.D.
Pauline Boss, Ph.D.
Rachel Bryant-Waugh
James Coyne, Ph.D.
Lawrence Fisher, Ph.D.
David M. Garner, Ph.D.
Madeline M. Gladis, Ph.D.
Henry Grunebaum, M.D.
Katherine Halmi, M.D.
David Herzog, M.D.
David C. Jimerson, M.D.
Allan S. Kaplan, M.D.
Nadine J. Kaslow, Ph.D.
Melanie A. Katzman, Ph.D.
Walter H. Kaye, M.D.
Dean Krahn, M.D.
Bryan Lask, M.D.
Jay Lebow, Ph.D.
Howard Liddle, M.D.
Marsha D. Marcus, Ph.D.
Patricia Minuchin, M.D.
James E. Mitchell, M.D.
J. Scott Mizes, Ph.D.
Marion P. Olmsted, Ph.D.
Candyce Russell, Ph.D.
M. Duncan Stanton, Ph.D.
Peter Steinglass, M.D.
Ruth H. Striegel-Moore, Ph.D.
Michael Strober, Ph.D.
Albert Stunkard, M.D.
Kelly Bemis Vitousek, Ph.D.
Froma Walsh, Ph.D.
Denise E. Wilfley, Ph.D.
Stephen Wonderlich, Ph.D.
Joel Yager, M.D.
Susan Yanovski, M.D.

Advisers for Sleep Disorders Measures

Sonia Ancoli-Israel, Ph.D.
David Avery, M.D.
Donald Bliwise, Ph.D.
Daniel Buysse, M.D.
Rosalind Cartwright, Ph.D.
Ronald Dahl, M.D.
David Dingers, Ph.D.
Paul Frederickson, M.D.
June Fry, M.D., Ph.D.
Donna Giles, Ph.D.
J. Christian Gillin, M.D.
Peter Hauri, Ph.D.
Yasuo Hishikawa, M.D.
Florian Holsboer, M.D., Ph.D.
Myriam Kerkhofs, Ph.D.
Peretz Lavie, Ph.D.
Alfred Lewy, M.D., Ph.D.
Alistair MacLean, Ph.D.
Bentson McFarland, M.D., Ph.D.
Wallace Mendelson, M.D.
Merril Mitler, Ph.D.
Barbara Parry, M.D.
R. T. Pivik, Ph.D.
Patricia Prinz, Ph.D.
Charles Reynolds, M.D.
Gary Richardson, M.D.
Carlos Schenk, M.D.
Michael Thorpy, M.D.
James Walsh, Ph.D.
Gary Zammit, Ph.D.
Vincent Zarcone Jr., M.D.

Advisers for Impulse-Control Disorders Measures

Ernest S. Barratt, Ph.D.
Donald W. Black, M.D.
Sheila Blume, M.D.
Don R. Cherek, Ph.D.
Gary Christenson, M.D.
Concetta M. DeCaria, Ph.D.
Jerry L. Deffenbacher, Ph.D.
Alan R. Felthous, M.D.
Wayne Goodman, M.D.
Jeffrey Halperin, Ph.D.
Martin Kafka, M.D.
Thomas A. Kent, M.D.
Markus Kruesi, M.D.
Markku Linnoila, M.D., Ph.D.
J. John Mann, M.D.
Paul Markovitz, M.D.
Terrie E. Moffitt, Ph.D.
Larry J. Siever, M.D.
Jonathan Silver, M.D.
Daphne Simeon, M.D.
Charles D. Spielberger, Ph.D.
James T. Tedeschi, Ph.D.

Advisers for Personality Disorders, Personality Traits, and Defense Mechanisms Measures

Arthur Alterman, Ph.D.
Lorna Benjamin, Ph.D.
Roger Blashfield, Ph.D.
Michael Bond, M.D.
James Butcher, Ph.D.
Lee Anna Clark, Ph.D.
John Clarkin, Ph.D.
Paul Costa, Ph.D.
Alv Dahl, M.D.
John Gunderson, M.D.
Robert Hare, Ph.D.
Leonard Horowitz, Ph.D.
Steven Hyler, M.D.
Daniel Klein, Ph.D.
Marjorie Klein, Ph.D.
Michael Lambert, Ph.D.
Armand Loranger, Ph.D.
Thomas McGlashan, M.D.
Theodore Millon, Ph.D., D.Sc.
Rudolph Moos, Ph.D.
Leslie Morey, Ph.D.
John Oldham, M.D.
Bruce Pfohl, M.D.
Paul Pilkonis, Ph.D.
James Reich, M.D., M.P.H.
Larry J. Siever, M.D.
Paul Soloff, M.D.
Timothy Trull, Ph.D.
Peter Tyrer, M.D.
Mark Zimmerman, M.D.

DSM-IV-TR Classification

NOS = Not Otherwise Specified.

An *x* appearing in a diagnostic code indicates that a specific code number is required.

An ellipsis (. . .) is used in the names of certain disorders to indicate that the name of a specific mental disorder or general medical condition should be inserted when recording the name (e.g., 293.0 Delirium Due to Hypothyroidism).

If criteria are currently met, one of the following severity specifiers may be noted after the diagnosis:

> Mild
> Moderate
> Severe

If criteria are no longer met, one of the following specifiers may be noted:

> In Partial Remission
> In Full Remission
> Prior History

DISORDERS USUALLY FIRST DIAGNOSED IN INFANCY, CHILDHOOD, OR ADOLESCENCE

Mental Retardation

Note: These are coded on Axis II.

317	Mild Mental Retardation
318.0	Moderate Mental Retardation
318.1	Severe Mental Retardation
318.2	Profound Mental Retardation
319	Mental Retardation, Severity Unspecified

Learning Disorders

315.00	Reading Disorder
315.1	Mathematics Disorder
315.2	Disorder of Written Expression
315.9	Learning Disorder NOS

Motor Skills Disorder

315.4	Developmental Coordination Disorder

Communication Disorders

315.31	Expressive Language Disorder
315.32	Mixed Receptive-Expressive Language Disorder
315.39	Phonological Disorder
307.0	Stuttering
307.9	Communication Disorder NOS

Pervasive Developmental Disorders

299.00	Autistic Disorder
299.80	Rett's Disorder

299.10	Childhood Disintegrative Disorder
299.80	Asperger's Disorder
299.80	Pervasive Developmental Disorder NOS

Attention-Deficit and Disruptive Behavior Disorders

314.xx	Attention-Deficit/Hyperactivity Disorder
.01	Combined Type
.00	Predominantly Inattentive Type
.01	Predominantly Hyperactive-Impulsive Type
314.9	Attention-Deficit/Hyperactivity Disorder NOS
312.xx	Conduct Disorder
.81	Childhood-Onset Type
.82	Adolescent-Onset Type
.89	Unspecified Onset
313.81	Oppositional Defiant Disorder
312.9	Disruptive Behavior Disorder NOS

Feeding and Eating Disorders of Infancy or Early Childhood

307.52	Pica
307.53	Rumination Disorder
307.59	Feeding Disorder of Infancy or Early Childhood

Tic Disorders

307.23	Tourette's Disorder
307.22	Chronic Motor or Vocal Tic Disorder
307.21	Transient Tic Disorder
	Specify if: Single Episode/Recurrent
307.20	Tic Disorder NOS

Elimination Disorders

—.–	Encopresis
787.6	With Constipation and Overflow Incontinence
307.7	Without Constipation and Overflow Incontinence
307.6	Enuresis (Not Due to a General Medical Condition)
	Specify type: Nocturnal Only/Diurnal Only/Nocturnal and Diurnal

Other Disorders of Infancy, Childhood, or Adolescence

309.21	Separation Anxiety Disorder
	Specify if: Early Onset
313.23	Selective Mutism
313.89	Reactive Attachment Disorder of Infancy or Early Childhood
	Specify type: Inhibited Type/Disinhibited Type

307.3	Stereotypic Movement Disorder
	Specify if: With Self-Injurious Behavior
313.9	Disorder of Infancy, Childhood, or Adolescence NOS

DELIRIUM, DEMENTIA, AND AMNESTIC AND OTHER COGNITIVE DISORDERS

Delirium

293.0	Delirium Due to . . . *[Indicate the General Medical Condition]*
—.–	Substance Intoxication Delirium (*refer to Substance-Related Disorders for substance-specific codes*)
—.–	Substance Withdrawal Delirium (*refer to Substance-Related Disorders for substance-specific codes*)
—.–	Delirium Due to Multiple Etiologies (*code each of the specific etiologies*)
780.09	Delirium NOS

Dementia

294.xx*	Dementia of the Alzheimer's Type, With Early Onset (*also code 331.0 Alzheimer's disease on Axis III*)
.10	Without Behavioral Disturbance
.11	With Behavioral Disturbance
294.xx*	Dementia of the Alzheimer's Type, With Late Onset (*also code 331.0 Alzheimer's disease on Axis III*)
.10	Without Behavioral Disturbance
.11	With Behavioral Disturbance
290.xx	Vascular Dementia
.40	Uncomplicated
.41	With Delirium
.42	With Delusions
.43	With Depressed Mood
	Specify if: With Behavioral Disturbance

Code presence or absence of a behavioral disturbance in the fifth digit for Dementia Due to a General Medical Condition:

| 294.1x | Dementia Due to HIV Disease (*also code 042 HIV infection on Axis III*) |
| 294.1x | Dementia Due to Head Trauma (*also code 854.00 head injury on Axis III*) |

**ICD-9-CM code valid after October 1, 2000

294.1x   Dementia Due to Parkinson's Disease (*also code 332.0 Parkinson's disease on Axis III*)

294.1x   Dementia Due to Huntington's Disease (*also code 333.4 Huntington's disease on Axis III*)

294.1x   Dementia Due to Pick's Disease (*also code 331.1 Pick's disease on Axis III*)

294.1x   Dementia Due to Creutzfeldt-Jakob Disease (*also code 046.1 Creutzfeldt-Jakob disease on Axis III*)

294.1x   Dementia Due to . . . [*Indicate the General Medical Condition not listed above*] (*also code the general medical condition on Axis III*)

——.–   Substance-Induced Persisting Dementia (*refer to Substance-Related Disorders for substance-specific codes*)

——.–   Dementia Due to Multiple Etiologies (*code each of the specific etiologies*)

294.8   Dementia NOS

Amnestic Disorders

294.0   Amnestic Disorder Due to . . . [*Indicate the General Medical Condition*]
          Specify if: Transient/Chronic

——.–   Substance-Induced Persisting Amnestic Disorder (*refer to Substance-Related Disorders for substance-specific codes*)

294.8   Amnestic Disorder NOS

Other Cognitive Disorders

294.9   Cognitive Disorder NOS

MENTAL DISORDERS DUE TO A GENERAL MEDICAL CONDITION NOT ELSEWHERE CLASSIFIED

293.89   Catatonic Disorder Due to . . . [*Indicate the General Medical Condition*]

310.1   Personality Change Due to . . . [*Indicate the General Medical Condition*]
          Specify type: Labile Type/Disinhibited Type/Aggressive Type/Apathetic Type/Paranoid Type/Other Type/Combined Type/Unspecified Type

293.9   Mental Disorder NOS Due to . . . [*Indicate the General Medical Condition*]

SUBSTANCE-RELATED DISORDERS

[a]*The following specifiers may be applied to Substance Dependence:*

> With Physiological Dependence/Without Physiological Dependence
>
> Early Full Remission/Early Partial Remission
>
> Sustained Full Remission/Sustained Partial Remission/In a Controlled Environment

The following specifier applies to Opioid Dependence:

> On Agonist Therapy

The following specifiers apply to Substance-Induced Disorders as noted:

> [I]With Onset During Intoxication/[W]With Onset During Withdrawal

Alcohol-Related Disorders

Alcohol Use Disorders

303.90   Alcohol Dependence[a]
305.00   Alcohol Abuse

Alcohol-Induced Disorders

303.00   Alcohol Intoxication
291.81   Alcohol Withdrawal
          Specify if: With Perceptual Disturbances
291.0   Alcohol Intoxication Delirium
291.0   Alcohol Withdrawal Delirium
291.2   Alcohol-Induced Persisting Dementia
291.1   Alcohol-Induced Persisting Amnestic Disorder
291.x   Alcohol-Induced Psychotic Disorder
    .5   With Delusions[I,W]
    .3   With Hallucinations[I,W]
291.89   Alcohol-Induced Mood Disorder[I,W]
291.89   Alcohol-Induced Anxiety Disorder[I,W]
291.89   Alcohol-Induced Sexual Dysfunction[I]
291.89   Alcohol-Induced Sleep Disorder[I,W]

291.9   Alcohol-Related Disorder NOS

Amphetamine (or Amphetamine-Like)–Related Disorders

Amphetamine Use Disorders

304.40   Amphetamine Dependence[a]
305.70   Amphetamine Abuse

Amphetamine-Induced Disorders

292.89   Amphetamine Intoxication
          Specify if: With Perceptual Disturbances
292.0   Amphetamine Withdrawal
292.81   Amphetamine Intoxication Delirium

292.xx   Amphetamine-Induced Psychotic Disorder
   .11   With Delusions[I]
   .12   With Hallucinations[I]
292.84   Amphetamine-Induced Mood Disorder[I,W]
292.89   Amphetamine-Induced Anxiety Disorder[I]
292.89   Amphetamine-Induced Sexual Dysfunction[I]
292.89   Amphetamine-Induced Sleep Disorder[I,W]

292.9   Amphetamine-Related Disorder NOS

Caffeine-Related Disorders

Caffeine-Induced Disorders

305.90   Caffeine Intoxication
292.89   Caffeine-Induced Anxiety Disorder[I]
292.89   Caffeine-Induced Sleep Disorder[I]

292.9   Caffeine-Related Disorder NOS

Cannabis-Related Disorders

Cannabis Use Disorders

304.30   Cannabis Dependence[a]
305.20   Cannabis Abuse

Cannabis-Induced Disorders

292.89   Cannabis Intoxication
     Specify if: With Perceptual Disturbances
292.81   Cannabis Intoxication Delirium
292.xx   Cannabis-Induced Psychotic Disorder
   .11   With Delusions[I]
   .12   With Hallucinations[I]
292.89   Cannabis-Induced Anxiety Disorder[I]

292.9   Cannabis-Related Disorder NOS

Cocaine-Related Disorders

Cocaine Use Disorders

304.20   Cocaine Dependence[a]
305.60   Cocaine Abuse

Cocaine-Induced Disorders

292.89   Cocaine Intoxication
     Specify if: With Perceptual Disturbances
292.0   Cocaine Withdrawal
292.81   Cocaine Intoxication Delirium
292.xx   Cocaine-Induced Psychotic Disorder
   .11   With Delusions[I]
   .12   With Hallucinations[I]
292.84   Cocaine-Induced Mood Disorder[I,W]
292.89   Cocaine-Induced Anxiety Disorder[I,W]
292.89   Cocaine-Induced Sexual Dysfunction[I]
292.89   Cocaine-Induced Sleep Disorder[I,W]

292.9   Cocaine-Related Disorder NOS

Hallucinogen-Related Disorders

Hallucinogen Use Disorders

304.50   Hallucinogen Dependence[a]
305.30   Hallucinogen Abuse

Hallucinogen-Induced Disorders

292.89   Hallucinogen Intoxication
292.89   Hallucinogen Persisting Perception Disorder
     (Flashbacks)
292.81   Hallucinogen Intoxication Delirium
292.xx   Hallucinogen-Induced Psychotic Disorder
   .11   With Delusions[I]
   .12   With Hallucinations[I]
292.84   Hallucinogen-Induced Mood Disorder[I]
292.89   Hallucinogen-Induced Anxiety Disorder[I]

292.9   Hallucinogen-Related Disorder NOS

Inhalant-Related Disorders

Inhalant Use Disorders

304.60   Inhalant Dependence[a]
305.90   Inhalant Abuse

Inhalant-Induced Disorders

292.89   Inhalant Intoxication
292.81   Inhalant Intoxication Delirium
292.82   Inhalant-Induced Persisting Dementia
292.xx   Inhalant-Induced Psychotic Disorder
   .11   With Delusions[I]
   .12   With Hallucinations[I]
292.84   Inhalant-Induced Mood Disorder[I]
292.89   Inhalant-Induced Anxiety Disorder[I]

292.9   Inhalant-Related Disorder NOS

Nicotine-Related Disorders

Nicotine Use Disorder

305.1   Nicotine Dependence[a]

Nicotine-Induced Disorder

292.0   Nicotine Withdrawal

292.9   Nicotine-Related Disorder NOS

Opioid-Related Disorders

Opioid Use Disorders

304.00   Opioid Dependence[a]
305.50   Opioid Abuse

Opioid-Induced Disorders

292.89   Opioid Intoxication
     Specify if: With Perceptual Disturbances
292.0   Opioid Withdrawal

292.81   Opioid Intoxication Delirium
292.xx   Opioid-Induced Psychotic Disorder
  .11   With Delusions[I]
  .12   With Hallucinations[I]
292.84   Opioid-Induced Mood Disorder[I]
292.89   Opioid-Induced Sexual Dysfunction[I]
292.89   Opioid-Induced Sleep Disorder[I,W]

292.9   Opioid-Related Disorder NOS

Phencyclidine (or Phencyclidine-Like)–Related Disorders

Phencyclidine Use Disorders

304.60   Phencyclidine Dependence[a]
305.90   Phencyclidine Abuse

Phencyclidine-Induced Disorders

292.89   Phencyclidine Intoxication
             Specify if: With Perceptual Disturbances
292.81   Phencyclidine Intoxication Delirium
292.xx   Phencyclidine-Induced Psychotic Disorder
  .11   With Delusions[I]
  .12   With Hallucinations[I]
292.84   Phencyclidine-Induced Mood Disorder[I]
292.89   Phencyclidine-Induced Anxiety Disorder[I]

292.9   Phencyclidine-Related Disorder NOS

Sedative-, Hypnotic-, or Anxiolytic-Related Disorders

Sedative, Hypnotic, or Anxiolytic Use Disorders

304.10   Sedative, Hypnotic, or Anxiolytic Dependence[a]
305.40   Sedative, Hypnotic, or Anxiolytic Abuse

Sedative-, Hypnotic-, or Anxiolytic-Induced Disorders

292.89   Sedative, Hypnotic, or Anxiolytic Intoxication
292.0   Sedative, Hypnotic, or Anxiolytic Withdrawal
             Specify if: With Perceptual Disturbances
292.81   Sedative, Hypnotic, or Anxiolytic Intoxication Delirium
292.81   Sedative, Hypnotic, or Anxiolytic Withdrawal Delirium
292.82   Sedative-, Hypnotic-, or Anxiolytic-Induced Persisting Dementia
292.83   Sedative-, Hypnotic-, or Anxiolytic-Induced Persisting Amnestic Disorder
292.xx   Sedative-, Hypnotic-, or Anxiolytic-Induced Psychotic Disorder
  .11   With Delusions[I,W]
  .12   With Hallucinations[I,W]
292.84   Sedative-, Hypnotic-, or Anxiolytic-Induced Mood Disorder[I,W]

292.89   Sedative-, Hypnotic-, or Anxiolytic-Induced Anxiety Disorder[W]
292.89   Sedative-, Hypnotic-, or Anxiolytic-Induced Sexual Dysfunction[I]
292.89   Sedative-, Hypnotic-, or Anxiolytic-Induced Sleep Disorder[I,W]

292.9   Sedative-, Hypnotic-, or Anxiolytic-Related Disorder NOS

Polysubstance-Related Disorder

304.80   Polysubstance Dependence[a]

Other (or Unknown) Substance–Related Disorders

Other (or Unknown) Substance Use Disorders

304.90   Other (or Unknown) Substance Dependence[a]
305.90   Other (or Unknown) Substance Abuse

Other (or Unknown) Substance–Induced Disorders

292.89   Other (or Unknown) Substance Intoxication
             Specify if: With Perceptual Disturbances
292.0   Other (or Unknown) Substance Withdrawal
             Specify if: With Perceptual Disturbances
292.81   Other (or Unknown) Substance–Induced Delirium
292.82   Other (or Unknown) Substance–Induced Persisting Dementia
292.83   Other (or Unknown) Substance–Induced Persisting Amnestic Disorder
292.xx   Other (or Unknown) Substance–Induced Psychotic Disorder
  .11   With Delusions[I,W]
  .12   With Hallucinations[I,W]
292.84   Other (or Unknown) Substance–Induced Mood Disorder[I,W]
292.89   Other (or Unknown) Substance–Induced Anxiety Disorder[I,W]
292.89   Other (or Unknown) Substance–Induced Sexual Dysfunction[I]
292.89   Other (or Unknown) Substance–Induced Sleep Disorder[I,W]

292.9   Other (or Unknown) Substance–Related Disorder NOS

SCHIZOPHRENIA AND OTHER PSYCHOTIC DISORDERS

295.xx   Schizophrenia

The following Classification of Longitudinal Course applies to all subtypes of Schizophrenia:

Episodic With Interepisode Residual Symptoms (*specify if:* With Prominent Negative Symptoms)/Episodic With No Interepisode Residual Symptoms

Continuous (*specify if:* With Prominent Negative Symptoms)

Single Episode In Partial Remission (*specify if:* With Prominent Negative Symptoms)/Single Episode In Full Remission

Other or Unspecified Pattern

.30   Paranoid Type
.10   Disorganized Type
.20   Catatonic Type
.90   Undifferentiated Type
.60   Residual Type

295.40   Schizophreniform Disorder
         Specify if: Without Good Prognostic Features/With Good Prognostic Features
295.70   Schizoaffective Disorder
         Specify type: Bipolar Type/Depressive Type
297.1   Delusional Disorder
         Specify type: Erotomanic Type/Grandiose Type/Jealous Type/Persecutory Type/Somatic Type/Mixed Type/Unspecified Type
298.8   Brief Psychotic Disorder
         Specify if: With Marked Stressor(s)/Without Marked Stressor(s)/With Postpartum Onset
297.3   Shared Psychotic Disorder
293.xx   Psychotic Disorder Due to . . . [*Indicate the General Medical Condition*]
    .81   With Delusions
    .82   With Hallucinations
——.–   Substance-Induced Psychotic Disorder (*refer to Substance-Related Disorders for substance-specific codes*)
         Specify if: With Onset During Intoxication/With Onset During Withdrawal
298.9   Psychotic Disorder NOS

MOOD DISORDERS

Code current state of Major Depressive Disorder or Bipolar I Disorder in fifth digit:

1 = Mild

2 = Moderate

3 = Severe Without Psychotic Features

4 = Severe With Psychotic Features
    Specify: Mood-Congruent Psychotic Features/Mood-Incongruent Psychotic Features

5 = In Partial Remission

6 = In Full Remission

0 = Unspecified

The following specifiers apply (for current or most recent episode) to Mood Disorders as noted:

[a]Severity/Psychotic/Remission Specifiers/[b]Chronic/[c]With Catatonic Features/[d]With Melancholic Features/[e]With Atypical Features/[f]With Postpartum Onset

The following specifiers apply to Mood Disorders as noted:

[g]With or Without Full Interepisode Recovery/[h]With Seasonal Pattern/[i]With Rapid Cycling

Depressive Disorders

296.xx   Major Depressive Disorder,
    .2x   Single Episode[a,b,c,d,e,f]
    .3x   Recurrent[a,b,c,d,e,f,g,h]
300.4   Dysthymic Disorder
         Specify if: Early Onset/Late Onset
         Specify: With Atypical Features
311   Depressive Disorder NOS

Bipolar Disorders

296.xx   Bipolar I Disorder,
    .0x   Single Manic Episode[a,c,f]
         Specify if: Mixed
    .40   Most Recent Episode Hypomanic[g,h,i]
    .4x   Most Recent Episode Manic[a,c,f,g,h,i]
    .6x   Most Recent Episode Mixed[a,c,f,g,h,i]
    .5x   Most Recent Episode Depressed[a,b,c,d,e,f,g,h,i]
    .7   Most Recent Episode Unspecified[g,h,i]
296.89   Bipolar II Disorder[a,b,c,d,e,f,g,h,i]
         Specify (current or most recent episode): Hypomanic/Depressed
301.13   Cyclothymic Disorder
296.80   Bipolar Disorder NOS

293.83   Mood Disorder Due to . . . [*Indicate the General Medical Condition*]

Specify type: With Depressive Features/With Major Depressive–Like Episode/With Manic Features/With Mixed Features

——.– Substance-Induced Mood Disorder (*refer to Substance-Related Disorders for substance-specific codes*)
Specify type: With Depressive Features/With Manic Features/With Mixed Features
Specify if: With Onset During Intoxication/With Onset During Withdrawal

296.90 Mood Disorder NOS

ANXIETY DISORDERS

300.01 Panic Disorder Without Agoraphobia
300.21 Panic Disorder With Agoraphobia
300.22 Agoraphobia Without History of Panic Disorder
300.29 Specific Phobia
Specify type: Animal Type/Natural Environment Type/Blood-Injection-Injury Type/Situational Type/Other Type
300.23 Social Phobia
Specify if: Generalized
300.3 Obsessive-Compulsive Disorder
Specify if: With Poor Insight
309.81 Posttraumatic Stress Disorder
Specify if: Acute/Chronic
Specify if: With Delayed Onset
308.3 Acute Stress Disorder
300.02 Generalized Anxiety Disorder
293.84 Anxiety Disorder Due to . . . [*Indicate the General Medical Condition*]
Specify if: With Generalized Anxiety/With Panic Attacks/With Obsessive-Compulsive Symptoms
——.– Substance-Induced Anxiety Disorder (*refer to Substance-Related Disorders for substance-specific codes*)
Specify if: With Generalized Anxiety/With Panic Attacks/With Obsessive-Compulsive Symptoms/With Phobic Symptoms
Specify if: With Onset During Intoxication/With Onset During Withdrawal
300.00 Anxiety Disorder NOS

SOMATOFORM DISORDERS

300.81 Somatization Disorder
300.82 Undifferentiated Somatoform Disorder

300.11 Conversion Disorder
Specify type: With Motor Symptom or Deficit/With Sensory Symptom or Deficit/With Seizures or Convulsions/With Mixed Presentation
307.xx Pain Disorder
.80 Associated With Psychological Factors
.89 Associated With Both Psychological Factors and a General Medical Condition
Specify if: Acute/Chronic
300.7 Hypochondriasis
Specify if: With Poor Insight
300.7 Body Dysmorphic Disorder
300.82 Somatoform Disorder NOS

FACTITIOUS DISORDERS

300.xx Factitious Disorder
.16 With Predominantly Psychological Signs and Symptoms
.19 With Predominantly Physical Signs and Symptoms
.19 With Combined Psychological and Physical Signs and Symptoms
300.19 Factitious Disorder NOS

DISSOCIATIVE DISORDERS

300.12 Dissociative Amnesia
300.13 Dissociative Fugue
300.14 Dissociative Identity Disorder
300.6 Depersonalization Disorder
300.15 Dissociative Disorder NOS

SEXUAL AND GENDER IDENTITY DISORDERS

Sexual Dysfunctions

The following specifiers apply to all primary Sexual Dysfunctions:

Lifelong Type/Acquired Type
Generalized Type/Situational Type
Due to Psychological Factors/Due to Combined Factors

Sexual Desire Disorders

302.71 Hypoactive Sexual Desire Disorder
302.79 Sexual Aversion Disorder

Sexual Arousal Disorders

302.72 Female Sexual Arousal Disorder
302.72 Male Erectile Disorder

Orgasmic Disorders

302.73 Female Orgasmic Disorder
302.74 Male Orgasmic Disorder
302.75 Premature Ejaculation

Sexual Pain Disorders

302.76 Dyspareunia (Not Due to a General Medical Condition)
306.51 Vaginismus (Not Due to a General Medical Condition)

Sexual Dysfunction Due to a General Medical Condition

625.8 Female Hypoactive Sexual Desire Disorder Due to . . . [Indicate the General Medical Condition]
608.89 Male Hypoactive Sexual Desire Disorder Due to . . . [Indicate the General Medical Condition]
607.84 Male Erectile Disorder Due to . . . [Indicate the General Medical Condition]
625.0 Female Dyspareunia Due to . . . [Indicate the General Medical Condition]
608.89 Male Dyspareunia Due to . . . [Indicate the General Medical Condition]
625.8 Other Female Sexual Dysfunction Due to . . . [Indicate the General Medical Condition]
608.89 Other Male Sexual Dysfunction Due to . . . [Indicate the General Medical Condition]
——.– Substance-Induced Sexual Dysfunction (refer to Substance-Related Disorders for substance-specific codes)
   Specify if: With Impaired Desire/With Impaired Arousal/With Impaired Orgasm/With Sexual Pain
   Specify if: With Onset During Intoxication

302.70 Sexual Dysfunction NOS

Paraphilias

302.4 Exhibitionism
302.81 Fetishism
302.89 Frotteurism
302.2 Pedophilia
   Specify if: Sexually Attracted to Males/Sexually Attracted to Females/Sexually Attracted to Both
   Specify if: Limited to Incest
   Specify type: Exclusive Type/Nonexclusive Type
302.83 Sexual Masochism

302.84 Sexual Sadism
302.3 Transvestic Fetishism
   Specify if: With Gender Dysphoria
302.82 Voyeurism
302.9 Paraphilia NOS

Gender Identity Disorders

302.xx Gender Identity Disorder
   .6   in Children
   .85   in Adolescents or Adults
      Specify if: Sexually Attracted to Males/Sexually Attracted to Females/Sexually Attracted to Both/Sexually Attracted to Neither
302.6 Gender Identity Disorder NOS

302.9 Sexual Disorder NOS

EATING DISORDERS

307.1 Anorexia Nervosa
   Specify type: Restricting Type; Binge-Eating/Purging Type
307.51 Bulimia Nervosa
   Specify type: Purging Type/Nonpurging Type
307.50 Eating Disorder NOS

SLEEP DISORDERS

Primary Sleep Disorders

Dyssomnias

307.42 Primary Insomnia
307.44 Primary Hypersomnia
   Specify if: Recurrent
347 Narcolepsy
780.59 Breathing-Related Sleep Disorder
307.45 Circadian Rhythm Sleep Disorder
   Specify type: Delayed Sleep Phase Type/Jet Lag Type/Shift Work Type/Unspecified Type
307.47 Dyssomnia NOS

Parasomnias

307.47 Nightmare Disorder
307.46 Sleep Terror Disorder
307.46 Sleepwalking Disorder
307.47 Parasomnia NOS

Sleep Disorders Related to Another Mental Disorder

307.42 Insomnia Related to . . . [Indicate the Axis I or Axis II Disorder]

307.44 Hypersomnia Related to . . . [*Indicate the Axis I or Axis II Disorder*]

Other Sleep Disorders

780.xx Sleep Disorder Due to . . . [*Indicate the General Medical Condition*]
.52   Insomnia Type
.54   Hypersomnia Type
.59   Parasomnia Type
.59   Mixed Type
——.–   Substance-Induced Sleep Disorder (*refer to Substance-Related Disorders for substance-specific codes*)
     Specify type: Insomnia Type/Hypersomnia Type/Parasomnia Type/Mixed Type
     Specify if: With Onset During Intoxication/With Onset During Withdrawal

IMPULSE-CONTROL DISORDERS NOT ELSEWHERE CLASSIFIED

312.34 Intermittent Explosive Disorder
312.32 Kleptomania
312.33 Pyromania
312.31 Pathological Gambling
312.39 Trichotillomania
312.30 Impulse-Control Disorder NOS

ADJUSTMENT DISORDERS

309.xx Adjustment Disorder
.0   With Depressed Mood
.24   With Anxiety
.28   With Mixed Anxiety and Depressed Mood
.3   With Disturbance of Conduct
.4   With Mixed Disturbance of Emotions and Conduct
.9   Unspecified
     Specify if: Acute/Chronic

PERSONALITY DISORDERS

Note: These are coded on Axis II.
301.0   Paranoid Personality Disorder
301.20   Schizoid Personality Disorder
301.22   Schizotypal Personality Disorder
301.7   Antisocial Personality Disorder
301.83   Borderline Personality Disorder
301.50   Histrionic Personality Disorder
301.81   Narcissistic Personality Disorder
301.82   Avoidant Personality Disorder
301.6   Dependent Personality Disorder
301.4   Obsessive-Compulsive Personality Disorder
301.9   Personality Disorder NOS

OTHER CONDITIONS THAT MAY BE A FOCUS OF CLINICAL ATTENTION

Psychological Factors Affecting Medical Condition

316 . . . [*Specified Psychological Factor*] Affecting . . . [*Indicate the General Medical Condition*]
Choose name based on nature of factors:

    Mental Disorder Affecting Medical Condition

    Psychological Symptoms Affecting Medical Condition

    Personality Traits or Coping Style Affecting Medical Condition

    Maladaptive Health Behaviors Affecting Medical Condition

    Stress-Related Physiological Response Affecting Medical Condition

    Other or Unspecified Psychological Factors Affecting Medical Condition

Medication-Induced Movement Disorders

332.1   Neuroleptic-Induced Parkinsonism
333.92   Neuroleptic Malignant Syndrome
333.7   Neuroleptic-Induced Acute Dystonia
333.99   Neuroleptic-Induced Acute Akathisia
333.82   Neuroleptic-Induced Tardive Dyskinesia
333.1   Medication-Induced Postural Tremor
333.90   Medication-Induced Movement Disorder NOS

Other Medication-Induced Disorder

995.2   Adverse Effects of Medication NOS

Relational Problems

V61.9   Relational Problem Related to a Mental Disorder
         or General Medical Condition
V61.20   Parent-Child Relational Problem
V61.10   Partner Relational Problem
V61.8   Sibling Relational Problem
V62.81   Relational Problem NOS

Problems Related to Abuse or Neglect

V61.21   Physical Abuse of Child (*code 995.54 if focus of
         attention is on victim*)
V61.21   Sexual Abuse of Child (*code 995.53 if focus of
         attention is on victim*)
V61.21   Neglect of Child (*code 995.52 if focus of attention
         is on victim*)
——.–   Physical Abuse of Adult
V61.12   (if by partner)
V62.83   (if by person other than partner) (*code 995.81
            if focus of attention is on victim*)
——.–   Sexual Abuse of Adult
V61.12   (if by partner)
V62.83   (if by person other than partner) (*code 995.83
            if focus of attention is on victim*)

Additional Conditions That May Be a Focus of Clinical Attention

V15.81   Noncompliance With Treatment
V65.2   Malingering
V71.01   Adult Antisocial Behavior
V71.02   Child or Adolescent Antisocial Behavior
V62.89   Borderline Intellectual Functioning
         Note: *This is coded on Axis II.*
780.9   Age-Related Cognitive Decline
V62.82   Bereavement
V62.3   Academic Problem
V62.2   Occupational Problem
313.82   Identity Problem
V62.89   Religious or Spiritual Problem
V62.4   Acculturation Problem
V62.89   Phase of Life Problem

ADDITIONAL CODES

300.9   Unspecified Mental Disorder (nonpsychotic)
V71.09   No Diagnosis or Condition on Axis I
799.9   Diagnosis or Condition Deferred on Axis I
V71.09   No Diagnosis on Axis II
799.9   Diagnosis Deferred on Axis II

MULTIAXIAL SYSTEM

Axis I   Clinical Disorders
          Other Conditions That May Be a Focus of
              Clinical Attention
Axis II   Personality Disorders
          Mental Retardation
Axis III General Medical Conditions
Axis IV   Psychosocial and Environmental Problems
Axis V   Global Assessment of Functioning

List of Measures Included on the CD-ROM

ALPHABETICAL LISTING

Abnormal Involuntary Movement Scale (AIMS)
Addiction Severity Index (ASI)
Alcohol Dependence Scale (ADS)
Alcohol Expectancy Questionnaire (AEQ)
Alcohol Outcomes Module (AOM)
Alcohol Timeline Followback (TLFB)
Alcohol Use Disorders Identification Test (AUDIT)
Alzheimer's Disease Assessment Scale (ADAS)
Anger, Irritability, and Assault Questionnaire (AIAQ)

Barnes Akathisia Rating Scale (BARS)
Barratt Impulsiveness Scale, Version 11 (BIS-11)
Behavior and Symptom Identification Scale (BASIS-32)
Behavior Pathology in Alzheimer's Disease Rating Scale (BEHAVE-AD)
Behavioral and Emotional Rating Scale (BERS)
Body Dysmorphic Disorder Examination (BDDE)
Body Shape Questionnaire (BSQ)
Brief Psychiatric Rating Scale (BPRS)
Brief Sexual Function Inventory (BSFI)
Brief Social Phobia Scale (BSPS)
Burden Interview (BI)
Buss-Durkee Hostility Inventory (BDHI)

CAGE Questionnaire
Calgary Depression Scale for Schizophrenia (CDSS)

Center for Epidemiologic Studies of Depression Scale (CES-D)
Child Dissociative Checklist (CDC)
Child Health Questionnaire (CHQ)
Children's Global Assessment Scale (CGAS)
Clinical Dementia Rating (CDR) Scale
Clinical Global Impressions (CGI) Scale
Clinical Institute Withdrawal Assessment for Alcohol (CIWA-AD)
Clinician Administered Rating Scale for Mania (CARS-M)
Clinician Alcohol Use Scale (AUS)
Clinician Drug Use Scale (DUS)
Columbia Impairment Scale (CIS)
COMPASS OP
Confusion Assessment Method (CAM)
Cornell Scale for Depression in Dementia (CSDD)
Crown-Crisp Experiential Index (CCEI) [often referred to as Middlesex Hospital Questionnaire (MHQ)]

Dartmouth COOP Functional Assessment Charts (COOP)
Defense Style Questionnaire (DSQ)
Depression Outcomes Module (DOM)
Diagnostic Interview for Borderline Patients—Revised (DIB-R)
Diagnostic Interview for DSM-IV Personality Disorders (DIPD-IV)
Dissociative Disorders Interview Schedule (DDIS)
Dissociative Experiences Scale (DES)
Drug Attitude Inventory (DAI)

Epworth Sleepiness Scale (ESS)

Excessive Daytime Sleepiness and Nocturnal Sleep Subscales of the Sleep/Wake Activity Inventory (SWAI)

Family Assessment Device (FAD)

Fear Questionnaire (FQ)

Functional Assessment Staging (FAST) Measures

Galveston Orientation and Amnesia Test (GOAT)

Geriatric Depression Scale (GDS)

Global Assessment Scale (GAS)

Global Deterioration Scale (GDS)

Health of the Nation Outcomes Scales (HoNOS)

Impact of Event Scale (IES)

Internal State Scale (ISS)

Inventory of Depressive Symptomatology (IDS)

Lawton Instrumental Activities of Daily Living Scale (Lawton IADL)

Life Skills Profile (LSP)

Massachusetts General Hospital (MGH) Hairpulling Scale

McGill Pain Questionnaire (MPQ)

MEDWatch

Middlesex Hospital Questionnaire (MHQ) [Crown-Crisp Experiential Index (CCEI)]

Mini-Mental State Examination (MMSE)

Mississippi Scale (MSS)

Mobility Inventory for Agoraphobia (MI)

Multnomah Community Ability Scale (MCAS)

Neurobehavioral Cognitive Status Examination (NCSE or COGNISTAT)

Obsessive Compulsive Drinking Scale (OCDS)

Overt Aggression Scale—Modified (OAS-M)

Padua Inventory (PI)

Panic Disorder Severity Scale (PDSS)

Patient Satisfaction Questionnaire (PSQ)

Penn State Worry Questionnaire (PSWQ)

Pittsburgh Sleep Quality Index (PSQI)

Primary Care Evaluation of Mental Disorders (PRIME-MD)

Psychiatric Institute Trichotillomania Scale (PITS)

Quality of Life Index (QLI)

Quality of Life Interview (QOLI)

Quality of Life Scale (QLS)

Questionnaire on Eating and Weight Patterns—Revised (QEWP-R)

Raskin Three-Area Severity of Depression Scale

Rating Scale for Extrapyramidal Side Effects (Simpson-Angus EPS Scale)

Recent Life Changes Questionnaire (RLCQ)

Scale for the Assessment of Negative Symptoms (SANS)

Scale for the Assessment of Positive Symptoms (SAPS)

Schedule for Affective Disorders and Schizophrenia for School Age-Children: Present and Lifetime version (K-SADS-PL)

Schizophrenia Outcomes Module (SCHIZOM)

Screen for Caregiver Burden (SCB)

Screener for Somatoform Disorders

Service Satisfaction Scale—30 (SSS-30)

Sexual Arousability Inventory (SAI)

SF-36 Health Survey (SF-36)

Sheehan Disability Scale

Simpson-Angus EPS Scale (Rating Scale for Extrapyramidal Side Effects)

Sleep/Wake Activity Inventory (SWAI), Excessive Daytime Sleepiness and Nocturnal Sleep Subscales

Somatoform Disorders Schedule (SDS)

Somatoform Disorders Symptom Checklist

South Oaks Gambling Screen (SOGS)

Systematic Assessment for Treatment Emergent Events—General Inquiry (SAFTEE-GI)

Three-Area Severity of Depression (Raskin) Scale

Treatment Services Review (TSR)

TWEAK Test

West Haven–Yale Multidimensional Pain Inventory (WHYMPI)

Whiteley Index of Hypochondriasis

Wisconsin Quality of Life Index (W-QLI)

Yale Global Tic Severity Scale (YGTSS)
Yale-Brown Obsessive Compulsive Scale (Y-BOCS)
Yale-Brown Obsessive Compulsive Scale Modified for Body Dysmorphic Disorder (BDD-YBOCS)
Young Mania Rating Scale (YMRS)

Zung Self-Rating Depression Scale (Zung SDS)

LISTING BY CHAPTER

Chapter 6: Diagnostic Interviews for Adults

Primary Care Evaluation of Mental Disorders (PRIME-MD)

Chapter 7: General Psychiatric Symptoms Measures

Behavior and Symptom Identification Scale (BASIS-32)
Crown-Crisp Experiential Index (CCEI) [often referred to as Middlesex Hospital Questionnaire (MHQ)]

Chapter 8: Mental Health Status, Functioning, and Disabilities Measures

Clinical Global Impressions (CGI) Scale
Global Assessment Scale (GAS)
Health of the Nation Outcomes Scales (HoNOS)
Life Skills Profile (LSP)
Multnomah Community Ability Scale (MCAS)
Sheehan Disability Scale

Chapter 9: General Health Status, Functioning, and Disabilities Measures

Dartmouth COOP Functional Assessment Charts (COOP)
Lawton Instrumental Activities of Daily Living Scale (Lawton IADL)
SF-36 Health Survey (SF-36)

Chapter 10: Quality of Life Measures

Quality of Life Index (QLI)
Quality of Life Interview (QOLI)
Quality of Life Scale (QLS)
Wisconsin Quality of Life Index (W-QLI)

Chapter 11: Adverse Effects Measures

Abnormal Involuntary Movement Scale (AIMS)
Barnes Akathisia Rating Scale (BARS)
MedWatch
Rating Scale for Extrapyramidal Side Effects (Simpson-Angus EPS Scale)

Systematic Assessment for Treatment Emergent Events—General Inquiry (SAFTEE-GI)

Chapter 12: Patient Perceptions of Care Measures

Patient Satisfaction Questionnaire (PSQ)
Service Satisfaction Scale—30 (SSS-30)

Chapter 13: Practitioner and System Evaluation

Alcohol Outcomes Module (AOM)
COMPASS OP
Depression Outcomes Module (DOM)
Schizophrenia Outcomes Module (SCHIZOM)
Treatment Services Review (TSR)

Chapter 14: Stress and Life Events Measures

Recent Life Changes Questionnaire (RLCQ)

Chapter 15: Family and Relational Issues Measures

Family Assessment Device (FAD)

Chapter 17: Child and Adolescent Measures for Diagnosis and Screening

Schedule for Affective Disorders and Schizophrenia for School Age-Children: Present and Lifetime version (K-SADS PL)

Chapter 18: Symptom-Specific Measures for Disorders Usually First Diagnosed in Infancy, Childhood, or Adolescence

Yale Global Tic Severity Scale (YGTSS)

Chapter 19: Child and Adolescent Measures of Functional Status

Behavioral and Emotional Rating Scale (BERS)
Child Health Questionnaire (CHQ)
Children's Global Assessment Scale (CGAS)
Columbia Impairment Scale (CIS)

Chapter 20: Behavioral Measures for Cognitive Disorders

Behavior Pathology in Alzheimer's Disease Rating Scale (BEHAVE-AD)
Burden Interview (BI)
Confusion Assessment Method (CAM)
Cornell Scale for Depression in Dementia (CSDD)
Screen for Caregiver Burden (SCB)

Chapter 21: Neuropsychiatric Measures for Cognitive Disorders

Alzheimer's Disease Assessment Scale (ADAS)
Clinical Dementia Rating (CDR) Scale

Functional Assessment Staging (FAST) Measures
Galveston Orientation and Amnesia Test (GOAT)
Global Deterioration Scale (GDS)
Mini-Mental State Examination (MMSE)
Neurobehavioral Cognitive Status Examination (NCSE or COGNISTAT)

Chapter 22: Substance Use Disorders Measures

Addiction Severity Index (ASI)
Alcohol Dependence Scale (ADS)
Alcohol Expectancy Questionnaire (AEQ)
Alcohol Timeline Followback (TLFB)
Alcohol Use Disorders Identification Test (AUDIT)
CAGE Questionnaire
Clinical Institute Withdrawal Assessment for Alcohol (CIWA-AD)
Obsessive Compulsive Drinking Scale (OCDS)
TWEAK Test

Chapter 23: Psychotic Disorders Measures

Brief Psychiatric Rating Scale (BPRS)
Calgary Depression Scale for Schizophrenia (CDSS)
Clinician Alcohol Use Scale (AUS)
Clinician Drug Use Scale (DUS)
Drug Attitude Inventory (DAI)
Scale for the Assessment of Negative Symptoms (SANS)
Scale for the Assessment of Positive Symptoms (SAPS)

Chapter 24: Mood Disorders Measures

Center for Epidemiologic Studies of Depression Scale (CES-D)
Clinician Administered Rating Scale for Mania (CARS-M)
Geriatric Depression Scale (GDS)
Internal State Scale (ISS)
Inventory of Depressive Symptomatology (IDS)
Raskin Scale (Three-Area Severity of Depression Scale)
Young Mania Rating Scale (YMRS)
Zung Self-Rating Depression Scale (Zung SDS)

Chapter 25: Anxiety Disorders Measures

Brief Social Phobia Scale (BSPS)
Fear Questionnaire (FQ)
Impact of Event Scale (IES)
Mississippi Scale (MSS)
Mobility Inventory for Agoraphobia (MI)
Padua Inventory (PI)
Panic Disorder Severity Scale (PDSS)
Penn State Worry Questionnaire (PSWQ)
Yale-Brown Obsessive Compulsive Scale (Y-BOCS)

Chapter 26: Somatoform and Factitious Disorders and Malingering Measures

Body Dysmorphic Disorder Examination (BDDE)
McGill Pain Questionnaire (MPQ)
Screener for Somatoform Disorders
Somatoform Disorders Schedule (SDS)
Somatoform Disorders Symptom Checklist
West Haven–Yale Multidimensional Pain Inventory (WHYMPI)
Whiteley Index of Hypochondriasis
Yale-Brown Obsessive Compulsive Scale Modified for Body Dysmorphic Disorder (BDD-YBOCS)

Chapter 27: Dissociative Disorders Measures

Child Dissociative Checklist (CDC)
Dissociative Disorders Interview Schedule (DDIS)
Dissociative Experiences Scale (DES)

Chapter 28: Sexual Disorders Measures

Brief Sexual Function Inventory (BSFI)
Sexual Arousability Inventory (SAI)

Chapter 29: Eating Disorders Measures

Body Shape Questionnaire (BSQ)
Questionnaire on Eating and Weight Patterns—Revised (QEWP-R)

Chapter 30: Sleep Disorders Measures

Epworth Sleepiness Scale (ESS)
Pittsburgh Sleep Quality Index (PSQI)
Sleep/Wake Activity Inventory (SWAI), Excessive Daytime Sleepiness and Nocturnal Sleep Subscales

Chapter 31: Impulse-Control Disorders Measures

Anger, Irritability, and Assault Questionnaire (AIAQ)
Barratt Impulsiveness Scale, Version 11 (BIS-11)
Buss-Durkee Hostility Inventory (BDHI)
Massachusetts General Hospital (MGH) Hairpulling Scale
Overt Aggression Scale—Modified (OAS-M)
Psychiatric Institute Trichotillomania Scale (PITS)
South Oaks Gambling Screen (SOGS)

Chapter 32: Personality Disorders, Personality Traits, and Defense Mechanisms Measures

Defense Style Questionnaire (DSQ)
Diagnostic Interview for Borderline Patients—Revised (DIB-R)
Diagnostic Interview for DSM-IV Personality Disorders (DIPD-IV)

Index of Measures

Page numbers in **bold** type refer to detailed discussions of measures.
Page numbers in *italic* type refer to tables.

Index of Abbreviations for Measures

Page numbers in **bold** type refer to detailed discussions of measures.
Page numbers in *italic* type refer to tables.

General Index

Page numbers in **bold** type refer to detailed discussions of measures.
Page numbers in *italic* type refer to tables or examples.